# Audubon Wildlife Report 1986

Audubon Wildlife Report 1986

The National Audubon Society, founded in 1905, is dedicated to conserving plants and animals and their habitats, to promoting wise use of land, water, and energy, and to protecting life from the many global environmental problems that now threaten it. With more than half a million members, 500 chapters, 10 regional offices, and a staff of nearly 300, the Audubon Society is a powerful force for conservation research, education, and action.

# Audubon Wildlife Report 1986

Amos S. Eno, Project Director
Roger L. Di Silvestro, Editor
William J. Chandler, Research Director

The National Audubon Society
New York, New York

Cover Photo: Fred Baldwin/Photo Researchers
Design by Caliber Design Planning, Inc.
Printed by R. R. Donnelley & Sons Company
Published by The National Audubon Society
950 Third Avenue, New York, New York 10022

ISSN 0885-6044
ISBN 0-930698-23-1 (1986 Volume)
     0-930698-20-7 (Volume Set)

# Acknowledgements

For their help in the preparation and review of material for this volume, thanks are due to the Marine Mammal Commission, U.S. Fish and Wildlife Service, National Marine Fisheries Service, National Park Service, Department of State, Department of the Interior Office of the Solicitor, U.S. Army Corps of Engineers, Environmental Protection Agency, Bureau of Land Management, Agricultural Stabilization and Conservation Service of the Department of Agriculture, Forest Service, Extension Service of the Department of Agriculture, House Merchant Marine and Fisheries Committee, Senate Environment and Public Works Committee, Senate Energy and Natural Resources Committee, House Interior and Insular Affairs Committee, Canadian Wildlife Service, Embassy of Canada, Columbia River Inter-tribal Fish Commission, North Atlantic Salmon Treaty Organization, International Union for the Conservation of Nature, American Horse Protection Association, *International Game Warden* magazine, Maryland Department of Natural Resources, Virginia Commission of Game and Inland Fisheries, Colorado Division of Wildlife, New Mexico Game and Fish Department, Tennessee Wildlife Resources Agency, New Hampshire Fish and Game Department, Illinois Department of Conservation, Oregon Department of Fish and Wildlife, International Association of Fish and Wildlife Agencies, Defenders of Wildlife, National Parks and Conservation Association, The Wilderness Society, National Wildlife Federation, Izaak Walton League of America, Natural Resources Defense Council, Sierra Club Legal Defense Fund, Environmental Defense Fund, Sport Fishing Institute, Wildlife Management Institute, Friends of the Earth, and the American Fisheries Society.

Thanks also go to the National Audubon Society's Mary McCarthy, for her excellent and imaginative work on the graphs that appear in this book; Lillian Labate, for her efforts above and beyond the call of a 40-hour work week; Claire Rusowicz, for meeting the many demands of proofreading the massive amount of material that went into this volume; Michele Ball, for her help with the proofreading of the appendices; Mercedes Lee, for help with the typing and proofreading; Jim Leape, who prepared while under the duress of a heavy work schedule the Legal Developments sections of the agency and program chapters; Ruth Norris, who helped with the promotions of the report and was always ready with a word of encouragement; Marcy Downs, who helped type many of the manuscripts in the shadow of looming deadlines; and Chris Wille, for guidance and advice. Appreciation also goes to Scott Groene, Laurie Lambrix, and Ellen S. Roberts, University of Colorado Law School students who helped Jim Leape with the legal sections; Diane Jukofsky for help with proofreading; Paula Weaver, for help with typing; and Defenders of Wildlife's Sara Vickerman for many helpful suggestions over the past year.

## Dedication

For Amos Eno, who walked through this world quietly yet with a joyful heart, listening for the birds that sing. My father, like many others, drew from an hour's bird walk the inspiration for grander visions of conservation and of a saner world. For me, it is enough that he pointed the way to the path to be taken. From that choice and his memory, I derived inspiration for this book.

# The Audubon Wildlife Report 1986

Preface    xiii
Foreword    xv
*Secretary of the Interior—Donald Hodel*
Introduction    xvii
*Amos S. Eno*


## PART 1.    The Featured Agency


The U.S. Forest Service    1
*Katherine Barton*
Wildlife Issues on the National Forest System    159
*Whit Fosburgh*


## PART 2.    Federal Agencies and Programs


Federal Grants for State Wildlife Conservation    177
*William J. Chandler*
Migratory Bird Protection and Management    215
*William J. Chandler*
Federal Marine Fisheries Management    267
*Michael Weber*
The Endangered Species Program    347
*Michael J. Bean*
Federal Wetlands Protection Programs    373
*Katherine Barton*

The National Wildlife Refuge System    413
*Wendy Smith Lee*
Wildlife and the National Park Service    463
*Chris Elfring*
Wildlife and the Bureau of Land Management    497
*Katherine Barton*
International Wildlife Conservation    543
*Michael J. Bean*

## PART 3.  Conservation and the States

State Wildlife Conservation: An Overview    579
*William J. Chandler*
State Wildlife Law Enforcement    593
*William J. Chandler*
State Nongame Wildlife Programs    631
*Susan Cerulean and Whit Fosburgh*

## PART 4.  Species Accouts

The Whooping Crane    659
*James C. Lewis*
The Common Loon    679
*Judy McIntyre*
The Atlantic Salmon    697
*Lawrence W. Stolte*
Chinook Salmon of the Columbia River Basin    715
*Lloyd A. Phinney*
The Spotted Owl    743
*Eric Forsman and E. Charles Meslow*
Sage Grouse    763
*Robert Autenrieth*
The Small Whorled Pogonia    781
*Richard W. Dyer*
The Polar Bear    791
*Steven C. Amstrup*
The Peregrine Falcon    807
*Gerald Craig*
The Hooded Warbler    827
*George V. N. Powell and John H. Rappole*

The Black Duck    855
*Howard E. Spencer, Jr.*
The Red Knot    871
*Brain Harrington*
The Osprey    889
*Mark A. Westall*
Lange's Metalmark Butterfly    911
*Paul A. Opler and Lee Robinson*
Kemp's Ridley Sea Turtle    919
*Jack B. Woody*
The Loggerhead Shrike    933
*James D. Fraser and David R. Luukkonen*
The Knowlton Cactus    943
*Peggy Olwell*
The Gray Wolf    951
*Rolf O. Peterson*

# PART 5. Appendices

Appendix A.    Forest Service Directory    971
Appendix B.    U.S. Fish and Wildlife Service Directory    976
Appendix C.    National Park Service Directory    986
Appendix D.    Bureau of Land Management Directory    994
Appendix E.    Wetlands Management Directory    997
Appendix F.    Federal Offices Involved in the Management of
               Marine Fisheries and the Conservation of Marine
               Mammals    1011
Appendix G.    Budget Information Contacts on Federal Fish and Wildlife
               Programs    1015
Appendix H.    Congressional Contacts and Addresses    1016
Appendix I.    Major Population Objectives, Status and Trends of
               Migratory Bird Species of Special Management
               Emphasis    1022
Appendix J.    The Development of Annual Waterfowl Hunting
               Regulations    1029
Appendix K.    Permit Requirements for Federally Protected Fish and
               Wildlife Species    1034
Appendix L.    Species and Special Goups for Which National Resource
               Plans Are Prepared by FWS    1059
Appendix M.    Fish and Wildlife Species for Which Regional Resource
               Plans are Prepared    1062
Appendix N.    National Forest System Acreage by State as of September
               30, 1984 (in acres)    1064

# Preface

FOR THE SECOND CONSECUTIVE year, this report was made possible by the extraordinary and timely generosity and support of numerous individuals and foundations. The *Audubon Wildlife Report* has been a special undertaking which owes its existence to the foresight and confidence of its supporters. We are indebted to and deeply appreciate the support of:

Avatar Properties, Inc.; Howard Burris; James A. Buss; the Clark Foundation; the James R. Dougherty, Jr. Foundation; Sophie Engelhard; the Jamee & Marshall Field Foundation; the Forbes Foundation; Edward H. Hamm; the Hershey Foundation; the W. Alton Jones Foundation; Robert H. Kanzler; Dan W. Lufkin; Louis Marx, Jr.; the G.H. Milliken Foundation; Clement C. Moore, II; the Northern Star Foundation; Mrs. Sumner Pingree; Peter Sharp; Mrs. Charlotte C. Weber; F.J. (Rick) Weyerhaeuser; John Winthrop; and Robert Winthrop.

# Foreword

THROUGHOUT much of our history, we have witnessed the conversion of wild lands to settlements, the change of forests and prairies to farm fields and suburban housing areas. As a people, we have accepted that the development of a civilization entails some loss or displacement of natural resources. But we also have grown to realize that without wise use and protection of that same resource base, the very civilization we have strived so hard to build could not continue to exist at all.

Conservation is the lesson of balance, of how to use a resource and of how to invest in the resource's future. In my tenure as secretary of the Interior, I have had the opportunity to meet with countless groups and individuals from all parts of the country, from all the varied economic strata this great nation represents. I am both impressed and humbled, time and time again, by the knowledge, interest, and sincerity of the people concerning our natural resources. I believe that as a people we have become one of the most environmentally knowledgeable, concerned, and committed citizenries in the world. Everywhere I go, I sense the public's growing appreciation for the values of wetlands and their strong support for our nation's parks, refuges, and forests. But most of all, I hear the public voicing deep interest in "wilderness."

Some people I meet use the term "wilderness" quite specifically and with reference to the federal Wilderness Act. To most citizens, though, the word summarizes a succinct upwelling of their feeling for the American landscape. They want the land protected, respected, and conserved as a legacy they can proudly pass along to future generations.

We all share responsibility for our diverse natural resources. And we all understand that good resource stewardship costs money and the federal government cannot afford to do it alone.

Indeed, we are once again in a period when the federal share of natural-resource funding cannot grow at the rate some wildlife and wilderness advocates would like. Regardless of the cyclic rise and fall of federal expenditures—an historic pattern necessitated, as at present, by increased concern over the federal budget and the overriding need to reduce deficits—the American people have always found a way to demonstrate their active commitment to our resources.

I believe Americans want to take an active role in helping to restore and replenish our natural bounty. I encourage them to take pride in our resources and to do all they can to safeguard them.

But first, I share with many of them another view of "wilderness"—another wilderness they must first confront and understand if they are to help wildlands and wildlife resources materially. This other wilderness is the vast and daunting tangle of rules and regulatory undergrowth that too often discourages innovative approaches to resource management.

The full array of federal agencies marshalled to safeguard our resources is the most impressive on Earth. But for the citizen or community groups trying to better the environment, that same complex of federal agencies frequently presents a bewildering and seemingly impenetrable barrier. I would hasten to note that public servants are far from being villains in this situation. In fact, most public servants are helpful and courteous and are the concerned citizen's greatest ally in advancing sound conservation efforts.

Fortunately, another ally—the National Audubon Society—has appeared to make the institutionilized conservation mechanisms of government more available to the general citizenry. This well-researched and fact-filled AUDUBON WILDLIFE REPORT is another way to make conservation issues and institutions more understandable and accessible.

With publication of this second volume in its series of reports, the Society reaffirms its commitment to conservation by providing a book that will help explain the "ecology" of government. It outlines how federal conservation systems work—and where at times they don't work as well as they might. It is fine example of the philosophy of conservation, in and of itself—it is balanced, it is a work of give and take—and out of it emerges, not a wilderness of rules and bureaus, but some of the order and harmony of process and law, the tools each of us can wield to save the wild lands, wildlife, and other natural resources that made—and make—this great nation our home.

Donald Hodel
Secretary of the Interior

# Introduction

In the dawning years of the 20th century, W.J. McGee and Gifford Pinchot popularized the term conservation, which they defined as "use of the natural resources for the greatest good of the greatest number for the longest time."

As we approach this century's final decade, our repositories of "good" are hard pressed. Exponential growth has swelled an already burgeoning human population. And time, a factor that once buffered man's impact on the environment, is an increasingly scarce commodity. Time is measured now as something that we are running out of, particularly for endangered species and for wildlife habitat.

The world has shrunk in terms of transportation, communication, and time, but has become phenomenally more complex. More nations have gained independence and, with it, the authority for managing resources. In this country, the agencies responsible for natural-resource management have multiplied. The laws and regulations guiding the management of our resources have proliferated a thousandfold. Resource management has become interwoven with all aspects of our society's social, economic, and political fabric.

Durward Allen insightfully pinpointed the multiple influences of complexity in his address, "These Fifty Years," to the 1985 North American Wildlife and Natural Resource Conference. He emphasized that the "main trouble in dealing with ecological issues is that we underestimate them. The ecosystems that support all living things are the most complex entities we know anything about in the universe. . . . Today, armed with all the devices of mechanical ingenuity, we are redoing the earth. We add confusion to complexity. Our 'developments' are a welter of discordant conditions that we sometimes dignify as a system. The biosphere has become a patchwork of disturbance communities maintained as unsightly back alleys of the human citadel. The occupation forces do not know what was there before or what is likely to come after. A look at what man hath wrought suggests that we got into the construction business without benefit of blueprinting."

Our numerous wildlife conservation laws and regulations should serve as guidelines for development, but enforcement lags while building proceeds. As the turtle is to the hare in fable, we know that ultimately we must win, though the race is daunting.

In 1934, during the height of the Depression, President Franklin Roosevelt appointed J.N. (Ding) Darling chief of the Biological Survey, the precursor of today's U.S. Fish and Wildlife Service. Darling was noted for his "sense of personal outrage that wildlife was either ignored or a consistent loser in the competition of resource decisions," as Durward Allen observed in his wildlife conference address.

Fifty years later, the National Audubon Society launched the Wildlife Report from similar concerns. Wildlife continues to get the short shrift in important resources decisions. And we still lack understanding of the increasingly complex and competitive nature of the world we live in, with its exponential growth and the urgency wrought by overpopulation, air and water pollution, tropical and old-growth deforestation, soil erosion, and the loss of genetic diversity.

We have prepared the *Wildlife Report* as an aid for the whole spectrum of professional and amateur decision-makers, as well as those simply interested in wildlife. A major purpose of the project is to attract more and more people into the fold of natural-resource policy. Wildlife has taken a back seat for too long primarily because no forceful constituency exists to advocate protection. Even today, wildlife advocates still are relegated to the rumble seat, far removed from the centers of policy and budget decision making.

This year, the first in which the implications of the Gramm-Rudman-Hollings balanced-budget legislation may be felt, does not bode well for federal and state wildlife programs. The specter of budget recissions and cutbacks, reminiscent of the Reagan administration cuts of 1981 that targeted wildlife and natural resource programs for disproportionately deep budget reductions, is real. As we go to press, the funding of many wildlife programs may be in jeopardy, and every federal agency is withholding four to five percent of its budget. Already, the president's Office of Management and Budget has revised its budget projections downward for both the Bureau of Land Management and the Forest Service to accommodate the president's decision not to raise grazing fees on public lands. Without the projected increase in fees to provide receipts to the Treasury, natural resource programs will be further reduced to balance the books.

A realistic appraisal indicates that the pre-eminent issue facing all federal and state wildlife programs for the remainder of the century will be funding. For this reason, it is important that conservationists—amateurs and professionals—join the fray and forcefully advocate adequate funding for wildlife programs. We can no longer permit the faceless whittlers of pencils and numbers in government budget offices to eviscerate wildlife and conservation programs in the name of fiscal austerity. We must demonstrate that wise management of our nation's wildlife resources is not a cost but an investment in the quality of life for the future.

With the completion of this volume, we have two years of research and analysis under our belts. We have learned that, with few exceptions, inadequate funding already is eroding vital wildllife programs. In both the Forest Service and the Bureau of Land Management, fiscal support for wildlife management and research programs has declined in contrast to increased funding for commodity production activities. As a result, on-the-ground wildlife managers have difficulty even keeping abreast of developments and have virtually no chance of coping with developmental impacts on important wildlife habitats.

The Reagan administration continues to target for elimination some of the Fish and Wildlife Service's successful and cost-effective wildlife programs. For the fourth time in six years, the endangered species grants program is targeted for elimination, and, similarly, for the fourth time in six years the administration is recommending no funds for land acquisition to protect critical endangered species and migratory bird habitats. The lack of a funding mechanism for a national nongame program seriously impedes the service's ability to address population declines of many important species and hinders coordination with state nongame programs.

A major issue confronting the National Park Service is the control of exotic species within its domains. This issue is one component of a larger institutional problem—the lack of programs for effective wildlife research, natural resource inventories, and resource training programs. This problem seriously handicaps the park service's ability to respond to threats posed by both exotic species in the parks and developmental activities on the borders.

The inability of state wildlife departments to control the rise in illegal wildlife activities also is a by-product of constricted budgets. Law enforcement programs could benefit from increased forensic research and data compilation capabilities, more undercover operations, and broader application of reward programs.

Dollars and cents are the driving force behind the successful implementation of wildlife policy in this country today. We must make wildlife programs more successful in the competition for government funds. Conservation, by definition, is an investment in the future not only for mankind, but for all the world's living things. If we cannot commit ourselves adequately to protecting the resources that sustain us, our future will be bleak indeed.

The *Audubon Wildlife Report 1986* is part of a continuing attempt to aid those working to protect the future of our natural resources. The 1985 volume was well received by the conservation community, and this volume will live up to that precedent.

This year's featured agency is the U.S. Forest Service. Included here as Part One, the Forest Service chapter could stand alone as a separate book in its thorough coverage of how the service is organized and operated, what its programs seek to attain, how it is funded, and how it contends with the controversial issues that surround it.

Part Two is a comprehensive review of the major federal wildlife programs and agencies. The 1986 volume updates coverage of the agencies and programs included in last year's book. Some material from last year is included in abridged form, but readers are referred to the 1985 book for more detailed treatment of agency history and structure. New additions to Part Two are chapters on the National Marine Fisheries Service and on international wildlife conservation efforts. The chapters in this section are organized according to the outline below, with some exceptions to allow flexibility in coverage of new subjects and in updating last year's text:

- Introduction—a brief statement describing the agency or program.
- History and Legislative Authority—an examination of the federal laws that underpin the agency or program.
- Organization and Operations—an outline of agency roles and responsibilities, including organizational structure, admission, budgeting, and research.
- Current Program Trends—an examination of significant management activities and trends.
- Current Issues—discussion of the specific problems and concerns that conservationists confronted in 1983 and 1984.
- Legislation—bills enacted during the 98th Congress (1983-1984) and how they affect wildlife programs.
- Legal Developments—a discussion of significant court cases decided in recent years.
- Status of the Resource—an assessment of the resources managed by the agency or program.

Part Three begins the Audubon Wildlife Report's coverage of state wildlife conservation with an overview of state management and chapters on nongame programs and state conservation law enforcement. Part Four focuses on selected wildlife species that illustrate a full range of conservation problems, solutions, and challenges.* Written by acknowledged experts, each chapter is divided as follows:

---

* Species covered in the *Audubon Wildlife Report 1985* were the: California condor, grizzly bear, striped bass, arctic geese, wood stork, desert bighorn, Puerto Rican parrot, woodland caribou, bald eagle, green pitcher plant, West Indian manatee, Hawaiian birds.

Species Description and Natural History—what the species looks like, where and how it lives.

Significance of the Species—a discussion of its biological importance and its value to man.

Historical Perspective—an examination of the developments that led to the species' current status.

Current Trends—a discussion of the problems and successes presently affecting the species.

Management—a description of what wildlife professionals are doing to protect and preserve the species.

Prognosis—a prediction about what could happen to the species within the near future.

Recommendations—a discusssion of what should be done to ensure the species' survival.

The 1986 volume closes with an extensive appendix that includes lists of personnel contacts and government offices, budget data, the complete list of endangered and threatened species, and other information.

Any suggestions or comments for making future editions more useful should be sent to:

Amos S. Eno  
Wildlife Report Project Director  
National Audubon Society  
645 Pennsylvania Avenue  
Washington, D.C. 20003

Roger Di Silvestro  
Wildlife Report Editor  
National Audubon Society  
950 Third Avenue  
New York, New York 10022

# PART 1

◆———————◆

# The Featured
# Agency

A forester uses a diameter tape to determine the number of board feet of lumber a tree will yield.

*U.S. Forest Service*

# The U.S. Forest Service

## Katherine Barton
## and
## Whit Fosburgh

## Introduction

THE FOREST SERVICE is the largest natural-resource agency in the federal government. It has an annual budget of approximately $2 billion and employs the equivalent of nearly 39,000 full-time personnel. Its research arm is one of the largest natural-resource research organizations in the world. The Service provides technical assistance for the management of private forest and range lands all across the nation. But most important, the Forest Service manages a wealth of natural resources on 191 million acres—the National Forest System.

The National Forest System is unmatched among federal lands in its importance for wildlife and recreation. It holds some of the largest pristine areas and the majority of designated wilderness in the lower 48 states. It supports 41 percent of the recreational use on federal lands, more than any other agency. It provides habitat for about 3,000 species of fish and wildlife, contains half of the big-game and cold-water-fish habitat in the nation, and is key to the survival and recovery of many threatened and endangered species, particularly those requiring large undisturbed areas such as the grizzly bear, California condor, and gray wolf, and those inhabiting old-growth stands, such as the red-cockaded woodpecker.

At the same time, the system contains a variety of resources that support commodity uses. It accounts for about 15 percent of the total annual U.S. timber harvest and for about 23 percent of the harvest of the more heavily used softwoods. It provides about five percent of the nation's livestock grazing forage and produces a small share of the nation's energy and mineral resources, although this production is on the increase. Unlike the National Park Service or the Fish and Wildlife Service, the Forest Service is required by law to manage its lands for all these uses, with no particular use specified to receive top priority.

Until the 1950s, demands on the National Forest System were low and the conflicts relatively minor. The Forest Service was regarded widely as a leader in conservation, and it sought to expand its role in meeting the nation's outdoor recreation needs. But over the past three decades or so, recreational demand skyrocketed, timber demand shot up, new concerns arose for development of U.S. energy supplies and strategic minerals, the wilderness movement took hold, and awareness of the need for increased environmental protection blossomed. These competing and conflicting demands on the National Forest System have forced the Forest Service to make complicated and often controversial decisions about how to balance the various uses.

As conflicting demands on the system have increased, conservationists believe the Forest Service has tilted National Forest System management heavily in favor of commodity uses, particularly timber harvest. The perception that the Forest Service would sacrifice wilderness areas for timber harvest caused conservationists to push to remove wilderness protection from the discretion of the Forest Service, an effort that culminated successfully in 1964 with the passage of the Wilderness Act. Just over a decade later, conservationist outrage over extensive clearcutting on the forest system ultimately led to the passage of the National Forest Management Act, which set certain limitations and restrictions on logging and required the Forest Service to prepare comprehensive, detailed forest plans, developed with public participation, to guide the management of the forest system.

Now, a decade after the passage of the National Forest Management Act, criticisms of Forest Service mismanagement of the system are on the rise again. Although the management act and other environmental laws of the 1970s have resulted in a broader, more ecological view toward fish and wildlife management in the forest system, fish and wildlife, as well as recreation, continue to take a back seat to logging. Timber management continues to receive a far greater portion of the Forest Service budget than does any other activity. Foresters and engineers, who primarily design the roads required for logging, dominate the service both in numbers and in their position in its power structure. The Forest Service is under attack for building extensive road systems for timber production in large roadless areas of the West, particularly in areas that provide important elk habitat, even though the lands in question are not profitable timber lands. The Service has been criticized for losing money on a great number of its timber sales, a practice the service has defended as providing important nonmonetary benefits for wildlife and recreation even though virtually all wildlife and recreation interests oppose the practice. In a recent survey of knowledgeable Forest Service constituents, representing a cross-section of interests, the number one complaint about Forest Service policy was that the Service's program overemphasizes timber harvest and road building. The most often cited recommendation for changing National Forest System Management is that the service should place all resources on the same level, increasing noncommodity uses and associated funding and staff to create a more balanced program (Forest Service 1985, pp. 3-6).

As the initial drafts of the forest plans required by the National Forest Management Act have been released over the past couple of years, this perceived pro-timber bias has been reinforced. Many of the draft plans project a doubling, tripling, or even quadrupling of timber-sales levels during the 40- to 50-year period addressed in the plans. Extensive road construction is projected for currently roadless areas in several regions. Plans have been criticized for a number of other reasons, including proposals for extensive use of clearcutting, making inadequate wilderness recommendations, increasing below-cost sales and failing to designate uneconomic timber stands as unsuitable for timber harvest, and giving inadequate attention to maintaining wildlife diversity.

Critical decisions about fish and wildlife management on the National Forest System are being made now and will continue to be made over the next several years. Questions about how much old-growth habitat will be maintained, the extent of roading in undisturbed areas, levels of timber sales and intensity of timber management, and what types of fish and wildlife species will be emphasized and at what population levels they will be maintained are being answered for the next 10 to 15 years in the forest plans. The finalization and implementation of the plans will show whether they can be used to restore balance to the system's management and provide the tool for resolving conflicts over competing demands on the system, as envisioned by the National Forest Management Act.

## History and Legislative Authority

When the first colonists arrived in America, half of the country was covered with forest—a vast and seemingly endless resource. As the nation grew and new areas of the continent came into the hands of the United States government, there was little thought of conserving them. Instead, to raise money for the new government and to encourage settlement of the growing country, Congress moved to dispose of these lands—initially by attempting to sell them and, when selling proved slow and ineffective, by simply granting lands to states, to railroad companies, and to settlers through myriad homesteading laws.

Although well intentioned, these policies often were unsound and poorly implemented. Land speculators, miners, and loggers abused the homestead laws to gain control of valuable resources or large blocks of land. In many cases, even legitimate use of the homesteading laws resulted in destruction of the land, especially in the arid West where the agricultural focus of the laws led to farming on erosion-prone lands and to extensive overgrazing on millions of acres of rangeland.*

## The Early Reserves

***The Forest Reserve Act of 1891.*** The movement to conserve the nation's natural resources began toward the latter half of the 19th century, focusing on the rapidly disappearing forests. As early as 1868, the commissioner of the General Land Office—the agency within the Department of the Interior that managed land disposals—predicted that in 40 to 50 years the forests of the United States would have disappeared and those of Canada would be approaching exhaustion. By the end of the century, the logging industry had cut over forests in the Northeast, the Great Lakes states, and the South, and moved into the Northwest.

Pressure for action began to build. By 1876, the first bill to reserve a portion of the public forests was introduced in Congress, and, in the same year, a rider on an appropriations bill authorized the secretary of Agriculture to conduct a study on future timber needs and methods for forest preservation and renewal. The Agriculture Department established a forestry division to carry out the study and, in 1878, the resulting report endorsed the concept of forest reserves. By 1886, Congress statutorily recognized the Division of Forestry. Bernhard H. Fernow, a German forester who had been secretary of the American Forestry Association, was made the division's first chief.

Congress debated the idea of forest reserves for more than a decade, during which more than 200 reserve bills were introduced. But when the Forest Reserve Act finally was enacted in 1891 (Act of March 3, 1891, Ch. 561, 26 Stat. 1103, repealed 1976), it passed without fanfare. The Reserve Act was added in conference to a lengthy statute revising the land laws and passed Congress with little debate. The reserve provision simply authorized the president to reserve any public lands covered with timber or undergrowth, whether of commercial value or not.

***The Organic Administration Act of 1897.*** Within two years after the passage of the Reserve Act, presidents William Henry Harrison and Grover Cleveland had established more than 17 million acres of reserves. The Reserve Act, however, lacked any provision for protection, administration, or use of the reserves and was interpreted by the Interior Department as prohibiting any type of utilization. Under pressure from settlers, miners, stock raisers, and loggers who wanted access to the reserves, Cleveland stopped reserving forest

* Much of the information in the following discussion is drawn from *Forest and Range Policy,* by Samuel Dana and Sally Fairfax, 1980.

lands to give Congress the opportunity to enact legislation providing for their management. But Congress was slow to act, and Cleveland, just before leaving office in 1897, created 13 new reserves totaling 21.3 million acres, more than doubling the existing acreage.

Cleveland's action angered Congress and brought immediate legislative action. During a special session convened under newly inaugurated President William McKinley to deal with lapsing appropriations, Congress added an amendment to the appropriations bill providing for administration of the forest reserves, the Organic Administration Act of 1897 (Act of June 4, 1897, Ch. 2, 30 Stat. 11, currently codified at 16 U.S.C.A. 473-475, 477-482, 551).

The Organic Act defined the purposes of the forest reserves: to improve and protect the forest, to secure favorable water flows, and to furnish a continuous supply of timber for the use of the citizens of the United States. It placed the reserves under the management of the secretary of the Interior, who was authorized to establish rules for their protection, occupancy, and use. The act authorized the president to modify or revoke existing reservations and extended the public domain mining laws to the forest reserves. It also authorized the selling of timber "for the purposes of preserving the living growing timber . . . under rules he shall prescribe." Cutting was limited to "the dead, matured or large growth of trees" found on the reserves—a limitation that came back to haunt the Service in the clear-cutting debate of the 1970s.

***The Early Forest Service.*** The Department of the Interior quickly implemented the new law, issuing regulations within a few months. Appropriations were first approved in 1898, and the General Land Office established a forestry division in 1901.

At the same time, the Department of Agriculture also was advancing its forestry research and technical assistance efforts under the energetic and charismatic leadership of Gifford Pinchot. Three years after Pinchot took charge of the Agriculture Department's Division of Forestry in 1898, he had increased its budget from $28,520 to $185,440 and its staff from 11 to 179. He began campaigning, with the support of his friend and fellow conservationist President Theodore Roosevelt, to have the reserves transferred to the Department of Agriculture. The exposure of land frauds carried out under the General Land Office's administration of the public land disposal laws aided Pinchot's arguments, and in 1905, Congress transferred administration of the reserves from Interior to Agriculture. It also provided a secure source of funding for their management by requiring that receipts from the forests be used for forest protection for the next five years. Later that year, the Department of Agriculture's Bureau of Forestry was renamed the Forest Service.

Pinchot moved quickly to carry out his new responsibilities. He reorganized the Forest Service to place responsibility for administration, as far as practicable, in the hands of local and regional officers, establishing the basic management structure that remains today. The Forest Service required permits for grazing livestock in the forests, began to charge grazing fees, and conducted timber sales.

With Pinchot managing the national forests, the philosophy of their use moved away from preservation toward "wise use," which Pinchot often described as "that which would provide the greatest good for the greatest number for the longest time." Pinchot's emphasis was on practical forestry through the silvicultural approach of planting and harvesting trees.

Pinchot's philosophy, as well as that of most foresters at the time, was based largely on the idea that forests should be managed for sustained yield—a concept that was drawn from European and especially German forestry. The first three chiefs of Agriculture's forestry program—Fernow, Pinchot, and Henry Graves—were all trained in Europe, and the early forestry schools at Cornell and Yale were headed by foresters trained on German forestry concepts. In Europe, with scarce forest resources and dense population, the basic assumptions in forest management were that wood was scarce and that there would always be a stable demand for its products, which led to the belief that the consumption of wood must be limited to the growth potential of the forest and that lands that are harvested would be replanted and managed under silvicultural practices for future reharvests.

The adoption by the American forestry profession of European forestry concepts, which continues to this day, has been criticized by many outside the Forest Service. Dana and Fairfax (1980) charge that the fear of "timber famine" led to the belief that every available acre had to be used for growing trees regardless of the investment necessary. This resulted in economically inefficient management practices on some Forest Service lands and unrealistic expectations by some Forest Service personnel—particularly Pinchot—as to how private landowners should manage their lands. They also charge that the emphasis on growing trees in the present day has overwhelmed consideration of other uses: "Nontimber uses of the forests have been covered by parity of logic or force of necessity, but the basic preoccupation with physical supply and unrelenting demand and remains" (Dana and Fairfax 1980, p. 53). Many environmentalists say that the Service throughout its history has called for increases in timber harvest to meet shortages that have never occurred, to the detriment of other forest uses. The Service, however, points to numerous current studies predicting sharp increases in demand for timber over the next 50 years.

*Attacks on the System.* In spite of some criticisms today of his practices, there is no question that Pinchot, teamed with President Roosevelt, significantly advanced the National Forest System, particularly by setting aside the bulk of the land that forms the system today. By the time Roosevelt left office, he had created 132 million acres of park and forest reserves.

But this aggressive administration of the national forests fostered hostility among many westerners, who now began to attack the system. First they began tapping national forest receipts, which the Forest Service was using to support the system. In 1907 and 1908, Congress directed that 75 percent of annual gross receipts be turned over to the federal treasury. The remaining 25 percent was to be turned over to the states or territories for the benefit of the public schools and roads of the counties in which the forests were located, and the use of national forest receipts by the Forest Service was abolished. Congress also prohibited the creation of forest reserves, except by act of Congress, in Colorado, Idaho, Montana, Oregon, Washington, and Wyoming, states containing the nation's heaviest timber stands. Roosevelt, who opposed this prohibition but did not want to veto the appropriations bill to which it was attached, first created another 16 million acres of reserves and then signed the bill.

In 1909, Roosevelt was succeeded by President William Howard Taft, and the aggressive conservation era of Pinchot and Roosevelt came to an end. Not only was Taft less assertive than Roosevelt in using his executive powers, but he also replaced Roosevelt's Interior Secretary James Garfield—a friend of Pinchot's—with Richard Ballinger, a former commissioner of the General Land Office. Pinchot went on the offensive to discredit Ballinger publicly over some land fraud problems and was dismissed by Taft in 1910. Attacks continued against the Forest Service, which was under pressure to open the forests to homestead entry and to cede land to the states. Several million acres of the national forests were lost through homesteading and boundary adjustments, but in general these attacks met with little success, and the system remained intact.

## Eastern National Forests

In the meantime, interest was growing in establishing national forests in the East. However, because little public domain acreage existed in the East, the land would have to be purchased by the federal government rather than simply reserved.

The idea to purchase large blocks of lands in the East first arose in the 1880s. Congress appropriated funds to investigate the possibility in 1900 and again in 1907. Numerous bills were introduced in the early 1900s to acquire various areas, including the southern Appalachians, the White Mountains, the watershed of the Potomac River, the Ozarks, the head of the Mississippi and Red Rivers, and the Hudson River highlands. In general, these lands had been cut over, farmed, and abandoned. They posed flood hazards because of their inability to retain water, and posed fire hazards because of heavy debris left from wasteful logging practices. The timber industry, now stuck with paying taxes on much of these cut-over, unreforested lands, generally pressed for government acquisition.

In 1911, Congress passed the Weeks Act (Act of March 1, 1911, Ch. 186, 36 Stat. [961 currently codified at scattered sections in 16 U.S.C.A. 480-563]), which authorized appropriations for Forest Service land acquisition. Acquisition authority was limited to lands located on the headwaters of navigable streams, since there was concern that unless this authority were limited to lands clearly related to interstate commerce, the legislation would be found unconstitutional. The secretary of Agriculture was authorized to establish purchase boundaries and, when sufficient acreage was acquired within an area, to declare it a national forest. Lands could be purchased only with the consent of the legislature of the state in which the lands were located, but such purchases generally were approved without conflict.

In 1924, the Clarke-McNary Act (Act of June 7, 1924, Ch. 348, 43 Stat. 653 [currently codified at scattered sections in 16 U.S.C.A. 499-570]) amended the Weeks law and expanded acquisition authority to include forested or cut-over lands *anywhere* within the watershed of navigable streams and permitted the purchase of land for timber production as well. Today, national forests in the East total approximately 24 million acres, most of them established prior to World War II.

## World War I to World War II

World War I brought hard times to the national forests. Rangelands were overgrazed for meat production, and all research investigations not concerned with the war effort were halted. But the 1930s were in many ways an active period for the National Forest System. In 1930, Congress passed the Knutson-Vandenberg Act (Act of June 9, 1930, Ch. 416, 46 Stat. 527 [currently codified at 16 U.S.C.A. 576-576B]) to speed up reforestation and improve silvicultural practices in the national forests. The law authorized appropriations for the operation of nurseries and the establishment of tree plantations. Most significantly, it authorized the secretary of Agriculture to require timber purchasers to make deposits to a special fund in the Treasury to cover the costs of reforesting the area they cut. The Knutson-Vandenberg Act was amended in 1976 by the National Forest Management Act (16 U.S.C.A. 576b) to allow use of these funds for other resource improvements, including improvements for fish and wildlife.

The Depression also proved a boon for the National Forest System, as efforts to get people back to work focused on America's public lands. Shortly after President Franklin D. Roosevelt's election in 1932, the Civilian Conservation Corps was established. More than 200,000 men were enrolled in forestry camps. They fought fires, planted trees, implemented soil and water conservation practices, and eventually moved into construction of trails and facilities.

This period, however, also was characterized by bitter feuding between the Forest Service and the Park Service as empire-building Interior Secretary Harold Ickes sought to raid the national forests. Ickes proposed to establish a Department of Conservation, which would include the Forest Service, an idea that has cropped up repeatedly in various forms ever since. When it became clear that he was not going to get wholesale authority over the National Forest System, Ickes expanded the Park Service's authority through a reorganization plan that placed all national monuments—including some managed by the Forest Service—and other historic sites under its purview, doubling the number of areas within its jurisdiction. Ickes further increased the animosity between the two agencies by assigning the National Park Service the authority for compiling a survey of national recreational resources, a report that identified 14 areas within national forests that should be added to existing parks or established as new ones.

## Recreation and Wilderness

In the end, the Forest Service lost only a few small areas to the Park Service, but the threat of massive land transfers helped prompt the Forest Service to increase and more heavily promote recreational use of its lands.* Interest in recreation on the national forests had blossomed after World War I, in part because of the new mobility provided by the automobile. As early as 1920, Forest Service chiefs had begun calling for a national recreation policy, but were unable to secure congressional appropriations to pay for recreational programs.

Also during the 1920s, some within the service—led by Arthur Carhart, the service's first landscape architect, and Aldo Leopold, then a forester on the Gila National Forest in New Mexico—began pressing for protection of forest roadless areas. The Gila was designated the first primitive area in 1924. In 1929, the Forest Service promulgated regulations, called the L-20 regulations, setting criteria and procedures for establishing primitive areas, although the regulations were unclear as to what uses were to be allowed on such areas.

By 1932, the Forest Service chief had issued a memorandum classifying recreation as a major use of the national forests equal to other uses. Pressure for wilderness designations continued to build through another famous conservationist, Bob Marshall, who headed the Service's newly established Recreation and Lands Division from 1937 to 1939. Under Marshall's guidance, the Service established tougher wilderness regulations—the U-Regulations—which established three categories of roadless areas and specified that no roads, timber harvesting, motorized transportation, or occupancy under special-use permits would be permitted on lands classified by the Forest Service as wilderness. Marshall died two months after the rules were adopted.

After World War II, the country experienced another recreation boom, and the Forest Service, not to be outdone by the Park Service's massive postwar rehabilitation effort known as Mission 66, undertook its own accelerated

* In fact, many who have studied federal bureaucracies believe that the competition between the Forest Service and the National Park Service has improved the performance of both.

The National Forest System

recreation program, Operation Outdoors, which brought the agency increased appropriations for recreation and put the program on sounder footing. The Forest Service was so intent on capturing the recreational high ground that when Congress passed the Multiple-Use Sustained-Yield Act in 1960, the service rewrote the list of multiple uses in the act to ensure that outdoor recreation would come first.*

At the same time, however, the Forest Service and wilderness advocates were parting ways. Wilderness classification proceeded slowly under the U-Regulations, although the primitive areas were managed in the interim as if they were protected by these rules. In addition, after World War II, pressures for commodity development as well as recreation increased, and the Forest Service began to increase timber-harvest levels rapidly. Wilderness supporters feared the Service would begin to allow cutting in roadless areas. The issue came to a head in 1954, when the Service proposed to eliminate 53,000 acres from the Three Sisters Primitive Area in Oregon to open it to timber harvest.

Wilderness advocates, now convinced they could not count on the Service to protect roadless areas, turned to Congress. The first wilderness bill was introduced in 1956, and the National Wilderness Preservation Act (16 U.S.C.A. 1131-1136) finally was passed in 1964. It provided instant wilderness designation for areas classified as wilderness or wild areas under the U-Regulations and directed the Service to survey for wilderness suitability any areas classified as primitive. In 1975, Congress ensured that the smaller, less pristine areas of the eastern national forests were eligible for wilderness protection with the enactment of the Eastern Wilderness Act (16 U.S.C.A. 1132 (note)).†

## Multiple Use and Modern Day Management

*Multiple-Use Sustained-Yield Act.* The growing pressures on the national forests after World War II to meet competing demands eventually caused the Forest Service to seek legislation confirming its multiple-use management authority, particularly since a number of forest uses, such as recreation and wildlife habitat, were not specifically provided for in the Organic Act. In 1960, Congress responded by passing the Multiple-Use Sustained-Yield Act (16 U.S.C.A. 528-531), which established the policy that the national forests be administered for outdoor recreation, range, timber, watershed, and fish and wildlife purposes. Mining was not included in the list, but the law specified that it was not intended to affect current policies allowing such use. The act directed the secretary of Agriculture to "develop and administer the renewable surface resources of the national forests for multiple use and sus-

---

* The order of the list in practice never has been given any weight by the Service, Congress, or the courts.
† See the Recreation and Wilderness Management section for more details on the Wilderness Act and subsequent wilderness reviews.

tained yield," and gave the definition of multiple-use that the Forest Service still uses today:

> ". . . the management of all the various renewable surface resources of the national forests so that they are utilized in the combination that will best meet the needs of the American people; making the most judicious use of the land for some or all of these resources or related services over areas large enough to provide sufficient latitude for periodic adjustments in use to conform to changing needs and conditions; that some land will be used for less than all of the resources; and harmonious and coordinated management of the various resources, each with the other, without impairment of the productivity of the land, with consideration being given to the relative values of the various resources, and not necessarily the combination of uses that will give the greatest dollar return or the greatest unit output."

*Other Environmental Laws Affecting Forest Management.* The Multiple-Use Sustained-Yield Act, while congressionally mandating multiple-use management of the forests, gave no standards as to how to resolve issues of competing and incompatible uses, and the controversy over national forest management continued and grew. In the meantime, the burgeoning environmental movement led to the passage of a number of environmental laws that affected forest management, including the Clean Water Act, the Clean Air Act, the Endangered Species Act, the Federal Insecticide, Fungicide, and Rodenticide Act, and amendments to the Sikes Act regarding wildlife management.*

Most important of these new laws was the National Environmental Policy Act of 1969 (42 U.S.C.A. 4321-4361), which required federal agencies to analyze in detail the environmental impacts of any "major federal action significantly affecting the quality of the human environment." This led to the environmental assessment process and the creation of environmental impact statements, which are incorporated today throughout the Forest Service's planning process. It also institutionalized public participation in decision making at all agency levels. In addition, the requirement that agencies review their programs and policies to determine if they are consistent with the National Environmental Policy Act eventually caused the Forest Service for the first time to regulate surface activities conducted under the 1872 Mining Law.†

*Forest and Rangeland Renewable Resources Planning Act.* In the same year that the National Environmental Policy Act was passed, timber prices increased dramatically, causing a new round of controversy over national forest management. The timber industry tried to push legislation that would ensure a steady timber supply and require long-range planning for national

---

* These laws are discussed further in subsequent sections.
† Covered in the Energy and Minerals Management section.

forest management by the Forest Service. Environmental groups blocked the timber proposals but supported the planning requirement, as did Congress, which wanted more accountability in the Forest Service budget.

The result was the Forest and Rangeland Renewable Resources Planning Act of 1974 (P.L. 93-378, 88 Stat. 476 [currently codified at 16 U.S.C.A. 1600-1614]), commonly called the Resources Planning Act. The act established the basic planning system under which the Forest Service operates today. The Resources Planning Act required the Forest Service to prepare three types of planning documents: an assessment of the status and needs of forest and rangeland resources every 10 years; a 50-year program projecting management levels and budget requests to be updated every five years; and individual land-management plans for units of the National Forest System to be updated every 15 years.*

***National Forest Management Act.*** While the Resources Planning Act generally addressed how the Forest Service should plan its management activities, it ignored the brewing controversy over the more serious question of what those activities should be. Public outrage grew as timber harvesting moved increasingly into previously uncut areas, and the controversy broke loose over extensive clearcutting, particularly on the Bitterroot National Forest in Montana and the Monongahela National Forest in West Virginia. After multiple congressional hearings on the issue, Senator Frank Church (R-ID) developed a set of nonbinding recommendations—urging moderation, care, and environmental protection in clearcutting—which were accepted by the Forest Service. But conservationists in West Virginia were not satisfied, and they went to court under the auspices of the Izaak Walton League of America. The plaintiffs argued that clearcutting was illegal under the provision of the Organic Act that limited harvesting to "dead, mature, or large growth of trees" that had been marked and designated by the Forest Service. The court agreed and enjoined the Forest Service from cutting on the Monongahela until the Service's practices matched the law. Similar cases were brought against clearcutting on other forests across the nation, leading some to fear that all harvesting would be halted if the law were not changed.

After a contentious battle, Congress passed the National Forest Management Act of 1976 (P.L. 94-588, 90 Stat. 2949, [16 U.S.C.A. 1601-1614]), which was primarily a series of amendments to the Resources Planning Act. In response to timber industry concerns, the National Forest Management Act deleted the language from the Organic Act that had been interpreted as prohibiting clearcutting. In response to environmentalists concerns, the act contained a number of restrictions on timber management—including requirements regarding clearcutting, logging on marginal lands, maintenance

---

* Resources Planning Act planning requirements are discussed in the Forest Administration section under "Planning."

of animal and plant species diversity, and rotation ages—although these requirements and restrictions are qualified by numerous exemptions and exceptions.*

Over the past 10 years, the Forest Service has moved to implement the planning requirements of the Resources Planning Act and the National Forest Management Act and currently is in the process of releasing drafts of the required forest plans for public comment and of finalizing others. On the legislative and legal front, the designation of wilderness dominated the center of controversy over the past several years, although this battle at least temporarily died down with the passage in 1984 of a number of state wilderness bills that added seven million acres to the National Forest Wilderness System.

As the individual forest plans are being released, public controversy is once again focusing on basic questions of how the forests should be managed. Already there have been some suggestions that the National Forest Management Act fails to provide sufficient guidance to the Forest Service and needs to be amended. There have been numerous appeals of Forest Service plans that could lead to lawsuits over the meaning of some of the law's basic provisions. The Forest Service is under fire for selling timber at a loss on a number of forests, for constructing roads in roadless areas released from wilderness study, for proposing substantially increased logging on many forests, and for continuing to harvest old-growth forests. It is a pivotal period for the Forest Service and the National Forest System—one that could determine whether the planning system alone can resolve the ongoing controversies over forest management or whether yet another round of litigation and legislation will follow.

## Forest Service Administration

### Organization and Responsibilities

Although the other major federal land-managing agencies are within the Department of the Interior, the Forest Service is within Department of Agriculture, due in part to historical accident: The first congressional mandate for study on the nation's forests was included in an amendment to a Department of Agriculture appropriations bill. The Service is headed by a chief, who has always been a forestry professional promoted through Forest Service ranks. The chief reports to the assistant secretary for Natural Resources and Environment, a political appointee who oversees the Soil Conservation Service as well.

The Forest Service chief is assisted in the Washington headquarters by five deputy chiefs. There is one deputy chief for each of the service's three main programs: Forest Research, the National Forest System, and State and

---

* Detailed requirements of the National Forest Management Act are discussed in subsequent sections.

Forest Service Staff Organization

Richard E. Lyng
Secretary of Agriculture
(202) 447-6158

Peter Myers
Assistant Secretary for Natural
Resources and the Environment
(202) 447-7173

Donald S. Girton
Director, Office of Information
(202) 447-3760

F. Dale Robertson
Associate Chief, Forest Service
(202) 447-7491

R. Max Peterson
Chief, Forest Service
(202) 447-6661

John H. Ohman
Deputy Chief, State and Private
Forestry
(202) 447-6657

J. Lamar Beasley
Deputy Chief, NFS
(202) 447-3523

Jeff M. Sirmon
Deputy Chief, Programs and Legislation
(202) 447-6663

Robert E. Buckman
Deputy Chief, Research
(202) 447-6665

Jerome A. Miles
Deputy Chief, Administration
(202) 447-6707

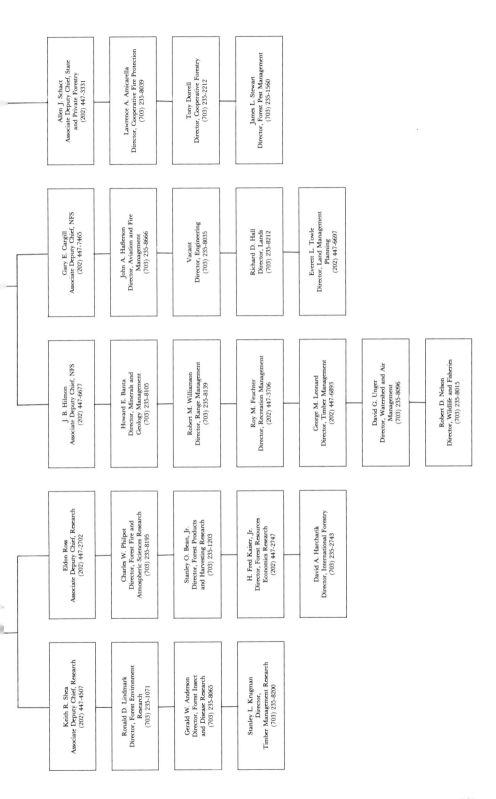

Allen J. Schact
Associate Deputy Chief, State
and Private Forestry
(202) 447-3331

Lawrence A. Amicarella
Director, Cooperative Fire Protection
(703) 235-8039

Tony Dorrell
Director, Cooperative Forestry
(703) 235-2212

James L. Stewart
Director, Forest Pest Management
(703) 235-1560

Gary E. Cargill
Associate Deputy Chief, NFS
(202) 447-7465

John A. Hafterson
Director, Aviation and Fire
Management
(703) 235-8666

Vacant
Director, Engineering
(703) 235-8035

Richard D. Hall
Director, Lands
(703) 235-8212

Everett L. Towle
Director, Land Management
Planning
(202) 447-6697

J. B. Hilmon
Associate Deputy Chief, NFS
(202) 447-6677

Howard E. Banta
Director, Minerals and
Geology Management
(703) 235-8105

Robert M. Williamson
Director, Range Management
(703) 235-8139

Roy M. Feuchter
Director, Recreation Management
(202) 447-3706

George M. Leonard
Director, Timber Management
(202) 447-6893

David G. Unger
Director, Watershed and Air
Management
(703) 235-8096

Robert D. Nelson
Director, Wildlife and Fisheries
(703) 235-8015

Eldon Ross
Associate Deputy Chief, Research
(202) 447-2702

Charles W. Philpot
Director, Forest Fire and
Atmospheric Sciences Research
(703) 235-8195

Stanley O. Bean, Jr.
Director, Forest Products
and Harvesting Research
(703) 235-1203

H. Fred Kaiser, Jr.
Director, Forest Resources
Economics Research
(202) 447-2747

David A. Harcharik
Director, International Forestry
(703) 235-2743

Keith R. Shea
Associate Deputy Chief, Research
(202) 447-4507

Ronald D. Lindmark
Director, Forest Environment
Research
(703) 235-1071

Gerald W. Anderson
Director, Forest Insect
and Disease Research
(703) 235-8065

Stanley L. Krugman
Director,
Timber Management Research
(703) 235-8200

Private Forestry. In addition, there is a deputy chief for Programs and Legislation who supervises budgeting, the National Environment Policy Act compliance, policy analysis, legislative matters, and the preparation of the Resources Planning Act Program and Assessment. There is also a deputy chief for Administration, who oversees the Service's various administrative functions as well as the Human Resources program.

*Major Programs.* The Forest Service categorizes most of its activities under three major program areas. The largest is the National Forest System, which includes all activities related to the system's management, such as the development of forest plans, land acquisition and administration, and management of the various resources—timber, energy and minerals, range, fish and wildlife, outdoor recreation and wilderness, and watersheds. The Forest Research Program, the second largest program, conducts and funds forest and rangeland research to aid in improved management of these resources throughout the United States, including but not limited to the National Forest System. Through the State and Private Forestry Program, the smallest of the three program areas, the Forest Service cooperates with state and local governments, forest industries, and other private landowners and forest users in the management, protection, and development of 877 million acres of forest and rangeland in nonfederal ownership. Activities carried out under each of these programs are covered in detail in subsequent chapters.

The Service also has a fourth, very small program—the Human Resources Program. Because it is a minor and declining program, it is not covered in detail elsewhere in this chapter, but is worth a mention here. The Human Resources program currently consists of three main efforts: The Job Corps, the Senior Community Service Employment Program, and the Youth Conservation Corps. Both the Job Corps and the Senior Community Service programs are funded through the Labor Department. Under the Job Corps, the Forest Service administers 18 Civilian Conservation Centers for disadvantaged youth between ages 16 and 22. In 1984, the $43.1 million program funded participation of more than 7,000 youths. The Senior Community Service Employment Program is designed to provide part-time employment and training for the low-income elderly while providing community service to the public. From July 1, 1983, to June 30, 1984, the $21.1 million program employed approximately 5,900 people. The Youth Conservation Corps has been nearly eliminated in recent years, but in the past two years, Congress directed the Forest Service to reprogram $3.5 million of National Forest System funds to keep this program going. In 1984, some 2,000 youths in Youth Conservation Corps summer jobs with the Forest Service accomplished $4.8 million worth of work.

In addition to these three programs, the Forest Service also conducts several efforts that receive no appropriated funds. This includes Volunteers in the National Forests, a general volunteer program that in 1984 attracted 43,500 participants who contributed work valued at $23.4 million. It also runs a special volunteer program, the Touch America Project, in which private organizations sponsor youths between the ages of 14 and 17 to gain job experience and environmental awareness while working on public lands. Some 7,000 youths participated in 1984. Finally, the Forest Service provides conservation work opportunities for participants in programs administered primarily by state and local governments, such as the Job Training Partnership Act, college work study, vocational work study, and work incentive. In 1984, more than 6,500 people participated in these programs, accomplishing 744 person-years of work worth $9.5 million.

*Organization of the National Forest System.* Each of the Service's three major programs has a slightly different staff and field structure. The organizational structure for the Forest Research and State and Private Forestry programs are covered in the sections on those topics. This section covers the organizational structure of the National Forest System, through which the vast majority of Forest Service activities take place.

The National Forest System includes 191 million acres in 156 national forests, 19 national grasslands, and a number of other smaller land units located in 44 states, Puerto Rico, and the Virgin Islands. The system comprises about a third of the federal land in the United States and includes such diverse areas as glacier fields, forests, range and grasslands, lakes and streams, and tropical rain forests. The national forests make up the bulk of the system, 186.4 million acres. The national grasslands comprise 3.8 million acres. The system also includes various other relatively small parcels of land that may or may not be near the national forests, including 46,000 acres of land-utilization projects purchased under the Bankhead-Jones Farm Tenant Act, 118,000 acres of research and experimental areas, and 111,000 acres of "purchase units"—government lands under the jurisdiction of Department of Agriculture and placed under the Forest Service for land-management purposes. Approximately 166.5 million acres, 87 percent of the system, are located in the West and Alaska; 24.2 million acres are in the East.

National forests in the East differ in some important ways from those west of the Mississippi. Most of the forest system in the West, with the exception of the national grasslands, was established by reserving lands from the public domain and consists of large blocks of federal holdings. Most of the forests in the East were purchased by the federal government from private owners and are still intermingled with numerous parcels of private land. In fact, only slightly more than half of the land within national forest boundaries in the East is owned by the federal government, a situation that often contributes to management problems. Management of eastern national forests is complicated further because even on many of those lands owned by the

Forest Service Field Staff Organization

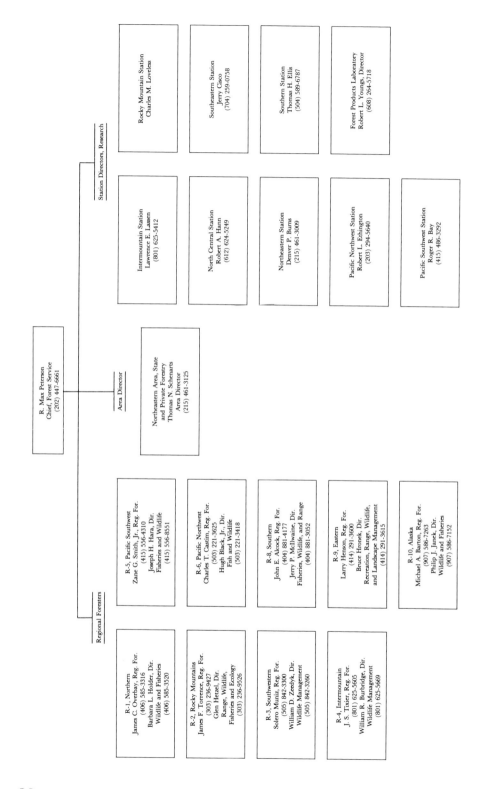

government, certain private rights were reserved at the time of purchase, giving private individuals right of access to certain resources, most notably coal, oil, and gas.

One other important difference is that in many western states, the National Forest System accounts for a substantial percentage of all forested lands—from 26 percent in Arizona to 80 percent in Idaho. In the East, the vast majority of forest land remains in private hands: six eastern states have no national forests;* in the other eastern states, national forests account for from 0.2 percent of the forest acreage in Maine to a high of 13.8 percent in Minnesota.

At the national headquarters, the National Forest System is overseen by a deputy chief, who supervises 10 staff divisions: air and watershed management—which also is responsible for soil management; wildlife and fisheries management; minerals and geology management; range management; recreation management—which includes wilderness and cultural resources; timber management; aviation and fire management; lands—which includes boundary disputes, exchanges, land classifications, and special-use permits; land management planning; and engineering. Activities of the various staffs are covered in subsequent sections.

The National Forest System is divided into nine regions, numbered 1 through 10:†

1. Northern Region (Montana, North Dakota, and parts of Idaho, South Dakota, and Wyoming).
2. Rocky Mountain Region (Colorado, Kansas, Nebraska, and parts of South Dakota and Wyoming).
3. Southwestern Region (Arizona and New Mexico).
4. Intermountain Region (Nevada, Utah, and parts of Idaho and Wyoming).
5. Pacific Southwest Region (California and Hawaii).
6. Pacific Northwest Region (Oregon and Washington).
8. Eastern Region (Illinois, Indiana, Maine, Michigan, Minnesota, Missouri, New Hampshire, New York, Ohio, Pennsylvania, Vermont, West Virginia, Wisconsin).
9. Southern Region (Alabama, Arkansas, Florida, Georgia, Kentucky, Louisiana, Mississippi, North Carolina, Oklahoma, Puerto Rico, South Carolina, Tennessee, Texas, Virginia).
10. Alaska Region (Alaska).

Each region is supervised by a regional forester, who is the line officer responsible for administration of all activities in the region except for research and, in

---

* Connecticut (which has only an experimental area), Delaware, Maryland, Massachusetts, New Jersey, Rhode Island.
† Region 7 recently was combined with Regions 8 and 9.

the East, state and private forestry, and has considerable authority over management on the National Forest System lands under his jurisdiction. Regional foresters report directly to the chief of the Forest Service. Below the regional foresters are the forest supervisors, who generally are responsible for a single forest, although a supervisor also may oversee a neighboring national grassland or land utilization project. In a few cases, two or more forests have been combined under the supervision of a single forest supervisor.

Each forest is divided into several ranger districts, the number of districts depending upon the size and needs of the forest. There are more than 600 districts with an average size of about 295,000 acres. The district is headed by a district ranger who is in charge of the daily management of his or her section of the forest.

At each of the field levels, the responsible supervisors are assisted by a variety of staff divisions. The regions, for example, have staff for timber, range and wildlife, fire control, lands, recreation, watersheds, and engineering. Below the regional level, staffs may be fairly small. Each forest has at least one fisheries or wildlife biologist, but less than half the districts have a biologist on staff.

*Congressional Oversight of Forest Service Programs.* Different congressional committees oversee Forest Service activities depending on the subject area and on whether the lands in question were reserved from the public domain or were acquired from private owners. In general, forests created from the public domain are overseen by the House Interior and Insular Affairs Committee and the Senate Energy and Natural Resources Committee. Within the House Interior Committee jurisdiction is split between the Subcommittee on General Oversight, Northwest Power and Forest Management and the Subcommittee on Public Lands. Within the Senate Energy Committee, the responsible subcommittee is the Subcommittee on Public Lands, Reserved Waters, and Resource Conservation. Acquired national forests and other general forestry matters are overseen in the House by the Agriculture Committee—specifically the Subcommittee on Forests, Family Farms, and Energy—and in the Senate by the Committee on Agriculture, Nutrition, and Forestry—specifically the Subcommittee on Agricultural Research, Conservation and Forestry, and General Legislation.

Forest Service appropriations, since they deal with land management and conservation issues, are included each year in the Interior and related agencies appropriations bill and are under the jurisdiction of the Interior Subcommittees of both the House and Senate Appropriations Committees. The annual Agriculture appropriations bill includes other Agriculture Department budget items, including the Soil Conservation Service, but does not include the Forest Service.

Other committees and subcommittees may share jurisdiction over questions dealing with specific resources on the National Forest System. For example, wildlife policy generally is handled by the Senate Subcommittee on Environmental Pollution of the Committee on Environment and Public Works and by the House Subcommittee on Fisheries and Wildlife Conservation and the Environment of the Committee on Merchant Marine and Fisheries. These committees may address matters of wildlife management and protection on the national forests as well as on other federal lands. Other committees may oversee issues such as mining, recreation, and water development on the national forests.

## Planning

The passage of the Forest and Rangeland Renewable Resources Planning Act in 1974 and the National Forest Management Act in 1976 launched the Forest Service on a massive effort to prepare long-range comprehensive plans for carrying out its responsibilities. Planning occurs at three levels within the Forest Service: national, regional, and forest. At the national level, the Forest Service is required to prepare two documents: a renewable-resource *assessment* describing the nation's overall renewable resource situation—including both private and government lands—and a renewable-resource *program* outlining 50-year goals and objectives for the Forest Service's three major programs: the National Forest System, State and Private Forestry, and Research. At the regional level, the *regional guides* tentatively allocate the Resources Planning Act program goals to the individual forests, establish standards and guidelines for forest planning within the region, and help coordinate management of the National Forest System with the state and private forestry and research programs. Below the regional level, the individual *forest plans* determine specifically how the lands and resources of the National Forest System will be managed to meet the goals of the Resources Planning Act program. The most important element of the planning effort for fish and wildlife is the preparation of land management plans for the individual forests. Critical decisions that will determine for the next decade or longer what types of fish and wildlife will thrive on a forest and at what population levels are being made now in these forest plans.

The Resources Planning Act program, the regional guides, and the forest plans all must follow several general requirements. They must meet the requirements of the National Environmental Policy Act and thus require the preparation of a draft and final environmental impact statement. Public participation in the development of each of the three documents is required by both Resources Planning Act and National Environmental Policy Act and is a critical part of the planning process. In addition, both regional guides and forest plans must be developed with the aid of "interdisciplinary teams" of Forest Service professionals to ensure that the physical, biological, economic, and social sciences and the environmental design arts are integrated in the planning process.

*National Planning.* National-level planning proceeds in two steps. First, the Forest Service prepares the "Resources Planning Act Assessment," which describes the nation's renewable resource situation, projects future supplies of and demands for these resources, and identifies opportunities to increase their yield. The most recent assessment was prepared in 1979 and was updated by a supplement in 1984 to aid in the development of the 1985 Resources Planning Act program. The next full-scale assessment is due in 1989 and must be updated every 10 years thereafter.

Based on the findings of the assessment, the Forest Service develops a recommended "Resources Planning Act Program." The program identifies annual program outputs and benefits over a 40- to 50-year period, including, for example, the amount of timber to be offered for sale, acres to be reforested, grazing to be permitted, recreation use, and wildlife and fish use. Similar targets are set for state and private forestry and research, and budget projections for meeting program goals are outlined.

The president transmits the recommended program to Congress along with a "Statement of Policy" intended to be used in framing budget requests over the next five to 10 years. Congress may reject or modify the president's recommendations. The Resources Planning Act requires subsequent Forest Service budget requests to be based on the act's program and to justify any deviations from the program, but this requirement has been largely ignored. Two Resources Planning Act programs have been issued so far, in 1975 and 1980. The 1985 program, due in early 1985, was still under review by the president's Office of Management and Budget at the end of 1985.

*Regional Guides.* Each Forest Service region is required to develop a regional guide that tentatively allocates the region's Resources Planning Act program goals and objectives for resource outputs to the individual national forests. It also identifies major issues and management concerns that need to be addressed in the forest plans and establishes standards and guidelines to be followed on a number of management issues, including prescriptions for silvicultural methods by forest type and general restrictions for clearcutting. The guide also sets requirements for monitoring and evaluating forest-plan implementation. The regional guides are prepared by the regional foresters and approved by the Forest Service chief. Guides have been approved for all regions, although portions of the Pacific Northwest regional guide are being reviewed as a result of an appeal by environmental groups over protection for the spotted owl.*

*Forest Plans.* The basic decisions about how the National Forest System will be managed are made in the forest plans. The forest plans determine

---

* Discussed further in the Forest Service wildlife issues chapter. See also the chapter on the spotted owl.

resource management practices for various management areas within the forest, set levels of production, and identify the availability and suitability of lands for various uses. For example, forest plans identify lands that are unsuitable for timber production, establish a 10-year timber-sale schedule identifying the specific areas where sales are planned, identify areas off limits to logging or other activities in order to protect wildlife, and prescribe wildlife habitat improvement measures as well as constraints on or mitigation required for various other forest uses and activities to protect fish and wildlife. Minimum requirements for how various resources are to be dealt with in the forest plans are outlined in Forest Service regulations (36 CFR 219.14 to 219.26.). Other planning criteria and guidelines are included in policy directives from the Washington office and in the Forest Service Manual and planning handbooks, which may be supplemented by regional guidance and handbooks. Details on planning requirements for specific resources are discussed in subsequent chapters.

Public participation is required throughout the forest planning process, and participation in plan development by interested parties can affect decisions about national forest management. Several guides are available that give detailed explanations of how the process works and outline important environmental considerations that are supposed to be covered by the plans.* In brief, forest planning begins with the identification of particular issues and concerns to be addressed in the plan and the development of criteria for selecting the preferred alternative from among various proposed plans. Then the Forest Service inventories forest resources and prepares an "analysis of the management situation" to determine the ability of the forest to meet local resource and user demands. Based on this information, the service formulates management alternatives and estimates their effects. After evaluating the alternatives, the forest supervisor recommends a preferred alternative and prepares a draft plan, which is issued for public comment along with a draft environmental impact statement. After public comments are reviewed, the regional forester approves the final plan. The most important steps for public input are during the development of issues and concerns, the formulation of alternatives, and the 90-day public review period for the draft plan and environmental impact statement.

*Developing Alternatives.* The process of developing alternatives is critical and complex. The forest staff begins by running a benchmark analysis to determine the maximum potential outputs of individual resources after the minimum management needs of other resources are met. For example, the analysis would determine the maximum timber-production capability of the

---

* The National Audubon Society and four other conservation organizations publish a 121-page handbook, *National Forest Planning: A Conservationists' Guide.* It can be ordered for $2.00 from the Wilderness Society.

forest as constrained by minimum habitat needs for fisheries and wildlife. Thus, the benchmark analysis defines the range within which alternatives can be constructed.

The National Forest Management Act requires the formulation of a broad range of reasonable alternatives, including a no-action alternative—which looks at what would happen on the forest if current management were continued—as well as an alternative that attempts to incorporate the Resources Planning Act program objectives assigned to the forest by the regional guide. Each alternative is required to represent the most cost-efficient combination of management prescriptions that will achieve the objectives of the alternative. The Forest Service calls this maximizing "present net value"—essentially the difference between the alternative's costs and benefits. In calculating present net value, the Forest Service considers priced benefits, such as timber sale receipts, and also attempts to factor in nonmarket values, such as recreation and wildlife use, by determining the public's "willingness to pay" for these uses.

To help generate alternatives and to find the most efficient mix of management measures for each alternative, the Forest Service uses a computer linear programming model called FORPLAN (for FORest PLANning). With FORPLAN, the planners can feed into a computer information on the goals of the alternatives, constraints on resource uses, resource capabilities, needs of management indicator species, and so forth, and the model will yield information on how much use of each resource can be provided, where, and when—all in the most cost-efficient manner. While Forest Service planners note that FORPLAN allows the service to generate multiple, detailed alternatives that simply could not be accomplished without a computer, the quality of the results of FORPLAN modeling depends on the quality of the information fed into the computer. It is important for planning-process participants to know what constraints were used in the FORPLAN modeling for the various alternatives, such as what fish and wildlife species were used to represent habitat needs and what management objectives were chosen. If this information is not included in the environmental impact statement, it should be available from the forest supervisor.

Forest Service regulations require forest plans to provide for multiple use and sustained yield of goods and services from the National Forest System in a way that "maximizes long-term net public benefits in an environmentally sound manner." There is no other guidance on how the regional forester is to choose the final plan. However, he must lay out his rationale in a "record of decision" accompanying the plan. The regional forester also is required by the National Environmental Policy Act to explain why he did not choose the environmentally preferable alternative and by Forest Service regulations to explain why he did not choose the alternative with the highest present net value.

*Appeals.* The public can appeal almost any decision made by a Forest Service officer—including final decisions on regional guides and forest plans—through the administrative appeal procedure (36 CFR 211.18). According to the Forest Service, this review is to be an informal process with a minimum of legalistic procedures.*

To start an appeal, the appellant must file a notice of appeal within 45 days of the date of the decision and must file a statement of reasons for seeking the appeal. Any request to make an oral presentation must be made within the same time period unless an extension is granted. Implementation of the decision in dispute is not automatically halted by an appeal, but the appellant can request and often can obtain a stay of actions.

The appeal is filed with the officer responsible for making the decision and is reviewed by the officer one level above him. Appeal decisions can be appealed to a second level, except that review of a decision by the secretary of Agriculture is discretionary. Thus appeals on forest plans, which are approved by the regional forester, are reviewed by the chief of the Forest Service. The secretary will not accept a second-level appeal of the chief's decision, but does have 10 days in which to decide if he will exercise his option to review the decision. Decisions on regional guides, made by the chief, may be appealed to the secretary who, again, has the option to accept the appeal or not. Once the appeal procedure has been exhausted, the appellant may have the option of taking the issue to court.

*Implementing the Plan.* Once a forest plan is approved and implemented, the Forest Service is required to monitor and evaluate it at established intervals to determine how well its guidance is being applied and how well objectives are being met. If necessary, the plan can be revised or amended. The forest supervisor also is required to review the forest's condition every five years to determine if plan revisions are necessary. The plans also may be amended to reflect new Resources Planning Act program policies and goals or other changes in objectives or to authorize new uses not specified in the plan.

To amend the plan, the forest supervisor first must determine if the amendment would result in a "significant" change in the plan. Significant changes require use of the standard planning procedures, including the preparation of an environment impact statement. Changes that are not significant can be made in a streamlined process that requires only public notification of the intent to change the plan and compliance with the National Environmental Policy Act requirements for environmental review. The Forest Service has not defined what constitutes a significant change, and this certainly will be a matter of controversy as changes to the plans become necessary. The Forest

---

* A guide to the appeals process is available from the U.S. Department of Agriculture, Forest Service, "A Guide to the Forest Service Appeal Regulation," FS-388.

Service says that no amendment will be needed for deviations from the plan due to insufficient appropriations, although public notification of such deviations might be made in some cases.

The forest plans are to be completely revised, preferably every 10 years but at least every 15. This revision is to take place through the standard planning procedures.

Only 25 final forest plans had been issued by September 30, 1985, the target set by the National Forest Management Act for the issuance of all 123 final forest plans. However, the service hopes to have completed at least internal review of all draft plans and environmental impact statements by the end of 1985 and to have issued all plans in proposed form by spring, 1986. It should take from six months to a year for the issuance of final plans, which means some will not be completed until 1987. Then, of course, the service will have to resolve appeals on the plans. All of the first 25 plans were appealed by various parties. Fifty appeals were filed on these plans by the end of FY 1985, and more were expected. Assuming the Forest Service attempts to adhere generally to the 10-year cycle, preparatory work for the second generation of plans will probably start in 1991 or 1992.

***The Resources Planning Act in Practice.***   While the Resources Planning Act and the National Forest Management Act set up a theoretically neat system of planning from the national to the local level, the process—at least so far—has not worked as envisioned.

One problem is the apparent irrelevance of the Resources Planning Act programs issued so far to the decision-making process. In 1980, President Carter sent to Congress a Resources Planning Act program that set high and low objectives for production levels of each resource—the low bound reflecting what would be possible at relatively low funding levels and the high bound requiring significantly increased funding levels. Congress rejected this approach, saying it failed to give sufficient guidance to the service, and added language to the fiscal year 1981 Interior appropriations bill accepting the high bound.*

However, Forest Service budget requests and actual appropriations since 1980 have had no apparent connection to Resources Planning Act program funding goals (see budget section). With the emphasis on reduced federal spending, total appropriations have never reached the target levels of the

---

* In fact, Congress encouraged even higher production levels than in the high-bound program, especially for timber harvest, which it specified should be increased to minimize the inflationary impacts of wood-product prices and to permit a net export of forest products by the year 2030. To accomplish this goal, Congress suggested all lands classified as commercial forest in the major timber-growing regions would have to be brought to and maintained at 90 percent of their potential level of growth.

Resources Planning Act program nor has funding been allocated among activities in proportion to program priorities. The extreme disparity between the 1980 Resources Planning Act goals and actual spending levels has rendered the program largely meaningless and, in practice, useless. In fact, the administration recently has ignored the requirement to explain why its budget request deviates from the planning act program, and Congress has not bothered to direct it to do so.

The Resources Planning Act process also has failed to achieve the "top-down, bottom-up" flow of information envisioned between the forest plans and the national Resources Planning Act program, and it is still unclear as to how these might mesh in the future. The main reason for the failure of this process is that the initial The planning act programs were prepared before the forest plans were even under way. Thus, the 1975 and 1980 programs were completely "top-down" directives. The 1985 program does have the benefit of some information from forest plans that were far enough along to have useful data available when it was being developed, but still this information was incomplete.

While the 1985 program was supposed to be issued by September 30, 1985—and could be issued at any time—the goals of the Resource Planning Act program that the forest plans must include among their alternatives are those of the 1980 program. It already appears that the plans in sum will not meet the objectives of the 1980 program,* and their relation to the 1985 program remains to be seen.

What if the national-level and forest-level goals do not match? No clear direction exists for resolving these differences, but a number of possible courses of action do exist. If it appears that the plans will fall short of national program goals, forests with uncompleted plans could be directed to try to meet increased resource outputs to make up the difference. Plans already completed could be adjusted to meet the goals, or the goals could be adjusted to reflect the forest plans, or some of both. Or revisions could be put off until the next Resources Planning Act program is developed and until the second generation of forest plans is prepared.

Finally, there are numerous more specific and technical criticisms of the process. With respect to wildlife, one issue of concern is the attempt to put dollar values on the benefits of wildlife use. In general, environmentalists have charged that the nonmarket values are set too low and that items such as wildlife and recreation consequently are undervalued in comparison to resource uses—such as timber and minerals—with clear economic returns. This charge was aggravated by a largely arbitrary Department of Agriculture decision in 1984 to make a 37.5-percent reduction in willingness-to-pay values

---

* For example, the Forest Service says initial draft and final plans are falling short of the 1980 program's timber-sale goals.

used in the 1985 Resources Planning Act to determine benefits of wildlife and other recreational activities. The Department of Agriculture recognizes that inadequacies do exist in its procedures for determining fish and wildlife recreational values and has established a working group to try to develop a better method for doing so, although it has not made much progress to date. Meanwhile, the Forest Service is studying what effect choosing different wildlife and recreation values might have on the planning process.

With the forest plans still in development, it is too early to judge the success of the Resources Planning Act planning process. The true test at any rate will not be whether the procedural quirks of the process can be addressed, but whether the planning process succeeds in providing a forum for resolving the basic resource management questions that have been at the heart of controversies over Forest Service programs since the 1960s.

## Budget

*Setting Annual Appropriations.* Funding levels for Forest Service programs are set each year in legislation passed by Congress and signed by the president. The process for determining what these levels will be begins within the administration approximately two years prior to the fiscal year in which the funds will be spent. The first step is the development of guidance by the Forest Service Washington office for the preparation of budgets at the field level. Over the past several years, the Washington office has assigned the regions actual production targets for developing budgets—how much timber to produce, how much grazing, and so forth. Beginning with the fiscal year 1988 budget, however, the regions will be expected to rely on long-term direction in the Resources Planning Act program and the forest plans to provide this kind of guidance.

The regions generally are asked to specify how they would allocate their funds at several different possible budget levels. In recent years, for example, the Service has asked the regions to prepare one alternative assuming a funding level of 80 percent of the president's request for the previous years, since the Department of Agriculture regularly asks to see such a lower-bound alternative.

Based on alternative budgets from the regions, the Washington office develops national budget alternatives. The Forest Service chief chooses several alternative budgets to meet Department of Agriculture requirements and proposes one of the alternatives as the Service's budget recommendation. The department makes any changes it considers necessary in the chief's proposal and submits it as part of the entire Agriculture Department budget to the Office of Management and Budget. The Office of Management and Budget, which coordinates and clears budget recommendations for all agencies through the executive branch, also may make changes in the agency's budget, changes that may be appealed by the Department of Agriculture. Whatever allowance the Office of Management and Budget finally approves becomes the president's budget request to Congress, which is submitted in January of the year in which the appropriations must be approved. Also at this time, the Forest Service Washington office sends tentative funding levels, personnel allocations, and program direction to the field so these units can begin preparing to carry out the president's budget.

Congressional work on the budget begins in February and March with hearings on the president's proposal. Hearings are held by both the relevant appropriations and authorizing subcommittees in the House and Senate, although the authorizing committees have no direct role in actual development of the appropriations bill. Unlike most legislation, which can originate in either the House or Senate, appropriations bills must begin in the House. Otherwise, the bill works its way through the standard legislative process: it is approved by the Interior Appropriations Subcommittee, by the Appropriations Committee, and by the full House of Representatives. After House passage, the Senate begins the development of its appropriations bill following the same procedures. Differences between the House and Senate bills are settled in a conference committee, and a final bill is passed in both bodies. Sometimes Congress fails to approve appropriations for the Service prior to the start of the fiscal year on October 1, in which case it may approve a "continuing resolution" that extends funding until a regular appropriations bill is finished. When the final bill is signed, the Forest Service adjusts the allocation of funds to the field as necessary.

The final appropriations bill establishes funding levels for several broad categories of programs. More detailed guidance on how Congress expects the agencies to spend the funds within these accounts is included in the House and Senate Appropriations Committee reports. These appropriations levels may be altered later in the fiscal year if the president requests and/or Congress approves supplements or rescissions in funding. In addition, the president may defer spending of appropriated funds until the following fiscal year.

Congress often makes numerous changes in the president's budget, but the changes usually are selective, and much of the president's request tends to be maintained. During President Reagan's term of office, two significant exceptions to this rule have been in the State and Private Forestry Program and in lands acquisition. Congress repeatedly has rejected administration proposals to scale down these programs dramatically. Congress also has generally approved less severe restrictions on spending for wildlife, soil and water, and recreation than the administration has proposed. Nevertheless, Congress has maintained the overall thrust of the President's proposals to increase funds for the timber and mining programs while cutting other aspects of Forest Service spending, particularly for conservation.

**Budget Structure and Comparative Spending Levels.\*** The Forest Service is a large agency, with a total budget for FY 1985 of roughly $2.3 billion† and personnel levels of 38,500 full-time equivalents.†† By comparison, the Bureau of Land Management—which manages more land, although less intensively— had a 1985 budget of about $575 million and fewer than 10,000 full-time equivalents. The Park Service in 1985 was budgeted at $920 million with 16,500 full-time equivalents.

The Forest Service budget can be broken into three main categories of spending, paralleling the Service's three major programs: the National Forest System; Forest Research; and State and Private Forestry. The vast majority of funds and personnel are allocated to the National Forest System. In 1985 the system received appropriations of $2 billion and more than 34,300 full-time

---

\* Throughout this discussion the numbers used represent actual appropriations, including supplemental and rescinded funds. Numbers used for permanent and trust funds represent actual funds available.

† Most budget documents show 1985 appropriations of $2.05 billion. This is because Congress deducted from the Forest Service budget $226 million in previously authorized but unused purchaser road credits in an accounting maneuver to get the credits off the books. This discussion does not deduct the credits, to allow more accurate comparisons with previous years.

†† Full-time equivalents are the total number of hours worked by an individual divided by the total number of compensable hours in a year. Work of part-time and intermittent employees is converted to full-time equivalents and, when added to the number of full-time employees, gives a measure of total employment.

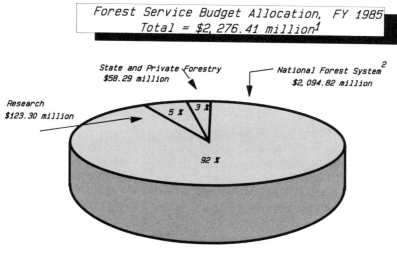

Forest Service Budget Allocation, FY 1985
Total = $2,276.41 million[1]

State and Private Forestry
$58.29 million

National Forest System[2]
$2,094.82 million

Research
$123.30 million

5 %   3 %

92 %

1) Purchaser credit offset not included.

2) Includes all permanent and trust funds and all appropriated line items except Forest Research, State and Private Forestry, Construction of Research Facilities.

Source: U.S. Department of Agriculture, Forest Service

equivalents, about 92 percent of total funding and 89 percent of the personnel. Forest Research, funded at $123.3 million and 2,400 full-time equivalents, accounted for just over five percent of the funding and six percent of the personnel. State and Private Forestry, at $58.29 million and 586 full-time equivalents, accounted for three percent of the funding and two percent of the personnel.*

A substantial portion of the Forest Service's budget—$665.66 million in 1985 or 29 percent of the total—is funded through permanent appropriations and trust funds. Expenditures of these funds are not set by Congress in the annual appropriations process, and often they are not even displayed in congressional appropriations documents.

Permanent and trust funds are split into three major categories: working funds, payments to states, and cooperative work. Working funds include receipts and deposits from a variety of sources that are allocated automatically to certain Forest Service activities. These include, for example, deposits by timber purchasers for use in disposing of brush after timber harvest; deposits from some small-business timber purchasers to finance logging-road construction by the Forest Service; and receipts from timber salvage sales used to prepare and administer future sales. Payments made to the states cover primarily the disbursement of 25 percent of national-forest earnings to the states

* The remaining three percent of personnel are supported by funds transferred to the Forest Service from other agencies, such as for the Job Corps and Senior Employment Service.

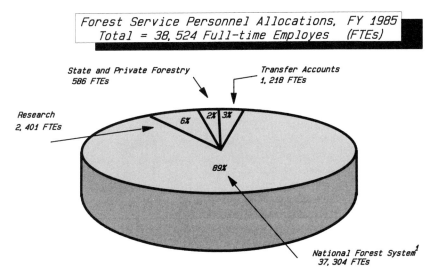

Forest Service Personnel Allocations, FY 1985
Total = 38,524 Full-time Employes (FTEs)

State and Private Forestry
586 FTEs

Transfer Accounts
1,218 FTEs

Research
2,401 FTEs

6%  2%  3%

89%

National Forest System[1]
37,304 FTEs

1) Includes all permanent and trust funds and all appropriated line items except Forest Research, State and Private Forestry, Construction of Research Facilities.

Source: U.S. Department of Agriculture, Forest Service

Forest Service Appropriations FY 1985 (in millions)

| | |
|---|---|
| Forest Research | $121.67 |
| State and Private Forestry | 58.30 |
| National Forest System: | |
|   Minerals Management[1] | 26.57 |
|   Real Estate Management[1] | 20.84 |
|   Land Line Location[1] | 29.09 |
|   Maintenance of Facilities[1] | 14.79 |
|   Forest Fire Protection[2] | 156.59 |
|   Forest Fire Fighting[2] | 62.23 |
|   Cooperative Law Enforcement[2] | 7.21 |
|   Forest Road Maintenance[2] | 65.41 |
|   Forest Trail Maintenance[2] | 9.26 |
|   Timber Sales Administration and Management | 194.70 |
|   Reforestation/Stand Improvement | 67.26 |
|   Recreation Management | 102.06 |
|   Wildlife & Fish Habitat Management | 36.73 |
|   Range Management | 28.17 |
|   Soil, Water, and Air Management | 31.81 |
|   General Administration | 258.84 |
| Total, National Forest System | 1,111.55 |
| Construction | 263.87 |
| Forest Roads Purchaser Construction | ( 192.30)[3] |
| Purchaser Credit Roads Funds | (−226.29)[4] |
| Land Acquisition-Land and Water Conservation Fund | 50.54 |
| Land Acquisition-Special Acts | .77 |
| Land Acquisition to Complete Exchanges | .02 |
| Range Betterment Fund | 3.97 |
| Miscellaneous Appropriated Trust Funds | .09 |
| TOTAL, APPROPRIATED FUNDS | 1,610.75 |
| Permanent Appropriations: | |
|   Working Funds | 157.93 |
|   Payments to States | 235.70 |
| Total, Permanent Appropriations | 393.63 |
| Cooperative Work: | |
|   Knutson-Vandenberg Funds | 194.75 |
|   Other | 39.88 |
| Total, Cooperative Work | 234.63 |
| Reforestation Trust Fund | 37.41 |
| TOTAL FOREST SERVICE | $2,276.41[5] |

Notes:

[1] These items are sometimes grouped in appropriations bills under "Minerals and General Land Activities."

[2] These items are sometimes grouped in appropriations bills under "Resource Protection and Maintenance."

[3] This item is not included in budget totals.

[4] Congress deducted previously authorized but unused purchaser road credits in an accounting maneuver. These funds are not deducted here in order to give a more accurate picture of actual spending levels.

[5] Numbers may not total due to rounding.

Source: U.S. Department of Agriculture, Forest Service

for school and road purposes, as required by law. Cooperative work consists primarily of Knutson-Vandenberg deposits—deposits made by timber purchasers for reforestation and resource improvements in the timber-sale area. In 1985, payments to the states accounted for about 35 percent of permanent and trust funds, cooperative work for 35 percent, and working funds for 24 percent. The remaining six percent was for the reforestation trust fund. Almost all expenditures in the permanent and trust funds are related to the National Forest System.

One item that involves significant dollar value but does not appear in the Forest Service budget is timber-purchaser road credits. These credits are the value of the national-forest timber given away to timber purchasers in exchange for their construction of logging roads. Congress sets an annual cap on the timber-purchaser credits, which has run between $190 million and $242 million during the 1980s, but since 1982 Congress has not included purchaser credits in budget totals.

Most congressional and public attention to Forest Service funding focuses on the items for which Congress does provide annual appropriations. Such appropriated funds totaled $1.6 billion in 1985.* These funds are distributed among nine major accounts: forest research, state and private forestry, the National Forest System, construction, land acquisition using Land and Water Conservation Fund monies, acquisition of lands—special acts, acquisition of lands to complete exchanges, appropriated trust funds, and the range betterment fund.

*$1.4 billion if the purchaser-road credit deduction for 1985 is included.

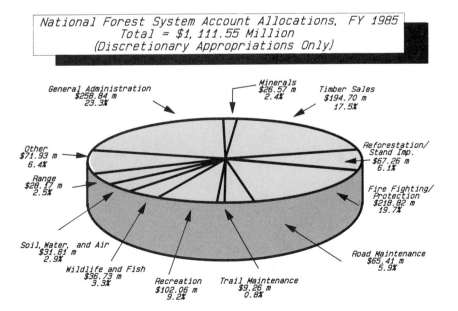

National Forest System Account Allocations, FY 1985
Total = $1,111.55 Million
(Discretionary Appropriations Only)

General Administration
$258.84 m
23.3%

Minerals
$26.57 m
2.4%

Timber Sales
$194.70 m
17.5%

Other
$71.93 m
6.4%

Reforestation/
Stand Imp.
$67.26 m
6.1%

Range
$28.17 m
2.5%

Fire Fighting/
Protection
$218.82 m
19.7%

Soil, Water, and Air
$31.81 m
2.9%

Road Maintenance
$65.41 m
5.9%

Wildlife and Fish
$36.73 m
3.3%

Recreation
$102.06 m
9.2%

Trail Maintenance
$9.26 m
0.8%

The National Forest System account is the largest of the nine—totaling $1.1 billion in 1985—and includes most of the projects directly related to National Forest System management plus general administration costs for the entire Forest Service. The projects receiving the most funding under this account are general administration at $258.84 million, fire fighting and protection at $218.82 million, and timber sales at $194.70 million. Together, these make up for 60 percent of the account. At a somewhat lower tier of funding are recreation management at $102.06 million and reforestation and timber-stand improvement at $67.26 million. Another tier below this is fish and wildlife habitat management at $36.73 million; soil, water, and air management at $31.81 million; range management at $28.17 million; and minerals management at $26.57 million.

Looking just at the National Forest System account, however, does not fully show how funds are allocated among the system's various activities. This is in part because the National Forest System account includes only the funds used in *management* activities on the National Forest System, while actually almost all the funds in the Forest Service budget—with the exception of the forest research account, the state and private forestry account, and a small amount of funding in the construction account allocated to research facilities—also are used to support the National Forest System. In addition, portions of funding for some activities are spent toward coordinating with or supporting other programs.

Thus, looking at spending across the board, and including support from other programs, timber receives by far the largest portion of the Forest Service's budget. In addition to the $187.55 million appropriated in 1984 for timber sales management and administration in the National Forest System account, approximately $85 million from other programs also were used for timber-sales support.* This includes activities that directly support timber sales, such as land-line location to locate and mark property lines, maintenance of logging roads, and forest fire protection. It also includes funds from various resource-protection programs—including wildlife; range; and soil, water and air—to allow program staff to coordinate with timber staff to plan the sale in an environmentally sound manner, to conduct activities to mitigate adverse impacts, and in some cases to achieve actual resource improvements. In 1984, 28 percent of the soil, water, and air budget and 24 percent of the wildlife and fish budget were spent on such activities. In addition, almost all road construction—more than $260 million—and several of the permanent working funds, totaling about $104 million, were spent on timber sales and harvesting. In 1984, the Service calculated total timber sales and support at nearly $630 million, about 30 percent of the total budget. But even this does not include purchaser credits for road construction, general administration costs, or reforestation and timber-stand improvements.

---

* This discussion uses 1984 figures because 1985 timber-support costs had not yet been calculated.

FY 1984 Timber Sales Program and Timber Support (in millions)

| | |
|---|---:|
| National Forest System | |
| Timber Management | $141.91 |
| Harvest Administration | 45.64 |
| Timber Support to Other Programs | 18.35 |
| Subtotal, Timber Sales Program | 179.19 |
| Support to Timber Sales Program: | |
| Minerals | .94 |
| Land Line Location | 22.10 |
| Forest Fire Protection | 4.05 |
| Forest Road Maintenance | 31.93 |
| Recreation | 8.35 |
| Wildlife and Fish | 8.41 |
| Range | .89 |
| Soil, Water, and Air | 8.52 |
| Subtotal, Timber Support | 85.19 |
| Total, National Forest System | 264.39 |
| Road Construction | |
| Forest Service Construction | 210.62 |
| Purchaser Construction | (240.00)[1] |
| Purchaser Roads Constructed by FS | 50.48 |
| Total, Road Construction | 261.10 |
| Special Accounts | |
| Brush Disposal | 48.30 |
| Timber Salvage Fund | 12.78 |
| Tongass Timber Supply Fund | 43.10 |
| Total, Special Accounts | 104.18 |
| TOTAL, TIMBER SALES PROGRAM | $629.66[2] |

[1] Purchaser construction is not included in total.
[2] Does not include reforestation or percentage of general administration costs.
Source: U.S. Department of Agriculture, Forest Service, 1986 Budget Explanatory Notes.

Fish and wildlife habitat management is another activity that receives funds from more than one account. Most of its funding is under the National Forest System account, which provided $36.73 million in 1985. This included $22.37 million for "support" (now called coordination), including funds for timber support, as described above, as well as funds for the participation of fish and wildlife biologists in forest planning, coordination with other activities such as minerals and range, and administrative work. The remaining $14.36 million was for direct habitat improvement, including about $2.5 million for threatened and endangered species and $3.8 million for anadromous fish. Additional wildlife funds come from Knutson-Vandenberg deposits, which provided $5.87 million for habitat improvement in 1985. In total, fish and wildlife funding was $42.6 million in 1985, or just under two percent of the total Forest Service budget. Fish and wildlife personnel totaled 877 full-time equivalents in 1985, two percent of the total, including 536 biologists.

***Budget Trends.*** In 1980, the total Forest Service budget was $2.05 billion. In 1985, it was $2.3 billion, about an 11 percent increase. However, using 1980 constant dollars in order to correct for inflation, the Forest Service budget in 1985 was $1.7 billion, nearly a 16 percent drop since 1980 in spending power.* During the same period, funding for the National Forest System account also dropped about 20 percent. Overall research funding dropped by four percent, while wildlife research dropped by nine percent. State and private forestry, although repeatedly rescued by Congress from massive cuts requested by the Reagan administration, has still dropped 38 percent.

The major trend in Forest Service spending has been an increase in funding for timber sales and minerals development, while funding for almost everything else has dropped in terms of constant dollars. From 1980 to 1985, funding for timber sales and administration increased seven percent, energy and minerals management funding increased 64 percent, and land-line location—which almost entirely supports timber and minerals—increased 30 percent. At the same time, recreation management decreased six percent, fish and wildlife habitat management funding decreased nine percent, range management funding dropped 27 percent, and funding for soil, water, and air management declined 36 percent.

\* Budget trends in this discussion are all based on constant dollars.

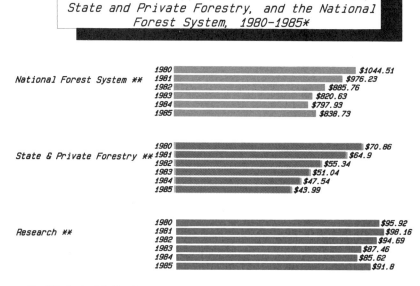

Forest Service Appropriations for Research, State and Private Forestry, and the National Forest System, 1980–1985*

National Forest System **
1980 $1044.51
1981 $976.23
1982 $885.76
1983 $820.63
1984 $797.93
1985 $838.73

State & Private Forestry **
1980 $70.86
1981 $64.9
1982 $55.34
1983 $51.04
1984 $47.54
1985 $43.99

Research **
1980 $95.92
1981 $98.16
1982 $94.69
1983 $87.46
1984 $85.62
1985 $91.8

\* (In 1980 Constant Dollars)
\*\* (Dollars in Thousands)

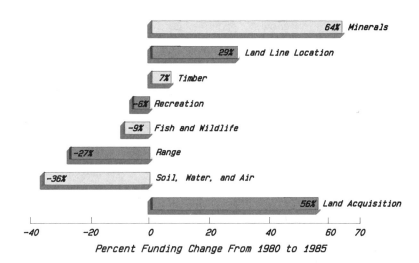

Percent Increase or Decrease in Appropriations Between 1980 and 1985 for Selected National Forest System Activities (in constant dollars)

Percent Funding Change From 1980 to 1985

The one significant exception to this trend favoring development activities is land acquisition. In spite of Reagan administration proposals to make deep cuts in land acquisition, Congress has appropriated increased amounts for this effort. In 1985, land acquisition funding was 56 percent higher than in 1980.

In addition to the funding declines, a shift has occurred in the allocation of funds within the range, wildlife, and soil, water and air programs, with an increasing share of each account going toward administration or support activities and decreasing shares toward resource improvements. Several factors account for this. As funding has become tight, the first priority in these programs has been to mitigate the adverse effects of other activities on these resources and to prevent their future degradation. This situation has been magnified by the fact that although funding for these programs has declined, timber sales have remained more or less steady and mineral leasing has accelerated, requiring increases in support efforts. In addition, forest planning has made increased demands on most Forest Service programs in the past several years. Thus, while fish and wildlife funding has decreased nine percent overall, support funding under the fish and wildlife budget item has increased 14 percent and habitat improvement funding has declined 31 percent. While range funding has decreased 27 percent overall, range management funding has declined 25 percent compared to a 35 percent decline in funding for range improvements.* While soil, water, and air management funding has decreased 36 percent overall, administration funding under that item has increased 12 percent and improvement spending has declined 72 percent.

*The Budget and Resources Planning Act.*   Forest Service appropriations over the past five years have been far below the funding levels anticipated in the 1980 Resources Planning Act program. For fiscal year 1985, the program projected funding levels of slightly more than $3 billion for the National Forest System, $175 million for state and private forestry, and $315 million for forest research. Actual funding for the forest system was less than half the Resources Planning Act goal, and funding for research and state and private forestry was about a third of their goals. The discrepancy is not surprising. The "high-bound" Resources Planning Act levels that Congress adopted were something of an ideal: what the Forest Service would do without budget constraints. Soon after Congress approved the Resources Planning Act, however, not only was federal spending constrained, but it began to decrease, and Planning Act goals and real spending rapidly diverged.

In addition, spending priorities in the 1980 Resources Planning Act program, prepared under the Carter administration, have not been followed un-

---

* In addition, range betterment funds have declined by 47 percent, but this is due to a decline in grazing fees, not to budget decisions.

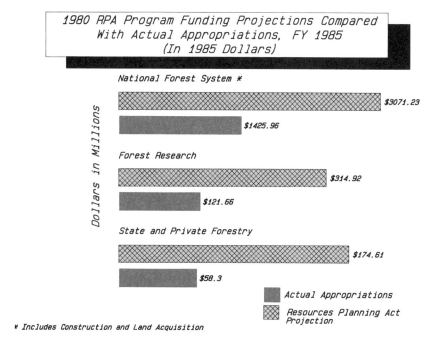

**1980 RPA Program Funding Projections Compared With Actual Appropriations, FY 1985 (In 1985 Dollars)**

National Forest System *
$3071.23
$1425.96

Forest Research
$314.92
$121.66

State and Private Forestry
$174.61
$58.3

*Dollars in Millions*

■ Actual Appropriations
▨ Resources Planning Act Projection

* Includes Construction and Land Acquisition

der the Reagan administration. The program aimed to balance the Forest Service's emphasis on timber by holding timber funding roughly level while increasing spending for almost everything else. The 1980 program projected significant increases in conservation-oriented programs, including soils, water, land acquisition, fish and wildlife, and wilderness, as well as in other programs, including state and private forestry, facilities, minerals, and research. For example, under the 1980 program, timber was projected to increase three percent between 1981 and 1985, while range spending was to increase 28 percent, recreation 42 percent, water 67 percent, fish and wildlife 112 percent, and soil 168 percent. In fact, timber has increased about seven percent, and almost all other programs have dropped, some substantially. Only minerals and land acquisition have had significant increases—minerals with the support of the Reagan administration and land acquisition in spite of it. However, both still have fallen short of their Resources Planning Act goals.

Meaningful comparisons of Resources Planning Act spending goals with actual expenditures, however, are difficult to make because the act's allocation of costs among programs differs from the allocation in the budget.* In part for this reason, the service prefers to compare Resources Planning Act projected accomplishments with actual accomplishments. By this measure as well, the commodity-oriented programs generally have been favored over the resource conservation programs: timber, minerals, and range have achieved from 97 to more than 100 percent of the goals, while wildlife, and soil, water and air have accomplished from 20 to 70 percent. Measuring these accomplishments, however, gives an incomplete picture of program achievements. For example, while the range program has met 100 percent of its goal in grazing *use,* the sharp decline in funding for range management and improvement funding suggests that range condition may be suffering; at the least it is clear that improvements have slowed. Likewise, while the recreation program has nearly achieved its Resources Planning Act visitor-use projections, reduced funding for recreational use has caused—especially in the face of such increased demand—reductions in the *quality* of recreational use as facilities have been closed or have been inadequately maintained and as seasons for some uses have been shortened.

## Land Acquisition and Management

From the earliest forest reservations established under the Forest Reserve Act in 1891, to acquisitions in the East during the 1920s and 1930s, to the addition of large amounts of Alaskan forests in 1980 under the Alaska National Interest

---

* For example, in the Resources Planning Act projections, timber costs include various support costs and road construction; soil and water are split into separate items; costs of wilderness management are not included under recreation; general administration costs are spread across the accounts, and so forth. The Forest Service does, however, attempt to make a comparison of actual and Resources Planning Act-recommended spending levels in its annual report.

Summary of National Forest System Accomplishments Compared to RPA goals—Fiscal Year 1984

| Resource area | Activity | Unit of measure[1] | 1984 | | | 1981-84 average | | |
|---|---|---|---|---|---|---|---|---|
| | | | RPA goal | Accomplished | Percent of RPA accomplished | RPA goal | Accomplished | Percent of RPA accomplished |
| Final output[2] | | | | | | | | |
| Timber | Sales offering | B bd. ft. | 12.2 | 11.9 | 98 | 12.0 | 11.6 | 97 |
| Recreation | Visitor use | MM RVD's | 247.0 | 227.6 | 92 | 233.3 | 231.1 | 99 |
| Range | Permitted grazing use | MM AUM's | 10.0 | 10.0 | 100 | 10.0 | 10.0 | 100 |
| Minerals | Applications, proposals and administration | Cases[3] | 22,793.0 | 27,310.0 | 120 | 20,303 | 28,028 | 138 |
| Intermediate output[4] | | | | | | | | |
| Timber | Reforestation | M acres | 469.0 | 376.0 | 80 | 464.8 | 385.8 | 83 |
| | Timber stand improvement | M acres | 408.0 | 361.5 | 89 | 393.0 | 379.1 | 96 |
| Wildlife | Habitat improvement | M acres | 626.0[7] | 365.9[8] | 58 | 517.2[7] | 364.7[8] | 71 |
| Wilderness | Maintenance | MM acres | 41.0 | 25.2[9] | 61 | 38.3 | 25.2 | 66 |
| Soil and water | Resource improvement | M acres | 32.0 | 8.9[10] | 28 | 24.5 | 12.3[11] | 50 |
| Trails | Construction/reconstruction | Miles | 2,238.0 | 528.0 | 24 | 1,841.5 | 412.8 | 22 |
| Roads | Construction/reconstruction[12] | Miles | 13,416 | 7,650 | 57 | 13,083 | 8,711 | 67 |
| Fire | Fuel management | M acres | 333.0 | 206.6[13] | 62 | 283.3 | 300.2 | 106 |
| Lands | Purchase and donation | M acres | 205.0 | 22.8 | 11 | 174.0 | 74.0 | 43 |

[1]M = thousand, MM = million, B = billion.

[2]Final output = Forest and rangeland goods and services purchased or consumed by the private sector or individual consumers.

[3]Reported as operating plans in the RPA.

[4]Intermediate output = Work performed by the Forest Service which contributes to the production of final outputs.

[5]Increased accomplishment due to 65,500 acres of site prep done in 1983 with Emergency Jobs Program Funds.

[6]K-V = Knutson-Vandenberg Act.

[7]Resources Planning Act goal for 1984 was 3,130 acre equivalents, which is approximately 626 acres, the RPA 1981-84 average was 2,586 acre equivalents which is approximately 517.2 acres.

[8]Includes 170,047 acres accomplished with Knutson-Vandenberg funds in 1984, and a 1981-84 average of 115,940 acres.

[9]Does not include 6.9 million acres added to the Wilderness Preservation System by the 98th Congress, after October 1, 1984.

[10]Includes 2,733 acres accomplished with K-V and other funds in 1984.

[11]Average for 1982-84; 1981 data not available. Includes a 1982-84 average of 4,677 acres accomplished with K-V and other funds.

[12]Total Forest Service road construction/reconstruction using purchaser construction, purchaser elect, and appropriated funds.

[13]In 1984, an additional 1,506 acres were accomplished through human resource programs and 315,175 acres using brush disposal funds. In 1981-84, the average was 9,394 acres accomplished through human resource programs and 337,276 using brush disposal funds.

Source: U.S. Dept. of Agriculture, Forest Service, *Report of the Forest Service, FY 1984.*

Lands Conservation Act, the National Forest System has continually grown to its current 191 million acres. And as it has grown, the complexities of federal land ownership have increased. Today the Forest Service must cope with numerous boundary disputes, inholdings, rights-of-way, condemnations, leases, land exchanges, new acquisitions, and the issuance of special-use permits. All of these are handled through the National Forest System's Lands Program.

*Acquisition.* The Forest Service first received authority to acquire lands in 1911 with the passage of the Weeks Act, which with subsequent amendments authorizes the Service to acquire forested or cutover lands necessary for the protection of the watersheds of navigable streams or for timber production within those watersheds. Some 24 million acres of eastern national forest were acquired under this authority. Although funding through the Weeks Act has not been used in recent years, it remains the Service's dominant acquisition authority.

Since the Weeks Act, the Service has been granted authority to acquire lands for a variety of purposes under several different laws, including the Department of Agriculture Organic Act of 1956 (7 U.S.C.A. 428a(a)), the Wilderness Act of 1964 (16 U.S.C.A. 1134), the Wild and Scenic Rivers Act of 1968 (16 U.S.C.A. 1277), the National Trails System Act of 1968 (16 U.S.C.A. 1246), the Endangered Species Act of 1973 (16 U.S.C.A. 1534), the Eastern Wilderness Act of 1975 (16 U.S.C.A. 1132 (note)), and certain other laws authorizing acquisition in specific areas.

Today, most land acquisition by the Forest Service is accomplished using funds under the Land and Water Conservation Fund Act of 1965 (16 U.S.C.A. 460l-4 to 460l-11), which provides funding to acquire lands or interests in land for outdoor recreation and protection of threatened and endangered species. These funds are derived from revenues from several sources, including receipts from outer continental shelf oil and gas leasing, proceeds from federal surplus property sales, certain user fees, and a motorboat fuels tax. Revenues from these sources are deposited into the fund up to a total of $900 million yearly, but monies in the Land and Water Conservation Fund can be expended only when appropriated by Congress.

Decisions on what lands should be purchased start within the various National Forest System programs. For example, if the wildlife and fisheries staff of a national forest decides that a given area needs to be acquired for wildlife protection, it notifies the lands staff, which gives its best estimate of the property's value. The forest supervisor determines where the property fits in the forest's acquisition priorities and whether to include it in work and budget plans.

The forest officer will try to negotiate the acquisition of the land by exchange first. If the owner is not interested in exchange, the forest supervisor will recommend that funds for the land's acquisition be included in the Forest Service budget request. However, with constrained budget levels in recent years, very little funding for land acquisition has been included in the annual budget requests. If funds are included in the budget request or if Congress adds funding for the acquisition of the property, the Forest Service will negotiate the purchase of the property. If funds are not included, the forest staff may continue to pursue acquiring the area by exchange through a third party.

While funding for most of the conservation-oriented programs in the National Forest System has declined in recent years, funding for land acquisition has increased dramatically because of congressional add-ons, from $24.39 million in 1980 to $50.54 million in 1985—a 56 percent increase even when inflation is taken into account. This increase comes in spite of repeated requests by the Reagan administration to curtail land acquisition expenditures sharply. The majority of recent acquisitions have been for recreational purposes, but many areas also have been acquired to provide critical habitat for endangered species, including the California condor, the Palmer chipmunk, the grizzly bear, the Virginia big-eared bat, and the bald eagle.

Under the Right of Eminent Domain Act of August 1, 1885 (40 U.S.C.A. 257), the secretary of Agriculture has authority to condemn land— that is to acquire the property through a court action, with the court determining the compensation that is to be paid to the owner. This authority is used rarely, however, and only as a last resort in situations where the land is considered essential for National Forest System purposes or if private actions on the parcel will threaten resources in the system. In some cases, Congress has limited this authority, such as in the Wilderness Act and the Wild and Scenic Rivers Act.

*Exchanges and Disposals.* The primary authorities for Forest Service land exchanges are the 1922 General Exchange Act (16 U.S.C.A. 485, 486) and the 1911 Weeks Act, which authorize exchanges of national forest lands or timber for inholdings within national-forest or purchase-unit boundaries. These laws were amended by the Federal Land Policy and Management Act to require that exchanges be of equal value or that payments be made to equalize value. In addition, under the Sisk Act of 1967 (16 U.S.C.A. 484(a)), the Service can exchange certain lands with public schools or state and local governments for land, cash deposits, or a combination of the two.

Exchanges are made to consolidate ownerships in the National Forest System with the goal of facilitating management and reducing costs. For example, the Service reports that 150 exchanges were made in 1984, resulting in a reduction of 1,800 miles of National Forest System property boundary and representing a savings of $10 million in surveying. Exchanges often benefit communities near national forests as well by trading isolated inholdings within the forest for national forest land adjacent to the community. Currently the Service is focusing its exchange program on consolidating wilderness areas.

The Forest Service authority to sell National Forest System lands is limited sharply by law. Under the Small Tracts Act of 1983 (16 U.S.C.A. 521c-521i), the Service is authorized to sell, exchange, or conduct a more informal "interchange" of certain small parcels of lands not worth more than $150,000. Under the Townsite Act (7 U.S.C.A. 1012(a); 16 U.S.C.A. 478a), the Forest Service can sell parcels of up to 640 acres in Alaska and the 11 western states if the parcel is adjacent to an established community. Under the Bankhead-Jones Act, miscellaneous parcels of land called land-utilization projects were transferred to the Forest Service. The Service can sell lands within the land-utilization projects to public authorities, such as state and local governments Except for these cases, the Service cannot sell National Forest System lands.

*Withdrawals.* At the request of the secretary of Agriculture, the secretary of the Interior can close lands in the National Forest System to settlement, sale, or mineral entry by withdrawing them under Section 204 of the Federal Land Policy and Management Act (43 U.S.C.A. 1714). In addition, the act requires the review of all withdrawals that existed in the national forests in the 11 western states at the time of the act's passage, with the purpose of revoking unnecessary or obsolete withdrawal orders. Withdrawals are considered and reviewed in the forest planning process. Withdrawal procedures and review are discussed further in the Energy and Minerals section.

*Special Use Permits.* The authority to issue special-use permits comes under 13 different laws—listed in 36 CFR 251.53—including the Organic Act of 1897, the Permit Act of 1915 (16 U.S.C.A. 497), and most recently, the Federal Land Policy and Management Act of 1976. A special-use permit authorizes the use of National Forest System lands by other federal, state, local, or private interests. Many of the permits, about 16,000 in 1984, are for summer homes. Other activities that require a special-use permit include road construction and power line rights-of-way. Ski area developments, grazing, and other resource activities also require special-use permits, but these are handled by the overseeing program, not the Lands Program staff. The Forest Service charges special-use fees, which vary depending on the nature and duration of the activity.

One activity requiring a special-use permit that recently has posed a particular threat to fish and wildlife on the National Forest System is the development of small hydroelectric facilities. The Public Utilities Regulatory Policies Act of 1978 (16 U.S.C.A. 823:2705 *et seq.*) provided a number of incentives for small hydropower development and allowed some hydroelectric dams under five megawatts to be exempt from licensing procedures as long as they maintain environmental review procedures and meet terms and conditions recommended by the Fish and Wildlife Service and the state fish and game department.

The Regulatory Policies Act has resulted in a substantial increase in applications for small hydro development on the National Forest System since the 1970s. An increase in small hydropower development has serious implications for fish. Dams can severely hinder anadromous fish migration, either because some fish are blocked from moving upstream—even at dams with advanced fish-passage systems—or because the fish are killed in downstream migration by the electricity-generating turbines or by pressure changes encountered in passing through the dam. Environmental groups, members of Congress, and fish and wildlife agencies have been highly critical of the Federal Energy Regulatory Commission's failure to adequately address environmental concerns in granting licenses and exemptions.

Currently, 26 permits have been issued for small hydro development on the National Forest System. After an initial rush in applications following the enactment of the Public Utilities Regulatory Policies Act, new applications have dropped significantly in recent years because of unrealized economic benefits and prolonged appeals and controversy at many sites. In addition, in 1984, the Ninth Circuit Court of Appeals found that the Federal Energy Regulatory Commission did not have the authority to extend the exemption for projects under five megawatts to projects at new dam sites, but only to projects at existing sites (*Tulalip Tribes* v. *The Federal Energy and Regulatory Commission*, 732 F. 2nd 1451 9th Cir. 1984).

One special use that could pose problems for fish and wildlife in the future is the diversion of water for irrigation and other purposes. Prior to the passage of the Federal Land Policy and Management Act, anyone who wished to divert water from the National Forest System for irrigation, diversion, or impoundment purposes could either get a special-use permit from the Forest Service or could get a permanent grant to the water rights from the Bureau of Land Management. The act changed the law by removing the opportunity for national forest water users to get a permanent water grant, requiring instead that all new users or those renewing their permits obtain a special-use permit from the Forest Service. In 1984, with support from livestock interests, Senator Bill Armstrong (R-CO) introduced legislation that again would have allowed users to bypass the National Environmental Policy Act and the Forest Service and receive permanent water grants from the Bureau of Land Management. That legislation did not pass, but two similar bills have been introduced in this Congress by Representative Michael Strang (R-CO).

## Timber Management

Approximately 87 million acres, slightly less than half of the National Forest System, are classified as commercial forest.* This is a relatively small portion,

---

* Defined by the Forest Service as forestland that is producing, or is capable of producing, crops of industrial wood and (a) has not been withdrawn by Congress, the secretary of Agriculture, or the chief of the Forest Service; (b) land where existing technology and knowledge is available to ensure timber production without irreversible damage to soil productivity or watershed conditions; and (c) land where existing technology and knowledge, as reflected in current research and experience, provides reasonable assurance that adequate restocking can be obtained within five years after final harvesting.

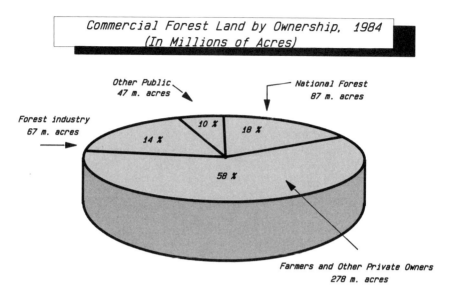

Commercial Forest Land by Ownership, 1984
(In Millions of Acres)

Other Public
47 m. acres

National Forest
87 m. acres

Forest industry
67 m. acres

10 %

18 %

14 %

58 %

Farmers and Other Private Owners
278 m. acres

Source: U.S. Department of Agriculture, Forest Service
Draft Environmental Impact Statement on the 1985-2030
Resources Planning Act Program, 1984, p. 3-2.

about 18 percent, of the total 481 million acres of commercial forest in the United States. The vast majority of commercial forest is in private owner-ship—with 14 percent owned by the forest industry and 58 percent by farmers and other private owners, most of the latter in plots of less than 10 acres. The remaining 10 percent is in other public and Indian ownership (U.S. Depart-ment of Agriculture, 1984b, p. 3-2).

In 1976, the national forests accounted for 15 percent of the total timber cut in the United States and 19 percent of the sawtimber* (U.S. Department of Agriculture, 1982, pp.423-426). The national forests are primarily impor-tant as softwood producers, providing 23 percent of the softwood-sawtimber production in the United States in 1976, but only three percent of the hard-wood. In terms of potential production, the national forests take on increased significance: They hold 41 percent of the nation's sawtimber growing stocks and more than half of the nation's softwood sawtimber, making the Forest Service the largest single holder of timber in the United States. Most of the national forest softwood is in old-growth stands in the western United States (U.S. Department of Agricutlure, 1981, pp. 229-231).

The most important timber area in the National Forest System is the Pacific Coast forest of northern California, Oregon, and Washington. The Forest Service's Pacific Northwest region (Oregon and Washington only) ac-counted for 4.962 billion board feet, or 47 percent of the total 10.662 billion

* Sawtimber is trees containing at least one 12-foot sawlog or two noncontiguous 8-foot logs.

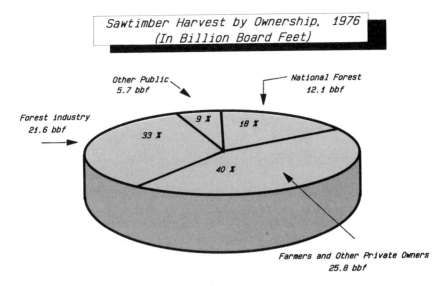

Sawtimber Harvest by Ownership, 1976
(In Billion Board Feet)

Other Public
5.7 bbf

National Forest
12.1 bbf

Forest industry
21.6 bbf

9 %

18 %

33 %

40 %

Farmers and Other Private Owners
25.8 bbf

Source: U.S. Department of Agriculture, Forest Service
An Analysis of the Timber Situation in the United
States. 1952-2030. 1982. p. 426

board feet sold from the national forests in 1984 (U.S. Department of Agriculture, 1985b, p. 79). The region holds 38 percent of the softwood-sawtimber growing stock in the national forests and 19 percent of the softwood in the nation. The other major supplies of softwood are found on private lands in the Pacific Northwest and the South. The major hardwood supplies—84 percent—are almost all located on private ownerships in the East and the South (U.S. Department of Agriculture, 1984b, p. 3-4).

The timber program is by far the dominant program in the Forest Service. In 1984, it accounted for $629.66 million, about 30 percent of the agency's total budget, not including $111.06 million in purchaser road credits, which are not included in Forest Service budget totals.* In 1982, half of Forest Service professionals were foresters; together, foresters and civil engineers—whose efforts largely support construction of logging roads—accounted for nearly two-thirds of Service professionals. Fish and wildlife biologists formed about five percent of the professional staff (Frome 1984, p. 48).

Another measure of the priority given to timber is that while most other programs generally have fallen substantially short of meeting Resources Planning Act goals, the timber program—as well as forest road construction, which is directly related to timber production—consistently has achieved nearly 100

* Purchaser road credits are discussed further under sections in this chapter on the budget and on roads.

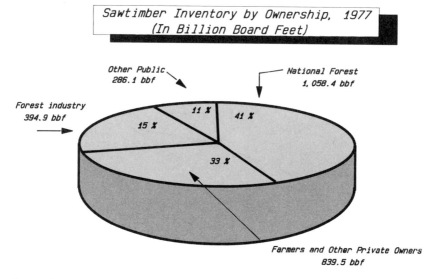

Sawtimber Inventory by Ownership, 1977
(In Billion Board Feet)

Other Public
286.1 bbf

National Forest
1,058.4 bbf

Forest industry
394.9 bbf

11 %

41 %

15 %

33 %

Farmers and Other Private Owners
839.5 bbf

Source: U.S. Department of Agriculture, Forest Service
An Assessment of the Forest and Rangeland Situation in the
United States, 1981, p. 230.

percent or more of Planning Act goals. Timber accomplished 98 percent of its goal in 1984 and averaged 97 percent of Planning Act targets from 1981 to 1984. Reforestation and timber-stand improvement have accomplished an average of 83 percent and 96 percent of their goals respectively. In contrast, wildlife habitat improvement achieved 24 percent of its 1980 Planning Act program goal in 1984 and accomplished an average of 29 percent of its goals from 1981 to 1984 because of inadequate funding* (U.S. Department of Agriculture, 1985a, p. 72).

The timber program has extensive implications for wildlife, since it involves direct manipulation of the habitat on which many wildlife species depend. Almost all aspects of timber management can affect wildlife. These include the type of silvicultural technique used to harvest timber, the size of the areas cut, the timing and location of cuts, the location and management of roads, the rotation age for timber harvest, the dispersal of cuts and effects on diversity of forests, erosion and stream siltation from road construction, choice of logging systems, the rate and method of regeneration, the types of trees chosen for reforestation, the use of herbicides in timber-stand improvement and regeneration, and the use of pesticides to protect timber stands.

In many cases, timber-management activities can be modified to reduce their negative impacts on fish and wildlife habitat and in some cases to produce significant wildlife benefits. With respect to fish habitat, however, timber

* Includes only direct habitat improvement accomplished with appropriated funds, not improvements associated with timber harvest.

harvesting usually has some negative impact and produces no benefits.* In addition, the decision to cut an area at all, regardless of the methods used, may have serious implications for species that need habitat in a certain successional stage, such as old-growth, or that need isolated, wilderness-type habitat free from human disturbance. Because much of the Forest Service's program is designed to meet timber-production needs, in many parts of the National Forest System the major decisions affecting fish and wildlife are made in the context of the timber program.

## Legal Authority and Requirements

The underlying legal criteria for and restrictions on timber sales and harvests are established primarily in the National Forest Management Act of 1976. These criteria are fleshed out in Forest Service regulations (36 CFR Parts 219, 221, and 223). The major limitations and requirements contained in the law and implementing rules are discussed below.

*Non-Declining Flow.* The underlying principle for the administration of all forest resources, as specified in the Multiple-Use Sustained-Yield Act, is that they be managed on a sustained-yield basis. Even before the Multiple-Use Act, however, the Forest Service attempted to ensure a continuous flow of timber from the national forests by allowing an increase in the amount of cut on a forest only if that higher level of cut could be maintained in the future. This policy, called "non-declining flow," developed out of concern for the stability of communities dependent on national-forest timber, under the assumption that accelerated cutting above sustainable levels would cause an economically damaging drop in timber supply for the community at sometime in the future.

The policy of non-declining even flow was made mandatory by Section 13 of the National Forest Management Act, which requires timber sales from each national forest to be limited to "a quantity equal to or less than a quantity which can be removed from such forest annually in perpetuity on a sustained-yield basis." However, as is typical of the act, there are a number of exceptions and qualifiers to this requirement:

1. Decade-long increases above non-declining flow harvest levels—called departures—may be allowed "in order to meet overall multiple-use objectives," provided the departure is consistent with the multiple-use management objectives of the forest's land use plan and that the decision is made with public participation.
2. Annual departures are allowed as long as the average sale quantity over

---

* On occasion, however, Knutson-Vandenberg deposits from a timber sale are used to fund improvements for fish habitat, such as a fish ladder.

the decade covered by the forest plan does not exceed non-declining flow limits.

3. Departures are allowed as necessary for timber stands damaged by fire or other catastrophes or in imminent danger from insect or disease attack.

Forest Service regulations direct forest plans to consider departures from non-declining flow in the following situations: if no other alternative provides a sale schedule that could achieve the Resources Planning Act program timber-sale goal assigned to the forest by the regional guide; if the departure would reduce high mortality losses, such as from disease, or would improve age-class distribution in the forest; if local communities would suffer adverse economic impacts without a departure; or if it is reasonable to expect that overall multiple-use objectives would be better attained by a departure. Wildlife and other environmental organizations generally have opposed departures, which usually have meant accelerated cutting of old-growth stands, particularly in the Pacific Northwest.

*Suitability.* During congressional debate on the National Forest Management Act, resource economists pointed out that a large portion of National Forest System timber sales failed to generate sufficient receipts to cover the government's costs in administering the sale. In part to address this issue, Section 6(k) of the act requires the Forest Service, in the development of land-use plans, to identify lands not suited for timber production, "considering physical, economic, and other pertinent factors to the extent feasible," where no harvesting will occur. Unsuitable areas are to be reviewed at least every 10 years and are to be returned to production if conditions change to make them suitable. More specifically, Forest Service regulations require that areas be identified as unsuitable if (a) technology is not available to insure timber production from the land without irreversible resource damage to soil productivity or watershed conditions, (b) there is no reasonable assurance that the lands can be reforested within five years after harvest, or (c) the land is withdrawn from harvest, such as in wilderness or research natural areas.* As debate has flared up again over below-cost timber sales, environmental groups have charged that the Forest Service has not adequately considered economic factors in making suitability determinations, a charge rejected in 1985 at the secretarial level in the Department of Agriculture in response to an appeal by environmentalists.†

In addition to these across-the-board criteria for determining areas unsuitable for timber harvest, Forest Service regulations outline a procedure for identifying additional areas that should be off-limits to logging in order to meet other management needs identified in the forest plan. In developing the

* Land where timber harvesting can meet these conditions is considered commercial forest under the Forest Service's definition.
† Discussed further in the Forest Service wildlife issues Chapter.

various plan alternatives, the Service identifies lands as "not appropriate" for timber production if the lands are proposed for a resource use that precludes timber production, such as endangered species protection or roadless area management; if other management objectives limit timber production activities to the point where Forest Service regulatory requirements cannot be met; or if harvesting the lands would not be cost-efficient in meeting forest objectives.* Lands identified as not appropriate are designated unsuitable for timber production when the final plan is approved.

*Harvesting Constraints.* The National Forest Management Act also includes a number of constraints on the location and methods of timber harvest:

*Clearcutting.* The National Forest Management Act grew out of controversy over extensive clearcutting on a number of national forests. Consequently it puts a number of constraints on the use of this and other even-aged-timber management techniques. The act specifies that clearcutting may be used only where it is determined to be the "optimum method" for meeting the objectives of the forest plan.† Even-aged techniques may be used for any given sale only after an interdisciplinary team has assessed the impacts of the sale and its consistency with the multiple use of the general area. Even-aged management must be accomplished by cut blocks, patches, or strips that are shaped and blended to the extent practicable with the natural terrain and must be carried out "in a manner consistent with the protection of soil, watershed, fish, wildlife, recreation, esthetic resources, and the regeneration of the timber resource." In addition, the National Forest Management Act prohibits the Forest Service from choosing a harvest method primarily because it will give the greatest dollar return or the greatest unit output of timber, a measure meant to prevent the use of clearcutting just because it is cheaper than other methods.

During debate on the National Forest Management Act, environmentalists pressed for the inclusion of specific limitations on the size of allowable clear cuts, but Congress deferred to the wishes of the Forest Service to leave such specific management decisions to its discretion. Thus the National Forest Management Act requires the Forest Service to establish maximum size limits for clearcuts by geographic area or forest type, although these limits can be exceeded for an individual sale after 60 days advance public notice and review by the regional forester. Forest Service regulations establish the following maximum size limits:

- 60 acres for Douglas fir in California, Oregon, and Washington;
- 80 acres for southern yellow pine in Alabama, Arkansas, Florida, Georgia,

---

* The cost-efficiency requirement does not preclude below-cost sales. Sales that lose money can still be considered cost-efficient if they are the most economic way of meeting the plan's goals.
† Other even-aged harvest methods need to meet the less rigorous standard of being "appropriate" in meeting plan objectives.

Louisiana, Mississippi, North Carolina, Oklahoma, South Carolina, and Texas;
- 100 acres for the hemlock-sitka spruce forest of coastal Alaska; and
- 40 acres for all other forest types.

The national forest regional guides outline more specific size limitations, as well as other requirements such as dispersion of openings, for areas and forest types in each region.

*Rotation Age.* Section 6(m) of the National Forest Management Act generally requires trees to have reached "the culmination of mean annual increment of growth" before they are eligible for harvest. Mean annual increment is a measure of tree growth-rate derived by dividing total growth by total age. The culmination of mean annual increment is the point at which a tree's growth rate no longer increases yearly. Exceptions to the rotation-age standards can be made on a case-by-case basis after consideration has been given to the multiple uses of the forest, including recreation, wildlife habitat, and range. Decisions to allow such exceptions must be made with public participation.

*Protection for Riparian Zones.* Of particular importance for fish is the National Forest Management Act requirement that logging occur only where protection is provided for streams, streambanks, wetlands, and other bodies of water if harvests are likely to have serious effects on water conditions or fish habitat. In such instances, Forest Service regulations prohibit management practices that would cause detrimental changes in water temperature or composition, blockages of water courses, or deposits of sediment within 100 feet from the edges of all perennial streams, lakes, and other water bodies (36 CFR 219.27(e)).

*Diversity.* Another provision that affects timber management is the requirement in the National Forest Management Act that forest plans provide for the diversity of plant and animal communities "based on the suitability and capability of the specific land area in order to meet overall multiple-use objectives." The plans, "where appropriate" and "to the degree practicable," are also to take steps to preserve the diversity of tree species similar to that existing in the region controlled by the plan. Forest Service regulations specify that reductions in the diversity of plant and animal communities and tree species may be prescribed *only where needed to meet overall multiple-use objectives*— that is, diversity cannot be reduced to meet a single-use objective such as timber production. The rules also require that any proposals to convert forest type must be justified by an analysis showing biologic, economic, social, and environmental design consequences as well as the relation of such conversions to the process of natural change.

**Timber Sales.** Specific procedures for making timber sales are outlined in Section 14 of the National Forest Management Act. The act forbids the Service to sell timber for less than the appraised value and to use bidding methods that ensure open and fair competition, ensure that the federal government will not receive less than the appraised value of the timber, and consider the economic stability of communities whose economies are dependent on national materials. Timber-sale contracts are not to exceed 10 years.

## Timber Sales Planning and Management

*Timber Planning.* Timber planning begins with the setting of 50-year national timber sale offering goals in the Resources Planning Act program. These goals are divided among the regions, which in turn tentatively allocate their assigned goals to each forest in the regional guide. The regional guide also establishes "standards and guidelines" for timber management, including harvest methods; maximum size, dispersal, and size variation of tree openings created by even-aged management; reforestation standards; and rotation ages. The standards and guidelines also may include some general prescriptions related to wildlife-habitat protection.

The forest plans identify areas suitable for timber harvest and set the annual allowable cut on the forest. At least one of the alternatives considered in the development of the plan must strive to meet the Resources Planning Act timber-sale goal assigned by the regional guide—keeping within biological limits and legal constraints—but there is no requirement to choose that alternative. The plans also allocate timber-sale levels among specific management areas on the forest and outline a 10-year timber sale schedule. Of course, actual timber-sale levels ultimately depend on a number of factors, including demand and annual program appropriations.

Plans usually also specify the timing of harvests, the miles of road construction associated with sales, the silvicultural methods to be used, and areas unsuitable for or otherwise excluded from timber sales. The timber section of the plan also may specify wildlife protection needs, such as prohibitions on harvests in riparian zones, requiring maintenance of wildlife travel corridors during reforestation, insuring protection of endangered species, and designating old-growth habitat to be managed to maintain old-growth characteristics.

The approval of a sale in the forest plan is only the first step toward making the sale, a process that normally takes from seven to 10 years. Actual work toward making the sale begins with the development of a "Position Statement." The statement, completed at least five years before the sale offering, identifies issues and concerns, outlines tentative sale alternatives, and contains an economic analysis to determine the sale's economic feasibility. The statement also serves as the initial "scoping" phase of the National Environmental Policy Act process—identifying potential environmental conflicts and concerns—and is intended to weed out environmentally unsound or uneconomic sales.* If the statement is approved by the forest supervisor, the sale

---

* However, many sales considered unsound by environmentalists frequently make it past this review and are often subsequently appealed. There were 116 appeals on road construction and timber sales decisions in 1984. (U.S. Department of Agriculture, 1985, p. 1004).

National Forest Timber Offered Sold, and Harvested by Region FY 1984 (in billion board feet)

| Region | Offered[1] | Sold[2] | Harvested[3] |
|---|---|---|---|
| Northern | 1.102 | .917 | .969 |
| Rocky Mountain | .495 | .414 | .340 |
| Southwestern[4] | .511 | .363 | .387 |
| Intermountain[4] | .458 | .396 | .380 |
| Pacific Southwest | 1.735 | 1.458 | 1.658 |
| Pacific Northwest | 4.926 | 4.962 | 4.539 |
| Southern | 1.424 | 1.325 | 1.275 |
| Eastern[4] | .810 | .774 | .740 |
| Alaska[4] | .478 | .052 | .262 |
| Total[5] | 11.939 | 10.662 | 10.549 |

[1] Sale volume offered for the first time.
[2] Does not include the volume of long-term sales released for harvesting. Includes miscellaneous small sales that were previously offered and/or sold and were reoffered and sold in FY 1984.
[3] Includes the volume harvested on large-term sales.
[4] Includes long-term sales volume prepared in the offered column.
[5] Columns may not add due to rounding.
Source: U.S. Department of Agriculture, Forest Service, *Report of the Forest Service,* FY 1981, p. 79.

may be added to the five-year timber-sale action plan, which lists the various sales in preparation and schedules steps toward their implementation.

One to three years prior to making a sale, the Service develops a sale-area plan, which includes major decisions about how the timber harvest will be conducted, including many decisions affecting wildlife. The sale area plan, also called, "sale area design," identifies the approximate location of the cut, preliminary silvicultural prescriptions, locations of roads, and areas on the sale with specific management constraints or mitigation measures. At the same time, a sale area improvement plan is prepared. This plan outlines potential resource improvements to be made with Knutson-Vandenberg deposits from the timber purchaser, including improvements for fish and wildlife.

The sale-area design is also the stage at which National Environmental Policy Act requirements are met by the preparation of an environmental analysis and sometimes an environmental impact statement. In early 1985, the Ninth Circuit Court of Appeals, reviewing a proposed timber sale in the Jersey Jack area of the Nez Perce National Forest in Idaho, found that the Service's current approach of doing separate environmental analyses on individual but related timber sales failed to consider the cumulative effects of the several sales taken together (*Thomas v. Peterson*). This may mean that in some cases the service now will have to do a cumulative environmental analysis on multiple sales in the same area. Forest Service personnel say that the environmental impact statements prepared in connection with the forest plans should serve this function in most cases in the future. Environmentalists disagree, however, saying that the forest-plan environmental impact statements are much too general to cover the actual on-the-ground impacts of a specific sale.

*Timber Sales.*　After the sale-area plan is approved, actual work toward implementing it can begin. The district ranger and his staff mark the timber, determine timber quantity and quality, locate roads on the ground, and so forth. Fish and wildlife biologists participate in actual on-the-ground decisions regarding the location of cuts and other activities affecting fish and wildlife. These decisions are documented in a "timber-sale report." The sale is then appraised, a sample contract is prepared, and the timber sale is advertised. Timber is sold by competitive bid, either through sealed bids or oral auction, and the sale generally is awarded to the highest bidder. With few exceptions, the minimum acceptable bid must be sufficient to cover essential reforestation costs, which are funded through Knutson-Vandenberg deposits. Funds remaining from the timber sale after reforestation and certain other costs are covered are used to carry out the resource improvements specified in the sale-area improvement plan.

Timber-sale contracts specifically spell out how the objectives of the sale, including wildlife mitigation, are to be met. Contracts for two years or more require the preparation of an operating plan outlining the timing of harvests and other sale activities. The purchaser generally is required to furnish a performance bond to assure that contract requirements are met. The Forest Service can revise or cancel contracts under certain circumstances, for example to prevent serious environmental damage, or if the contracts are inconsistent with new or revised forest plans, or if the purchaser commits serious or continued violations of contract terms.

*Timber Buy-Back.*　Timber sales from the national forests have averaged about 11 billion board feet a year since the 1970s. Actual harvesting of a particular area lags behind the sale. In fact, the timber industry prefers to have two-and-a-half to three-years worth of timber under contract at any one time to provide some flexibility and lead time for activities such as road construction. In recent years, however, this backlog of sold but unharvested timber grew to about 38 billion board feet, nearly a four-year supply. This situation arose because in the late 1970s and early 1980s, when inflation was on a rapid rise, the timber industry contracted for substantial volumes of national-forest timber at high prices, speculating that lumber prices would continue to increase. When timber demand and prices slumped with the 1982 recession, harvest levels also dropped.

In 1984, Congress passed the Timber Contract Modification Act (16 U.S.C.A. 619) allowing timber companies to turn back to the federal government a portion of their timber contracts to prevent the companies from having to sell the timber at a substantial loss. Each company turning back timber is required to make a payment to the government depending on the company's financial status.

Approximately 9.6 billion board feet were turned back to the Forest Service under this law, reducing the unharvested backlog under contract to more normal levels. This timber, or much of it, will be offered for resale by the Service under standard timber-sale procedures, although the Service estimates the cost of reoffering about 25 percent of this timber will be reduced substantially since most of the preparatory sales work will not have to be redone. The buy-back has been criticized as a government bail-out for the unwise speculation practices of the timber industry. It does, however, provide some positive management opportunities. For example, some old-growth stands returned in the Pacific Northwest could be preserved for spotted owl habitat. Environmental planning on some sale areas may be improved, and new road construction in the Pacific Northwest could be reduced in the short term, since some of the roads for these sales already have been built.

*Salvage and Fuelwood Sales.* In addition to the regular timber sales planned primarily for timber production, the National Forest Management Act authorizes the Forest Service to sell timber that has been damaged by fire, insects, disease, windthrow, and other natural catastrophes without meeting some of the restrictions in the law. Income from these sales are deposited to the salvage sale fund, which the Service may use to cover the cost of preparing and administering future salvage sales. About 1.1 billion board feet of salvageable timber was sold in 1984.

The Forest Service also may allow public cutting of timber for fuelwood. Beginning in 1983, the Forest Service instigated a $10 minimum charge for a fuelwood permit in some areas, while continuing to allow free use in areas where supply significantly exceeds demand. In 1984, the equivalent of 1.4 billion board feet of fuelwood was harvested, 0.8 billion board feet of which was sold for more than $5.7 million.

*Timber Receipts and Below-Cost Sales.* Timber sale receipts fluctuate significantly with the level of timber harvest, but they consistently form the largest share of receipts from national forest lands. In 1984, receipts from timber sales were $526 million, plus $165.5 million in deposits to the Knutson-Vandenberg Fund for reforestation and resource improvements. The total, $691.5 million, constituted 67 percent of total receipts from Forest Service lands that year. In 1985, timber harvest levels were expected to increase, yielding timber receipts of $1.1 billion, nearly 80 percent of total Forest Service receipts.

Not all timber receipts, however, are returned to the federal treasury. Twenty-five percent of these funds (plus 25 percent of most other national forest receipts) are transferred to the states* for support of public schools and

---

* The Reagan administration has proposed to change payments to states from a sharing of gross receipts to a sharing of the receipts that remain after deducting the costs of managing the lands from which the receipts are generated.

roads in the counties from which the receipts were derived.* In addition, the Forest Service incurs costs in making a sale—for doing the planning, marking the timber, overseeing the work and contract, planning and engineering the roads, timber-stand improvement, pest control, and so forth. In fact, several reports in recent years have found that numerous sales lose money and that the Service seems consistently to lose more money than it makes on sales in several forest system regions. The Congressional Research Service, for example, calculated that from 1972 to 1982, sales programs in 23 states lost $140 million to $155 million yearly (Congressional Research Service 1984). The Forest Service maintains that the overall value of timber sold from the National Forest System consistently exceeds costs, and defends numerous individual below-cost sales as achieving other forest management objectives, such as providing benefits for recreation, fire protection, and wildlife.

In part because many below-cost sales are in isolated, unroaded areas that conservationists believe have potential for future wilderness designation or management as unroaded areas, the below-cost sale practice has caused a public uproar leading to numerous congressional hearings. The Forest Service has established a task force to review its accounting system. In addition, the Agriculture secretary's office, in response to a Natural Resources Defense Council appeal of plans for four Colorado forests, found that these plans had not done sufficient economic analysis or provided adequate justification for allowing increased levels of below-cost sales on these forests. Agriculture's Deputy Assistant Secretary for Natural Resources and Environment Douglas MacCleery directed the Forest Service to review the plans, to consider additional alternatives, and to address a number of specific questions about the necessity and wisdom of using extensive below-cost sales to achieve plan objectives. This directive should influence how other forest plans are prepared. Nevertheless, it seems unlikely that these measures will be sufficient to end this brewing controversy, which has been compared to the clearcutting debate in the early 1970s that led to the passage of the National Forest Management Act.†

## Reforestation and Timber-Stand Improvement

Reforestation is needed for lands that have been logged as well as for lands that have suffered previous regeneration failures natural disasters such as fire, storms, insects and disease. The method of regeneration for logged areas is determined as part of the overall silvicultural system specified in the timber sale plan. The National Forest Management Act specifies that timber can be

* Timber-purchaser road credits also are counted as receipts to the government for purposes of calculating the states' 25-percent share.
† Below-cost sales are discussed further in the Forest Service wildlife issues chapter.

harvested only where "there is assurance that such lands can be adequately restocked within five years after harvest." The regional guides establish standards for what qualifies as "adequate" restocking.

Most of the costs of reforesting logged areas are covered by deposits made by timber purchasers under the Knutson-Vandenberg Act. Additional reforestation costs are covered with appropriated funds. In FY 1986, the Forest Service expected about half of reforestation costs to be paid with Knutson-Vandenberg funds.

In the mid-1970s, the Forest Service reported that it had accumulated a 3.1-million-acre backlog of unreforested lands. In 1975, Congress instituted a 10-year program of accelerated funding to reduce the backlog, a program formalized the following year in the National Forest Management Act. In 1980, Congress boosted funding for the effort even further by establishing the Reforestation Trust Fund (P.L. 96-451, 94 Stat. 1983, codified as amended in scattered sections of 26 U.S.C.A.), with money paid into it from certain tariffs.

As of the end of FY 1985, the Forest Service declared that the backlog of unreforested lands had been eliminated. Some have challenged this claim, pointing out that Forest Service records show that only about one million acres were reforested and that 63 percent of the backlog was eliminated through "adjustments" (U.S. Congress, 1985, p. 812). The Forest Service says the discrepancies arose in part because the initial estimates of the need were inaccurate and greatly exaggerated the problem and in part because reforestation

**Softwood and Hardwood Sawtimber Inventories by Ownership and Forest Service Region, 1977**

| Region | Softwood Sawtimber Inventory (BBF) | | | | Hardwood Sawtimber Inventory (BBF) | | | |
|---|---|---|---|---|---|---|---|---|
| | NFS | Other | Total | NFS% of total nationwide | N.F.S. | Other | Total | NFS% of total nationwide |
| Northern | 107.8 | 57.9 | 165.7 | 5.4% | 0.2 | 1.7 | 1.9 | — |
| Rocky Mntns. | 55.3 | 14.9 | 70.2 | 2.8% | 3.1 | 5.0 | 8.1 | 0.5% |
| Southwestern | 27.5 | 18.9 | 46.4 | 1.4% | 0.9 | 1.3 | 2.2 | 0.2% |
| Intermountain | 70.4 | 28.3 | 98.7 | 3.5% | 0.9 | 0.8 | 1.7 | 0.2% |
| Pacific S.W. | 158.6 | 97.6 | 255.6 | 8.0% | 3.0 | 6.1 | 9.1 | 0.5% |
| Pacific N.W. | 386.6 | 340.9 | 727.5 | 19.5% | 5.4 | 28.6 | 34.0 | 0.9% |
| Southern | 34.4 | 308.7 | 343.1 | 1.7% | 20.2 | 280.3 | 300.5 | 3.4% |
| Eastern | 7.5 | 86.3 | 93.8 | 0.4% | 14.8 | 216.8 | 231.6 | 2.5% |
| Alaska | 161.9 | 22.5 | 184.4 | 8.2% | 0.8 | 3.7 | 4.5 | 0.1% |
| TOTAL | 1009.3 | 976.1 | 1985.4 | 50.8% | 49.1 | 544.4 | 593.5 | 8.3% |

Source: U.S. Department of Agriculture, Forest Service, *Draft Environmental Impact Statement for 1985 Resources Planning Act Program*, 1984, p. 3-4.

needs were reduced as some areas naturally regenerated and others were designated as wilderness.

Timber-stand-improvement activities include removal of vegetation that competes with desirable timber trees, thinning of stands, and fertilizing stands for additional growth. The Forest Service has been accruing a backlog in timber-stand-improvement needs. As of October 1984, 1.4 million acres needed timber-stand-improvement treatment, but the administration requested funds for FY 1986 to conduct only 165,600 acres of stand improvement work. The Forest Service does not consider this a true backlog, since the needs are transitory—if treatment does not occur at the correct times, opportunities for accelerating stand growth are lost.

## Road Construction and Management

The Forest Service road-construction program provides a transportation network for a variety of purposes—including access for recreation, mineral development, and fire protection—but the overwhelming majority of roads are built to provide timber access. In 1984, 99 percent of all road mileage constructed was for timber access.

Road construction and management have significant implications for wildlife. Road construction can have particularly serious impacts on fish. Erosion can cause stream siltation, and sedimentation and stream crossings may interfere with fish passage. In some cases, the failure to close roads after initial use can disturb sensitive wildlife and increase hunting pressure or access for poachers. On the other hand, roads can provide clearings and edge habitat, benefits to wildlife in some cases. In South Carolina, for example, the Forest Service has had good success in using closed roads as food plots to enhance wild turkey populations.

Several different categories of roads provide access in and through the National Forest System for different purposes. Primary access to the national forests is from forest highways that link the federal-aid highway system with forest roads. Forest highways are financed through the Federal Highway Act Trust Fund, are administered by the Federal Highway Administration, and are maintained by state or local governments. They are not discussed further here.

Roads funded by or constructed under the authority of the Forest Service are called forest development roads and are divided into three categories: arterials, collectors, and local roads. Arterial roads are the highest grade roads—they generally are two lanes and paved—and comprise five percent of the total forest development road mileage. Collector roads, which make up 20 percent of the road system, serve smaller land areas than arterial roads. They may be two-lane or single-lane and may be surfaced or unsurfaced. The most common roads are local roads, comprising 75 percent of total forest development road mileage. Local roads generally serve a single resource need, usually a timber sale. Their design varies according to the intended use, but they usually are single lane and unpaved. They may be constructed for short-term or long-term service.

*Road Construction Funding.* Forest development roads can be built and funded under several different mechanisms. The Forest Service itself can construct the roads, using funds appropriated by Congress under the Forest Road Program. Roads providing access to timber-sale areas frequently are constructed by timber purchasers under the Purchaser Credit Program. Finally, small-business timber-sale roads are constructed under the Purchaser Election Program.

The vast majority of road mileage is constructed under the Purchaser Credit Program. Under this program, the Forest Service requires the timber purchaser to construct any roads needed to remove the timber purchased. Road-construction costs, established by the Service prior to the sale, are deducted from the price the purchaser pays for the sale, allowing him to recover his construction costs in national forest timber. In essence, the government exchanges timber for roads.

The value of the timber used in this exchange can be significant, but it is not included in Forest Service budget totals, although Congress does set a spending limitation on timber-purchaser credits each year in the Forest Service appropriations bill. To get an accurate picture of how much of its resources—be they dollars or timber—the Service spends on road construction, timber-purchaser credits must be added to road-construction appropriations. In 1984, purchaser credits totaled $111.06 million, accounting for about 30 percent of total road construction costs, and funded the construction of 5,507 miles of road, nearly 72 percent of total mileage constructed that year.*

The Purchaser Election Program covers a very small portion of road construction. Under Section 14(i) of the National Forest Management Act, small business timber purchasers, except in Alaska, can request the Forest Service to directly finance and construct the necessary timber roads, provided construction costs do not exceed $20,000. Costs in excess of $20,000 are included in the timber sale contract. This provision is meant to help small businesses that may not have the personnel or expertise to undertake the construction job themselves. Funding for this program shows up under the "Permanent Appropriations" section of the Forest Service budget. Purchaser-election roads accounted for $10.67 million in 1984, about three percent of road-construction costs, and funded construction of 475 miles of road, about six percent of total mileage.

---

* Purchaser credits, at only 30 percent of total road funding, can cover such a large share of construction because they do not include planning and engineering costs and because logging roads are the cheapest type of road to construct.

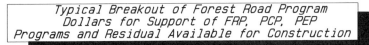

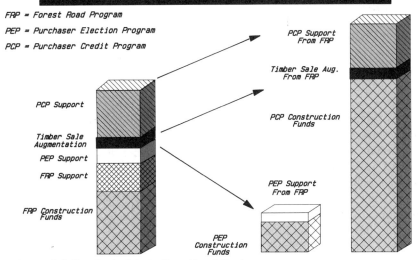

Typical Breakout of Forest Road Program
Dollars for Support of FRP, PCP, PEP
Programs and Residual Available for Construction

FRP = Forest Road Program

PEP = Purchaser Election Program

PCP = Purchaser Credit Program

PCP Support

Timber Sale
Augmentation

PEP Support

FRP Support

FRP Construction
Funds

PCP Support
From FRP

Timber Sale Aug.
From FRP

PCP Construction
Funds

PEP Support
From FRP

PEP
Construction
Funds

Source: U.S. Department of Agriculture, Forest Service
1986 Budget Explanatory Notes for Committee on Appropriations

The remaining road-construction costs are covered by the Forest Road Program. This program finances the multi-purpose road system on or adjacent to national forests. But most road program funds are used to support or construct timber roads. For example, the program funds all planning, management, and project engineering costs for the Purchaser Credit and Purchaser Election Programs, which cover construction and reconstruction costs only. It also provides supplemental funds for purchaser credit and election roads if the Forest Service wants the road constructed to a higher standard than is necessary for timber removal. And it may provide funds or materials for timber roads where a deficit timber sale is made and the timber value is too low to cover purchaser credits.

The Forest Road Program is funded by appropriations under the construction account of the Forest Service's budget. Program expenditures were $230.05 million in 1984, 65 percent of road construction costs, and funded construction of 1,567 miles of roads, 21 percent of total mileage.* All but about 100 miles of these roads were for timber.

*Road Planning and Management.* The basic goal of road construction, specified in the National Forest Management Act, is to design roads "to standards appropriate for intended use, considering safety, cost of transportation,

* In addition, 101 miles of road were constructed in Alaska through Tongass timber-supply funds.

and impacts on land and resources." The needs for road construction and management are determined by decisions made in the forest plan about resource objectives for the various management areas on the forest. These objectives help identify the types and mileage of necessary roads as well as areas in which roading will be prohibited or constrained. The forest plans generally identify the arterial and collector roads to be constructed during the life of the plan and describe the ultimate road system for the forest. The plan also outlines standards and guidelines for road management, such as constraints on construction near riparian areas and closures after use in sensitive wildlife areas.

Specific decisions on where and how the road should be built are made at the project-plan level, such as during planning for a specific timber sale. Environmental impacts are considered in the environmental assessment of the project in question. Design criteria, including environmental constraints, are set by the forest supervisor with assistance from the resource and engineering staff. The engineers take major responsibility for determining how those criteria can be met. The Forest Service recently has conducted a national assessment of its procedures for planning and designing roads and is developing national, regional, and forest action plans—targeted for completion in 1988— to improve these processes.

How forest roads are managed can have serious implications for wildlife. Decisions to restrict the use of roads or close them in order to protect wildlife are made in the forest plans based on the management needs and objectives of the area in question. Roads may be closed only to certain types of use or during just certain times of year. Of the 342,000 miles of roads in the National Forest System, 31 percent are open to all traffic, 50 percent are open only to "high-clearance" vehicles, and 19 percent are closed. Most of the road closures are intended to protect resource values, but a small portion is due to insufficient maintenance funds.

The Forest Service has moved to reduce road costs over the past several years by constructing roads to the minimum standards necessary to achieve their purposes and to meet environmental requirements. As construction of these lower-cost roads increases, the Service expects that the proportion of roads closed to use will increase as well, since the cheaper roads often are impassible in bad weather, difficult for many vehicles to use, and expensive to maintain.

## Trends and Issues

The basic questions about how much timber will be harvested and where will not be answered until the forest plans are completed, but environmentalists and wildlife conservationists are concerned about two apparent trends revealed in early drafts of the plans: a substantial increase in timber harvest over the next 40 to 50 years and the construction of tens of thousands of miles of new roads, many in currently unroaded areas. Another possible problem could be departures from non-declining flow. Each would have important impacts on wildlife.

*Increased Timber Harvest.* Substantial timber harvests are recent in the national forests' history. For the first 50 years, timber sales and harvests were quite low, and the Forest Service's management role during this period frequently is described as custodial. But with the unprecedented population growth and economic expansion that followed World War II, timber demand boomed and timber sales from the national forests rapidly increased. Sales rose from 3.5 billion board feet in 1950 to 10.1 billion in 1955 to 13.3 billion in 1958. Timber sales settled in the 1960s at an elevated level averaging more than 11 billion board feet yearly and have fluctuated between 10 and 12 billion board feet since 1970, following no clear trend. Over the past five years, timber sales dipped slightly with the recession but now appear to be on the rise.

Looking to the future, Forest Service studies project substantial increases in timber demand over the next 50 years. To help meet this demand, the 1980 Resources Planning Act program set goals of increasing timber sale offerings from 11.9 billion board feet in 1981 to 13.1 billion in 1990 and to 16.4 billion by 2030, almost a 40 percent increase. Congress reinforced this push to increase timber harvest in its revisions of the Statement of Policy accompanying the Resources Planning Act program, which urged the management of all commercial timberlands at 90 percent of their productive potential. In the first term of the Reagan Administration, support for increased harvests got a boost within the Agriculture Department from then-Assistant Secretary John Crowell, who vowed to double timber sales from the National Forest System.

Since the development of the 1980 Resources Planning Act program, information from two sources indicates these goals may have been overly ambitious. First, as the forest plans have yielded more information on the capability of the national forests, the Forest Service has found that the system cannot meet the 1980 program's timber-sale goals while still trying to achieve the program's other resource goals. Thus the timber program goals have been revised to reflect an attainable level of timber sales. The projected sale level in 2030 has been reduced from 16.4 billion board feet to 15.4 billion, still a 30 percent increase from 1981.

In addition, the Forest Service has reduced its projections for increases in U.S. timber demand. In the 1979 Resources Planning Act Assessment, the Forest Service projected an 80-percent overall increase in demand by 2030, compared to 1970 consumption levels, and a 75 percent increase in demand for softwood, the type of timber that predominates on the National Forest System. In a 1984 update of the 1979 Assessment, the Service reduced these figures, projecting instead a 61 percent increase in timber demand overall and a 41 percent increase for softwood (U.S. Department of Agriculture 1984a).

Timber Sold and Harvested on the National Forest System, 1950–1984

| Fiscal Year | Volume Sold (bbf) | Average Price per thousand board feet | Volume Harvested (bbf) |
|---|---|---|---|
| 1950 | 3.4 | $ 5.93 | 3.5 |
| 1951 | 4.9 | 12.31 | 4.7 |
| 1952 | 4.7 | 16.91 | 4.8 |
| 1953 | 4.7 | 12.08 | 5.4 |
| 1954 | 6.4 | 9.31 | 5.9 |
| 1955 | 10.1 | 9.34 | 6.9 |
| 1956 | 6.8 | 19.83 | 6.9 |
| 1957 | 6.5 | 17.03 | 7.0 |
| 1958 | 13.3 | 7.77 | 6.4 |
| 1959 | 9.4 | 13.83 | 8.3 |
| 1960 | 12.2 | 14.05 | 9.4 |
| 1961 | 8.9 | 14.13 | 8.4 |
| 1962 | 10.3 | 12.94 | 9.0 |
| 1963 | 12.2 | 13.02 | 10.0 |
| 1964 | 11.7 | 14.72 | 10.1 |
| 1965 | 11.5 | 17.30 | 11.2 |
| 1966 | 11.3 | 19.69 | 12.1 |
| 1967 | 11.6 | 18.01 | 10.8 |
| 1968 | 11.7 | 23.47 | 12.1 |
| 1969 | 19.5 | 25.77 | 11.9 |
| 1970 | 13.4 | 23.71 | 11.5 |
| 1971 | 10.6 | 20.24 | 10.3 |
| 1972 | 10.3 | 31.77 | 11.7 |
| 1973 | 10.2 | 62.37 | 12.4 |
| 1974 | 10.2 | 88.14 | 11.0 |
| 1975 | 10.8 | 60.72 | 9.2 |
| 1976* | 11.8 | 65.02 | 13.0 |
| 1977 | 9.9 | 99.54 | 10.5 |
| 1978 | 11.0 | 120.81 | 10.1 |
| 1979 | 11.3 | 173.22 | 10.4 |
| 1980 | 11.3 | 172.60 | 9.2 |
| 1981 | 11.5 | 154.30 | 8.0 |
| 1982 | 10.0 | 61.24 | 6.7 |
| 1983 | 11.1 | 70.01 | 9.2 |
| 1984 | 10.7 | 65.54 | 10.5 |

*Includes transition quarter to new fiscal year.
Source: U.S. Department of Agriculture, Forest Service.

The new information from the forest plans and the revised demand projections may lead to reduced timber-sale goals in the 1985 Resources Planning Act program if and when it is released.

The most significant decisions on timber-sale levels, however, will be made in the forest plans, currently in preparation. As drafts of the plans have been released, environmental groups have protested proposals to double or triple timber sales on some forests over the next 50 years and have feared these

1980 Revised RPA Program Timber Sale Offering Goals by Region[1]
(in billion board feet)

| Region | 1984 actual (for comparison) | 1986 | 1990 | 2000 | 2030 |
|---|---|---|---|---|---|
| Northern | 1.1 | 1.2 | 1.2 | 1.6 | 2.2 |
| Rocky Mtn. | 0.5 | 0.4 | 0.4 | 0.5 | 0.5 |
| Southwestern | 0.5 | 0.4 | 0.5 | 0.5 | 0.5 |
| Intermountain | 0.5 | 0.4 | 0.4 | 0.4 | 0.4 |
| Pac. Southwest | 1.7 | 1.9 | 2.0 | 2.4 | 2.2 |
| Pac. Northwest | 4.9 | 5.7 | 5.9 | 5.6 | 5.1 |
| Southern | 1.4 | 1.2 | 1.4 | 1.8 | 2.8 |
| Eastern | 0.8 | 0.7 | 0.8 | 1.0 | 1.2 |
| Alaska | 0.5 | 0.5 | 0.5 | 0.5 | 0.5 |
| Total | 11.9 | 12.4 | 13.1 | 14.3 | 15.4 |

[1]Since the development of the 1980 Resources Planning Act program, areas have been designated wilderness and thus off-limits to timber production and new and better information on the forests' capabilities have become available as forest plans are prepared. The 1980 RPA timber goals have been revised to reflect this new information. They represent the closest the forests can come to meeting the timber 1980 RPA goals while attempting to also attain RPA goals for other resources.
Source: U.S. Department of Agriculture, Forest Service

plans reflect an overall trend. The Forest Service has downplayed these long-range timber-sale increases and has pointed out that most plans propose timber-sale levels below their assigned 1980 Resources Planning Act goals.

Part of the difference between environmentalist charges and Forest Service claims is due to a difference in the time period considered. The Forest Service emphasizes that the plans, although they project activities over a 50-year period, will be revised in 10 to 15 years. The Service believes critics should focus primarily on this time period and has prepared a summary of 62 plans that are in draft or final form. According to this summary, these plans propose on the average a 10-percent increase in the allowable timber-sale quantity over the next decade.

The Forest Service compilation, however, does not show projections for sale levels beyond the next decade. These long-term projections often show much larger increases in timber harvest. For example, timber sales on the Beaverhead National Forest in Montana are projected to drop in the next decade, but increase 16 percent thereafter. Likewise, the White Mountain National Forest in New Hampshire projects a drop in timber harvest in the first decade but would nearly double its harvest by the end of the third decade. The Cherokee National Forest in Tennessee shows a 30-percent increase in harvest in the first decade, but projects harvest to more than double by the second decade and nearly quadruple in four decades. Environmentalists believe these long-term projections are significant because a number of activities, particularly road construction, will begin in the next decade to gear up for increased harvests in the decades beyond.

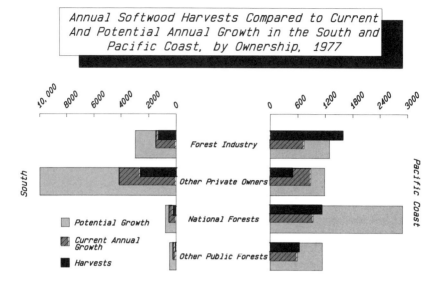

Annual Softwood Harvests Compared to Current
And Potential Annual Growth in the South and
Pacific Coast, by Ownership, 1977

With almost all the plans still in development, it is impossible to tell what levels of timber sales the final plans will project. Public comments on and complaints about various aspects of the draft plans, including increases in timber sales, have forced complete revisions of some plans and alterations to others. Multiple appeals have been filed on every final plan issued to date, prompting further changes. As discussed earlier, an appeal by the Natural Resources Defense Council filed on plans for four Colorado forests that proposed increased deficit timber sales resulted in instructions from the secretary's office to review the justification and wisdom of the proposal, a directive that should influence other forests to more carefully analyze proposals for increased timber sales. The final plans may propose timber-sales increases, but because of the public participation process, these increases almost certainly will be lower than originally proposed.

*Roads.* Currently the forest road development system includes 342,000 miles of roads.* The Forest Service expects to construct an additional 58,000 miles of new roads over the next 15 years, for a total of 400,000 miles by the year 2000. This is an average of 3,900 miles of new roads per year, roughly the

* For comparison, the interstate highway system has 42,500 miles.

Recent and Projected Miles of New Road Construction by Region
(based on final forest plans and approved preferred alternatives)

| Region | 1979-1984 Average Annual Mileage | 1986-1995 Projected Average Annual Mileage | % increase or decrease over current average | Projected Ave. Annual Mileage in Unroaded Areas[1] | Unroaded mileage as % of total projected |
|---|---|---|---|---|---|
| Northern | 804.6 | 890.0 | +11% | 191.9 | 21% |
| Rocky Mtn. | 283.9 | 311.3 | +10% | 112.1 | 36% |
| Southwestern | 106.9 | 101.0 | −6% | 6.5 | 6% |
| Intermountain | 230.8 | 280.4 | +22% | 75.6 | 27% |
| Pac. Southwest | 477.8 | 299.8 | −37% | 171.2 | 57% |
| Pac. Northwest | 1131.2 | 922.0 | −18% | 202.4 | 22% |
| Southern | 506.8 | 659.5 | +30% | 32.5 | 5% |
| Eastern | 310.8 | 316.0[2] | +2% | 19.7[2] | 6% |
| Alaska | 128.1 | 180.0 | +41% | – | – |
| TOTAL | 3,980.9 | 3,960.0 | −0.5% | 811.9 | 21% |

[1] Unroaded Areas include Released RARE II areas or areas recommended by Forest Service for development.
[2] Estimate understated because projections from four forests are unavailable.
Source: House Committee on Appropriations, Surveys and Investigations Staff, "Selected Aspects of the U.S. Forest Service Timber and Road Construction Programs," April 15, 1985, p. 5.

same as the average annual rate of construction from 1979 to 1984. In addition, the Service expects to continue reconstruction of roads at the current average rate of approximately 4,500 miles per year.

The projected new construction is not evenly distributed among the regions. According to Forest Service projections, several regions are slated for significant increases. Average annual construction is projected to increase in the Rocky Mountain region by 10 percent, in the Northern region by 11 percent, in the Intermountain region by 22 percent, in the South by 30 percent, and in Alaska by 41 percent.

One of the greatest conservationist concerns is that many of these new roads are targeted for roadless areas recently released from wilderness protection by Congress or recommended for uses other than wilderness by the Forest Service. On the average, 20 percent of annual new-road mileage is planned for roadless areas, for a total of 8,100 miles over the next decade. Again, however, Forest Service projections show this mileage will be concentrated in a few regions. Road construction in roadless areas accounts for 27 percent of new construction in the Intermountain region, 36 percent in the Rocky Mountains, and 57 percent in California. In the Northern region, the stated first priority for use of capital investment funds is to provide new road and bridge access to commercial timberlands in RARE II and other unroaded areas released for development (National Wildlife Federation 1985).

Road construction in roadless areas is planned primarily to support increases in timber harvest. But the Forest Service says many of these new roads are needed simply to maintain existing harvest levels. During the past decade, when millions of acres of the National Forest System were off-limits to timber cutting because of the wilderness review, the Service continued to calculate allowable sale quantities as if many of these lands were available for harvesting. In reality, however, timber sales were limited to already roaded areas, resulting in intensive cutting on many of these lands. In testimony before the House Interior Appropriations Subcommittee in 1985, Forest Service Chief Max Peterson said the Forest Service is nearing the point where it either must move timber harvest into new unroaded areas, reduce harvest level, or risk violating the resource protection requirements of the National Forest Management Act (U.S. Congress 1985, p. 894).

*Departures from Non-Declining Flow.* In addition to an overall harvest increase, the Forest Service also has been considering departures from non-declining flow harvest levels on some old-growth forests to temporarily boost harvest levels. This push began in 1979, when President Carter—searching for a way to cut rapidly rising housing costs—directed the Agriculture Department to identify forests that temporarily could raise timber harvests above non-declining flow levels and to accelerate development of their plans. With the drop in the inflation rate, immediate concern about a rapid rise in housing costs has waned. But with the continued push for increased timber harvest, such departures from non-declining flow can be attractive because they provide a rapid boost in harvest levels in the short-term and can speed up the conversion of the forest into regulated, regenerating stocks over the long-term. In addition, particular interest exists in allowing departures in the Pacific Northwest in order to promote community stability. The forest industry in this region is rapidly depleting the old-growth inventory on its lands, and the Forest Service says harvest from second-growth stands will not be able to significantly offset this decline for some time. Forest Service documents say a temporary boost in timber harvest from the national forests during this period could help maintain a more steady flow of timber to support the economies of these communities—although with or without departures, timber harvest overall is expected to decline in the Northwest as the old-growth is eliminated (U.S. Department of Agriculture 1982, p. 156).

Of the 70 or so forest plans reviewed so far by Forest Service timber management staff in Washington, the vast majority—some 80 to 90 percent—have considered a departure in one of their alternatives. As of October 1985, four forests had proposed a preferred alternative that includes a departure: the Deschutes in Oregon, the Klamath in California, the Targhee in Idaho, and the Ashley in Utah. The Deschutes and Klamath plans, however, are being extensively revised and could change substantially before final issuance.

*Summary.* Wildlife conservationists are concerned about all three of these issues. Increased or more intensive timber harvests can mean shorter rotation ages and accelerated cutting of old-growth and mature forests;* increased use of herbicides and insecticides; conversion from hardwoods to pines in the East, reducing biological diversity; and disturbance of wildlife that is sensitive to human intrusion. More roads and intrusion of roads into roadless areas may reduce wildlife cover, disturb sensitive wildlife, and increase hunting pressure and other human activity. Roading in elk habitat has been particularly controversial in Idaho, Montana, and Wyoming, since elk need extensive cover and are sensitive to disturbance. Departures from non-declining flow have not been much at issue in recent years, but have the potential to further aggravate concerns about the cutting of old-growth.

Even existing harvest levels are of concern to many environmental groups who believe that to provide true multiple use, timber harvest on the National Forest System should be *reduced* to five or six billion board feet per year. With such lowered levels of harvest, they say, not only could threats to old-growth be reduced, but areas with almost no old-growth remaining—particularly the East—could be allowed to grow into old-growth forests. Large areas of undisturbed fish and wildlife habitat could be maintained to help protect species that suffer from human activity, to serve as a benchmark for

* Loss of old-growth habitat is one of wildlife conservationists top concerns and is discussed in detail in the Forest Service Status Chapter.

studying and understanding wildlife in an undisturbed setting, and to provide pure, unspoiled watersheds for fish spawning. The forests also could preserve ecological diversity—protecting gene pools, providing natural laboratories for medical and scientific study and providing an ecological baseline against which to measure environmental change.

Some environmental groups suggest that rather than try to meet increased timber demand from the national forests, the United States should focus more on those lands with the greatest potential for timber production— farmer and other private lands, primarily in the South. In fact, the Forest Service has projected that the South will outproduce the Pacific Northwest in softwood sawtimber production by 2030, with the South producing 50 percent of the softwood and the Northwest 35 percent (U.S. Department of Agriculture 1982, p. 156). More recent studies, however, show that only 40 percent of nonindustrial private forests in the South are being reforested and that net annual growth of softwood timber in the southern United States has peaked and turned downward after a long upward climb (U.S. Congress, 1985, p. 904). The Service says the reasons for the decline are not clear and has initiated a special study of the southern timber supply situation. In the meantime, the Forest Service program that could help increase timber supply on these lands, the State and Private Forestry Program, is being reduced, and the administration has proposed eliminating such assistance.

# Range Management

More than half of the National Forest System—104 million acres—is in allotments for livestock grazing. Not all the land within these allotments is suitable for grazing—some of it has unstable soils, steep slopes, or inherently low forage production—but 51 million acres, nearly 30 percent of the system, is considered suitable land.* In 1984, the Forest Service administered 14,600 grazing permits for approximately 2.5 million cattle, sheep, and horses on 10,300 allotments.

The National Forest System plays a minor role in overall U.S. livestock production. It encompasses only six percent of the rangeland in the United States and accounts for only five percent of the total animal unit months (AUMs)—a measure that equals the amount of forage grazed by a 1,000 pound cow for one month. This use is concentrated in the West, primarily in the Northern, Intermountain, Rocky Mountain, and Southwestern regions. However, these lands do supply an average of 25 percent of annual livestock feed requirements for those that use them and often are economically important on a local or regional scale.

---

* Suitable lands are those that are accessible to livestock, can produce forage, and can be grazed on a sustained-yield basis under reasonable management goals.

Grazing Use on the National Forest System by Region, 1984 Acreage in Allotments, Suitable Acres, Authorized and Actual Use in AUMs

| Region | Total acres in allotments[1] | Suitable Acres[1] | Authorized Use (in millions of AUMs)[2] | Actual Use (in millions of AUMs) |
|---|---|---|---|---|
| Northern | 11,884,397 | 4,133,572 | 1.402 | 1.350 |
| Rocky Mountain | 18,910,803 | 8,605,998 | 2.214 | 1.941 |
| Southwestern | 18,989,926 | 13,089,163 | 2.513 | 2.144 |
| Intermountain | 26,016,559 | 11,337,738 | 2.262 | 1.932 |
| Pacific Southwest | 13,114,627 | 5,000,545 | .609 | .560 |
| Pacific Northwest | 11,975,715 | 6,754,348 | .740 | .636 |
| Southern | 3,714,544 | 2,224,857 | .247 | .203 |
| Eastern | 93,128 | 45,508 | .077 | .073 |
| Total | 104,699,699 | 51,191,729 | 10.064 | 8.839 |

[1]Source: U.S. Department of Agriculture, Forest Service, *Report of the Forest Service, FY 1984.*
[2]Source: USDA, Forest Service, *Grazing Statistical Summary, FY 1984.*

These lands also provide important wildlife habitat and, in some areas, provide forage for herds of wild horses and burros, animals that are not native to the United States but that the Forest Service is required by law to manage and protect. Livestock grazing can cause numerous conflicts with wildlife. Due in part to a long history of overgrazing, only 24 percent of the range in the National Forest System is classified as being in "good" condition, that is, producing at greater than 60 percent of its ecological potential.

Even on good range, heavy grazing levels can mean that not enough forage is available for wildlife. Conflicts can occur if grazing periods coincide with important wildlife uses of an area. Range "improvements" such as fences and planting of non-native grasses can have detrimental effects on some wildlife species. The most serious current conflict is damage to riparian zones—vital fish and wildlife zones—by cattle grazing on national forests and other public lands. However, with the use of good management techniques, reasonable grazing levels, and carefully crafted grazing systems and range improvements, many of these conflicts can be minimized and range condition can be

National Forest System Range Condition, 1977

| Condition[1] | Millions of Acres | Percent |
|---|---|---|
| Good | 13.1 | 24% |
| Fair | 25.0 | 46% |
| Poor | 14.2 | 26% |
| Very Poor | 2.1 | 4% |

[1]The four condition classes are based on the degree of departure of the present vegetation on the site from the site's ecological potential. Good condition rangelands are those with vegetation between 61 and 100 percent of potential; fair, 41 to 60 percent; poor, 21 to 40 percent; and very poor, less than 20 percent.
Source: U.S. Department of Agriculture, *1980 Resource Conservation Act Assessment*

improved.* In some cases, improvements made for livestock, such as the development of water sources, can improve habitat for wildlife as well.

## Legal Authority and Requirements

Management of the national-forest rangelands generally is carried out under the basic multiple-use and planning laws that guide the operation of all Forest Service lands: the Multiple-Use Sustained-Yield Act, which includes range as one of five basic uses of the land; the Resources Planning Act; and the National Forest Management Act. In addition, the management of livestock grazing on the national forests is conducted under the authority of the Organic Act of 1897; the Federal Land Policy and Management Act of 1976 (43 U.S.C.A. 1701 *et seq.*); and the Public Rangelands Improvement Act of 1978 (43 U.S.C.A. 1901 *et seq.*). Grazing on national grasslands is managed primarily under the authority of Title III of the Bankhead-Jones Farm Tenant Act of 1937 (7 U.S.C.A. 1010-1012). In addition, the Forest Service is required by the Wild Free-Roaming Horses and Burros Act of 1971 (16 U.S.C.A. 1331 *et seq.*). to manage and protect wild horses and burros on the national forest system.

*Early Grazing Administration.* The Forest Service began to regulate grazing on the national forests when it took charge of the forest reserves in 1905. The Service based this authority on the provision in the 1897 Organic Act that authorized the secretary of Agriculture to regulate the use and occupancy of the national forests. The Service drew up grazing allocations to protect water supply, tree growth, and the range; imposed the first fees for grazing use of public land; and recognized livestock advisory boards. The Service's authority to regulate grazing and charge grazing fees was challenged by stock operators all the way to the Supreme Court. In 1911, the court found in favor of the Forest Service, but this did not end the controversy over regulating grazing on public lands. Instead, the protests generated by the Forest Service's actions were diverted toward the Department of the Interior, which consequently was unable to get authority to manage grazing on its lands until 1934.

During the early 1900s, the Service initiated removal of excess animals from the range. World War I, however, brought pressure for increased and even unrestricted use of the range, causing range management to deteriorate. After the war, the Forest Service made some headway on reducing grazing when the Depression and the Dust Bowl drought caused some livestock operators to go bankrupt. World War II brought new pressures on the range, but

---

* In some severely degraded areas, however, conservationists believe livestock grazing must cease completely for a period of time to allow the range to recover.

this time the Service fought with success to prevent a repetition of World War I overgrazing.

After World War II, the 10-year grazing permits came up for renewal, and the Forest Service began reviewing them with the intent of shortening grazing seasons, reducing the number of livestock on the range, and excluding grazing in some areas. The stock operators rebelled once again, this time by proposing to transfer Forest Service grazing lands to the Department of the Interior and by pressing for legislation to allow permittees to purchase the federal property on which they grazed. Public outcry against this "great land grab" forced the proposal to be withdrawn, but stock operators did instigate a congressional investigation of the Forest Service grazing program that culminated in the passage of the Granger-Thye Act of 1950 (16 U.S.C.A. 490 *et seq.*). The Granger-Thye Act did not, however, make significant changes in the Forest Service program. The one provision that somewhat strengthened the hand of the livestock industry was the legal establishment of grazing advisory boards, composed of up to 12 livestock permittees plus one optional wildlife representative.

***The Federal Land Policy and Management Act.*** Subsequent Forest Service legislation—the Multiple-Use Sustained-Yield Act, the Resources Planning Act, and the National Forest Management Act—had no substantive management provisions dealing directly with grazing. But in 1976, Congress passed the Federal Land Policy and Management Act—the "Organic Act" of the Bureau of Land Management—and extended certain of its provisions regarding grazing to the national forests in the West.*

The Federal Land Policy and Management Act continued the requirement for grazing permits, emphasizing that permits generally should be issued for a period of 10 years. The act gives the holder of a permit first priority for its renewal as long as he has complied with previous permit terms and regulatory requirements. Grazing permits must specify, at a minimum, the numbers of animals that may be grazed and seasons of use allowed. Additional requirements for use of specific grazing management systems or installation of range improvements may be outlined in allotment management plans.

The Federal Land Policy and Management Act restructured the grazing advisory boards by extending the maximum number of members from 12 to 15, eliminating the wildlife representative seat, and authorizing the boards to make recommendations only on the development of allotment management plans and the use of range-improvement funds. The act extended the boards through December 31, 1985, at which time they expire unless Congress authorizes their continuation.†

---

* Most of these provisions apply to national forests in the "16 western states:' Arizona, California, Colorado, Idaho, Kansas, Montana, Nebraska, Nevada, New Mexico, North Dakota, Oklahoma, Oregon, South Dakota, Utah, Washington, and Wyoming.

† The government may find authority in other laws to continue the boards administratively.

The Federal Land Policy Management Act also set up a "range betterment fund," into which 50 percent of the grazing receipts are deposited. Half of the receipts—25 percent of the total—are to be distributed back to the forest from which they were collected and half as the secretary of Agriculture determines.* The funds are to be used for range improvements, which the Federal Land Policy and Management Act defines to include fish and wildlife habitat enhancement as well as seeding and reseeding, fence construction, weed control, and water development. The range betterment fund is not strictly a trust fund, since it is only available for expenditure if appropriated by Congress, but Congress consistently has appropriated the full amount authorized by law.

*Public Rangelands Improvement Act.* At the time of the Federal Land Policy and Management Act's passage, the departments of the Interior and Agriculture were phasing in grazing-fee increases in an attempt to raise the fee to a rate relatively comparable to that for private lands, although this perennially controversial effort had been stalled several times by congressional moratoria on further increases. The Federal Land Policy and Management Act ducked the issue of grazing fees by freezing the fee at 1976 levels for a year and requiring the two departments to conduct a study. As a result of that study, Congress, in the Public Rangelands Improvement Act of 1978, for the first time legislatively prescribed a fee formula. Under the Public Rangelands Improvement Act formula, which applies to all Forest Service lands in the 16 western states except the national grasslands, the grazing fee varies with the cost of production and the price of beef and is thus essentially based on the livestock operator's ability to pay. Like the grazing advisory boards, the fee formula is scheduled to expire December 31, 1985, although the current fee actually will extend through the grazing-permit year ending February 28, 1986. Unless Congress acts to extend the formula or set a new one, the decision of how to set grazing fees once again will be up to the Reagan administration.

The Public Rangelands Improvement Act contains several other grazing provisions that affect the Forest Service. It directs the secretary of Agriculture to maintain an inventory on range condition and trends on the national forests and calls for the development of an Experimental Stewardship Program to explore innovative grazing management practices to encourage livestock operators to improve range conditions.

*National Grasslands.* The national grasslands include approximately 3.8 million acres in the West, primarily in the Great Plains. These originally were private lands farmed by homesteaders who abandoned the drought-prone Dust Bowl lands in the 1930s. Under various emergency relief programs, the federal government purchased these lands from 1933 to 1942. The

---

* Currently the Forest Service distributes this discretionary portion back to the regions from which they were collected, to be distributed as the regional forester sees fit.

major authority for such purchase was the Bankhead-Jones Farm Tenant Act of 1937, which authorized the federal government to purchase submarginal lands and directed the secretary of Agriculture to develop a conservation and utilization program to correct the former misuse of the lands. The ambitious goal was to "assist in controlling soil erosion, reforestation, preserving natural resources, protecting fish and wildlife, developing and protecting recreational facilities, mitigating floods, preventing impairment of dams and reservoirs, developing energy resources, conserving surface and subsurface moisture, protecting the watersheds of navigable streams, and protecting the public lands health, safety, and welfare . . . "

These lands initially were placed under the jurisdiction of the Soil Conservation Service. The Soil Conservation Service worked with ranchers and farmers to restore and use these lands, which generally are best suited to producing forage and are used primarily for livestock grazing. In 1954, the lands were transferred to the Forest Service and, in 1960, most of the Bankhead-Jones lands in large parcels were designated as national grasslands.

The grasslands, as part of the National Forest System, are subject to the planning requirements of the Resources Planning Act and the National Forest Management Act and are covered by national forest land management plans. The grasslands generally are not covered by the grazing provisions of the Federal Land Policy and Management Act, which in most cases apply only to national forests, or by the provisions of the Public Rangelands Improvement Act, which specifically exempts the grasslands from its provisions.

*Wild Free-Roaming Horses and Burros Act.* Horses and burros are not native to the western range, but were brought to the area by the earliest Spanish explorers and have roamed these lands for as long as 400 years in some areas. As the range became settled, the animals were captured for various uses or shot as nuisances. Population levels dropped from an estimated high of two to seven million in the early 1800s to 150,000 by the 1930s. Increasing settlement and round-ups of these animals for sale as pet food caused further population declines to an estimated 25,000 animals by the early 1970s.*

The declining populations and the brutal methods used to round up the animals caused a public outcry. In 1959, Congress prohibited the use of aircraft and motor vehicles to hunt wild horses or burros on the public lands, but the round-ups and controversy continued. In 1971, Congress passed the Wild Free-Roaming Horses and Burros Act to halt the killing and to ensure long-term protection. The act applies to wild horses and burros on both Bureau of Land Management and Forest Service lands, but 98 percent of these animals are on Bureau lands. The management of wild horses and burros is only a minor program for the Forest Service.

* Bureau of Land Management estimate.

The act protects wild horses and burros from capture, branding, harassment, or death and directs that they be considered "an integral part of the natural system of the public lands" in areas where they existed at the time of the act's passage. At the same time, however, Congress realized that management of these non-native animals could pose problems for wildlife conservation and directed that all management activities be conducted in consultation with state wildlife agencies to protect the natural ecological balance of wildlife species. Congress also required that in making forage allocations for wild horses and burros, the agencies must consider the forage needs of native wildlife.

To assure that these non-native animals do not overrun the range, the act gives the secretaries authority to remove or destroy excess animals. This authority was modified by amendments to the Wild Free-Roaming Horses and Burros Act included in the Public Rangeland Improvement Act of 1978, which direct that old, sick, or lame animals are to be destroyed as humanely as possible, while other excess animals are to be put up for adoption. Healthy animals can be killed using humane methods if no adoption demand exists, but because of public opposition to such killing, the federal government for several years has had a moratorium on destroying any animals.

Wild horses and burros on the National Forest System are managed essentially in the same manner as on Bureau of Land Management lands. By law, the Service must limit these animals to locations where herds existed when the Wild Free-Roaming Horses and Burros Act was passed in 1971. These areas are called territories by the Service. The Forest Service has identified 47 territories totaling 1.9 million acres in 10 western states.* Nearly 60 percent of the territory acreage is in Nevada. Not all original territories, however, must be managed for continued horse and burro populations.

By 1983, the Forest Service had completed management plans for 27 of the 47 identified territories. Of the remaining 20, 10 had no animals and five had fewer than eight animals each. Decisions on the management of these remaining areas will be made in the land use plans. In addition to designating areas for management, the plans establish population management levels which generally are somewhat below maximum carrying capacity to allow other uses of the forage. Some deviations are allowed in population levels, but if populations are determined to have excess animals, the Service removes them. The Forest Service consults and cooperates with state wildlife agencies in establishing appropriate population levels, determining the effects of horses and burros on wildlife, and developing measures to mitigate adverse effects. Horses and burros are believed to compete with some species of wildlife and to degrade habitat—the most prominent case is wild burros and desert bighorn

---

* Arizona, California, Colorado, Idaho, Montana, Nevada, New Mexico, Oregon, Utah, and Wyoming.

Biennial Population Estimates for Wild Horses and Burros on National Forests

|  | 1974 | 1976 | 1978 | 1980 | 1982 | 1984 |
|---|---|---|---|---|---|---|
| Horses | 2,541 | 3,025 | 3,172 | 2,947 | 2,894 | 1,387 |
| Burros | 282 | 311 | 390 | 204 | 416 | 283 |
| Total | 2,823 | 3,336 | 3,562 | 3,151 | 3,310 | 1,670 |

[1]Some of the difference between 1982 and 1984 population estimates is due to an aggressive capture program to bring populations in line with management plan levels, elimination of duplicate counting by BLM and FS on overlapping territories, and improved census techniques.

Source: U.S. Department of the Interior, Bureau of Land Management, and U.S. Department of Agriculture, Forest Service, *Administration of the Wild and Free-Roaming Horse and Burro Act,* 5th Report to Congress, June 1984.

sheep—but with so few horses and burros on system lands and fairly good population control, this is not a major problem in the National Forest System.

The Forest Service's long-term population goals for these animals are 1,248 horses and 112 burros, for a total of 1,360 animals. During the early 1970s, horse and burro populations increased on Forest Service lands, as they did on Bureau of Land Management lands, to an estimated high of 3,562 animals in 1978, more than two and a half times the management goal. Concerns about excess populations, however, led to increased appropriations for horse and burro round-ups in the late 1970s and to a 1976 amendment to the Horses and Burros Act that allows the use of helicopters and motorized vehicles in government removal programs. In 1985, the Forest Service estimated population levels at 1,326 horses, almost down to the management goal, and 261 burros, more than double the management goal but still a significant reduction from previous levels. Some of this reduction is due to aggressive capture programs, but some also is due simply to improved census techniques and the elimination of double counting by the Bureau of Land Management and the Forest Service in overlapping areas.

The Forest Service, through the Adopt-a-Horse program, cooperates with the Bureau of Land Management to find homes for excess animals from National Forest System lands. Most of these adoptions are handled by the Bureau of Land Management, although the Forest Service does have a few of its own adoption centers in areas far from Bureau of Land Management programs.

In recent years, the number of available animals has exceeded the adoption demand, creating some problems for the federal government. Demand declined apparently in part because of the recession in the early 1980s and in part because in 1982 the Bureau of Land Management and the Forest Service raised adoption fees sharply and required adopters to pay the costs of moving the animals between adoption centers. The fees have since been reduced somewhat, but in the meantime the government has had to pay for the upkeep of thousands of animals awaiting adoption, which has reduced the funds available for continued round-ups. And although the government has authority to destroy unadopted animals, the Bureau of Land Management and the Forest Service have had a moratorium on destroying healthy animals since 1982. At least on Bureau of Land Management lands, horse and burro populations appear to be on the increase again, although Congress did provide a one-time increase in funds in 1985 for an accelerated round-up.

The upshot of all this has been to heighten controversy over an issue that always has generated strong emotions. The administration has been pushing for legislative authority to sell excess horses and burros as a way to help reduce the numbers of animals in government corrals and to offset the costs of running the program. Groups concerned with the protection of these animals, such as the Animal Horse Protection Association and the Humane Society of the United States, oppose this legislation and have long argued that the Forest Service and the Bureau of Land Management exaggerate the population levels on public lands as well as the impacts these animals have on the resources and the need to remove them. For example, wild horses and burros account for 17,800 animal unit months of grazing on the National Forest System, less than a tenth of a percent of the total. Nevertheless, wildlife and conservation groups generally believe that of horses and burros, which are not native species, must be reduced for the good of the range and native wildlife.

## Range Planning and Management

The Forest Service makes general plans for grazing management in the forest plans, which are supplemented by more specific plans developed for each allotment. At the forest-plan level, Forest Service regulations require that the plan identify lands suitable for grazing and determine their condition and trend, estimate the present and potential supply of forage for livestock and wild horses and burros as well as the capability of the lands to produce food and cover for selected wildlife species, estimate the use of forage by grazing and browsing animals, and identify lands that are in less than satisfactory condition and outline a plan of action for their restoration. The plans divide the range into management areas called allotments and identify the intensity of management for the various allotments.

Other elements of the plans also may affect grazing and range use. For example, fish and wildlife portions of the plan may require management of certain rangelands specifically for wildlife or may place conditions on grazing management to protect wildlife habitat. Requirements for riparian management outlined in the watershed portion of a plan also can have important range-management implications.

*Grazing Permits.* Livestock grazing is managed through grazing permits and leases, which are accompanied by either an allotment management plan or an annual operating plan. To qualify for a grazing permit, the operator must have a certain amount of base property capable of supporting grazing and a certain minimum amount of livestock as determined by the forest supervisor. Permits are issued generally for 10 years, although the Service can authorize shorter term permits on national grasslands. Permits can be terminated if they need to be revised, but the reissued permit must then extend for another 10 years. Permits can be cancelled, suspended, or modified for a variety of reasons, including failure of the permittee to comply with permit terms or to pay required grazing fees. Permits also can be cancelled to devote land to other public purposes, but the permittee must be given two years advance notice and must be compensated for any interest in range improvements constructed by him. Permit terms can be modified because of resource conditions, but, except in emergencies, the permittee must be given a year's notice before the modification takes effect. The Forest Service also grants temporary permits, such as to allow the use of increased forage in a productive year, and other miscellaneous permits for limited or one-time use of the National Forest System range.

The forest supervisor is responsible for issuing permits and determining grazing levels. In contrast to the Bureau of Land Management, the Forest Service generally does not allocate certain amounts of forage among the various range animals, such as livestock, horses and burros, and wildlife. Instead, the Service considers the current condition and use of the range and determines whether it is understocked, at acceptable levels, or overstocked. In setting grazing levels, the forest supervisor also is to consider the use of the range by big game and other fish and wildlife. According to the Forest Service manual, grazing levels are to be set low enough to prevent damage to soil or vegetation, provide a margin of safety for seasons of subnormal forage productivity, and allow recovery of ranges in unsatisfactory condition. If grazing reductions are deemed necessary, the permittee must be given a year's advance notice, with yearly reductions limited to no more than 20 percent of the herd. Some year-to-year adjustments needed because of fluctuating weather may be worked out between the permittee and the district ranger.

*Allotment Management Plans.*   For most allotments, the Forest Service prepares an allotment management plan in consultation with the permittee. Many important on-the-ground management decisions may be made in these plans, and they generally are prepared through an interdisciplinary approach. Fish and wildlife biologists, for example, may be consulted in the development of a plan if wildlife resources may be affected significantly.

Allotment management plans are approved by the forest supervisor and normally are designed for a four-year to eight-year period. The plan establishes seasons of use, the number of livestock, and the grazing system to be used. It includes a schedule for rehabilitating range in unsatisfactory condition, and a schedule for initiating and maintaining range improvements and sets forth monitoring and evaluation procedures. An allotment management plan, for example, may specify a grazing system designed to protect riparian zones, such as through restoration, location of salt licks away from water areas, or fencing. Allotments without a current long-term plan may be managed under year-to-year operating plans.

As of 1984, the Forest Service reported that 68 percent of the allotments were in improved management with adequate maintenance. By definition, these are allotments where at least one of the management actions prescribed in an allotment plan has been completed and where the plan is continuing to be implemented on a schedule that prevents deterioration of the range.

***Range Improvements.*** Range improvements may be structural, such as fences or water developments, or nonstructural, such as plant control to improve forage condition. Livestock operators or other organizations or individuals may initiate or help install range improvements through agreements with the Forest Service, but the Service retains title to all permanent structural improvements, all nonstructural improvements, and all temporary structural improvements that involved government funds. Once the improvements are installed, the livestock permittee is required to maintain them. On national forests, the Service may not adjust either grazing fees or grazing allotments to compensate permittees for the cost of range improvements. Such costs may be considered on national grasslands, as discussed later.

Range improvements on the national forests in the 16 western states are funded primarily by the range betterment fund—the fund derived from 50 percent of grazing fee receipts. Only on-the-ground improvement costs are covered by the fund. Planning and administrative costs are funded out of the range management line item in the Forest Service budget. Because range betterment funds are directly proportional to the price of grazing fees, these funds have fallen from a high of $6.9 million in 1980 to $4.0 million in 1984 as grazing fees have declined.

The Federal Land Policy and Management Act directs that one of the uses of the range betterment funds is for fish and wildlife habitat enhancement, but it is Forest Service policy not to use these funds solely for that purpose. However, wildlife may benefit indirectly from range improvements intended for livestock. Conservation groups recently have charged that livestock improvements can in fact harm wildlife, but Forest Service wildlife officials say they do not believe this is a significant problem on the National Forest System. Range improvements are to be planned through an interdisciplinary approach, must reflect forest-plan direction, and are included in the grazing permit or an allotment management plan. State wildlife agency personnel review any revegetation plans prior to approval. The grazing advisory boards also may make recommendations on range improvements.

***Special Provisions for National Grasslands and Other Areas.*** Grazing management on national grasslands, land-utilization projects, and national forests east of the Mississippi is generally similar to that for the national forests in the 16 western states, but there are some significant differences. The Service has more flexibility in the permit system on these lands. For example, the Federal Land Policy and Management Act generally requires that permits in the 16 western states be issued for 10 years, a requirement that does not pertain to other lands. In addition, grazing fees on these lands are not mandated to follow the formula specified in the Public Rangelands Improvement Act for other federal grazing land. The Service uses the same basic criteria for setting the fees on these lands, but there are some differences in the index or the formula used, depending on the type and location of the lands. Thus fees on national grasslands and in the Northeast tend to be higher than the fees based on the Public Rangelands Improvement Act, while fees in the Southeast are somewhat lower.

In addition, the majority of national grasslands are intermingled with private lands, and grazing associations and the Forest Service often cooperate to manage the national grasslands under grazing agreements.* These agreements are intended to better coordinate and integrate grazing and other uses on these patchwork areas by operating them under a single management plan. They also are meant to encourage the use of sound management practices on other lands in the area through demonstration projects on the lands covered by the agreement. Once the agreement is signed, the grazing association is responsible for issuing permits, administering the resource, and constructing range improvements. Grazing must be done in accordance with approved allotment management plans developed by the Forest Service and the permittee. Any special range management adopted by the grazing association and approved by the Forest Service must be included in all permits issued by the associations.

Permittees on national grasslands take an active role in managing the land and generally are responsible for carrying out conservation practices and installing range improvements under the authority of the Bankhead-Jones Act. Under this Conservation Practices Program, the permittee's costs for such activities can be deducted from the grazing fee. The grasslands also include some wildlife habitat demonstration projects intended to show private landowners how they can develop habitat on their lands to their own benefit, since they can charge for hunting on private lands.

## Trends and Issues

*Grazing Trends.* Since 1980, actual grazing use of the National Forest System range has remained steady at 8.8 million animal unit months. Permitted use has increased slightly, from 9.8 million to 10.1 million animal unit months, as demand has increased in certain areas, but actual use has not risen

---

* Grazing agreements can be used on the national forests as well, but this is infrequent.

Status of Range Allotments in National Forest System, 1980–1984

|  | 1984 | 1983 | 1982 | 1981 | 1980 |
|---|---|---|---|---|---|
| Total # of Allotments | 10,296 | 10,417 | 11,069 | 10,871 | 10,754 |
| Improved Management Started ( # of Allotments) | 471 | 534 | 705 | 677 | 1,236 |
| Improved Management Maintained ( # of Allotments) | 7,018 | 7,125 | 6,886 | 6,705 | 6,378 |
| Percent of Allotments with Improved Management Maintained | 68% | 68% | 62% | 62% | 59% |
| Total Acres in Allotments (million acres) | 105 | 104 | 105 | 105 | 112 |
| Suitable Acres (million acres) | 51 | 52 | 52 | 56 | 58 |
| Permitted Use (million AUMs) | 10.1 | 10.1 | 9.9 | 9.8 | 9.8 |
| Actual Use (million AUMs) | 8.8 | 8.8 | 8.8 | 8.8 | 8.8 |

Source: U.S. Department of Agriculture, Forest Service, *Report of the Forest Service, FY 1984*

due to offsetting reductions in other areas. At 10.1 million animal unit months, the range program achieved 100 percent of its 1980 Resources Planning Act program goal for authorized grazing use in 1984 and has averaged 100 percent of its goals over the past four years.

The 1980 Resources Planning Act program projected grazing use on the National Forest System to stay fairly steady through the end of the century and then to increase to 10.6 million animal unit months by 2030. The forest plans issued so far* are following this general pattern (U.S. Department of Agriculture, 1984). At present little pressure exists to increase grazing since the livestock industry, in poor economic shape because of rising production costs and the decline in demand for red meat, is moving to reduce U.S. livestock numbers in an effort to bolster prices. Environmentalists generally are pressing for reductions in grazing levels on the public lands, though the focus of this effort is primarily Bureau of Land Management lands.

*Reductions in Range Improvements.* From 1980 to 1984, the percent of allotments in improved management increased from 59 to 68 percent. This is due in part to a drop in the total number of allotments and in part to an increase of 640 allotments maintained under improved management. But the number of new allotments on which improved management is started each year has declined by more than 60 percent since 1980, from 1,236 allotments in 1980 to 471 in 1984. This is due primarily to reductions in personnel and available funds during this period. Overall funding for range management has dropped 25 percent in spending power since 1980, and funds appropriated specifically for range improvements have dropped 35 percent when inflation is

* Plans issued in final form or draft plans for which the preferred alternative has been selected.

Grazing Fees and Range Betterment Funds, 1981–1985

| Fiscal Year | Fee (dollars per AUM) | Range Betterment Funds (in millions of dollars) |
|---|---|---|
| 1980 | $2.41 | $5.633 |
| 1981 | $2.31 | $6.940 |
| 1982 | $1.86 | $6.583 |
| 1983 | $1.40 | $5.378 |
| 1984 | $1.37 | $4.028 |
| 1985 | $1.35 | $3.665 |

Source: U.S. Department of Agriculture, Forest Service

considered. In addition, grazing fees have dropped steadily since 1980, resulting in a 47-percent drop in range betterment funds. It is administration policy to encourage livestock permittees to assume more responsibility for implementing and maintaining allotment management plans, but this effort has not made up for reductions in Forest Service activity and funding.

*Grazing Fees and Riparian Management.* The major concern of wildlife interests is the poor condition of the range in general and, most important, livestock damage to riparian areas. With the grazing-fee formula up for renewal in 1985, environmental groups pushed for an increased fee, which is now far below fees charged on similar private lands. Environmentalists support a higher fee because they believe the low fee encourages overgrazing and because a higher fee would yield higher receipts and more funds for range improvement, a portion of which they believe should be dedicated specifically to enhancing fish and wildlife habitat. In addition, environmental groups called for the inclusion of range improvement measures in any legislation that extends the fee or establishes a new formula, with top priority on establishing a program to restore and protect riparian areas. Negotiations in Congress to develop such a bill failed to produce any legislation in 1985. These issues are discussed further in the Bureau of Land Management chapter.

# Energy and Minerals Management

The National Forest System overlies a variety of energy and mineral resources, some in significant amounts. Approximately 45 million acres—a quarter of the system—have potential for oil and gas, primarily in the overthrust belts of the Rockies and the Appalachians. Six-and-a-half-million acres are known to be underlain by an estimated 50 billion tons of coal in Montana, Utah, and Wyoming. Some 300,000 acres have potential for oil shale, and the system holds promising areas for geothermal development within 17 million acres in the Great Basin and in the Pacific Coast states. The system also holds mineral resources of strategic importance, including chromium, nickel, tungsten, and molybdenum, and significant amounts of other minerals including gold, copper, silver, and phosphate. Currently about 34 million acres are under lease for oil, gas, geothermal resources, and other minerals.

Mineral activities may have numerous impacts on fish and wildlife. Land clearing for mineral operations, roads, and facilities directly destroys habitat. Construction of roads and facilities may cause soil erosion, with damage to riparian and aquatic habitat, and access into new areas by roads may increase hunting and harassment of wildlife. Streams and lakes may be polluted—for example by brine and hydrocarbons from oil and gas and by acid drainage from coal development—damaging aquatic habitat and water supplies. Soils may be rendered unproductive by oil and brine spills; non-native plants may be introduced into rights-of way; and the activity and noise of mineral activities can disturb wildlife that needs relatively undisturbed habitat. The type and degree of impacts on wildlife depend on a number of factors, such as the species involved, location of the development, size of the area disturbed, types and extent of facilities required, timing and duration of operations, density of development, and types of mitigation measures employed. It is the Forest Service's role to assess the potential environmental impacts of mineral activities on the National Forest System, to determine how these impacts can be minimized or mitigated—including a determination of whether the activity should be allowed to proceed at all—and to attempt to assure that mineral activities comply with the various environmental laws, including the Endangered Species Act, the Clean Water and Clean Air acts, and the National Environmental Policy Act.

Mining on the National Forest System is governed by a multitude of laws, depending on what kind of mineral resource is involved and where it is located. Mineral resources are divided into three main types: locatable, leasable, and salable. Locatable minerals are those for which an individual can stake or "locate" a claim and obtain rights to its development. Leasable minerals are those that can be developed only after obtaining a lease from the Department of the Interior. Salable minerals generally are construction materials, such as sand and gravel, that can be sold or otherwise disposed of by the Forest Service. In addition, different laws may apply depending on whether the minerals are located on National Forest System lands that were reserved from the public domain or on lands that were acquired by purchase from private owners.

Except for some exploration activities and common variety minerals, all mineral activities on the National Forest System are administered by the Department of the Interior. The Forest Service is responsible for ensuring the protection of the system's surface resources from mineral activities. In some cases, the Forest Service merely makes recommendations to the Interior Department on whether a mineral activity should be allowed and how it should be conducted to minimize adverse impacts. In other cases, the Interior Department can authorize mineral activities only with the consent of the Forest Service and in the manner the Service prescribes. In practice, however, the Forest

Service has substantial control over how and in many cases whether development of federally owned minerals will proceed on the National Forest System.*

## Locatable Minerals

*1872 Mining Law.* "Locatable" minerals are those minerals covered by the General Mining Law of 1872 (30 U.S.C.A. 22, 28, 28b), which allows qualified prospectors to search for minerals on certain federal lands and, upon finding a valuable deposit, to "locate" a claim. This law applies to hardrock mineral activities on all public domain lands, including on National Forest System lands reserved from the public domain. It does not apply to acquired National Forest System lands. Hardrock minerals include metallic minerals—such as gold, silver, lead, copper, molybdenum, and uranium—and nonmetallic industrial minerals—such as fluorspar, asbestos, limestone, and mica. The 1872 Mining Law was enacted at a time when the nation was encouraging private ownership and development of public resources, and it essentially declares all public domain lands free and open to hardrock mineral exploration, development, and purchase unless they are specifically withdrawn by statute or administrative action.

A mining claim comes into existence in a series of steps and reaches full cycle when the discovery of a valuable deposit has been established and various other requirements have been met. Upon finding some indication of mineral presence, the miner can protect his right to the claim by staking its boundaries, recording the claim with the Bureau of Land Management and the county in which it is located, and conducting a minimum amount of work on it each year. The Mining Law gives the prospector the right to "reasonable" access across public lands to prospect for minerals and to maintain and mine his claim, although he must comply with Forest Service regulations when crossing and working on National Forest System lands. In working his claim, the miner may use only as much of the surface and surface resources as are "reasonably necessary" to carry out mining operations and must have an operating plan approved by the Forest Service for any activities likely to cause significant disturbance of surface resources, as discussed below. The federal government charges no fee and requires no royalty payments for locatable minerals extracted from its lands.

To establish that he has a valid claim, the miner must find a valuable deposit. However, the miner can spend many years and can conduct a substantial amount of activity attempting to make such a discovery. Generally a miner does not need to establish that he has a valid claim until special circumstances arise, such as if he wishes to patent his claim, establish a valid existing right in the face of administrative or legal withdrawal, or propose operations that will have major impacts on surface resources. To determine if a finding is

---

* This is less true for the development of privately owned minerals underlying the National Forest System, which are discussed at the end of this section.

valuable, the government uses a standard called the "prudent man and marketability test," which is met

> . . . where minerals have been found and the evidence is of such a character that a person of ordinary prudence would be justified in further expenditure of his labor and means, with a reasonable prospect of success in developing a valuable mine, and the minerals can be extracted, removed, and marketed at a profit.

If the claimant meets certain additional criteria, he can patent the claim and purchase the lands for $2.50 to $5 an acre. Mineral patent applications are considered exempt from National Environmental Policy Act requirements and no environmental analysis of the impacts of patenting is conducted. Once the claim is patented, the claimant receives full title to both the land and its minerals, and the Forest Service has no authority over their use.

***Regulations for Locatable Minerals.*** The 1872 Mining Law is administered by the Department of the Interior and gives the Forest Service no direct statutory authority to oversee mining activities. Since 1957, however, the Bureau of Land Management and the Forest Service have operated under a memorandum of understanding providing for joint administration of the mining laws on the National Forest System lands. In addition, in 1974 the Forest Service promulgated regulations to protect surface resources in the National Forest System during mineral operations (36 CFR 228 Subpart A). These regulations were prompted by the National Environmental Policy Act, which required federal agencies to review their legal and regulatory authorities in light of national goals for environmental protection. The Forest Service determined that the provisions in the Organic Act authorizing the secretary of Agriculture to protect forests from destruction and to regulate their occupancy and use gave the Service authority to regulate hardrock mining as it affected national forest surface resources.

Under the Service's locatable mineral regulations, anyone proposing prospecting or mining operations under the 1872 Mining Law that might disturb surface resources—such as the use of earthmoving equipment or the cutting of trees—is required to give the appropriate district ranger a "notice of intent to operate." If the district ranger determines that such operations are likely to cause "significant disturbance" of surface resources, the prospector must submit a plan describing the type of operation proposed. The plan must include specific descriptions of how the operation will be conducted, what roads or access routes will be needed, transportation to be used, the period during which the proposed activities will take place, and how environmental protection requirements will be met. The operator must minimize adverse environmental impacts on the national forests and take all "practicable" measures to maintain and protect fisheries and wildlife habitat.

In analyzing each operating plan, the district ranger must assess the environmental impacts of the proposed operation and determine if an environmental impact statement is required. Individuals have a statutory right to prospect and mine on National Forest System land, but they still must comply with all applicable rules and regulations, including the various environmental laws. If the proposed plan does not meet these requirements, the district ranger can negotiate changes with the applicant or, if necessary, disapprove the plan. Once the plan is approved, the district ranger may ask the operator to modify it to minimize unforeseen significant disturbance of surface resources. The operator generally must reclaim the area and may be required to furnish a bond commensurate with the expected cost of rehabilitation. Of course, if the claim is patented, these regulations do not apply.

## Leasable Minerals

With the exception of locatable hardrock minerals on public domain national forests and common variety minerals, which the Forest Service can sell directly, energy and mineral development on national forests is authorized through leases issued by the Department of the Interior. Leasable minerals are governed by several different laws, and Forest Service statutory authority over leasing depends on which law applies. The mineral-leasing laws as a group, however, give the federal government more control over mineral development on federal lands than does the General Mining Law. Under the leasing laws, rights to minerals are granted at the discretion of the secretary of the Interior, who has clear authority to deny the development of leasable minerals and to place conditions on the lease to protect surface resources. The lessee does not get rights to purchase the overlying land and is required to pay an annual rental fee and a percentage of his proceeds to the federal government.

***Leasing on the Public Domain—the Mineral Leasing Act of 1920.*** Mineral leasing on public-domain lands, including National Forest System lands reserved from the public domain, is governed by the Mineral Leasing Act of 1920 (30 U.S.C.A. 131). This law covers the leasing of coal, oil, gas, oil shale, other bitumens, potassium, sodium, phosphate, and, in New Mexico and Louisiana, sulfur. With the exception of coal, the 1920 Leasing Act gives the Forest Service no statutory authority over the issuance of leases on national forests, and the secretary of the Interior can issue a lease without the Service's consent. However, under a series of agreements since 1945 between the secretaries of the Interior and Agriculture, applications for prospecting permits and leases on national forests are referred by the Bureau of Land Management to the Forest Service. The Service analyzes the possible environmental impacts of mineral development and, if necessary, works with the Bureau of Land Management to prepare an environmental impact statement. The Forest Service recommends whether the permit or lease should be issued and suggests measures necessary to protect surface resources and reclaim disturbed lands. The secretary of the Interior almost invariably accepts Forest Service recommendations.

# Mining Administration on the National Forest System

| Mineral Category | Authority | Administration |
|---|---|---|
| Hardrock minerals on public domain nat. forests | 1872 Mining Law 1957 USDI-USDA memorandum of understanding Organic Administration Act of 1897 | Lands open to claim location and patenting Joint USDI-USDA administration Surface disturbance regulated by FS rules at 36 CFR 228 Subpart A |
| Leasable minerals on public domain nat. forests (except coal, geothermal) | Mineral Leasing Act of 1920 1945 USDI-USDA agreement | Leasing by USDI. Applications reviewed by FS, but USDI does not have to accept FS recommendations |
| Leasable minerals on acquired nat. forests (except coal, geothermal) | Hardrock minerals—Act of March 4, 1917; Reorganization Plan of 1946 Other minerals—1947 Mineral Leasing on Acquired Lands Act | Leasing by USDI only with FS consent and conditions |
| Coal mining on all nat. forest system lands | Public domain forest—1920 Mineral Leasing Act, 1975 Coal Leasing Amendments Act Acquired forest—1947 Mineral Leasing on Acquired Lands Act Surface mining on all lands—Surface Mining Control and Reclamation Act of 1977 | Exploration licensing and Leasing by USDI only with FS consent and conditions |
| Geothermal steam on all nat. forest system lands | Geothermal Steam Act of 1970 | Leasing by USDI only with FS consent and conditions |
| Common variety "salable" minerals on all nat. forest system lands | Public domain—Common Varieties of Mineral Materials Act of 1947 Acquired nat. forests—1947 Mineral Leasing on Acquired Lands Act; 1960 Transfer Functions law | FS disposal through sale or free use permits Regulations at 36 CFR 228 Subpart C |

*Mineral Leasing on Acquired Lands.* On acquired National Forest System lands, all minerals except common variety minerals are managed through leases issued by the Department of the Interior. This includes hardrock minerals as well as the mineral resources leased on public domain lands under the 1920 Leasing Act. The 1872 Mining Law does not apply to acquired lands.

Different laws apply to the different mineral types. On acquired lands, minerals that would be leasable under the 1920 Leasing Act if they were on public domain lands—oil, gas, oil shale, phosphate, sodium, potassium, and sulfur—are covered by the 1947 Mineral Leasing Act for Acquired Lands (30 U.S.C.A. 351-359). This law extended the provisions of the 1920 Leasing Act to acquired lands, but authorized the secretary of the Interior to lease such minerals *only* with the consent of the secretary of Agriculture and *only* in accordance with conditions he specifies to protect surface resources.

Hardrock minerals, which would fall under the 1872 Mining Law on public domain lands, are administered under the Act of March 4, 1917 (16 U.S.C.A. 520), which gave the secretary of Agriculture authority to issue leases for hardrock mineral development on acquired lands. Under a 1946 reorganization plan, responsibility for issuing such leases was transferred to the secretary of the Interior, but again their issuance is subject to the consent and conditions specified by the secretary of Agriculture. Thus, unlike most leasing on public domain lands, where the Forest Service has only advisory authority over mineral leasing, leasing on acquired lands can proceed only with the Service's consent.

*Coal Mining.* Leasing of federal coal on all National Forest System lands, both acquired and public domain, is conducted by the Department of the Interior, but requires the consent of the secretary of Agriculture and must be done in accordance with conditions he may prescribe. Coal leasing on public domain lands is governed by the Coal Leasing Amendments Act of 1975 (30 U.S.C.A. 201(1), 201(b), 207; 16 U.S.C.A. 1276) and on acquired lands by the 1947 Mineral Leasing Act for Acquired Lands. Leasing procedures are similar on both types of land. However, the coal-leasing amendments contain some special provisions, such as giving the governor of the state in which leasing is proposed an opportunity to review and object to leasing plans and requiring that lease sales be compatible with comprehensive land-use plans, although leasing can still proceed regardless of the status of the Resources Planning Act planning process.

In addition, the Surface Mining Control and Reclamation Act of 1977 (30 U.S.C.A. 1201 *et seq.*) provides for cooperation between the secretary of the Interior and the states in the regulation of surface-mining operations and reclamation and has detailed provisions regarding permit requirements, environmental protection standards, reclamation-plan requirements, and reclamation of abandoned mines. Although the Department of the Interior and the states have responsibility for administering the program, the Forest Service is involved wherever there are operations on National Forest System lands.

The Surface Mining Act contains special provisions pertaining to the National Forest System that placed much of the system off limits to surface-mining operations. Section 522(e)(2) of the act prohibits surface coal mining within any national forest unless the secretary of the Interior finds there are no significant recreational, timber, economic, or other values that may be incompatible with surface mining *and* (a) surface operations and impacts are incident to an underground mine or (b) the secretary of Agriculture determines, with respect to national forests west of the 100th meridian that lack significant forest cover, that surface mining is in compliance with other relevant laws, including the Multiple-Use Sustained-Yield Act, the National Forest Management Act, the 1975 Coal Leasing Amendments, and other provisions of the Surface Mining Control and Reclamation Act.

This complicated provision essentially means that aside from surface operations incidental to underground mining, there can be no surface mining on national forests in the East* and that in the West, surface mining is restricted to the national grasslands, which are not covered by this section, and to national forests lacking significant forest cover. In both cases, surface mining can be allowed only if there are no significant values incompatible with surface mining.†

As with most provisions of the Surface Mining Act, which has been in litigation almost since its enactment, the interpretation of this provision is still in flux. At issue is the prohibition of mining unless there are no significant values that are incompatible with surface coal mining operations. In regulations issued under former Interior Secretary James Watt, the Department of the Interior interpreted this provision as prohibiting surface-mining operations only if other resource values would be irreparably damaged—that is, if the area could not be reclaimed. In the summer of 1985, a federal court overturned this interpretation as not affording sufficient consideration to other forest resources (*In Re: Permanent Surface Mining Regulation Litigation*). New rules have yet to be promulgated.

**Geothermal Steam.** The Geothermal Steam Act of 1970 (30 U.S.C.A. 1001 *et seq.*) authorizes the secretary of the Interior to issue leases for the

---

* It is unclear whether valid existing rights to private coal within National Forest System boundaries can be exercised under this provision. A recent court decision determined that surface mining of private coal even on private lands within the Daniel Boone National Forest in Kentucky was prohibited. If this decision is upheld or appealed, the federal government would be required to purchase the coal to extinguish the right to mine it.

† Even those areas not exempted by this provision may be off-limits to surface-mining under other environmental criteria in the Surface Mining Control and Reclamation Act and Bureau of Land Management regulations, which apply to all federal lands, or may be classified for other uses in forest plans.

Existing Licenses, Prospecting Permits or Leases for Energy and Mineral Activities on the National Forest System as of March 31, 1985

| Region | Oil and Gas | | Geothermal | | Coal | | Other Mineral | |
|---|---|---|---|---|---|---|---|---|
| | # | Acres | # | Acres | # | Acres | # | Acres |
| Northern | 3,939 | 7,688,327 | — | — | 2 | 90 | 65 | 18,709 |
| Rocky Mountain | 5,579 | 5,321,062 | 4 | 5,121 | 46 | 39,298 | 32 | 37,813 |
| Southwestern | 1,089 | 1,916,176 | 15 | 25,878 | — | — | — | — |
| Intermountain | 4,730 | 7,932,730 | 38 | 59,072 | 81 | 134,835 | 74 | 37,035 |
| Pac. Southwest | 345 | 577,800 | 238 | 393,000 | — | — | 4 | 3,331 |
| Pac. Northwest | 771 | 1,980,904 | 287 | 564,837 | — | — | — | — |
| Southern | 5,340 | 6,093,317 | — | — | 1 | — | 29 | 19,620 |
| Eastern | 891 | 626,577 | — | — | — | — | 213 | 216,488 |
| Alaska | — | — | — | — | — | — | — | — |
| TOTAL | 22,684 | 32,136,893 | 582 | 1,047,908 | 130 | 174,223 | 417 | 332,996 |

Source: U.S. Department of Agriculture, Forest Service, *Lease Status Report,* March 31, 1985

development and utilization of geothermal resources, including on the National Forest System. As for coal, geothermal leases can be issued only with the consent of and under conditions prescribed by the Forest Service on both acquired and public domain national forests.

***Leasable Minerals Management.*** The overwhelming majority of leasing on the National Forest System is for oil and gas. As of March 31, 1985, 32.1 million acres were under an oil and gas lease or exploration permit, about one million acres were leased for coal, and 333,000 acres were leased for other mineral resources. Because of its predominance on the National Forest System, this section focuses on oil and gas leasing.

Oil and gas activities require Forest Service review at several different stages—for conducting prospecting activities either prior to or after the issuance of a lease, for the issuance of a lease itself, and for the approval of operating plans for working the lease.

The Forest Service has sole authority for authorizing prospecting for oil and gas on the National Forest System through the issuance of geophysical permits. These permits are issued directly by the Forest Service under its general authority to regulate the use of the National Forest System to protect surface resources. These permits do not authorize the removal of oil and gas and do not give the prospector any rights to a federal oil and gas lease.* Either the forest supervisor or the district ranger can issue a geophysical permit after

* This is in contrast to prospecting permits issued by Bureau of Land Management for phosphate, sodium, potassium, sulfur, gilsonite, and asphalt, which allow the prospector, upon discovery of a valuable mineral deposit, to get a "preference right lease" without the consent of the Forest Service.

preparing an environmental analysis, collecting fees, and obtaining a performance bond if necessary to assure reclamation. Routine geologic activities that cause no significant surface disturbance do not require a permit.

Oil and gas leases can be initiated in three ways. When lands are classified by the Bureau of Land Management as being within the known geologic structure of a producing well, they can be leased only at the Bureau of Land Management's initiation and only through competitive bidding. Lands outside of such known producing areas may be leased noncompetitively to the first qualified applicant. These are called over-the-counter sales. Lands on which leases have expired and that are not within a known geologic structure are leased noncompetitively by the Bureau of Land Management through a lottery and are referred to as simultaneous oil and gas leases.

In all cases, the Bureau of Land Management is responsible for issuing the lease. Prior to doing so, the Bureau notifies the Forest Service and requests a "mineral report." The Bureau of Land Management and the Forest Service work together to prepare the necessary environmental analyses. For leasing of National Forest System lands reserved from the public domain, the regional forester makes recommendations to the Bureau of Land Management on lease issuance or denial and on necessary stipulations to protect surface resources. For leases on acquired lands, the regional forester either consents or denies to consent to lease issuance and specifies required lease stipulations. Stipulations generally include restrictions on the location of mineral activities, such as prohibiting development on steep slopes or stipulating that there can be "no surface occupancy" in critical wildlife areas, or their timing, such as prohibiting operations in certain areas during a species' breeding season.

The issuance of a lease gives the leaseholder the right to develop the mineral resources covered in the lease, but the activities must be conducted according to general lease terms, regulations, and Bureau of Land Management and Forest Service stipulations. Prior to actually drilling on the lease, the leaseholder must submit an operating plan to the Bureau of Land Management and receive a permit to drill. For drilling on National Forest System lands, the Bureau of Land Management and the Forest Service again cooperate in conducting an environmental analysis, and the Service makes recommendations on or gives or withholds consent for the portion of the plan addressing surface-resource protection. If the operator makes a discovery and plans to fully develop the lease, another operating plan and environmental review may be required. When the operator wishes to abandon the lease, the Bureau of Land Management, before terminating the lease, again consults with the Forest Service to assure that the lands have been reclaimed properly.

The issuance and development of a lease is a step-by-step process, proceeding from extensive activities with relatively light environmental impacts to intensive development covering a smaller area with more severe environmental impacts. According to the Forest Service, most leases are purchased on pure speculation and never are developed. The Service says that only about five to 10 percent of leases are ever operated on, that only about five percent of leases operated on result in a discovery, and that in the event of a discovery, only small portions of the lease are disturbed. Thus it is difficult to predict at the lease stage whether a lease will ever be developed and, if it is, where development will occur and how intensive it will be. The Forest Service in the past has conducted rather broad environmental reviews and included relatively general stipulations at the lease stage, focusing on specifics as development of the lease proceeds. However, this approach recently has been challenged in the courts by environmentalists—so far with some success—and the Forest Service is likely to have to conduct more intensive environmental analyses at earlier stages in the future. This issue is discussed further under Policies and Trends.

## Common Variety Minerals

Common variety minerals—also called mineral materials—include sand, gravel, clay, pumice, cinders, and other construction materials. Under the Common Varieties of Mineral Materials Act of 1947 (30 U.S.C.A. 601, 602, 611), the Forest Service has authority to sell these materials from the public domain national forests if the sale is not detrimental to the public interest. For acquired national forests, such disposal is governed by the 1947 Mineral Leasing Act for Acquired Lands. After several transfers of authority, this authority was vested in the secretary of Agriculture under the 1960 Transfer Functions Law (7 U.S.C.A. 2201). In addition, the Forest Service can authorize local, state, and federal units of government as well as nonprofit organizations to remove such minerals without charge as long as they are not used for commercial purposes or industrial resale. Most disposals are by such free-use permits. In fact, most of the use of these materials is by the Forest Service itself for road construction.

Requirements regarding common-variety-minerals prospecting and removal are covered in Forest Service regulations (36 CFR 228 Subpart C). The Service conducts an environmental analysis for all planned disposals, which must conform to approved forest land management plans. Activities causing surface disturbance may require an approved operating plan that includes conditions to protect the environment. All contracts or permits must include requirements for reclamation of disturbed areas, except for disposals from community sites or common-use areas, from which nonexclusive disposals may be made to low-volume and/or noncommercial users. Operations by the Forest Service also require an operating plan.

## Protected Areas

Certain areas within the National Forest System are off-limits to new mineral development or are restricted from certain types of development, as described below. In all cases, however, valid existing rights may be developed, although the Forest Service may place restrictions on how those rights are exercised in order to protect the character of the area. The government can extinguish valid existing rights only by acquiring the mineral resources in question.

*Wilderness.* As of January 1, 1984, National Forest System lands designated as wilderness were off-limits to mineral entry, location, and leasing as specified in the National Wilderness Preservation Act of 1964. In addition, for the past several years Congress has specified annually that lands recommended for wilderness designation by the Forest Service under its roadless area review process and congressionally designated wilderness study and further planning areas are off-limits to oil and gas leasing. Valid mining claims in wilderness may be developed, but operations must be conducted in a manner to protect and preserve wilderness values where possible, and patents may be issued only for mineral rights, not for the surface. Prospecting and other activities to gather information about mineral resources can be allowed if they are carried out in ways compatible with preservation of the wilderness environment. Under the Surface Mining Control and Reclamation Act, no surface-coal development has been allowed in wilderness since 1977.

*National Recreation Areas.* All national recreation areas in the National Forest System are withdrawn from mineral entry, location, and patent by their enabling legislation, which also may contain certain restrictions on the development of valid claims. Provisions regarding mineral leasing vary and are specified in the enabling legislation. The Surface Mining Act prohibits surface-coal mining in these areas.

*Wild and Scenic Rivers.* National forest lands within the boundaries of rivers designated as wild within the Wild and Scenic Rivers System are withdrawn from mineral entry and leasing as of the date the river was added to the system. Congressionally designated study rivers also are withdrawn from mineral entry and location generally for three years, but normally are not withdrawn from mineral leasing. Patents to surface rights for valid existing claims can be issued only to the extent reasonably required to carry on mining operations. Scenic and recreation rivers are not withdrawn from mineral operations, but mining proposals are to be evaluated carefully to prevent pollution or other degradation of the area. All designated rivers and study rivers covered in the Wild and Scenic Rivers Act are off-limits to surface coal mining.

*Withdrawals.* Under Section 204 of the Federal Land Policy and Management Act, the secretary of the Interior can make "withdrawals" of federal land to withhold it from settlement, sale, and mineral location and entry in order to maintain other public values in the area or to reserve the area for a particular public use. The secretary of Agriculture can request a withdrawal within the National Forest System, but only the seretary of the Interior can approve it. However, the secretary of the Interior cannot make, modify, or revoke a withdrawal on the National Forest System without the approval of the secretary of Agriculture, except in emergency situations. The secretary of the Interior must notify both houses of Congress if he withdraws an area of 5,000 acres or more. Congress can terminate the withdrawal by passing within 90 days a concurrent resolution stating its disapproval. Withdrawals of this size can be made for a period of no longer than 20 years.

It is Forest Service policy to request withdrawals only where there are sensitive, unique resources that cannot be protected adequately under current public laws. The Forest Service manual states there should be relatively few withdrawals from mineral leasing, on the grounds that surface resources generally can be protected from mineral operations by stipulation and that leasing can be prevented by recommending against the lease or by refusing consent for its issuance.

Nearly 2.2 million acres within the National Forest System are withdrawn from appropriation under the mining laws. The Federal Land Policy and Management Act directs that all lands withdrawn from the mining laws in the 11 western states—except those in wilderness, natural areas, or national recreation areas—be reviewed by 1991 to determine whether or how long the lands should continue to be withdrawn. Beginning in fiscal year 1985, the Forest Service plans to review 20 percent of its withdrawn acreage yearly, about 455,000 acres, in order to complete its recommendations to the Interior Department by 1989. Withdrawal recommendations must be consistent with the forest plans, and a recommendation to discontinue a withdrawal may require an amendment or supplement to the plan.

## Outstanding and Reserved Rights

In many cases where the U.S. government purchased lands for inclusion in the National Forest System, it purchased only the surface rights. The subsurface rights sometimes belonged to a third party, called outstanding rights, or were retained by the owner at the time of sale, called reserved rights. Approximately a third of the mineral rights on eastern national forests are in private hands, and on some forests the proportion is much higher. On the Allegheny National Forest in Pennsylvania, private parties own 97 percent of the oil and gas rights.*

As a general rule, the Forest Service does not have authority to prevent the reasonable exercise of mineral reservations or outstanding rights, but it can require the protection of surface resources. These requirements are somewhat

---

* In many cases, mineral rights were reserved only for a period of 50 years. Since much of the acquisition occurred in the 1930s, mineral rights on several million acres are scheduled to expire over the next decade.

different for outstanding rights than for reserved rights, and requirements for exercising reserved rights differ depending on when the rights are reserved. Mineral rights reserved after May 3, 1963, are governed by Forest Service regulations (36 CFR 251.15). For mineral rights reserved prior to 1963, the rules and regulations in existence at the time of purchase were incorporated into the deed, and they control mining operations today. No regulations cover the exercise of outstanding rights. However, all mining operations must meet the requirements of state and federal environmental laws, such as the Clean Water Act, and surface-coal mining operations must comply with the Surface Mining Control Act.

In practice, the requirements for protection of surface resources in the exercise of any of these rights are much the same. In general, the mineral owner or lessee must submit a plan to the forest supervisor specifying how the mineral operations will be carried out and how the area will be reclaimed. The Forest Service requires the posting of a bond to the extent that it may be required under the terms of the deed or applicable law. Reserved mineral permits are issued only after questions concerning the mineral owner's title and rights have been resolved. Only as much of the surface as is necessary for mining operations is to be disturbed.

## Minerals Planning

The Forest Service has less control over mineral development than it does over most other activities and resources on the National Forest System. The level of mineral activity is dependent largely on market and economic factors rather than Forest Service priorities. In addition, the Forest Service has only limited authority to condition or prevent development in areas where the Service does not own the mineral rights. Furthermore, the Service often lacks data on national forest mineral resources, and predicting where and what type of mineral operations eventually may take place can be difficult. In part for these reasons, planning for mineral development in the forest plans is generally less specific than for other resources, such as timber, recreation, and fish and wildlife habitat.

In general, the forest plans consider the potential for mineral development and the need to withdraw areas from mineral activities or the need for access for mineral exploration and development. Forest Service regulations also require forest plans to consider the probable effect of renewable resources management proposals on mineral development. The plans also may identify areas that are off-limits to certain mineral activities; require restrictions on mineral development in certain areas—such as prohibiting surface occupancy in key wildlife habitat; and define how often valid existing claims are to be inspected in areas intended for strict protection, such as wilderness. The plans generally leave as much area open to mineral exploration and development as possible, subject to constraints imposed by other resource uses. More specific determinations on types of stipulations and conditions to be required for various activities are made when specific exploration or development proposals are generated. Environmental groups have criticized some forest plans for failing to anticipate likely mineral activities adequately, assess their potential impacts, and develop sufficient prescriptions or stipulations to protect other resources, especially in order to anticipate the cumulative impacts of multiple leases or other development. The Service's minerals planning staff say they are now working to develop more detailed guidance for the next round of planning.

## Trends and Issues

*Accelerated Mineral Activity.* Congress repeatedly has granted energy and mineral development high priority on the public lands, including on the National Forest System. The 1872 Mining Law essentially declares mineral development to be the highest and best use of the public domain. The 1920 Mineral Leasing Act weighs heavily in favor of mineral development. And in the 1970 Mining and Minerals Policy Act (30 U.S.C.A. 21a), Congress reiterated this emphasis, declaring it to be the policy of the federal government to foster and encourage energy and mineral development in general.

With the growing concern for reducing America's dependence on foreign oil supplies, as well as increased interest in developing U.S. sources of strategic minerals, interest in developing the nation's energy and mineral resources grew in the 1970s and early 1980s. The 1980 Resources Planning Act program declared it was Forest Service policy "to accelerate the development of National Forest System resources with appropriate environmental safeguards," with priority on development of energy resources. The 1980 program projected the number of operating-plan approvals to increase from 14,500 yearly

Energy mineral workload and production—fiscal years 1980–84

| Fiscal year | Acres under lease *Millions* | Energy-related cases | Energy-related cases in inventory | Oil production | Gas production | Coal production |
|---|---|---|---|---|---|---|
| | | | | *Barrels* | *1,000 cubic feet* | *Short tons* |
| 1980 | 25.0 | 13,980 | 7,300 | 12,200,000 | 213,800,000 | 7,100,000 |
| 1981 | 25.2 | 15,037 | 5,200 | 13,350,000 | 214,100,000 | 12,400,000 |
| 1982 | 25.0 | 16,380 | 7,200 | 13,000,000 | 214,000,000 | 13,000,000 |
| 1983 | 34.4 | 15,940 | 4,400 | 13,000,000 | 205,000,000 | 14,300,000 |
| 1984[1] | 34.0 | 13,103 | 2,805[2] | 12,000,000 | 205,000,000 | 15,100,000 |

[1] All figures are estimated.
[2] Estimate includes 1,386 unprocessed lease applications in wilderness study areas, RARE II recommended wilderness areas, and RARE II further planning areas.
Source: U.S. Department of Agriculture, Forest Service, *Report of the Forest Service, FY 1984.*

in 1978 to 24,000 in 1985 to almost 43,500 by 2030. The Forest Service, in an attempt to promote mineral development to many field officers skeptical about it, began stressing that mineral development could be consistent with multiple use. In this vein, the Forest Service manual states that the Service "recognizes that mineral exploration and development are ordinarily in the public interest and can be compatible in the long-term, if not immediately, with the purposes for which the National Forest System lands are managed" (*Forest Service Manual*, 2822.03).

As a result of increased demand for mineral development and the federal government's efforts to accommodate it, mineral activity increased on the National Forest System, and the minerals program has grown while most other programs, except timber, have shrunk. Acres under lease increased from 25 million in 1980 to 34 million in 1984. In 1984, the minerals program processed 27,300 mineral cases, exceeding its 1980 Resources Planning Act program goal by 20 percent. From 1981 through 1984, the mineral program accomplished an average of 138 percent of 1980 Planning Act program goals, more than any other program. Funding for minerals management has increased more than 100 percent since 1980, from $12.2 million to $26.57 million in 1985. This is a 64 percent increase even when inflation is taken into account. From 1982 to 1985, personnel levels for minerals *increased* 14 percent, while total personnel for the National Forest System decreased 10 percent. Some of the increased funding and staff are to be used to conduct more rigorous environmental assessments and to mitigate mining impacts. In spite of this, the minerals program still receives a relatively small portion of National Forest System funding, less even than fish and wildlife.

*Oil and Gas Leasing.* The greatest increase in mineral activity has been in oil and gas leasing, and some conservationists are concerned that operations on these leases could have adverse impacts on wildlife populations. More than 32 million acres of the National Forest System are under lease for oil and gas, most of it in the Northern, Intermountain, Rocky Mountain, and Southern regions. Environmental groups watching this growing trend report that up to 96 percent of available federal land currently is under lease in some states with significant oil and gas potential, such as Utah and Wyoming. Some conservationists have been particularly concerned about intensive leasing around Yellowstone and Glacier National Parks, which they believe could jeopardize habitat for endangered and threatened species such as the grizzly bear, the gray wolf, and the bald eagle.

Leasing in these areas has generated substantial controversy. Conservation groups have challenged the adequacy of the Forest Service's assessment of the environmental impacts of oil and gas leasing and development, claiming in various instances that the Service has not met its obligations under the Endangered Species Act; has determined, based on stipulations that it cannot enforce, that leases would not have substantial environmental impacts; has prepared only environmental assessments when more comprehensive impact statements should have been completed; did not conduct proper cumulative impact analyses; and leased areas without sufficiently considering what the impacts of future development would be. The Forest Service argues that only a small percentage of leases are ever operated and that even a smaller percentage of total lease acreage is ever affected, making extensive assessments of environmental impacts at the leasing stage difficult, costly, and often unnecessary.

Federal courts have upheld some of environmentalists charges in recent lawsuits—most recently in March 1985, when a federal district court in Montana directed the Forest Service and the Bureau of Land Management to reconsider hundreds of leases issued on the Gallatin and Flathead National Forests in Montana. The government, however, has appealed the decision. While these challenges continue through the courts, it is unclear what the Forest Service must do to meet National Environmental Policy Act requirements when issuing leases. Court rulings in different parts of the country do not yet add up to any comprehensive guidance, and some rulings could be changed by appeals. However it is clear that the trend is toward requiring more thorough analyses than have been conducted to date. In the meantime, it is up to the regional foresters to determine how extensive an environmental assessment is needed at the leasing stage.

***Coal.*** The federal government has not leased federal coal since the fall of 1983 when Congress, in reaction to coal-leasing practices under then-Secretary of the Interior James Watt, placed a moratorium on federal coal leasing and established a commission to study the program. The major complaint was that extensive amounts of coal had been leased for less than fair market value, although concern also existed that leases were being issued without adequate environmental assessment. In response to recommendations made by the commission, as well as a report on environmental requirements by the congressional Office of Technology Assessment, the Department of the Interior has moved to revise the coal-leasing program. A final environmental impact statement on the revised program was issued in October 1985, presumably meaning that federal coal leasing could resume again soon.

***Bureau of Land Management/Forest Service Interchange.*** One pending proposal that could affect minerals policy on the national forests is a Reagan administration proposal to exchange some 35 million acres of land between the Bureau of Land Management and the Forest Service to consolidate land ownerships and reduce administrative duplication. As part of this proposal, administrative responsibility over mineral activities on the National Forest System would be transferred from the Bureau of Land Management to the Forest Service, giving the Forest Service full authority over mineral development on National Forest System lands. The goal of this change is to provide "one-stop" service for mineral operators applying for leases or permits. The exchange proposal, however, would require legislative changes by Congress, which has shown little enthusiasm for the idea. In fact, until specific details of the exchange are outlined, Congress has moved to block the administration from implementing even the elements of the exchange that do not require changes in law.*

# Fish and Wildlife Habitat Management

The 191 million acres of the National Forest System contain forest, rangeland, and aquatic habitats supporting more than 3,000 wildlife species. The system provides habitat crucial for the survival and recovery of 185 federally listed threatened or endangered species, including such animal species as the bald eagle, woodland caribou, grizzly bear, red-cockaded woodpecker, gray wolf, Lahontan cutthroat trout, and Kirtland's warbler, plus an additional 15 species proposed for listing and a growing list of plants. It provides more than 50 percent of the spawning and rearing habitat for salmon and steelhead in the Pacific Northwest, habitat that supports the annual production of more than 118 million pounds of fish, with a direct economic value of approximately $123 million. The National Forest System also contains more than half the big-game habitat in the United States, supporting deer, moose, black bear, bighorn sheep, and mountain goats, among others, and produces nearly 80 percent of all elk killed by hunting in the United States each year.

The National Forest System supports extensive fish and wildlife recreational opportunities. In 1984, hunting and fishing alone accounted for 30.8 million user days.† And as the population increases, access to private land becomes more restricted, and habitat on private land continues to be lost to development, the Forest Service predicts a substantial increase in recreational demand on the national forests—up by 20 percent for hunting and 40 percent for fishing by the year 2000.

The Multiple-Use Sustained-Yield Act of 1960 requires the Forest Service to give fish and wildlife due consideration in National Forest System management, and Forest Service policy requires that fish and wildlife receive "co-equal" consideration with other resources (*Forest Service Manual*, Sec. 2603, #7). But in fact, wildlife and fish have minor roles in the system's management compared to commodity uses. In 1984, for example, timber met 98 percent of its Resources Planning Act accomplishment goals and minerals 120 percent, while wildlife and fish habitat improvement achieved only 25 percent. From 1981 to 1984, wildlife and fish habitat improvement achieved an aver-

---

* For further discussion, see the Bureau of Land Management Status Chapter.
† A user day equals 12 visitor hours.

age of 28 percent of its Resources Planning Act goals*, program compared to 97 percent for timber and 138 percent for minerals. Though funding for wildlife and fish has remained fairly constant in recent years, accounting for inflation shows that a nine percent decline in spending power since 1980. Furthermore, the allocation of these funds has shifted. Dollars for habitat improvement have declined continually as more money is needed to mitigate the effects of other resource activities such as timber harvest, grazing, or oil and gas leasing and development. Extensive legal requirements, increased public demand, mounting development pressures and limited staff and funding make wildlife and fish habitat management on the National Forest System an extremely important and increasingly complex and difficult task.

## Legal Authority and Requirements

Indirect protection for wildlife and fish on the nation's forests began with the passage of the 1891 Forest Reserve Act, which authorized the creation of forest reserves from public domain. Because the act contained no provision for management or use of the reserves, they were theoretically inviolate—off limits to mining, logging, hunting, and fishing. In practice, however, enforcement of these limitations was nearly non-existent. With the passage of the Organic Act in 1897, the forest reserves were opened to a variety of uses, including timber harvesting and mining. The act, however, made no mention of fish or wildlife, leaving their management largely to the discretion of forest rangers.

Many early conservationists had championed the idea of forest reserves as inviolate game sanctuaries, but passage of the Organic Act shifted the focus to creating smaller game refuges inside the forests. The precedent for establishing game refuges on federal land was set in 1903 by the designation of what is today the Pelican Island National Wildlife Refuge, the start of the National Wildlife Refuge System. The first game refuge on the forest system was established in 1905, when Congress authorized President Theodore Roosevelt to set aside part of the Wichita Forest Reserve† in Oklahoma as a "breeding place and refuge for game animals and birds." (Trefethan 1975, p. 71). In 1916, Congress authorized the president to designate game refuges on lands acquired for the National Forest System as well (Act of Aug. 11, 1916, ch. 313, 39 Stat. 446 as amended; 16 U.S.C.A. 683).

---

* This includes only those direct habitat improvements made at the initiation of the fish and wildlife habitat management program. If indirect habitat improvements associated with timber sales and other development activities are included, habitat improvement achieved 34 percent of its goals; if improvements made with Knutson-Vandenberg timber purchaser deposits are included, it achieved 58 percent.

† Today it is the Wichita Mountains National Wildlife Refuge managed by the Fish and Wildlife Service.

Hunting initially was prohibited in these refuges, which were intended to provide natural breeding areas. In general, the refuges were a success, allowing species to reproduce and restock healthy populations on surrounding forest lands. Eventually, however, forest managers realized that the game refuges could not support the unchecked populations, and hunting was allowed. Today, the Forest Service manages 21 game refuges in 12 states, totaling 1.23 million acres. Management of the refuges does not differ significantly from that of the general forest.

Aside from the designation of game refuges, fish and wildlife received little attention on the National Forest System until 1960 when the Multiple-Use Sustained-Yield Act established fish and wildlife as one of several purposes for which the system is to be managed. Although the act gives no guidance as to how the Service should balance these various uses, it clearly authorized and directed the Service to manage for fish and wildlife and required consideration of fish and wildlife values in administering the National Forest System.

The 1960s yielded other legislation with significant implications for fish and wildlife management on the national forests. This included the Wilderness Act of 1964, which created a system of protected areas where wildlife and fish would be largely free from resource development, and the National Environmental Policy Act of 1969, which requires federal agencies to consider the environmental impacts of their proposed actions and to prepare environmen-

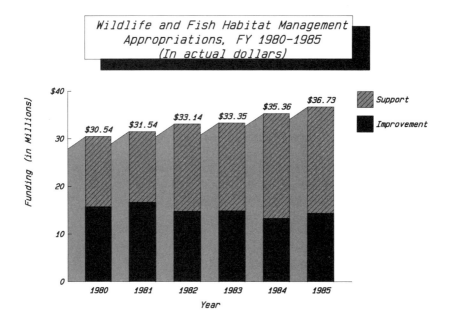

Wildlife and Fish Habitat Management Appropriations, FY 1980–1985 (In actual dollars)

tal impact statements for any major federal actions significantly affecting the human environment.

The Endangered Species Act of 1973 (16 U.S.C.A. 1531-1543) greatly expanded the Forest Service's wildlife management requirements. The stated purpose of the act is "to provide a means whereby the ecosystems upon which endangered species and threatened species depend may be conserved." To achieve this goal, the act directs that all federal departments and agencies "shall use their authorities in furtherance of the purposes of this Act." Section 5 of the act directs the secretary of Agriculture to implement programs on the National Forest System to conserve fish, wildlife, and plants, including federally listed species, and authorizes the use of the Land and Water Conservation Fund to acquire lands to carry out such a program. Under Section 7, the Forest Service is required to consult with the Fish and Wildlife Service to ensure that any actions authorized, funded, or carried out by the Forest Service are not likely to jeopardize the continued existence of threatened or endangered species or to cause the destruction or adverse modification of critical habitat.

The Endangered Species Act led to substantial changes in wildlife and fish management on the National Forest System. It required a more thorough review of project impacts in the planning stages, thus often forcing project modifications to minimize impacts on listed species. It provided a legal tool for environmentalists in protecting fish, wildlife, and plants from the impacts of development. And it ended fish and wildlife management that focused mostly on game species, such as elk, deer, turkey, trout, and salmon.

In 1974, amendments to the Sikes Act (16 U.S.C.A. 670g, 670h, 670o) addressed the need to better coordinate state and federal fish and wildlife management, especially on federal lands. The amendments directed the secretaries of Interior and Agriculture to develop comprehensive plans with state fish and wildlife departments in order "to develop, maintain and coordinate programs for the conservation and rehabilitation of wildlife, fish, and game." In addition, the Sikes Act authorized the implementation of user fees for hunting and fishing on national forests, with receipts to go to the respective states for fish and wildlife conservation and rehabilitation. As of 1985, only the Santa Fe National Forest in New Mexico had a Sikes Act user fee area. Several states use state authorities for implementing fees. Although the Sikes Act did lead to cooperative agreements for fish and wildlife management with nearly every state, it resulted in little active change in Forest Service management as it merely strengthened state-Forest Service cooperative efforts already in place.

The Resources Planning Act of 1974 and the National Forest Management Act of 1976 added more specific requirements for fish and wildlife management on the National Forest System. The National Forest Management Act clarified and built on the multiple-use requirements of the Multiple-Use Sustained-Yield Act, specifically calling for the maintenance of a diversity of plant and animal communities. It also placed limits on timber harvest practices that could harm fish and wildlife populations, including a prohibition on logging likely to affect water quality and fish habitat seriously.* These laws also established a more comprehensive planning process than did the Sikes Act, in which fish and wildlife must be considered along with other resource uses. Today, Sikes Act agreements primarily provide specific implementation schedules for habitat work broadly outlined in forest plans.

Another important provision of the National Forest Management Act was an amendment of the 1930 Knutson-Vandenberg Act that allows funds deposited by timber purchasers for the protection and improvement of fish and wildlife habitat. Knutson-Vandenberg monies can provide a substantial amount of habitat improvement in addition to that accomplished with funds appropriated to the Wildlife and Fish Program.† In 1984, for example, Knutson-Vandenberg deposits funded improvements on 130,000 acres, almost as much as the 158,000 acres of improvements accomplished with appropriated funds. However, the use of Knutson-Vandenberg funds is limited to the actual timber sale area. The funds cannot be used to improve adjacent areas affected by the sale, a provision that particularly limits fish-habitat improvement since many timber sales bound, but do not cross, rivers and streams. Knutson-Vandenberg funds are discussed further under Timber Management.

## Wildlife and Fish Planning and Management

Habitat management on the National Forest System is a cooperative venture between the Forest Service and the states and often other federal agencies as well. The general division of responsibilities is outlined in memoranda of understanding between the Forest Service and each state. The memoranda formally give the states the lead in managing species populations and gives the service the lead in managing habitat. In practice, however, effective management dictates that the Service provide recommendations in setting seasons and that the states provide input in habitat management decisions. While forest plans set objectives for habitat management, actual scheduling of habitat improvements is contained in the Sikes Act agreements, which the Forest Service has signed with 42 states. In some cases, the service works cooperatively with several other state, federal, and private interests to coordinate management efforts on a regional basis, including participation in the Oregon-Washington Interagency Wildlife Committee in the Pacific Northwest and the Interagency Grizzly Bear Committee, discussed later. Volunteer labor and private funding from local conservation groups such as Trout Unlimited, Ducks Unlimited, and National Audubon Society chapters, also is important in contributing to habitat-improvement objectives.

* Discussed in more detail under Timber Management.
† Although Knutson-Vandenberg funds technically are to be used for resource *improvements,* some funds are used for mitigation of adverse impacts.

*Fish and Wildlife Planning.*   To meet the National Forest Management Act's mandate to maintain a diversity of plant and animal communities on the National Forest System, the Forest Service is required by Department of Agriculture regulations to maintain "viable" populations. Viable populations are defined as having sufficient numbers and distribution to ensure that they will continue to exist in a well-distributed pattern throughout the planning area.

To ensure that viable populations are maintained, the Service requires the forests to select "management indicator species." Indicator species may include species with special protection needs, such as endangered species; species with special habitat requirements that could be affected seriously by proposed management activities; game or nongame species of special public interest; or species whose populations fluctuate in response to certain activities and are thought to be indicators of biological change. In general, indicator species are presumed to indicate the welfare of groups of other species. For example, the spotted owl is monitored as a representative of Pacific Northwest old-growth coniferous forest species, and a decline in its population is likely to represent a decline in other species associated with that habitat, including the goshawk, pine marten, pileated woodpecker, and flying squirrel. Indicator species are used both to estimate the effects of the various proposed management alternatives on fish and wildlife and, subsequent to the planning process, to monitor the effects of management activities on viable populations. In addition, national management indicator species are listed in the Resources Planning Act program. The national list includes mule deer, white-tailed deer, black-tailed deer, elk, wild turkey, cavity-nesting birds, resident trout, and anadromous fish.

The forest plans establish standards and guidelines for maintaining viable populations of each of the indicator species. These guidelines generally specify the types and distribution of vegetation or other habitat components that are to be maintained throughout the planning area. For example, for cavity-nesting bird species, the plan might specify the size and number of snags to be maintained per acre. The plan may include certain constraints to ensure the distribution of a species; for example, old-growth stands managed for spotted owl habitat in the Pacific Northwest must be within a certain distance of each other to allow the owls to fly from one area to another. The plans also identify certain indicator species to receive special emphasis and to be managed to increase rather than just maintain their populations. These generally are game species such as deer and elk.

In addition to establishing objectives for maintaining and improving the habitat of indicator species, forest plans also must identify habitat considered critical for endangered and threatened species, and measures must be prescribed to prevent the adverse modification of such habitat. Where possible, the plans are to establish appropriate conservation measures, including the designation of special protection areas, for the recovery and removal of species from the endangered and threatened list. Finally, federal regulations require the Forest Service to consult with state and other federal agencies to coordinate wildlife management planning efforts.

As development pressures have increased and planning and legal requirements have multiplied, the Forest Service has had to develop new information and new management and data base systems. The most significant of these is the Wildlife and Fish Habitat Relationships program, which is becoming the backbone of wildlife management on the National Forest System. Under this program, the regions and forests have adopted or developed database systems and predictive models to assess the consequences of land-management decisions on wildlife populations. Implementing the program requires information about an individual species' relationship with its habitat, from which the effects of potential habitat alterations can be predicted. This new management system has given the Forest Service greater latitude in wildlife-habitat management, allowing it to go beyond managing for high-visibility game species, such as elk and deer, to management of whole species complexes. In addition, the predictive function of the system allows managers to foresee resource-development conflicts and tradeoffs and to move away from the purely reactive management of the past.

*Wildlife Coordination.* The greatest portion of the Fish and Wildlife Program's efforts is in wildlife and fish coordination (previously called "support") which is intended to minimize adverse impacts on fish and wildlife habitat from other resource activities, such as grazing, logging, and mining. Coordination activities may include streamside protection measures for fish habitats affected by roading, timber harvesting, or grazing; designing timber sales to meet wildlife habitat needs; and modifying livestock grazing plans to protect critical riparian zones. Whenever possible, such projects are designed not only to mitigate adverse impacts, but also to produce concurrent fish and wildlife benefits, often referred to as indirect habitat improvements. Wildlife and fish budget funds expended for coordination in 1985 amounted to $22.37 million, 61 percent of the fish and wildlife habitat management budget. Knutson-Vandenberg deposits are a separate source of funding, and are not included in support.

*Direct Habitat Improvement.* The other major category of activities carried out under the wildlife program is direct habitat improvement. Direct habitat improvement projects differ from indirect habitat improvement efforts in that they are not carried out in conjunction with another resource project, such as a timber sale. Direct improvements include activities such as prescribed burning to create openings and early successional vegetation for such species as white-tailed deer and the endangered Kirtland's warbler, installing nesting boxes for waterfowl, developing lake and stream spawning beds and cover for fish, and installing gates or other barriers to limit vehicle access to grizzly bear and elk habitat at critical periods. Direct habitat improvement

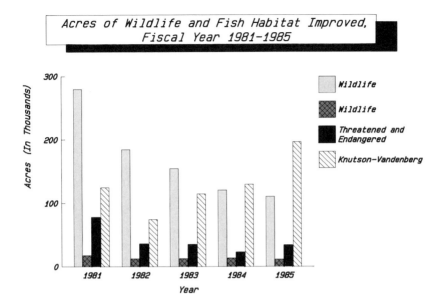

Acres of Wildlife and Fish Habitat Improved, Fiscal Year 1981–1985

currently is a secondary priority in the habitat management program and was funded at $14.36 million in 1985, 39 percent of the habitat management budget.

The majority of wildlife habitat improvement is accomplished by prescribed burning. Many wildlife species depend on early successional vegetation types, including the Kirtland's warbler, bighorn sheep, certain woodpeckers, and, to an extent, the grizzly bear. But throughout its history, the Forest Service's fire suppression efforts have been so successful that vegetative types representing later successional stages have occurred in many areas where they probably would not if left to natural forces. In order to promote early successional species, prescribed fire often is necessary.

When burning is prescribed by wildlife biologists, members of the service's fire management staff are brought in to determine the feasibility and mechanics of the burn. Biological evaluations are required when threatened, endangered, proposed, and sensitive species are present, and an environmental assessment is prepared for larger burns. Although the Service's prescribed burning has by and large been very successful, it is not without risks. For example, after conducting 56 successful burns to improve Kirtland's warbler habitat, a 25,000-acre blaze occurred in central Michigan when the service lost control of what was to be a 200-acre burn.

***Endangered, Threatened and Sensitive Species.*** Eighty-five threatened or endangered species occur on the National Forest System, including 60 animal species and 25 plant species. The Forest Service consults with the Fish and

Wildlife Service to ensure that activities on the National Forest System do not jeopardize listed species. In addition, the Service works to recover listed species, for example by assisting the Fish and Wildlife Service in preparing recovery plans for species with habitat on the National Forest System and by developing "implementation strategies" to carry out actions assigned to the service in recovery plans. Although 64 listed species on the National Forest System have recovery plans, budget and personnel constrictions limit most recovery efforts to 13 high-priority species: the grizzly bear, California condor, Kirtland's warbler, red-cockaded woodpecker, Lahonton cutthroat trout, greenback cutthroat trout, woodland caribou, bald eagle, peregrine falcon, Puerto Rican parrot, and, to a lesser degree, the gray, Indiana, and Virginia big-eared bats. Funding for endangered species recovery has increased steadily in recent years, from $865,000 in 1980 to $2.46 million in 1985, but still amounts to only seven percent of the habitat management total.

In some special management situations, the Forest Service works closely with other federal and state agencies, going beyond mandatory consultation with the Fish and Wildlife Service. This is the case with the grizzly bear, a federally listed threatened species in the Lower 48 that survives on lands in various state, federal, and private ownerships in Wyoming, Idaho, Montana, and perhaps Washington. The Forest Service has joined with the National Park Service, the Fish and Wildlife Service, state fish and wildlife departments, and interested private organizations to form the Interagency Grizzly Bear Committee for the coordination of research and recovery efforts. Similar cooperative efforts have occurred in California for the recovery of the endangered California condor, for the northern spotted owl in Oregon, Washington, and California, and for the Puerto Rican parrot.

In addition to providing protection for federally listed threatened and endangered species, the Forest Service places special management emphasis on "sensitive species." Although this designation carries no legal weight, it is used by the Forest Service to identify species that may need special management attention to prevent their listing by the Fish and Wildlife Service as threatened or endangered species.

***Anadromous Fish.*** In 1982, the Forest Service embarked on a major initiative to restore instream habitats in the Northwest, where salmon stocks are at all-time lows due in part to habitat degradation. Some 50 percent of the salmon and steelhead spawning and rearing habitat in California, Oregon, Washington, and Idaho is on national forests; in Alaska the figure is 27 percent. Because of the combined commercial and recreational value of these fisheries, estimated at $349 million in 1983, and the willingness of the states, the Northwest Power Planning Council, individual Indian tribes, and private organizations to provide additional funding and manpower, the Forest Service has accelerated a program of instream habitat improvements. Examples of such improvements include barrier removal, spawning-bed improvement, pool development, and cover enhancement. Although the Service has identified anadromous-fish habitat improvement as a priority, to date, this initiative has been hampered by inadequate federal funding.

*Resident Fish.* The National Forest System contains or directly affects most of the nation's premier trout streams and supports significant warm-water fisheries as well. In all, the national forests contain 128,000 miles of fishable streams and 2.2 million acres of lakes and reservoirs. These areas contribute significantly to public-angling opportunities, commercial-fishing success, and subsistence fishing by Native Americans. In 1985, the National Forest System supported 15.7 million fish-user days, of which more than 14 million were related to resident fish.

The productivity of fish habitat on the National Forest System has declined over the last decade, particularly in the West, because of timber harvesting and livestock grazing. Although techniques to mitigate the impacts of these activities have been successful in many cases, mitigation efforts have not been funded sufficiently to support full compensation of the losses. To reverse this trend, additional emphasis is needed on the protection and enhancement of fish habitat. The Forest Service estimates that habitat improvements have the potential to support a 25-percent increase in fish populations, but only if funding is increased.

*Wildlife Damage Control.* Department of Agriculture policy directs that wildlife damage control be initiated when animal populations threaten public health, safety, or threatened and endangered species or when they threaten to cause excessive damage to other resources. Jurisdiction for wildlife damage control on the National Forest System is divided among the Forest Service, the Fish and Wildlife Service, and the states, although the Forest Service recognizes the Fish and Wildlife Service as the lead agency.* The Forest Service conducts routine wildlife damage control activities such as controlling pocket gopher damage to tree seedlings, but by agreement, only the Fish and Wildlife Service or state agencies conduct predator control activities, such as control of coyote, mountain lion, or bobcat depredation on livestock. Forest Service responsibilities for wildlife damage control are handled by the wildlife staff. An environmental assessment must be done for any wildlife damage control, and if threatened, endangered, proposed, or sensitive species are present, a biological evaluation must be prepared.

In 1984, the majority of the damage to forest and range resources was done by pocket gophers, deer, elk, mountain beaver, and prairie dogs. Wildlife damage control is not limited to the use of direct control measures, such as

---

* Responsibilty for wildlife damage control was transferred at the end of 1985 by an amendment to the 1986 continuing resolution from the Fish and Wildlife Service to the Animal, Plant and Health Inspection Service in the Department of Agriculture.

poisoning and trapping. For example, the program may protect new, regenerating trees from grazing wildlife through use of chemical repellants, plastic seedling protectors, or fencing.

## Trends and Issues

The overall trend in fish and wildlife management on the National Forest System over the past decade has been a shift in emphasis from game-species management to a broader management approach based on whole species complexes. The new management systems already described illustrate this shift. The most significant trend has been the growing proportion of habitat-management funds spent on resource coordination rather than improvement. In addition, two areas of habitat management recently have become priorities within the Forest Service's habitat management program: wetlands and anadromous fish habitat. In both, cases the Forest Service is using private support to augment its own limited budget and field staff.

*Drop in Habitat Improvement.* Since 1982, the number of acres of habitat improvement have declined steadily as mitigation and planning needs have increased. In 1981, habitat improvement received more funding than fish and wildlife coordination, but by 1985, coordination funding was nearly double that for direct improvement. Acres directly improved for wildlife decreased from 280,140 in 1981 to 158,100 in 1984, to 110,973 acres in 1985, nearly a 61-percent reduction over five years. The drop in habitat improvement is due to an emphasis on planning and on revenue-producing activities, such as timber harvest and energy and mineral development, with decreasing funds for habitat management.

*Wetlands and Anadromous Fish.* There is a growing interest, both inside and outside of the Forest Service in increasing efforts to improve anadromous-fish habitat in the National Forest System. A compilation of the habitat-improvement aspects of the various Sikes Act plans indicates a significant opportunity to increase anadromous fish production in the national forests. To increase fish production 60 percent, the Forest Service would need to spend an estimated $7.7 million in 1985, rising to $14.2 million in five years. Administration budget requests, however, have fallen far short of these levels, and although Congress recently has added some funds to the Forest Service budget specifically for anadromous fish, the current program is still small. In 1985, anadromous-fish habitat improvement was funded at $3.8 million, about half the necessary funds. If this level of funding is continued, it is estimated that habitat quality will at best stay the same and could decline as much as an additional 10 percent by the year 2000.

Since the Forest Service has had considerable success enlisting the support of private organizations such as Trout Unlimited to help provide funding and manpower for stream improvement, it is now trying to do the same to help preserve its portion of the nation's vanishing wetlands. In 1984, the Department of Agriculture and the Department of the Interior signed a cooperative agreement with Ducks Unlimited for that organization to expand its efforts to preserve wetlands on the national forests and other public lands. Later that year, the Chippewa National Forest, in cooperation with Ducks Unlimited, built three impoundments designed to improve waterfowl habitat at a cost to Ducks Unlimited of $105,000.

## Recreation and Wilderness Management

Much of the land originally designated as national forests was considered undesirable by those who opened the West. By and large these were rough and forested lands, often at high elevations and far from the burgeoning population centers. But the remoteness and spectacular scenery of these areas has made the National Forest System the leader among federal lands in recreation use. More outdoor recreation occurs on the National Forest System than on any other single landholding. Approximately 228 million recreational visitor days* were registered on the National Forest System in 1984, accounting for 41 percent of all visitor days on federal lands. In contrast, the National Park

* A recreational visitor day is 12 visitor hours, which may be calculated as continuous, intermittent, or simultaneous use by one or more persons.

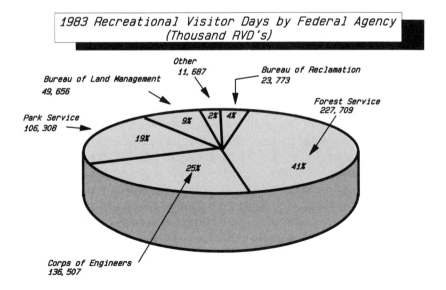

**1983 Recreational Visitor Days by Federal Agency (Thousand RVD's)**

Other
11, 687

Bureau of Land Management
49, 656

Bureau of Reclamation
23, 773

Forest Service
227, 709

Park Service
106, 308

2% 4%

9%

19%

25%

41%

Corps of Engineers
136, 507

*Total Recreation Visitor Days—555, 640 Thousand*

System accounted for 19 percent. Activities on the National Forest System include camping at more than 5,000 overnight campgrounds, hiking on 98,500 miles of trails, canoeing on 20,000 miles of rivers and 1.4 million acres of lakes, snowshoeing, off-road vehicle use, and trail-riding. About two-thirds of the recreation occurs in undeveloped forest areas.

Recreational use of the national forests has increased dramatically since the 1950s, and recreational demand is expected to continue to increase at a strong although somewhat slower rate. The Forest Service predicts that in the next 50 years overall recreational demand in the United States will increase 61 percent for land-based recreation such as camping, hiking, and nature study; 206 percent for water-based recreation; and 240 percent for snow and ice-related recreation, particularly skiing. The National Forest System will have to meet much of this demand.

Wildlife and recreation are interrelated in both positive and negative ways. Wildlife-related recreation is a significant portion of total recreational use. Hunting and fishing alone accounted for 30.8 million user days in 1984 or 13.6 percent of total recreational use. Thus wildlife habitat management can provide important recreation benefits. At the same time, elements of the recreation program, such as protection of wilderness areas and maintaining free-flowing wild rivers, can provide wildlife benefits. On the other hand, some recreational uses, including off-road vehicles and the construction of large facilities such as downhill ski areas, can cause conflicts with fish and wildlife conservation. As recreational demand increases, wildlife enhancement will be increasingly necessary to meet the demand, and efforts to minimize recreation-wildlife conflicts will become increasingly important.

## Legal Authority and Requirements

Although the Forest Service began to address the demand for recreational use of the forests as early as the 1920s, it had no specific authority to manage the forests for recreation until the passage of the Multiple-Use Sustained-Yield Act in 1960.* In fact, this act was prompted in part by the increasing demand for recreation on the forests at the same time that demand was rising for commodity uses, particularly timber. The Multiple-Use Sustained-Yield Act gives no guidance regarding recreation management, but does specify that outdoor recreation must be considered along with other forest uses in administering the National Forest System.

The other general authority for recreational use on the system comes from the 1974 Forest and Rangeland Resources Planning Act as amended by the 1976 National Forest Management Act. Again, these laws do not establish any particular standards and criteria for outdoor recreation management, but

---

* A brief history of recreation management on the National Forest System is covered in the section on History and Legislative Authority.

Estimated Wildlife- and Fish-related Recreation Visitor Days on the National Forest System—Fiscal Year 1984

| Region | | Cold Water Fishing | Warm Water Fishing | Salt Water Fishing | Ice Fishing | Big Game Hunting | Small Game Hunting | Upland Game Bird Hunting | Waterfowl Hunting |
|---|---|---|---|---|---|---|---|---|---|
| 1 | RVDs | 894,500 | 11,900 | 0 | 16,500 | 1,089,300 | 73,000 | 188,000 | 55,200 |
|   | Percent | 96.9 | 1.3 | 0 | 1.8 | 77.5 | 5.2 | 13.4 | 3.9 |
| 2 | RVDs | 1,628,000 | 38,500 | 0 | 11,200 | 1,324,600 | 101,700 | 54,200 | 29,900 |
|   | Percent | 97.0 | 2.3 | 0 | .7 | 87.7 | 6.7 | 3.6 | 2.0 |
| 3 | RVDs | 659,000 | 296,500 | 0 | 1,500 | 820,300 | 154,200 | 110,800 | 61,800 |
|   | Percent | 68.9 | 31.0 | 0 | .2 | 71.5 | 13.4 | 9.7 | 5.4 |
| 4 | RVDs | 2,184,300 | 4,200 | 0 | 2,100 | 1,327,600 | 76,800 | 123,800 | 49,400 |
|   | Percent | 99.7 | .2 | 0 | .1 | 84.3 | 4.9 | 7.9 | 2.9 |
| 5 | RVDs | 2,339,900 | 390,700 | 43,900 | 12,500 | 850,300 | 134,000 | 103,500 | 28,200 |
|   | Percent | 84.0 | 14.0 | 1.6 | .4 | 76.2 | 12.0 | 9.3 | 2.5 |
| 6 | RVDs | 1,743,500 | 10,400 | 27,200 | 2,200 | 1,866,100 | 99,300 | 136,300 | 46,500 |
|   | Percent | 97.8 | .6 | 1.5 | .1 | 86.9 | 4.6 | 6.3 | 2.2 |
| 8 | RVDs | 787,400 | 1,966,900 | 11,500 | 700 | 2,006,600 | 1,278,700 | 411,600 | 100,200 |
|   | Percent | 28.5 | 71.1 | .4 | 0 | 52.8 | 33.7 | 10.8 | 2.6 |
| 9 | RVDs | 639,500 | 1,327,600 | 300 | 161,200 | 1,222,500 | 584,500 | 399,700 | 188,300 |
|   | Percent | 30.4 | 62.4 | 0 | 7.6 | 51.0 | 24.4 | 16.7 | 7.9 |
| 10 | RVDs | 249,500 | 0 | 137,300 | 3,200 | 104,700 | 12,300 | 13,300 | 19,300 |
|   | Percent | 64.0 | 0 | 35.2 | .8 | 70.0 | 8.2 | 8.9 | 12.9 |
| TOTAL | RVDs | 11,125,600 | 4,046,700 | 220,200 | 211,100 | 10,612,000 | 2,515,300 | 1,541,200 | 575,800 |
|   | Percent | 71.3 | 25.9 | 1.4 | 1.4 | 69.6 | 16.5 | 10.1 | 3.8 |

Use expressed in recreation visitor days (RVDs) as provided by the recreation information management data base (RIM).

State Summary of Total Recreation Use on National Forest System Lands by Activity—Fiscal Year 1984

| State,[1] Territory, or Commonwealth | Camping | Picnicking | Travel (mechanized) | Water sports | Winter sports | Fishing | Hunting | Hiking & mountain climbing |
|---|---|---|---|---|---|---|---|---|
| | | | | 1,000 RVDs[2] | | | | |
| Alabama | 192.2 | 59.1 | 211.8 | 145.9 | 0 | 61.1 | 236.7 | 63.9 |
| Alaska | 275.2 | 49.7 | 343.5 | 1,112.9 | 106.1 | 390.0 | 149.6 | 230.0 |
| Arizona | 3,776.2 | 671.8 | 6,287.0 | 1,137.1 | 121.5 | 580.8 | 590.6 | 625.9 |
| Arkansas | 449.4 | 102.6 | 376.6 | 260.5 | 0 | 311.6 | 466.4 | 102.3 |
| California | 14,478.9 | 1,460.1 | 14,104.8 | 4,060.3 | 3,063.2 | 2,943.1 | 1,157.5 | 2,771.8 |
| Colorado | 4,333.5 | 424.1 | 4,312.9 | 214.2 | 4,459.2 | 1,317.6 | 1,045.6 | 1,513.2 |
| Florida | 1,035.6 | 262.4 | 261.8 | 350.4 | 0 | 135.6 | 189.6 | 39.5 |
| Georgia | 490.7 | 84.7 | 505.2 | 163.0 | 3.3 | 225.9 | 312.4 | 197.9 |
| Idaho | 2,753.0 | 335.5 | 2,280.6 | 577.9 | 612.3 | 845.2 | 817.6 | 437.1 |
| Illinois | 102.0 | 42.2 | 160.3 | 60.0 | .1 | 39.3 | 116.5 | 83.1 |
| Indiana | 127.3 | 17.7 | 40.6 | 45.9 | 0 | 53.0 | 43.7 | 18.1 |
| Kansas | 1.1 | 2.6 | 8.2 | 0 | .1 | .5 | 2.4 | .5 |
| Kentucky | 352.6 | 110.2 | 352.6 | 463.1 | .9 | 229.5 | 150.0 | 189.9 |
| Louisiana | 102.7 | 39.6 | 72.1 | 34.4 | 0 | 46.0 | 102.7 | 20.4 |
| Maine | 10.9 | 2.2 | 1.8 | 2.5 | .8 | 2.7 | 7.4 | 10.5 |
| Michigan | 957.6 | 89.5 | 1,542.5 | 345.4 | 131.0 | 440.3 | 640.1 | 117.7 |
| Minnesota | 1,298.7 | 47.1 | 544.1 | 751.8 | 104.8 | 667.7 | 291.9 | 70.4 |
| Mississippi | 174.7 | 43.8 | 315.8 | 83.3 | 0 | 71.4 | 429.0 | 65.0 |
| Missouri | 343.0 | 93.7 | 392.7 | 246.6 | .1 | 85.9 | 283.8 | 77.4 |
| Montana | 1,720.8 | 299.7 | 2,257.2 | 320.4 | 586.5 | 693.6 | 958.5 | 619.3 |

| | | | | | | | |
|---|---|---|---|---|---|---|---|
| Nebraska | 23.8 | 13.7 | 18.0 | 4.3 | .2 | 5.8 | 17.8 | 6.6 |
| Nevada | 432.6 | 155.8 | 309.2 | 119.5 | 125.2 | 106.0 | 123.1 | 98.8 |
| New Hampshire | 540.2 | 51.8 | 372.3 | 32.0 | 431.8 | 21.5 | 34.1 | 448.8 |
| New Mexico | 1,499.4 | 532.5 | 1,044.4 | 146.6 | 519.2 | 358.8 | 549.2 | 512.1 |
| New York | 7.9 | 1.9 | .8 | 0 | .8 | 1.3 | 5.3 | 1.5 |
| North Carolina | 912.4 | 175.1 | 940.3 | 266.1 | 1.6 | 284.6 | 469.4 | 496.1 |
| North Dakota | 13.6 | 236.4 | 18.8 | 2.5 | 1.3 | 4.1 | 60.6 | 2.4 |
| Ohio | 34.7 | 28.4 | 87.1 | 19.9 | .3 | 24.4 | 98.6 | 34.5 |
| Oklahoma | 55.7 | 27.2 | 141.1 | 27.9 | 0 | 20.5 | 57.9 | 17.5 |
| Oregon | 6,013.1 | 737.1 | 4,043.5 | 1,118.2 | 953.4 | 1,152.0 | 1,290.2 | 996.6 |
| Pennsylvania | 425.1 | 29.1 | 353.2 | 132.1 | 5.4 | 263.2 | 462.9 | 85.5 |
| Puerto Rico | 13.5 | 200.1 | 35.8 | 69.0 | 0 | 0 | 0 | 97.2 |
| South Carolina | 178.9 | 54.7 | 268.9 | 76.5 | 0 | 68.3 | 203.3 | 41.9 |
| South Dakota | 148.3 | 47.3 | 1,570.0 | 56.5 | 38.5 | 68.5 | 158.8 | 63.6 |
| Tennessee | 709.5 | 243.5 | 507.7 | 290.3 | .5 | 172.6 | 244.8 | 125.5 |
| Texas | 426.3 | 53.1 | 150.6 | 150.5 | 0 | 870.0 | 188.0 | 30.3 |
| Utah | 4,277.2 | 586.5 | 2,673.4 | 352.1 | 901.2 | 1,169.7 | 817.0 | 773.9 |
| Vermont | 43.8 | 12.9 | 104.6 | 12.1 | 309.5 | 5.1 | 30.8 | 14.9 |
| Virginia | 711.8 | 186.6 | 604.5 | 169.9 | 4.8 | 277.4 | 638.2 | 260.1 |
| Washington | 3,728.5 | 364.3 | 3,146.1 | 301.5 | 1,076.1 | 620.4 | 853.3 | 783.0 |
| West Virginia | 405.3 | 42.9 | 192.9 | 35.2 | 2.2 | 143.3 | 280.7 | 67.0 |
| Wisconsin | 440.6 | 29.0 | 535.3 | 157.0 | 21.0 | 390.3 | 215.2 | 33.3 |
| Wyoming | 1,435.7 | 150.3 | 1,237.8 | 157.9 | 317.5 | 435.0 | 453.1 | 326.2 |
| Total | 55,454.0 | 8,198.5 | 52,728.4 | 14,073.2 | 13,900.4 | 15,603.6 | 15,244.3 | 12,571.2 |

[1]States not listed have no Forest Service recreation program.

[2]One recreation visitor-day (RVD) is the recreation use of National Forest land or water that aggregates 12 visitor-hours. This may entail one person for 12 hours, 12 persons for one hour, or any equivalent combination of individual or group use, either continuous or intermittent.

State Summary of Total Recreation Use on National Forest System Lands by Activity—Fiscal Year 1984—continued

| Horseback riding | Recreation cabin use | Nature study | Sightseeing | Visitor information service users | Other developed site use | Total use | State,[1] Territory, or Commonwealth |
|---|---|---|---|---|---|---|---|
| | | | | 1,000 RVDs[2] | | | |
| 9.4 | 0 | 29.6 | 17.7 | 22.9 | 3.4 | 1,053.7 | Alabama |
| 2.9 | 101.5 | 79.7 | 546.2 | 97.3 | 35.0 | 3,519.6 | Alaska |
| 251.7 | 280.1 | 545.9 | 513.6 | 269.3 | 725.2 | 16,376.7 | Arizona |
| 30.1 | 7.6 | 54.2 | 25.5 | 34.4 | 30.1 | 2,251.3 | Arkansas |
| 585.1 | 3,205.8 | 1,120.3 | 2,015.0 | 661.0 | 3,849.4 | 55,476.3 | California |
| 428.6 | 221.9 | 490.1 | 1,212.1 | 189.1 | 572.8 | 20,734.9 | Colorado |
| 24.7 | 132.0 | 46.3 | 32.8 | 33.4 | 85.9 | 2,630.0 | Florida |
| 29.5 | 28.5 | 56.0 | 117.0 | 20.0 | 41.5 | 2,275.6 | Georgia |
| 267.4 | 255.0 | 615.0 | 275.7 | 134.5 | 299.1 | 10,505.9 | Idaho |
| 50.3 | 0 | 42.1 | 88.1 | 11.8 | 5.6 | 801.4 | Illinois |
| 27.6 | 0 | 8.7 | 1.3 | 4.8 | 0 | 388.7 | Indiana |
| .2 | 0 | .8 | 0 | 0 | .1 | 16.5 | Kansas |
| 28.3 | 11.2 | 51.5 | 93.9 | 33.3 | 23.4 | 2,090.4 | Kentucky |
| 4.9 | 9.8 | 17.7 | 2.9 | 9.9 | 17.1 | 480.2 | Louisiana |
| 0 | 0 | 2.4 | 3.3 | 1.1 | 6.0 | 51.6 | Maine |
| 22.0 | 74.9 | 160.4 | 84.3 | 29.8 | 17.0 | 4,652.5 | Michigan |
| 7.3 | 204.4 | 112.5 | 18.2 | 37.8 | 145.8 | 4,302.5 | Minnesota |
| 16.5 | 0 | 23.1 | 7.5 | 14.8 | 1.1 | 1,246.0 | Mississippi |
| 27.1 | 0 | 78.2 | 46.2 | 12.4 | 19.8 | 1,706.9 | Missouri |
| 391.5 | 209.2 | 538.2 | 330.6 | 224.3 | 238.3 | 9,388.1 | Montana |

| | | | | | | | |
|---|---|---|---|---|---|---|---|
| 5.8 | 0 | 13.8 | .3 | 9.4 | 9.9 | 129.4 | Nebraska |
| 47.1 | 25.7 | 105.9 | 54.8 | 205.2 | 150.2 | 2,059.1 | Nevada |
| .2 | 0 | 12.8 | 243.9 | 22.5 | 74.3 | 2,286.2 | New Hampshire |
| 139.5 | 90.1 | 458.7 | 232.1 | 163.4 | 170.1 | 6,416.1 | New Mexico |
| 1.2 | 0 | 1.6 | 0 | 0 | 0 | 22.3 | New York |
| 47.4 | 6.7 | 92.0 | 273.0 | 97.0 | 24.0 | 4,085.7 | North Carolina |
| 3.7 | 0 | 3.1 | 9.2 | 1.8 | 0 | 357.5 | North Dakota |
| 14.1 | 0 | 17.5 | 4.2 | 10.6 | 2.0 | 376.3 | Ohio |
| 3.5 | 0 | 7.8 | 30.1 | 9.4 | .2 | 398.8 | Oklahoma |
| 245.3 | 380.8 | 1,002.3 | 988.9 | 406.1 | 812.0 | 20,139.5 | Oregon |
| 5.3 | 48.8 | 51.5 | 117.1 | 12.0 | 9.6 | 2,000.8 | Pennsylvania |
| 0 | 3.5 | 12.3 | 24.8 | 45.8 | 28.2 | 530.2 | Puerto Rico |
| 21.7 | 0 | 37.9 | 23.8 | 18.2 | 10.0 | 1,004.1 | South Carolina |
| 16.7 | 80.8 | 50.3 | 122.8 | 88.4 | 45.6 | 2,556.1 | South Dakota |
| 26.2 | 39.1 | 31.4 | 51.1 | 25.2 | 57.8 | 2,525.2 | Tennessee |
| 7.3 | 0 | 16.3 | 36.7 | 15.4 | 20.7 | 1,965.2 | Texas |
| 293.8 | 198.7 | 345.8 | 354.0 | 126.0 | 751.8 | 13,621.1 | Utah |
| 1.3 | .3 | 5.1 | 45.6 | 3.0 | 20.2 | 609.2 | Vermont |
| 80.2 | 0 | 137.9 | 370.9 | 36.2 | 37.9 | 3,516.4 | Virginia |
| 174.9 | 407.2 | 448.2 | 955.6 | 447.9 | 679.8 | 13,986.8 | Washington |
| 4.0 | .2 | 25.0 | 114.0 | 21.5 | 36.2 | 1,370.4 | West Virginia |
| 3.6 | 15.8 | 66.9 | 7.6 | 5.4 | 7.9 | 1,928.9 | Wisconsin |
| 197.5 | 180.1 | 175.5 | 265.8 | 60.0 | 327.4 | 5,719.8 | Wyoming |
| 3,545.4 | 6,219.7 | 7,192.3 | 9,758.2 | 3,672.3 | 9,392.4 | 227,553.9 | Total |

they do require that the forest plans provide for multiple use, including outdoor recreation.

A number of other laws give the service authority or mandates to protect particular recreation-related resources and are discussed below.

*Wilderness.* The Forest Service began providing protection for roadless areas early in its history. The Service designated the first primitive area by administrative fiat in 1924, and by 1929 had established regulations setting criteria and procedures for creating a system of such areas. But by the 1950s, increased timber harvesting and agency intentions to decrease the size of some wilderness areas led many to the fear that the Service would remove protection from areas that had commercial timber resources. Conservationists began to push for a law that would take wilderness protection out of the Service's discretion and permanently protect roadless areas designated as wilderness by Congress. After nearly a decade of debate, Congress passed such a law, the Wilderness Act of 1964 (16 U.S.C.A. 1131 et seq.).

The Wilderness Act established the National Wilderness Preservation System composed of areas designated as wilderness on federal lands—including the national forests and national parks—to be managed to "leave them unimpaired for future use and enjoyment." The act defined wilderness as an area that:

> . . . in contrast with those areas where man and his own works dominate the landscape, is hereby recognized as an area where the earth and community of life are untrampeled by man, where man himself is a visitor who does not remain. An area of wilderness is land retaining its primeval character and influence, without permanent improvements or human habitation, which is protected and managed so as to preserve its natural conditions.

In addition, wilderness areas were to:

1. appear to be affected primarily by the forces of nature, with the imprint of man substantially unnoticeable;
2. provide outstanding opportunities for solitude or a primitive and unconfined type of recreation;
3. have at least 5,000 acres of land or be of sufficient size to be preserved in unimpaired condition; and
4. if possible contain ecological, geological, or other features of scientific, educational, scenic, or historical value.

With respect to the National Forest System, the act automatically designated as wilderness all areas that had been classified previously by the Forest Service as wilderness, wild, or canoe areas. This included 54 units covering 9.1 million acres (Frome 1984). In addition, it required the Forest Service to survey its 34 primitive areas, totaling 5.5 million acres, and to provide recommendations to Congress within 10 years as to whether they should be designated as wilderness under the act—a requirement that the Forest Service eventually expanded, under considerable outside pressure, to include a review of all roadless areas in the system, as discussed later.

The Wilderness Act prohibits numerous activities on designated areas, but at the same time allows a number of uses that apparently are incompatible with the goal of leaving the areas unimpaired. Prohibited activities include commercial enterprise, permanent and temporary roads except as needed to meet minimum requirements for administration of the areas, motorized travel including boats and landing of aircraft, other forms of mechanical transport, and structures and installations. These restrictions, however, are subject to valid existing rights, and people with inholdings or valid mining claims within a designated wilderness area are allowed adequate access to these sites. In addition, the act allows the Service to permit livestock grazing where it existed prior to an area's designation and authorizes the president to allow prospecting for water resources and water-related developments. Finally, the act allowed mineral entry and leasing to continue in wilderness until December 31, 1983, and certain types of mineral exploration still may be allowed.

As the Forest Service conducted its roadless-area review, it decided that most lands in the eastern national forests, some of which had been heavily timbered and settled in the 1800s, did not qualify for wilderness protection under the 1964 act, causing another round of controversy. In response, in 1975 Congress passed the Eastern Wilderness Act (16 U.S.C.A. 1132 [note]). The act stated that it was in the national interest to designate wilderness in the East in general and in the eastern national forests in particular. It automatically added a number of areas to the wilderness system and designated other areas for further study for wilderness suitability.

***Wild and Scenic Rivers.*** In 1968, Congress passed the Wild and Scenic Rivers Act (16 U.S.C.A. 1271 *et seq.*) in order to protect rivers possessing "outstandingly remarkable" scenic, recreation, geologic, fish and wildlife, historic, cultural, or other similar values in free-flowing condition. The act established three possible designations for a river: wild, scenic, or recreational. Wild rivers are essentially undeveloped and inaccessible by road. Scenic rivers can be reached or even crossed by car and can have limited development on the shoreline. Recreational rivers may have parallel roads and shoreline development, but still are free-flowing, thus allowing nonpristine rivers to be eligible for protection (Babcock 1984). The Wild and Scenic Rivers Act immediately added a number of rivers to the system and identified other specific rivers for study by the secretaries of Agriculture and Interior. Unlike the Wilderness Act, the Wild and Scenic Rivers Act did not authorize a broad survey of rivers on the National Forest System, restricting studies to rivers designated by Congress. However, rivers may be added to the system without congressional approval by the secretary of the Interior if the river segment has been designated for protection by the legislature of the state in which it is located, if the secretary is petitioned by the governor to do so, and if the river meets the criteria of the act.

The aim of the act is to maintain these rivers as free-flowing and to protect their natural surroundings and water quality. The act prohibits the Federal Energy Regulatory Commission from licensing dams or other projects on, or that would directly affect, designated rivers and prohibits all federal agencies from providing any assistance to such water-resource projects. This provision of the act is the only federal law preventing federal diversion or

Wild And Scenic River System As Designated By Congress (as of 12/85)

| | Name and State | National Forest(s) | P.L. | Year | National Forest Acres |
|---|---|---|---|---|---|
| 1 | Middle Fork-Feather, CA | Plumas N.F. | 90–542 | 10/2/68 | 16,415 |
| 2 | Middle Fork-Clearwater, ID | Bitterroot N.F. | 90–542 | 10/2/68 | 12,800 |
| | | Clearwater N.F. | | | 25,540 |
| | | Nezperce N.F. | | | 12,488 |
| 3 | Middle Fork-Salmon, ID | Boise N.F. | 90–542 | 10/2/68 | 9,007 |
| | | Challis N.F. | | | 9,660 |
| | | Payette N.F. | | | 626 |
| | | Salmon N.F. | | | 12,608 |
| 4 | Eleven Point, MO | Mark Twain N.F. | 90–542 | 10/2/68 | 5,970 |
| 5 | Rio Grande, NM | Carson N.F. | 90–542 | 10/2/68 | 2,065 |
| 6 | Rogue, OR | Siskiyou N.F. | 90–542 | 10/2/68 | 11,731 |
| 7 | Namekegon-St. Croix | Chequamegon N.F. | 90–542 | 10/2/68 | 826 |
| 8 | Chattooga, GA | Chattahoochee N.F. | 93–621 | 1/3/75 | 8,270 |
| | Chattooga, NC | Nantahala N.F. | 93–621 | 1/3/75 | 946 |
| | Chattooga, SC | Sumter N.F. | 93–621 | 1/3/75 | 6,317 |
| 9 | Rapid, ID | Nezperce N.F. | 94–199 | 12/31/75 | 4,500 |
| | | Payette N.F. | | | 4,105 |
| 10 | Snake, ID | Nezperce N.F. | 94–199 | 12/31/75 | 8,700 |
| | | Payette N.F. | | | 395 |
| | Snake, OR | Wallowa N.F. | 94–199 | 12/31/75 | 4,081 |
| 11 | Flathead, MT | Flathead N.F. | 94–486 | 10/12/76 | 36,540 |
| 12 | North Fork of the American, CA | Tahoe N.F. | 95–625 | 10/10/78 | 5,769 |
| 13 | St. Joe, ID | St. Joe N.F. | 95–625 | 10/10/78 | 20,857 |
| 14 | Pere Marquette, MI | Huron N.F. | 95–625 | 10/10/78 | 2,193 |
| 15 | Skagit, WA | Mt. Baker N.F. | 95–625 | 10/10/78 | 16,615 |
| 16 | Salmon, ID | Bitterroot N.F. | | 7/23/80 | 3,035 |
| | | Nezperce N.F. | | | 8,785 |
| 17 | Verde, AZ | Coconino N.F. | 98–406 | 8/28/84 | 12,614 |
| | | Prescott N.F. | | | |
| 18 | Tuolumne, CA | Stanislaus N.F. | 98–425 | 9/25/84 | 6,115 |
| 19 | Au Sable, MI | Huron-Manistee N.F. | 98–444 | 10/4/84 | 4,810 |
| 20 | Illinois, OR | Siskiyou N.F. | 98–494 | 10/19/84 | 13,926 |
| | TOTAL ACREAGES | | | | 288,309 |

impoundment of rivers.* In addition, the act authorizes the use of the Land and Water Conservation Fund to acquire lands along the banks of designated rivers, although the amount of acquisition and the government's condemnation authority is limited. Mineral activity is restricted along designated rivers, depending on the category in which they are included.† Other management restrictions or requirements may be included in a river's enabling legislation. Currently, 20 wild and scenic rivers run through the National Forest System, totaling 1,800 miles.

*Land and Water Conservation Fund.* The Land and Water Conservation Fund Act of 1965 (16 U.S.C.A. 4601-4-4601-11) established the Land and Water Conservation Fund, which among other things provides money for the acquisition of outdoor recreation lands and endangered species habitat by the Forest Service. The Land and Water Fund is the primary source of Forest Service acquisition funding and is discussed further under Lands Acquisition and Management. The act also authorizes the Forest Service to charge fees for the use of recreational facilities that meet certain criteria, including highly developed campgrounds and swimming sites. These receipts, however, are not returned to the forests, but instead go to the federal treasury and the states.

*National Trails System.* In 1968, Congress passed the National Trails System Act (16 U.S.C.A. 1241 *et seq.*) recognizing the value of maintained hiking trails both near urban areas and in more isolated scenic areas. The act established two categories of trails that could be designated only by act of Congress—historic and scenic trails—and established the Appalachian Trail and the Pacific Crest Trail as the first elements of the system. These trails were nearly complete at the time of their designation, but the act consolidated their management, giving the National Park Service the lead on the Appalachian Trail and the Forest Service the lead on the Pacific Crest Trail, despite the fact that the Forest Service administers the vast majority of federal land traversed by both. The act also required the study of 14 possible additions to the system. The act encourages states and localities to protect the scenic trails outside of federal landholdings, but provides no funds for this purpose. Today, the National Trails System consists of three trails within the National Forest System—the Pacific Crest, Continental Divide, and Florida National Scenic Trails. These trails cover 6,750 miles, 60 percent of which are in the National Forest System.

In addition, the National Trails System Act authorizes the secretaries of Agriculture and the Interior to designate "recreation" trails located entirely on

---

* In addition, the Federal Power Act requires Federal Energy Regulatory Commission to comply with environmental restrictions imposed by the Forest Service on hydroelectric projects developed on the National Forest System.
† Discussed further under Energy and Minerals.

federal lands. As of 1981, the Forest Service had used this category to establish 374 national recreation trails totaling 1,300 miles.

*Historic Preservation.* The Historic Preservation Act of 1966 (16 U.S.C.A. 470a, 470f, 470j) and the Archeological Resources Preservation Act of 1979 (16 U.S.C.A. 470aa-11) provide the authority for the Service's cultural resources program. These acts generally direct the Forest Service to protect important cultural or historical resources during activities that disturb the land, such as road building and mineral exploration. These programs have little impact on wildlife and are not covered further in this chapter.

## Recreation Planning and Management

*General Recreation Use.* Historically, recreation management on the National Forest System has been very casual. Few forests and far fewer ranger districts have staff that specialize exclusively in recreation. Instead, recreation may be one of several responsibilities entrusted to a single staff person. Unlike the National Park System, national forests have simple and often very few facilities—although as the national forests have become more popular, more facilities have been built to accommodate visitors and to protect the environment. There are few visitor restrictions: hunting and fishing are allowed subject to state law; firewood gathering is permitted; semi-precious stones and nonprotected plant species may be collected. Today the Forest Service operates more than 5,000 campgrounds, 1,300 picnic grounds, and 1,000 boating sites.

The Forest Service also issues and administers "special-use" permits to the private sector to provide additional recreational opportunities on the National Forest System. Privately operated facilities account for 10 percent of total recreational use on system lands and include more than 15,000 private "recreation" residences, 500 lodges and resorts, 490 organization camps, and 165 downhill ski areas. Construction of new ski areas is the most controversial activity of private recreation because it can cause extensive disturbances to wildlife, increased air pollution due to the influx of cars and, in the East, increased pressure on water resources from making artificial snow.

To obtain permission for such uses, developers submit bids to the Forest Service. Upon awarding the contract and issuing the necessary special-use permit, the service receives an annual percentage of the area's gross receipts. Although the Recreation Management staff has the lead in developing contracts of this type, it works closely with the Lands staff, which otherwise has the lead in the preparation of special-use permits.

In 1984, recreation on the National Forest System returned $27.5 million in receipts, derived from both public and private facilities. Although most Forest Service-operated facilities are open to the public free of charge, about 2,000 campsites and 85 swimming areas do charge user fees as authorized by the Land and Water Conservation Fund Act. These uses generated $11.9 million in 1984. The remaining $15.7 million came from fees for privately operated special uses, primarily recreation residences and ski areas.

In contrast to the $27.5 million generated from recreational use, the cost of operating and managing recreation facilities was $100.9 million in 1984. With the current emphasis on reducing federal spending, the Forest Service has moved to expand and increase its use of fees where it has the authority to do so. As a result, recreation receipts increased 42 percent between 1981 and 1984. In addition, the Reagan administration repeatedly has proposed to amend the Land and Water Conservation Fund Act to remove limitations on the ability of the Forest Service, as well as other federal agencies, to expand recreation fees. This proposal has made little headway in Congress, although there appears to be substantial support for additional fees if the receipts would be used to provide additional funding for Forest Service recreation management.

*Trails Management.* Among the most popular aspects of the Forest Service's recreation program is its trail system. In 1985, 98,500 miles of trails existed on the National Forest System. In 1984, these trails provided nearly 13 million visitor days of recreation.

Maintaining this vast trails network is a costly and time-consuming responsibility. Over-use can cause erosion and drainage problems which may make trails unusable in certain periods of the year and visually unappealing at others and also may cause resource damage. Less-used trails may need repeated clearing and blazing. Some trails must be closed at certain periods of the year to prevent disturbance of wildlife or to keep people away from potentially dangerous animals, such as grizzly bears with cubs. These responsibilities fall to the district rangers and their staffs. To aid forest personnel in recreation maintenance in general, and trail maintenance in particular, the Forest Service recruits substantial seasonal and volunteer help. In 1984, 43,496 people donated their time to the Forest Service, worth an estimated $23.4 million.

*Wilderness.* Taking a broad view, wilderness management on the National Forest System consists of three important aspects: the management of areas designated as wilderness; the study of areas with potential for wilderness designation; and the management of roadless areas released from wilderness consideration. To understand the current status of each of these, it is necessary to describe the Forest Service's survey of its lands for wilderness potential.

Although the Wilderness Act required the Service to study only its primitive areas for wilderness suitability, soon after the act was passed environmentalists began to press for wilderness designation of other roadless areas that the Service had not classified as primitive. In 1971, the Forest Service agreed to survey these areas—sometimes called "de facto" wilderness—embarking on its first Roadless Area Review and Evaluation (RARE I). After the initial survey of 56 million acres under RARE I, the Service decided that 12 million acres of roadless areas deserved further wilderness study. It proposed to protect these acres while continuing the surveys, but to make the remaining 34 million acres of roadless areas available for timber harvest and other use. The Sierra Club sued the Service over the adequacy of its RARE I environmental impact statement and, in an out-of-court settlement, the Service agreed to continue protection for all 56 million acres, opening units to other uses only as individual environmental impact statements were completed.

The timber industry protested this indefinite "lock-up" of so much acreage, and in 1977, in order to speed up a decision on how these lands should be managed, the Carter administration began a second wilderness survey covering some 65 million acres, called RARE II. In spite of initial high hopes, environmentalists also objected to the results of RARE II, which dropped 36 million acres from further wilderness consideration and released them to development. The state of California took the Forest Service to court, charging that RARE II had assessed inadequately the environmental impacts of releasing California's supposed nonwilderness areas to development. In 1982, the Ninth Circuit Court of Appeals in California found in favor of the state and enjoined any devlopement of the non-wilderness recommendations in California (*California v. Block*).

The threat of similar lawsuits in other states and lingering uncertainty about the use of these lands spurred Congress to act. Also, environmentalists did not want to see a RARE III conducted under the pro-development Reagan administration. Congress quickly got to work on a number of statewide wilderness bills, but industry still feared that environmentalists would legally block the opening of areas not designated as wilderness in these bills and insisted on specific congressional authorization for their release. Initially, some bills passed Congress with language designed to modify California-type decisions by declaring the RARE II Environmental Impact Statement to be sufficient. But the nervous timber industry wanted more assurance that the areas would not be forced immediately back into wilderness review and in 1984, compromise language was developed specifying that released areas would not be reconsidered for wilderness designation until the Forest Service revises its forest-management plans, which it does every 10 to 15 years. This language does not, however, prohibit the service from managing these areas to protect their wilderness characteristics in the interim if it determines in the planning process that such management is appropriate.

With the release issue resolved, the 98th Congress (1983-1984) added another 6.8 million acres of wilderness to the national forest wilderness system and released 13.8 million acres from wilderness management. Today, the National Forest System's 32.1 million acres of designated wilderness comprise 16.8 percent of national-forest acreage. Of this, 26.6 million acres are in the lower 48 states. Of the 46 million acres of RARE II study lands in the lower 48 states, 8.6 have been designated wilderness, 19.9 have been released to other uses, and the status of 17.3 million acres remains unresolved, primarily in Idaho, Montana, and Nevada.

Decision making on what to do with the unresolved RARE II acreage—lands that have been neither released nor designated as wilderness—is proceeding on two tracks. Congress continues to consider bills to designate wilderness. In 1985, major statewide bills were introduced for Kentucky, Michigan, Nebraska, and Nevada. The Forest Service, for its part, has revised its planning regulations to require the forest plans to re-evaluate roadless areas that have been neither designated as wilderness nor released to other uses. The goal of this re-evaluation is to prepare environmental studies that can withstand a legal challenge and allow the Service to release administratively to any development areas it does not want to recommend for wilderness status. The future management of newly released areas is also being addressed in the plans.

Since many of the wilderness bills have cleared Congress, the wilderness debate has somewhat refocused on how the service will manage roadless areas not designated as wilderness. Wilderness supporters would like the Service to continue to manage some of these areas to maintain their wilderness characteristics so that they would be eligible for wilderness recommendation in the next forest-planning cycle. Initial forest plans, most still in draft stage, contain plans for more than 8,000 miles of new roads in roadless areas, which would make these areas ineligible for future wilderness designation. In addition, many of the proposed new roads, particularly in the Rocky Mountain region, could seriously disturb wildlife species, such as the elk and woodland caribou. The increase in roading is linked to projected increases in timber harvests and is discussed further in the section on timber management.*

Wilderness management has been far less controversial than wilderness designations. The major management limitations in the law were discussed earlier. With respect to wildlife, habitat management is restricted severely on wilderness. Prescribed burns, planting and seeding, access roads, and motorized travel are prohibited.† Some activities, however, are permitted, such as removing debris from critical spawning streams; operating wildlife-oriented water developments, dams, and irrigation ditches that existed prior to designation; chemically treating waters to remove undesirable non-native fish; and even using helicopters and fixed-wing aircraft to complete existing research work. In addition, hunting, fishing, animal damage control, and transplanting endangered or threatened species to a wilderness area can be permitted. Some activities that can conflict with wildlife, including mining of valid claims and livestock grazing, can continue in wilderness. Despite management limitations, however, wilderness generally benefits wildlife. It protects watersheds for fish and provides large undisturbed tracts of land required by some species, such as

---

* See also the discussion of roads in the Forest Service wildlife issues chapter.

† The Forest Service may issue regulations that would allow prescribed burning in certain circumstances.

the grizzly bear. In the long run, wilderness provides a baseline against which to measure environmental change, such as impacts on disturbed watersheds and changes in wildlife populations and behavior in less-protected areas. And as development pressures increase, wilderness provides wildlife an oasis of protection from neighboring multiple-use activities.

The most controversial management provision in the Wilderness Act has been Section 4(d), which prohibited the staking of mining claims and the operation of mineral leasing laws in national forest wilderness after January 1, 1984.* In late 1982, as the deadline for such activity neared, then-Secretary of the Interior James Watt announced his intention to issue numerous oil and gas leases in national forest wilderness areas. Congress, in response, imposed a temporary ban on energy and mineral leasing in wilderness areas as well as in wilderness study areas and areas under further planning to determine their wilderness potential. Congress extended the ban on mineral leasing on wilderness until authority for such activity expired under the Wilderness Act at the end of 1983. In addition, Congress has continued to include a ban on leasing in study and further-planning areas each year in the Interior-and-related-agencies appropriations bill, which covers the Forest Service.

*Off-Road Vehicles.* The Forest Service estimates that five percent of all recreational use is done with off-road vehicles, including snowmobiles, four-wheel drive vehicles, motorcycles, dune buggies, and recently, three-wheeled vehicles. Off-road-vehicle use has caused some bitter disputes, in part because some forest users, such as hikers and cross-country skiers, find it incompatible with their recreational uses, and in part because it can destroy vegetation, accelerate erosion, disturb wildlife, and cause air and noise pollution.

Off-road-vehicle use on public lands increased rapidly in the 1960s and quickly became controversial. In 1972, President Nixon issued Executive Order 11644 directing federal land-managing agencies to develop and issue regulations and administrative instructions to designate specific areas and trails where off-road-vehicles could and could not be used. Conservationists protested that this order, by requiring the issuance of regulations for designating areas off-limits to the vehicles, opened millions of acres to off-road vehicle use while the agencies developed the rules. In 1977, President Carter issued an Executive Order 11989 modifying this requirement by directing the federal agencies to immediately close areas where off-road vehicles cause considerable adverse effects on the environment. The President's Council on Environmental Quality further instructed the agencies that even areas where adverse impacts are anticipated but have not yet appeared are to be closed to off-road-vehicle use.

---

* Restrictions on mineral activity in wilderness are discussed further under Energy and Minerals Management.

The Forest Service reports that, in response to these orders, many national forests have closed much of their lands to off-road-vehicle use. Further determinations as to whether to open, restrict, or prohibit areas to certain types of off-road-vehicle use are being made in the forest plans. The plans are to evaluate current and potential impacts of off-road-vehicle use on soil, water, vegetation, fish and wildlife, forest visitors, and cultural and historic resources and to restrict or prohibit any use likely to cause adverse effects on these resources. Furthermore, areas and trails are to be located to minimize damage to soil, watershed, and vegetation and to minimize harassment of wildlife or significant disruption of wildlife habitats. The regulations required by the Nixon executive order will be included in the upcoming forest plans.

## Trends and Issues

*Reduced Recreation Management.* The major recent trend in the recreation program is a reduction in spending power, cutbacks in available facilities, and diversion of limited funds to planning, all while recreational use continues to increase. Recreational management was funded at just over $100 million in 1985, about five percent of the Forest Service's total budget. The recreational-management budget includes recreation use, wilderness management, and cultural resources management. Since 1980, the recreation-management budget as a whole has declined by six percent in constant dollars, and the general recreational use portion of the budget has declined 13 percent. In addition, as funding has been constrained, an increasing portion of the recreation budget has been used for forest planning, further reducing funds for recreation management and facilities. In 1984, recreation met 92 percent of its Resources Planning Act program accomplishment goals as measured in visitor days, but other measurements indicate that the quality of this use is declining. For example, in 1978, the Service estimated that 74 percent of the recreational facilities on the system were maintained at the standard service level, which is the level of service at which a facility is expected to last its designated project life. Since that time, in response to limited budgets, the Service has had to defer or reduce the standard of maintenance and cleanup and to shorten the length of time some facilities are open for public use. By 1984, only 27 percent of facilities were operated at standard level. In addition, as maintenance of facilities has been postponed, the deferred maintenance backlog has grown to $295.7 million.

*Deteriorating Trails System.* Another deteriorating element of national forest recreation is the trails system. Trail-system mileage peaked in the 1940s at 144,000 miles. Since then, the mileage has declined steadily to 98,500 miles in 1984. This is due both to the inability of forest personnel to keep up with natural deterioration and to loss from road construction, mainly for logging.

The trail-construction budget is a small portion of the Service's budget at $7.09 million in 1985, and it has declined 19 percent in constant dollars since 1980. Trail construction also fell far below its 1984 Resources Planning Act goal of 2,238 miles. The actual 1984 total was 528 miles, just 24 percent of the goal, and of these, 175 miles were constructed by volunteers. As trail mileage has decreased, visitor use of trails has surged. Between 1969 and 1983, visitor days went from 5.6 million to 13 million, an increase often resulting in increased trail erosion.

# Soil, Water, and Air Management Program

Among the original purposes of the National Forest System was watershed protection, which is strongly linked to soil maintenance and prevention of erosion. Today on the National Forest System, these resources, together with air-quality monitoring, are the charge of the Service's Watershed and Air Management staff. Soil, water, and air are the basic resources on which the rest of the forest resources depend and their management ultimately has significant effects on the quality of fish and wildlife habitat in the National Forest System.

## Legal Authority and Requirements

The initial, basic authority for watershed management on national forest lands was established in the 1897 Organic Act, which specified securing favorable water flows as one of the principal reasons for establishing forest reserves. The Weeks Act of 1911 and the Clarke-McNary Act of 1924, in authorizing the Service to acquire private lands into the system, specified that the goal of such purchases was watershed protection. The Multiple-Use Sustained-Yield Act of 1960 reiterated watershed maintenance as a basic tenet of National Forest System management.

*Resources Planning Act/National Forest Management Act.* Soil and watershed protection have long been important components of national forest management. But it was not until the 1970s that various laws placed specific requirements on their protection and expanded the service's responsibilities to include air quality. The Resources Planning Act of 1974 and the National Forest Management Act of 1976 contain many references to the suitability and capability of specific land areas for management activities, to maintaining the productivity of the land, and to the need to protect and improve the quality of the soil and water resources. This imposed an increased duty on the Service to develop and maintain information on the condition of the basic soil and water resources and to assess and mitigate the impacts of other activities on them.

These laws require the Forest Service's recommended national Resources Planning Act program to "recognize the fundamental need to protect and where appropriate improve the quality of soil, water and air resources." The National Forest Management Act permits timber harvest only where soil, slope, or other watershed conditions will not be irreversibly damaged and only where protection is provided to prevent damage to fish habitat. In addition, amendments to the Knutson-Vandenberg Act included in the National Forest Management Act authorized the use of Knutson-Vandenberg deposits made by timber purchasers to protect and improve renewable resources, including soil and water.

*Clean Water Act.* The Clean Water Act of 1977 (33 U.S.C.A. 466 *et seq.*), which amended the Federal Water Pollution Control Act of 1972, imposes requirements with respect to both point-source and nonpoint-source pollution and dredge-and-fill activities in the waters of the United States. Point-source discharges (i.e., those discharges of pollution from a discrete conveyance, pipe, or conduit) on the National Forest System come most commonly from administrative sites or recreational facilities and require the service to obtain a discharge permit from either the Environmental Protection Agency or from a state, if the state has been delegated the permitting authority. Nonpoint-source pollution is a far greater problem on the National Forest System. Resource activities, such as timber harvesting and mining, must comply with state requirements as well as with guidelines set by the Forest Service itself in its forest plans. Guidelines set by the Forest Service and approved by the state and the Environmental Protection Agency are known as "best management practices" and are developed and implemented on the forest level. In addition, the Service must comply with Section 404 permitting requirements for any dredge or fill activities in waterways or wetlands, including building any road that crosses a stream. However, the Service does not have to apply for a specific permit at many small stream crossings because of a blanket "nationwide permit" which covers small streams with small water flows.

Several laws, executive orders, and federal regulations exist that focus on particular local watersheds and water rights problems.

*Clean Air Act.* The Clean Air Act (42 U.S.C.A. 7401 *et seq.*) originally was passed in 1955 and amended in 1963, 1970, and 1977. The 1977 amendments provide the dominant authority for the Service's air-management role. This act designated certain federal lands as Class I air quality areas, where any increases in pollution levels are forbidden, to protect many large national parks, national monuments, wilderness areas, and wild and scenic rivers. There are 88 Class I areas on the National Forest System, and these are monitored to determine sulfur dioxide and particulate levels. Except for three Indian reservations in Montana, there have been no Class I areas designated in the United States since 1977. Although the act allowed some areas to be designated as Class III, where high pollutant levels would be allowed; currently, none exist. Class I areas designated by the 1977 act cannot be downgraded, and the states have the authority to upgrade Class II areas, where moderate increases in pollution are allowed.

The Forest Service and other land managing agencies ensure air quality compliance in the planning stages of new industrial sources. The Environmental Protection Agency, or individual states following federal guidelines, sets emissions standards for industry compliance. Any new emissions source within 100 kilometers of a Class I area that may affect air quality related values must get specific permission from the state regarding their proposed pollutants. If the Forest Service determines that a proposed facility may cause or contribute to a change in the air quality, including visiblity, of a Class I area under its jurisdiction, it must present its case before the state for the state to either deny the permit altogether or, more likely, force modifications in the proposed emissions level. If the owner or operator of the proposed facility wants to exceed the Class I emissions requirements, the proponent must show that the emissions will cause no adverse environmental impacts. To date, no new industry has been denied a construction permit, although design modifications have been required in numerous cases.

## Soil, Water, and Air Planning and Management

*Watershed Management.* Watershed management includes managing both water and soil. The Forest Service integrates water-resource management into its planning process and coordinates national forest water programs with similar local, state, and federal programs. Management may involve watershed condition surveys; water-resource inventories, analyses, prescriptions,and monitoring; or management support services to other National Forest System programs. The support function may have direct bearing on fish or wildlife. For example, hydrologists coordinate with fisheries biologists on the construction of fish ladders or spawning cribs or in creating models of anticipated stream sedimentation in proposed timber-sale or road-building areas. Water-resource management also includes floodplain and wetlands evaluations, designed to aid any development activities in these areas and to offset their impacts.

*Water Rights.* The watershed management staff is responsible for securing water rights for national forest purposes. To do this, it applies to the states for a water permit. Under a 1978 Supreme Court decision, the Forest Service is not guaranteed water for fish and wildlife. In *U.S. v. New Mexico* (438 U.S. 696, 98 S.Ct. 3012, 57 L.Ed.2d 1052 (1978)), the court rejected Forest Service claims of reserved rights to water for wildlife, recreation, aesthetics, and stock watering, stating that the Organic Act of 1897 only ensured water for timber production and watershed protection. The Forest Service has taken watershed protection to mean maintaining channels that will keep sediment moving, retard encroaching vegetation, and allow adequate water for areas downstream from national forests. Justice Powell echoed the concern of environmentalists in his dissenting opinion. He found that the forests the National Forest System was created to protect are not "the still, lifeless places envisioned by the court. In my view the forests consist of the birds, animals, and fish—the wildlife—that inhabits them, as well as the trees, flowers, shrubs, and grasses," therefore arguing that the United States should be entitled to the water necessary to sustain wildlife and plants. Though at best the New Mexico decision gave the service a limited water right, it applied only to forests created out of public domain. Acquired forests do not have even this right and must apply to the states for any rights.

Currently, no legal basis supports the service's interpretation of how much water is required for watershed protection. Instead, each state has its own water-rights policy. In the absence of water rights for fish and wildlife, the Service does have some control of its water through the issuance of special-use permits, by which the Service can deny the diversion of water out of the system.

*Soil Management.* Watershed management and soil management go hand in hand. Few management activities are not influenced by, or do not have impacts on, the soil. Timber harvesting on a wooded hillside with poor quality soils is very apt to cause erosion, flooding, and subsequent loss of instream and riparian habitat. Thus, these areas must be identified and management precautions must be recommended. For areas already impaired, a knowledge of the soils can lead to successful reclamation efforts and to improvement of fish and wildlife habitat. To provide the basic knowledge necessary for such efforts, the Forest Service's soil scientists inventory, monitor, and study the soils of the National Forest System. The resulting data is applied in land and resource planning and management in order to provide a sustained yield of goods and services without impairing the productivity of the land.

The Forest Service's top priority in soil management is providing data and technical support for other resource-management activities, but some direct soil improvements are made as well. The most common improvement is chemical fertilization to improve soil quality and increase production. Other improvements include installing erosion control structures, revegetating denuded areas, and breaking up overly compacted soils. In addition, emergency soil management measures often are required following natural alterations such as flooding or fire.

*Air Management.* The Watershed and Air staff has two responsibilities in air management: to protect surrounding environments from airborne pollutants originating inside the National Forest System and to protect the National Forest System from pollutants generated outside the system.

Particulate matter in smoke from prescribed burns is the principal air pollutant produced within the National Forest System. To limit this pollution, the Forest Service works with the states to ensure conditions are proper for burning—for example that atmospheric conditions will allow the smoke to rise and dissipate. The primary goal of the smoke management program is to maintain high visibility on and adjacent to the National Forest System.

The air management program also protects the national forests from outside pollutants, a far more difficult task. The Forest Service currently uses lower plant forms such as lichens as a monitoring tool for airborne pollutants. Not only are lichens very susceptible to pollutants, providing an early warning sign of pollution, but they also accumulate pollutants, allowing scientists to identify possible sources of the pollutants.

All 88 of the 156 Class I areas designated by the Clean Air Act on the National Forest System are wilderness areas. To monitor these areas, the service employs only four full-time air specialists, located in Fort Collins and Denver, Colorado, in Portland, Oregon, and in Washington, D.C. Ensuring that air-quality standards are maintained requires an understanding of air chemistry, control technologies, computer modeling, and a particular pollutant's affect on the environment. This extremely complex task is a new technical field for most of those who must assume this responsibility. The Watershed and Air staff has been given Forest Service approval to hire at least one qualified air specialist for each National Forest System region and to strengthen its Washington, D.C. staff, but lack of funding continues to hamper its ability to meet air resource management responsibilities adequately.

## Trends and Issues

Soil, water, and air has suffered greater funding declines than any other resource management program within the National Forest System in the past six years. Funding dropped from $37.23 million in 1980 to $28.71 million in 1983, although it has had a slight boost over the past two years to $30.98 million in 1985. This is approximately a 36-percent decline in spending power since 1980.

As funding has declined, an increasing proportion of the funds for soil, water and air management have been allocated for providing support to other resource activities, causing even sharper drops in improvements and inventories. From 1980 to 1985, funding for the administration of soil, water and air support programs increased from $14.81 million to $21.47 million, while funding for improvements dropped from $8.29 million to $3.02 million, a 72 percent decline in spending power. In 1984, 8,931 acres were improved under the program, compared to 27,700 acres in 1980. In 1984, soil, water, and air accomplished just 28 percent of its Resources Planning Act improvements goal.

The Forest Service, in conjunction with the Soil Conservation Service, is conducting an inventory of the nation's soils. Begun in the 1960s, the inventory is scheduled for completion by the year 2000. But as with soil improvements, the inventory has been slowed by a lack of funding as resources are first allocated to preventing further damage. Funding for inventories dropped from $14.13 million to $6.49 million, a 64 percent decline in spending power.

*Resource Conditions.* The primary cause of soil and water quality decline on the National Forest System has been livestock grazing. Grazing occurs on 51 million acres of the system, and in many areas has caused extensive overgrazing, soil compaction, riparian zone destruction, and erosion. Timber harvest, road building, and mining also have affects on soil and water qualitiy. The Service says, however, that the situation has improved in most areas during the past 20 years because of an increased awareness of the problem. Nevertheless, the impact of livestock grazing on riparian habitat is still one of the major threats to fish and wildlife on rangelands, and conservation groups are trying to strengthen requirements for protecting these areas on Forest Service lands. This is an even more serious issue on Bureau of Land Management lands and is discussed in the Bureau of Land Management chapter.

*Acid Rain.* In general, water quality on the National Forest System has improved because of the Clean Water Act and provisions in the National Forest Management Act that restrict timber harvesting that seriously affects watershed integrity. But a new water-quality threat has emerged in the form of acid rain, which poses a particular problem for national forests since many are at high elevation where soils have poor buffering capabilities. Aside from affecting water quality, acid rain affects soil quality as well. Five Forest Service research work units currently are involved in acid rain research, and acid rain has become a major Forest Service concern. However, any government action to reduce the emissions that contribute to acid rain is out of the Forest Service's control. The Environmental Protection Agency has refused to take substantive action limiting sulfur dioxide and nitric oxide emissions, preferring instead more research. For several years, Congress has considered legislation to force emissions reductions, but regional conflicts over the required level of reductions, who pays for these reductions, and by what means the reductions should be achieved have blocked legislation continually.

# Forest Research

The Research Program of the Forest Service is responsible for developing scientific and technical knowledge to enhance management of the nation's 1.6 billion acres of forests and associated rangelands and, in particular, management of the 191 million acres of the National Forest System. Forest Service research covers a wide spectrum of biologic, economic, engineering, and social disciplines. It ranges from regional to international in scope. The Forest Service's research program has develop into one of the largest natural resource research organizations in the world, with an annual budget of $121 million in 1985 and as many as 2,800 different studies under way at one time.

The Forest Research program is divided into seven functional areas: Forest Environment Research, Fire and Atmospheric Sciences Research, Forest Insects and Disease Research, Timber Management Research, Resource Economics Research, Forest Products and Harvesting Research, and International Forestry. Research on wildlife and fish habitat, as well as range research, which also has important implications for wildlife, are part of Forest Environment Research. Washington staff for each of the seven functional branches of research, along with the Forest Products Laboratory, work closely with National Forest System personnel and other federal, state, and private researchers.

With the recent enactment of laws such as the Endangered Species Act and the National Forest Management Act, which required the Forest Service to undertake increased planning for and management of wildlife in the National Forest System, the need for data on fish and wildlife and their habitats has increased. In addition, as development pressures grow, particularly from increased timbering and energy development, the need for a better understanding of habitat needs and complex multiple-use interactions becomes more urgent.

## Legal Authority and Requirements

Research and federal forestry began together in 1876, when Congress appropriated $2,000 for the Department of Agriculture to conduct a study and report on the best means to preserve and renew forests (Frome 1984). With the creation of the Forest Service in 1905, forestry research received new emphasis under the Department of Agriculture's general charter. In 1908, the first regional forest experiment station was set up in the Southwest, which pioneered studies on forests, rangelands, and watersheds. Experiment stations in other regions soon followed. The Forest Products Laboratory in Madison, Wisconsin, was established in 1910 in cooperation with the University of Wisconsin. Research in the Forest Service made its greatest strides in 1915, when Earle H. Clapp successfully took the research function out of the National Forest System, making it an autonomous branch of the Forest Service and expanding the scope of its work.

Forestry schools and state experiment stations began to blossom in the early 1900s, and cooperation between these groups and universities, private timber industries, and the Forest Service became a key ingredient in the service's research program. This relationship was recognized in the 1928 McSweeney-McNary Research Act (Act of May 22, 1928 45 Stat. 699-702;

Repealed 1978), which along with later amendments and the 1962 McIntyre-Stennis Act (16 U.S.C.A. 582a) enabled the Department of Agriculture to support non-federal research efforts. The McSweeney-McNary Act also outlined the basic elements of Forest Research, which even today remain largely unchanged. It authorized and directed the service to:

> . . . conduct a comprehensive program of investigations to determine, demonstrate, and promulgate the best methods of reforestation and of growing, managing, and utilizing timber, forages and other forest products, of protecting timber and other forest growth from fire, insects, disease, or other harmful agents, of obtaining the fullest and most effective use of forest lands, and to determine and promulgate the economic considerations which should underlie the establishment of sound policies for the management of forest lands and the utilization of forest products.

The act also authorized the establishment of a full system of regional experiment stations which today includes eight stations across the country.

The Resources Planning Act of 1974 and the National Forest Management Act of 1976 made no direct changes in the research program per se, but the extensive planning process they established forced changes in research. Research data is needed for the preparation every five years of the national assessment and for the development and maintenance of the forest plans. These plans require information on the present and prospective availability of resources, demands for their use, and opportunities to improve yields. With respect to fish and wildlife, the National Forest Management Act required the Forest Service to provide for diversity of plant and animal communities on the National Forest System, and the act's regulations require the Service to maintain viable populations of all existing native and non-native vertebrate species. In essence, this mandate requires Forest Service land managers to be knowledgeable about the entire vertebrate fauna in their planning units and to be able to predict the fauna's response to habitat changes caused by other planned activities. This meant the Forest Service needed more information on a broader range of species and better data on their relationships with their habitat, substantially increasing research needs.

In 1978, Congress enacted a comprehensive research law, the Forest and Rangeland Renewable Resources Research Act of 1978 (16 U.S.C.A. 1641-1647). This act updated, clarified, and consolidated existing forest-research and range research authorities. Among other provisions, the act requires renewable resources environmental research to include research activities related to maintaining and improving wildlife and fish habitat and also requires research on endangered and threatened fauna. Today, this act is the dominant authority for Forest Research.

## Forest Research Planning and Management

Forest Research had a 1985 budget of over $120 million, underwriting more than 2,800 ongoing studies. These studies currently are conducted by 199 research work units, comprised of nearly 800 scientists and their assistants at 75 locations throughout the United States, Puerto Rico, and the Pacific Trust Islands. Research work is coordinated through a system of regional experiment stations. Each station is supervised by a director, who oversees research work in that region. There are eight research regions, compared to nine regions for the National Forest System, and they have different boundaries from the system's regions. The seven functional areas of forest research are represented by seven staff divisions within the Washington, D.C., office. The staff director for each of the functional areas supports the deputy chief for Research and provides overall leadership, direction, and coordination in each given area.

***Research Planning.*** In setting research direction and priorities, Forest Research works closely with the National Forest System staffs in the Washington office and in the field and with various user groups. These user groups often include other federal agencies, such as the Bureau of Land Management and the Fish and Wildlife Service; state agencies; private industry; or other interest groups. To determine what research work is needed, Forest Research may informally survey these groups, or the groups may come to the Forest Service. Local input is consolidated in the forest plans, which include research needs identified during the planning process. Needs identified in the various forest plans are evaluated by the regional forester for possible inclusion in a regional research proposal.

Forest Service research staff, including project scientists, survey suggested research areas to determine what should and can be done. In making this determination, they consider whether or not adequate information is already available, whether research work on the subject already is under way someplace else, and whether the money and qualified personnel are available. Finally, selected areas of research are approved by the station director with the concurrence of the deputy chief for Research in the Washington headquarters. Research work plans generally receive a five-year authorization, at the end of which they are reviewed and either revised, updated, or terminated. Changes in administration policies or funding cutbacks, however, can cause the abrupt ending of "lower priority" work plans.

***General Research Efforts.*** Although only a portion of Forest Research is directly aimed at fish and wildlife, other aspects of the service's research program can have indirect wildlife benefits—for example, by finding alternatives to chemical pest control, identifying ways to make more efficient use of wood, and investigating environmental contaminants that eventually could cause adverse impacts on fish and wildlife. Other aspects of the research program, of course, produce no wildlife-related benefits. A brief description of some of the recent efforts of the seven functional research areas are described below.

*Forest Environment Research.* This includes research on recreation, mineland rehabilitation, watershed management, atmospheric chemical deposition, range, and fish and wildlife habitat, the latter discussed later. Recent projects include studying the effects of acid deposition on forest vegetation, soils, and water quality; development of a mathematical model to predict landslides; publication of a guide to assist forest managers in soliciting public opinion on river uses; and development of standards and treatments for reducing erosion from road construction.

*Fire and Atmospheric Sciences Research.* This research is intended primarily to prevent and control wildfires, reduce weather-related forest-resource loss, and reduce certain management costs by using prescribed burning. Recent efforts include the development of a computerized system to predict spread, intensity, and control of fires; identifying how to vary prescribed burning techniques to reduce smoke emissions; and development of a system to assess air-pollution potential in mountain areas.

*Forest Products and Harvesting Research.* The goals of this program include providing technogy to harvest and use timber more efficiently, improving the performance of wood products, and reducing costs and energy consumption in wood processing. Recently, this effort has resulted in the identification of enzymes that break down a noxious woodwaste product and convert it to a useful chemical, the use of fungi in some elements of wood processing with the goal of reducing chemical and energy usage and demonstrating that certain unused sawmill residues can be used in manufacturing processes.

*Forest Insect and Disease Research.* This program focuses on ways to protect trees on the forests and to protect wood in use or in storage. It is developing plant-breeding techniques to produce disease-resistant trees; methods to transfer genes from disease-resistant trees to susceptible ones; and strategies to control spruce-budworm damage that rely less on chemicals. Such research recently has developed, for use against termites, an insecticide with lower toxicity to mammals than other available chemicals.

*Resource Economics Research.* Research in this area recently has produced a comprehensive review of the value of all forest-resource outputs, including recreation, to guide future resource-valuation studies; identified a reduction in the rate of pine growth in several southern states; and determined that investments in timber management in the South could lead to a doubling in timber production over 1970 levels while yielding a four percent return on the investment.

*Timber Management Research.* Focusing primarily on silvicultural techniques, research in this area has resulted in the publication of a comprehensive manual on how to choose silvicultural systems for all major United States forest types and the development of a computerized system for prescribing silvicultural treatments on certain discrete forest types.

*International Forestry.* Through this program, the Forest Service participates in international forestry bodies, has helped initiate a program to strengthen forestry-research in developing countries, and conducts scientific exchanges.

*Fish, Wildlife, and Range Research.* Research on fish and wildlife currently is done at 28 locations in 30 research work units employing more than 67 Forest Service biologists—about eight percent of all scientists—plus supporting university cooperators. Funding for fish, wildlife, and range totaled $9.11 million in 1985, about seven percent of the research budget. Within this program, wildlife gets roughly 65 percent of the funding, range 25 percent, and fish 10 percent.

There are four broad program areas within fish and wildlife research: threatened, endangered, and sensitive species; anadromous and cold water fish habitats; livestock grazing and wildlife and fish relationships; and intensive forest management and wildlife. Threatened, endangered, and sensitive species research highlights species that have come into direct conflict with other forest resouce use such as timber harvest and to a lesser degree, livestock grazing. For example, researchers are studying the linkage between old-growth forest, which is being reduced by logging, and habitat requirements for the endangered red-cockaded woodpecker and the spotted owl, a sensitive species. Other research focuses on the endangered Puerto Rican parrot and Kirtland's warbler and the threatened bald eagle. In addition, several research locations are investigating habitat requirements and developing management methods for cavity-nesting species, a group whose habitat is sensitive to intensive forest management.

Anadromous and cold-water fish research focuses on chinook, coho, sockeye, pink and chum salmon; steelhead and cutthroat trout; and one species of char, the Dolly Varden. All depend heavily on the forested watersheds of the Pacific Northwest, Alaska, the Intermountain West, and northern California to complete their life cycles. This research is attempting to clarify the often confusing relationships between land-management activities and the anadromous fish and its habitat. A predictive relationship between habitat quality and fish populations can be established only if the fish's habitat requirements are known thoroughly. Current research focuses on identifying habitat needs for fish rearing; determining the influence of timber harvesting activities on habitat; identifying processes involved in pool and riffle formation; and developing cost-effective methods to improve habitat. In addition, a small cold-water fish program is located in the southern Appalachian Mountains.

Research on the interrelationships of wildlife and fish with livestock grazing splits into two areas of concentration. One major effort is examining the interactions between cattle and wildlife and fish in critical riparian zones of the Intermountain West and Southwest. The other is assessing dietary competition and other kinds of direct interaction between livestock and wild ungulates, such as deer and elk, in nonriparian areas.

Because of the National Forest System's emphasis on timber production, wildlife research focusing on intensive forest management has attempted to understand how the multiple-species complexes that make up forest wildlife communities change after logging. In connection with this effort, species identified in the forest plans as management indicator species are being studied to determine the effects of timber harvesting on their populations. Research also is helping to develop methods to monitor the effects of logging on wildlife.

In addition to their role in the discovery and publication of new information, Forest Service scientists frequently act in other ways to promote application of research findings. These activities include consultation and technical assistance, participation in workshops and symposiums, establishment of demonstration areas, and development and publication of management guides. The 1979 Forest Service publication, *Wildlife Habitats in Managed Forests: The Blue Mountains of Oregon and Washington,* is an example of one such effort. This book, which for the first time presented a framework for management of all wildlife on an area as large as a national forest, formed the basis of the current Forest Service Wildlife and Fish Habitat Relationship Program.

The benefits of fish and wildlife habitat research on the National Forest System can be great. Data on fish and wildlife habitat requirements is essential for the service to meet its legal mandate under the Endangered Species Act to protect endangered and threatened species and under the National Forest Management Act to maintain species diversity. In addition, understanding how to improve habitat for popular species such as anadromous fish, furbearers, and game animals can yield substantial economic benefits. Moreover, the better the Service understands habitat needs, the more accurately it can tailor management and mitigation efforts, often eliminating unnecessary costs and reducing risks to the species. With a sounder technical base, delays and costs of appeals and litigation may be reduced.

***Experimental Forests and Ranges and Research Natural Areas.*** The Forest Service sets aside small portions of National Forest System land for research purposes, either as experimental forests and ranges or as research natural areas. No statutory requirement exists for the designation, protection, or management of such areas. The Forest Service derives its authority to do so from the provision in the Organic Act that authorizes the Forest Service to regulate the occupancy and use of National Forest System lands.

Experimental forests and ranges are established by the chief of the Forest Service for research purposes. As of November 1985, there were 83 experimental forests and ranges totaling more than 608,000 acres. Two of the areas exceed 50,000 acres, but overall they average 7,328 acres each. The Forest Service limits their use primarily to forest, watershed, rangeland, recreation, and wildlife and fish habitat.

Research natural areas are established to preserve a wide spectrum of pristine areas that typify important forest, shrubland, grassland, alpine, aquatic, geologic, and similar natural situations for research, study, observation, monitoring, and those educational activities that maintain unmodified conditions. They are established to preserve natural diversity; to serve as reference areas for the study of succession, baseline areas for measuring long-term ecological change, and central areas for manipulative research; to monitor effects of resource-management practices; and to provide on-site educational activities.

There are currently 150 research natural areas ranging in size from fewer than 20 acres to more than 2,000 acres and averaging about 1,150 acres each. In all, they total fewer than 175,000 acres. Forest Service regulations (36 CFR 251.19) require that the areas be maintained in a virgin or unmodified condition, and generally only non-manipulative research is allowed—although management necessary to maintain the plant community that the area was designed to protect is allowed. Neither construction of permanent improvements nor occupancy by special-use permits is allowed. Few research natural areas are even posted, for if too much public attention is drawn to them, the possibility exists that they may be used for other than designated purposes and lose their pristine condition and value.

Selection and establishment of research natural areas within the National Forest System is part of the continuing land and resource management planning process. The Forest Service cooperates with universities, private and professional organizations, and state and other public agencies to establish and maintain a national network of these areas. The process of identifying and establishing a research natural area on a national forest starts within a regional committee set up for this purpose. Candidate areas are reviewed and examined. If one meets all criteria, an establishment record is prepared, complete with a biological description of the area and an environmental assessment. The establishment record is reviewed by concerned Forest Service staffs in Washington and, if deemed suitable, the candidate area is recommended to the chief for approval. Only the chief may approve establishment of Forest Service natural areas.

The current round of forest plans are identifying hundreds of candidates for the research natural areas network. By first identifying candidate research natural areas in individual forest plans, the overall review and approval process ultimately will be expedited because the environmental impact statement of an approved forest plan precludes the need for developing environmental impact statements for every candidate area.

## Trends and Issues

***Expansion and Increased Complexity of Research Needs.*** Throughout most of its history, Forest Service research on fish and wildlife—like the habitat management program—focused heavily on game species. In the 1970s, however, there was a growing concern for and awareness of the need to protect nongame species, to anticipate and moderate the effects of land management on wildlife habitat, and to achieve greater productivity of all forest and rangeland resources. This led to the passage of such laws as the Endangered Species

Act and the National Forest Management Act, which greatly expanded the legal and regulatory requirements for fish and wildlife management on the National Forest System.

The emerging program of wildlife and fisheries research is focusing heavily on providing the information that will be needed to meet these legal and regulatory requirements. As a result, wildlife and fisheries research has become more holistic, studying whole species complexes and the integration of wildlife and fisheries resources with other uses and products of forests and rangelands. At the same time, limited resources have been redirected to address higher priority needs, such as determining how to maintain diverse and well-distributed viable populations of old-growth wildlife while achieving timber-production objectives.

In the future, research will continue to address information needs to better meet legal and regulatory requirements and will increase its emphasis on methods integrating and producing wildlife and fish in concert with increased production of the other goods and services of forests and rangelands. As research establishes the correlation between certain activities and increases or decreases in wildlife populations, it will focus on discovering the fundamental causes of these changes. Some emerging trends in wildlife and fish research include:

- continued study of methods to increase stream productivity for anadromous fish, a multimillion-dollar commercial and recreational resource, which over the life of a rotation can produce more value than the timber on a stream's drainage system;
- development of new concepts and methodologies for efficient and cost-effective monitoring of wildlife populations over large land areas;
- determination of the quantitative relationship between management indicator species abundance and habitat in order to determine habitat carrying capacity and maintain viable populations;
- development of new concepts, tools, and methodologies to model the relationships of wildlife and fish abundance and habitat; and
- study of the extension and application of the basic ecological concepts emerging from the requirements of the National Forest Management Act, including diversity, edge effect, island biogeography, ecological indicators, and viable populations.

***Research Funding.*** As the Forest Service's research needs have increased, spending power in the research program overall as well as in fish, wildlife, and range research has decreased. Research funding increased from $108.45 million in 1981 to $121.66 million in 1985 in actual dollars, but declined 13 percent in spending power. In 1981, there were 242 research work units, down to 199 in 1985. The number of Forest Service scientists had dropped from 965 in 1981 to 794 by the end of 1984. Wildlife, fish, and range research has followed a similar pattern, suffered nearly a 10-percent decline in constant dollars during this same period. In 1981, there were 39 wildlife, range, and fish research work units, down to 28 in 1985, and it suffered a corresponding decline in scientists from 78 to 67. Within the wildlife, fish, and range research program, however, some funds have been shifted from lower priority range research to fish and wildlife studies, somewhat softening the impacts of the budget reductions on wildlife research.

# State and Private Forestry

Although public attention and debate over forest management focuses primarily on the National Forest System, the majority of the nation's forests and a substantial amount of the rangelands are in private or other nonfederal ownership. About 1.6 billion acres in the United States, approximately 66 percent of the nation's area, arc classified as forest or rangeland or are covered by water. More than half of this, about 887 million acres are in private or other nonfederal ownership. The Forest Service's State and Private Forestry program cooperates with several other agencies in the Department of Agriculture and with state foresters to provide a variety of assistance toward the management of these lands.

Of particular importance are the forestlands in private ownership. In total, about 721 million acres throughout the United States are classified as forest or transition land—land that is at least 10 percent stocked with trees or that previously had such cover and has not been developed for other uses. Approximately 445 million acres, or 61 percent of the total are in non-federal ownership. Moreover, of the 481 million acres in the United States classified as commercial forests,* 280 million acres or 58 percent are in nonindustrial private ownership. These non-industrial forests range in size from one acre to well over 10,000 acres, with an average size of about 70 acres. They are located primarily in the East and have a broad diversity of types of owners.

State and private lands are important in meeting many of the nation's needs for natural resources, especially for timber and fish and wildlife. For example, lands in non-industrial private ownerships accounted for 40 percent of the total United States sawtimber harvested in 1976, and the Forest Service reports that the 74 percent of the opportunities for increasing timber supplies are on farm lands and other private ownerships, which have the potential to yield an additional nine billion cubic feet of timber yearly (U.S. Department of Agriculture 1982). Privately owned forest and range lands play a major role in providing key habitats for waterfowl and for warm-water fish and in providing opportunities for hunting, especially for small game mammals, upland

* See the Timber Management section.

game birds, and waterfowl. In the 1979 Resources Planning Act Assessment, the Forest Service reported that one of the major opportunities for maintaining and enhancing fish and wildlife resources lies in improving federal-state-private cooperative programs aimed at enhancing the resources on private lands.

The Forest Service's State and Private Forestry Program has three basic roles: to cooperate with the states on fire prevention and control on non-federal forest and rangelands; to assist in pest management on both private and federal lands, including on the National Forest System; and to work with the states to improve management and productivity of non-industrial private forests. The latter effort, generally referred to as cooperative forestry, can benefit wildlife through better forest management in general and habitat improvements specifically. However, funding cutbacks in recent years have severely curtailed technical assistance in cooperative forestry in general and in wildlife and fisheries in particular.

## History and Legal Authority

Efforts to conserve and manage federal forest lands bore fruit at the end of the 19th century with passage of the Forest Reserve Act of 1891 and the Organic Administration Act of 1897, which established the authority and framework for the National Forest System. Once the conservation of these lands seemed assured, forestry experts turned their attention to non-federal forest lands. The frequently wasteful use of the nation's forest lands was the cause of growing concern at the turn of the century. The practice of "cut and run" was the rule, and slash left behind provided the fuel for massive forest fires, often set by lightning or sparks from trains and steam-powered log skidders. By the 1920s, many voices—led by former Forest Service Chief Gifford Pinchot—began to call for federal regulation of private forests, initiating a debate that continued until the 1940s.

*Cooperation vs. Regulation.* The first legislation passed by Congress involving cooperative forestry was the 1911 Weeks Act, which offered the states federal assistance in fire control, reforestation, and forest protection,* but the act's effectiveness was hurt by inadequate funding (Dana and Fairfax 1980).† In 1919, Pinchot—who had left the Forest Service nine years earlier—began in earnest his drive for federal regulation of forest practices on private lands. As the head of the Society of American Foresters, Pinchot was behind a report, called "Forest Devastation: A National Danger and How to Meet It," released

* Repealed and replaced by the Cooperative Forestry Assistance Act of 1978, except for authority to cooperate in fire control.
† Much of the information for this history is drawn from Forest and Range Policy by Samuel Dana and Sally Fairfax.

by the group. The report emphasized the nation's need for wood, the danger of a severe timber shortage resulting from the devastation of private lands, and the need to keep all forest lands in production. To achieve improved production, the report made several detailed recommendations, among them the establishment of a Federal Forest Commission to set and promulgate regulations over private forest lands.

During the debate over federal regulation, the position of the Forest Service varied depending on who was chief. Around the time of the Society of American Foresters report, the Service was headed by William Greeley, a staunch supporter of cooperation rather than regulation. In 1920, the Forest Service, at the request of Senator Arthur Capper of Kansas, issued its own report on the issue, called "Timber Depletion, Timber Exports, and Concentration of Timber Ownership." Although the report was issued in Capper's name, who supported Pinchot's regulatory approach, the study's findings reflected Greeley's position in favor of cooperation. The so-called "Capper Report" recommended immediate legislation permitting "effective cooperation between the Federal Government and the several states in preventing forest fires and growing timber on cut-over lands . . . " (Dana and Fairfax 1980).

Unhappy with the report's results, Capper introduced legislation in 1920 that included nearly all of the recommendations Pinchot had made in the earlier Society of American Foresters report, including a process for federally regulating private forestry. Congressman Bertrand Snell of New York countered with several bills supporting Greeley's emphasis on federal encouragement of state regulation. Pinchot's influence was sufficient to block Snell's bills, but not to pass Capper's.

The congressional stalemate was broken by the 1924 Clarke-McNary Act, which avoided the question of either state or federal regulation and took a cooperative approach. This law included two provisions of particular importance for today's cooperative forestry program: cooperation in fire control and cooperation in reforestation and management. The provisions of the Clarke-McNary Act* regarding fire control authorized the secretary of Agriculture to recommend regional systems of fire prevention and suppression and to enter into cooperative control programs with the states. To do this, up to $2.5 million annual appropriations were authorized. The act also allowed the money to be used to study tax breaks as an incentive to better forest management, a concept which flourishes today on the state and federal level. The provisions concerning reforestation and management authorized congressional appropriations to be used on a 50-50 matching basis with the states. The initial appropriation under this authority was only $100,000, but marked the first direct federal involvement in state and private reforestation. Another small appropriation was authorized for education and assistance programs, again on a matching basis.

---

* Repealed and replaced in part by the Cooperative Forestry Assistance Act of 1978.

*The Lumber Code.* The last major attempt at federal forest regulation came in the 1930s. During the Depression, many businesses and farms failed and became available for purchase at reduced prices. Many advocated expanding federal land acquisition during this period and, at the same time, expanding federal forest regulation on non-federal lands. This position was aided by a new string of Depression-era Forest Service chiefs who reversed the service's position and advocated federal regulation. The most adamant of these was Earle Clapp, acting chief between 1939 and 1943.

In 1933 Clapp, then director of Forest Research, and Robert Marshall of the Bureau of Indian Affairs' forestry department and later the director of the Forest Service's recreation program, authored a report titled "A National Plan for American Forestry," better known as the Copeland Report. The Copeland Report contained two important proposals: It called for greatly increasing public ownership of forests, and it advocated intensive management of public forests. The report demonstrated that private forestry had not adequately contributed to "human happiness" despite the assistance of federal and state governments and recommended massive federal acquisition of private forest land and an increased federal role in cooperative forestry. Although acquisition never was funded to the recommended level, the report presented an impressive empirical base that supported the need for federal leadership in private forestry.

The forest industry was too poorly organized during this period to resist the growing support for regulation. In fact, some leaders actually favored regulation as a solution to relieve the chaos. This disarray in the forest industry, combined with the findings of the Copeland Report, helped pave the way for a provision of the New Deal's National Industrial Recovery Act that required the development of a federal "Lumber Code." The act, primarily concerned with public works, labor, and trade, also attempted to conserve natural resources, in part by implementing forest rules. Article X of the act required the forest industries, in cooperation with government agencies, to develop regulations based on broad principles of forest conservation. Although the president approved the resulting Lumber Code, various regions were slow to adopt the rules and the government refused to prosecute violators. The Industrial Recovery Act's attempt at regulating private forestry died in 1935, when the Supreme Court declared the act unconstitutional.

Because the Lumber Code was in effect for less than a year, it is difficult to assess how well the regulations would have worked over time. The act did, however, succeed in hastening private-forestry reforms. Partly as an effort to head off further calls for federal regulation, industry often encouraged state regulation of forest practices, and numerous such bills were passed in the 1940s. A final attempt at federal regulation by President Roosevelt and Acting Forest Service Chief Earle Clapp failed in 1939 when the Joint Congressional Committee on Forestry—established at Roosevelt's request to review the situation—failed to recommend strong forest regulatory measures.

After suffering a serious decline during the Depression, the forest products industry was reborn during World War II. The demand for wood, technological advances, and the need for the first time to manage land for forest production as virgin forests in the South gave way to second growth, all contributed to the industry's growth and consequent development into an effective political block. The industry also adopted a more professional orientation. From 1933 to 1951, the number of professional foresters employed by the industry grew from 136 to 4,400. This evolution effectively prevented any further serious attempts at overall forest regulation.

*Nonindustrial Private Forests.* With industry lands under improved management, forestry experts began to focus on the nation's 278 million acres of non-industrial private forests. Reports from the Eisenhower administration through the Carter administration predicted shortfalls in timber, and bemoaned the low productivity rate of most small private forests. However, in part because the small size of these ownerships—70 acres on the average—would make these forests difficult to regulate, the federal government generally has attempted to encourage improved management through incentives and cooperation.

The cooperative approach was embodied in the Cooperative Farm Forestry Act of 1937 and the Cooperative Forest Management Act of 1950,* which authorized the Department of Agriculture to aid states and private landowners through technical assistance, education, and research. The incentives approach was first embodied in the Agricultural Conservation Program, started under the Soil Conservation and Domestic Allotment Act of 1936, which provided direct financial assistance for tree planting and timber-stand improvement. However, because the Agricultural Conservation Program was designed primarily as an agricultural incentives program, few outlays were made to forest owners. More recently, Congress provided financial incentives specifically for forest management with the enactment of the Forestry Incentives Program under Title X of the Agriculture and Consumer Protection Act of 1973.† Enacted in the regulatory climate of the 1970s, the Forest Incentives Program again showed the congressional preference for incentives over regulation.

*Cooperative Forestry Assistance Act of 1978.* The State and Private Forestry Program in the Forest Service began to take its present form in 1966, when two area offices were established to serve the 33 eastern states, where most private forest land is located. Recent laws that guide the program include the 1974 Resources Planning Act and 1976 National Forest Manage-

---

* Both repealed. The 1950 act was replaced by the Cooperative Forestry Assistance Act of 1978.
† The Forestry Incentives Program currently is embodied in the Cooperative Forestry Assistance Act of 1978, discussed below.

ment Act, which authorized Forest Service assistance in intensive state and regional planning.

In 1978, Congress repealed earlier authorities, consolidated the Service's authority for assistance programs, and reaffirmed the basic principles of cooperation in forestry with the passage of the Cooperative Forestry Assistance Act (16 U.S.C.A. 2101-2110, 1606, 2111). Today, this act provides the basic underpinnings for the Forest Service's State and Private Forestry Program. The act authorizes the secretary of Agriculture to cooperate with state foresters to provide assistance for a wide variety of forest-related activities: the advancement of forest-resources management; the encouragement of timber production; the prevention and control of insects and disease; the prevention and control of rural fires; the efficient use of wood; the planning and implementation of urban forestry programs; and the improvement and maintenance of fish and wildlife habitat. Of most significance for wildlife and fisheries, the act authorized the service to provide financial and technical assistance to state foresters for the protection of soils, water quality and quantity, and fish and wildlife habitat improvement and to assist the states in providing information to landowners on these topics.

## Program Management

State and Private Forestry, one of the Forest Service's three major programs, is supervised at the Washington level by a deputy chief who is supported by three staff directors, one each for cooperative fire protection, forest-pest management, and cooperative forestry. In the field, state and private forestry offices are located in the regional headquarters and are under the supervision of the regional forester. The one exception to this arrangement is in the eastern region, which has a separate northeastern area office headed by an area director who oversees the program in 20 northeastern states.

Although the State and Private Forestry Program assists in activities on the 877 million acres of nonfederal land, it is not a large portion of Forest Service efforts. In 1985, it was funded at $58.3 million, about three percent of the total service budget, and had about two percent of the full-time-equivalents. The major activities under the current programs are outlined below.

*Cooperative Fire Management.* The primary role of Cooperative Fire Management is to help the states develop effective fire prevention and control programs on nonfederal land. The Service provides technical and financial assistance for activities such as planning and training. Cooperative Fire Management was funded at $13.7 million in 1985, accounting for about 23 percent of State and Private Forestry funding.

*Forest Pest Management.* The Forest Service, through the Forest Pest Management Program, has the lead in pest management on all federal lands, including the National Forest System, and also works closely with state and private organizations that control pests on nonfederal lands. Because it includes this federal component, pest management is the largest part of the State and Private Forestry Program, funded at about $29 million in 1985, nearly half the program budget. About two-thirds of these funds were spent on pest control on federal lands.

In 1984, the program assisted in suppression activities on 329,000 acres of federal lands and nearly 700,000 acres of private lands. In recent years, major suppression projects have been conducted against the spruce budworm and the gypsy moth in the East, the southern pine beetle in the South, and the dwarf mistletoe mountain pine beetle and the spruce budworm in the West. The Forest Service estimates that these projects protected 798 million cubic feet of merchantable timber in 1984 and permitted salvage of 32 million feet of infested timber, resulting in approximately $70 million in direct benefits.

Pesticide use on the National Forest System from 1980 to 1984 averaged 40 percent for insect and disease control, 43 percent for vegetation control, and 17 percent for animal damage control and other minor uses.

In recent years, the Forest Service has reduced the use of conventional chemical pesticides through integrated pest management, which uses the best combination of pest suppression tactics—including silvicultural, biological, chemical, mechanical, and manual means—to achieve the management goal while minimizing environmental impacts and considering costs. The Forest Service emphasis on integrated pest management began during the Carter administration and has been accelerated recently as a result of lawsuits, and threats of lawsuits, by environmental groups concerned about the adverse effects many of these chemicals may have on fish and wildlife. In fact, since 1984, Forest Service pesticide use on the national forests has dropped because of court injunctions against the application of certain chemicals, principally herbicides, in parts of the West. In addition, the Forest Service has voluntarily halted aerial spraying nationwide until the legal issues are resolved. In its 1986 budget request, however, the administration has sought to cut the program's costs by concentrating on conventional pesticides and mechanical treatments rather than integrated pest management techniques, although Forest Service staff generally do not favor such a switch (U.S. Department of Agriculture 1985b).

*Cooperative Forestry.* Cooperative Forestry is the State and Private Forestry Program with the greatest potential for providing direct benefits for fish and wildlife habitat. The Forest Service provides cooperative forestry assistance through state foresters, who in turn work with private landowners to do the actual cooperative work. The Cooperative Forestry Program provides several forms of assistance, including technical advice and direct financial assistance. Cooperative Forestry was funded at $10.7 million in 1985, the smallest share of funding of the three State and Private Forestry programs, about 18 percent.

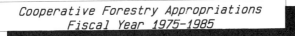

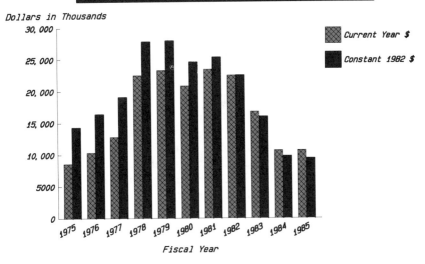

Cooperative Forestry Appropriations
Fiscal Year 1975-1985

Dollars in Thousands

Current Year $

Constant 1982 $

Fiscal Year

One of the most important cooperative forestry activities is state-forest-resource planning. Planning is important to help state and private forests meet state, regional, and national priorities and to coordinate land management on the federal level with that on nonfederal lands. The State Forest Resource Plans, prompted by the Resources Planning Act and the National Forest Management Act, are commonly supported by matching Forest Service grants. Compared to other federal planning grants for air quality, water quality, outdoor recreation, urban renewal, and similar efforts, the amounts of money allocated to state forest planning are small. Thus, state forest-planning staffs are very small. Total federal spending related to state planning was under $1 million in 1985.

The Service also provides technical assistance, primarily information on forest technology, to state foresters, who in turn convey it to the private landowner. This might include, for example, information on new silvicultural techniques or booklets on improving wildlife habitat. About two percent of the nation's 7.7 million non-industrial private forest landowners receive such assistance each year. This aspect of the program received just over $5 million in 1985. Cooperative Forestry also includes assistance to loggers, processors, and states for improved wood utilization; assistance in providing genetically improved tree-seed and planting stock for reforestation on non-federal lands; and help to local governments in planning and implementing urban-forestry programs.

*Cooperative Forestry and Wildlife and Fisheries.* Many studies have demonstrated that the majority of non-industrial private landowners consider wildlife-related outputs, such as hunting and fishing, as primary objectives of the management of their lands, while only a very small percentage cite timber production as a priority. In addition, the Service has identified these lands as holding substantial potential for habitat improvement, and fish and wildlife habitat improvement and maintenance were cited as a cooperative goal in the Cooperative Forestry Assistance Act. However, the staff position for the national coordinator of fish and wildlife concerns in the Cooperative Forestry Program was eliminated in 1984 in budgetary and personnel cutbacks. In conjunction with this cutback, a wildlife-management plan for the northeastern area was shelved after completion in 1981. This plan provides a model for what could be done if the Service reinstated this effort. The goals of the never-implemented report were: (1) to educate resource managers to develop a sensitivity to the needs of fish and wildlife for integration into management activities; (2) to recognize the needs of threatened, endangered, and sensitive plants and animals and to provide safeguards for their management and protection; (3) to transfer new information and technology to the states; (4) to develop a habitat management incentives program and establish evaluation criteria for accomplishments; and (5) to conduct surveys and data collection for planning and management.

## Trends and Issues

The major trend in the State and Private Forestry Program has been a cut in funding and personnel. Funding has dropped from $70.86 million in 1980 to $58.3 million in 1985, an 18 percent decline in actual dollars, a 38 percent decline in spending power when inflation is taken into account. Full-time equivalents have dropped from 688 in 1982* to 567 in 1985, also about an 18 percent drop.

This trend is even sharper in the program of most significance to wildlife and fisheries, Cooperative Forestry. After a 1977 report by the President's Advisory Panel on Timber and the Environment found that incentives to small forest owners were having "no significant effect on the intensity of forest practice," President Carter made significant increases in the Cooperative Forestry budget. But in recent years, budget cutbacks have reduced the scope of the program as the Reagan administration has attempted to scale back sharply the entire program. Funding has gone from a high of $23.45 million in 1981, to $10.76 million in 1985, a 54-percent decline in real dollars and a 62-percent decline in spending power. The administration's request for Cooperative Forestry for FY 1985 was $3.98 million.

* Full-time-equivalents are not available for years prior to 1982.

Forest Service reports have found that by far the greatest potential for increasing timber production is on the private non-industrial forests (U.S. Department of Agriculture 1981). In fact, in the past decade, the service has predicted that the South—which contains predominantly private lands—will outproduce the Pacific Northwest, even in the critical softwoods, by the turn of the century (U.S. Department of Agriculture 1981). The 1980 Resources Planning Act program had recommended a substantial growth in the State and Private Forestry Program to help achieve this potential, but funding for Cooperative Forestry is now less than a quarter of what the Resources program had projected.

Recent Forest Service inventories, however, indicate that the non-industrial private forests may not be producing at the rate originally projected. One problem is that growth rates on the southern forests appear to have slowed. Some have suggested that this may be an effect of acid rain, but Forest Service researchers say they do not have the information to show what has caused the reduction. In addition, the non-industrial private forests are not being restocked with softwoods, the type of timber most in demand, as the service had anticipated. The Service believes this is due to management ignorance or neglect by landowners who expected softwoods to regenerate naturally after timber harvest and therefore did not actively reforest their lands. Consequently, on about 60 percent of naturally regenerated areas, hardwoods are predominant, causing the Forest Service to lower its projections for the amount of softwood demand that will be met from these lands.

# References

Babcock, H. 1984. "Rivers: our vanishing heritage." *The Environmental Forum,* vol. 2, no. 10 (February 1984). p. 40.

Dana, S.T. and S.K. Fairfax. 1980. *Forest and Range Policy: It's Development in the United States.* McGraw-Hill, New York. 458 pp.

Emerson, P.M., A.T. Stout and D. Kloepfer. 1984. Wasting the National Forests: Selling Timber Below Cost. Unpublished manuscript. The Wilderness Society. Washington, D.C.

France, T.M. 1985. Statement on Behalf of the National Wildlife Federation Before the Subcommittee on Public Lands and General Oversight, Northwest Power and Forest Management, June 13, 1985. Unpublished manuscript. National Wildlife Federation. Washington, D.C.

Frome, M. 1984. *The Forest Service.* Westview Press. Boulder, Colorado. 364 pp.

Trefethan, J.B. 1975. *An American Crusade for Wildlife.* Winchester Press and the Boone Crockett Club. New York. p. 71.

U.S. Congress, House, Committee on Appropriations, Survey and Investigations Staff. 1985. "Selected aspects of the U.S. Forest Service timber and road construction program," in U.S. Congress, House, Committee on Appropriations. 1985. *Department of the Interior and Related Agencies Appropriations for 1986, Part II.* Government Printing Office. Washington, D.C. pp. 991-1029.

U.S. Department of Agriculture, Forest Service. 1980. *A Recommended Renewable Resources Program—1980 Update.* FS-346. Government Printing Office. Washington, D.C.

————. 1981. *An Assessment of the Forest and Range Land Situation in the United States,* Forest Resource Report No. 22. Government Printing Office. Washington, D.C. 352 pp.

————. 1982. *An Analysis of the Timber Situation in the United States, 1952-2030,* Forest Resource Report No. 23. Government Printing Office. Washington, D.C. 499 pp.

————. 1984a. *America's Renewable Resources: A Supplement to the 1979 Assessment of the Forest and Range Land Situation in the United States,* FS-386. U.S. Department of Agriculture. Washington, D.C. 84 pp.

————. 1984b. Draft Environmental Impact Statement on the 1985-2030 Resources Planning Act Program. U.S. Department of Agriculture. Washington, D.C.

————. 1984c. *Grazing Statistical Summary, FY 1984.* U.S. Department of Agriculture. Washington, D.C. 97 pp.

————. 1984d. *Land Areas of the National Forest System as of September 30, 1984,* FS-383. Government Printing Office. Washington, D.C. 88 pp.

————. 1985a. *Report of the Forest Service—Fiscal Year 1984.* U.S. Department of Agriculture. Washington, D.C. 153 pp.

————. 1985b. *1986 Budget Explanatory Notes for Committee on Appropriations.* U.S. Department of Agriculture. Washington, D.C. 377 pp.

U.S. Department of the Interior, Bureau of Land Management and U.S. Department of Agriculuture, Forest Service. 1984. *Administration of the Wild Free-Roaming Horse and Burro Act: 5th Report to Congress.* Government Printing Office. Washington, D.C. 25 pp.

Wilderness Society, Sierra Club, National Audubon Society, Natural Resources Defense Council, National Wildlife Federation. 1983. *National Forest Planning: A Conservationist's Guide.* Published by authoring groups. Washington, D.C. 121 pp.

# Table of Statutes

Archaeological Resources Protection Act of 1979, P.L. 96-96, 93 Stat. 721; 16 U.S.C.A. 470aa-11.

Bankhead-Jones Farm Tenant Act of 1937, Act of July 22, 1937, Ch. 517, 50 Stat. 522, as amended; 7 U.S.C.A. 1010-1012.

Clarke-McNary Act of 1924, Act of June 7, 1924, Ch. 348, 43 Stat. 653, as amended; 16 U.S.C.A. 499-570.

Clean Air Act Amendments of 1977, P.L. 95-95, 91 Stat. 685, as amended; 42 U.S.C.A. 7401-7642.

Clean Water Act, P.L. 92-500, 86 Stat. 816, as amended; 33 U.S.C.A. 1251-1376.

Common Varieties of Mineral Materials Act of 1947, Act of July 31, 1947, Ch. 406, 61 Stat. 681; 30 U.S.C.A. 601-602, 611.

Eastern Wilderness Act, P.L. 93-622, 88 Stat. 2096; 16 U.S.C.A 1132 (note).

Endangered Species Act of 1973, P.L. 93-205, 87 Stat. 884, as amended; 16 U.S.C.A. 1531-1540.

Federal Coal Leasing Amendments Act of 1975, P.L. 94-377, 90 Stat. 1083, as amended; 30 U.S.C.A. 201-207.

Federal Land Policy and Management Act of 1976, P.L. 94-579, 90 Stat. 2743, as amended; 43 U.S.C.A. 1701-1782.

Forest and Rangeland Renewable Resources Planning Act 1974, P.L. 93-378, 88 Stat. 476, as amended; 16 U.S.C.A. 1600-1614.

Forest and Rangeland Renewable Resources Research Act of 1978, P.L. 95-307, 92 Stat. 353, as amended; 16 U.S.C.A. 1641-1647.

Forest Reserve Act of 1891, Act of March 3, 1891, Ch. 561, 26 Stat. 1103 (repealed 1976).

Forest Service Organic Administration Act of 1897, Act of June 4, 1897, Ch. 2, 30 Stat. 11, as amended; 16 U.S.C.A. 473-475, 477-482, 551.

General Exchange Act, Act of March 20, 1922, Ch. 105, 42 Stat. 465, 16 U.S.C.A. 485, 486.

Geothermal Steam Act of 1970, P.L. 91-581, 84 Stat. 1566; 30 U.S.C.A. 1001-1024.

Granger-Thye Act of 1950, Act of April 24, 1950, Ch. 97, 64 Stat. 82; 16 U.S.C.A. 490-581.

Knutson-Vandenberg Act of 1930, Act of June 9, 1930, Ch. 416, 46 Stat. 527, as amended; 16 U.S.C.A. 576-576b.

Land and Water Conservation Fund Act of 1965, P.L. 88-578, 78 Stat. 897, 16 U.S.C.A. 460l-4—460l-11.

McIntire-Stennis Act, P.L. 87-788, 76 Stat. 806, as amended; 16 U.S.C.A. 582a.

McSweeney-McNary Act, Act of May 22, 1938, 45 Stat. 699-702 (repealed 1978).

Mineral Leasing Act for Acquired Lands, Act of August 7, 1947, Ch. 513, 61 Stat. 913; 30 U.S.C.A. 351-359.

Mineral Leasing Act of 1920, Act of February 25, 1920, Ch. 85, 41 Stat. 437, as amended; 30 U.S.C.A. 181.

Mineral Resources on Weeks Law Lands Act, Act of March 4, 1917, Ch. 179, 39 Stat. 1134; 16 U.S.C.A. 520.

Mining Law of 1872, Act of May 10, 1872, Ch. 152, 17 Stat. 91; 30 U.S.C.A. 22, 28, 28b.

Multiple-Use Sustained-Yield Act of 1960, P.L. 86-517, 74 Stat. 215; 16 U.S.C.A. 528-531.

National Environmental Policy Act of 1969, P.L. 91-190, 83 Stat. 852; 42 U.S.C.A. 4321-4361.

National Forest Management Act of 1976, P.L. 94-588, 90 Stat. 2949, as amended; 16 U.S.C.A. 1601-1614.

National Trails System Act, P.L. 90-543, 82 Stat. 919, as amended; 16 U.S.C.A. 1241-1249.

Public Rangelands Improvement Act of 1978, P.L. 95-514, 92 Stat. 1806; 43 U.S.C.A. 1901-1908.

Right of Eminent Domain Law, Act of August 1, 1888, Ch. 782, 25 Stat. 357, as amended; 40 U.S.C.A. 257.

Sikes Act Extension, P.L. 93-452, 88 Stat. 1369, as amended; 16 U.S.C.A. 670g-670o.

Sisk Act, P.L. 90-171, 81 Stat. 531, as amended; 16 U.S.C.A. 484a.

Small Tracts Act of 1983, P.L. 97-465, 96 Stat. 2535; 16 U.S.C.A. 521c-521i.

Statement of Policy (Interior Department and Related Agencies, Appropriations for Fiscal Year 1981), P.L. 96-514, 96 Stat. 2957.

Surface Mining Control and Reclamation Act of 1977, P.L. 95-87, 91 Stat. 445; 30 U.S.C.A. 1201-1272.

Townsite Act of 1958, P.L. 85-589, 72 Stat. 438, as amended; 7 U.S.C.A. 1012a; 16 U.S.C.A. 478a.

Weeks Act of 1911, Act of March 1, 1911, Ch. 186, 36 Stat. 961, as amended; codified at scattered sections in 16 U.S.C.A. 480-563.

Wild and Scenic Rivers Act of 1968, P.L. 90-542, 82 Stat. 906, as amended; 16 U.S.C.A. 1271-1287.

Wild Free-Roaming Horse and Burros Act, P.L. 92-195, 85 Stat. 649, as amended; 16 U.S.C.A. 1331-1340.

Wilderness Act of 1964, P.L. 88-577, 78 Stat. 890; 16 U.S.C.A. 1131-1136.

*Katherine Barton, a freelance writer who specializes in conservation issues, is based in Washington D.C.*

*Whit Fosburgh is on the National Audubon Society's Washington D.C. staff.*

The grizzly bear, to many a symbol of unspoiled wilderness, is one of some 60 threatened and endangered species whose fate is closely linked to Forest Service policies.

*Tom McHugh/ Photo Researchers*

# Wildlife Issues in the National Forest System

## Whit Fosburgh

THE FOREST SERVICE is a multiple-use agency, and its lands are used for a variety of competing purposes. As a result, conflicts regularly arise over what land use is most appropriate for a given area. In the *Audubon Wildlife Report 1985*, five issues relating to the National Forest System and wildlife and fish were covered: the effects of old-growth timber harvest on wildlife (illustrated by three examples—the spotted owl, the red-cockaded woodpecker, and the Sitka black-tailed deer); below-cost timber sales and their effect on wildlife and fish; road building; conflicts over grizzly bear management; and the effects on wildlife and fish of grazing in riparian zones. These issues, except for protection of riparian areas (which is covered in detail in the Bureau of Land Management chapter), will be updated in this chapter, but for background information, the 1985 volume should be consulted. In addition, one new issue has been added: the woodland caribou and the controversy surrounding its recovery in the northern Rocky Mountains.

## Old-Growth Timber Harvest and Wildlife

### The Spotted Owl

The northern spotted owl (*Strix occidentalis*) is a medium-sized owl native to the coniferous old-growth forests of the Pacific Northwest. As timber harvest has

159

reduced the amount of old-growth habitat available to the owl, conservation-ists have raised concerns about the survival of the spotted owl (for more infor-mation on the biology and management of the spotted owl, see this volume's species account by Charles Meslow and Eric Forsman).

The Forest Service, which manages the great majority of occupied spot-ted owl habitat, estimates that approximately 2,500 pairs currently remain in lands of all jurisdictions. In 1984, the Forest Service issued its guide for the Pacific Northwest Region—a document outlining overall management objec-tives for the region. In order to maintain species viability in Oregon and Washington, the guide called for maintaining 500 pairs of spotted owls with 1,000 acres of old growth per pair. On October 22, 1984, conservationists, led by the National Wildlife Federation and including the Oregon Wildlife Feder-ation, the Lane County Audubon Society, and the Oregon Natural Resources Council, appealed the adoption of the regional guide on the basis that no environmental impact statement had been completed regarding the effects of continued timber harvest on the spotted owl.

On March 8, 1985, the federation's appeal was upheld by Assistant Secretary of Agriculture Douglas MacCleery. Citing the lack of concrete scien-tific data on the owl, MacCleery directed the region to prepare a supplemen-tal environmental impact statement that would address the current population and habitat requirements of the spotted owl, inventory old growth and suit-able spotted owl habitat, predict the current timber harvest schedule's effect on the overall population of the owl; and determine the minimum number of spotted owls that must be maintained to assure the species' viability. The supplementary statement, which is expected to be released in February or March 1986, Preliminary findings from the supplemental environmental impast statetment indicate that the 1,000-acre requirement is inadequate.

Pending completion of the supplementary environmental impact state-ment by the Forest Service, the federation asked for a halt to further timber sales in suitable spotted owl habitat. In his decision, MacCleery denied this portion of the appeal on the grounds that "Any reduction in the amount of suitable spotted owl habitat during the time necessary to prepare a supple-mental environmental statement will have an insignificant impact on the via-bility of the spotted owl" (U.S. Department of Agriculture 1984). The federation requested but failed to obtain a reversal of this portion of the deci-sion from MacCleery, so timber sales continue. Warned of probable lawsuits, the Forest Service has canceled or postponed some controversial sales pending the outcome of the supplemental environmental impact statement.

Adding fuel to the fire, a report released by University of Chicago scien-tist Russell Lande concluded that "under current conditions the population of the spotted owl may already be declining and in danger of extinction within the next century" and that "Further habitat alteration, as planned by the U.S. Forest Service, is very likely to cause the extinction of the spotted owl from the management area on a shorter time scale" (Lande 1985, p. 26). Although Lande's prognosis is very grim, there is little agreement among scientists as to what constitutes a minimum viable population, and how large a home range each pair needs.

In order to produce a sound and more unified scientific opinion, the National Audubon Society, along with the American Ornithologists' Union and the Cooper Ornithological Society, assembled a blue ribbon panel of eminent ornithologists and biologists. The charge of the panel is to review all existing information regarding the current population of the spotted owl and its biology and habitat requirements, and then make concrete research and management recommendations. The report of the panel is expected to be issued by May 1986.

## Red-Cockaded Woodpecker

The old-growth forests of the southeastern United States are the setting for a continuing dispute over the conservation of the red-cockaded woodpecker (*Picoides borealis*). The woodpecker, a colonial-nesting bird federally listed as endangered, is threatened by the harvest of mature softwood forests, predominately longleaf and loblolly pine, and continued harvest on shorter rotation schedules. While a tentative settlement has been reached in the appeal by the National Wildlife Federation over the Forest Service's red-cockaded woodpecker management guidelines, a new controversy has erupted over the service's southern pine beetle suppression methods, which directly involves the red-cockaded.

In 1984, the National Wildlife Federation filed a notice of violation with the U.S. Fish and Wildlife Service (FWS) and the Forest Service under the Endangered Species Act. The federation claimed that the Forest Service's regional management guidelines for the red-cockaded were not based on the best scientific information available, and consequently, the guidelines jeopardized the continued viability of the species. The federation demanded that consultation between FWS and the Forest Service be reinitiated in order to prepare new and acceptable management guidelines. Under the spectre of a lawsuit, consultation was reinitiated, and in February 1985 the Forest Service issued new management guidelines, which FWS found did not jeopardize the species.

The new red-cockaded guidelines are similar to the old ones in that two management alternatives are given. The first is that rotation ages of 100 years for longleaf pine and 80 years for loblolly and other pines be maintained within one mile of a woodpecker colony site. The second alternative is that rotation ages be maintained at 80 and 70 years and that recruitment/replacement stands (areas managed if they contained colonies in the hope of attracting more woodpeckers) be used to expand the population, or to give a colony a place to go if natural causes force it from an existing colony site. The difference in the new guidelines is that they set specific population goals for all the forests with red-cockaded populations and describe the amount and composition of foraging habitat to be associated with each colony site. In each of the 23 national forests with red-cockaded populations, the new guidelines propose population increases. In total, the population increase called for exceeded 100 percent. One way this increase is to be achieved is by establishing 125-acre foraging areas within a half mile of each colony site. Foraging areas must contain trees 30 years of age or older, with at least 40 percent 60 years or older. In addition, the guidelines provide for the placement of additional recruitment/replacement stands around active colonies depending on what the population density objective is for the given area. Although the federation has concerns that the criteria for declaring a population "recovered"—the existence of 250 colonies—may be inadequate*, and that the number of forests striving for recovered populations may be too low, the new guidelines are seen as a definite improvement over the previous ones. The federation has not challenged the new guidelines, but implementation and subsequent results will be watched closely.

While the controversy over the management guidelines lessened in 1985, two lawsuits were filed against the Forest Service regarding southern pine beetle suppression in wilderness areas. Wilderness areas are by definition inviolate, to be left undisturbed and free from any evidence of man's presence. But the southern pine beetle knows no jurisdictional boundaries and has swept through large areas of wilderness. Throughout the South, the beetle has infested some 200,000 acres. Among the casualties of the beetle is the red-cockaded woodpecker, which depends on live trees infected with red heart fungus. The beetle kills the trees, and thus forces the woodpecker to relocate.

In order to protect the woodpecker, which it is required to do under the Endangered Species Act, the Forest Service has adopted a policy of cutting all infested trees, including cavity trees where necessary. The basis of the suits (*Sierra Club et al v. Block et al*, 614 F.Supp. 488 [D. Tex 1985] and *Sierra Club and the Wilderness Society v. Block, et al*, 614 F.Supp. 134 [D.D.C. 1985]) is that the Forest Service is violating the Wilderness Act by cutting these trees. Furthermore, the plaintiffs allege that the Forest Service's strategy of cutting infected trees is damaging woodpecker habitat. The Forest Service says that if it does not stop the spread of the beetle, far more woodpecker habitat would be lost than is being lost through preventative cuts. Final decisions in the cases are expected in 1986. In addition, the Forest Service will release a new environmental impact statement on pine beetle suppression in early 1986.

## Sitka Black-Tailed Deer

The Sitka black-tailed deer (*Odocoileus hemionus sitkensis*) is only one species in a broad controversy surrounding the Tongass National Forest in southeast

* The federation cites research done by Phillip Doerr of North Carolina State University. Doerr states that demographic studies from North Carolina red-cockaded populations suggest that the Forest Service's current population goal of 250 colonies is substantially below levels that would ensure viability. Doerr believes that an adequate goal is more likely 500 to 700 colonies.

Alaska. The controversy involves the impacts of intensive timber harvest on old-growth associated species, such as the Sitka deer, marten, cavity-nesting birds, brown bear, and anadromous fish. Unlike other old-growth controversies, in which the economics of cutting are rarely an issue, the Tongass harvest is a prime example of the below-cost timber sale issue (discussed later in this chapter in greater detail). Though the Sitka deer population is still healthy, scientists, conservationists, sportsmen, and Native subsistence hunters fear that further depletion of the old-growth forests will lead to a decline in the deer population.

The Tongass National Forest represents 93.8 percent of southeast Alaska's total land area (excluding the Glacier Bay National Park and Preserve). The State of Alaska owns 482,000 acres, or 2.7 percent, and Native Corporations 630,000 acres, or 3.5 percent. In the 16.9 million acre Tongass National Forest, 34 percent or 5.7 million acres is classified by the Forest Service as commercial forest. Of this, 635,000 acres, or 12 percent of the commercial forest, is considered "high-volume stands" capable of producing greater than 30,000 board feet of timber per acre. Nearly half of this already has been harvested.

The high-volume forest land is also the most important habitat for the Sitka black-tailed deer. The deer will use whatever habitat is available during the spring, summer and fall in order to find food, but studies show that deer use old growth more than five times as much as young growth during this period. During winter, the ratio increases to seven times as much (Wallmo and Schoen 1980). In winter, the deer are dependent upon old-growth areas because the uneven canopies of these high-volume stands of large trees intercept snowfall and yet allow light to reach the forest floor, which results in shallower snow depths and more available forage during the winter (Schoen et al 1981, Schoen et al 1985, Territorial Sportsman 1985). Generally, these high-volume stands are found near the coast at low elevations and along broad valley bottoms.

Commercial logging began on the Tongass in 1833 when the first Alaskan sawmill was built near the town of Sitka (Territorial Sportsman 1985). As the local economies expanded during the 19th and early 20th centuries, primarily through fishing and fish processing, so did the local demand for timber. By 1926, six sawmills were cutting lumber both for local use and export, and, by 1930, most easily accessible timber had been logged.

It was not until the 1950s that large-scale industrial logging as it exists today came to southeast Alaska. Lured by the prospect of 50-year contracts from the Forest Service worth billions of board feet, two companies became the dominant purchasers of Tongass timber—the Ketchikan Pulp Company (now Louisiana Pacific-Ketchikan) and the Japanese-owned Alaska Lumber and Pulp Co. The method of harvest was large-scale clearcuts concentrating on the remaining high-volume forests near the coast and in the valleys. Between 1956 and 1972, the areas harvested averaged in excess of 50,000 board feet per acre, and from 1972 through 1981, the figure was 48,000 board feet per acre. Today, 317,000 acres, or about half the high-volume forest land, have been cut. Nearly all of this was high-density old growth.

The Sitka deer and Tongass timber-harvest controversy currently stems from Section 705 of the Alaska National Interest Lands Conservation Act of 1980. Section 705 mandates that the secretary of Treasury annually provide the secretary of Agriculture $40 million, or as much as the Agriculture secretary finds necessary, to maintain the timber supply from the Tongass to dependent industry at a rate of 4.5 billion board feet per decade, or approximately 450 million board feet yearly. The act does not mandate the harvest of this timber, merely that it be made available should timber companies care to harvest it.

The original goal of Section 705 was to aid the local timber industry and to provide jobs, and it was strongly supported by Louisiana Pacific-Ketchikan and Alaska Lumber and Pulp. In effect, Section 705 has provided the companies with enormous subsidies for cutting the Tongass. In a 1983 Wilderness Society report, timber harvesting in the Tongass is shown to return only two cents to the Treasury for every dollar expended. The costs of administering the sales are high and demand and prices paid for Alaskan timber are low. Nearly all the timber harvested on the Tongass is exported to Japan.

In addition, Louisiana Pacific-Ketchikan and Alaska Lumber and Pulp have been convicted of fraud and collusion. In 1981, Alaska Lumber and Pulp and the Ketchikan Pulp Co. (now Louisiana Pacific-Kechikan) were found guilty in U.S. District Court of conspiring in restraint of trade and attempt to monopolize in violation of the Sherman Antitrust Act (*Reid Brothers v. Ketchikan Pulp Co. and Alaska Lumber and Pulp Co.* 1981), a decision that was upheld by the Ninth Circuit Court of Appeals, and let stand by the Supreme Court. The Reid Brothers case showed many improprieties in the companies' harvest of Tongass timber. Not only were the companies keeping prices artificially low, thus effectively discouraging new companies interested in Tongass timber, but they also overestimated logging and mill costs, thus further lowering stumpage prices, and thereby increasing the government subsidy and their own profits.

As early as 1968, and again in 1970 and 1974, the Forest Service notified the Justice Department of possible antitrust violations, but little action was taken by the Justice Department, and the Forest Service failed to follow up with its own investigation until after the Reid Brothers decision in 1981. Among the recommendations then made by the Forest Service investigation team was that Alaska Lumber and Pulp and Louisana Pacific-Ketchikan be debarred from future timber sales on the Tongass in order to allow competititive bidding to begin again.

Since the Forest Service's review team's recommendations, little has happened. Debarment action was not taken. The Justice Department has not attempted to recover damages, estimated by the Forest Service to be between $76 and $81 million. Nor has the Justice Department pursued criminal charges against the companies. In both cases, the department concluded that there was no basis for action because the statutes of limitations, four and five years, respectively, had passed. Claims of fraud and breach of contract, which have longer statutes of limitations, still are being considered.

In addition, the Forest Service granted Louisiana Pacific-Ketchikan and Alaska Lumber and Pulp large reductions in the cost of timber. Under the Alaskan National Interests Lands Conservation Act, the Forest Service is required to recalculate timber-sale prices in the 50-year contracts every five years in order to ensure industry profits if markets decline. There is no reciprocal agreement for rising markets. Emergency rate redeterminations—made because of recent declining market prices—have cost the loss of additional moneys. For example, in 1984 redeterminations retroactive to July 1, 1982, Alaska Lumber and Pulp had the 1981-86 appraisal rate per thousand board feet reduced for spruce sawlogs from $215.98 to $2.26 and for Alaska cedar sawlogs from $1,058.27 to $1.22. For Louisiana Pacific-Ketchikan, the 1979-84 appraisal rate for spruce sawlogs was reduced from $114.96 to $2.87, retroactive to December 1, 1981 (Territorial Sportsman 1985).

Another problem with timber harvest practices is that the companies have very large contracts, which were appraised on the basis of all the timber present. But in practice only the highest volume stands were being cut while lower-quality stands often were being overlooked. Thus, not only were stumpage fees less than what should have been paid for the timber cut, but more importantly, the most valuable wildlife habitat was being affected heavily.

Often lost in the controversy over economics and fair practices are the effects of logging on wildlife and fish. The Alaska Department of Fish and Game has recommended that wildlife and fish be given greater consideration in the management of the Tongass, but conservationists feel that the Forest Service has largely ignored these recommendations (Wilderness Society 1985). Research by the Alaska Department of Fish and Game predicts a significant decrease in the carrying capacity of the habitat for the deer as old-growth harvest continues. A 1985 report by the Southeast Alaska Conservation Council predicts that half the deer habitat currently available will be lost as the Forest Service completes the first 100-year rotation now under way. The report also predicts serious damage to the anadromous fish resource of the Tongass. The Forest Service and the Alaskan Department of Fish and Game have not estimated the losses. To determine if second growth can be managed for the deer, the Forest Service is continuing research in its Second Growth Management Project.

## Below-Cost Timber Sales

Controversy over the Forest Service's practice of selling timber in certain regions at a loss to the federal treasury reached a new high in 1985. Congressional hearings were held on the subject, and the Forest Service continued revising its timber accounting system. But the action with the most potential to change the current practice was a successful appeal by the Natural Resources Defense Council *et al* against plans proposing timber harvest increases on two Colorado national forests. Assistant Secretary of Agriculture Douglas Mac-Cleery upheld the appeal, a ruling that environmentalists hope will set a national precedent.

The appeal by Natural Resources Defense Council and nine other local and national environmental groups, centered on the forest plans of the San Juan and Grand Mesa/Uncompaghre/Gunnison (GMUG) national forests. The plans proposed an increase in timber-harvest levels from a recent average of 26 million board feet to an allowable harvest level of 38 million board feet on the San Juan, and an increase from 29 million board feet to 35 million board feet on the GMUG. Though the new harvest levels are merely allowable, not required, harvest limits, it is agreed that the plan is an increase in the existing timber program.

The Wilderness Society estimated that the San Juan and the GMUG returned to the treasury three and four cents, respectively, for every dollar spent (Wilderness Society 1984).

The Natural Resources Defense Council appeal cited, among other things, Section 6 of National Forest Management Act, which states, "[i]n developing land management plans pursuant to this Act, the Secretary shall identify within the management area lands which are not suited for timber production, considering physical, economic and other pertinent factors to the extent feasible . . . " In his decision, the assistant secretary noted that if current costs and prices are considered alone, the timber-sale level that would be economically efficient would be only seven to nine million board feet on the San Juan and four to nine million board feet on the GMUG. But the decision stated that the National Forest Management Act regulations did not require that economic suitability be the only criterion for timber harvest. The Forest Service has long claimed that many benefits of harvest do not easily show up on a balance sheet. Timber roads also may serve as fire roads and as access roads for hunters and fishermen. In addition, some timber sales may be done to improve wildlife habitat or to remove diseased trees. But in recognizing that most of the benefits incurred by the proposed timber sales would not be economic, the decision recommends "exploration of the question of whether it is possible to achieve the non-timber benefits more cost effectively through a management program of a different nature than presently proposed." The decision goes on to ask, as environmentalists have long asked, "Are the non-timber multiple-use benefits achieved through the timber program really needed?" Wildlife groups, such as the National Audubon Society and the National Wildlife Federation, have questioned whether road building and timber harvest do in fact help wildlife, noting that the benefit for species such as deer is more than offset by damage done to other species such as cavity-nesting birds, elk, and fish.

MacCleery agreed with the appellants that "the planning documents for both the San Juan and GMUG provide inadequate information on, or discussion of, the economic implications of continuing and increasing a timber sales program where costs substantially exceed revenues . . . " His decision directs the regional forester to reconsider the existing alternatives, and, if necessary, develop new ones, to ensure that questions regarding economics and public benefits are adequately considered.

MacCleery agreed that lands that really are unsuitable for timber production (low productivity lands) may be classified as suitable if the timber production goals assigned to the forest or region are set unrealistically high, as environmentalists had charged, but he reiterated the difficulty in assigning cost/benefit figures in dollar terms. In the report accompanying the 1985 appropriations bill language, Congress directed the Forest Service to adjust its accounting system to take account of the benefits which it claims make uneconomic sales worthwhile. The service has yet to release this new system.

Extensive oversight hearings were held in Congress in 1985 on the subject of below-cost timber sales, but no major actions were taken to stop the practice. The Natural Resources Defense Council and its co-appellants hope the San Juan/GMUG decision will set a precedent upon which a more balanced approach to resource allocation will be achieved.

## Road Building

The effects on wildlife and the environment of Forest Service road building continued to be a major issue in 1985. The issue was debated in the courts and in Congress as environmentalists sought to curb what they view as ambitious plans by the Forest Service to expand roads into currently roadless areas. As more forest plans are released, 1986 promises to be another important year in the debate.*

The road-construction plans in the Idaho-Montana region were appealed by the National Wildlife Federation, which sought an injunction on the grounds that the plans violated National Environmental Policy Act requirements. The Forest Service plans 30 new road projects in the region, 15 in currently roadless areas. The Ninth Circuit Court (*NWF v. Coston*, 9th Cir. No 84-4198 October 15, 1985) denied the federation's appeal, stating that the Forest Service had followed the National Environmental Policy Act requirements adequately and, moreover, that the issue was essentially a budgetary one and therefore exempt from NEPA.

But in a separate decision, the Ninth Circuit court decided against the Forest Service in a case that could have important implications nationwide. This case, *Northwest Indian Cemetary Protective Association*, et al., *v. Peterson* (9th

* See the *Audubon Wildlife Report 1985* for a more detailed discussion of road building and its impacts on wildlife.

Cir. No. 83-2225, 1985), challenged the Forest Service's timber harvest and road-building plans on the Blue Creek Unit of the Six Rivers National Forest in California. The unit includes a sacred area for the Yurok, Karok, and Tolowa Indians. The court found that the proposed road, known as the G-O Road, violated not only federal environmental laws but also California water-quality statutes, even though the plan specified the use of "best management practices," which generally are assumed to prevent undue environmental damage during forestry operations. The decision casts doubt on whether current management strategies in nonpoint-source pollution areas are adequate and may set a new precedent for the relationship between state water-quality standards and generally accepted methods of forest management (*American Forests* 1985, p.8).

In the appropriations hearings for the 1986 budget, roading was a major issue. The administration proposed a budget of $195.56 million for road construction on the National Forest System. The House reduced this to $151.29 million, pointing out that nearly every completed forest plan has been appealed, largely because of timber-sale and roading plans, and to continue funding an ambitious roading program does not make sense, especially in times of fiscal austerity. But the Senate supported the president's request and recommended that road construction be funded at the original level. In conference committee, a compromise of $188.21 million was reached. This represents a significant decrease from the 1985 total of $228.91 million.

# The Grizzly Bear

1985 was a year of significant progress for the Forest Service and its efforts to restore the threatened grizzly bear (*Ursus arctos horribilus*) in the lower 48 states. The grizzly bear, once native to most of the western United States, now exists only in a limited area in Montana, Wyoming, Idaho, and Washington. The Forest Service manages more grizzly bear habitat than any other land-management agency, and is at the forefront of the bear's management. On-the-ground bear management improved and strides were made in the internal organization of state-federal cooperative management, but opposition to augmentation of existing grizzly populations continued in Congress.

In 1985, the Forest Service continued mapping bear habitat. Mapping is a part of the cumulative effects analysis that is being implemented throughout grizzly bear habitat in the Rocky Mountain region. Cumulative effects analysis looks at the value of a given area to the bear and forecasts the effects of a proposed alteration of habitat on the bear. In addition, prescribed burning and timber cutting were conducted to encourage the growth of herbs and shrubs and thus improve habitat for the bear. To reduce bear/human conflicts, public education programs continued, and new camp sanitation regulations were implemented and enforced by interagency law enforcement teams.

Grizzly bear management in the lower 48 states is headed by the Interagency Grizzly Bear Committee, consisting of five federal agencies (the Forest Service, Fish and Wildlife Service, Bureau of Land Management, National Park Service, and the Bureau of Indian Affairs) and four state fish and wildlife agencies (Idaho, Montana, Washington, and Wyoming). Among the committee's main accomplishments in 1985 was extending the management guidelines currently being used in the Yellowstone Ecosystem—seen as the best management guidelines currently known—to the other grizzly bear ecosystems (namely the Northern Continental Divide and Cabinet-Yaak ecosystems). Directorship of the committee also changed in 1985, giving the Forest Service a greater voice, as Stan Tixier, regional forester for the Forest Service's Intermountain Region, replaced Galen Buterbaugh of the Fish and Wildlife Service. The Forest Service also created a new position—grizzly bear habitat coordinator—to oversee management of the bear on the National Forest System, and named John Weaver to the post.

The same fears and debate that marred the 1985 appropriations bill hearings for the Forest Service again arose in 1985 when the 1986 bill was being debated. Under pressure from local constituents and landowners, Senator James McClure (R-ID) inserted language into the bill limiting bear population "augmentation" (management to increase the number bears in local populations). No federal funds can be used for augmentation unless "an augmentation plan has been developed and made available for public review and comment in full compliance with the National Environmental Policy Act by all participating agencies . . ." But whereas last year's language was interpreted to mean that no augmentation or studies for augmentation could take place, Senator Max Baucus (R-MT) worked with Senator McClure to alter this year's language to allow expressly for the augmentation of bears in the Cabinet-Yaak Ecosystem in Montana and Idaho. The Forest Service hopes that the necessary environmental assessment and final forest plan for the Kootenai National Forest—located in the Cabinet-Yaak ecosystem—will be finished by July 1986, allowing the addition of two to three bears to the area. Augmentation is scheduled to take place in August, to coincide with the period when berries and other foods are at their peak, making a translocated bear less likely to wander from its new home.

## The Woodland Caribou

The woodland caribou (*Rangifer tarandus caribou*) was the subject of a great deal of controversy in 1985 as the Forest Service approved a plan to augment the species in northwestern Idaho. Because the caribou depends in part on old-growth forest for habitat, the timber industry and other local interests fear that the augmentation of caribou populations could further slow the region's ailing timber-based economy. On the other side, conservationists are concerned that the Forest Service is delaying implementation of the augmentation plan un-necessarily. In spite of this controversy, however, recovery of the woodland caribou may proceed more smoothly than for certain other species. In report-ing on the woodland caribou in the *Audubon Wildlife Report 1985*, Michael Scott noted:

> Caribou in a sense are more fortunate than other threatened or endangered species in the West . . . they capture the public's imagination yet are not viewed as potentially dangerous as are the wolf and grizzly bear . . . Most of the opposition comes from those who see caribou as a threat to their economic well-being.

The woodland caribou exists in healthy populations across central Can-ada, but has disappeared from the conterminous United States except for a small remnant population in the southern Selkirk Mountains of northeastern Washington, northern Idaho, and southern British Columbia. Although there is no record of the caribou's historical population levels in the lower 48 states, this large ungulate ranged far south of its current location. Populations were reduced primarily by habitat destruction from timber harvest, road building and other construction, disease, and hunting. The single U.S. population was listed as an endangered species in 1983. Today, the Selkirk herd consists of approximately 25 animals located in southern British Columbia. Recent re-search indicates two to three mature bulls spend at least a few months of the year in the United States.

On September 19, 1985, Regional Forester Tom Coston signed a Deci-sion Notice to augment the woodland caribou population. Originally, the Forest Service had planned to commence augmentation in 1985—a move generally supported by environmentalists and the Idaho Fish and Game De-partment. The Forest Service subsequently postponed the date to 1986, stating that recent research findings required revision of the caribou-management perscriptions in the Idaho Panhandle National Forest Plan before augmenting current populations (see below).

The decision to augment the U.S. caribou population follows several years of interagency study and the completion of an environmental assessment which determined that: 1) the caribou population is existing at subviable levels; 2) recolonization of the U.S. herd by excess animals in the Canadian herd is unlikely; and 3) augmentation is the only reasonable choice to meet the primary goal of 100 animals as established in the recovery plan. This popula-tion target is based on theoretical genetic considerations, and is felt to repre-sent the minimum number of animals necessary for short-term maintenance of species vigor and herd size.

The augmentation plan calls for transplanting six to 12 animals yearly for three years, which are to be captured from the Revelstoke, British Colum-bia, herd, to a release site west of Bonners Ferry, Idaho. The captured animals would consist of mature females and a few young bulls, with an ideal ratio of four females to one bull.

As expected, the announcement of a 1986 augmentation drew strong reaction. In October, the Bonners Ferry Chamber of Commerce appealed the decision, citing economic impacts (e.g., reduction in timber harvest) and the lack of an environmental impact statement. On the opposite side, a group of environmental organizations appealed the decision to delay augmentation until 1986 contending that such a delay was inconsistent with the spirit of the Endangered Species Act. As of the end of 1985, Forest Service Chief R. Max Peterson had not acted on these appeals. A major concern of all parties interested in caribou recovery is that any delay may prevent augmentation in the future because of political and finanical pressures. One potential problem is that personnel charged with caribou augmentation are temporary employees who may not be available in 1986.

Fears that caribou will preclude timber harvesting and other uses of the national forest lands appear to be misplaced. While the proposed Idaho Panhandle National Forest Plan calls for 40 percent more habitat for the caribou than originally proposed, recent research indicates that woodland caribou can coexist with carefully planned timber harvesting and recreation. New research findings suggest that the importance of cedar/hemlock old-growth timber for summer habitat may not be as limiting as originally believed. It also appears that carefully managed logging of spruce/fir stands, which provides the caribou's early winter habitat, actually can benefit the caribou, which browse lichens off the fallen tree tops. As scientific knowledge of the caribou increases, a more careful balancing of resource needs can be achieved. For example, scientists only recently have discovered the importance of early summer calving areas located at high, exposed elevations where cows can escape predation pressures. These areas generally are of low timber value and limited importance for recreation at this time of year.

As is true of many endangered species, the controversy surrounding recovery of the woodland caribou has moved beyond the biological and species-specific issues to become the symbol of larger conflicts involving an ailing regional timber industry, local public distrust of the Forest Service, and suspicion of conservationists and their efforts to "lock-up" wildlands in the name of endangered species. As with the grizzly bear and timber wolf, many local residents believe that the woodland caribou should not be listed as an endangered species and believe that efforts to protect the caribou are another example of outside interests dictating policy at the expense of the local economy. Any succesful augmentation of the woodland caribou requires the cooperation of all parties, including local residents, land-management agencies, and the conservation organizations, yet for much of 1985 the parties remained apart. In an effort to seek agreement, Senator James McClure (R-ID) sponsored several meetings which, while the parties still remained fundementally opposed, have helped foster a fragile compromise that currently calls for the augmentation effort to begin in the fall of 1986. It is hoped that Bonners Ferry, the State of Idaho, the Forest Service, and the conservation community can maintain the current fragile truce as all parties work toward recovery of the woodland caribou and coexistence of other traditional uses.

## Funding for Wildlife and Fish Habitat Management

Congress appropriated $38,799,000 to the Forest Service for wildlife and fish habitat management on the National Forest System for FY 1986.* This total represents more than a $2 million increase over the 1985 total of $36,607,000. The presidential request for 1986 was $35,977,000. The following is a breakdown of the budget:

| Program | Presidential Request | Appropriation |
|---|---|---|
| Wildlife & Fisheries Admin. & Support | $23,927,000 | $23,751,000 |
| Wildlife Habitat Improvement | $6,023,000 | $6,719,000 |
| Resident Fish Habitat Improvement | $1,764,000 | $1,988,000 |
| Endangered, Threatened, & Sensitive Species Habitat Improvement | $1,585,000 | $2,470,000 |
| Anadromous Fish Habitat Improvement | $2,678,000 | $3,855,000 |
| Total | $35,977,000 | $38,799,000 |

The 1986 budget follows a familiar pattern in recent years: the administration proposes a budget that is below the previous year's total, and Congress steps in to restore, and slightly increase, the total. The following table shows administration requests and actual Congressional appropriation from the years 1981 through 1986. In 1981, the only year where the request was higher than the appropriation, the budget was submitted by the Carter administration.

| Year | Request | Appropriation | Difference |
|---|---|---|---|
| 1981 | $32,934,000 | $31,542,000 | −$1,392,000 |
| 1982 | $30,224,000 | $33,136,000 | +$2,912,000 |
| 1983 | $32,520,000 | $33,349,000 | +$829,000 |
| 1984 | $33,508,000 | $35,008,000 | +$1,500,000 |
| 1985 | $33,963,000 | $36,607,000 | +$2,644,000 |
| 1986 | $35,977,000 | $38,799,000 | +$2,822,000 |

* This appropriation subsequently was reduced by the Interior Appropriations Committee to $38,694,000. This amount was reduced further by the Gramm-Rudman deficit-reduction plan to $36,759,300.

Environmental organizations see these figures as evidence of the Reagan administration's lack of regard for natural resources programs while favoring development activities, such as timber harvesting and mining, which continually have received budgetary priority.

# References

Doerr, P. 1985. Comments on proposed management plan for the National Forest in Florida. July 3, 1985.

Laude, R. 1985. Report on the Demography and Survival of the Northern Spotted Owl. University of Chicago. June 1985.

Schoen, J.W., M.D. Kirchhoff, and M.H. Thomas. 1985. *Seasonal Distribution and Habitat Use by the Sitka Black-Tailed Deer in Southeastern Alaska.* Alaska Department of Fish and Game. April, 1985.

Schoen, J.W., O.C. Wallmo, and M.D. Kirchhoff. 1981. "Wildlife—forest relationships: Is a reevaluation of old growth necessary?" *Transactions of the 46th North American Wildlife and Natural Resources Conference.* Wildlife Management Institute. Washington, D.C.

Southeast Alaska Conservation Council. 1985. *Last Stand for the Tongass National Forces. November 1, 1985.*

Territorial Sportsman, Inc. 1985. *Logging in Southeast Alaska and Its Relationship to Wildlife, Fisheries and Economics.* February 1985.

U.S. Department of Agriculture. Letter, March 8, 1985, from Douglas MacCleery to R. Max Peterson.

Wallmo, O.C. and J.W. Schoen. 1980. "Response of deer to secondary forest succession in southeast Alaska." *Forest Science* 26, No. 3.

Wilderness Society. 1985. *Below Cost Timber Sales on the National Forests.* July 1984.

*Whit Fosburgh is on the National Audubon Society's Washington D.C. staff.*

# PART 2

◆————————————————————◆

# Federal
# Agencies
# and Programs

Federal grants help support the work of state researchers, such as these Alaskan
biologists who are radio-collaring a Dall ewe in a study of sheep movements.

*Larry B. Jennings/Photo Researchers*

# Federal Grants for State Wildlife Conservation

## William J. Chandler

### Introduction

THE FEDERAL GOVERNMENT makes annual matching grants to states and territories* for the restoration and management of birds, and mammals and sport fish, and for public recreational use of these biological resources. The legal authorities for such assistance are:

- The Federal Aid in Wildlife Restoration Act, also referred to as the Pittman-Robertson Act.
- The Federal Aid in Fish Restoration Act, also known as the Dingell-Johnson Act.
- The Fish and Wildlife Conservation Act, also called the Forsythe-Chafee Act or the Nongame Act.

All three laws are administered by the U.S. Fish and Wildlife Service (FWS), Department of the Interior, through its Federal Aid Program.

The Federal Aid Program budget for FY 1986, $242.9 million, constituted 37.3 percent of total FWS budget authority for fish and wildlife management. All of this federal aid money, less a small amount for program administration, is apportioned directly to the states for their use.

Federal aid funds make up a significant proportion of state fish and

---

* Referred to hereafter as states for the purpose of brevity.

177

wildlife agency budgets. On average, 17.8 percent of state wildlife budgets were financed by federal assistance in the late 1970s. State wildlife agencies received a total of $107 million in federal grants at that time. Of this amount, most was provided through the Federal Aid Program. (The Wildlife Conservation Fund of America, 1980).

Federal grants under the Pittman-Robertson Act are used by states principally to benefit game animals, including migratory waterfowl (e.g., ducks, geese, and swans), big game (such as deer, elk, bear, moose), small game (such as squirrel, rabbit, fox), and nonmigratory birds (e.g., quail, pheasant). Dingell-Johnson grants are used to benefit 30 to 40 species of sport fish. Although conservation actions taken on behalf of game species and sport fish have provided benefits for some nongame species, such benefits have been largely serendipitous. The Forsythe-Chafee Act was passed to encourage direct state conservation actions for hundreds of nongame species, but no appropriations ever have been made to implement the law.

In addition, both the Pittman-Robertson and Dingell-Johnson acts promote the recreational use of game species and sport fish. Funds under both programs are used by the states to gather information on the public use of, and demand for, fish and wildlife recreation; to provide facilities for access and use of fish and wildlife resources; and to educate hunters and fishermen in equipment safety and ethical conduct afield.

# History and Legislative Authority

## Pittman-Robertson Act

The Pittman-Robertson Act (16 U.S.C.A. 669 *et seq.*), passed in 1937, established a program of federal matching grants to state wildlife agencies for "wildlife restoration projects." The program was conceived as a collaboration between the federal and state governments with voluntary state participation. This approach was based on the fact that under the Constitution the states have primary authority to manage resident wildlife species.

Although state participation is voluntary, eligibility to participate was conditioned on state passage of conservation laws that include a prohibition against the diversion of hunting license fees for any purpose other than the administration of the state fish and game department. This requirement ensured that the states would have sufficient funds to put up their share of wildlife project costs and ended the then frequent practice of diverting a portion of license revenues to finance nonwildlife programs.

The impetus for the Pittman-Robertson Act was marked decreases in certain wildlife populations. The purpose of the act was to augment existing approaches to wildlife conservation by emphasizing the preservation and restoration of wildlife habitat.* The Senate report on the bill states: "The problems of wildlife are unescapably and inherently linked with the land. We must restore the environment for wildlife if we are to have more of it" (U.S. Congress, Senate, 1937).

The original goal of the act was to achieve a "continent-wide restoration for all species of wildlife" (U.S. Congress, Senate, 1937). However, since the statute did not define the term "wildlife" precisely, determining which species would become the primary beneficiaries of the program was left up to the Secretary of the Interior and the states. Since its inception, the Pittman-Robertson program has focused almost exclusively on game animals.**

The initial emphasis of the program was on big game species, such as deer, elk, and antelope, and on migratory birds which had been extirpated from certain states, were in danger of extirpation, or were threatened with extinction nationally. As these depleted game species gradually were stabilized and restored, the emphasis of state programs shifted to augmenting and maintaining populations of big and small game species, primarily for sport hunting. It was not until 1956 that FWS issued its first administrative definition of the term "wildlife," restricting the application of Pittman-Robertson grant funds to any species of wild bird or mammal (Bean 1983).† While this action clarified the potential biological scope of the program—a scope much broader than that pursued by state wildlife agencies—most states continued to focus their projects on game species.††

The act is more precise in defining "restoration project:"

> . . . the term "wildlife-restoration project" shall be construed to mean and include the selection, restoration, rehabilitation, and improvement of areas of

---

* The principal methods of wildlife conservation employed at the time included bans on the hunting of certain species, regulation of hunting and fishing, some stocking, and the management of wildlife refuges.

** No language in either the House or Senate reports or in floor debate interprets the act as applying only to game species in general or to certain groups of game species in particular. The legislative history indicates that Congress apparently intended the act to apply to a broad range of wildlife species. The Senate report, in discussing the rationale for the bill and the wildlife to be benefitted by the program, refers to "wildlife resources," "wildlife species," "fresh water fishes," and "migratory birds." The House report (U.S. Congress, House, 1937), like the Senate report, speaks of restoring "all species of wildlife." During Senate floor debate, Senator Clark of Missouri stated: "The enjoyment of wildlife areas is an important factor in the happiness and contentment of our people. We must preserve these values for posterity. We must not permit a further depletion of our wildlife population, nor the extinction of any more species." (U.S. Congress, Senate, 1937b).

† The act nowhere compels this limited definition of wildlife.

†† It is often asserted by FWS and state wildlife officials that the Pittman-Robertson program benefits nongame species in a variety of ways, for example by conserving habitat vital to more than just game species. While true, such nongame benefits are random and serendipitous in nature and cannot be equated with the benefits to be derived from a purposeful conservation program for the hundreds of nongame species that inhabit all states. In its *Environmental Impact Statement, Federal Aid in Fish and Wildlife Restoration Program* (Interior 1978), due to lack of data FWS could not quantify what percent of state expenditures benefitted nongame species.

land or water adaptable as feeding, resting, or breeding places for wildlife, including acquisition by purchase, condemnation, lease, or gift of such areas or estates of interests therein as are suitable or capable of being made suitable therefor, and the construction thereon or therein of such works as may be necessary to make them available for such purposes and also including such research into problems of wildlife management as may be necessary to efficient administration affecting wildlife resources. . . . * (16 U.S.C.A. 669a)

The act later was amended to allow federal matching grants for purposes other than restoring depleted species, including the "maintenance of completed projects" (1946); the "management (exclusive of law enforcement and public relations) of wildlife areas and resources" (1955); to help pay for "a hunter safety program and the construction, operation, and maintenance of public outdoor target ranges" (1970); and for the preparation of a "comprehensive fish and wildlife resource management plan which shall insure the perpetuation of these resources for the economic, scientific, and recreational enrichment of the people" (1970).

***Projects Eligible for Federal Assistance.***   For administrative purposes, FWS classifies projects eligible for Pittman-Robertson funds into one of seven categories:

1. *Surveys and Investigations.* Research for the restoration, conservation and management of wildlife or their habitat; field inventories and surveys.
2. *Land Acquisition.* The purchase or lease of lands or waters or interests in lands or waters (e.g. conservation easements). Title to acquired interests is given to the state.†
3. *Development.* Includes capital improvements such as dikes, roads, and trails, operation and maintenance of lands and facilities, the manipulation of habitat for wildlife, and the trapping and stocking of wildlife.
4. *Coordination.* Administrative activities conducted to ensure that state Pittman-Robertson projects are carried out in accordance with the act's requirements and with other applicable federal laws and regulations and that these projects do not duplicate or conflict with other state or federal programs.
5. *Planning.* The development and implementation of plans and management systems for wildlife programs. A state has the option of preparing "modular" conservation plans for distinct segments of its wildlife program or a "comprehensive" conservation plan that covers its entire activities. States

---

* This definition of restoration project appeared in the original act passed in 1937; it has not changed.

† Federal aid funds may be used by the state wildlife agency to purchase land owned by another state agency. Conservation easements may be for a limited term or perpetual. The sale by the state of land originally acquired with Pittman-Robertson funds is permitted, but the state must reimburse the federal share of the purchase price when such a transfer is made.

also may design management systems through which planning, programming, budgeting, implementation, and evaluation activities are conducted in a uniform and integrated manner.

6. *Technical Assistance.* The provision of technical assistance to other state or federal agencies or to private landowners for the purpose of improving environmental conditions, protecting or creating habitat, or managing wildlife populations, areas, and habitats for increased production or for public use.

7. *Hunter Education.* Training programs for educating hunters in the safe handling and use of firearms and archery equipment, hunter ethics, responsibilities and outdoor survival, and basic wildlife management. Funds also may be used for the construction, operation and maintenance of public target ranges.

Funds for Pittman-Robertson grants are derived from an 11 percent federal excise tax on firearms, ammunition, and archery equipment and a 10 percent tax on handguns.* The full amount of the tax receipts are automatically appropriated in the fiscal year following their collection. Monies for wildlife restoration are apportioned to each state under a formula that considers both the land area of the state and the number of licensed hunters relative to other states. No state may receive more than five percent or less than 0.5 percent of the total sum apportioned in any year.

One-half of the taxes collected on pistols and archery equipment is allocated to the states solely on the basis of population. These funds, at the state's discretion, may be used either for hunter education programs or for wildlife projects. Apportioned funds are obligated to the states to reimburse them for the cost of executing approved projects. The federal matching share may not exceed 75 percent of the total cost.†

Up to eight percent of excise-tax revenues may be withheld by FWS to administer the program. FWS uses these funds to pay for its federal aid program staff and associated expenses and to finance special studies, projects, and symposia that provide benefits to the overall program. On average, FWS use of excise tax revenues for administrative purposes does not approach the eight percent limit.†† The states have two years to obligate and spend their annual apportionment. Funds not used in this period revert back to FWS and are used as specified in the law to finance migratory bird conservation activities.†††

* Both taxes are levied at the manufacturer or wholesale level.
† The 75 percent (federal)-25 percent (state) cost share ratio is not used on all projects. In certain cases, especially land acquisition, a state may agree to pay a higher share of the cost, thus reducing the federal share. It is general practice, however, for FWS to pay 75 percent of costs for any type of project if the state requests this amount.
†† For example, FWS administrative deductions were four percent of all tax receipts in FY 1982, 3.9 percent in FY 1983, 5.6 percent in FY 1984, and 7.9 percent in FY 1985.
††† Between FY 1939 and 1984, a total of $13,508,172 of state apportionments reverted to FWS.

## Dingell-Johnson Act

The Dingell-Johnson Act (16 U.S.C.A. 777 *et seq.*), passed in 1950, was the "culmination of many years of effort by conservationists, enlightened sportsmen, and . . . the fishing industry who saw the need to bolster efforts of state fish and wildlife agencies in managing recreational fisheries" (Interior undated). Modeled after the Pittman-Robertson Act, the law authorized federal matching grants to the states for fish restoration and management projects and their maintenance. The act defines a fish restoration and management project to include:

(a) such research into problems of fish management and culture as may be necessary to efficient administration affecting fish resources;

(b) the acquisition of such facts as are necessary to guide and direct the regulation of fishing by law, including the extent of the fish population, the drain on the fish supply from fishing and/or natural causes, the necessity of legal regulation of fishing, and the effects of any measures of regulation that are applied;

(c) the formulation and adoption of plans of restocking waters with food and game fishes according to natural areas or districts to which such plans are applicable, together with the acquisition of such facts as are necessary to the formulation, execution, and testing the efficacy of such plans;

(d) the selection, restoration, rehabilitation, and improvement of areas of water or land adaptable as hatching, feeding, resting, or breeding places for fish, including acquisition by purchase, condemnation, lease, or gift of such areas or estates or interests therein as are suitable or capable of being made suitable therefor, and the construction thereof or therein of such works as may be necessary to make them available for such purposes. . . . (16 U.S.C.A. 777a)

Whereas the Pittman-Robertson Act aimed to restore "all species of wildlife," the Dingell-Johnson Act limited its biological scope to "all species of fish which have material value in connection with sport or recreation in the marine and/or fresh waters of the United States" (16 U.S.C.A. 777a). In 1970, the act was amended to allow a state the option of preparing comprehensive plans to guide fish conservation efforts. A 1984 amendment required the states to use 10 percent of their program allocation to develop recreational boating facilities and gave them the option of using another 10 percent of their money for "aquatic resource education programs."

Projects eligible for funding are classified in the same categories as those used for the Pittman-Robertson program: surveys and investigations; land acquisition; development; coordination; planning; technical assistance; and aquatic resources education. As is the case with Pittman-Robertson Act, no funds may be spent for state law enforcement or public relations activities.

Funds for the Dingell-Johnson program are derived from a combination of sources, including a 10 percent federal excise tax on the major types of equipment used in sport fishing; import duties collected on yachts, pleasure craft and imported fishing equipment; and a portion of the federal excise tax on gasoline attributable to the sale of fuel for motorboats.

Revenues for the Dingell-Johnson program are apportioned yearly to the states, 40 percent on the basis of geographical area* and 60 percent on the basis of the number of each state's fish-license holders relative to those of other states. Each coastal state is required, to the extent practical, to spend its annual apportionment on both marine and freshwater fish projects in the same ratio as the number of resident fishermen who participate in each type of fishing.

FWS is authorized to withhold up to six percent of Dingell-Johnson revenues for program administration and to fund special projects that benefit the overall program. Funds that have not been spent by the states within two years of apportionment revert back to FWS to fund fishery research related to sport fish species.

## The Forsythe-Chafee Act

In 1980, Congress passed the Fish and Wildlife Conservation Act, (16 U.S.C.A. 2901 *et seq.*) also referred to as the Forsythe-Chafee Act, to promote the conservation of nongame species of fish and wildlife that receive relatively little assistance under the Pittman-Robertson and Dingell-Johnson statutes. The Forsythe-Chafee Act authorizes federal technical and financial assistance to the states, generally on a 75 percent federal—25 percent state basis, for the development of plans, programs, and projects for the conservation of nongame species of vertebrate wildlife.† Nongame species are defined as those "not ordinarily taken for sport" and which are not listed as threatened or endangered species under the Endangered Species Act or covered under the Marine Mammal Protection Act.††

The Forsythe-Chafee Act authorizes federal grant assistance to the states for the

- development or revision of a conservation plan for nongame and other fish and wildlife species that the states deem appropriate;
- implementation of projects for nongame species identified in the plan;
- implementation of nongame projects not covered in a plan if the project meets certain criteria;

* Such areas includes coastal and Great Lakes waters under state jurisdiction, i.e, the territorial waters of the states.
† Excluded from the Forsythe-Chafee Act's coverage are other key elements of biological diversity including all invertebrates such as anthropods (insects, crustaceans, arachnids) and mollusks.
†† Domesticated animals such as pigs and goats that have reverted to a feral existence also are excluded from eligibility.

- coordination, consolidation, or implementation of the conservation plan or nongame plan actions with plans and projects authorized by the Pittman-Robertson and Dingell-Johnson acts.

The Forsythe-Chafee Act is financed by general revenues that must be appropriated annually by Congress. Although the statute authorized the appropriation of up to $5 million for each of fiscal years 1982-85, no monies ever have been requested by the executive branch or appropriated by Congress for implementing the act.* In 1985, the Reagan administration completed a report evaluating various alternative methods that would be "equitable and effective" in financing the Forsythe-Chafee Act, but declined to request new authority for financing the program (the report is covered in the legislative section of this chapter).

Although no funds for implementation of the Forsythe-Chafee Act have been appropriated, FWS has implemented the planning provisions of the act and integrated the provisions with those of the Pittman-Robertson and Dingell-Johnson programs. The states now have the option of obtaining federal aid funds to finance the development of either modular or comprehensive plans. Modular plans address one or more of the agency's resource management responsibilities (e.g. big game, warm-water fish, nongame, hunter education). Comprehensive plans cover all species of wildlife for which the agency has responsibility, but usually focus on a selected number of species which the state wants to manage. All state planning efforts financed with Pittman-Robertson or Dingell-Johnson funds must, in accordance with a provision of the Forsythe-Chafee Act and the National Environmental Policy Act, provide for public participation.

## Organization and Operations

The Federal Aid Program is administered by FWS Associate Director for Federal Assistance Rolf Wallenstrom. National coordination of the program is handled by the Division of Federal Aid, which develops program standards and guidelines, ensures that funds are allocated properly to the states, provides technical assistance to the states, and identifies and reports program accomplishments.

The program is highly decentralized. Day-to-day supervision of the program was delegated in 1958 to the seven FWS regional offices, each of which

---

* Although no federal funds have been made available for nongame projects under the Forsythe-Chafee Act, states do have the authority to utilize Pittman-Robertson grant funds for the conservation of nongame bird or mammal species. However, since the states view Pittman-Robertson funds as the hunter's contribution to wildlife, they have elected to spend such funds principally for the benefit of hunted species. To finance nongame conservation efforts, many states have set up separate nongame programs that are state financed. These nongame programs are covered in a separate chapter in this report.

Table of Organization, Federal Aid Program, Fish and Wildlife Service

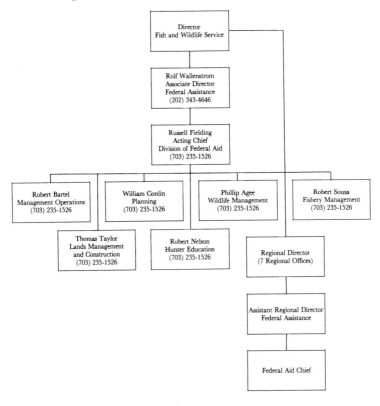

has a federal aid chief who reports to the assistant regional director for federal assistance, who in turn reports to the regional director. The regional federal aid staff reviews and approves all state grant requests, monitors the implementation of approved projects, assures state compliance with national standards and regulations, provides technical assistance to the states, and maintains project records.

In implementing the program, FWS gives heavy emphasis to the desires and needs of state wildlife agencies. FWS views its role as one of cooperation with the states to carry out state responsibilities for fish and wildlife. Its mission is to strengthen the ability of state fish and wildlife agencies to "meet effectively the consumptive and nonconsumptive needs of the public for fish and wildlife resources" (Interior 1985a). The specific goals of the federal aid program are:

1. To ensure that all states desiring to participate maintain eligibility.
2. To ensure that funds are apportioned promptly and accurately to the states and that accountability for unused balances are documented properly.
3. To fund only those eligible state projects that the state and FWS agree will provide significant program benefits.

4. To ensure that approved projects are executed in accordance with project design and that accomplishments are in accordance with the desired results.
5. To ensure that information and plans generated by the states and FWS are used effectively and cooperatively in managing fish and wildlife resources.

## The Grant Process

States continually submit fish and wildlife projects or plans to FWS regional offices for approval. To be approved, FWS must determine that the plan or project is "substantial in character and design"—a requirement of both the Pittman-Robertson and Dingell-Johnson laws. FWS regulations define a substantial project as one that:

(a) identifies and describes a need within the purposes of the relevant act to be utilized;
(b) identifies the objectives to be accomplished based on the stated need;
(c) utilizes accepted fish and wildlife conservation and management principles, sound design, and appropriate procedures; and
(d) will yield benefits pertinent to the identified need at a level commensurate with project costs" (50 CFR 80.13).

FWS does not attempt to set priorities as to which species deserve the highest priority for state conservation work or which types of projects—land acquisition, research, etc.—are needed more than others. These decisions are left up to each state. So long as a project is demonstrably "substantial," FWS will fund it.

The project application must contain an environmental assessment or environmental impact statement, unless the project has limited or no environmental impact. For example, research studies do not require environmental assessments nor would minor development activities such as the installation of cattle guards to protect wildlife areas.

If a project is approved by the FWS regional office, a "project agreement" is signed that obligates funds for the various work segments of the project. Finally, the state must submit annual progress reports to show how well project objectives have been met. The FWS regional office is responsible for monitoring projects during and after their completion to insure compliance with all requirements.

The FWS project review process has both formal and informal components. Although not required by program regulations, a state ordinarily will go through several steps in seeking project approval. First, the state will propose a project informally to the regional federal aid chief. At this point, FWS attempts to discourage unacceptable projects by arguing against them, while acceptable projects are encouraged. Next, a preliminary draft proposal may be submitted by the state for review. At this juncture, FWS will provide the state with an informal response as to its acceptability. Finally, a formal application for federal assistance is submitted with the full documentation required by FWS regulations.

## Budget and Staff

The FY 1986 Federal Aid Program budget of $242.9 million constituted 37.3 percent of the total FWS budget for the fiscal year. The federal aid budget includes $120.8 million for Pittman-Robertson activities and $122.2 million for Dingell-Johnson activities. Pittman-Robertson revenues have increased $35 million over the FY 1985 budget of $85.8 million. While this substantial increase obviously is attributable to an increase in excise tax receipts, the reasons for the increase are not documented.

Dingell-Johnson revenues have increased dramatically, rising from $38 million in FY 1985 to $122.2 million in FY 1986. This increase represents an influx of funds caused by the 1984 legislative expansion of program revenue.

No changes occurred in the number of full-time-equivalent positions for the federal aid division between 1985 and 1986. The Pittman-Robertson staff held steady at 74, the Dingell-Johnson staff at 26, for a total of 100 positions.* Of these positions, 15 are in the FWS national office, 85 in the seven regional offices.

* Ten new full-time-equivalents were added to the federal aid program in FY 1985 as a result of the expansion of the Dingell-Johnson program.

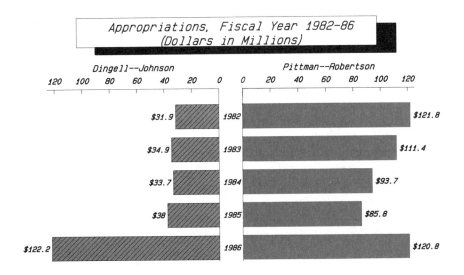

### Appropriations, Fiscal Year 1982-86 (Dollars in Millions)

| Dingell--Johnson | Year | Pittman--Robertson |
|---|---|---|
| $31.9 | 1982 | $121.8 |
| $34.9 | 1983 | $111.4 |
| $33.7 | 1984 | $93.7 |
| $38 | 1985 | $85.8 |
| $122.2 | 1986 | $120.8 |

*Source: FWS, Division of Federal Aid*

BLACK

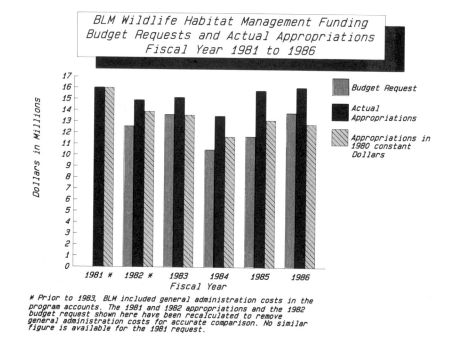

BLM Wildlife Habitat Management Funding
Budget Requests and Actual Appropriations
Fiscal Year 1981 to 1986

* Prior to 1983, BLM included general administration costs in the
program accounts. The 1981 and 1982 appropriations and the 1982
budget request shown here have been recalculated to remove
general administration costs for accurate comparison. No similar
figure is available for the 1981 request.

# Current Program Trends

## Accomplishments

The Federal Aid Program, according to federal and state wildlife management professionals, has been a resounding success. Using federal assistance, states have substantially increased populations of game animals such as elk, deer, and turkey; protected or improved millions of acres of wildlife habitat; expanded the distribution of many game species; and significantly improved state wildlife management efforts through surveys, inventories, and research. In addition, all states have established hunter education programs.

The Pittman-Robertson and Dingell-Johnson acts are credited with impelling the professionalization of wildlife management in the United States. A major factor contributing to that professionalization is the guaranteed funding established by both statutes. Each year, the states can count on a more or less known quantity of federal funds for their fish and wildlife programs. This steady stream of funding, combined with state revenues, has allowed the progressive development of state fish and wildlife programs.

***Biological Achievements.*** While the general accomplishments of the Federal Aid Program are universally recognized, a quantifiable assessment of its biological achievements is difficult to obtain. Even though the Pittman-Robertson and Dingell-Johnson acts specifically call for the restoration and maintenance of wildlife and fish species—clear resource objectives—the Division of Federal Aid does not keep adequate records at the national level to show precisely how the many species eligible for assistance are faring.

A major reason such quantitative biological data have not been collected is FWS' perception of the role of the federal aid program. FWS views it as helping the states achieve state wildlife goals. FWS officials emphasize that they do not try to guide states in setting biological conservation priorities in the Federal Aid Program. The major FWS role, say FWS officials, is to ensure that federal grant funds are used for the types of conservation activities specified by the law and to ensure that the states use effective tools, methods, and strategies in their conservation work.*

The difficulty of obtaining a precise assessment of the program's biological impact is compounded by the way funds are distributed and used. States have the option of requesting federal matching assistance for whatever types of projects they choose. One state may use its entire federal aid allocation on just a few types of activities, such as land acquisition and research, and spend its own funds on planning, technical assistance activities, and the like. Another state may do just the opposite. Furthermore, a state may vary over time the amount of federal-aid funds it uses to conserve any particular species. For example, during the early stages of a restoration project, the state may match all of its work with federal funds. Later, the state may rely minimally on federal assistance to manage the restored species. Thus, it is difficult to determine whose dollar benefited which species and to what degree over time.

In view of these limitations in assessing the Federal Aid Program's biological benefits and shortcomings, the Division of Federal Aid has kept records that show only by project type (e.g. land acquisition, planning, development) how the states have spent their funds. Unfortunately such statistics, for the most part, offer few clues to the biological status of the many species the states are supposed to be conserving with federal assistance.

*State Use of Pittman-Robertson Funds by Project Type.* During the period 1939-84, a total of $1.35 billion in federal aid funds were expended by state fish and wildlife agencies under the Pittman-Robertson Act. Of this amount, $372 million (27.6 percent) was spent on surveys and research; $196

---

* FWS' inactive role in setting guidelines for species conservation priorities is not compelled by law. The Pittman-Robertson Act calls for the restoration and maintenance of all wildlife species, a term defined by FWS to include all birds and mammals. The Dingell-Johnson Act calls for the restoration and maintenance of all sport-fish species. Both laws give the secretary of the Interior the power to reach *mutual agreements* with the states regarding the implementation of wildlife projects that conform with the acts' purposes and objectives and with standards fixed by the secretary of the Interior. While neither act specifically addresses the secretary's role in determining species priorities, neither do they require that he play absolutely no role in the establishment of resource priorities for use of federal funds by states that elect to participate in the program. In fact, the laws' requirements that the secretary and the states reach mutual agreement on projects that conform with the acts' purposes could be construed as giving the secretary a strong voice in determining which species should benefit from federal grant funds, if he chose to exercise such authority.

Percent of State Pittman-Robertson Expenditures
by Project Type for Selected Years

| | Surveys and Research | Land Acquisition | Development | Coordination | Hunter Eduction* | Planning* | Tech. Guidance |
|---|---|---|---|---|---|---|---|
| 1949 | 19.3 | 22.9 | 51.9 | 5.9 | 0 | 0 | 0 |
| 1959 | 21.7 | 23.6 | 50.3 | 4.4 | 0 | 0 | 0 |
| 1969 | 28.7 | 18.1 | 47.3 | 5.8 | 0 | .0005 | .001 |
| 1979 | 29.5 | 9.6 | 45.8 | 5.4 | 7.0 | .01 | .01 |
| 1984 | 25.3 | 8.2 | 49.6 | 4.4 | 9.0 | 1.1 | 2.4 |
| Percent of all expenditures during the period 1939-1984 | 27.6 | 14.5 | 46.5 | 4.8 | 4.7 | .7 | 1.0 |

* Hunter education and planning uses authorized in 1970.

Source: Based on expenditure statistics supplied by FWS, Division of Federal Aid.

million (14.5 percent) on land acquisition; $628 million (46.5 percent) on development of acquired or leased lands; $64 million (4.8 percent) on coordination of program activities; $64 million (4.7 percent) on hunter education; $10 million (0.7 percent) on planning; and $13 million (one percent) on providing technical guidance to federal and state agencies and private landowners.

The sums expended by the states for various project types have shifted over the years. The major discernible trends are a decline in the percentage of funds used for surveys and investigations and for land acquisition. Survey and investigation expenditures have dropped from a high of 29.5 percent in 1979 to 25.3 percent in 1984. Land acquisition has dropped from over 20 percent in 1949 and 1959 to 8.2 percent in 1984. Meanwhile, expenditures for development have hovered around 50 percent, with a 1949 high of 51.9 percent and a 1979 low of 45.8 percent.

FWS officials say that research expenditures have dropped partly because the Division of Federal Aid has developed a computerized data base that helps screen out duplicative research. The decrease in land acquisition may mean only that the states are buying less land with federal matching monies, not that total land acquisition overall by state wildlife agencies has dropped. But FWS has no definitive data to explain either trend.

***Dingell-Johnson Expenditures by States.*** Between 1952 and 1985, $467.23 million was transferred to the states under the Dingell-Johnson Act for sport-fish management and recreation projects. The Division of Federal Aid does not keep readily available records that show how these funds have been allocated by project type over the years.

***Pittman-Robertson Research Expenditures.*** The most recent evaluation of the use of Pittman-Robertson research grants was made by division staff member Robert J. Sousa (1982a). Such evaluations are not routinely conducted by FWS, so no comparable analysis exists for more recent years.

Sousa selected all "management-oriented" research studies under way in 1981 and categorized these investigations into four research types: "discipline-type" wildlife studies, environmental surveys and habitat studies, planning and user studies including recreational surveys and opinion polls, and miscellaneous. He then compared total expenditures for the various types of studies and the percent of total funds spent on each.

The data show that 61.3 percent of all management-oriented research funds were spent on discipline-type wildlife studies, 27.8 percent on environmental and habitat investigations, and 10.3 percent on planning and user studies. The most frequently conducted studies were harvest studies (25.8 percent), population surveys (17.3 percent), and environmental surveys (17.9 percent). Relatively little effort was devoted to studying the effects of environmental pollution on wildlife and the effects of development on wildlife habitat, or to habitat-related research studies.

Pittman-Robertson Research Obligations in 1981 by Study Type

| Category | Amount obligated ($1,000s) | % of total |
|---|---|---|
| **Planning and User Studies** | | |
| Planning | 1,355 | 6.4 |
| Research techniques | 603 | 2.8 |
| Users | 198 | 0.9 |
| Economic studies | 46 | 0.2 |
| Subtotal | 2,202 | 10.3 |
| **Discipline Wildlife Studies** | | |
| Harvest | 5,527 | 25.8 |
| Populations | 3,692 | 17.3 |
| Life history | 1,019 | 4.8 |
| Stocking | 667 | 3.1 |
| Diseases/parasites | 491 | 2.3 |
| Mortality | 380 | 1.8 |
| Migration | 307 | 1.4 |
| Food habits | 215 | 1.0 |
| Reproduction | 189 | 0.9 |
| Age/growth | 183 | 0.9 |
| Culture/rearing | 131 | 0.6 |
| Anatomy/physiology | 106 | 0.5 |
| Animal control | 92 | 0.4 |
| Systematics | 83 | 0.4 |
| Behavior | 21 | <0.1 |
| Subtotal | 13,103 | 61.3 |
| **Environmental Surveys/Habitat Studies** | | |
| Environmental surveys | 3,828 | 17.9 |
| Habitats | 634 | 3.0 |
| Management techniques | 518 | 2.4 |
| Development-degradation | 215 | 1.0 |
| Food production | 196 | 0.9 |
| Plant production | 149 | 0.7 |
| Mining pollution | 128 | 0.6 |
| Heavy metals | 73 | 0.3 |
| Plant control | 71 | 0.3 |
| Forest-degradation | 66 | 0.3 |
| Water quality | 42 | 0.2 |
| General pollution | 7 | <0.1 |
| Water quantity | 7 | <0.1 |
| Pesticide pollution | 6 | <0.1 |
| Reproduction aids | 6 | <0.1 |
| Subtotal | 5,946 | 27.8 |
| Miscellaneous | 141 | 0.7 |
| Total | $21,392 | 100% |

Source: Sousa (1982a) Copyright, The Wildlife Society.

Sousa also categorized 1981 research studies by species or resource group. The results show the overwhelming predominance of game species in state research studies financed with federal aid funds. Research expenditures on nongame wildlife, endangered wildlife, and raptors were $0.48 million, or just 2.2 percent of total expenditures for all types of wildlife and resource studies.

***Dingell-Johnson Research.*** Sousa (1982b) also made a review of Dingell-Johnson research expenditures in 1981 similar to his analysis of Pittman-

Pittman-Robertson Research Obligations in 1981 by Species Group

| Component | Amount obligated ($1,000s) |
|---|---|
| Resource Component Distribution | |
| General Category | |
| Game mammals | 3,083 |
| Game birds | 2,516 |
| Waterfowl | 2,134 |
| Game species | 2,039 |
| All wildlife species | 963 |
| Furbearers | 925 |
| Migratory birds | 483 |
| Nongame wildlife | 333 |
| Endangered wildlife | 91 |
| Mammalian predators | 66 |
| Raptors | 60 |
| Species Category | |
| Dear/moose/elk/caribou | 4,894 |
| Bison/muskoxen/goats/sheep | 691 |
| Bears | 656 |
| Pronghorns | 319 |
| Cats | 235 |
| Peccaries/feral pigs | 225 |
| Doves | 211 |
| Canines | 197 |
| Miscellaneous wildlife species | 363 |
| Other | |
| Ecological/habitats | 414 |
| Nonspecies oriented | 205 |
| Vegetation | 148 |
| Diseases | 141 |
| Total | $21,392 |

Some overlap between components is acknowledged, e.g., bears are considered game mammals. However, because the assignment of a dollar figure to a resource component is based on the CFAR worksheet designation, dollar amounts represent a distinct quantity and are additive.
Source: Sousa (1982a) Copyright, The Wildlife Society.

Robertson research. Dingell-Johnson program expenditures are by law limited to sport-fish species. Of the $20.1 million in Dingell-Johnson funds obligated for research in 1981, 52.8 percent were for fishery studies, 40.3 percent for environmental studies and surveys, and 6.8 percent for planning and user studies. Research studies receiving the largest amount of funds were:

|  | Millions Obligated | Percent of Total Obligations |
|---|---|---|
| Environmental surveys | $5.1 | 25.6 |
| Harvest surveys | 3.9 | 19.4 |
| Population surveys | 2.3 | 11.7 |
| Life-history studies | 1.4 | 7.2 |
| Stocking methods | 1.4 | 7.0 |
| Management techniques | 1.1 | 5.5 |

Very little money was obligated for pollution, water quality or quantity, or stream-improvement and lake-improvement research.

Sousa's categorization of research costs allocated by species or species group shows that salmonids* received approximately a fourth of all research dollars. Bass were the next most popular species, receiving 13.5 percent.

According to Sousa, a comparison of his 1981 data with similar statistics compiled in 1969 and 1974 shows that while the amounts obligated for planning and fishing-oriented research have fluctuated up and down, there has been a 92 percent growth in allocations for environmental studies since 1969. According to Sousa, this suggests that:

> fishery managers are demonstrating their concern about ecological matters. . . . Further evidence of this trend is exhibited in the apparent decrease in species-specific research. More effort is currently going toward determining information relating to multiple species and systems than previously manifested. Perhaps there is the realization that no longer can fishery managers afford the luxury of studying a single species while the demands of other species or systems remain unfilled. (Sousa, 1982b, pp. 5-6.)

*Land Acquisition Expenditures.* In FY 1984, the states spent a total of $18,116,530 on land and water acquisitions totaling 39,705 acres using federal aid matching funds†. During the period FY 1938-84, four million acres were acquired at a cost of $284 million.

In addition to acquiring land, federal aid funds are used to acquire and develop access sites to public hunting and fishing areas. Twenty-seven sites were acquired in FY 1984, and another 28 were developed. These actions opened up another 84 miles of fishing streams, 11,704 acres of fishing lakes,

---

* There are approximately 40 species of salmonids found in the United States.
† Average cost per acre equals $456, not including the acquisition overhead.

Dingell-Johnson Research Obligations in 1981 by Species or Resource Component

| General Categories: | |
|---|---:|
| Salmonids | $ 5,032 |
| Bass | 2,723 |
| Warmwater fish | 2,692 |
| Freshwater fish | 2,080 |
| Marine fish | 1,249 |
| Game fish | 1,124 |
| Nonspecies oriented | 864 |
| Miscellaneous fish | 756 |
| All fish & wildlife species | 571 |
| Diseases | 432 |
| Coldwater fish | 270 |
| Anadromous fish | 128 |
| Exotic fish | 24 |
| Endangered fish | 17 |
| Nongame fish | 16 |
| Forage fish | 11 |
| *Specific Categories:* | |
| Herring/Shad | 439 |
| Walleye | 328 |
| Catfish | 309 |
| Muskellunge/Pike | 266 |
| Crappie | 236 |
| Carp/Carp hybrids | 219 |
| Bluegill/Sunfish | 201 |
| Perch | 183 |
| Total | $20,170 |

Source: Sousa (1982b). Used by permission.

and 13,195 acres of hunting lands in 10 states. A total of 1,348 hunting and fishing access sites totalling 90,347 acres have been acquired through FY 1984 and 2,825 sites developed. These actions opened 289,656 acres to hunting and 982,186 lake acres and 3,156 stream miles to fishing.

Pittman-Robertson funds are used not only to acquire land outright, but also to acquire conservation easements on private lands and to lease or rent private lands for public hunting. As of the end of FY 1984, the states had acquired, developed, or placed under management 4,385 areas totaling 38,232,858 acres. Nearly all of this acreage is open to hunting.

***Fishing Lakes.*** Ten fishing lakes were constructed or restored in FY 1984 in five states. During the period 1951 through 1984, a total of 283 lakes were constructed or restored.

***Expenditures for Waterfowl.*** The only species group for which the FWS tracks total federal aid expenditures is waterfowl. In FY 1984, FWS obligated

Status of State Planning Efforts

| | Comprehensive Plan | One or More Modular Plans |
|---|---|---|
| Alabama | N | N |
| Alaska | N | YD |
| Arizona | N | YD |
| Arkansas | N | N |
| California | N | YC |
| Colorado | YC(FA) | |
| Connecticut | N | YD |
| Delaware | N | YD |
| Florida | YD | |
| Georgia | N | N |
| Hawaii | N | N |
| Idaho | N | YC |
| Illinois | YD(FA) | |
| Indiana | YD | |
| Iowa | N | N |
| Kansas | YC(FA) | |
| Kentucky | N | N |
| Louisiana | N | N |
| Maine | N | YC(FA) |
| Maryland | N | YC(FA) |
| Massachusetts | N | N |
| Michigan | N | YD |
| Minnesota | YD(FA) | |
| Mississippi | N | N |
| Missouri | N | YC |
| Montana | YD(FA) | |
| Nebraska | N | N |
| Nevada | N | YD |
| New Hampshire | N | N |
| New Jersey | N | YD |
| New Mexico | YC | |
| New York | N | N |
| North Carolina | N | N |
| North Dakota | N | N |
| Ohio | N | N |
| Oklahoma | N | N |
| Oregon | N | YD |
| Pennsylvania (Game) | N | N |
| Pennsylvania (Fish) | N | N |
| Rhode Island | N | N |
| South Carolina | N | N |
| South Dakota | N | N |
| Tennessee | YC(FA) | |
| Texas | N | YD |
| Utah | N | N |
| Vermont | N | N |
| Virginia | N | N |
| Washington | YC | |
| West Virginia | YD(FA) | |

Status of State Planning Efforts—continued

| | Comprehensive Plan | One or More Modular Plans |
|---|---|---|
| Wisconsin | N | YC(FA) |
| Wyoming | YC(FA) | |
| American Samoa | N | N |
| Guam | N | N |
| Puerto Rico | N | YD(FA) |
| Virgin Islands | N | N |

Legend: N–No
Y–Yes
C–Complete
D–Developing
FA–Federal Aid Funds Used

Source: Division of Federal Aid, FWS, December 1985

$23.7 million for state waterfowl projects, about 25 percent of all Pittman-Robertson obligations that year. Since the program began operating, the states have acquired 1.5 million acres of land for waterfowl conservation purposes, and expended $201 million in developing waterfowl areas.

***Status of State Planning Efforts.*** To improve the efficiency and comprehensiveness of state fish and wildlife agency conservation programs, Congress amended the Pittman-Robertson and Dingell-Johnson acts in 1970 to allow use of federal aid funds for the preparation of comprehensive fish and wildlife resource management plans. Comprehensive planning was needed, said the Senate report on the legislation, to promote the efficient use of federal aid funds and to enable the state fish and wildlife department to protect fish and wildlife resources adequately from the impacts of growing development activities such as urbanization, road-building and timber harvest (U.S. Congress, Senate, 1970.)

When the Forsythe-Chafee Act was passed in 1980, Congress again emphasized the need for planning. The Forsythe-Chafee Act called for the preparation of conservation plans that covered game and nongame species, and regular assessments of the state's effectiveness in conserving plan species.

Congress did not require the states to develop plans as a condition for receiving wildlife project funds under the Pittman-Robertson, Dingell-Johnson, or Forsythe-Chafee acts. Nor is any state's share of funds under those laws reduced if it does not operate with a comprehensive fish and wildlife plan.

Progress toward the use of planning as a modern wildlife management tool has been slow. Fifteen years after the planning option was made available, only four states—Colorado, Tennessee, Kansas, and Wyoming—have approved comprehensive plans; only Maryland has an approved modular plan. Altogether 27 states and territories have initiated planning efforts of one type or another, but 27 still have no formal planning effort of any kind, federally funded or not, according to federal aid officials.

Several reasons lie behind the states' failures to adopt formal planning processes say FWS officials. These include inertia, hostility to planning by state fish and wildlife personnel who do not appreciate the importance of planning in conserving a state's wildlife heritage, and the failure of university wildlife management programs to teach management science skills. In addition, some states fear that the adoption of a formal planning process would require the state wildlife agency to deal with certain wildlife organizations whose outlook on state goals and priorities may not be the same as those of the agency's traditional constituency groups: hunters and fishermen. In sum, say FWS officials, state planning efforts—even many of those now under way—have yet to measure up to the sound goals originally promulgated by Congress: promoting efficient use of federal aid funds and protecting wildlife resources from development impacts.

## Program Trends

Recent management trends in the FWS Federal Aid Program include the continuing devolution of program responsibilities to the states; an expansion of the eligible uses of Dingell-Johnson funds; more stringent standards for hunter education programs; and a clarification of the use of Pittman-Robertson funds for trapper education. Each of these developments is discussed below.

*Reliance on State Administration.* Since 1979, FWS has worked purposefully to give the states greater responsibility in administering the federal aid program and to limit federal involvement to providing technical assistance and periodic monitoring for oversight purposes. The states have been encouraged to develop their own administrative control systems for monitoring expenditures, reporting results, and accounting for program funds.

FWS has moved in the direction of turning over more responsibility to the states for two reasons, say Division of Federal Aid officials. First, the states have developed stronger capabilities for running their programs without FWS surveillance. Second, a 1981 report by the Interior Department's Inspector General recommended that FWS eliminate its detailed review and monitoring of individual projects because this approach imposed excessive and generally nonproductive paperwork burdens on the states (Interior 1981).

Placing greater reliance upon the states for grant administration is viewed by FWS as a way to improve the efficiency of the program and reduce federal costs. The savings that accrue are used to increase the annual grant allocations to the states.

*New Uses of Dingell-Johnson Funds.* Legislation passed in 1984 (Pub. L. 98-269) significantly changed the Dingell-Johnson program by expanding the sources and amounts of revenue for the program and authorizing the expenditures of funds for several new activities. In addition, FWS has made changes in its policies on the use of federal aid funds for fish rearing and stocking and hatchery construction and operation under the Dingell-Johnson program.

Amendments made to the Dingell-Johnson Act in 1984 are expected to more than triple the amount of grant funds available to the states for sport-fish restoration and maintenance projects. Grant revenues jumped from $38 million in FY 1985 to $122 million in FY 1986. State-share allocations will more than double for every state.

This large infusion of funds was approved by Congress because of the inability of state fish and wildlife agencies to maintain adequate sport-fishery resources in the face of increased numbers of fishermen using more advanced fishing technology. A 1982 survey conducted by the American Fisheries Society reported unmet state fishery-management needs of $134 million yearly (U.S. Congress, House, 1983).

The states are expected to use the increase in Dingell-Johnson grant funds in a variety of ways. Arizona, for example, intends to use its increase on hatchery renovation, dam repair and maintenance, and construction of boat access facilities. Florida will use its funds to build boat access ramps, to establish a permanent biological research team on Lake Okeechobee, to poll fishery users regarding their needs, to conduct an urban fisheries program in coordination with metropolitan recreation departments, to increase the number of fish in several impoundments, and to develop an aquatic education program for public schools.

Some observers have questioned whether or not some states can use their share increases effectively. Senator James McClure (R-ID), Chairman of the Senate Appropriations Subcommittee for the Department of the Interior, warned a meeting of state fish and game directors that failure to use their money wisely would jeopardize the program (American Fisheries Society 1985).

*New Stocking and Hatchery Guidelines.* FWS in 1985 proposed new fish-stocking and hatchery guidelines that would have permitted more liberal use of Dingell-Johnson funds for put-and-take recreational fishing programs. Under its old policy, FWS provided federal funds for the stocking of fish when "necessary to establish a fishery in waters devoid of fish (such as new and renovated waters) or to manage an existing fishery by introducing species not presently found in that fishery or maintain species having insufficient natural reproduction"* (Interior 1982 Section 11.15). The old policy prohibited the use of Dingell-Johnson funds for the stocking of fish anywhere for "immediate and temporary fishing," that is for put-and-take fishing.†

---

* Examples of actions allowed by the policy include stocking alpine lakes that lose their fish populations in winter, the stocking of regulated reservoirs which can hold fish only during certain times of the year, and the stocking of newly impounded waters.

† States, of course, can use their own funds for put-and-take fishing if they wish.

In response to the requests of a few states interested in put-and-take fishing, the Division of Federal Aid proposed new guidelines that would have enabled more put-and-take stocking. However, this proposal was rejected by the majority of state representatives at the 1985 annual meeting of state fish and wildlife agencies because it was feared the more liberal guidelines could undermine the efforts of states to resist angler pressure for put-and-take stocking programs that could displace more important fishery management activities.

Under the policy finally approved, federal funds will be available for the propagation, rearing and distribution of fish in support of these state-program purposes:

1. To establish fish species, types, or strains in new or existing waters;
2. To re-establish fish species, such as in winter-killed or renovated lakes;
3. To maintain fish populations that have insufficient natural reproduction. The take of stocked fish must exceed 110 percent of the weight of the fish stocked.

The 110 percent requirement represents the first time FWS has used specific criteria for defining the amount of fish growth required for a stocking project to qualify as a put-grow-take fishery. It is a standard, say FWS officials, that because of its stringency essentially precludes put-and-take stocking in nearly all cases.

On the other hand, changes in FWS hatchery construction, maintenance, and operations guidelines would help those states who conduct put-and-take operations. Under the new policy, FWS allows Dingell-Johnson fund use for the construction, improvement, or renovation of any state fish hatchery even if the hatchery produces fish for put-and-take stocking purposes. FWS also allows the use of federal funds to help pay cyclical maintenance costs of these facilities. Cyclical maintenance is defined as maintenance tasks such as painting that recur at intervals greater than one year. However, FWS will not help pay for the custodial maintenance costs of hatcheries that raise fish for put-and-take operations. Custodial maintenance is defined as those routine tasks required to operate a facility from day to day such as cleaning hatchery tanks. In sum, the changes in hatchery policy made by FWS represent a modest concession to states that have sought to obtain more federal funding support for their put-and-take recreational fisheries.

*Hunter Education.* All states conduct hunter education programs,* and 48 states use federal aid funds to help pay for them. In the past, the quality of these programs has varied considerably, ranging from those that provided a minimal amount of instruction, primarily in firearms safety, to more highly developed programs taught by professional educators.

---

* Thirty-four states require hunters to attend a hunter education course, while 16 provide such courses on a voluntary basis.

Effective October 1, 1985, all states using federal aid funds for hunter education must conduct a ten-hour course. The states are encouraged to review existing programs to ensure their needs are being met. Course content is supposed to be designed to help the states alleviate problems associated with hunting or resources affected by hunters. According to FWS officials, the increased training will help to ensure that hunters conduct themselves properly in the field, respect the rights of property owners and other recreationists, and abide by fish and wildlife laws. FWS also is striving to increase the qualifications of the hunter education specialists in its regional offices so that they can provide more effective technical assistance to the states.

*Trapper Education.* FWS considers trapping to be a form of hunting and has in the past allowed the states to provide introductory instruction in trapping as part of hunter education programs.* In 1985, the Division of Federal Aid clarified the use of Pittman-Robertson funds for trapping instruction. Effective October 1, 1985, trapper education is an eligible activity only to the extent that it relates to safety, ethics, hunter responsibility, and avoidance of nontarget species. The development of trapping skills and instruction in the grading, treatment, and marketing of pelts are ineligible activities.

# Current Issues

## Diversion of License Revenues

A major goal of the Federal Aid Program is to ensure that all states desiring to participate maintain their eligibility to do so. Both the Pittman-Robertson and Dingell-Johnson acts require the states to have statutes prohibiting the diversion of state hunting and fishing license fees to any use other than the administration of state fish and wildlife programs. All states passed such laws years ago, but occasionally a state will take an action or pass legislation that violates the diversion prohibition. Some examples:

- The Oklahoma legislature passed a law in 1971 that would have transferred lands from the state wildlife commission to the Industrial Development and Park Commission without payment. While the lands in question were not acquired with Pittman-Robertson or Dingell-Johnson funds, the Department of Interior ruled that the transfer would violate the Pittman-Robertson Act because the wildlife lands represented assets of the agency that had been acquired with the license revenues.

---

* Trapping is nowhere mentioned in the Pittman-Robertson Act. FWS officials say that since trapping occurs, they should attempt to prevent any abuses to wildlife by giving trappers minimal instruction. The hunter education course neither promotes nor discourages trapping as an activity, according to FWS officials.

- In 1984, the Idaho legislature sought to earmark an additional $30,000 in the Fish and Game Department budget to help finance the state's contribution to the FWS animal damage control program. At that time, the department contribution to the control program was already $21,000. Since these additional funds could have come from license revenues collected by the Fish and Game Department, FWS warned the state that it could lose approximately $2 million in Pittman-Robertson grants if license funds were used. Eventually, the game department did increase its contribution to $50,000, but used only nonlicense revenues to do so.

Generally, FWS relies on its interactions with state fish and wildlife agencies to learn of potential diversion problems. FWS then works informally with the appropriate parties to head off diversion actions. Only rarely is a state formally notified that it is in violation of the diversion prohibition. Should this occur, FWS would withhold further grants until the situation was corrected.

## Incompatible Use of Areas Acquired with Federal Aid Funds

When land and waters are acquired or leased by the states with federal-aid funds, the property must be operated and maintained in accordance with the uses described in the application for project assistance. Since 1937, thousands of fish and wildlife areas have been acquired or leased. These include 4,385 wildlife areas and refuges, 361 constructed or restored fishing lakes, and 1,348 access sites to fish and wildlife resources.*

Increasing development pressures and growth in the number of people participating in all types of outdoor recreation, combined with the inherent difficulty of monitoring project lands—many of them small tracts—scattered throughout a state, have led to the conversion for nonwildlife uses of some areas acquired or leased with federal aid funds. Some examples:

- A private ski resort located on Forest Service property in Washington wants to expand its operations onto a Pittman-Robertson wildlife area that provides summer and winter range for elk.
- Areas purchased for hunting areas have been closed to hunting and used for purposes such as tree nurseries.
- Wildlife on project areas has been disturbed by the unauthorized use of the property by horseback riders and skimobilers.
- A large storage building recently was constructed on five acres of the Flat River State Management Area by the Michigan Waterways Division.
- Two hundred forty-six acres of elk winter range in Baker County, Oregon, were sold by the state to an irrigation district for a reservoir site.

* Statistics are current through FY 1984.

FWS requires the states to "maintain adequate control of federally funded real property" and encourages the states to develop and use their own property control systems provided they meet certain minimum requirements, including the "physical verification at reasonable intervals, that all real property serves its intended purpose and is properly maintained" (Interior 1982 section 10.19). If federal-aid properties are converted to non-program uses, either deliberately or unknowingly, the state is required either to correct the problem or replace the property with land of equal value and with equal wildlife benefits.*

According to FWS officials, only about half the states have adequate systems to monitor the status of real property acquired with federal-aid funds. That theoretically leaves FWS regional offices with the ultimate responsibility of directly monitoring hundreds of areas, a responsibility that is not being adequately discharged. FWS officials state that field offices simply do not have the personnel or travel budgets to allow them to inspect all previously acquired sites in addition to their more pressing duties of administering current projects.

The Division of Federal Aid does not keep nationally aggregated records on how often completed project areas are checked by its regional staff or the states themselves, how many cases of incompatible use come to light annually, or how such cases are resolved. Thus, there is no way to determine accurately the exact status of these areas or how serious the problem of incompatible use is. FWS officials say that current procedures for monitoring federal-aid properties are sufficient to uncover most cases of incompatible use and that more intensive review of properties by FWS personnel is not warranted.

## Research Coordination

According to FWS officials, no mechanism exists at the national level for coordinating fish and wildlife research undertaken by federal, state, and private entities. The Division of Federal Aid has taken the lead in correcting this deficiency by establishing computerized data bases for all research studies undertaken and completed with federal aid funds.

The Divisions' Current Federal Aid Research System (CFAR) became functional in 1980. It is a computerized data base that summarizes all current research being undertaken by the states with Pittman-Robertson and Dingell-Johnson funds. Each spring, the division also publishes two reports—one for fish and one for wildlife—that summarize and categorize current research studies. Additional information can be found in the Fish and Wildlife Refer-

---

* A state may dispose of federal-aid property that is no longer needed if it receives the approval of the FWS regional director and reimburses the program for the federal share of the current market value of the property.

ence Service (FWRS), a computer data base of all significant reports and publications completed under federal aid projects. Both the Current Federal Aid Research System and the Fish and Wildlife Reference Service may be accessed by telephone or computer terminal to initiate information searches or to obtain copies of stored materials.

The division has encouraged all FWS offices and other federal agencies to enter their research studies into both data systems. The FWS Cooperative Research Unit program already has done so. The various FWS and National Marine Fisheries Service research divisions also have agreed to enter their data, though no deadline has been set for completion. The establishment of a comprehensive national data base on current and completed research will increase the efficiency of fish and wildlife researchers everywhere, as well as avoid duplication of effort.

# Legislation

## Reagan Initiative to Cut Dingell-Johnson Spending

In its proposed FY 1985 budget for FWS, the Reagan administration surprised fishing, boating, and conservation organizations by requesting a drastic cutback in funds to be spent under the Dingell-Johnson Act. The cutback proposal was totally unexpected, since the administration had supported legislation in 1984 that substantially expanded revenue for the program.

A provision of the omnibus tax bill of 1984 (known as the Deficit Reduction Act) merged the federal boating safety program with the Dingell-Johnson program. The act created an Aquatic Resources Trust Fund, to be called the Wallop-Breaux Fund, composed of the two accounts, each with its own distinct revenue sources: the Boating Safety Account funded by a portion of the federal tax on motorboat fuel; and the Sport Fish Restoration Account (equivalent to the old Dingell-Johnson fund), funded by excise taxes on sport-fishing equipment. In addition, the legislation expanded the items of fishing equipment taxed and created two new sources of revenue for the sport-fish account: import duties on yachts and pleasure craft and a portion of the tax receipts from motorboat-fuel sales. As a result, total revenues for the sport-fish account, or Dingell-Johnson fund, more than tripled, from $38 million in FY 1985 to $122 million in FY 1986.

The Reagan administration in 1985 attempted to reverse these financial gains by proposing to spend in FY 1986 only that portion of the Dingell-Johnson fund derived from excise taxes on fishing equipment, an estimated $44 million. In addition, the administration asked Congress to make Dingell-Johnson funds subject to the annual appropriations process by repealing the permanent-indefinite appropriation authority for the program. This would have enabled the administration to increase or decrease expenditures from year to year as it deemed necessary rather than have these monies spent automatically each year by FWS and the states.

Before the President's proposal had even been submitted to Congress, sport-fishing, boating, and conservation organizations, led by the Sport Fishing and Boating Enhancement Committee,* launched a counter attack to block it. Senator Malcolm Wallop (R-WY) and Representative John Breaux (D-LA), prime movers behind the 1984 law that created the Aquatic Resources Trust Fund, each introduced nonbinding resolutions (S. Res. 130, H. Res. 165) calling on President Reagan to drop his cutback proposal, and both worked hard to protect the program in the congressional budget process. Their resolutions gained substantial support—57 cosponsors of the Wallop measure, 159 cosponsors of the Breaux resolution—but never were brought to a floor vote because action taken on other bills settled the matter. Both the House and Senate appropriations committees included language in their reports on the 1986 Appropriations Bill for the Department of the Interior and Related Agencies which rejected the administration's proposed changes. The Senate report stated:

> The Committee recommends that the Wallop-Breaux amendments to the Federal Aid in Fish Restoration Act of 1950 (the Dingell-Johnson Act) should be adhered to and does not agree with the budget proposal to appropriate the excise tax receipts. Rather, the Committee recommends that this program of user fees continue as a permanent, indefinite appropriation, as was anticipated when the sport fishermen and recreational boaters agreed to excise taxes on additional items (U.S. Congress, Senate, 1985).

Given this strong endorsement of the Dingell-Johnson program, any renewed attempt to repeal the program's automatic appropriations appears to stand little chance of success.

## Nongame Act Funding Study and Reauthorization Legislation

When the Forsythe-Chafee Act was passed in 1980, Congress authorized up to $5 million yearly in general appropriations to fund the program through FY 1985. However, no funds were ever requested by FWS to implement the act because of a general policy of budget restraint pursued by presidents Carter and Reagan. Nor has Congress taken the initiative in appropriating funds.

Section 12 of the act requires FWS to prepare a study of various ways to

---

* The committee was composed of these members in January, 1985: American Fisheries Society, American Recreation Coalition, Atlantic States Marine Fisheries Commission, Bass Anglers Sportsman Society, Boat Owners Association of the U.S., International Association of Fish and Wildlife Agencies, Izaak Walton League of America, National Association of State Boating Law Administrators, National Boating Federation, National Marine Manufacturers Association, National Wildlife Federation, Sport Fishing Institute, Trout Unlimited, and Wildlife Management Institute. This committee has re-formed and is now called the American League of Anglers and Boaters.

provide federal financing of state nongame conservation projects. The report, *Potential Funding Sources to Implement the Fish and Wildlife Conservation Act of 1980* (Interior 1985b), was submitted in February 1985, but with no Reagan administration recommendation for implementing any of the funding alternatives discussed.

A total of 25 potential funding methods, including general appropriations, fees, and excise taxes, were considered by FWS. The 18 deemed most appropriate and feasible were examined in detail.* Each potential funding method was evaluated for its revenue-raising potential, economic impact, benefits received by those paying a tax, and the ability of the public to pay a tax or fee. The pros and cons of each financing method were presented in detail, as were summaries of public comments on each alternative.

Only eight of the 18 funding methods studied would each provide $10 million or more annually. A five to 10 percent excise tax on bird seed, houses, and feeders would raise considerably less. At the recommended maximum 10 percent tax rate, a bird-seed tax would generate $7.3 million yearly; a bird house tax, $0.9 million; a feeder tax, $2.5; and a tax on bird baths and other equipment, $1.2 million.

During the course of the study, FWS solicited written comments from manufacturers, trade associations, user groups, conservation organizations, wildlife agencies, and the general public. Only four funding methods received more favorable than negative responses: (1) use of general appropriations; (2) a tax on wildlife identification books; (3) a voluntary tax check-off; and (4) sale of semi-postal stamps.

* In addition, the report includes an addendum that discusses the potential of levying "developer fees" for various economic uses of federal lands— including grazing, timber harvesting, mineral extraction, recreation and tourism, and use of lands for power-generation sites—and for other development activities that involve the federal government.

Estimated Revenues from Potential
Nongame Act Funding Methods

| Funding Method | Estimated Annual Revenue in Millions (1980 Dollars) |
|---|---|
| 5-10% tax on wild animal furs | $11.2-21.4 |
| 5-10% tax on hiking/camping items | $14.3-28.1 |
| 2-5% tax on off-road vehicles | $76.8-147.3 |
| Fees ($.50-$2.00) for use of federal lands | $103.1 |
| Voluntary contribution, income tax check-off | $40 |
| Sale of semi-postal stamps (25-50% of face value) | $11.3-203.4 |
| 1-5% tax on photographic equipment and film | $25.2-124.0 |
| Mining claim renewal fee ($10-$15) | $12.1-30.2 |

Source: Potential Funding Sources to Implement the Fish and Wildlife Conservation Act of 1980 (Interior, 1985b)

Irrespective of the study results, the Reagan administration declined to promote any new funding proposal. In his letter transmitting the report to the Congress, FWS Director Robert Jantzen cited the "present fiscal situation and Administration policies on Federal spending and taxation" (Jantzen 1985) as reasons for inaction. On the other hand, Jantzen hinted that the sale of semi-postal stamps was a voluntary financing method worthy of consideration, but that the U.S. Postal Service opposed it.

The House held one day of hearings on nongame reauthorization legislation (H.R. 1406) and the financing study. At the House hearings, Eugene Hester, deputy director of FWS, speaking for the Reagan administration, opposed the reauthorization of appropriations for the act on four grounds:

1. No funds have yet been appropriated under this act;
2. The current emphasis on federal deficit reduction would not allow room in the budget for this program for several years into the future;
3. Existing Pittman-Robertson funds can be used for certain nongame purposes at the discretion of the states; and
4. The states are moving ahead on their own to expand nongame wildlife management efforts.

In lieu of federal funding, Hester recommended that the states be encouraged to use their own funds to expand their nongame conservation efforts, since they have primary jurisdiction over nongame wildlife species. The states, on the other hand, supported a combination of federal financing methods, including the sale of semi-postal stamps and the levying of excise taxes on selected photographic equipment, backpacking and camping equipment, binoculars, and wild bird feeds. A spokesman for the American Recreation Coalition opposed excise taxes on outdoor recreation equipment and instead urged that monies be derived from development activities that destroy wildlife habitat.

Ultimately the House approved a simple, three-year reauthorization of the act through FY 1988, with authority for annual appropriations set at $5 million. The Merchant Marine and Fisheries Committee, while interested in voluntary financing plans such as the sale of semi-postal stamps, declined to pursue this avenue further. Other factors influencing the committee's action were the lack of overwhelming support for any one financing mechanism, as well as the Reagan administration's general opposition to new taxes and increases in federal spending. In addition, nonprofit conservation organizations demonstrated little visible support for a nongame fund.

The Senate Environment and Public Works Committee did not hold hearings on the nongame program in 1985, but did report legislation, S. 1353, reauthorizing the act. The committee intends to hold hearings on the measure sometime in 1986 and eventually to bring the measure to the Senate floor for approval.

Status of Game Populations in the Southeastern States, 1982

| SPECIES | AL | AR | FL | GA | KY | LA | MD | MS | MO | NC | OK | SC | TN | TX | VA | WV |
|---|---|---|---|---|---|---|---|---|---|---|---|---|---|---|---|---|
| WHITETAIL DEER | I | S | S | I | I | S | I | I | S? | I | S | I | I | S | S | I |
| BLACK BEAR | I | I | I | I | I | S | | | | S | I | S | S | U | S | I |
| WILD HOG AND PECCARY | | | S | U | | | | | | | N/A | S | I | I | | |
| TURKEY | S | I | I | I | I | I | I | I | I | I | I | I | S | I | I | I |
| SQUIRREL (ALL SPECIES) | S | S | N/A | S | S | D | S | S | S | S | S | S | S | U | S | S |
| GROUSE | U | | N/A | F | S | | S | | I | S | N/A | S | S | U | I | S |
| RACCOON | S | S | U | S | S | S | S | D | S | S | S | S | S | U | S | S |
| OPOSSUM | S | S | U | S | S | S | S | | S | S | S | S | S | U | S | S |
| RED FOX | S | I | S | S | S | S | S | | I | S | S | D | S | U | S | D |
| GRAY FOX | S | S | S | S | I | | S | | S | S | S | S-I | S | U | S | I |
| COYOTE | I | I | I | I | I | I | | | S | U | F | N/A | I | U | N/A | S |
| BOBCAT | D | S | S | S-I | I | S | U | | S | U | F | I | S | U | S | S |
| QUAIL | S | S | U | D | I | S | I | S | D | S | F | S | S | U | S | I |
| RABBIT (ALL SPECIES) | S | S | U | D-S | I | S | I | D | S-D | S | F | S | S | U | S | S |
| DOVE | S | U | U | F | S | S | I | S | S | S | S | I | S | U | U | S |
| GROUND HOG | I | U | N/A | U | S | | I | | D? | I | I | U | S | S | S | S |
| ARMADILLO | I | I | I | I | | I | | | S | | I | U | U | U | N/A | N/A |
| CROW | S | S | S | U | S | S | I | | F | S | I | S | U | U | S | S |
| DUCKS | S | I | S | F | S | S | D | S | F | S | D | S | S | U | S | S |
| GEESE | S | I | D | I | S | S | I | | U | D | D | | I | S | I | I |
| WOODCOCK | S | S | S | F | S | S | S | U | U | S | S | S | S | U | U | S |
| SNIPE | S | S | S | S | U | S | S | | U | U | S | S | S | U | U | S |
| RAILS | U | S | S | F | U | S | S | | U | S | S | I | S | U | S | S |
| CRANES | D | | N/A | | | | | | | | I | U | U | U | | |
| ANTELOPE | | | N/A | | | | | | | | I | | | I | | |
| PHEASANT | | I | N/A | | | | | | I | | S | | I | U | | |
| GREATER PRAIRIE CHICKEN | | | N/A | | | | | | S | | D | | | U | | |
| LESSER PRAIRIE CHICKEN | | | | | | | | | | | D | | | U | | |
| BEAVER | I | I | I | I | I | I | I | | S | I | I | | I | U | S | S |

| | | | | | | | | | | | |
|---|---|---|---|---|---|---|---|---|---|---|---|
| OTHER | | | | | | | | U | | | |
| WEASEL | S | U | | S | S | U | S | | U | S | |
| MINK | S | I | U | I | I | S | S | | U | S | N/A |
| OTTER | D | S | U | D | I | S | S | | U | I | N/A |
| SKUNK | | I | N/A | S | S | D | S | | U | S | I |
| MUSKRAT | | I | U | S | S | F | S | D | U | S | |
| NUTRIA | | I | | D | D | N/A | D | D | U | N/A | |

LEGEND: D-DECREASING, F-FLUCTUATING, I-INCREASING, S-STABLE, U-UNKNOWN, N/A-NOT APPLICABLE.

Source: Southeastern Association of Fish and Wildlife Agencies, *Vital Statistics '82* (1983).

# Legal Developments

There has been relatively little litigation concerning the Federal Aid Program, a circumstance that wildlife law specialist, Michael J. Bean of the Environmental Defense Fund, finds "striking" given the "duration and magnitude of the Pittman-Robertson program and the widely divergent views of those interested in its administration. . . . " (Bean 1983). This dearth of legal activity continues in the 1980s. There were no court decisions pertaining to either the Pittman-Robertson or Dingell-Johnson statues in 1985 and no suits filed. A discussion of previous litigation regarding these laws can be found in *The Evolution of National Wildlife Law* (Bean 1983).

# Resource Status

The Division of Federal Aid does not keep records on the local, regional, or national biological status of the fish and wildlife species that are eligible for assistance under the Federal Aid Program. Nor does the division require that the states provide it with such data. Thus it is impossible to easily determine how effective the states have been in restoring and maintaining all eligible species. While it is clear that certain game species and sport fish have benefitted greatly from state wildlife management projects assisted with federal funds, the status of many other species is unknown.

The only state fish and wildlife association that collects and publishes data on the biological status of species is the Southeastern Association of Fish and Wildlife Agencies. The association asks its member states to classify the status of 35 game species or species groups in terms of whether the numbers of a species or group are decreasing, fluctuating, increasing, stable, or unknown. The status assessment for 1982 shows that most species are either stable or increasing.

Other states maintain records on the status of selected resident bird, mammal, and fish species. However, it is beyond the scope of this report to collect and summarize that data.

# References

American Fisheries Society. 1985. *The AFS Diary,* Vol. 11, No. 22 (June 7, 1985).

Bean, M.J. 1983. *The Evolution of National Wildlife Law.* Praeger Publishers. New York. 449 pp.

Jantzen, R. 1985. Letter to Senator Robert T. Stafford, Chairman, Senate Committee on Environment and Public Works, February 8, 1985.

Sousa, R.J. 1982a. "A National Overview of Wildlife Management Investigations Funded by the Pittman-Robertson (P-R) Program." *Wildlife Society Bulletin*, Vol. 10, No. 3, 1982: p. 254.

——. 1982b. "A National Overview of Fishery Research Funded by the Dingell-Johnson Program." *Fisheries*, Vol. 7, No. 1 (January-February 1982): p. 3.

Southeastern Association of Fish and Wildlife Agencies. 1983. *Vital Statistics '81*. Southeastern Cooperative Fish and Game Statistics Project, Institute of Statistics. North Carolina State University. Raleigh, N.C.

The Wildlife Conservation Fund of America. 1980. "Fish and Wildlife Agency Funding." The Wildlife Conservation Fund of America. Columbus, Ohio.

U.S. Congress, House, Committee on Agriculture, Aid to States in Wildlife Restoration Projects. 1937. Report to Accompany S. 2670, 75th Congress, 1st Session, H. Rpt. 1572.

U.S. Congress, House, Committee on Merchant Marine and Fisheries, Federal Boat Safety Act Amendments. 1983. Report to Accompany S. 2163, 98th Congress, 1st Section, H. Rpt. 98-133 Part 1.

U.S. Congress, Senate, Special Committee on Conservation of Wildlife Resources, United States Aid to States in Wildlife Restoration Projects. 1937a. Report to Accompany S. 2670, 75th Congress, 1st Session, S. Rpt. 868.

U.S. Congress, Senate. 1937b. *Congressional Record*, 75th Congress, 1st Session: pp. S 8582-86.

U.S. Congress, Senate, Committee on Commerce. 1970. Report to Accompany H.R. 12475, 91st Congress, 2nd Session, S. Rpt. 91-1289.

U.S. Congress, Senate, Committee on Appropriations, Department of the Interior and Related Agencies Appropriations Bill, 1986. 1985. Report to Accompany H.R. 3011, 99th Congress, 1st Session, S. Rpt. 99-141.

U.S. Department of the Interior, Fish and Wildlife Service. Undated. *25 Years of Federal-State Cooperation for Improving Sport Fishing*. U.S. Government Printing Office. Washington, D.C. 38 pp.

U.S. Department of the Interior, Fish and Wildlife Service. 1978. *Environmental Impact Statement: Federal Aid in Fish and Wildlife Restoration Program*. U.S. Department of the Interior. Washington, D.C.

U.S. Department of the Interior, Office of the Inspector General. 1981. "Review of Fish and Wildlife Service Administration of the Federal Aid in Fish and Wildlife Restoration Programs." U.S. Department of the Interior. Washington, D.C.

U.S. Department of the Interior, Fish and Wildlife Service. 1982. *Federal Aid Manual*. U.S. Department of the Interior. Washington, D.C.

U.S. Department of the Interior, Fish and Wildlife Service. 1984. *Federal Aid in Fish and Wildlife Restoration 1984*. U.S. Department of the Interior. Washington, D.C.

U.S. Department of the Interior, Fish and Wildlife Service. 1985a. "Federal

Aid Program: Interim Program Management Document." U.S. Department of the Interior. Washington, D.C.

U.S. Department of the Interior, Fish and Wildlife Service. 1985b. *Potential Funding Sources to Implement the Fish and Wildlife Conservation Act of 1980.* U.S. Department of the Interior. Washington, D.C.

*William J. Chandler is president of W. J. Chandler Associates, a Washington D.C. environmental policy and government relations consulting firm, and publisher of* Land Letter, *a newsletter for natural-resources professionals.*

A biologist frees a netted duck during a banding project, one of many programs instrumental to the management of the 813 federally protected migratory bird species.

*U.S. Fish and Wildlife Service*

# Migratory Bird Protection and Management

## William J. Chandler

## Introduction

THE FEDERAL GOVERNMENT has treaty and legislative authority to protect, manage, and conserve 813 species of native migratory birds that are identified in four bird-protection treaties between the United States and the nations with which it shares these migrants. Authority over migratory birds was assumed by the federal government in 1916 when it became clear that the states were not adequately protecting waterfowl or other migratory species. The states, however, retain authority over nonmigratory birds, principally members of the order Galliformes (pheasants, quails, and grouse) and introduced, nonnative species such as the European starling.

Migratory bird conservation is the responsibility of the U.S. Fish and Wildlife Service (FWS), an agency of the Department of the Interior. FWS classifies migratory birds into two categories, game and nongame. Game includes 162 species that may be hunted legally, but only 59 actually are at present. Game species are further subdivided into waterfowl and migratory shore and upland game birds. Nongame (unhunted) birds include 669 species, some 80 percent of all migratory species under federal authority, but since 103 game species no longer are hunted, the effective number of nongame birds is 772, 93 percent of all federally protected species.

By necessity, the management of wide-ranging birds is accomplished through a partnership between FWS and its counterpart agencies at the state level. State fish and wildlife agencies have established four flyway councils (Atlantic, Mississippi, Central, and Pacific) to provide advice and cooperative assistance to the federal government in the management of waterfowl species that pass through or occupy their territories. The states also conduct research and banding programs, acquire and manage habitat, manage a few federally acquired waterfowl refuges, and assist in the enforcement of federal hunting regulations and bird-protection laws.

Several private, nonprofit organizations conduct programs that complement FWS migratory-bird activities. Ducks Unlimited leases and manages habitat for migratory waterfowl, primarily in Canada. The Nature Conservancy acquires significant wetlands within the United States in order to protect them from development, and either resells the lands to federal or state conservation agencies or retains them as nature reserves. The National Audubon Society acquires and manages bird refuges and conducts bird research projects.

Certain game birds have received intensive study and management over the years. FWS officials say this is because more information is needed about hunted species to ensure that they are not overhunted and because federal wildlife laws tend to emphasize game species. Nongame species have received considerably less attention from FWS. Although these birds have been totally protected from all hunting since 1916, relatively little has been done by the federal government to gather a comprehensive body of information on their biological status or habitat needs. In 1965, FWS took a step toward remedying this situation by establishing a breeding-bird survey that monitors yearly population trends for about 500 nongame species. However, adequate information is obtained for only 250 of these.

Today, FWS focuses its management activities on 44 species of ducks, geeses, and swans; six species of doves; coots; woodcock; sandhill cranes; rails; and gallinules. While FWS conducts a few activities to benefit nongame species, the budget for these activities is only a tiny fraction of that devoted to game birds.

# History and Legislative Authority

Most of the major federal statutes dealing with migratory birds were passed between 1918 and 1934, a time when the public recognized that America's wildlife resources could not withstand unregulated hunting and unlimited habitat destruction. Although these early laws have been amended, their principal emphasis remains much the same as when originally enacted. The principal authorities for federal migratory bird management include:

- The Migratory Bird Treaty Act (16 U.S.C.A. 703 *et seq.*), which prohibits the hunting of any migratory bird species unless open seasons are declared and hunting regulations are issued by the secretary of the Interior. This act was passed in 1918 to implement a 1916 migratory-bird protection treaty signed with Canada.

- The Migratory Bird Conservation Act (16 U.S.C.A. 715 *et seq.*), which authorizes the purchase of land for federal migratory-bird refuges.
- The Migratory Bird Hunting Stamp Act (16 U.S.C.A. 718 *et seq.*), which requires each hunter to buy a federal "duck stamp." The proceeds are placed in a special fund and used exclusively for the purchase of refuge lands.
- The Wetlands Loan Act (16 U.S.C.A. 715 k-3 *et seq.*), which authorizes the appropriation of up to $200 million dollars from the general Treasury to purchase migratory-bird refuges. The appropriations are considered an "advance" against future duck-stamp receipts and eventually must be repaid.
- The Fish and Wildlife Coordination Act (16 U.S.C.A. 611 *et seq.*), which requires water-resource agencies to consult with the secretary of the Interior regarding the impact of proposed development projects on fish and wildlife and to include wildlife protection or enhancement measures in these projects where feasible and to mitigate losses that occur.

These laws and their development were covered in detail in the *Audubon Wildlife Report 1985*. See that volume for a full discussion.

## Organization and Operations

FWS has sole authority for coordinating and supervising all federal migratory-bird management activities. Its principal functions include conducting population and harvest surveys, research, development of annual hunting regulations, acquisition and management of migratory-bird refuges, control of bird depredations on private lands, review of federal water-resource projects to prevent or mitigate their damage to migratory-bird habitat, the provision of grants to states for wildlife-restoration projects, and enforcement of all federal migratory-bird statutes regulating the taking of, and commerce in, protected species.

FWS encourages state cooperation in all aspects of federal wildlife programs, and the states play an active role in migratory-bird management through four flyway councils. The states work closely with FWS in developing annual hunting regulations for both waterfowl and migratory shore and upland game birds and play a major role in enforcing federal laws, since states collectively are able to field a much larger number of law enforcement officers than is the federal government. States also acquire and manage waterfowl refuges, conduct research and population surveys, and control bird depredations on private lands under cooperative agreements with FWS.

Wildlife Resources Program, FWS

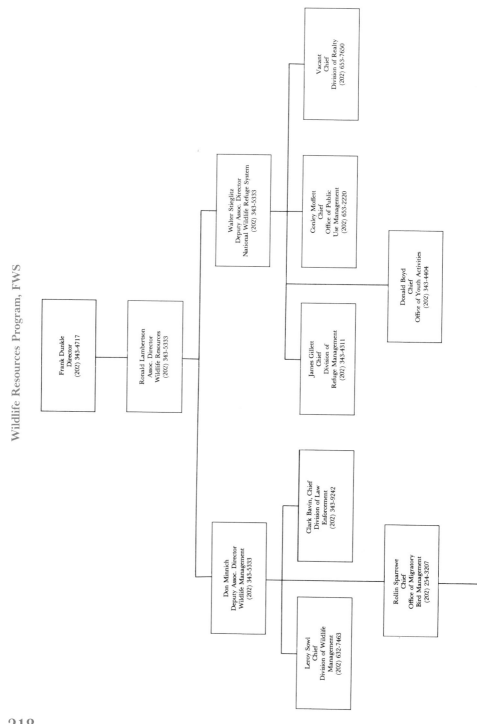

Frank Dunkle
Director
(202) 343-4717

Ronald Lambertson
Assoc. Director
Wildlife Resources
(202) 343-5333

Don Minnich
Deputy Assoc. Director
Wildlife Management
(202) 343-5333

Walter Stieglitz
Deputy Assoc. Director
National Wildlife Refuge System
(202) 343-5333

Leroy Sowl
Chief
Division of Wildlife
Management
(202) 632-7463

Clark Bavin, Chief
Division of Law
Enforcement
(202) 343-9242

James Gillett
Chief
Division of
Refuge Management
(202) 343-4311

Conley Moffett
Chief
Office of Public
Use Management
(202) 653-2220

Vacant
Chief
Division of Realty
(202) 653-7650

Rollin Sparrowe
Chief
Office of Migratory
Bird Management
(202) 254-3207

Donald Boyd
Chief
Office of Youth Activities
(202) 343-4404

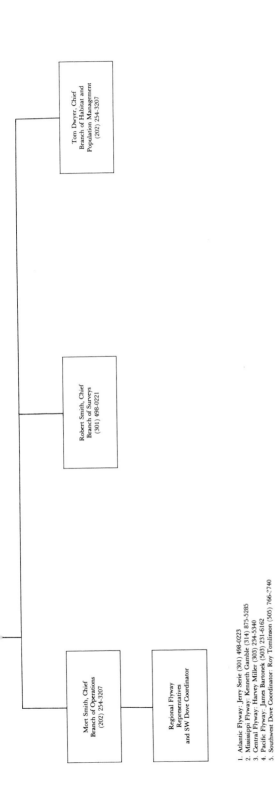

Tom Dwyer, Chief
Branch of Habitat and
Population Management
(202) 254-3207

Robert Smith, Chief
Branch of Surveys
(301) 498-0221

Mort Smith, Chief
Branch of Operations
(202) 254-3207

Regional Flyway
Representatives
and SW Dove Coordinator

1. Atlantic Flyway: Jerry Serie (301) 498-0223
2. Mississippi Flyway: Kenneth Gamble (314) 875-5285
3. Central Flyway: Harvey Miller (303) 234-5340
4. Pacific Flyway: James Bartonek (503) 231-6162
5. Southwest Dove Coordinator: Roy Tomlinson (505) 766-2740

219

## Agency Structure

FWS organizes its fish and wildlife management activities into eight programs, each supervised by a national program manager. Planning, budgeting, and evaluation are carried out within this program structure.

The Wildlife Resources Program, directed by Associate Director for Wildlife Resources Ronald Lambertson, has responsibility for migratory birds as well as for certain other wildlife species of federal interest that are not listed as threatened or endangered under the Endangered Species Act. (All listed species are the responsibility of the Federal Assistance Program and the Office of Endangered Species.)

The associate director is responsible for setting national program goals, providing policy guidance to FWS regional and field offices, preparing the annual program budget, and evaluating performance. The associate director is assisted by two deputy associate directors who in turn supervise various offices and divisions of the Wildlife Resources Program. Migratory bird responsibilities are spread throughout these units.

The Office of Migratory Bird Management, contrary to its name, does not coordinate all migratory-bird activities. The office's principal functions are to conduct national population and hunting-harvest surveys, coordinate the national bird-banding program for game and nongame birds and the annual breeding-bird survey, monitor raptor migration, assist in the preparation and implementation of migratory-bird management plans (including the National Waterfowl Management Plan and the North American Waterfowl Management Plan), develop federal hunting regulations for migratory game birds, and provide liaison with state migratory-bird programs. Other FWS offices with migratory-bird responsibilities are the Division of Refuge Management, which coordinates management of the national wildlife refuge system; the Division of Realty, responsible for acquiring land for any type of refuge; the Division of Law Enforcement, which enforces migratory bird statutes as well as other wildlife laws; and the Division of Wildlife Management, which controls problems or depredations caused by waterfowl, blackbirds, and other birds* and which coordinates the preparation of habitat-conservation strategies for private lands used by waterfowl.

In addition, other FWS offices that are not supervised by the associate director for Wildlife Resources have significant migratory-bird responsibilities. The Division of Wildlife Research conducts or coordinates basic and applied research on migratory birds. The Office of Ecological Services in the Habitat Resources Program reviews all federal actions and federal permits for water resource and other development projects to identify impacts on migratory birds and other species and makes recommendations for preventing or mitigat-

---

* The division's animal damage control function was transferred to the U.S. Department of Agriculture, effective April 1, 1986 (see chapter on animal damage control).

ing damage to wildlife. The Division of Federal Aid supervises the distribution of federal financial assistance to the states under the Pittman-Robertson Act. These funds may be used for migratory-bird management activities, including habitat acquisition.

The actual implementation of Wildlife Resources program activities is carried out by personnel in FWS regional and field offices. Each regional director is assisted by an assistant regional director for Wildlife Resources and by a special agent-in-charge who runs law enforcement activities. At the field level, migratory-bird activities are conducted by refuge managers and other field personnel.

## Migratory Bird Plans

Objectives for migratory-bird conservation operations are identified in a series of interrelated plans prepared by FWS at the national, regional, and field levels. The Office of Migratory Bird Management prepares national resource plans for 54 species or specific populations of migratory birds that are consid-

**Principal Offices Responsible for Migratory Bird Activities of the U.S. Fish and Wildlife Service**

| Activity | Office and Supervisor |
| --- | --- |
| 1. Annual population and harvest surveys | Office of Migratory Bird Management, Associate Director—Wildlife Resources |
| 2. Bird banding program | Office of Migratory Bird Management, Associate Director—Wildlife Resources |
| 3. Breeding bird survey | Office of Migratory Bird Management, Associate Director—Wildlife Resources |
| 4. Basic and applied research | Division of Wildlife Research and Division of Cooperative Fish and Wildlife Research Units, Assistant Director—Research and Development |
| 5. Annual hunting regulations | Office of Migratory Bird Management, Associate Director—Wildlife Resources |
| 6. Land acquisition | Division of Realty, Associate Director—Wildlife Resources |
| 7. Management of migratory bird refuges | Division of Refuge Management, Associate Director—Wildlife Resources |
| 8. Enforcement of migratory bird laws | Division of Law Enforcement, Associate Director—Wildlife Resources |
| 9. Control of bird depredations | Division of Wildlife Management, Associate Director—Wildlife Resources |
| 10. Review of federal actions and permits impacting migratory birds. | Division of Ecological Services, Associate Director—Habitat Resources |
| 11. Provision of grants to states for migratory bird conservation projects. | Division of Federal Aid, Associate Director—Federal Assistance |

Source: U.S. Fish and Wildlife Service, 1985.

ered significant. The Office of Migratory Bird Management also works with state flyway councils to prepare management plans for each distinct waterfowl population in each flyway. These flyway plans guide the day-to-day management efforts of both FWS and state wildlife personnel.

In addition, the Office of Migratory Bird Management, in cooperation with the Canadian Wildlife Service, has prepared a draft North American Waterfowl Plan. This document focuses on species of waterfowl for which international coordination is essential to achieve population objectives. Both the national resource plans and flyway plans are coordinated with the North American plan (see the Current Program Trends section for more details on the North American plan).

Planning objectives and management strategies identified in national plans are broken down into more specific objectives, strategies, and activities at the regional and field levels. Each of the seven FWS regional offices prepares a regional resource plan to guide the operations of the field units and personnel that it supervises. A regional plan covers five years and focuses FWS efforts on the management of both species of national significance and other species considered only regionally significant. The regional plan takes into account endangered species recovery plans to ensure that management activities for migratory birds and other wildlife do not affect endangered species adversely.

Field plans provide operational guidance to FWS personnel who operate refuges and research laboratories or who conduct resource management programs at the regional or subregional level. Field plans that must incorporate national and regional migratory-bird objectives include refuge master plans, the long-range management documents for national wildlife refuges; refuge management plans, prepared for specific refuge-management activities such as waterfowl production; research and development plans, which guide the work of each research facility; animal damage control plans, formulated for each state where waterfowl and other species cause economic loss or human health or safety problems; fish and wildlife management plans, which establish recommended goals and actions for species on federal lands in cases where a federal agency has requested FWS assistance; the Bristol Bay Cooperative Management plan, an economic development and natural-resources management plan for the Bristol Bay region of Alaska prepared by several cooperating federal, state, and local agencies; and law-enforcement strategy plans, developed to protect waterfowl and other fish or wildlife that are hunted illegally or taken from the wild.

## Research

The role of all FWS research units is to support the needs of the agency's various resource management programs. With regard to migratory birds, the

Wildlife Resources Program establishes research needs and objectives to be carried out by the Division of Wildlife Research and provides the necessary funds from the Wildlife Resources budget. Actual supervision of research, however, is the responsibility of the associate director for FWS Research and Development, who oversees all FWS research activities and personnel.

A substantial amount of the Wildlife Resources research budget—about 75 percent—is spent on migratory birds. The principal areas of research are:

(1) Waterfowl population status: Studies on population status, including the development of census and survey techniques, investigation of factors affecting the productivity and mortality of birds, and the effects of environmental factors and hunting regulations on waterfowl populations.

(2) Waterfowl ecology, habitat requirements, and habitat manipulation: General research aimed at increasing the productivity of waterfowl on both national wildlife refuges and other lands.

(3) Waterfowl health: Research on the causes, diagnosis, control, and prevention of migratory-bird diseases such as avian cholera, duck plague, and lead poisoning. Research results are conveyed to refuge personnel in order to train them in how to reduce the likelihood of disease outbreaks.

(4) Nongame migratory birds: The primary research emphasis is on monitoring nongame-bird populations to identify population trends. Study areas include improvement of survey methods and identification of significant habitats for nongame species.

(5) Bird damage control: Studies to define and develop standard methods for measuring bird-caused damage, to develop chemical and nonchemical wildlife-control methods, and to assess the ecological effects of these methods on the controlled species and the general environment.*

Migratory bird research is conducted at four facilities. The Patuxent Wildlife Research Center, in Laurel, Maryland, specializes in migratory-bird population-survey and status assessment work; the Northern Prairie Wildlife Research Center, in Jamestown, North Dakota, addresses waterfowl habitat and management requirements; the National Wildlife Health Laboratory, in Madison, Wisconsin, specializes in disease prevention and control; and the Denver Wildlife Research Center, in Colorado, conducts research on Alaska-nesting geese, seabirds, and riparian ecology and maintains the North American bird collection in cooperation with the Smithsonian Institution.

In addition, considerable research on migratory birds is conducted by FWS "cooperative units" located at various state universities. Such research frequently is executed in cooperation with the state fish and wildlife agency and FWS.

---

* Bird damage control research has been transferred to the Department of Agriculture, effective April 1, 1986.

## Budget and Staff

For FY 1986, the $135.1 million appropriated for the Wildlife Resources Program constituted 20.7 percent of total FWS budget authority. Of this amount, a substantial portion is spent on migratory-bird management, but the exact sum is unknown since FWS no longer divides its budget into species accounts, as it did during the period FY 1974-83. In its FY 1984 budget justification, FWS stated that 65 percent of its Wildlife Resources budget request was for migratory birds. This proportion undoubtedly has increased since then because of an emphasis on migratory birds and because animal damage control functions (about $20 million) have been transferred from the wildlife resources budget to the Department of Agriculture commencing in FY 1986.

Administration budget requests for the Wildlife Resources Program have increased steadily since FY 1984, as have the amounts appropriated by Congress. The only exception to this trend is FY 1986, when Congress appropriated less than the budget request principally because of the transfer of animal damage control activities.

Statistics for the number of employees engaged primarily in migratory-bird management activities is not available.

# Current Program Trends

The Reagan administration has made waterfowl its top management priority, to the virtual exclusion of all other migratory-bird species. FWS is reorganizing its staff, rethinking management issues, and launching new initiatives designed to increase and maintain duck and goose populations at predetermined levels. Meanwhile, FWS efforts on behalf of other migratory species have been reduced or ended. FWS has identified 54 bird species, species populations, or species groups as nationally significant. Of these, 39 are waterfowl, nine are migratory shore and upland game birds, and six are nongame birds.

## Restructuring Waterfowl Management

FWS has been managing migratory birds since 1918. Over the years, management responsibility for the resource has been fractionated among various headquarters and regional and field units, with the result that it has become increasingly difficult to determine who, in fact, runs the program and to assess what is being achieved.

There is now a movement to end this confusion by clarifying management roles, merging functions, and augmenting staff to cope with new problems. In FY 1985, the Office of Migratory Bird Management was given the responsibility of developing national conservation plans for migratory birds, including habitat conservation, in addition to its traditional role of surveying and estimating waterfowl populations and establishing hunting regulations. A

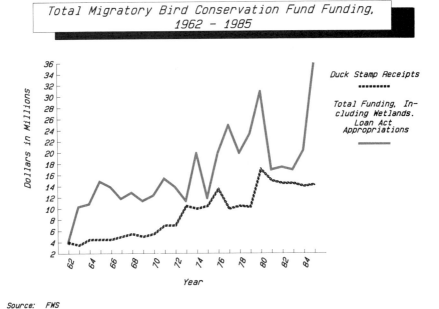

Total Migratory Bird Conservation Fund Funding,
1962 - 1985

Source: FWS

new Branch of Population and Habitat Management was added to the office
in FY 1986 to help it carry out its expanded role.

In addition, the Office of Migratory Bird Management has expanded its
population survey staff in a move to improve waterfowl survey methods and
research results. Concurrently, the Division of Wildlife Research has been
instructed to place more emphasis on waterfowl and migratory game-bird
problems, especially on techniques to improve hunter success and population
estimates.

At the regional level, directors will continue to serve as FWS spokespersons on federal migratory bird policy and issues. Flyway representatives, who
report to the Office of Migratory Bird Management, are to ensure that the
directors have sufficient information to fulfill their roles competently.

Budget Requests and Appropriations Wildlife Resources Program* (in millions)

|  | Requested | Appropriated |
|---|---|---|
| FY1984 | $126.14 | $131.84 |
| FY1985 | 135.73 | 146.58 |
| FY1986 | 148.44 | 135.11 |

*Includes president's budget request and congressional action in the Interior and Related Agencies Appropriations Bill (not subsequent adjustments).
Source: FWS Budget Office

## Increasing Waterfowl Production

A major goal of FWS is to increase waterfowl production in accordance with population objectives defined in flyway, national, and international plans. FWS is developing coordinated strategies for increasing production both on FWS-managed refuges and waterfowl production areas and on privately owned lands. While FWS has long recognized that it could not own all waterfowl habitat, it has never before developed a specific strategy for getting private landowners to manage their property for waterfowl conservation.

FWS has assigned waterfowl production objectives to most of its refuges and waterfowl production areas, although collectively FWS-managed refuges and Wetland Production Areas contribute only a fraction of the yearly North American production of ducks and geese. The program is in its early phase, and FWS officials say it will take several years to get it running smoothly, develop methods for accurately measuring production increases, and determine which combination of management practices (control of predators, plantings, water manipulation, etc.) works best. FWS intends to initiate several research projects in FY 1986 in support of the program, but may be constrained from doing so due to impending budget cuts.

FWS also would like to obtain conservation assistance from private landowners who own wetlands and associated upland habitat areas used by breeding waterfowl. The Mid-Continent Waterfowl Management Project, run by Region 3, is successfully developing and applying new and innovative techniques to increase duck production on private agricultural lands in western Minnesota. Most of these techniques could be applied throughout the Midwest.* In addition, the Division of Wildlife Management is coordinating FWS involvement in the implementation of the land-conservation provisions of the 1985 farm bill, which could help protect waterfowl habitat (see the Legislation section for further details).

## Population and Harvest Surveys

Although FWS employs the most sophisticated wildlife and harvest survey techniques in the world, FWS officials say there is much room for improving the accuracy and reliability of the data collected. The Office of Migratory Bird Management will continue to focus its data collection activities so as to provide national and continent wide estimates of breeding and migrating flock size and hunter take. Where necessary, this effort will be complemented by surveys undertaken by FWS regions or the states. Currently, FWS is working to improve its survey techniques, population and kill estimates, and measurements of waterfowl recruitment.†

---

* These techniques include the use of 10-year lease agreements that enable FWS to renovate marshes, build nesting structures, and carry out predator-control measures on private lands.
† Recruitment refers to the number of new birds added to the population each year after breeding takes place.

## Waterfowl Disease Research

Waterfowl disease research within FWS has focused on the causes, diagnosis, control, and prevention of disease outbreaks in migrating birds and on the lead-poisoning problem. In order to make major progress in preventing and managing disease outbreaks, FWS says it will need a larger commitment of funds (averaging $600,000 yearly) and more personnel over a six-year period. In the FY 1986 budget, FWS received $600,000 to accelerate research on lead-shot substitutes and $1 million for studying contaminant-disease relationships in waterfowl, especially in populations that winter in California, where selenium poisoning has killed birds on the Kesterson National Wildlife Refuge.

## Wetlands Acquisition

Even though FWS has been acquiring lands for migratory birds since the 1930s, it has not been able to acquire sufficient acreage to protect waterfowl populations adequately. The number and size of federal refuges and Wetland Production Areas needed to protect migratory birds is related directly to the amount of privately owned wetlands that are destroyed by private agricultural and development activities. The greater the destruction of privately owned wetlands, the more important it becomes for FWS to own and manage more land to protect waterfowl breeding, migration, and wintering habitat in order to keep populations from declining.

So far, Congress has eschewed regulatory methods to prevent the destruction of waterfowl habitat, leaving land acquisition as the only alternative. But despite several previous attempts by Congress to accelerate wetlands acquisition, FWS has not received sufficient appropriations to meet its acquisition goals.

In the 1950s, FWS and state fish and wildlife agencies jointly determined that 12.5 million acres of waterfowl habitat in the conterminous United States should be protected in federal and state refuges in order to maintain species populations at then-existing levels. FWS took responsibility for eight million acres, 3.5 million of which already were owned, and the states took responsibility for 4.5 million acres, of which two million were owned.

In 1976, FWS revised its acquisition strategy to target 33 types of wetlands that should be protected to save significant migratory-bird habitat. The total acreage goal was 3,825,000, of which 1,878,000 already had been acquired during FY 1962-76. That left 1,947,000 acres to be acquired either in fee or by easement from FY 1977 to FY 1986. FWS did not meet this goal. At the end of FY 1985, it had acquired only 60.5 percent of the original 3,825,-000-acre objective.

In connection with its newly developed strategies for waterfowl conservation, FWS has designed a new, 10-year acquisition plan to guide its habitat-acquisition efforts (Interior 1985a). The new plan identifies 12 regions of the country where FWS intends to protect more than 2.6 million acres through purchases of land or conservation easements during FY 1987-96. The estimated cost of the program is at least $563 million. The acquisition program is designed especially to benefit these species: northern pintails, mallards, black ducks, ringed-neck ducks, wood ducks, canvasbacks, redheads, and goose populations in the Pacific Flyway (cackling Canada goose, Pacific white front, and Pacific brant).

## Stabilized Hunting Regulations Study

The 1985-86 hunting season marks the end of a five-year study conducted by FWS in cooperation with the states and the Canadian Wildlife Service to determine the effects of "stabilized hunting regulations" on duck populations and take. Prior to the beginning of the study, open seasons, daily bag limits, and other hunting regulations were adjusted yearly in accordance with population fluctuations on the theory that these adjustments had a significant impact on the survival rate of duck-breeding populations from year to year. However, some studies indicate that hunting mortality, at a certain level, does not reduce the following year's breeding population of mallards. Hunters, it is believed, simply kill birds that otherwise would die from other natural causes. This might be true for other duck species, too. If so, it may not be necessary to adjust hunting regulations on a yearly basis if it can be shown that factors such as environmental conditions and habitat availability are the major determinants of population size. However, some studies suggest that hunting is a factor in black duck declines (see the Black Duck chapter in this volume).

A "stabilized regulations study" was launched in 1980 by Canada and the United States for the purpose of evaluating the significance of non-hunting

### Waterfowl Habitat Acquisition Objectives FY 1987-97

| Priority | Area | Acres | Estimated Cost |
|---|---|---|---|
| 1 | Central Valley, California | 80,000 | $57.00M |
| 2 | Prairie Potholes and Parklands | 838,000 | 237.43M |
| 3 | Bottomland Hardwoods | 300,000 | 45.00M |
| 4 | Atlantic Coastal Plain | 50,000 | 15.30M |
| 5 | Gulf Coast | 386,000 | 115.80M |
| 6 | Alaska | 900,000 | 30.00M |
| 7 | Intermountain West | 35,000 | 10.00M |
| 8 | Playa Lakes | 48,000 | 12.00M |
| 9 | Klamath Basin | 1,500 | .50M |
| 10 | Upper Pacific Coast | 50,000 | 40.00M |
| 11 | San Francisco Bay | 3,000 | 5.60M |
| 12 | Additions to existing national wildlife refuges (including inholdings) | Undetermined | Undetermined |
| | | 2,678,500 | $563.85M |

FWS, 1985

mortality on duck populations, the relationship between hunting mortality and other causes of death, and the role of recruitment in affecting population size. Preliminary results of the study are expected to be available beginning in 1986, but the final report will not be issued until 1987. The study will help FWS refine its strategy for setting hunting regulations for the 1987-88 hunting season.

## Migratory Shore and Upland Game Species Management

Migratory shore and upland game birds have never received the same level of attention that FWS devotes to waterfowl. The perception has been that birds in this category are not as greatly threatened by hunting pressure or habitat loss as are waterfowl.

Historically, FWS has paid the most attention to three bird species— woodcock, mourning dove, and sandhill crane—all avidly sought by hunters. FWS conducts annual population-trend surveys for these species. In addition, the states conduct their own population and hunter-take surveys for species such as the band-tailed pigeon and white-winged dove. As it does for waterfowl, FWS, with the advice of the states, promulgates annual regulations for migratory shore and upland game birds that are hunted.

Four species are considered nationally significant: woodcock, mourning dove, white-winged dove, and six distinct populations of sandhill crane, only two of which are hunted. The woodcock is of special concern, since the population-trend survey shows a gradual but continuing decline in the eastern population.

In the mid-1960s, FWS initiated a modest accelerated-research program for migratory shore and upland game birds to collect basic data on their population size, biology, and habitat needs. Commencing in FY 1968, $250,000 was budgeted yearly: $175,000 for state research grants and $75,000 for FWS research and program coordination. The program was terminated in FY 1982 as part of an FWS budget-reduction effort because it was not viewed as a pressing need. Presently, no FWS-sponsored research of any magnitude is being conducted on any migratory shore and upland game species even though significant gaps in knowledge exist.

## Nongame Management

FWS is responsible for managing 772 nongame migratory-bird species. In the late 1970s and early 1980s, FWS expanded its nongame activities and identified several objectives it intended to pursue to improve its understanding and management of these species. One major objective was the identification of birds in danger of decline and the causes for their predicament. Another was the preparation of a national nongame management plan patterned after the national plan for waterfowl.

In July 1982, the Office of Migratory Bird Management released a report, *Nongame Migratory Bird Species with Unstable or Decreasing Population Trends in the United States* (Interior 1982). The report identifies 28 birds "with some evidence of unstable or declining populations in significant portions of their range during the past 10-15 years." The list includes nine wading birds, five raptors, three marine birds, four shore birds, and seven passerines. Five of these have been selected as nationally significant species (see the Status of the Resource section for details).

The list is only a preliminary step in assessing the true status of these birds. FWS used a wide variety of available data in compiling the list, not all of which is considered definitive. Furthermore, little information on the causes of population declines was obtained. The study recommended a number of additional measures to refine the list, including the incorporation of new data sources, periodic updating of the list, development of practical survey programs for species not adequately monitored by the breeding-bird survey, and special investigations of species such as the common loon, roseate tern, and loggerhead shrike. However, no action has been taken to implement most of these recommendations.

FWS has prepared national resource plans for five of the 28 declining species—interior least tern, roseate tern, piping plover, northern spotted owl, and trumpeter swan. In addition, two raptors not on the declining list, the western population of the golden eagle and the osprey, also are the subject of national resource plans. Nongame species also may be designated "regional species of special emphasis" by FWS regional offices, a designation that provides increased management attention at that level. Regionally significant species include the mottled duck (Region 2); common tern and great blue heron (Region 3); snail kite, wood stork, yellow-shouldered blackbird, eastern bluebird, Florida duck, mottled duck, redheaded woodpecker, Caribbean waterfowl, seaside sparrow, and white-crowned pigeon (Region 4); colonial-nesting waterbirds (Region 5); and emperor goose (Region 7).

A draft "Nongame Migratory Bird Management Plan for the United States" (Interior 1983a) was completed in 1983 and cited as an FWS accomplishment in its FY 1985 budget request to Congress. The draft plan identifies general goals, objectives, policies, and strategies for the conservation and management of nongame migratory birds to achieve compliance with the objectives of migratory-bird treaties and legislation. The plan represents the first synthesis of what FWS does or intends to do for nongame birds. Since its submittal, however, FWS has taken no action to seek public comment on the draft plan, to revise it, or, ultimately, to implement it.

In conclusion, FWS has no special program or approved comprehensive plan to guide its efforts in complying with clear treaty and legislative requirements that call for the protection and conservation of nongame migratory birds as well as game species. The modest nongame research program undertaken in the 1970s has been eliminated. While FWS recognizes the need for better monitoring and research on nongame populations and the need for national coordination of nongame migratory-bird conservation efforts, it has been unwilling to reallocate some of its resources from either waterfowl or other resource-management activities to nongame bird species.

Meanwhile, 46 states have established nongame wildlife programs, many of them financed by special funds. These programs cover the full spectrum of nongame wildlife, including migratory birds. The states may conduct conservation activities for bird species under federal authority as long as the activities are consistent with federal laws and regulations. FWS does not coordinate these individual state activities nor does it provide the states with any financial assistance for nongame projects as authorized by the Fish and Wildlife Conservation Act. (For further details on nongame activities, see the federal aid and state nongame chapters).

## Accomplishments

FWS achieved several milestones in its migratory-bird management activities in FY 1985. These included preparation, in cooperation with Canada, of a draft "North American Waterfowl Management Plan," issuance of a supplemental environmental impact statement on lead-shot use in waterfowl hunting, the development of a new cooperative agreement to conserve and manage certain goose populations that breed in Alaska, and the promulgation of new criteria for identifying areas where lead poisoning is a serious problem. Only the North American plan is discussed here. The other accomplishments are covered in the "Problems and Issues" section of this chapter.

*North American Waterfowl Management Plan.* Although the United States and Canada signed the Convention for the Protection of Migratory Birds in 1916, the two nations have never agreed to a common plan of action. However, as wetlands destruction and other threats to migratory birds have increased, and some waterfowl populations have declined, it became imperative for Canada and the United States to develop a more competent approach to resource management. The result is the draft "North American Waterfowl Management Plan," released in December 1985 for public comment (Environment Canada and U.S. Department of the Interior 1985).

The plan identifies major waterfowl-management problems and establishes specific strategies and objectives to solve them. Duck-population objectives are based on population levels that pertained from 1970 to 1979, a time when environmental conditions were good and the fall flight size was estimated to be in excess of 100 million ducks. Objectives for geese and swan populations were set at 1980-84 levels, except for the four species with declining populations and the Aleutian Canada goose, which is listed as endangered.

To reach the population objectives, the plan calls for an ambitious habi-

Breeding Duck Population Status, Trends and Objectives for the 10 Most Common Species in the Surveyed Area.[a]

| Species | Status (1985)[b] | | | Population Trend (1970-1985)[c] | Objectives (year 2000)[d] |
| | United States | Canada | Total | | |
| --- | --- | --- | --- | --- | --- |
| Mallard | 1,597 | 3,878 | 5,475 | Decreasing | 8,700 |
| Pintail | 1,339 | 1,596 | 2,935 | Decreasing | 6,300 |
| Gadwall | 464 | 946 | 1,410 | No change | 1,600 |
| Wigeon | 969 | 1,537 | 2,506 | No change | 3,300 |
| Green-winged teal | 433 | 1,440 | 1,873 | No change | 2,300 |
| Blue-winged and cinnamon teal | 1,190 | 2,566 | 3,756 | Decreasing | 5,300 |
| Shoveler | 769 | 1,156 | 1,925 | No change | 2,100 |
| Redhead | 167 | 539 | 701 | No change | 760 |
| Canvasback | 126 | 285 | 411 | No change | 580 |
| Scaup | 1,339 | 4,893 | 6,235 | No change | 7,600 |

[a] The surveyed area includes Strata 1-50 and data from the six states that contribute information to the annual "Status of Waterfowl and Fall Flight Forecast."
[b] In thousands of ducks.
[c] Status of several species declined significantly in 1985 from previous trends.
[d] The average of 1970-1979 for Strata 1-50 plus six cooperating states.
Source: "North American Waterfowl Management Plan" (Draft 1985)

tat-conservation program estimated to cost Canada $239 million (Canadian dollars) and the United States $717 million (Canadian dollars) over the next 15 years. These expenditures would protect and improve 3.6 million acres of key waterfowl habitat.

In addition, the United States would protect an additional 1,084,000 additional acres of pintail and mallard breeding habitat in the prairie pothole region of the northcentral states; 686,000 acres of mallard and pintail migration and winter habitat in the lower Mississippi Valley; 80,000 acres of wintering habitat in the Central Valley of California; and 50,000 acres of migration and wintering habitat for the black duck on the East Coast and 10,000 acres in the Great Lakes region. These measures would cost an additional $477 million (U.S. dollars). Canada also would protect an additional 70,000 acres at a cost of $25 million (Canadian dollars) for the black duck.

The plan also proposes a new strategy of "stabilized regulations" for duck hunting in the United States and Canada. Under this scheme, hunting regulations would remain fixed for a period of years unless population levels of individual species reached levels that triggered predetermined corrective changes to increase or lower the hunter kill. The precise details of the fixed regulations strategy will be based on the conclusions of the stabilized regulations study. The main reason for this approach is to minimize the amount of time and resources devoted to the annual fine-tuning of regulations—time and resources that could be directed toward other conservation tasks.

FWS expects final approval of the plan sometime in 1986. Once

## Status of and Objectives for North American Goose Populations.[a]

| Species and population | Estimated winter populations (1984-1985) | Recent trend (1980-1984) | Winter population objective (Year 2000) |
|---|---|---|---|
| Canada Goose | | | |
|   Atlantic Flyway | 830,000 | Increasing | 900,000 |
|   Tennessee Valley | 130,000 | Stable | 150,000 |
|   Mississippi Valley | 477,000 | Increasing | 500,000 |
|   Eastern prairie | 168,000 | Stable | 200,000 |
|   Western prairie | 233,000 | Increasing | 200,000[b] |
|   Great Plains | 17,000[c] | Increasing | 50,000[d] |
|   Tallgrass prairie | 279,000 | Increasing | 255,000 |
|   Shortgrass Prairie | 158,000 | Stable | 175,000 |
|   Hi-line | 80,000 | Stable | 80,000 |
|   Rocky Mountain | 73,000 | Stable | 75,000 |
|   Pacific | 24,700[c] | Increasing | 29,000[c] |
|   Lesser Pacific Flyway | 150,000 | Stable | 125,000 |
|   Dusky | 9,000 | Decreasing | 20,000 |
|   Cackling | 23,000 | Decreasing | 250,000[b] |
|   Aleutian | 3,800 | Increasing | Delist[e] |
| Snow Goose | | | |
|   Greater | 200,000 | Increasing | 185,000 |
|   Midcontinent lesser | 1,504,000 | Increasing | 1,000,000[d] |
|   Western Central Flyway | 107,000 | Increasing | 110,000 |
|   Wrangel Island (U.S.S.R.) | No estimate | Stable | 120,000 |
|   Western Canadian Arctic lesser | 185,000[c] | Stable | 120,000[d] |
| Ross' Goose | 106,000 | Increasing | 100,000 |
| White-fronted goose | | | |
|   Eastern midcontinent | 70,000 | Increasing | 80,000 |
|   Western midcontinent | 201,000 | Increasing | 250,000 |
|   Tule | 5,000 | Stable | |
|   Pacific Flyway | 100,000 | Decreasing | 300,000 |
| Black Brant | | | |
|   Atlantic | 124,000 | Increasing | 124,000 |
|   Pacific | 145,000 | Decreasing | 185,000 |

[a]The emperor goose is found only in Alaska and will not be considered in this plan. The Vancouver Canada goose population is also not considered.

[b]Long-term objective fall flight as measured by a fall inventory.

[c]Breeding population information only available.

[d]Breeding population objectives.

[e]Currently listed as an endangered species. Recovery plans specify maintaining a wild population at a level of 1,200 or greater and to re-establish self-sustaining populations of geese (50 breeding pairs per area) on three former breeding areas in addition to Buldir Island.

Source: "North American Waterfowl Management Plan" (Draft 1985)

adopted, the next step is to ensure that FWS waterfowl-management efforts are consistent with the plan and to obtain sufficient resources from private and public sources to implement it.

# Current Issues

Disputes over the management of migratory birds are common among federal and state wildlife agencies, sport-hunting organizations, and wildlife-conservation groups. Some of these disputes, such as that over lead poisoning in waterfowl, have dragged on for years. In 1985, the most controversial issue was the promulgation of duck-hunting regulations that required a 25 percent reduction in the hunter take from the previous year. Other issues include the continuing debate over how to reverse the decline of goose populations in the Pacific Flyway and the effects of tropical deforestation on nongame birds.

## 1985–86 Duck-Hunting Regulations

Hunting regulations promulgated in 1985 by FWS to reduce the number of ducks killed by hunters in the United States by approximately 25 percent proved to be the single most controversial issue of the year. Opponents of the regulations attacked FWS for faulty duck-management strategy and for unnecessarily penalizing hunters for a duck decline not of their making. The debate even led to a hearing before a congressional committee. But in the end, after making some minor modifications to the regulations, FWS prevailed.

Each year, FWS, the Canadian Wildlife Service, and the states conduct surveys of duck breeding grounds to assess environmental conditions, the number of breeding ducks, and their reproductive success. These data are used by FWS to estimate the fall flight size of 14 duck species, and this number in turn is used to determine how many or how few ducks should be taken that season. Hunting regulations are then promulgated which would achieve acceptable hunter kill levels.

The 1985 survey indicated that the duck breeding population had declined from about 38 million in 1984 to 30 million, a 19 percent reduction, and the lowest level in the 31 years that the survey has been made. Numbers of breeding mallards fell to 5.4 million, and pintails dropped to 2.9 million, both record lows for these avidly hunted species. All other species declined as well, except for green-winged teal, which increased by four percent. The overall decline in the breeding population is attributed to a long drought in the breeding area, which has dried up ponds and wetlands needed by breeding ducks, and to the extensive modification of ponds, wetlands, and contiguous uplands by agricultural practices.

The estimated 1985 fall flight of ducks, 62 million, was 22 percent less than the 1984 estimated flight of 80 million, and the lowest on record in the 16 years FWS had been estimating fall-flight size. The largest fall flight of ducks, 100 million, occurred in 1972.

In response to this situation, the Canadian Wildlife Service proposed hunting regulations for the 1985-86 season designed to reduce by 25 percent the number of ducks that would be killed if the 1984-85 regulations remained unchanged. FWS agreed with the Canadian assessment of the situation and proposed similar regulations. The reduction was to be achieved by changing the opening and closing dates of the hunting season and reducing the daily bag limit, with the changes varying from flyway to flyway. The principal reason for reducing the total take, said FWS, was to ensure that duck populations could recover more rapidly when environmental and habitat conditions become more favorable. FWS feared that a continued U.S. take of 12 million ducks yearly—the 1984-85 estimated take—would reduce the total number of breeding pairs that survived the hunting and winter seasons, and that this in turn would hinder population increases in ensuing years.

The FWS proposal quickly drew praise from some states, hunter organizations, and conservation groups, but criticism from others. Among other charges, the FWS strategy was said to be too restrictive in certain flyways where winter duck populations did not originate in the prairie potholes and were alleged to be stable or increasing, such as in the Atlantic Flyway. The shortening of the season length was criticized for unfairly restricting hunting opportunity in states where a higher percentage of the take occurred at either the beginning or end of the season. Also, it was alleged that the FWS objective of protecting mallards and pintails could be achieved by limiting the take of females without restricting the take of males. In addition, Ducks Unlimited opposed any reduction in hunter take from the 1984 level on the grounds that the birds killed by hunters otherwise would die of other environmental or natural causes; that FWS had no evidence to show that reducing hunter take would, in fact, produce more breeding birds the following year; and that FWS estimates of the 1985 breeding population were based on an unexplained, exceptional loss of ducks, from the 1984 fall-flight estimate of 80 million to the 1985 breeding population of 30 million, a 62.5 percent reduction (Shepherd 1985).*

Under severe pressure, FWS modified its final hunting regulations to accommodate some of its critics as follows:

- An experimental Northeast hunting zone was established in the Atlantic Flyway with a daily bag limit of five instead of the proposed four, and no restrictions were placed on mallards. The states had argued that the wintering population of mallards in the Atlantic Flyway was increasing and that the source of these birds was eastern Canada, not the prairie region where duck populations had declined.

* FWS officials say that a change of this magnitude has occurred three times since 1969 and that the decline is not due to faulty survey procedures.

- The hunting season opening date was advanced by three days in the Central and Mississippi flyways.
- Daily bag limits in the Pacific Flyway were modified to allow five mallards or five pintails or any combination of the two, provided that no more than one hen mallard and one hen pintail are included in the daily bag.

The changes, say FWS officials, had minor influences on the overall 25 percent reduction goal, but probably will result in unequal levels of take reductions in each flyway.

To cap the whole process, the House Subcommittee on Fisheries and Wildlife held a hearing September 17, 1985, on the formulation of the hunting regulations at which FWS was pummeled by its critics and upheld by its supporters. The hearing elicited virtually the same points, arguments, and complaints raised throughout the regulations development process and in the end resulted in no congressional pressure to change the regulations. In defending FWS actions, Director Robert Jantzen underscored the need for prudence in dealing with a complex biological resource about which much remains to be learned:

> While the Service recognizes that long-term declines in habitat have contributed to the present status of duck populations, we also feel that recent populations of ducks have declined to such levels that regulations must be conservative to allow the birds the best chance of recovery when habitat conditions improve in the primary breeding areas. Our decision to recommend restrictive regulations was not based on the single indication of a greatly reduced fall flight, but instead from many long- and short-term indicators that duck populations and their habitats are presently in poor condition.

> The Service feels that protecting a depleted breeding population requires positive action. Therefore, we recommended, based on our best biological judgment, a 25 percent reduction in harvest as the minimum level likely to produce a positive, measurable impact on the population. Attempts at lesser reductions might prove cosmetic or too small to detect trends, and could well be overwhelmed by climatological or other variables which affect harvest profoundly. We hope that such a reduction will assist the recovery of duck populations. The risk that a high harvest will have a detrimental effect on the low populations we have observed is too great to take while populations and their habitats are under stress (Jantzen 1985).

## Toxic Poisoning from Lead Shot

For some 10 years, the issue of how to prevent the poisoning of waterfowl by spent lead shot has kept FWS, state wildlife agencies, and conservation and hunter organizations at loggerheads. As yet, no satisfactory resolution of the controversy appears to be in sight.

It has been known for decades that migratory waterfowl may be poisoned by spent lead shot ingested while feeding. FWS estimates that 1.6 million to 2.4 million waterfowl die yearly from lead poisoning (Interior 1976). More recently, it has been recognized that other migratory species have been poisoned as well, either from direct ingestion or, as is the case for scavenging birds such as the bald eagle, from eating the flesh of other birds that contain lead pellets.

In 1976, FWS decided to ban the use of lead shot for waterfowl hunting only in areas, including national wildlife refuges, determined to have high accumulations of spent shot. The principal rationale for this limited "hot spot" approach, say FWS officials, was that a total ban on lead-shot use would be economically costly to hunters generally, and noticeably so for individual hunters who would have to buy new shotguns that can use steel shot. In addition, the killing efficiency of lead shot was believed to be better than steel, and numerous studies were conducted in an attempt to obtain conclusive evidence.* FWS "hot-spot" strategy has remained in place ever since, but even the closure by FWS of a limited number of problem areas to lead-shot use has provoked strong and continuing hunter opposition in a few states.

A number of conservation organizations believe that the only way to end the lead-poisoning problem is to require the use of steel shot nationwide for all waterfowl hunting. Proponents of a national lead-shot ban argue that dealing only with the most contaminated areas still leaves waterfowl and other birds, especially raptors, at risk, since they may still ingest pellets deposited on less contaminated areas. In short, say critics of the FWS strategy, too many birds still are dying from lead poisoning. The National Wildlife Federation has been continually in the vanguard of lead-shot opposition. Other organizations favoring a total switch from lead to steel shot for waterfowl hunting include the Wildlife Society, the National Audubon Society, and the Atlantic, Mississippi, and Central flyway councils.

Opponents of steel-shot use gained an advantage when Senator Ted Stevens (R-AK) added a directive to the FY 1978 Interior Appropriations Bill that requires FWS to obtain state approval before designating steel-shot zones on any lands within a state, including zones on federal refuge lands. This provision has been included in each subsequent appropriation bill.

Gradually, FWS has been documenting the need to identify more areas as steel-shot zones, but the Stevens amendment has played havoc with FWS' ability to protect migrating birds from lead-shot poisoning, even on its own refuge lands. On October 30, 1984, FWS proposed the use of steel shot in portions of 32 states, including 65 national wildlife refuges, five of which were requiring steel shot for the first time. Three states—Nevada, Montana, and California—rejected the designation of any steel-shot zones within their borders. Thus, the FWS attempt to protect birds on its own refuge lands in

---

* The killing-efficiency debate continues to the present. However, some observers say that the difference between lead and steel are not that great, certainly not great enough to outweigh the bird-death-prevention benefits than a total ban on lead shot would achieve.

Nevada (Stillwater National Wildlife Refuge), California (Tule Lake and Lower Klamath national wildlife refuges), and Montana (Benton Lake National Wildlife Refuge) was thwarted.

Believing that it had adequate data to justify the use of steel shot on the disputed refuges, FWS in 1985 notified the states that it would use its authority under the Migratory Bird Treaty Act to close selected refuges to waterfowl hunting for the 1986-87 season if the states concerned did not approve the designation of steel-shot zones on those refuges. The possibility of a hunting closure quickly led to approvals by California, Nevada, and Montana.

*Bald Eagles and Lead Shot.* In a related development, FWS took action in 1985 to protect the bald eagle—an endangered or threatened species in 48 states—from lead poisoning. The action was prompted by steady pressure, and ultimately a lawsuit, from the National Wildlife Federation.

Bald eagles become susceptible to lead poisoning when they ingest lead pellets imbedded in the flesh of crippled and dead waterfowl. Data collected by FWS indicate that since 1966, 105 bald eagles have died from lead poisoning and another 91 have been diagnosed as dying of other causes but with elevated levels of lead in their bodies.

The federation in August 1984 petitioned FWS to designate six counties as steel-shot areas to protect the eagle for the 1984-85 hunting season, and another 89 counties for the 1985-86 season. After seeking comments on the federation proposal, FWS on February 13, 1985 proposed steel shot zones to help protect bald eagles in 30 counties in California, Illinois, Iowa, Kansas, Missouri, Oklahoma, Oregon, and South Dakota.

After Illinois, Missouri, Oklahoma, California, and Oregon failed to give their approval to the designations, FWS in May 1985 designated 12 counties in three states as steel-shot zones. However, at the same time, it issued a notice of intent not to open state-vetoed areas to waterfowl hunting in 1987-88, unless such areas were approved by the states as steel-shot zones.

Citing FWS action as unacceptable and inconsistent with the Interior Department's stewardship responsibilities under the Migratory Bird Treaty and Endangered Species acts (Hair 1985), the National Wildlife Federation filed suit to obtain a court order to require the use of steel shot on, or the federal closure of hunting in, the areas in 30 counties originally proposed by FWS on February 13. On August 26, 1985, the federal District Court for the Eastern District of California issued an order requiring the use of steel shot in the 30 counties (*National Wildlife Federation v. Hodel*, 23 ERC 1089). The court found that the FWS failure to require steel shot was a violation of the Endangered Species Act prohibition against the taking of an endangered species and also a violation of the act's mandate that all reasonable actions be taken to recover a species to a more sound biological status. A last minute attempt by the National Rifle Association and the Wildlife Legislative Fund of America to stay the injunction was rejected by the U.S. Court of Appeals, 9th Circuit, on October 3.

It is unclear whether or not the federation suit will have a significant impact on the FWS steel-shot-zone designation process or whether FWS will continue to designate more areas to protect eagles. However, what is clear is that states that use their power under the Stevens amendment to block steel-shot-zone designations will face a double threat: If the use of steel-shot zones is justified to protect the bald eagle or any other endangered species, FWS can unilaterally invoke the designations under the Endangered Species Act; alternatively, FWS can use its authority under the Migratory Bird Treaty Act to protect migratory birds from lead-shot hazards by closing areas to hunting. And if FWS fails to use these authorities, private organizations such as the National Wildlife Federation, can always drag it back into court.

*New Criteria for Identification of Lead-Shot Problem Areas.* In 1985, FWS promulgated new guidelines which specify criteria for determining whether or not an area should be considered a lead-shot hazard area and hence suitable for designation as a steel-shot zone. According to FWS, the new guidelines were necessary because no uniform methodology was being applied by FWS and the states nationwide, some of the methods in use are controversial, and many states and conservation organizations have requested clearer guidance from FWS regarding the scientifically objective identification of problem areas.

The guidelines were issued July 30, 1985, (50 FR 30849) after extensive consultation with interested parties. The guidelines include "triggering" criteria for initial selection and monitoring of counties or areas that have the potential for a lead-shot poisoning problem and "decision" criteria for determining whether or not a problem actually exists.

A county or area will be triggered for monitoring by the states if there are large numbers of waterfowl killed (and hence a high incidence of spent lead shot) or if three waterfowl are diagnosed as having died there of lead poisoning during the year. Since the states with large areas open to waterfowl hunting may not have the resources to monitor all areas with high kill levels, FWS established a phased monitoring program:

| Kill Level (birds per square mile) | Hunting Season Monitoring to Begin |
|---|---|
| 20 | 1985-86 |
| 15 | 1986-87 |
| 10 | 1987-88 |
| 5 | 1988-89 |

States with less than five birds killed per square mile would not be expected to monitor for lead-shot problems.

If either of the triggering criteria are met, then monitoring is to begin to determine whether a lead-shot problem does in fact exist. An area is considered to have a significant lead-shot problem if, based on a sample size of 100 birds, one or more lead pellets is found in five percent or more gizzards examined; lead levels in five percent or more of the liver tissues sampled are two part per million or greater; or 0.2 parts per million of lead is found in five percent or more of the blood samples taken (or alternatively, a protoporphyrin level of 40 ug/dl exists).

If study results are positive for the gizzard criterion plus either the liver blood or photoporphyrin criteria, the area will be proposed as a nontoxic zone. If the results are negative, the area will be considered not to pose a significant lead-poisoning problem unless at a future date three or more birds are diagnosed as having died of lead poisoning, at which time the area would be remonitored.

FWS expects the states to conduct the monitoring program outlined in the guidelines. If they do not, FWS has indicated that it will propose areas targeted for monitoring as steel-shot zones and may not open the areas to waterfowl hunting if the states refuse to approve the zones.

The FWS guidelines do not prevent the states from designating steel-shot zones where lead levels are below the "decision" criteria. Also, FWS will continue to honor state requests that FWS declare steel-shot zones on refuges or other areas that are below the minimum-decision criteria.

*Supplemental Environmental Impact Statement on Lead Poisoning.* FWS issued an "Environmental Impact Statement on Lead Shot Poisoning" in 1976 (Interior 1976) when it adopted its "hot-spot" approach to selecting areas for steel-shot designation. Since then, significant amounts of new data on the lead-poisoning problem have been developed, including state surveys and clinical studies, ballistics studies comparing the killing efficiency of steel vs. lead shot, and information on lead poisoning in migratory birds other than waterfowl, such as the bald eagle. In addition, FWS has revised its criteria for identifying areas with lead shot problems and has taken new measures to protect areas where bald eagles are likely to be poisoned.

Because of these developments, FWS in December 1985 issued a "Draft Supplemental Environmental Impact Statement on the Use of Lead Shot for Hunting Migratory Birds in the United States" (Interior 1985b). After a round of public hearings and opportunity for written comments, FWS intends to issue a final version of the report in 1986. The draft recommends that FWS continue with its current hot-spot strategy for identifying lead-shot problem areas.

## The Effects of Tropical Deforestation on United States Birds

An issue of growing interest to conservation organizations in the United States is the effect that tropical deforestation is having on 332 Nearctic species, birds that breed in the United States in the summer and winter in the tropics (see the chapter on the hooded warbler in this volume). A few studies have shown that populations of certain Nearctic migrants have disappeared from areas in the United States where they once were present. The reason for their disappearance has not been adequately explained. One theory holds that the disappearance is a result of habitat disturbance and resultant forest fragmentation in North America. A conflicting theory states that land-use changes—especially deforestation—in the tropics of Mexico and of Central and South America are the major reason for the disappearance.

The FWS has devoted some resources to documenting the problem, but the level of commitment is inadequate. In cooperation with the World Wildlife Fund, FWS in 1983 published a report, *Nearctic Avian Migrants in the Neotropics* (Interior 1983b), which synthesizes known information about these species. FWS also initiated in 1983 a modest, three-year research and training program to gather field data on forest fragmentation in the neotropics in cooperation with Latin American biologists. The total cost of the study is estimated to be about $150,000, of which $30,000 is provided by the FWS International Affairs Office with a portion of its appropriation for implementing the Western Hemisphere Convention. The study is designed to determine whether or not there is a statistically relevant correlation between forest size and the abundance of certain bird species. The study will be completed in 1986 or 1987, but there is no guarantee that further investigations will continue.

Without a credible research effort, FWS cannot fully meet its treaty and statutory responsibilities to protect and conserve all species of migratory birds. Obtaining adequate scientific evidence on Nearctic migrants will require a much larger commitment of research dollars than currently is being expended.

## Reversing the Decline of Pacific Flyway Geese

A steady decline over the past 20 years in the breeding populations of four goose species—greater white front, Pacific brant, emperor, and cackling Canada—that breed in Alaska's Yukon-Kuskokwim (Y-K) Delta and winter in Pacific Flyway states and Mexico has prompted a cooperative effort by FWS, the Alaska Department of Fish and Game, Native Alaskan Eskimos, and the California Department of Fish and Game to correct the problem. Cackling Canada geese have declined 94 percent since 1965, Pacific white-fronted geese have dropped 78 percent since 1967, black brant 23 percent since 1979, and emperor geese 49 percent since 1964.

The "The Yukon-Kuskokwim Delta Goose Management Plan," which replaced the "Hooper Bay Agreement," was signed in March, 1985. (Interior 1985c) The purpose of the new plan is to restore goose populations to specified higher levels. Specifically, the Yukon-Kuskokwim plan:

- Prohibits any hunting of the cackling Canada goose, or the collection of its eggs, until the breeding population exceeds 110,000. The cackler's 94 percent decline, from its 1965 population estimate of 350,000 to 21,800 in 1984, is so drastic that some biologists believe the bird should be listed as an endangered species.*

- Establishes optimum-population objectives for all four species, and minimum-population levels below which any hunting of the species would be prohibited.
- Prohibits the collection of eggs of all four species.
- Prohibits the hunting by Eskimos of white fronts, emperors, and Pacific brants during the nesting season.
- Expands and improves harvest surveys.
- Establishes a plan for monitoring, verifying, and enforcing hunting restrictions.

In addition, FWS, with the assistance of the National Audubon Society, has launched an educational program to inform Eskimos and Pacific Flyway hunters about the need for the plan and has intensified its research efforts to learn more about the habitat requirements and biological status of the geese and more about the threats to goose survival.

Meanwhile, a suit was filed in 1984 by Alaska sportsmen groups to void both the Hooper Bay and subsequent Yukon-Kuskokwin agreements (*Alaska Fish and Wildlife Federation and Outdoor Council v. Jantzen, et al*). The plaintiffs sought to require FWS to prohibit the killing of geese by Alaskan Eskimos during the spring and summer, an action they maintained was required by the Migratory Bird Treaty Act. However, in January 1986 the federal judge rejected the plaintiff's suit and ruled that FWS has the legal authority to permit subsistence hunting of the geese by Natives.

FWS officials acknowledge that subsistence hunting is one contributing factor in the decline of goose populations, but they contend that the strict enforcement called for by sport hunters would be difficult to achieve and counterproductive to the long-term survival of the geese. The Yukon-Kuskokwim Delta alone covers some 20 million acres, an area larger than South Carolina. Past FWS attempts to arrest and fine Eskimos for hunting violations have brought little success and have resulted in a deterioration of relations between Eskimos and government agencies. Another reason FWS also has been reluctant to enforce the treaty is because it recognizes the traditional, cultural, and subsistence importance of the spring/summer goose hunt to the Eskimos. Sport-hunting groups take special exception to this argument, claiming that subsistence hunting is an anachronism, since Alaskan Natives use modern weapons to pursue their quarry and Eskimo communities are expanding rapidly and modernizing.

So far, the Yukon-Kuskokwim plan is working, according to an FWS report to the federal judge hearing the case:

---

* A recent FWS-sponsored study of the cackler indicates the 1984-85 wintering population may be as high as 38,500, and the 1985 fall staging population, 41,200.

The 1985 Y-K Delta Goose Management Plan has been highly successful in virtually all respects. It led to the acquisition of new biological information already being used to refine the direction of future management actions. It resulted in excellent cooperation by subsistence hunters in a systematically designed waterfowl harvest survey that provides a firm baseline from which to compare numbers of geese taken in future years. It has substantially reduced egg gathering activities and appears to have reduced hunting for the species covered by the plan. It provided impetus and a mechanism for development and implementation of an expanded cooperative program to inform hunters on the Y-K Delta and elsewhere about the status of arctic nesting geese and the flyway-wide restrictions on harvest of those species. Finally, by recognizing Y-K Delta residents as necessary participants in the management of the resource, the plan has increased their motivation to share responsibility for the protection of the four species of geese.

With increased involvement in management comes increased accountability. On the Y-K Delta, increased accountability already has been translated into changes in attitudes and behavior. The emphasis on obtaining voluntary compliance with harvest restrictions and the degree of commitment that appears to be surfacing is unprecedented in waterfowl management. It sets the stage for wise use of the resource as we collectively begin the task of rebuilding populations of geese on the Delta (Interior 1985d).

In the long-run, FWS wants to legitimize Eskimo subsistence hunting allowed by the Yukon-Kuskokwim plan by amending the 1916 Convention for the Protection of Migratory Birds. The treaty was negotiated without consideration of Eskimo subsistence practices, and FWS believes that the Eskimos must be included as cooperative partners in wildlife management if goose populations are to be protected. The United States and Canada negotiated a protocol amending the treaty in 1979, but objections by the International Association of Fish and Wildlife Agencies and hunting organizations over the vague wording of the document have sent FWS and Canadian officials back to the negotiating table.

In addition to the Yukon-Kuskokwim plan, another idea that could help the geese is the creation of nesting sanctuaries where no hunting would be allowed. Such refuges could be created by the Eskimos on their own lands, by FWS on the Yukon Delta National Wildlife Refuge, and by Alaska on state lands. This concept is just starting to be discussed, but has obvious potential. All species of geese are fairly prolific, given good nesting, migration, and wintering habitat, so there appears to be no reason why the Yukon-Kuskokwim Delta populations can not be brought back (Laycock 1985).

## Legislation

During the first session of the 99th Congress (1985-86), several proposals were considered to protect migratory bird habitat:

## Emergency Wetlands Resources Act

Declining waterfowl populations and the continued destruction of interior wetlands and associated upland areas that provide breeding habitat for North American duck species have rekindled congressional interest in conserving more duck habitat before it is degraded or destroyed. A comprehensive wetlands conservation measure, the Protect Our Wetlands and Duck Resources Act (S. 978, H.R. 2268), was submitted by the Reagan administration in early 1983. Eventually, the House passed H.R. 3082, the Emergency Wetlands Resources Act, and two Senate committees reported a similar measure, S. 1329, but that was as far as either bill went.

In 1985, emergency wetlands measures similar to those reported in 1984 were reintroduced in both houses. The House Merchant Marine Committee reported its bill, H.R. 1203, in May 1985, but did not bring the measure up for a floor vote. The House measure, sponsored by Representative John Breaux (D-LA), would:

- Increase the amount of revenue going into the migratory bird conservation fund by authorizing the collection of admission fees at certain national wildlife refuges and gradually increasing the cost of the federal duck stamp from $7.50 to $15.00 over a five-year period.
- Establish a new federal-state cooperative program to acquire, preserve, and enhance wetlands. The program would be financed by a new Wetlands Conservation Fund established by the legislation and financed by the transfer of $75 million yearly from the Land and Water Conservation Fund. Up to two-thirds of the amount appropriated from the fund each year would be made available for matching grants to the states on a 75-percent-federal/25-percent-state basis. The remainder would go to the secretary of the Interior to acquire wetland areas identified in a national wetland priority conservation plan prepared by him.
- Require that half the amount appropriated for state grants be allocated on the basis of each state's past expenditures for wetlands conservation. Allocation of the other half would be based on the need to fund priority projects identified in the national priority plan. The states may become eligible to receive federal assistance either by preparing a comprehensive wetlands conservation plan or by submitting individual projects for approval by the secretary.
- Provide additional funding authority to accelerate the National Wetlands Inventory Project, the purpose of which is to classify and map all the wetland and deepwater habitat in the United States. Top priorities for mapping are the entire coastal zone, flood plains of major river systems, and the prairie pothole region, where a large portion of North American ducks nest and breed.
- Mandate a comprehensive report to Congress on the causes of wetlands destruction and loss to include an analysis of federal laws and programs

that induce wetlands destruction, a discussion of the costs of these losses to the federal government, and recommended management alternatives for wetlands.

- Repeal the provision of the Wetlands Loan Act that calls for repayment of all appropriations made under the act—about $175 million through FY 1985—with future duck-stamp receipts.

The Senate bill, S. 740, introduced by Senator John Chafee (R-RI), is similar to the House measure with these exceptions:

- In addition to repealing the repayment requirement for appropriations advanced to the migratory bird conservation fund, S. 740 extends the Wetlands Loan Act another 10 years. The act expires at the end of FY 1986.
- The Senate bill provides an additional source of revenue for the migratory bird conservation fund by diverting import duties collected on firearms and ammunition from the general Treasury to the fund.

Passage of wetlands legislation in 1986 has been clouded by potentially large-scale cuts in domestic spending programs that would occur under the Gramm-Rudman-Hollings balanced-budget law. If such cuts do occur, the political climate for enacting new spending measures is likely to be highly unfavorable.

## Tax-Code Changes That Promote Conservation

During the 98th Congress, hearings were held on two different measures, S. 1675 and H.R. 5900, that would have provided tax incentives for private landowners who sell or donate their land, including wetlands, for conservation purposes or who undertake conservation measures on their property. Neither of these measures was reintroduced in 1985. However, Senator John Chafee (R-RI) has introduced a new measure, S. 1839, that would deny tax deductions or credits to individuals or corporations that develop designated areas of ecological significance called "environmental zones."

The purpose of the bill, says Chafee, is to end federal support for development activities that take place within certain environmental zones that the government is trying to protect under other programs. The measure defines "environmental zone" to include any area:

- within a critical habitat designated under the Endangered Species Act;
- authorized by Congress or designated by the secretaries of the Interior or Agriculture for inclusion, but not yet included in, the national park, wildlife refuge or forest systems;
- within a unit of the Coastal Barrier Resources System;
- designated as a national natural landmark under the Historic Sites, Buildings, and Antiquities Act;

- authorized by Congress for study as a potential unit of the Wild and Scenic River System.

Although the Chafee bill would deny certain tax subsidies for development activities on private lands within environmental zones, it does not prohibit a private party from undertaking the development activity. Chafee hopes that if passed, the bill would discourage the development of wetlands and other significant ecological areas by making such development more uneconomical.

The measure has been referred to the Senate Finance Subcommittee on Taxation, which Chafee chairs. Thus, the prospects are good that the bill will at least receive a fair hearing. However, the track record for tax bills promoting conservation has not been good. A conservation tax measure has not been approved since 1980, when Congress reauthorized on a permanent basis the conservation-easement law. Since that time, several other tax bills have been introduced, but none of them has ever been reported out of committee.

## Fish and Wildlife Coordination Act Amendments

In 1985, the House passed a bill, H.R. 2704, sponsored by Representative John Breaux (D-LA) that would make several changes in fish and wildlife planning and mitigation activities conducted under the Fish and Wildlife Coordination Act. Among other things, the bill would:

- Make clear that water-resource agencies must consult with both FWS and the National Marine Fisheries Service over the impacts of water projects on fish and wildlife resources.
- Mandate the transfer of funds from water-development agencies to FWS and the National Marine Fisheries Service as appropriate, to pay for biological studies. Although the transfer of the funds is authorized by current law, the mandatory requirement has been added because "transfer of funds has not always proceeded in a consistent and reliable fashion" (U.S. Congress, House 1985).
- Authorize fish and wildlife mitigation measures on lands outside a project area and define mitigation to be consistent with regulations implementing the National Environmental Policy Act. This provision, according to the House Merchant Marine and Fisheries Committee, would facilitate the use of innovative conflict-resolution techniques such as mitigation banking. Mitigation banking is a procedure whereby a private developer is allowed to establish "habitat credits" by protecting or managing certain areas for the benefit of wildlife. These credits then may be used to offset habitat losses caused by the developer in another location. The report accompanying H.R. 2704 states that "mitigation banking" cannot "be used to circumvent existing regulations or policies relative to development in wetlands areas." (U.S. Congress, House 1985).

- Require follow-up studies by FWS, the National Marine Fisheries Service, and water-resource agencies to determine the extent to which recommended fish and wildlife measures are incorporated in project plans and actually carried out. A 1982 study by the National Marine Fisheries Council showed that noncompliance with its recommendations for projects in the southeastern region ran as high as 25 percent.
- Authorize the secretaries of Commerce and the Interior to negotiate long-term plans that reconcile fish-conservation and wildlife-conservation objectives with water-resource development objectives. The goal is to provide assurance to biological-resource agencies, private developers and government development agencies that once designed and under way, a project will proceed without further delays, and each party will know precisely what its obligations and responsibilities are. A similar planning provision was added to the Endangered Species Act in 1982.

According to one FWS official, the effect of the legislation would be minor because it does not address the central defect of the Coordination Act: providing FWS equal status with the water-development agencies, which in turn would give FWS better clout for promoting wildlife conservation throughout the project planning process. No companion bill to H.R. 2704 was introduced in the Senate in 1985, and there is no guarantee that the Senate Environment and Public Works Committee will report Coordination Act amendments in 1986. The Committee failed even to consider a similar measure passed by the House in 1984.

## Farm-Bill Provisions for Land Conservation

The Food Security Act, also called the Farm Bill, passed by Congress and enacted into law in 1985 (P.L. 99-198), has the potential to restore millions of acres of migratory-bird habitat. The conversion of wetlands and associated upland areas to cropland is a major cause of the loss of migratory bird habitat. The main conservation features of the Farm Bill penalize farmers who convert this important habitat into cropland and pay farmers to return cropland to grassland. The utility of these provisions to migratory waterfowl, however, will depend a great deal on how the Department of Agriculture interprets the law in the regulations it will issue in 1986 and on its subsequent ability and willingness to enforce the regulations.

Two of the most important conservation components of the Farm Bill are its so-called "swampbuster" and "sodbuster" provisions. They deny federal farm subsidies (price supports, crop insurance, disaster payments, loans) to farmers who, after enactment of the law,* convert wetlands or highly erodible land (often grasslands) into cropland. It is hoped that farmers will decide

---

* By 1995, all highly erodible lands, even those cropped prior to enactment of the law, must be tilled under an approved conservation plan or the farmer will be denied federal subsidies.

that it is ecomonically more valuable to maintain federal subsidies for their entire farm than it is for them to convert wetlands or erosion-prone acres to cropland. The sodbuster and swampbuster provisions are expected to reduce significantly the rate of interior-wetlands drainage nationwide and save grass-land areas needed by migratory birds for nesting habitat.

Another significant component of the Farm Bill is the Conservation Reserve Program. The secretary of Agriculture is authorized to sign long-term contracts (at least 10 years) with farmers to take erosion-prone acreage out of production. Under these contracts, the Department of Agriculture would make annual rental payments, provide technical assistance, and pay up to 50 percent of the cost of converting the land to less intensive uses than cropland. Most of the reserved land will be converted to grasses. The 40 to 45 million acre reserve program presents a unique opportunity to restore millions of acres of upland migratory-bird nesting habitat.

Finally, hundreds of thousands of wetlands could be restored and protected by the conservation easement program authorized by the Farm Bill. Section 1318 of the statute authorizes the secretary of Agriculture to reduce the debts of farmers close to defaulting on their Farmers Home Administration loans in return for the donation of conservation easements of 50 years or more on portions of their lands suitable for wildlife. The secretary must consult with FWS in selecting land suitable for easements, formulating the management terms of the easement, and enforcing the terms. Many farmers near default are located in key states of the Central and Mississippi flyways. According to FWS, the provision could be used to return to wetlands status thousands of acres that have been drained in the Mississippi Delta.

# Legal Developments

Court cases involving migratory-bird law continue to arise principally in the context of criminal prosecutions. Of these, *U.S. v. Dion* (762 F.2nd [8th Cir. 1985]) is discussed in the endangered species chapter.

In *U.S. v. Wulff* (758 F.2nd 1121 [6th Cir. 1985]), the court of appeals found a provision of the Migratory Bird Treaty Act unconstitutional. Robert Wulff had been indicted under the act for selling to an FWS agent a necklace made of red-tailed hawk and great-horned owl talons. The circuit court upheld a previous decision to dismiss the charges, even though under the Migratory Bird Treaty Act sale of such a necklace is a felony even if the seller does not know he is breaking the law. The circuit court reasoned that, as the offense was not one recognized under common law, it would be a violation of due process to impose the heavy penalties of a felony convinction for a crime that, by statute, does not require the prosecutor to prove the defendant acted with criminal intent.

In *U.S. v. Chandler* (753 F2nd 360 [4th Cir. 1985]), the court affirmed the criminal convictions of defendants charged with attempting to take waterfowl by baiting them, a violation of Migratory Bird Treaty Act regulations. Reviewing the criminal convictions of hunters charged with taking waterfowl over a baited area, the court upheld FWS regulations that require no proof that the hunters had done the baiting themselves or that the hunters could reasonably have known the area was baited.

In the past few years, the courts have repeatedly affirmed the broad authority of FWS to manage migratory birds. In a series of criminal prosecutions under the Migratory Bird Treaty Act, the courts upheld convictions for offenses ranging from hunting waterfowl over baited fields (*United States v. Brant*) to abrogation of conservation easements held by FWS (*United States v. Seest*).

In civil litigation, the courts have upheld FWS migratory-bird-management decisions. The courts approved an FWS decision to allow continued hunting of black ducks, despite recent population declines (*Humane Society of the United States v. Watt*), and rebuffed Nevada's challenge to FWS authority to protect migratory birds on the Ruby Lake National Wildlife Refuge (*Nevada v. United States*). The Supreme Court also rejected an attempt by North Dakota to limit the FWS authority to acquire interests in land under the Migratory Bird Hunting Stamp Act of 1934 and the Wetlands Loan Act of 1961. The prairie potholes of North Dakota are some of the richest waterfowl breeding areas in the United States. In 1961, FWS began acquiring easements to protect these wetlands, using duck-stamp funds. These areas, known as waterfowl production areas, became part of the National Wildlife Refuge system. The Wetlands Loan Act requires the governor's approval for the acquisition of lands or interests in lands and water, and for 16 years, a succession of North Dakota governors had approved the easement purchase program. In 1977, however, the state enacted statutes attempting to limit the acquisition program. The United States filed suit, arguing that the North Dakota statutes were an unconstitutional infringement on federal authority. The Supreme Court agreed, holding that a state's consent, once given, to allow easement purchases, could not be conditioned or withdrawn (*North Dakota v. United States*).

## Status of the Resource

FWS does not have a centralized, comprehensive system for monitoring the 831 migratory birds under its authority, but it does attempt to monitor the population trends of several hundred species. Certain species of ducks, all goose populations, and some swans are monitored intensively through a variety of survey methods and census techniques. Three migratory shore and upland game birds—woodcocks, mourning doves, and sandhill cranes—also are surveyed annually.

An effort is made with a national breeding-bird survey to develop annual population-trend information for other game and nongame birds. Coordinated by FWS, but conducted principally by volunteers, the breeding-bird survey provides population and distribution information on about 500 birds. FWS also coordinates counts of migrating raptors at six different locations around the country.

FWS has selected 54 species or distinct populations of species—39 waterfowl, nine shore and upland game birds, and six nongame birds—as significant species for which it has prepared national resource plans. These species are the foci of FWS migratory-bird-management efforts. The Office of Migratory Bird Management coordinates the preparation of population objectives and management strategies for each of the 54 species. A brief summary of the population status and FWS objectives for each species is given in the appendix. Highlights of the status of major species groups are provided here. The *Audubon Wildlife Report 1985* contains more extensive discussions of individual species of waterfowl and migratory shore and upland game birds.

## Ducks

FWS, in cooperation with the Canadian Wildlife Service, various provinces, and states, conducts aerial surveys and collects other data to develop annual

Duck Breeding Population Estimates, 1984-85 (excludes scoters, eiders, oldsquaws, and mergansers).

| Survey area | (estimates in thousands) | | Percent Change |
| --- | --- | --- | --- |
| | 1984 | 1985 | |
| Alaska-Old Crow | 5,109 | 3,564 | −30 |
| N. Alberta-Northwest Territories | 10,661 | 6,852 | −36 |
| N. Saskatchewan-N. Manitoba-W. Ontario | 3,364 | 3,685 | +10 |
| S. Alberta | 2,860 | 3,406 | +19 |
| S. Saskatchewan | 5,355 | 6,060 | +13 |
| S. Manitoba | 838 | 1,050 | +25 |
| Montana | 750 | 492 | −34 |
| Wyoming | 585 | 288 | −51 |
| Colorado | 110 | 110* | NC |
| North Dakota | 3,972 | 2,459 | −38 |
| South Dakota | 3,301 | 1,765 | −47 |
| Nebraska | 154 | 75 | −51 |
| Minnesota | 621 | 644 | +4 |
| California | 123 | 168 | +37 |
| Wisconsin | 249 | 263 | +6 |
| Total | 38,052 | 30,881 | −19 |

* No survey in 1985; figure represents 1984 survey results.

breeding-population estimates for 14 species of ducks on selected breeding grounds in Alaska, Canada, and the United States: mallard, gadwall, American wigeon, green-winged teal, blue-winged teal, northern shoveler, northern pintail, redhead, canvasback, scaup,* bufflehead, common golden eye, ruddy duck, and ring-necked duck. Survey findings are published yearly in a report, "Status of Waterfowl and Fall Flight Forecast" (Interior 1985e). Since these surveys do not cover all breeding areas for each species, the population estimates do not represent the total breeding population of each species. Nonetheless, when aggregated, these estimates cover a substantial portion of all breeding ducks for these 14 species and hence are used as an annual index to duck-population size.

The 1985 duck breeding population estimate of 30.8 million represents a 19 percent decline from the 1984 total of 38 million and is the lowest duck count since the survey began in 1955. The 1985 population estimate is 24 percent below the average annual estimate for the 1955-84 period.

FWS tracks the long-term trend of duck populations by using total-population estimates for the 14 species of ducks that breed in the 50 areas which FWS itself surveys yearly by air. The total number of ducks varied from

* Greater and lesser scaup are counted as one species since it is extremely difficult to tell them apart.

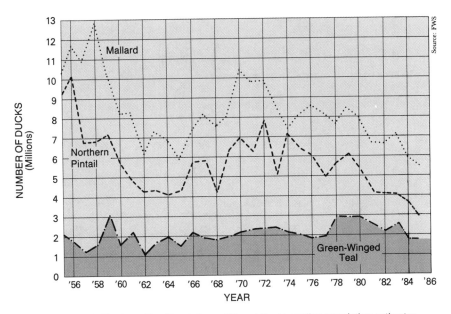

Mallard, Northern Pintail and Green-Winged Teal breeding population estimates, 1955-85, adjusted for birds not recorded by aerial crews; includes areas with comparable annual surveys

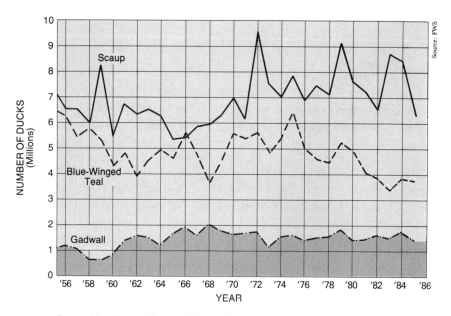

Scaup, Blue-Winged Teal and Gadwall breeding population estimates, 1955-85, adjusted for birds not recorded by aerial crews; includes areas with comparable annual surveys

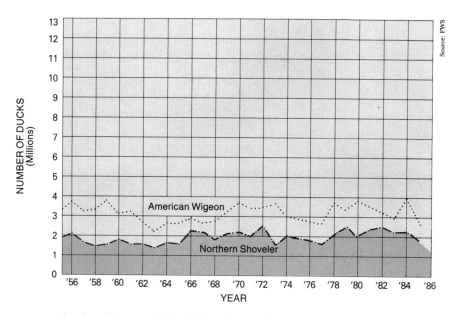

American Wigeon and Shoveler breeding population estimates, 1955-85, adjusted for birds not recorded by aerial crews; includes areas with comparable annual surveys

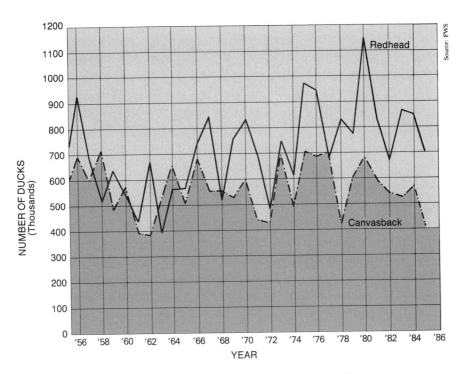

Source: FWS

Redhead and Canvasback breeding population estimates, 1955-85, adjusted for birds not recorded by aerial crews; includes areas with comparable annual surveys

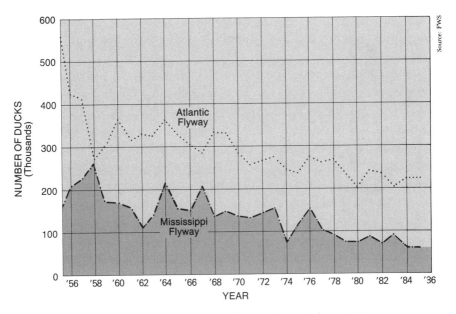

Source: FWS

Trends in Black Duck populations as shown by the mid-winter survey, 1955-85

Breeding Population Estimates for 10 Species of Ducks, 1955-85 (in thousands)

| Year | Mallard | Gadwall | American wigeon | Green-winged teal | Blue-winged teal | Northern shoveler | Northern Pintail | Redhead | Canvasback | Scaup |
|---|---|---|---|---|---|---|---|---|---|---|
| 1955 | 10,345 | 1,106 | 3,333 | 2,076 | 6,436 | 1,965 | 9,251 | 733 | 595 | 7,100 |
| 1956 | 11,711 | 1,202 | 3,712 | 1,898 | 6,267 | 2,084 | 10,124 | 928 | 692 | 6,595 |
| 1957 | 10,946 | 1,102 | 3,208 | 1,293 | 5,449 | 1,744 | 6,856 | 684 | 600 | 6,535 |
| 1958 | 12,904 | 687 | 3,372 | 1,618 | 5,799 | 1,515 | 6,889 | 524 | 713 | 6,040 |
| 1959 | 10,292 | 683 | 3,779 | 3,153 | 5,300 | 1,649 | 7,228 | 641 | 481 | 8,220 |
| 1960 | 8,206 | 873 | 3,165 | 1,630 | 4,303 | 1,859 | 5,769 | 542 | 575 | 5,566 |
| 1961 | 8,290 | 1,422 | 3,219 | 2,216 | 4,833 | 1,625 | 4,860 | 437 | 396 | 6,764 |
| 1962 | 6,144 | 1,610 | 2,721 | 1,119 | 3,890 | 1,633 | 4,299 | 664 | 385 | 6,398 |
| 1963 | 7,360 | 1,578 | 2,209 | 1,754 | 4,587 | 1,435 | 4,361 | 396 | 523 | 6,564 |
| 1964 | 6,974 | 1,223 | 2,630 | 2,051 | 4,943 | 1,685 | 4,111 | 560 | 658 | 6,326 |
| 1965 | 5,948 | 1,692 | 2,695 | 1,526 | 4,628 | 1,607 | 4,301 | 568 | 505 | 5,383 |
| 1966 | 7,401 | 1,976 | 2,901 | 2,219 | 5,616 | 2,272 | 5,777 | 747 | 683 | 5,421 |
| 1967 | 8,205 | 1,638 | 2,637 | 1,944 | 4,715 | 2,244 | 5,870 | 846 | 556 | 5,877 |
| 1968 | 7,586 | 2,098 | 2,783 | 1,805 | 3,697 | 1,811 | 4,225 | 502 | 557 | 5,971 |
| 1969 | 8,065 | 1,837 | 3,192 | 1,991 | 4,514 | 2,150 | 6,390 | 759 | 530 | 6,338 |
| 1970 | 10,379 | 1,698 | 3,752 | 2,259 | 5,633 | 2,269 | 7,004 | 834 | 601 | 6,930 |
| 1971 | 9,843 | 1,733 | 3,425 | 2,352 | 5,426 | 2,052 | 6,291 | 693 | 441 | 6,149 |
| 1972 | 9,867 | 1,776 | 3,428 | 2,407 | 5,673 | 2,505 | 7,875 | 489 | 429 | 9,527 |
| 1973 | 8,781 | 1,198 | 3,665 | 2,444 | 4,866 | 1,657 | 5,114 | 754 | 696 | 7,535 |
| 1974 | 7,392 | 1,562 | 3,003 | 2,221 | 5,437 | 2,060 | 7,165 | 613 | 493 | 7,045 |
| 1975 | 8,109 | 1,672 | 2,862 | 2,038 | 6,441 | 1,994 | 6,387 | 974 | 706 | 7,846 |
| 1976 | 8,637 | 1,478 | 2,699 | 1,844 | 5,023 | 1,818 | 6,045 | 946 | 686 | 6,973 |
| 1977 | 8,226 | 1,546 | 2,678 | 1,952 | 4,626 | 1,616 | 4,971 | 688 | 702 | 7,490 |
| 1978 | 7,695 | 1,593 | 3,808 | 2,978 | 4,497 | 2,162 | 5,664 | 833 | 423 | 7,125 |
| 1979 | 8,444 | 1,889 | 3,388 | 2,920 | 5,278 | 2,555 | 6,070 | 774 | 606 | 9,135 |
| 1980 | 8,003 | 1,459 | 3,857 | 2,925 | 4,903 | 2,050 | 5,420 | 1,146 | 688 | 7,690 |
| 1981 | 6,757 | 1,479 | 3,555 | 2,515 | 4,076 | 2,403 | 4,227 | 825 | 594 | 7,253 |
| 1982 | 6,684 | 1,690 | 3,159 | 2,247 | 3,879 | 2,540 | 4,112 | 674 | 543 | 6,549 |

| | | | | | | | | | |
|---|---|---|---|---|---|---|---|---|---|
| 1983 | 7,107 | 1,536 | 2,923 | 2,574 | 3,381 | 2,237 | 4,086 | 866 | 528 | 8,788 |
| 1984 | 5,974 | 1,799 | 3,979 | 1,804 | 3,870 | 2,222 | 3,664 | 849 | 569 | 8,402 |
| 1985 | 5,475 | 1,410 | 2,506 | 1,873 | 3,756 | 1,925 | 2,935 | 701 | 411 | 6,235 |
| 1955-84 Ave. | 8,409 | 1,494 | 3,191 | 2,126 | 4,933 | 1,981 | 5,814 | 716 | 572 | 6,984 |
| Percent Change in 1985 from: | | | | | | | | | | |
| 1984 | -8 | -22 | -37 | +4 | -3 | -13 | -20 | -17 | -28 | -26 |
| 1955-84 Ave. | -35 | -6 | -21 | -12 | -24 | -3 | -50 | -2 | -28 | -11 |

Source: FWS, "Status of Waterfowl and Fall Flight Forecast 1985"

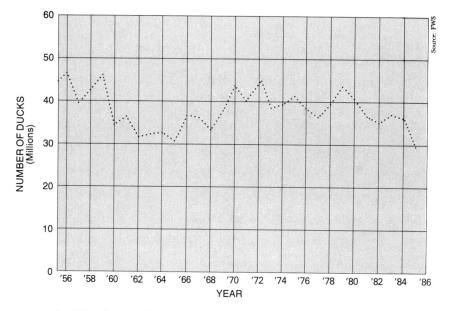

Duck breeding populations in North America, 1955-85, adjusted for
birds not recorded in aerial crews; includes areas with comparable
annual surveys; excludes Scoters, Eiders, Mergansers and Oldsquaws

a low of about 29 million in 1985 to a high of 47 million in 1956 in the 50
surveyed areas.

FWS also makes population estimates for the 10 most heavily hunted
duck species. The long-term population trends for each of these species have
been monitored yearly since 1955. In 1985, the estimated breeding population of each of the 10 species, except green-winged teal, declined from 1984
estimates. More significant, the 1985 populations of all 10 species below their
average annual size for the 30-year period 1955-84: mallard, −35 percent;
green-winged teal, −12 percent; blue-winged teal, −24 percent; pintail, −50
percent; canvasback, −28 percent; gadwall, −6 percent; wigeon, −21 per-
cent; northern shoveler, −3 percent; redhead, −2 percent; scaup, −11 per-
cent.

One other species of duck, the black duck, is monitored yearly by FWS
through winter surveys and evaluations of habitat conditions and production
on selected breeding grounds. The 1985 overall estimate of black ducks decreased three percent from that of 1984. Black duck populations continue to
decline in both the Atlantic (−2 percent from last year's estimate) and Mississippi flyways (−6 percent).

## Geese

The six species of native North American goose are the Canada, greater white-fronted, snow, Ross', emperor, and brant. All breed principally in Alaska and Canada. The emperor goose winters primarily along the Alaska coast. The other five species migrate to the United States and Mexico. Twenty-six distinct populations of various goose species have been identified, and national resource plans have been prepared for each.

Generally, most goose populations are in good shape. FWS, in cooperation with the states and Canada, conducts spring, fall, and winter surveys to estimate the size of goose populations in selected areas and to monitor population trends from year to year. FWS uses these estimates along with climate, weather, and reproductive information to forecast changes in the size of the fall-flight level of each goose population relative to that of the previous year.

The estimated mortality of all geese killed by hunters in the United States during the 1984-85 season was 1.83 million. This represented a six percent decrease from the 1.95 million estimated kill level of 1983-84.

It is beyond the scope of this report to discuss the status of each distinct goose population. Instead, trends and problems are identified by administrative flyway (further information on the status of individual populations may be found in the appendix).

***Atlantic Flyway.*** No major declines affect any goose species that winters along the East Coast, but distribution problems exist. The Canada goose is deserting its more southern winter range and spending more time farther

Estimated Numbers of Geese in Selected Areas From Fall, Winter and Spring Surveys (in thousands)

| | FLYWAY | | | | | | | |
|---|---|---|---|---|---|---|---|---|
| | Pacific Jan. | | Central Dec. | | Mississippi Dec. | | Atlantic Jan. | |
| Species | 1984 | 1985 | 1983 | 1984 | 1983 | 1984 | 1984 | 1985 |
| | | | | | | | 822 | 814 |
| Canada geese | 223 | 307 | | | | | 127 | 146 |
| Brant | 133[1] | 145[1] | 661 | 735 | 729 | 907 | May | |
| Snow Geese | 515[2] | 371[2] | 966 | 1043 | 589 | 993 | 180[3] | 250[3,4] |
| | Nov. | | | | | | | |
| | 1983 | 1984 | | | | | | |
| White-fronted geese | 113 | 100 | 140 | 156 | 70 | 81 | | |

[1] Includes Mexico
[2] Includes Ross' geese
[3] Greater snow geese from St. Lawrence River photo surveys
[4] Preliminary Figure

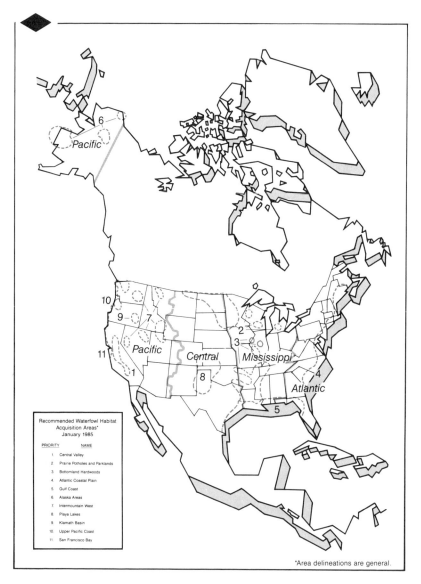

Recommended Waterfowl Habitat
Acquisition Areas*
January 1985

| PRIORITY | NAME |
| --- | --- |
| 1. | Central Valley |
| 2. | Prairie Potholes and Parklands |
| 3. | Bottomland Hardwoods |
| 4. | Atlantic Coastal Plain |
| 5. | Gulf Coast |
| 6. | Alaska Areas |
| 7. | Intermountain West |
| 8. | Playa Lakes |
| 9. | Klamath Basin |
| 10. | Upper Pacific Coast |
| 11. | San Francisco Bay |

*Area delineations are general.

Administrative waterfowl flyways of the United States

north. This means hunting opportunities have declined in North Carolina and other southern states. The Atlantic Flyway Council is conducting a three-year study to determine the causes of the distribution changes.

The Atlantic brant population declined precipitously in the mid-1970s because of poor nesting and wintering conditions. The majority of this flock winters in New Jersey, where biologists fear that its coastal habitat is being lost and degraded by development. Brant hunting has been allowed since 1982, but would be prohibited if the population dropped below 100,000. An estimated 146,000 wintering birds were reported in January 1985, an increase of 15 percent from the 1984 estimate of 127,000.

*Mississippi Flyway.* Goose populations in the Mississippi Flyway are considered to be in satisfactory to excellent shape. No species is suffering severe population declines or habitat problems. Mississippi Valley goose populations have increased significantly since their low numbers in the 1940s. However, allocation of the Mississippi Valley population of Canada goose take is currently disputed among the flyway states. States in the southern portion of the flyway would like to increase the number of birds wintering in their states.

*Central Flyway.* No goose population in the Central Flyway has declined or has serious habitat problems. One flock, the Great Plains population of the giant Canada goose, is under intensive management to restore it to its former size and range in 10 midwestern states. The initial population objective is to have 15,000 breeding pairs by 1990. In 1985, breeding pairs were estimated to be 7,500.

Concern exists that the mid-continent snow goose population is damaging its own breeding habitat in the arctic because of its large flock size. Some reports indicate that annual grasses in some heavily used breeding areas have not seeded for nearly a decade. This situation conceivably could lead to a sudden drop in population in the future, but recent data show that the flock is spreading out to other nesting areas and increasing in total size. The 1984 flock size estimate was 1.9 million. The Canadian Wildlife Service has initiated research to determine the magnitude of the problem.

*Pacific Flyway.* In contrast to the goose populations of other flyways, some Pacific Flyway populations have suffered serious declines from earlier levels. These include the cackling and dusky races of the Canada goose and the Pacific population of the greater white-fronted goose, the Pacific brant, and the emperor goose, which breeds and winters principally in Alaska. Two other populations, the Aleutian Canada goose and the tule race of the greater white-fronted goose, have increased, but remain small in total number.

A major threat to Pacific goose populations is the destruction of California wintering habitat. For instance, 93 percent of the Central Valley wetlands have been destroyed since 1900, and the attrition continues. Approximately

120,000 acres of private agricultural lands currently are managed for water-fowl by private sporting clubs but are susceptible to conversion to other in-compatible uses.

Another problem is the overhunting of Pacific goose populations by both Alaskan Eskimos and sportsmen. The amount of subsistence hunting of goose species that nest in Alaska is not well documented, but is believed to be high (see the Current Issues section for further details on declining Pacific Flyway goose species).

The portion of the Pacific brant population wintering in the United States has decreased because of the movement of birds south into Mexico. The causes for this shift are not well documented or understood. In addition, some nesting colonies in Alaska have experienced serious declines. FWS would like to maintain a winter population of 185,000, with 58,000 of those wintering in the United States. The 1985 winter count was 145,000.

## Swans

Only two species of swans are native to North America. One, the tundra swan (formerly called the whistling swan) is hunted; the other, the trumpeter swan, is not. The mute swan, introduced from Europe, is commonly seen in parks and is not hunted.

The tundra swan breeds in Alaska and the Canadian arctic and winters in large flocks in fresh or brackish shallow water, principally in three Pacific and three Atlantic coastal states. If adequate natural foods are not available, it will eat agricultural crops and forage for shellfish.

There are two distinct populations of tundra swans, eastern and western. The size of both flocks has grown substantially since FWS began making annual surveys. The eastern population increased from 81,000 in 1984 to 94,000 in 1985. FWS would like to keep this flock in the 60,000 to 80,000 range to hold down swan depredations on agricultural lands. The western population dropped from 62,000 in 1984 to 49,000 in 1985. The tundra swan is hunted under tight restrictions in just four states—Utah, Montana, Nevada, and North Carolina—and the number killed is low.

## Migratory Shore and Upland Game Birds.

In addition to waterfowl, the Department of the Interior allows hunting of sandhill cranes, four species of rails (king, clapper, Virginia, and sora), purple and common gallinules, coot, woodcock, snipe, and six species of pigeons and doves (white-crowned pigeon, band-tailed pigeon, scaly-naped pigeon, mourn-ing dove, zenaida dove, and white-winged dove). These species are referred to as "migratory shore and game birds" because of their habitat preferences. Annual hunting regulations are prescribed by FWS for each of these species. FWS has designated four upland game species as significant for management purposes: the mourning dove, woodcock, sandhill crane, and white-winged dove. Estimates of the status of these species may be found in the appendices.

FWS has expressed greatest concern about the woodcock, which has declined in abundance throughout its range, but especially in the eastern states. Over the next few years, the total woodcock population is expected to remain stable or decrease. A principal factor believed to be responsible for this trend is the loss of favorable breeding habitat. The woodcock prefers early successional stages of forests, but many of these are being replaced with climax vegetation. Increased development of woodcock habitat also is thought to be a factor in the decline. Continued loss of southeastern bottomland forests to agriculture may become a serious problem for the central population.

FWS would like to maintain the breeding index at 2.25 males per route in the eastern region and 3.5 in the central, but since it controls so little of the woodcock's habitat reaching this goal will be difficult. The estimated hunter take is about two million birds annually. However, a survey of hunter success indicates a downward trend that follows the population decline. In 1985, FWS issued more restrictive hunting regulations that were designed to decrease the hunter kill by approximately 25 percent from that of the previous year.

## Nongame Migratory Birds

Since 1965, FWS has conducted a breeding-bird survey designed to detect population trends for about 500 species. The survey does not provide a total count of bird populations or even estimates of the breeding population of each species. Rather, the survey samples the number of different birds heard or observed along 1,850 randomly selected road routes throughout the United States during one morning each spring. The number of birds per species heard

### Status of Raptors Monitored At Six Eastern Locations, 1980 to 1985

| Species | Statistically Verified Trend | Average Annual Number Counted | Average Annual Rate of Change (compounded) |
|---|---|---|---|
| Bald eagle | increase | 222 | +30% |
| Peregrine falcon | increase | 340 | +21% |
| Turkey vulture | increase | 2,724 | +12% |
| Merlin | no change | 1,722 | +15% |
| Osprey | no change | 2,700 | +6% |
| Red-tailed hawk | no change | 19,893 | +2% |
| Northern goshawk | no change | 1,285 | +21% |
| Golden eagle | no change | 94 | +1% |
| Northern harrier | no change | 3,853 | +2% |
| Rough-legged hawk | no change | 1,481 | +<1% |
| Broad-winged hawk | no change | 81,289 | −2% |
| Sharp-shinned hawk | no change | 82,249 | −1% |
| Cooper's hawk | no change | 2,851 | −5% |
| American kestrel | no change | 17,423 | −13% |
| Red-shouldered hawk | decrease | 1,712 | −7% |

Source: Office of Migratory Bird Management, FWS

Nongame Migratory Bird Species with Unstable or Decreasing Population Trends in the United States

| Species | FWS Regions Where Status is of Concern | Basis for Listing | | | Primary Reason for Listing | | |
|---|---|---|---|---|---|---|---|
| | | Significant or Negative BBS Trend | BBS or Other Data Indicating Decline | No BBS Data Available | Apparent Population Decline | Small Population Size | Restricted Habitat |
| Common Loon | 5 | | x | | x | | |
| Reddish Egret | 2, 4 | | x | | | x | x |
| Least Bittern | 1, 3, 4, 5, 6 | | | x | x | | x |
| American Bittern | 3, 5 | x | | | x | | x |
| Wood Stork | 4 | | x | | x | | x |
| White-faced Ibis | 1, 6 | | | x | | x | x |
| Trumpeter Swan | 1, 6 | | | | | x | x |
| Red-shouldered Hawk | 3, 5 | | | x | x | | x |
| Ferruginous Hawk | 1, 2 | | | x | x | x | |
| Northern Harrier | 1, 2, 3, 5, 6 | x | | | x | | x |
| Black Rail | 1, 2, 4, 6 | | | x | x | | x |
| Piping Plover | 3, 5, 6 | | | x | x | | x |
| Snowy Plover | 1, 2, 4, 6 | | | x | x | | x |
| Long-billed Curlew | 1, 6 | | | x | | | x |
| Upland Sandpiper | 3, 5 | | x | | x | | x |
| Gull-billed Tern | 4, 5 | | | x | x | | x |
| Roseate Tern | 4, 5 | | x | | x | x | x |
| Least Tern | 2, 3, 6 | | | x | x | x | x |
| Black Tern | 3, 6 | x | | | x | | x |
| Barn Owl | 4, 5 | | | x | x | | x |
| Spotted Owl | 1, 2 | | | x | | | x |
| Loggerhead Shrike | 3, 5 | | x | | x | x | |
| Bell's Vireo | 1, 6 | | x | | x | | |
| Golden-cheeked Warbler | 2 | | | x | | | x |
| Baird's Sparrow | 6 | | x | | x | | x |

| | | | | | |
|---|---|---|---|---|---|
| Henslow's Sparrow | 3, 5 | x | | x | |
| Seaside Sparrow | 4 | | x | x | |
| Bachman's Sparrow | 3, 4 | x | | x | x |

BBS = Breeding Bird Survey
Source: Fish and Wildlife Service, 1982.

calling per route is the yearly index that is used to determine population trends. By analyzing survey data over a number of years it is possible to determine significant increases or decreases in some species. The breeding-bird survey also provides a fairly precise measure of birds that are expanding or decreasing their range.

Although the survey collects information on about 500 species, adequate population data is obtained for only about 250 species. The survey inadequately samples certain habitats, such as marshes and other areas with no vehicular access, and collects insufficient information on rare birds and certain species whose habits make them hard to find on a regular basis.

Based on an analysis of breeding-bird survey data and other information, FWS prepared a 1982 report that identified 28 species with unstable or decreasing population trends during the past 10 to 15 years: nine wading birds, five raptors, three marine birds, four shorebirds, and seven passerines. Eighteen of the species are associated with coastal and wetland habitats, three are open woodland and forest species, six inhabit fields or grasslands, and three occupy mixed habitats. FWS has prepared national resource plans on five of the 28 birds —the interior population of the least tern, and the roseate tern, piping plover, spotted owl, and trumpeter swan. These plans state populations objectives and habitat conservation goals.

## Raptors

FWS conducts counts of migrating raptors at six different eastern locations. These surveys, in effect since 1977, are made in collaboration with several private conservation organizations.* About 250,000 raptors are monitored yearly.

Most monitored raptor populations in the East are stable or increasing. The red-shouldered hawk has shown declining numbers at several locations, but no long-term decline can be confirmed until several more years' data are accumulated. Significantly, raptors affected by pesticides in the 1960s and 1970s no longer show declines. These include the bald eagle, peregrine falcon, merlin, and Cooper's hawk.

# References

Environment Canada and U.S. Department of the Interior. 1985. Draft North American Waterfowl Management Plan. U.S. Department of the Interior. Washington, D.C.

Letter from Jay Hair to Donald P. Hodel, Secretary of the Interior, May 24, 1985.

* These are the Duluth, Michigan, New Jersey, and Onondaga Audubon societies and the Hawk Mountain Sanctuary Association.

Jantzen, Robert, 1985. Statement before the House Merchant Marine and Fisheries Committee, Subcommittee on Fisheries and Wildlife Conservation and the Environment, Concerning the 1985-86 Migratory Waterfowl Hunting Regulations, September 17, 1985.

Laycock, George. 1985. "Doing What's Right for the Geese." *Audubon,* Vol. 87, No. 6, November, 1985. p. 118.

Shepherd, James. 1985. Statement before the House Merchant Marine and Fisheries Committee, Subcommittee on Fisheries and Wildlife Conservation and the Environment, September 17, 1985.

U.S. Congress, House, 1985. Report to Accompany H.R. 2704, 99th Congress, 1st Session, H. Rpt 99-392.

U.S. Department of the Interior, Fish and Wildlife Service. 1976 Final Environmental Impact Statement: Proposed Use of Steel Shot for Hunting Waterfowl in the United States. U.S. Department of the Interior. Washington, D.C.

U.S. Department of the Interior, Fish and Wildlife Service. 1982. Nongame Migratory Bird Species with Unstable or Decreasing Population Trends in the United States. U.S. Department of the Interior. Washington, D.C.

U.S. Department of the Interior, Fish and Wildlife Service. 1983a. Nongame Migratory Bird Management Plan for the United States (draft). U.S. Department of the Interior. Washington, D.C.

U.S. Department of the Interior, Fish and Wildlife Service. 1983b. Nearctic Avian Migrants in the Neotropics. U.S. Department of the Interior. Washington, D.C.

U.S. Department of the Interior, Fish and Wildlife Service. 1985a. Unpublished memorandum: Waterfowl Habitat Acquisition Recommendations, January 17, 1985. U.S. Department of the Interior. Washington, D.C.

U.S. Department of the Interior, Fish and Wildlife Service. 1985b. Draft Supplemental Environmental Impact Statement on the Use of Lead Shot for Hunting Migratory Birds in the United States. U.S. Department of the Interior. Washington, D.C.

U.S. Department of the Interior, Fish and Wildlife Service. 1985c. The Yukon-Kuskokwim Delta Goose Management Plan. U.S. Department of the Interior. Washington, D.C.

U.S. Department of the Interior, Fish and Wildlife Service. 1985d. U.S. Fish and Wildlife Service Report on the Effectiveness of the 1985 Yukon-Kuskokwim Delta Goose Management Plan. U.S. Department of the Interior. Washington. D.C.

U.S. Department of the Interior, Fish and Wildlife Service. 1985e. Status of Waterfowl and Fall Flight Forecast 1985. U.S. Department of the Interior. Washington, D.C.

*William J. Chandler is president of W. J. Chandler Associates, a Washington D.C. environmental policy and government relations consulting firm.*

Alaska king crabs are sorted at a Kodiak Island fishery. Protection of the nation's marine fishery resources is among the responsibilities of the National Marine Fisheries Service.

*Shirley Richards/Photo Researchers*

◆————————————————————————————◆

# Federal Marine Fisheries Management

## Michael Weber

### Introduction

THE MANAGEMENT OF the nation's marine fisheries, including both finfish and shellfish, is one of the most complex areas of national wildlife policy. Fishery management decisions frequently are complicated by lack of information on fish populations by competing demands for use of the resource among commercial and sport fishermen, by regional, national, and international economic considerations, and by inconsistent management measures among federal, state, and international jurisdictions.

As the Strategic Plan for the National Marine Fisheries Service states (U.S. Department of Commerce 1985):

> Fish are the only modern food resource still considered a common property resource available for utilization by all who wish to pursue them, and which are substantially hunted and harvested from the wild state. The failure of fisheries managers to monitor and predict variations in the abundance of the various fishery stocks can result in either their severe depletion, or a substantial wastage and loss of economic potential to the U.S. industry.

Marine fisheries have played a significant economic and cultural role in the history of the United States. Nearly two centuries before the United States gained independence, Britons, Normans, Basques, and Portuguese fished for cod off Newfoundland. The early colonists used menhaden to fertilize their croplands, and by 1811 menhaden were being used for oil as well as fertilizer. During the 19th century and beyond the turn of the 20th century, U.S. landings of fish and shellfish increased erratically (Alverson 1978). By 1930, about 2.5 billion pounds of fish and shellfish were landed in the United States. During the 1930s and 1940s decade, the United States ranked second only to Japan in the production of fish and shellfish. In the 1950s, the total catch levelled off at nearly five billion pounds. By the late 1950s, more than half of this catch was converted to industrial products, such as fertilizer and fish meal (Alverson 1978).

In 1977, the year after the passage of the Fishery Conservation and Management Act (16 U.S.C.A. 1801-1882 [1976 & Supp. 1981]), 182,000 U.S. commercial fishermen, using more than 106,000 boats and vessels, landed 5.3 billion pounds of fish and shellfish for which the fishermen were paid $1.6 billion (U.S. Department of Commerce 1978a). More than half of these landings were for human consumption.

In 1984, the most recent year for which statistics are available (U.S. Department of Commerce 1985b), more than 223,000 commercial fishermen using more than 125,000 fishing craft landed about 6.4 billion pounds of fish and shellfish valued at $2.4 billion. Finfish made up 85 percent of the total landings but only 51 percent of the total value of U.S. landings. U.S. fishermen landed an additional 1.9 billion pounds valued at $287.3 million, which were transferred to foreign vessels or landed at ports outside the 50 states. Even with this expansion in fishing effort, the United States now ranks only fourth among the world's fishing nations, well behind Japan and the Soviet Union.

About 300 different species of fish and shellfish are landed in the United States. However, only a few species groups, including menhaden, salmon, crabs, shrimp, and flounders, account for the largest part of these landings. Menhaden alone, sought primarily in the territorial sea* for rendering into oil and meal, accounted for 45 percent of the volume of all commercial fish landings in 1984. More than 48 percent of the U.S. catch was used for industrial purposes. Shrimp species led all others in value. More than half of the fish and shellfish caught in U.S. waters by U.S. fishermen is caught within state waters. U.S. commercial fishermen caught more than 4.7 billion pounds in state waters in 1984 and nearly 3 billion pounds in federal waters.

In federal waters, foreign fishermen caught a little more than three bil-

* The territorial sea extends three nautical miles from the shores of all states except Texas and the Gulf Coast of Florida, where the seaward boundary is nine nautical miles. The states exercise primary management responsibility over living marine resources within these state waters. The fishery conservation zone, established by the Fishery Conservation and Management Act, extends beyond the boundary of the territorial sea to 200 miles offshore. The fishery conservation zone, often referred to as federal waters, and the territorial sea or zone, often referred to as state waters, comprise U.S. waters. Seaward of U.S. waters are the high seas, over which the United States does not exercise management responsibility for living marine resources.

lion pounds of fish and shellfish in 1984. By comparison, the foreign catch in federal waters in 1971, the peak year, was 7.7 billion pounds. Federal waters off Alaska supplied 96 percent of the foreign catch. The major foreign operators in 1984 were Japan, the Republic of Korea, East and West Germany, and the U.S.S.R.

Fish processors also have played an important role in the U.S. commercial fishing industries. As is the case with the fishing sector, the processing sector is characterized by many small operators. In 1983, processors and wholesalers operated 3,891 plants and employed some 80,000 people during the year.

In 1984, the U.S. supply of edible fish, which includes imports, amounted to 8.5 billion pounds. The supply of industrial fish products was 4.1 billion pounds. Of this total supply, the United States imported $3.7 billion worth of edible fishery products and $2.1 billion of industrial fishery products, setting records in both categories. In the same year, the United States exported $948.8 million of edible fishery products and $106.5 million of industrial fishery products. As a result, the U.S. trade deficit in fishery products set another record, amounting to about $5 billion. Fishery imports are one of the top five sources of the nation's trade deficit.

Increasing attention is being paid to the role and effect of marine recreational fishing on U.S. fisheries. In 1984, about 17 million marine recreational anglers caught more than 420 million fish, weighing more than 650 million pounds, or about 30 percent of the total landings of finfish used for food. In 72.8 million fishing trips, marine recreational anglers spent more than $7.5 billion. More than 75 percent of the recreational catch was from state waters.

Fishing affects other resources. The incidental capture of marine mammals, sea turtles, sea birds, and non-target species of fish and shellfish affects the abundance of these species, some of which are in danger of extinction. Fishing itself is affected both directly and indirectly by development along the coastline. Harvesters and processors may find themselves directly competing for space on waterfronts with other water-dependent industries. Development within the coastal zone may indirectly affect fisheries by altering or destroying estuarine and wetland areas in which commercially and recreationally valuable fish and shellfish spend critical stages in their lives.

As a final measure of the continuing significance of marine fisheries, annual per capita consumption of seafood products in the United States has increased from 11 pounds in 1968 to more than 13 pounds in 1984. The greatest growth has occurred in the consumption of fresh and frozen fish, from about six pounds in 1968 to more than eight pounds in 1984.

Management of such important renewable resources has evolved very slowly and only in reaction to the depletion of fish populations and the economic collapse of particular fisheries in the United States and abroad. Fishery managers in the United States and elsewhere must contend with a long history of management-free resource exploitation. One reviewer of U.S. fisheries concluded that each individual fishery generally exhibited at least some of the following problem-causing features:

- the fishery developed in an unregulated manner, responding only to economic factors in an open access (common property) environment;
- the fishery started in a restricted geographical area and eventually expanded throughout the exploitable range of the species;
- the fishery had an extended growth period of 50 to 100 years during which landings gradually increased, then sharply declined as a result of overfishing or environmental degradation;
- the fishery was sharply affected by technological innovations;
- the fishery eventually developed excess fishing capacity, leading to declining catches by individual fishermen (Alverson 1978).

With declining catches and increased competition among U.S. fishermen and between U.S. fishermen and foreign fishermen, conflicts developed requiring the intervention of federal and state governments. Initially, the federal government's role in marine fisheries generally was limited to providing research support and to representing U.S. interests in international fisheries negotiations. In the late 1960s and early 1970s, however, there were increasing complaints that large foreign factory trawlers were depleting U.S. offshore fishery resources. With the passage of the Fishery Conservation and Management Act in 1976, foreign fishing without U.S. permits was prohibited within 200 miles of the U.S. coast. The act also established eight regional fishery management councils and gave them the role of developing regional fishery management plans in order to provide for the development of the U.S. fishing industry and for the conservation of fish stocks.

## History and Legislative Authority

The federal government not only has exercised responsibility for the conservation and management of fish populations during the past century, but also has sought to promote the development of the fishing industry. The following discussion of federal marine fisheries programs treats these two activities separately.*

### Fisheries Management: Early Legislative History

With the passage of the Act of February 9, 1871 (Act of February 9, 16 Stat. 593 [repealed 1964]), Congress established a federal role in the management

* One of the principal sources for this section is "List of Legislative Authorities for NOAA" by Kip Robinson and Beverly B. Carter, September 1982.

of the nation's coastal fisheries. The act created the office of a Commissioner of Fish and Fisheries, which was ordered to study and suggest remedies for a decline in food fishes of U.S. seacoasts and lakes.

The Fish Commission and the Office of the Commissioner of Fish and Fisheries were moved to the Department of Commerce and Labor in 1903 (Act of February 14, 1903, 32 Stat. 827). In creating the Bureau of Fisheries, the act also transferred to Commerce and Labor the management of fur seals, salmon, and other Alaska fisheries previously administered by the Department of Treasury.

The first act specifically authorizing the regulation of a fishing activity was the Sponge Act (Act of June 20, 1906, 34 stat. 313 [repealed 1914]), which allowed for the regulation of the sponge fishery in the Gulf of Mexico and the Straits of Florida. The federal government's enforcement of this act's prohibition against the taking of sponges by means of a diving apparatus brought the celebrated *Abby Dodge* case before the Supreme Court (223 U.S. 166 [1912]) in 1912. The Supreme Court ruled that the federal government could regulate the taking of sponges, but only beyond Florida's territorial waters (Bean 1983).

The Sponge Act was subsequently amended in 1914 (38 Stat. 692, P.L. 63-172, Act of August 15, 1914) to apply to the taking or catching of sponges outside state jurisdiction. The act regulates the landing, delivery, curing, selling, or possession of sponges and allows the secretary of Commerce to request the assistance of the Coast Guard and the Customs Service in enforcing the act.

The next major development in federal fisheries management came with the Treaty for the Preservation and Protection of Fur Seals, which the United States concluded with Russia, Japan, and Great Britain in July 1911 (37 Stat. 1542, T.S. 564). This treaty (described in greater detail in this volume's Marine Mammal Protection chapter and in the International Wildlife Conservation chapter) halted pelagic hunting of northern fur seals during their migration through the Pacific Ocean to rookeries on islands owned by Japan, Russia and the United States. Besides being very wasteful, such pelagic sealing by one nation inevitably intercepted seals bound for rookeries owned by another country. Interestingly, the Fur Seal Treaty included no provisions for determining an appropriate level of take.

***The Halibut Fishery.*** U.S and Canadian fishermen began commercial fishing for Pacific halibut in about 1890. Landings peaked at about 65 million pounds in 1915, then plummeted to less than 40 million pounds in 1916 even though fishing had been expanding into new areas. Alarms were sounded and the United States and Canada undertook negotiations that in 1923 resulted in the first of four treaties concerning Pacific halibut (Bell 1970). The International Fisheries Commission established by these treaties, had powers limited largely to the investigation of the causes of the halibut fishery decline, although the initial treaty did include a winter closed season.

Investigations conducted by the International Fisheries Commission indicated that the primary cause for the decline in the halibut catches was overfishing. By 1930, a new treaty expanded the regulatory powers of the International Fisheries Commission, as did a 1937 treaty implemented by the Northern Pacific Halibut Act (50 Stat. 325, P.L. 75-169, Act of June 28, 1937). A regulatory scheme recommended by the commission led to restoration of the stock and improved catches (Alverson 1978). In 1953, the United States and Canada concluded the convention for the Preservation of the Halibut Fishery of the North Pacific Ocean and Bering Sea (5 U.S.T. 5, T.I.A.S. No. 2900), which is implemented by the North Pacific Halibut Act (16 U.S.C.A. 772-772j [1976 & Supp. V 1981]). This convention set up a quota system for the halibut fishery.

*Pacific Salmon Treaties.* From the first canning of salmon in 1864 in California's Sacramento River, the Pacific salmon industry grew rapidly until it supported more fishermen, vessels, and canneries than any other U.S. fishery (Alverson 1978). Because they are migratory, salmon spawned in one country's rivers might be caught on the high seas by fisherman of other countries. Competition for these migratory fish created the need for an allocation system.

In 1930, the United States and Canada concluded the Convention for the Protection, Preservation, and Extension of the Sockeye Salmon Fishery of the Fraser River System (50 Stat. 1355, T.S. No. 918). The management of pink salmon was added by protocol in December 1956. This treaty, implemented by the Sockeye Salmon or Pink Salmon Fishing Act of 1947 (16 U.S.C.A. 776-776f [1976 & Supp. V 1981]), established the International Pacific Salmon Fisheries Commission. Its purpose is to study sockeye and pink salmon of the Fraser River system and to recommend regulatory measures that will make possible the maximum sustainable yield of the fishery.

Congress also addressed the decline of Pacific salmon stocks by establishing the Columbia River Basin Fishery Development Program in 1938 (16 U.S.C.A. 755-757). This legislation authorized salmon hatcheries in Washington, Oregon, and Idaho and studies to conserve the fishery resources of the Columbia River and its tributaries.

*Early Legislation on Management Jurisdictions.* In 1940, Congress attempted to provide a foundation for cohesive state management of fishery resources shared by various states. By joint resolution and subsequent acts, Congress authorized the Atlantic states to enter into a compact of cooperation and mutual assistance in the regulation of fishing in the territorial waters and in the bays and inlets of the Atlantic Ocean (54 Stat. 261 [1940]; amended by 56 Stat. 267, P.L. 77-539 [1942], and 64 Stat. 467, P.L. 81-721 [1950]). This effort to solve problems caused by a lack of management coordination among states sharing a resource was repeated in 1947 and 1949, when Congress authorized the establishment of the Pacific States Marine Fishery Commission and the Gulf States Marine Fisheries Commission (61 Stat. 418, P.L. 80-232 [1947]; 63 Stat. 70, P.L. 81-66, [1949]). In 1962, Congress amended the Pacific States Fishery Commission charter to include Alaska and Hawaii and any other states having rivers or streams tributary to the Pacific Ocean (76 Stat. 763, P.L. 87-766 [1962]).

Congress supplemented these efforts to improve interjurisdictional fisheries management by mandating studies of regional fisheries resources. In 1949 and 1950, Congress also authorized several studies of regional fishery resources, including Atlantic shad (16 U.S.C.A. 759). Under the Atlantic Coast Fish Study for Development and Protection of Fish Resources (16 U.S.C. 760a-760c), the secretary of Commerce was to provide the eastern seaboard states with the results of studies on the fish of the Atlantic Coast. In 1947, Congress had given similar authorization to the secretary of Commerce for the development and use of the fisheries in the tropical and subtropical Pacific territories of the United States (16 U.S.C.A. 758).

Fishery management problems arising from jurisdictional issues were not confined to state and federal waters. In 1945, President Harry S Truman issued a declaration that the United States considered it within its rights to establish conservation zones on the high seas contiguous to the territorial seas of the United States where fishing activities might be regulated (Presidental Proclamation No. 2667, 59 Stat. 884, 10 *Federal Register* 12303 [September 28, 1945]). The Truman proclamation was issued in response to increasing difficulties in establishing international agreements for the management of fisheries on the high seas off U.S. shores. Chile reacted by declaring a conservation zone extending 200 miles from its shores (Bean 1983). Soon, the right of a coastal country to declare a conservation zone in what was once the high seas had become an accepted tenet of law.

Early in the 1950s, the United Nations began sponsoring an International Conference on the Law of the Sea. In 1958, the Conference of Parties concluded a Convention on Fishing and Conservation of the Living Resources of the High Seas ([1966] 17 U.S.T. 138, T.I.A.S. No. 5969). This convention provided that if a nation were unsuccessful in reaching an agreement with nations fishing in waters adjacent to it, that nation could take unilateral measures. At the same time, in response to the conclusion of the Convention on the Territorial Sea and Contiguous Zone ([1964] 15 U.S.T. 1606, T.I.A.S. No. 56390), most nations claimed territorial seas of three miles and conservation zones of 12 miles. With the Bartlett Act (16 U.S.C.A. 1081-1086 and 1091-1094 [1976], repealed March 1, 1977), the United States followed this pattern, prohibiting any foreign vessel from fishing within the U.S. conservation zone or from taking sedentary living resources from the continental shelf without a permit from the secretary of the Treasury or pursuant to an international agreement.

*The Pacific Tuna Fisheries.* One of the fisheries most affected when other countries (53 by 1983) adopted 200-mile conservation zones was the tuna fishery in the eastern tropical Pacific (Alverson 1978). This fishery began developing after the first canning of tuna in California in 1903. By 1940, the catch by U.S. tuna boats amounted to more than 175 million pounds, and the fishery extended south to the Galapagos Islands off Ecuador. In 1949, the United States and Costa Rica concluded the Convention between the United States of America and the Republic of Costa Rica for the Establishment of an Inter-American Tropical Tuna Commission (1 U.S.T. 230, T.I.A.S. No. 2044), implemented by the Tuna Conventions Act of 1950 (16 U.S.C.A. 951-961, 22 U.S.C.A. 2672). Panama, Ecuador, Mexico, and Canada later joined the convention.

The convention established the Inter-American Tropical Tuna Commission, which included a professional research staff. The inter-American commission was empowered to study the biology of tropical tuna species and other associated species and to recommend conservation measures. No regulations were actually implemented until 1966. By this time, a number of countries in the eastern tropical Pacific had declared 200-mile conservation zones and were seizing U.S. tuna boats fishing within these areas. The United States refused to recognize the conservation zones of these countries, declaring that tuna were highly migratory and therefore not subject to management by countries in whose waters they might occur. As we shall see, this policy remains controversial both within and without the United States.

Like other international fisheries agreements, the tuna convention's effectiveness is limited by the lack of means to enforce the recommendations of the Inter-American Tropical Tuna Commission. Congress attempted to address this problem by amending the Tuna Convention Act in 1962, and authorizing the secretary of State to prohibit the entry into the United States of fish from any country whose vessels are being used in a manner that tends to diminish the effectiveness of the commission's recommendations (16 U.S.C.A. 951-961). This provision, which empowers the federal government to enforce the recommendations of an international fisheries commission, became a model for similar provisions in other laws implementing international treaties.

*Fisheries of the Northwest Atlantic and North Pacific.* The fisheries of the Northwest Atlantic also were the subject of negotiations in the late 1940s. Even before the turn of the twentieth century, concern was expressed about the fisheries of the northwest Atlantic. The cod fisheries reached a peak of about 200 million pounds at the turn of the century then declined after 1902. In 1930, the haddock fishery reached nearly 264 million pounds. Only two years later the catch fell to 150 million pounds (Alverson 1978).

Like other fisheries, those of the northwest Atlantic were drastically affected by several technological innovations after World War II, including the use of synthetic fibers in nets, electric and hydraulic power for deck equipment, and new navigational and communications equipment. These improvements increased the pressure on the fishery stocks of the northwest Atlantic. In 1949, 12 nations fishing in this area met in Washington and signed the International Convention for the Northwest Atlantic Fisheries (1 U.S.T. 477, T.I.A.S. No. 2089), which was implemented in the United States by the Northwest Atlantic Fisheries Act (16 U.S.C.A. 981-991).

This convention provided for the "investigation, protection and conservation of the fisheries of the Northwest Atlantic Ocean, in order to make possible the maintenance of a maximum sustained catch from those fisheries." With further advancements in technology, however, the pressure on the haddock and other stocks in the convention area exceeded the ability of the commission to control it. The entry of several eastern European countries and the Soviet Union into these fisheries, as well as into other fisheries off the mid-Atlantic states, provided much of the impetus that led to the passage of the Fishery Conservation and Management Act in 1976.

Technological innovations after World War II also expanded capabilities in North Pacific fisheries early in the 1950s. Japan deployed fleets of catcher boats using drift nets miles long to catch salmon in the North Pacific Ocean. Although some of these salmon were of Asian origin, others were from North America rivers (Alverson 1978, Larkin 1970). The U.S. salmon industry brought pressure to bear, and by 1954, Japan, Canada and the United States had signed the International Convention for the High Seas Fisheries of the North Pacific Ocean (4 U.S.T. 380, T.I.A.S. No. 2786), implemented in the United States by the North Pacific Fisheries Act (16 U.S.C.A. 1021-1032). The treaty established the International North Pacific Fisheries Commission, whose objective was the rational exploitation and management of common fishery resources. Among other measures, the treaty included a prohibition on fishing by the Japanese east of longitude 175 west.

## Industry Assistance

Except for the domestic sponge fishery and international fisheries for northern fur seals, Pacific halibut, and Pacific salmon, the principal role of the federal government in fisheries management until after World War II was to collect and analyze scientific and statistical information, to develop fish culture techniques, and to rehabilitate depleted fisheries (Alverson 1978). Federal efforts to enhance and restore commercially valuable fish and shellfish to the nation's waters began in 1922, when Congress authorized the establishment of a station on the Mississippi River which was to protect fishes and propagate mussels (16 U.S.C. 750-751). Under the Federal Power Act (16 U.S.C.A. 811), the secretary of Commerce might prescribe the construction of fishways in projects approved by the Federal Power Commission.

Beginning in the late 1930s, the federal government initiated several programs to assist the development of the domestic commercial fishing industry. For instance, in 1937 Congress authorized the Department of Commerce to collect, publish, and distribute information regarding such matters as fish-market supply and demand and market prices of fishery products (50 Stat. 296, P.L. 75-169 [1937]). In 1939, Congress authorized the secretary of Agriculture to buy surplus domestic fishery products and distribute them through federal, state, and private relief channels (15 U.S.C.A. 713c-2 and 3, 7 U.S.C.A. 612c, 16 U.S.C.A. 742e).

In 1954, Congress amended the 1939 legislation with the Saltonstall-Kennedy Act of 1954 (15 U.S.C.A. 713c-3). This amendment directs the secretary of Agriculture to transfer to the secretary of Commerce an amount equivalent to 30 percent of the gross receipts from customs duties collected on fishery products. These monies are to be maintained in a separate fund and used by the secretary of Commerce to fund a fishery educational service and technological, biological, and related research programs for the promotion of the free flow of domestically produced fishery products. Also, these funds may be used for construction, operation, and maintenance of research vessels. The act encourages the secretary to cooperate with other federal and state agencies and private organizations in carrying out this program.

*The Fisheries Protective Act.* Congress also passed the 1954 Fishermen's Protective Act (22 U.S.C.A. 1971) in response to the seizure of U.S. fishing boats in waters claimed by other countries as their exclusive management zones. Under the act, which has been amended as discussed below, the secretary of State is authorized to take whatever actions he deems appropriated to protect a seized vessel and crew and to secure their release. The secretary of the Treasury also is directed to reimburse the vessel owner for any fines paid to secure their release.

Continued seizures of U.S. fishing boats in foreign waters led Congress in 1968 to amend the Fishermen's Protective Act. The amendments allow the secretary of Commerce to enter into contracts with fishing-vessel owners under which the secretary is to reimburse the owner for damages suffered in a seizure. In return, the vessel owners were required to pay for these guarantees. The secretary of State is empowered to collect claims against a foreign country that has seized a U.S. boat and to withhold any foreign aid funds if the country refuses to satisfy the claims.

In 1971, Congress further strengthened the Fishermen's Protective Act by adding the Pelly Amendment, which gives the president discretionary authority to prohibit the importation of fishery products from nations that conduct fishing operations in a manner that diminishes the effectiveness of any multilateral international fishery conservation program in which the United States participates (85 Stat. 786, P.L. 92-219, Act of December 23, 1971). The secretary of Commerce is to certify to the president when such operations are being conducted.

*The Fish and Wildlife Act.* In passing the Fish and Wildlife Act of 1956 (16 U.S.C.A. 742), Congress declared it as a national policy that the fishing industry must enjoy freedom of enterprise, protection or opportunity, and assistance consistent with that provided by government for industry generally. The original act established two fisheries bureaus within the U.S. Fish and Wildlife Service (FWS) in the Department of the Interior. The Bureau of Commercial Fisheries was responsible for commercial fisheries, whales, seals, and sea lions; the Bureau of Sport Fisheries and Wildlife was responsible for migratory birds, game management, wildlife refuges, sport fisheries, and other marine mammals. As a result of the act, some fisheries functions in other departments, such as Agriculture's surplus fishery products distribution program, were transferred to Interior.

The Fish and Wildlife Act also established a program that enables the secretary to make loans for financing or refinancing the purchase, construction, equipping, maintaining, repairing, or operating of new or used commercial fishing vessels or gear. Some of the other authorities and responsibilities of the secretary under this act are:

- to conduct research and disseminate information concerning the production and flow to market of fishery products;
- to collect and disseminate statistics on fishing;
- to conduct educational and extension service about commercial and sport fisheries;
- to develop and recommend measures to ensure maximum sustainable production of fish and fishery products.

*Industry Assistance Legislation in the 1960s.* In the 1960s, Congress continued to encourage the development of the domestic fishing industry. The United States Fishing Fleet Improvement Act of 1960 (46 U.S.C.A. 1401-1413), for instance, authorized the secretary to provide 35 to 50 percent of the construction of a new vessel in a U.S. shipyard, based upon the estimated difference in the cost of such construction in U.S. shipyards and foreign shipyards. This program, which expired in 1972, also subsidized the reconditioning of fishing vessels in U.S. shipyards.

Congressional interest in improving domestic commercial fishing capabilities continued in 1964 with the passage of the Commercial Fisheries Research and Development Act (16 U.S.C. 779). Under this act and the Anadromous Fish Conservation Act of 1965 (16 U.S.C. 757), the secretaries of Commerce and Interior may enter into cooperative agreements with and make grants to states for carrying out research and development projects on commercial fisheries.

One of the nation's principal fisheries research and extension program began in 1966 with passage of the National Sea Grant College and Program

Act (33 U.S.C. 1121). Under this act, originally administered by the National Science Foundation, the Commerce Department provides support to sea-grant colleges for necessary research, education, and advisory services in the field of marine resources.

During this period, Congress established other industry assistance programs, including continuing study of migratory marine fish of interest to recreational fishermen to develop conservation policies and management (16 U.S.C.A. 760e-g). In 1961, Congress authorized a research center at Milford, Connecticut, at which basic research on the physiology and ecology of commercial shellfish and on the development of hatchery methods was to be conducted (16 U.S.C.A 760h-i). In 1962, Congress authorized the secretary to acquire oyster brood stock resistant to disease for distribution to states where disease was jeopardizing the industry's economic stability (16 U.S.C.A. j-i). The act also authorized grants to states to conduct research on the development of disease-resistant strains of oysters.

*Other Fisheries Related Legislation.* Several other pieces of legislation, passed before the Fishery Conservation and Management Act, continue to provide authority for important federal activities affecting marine fisheries.

With passage of the Fish and Wildlife Coordination Act of 1934 (16 U.S.C.A 661-666c), federal agencies for the first time were required to consider the impacts of their projects on wildlife. As a result of amendments in 1946 and 1958, the act now focuses on mitigation of those impacts. Under this act, federal agencies sponsoring water development projects must give full consideration to the recommendations of state wildlife agencies and the National Marine Fisheries Service (NMFS, pronounced "nymphs') and mitigate damages caused by the projects. Also, the act allows NMFS and Interior's Fish and Wildlife Service to recommend the denial of requests for permits to dredge and fill wetlands under Section 404 of the Clean Water Act.

The Agricultural Trade Development and Assistance Act of 1954, also know as P.L. 480 (7 U.S.C. 1704b-3), authorizes federal agencies to use foreign currencies, accrued from the sale of surplus agricultural products, for the support of scientific and educational activities overseas. The Bureau of Commercial Fisheries received its first P.L. 480 funding in the budget year ending June 1962.

A seemingly minor but significant expansion of the role of federal fish agencies occurred in 1969, when Congress amended the Lacey Act to include "mollusk or crustacean" in the act's prohibition against the importation of foreign wild animals taken in violation of foreign, national, or state law. FWS and NMFS enforcement agents have used this authority recently to arrest fishermen selling striped bass illegally caught in Maryland waters and fishermen landing shrimp caught in Mexican waters.

## The Transition Years

As the decade of the 1960s came to a close, the nation's management of marine fisheries and of ocean resources generally came under increasing review. In March 1968, for instance, the University of Washington hosted a conference entitled "The Future of the Fishing Industry of the United States" (Stroud 1970). Among other things, the conference concluded:

- that a number of fisheries had too many fishermen with too many boats;
- that the principal target stocks of commercial fishing efforts were already near their sustainable limit of production;
- that the lack of effective coordination among the states led to confusion in fisheries management;
- that no effective means existed for managing domestic and foreign fisheries beyond territorial waters; and,
- that aquaculture did not seem to offer significant promise in the near future.

## The Stratton Commission

In January 1969, the Commission on Marine Science, Engineering, and Resources submitted to Congress its report on the nation's marine resources and their management (Commission on Marine Science, Engineering, and Resources 1969). This commission, named the Stratton commission after chairman Julius A. Stratton, was established by Congress in 1966 through the Marine Resources and Engineering Development Act. The work of the commission was paralleled by work on administrative concerns conducted by the National Council on Marine Resources and Engineering Development. To this day, the Stratton commission report remains a standard by which the nation's marine resource management programs can be measured.

The Stratton commission made a number of recommendations regarding the management of the nation's fisheries and habitat. Among these are the following:

- that instead of maximum sustainable yield, a major objective of fisheries management be "production of the largest net economic return consistent with the biological capabilities of exploited stocks" (Stratton 1969);
- that voluntary steps be taken, and government action if necessary, to reduce excess fishing effort;
- that an independent federal agency, called the National Oceanic and Atmospheric Agency (NOAA) by the commission, be created to coordinate the nation's ocean programs, including fisheries management;
- that NOAA be able to preempt state jurisdiction of endangered fisheries;
- that restrictions on the use of foreign-built vessels by U.S. fishermen in domestic fisheries be removed;

- that NOAA expand research on fishing technology and programs of technology transfer;
- that the federal government undertake a more aggressive program of promoting aquaculture.

The Stratton commission also made extensive recommendations regarding international fisheries management, which was becoming an area of increasing concern with the expansion of foreign fishing effort beyond the United States' 12 nautical mile fisheries zone. Among the commission's recommendations were:

- that national quotas be established for the fisheries of the Northwest Atlantic and the North Pacific;
- that an attempt be made to reach international agreement on the breadth of the territorial sea;
- that the geographical area subject to international fisheries management be large enough to permit regulation on the basis of ecological units rather than of species;
- that an existing international organization evaluate current international fisheries agreements and suggest new ones if necessary;
- that member nations provide funding for adequate research and management staff for international fisheries commissions;
- that the United States support compulsory arbitration of disputes.

Some of the commission's recommendations were adopted. The most significant of these was the creation of NOAA in the Department of Commerce under Executive Re-organization Plan No. 4 of 1970 (84 Stat. 2090). This reorganization also moved the Bureau of Commercial Fisheries and the marine recreational activities of the Bureau of Sport Fisheries and Wildlife from the Department of the Interior to NOAA, where it became known as the National Marine Fisheries Service.

Beyond approving the executive reorganization, Congress initially did little to implement the fisheries recommendations of the Stratton commission, although several fisheries laws were passed and programs established before passage of the Fishery Conservation and Management Act in 1976.

In 1970, international negotiations did conclude with the International Convention for the Conservation of Atlantic Tuna (20 U.S.T. 2887, T.I.A.S. No. 6767), which established the International Commission for the Conservation of Atlantic Tunas. Besides coordinating the collection of information on tuna and tuna-like fisheries in the Atlantic Ocean, the Atlantic Tuna Commission also formulates regulatory proposals, which are submitted to the individual governments for approval. The recommendations become effective within six months if no objections are made.

Implementing legislation for this treaty was not passed until 1975 (16 U.S.C. 971). The implementing legislation requires that regulations recommended by the Atlantic Tuna Commission must be published in the *Federal Register* for comment. If a member country is fishing in a manner that conflicts with the commission's recommendations, the regulations will be suspended for U.S. fishermen. The act also includes provisions for embargos, cooperative enforcement of commission regulations, and penalties.

In order to promote the modernization and expansion of the U.S. fishing fleet, Congress amended the Merchant Marine Act of 1936 to create the Capital Construction Fund for Fishing Vessels (46 U.S.C.A. 1177). Under this program, owners of commercial fishing vessels built in the United States may, with the approval of the secretary of Commerce, make deposits to a capital construction fund for fishing vessels. Taxes on the deposits are deferred. Withdrawals may be made for acquisition, construction, or reconstruction of qualified vessels. In 1972, Congress again amended the Merchant Marine Act of 1936 by replacing authority to insure vessel mortgages and loans on vessels, including fishing vessels of five net tons or more, with authority to guarantee obligations (46 U.S.C.A. 1271-1280).

## Legislation Indirectly Related to Marine Fisheries

The Marine Mammal Protection Act of 1972 (16 U.S.C.A. 1361-1407) as amended established a moratorium on the taking of marine animals. Taking, which is defined to include direct and indirect harm, is prohibited except by permit. The Marine Mammal Protection Act provides a number of exceptions to the prohibitions on taking, including limited allowance of the incidental capture of porpoises in tuna purse seine nets and of other marine mammals in other commercial fishing activities. It provides for an embargo on imports of fish and fish products from countries that allow fishing methods that U.S. fishermen are forbidden to use or which result in incidental killing or serious injury of marine mammals in excess of U.S. standards.

In some ways similar to the Marine Mammal Protection Act, the Endangered Species Act prohibits the taking of species listed as being in danger of extinction (16 U.S.C.A 1531 *et seq.*). While the Endangered Species Act does not specify prohibited activities for the threatened species, it allows the secretaries of Commerce and Interior to establish regulations for the conservation of such species. These regulations may include prohibitions on taking. The secretary of Commerce has delegated to the administrator of NOAA his responsibility for marine species listed under the Endangered Species Act. These include all species of sea turtles, some species of marine mammals, and several species of fish, including shortnose sturgeon. Under Section 7 of the act, agencies sponsoring activities that may conflict with the conservation of listed marine species must consult with the Department of Commerce. Section 10 of the act allows for the incidental taking of endangered species in the course of an otherwise legal activity provided certain conditions are met.

Under Section 404 of the Clean Water Act, the United States Army

Corps of Engineers regulates the discharge of dredge or fill material into the nation's waters (33 U.S.C.A 1344). Under the Fish and Wildlife Coordination Act, the Corps is required to consult with NMFS regarding 404 permit applications for dredge and fill activities that may affect marine fisheries. Although NMFS may recommend denial of a permit, the Fish and Wildlife Coordination Act does not require the Corps to heed this recommendation (Bean 1983).

Title III of the Marine Protection, Research, and Sanctuaries Act of 1972 establishes the National Marine Sanctuary Program in the Department of Commerce (16 U.S.C.A. 1431). The secretary of Commerce is authorized to designate as national marine sanctuaries certain areas in U.S. waters and may regulate activities to protect the resources in a sanctuary.

The Coastal Zone Management Act of 1972 (16 U.S.C.A 1451 note) authorizes the secretary of Commerce to make grants to coastal states to develop and implement coastal zone management plans consistent with national standards. The act also allows the secretary to make grants to states to acquire estuarine areas as National Estuarine Sanctuaries to serve as sites for estuarine research.

## The Fishery Conservation and Management Act of 1976

As early as the 1950s, foreign nations were launching factory-equipped freezer stern trawlers. These ships, capable of remaining at sea for months, could not only catch much larger amounts of fish than traditional fishing vessels, but could also process and freeze the catch. Furthermore, with increasingly sophisticated devices for locating schools of fish, fleets of these factory trawlers could overfish stocks in a particular area for several years, then leave for other areas. If fishermen using more traditional fishing activities continued to take from these overfished populations, as occurred in the Northwest Atlantic, the populations could not recover.

In waters off the United States, the effect of these factory trawlers was felt most acutely in the Northwest Atlantic, where cod and haddock were being managed by the International Commission for the Northwest Atlantic Fisheries. The Soviet Union, for instance, began fishing in the ICNAF area off Canada and the United States in 1956, catching about 38 million pounds of cod and haddock. By 1967, the Soviet Union ranked second behind Canada in its take, reporting a catch of nearly 1.3 billion pounds. By comparison, U.S. fishermen caught just half that amount. When the Northwest Atlantic commission was formed in 1949, the United States had had the area to itself (Graham 1970). The increase in fishing effort in the area also led to a 50 percent decline in the finfish stock from 1961 to 1973 (Council on Environmental Quality 1981). Foreign fleets also were operating elsewhere off the shores of the United States. The foreign catch within 200 miles of our shores reached a peak of nearly 7.7 billion pounds in 1971.

The failure of several international fisheries agreements to conserve fish contributed to calls for the right of coastal nations to exercise greater control over the exploitation of fisheries off their shores. In response to these calls, among other things, the United Nations convened a Third Conference on the Law of the Sea in 1974. As the conference wore on, it appeared that the parties would agree to allow coastal nations to claim a 200-mile resource conservation zone. By 1976, however, 36 nations had unilaterally declared so-called exclusive fishing zones beyond 12 miles and consensus on this crucial issue was disintegrating as nonfishing issues, such as seabed-mineral use, divided the nations (Bean 1983).

In an attempt to address these problems and the politically unacceptable depletion of fisheries off U.S. shores, among other things, Congress passed the Magnuson Fishery Conservation and Management Act in 1976 (16 U.S.C.A. 1801 *et seq.*). Passage of the act radically changed the management of fisheries and the conduct of foreign and domestic fisheries in U.S. waters. The act also introduced innovations in federal wildlife law (Bean 1983).

## The Fishery Conservation Zone

With the passage of the Fishery Conservation and Management Act, the United States joined a growing number of nations that had expanded their exclusive zones from 12 to 200 nautical miles. Within this fishery conservation zone the United States claims exclusive management over:

- all fish, except highly migratory species of tuna;
- all anadromous species throughout their migratory range beyond the conservation zone, except when they are within another nation's territorial sea or Fishery Conservation Zone as recognized by the United States; and
- all sedentary continental shelf fishery resources beyond the Fishery Conservation Zone, such as American lobster.

Besides the exception for highly migratory species of tuna, excluded for the benefit of U.S. tuna boats operating within 200 miles of the shores of several South and Central American countries, the Fishery Conservation and Management Act also excludes from its management provisions both marine mammals and seabirds.

Each coastal state maintains management control over fish and shellfish resources within its territorial waters unless the secretary of Commerce, who is responsible for implementing most federal activities under the Fishery Conservation and Management Act, finds that state management substantially and adversely affects a fishery management plan developed under the fishery act. Only in such a case may the federal government preempt state management authority for fish and shellfish in territorial waters.

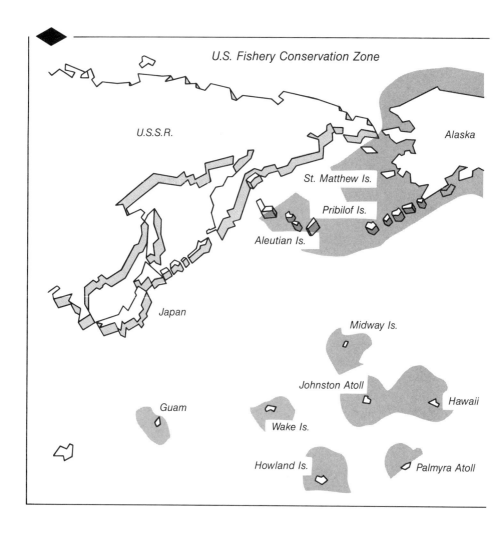

The U.S. Fishery Conservation Zone, the single largest pool of living resources
possessed by any country

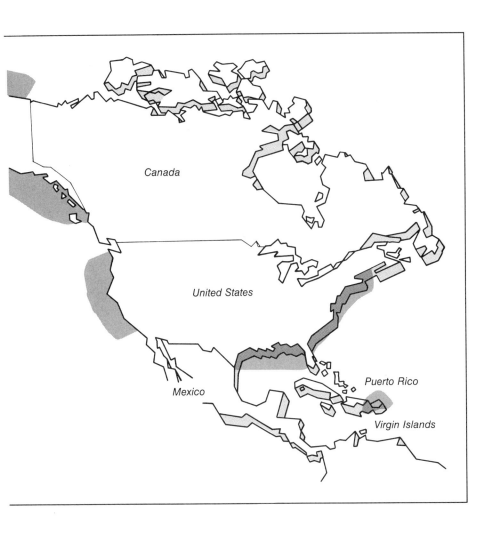

285

# Fishery Management Plans

The principal tool of fisheries management under the Fishery Conservation and Management Act is the development of fishery management plans, in accordance with national standards, by one or more of eight regional fishery management councils.* In order to meet the national standards, the act requires that fishery management plans:

- prevent overfishing and ensure an optimum yield from each fishery;
- be based on the best scientific information available;
- treat individual fish stocks as management units;
- not discriminate between residents of different states;
- promote efficiency;
- allow for contingencies; and
- minimize costs and avoid duplication.

The basic management determination under the Fishery Conservation and Management Act is a widely questioned theory of population dynamics called maximum sustainable yield (MSY). A recent critique of fisheries management under the act provides a fair description of the maximum sustainable yield concept:

> The principle behind MSY is based on observations that up to a point, the more fish of a given species that are caught, the more there are to catch. The reasoning is that when fish are harvested, more food resources are available to be used more efficiently by the remaining fish stock. Thus, they grow faster. At low fishing effort, the total amount of fish caught is also low. As the effort increases, the catch increases up to a point of leveling off. . . . Beyond this point, increased fishing effort results in a declining catch at the high point of the curve, which is defined as the maximum sustainable yield (Council on Environmental Quality 1981).

Partially because of the many limitations of this theory, some of which will be discussed later, Congress adopted "optimum yield" as a management goal of the fishery act. The act defines optimum yield as the amount of fish that will provide the greatest overall benefit to the nation, with particular reference to food production and recreational opportunities, and as maximum sustainable yield modified by relevant social, economic, and ecological factors (16 U.S.C.A. 1802[18]). Since these later determinations depend upon information that often is not available, optimum yield determinations often are controversial.

Nonetheless, a fishery management plan must include a determination of optimum yield for the fish stock and a determination of the "capacity and extent to which fishing vessels of the United States, on an annual basis, will

---

* The mechanism for developing plans is described in detail in another section of this chapter, as is the composition of the fishery management councils.

harvest the optimum yield" (16 U.S.C.A. 1853[a][4][a]). Whatever portion of optimum yield will not be taken by domestic fishermen is available to foreign fishermen under permit. A fishery management plan may include "the relevant fishery conservation and management measures of the coastal states nearest to the fishery" (16 U.S.C.A. 1853 [b]5) and other provisions, such as forms of limited access, gear restrictions, limitations on incidental catch, permits, and fees.

Although the fishery management councils are responsible for the development of fishery management plans for fisheries in their geographical areas, the secretary of Commerce is given the ultimate authority to review and approve a fishery management plan and to issue regulations implementing it. In addition, the secretary may prepare a fishery management plan if a fishery management council has failed to do so. Finally, the Fishery Conservation and Management Act directed the secretary of Commerce to prepare preliminary management plans for fish stocks in the U.S. conservation zone that were being fished by foreign but not domestic fishermen. These stocks included sharks in the Atlantic and Pacific and snails in the Bering Sea.

## Foreign Fishing

After February 28, 1977, foreign fishing for species over which the United States exercises management authority was prohibited unless:

- the fishing is authorized by an international fishery agreement;
- reciprocal privileges are granted to U.S. vessels to fish in foreign waters;
- each foreign vessel has on board a valid permit.

Even with a permit, foreign fishermen are allowed to take only whatever fish the domestic industry cannot catch. This total allowable level of foreign fishing is determined in the development of fishery management plans.

The total allowable level is allocated quarterly by the secretary of State, with the advice of NMFS and the regional fishery management councils, to those countries that have entered into a governing international fishery agreement with the United States. Negotiated by the State Department with the advice of NMFS, the agreements become effective 60 days after being submitted to Congress unless either house of Congress passes a resolution of disapproval.

Once a governing international fishery agreement is in force, the foreign nation submits individual applications for each vessel that will operate in the U.S. fishery conservation zone. These applications are reviewed by other federal agencies, the fishery management councils, and the public. If they are approved by the assistant administrator for Fisheries in NOAA, the permits are issued by the secretary of State. Foreign nations also pay permit fees, a poundage fee for fish caught, and a fee for maintaining U.S. observers aboard foreign fishing vessels while in the U.S. fishery conservation zone.

# Other Provisions

In passing the Fishery Conservation and Management Act, Congress amended a number of statutes in order to bring them in compliance with the act, principally with respect to the newly established 200-mile limit. These acts include the Marine Mammal Protection Act, Fishermen's Protective Act, and the Atlantic Tuna Convention Act. Congress also directed that any existing bilateral or multilateral fisheries agreements that conflict with the management concepts of the fishery act should be renegotiated and reviewed by Congress.

The fishery act identifies prohibited acts, civil penalties, criminal offenses, and civil forfeitures. The secretary of Commerce and the secretary of the department in which the Coast Guard is operating are responsible for enforcement of the act*. In addition, the act authorized the secretary of Commerce to change regulations promulgated under the act to bring them into compliance with any comprehensive treaty that might be concluded at the United Nations Law of the Sea Conference. A comprehensive treaty did emerge in 1982, but the United States did not sign it for reasons largely unrelated to fisheries management.

## Amendments to the Fishery Conservation and Management Act

Since 1976, Congress has passed other legislation amending the Fishery Conservation and Management Act or affecting its implementation. For instance, the Fishery Conservation Zone Act of 1977 (91 Stat. 14, P.L.95-6 [1977]) repealed the implementing legislation for the International Convention for the Northwest Atlantic Fisheries and gave congressional approval to governing international fishery agreements with Bulgaria, Romania, Taiwan, East Germany, Korea, the U.S.S.R., and Poland.

The Fishery Conservation Zone Act was amended in March 1977 to give congressional approval to fishing agreements with Japan, South Korea, Spain, and the European Economic Community (91 Stat. 18, P.L. 95-8 [1977]). In December 1977, the Fishery Conservation Zone Act was amended to approve an agreement with Mexico (91 Stat. 1613, P.L. 97-219 [1977]). The 1977 law also amended the Executive Reorganization Plan of 1970, which created NOAA, to authorize five NOAA assistant administrators, including one for fisheries.

The zone act was amended again by an omnibus fishing bill in 1984 (P.L. 98-623 [1984]) to include a governing international fishery agreement with Iceland and a renewal of the agreement with the European Economic Community. Another fishery agreement, this one with the Faroe Islands, was

---

* During times of peace the Coast Guard is in the Department of Transportation; during times of war it is in the Department of Defense.

approved as part of the Marine Sanctuaries Reauthorization bill (P.L. 98-498 [1984]). Finally, the 1984 reauthorization of the Marine Mammal Protection Act (P.L. 98-364 [1984]) also extended the agreements with Poland and the U.S.S.R. for an 18-month period ending December 31, 1985.

In 1978, Congress reauthorized and amended the Fishery Conservation and Management Act in an attempt to encourage the development of the domestic fishing fleet (92 Stat. 519, P.L. 95-354 [1978]). To this end, Congress provided the secretary of Commerce with the authority to regulate foreign processing vessels that receive fish from U.S. fishing vessels within the fishery conservation zone. Only excess fish that will not be used by domestic fish processors may be transferred to foreign processing vessels, which must have a permit from the secretary of Commerce. The legislation also required the secretaries of Commerce and State to submit to Congress and the president an annual report setting forth:

- a list, by species, of all allocations made to foreign nations;
- all permits issued to foreign nations; and
- all tariff and nontariff trade barriers imposed by these nations on the importations of these species from the United States.

The amendments also require that fishery management plans include a finding regarding the capacity of domestic processing facilities and the extent to which these facilities will process the catch of domestic fishing vessels on an annual basis.

In 1979, Congress also inserted into the Fishery Conservation and Management Act a provision very similar to the "Pelly Amendment" to the Fishermen's Protective Act. According to the "Packwood-Magnuson Amendment," the secretary of State must reduce by at least 50 percent the allocation of fish from the fishery conservation zone to any nation certified by the secretary of Commerce as jeopardizing the effectiveness of the international Convention for the Regulation of Whaling. This certification also triggers the provisions of the Pelly Amendment to the Fishermen's Protective Act, which provides for an embargo of fish and fish products from offending countries.

In June 1980, Congress amended the Fishery Conservation and Management Act to authorize the National Oceanic and Atmospheric Administration administrator to consult with the fishery management councils regarding any deep-seabed mining permitted by NOAA, if the mining could adversely affect fisheries protected under the fishery act.

In December 1980, Congress passed the American Fisheries Promotion Act (16 U.S.C.A. 1801 Note). This act amended the Fishery Conservation and Management Act to provide a means for reducing foreign fishing within the fishery conservation zone. The American Fisheries Promotion Act revised the criteria upon which the secretaries of State and of Commerce are to base determination on the allocation of allowable levels of foreign fishing. The act also increased the fees for foreign fishing and required that an observer be aboard each foreign vessel while it is fishing within the U.S. conservation zone.

Lastly, the act changed the name of the Fishery Conservation and Management Act to the Magnuson Fishery Conservation and Management Act in honor of the former senator from Washington who, as chair of the Senate Commerce Committee, had played a critical role in passing the original legislation.

In 1982, Congress amended and reauthorized the Magnuson Fishery Conservation and Management Act through FY 1985 (P.L. 97-453). Among other things, this legislation:

- established a program for placing observers on all foreign fishing vessels while operating in the U.S. conservation zone, thus providing a means for putting observers on the boats as required in the American Fisheries Promotion Act;
- provided for a partial allocation system whereby the initial release of foreign allocations to each nation in a given year would be limited and future releases would depend upon whether the country is providing access for U.S. fish products to its markets;
- exempted fishery management councils from the Federal Advisory Committee Act;
- changed the timing and procedures involved in the development, review, approval, and implementation of fishery management plans and regulations;
- provided that guidelines interpreting the Magnuson act's national standards do not have the force and effect of law.

In 1984, Congress amended the Magnuson Fishery Conservation and Management Act as part of an omnibus fishing bill (P.L. 98-623). These amendments determined that the state of Alaska would exercise management authority over fish and shellfish in certain partially enclosed Alaskan waters. The bill also changed the process by which foreign allocations are used to gain advantages for U.S. fishermen in foreign conservation zones and markets.

## International Fisheries Agreements After Passage of the Fishery Conservation and Management Act

One of the primary forces behind passage of the Magnuson Fishery Conservation and Management Act in 1976 was to "get the foreigners out" of fishing grounds which U.S. fishermen considered their own. This remains a principal driving force behind U.S. policy. At the same time, however, the United States has continued to enter or amend international fisheries agreements which may or may not comport with the standards of the act.* Management of fisheries that are subject to international fisheries agreements has changed both in

---

* Much of the following discussion is based upon an August 1985 memorandum regarding international fisheries agreements by Henry R. Beasely, Director, Office of International Fisheries, NMFS.

response to and in spite of the Magnuson Fishery Conservation and Management Act.

## International Fisheries in the Pacific Ocean

In 1977, Mexico and Costa Rica, in an effort to secure greater control of their fisheries, sought to renegotiate the convention establishing the Inter-American Tropical Tuna Commission. Mexico, Costa Rica, and Canada withdrew in 1978, 1979, and 1984 respectively. As negotiations stalled, attention became concentrated on the development of a regional licensing scheme and culminated on March 15, 1983, in the conclusion of the Eastern Pacific Ocean Tuna Fishing Agreement by the United States, Costa Rica, and Panama. The agreement will not come into effect until five coastal countries in the region have ratified it. By August 1985, only the United States, Panama, and Honduras had ratified the treaty.* The agreement established an international authority to issue regional licenses for fishing tuna in a broad area of the eastern Pacific Ocean, with licensing fees to be distributed among the coastal states in proportion to the amount taken within 200 miles of each contracting party.

The 1978 amendments to the North Pacific Fisheries Act of 1954 implemented a protocol amending the International Convention for the High Seas Fisheries of the North Pacific Ocean. Among other things, the act allows the Japanese salmon-fishing fleet operating within the U.S. fishery conservation zone to take marine mammals incidental to their fishing activities without first obtaining a permit under the Marine Mammal Protection Act. At the end of 1982, Congress amended the North Pacific Fisheries Act (96 Stat. 1949, P.L. 97-389). The amendments extended until 1987 the general permit issued to the Japanese mothership salmon fleet for the taking of marine mammals.

Canada and the United States in 1984 concluded a treaty concerning Pacific salmon that is implemented in the United States by the Pacific Salmon Treaty Act of 1985 (P.L. 99-5). This treaty, which came into effect on March 18, 1985, establishes the Pacific Salmon Commission as a successor to the International Pacific Salmon Fisheries Commission. The commission will be responsible for managing intercepting fisheries, i.e. fishermen of one country who intercept salmon originating in the waters of the other country.

## International Fisheries in the Atlantic Ocean

In January 1979, the Northwest Atlantic Fisheries Organization replaced the International Commission for the Northwest Atlantic Fisheries. The United States is considering membership in the organization, which was established by the Convention on Future Multilateral Cooperation in the Northwest At-

---

* In 1984, Congress passed P.L. 98-445 implementing this agreement domestically.

lantic Fisheries. Bulgaria, Canada, Cuba, the European Economic Community, the Faroe Islands (Denmark), East Germany, Iceland, Japan, Norway, Poland, Portugal, Romania, Spain, and the U.S.S.R. are members. The convention sets species quotas for all fishery resources outside the fishery conservation zone of the member nations in the Northwest Atlantic. The convention does not apply to salmon, tuna, marlin, and whales under the management of the International Whaling Commission, and sedentary species of the continental shelf.

The United States, Canada, Denmark, the European Economic Community, Finland, Iceland, Norway, and Sweden in 1983 concluded the Convention for the Conservation of Salmon in the North Atlantic Ocean (T.I.A.S. 10789). The principal purpose of the convention, implemented in the United States by the Atlantic Salmon Convention Act of 1982 (16 U.S.C.A. 3601), is to promote the conservation, restoration, enhancement, and rational management of salmon stocks in the north Atlantic Ocean. The treaty establishes a council, three regional commissions, and a secretariat. The United States and Canada belong to the North American Commission. The United States also belongs to the West Greenland Commission, along with Canada, the European Economic Community, and Denmark.

Salmon fishing is prohibited on the high seas, the area beyond the fishery conservation zones of the member states. Within the conservation zones of coastal states, salmon fishing generally is prohibited beyond 12 nautical miles from shore.

## The Antarctic Treaty

In 1982, the Convention for the Conservation of Antarctic Marine Living Resources became effective for the United States (T.I.A.S. 10240). This treaty, to which 18 other nations and the European Economic Community now belong, established a commission for the purpose of conserving marine living resources found in the waters surrounding Antarctica. Quite possibly the most ambitious of marine living resource treaties, the convention is based upon an ecosystem-wide approach to the conservation of marine living resources and incorporates standards designed not only to ensure the conservation of individual populations and species, but also to maintain the breadth of the Antarctic marine ecosystem as a whole.

## Fisheries Legislation Since Passage of the Fishery Conservation and Management Act

While the Fishery Conservation and Management Act revolutionized federal fisheries management, by no means did it exhaust congressional action on fisheries. Amendments to the Fishermen's Protective Act in 1977, 1978, and 1980 authorized the secretary of Commerce to make loans to domestic fishermen whose vessels or gear are damaged by foreign fishing operations in the U.S. fishery conservation zone. In 1981, Congress authorized a cooperative insurance program to allow American fishing vessel owners to recoup economic losses resulting from illegal seizure of their vessels.

In 1978, Congress also established a Fishermen's Contingency Fund under the Outer Continental Shelf Lands Act (43 U.S.C.A. 1801). Title IV of the act authorizes the secretary of Commerce to establish a $1 million fund in the U.S. Treasury to be used as a revolving fund for the purpose of compensating fishermen for damages to fishing vessels, gear, and any resulting economic loss due to offshore oil and gas exploration, development, and production. Besides establishing procedures, the act requires an annual report to Congress. In 1984, Congress amended this provision to provide for compensation equal to 50 percent, instead of 25 percent, of the economic loss suffered.

The 1980 American Fisheries Promotion Act not only amended the Magnuson Fishery Conservation and Management Act but also the Saltonstall-Kennedy Act of 1954 regarding the availability and use of funds for fisheries research and development projects. It also authorized the secretary of Commerce to appoint six U.S. fishery trade officers to promote U.S. fishing interests. The promotion act also amended the Merchant Marine Act of 1936 to extend its coverage to include fishery facilities on land and authorized the secretary to guarantee obligations for fishing vessels and facilities used for underutilized fisheries. Finally, the promotion act extended the Fisheries Loan Fund under the Fish and Wildlife Act of 1956 through fiscal year 1982 to provide loans to fishermen to avoid defaults on obligations covering fishing vessels*.

## Aquaculture

Living marine resources were the subject of a flurry of other legislative activities during 1980 and 1981†. Although government, industry, and academia had for years been touting the promise of aquaculture to feed the earth's expanding human populations, the U.S. activities in this area were not coordinated. In May 1977, NOAA issued its own Aquaculture Plan, and by 1980, some momentum had built toward a national aquaculture effort.

The National Aquaculture Act of 1980 promotes aquaculture in the United States by mandating a National Aquaculture Plan to coordinate do-

---

* In 1984 the Fisheries Loan Fund was extended through 1986.

† Included here but not discussed are amendments to the Commercial Fisheries Research and Development Act (16 U.S.C.A. 779), the Federal Crop Insurance Act (7 U.S.C.A. 1501), the Consolidated Farm and Rural Development Act (7 U.S.C.A. 1923), the Farm Credit System Act (12 U.S.C.A. 2001), and the Lacey Act (18 U.S.C.A. 43-44, 16 U.S.C.A. 3401). For discussion of the Salmon and Steelhead Conservation Act (16 U.S.C.A 3301) see the "Inland Fisheries Management" chapter in the *Audubon Wildlife Report 1985*.

mestic programs (16 U.S.C.A. 2801 Note). The Department of Commerce was designated the lead agency for the development and implementation of the plan in consultation with the secretaries of Agriculture and the Interior and the states, fishery management councils, and private industry. The act also establishes an interagency aquaculture coordinating group. It authorizes the secretaries to provide financial grants for demonstration projects and provides for the establishment of a loan guarantee program. Congress never appropriated funds for the implementation of the act, although the department did develop a National Aquaculture Plan (Joint Subcommittee on Aquaculture 1983). In 1984, Congress reauthorized the National Aquaculture Act for the fiscal years 1984 and 1985, but still failed to appropriate funds.

## Congressional Action in 1984

Congress passed a large number of bills affecting the programs of NMFS in 1984.* P.L. 98-623, an omnibus fishing bill mentioned previously, established national standards for the design, construction, and siting of artificial reefs in U.S. waters and implemented the Convention on the Conservation of Antarctic Marine Living Resources.†

The failure of the Atlantic states to implement the restrictions on catching striped bass recommended by the Atlantic States Marine Fisheries Commission led Congress to pass the Atlantic Striped Bass Conservation Act (16 U.S.C.A. 1851). Under the act, the secretary of Commerce was authorized to declare a moratorium on the catching of striped bass in the territorial waters of any coastal state from Maine to North Carolina that failed to implement the fisheries commission's recommendations by July 1, 1985. No federal moratorium was imposed, however, because all states complied. The act also extended the authorization of the Emergency Striped Bass study through fiscal year 1986.

In 1984, Congress also reauthorized the National Marine Sanctuary program under Title III of the Marine Protection, Research, and Sanctuaries Act and amended the enabling legislation in several important ways (P.L. 98-498). Of greatest interest for fisheries is a requirement that the responsibility

---

* Included here are P.L. 98-595, which amended Title XI of the Merchant Marine Act of 1936; P.L. 98-541, the Trinity River Basin Fish and Wildlife Restoration Act, which established a cost-sharing mechanism to restore salmon spawning areas in that river basin; P.L. 98-454, which permits U.S. documentation for foreign-built vessels in some U.S. territories; P.L. 98-371, which appropriated funds for a cooperative National Oceanic and Atmospheric Administration-Environmental Protection Agency study of water quality in four bays; and P.L. 98-369, which increased Dingell-Johnson support to fisheries management and recreational boating programs nationwide.

† This bill also extended the export promotion authority of the secretary of Agriculture and the Commodity Credit Corporation to include fish and fish products and reauthorized the National Sea Grant College Program for fiscal years 1984-1987.

for developing draft regulations on fishing within a proposed national marine sanctuary rest with the appropriate fishery management council, giving the fishing industry a formal and more explicit say in regulation planning. Under the amendments, the secretary of Commerce may accept or reject the draft regulations and prepare regulations if a fishery management council has not done so.

The Marine Mammal Protection Act Reauthorization (P.L. 98-364) extended the act through fiscal year 1988 and amended it by requiring any nation exporting fish or fish products to the United States to show the effects of its commercial fishing technology upon marine mammals. Specifically, any nation exporting yellowfin tuna caught with purse seine nets in the eastern tropical Pacific Ocean must show that it has a marine mammal protection program and average rate of incidental catch comparable to that of the United States.

## Organization and Operations

Although the focus of this chapter is upon the Commerce Department's National Marine Fisheries Service, other federal, quasi-federal, state, interstate, and international agencies play important roles in the management of U.S. marine fisheries. The functions, roles, and responsibilities of the principal agencies are discussed here.

### National Marine Fisheries Service

The Magnuson Fishery Conservation and Management Act vests the secretary of Commerce with the responsibility for managing marine fisheries within the U.S. fishery conservation zone. The secretary has delegated much of this authority to the administrator of the National Oceanic and Atmospheric Administration, who has in turn delegated authority to the assistant administrator for Fisheries. The assistant administrator for Fisheries oversees all NMFS activities and is assisted by three deputy assistant administrators.*

*Fisheries.* The deputy assistant administrator for Fisheries coordinates the work of three staff offices:

1) the management and budget staff, responsible for tracking NMFS expenditures, among other things;
2) the Office of Policy and Planning, which oversees NMFS policy development, internal program management and reporting systems, and budget formulation;

---

* Besides NMFS, the National Oceanic and Atmospheric Administration includes the National Ocean Service; the National Weather Service; the National Environmental Satellite, Data, and Information Service; and the Office of Oceanic and Atmospheric Research.

# National Marine Fisheries Service

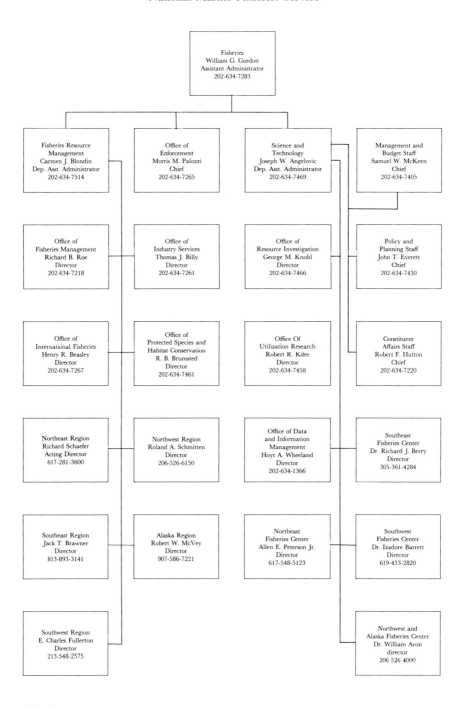

Fisheries
William G. Gordon
Assistant Administrator
202-634-7283

Fisheries Resource
Management
Carmen J. Blondin
Dep. Asst. Administrator
202-634-7514

Office of
Enforcement
Morris M. Palozzi
Chief
202-634-7265

Science and
Technology
Joseph W. Angelovic
Dep. Asst. Administrator
202-634-7469

Management and
Budget Staff
Samuel W. McKeen
Chief
202-634-7405

Office of
Fisheries Management
Richard B. Roe
Director
202-634-7218

Office of
Industry Services
Thomas J. Billy
Director
202-634-7261

Office of
Resource Investigation
George M. Knobl
Director
202-634-7466

Policy and
Planning Staff
John T. Everett
Chief
202-634-7430

Office of
International Fisheries
Henry R. Beasley
Director
202-634-7267

Office of
Protected Species and
Habitat Conservation
R. B. Brumsted
Director
202-634-7461

Office Of
Utilization Research
Robert R. Kifer
Director
202-634-7458

Constituent
Affairs Staff
Robert F. Hutton
Chief
202-634-7220

Northeast Region
Richard Schaefer
Acting Director
617-281-3600

Northwest Region
Roland A. Schmitten
Director
206-526-6150

Office of Data
and Information
Management
Hoyt A. Wheeland
Director
202-634-1366

Southeast
Fisheries Center
Dr. Richard J. Berry
Director
305-361-4284

Southeast Region
Jack T. Brawner
Director
813-893-3141

Alaska Region
Robert W. McVey
Director
907-586-7221

Northeast
Fisheries Center
Allen E. Peterson Jr.
Director
617-548-5123

Southwest
Fisheries Center
Dr. Izadore Barrett
Director
619-453-2820

Southwest Region
E. Charles Fullerton
Director
213-548-2575

Northwest and
Alaska Fisheries Center
Dr. William Aron
director
206 526 4000

3) the Office of Constituent Affairs, which coordinates NMFS relations with industry and the general public.

Three departmental-level offices provide legal, congressional liaison, and public affairs services through branch offices within NMFS. The Office of General Counsel—Fisheries represents NMFS in legal actions and provides legal advice and recommendations on the broad array of NMFS activities. The Office of Congressional Affairs coordinates the presentation of NMFS positions on legislation to Congress and responses to congressional inquiries regarding NMFS activities. The Office of Public Affairs assists in presenting NMFS activities and positions to the press.

***Fisheries Resource Management.*** The second deputy assistant administrator heads the fisheries resource management program, which includes five offices at the NMFS Washington D.C. headquarters, each headed by a director.

The Office of Fisheries Management is divided into the Fishery Management Operations Division and the Fees, Permits, and Regulations Division. The Fishery Management Operations Division coordinates the review of fishery management plans, assists the regional fishery management councils in developing fishery management plans, and recommends decisions on regulations and other regulatory actions. The Fees, Permits, and Regulations Division coordinates the development of regulations, the collection of fees such as poundage fees from foreign fishermen, and the review and issuance of permits as for foreign fishing.

The NMFS Office of Industry Services is divided into an Industry Development Division and a Financial Services Division. The Industry Development Division administers the Saltonstall-Kennedy program of fisheries development grants, participates in international trade processes relating to fisheries, advises industry regarding programs such as the Commodity Credit Corporation or government purchases of fishery products under the Surplus Commodity Program, and assists industry with the regulatory programs of other agencies.

The Financial Services Division administers several programs for financing fisheries production equipment, including the Fishing Vessel Obligation Guarantee Program and the Fishing Vessel Capital Construction Fund, two programs that help commercial fishermen with the purchase and maintenance of their boats.

The Office of International Fisheries is divided into two divisions. The International Organizations and Agreements Division assists in developing the position of the U.S. government in meetings of the nine international fisheries commissions to which the United States belongs and in bilateral fisheries agreements, where the State Department has the lead. The International Fisheries Development and Services Division participates with the regional fishery management councils, other divisions of NMFS, and the State Department as a member of the Allocations Board that sets allocations of fishing rights and catch quotas for foreign fishing operations within the U.S. fishery conservation zone. This division also evaluates joint ventures with foreign fishermen, assists in marketing U.S. fishery products abroad, provides advice for negotiations with other countries, and provides technical assistance to other countries through projects of the Agency for International Development.

Of the various international fisheries agreement to which the United States is a party, several have commissions that make decisions or recommendations regarding the allocations of fish stocks. The NMFS deputy assistant administrator for Fisheries Resource Management represents the United States in the International Commission for the Conservation of Atlantic Tunas. NMFS regional directors serve on the North Atlantic Salmon Conservation Organization, the International North Pacific Fisheries Commission, and the International Pacific Halibut Commission. In general, these commissions rely upon member countries to conduct research necessary for carrying out the conservation and management mission of the treaties.

The Office of Protected Species and Habitat Conservation is divided into a Protected Species Division and a Habitat Conservation Division. The Protected Species Division coordinates NMFS research and management programs under the Endangered Species Act and the Marine Mammal Protection Act (see the Marine Mammal Protection chapter for more detail). The Habitat Conservation Division provides coordination, liaison, policy guidance, and other oversight for a national program designed to minimize fishery-related habitat losses by reviewing permits. This division conducts research in order to obtain data upon which to base recommendations for coastal and marine development.

The NMFS Office of Enforcement sets overall enforcement policies. Each regional office's enforcement efforts are headed by a special agent-in-charge, who reports to the regional director. All NMFS agents, as federal representatives, may take part in non-fishing enforcement actions, such as drug-smuggling arrests. The activities of the Washington office include review of fishery management plans and other regulatory actions, coordination of the foreign observer program, and liaison with the Drug Interdiction Task Force.

*Science and Technology.* A third NOAA deputy assistant administrator coordinates the NMFS science and technology activities and oversees three offices at Washington headquarters, each headed by a director:

The Office of Resource Investigations coordinates NMFS research on living marine resources and their habitats. Research is conducted at four NMFS regional centers and at 28 different field facilities.

The Office of Data and Information Management collects statistics on fishing efforts and market prices, among other things, through 43 different offices around the country. This effort relies in some cases upon state data-collection programs.

The Office of Utilization Research serves as the principal source of advice and guidance on scientific and technological matters related to fish-product quality, safety, and use. This office also operates a voluntary inspection program for fish and fishery products.

## Regional Organization

Many of the daily decisions regarding fisheries management and industry assistance are delegated to five regional NMFS offices: Northeast, Southeast, Southwest, Northwest, and Alaska. NMFS regional directors have been given the authority to approve or disapprove fishery management plans and amendments to them, while regulations are approved by the Washington office. Regional directors are the primary contact with the fishery management councils and must coordinate with NMFS Fisheries Centers on research and with General Counsel Offices in the review and approval of fishery management plans.

NMFS research, similarly decentralized, is directed through the four fisheries centers: Northeast, Southeast, Southwest, Northwest, and Alaska. The center directors oversee numerous research laboratories and facilities in the various regions.

## Regional Fishery Management Councils

Under the Magnuson Fishery Conservation and Management Act, eight fishery management councils are responsible for the development of fishery management plans for both domestic and foreign fishing within the fishery conservation zone. These fishery management councils are: New England, Mid-Atlantic, South Atlantic, Gulf of Mexico, Caribbean, Pacific, North Pacific, and Western Pacific.

Each of the eight fishery management councils is composed of voting and nonvoting members. Voting members include the principal state marine-fishery managers from each member state in a region, the NMFS regional director, and "qualified individuals" recommended by the governors of each member state and appointed by the secretary of Commerce for three-year terms.

Nonvoting members include the regional or area director of the U.S. Fish and Wildlife Service, the commander of the U.S. Coast Guard district, the executive director of the relevant interstate Marine Fisheries Commission, and a representative of the U.S. Department of State. The Pacific Fishery Management Council has one additional nonvoting member who serves at the pleasure of the governor of Alaska.

Each fishery management council has established a science and statistical committee to assist in the identification and analysis of the scientific and socio-economic information needed for the development and monitoring of fishery management plans. Fishery management councils also have estab-

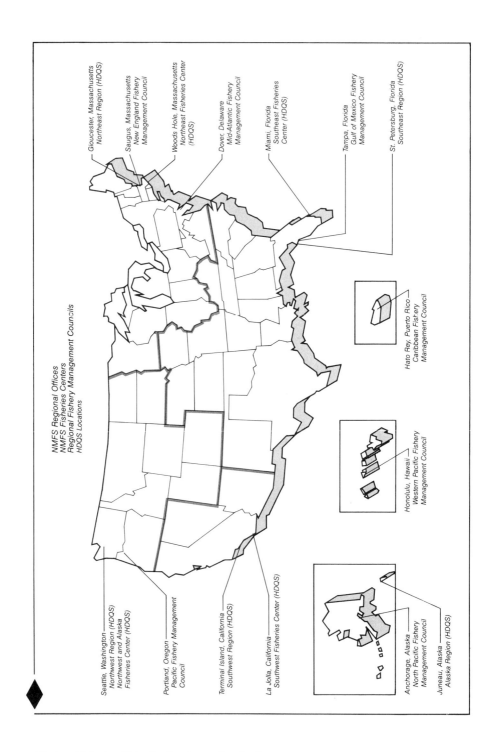

Seattle, Washington
Northwest Region (HDQS)
Northwest and Alaska
Fisheries Center (HDQS)

Portland, Oregon
Pacific Fishery Management
Council

Terminal Island, California
Southwest Region (HDQS)

La Jolla, California
Southwest Fisheries Center (HDQS)

Anchorage, Alaska
North Pacific Fishery
Management Council

Juneau, Alaska
Alaska Region (HDQS)

Honolulu, Hawaii
Western Pacific Fishery
Management Council

Hato Rey, Puerto Rico
Caribbean Fishery
Management Council

NMFS Regional Offices
NMFS Fisheries Centers
Regional Fishery Management Councils
HDQS Locations

Gloucester, Massachusetts
Northeast Region (HDQS)

Saugus, Massachusetts
New England Fishery
Management Council

Woods Hole, Massachusetts
Northeast Fisheries Center
(HDQS)

Dover, Delaware
Mid-Atlantic Fishery
Management Council

Miami, Florida
Southeast Fisheries
Center (HDQS)

Tampa, Florida
Gulf of Mexico Fishery
Management Council

St. Petersburg, Florida
Southeast Region (HDQS)

National Marine Fisheries Service regional offices, fisheries centers, and regional fishery management councils (headquarters locations)

lished advisory panels, often composed of individuals outside the council, to advise on a wide range of matters. Some councils have established multidisciplinary teams to draft fishery management plans and amendments to fishery management plans, to monitor fisheries, and to make recommendations to the councils. Each council has an executive director who coordinates clerical and technical support of the council's work. Council meetings may be called by the executive director or the council chair.

Besides developing, monitoring, and revising fishery management plans, each fishery management council also prepares comments on applications for foreign fishing within the fishery conservation zone and for other purposes, conducts public hearings regarding fishery management plans and amendments, and reviews and revises population estimates and fishing quotas.

## Other Federal Agencies

NMFS fisheries management efforts rely upon the support of other services within the National Oceanic and Atmospheric Administration. For instance, some NMFS research is conducted on NOAA research vessels operated under the direction of the National Ocean Service. Other research, requiring remote sensing from satellites, is conducted with the help of the National Environmental Satellite, Data, and Information Service and the Office of Oceanic and Atmospheric Research.

The NOAA National Sea Grant Office coordinates programs of research at various sea-great colleges and universities around the United States. Much Sea Grant research relates to commercial and recreational marine fisheries. Through its Marine Advisory Program, conducted in 28 states and Puerto Rico, Sea Grant conveys the results of scientific research to the fishing community and communicates fishermen needs and problems to Sea Grant researchers. NMFS periodically reviews Sea Grant proposals and programs so as to avoid duplication of effort.

Under a memorandum of understanding, the Department of Agriculture and the Sea Grant Advisory Program coordinate their efforts in providing educational information and technology transfer assistance to the fishing community. Under another memorandum of understanding with the Department of Commerce, Agriculture's Cooperative State Research Service coordinates its research and education programs on aquaculture.

The Department of State, through its Bureau of Oceans and International Environmental and Scientific Affairs, participates as a nonvoting member in the deliberations of fishery agreements under the Magnuson Fishery Conservation and Management Act, and allocates the total allowable level of foreign fishing in the fishery conservation zone. The State Department also represents the United States on international fishery commissions and negotiates access for U.S. fishermen to the exclusive economic zones of other countries.

The fishery management and conservation regulations issued under the Magnuson Fishery Conservation and Management Act and other laws are enforced principally by the U.S. Coast Guard and NMFS. The U.S. Coast Guard coordinates its enforcement of regulations issued under the act through its Operational Law Enforcement Division's Fisheries Enforcement Branch. Day-to-day enforcement decisions are made at the Coast Guard District level in coordination with NMFS special agents, whose efforts are coordinated in turn through NMFS regional and headquarters enforcement offices. NMFS and the Coast Guard have entered into memorandum of understanding with coastal states under which the states may enforce federal regulations. The Coast Guard also provides advice to the State Department on the enforcement issues that may arise during negotiation of fisheries treaties and the review of foreign fishing-permit applications. The Department of Justice provides legal support for enforcement of federal fishery regulations.

The Food and Drug Administration acts to ensure that fish and shellfish products are safe for human consumption, wholesome, and properly labeled. The Food and Drug Administration has entered into memoranda of understanding with NMFS regarding research for fishery products, with the Department of Commerce regarding inspection programs for fishery products, with the Interstate Shellfish Sanitation Conference regarding improvement of shellfish sanitation and quality, and with the countries of Japan, Republic of Korea, Iceland, United Kingdom, Canada, Mexico, and New Zealand regarding importation of shellfish into the United States. The Food and Drug Administration also works with the State Department and the Customs Service regarding shellfish imports and with the Environmental Protection Agency regarding environmental contaminants that may enter the food chain.

The U.S. Army Corps of Engineers of the Department of the Army undertakes projects that affect commercial and recreational fisheries in a variety of ways. First, the Corps administers a permitting system under Section 404 of the Clean Water Act that provides for dredging and dredge-spoil disposal in wetlands, including coastal wetlands. Review of Section 404 permit requests is a significant NMFS activity, particularly in the Southeast Region, where most of the Section 404 projects affecting coastal wetlands occur. The Corps also designs and constructs dam by-pass facilities for anadromous fish, hatchery facilities, and boat harbors for commercial and recreational boats.

The U.S. Fish and Wildlife Service, in the Interior Department, shares responsibility with the states for the management of inland fisheries and shares responsibility with NMFS for anadromous fisheries and some species protected under the Endangered Species Act. The U.S. Fish and Wildlife Service also has a memorandum of understanding with NMFS regarding a state grants-in-aid program for anadromous fish.

Interior's Office of Territorial and International Affairs participates with U.S. territories and the State Department in resolving fishing violations of territorial waters by U.S. or foreign fishing vessels. The office also promotes the development of the fishing industry in U.S. territories such as American Samoa and Puerto Rico.

## Nonfederal Agencies and Organizations

Congress has established three interstate Marine Fisheries Commissions (Atlantic States, Pacific States, and Gulf States) to coordinate the regulation of fishing in the territorial seas of the coastal states. Each member state of an interstate marine fisheries commission is represented by a member of the administrative agency in charge of marine fisheries, a legislative member, and an appointee of the governor. Each commission's daily activities are coordinated by an executive director and staff. Federally funded, these commissions rely upon NMFS and FWS for research data on which to base their recommendations, but these recommendations are not binding.

Since most of the catch in many fisheries occurs within state waters, state marine resource programs play a crucial role in the management of marine fisheries. The organization of state marine fisheries management efforts varies considerably. In California, for instance, the Department of Fish and Game enforces regulations adopted by the Fish and Game Commission. In Maine, by contrast, the Department of Marine Resources is a separate agency which is responsible for research, development, and enforcement of laws pertaining to Maine's marine resources.

Eight private fisheries development foundations conduct industry-related research with Saltonstall-Kennedy funds and other funds and serve to focus the identification of industry research and development needs. Saltonstall-Kennedy funds are awarded by NMFS after a review of projects submitted by the foundations and other organizations.

Several industry and professional associations regularly participate in the development of fisheries management policy. The International Association of Fish and Wildlife Agencies, for instance, represents state fish and wildlife managers at the national level. The National Fisheries Institute principally represents the interests of fish importers and processors. National organizations, such as the National Federation of Fishermen, and regional organizations, such as Texas Shrimp Association, Southeastern Fisheries Association, and the Pacific Coast Federation of Fishermen's Associations, represent commercial interests. The Sport Fishing Institute has long championed the cause of marine recreational fisheries. The American Fisheries Society addresses both freshwater and saltwater fisheries biology and promotes the conservation and wise management of fish resources.

## Congressional Committees

Several congressional committees have jurisdiction over marine fisheries issues. The Senate Committee on Commerce, Science, and Transportation and the

House Committee on Merchant Marine and Fisheries are responsible for all authorizing legislation regarding marine fisheries matters. Within the House Committee, the Subcommittee on Fisheries and Wildlife Conservation and the Environment exercises special influence over federal marine fishery programs. In the Senate, the National Ocean Policy Study, a subunit of the Commerce Committee, has the lead role.

Appropriations for marine fishery programs of NMFS are set by the Senate Subcommittee on Appropriations for Commerce, Justice, State and the Judiciary and Related Agencies and the House Subcommittee on Appropriations for Commerce, Justice, State and Judiciary and Related Agencies.

Authorizing legislation for the anadromous fish programs of the U.S. Fish and Wildlife Service is under the jurisdiction of the Senate Committee on Environment and Public Works and the House Committee on Merchant Marine and Fisheries. Appropriations for Fish and Wildlife Service anadromous fisheries programs are set by the House and Senate Appropriations Subcommittees on Interior and Related Agencies

## Planning in Federal Fisheries Management

Planning is central to the federal fisheries management effort. Strategic planning has been playing an increasingly important role at NMFS in recent years. The Magnuson Fishery Conservation and Management Act also depends upon regional planning to achieve many of its objectives, and fishery management planning is a principal activity of the fishery management councils.

*Planning within the NMFS.* The Office of Policy and Planning coordinates NMFS planning. The central planning document is the *Strategic Plan of the National Marine Fisheries Service,* which establishes the goals and objectives of NMFS consistent with:

> the agency mission, which is:
> "to achieve a continued optimum utilization of living marine resources for the benefit of the Nation" (48 Federal Register 531-42);
> national program stategies based on this mission;
> assessments of the status and future trends of fisheries and protected species stocks and their habitats; and
> regional program strategies, based on these assessments, for realizing the potential of individual marine resources to contribute socio-economically to the nation.

The goals of the NMFS strategic plan must be consistent with those set by the National Oceanic and Atmospheric Administration and the Department of Commerce. The relevant goals of the Department of Commerce are: to increase America's competitiveness in the world economy and to manage effectively the nation's oceanic and atmospheric resources. NMFS reports on progress toward departmental goals at quarterly Commerce Department meetings on strategic planning objectives, and reports on progress toward its 29 resource-based objectives at monthly National Oceanic and Atmospheric Administration management by objectives meeting.

The assumptions and strategies in the plan are revised and updated as needed on the basis of the operational decisions made during each year and of changes in NMFS priorities for the future. NMFS consults with interested groups, fishery management councils, state governments, and industry in developing its program goals and objectives.

Each NMFS region is responsible for developing its own strategic plan as part of this planning process. In establishing its objectives, each region determines the status of fisheries, protected species, and habitat in the region; take and marketing capacities; and outstanding issues and needs. Each stategic plan then identifies five to ten objectives. The regional plan discusses the significance of each objective, method of accomplishment, milestones for the current and future years, budgetary sources, performance measures, and major milestones for the year 2000. Most objectives focus upon specific commercial fisheries, although protected species and habitat objectives also are set.

Programmatic milestones, such as specific events, products, or services, leading toward the achievement of these objectives are detailed in the agency's *Current Year Operating Plans,* which are prepared every year. These milestones are incorporated into senior executive service contracts and merit pay plans for NMFS personnel.

*The Fishery Management Plan Process.*  A central feature of the Magnuson Fishery Conservation and Management Act is reliance upon fishery management plans, developed by the regional fishery management councils, to insure that fish are taken consistent with the best available scientific information and with the national standards.

In 1983, Congress amended the act, altering the process by which fishery management councils develop fishery management plans and receive approval from the secretary of Commerce. Previously, the law required the councils to develop plans for all fisheries. Under the amendments, Congress determined that fishery management councils need to develop fishery management plans only for those fisheries that "require conservation and management." The first step in the fishery management plan process is therefore the determination of whether or not there is a need for management. Once a fishery management council determines that a need exists, the council must conduct a scoping process as required by the National Environmental Policy Act. At this stage, the application of the Endangered Species Act, the Marine Mammal Protection Act, and the Coastal Zone Management Act is first considered.

The fishery management council then determines whether the development of the fishery management plan or fishery management plan amendment is a major federal action requiring an environmental impact statement or whether it need prepare only an environmental assessment and finding of no significant impact. The fishery management council next submits a work plan to the assistant administrator for Fisheries in the NOAA. This work plan outlines the need for a fisheries management plan, a description of environmental and economic issues, a timetable, means of ensuring public participation, etc.

In the second phase, the fishery management council develops draft documents, including the draft fishery management plan or amendment, draft implementing regulations, draft National Environmental Policy Act documents, and a draft regulatory impact analysis.

In the third phase, these documents are reviewed by the public and by state and federal agencies. The fishery management councils conduct public hearings, as required by the Magnuson Fishery Conservation and Management Act, in which NMFS participates. The National Environmental Policy Act and the various regulatory impact assessment orders and laws may require further measures, such as an environmental impact statement. Public comments are accepted for 45 days after notice of the availability of draft documents has been published in the *Federal Register*. The NMFS regional offices also distribute notices to newspapers, industry associations, and interested individuals to insure wide awareness of the documents.

The fishery management council then reviews the public comments and prepares the final fishery management plan, together with proposed regulations, and determines whether the fishery management plan complies with the Coastal Zone Management Act, the Marine Mammal Protection Act, and the Endangered Species Act. The fishery management council then adopts the fishery management plan or amendment, together with proposed regulations, and submits it for review by the secretary of Commerce.

In the fourth phase, the secretary of Commerce has 95 days to review the fishery-management-plan package. The secretary has 30 days to issue proposed rules. The public then has 45 days to comment upon the fishery management plan and the proposed rulemaking. Once this comment period is ended, the NMFS regional director may approve the fishery management plan and the secretary of Commerce may prepare final rules. In any event, the secretary of Commerce must inform the fishery management council of his final approval or disapproval, otherwise the fishery management plan becomes effective automatically. The Magnuson Fishery Conservation and Management Act requires that the secretary of Commerce publish final regulations 110 days after receiving a fishery management plan adopted by a fishery management council, unless the secretary has disapproved the fishery management plan or amendment.

In order to allow for continued foreign fishing while fishery management plans are being developed, the Magnuson Fishery Conservation and Management Act allows the secretary of Commerce to develop preliminary management plans for any fishery for which a foreign nation requests a permit. These preliminary management plans govern only foreign fishing and may be supplanted by fishery management plans developed by the fishery management councils. Seven preliminary management plans were in effect at the beginning of 1985.

The Magnuson Fishery Conservation and Management Act, implementing regulations, and other laws require that fishery management plans contain certain elements. Among these are the following:

- conservation and management measures, applicable to U.S. and foreign vessels, which are necessary and appropriate;
- a description of the fishery, including the number of vessels, types and quantity of fishing gear used, and species to be taken and location or distribution of the species;
- costs likely to be incurred in management of the fishery, and actual and potential revenues from the fishery;
- recreational interest in the fishery;
- nature and extent of foreign fishing;
- Indian treaty fishing rights, if any;
- assessment and specification of the present and probable future condition of the fishery;
- assessment and specification of the optimum yield from the fishery, including the social, economic, and ecological considerations used for this assessment and specification;
- summary of information used in making maximum-sustainable-yield and optimum-yield specifications;
- assessment and specifications of the annual capacity and estimated extent to which U.S. fishing vessels will reach the optimum yield;
- assessment and specifications of the portion of optimum yield which U.S. vessels will not catch annually and which can be made available for foreign fishing;
- assessment and specifications of the capacity and extent to which U.S. processors will process annually that portion of optimum yield caught by U.S. vessels; and
- specification of fishery data to be collected by or submitted to the secretary, including type and quantity of fishing gear used, catch by species (number and weight), areas and time of fishing, number of hauls, estimated processing capacity of U.S. processors, and actual processing capacity used by U.S. processors (U.S. Department of Commerce 1983b).

Besides satisfying these requirements, fishery management plans also must satisfy the procedural requirements of the Administrative Procedures Act, Marine Mammal Protection Act, the Endangered Species Act, Coastal Zone Management Act, Executive Order 12291 regarding federal regulations, Paperwork Reduction Act, Regulatory Flexibility Act, and National Environmental Policy Act.

Under the Magnuson Fishery Conservation and Management Act, a fishery management plan may include other optional features. These include fishing permits and fees, zones or periods within which fishing may be prohibited or permitted only with gear restrictions, specific limitations on the catch of fish, requirements for the use of specific types of gear, and incorporation of the conservation and management measures of the coastal states in the region. Fishery management plans may limit access to a fishery, taking into account a number of considerations discussed later.

As the federal government and the fishery management councils have gained practical experience in implementing the Magnuson Fishery Conservation and Management Act, the need for flexibility in managing fisheries has become clear. Limitations on the ability of fishery scientists to predict population levels and the sensitivity of some marine fish populations to environmental perturbations make it difficult to determine specific management measures in some fisheries until a fishing season is under way. Currently, NMFS and the fishery management councils are trying to meet the needs for flexibility and accountability by developing "framework" fishery management plans.

Generally, framework fishery management plans do not contain numerical management measures, such as fixed quotas, allocations, times, and areas. Rather, a framework plan describes the types of actions that the NMFS regional director, acting on behalf of the secretary of Commerce and with the advice of the appropriate fishery management council, should take given certain conditions in the fishery. Thus, a regional director might make annual or in-season determinations of optimum yield based upon specified levels of current catch and effort data.

Framework fishery management plans generally contain the following provisions:

- definition of the circumstances, such as the fulfillment of a catch quota, that will trigger a change in management;
- criteria for determining if a change is needed and for selecting among management options; and
- definition of the procedures to be used in making changes.

Where framework fishery management plans have been implemented by regulations issued by the secretary of Commerce, in-season adjustments undertaken by the appropriate NMFS regional director according to the criteria set out in the fishery management plan do not constitute an amendment of the fishery management plan or its regulations and therefore do not require public notice, although views may be solicited.

Often, a fishery management council has identified a potential issue, such as a conflict between two types of fishing gear, within a plan but has not been able to specify the exact circumstances in which the issue would affect the fishery nor the means by which the conflict should be resolved. When the nature and extent of an issue become clear, the fishery management council and NMFS may undertake to amend the regulations implementing the fishery management plan. This requires observing the normal rule-making procedures of the Administrative Procedures Act, but does not require amending the fishery management plan itself and following all the attendant procedures.

If, however, an issue arises that was not foreseen in a fishery management plan, the plan itself as well as its implementing regulations generally must be amended. This often requires issuance of a full environmental impact statement and public hearings.

If the secretary or a fishery management council by a unanimous vote determines that an emergency exists under Section 305(e)(2) of the Magnuson Fishery Conservation and Management Act, the secretary immediately must issue emergency regulations, which become effective upon publication or soon afterwards. These regulations remain in effect for 90 days and may be extended for another 90 days.

## NMFS Research

NMFS conducts stock assessments of the nation's renewable living marine resources and their supporting environment, as well as research on the commercial and recreational take, processing, and marketing of living marine resources. NMFS develops this information in order to assist state and federal fishery managers, the fishery management councils, and international commissions in implementing conservation and management measures. NMFS also provides scientific assessments of the impact of other human activities upon the marine environment.

NMFS currently conducts assessments of 139 different stocks of fish, marine mammals, and endangered species. Stock assessments rely upon information from field surveys conducted by NMFS itself and upon industry catch statistics. Cooperative surveys also are conducted with foreign governments, state governments, universities, and private organizations.

NMFS habitat research focuses upon the effects of natural and human-caused changes to the habitat of living marine resources, including the effects of dams, power plants, effluents, dumping, dredging, and logging on marine species. Recently, NMFS has sought to develop a methodology for evaluating the importance of nearshore habitats to the productivity of commercially valuable fisheries. About 90 percent of commercially valuable fish and shellfish in the southeastern United States depend upon estuarine areas during critical life stages.

Other areas of NMFS research include anadromous fisheries and hatcheries, advanced technology such as remote sensing of fish populations from satellites, and aquaculture of finfish and shellfish. These research programs are all part of the Office of Resource Investigations.

The Office of Data and Information Management coordinates the collection of a wide range of statistical information, including volume and value of catch in domestic and foreign fisheries by species, region, state, and type of gear; production of industrial finfish products; imports and exports of fishery products; number of marine recreational fishermen and their catches; effort and expenditures; and fishing effort and costs associated with catch. This socio-economic information is required by the Magnuson Fishery Conservation and Management Act in determining optimum yield in a fishery.

Each NMFS Fisheries Center coordinates research programs at various laboratories and facilities. The Northeast Fisheries Center maintains programs at eight fisheries laboratories. The Southeast Fisheries Center coordinates efforts at six laboratories and the Southwest Fisheries Center at four. The Northwest and Alaska Fisheries Center supports 14 different research facilities. The base programs at these laboratories range from $50,000 to more than $7 million per year.

The setting of NMFS research priorities begins with discussions between the regional offices and the fisheries centers. The regional management and research directors identify management research priorities in consultation with the regional fishery management councils, industry, and other interested people. The research priorities are incorporated in the current year's operating plan, the annual budget request, and the strategic plan.

Available funding for NMFS information collection and analysis programming has increased from $70.5 million in fiscal year 1982 to $82.2 million in fiscal year 1985. Since 1982, resource-information research's share of this funding has increased from 57 percent to 66 percent. Funding for information analysis and dissemination has declined from 31 percent in fiscal year 1982 to 22 percent in fiscal year 1985. Research on the fishing industry itself has continued to receive about 12 percent of the research funding within NMFS.

## Marine Fisheries Research Outside NMFS

Besides NMFS, a number of federal, state, and nongovernmental organizations conduct research relevant to the NMFS mission. The National Sea Grant College Program funds university programs in aquaculture, fisheries, general marine ecosystems, and marine pollution investigations; NMFS liaison helps ensure that this research does not duplicate, but enhances, NMFS research efforts. Both NMFS and the Food and Drug Administration conduct research aimed at ensuring that domestic and imported fish and shellfish products will be safe and wholesome.

The Minerals Management Service in the Department of the Interior, as part of Interior's program of outer-continental-shelf oil and gas leasing on federal submerged lands, sponsors research regarding living marine resources and their habitats. The Environmental Protection Agency also conducts considerable research on the habitat and environment of marine fish and shellfish. The Marine Mammal Commission has provided funding for studies on the incidental capture of marine mammals in fisheries. The National Science Foundation conducts basic research regarding the biology of marine organisms.

Finally, nongovernmental organizations also conduct research on marine fish and shellfish. Most prominent among these are the industry's fishery development foundations, which represent the interests of the fishing industry. The foundations rely to a considerable extent upon funds from the Saltonstall-Kennedy Fund for their research.

## Budgeting

The NMFS budget is developed as part of the budget request of the National Oceanic and Atmospheric Administration within the Department of Commerce. Formulation of the budget request within NMFS goes hand in hand with other planning efforts and is decentralized, although coordinated by the Washington Office of Policy and Planning.

At the beginning of the budget process, the directors of the NMFS regional offices and fisheries centers propose any changes to be made in existing management and research programs in the regions. These recommendations are then reviewed by the agency's board of directors, which includes the directors of the regional offices and fisheries centers and senior NMFS officials in Washington, D.C. The resulting budget request is sent up through the National Oceanic and Atmospheric Administration and the Department of Commerce to the Office of Management and Budget for review and revision before being submitted to Congress as part of the president's annual budget request.

The National Oceanic and Atmospheric Administration budget, of which the NMFS budget is a relatively small part, accounts for more than half the budget of the Department of Commerce, some $1 billion. Within the atmospheric administration's budget estimate, the principal NMFS marine fishery management programs appear under the activity "marine fishery resource programs" in the Operations, Research and Facilities budget. This activity includes three subactivities: information collection and analysis, conservation and management operations, and state and industry assistance programs. The Operations, Research and Facilities budget of NMFS has increased from $129.2 million in fiscal year 1982 to $167.4 million in FY 1986.

Within this total, the budget for information collection and analysis increased from $70.5 million to $92.4 million, while the budget for conservation and management operations decreased from $50.8 million to $49.8 million between 1982 and 1986. During the same period, the budget for state and industry programs increased from $7.8 million to $25.2 million.

Fiscal year 1986 funding for the information collection and analysis subactivity was $92.4 million, with a staffing level of 1,240 full-time-equivalent positions. Of this funding and staffing, the resource-information line item received $65.7 million and 642 positions, the fisheries-industry-information line item received $9.1 million and 82 positions, and the information-analysis-and-dissemination line item received $17.6 million and 253 positions.

The conservation and management operations subactivity received funding of $49.8 million and staffing of 453 full-time-equivalent positions in FY1986. Within this subactivity, the fisheries-management-programs line item

National Marine Fisheries Service Funding (000s) Fiscal Years 1982—1985

| Budget Category (Subactivity or line item) | Appropriation 1982(a) | Appropriation 1983(a) | President's Request 1984(a) | Appropriation 1984(b) | President's Request 1985(b) | Appropriation 1985(c) | President's Request 1986(c) | Appropriation 1986(d) |
|---|---|---|---|---|---|---|---|---|
| MARINE FISHERY RESOURCE PROGRAMS (OR&F) | 129,160 | 162,739 | 92,444 | 143,595 | 92,631 | 152,618 | 84,201 | |
| Information Collection and Analysis | | | | | | | | |
| Resource Information | 70,554 | 71,225 | 55,752 | 71,841 | 59,133 | 82,164 | 51,942 | |
| Fishery Industry Information | 40,316 | 43,931 | 29,202 | 44,322 | 35,296 | 54,186 | 29,304 | |
| Information Analysis and Dissemination | 8,801 | 9,435 | 7,382 | 9,696 | 6,879 | 9,742 | 6,026 | |
| Conservation and Management Operations | 21,437 | 17,859 | 19,168 | 17,823 | 16,958 | 18,236 | 16,612 | |
| Fishery Management Programs | 50,832 | 73,362 | 33,466 | 50,495 | 29,411 | 48,337 | 28,614 | |
| Protected Species Management | 28,655 | 30,965 | 18,408 | 33,740 | 13,517 | 30,060 | 13,606 | |
| Habitat Conservation | 7,650 | 30,149 | 3,439 | 4,352 | 4,595 | 5,301 | 4,301 | |
| Enforcement and Surveillance | 4,958 | 4,763 | 3,315 | 4,739 | 3,451 | 5,328 | 3,059 | |
| State and Industry Programs | 9,569 | 7,755 | 8,304 | 7,664 | 7,848 | 7,648 | 7,648 | |
| Grants to states | 7,774 | 17,882 | 3,226 | 21,259 | 4,087 | 22,117 | 3,645 | |
| Fisheries Development Program | 7,375 | 7,000 | — | 9,700 | — | 8,000 | — | |
| Financial Services Program | — | 10,341 | 2,750 | 10,996 | 3,200 | 13,595 | 2,836 | |
| Administration | 399 | 541 | 476 | 563 | 887 | 522 | 809 | |

## OTHER FUNDS (NON-OR&F)

| | | | | | | | |
|---|---|---|---|---|---|---|---|
| Fish Vessel Gear Damage Compensation Fund | 3,500 | 1,750 | 1,750 | 1,732 | — | 5,315* | — |
| Fishermen's Contingency Fund | 900 | 250 | 250 | 294 | 250 | 250 | 750 |
| Fishermen's Guaranty Fund | 1,800 | 1,800 | 1,800 | 2,079 | 1,800 | 1,800 | 1,800 |
| Foreign Fishing Observer Fund | 4,000 | 6,950 | 12,000 | 11,880 | 4,500 | 4,500 | 4,500 |
| Fisheries Loan Fund | — | 10,000 | — | 3,000 | 89,882† | 2,500 | 115,854† |
| Saltonstall-Kennedy Fund | 16,186 | 8,023 | — | 9,986 | — | 9,051* | — |
| Saltonstall-Kennedy Offset Against OR&F | (10,000) | (22,600) | (31,500) | (23,600) | (23,000) | (25,900) | (40,000) |

\* These figures include funds carried over from fiscal year 1984.

† These funds were to be used to offset NOAA operation costs and some costs of the Coast Guard.

(a) These figures are from the NMFS Congressional budget submission for fiscal year 1984.

(b) These figures are from the NOAA Budget Estimate for fiscal year 1985.

(c) These figures are from the NOAA Budget Estimate for fiscal year 1986.

(d) Based on H.R.2965 and House Conference Report 99-414.

received $31.3 million and staffing of 194 positions, while the protected-species-management line item received $5.6 million and staffing of 66 positions. Habitat conservation received $5.3 million and 71 positions, while enforcement and surveillance obtained $7.6 million and 122 positions.

The state and industry assistance programs subactivity received a total of $25.2 million and 239 positions in FY 1986. Within this subactivity, the grants-to-states line item received $10.5 million with no staff positions, while the fisheries-development-program line item was given $13.9 million and 226 positions. Finally, the financial services program administration line item received $809,000 and 13 positions.

Besides these Operations, Research and Facilities appropriations, NMFS also administers appropriations made under specific industry-assistance acts. These funds include the Saltonstall-Kennedy Fund, the Fishing Vessel and Gear Damage Compensation Fund, the Fishermen's Contingency Fund, the Foreign Fishing Observer Fund, the Fisheries Loan Fund, and the Fishermen's Guaranty Fund. Several of these funds, such as the Fisheries Loan Fund and Foreign Fishing Observer Fund, are based upon the collection of poundage and other fees from foreign fishermen and duties on fishery products imported into the United States. In recent years, the administration has sought to use some funds to offset expenses in the Operations, Research and Facilities accounts. The other funds are compensation programs funded by fees paid by offshore oil and gas producers, for instance.

Administration of the budget and implementation of program activities have been jeopardized in recent years by marked differences between the president's budget and the final congressional appropriations. As in previous years, the Reagan administration requested less than $100 million for NMFS marine-fishery-resource programs in FY 1986. The Reagan administration proposed the elimination of several programs, including aquaculture, grants to states, and Saltonstall-Kennedy grants for fisheries research and development. Elsewhere in the budget, the Reagan administration proposed a 49 percent reduction in resource-information activities, including a 55 percent reduction in protected-species research, a 57 percent reduction in fish-habitat research, and a 24 percent reduction in resource surveys. These reductions were accompanied by proposed increases of 55 percent in fisheries-management programs, 19 percent in protected-species management, and 43 percent in habitat-conservation activities.

Since 1982, Congress has regularly ignored the Reagan administration's NMFS budget requests. Congress generally has restored funding proposed for reduction to historical levels and sometimes has added funding. Nonetheless, the spending power of the NMFS budget has been decreasing in the face of inflation.

Fishery management councils receive federal funds through cooperative agreements for two basic types of expenditures: administrative funds to cover general operating expenses and programmatic funds for the development of fishery management plans. Each year, a fishery management council submits a funding request to NMFS, which is forwarded to NMFS headquarters if it receives the approval of the NMFS regional director. The work of the fishery management councils is then funded as a cooperative agreement. From 1977 through 1984, the eight fishery management councils received from the federal government $47.1 million in operating and program funds (U.S. Department of Commerce 1985a).

# Current Program Trends

## Management Under the Magnuson Fishery Conservation and Management Act

The development and implementation of fisheries management plans are useful measures of federal fisheries management since passage of the Magnuson Fishery Conservation and Management Act. Within two years after the act became effective, the secretary of Commerce issued a number of preliminary management plans for fish stocks that were the target of foreign fishing only. Seven preliminary management plans remain in effect, each of which has been amended at least twice and some as many as five times. These are:

> Atlantic Billfishes and Sharks
> Northwest Atlantic Ocean Fishery
> Hake Fisheries of the Northwest Atlantic
> Bering Sea Snails
> Pacific Billfish and Sharks
> Bering Sea Trawl and Herring Gill Net

The process of developing fishery management plans, of course, can require a considerable amount of time. By March 1978, there were three fishery management plans, two for Atlantic fisheries and one for the salmon fishery off Washington, Oregon and California. Five years later, 16 fishery management plans had been implemented fully. As of July 1, 1985, 23 fishery management plans had been fully implemented.

Of the 23 current fishery management plans, all but one involve domestic commercial fishing. Of these, 14 also involve recreational fishing. Only five of the fishery management plans concern foreign fisheries. Twenty of the fishery management plans manage fisheries where species either migrate between coastal waters of two or more contiguous states or migrate between territorial waters and the fishery conservation zone.

The following fishery management plans are currently in effect and listed in the order in which they became effective. The month and year in which a fishery management plan became effective are in parentheses.

> Commercial and Recreational Salmon (4/77)
> Atlantic Surf Clam and Ocean Quahogs Fisheries (2/78)

Northern Anchovy (9/78)
Tanner Crab (12/78)
Gulf of Alaska Groundfish (1/79)
High Seas Salmon (5/79)
Gulf of Mexico Stone Crab (9/79)
Gulf of Mexico Shrimp (5/81)
Bering Sea and Aleutian Island Groundfish (12/81)
Atlantic Sea Scallops (5/82)
Gulf and South Atlantic Spiny Lobster (7/82)
Interim Atlantic Groundfish (10/82)
Pacific Groundfish (10/82)
Coastal Migratory Pelagics (2/83)
Western Pacific Spiny Lobster (3/83)
Atlantic Mackerel, Squid, and Butterfish (4/83)
American Lobster (9/83)
Snapper/Grouper Fishery (9/83)
Western Pacific Precious Corals (9/83)
Gulf and South Atlantic Corals (7/84)
Gulf of Mexico Reef Fish (9/84)
Alaskan King Crab (12/84)
Caribbean Spiny Lobster (1/85)

NMFS anticipates that another 13 fisheries may be managed under the Magnuson Fishery Conservation and Management Act by the end of 1986. Nine of these involve both domestic commercial and recreational fishing. Three involve both domestic and foreign commercial fishing. These 13 fisheries are:

Northeast Multispecies Groundfish
Summer Flounder in the Mid-Atlantic
Black Sea Bass in the Mid-Atlantic
Atlantic Swordfish
South Atlantic Shrimp
Gulf Herring
Caribbean Shallow Water Reef Fish
Caribbean Ecosystem
Tilefish in the Mid-Atlantic
Bering Sea/Chukchi Sea Herring
Bottomfish/Seamount Groundfish in the Western Pacific
Striped Bass in the Northeast and Mid-Atlantic
Western Pacific Billfish

Finally, another 21 fisheries are being considered for management under the Magnuson Fishery Conservation and Management Act, including menhaden, tunas, squid, blue crab, and dogfish sharks.

As a greater and greater percentage of the fisheries in the U.S. fishery conservation zone come under fishery management plans, the effort of the fishery management councils has shifted to monitoring the effectiveness of existing fishery management plans.

## Habitat Conservation

The effects of habitat degradation upon commercial and recreational fishery stocks have gained increasing attention in recent years. Although efforts within NMFS to quantify the relationship between habitat requirements, fish-stock productivity, and commercial and recreational fishery yields have begun only recently, the general importance of coastal wetlands and estuaries to marine fish is well established. For instance, in the Southeast Region, 96 percent of the commercial and more than 50 percent of the recreational fishery landings consist of fish and shellfish that use estuarine areas for part or all of their lives. For the period 1978-80, estuarine-dependent species in the Southeast Region accounted for about 43 percent of all commercial landings in the United States (Lindall and Thayer 1982). Of these estuarine-dependent species, menhaden supports the top fishery in pounds landed, and shrimp supports the most economically valuable fishery in the United States.

The Southeast Region contains about 29,900 miles of tidal shoreline and 17.2 million acres of marsh/estuarine habitat, including more than 300 estuarine systems representing about 60 percent of the total remaining estuarine systems in the contiguous United States (46 percent if Alaska is included). Thus, it is hardly surprising that the Southeast Regional Office reviews the bulk of the permit applications referred to NMFS under the Fish and Wildlife Coordination Act and the National Environmental Policy Act.

The volume of permit applications evaluated nationally by the five NMFS regional offices has been declining. Until 1981, these offices annually evaluated about 25,000 notices of proposed federal actions that could have affected fishery or protected species habitats. In 1981 the number of proposed federal actions reviewed by NMFS dropped to about 14,000. The largest group of these were dredge and fill permit applications filed with the Corps of Engineers.

By 1983, NMFS was reviewing approximately 8,000 Corps of Engineers permits, most in the Southeast Region. In 1983, such applications covered more than 40,000 acres of coastal habitat with annual fisheries values estimated in excess of $8 million (U.S. Department of Commerce 1985e). In 1984, NMFS provided recommendations on more than 7,500 permits. Follow-up studies in the Southeast Region have shown that some 90 percent of the NMFS recommendations were included as legally binding stipulations in permits issued by the Corps of Engineers, but that one out of every five permit holders did not comply with the conditions and went unpunished (Lindall and Thayer 1982).

In 1983 NMFS published habitat conservation policy to focus its activities in this area. According to this policy, NMFS directs its habitat conservation activities to assist in:

> (1) meeting its resource, management, conservation, protection, or development responsibilities contained in the Magnuson Fishery Conservation and Management Act, the Marine Mammal Protection Act, and the Endangered Species Act; and
>
> (2) carrying out its responsibilities to the U.S. commercial and marine recreational fishing industry, including fishermen, and the States pursuant to the programs carried out under other authorities (48 *Federal Register* 53145 [1983]).

Each NMFS Regional Office, Fisheries Center, and NMFS headquarters office is responsible for implementing this policy. Among other things, the Regional Offices and Fisheries Centers are to identify the living marine resources of importance and the major habitat threats to these resources. They are to work with other NOAA offices, other federal agencies, state agencies, and the fishery management councils in doing so. The Fisheries Centers are to conduct environmental and ecological research in support of the policy. Also, the fishery management councils are to address habitat considerations in the development of fishery management plans, and NMFS is to assist them by providing habitat information.

## Marine Recreational Fisheries

Recognition of the importance of recreational fisheries in the management of marine fish populations has been increasing in recent years. Marine fishing did not become a significant recreational activity until after World War II when, among other things, a variety of technological improvements in boats and fishing gear made marine fishing more accessible to the growing number of coastal inhabitants.

In 1955, an estimated 4.5 million saltwater sport fishermen spent nearly 59 million sport fishing days and nearly $500 million. By 1965, there were an estimated 8.3 million saltwater anglers who spent nearly $800 million. Over the next 10 years, the number of recreational saltwater fishermen doubled and their expenditures had increased to $3.45 billion yearly (U.S. Department of Commerce 1981c).

Because earlier surveys yielded information of limited reliability and did not collect information on the species caught, NMFS undertook a revision of its survey techniques. In 1979, NMFS began a new survey of marine recreational fisheries, relying upon surveys of fishermen in the field and an independent telephone survey of households. Surveys were conducted in the Atlantic and Gulf of Mexico in 1979 through 1984, in the Pacific in mid-1979 through 1984, in the Western Pacific in 1979 through 1981, and in the Caribbean in 1979 and 1981. Based on these surveys, NMFS estimates that in 1984, 17 million saltwater fishermen caught about 653 million pounds of finfish on 72.8 million fishing trips and spent about $7.5 billion* (U.S. Department of Commerce 1985b).

As a result of this growth, marine recreational fishing has become an area of increasing attention within NMFS. In 1981, for instance, a special Task Group assembled by NMFS proposed a policy for marine recreational fisheries (U.S. Dept. of Commerce 1981c). The proposed policy was adopted by the agency on February 4, 1982. Declaring previous NMFS activities in the area of marine recreational fisheries fragmented and limited, the policy states that:

> NMFS, through it various programs, will protect, conserve, enhance, manage, and develop fishery resources of importance to the Nation in order to increase the Nation's food supply; promote increased opportunity of both commercial and marine recreational fishermen consistent with the concept of optimum yield; and promote activities which will assist the commercial and marine recreational fishing industries to thrive and expand (47 *Federal Register* 5926 [1982]).

The Task Group recommended that the policy be implemented through the NMFS strategic planning mechanism by making appropriate amendments to the goals of the agency.

Although more than half of the recreational catch is taken within the territorial sea and not in the federal fishery conservation zone, many sport species move between these two areas. Some of these fish are also the target of commercial fishing in both state and federal waters. Thus, three of the seven operational preliminary management plans and 14 of the 23 fishery management plans address recreational fishing. Of the 12 fishery management plans being developed for 1986, nine involve recreational fishing. And of these, five are principally recreational fisheries.†

## Shifts in Other NMFS Activities

As the agenda of the Reagan administration emerged in 1981, NMFS, as did other federal wildlife agencies, began re-evaluating its programs and activities. Under the direction of the Reagan administration, NMFS emphasizes reducing government regulation. Assisting U.S. industries, particularly in international markets, and turning federal activities over to state and local

---

*This increase in recreational fishing effort is less than might have been anticipated based upon the rate of growth in the recreational fishing sector before 1981, when the rate was 6.6 percent a year. Had this rate been maintained, there would have been 31 million saltwater anglers in 1985.

† Fishery management plans are expected to be developed in 1986 for the following fisheries that are primarily recreational: summer flounder, black sea bass, Caribbean shallow-water reef fish, striped bass, and Caribbean ecosystem. Of implemented preliminary management plans and fishery management plans, only the preliminary management plan for Atlantic billfishes and sharks is considered primarily recreational.

governments were accompanied by proposals for a drastic reduction in the federal budget for NMFS traditional activities. In NMFS, much of the re-evaluation was expressed in the strategic plan described above.

Since colonial times, the fishing industry has enjoyed a close relationship with the federal government. Congress has established a number of loan, loan guarantee, and tax deferral programs to assist the U.S. commercial fishing industry. Within Congress and NMFS, these "subsidy" programs are coming under increasing scrutiny as targets for reducing the federal budget.

Likewise, other NMFS industry assistance programs have been undergoing review. In some cases in the past, NMFS not only identified problems hindering the competitiveness of U.S fish products but also tried to solve those problems for industry. Current thinking within NMFS is that the appropriate role of the agency is to identify the problems and if possible identify means for solving them. The emphasis is less on directly assisting industry in marketing fisheries products in domestic and foreign markets and more on creating opportunities and assisting business to identify opportunities and overcome obstacles. For example, NMFS has sought to help industry gain approval from other federal agencies for marketing certain fish oils for human consumption.

Emphases are changing elsewhere within NMFS. For instance, the emphasis in fisheries enforcement has moved from patrol and inspection of recreational and commercial fishery activities to investigations of suspected violations. The emphasis within NMFS aquaculture program also has shifted from developing techniques for private-sector food production to developing techniques for public sector restoration and enhancement of wild populations. For instance, the NMFS Galveston laboratory has for several years been developing techniques for rearing endangered Kemp's ridley sea turtles for release into the wild as part of the NMFS aquaculture program.

## Current Problems and Issues

The range of current marine fisheries problems and issues is considerable. Some of the issues identified for planning purposes in the *Strategic Plan for the National Marine Fisheries Service* issued in April 1985 included:

- competition for fishery resources among domestic users will continue to increase;
- catch capacity will exceed available allocations, with overcapitalization continuing to be a problem in many traditional fisheries;
- management decisions will continue to reduce foreign allocation within the U.S. fishery conservation zone in order to encourage domestic industry expansion;
- joint ventures and direct foreign investment will increase as foreign fishing allocations are reduced, changing the structure of the domestic industry;

- more living-marine-resource conflicts will require interjurisdictional resolution involving cooperative actions with the states and with other nations;
- nonpoint-source pollution and a general deterioration of coastal environments will pose an increasing threat to fishery resource productivity;
- decisions in favor of fishery resources in issues involving incompatible use of the marine environment by other interests will require an evaluation that supports the economic value of the fishery; and
- growing public concern about the effects of pollution on the quality and safety of seafood products could dampen potential growth of domestic and foreign markets.

Several of these issues are discussed here.

## Foreign Competition

Foreign competition with the U.S. fishing industry has a significant effect upon U.S. policy on a wide variety of controversial issues and affects national marine fisheries management. The Magnuson Fishery Conservation and Management Act itself is a clear demonstration of this, since the outrage generated by the depletion of fish stocks off the United States by foreign trawlers provided a good deal of the political punch that led to passage of the act.

Although the foreign catch in the U.S. fishery conservation zone has declined since the passage of the act, the three-billion-pound foreign take of fish and shellfish in 1984 still accounted for more than half of the catch in the U.S. zone. By comparison, in 1971 foreign fishermen caught an estimated 7.7 billion pounds within 200 miles of U.S. shores. The bulk of the foreign catch—96 percent of it in 1984—came from waters off Alaska.

Some critics believe the increase in the take by U.S. fishermen is occurring too slowly. Both Senator Stevens (R-AK) and Senator Gorton (R-WA) introduced amendments to the Magnuson Fishery Conservation and Management Act in 1985 that would accelerate a phase-out of foreign fishing initiated by the Fishery Conservation Act in the U.S. fishery conservation zone.

Other observers believe that allocations of rights to fish within the U.S. fishery conservation zone provide an important negotiating tool in extracting from other nations assistance for the U.S. fishing industry. For instance, there has been some success in inducing foreign governments to open their markets to U.S. fish products or to assist in the development of the U.S. fishing industry in return for the granting of fishing allocations in the U.S. zone. For example, foreign nations, principally Japan, have provided capital for the construction of facilities that could process fish that U.S. processors cannot now handle. In Alaska, for instance, Japanese business has funded the construction of facilities to process Alaska pollock into "surimi." Until these facilities were built, U.S. fishermen were hampered in catching and processing this fish. However, even the apparent benefit of foreign investment has its disadvantages. As a recent report on the export problems of the U.S. fishing industry observed, "the U.S. fisheries assets will be almost wholly funded and operated by foreign interests, primarily Japan" (*Marine Fish Management* August 1985). Indeed, within Alaska, 65 percent of the shore-based processing facilities are now owned by Japanese interests (U.S. Department of Commerce 1985b). Such foreign control of U.S. harvesting and processing businesses may alter profoundly the politics of managing fisheries in the United States.

Research by the University of Washington's Fisheries Research Institute indicates that between 1978 and 1983 the Japanese mothership fleet caught between 200,000 and 700,000 Alaska chinook salmon yearly. In response to protests from Alaska fishermen and the North Pacific Regional Fishery Management Council, the State Department has sought a promise from the Japanese to stop these interceptions of North American salmon. The Japanese have rebuffed such efforts, provoking the State Department to consider reducing Japanese fishery allocations (*The Anchorage Times,* October 1985).

Demands for eliminating foreign fishing in the U.S. fishery conservation zone also have been blunted somewhat by so-called joint ventures. Since 1979, U.S. fishermen have caught and sold to foreign vessels certain relatively abundant species for which U.S. demand is low. Joint-venture catches of species such as cod, flounder, hake, squid, and Alaska pollock have grown from 23.3 million pounds in 1979 to 1.5 billion pounds in 1984 (U.S. Department of Commerce 1985b). Some observers view these joint ventures as a transition to full use of these fish stocks by U.S. fishermen and processors. Whether the U.S. fleet will be able to exploit these resources fully and eliminate foreign fishing vessels from these fisheries is somewhat contingent upon U.S. processors being able to process the U.S. catch. It is cheaper for some U.S. fishermen to send their pollock catch to South Korea for initial processing, after which it is exported to the United States for final processing.

Another aspect of foreign competition places fisheries issues in the midst of broader trade considerations. The U.S. fisheries trade deficit has increased from $2 billion in 1976 to $5 billion in 1984. Domestic fishermen object that some of the fish-product imports into the United States are subsidized by foreign governments, making it difficult for unsubsidized American fishermen to compete. On August 5, 1985, a coalition of northeastern fishing industry leaders filed a petition with the International Trade Commission asking for a 10 to 20 percent countervailing duty on fresh whole and filleted Canadian cod, flounder, haddock, pollock, and hake (*National Fisherman,* September and October 1985). Imports of these fish increased from a value of $38 million in 1983 to $53 million in 1985. The Canadian share of the U.S. market for some types of groundfish products has more than doubled.

On September 11, the trade commission ruled unanimously that there was a reasonable indication that U.S. fishermen and processors had suffered "material injury or threat thereof" from Canadian imports. If the Commerce Department determines that Canadian imports have been subsidized by the Canadian government, the International Trade Commission and the Commerce Department will conduct a more extensive investigation. Duties on Canadian fresh fish imports will be imposed only if the trade commission and the Commerce Department agree that the imports are subsidized and are injuring U.S. fishermen and processors (*National Fisherman* 1985).

The International Trade Commission is conducting a similar study regarding tuna and recently completed a study regarding shrimp imported from Mexico, Ecuador, and other South American countries. U.S. imports of aquacultured shrimp from Ecuador increased from slightly more than nine million pounds in 1976 to more than 50 million pounds in 1983, declining to about 46 million pounds in 1984 as the Ecuadorian government withdrew subsidies. The last year in which U.S. fishermen supplied more shrimp than did foreign imports was 1978. In 1984, U.S. harvesters supplied nearly 190 million pounds of shrimp, and imports supplied more than 422 million pounds.

## Limiting Access to Domestic Fisheries

One of the most hotly debated issues in fisheries management, particularly in the United States, is limiting access to domestic fisheries*. Unlike management measures aimed at achieving biological goals, limiting access to a fishery generally is aimed at achieving social or economic goals, although it may have biological and administrative advantages as well.

Those who espouse the limiting of fisheries access argue that the economic efficiency of some U.S. domestic fisheries has been reduced by excessive numbers of fishermen. More fishermen working a stable or declining fishery resource reduces the catch per unit effort of each fisherman and of the fleet as a whole. According to some estimates, the annual catch of certain fish stocks could be taken by as few as one-third of the vessels now fishing (U.S. Department of Commerce 1985b).

Three types of limited entry are discussed most often. The most common form is a limitation on the number of licenses for each fishery†. Under a second option, each participant is allocated the formal privilege to take a particular portion of the allowable catch and the privilege can be sold or leased. Finally, participants may be taxed by the fisheries managers on the basis of the poundage or value of their catch. This theoretically will discourage overfishing by reducing the rewards of increased fishing.

Despite its unpopularity among fishermen who oppose fishing restric-

---

* The industry publication *National Fisherman,* for instance, featured a debate on the subject in its August through November 1985 issues, articles that serve as the basis for this discussion.

† There are no fishery management plans issued under the Magnuson Fishery Conservation and Management Act that formally include limited entry as a management tool. Under the fishery management plan for the mid-Atlantic surf clam and ocean quahog fisheries, there is a moratorium on the issuance of licenses to take Atlantic surf clams. The Department of Commerce rejected an amendment to the fishery management plan, proposed by the Mid-Atlantic Fishery Management Council, that attempted to turn the moratorium into a formal limited-entry licensing system.

tions, limited entry once again has surfaced as an option under consideration by fishery management councils, Congress, and NMFS. The National Oceanic and Atmospheric Administration assistant administrator for Fisheries, believes that some form of limited entry will be imposed in some fisheries within the next five years (*National Fisherman* 1985). However, some fishery managers disagree.

A recently circulated draft NMFS paper suggests that traditional fishing restrictions, such as requirements for the use of particular types of gear or seasonal or area closures, have led to complex and costly management, placing unnecessary burdens on fishermen. If open-access fisheries are like other public resources, such as rangeland grazing, coal, and timber, potential exists for overuse or inefficient use. According to limitation proponents, limiting access to such resources can increase the economic efficiency of the fishing industry and reduce regulatory costs (*National Fisherman* August 1985).

Limited entry does not receive so favorable a review in Congress, however. When considering legislation to implement the U.S.-Canada Halibut Convention in 1982, Congress restricted the authority of the North Pacific Fishery Management Council to limit access. Indeed, the Office of Management and Budget rejected a halibut moratorium later proposed by the management council. Some congressional opponents saw the limited-entry proposal as unfairly benefiting fishermen already in the fishery.

Congressional opposition to limited entry surfaced again in January 1985, when the House Subcommittee on Fisheries and Wildlife Conservation and the Environment circulated draft amendments to the Magnuson Fishery Conservation and Management Act that would have set up a program to compensate fishermen excluded from a fishery by a limited-entry system.* What emerged from the subcommittee, however, was a bill that would make the imposition of a limited-entry system more difficult. The provision would require that any fishery management plan including a limited-entry system be approved by three-quarterers of the relevant fishery management council and two-thirds of the affected fishermen (*National Fisherman* September 1985).

Congressional and industry opposition stems from several concerns. Some members of Congress, such as Representative Don Young (R-AK), say that limiting entry "benefits the few and takes away the responsibility for many" and suspect that some fishery management councils and NMFS see limited entry as a means of exerting more control over the fishing industry.

---

* Currently, the Magnuson act allows a fishery management council to establish a limited access system in order to achieve optimum yield, if it takes into account:

- present participation in the fishery;
- historical fishing practices in, and dependence on, the fishery,
- the economics of the fishery;
- the capability of fishing vessels used in the fishery to engage in other fisheries;
- the cultural and social framework relevant to the fishery, and
- any other relevant considerations (16 U.S.C. 1853 (b)(6).

The National Federation of Fishermen says that foreign experience with limited entry suggests that it will not necessarily work in the same way in the United States and that limited-entry schemes can end up being more costly than traditional management measures. Other players object that the government should not be in the business of ensuring high incomes for fishermen or protecting marginal operations. Fishermen should be free to fail (*National Fisherman* September 1985).

Finally, some fishermen believe that the problem of excessive take has been created by the government through programs such as the Capital Construction Fund and the Fishing Vessel Obligation Fund. These funds, together with tax credits, allowed outside investors to build up the industry to the point at which fishery resources no longer can be used efficiently, according to this view. Rather than limiting access, these fishermen suggest eliminating indirect and direct federal subsidies (*National Fisherman*, November 1985).

## Jurisdictional Controversies

One of the problems that the Magnuson Fishery Conservation and Management Act sought to correct was the inconsistent management of fish caught in several different jurisdictions. It was hoped that consistent management of fish in the federal fishery conservation zone would be achieved by including state officials on the fishery management councils and making them responsible for the development of fishery management plans. However, the Magnuson Fishery Conservation and Management Act did not address conflicting management of fisheries in state waters. Nor did it resolve controversies over the management of fisheries crossing international boundaries.

One of the clearer cases of the jurisdictional problems in federal waters is exemplified by the Swordfish Fishery Management Plan. Swordfish migrate through the jurisdictions of five regional fishery management councils in the Atlantic Ocean, the Gulf of Mexico, and the Caribbean. Six years ago, the South Atlantic Fishery Management Council took the lead in preparing the Swordfish Fishery Management Plan, which was submitted to the secretary of Commerce for review in the summer of 1985. Prompt implementation of the plan, however, remains problematic since the fishery management councils still disagree over the plan's management objectives and over closure dates for fishing in some regions (*National Fisherman*, August 1985).

Further complicating implementation of the swordfish plan is the objection of the Department of State to two of the plan's proposed restrictions on foreign fishing. The State Department maintains that the fishery management plan will make it difficult for the United States to negotiate fishing agreements on tunas, the only species caught in the U.S. fishery conservation zone that are managed internationally rather than under the Magnuson act. It is feared that this could jeopardize the tuna-fishing industry.

Conflicting management measures among states within the range of a species can jeopardize seriously the effectiveness of fisheries conservation. For instance, in recent years, great attention has been paid the decline of the Atlantic striped bass, a species that spawns principally in the Chesapeake Bay but migrates as far north as Maine and as far south as North Carolina. Between 1973 and 1983, commercial landings of Atlantic striped bass fell from 14.7 million pounds to only 1.7 million pounds.

Passing through the jurisdiction of 12 states, three fishery management councils, and the Atlantic States Marine Fisheries Commission, the striped bass probably is the most studied of all marine fish. After considerable research and discussion, the Atlantic states commission recommended size limits, seasonal closures, and a 55 percent reduction in the mortality rate of striped bass, including both fish caught and fish that are hooked and probably die without being landed. Yet, member states of the commission, from Maine through North Carolina, did not fully adopt the commission's recommendations.

In 1984, however, Congress stepped in and passed the Atlantic Striped Bass Conservation Act, authorizing a federal moratorium on fishing for striped bass in the coastal waters of any state that fails to implement the commission's striped bass plan. This unusual imposition of federal over state authority in fisheries management has been successful in forcing the states to implement the commission's recommendations. More recently, the Mid-Atlantic, New England, and South Atlantic fishery management councils released a draft Striped Bass Fishery Management Plan and environmental assessment which is intended to apply to the seven percent of the commercial striped bass catch that occurs in the fishery conservation zone. The management measures proposed reinforce those of the Atlantic states commission (Mid-Atlantic Fishery Management Council 1985).

A third type of boundary issue concerns so-called transboundary fish stocks that overlap or cross international boundaries. Although the extension of the U.S. fishery conservation zone to 200 miles offshore placed many fish stocks well within U.S. jurisdiction, other stocks remained partially outside. The transboundary fish stocks on the Georges Bank, off New England, have not been subject to an international agreement since the demise of the International Commission for the Northwest Atlantic Fisheries. Some U.S. fishermen have been apprehended by the Canadians for fishing in Canadian waters. The lack of an agreement between the United States and Mexico on management of transboundary shrimp populations also has closed Mexican waters to U.S. shrimp fishermen. Undeterred, some U.S. shrimp fishermen have ventured into Mexican waters and have been cited by NMFS under the Lacey Act upon their return.

## Incidental Catch

The dramatic innovations in fishing technology that followed World War II have aggravated the problem of incidental catch. New synthetic fibers enabled gear manufacturers to produce much larger nets. Because of their size, these nets are much less selective than the smaller natural-fiber nets in what they catch. This catch is made up of target species—those the fisherman is seeking—and by-catch—species captured incidental to the target species. By-catch may include species of no or little commercial worth and species of special status, such as marine mammals or endangered or threatened species. Quite often, the by-catch is thrown overboard before vessels return to shore. The discarded catch includes target fish too small to process, target fish over or under the legal size limit, target fish whose retention would exceed a quota, and target fish that drop out of nets before being landed (Bricklemyer and Hartmann 1985).

Every year, commercial marine fishermen around the world catch 14 to 20 billion pounds of marine organisms that they then throw back overboard. Every year, in the world's shrimp fisheries alone, from 10 billion to 40 billion pounds of by-catch fish and other marine life are caught with the 2.2 billion to 3.0 billion pounds of shrimp landed. Of this by-catch, a quarter to a half is discarded (Bricklemyer and Hartmann 1985).

In the United States, enormous amounts of marine life are discarded as by-catch. For instance, during summer in the New England groundfish fishery, dogfish, a slow-growing shark, may make up 30-40 percent of the total catch per haul. Because dogfish become entangled in the nets and have no commercial value, their heads are cut off and the fish are thrown overboard (Brickelmeyer and Hartman 1985). Off the West Coast, incidental capture and discard of halibut in the crab and groundfish fisheries equals or exceeds halibut catch, which in 1983 totaled about 27 million pounds (Bricklemyer and Hartmann 1985).

In the Japanese gillnet fishery for salmon in the North Pacific, much of which is conducted within the U.S. fishery conservation zone, 21 species of seabirds become entangled in the nets and drown, together with about 5,500 Dall's porpoise yearly*. The fishing fleet includes four "motherships" and 172 catcher boats that deploy nets 10 miles long. Although exact figures are not known, it is conservatively estimated that 100,000 to 250,000 seabirds are killed yearly by Japanese gillnet fishermen working in the U.S. fishery conservation zone (King 1985).

In the past, incidental capture has led to controversy only when species with a special status have been involved. The most commonly known example is the incidental capture and drowning of porpoises in the purse-seine nets of the U.S. tuna fleet operating in the eastern Tropical Pacific.† Reports of the

---

* Most of the incidental catch is made up of short-tailed shearwater (*Puffinus tenuirostris*) and the tufted puffin (*Lunds cirrhata*). Short-tailed shearwaters comprised nearly half of the total seabird kill in some years. The Fish and Wildlife Service estimates that in an average year, 27 percent of the tufted puffins in the U.S. fishery conservation zone are killed in the Japanese salmon gillnet fishery (King 1985).

† Porpoise also are captured incidentally and drowned in the purse-seine nets of other nations' tuna fleets operating in the region.

drowning of several hundred thousand porpoise in the tuna fishery in the early 1970s created a public outrage that contributed to the passage of the Marine Mammal Protection Act in 1972. After much litigation, the U.S. tuna fleet adopted new gear that considerably reduced the incidental capture of porpoises. Indeed, mortality is now estimated to be below 17,000 porpoise each year.

A simmering controversy over incidental capture of protected species in the shrimp fishery may burst into the open in the next year. Each year, about two billion pounds of small shrimp, other invertebrates, and finfishes are discarded in the U.S. shrimp fishery. In the Gulf of Mexico, some 150 species of finfishes are caught incidentally. On the average, nine-pounds of finfish are caught and discarded for each pound of shrimp landed. Together with this discarded by-catch an estimated 45,619 sea turtles are caught. Of these more than 12,615 drown (U.S. Department of Commerce 1983d).

All sea-turtle species are listed as threatened or endangered under the Endangered Species Act, which prohibits taking species listed as endangered. In response to public concerns about the incidental capture of endangered Kemp's ridley sea turtles and other sea-turtle species listed under the Endangered Species Act, NMFS undertook a program of research in 1978 to develop fishing gear that would reduce the incidental capture of sea turtles while maintaining shrimp catch. By 1981, this research had led to the Turtle Excluder Device, which later became known as the Trawling Efficiency Device because of its ability to increase shrimp catch and eliminate other by-catch such as finfish and jellyfish. The device has since undergone substantial improvements, reducing by 97 percent incidental capture of sea turtles in the southeastern shrimp fishery (U.S. Department of Commerce 1985d).

In 1982, the federal government, with the assistance of some parts of the shrimp industry and the environmental community, undertook a program of encouraging voluntary use of the Trawling Efficiency Device by U.S. shrimp fishermen. This effort appears to be faltering. Fewer than 200 of the more than 6,000 shrimp vessels used the device at any time during the 1985 season. The lack of progress in the voluntary adoption program, together with the continued decline of the endangered Kemp's ridley sea turtle population (see the Kemp's chapter in this volume), has led the U.S. Sea Turtle Recovery Team, among other interested groups, to re-evaluate the voluntary program and to call for mandatory use. Such demands probably will be met with considerable resistance by the shrimp industry, which is reluctant to take on the extra tasks of working with the device, and by NMFS, which does not want to conflict with the shrimp industry.

## Efficient Implementation of the Magnuson Fishery Conservation and Management Act

With the Congressional emphasis on reducing the federal deficit has come greater scrutiny of the cost of implementing of the Magnuson Fishery Conservation and Management Act in particular and of the federal role in marine fisheries management in general. A recently released report by the Commerce Department's Office of the Inspector General examines the costs associated with implementation of the act (U.S. Department of Commerce 1985a).

Among other things, the Inspector General's report concluded that the Western Pacific and Caribbean fishery management councils should be merged into other councils. The Inspector General argued that the $1 million spent by the federal government on each of these two fishery management councils exceeded the importance of their fisheries.

The Inspector General also concluded that the development of sound fishery management plans would continue to be jeopardized by inadequate data on the size and distribution of fish populations and by the effect of commercial and recreational fishing on them. The Inspector General surmised that the fishery management councils "have been developing plans without all the data necessary for proper decisions. . . . One reason for this is that most Councils and National Oceanic and Atmospheric Administration research activities do little or no mutual planning of long-range data needs" (U.S. Department of Commerce 1985a). In addition, the Inspector General found that some fishery management council plans require continual collection of information for monitoring purposes, but that the lack of uniform requirements for gathering the data can prevent the monitoring in some cases.

The Inspector General also criticized failure of fishery councils to have fishery management plans reviewed by enforcement specialists. Lacking enforcement review, fishery management councils have adopted unenforceable regulations or regulations in conflict with those of the states. As an example, the fishery management plan for American lobster prohibits fishermen from possessing butchered lobster parts, although in adjacent state waters fishermen are allowed to possess butchered parts. It is almost impossible to determine whether fishermen caught the lobsters in state or federal waters (U.S. Department of Commerce 1985a.)

Finally, the Inspector General recommended that the administrative staffs of the fishery management councils be reduced and some support activities be provided by NMFS. The Inspector General also recommended that grants to fishery management councils for the development of plans include specific objectives or specific work statements (U.S. Department of Commerce 1985a). Although NMFS and the fishery management councils did not agree with all of the Inspector General's conclusions and recommendations, NMFS already has adopted some of them.

## Legislation

The current authorization of the Magnuson Fishery Conservation and Management Act expired October 1, 1985. In the first week of May, the House Merchant Marine and Fisheries Committee reported out a bill (H.R. 1533) which has not been acted upon by the full House. Besides maintaining current authorization levels at $69 million, the House bill makes it more difficult for fishery management councils to impose limited-entry programs by requiring support of such programs from three-quarters of the management council and two-thirds of the affected fishermen.

The House bill also limits the State Department to considering, in the determination of foreign fishery allocations, only "the conservation of living marine resources." This measure was initiated because some fishermen had complained that fisheries allocations were being used to achieve foreign policy objectives rather than fishery objectives.

Meanwhile, the Senate Committee on Commerce, Science, and Transportation has reported a straight two-year reauthorization, but continues to consider several bills written by members of the committee. Senator Ted Stevens (R-AK) introduced S. 1245, which would make a number of changes in the Magnuson Fishery Conservation and Management Act regarding foreign fishing. For instance, it would include so-called "straddling stocks"—that is, species whose distribution extends beyond the 200-mile limit—in U.S. management jurisdiction. Senator Stevens' bill also would phase out foreign fishing in the North Pacific by cutting 1986 allocations by 40 percent, and gradually eliminating foreign fishing over the succeeding four years.

A somewhat similar bill (S. 1386) has been introduced by Senator Slade Gorton (R-WA) under which fishing by Japan and Korea would be cut 40 percent in 1986 and eliminated by 1989. A longer-term phase out would be possible for these countries if they were to sign a bilateral agreement with the United States providing for aid in the development of the U.S. fishing industry. Other foreign nations would continue to be phased out as the domestic fishing and processing sectors are able to use all of the available fish.

A final reauthorization bill (S.747), introduced by Senator Frank Lautenberg (D-NJ), requires among other things that all fishery management plans identify habitat necessary for fish production and means of conserving that habitat. All federal agencies would then have to give full consideration to these concerns. The bill also would establish a regional planning process to identify and address marine fisheries habitat needs. Senator Lautenberg's bill also would place tuna under management of the Magnuson Fishery Conservation and Management Act and would establish a vessel dislocation fund, through fishing permit fees, to buy boats from fishermen who may be driven out of business by the limited-entry plans.

## Fishery Marketing Councils

The House Merchant Marine and Fisheries Committee reported another House bill, H.R. 2935, that would establish a mechanism under which fishermen and processors could form seafood marketing boards. If the marketing boards are approved in a referendum funded initially by the federal government, they could collect fees from businesses within the board's regional or fishery jurisdiction in order to fund operations such as promoting seafood and establishing quality standards. Whether or not the referendum was approved, the federal government would be reimbursed for the costs of the referendum by the organizations calling for it. Although the Senate has not taken up a companion bill, it is expected that the Senate will do so once the House has passed its bill.

## National Aquaculture Improvement Act

The National Aquaculture Improvement Act, a part of the Food Security Act (Farm Bill), passed Congress in 1985 (subtitle D of title 17 H.R. 2100). The bill authorizes appropriations of $3 million each to the departments of Agriculture, Interior, and Commerce for fiscal years 1986 through 1988. Besides reducing federal spending authority by 40 percent, the bill also makes the Agriculture Department the lead agency on aquaculture and establishes a National Aquaculture Information Center in Agriculture. The act also requires the Commerce Department to report by December 1987 on adverse impacts on the domestic fishing industry from imports of maricultured products. By the same date, the Interior Department must report on "exotic" species introduced into U.S. waters as a result of aquaculture activities. Between 1980, when the first National Aquaculture Act was passed, and 1984, aquaculture production increased from 207 million pounds to 458 million pounds. Only a very small amount of this production is of marine species.

## Interjurisdictional Fisheries Research Act

The House also passed the Interjurisdictional Fisheries Research Act (H.R. 1028) in the summer of 1985. The bill authorizes $5 million in fiscal years 1986 through 1988 to provide matching grants with the states to support research on species that:

- migrate between state and federal waters and are subject to a fishery management plan under the Magnuson Fishery Conservation and Management Act;
- migrate across state waters and are subject to a fishery management plan developed by one of the interstate marine fisheries commissions; or
- migrate across the waters of the Great Lakes states.

The bill also provides $350,000 for three years to support the three interstate fishery commissions. Programs established under the Commercial Fisheries Research and Development Act (16 U.S.C. 779), which this bill would replace, could continue for another year. For several reasons, including lack of enthusiasm for the bill from the fishing industry, the Senate is not likely to consider it.

## Legal Developments

No major legal developments involving federal marine fisheries management occurred in 1985.

## Status of the Resource

The National Marine Fisheries Service conducts assessments of 139 stocks, of which 111 are marine fish and shellfish stocks. In assessing commercially or recreationally valuable stocks, NMFS attempts to gather two basic types or information: measures of fishing effort and fishing mortality levels. NMFS relies upon two types of information regarding fishing levels. Fishery dependent data are obtained from the catch and include biological information, such as age of fish caught, as well as information on the amount and species in the catch. Fishery independent data on a stock is gathered from National Oceanic and Atmospheric Administration survey vessels.

These data are entered into computer systems affiliated with NMFS Fisheries Centers in Seattle, Washington; La Jolla, California; and Woods Hole, Massachusetts. In the last 10 years, NMFS has undertaken the development of increasingly sophisticated population models using these data. Each of the regional fisheries centers maintains population assessments for stocks in the region. A brief description of the status of selected stocks of commercially and recreationally valuable fish and shellfish in each of the five NMFS regions is presented here. In general, these descriptions are based upon the regional strategic plans contained in the *Strategic Plan for the National Marine Fisheries Service* of April 1985 and on *Fisheries of the United States, 1984.*

### Northeast Region

The Northeast Region's fisheries are supervised by the New England and Mid-Atlantic fishery management councils, 11 states, and the Atlantic States Marine Fisheries Commission. The region's two major commercial fisheries—for groundfish and scallops—are centered on Georges Bank, one of the world's richest fishing grounds. The number of fishing vessels in the New England fishing fleet has grown by some 50 percent since passage of the Magnuson Fishery Conservation and Management Act. The size of the vessels also has grown. As a result, pressure has become extreme on traditionally sought finfish and shellfish, and catch and earnings per vessel have dropped significantly in recent years.

Very little foreign fishing is conducted in this region. The domestic industry has entered into joint ventures with foreign vessels that buy the domestic catch of species, such as squid, mackerel, whiting, and red hake, for which there is little or no market in the United States at this time.

Demersal species of finfish, those living on or near the seabed, are caught by nets trawled through the water and by stationary gill nets. As many as 10 species may be landed in a single haul. Sedentary species are caught primarily by trawlers. Lobster are caught in lobster traps, primarily in state waters.

Many species of finfish and shellfish are distributed in discrete areas and show a preference for specific spawning and nursery grounds. Deepwater pelagic species are more migratory and more vulnerable to fishing when populations are low because they concentrate in schools. The size of year-classes within populations of these species vary more than do demersal species.

The exploited finfish and shellfish stocks in the northeast Atlantic (from Cape Hatteras, North Carolina, to Nova Scotia) number some 100 species. About 2.2 billion pounds of about 30 finfish and squid species and ten shellfish species are caught yearly by domestic commercial fishermen. An estimated 330 million pounds of finfish are caught by recreational fishermen.

Current estimates indicate that traditionally exploited finfish and squid stocks have a long-term annual yield of about 2 billion pounds for commercial fisheries and another 220 million to 440 million pounds for recreational fisheries. These estimates do not include a potential catch of 1.1 billion pounds of menhaden. Additionally, there is currently little or no commercial fishing for saury or sand lance, which have a potential yield as high as 2.2 billion pounds. These last two species are very important sources of food for larger species.

Some estimates have been made for large oceanic pelagic fish, such as swordfish and tunas. The stock of bluefin tuna, which are caught on long-lines, purse-seine nets, and harpoons, is seriously depleted. Most bluefin tuna caught by domestic fishermen is exported to Japan.

The principal demersal species of economic importance are cod, haddock, redfish, pollock, silver hake, red hake, yellowtail flounder, American plaice, winter flounder, and summer flounder. The foreign and domestic catch of this group in 1983 was about 445 million pounds or about half their estimated long-term potential. Except for silver and red-hake, all species are under intensive fishing pressure.

Although the haddock populations of Georges Bank seemed to recover in the late 1970s, the population now is declining toward levels that followed heavy overfishing by foreign operations in the 1960s. The cod populations of Georges Bank and the Gulf of Maine have remained abundant, although catches have been very high in recent years. The Georges Bank herring populations remain commercially extinct. However, mackerel has recovered significantly. Herring, mackerel, butterfish, and bluefish, all important pelagic species, have a combined long-term annual yield of about 815 million pounds. In 1983, the total catch was about a third of this. Recreational fishermen are taking close to the potential yield of bluefish.

The spiny dogfish catch in 1983 totalled about 10 million pounds, but has a potential yield estimated at nearly 150 million pounds. Long-finned and short-finned squid populations are highly variable as a result of their short lifespan. NMFS estimates a potential yield of about 165 million pounds yearly. In 1983, the foreign joint venture and domestic catch was nearly 87 million pounds. Domestic landings of squid have increased significantly in recent years.

The striped bass population, which has been the object of both commercial and recreational fishing, is extremely depleted. Commercial landings fell from a high of 14.7 million pounds in 1973 to 1.7 million pounds in 1983. Under congressional pressure, the states of the striped bass range have severely limited recreational and commercial striper catches.

Atlantic salmon, once one of the most abundant anadromous fish of the Atlantic seaboard, now is so depleted that it is rarely landed in the United States Excessive take and habitat degradation of spawning habitats are responsible.

The major shellfish species are sea scallops, surf clams, ocean quahogs, and lobsters. NMFS estimates a combined long-term yield of about 154 million pounds. In 1983, combined landings for these species were about 198 million pounds. With the possible exception of surf clams and ocean quahogs, commercial landings are exceeding long-term yields of these species. Surf clam populations only recently have begun recovering from overexploitation in the mid-1970s. Surf clam and quahog fishing are located along the New Jersey and Delmarva coasts.

The fishery for American lobster, which is conducted mostly in state waters, had landings of more than 44 million pounds in 1983, valued at $106.7 million. NMFS believes that the lobster resource is in danger of being overfished and suggests that minimum size limits are so low in most of the range that most females do not reproduce.

Demand for specific species of fish, including cod, haddock, and lobster, has led to overfishing of some species and underutilization of other species. There is concern that this selective pressure may disrupt the balance of species within the ecosystem, resulting in the decline of some species during the next five years. Shifts of unknown origin already have occurred on the Georges Bank, where herring, mackerel, and silver hake have been replaced as dominant species by short-finned and long-finned squid, dogfish, and sand lance.

## Southeast Region

The Southeast Region, which includes eight states, the Mid-Atlantic, South Atlantic, and Gulf of Mexico fishery management councils, and both the Gulf and Atlantic States marine fisheries commissions, hosts the largest and most valuable fisheries in the United States. From 1978 through 1980, domestic commercial landings in the Southeast Region represented 43 percent of the national volume of landings and 32 percent of the national value. Recreational landings for many species are equal to commercial landings.

Many of the commercially and recreationally valuable finfish and shellfish in the Southeast Region are short lived. As a result, the abundance of these species is extremely sensitive to environmental fluctuations, both natural and anthropogenic. Since 90 percent of the fishery yield in the region is based on species that are estuarine-dependent, degradation of estuarine areas is a major concern.

More than 6,000 boats and vessels participate in the shrimp fishery, the nation's most valuable at more than $474 million in 1984. That year nearly equal amounts of the five species of shrimp were caught in state waters (139 million pounds) and in federal waters (133 million pounds). In the last 11 years, the catch has fluctuated between 194 and 284 million pounds. NMFS estimates that shrimp populations are fully exploited in the region. The share of the catch per boat has declined.

The menhaden fishery, which is like the shrimp fishery in being more productive in the Gulf of Mexico than in the Atlantic, is the nation's most productive fishery. About 2.9 billion pounds were landed in 1984, 45 percent of the total weight of U.S. commercial fishery landings. However, the dockside value of $117.3 million is low because most menhaden is converted into fishmeal. Atlantic and Gulf menhaden landings are thought to be fully used. Atlantic menhaden landings increased through the 1950s, then fell off rapidly. Since the mid-1960s, landings have increased to a little more than half of the peak landings in the 1950s. The 1984 Gulf landings were three times the size of the Atlantic landings. NMFS scientists do not believe that the menhaden populations can sustain these levels of catch.

The third most valuable fishery in the region is for reef fish, such as spiny lobster, snapper, and grouper. Based upon limited information on catch and effort, NMFS believes that many stocks are overfished, particularly in in-shore areas.

Oceanic pelagic (openwater) species include blue marlin, white marlin, sailfish, spearfish, and swordfish. Japan, Cuba, Taiwan, Korea, and Venezuela operate high-seas longline fisheries that are directed at tuna but that incidentally take significant numbers of billfish. Catches of billfish in the Atlantic were about 10 million pounds in 1981, 14 percent less than the previous five-year average. The U.S. fishery for swordfish has increased rapidly in recent years. The total domestic and foreign catch of swordfish in 1982 was roughly 40 million pounds. Concern exists at NMFS that billfishes and swordfish are being fished at their maximum yield or already are being overexploited.

The fishery management plan for mackerels sets a maximum sustainable yield at 37 million pounds for king mackerel and 27 million pounds for Spanish mackerel in 1983. New information led to the reduction of the maximum sustainable yield for king mackerel to 26.2 million pounds. In addition, the new information indicated that there were at least two separate stocks of king mackerel, an Atlantic and a Gulf stock. As a result, it appears that the Gulf stock was being overfished and is near collapse (*National Fisherman,* November

1985). Even with a moratorium on the catch of this stock, it is likely that the population will not recover for at least 10 years. Also, the Mexican fishery for king mackerel has increased from seven million pounds in 1980 to 13.1 million pounds in 1982. Some evidence indicates that both the United States and Mexico are fishing the same stock of king mackerel.

Several populations of fish are not being fished heavily at this time. Sharks, for instance, are a focus for increasing attention. There is concern lest the effort increase too rapidly, since sharks are easily overfished. Small coastal openwater fishes, squid and bottomfish are also being investigated for exploitation.

The incidental capture of bottomfish, such as croaker, in shrimp trawls in the Gulf of Mexico is estimated to exceed one billion pounds annually. This bycatch is generally discarded. Since 1972, the mean weight of croaker has declined roughly 42 percent in the northcentral Gulf of Mexico. Bycatch in shrimp trawls has been implicated. The Trawling Efficiency Device, a device developed by NMFS originally to eliminate incidental capture of endangered and threatened sea turtles, could reduce the bycatch of bottomfish by 50 percent. Use of the device by Gulf shrimp fishermen, however, is minimal.

The most important recreational species are king mackerel, snappers and groupers, spotted seatrout, croakers, and bluefish. More than nine million recreational anglers catch about 180 million pounds of fish yearly in the region.

## Southwest Region

The Southwest Region includes California, Hawaii, Guam, American Samoa, the Northern Mariana Islands, and the Trust Territory of the Pacific Islands. California is represented on the Pacific Regional Fisheries Management Council, and Hawaii and the territories are represented on the Western Pacific Fishery Management Council. The Pacific States Marine Fisheries Commission also represents the region.

Three different climatic regimes occur in the region, with different species assemblages in each. Northern and central California are characterized by cold, productive waters supporting large populations of demersal and anadromous fishes as are found farther north. The southern California Bight, from Point Conception south, is characterized by warmer, less productive water, where warm-water, open-ocean species dominate. The third regime surrounding the tropical and subtropical islands is characterized by openwater species and highly diverse reef fish communities.

The fisheries in the region are quite diverse. The highly sophisticated California tuna fleet historically has been the largest in the region and one of the largest in the country. Many of these vessels have moved to Panama and the western Pacific as all of the San Diego canneries have closed and moved their operations to Puerto Rico and Samoa. The region, however, also supports handline fisheries for rockfish in southern California, Indian subsistence salmon fishery in northern California, and commercial, recreational, and subsistence fisheries of low volume in the Pacific island areas.

The major fishery resources in the region include skipjack, yellowfin, and albacore tunas, billfishes, and coastal pelagics, including squid, anchovy, Pacific and jack mackerels, bonito, and sardine. Nearshore fish and shellfish include salmon, spiny lobster, pink shrimp, dungeness crab, and groundfish. Sea bass, barracuda, and yellowtail are important off southern California. Landings by domestic vessels in the region amounted to more than 800 million pounds in 1983. Foreign catches in the region were quite small.

Evidence indicates that the West Coast trawl fishery has an excessive number of fishermen. The number of groundfish trawl vessels increased from 280 in 1976 to 430 in 1983. Many of these vessels moved into the fishery as pink shrimp and dungeness crab stocks off Washington, Oregon, and California and king and tanner crab stocks off Alaska declined.

The domestic catch of groundfish off the West Coast increased from 132 million pounds in 1977 to nearly 375 million pounds in 1983. NMFS estimates an optimum yield of about 685 million pounds. In NMFS' view, stocks of Pacific whiting, shortbelly rockfish, and jack mackerel are underfished. NMFS estimates a long-term yield of more than 220 million pounds of Pacific whiting annually. Stocks of Pacific ocean perch, sable fish, and widow rockfish, among others, must be rebuilt.

Some California chinook salmon stocks are depressed. Nonetheless, record landings were made in 1982. The 1982-83 El Niño climatic phenomenon apparently contributed to very low catches in 1983 and 1984.

Coastal pelagics, including mackerel, anchovy, squid, and bonito have an estimated potential catch of more than 880 million pounds yearly. However, abundance and availability of this group of species is highly variable. Only the anchovy fishery is managed under a fishery management plan, although anchovy fishermen also fish for other species in the group. Further complicating management of this group is the fact that both the United States and Mexico fish northern anchovy, although no management agreement exists between the two nations.

A moratorium on commercial fishing appears to have contributed to some recovery in Pacific sardine and Pacific mackerel populations which have been depressed for many years. Pacific mackerel are captured incidentally with the more abundant jack mackerel.

The offshore fisheries of the central and western Pacific are expanding as more vessels leave depressed Alaskan and West Coast fisheries. Interest is being directed at deepwater bottomfish, such as opakapaka, onaga, and ehu, shallow water snappers, reef predators, and deepwater shrimp and spiny lobster. Extensive resource surveys completed in recent years have not clarified fully the abundance and distribution of stocks in the Pacific islands. The near-shore fish stocks are fully exploited by commercial, recreational, and traditional subsistence fishing.

The eastern tropical Pacific Ocean has been the preferred fishing grounds of the U.S. distant-water, tropical tuna fleet. In 1983, about 134 U.S. vessels—51 percent of the total fleet—landed more than 130 million pounds of yellowfin tuna (down 30 percent from 1982) and nearly 80 million pounds of skipjack tuna (down 33 percent from 1982). The total catch in the eastern tropical Pacific Ocean was down in 1983, perhaps because of El Nino. The U.S. fleet continued to dominate the fishery, catching 55 percent of the total. NMFS estimates suggest that yellowfin tuna populations in the eastern tropical Pacific Ocean are close to being overfished.

The U.S. distant-water, tropical tuna fleet has been increasingly interested in pursuing tuna in the western Pacific territories of American Samoa, Guam, and the Northern Mariana Islands. About 25 U.S. purse seiners operated in the western Pacific in 1982, landing 133.7 million pounds of skipjack and yellowfin tuna. In 1983, about 60 vessels participated in the fishery and landed about 109 million pounds of yellowfin and about 230 million pounds of skipjack tuna. Estimates on the potential yield in this fishery range from about 440 million pounds to 1.1 billion pounds.

A highly migratory stock of north Pacific albacore is fished by several nations, principally the United States and Japan. Japanese gillnetting of albacore is increasing in the western and central Pacific. Increasing landings and decreasing catch per unit effort indicate that fishing effort could exceed sustainable yield. Continued declines may trigger negotiations to establish international management of the stocks.

Conflicts between marine mammals and commercial and recreational fishing activities are increasing in the region. More details are available in the Marine Mammal Protection chapter.

## Northwest Region

Oregon and Washington make up the Northwest Region and are represented on the Pacific and North Pacific fishery management councils and on the Pacific Marine Fisheries Commission. Along this coastline are 19 major estuaries, excluding Puget Sound, comprising nearly 200,000 acres of tidelands and submerged lands. The principal fishery in the region is the salmon fishery, although fishing also is focused on albacore, jack mackerel, herring, anchovy, shad, whiting, flounder, sole, rockfish, sablefish, lingcod, dungeness crab, shrimp, scallops, oysters, clams, and mussels. However, the vast majority of the 12,000 vessels registered in the region participate in local and Alaska salmon fisheries.

Current estimates for the various groundfish species indicate that rockfish populations are substantially below maximum sustainable yield. Whiting, flounder, sablefish, and lingcod appear to be producing at maximum sustainable yield. Of the pelagic species, jack mackerel appear to be producing at maximum sustainable yield, while anchovy stocks are below maximum sustainable yield. Dungeness crab catches have remained at their lowest levels in a decade.

NMFS estimates show both chinook and coho salmon stocks well below maximum sustainable yield, while pink and sockeye salmon stocks are increasing, and chum salmon stocks are stable. For more details on the status of salmon stocks, see the Inland Fisheries chapter, in this volume and in the *1985 Audubon Wildlife Report;* see also the chinook salmon chapter in this volume.

Conflicts between marine mammals and commercial and recreational fisheries are increasing in the region. About 500 harbor seals are killed yearly in the Columbia River and adjacent waters. For more details see the Marine Mammal Protection chapter in this and in the *Audubon Wildlife Report 1985.*

## Alaska Region

With 65 percent of the continental shelf of the United States off its shores, numerous large rivers, and 33,000 miles of coastline, Alaska provides a productive habitat for marine wildlife of all kinds. Besides the staggering marine fish and shellfish populations, the fishery conservation zone off Alaska also provides habitat for 95 percent of the marine mammals found in the U.S. fishery conservation zone. Ninety-six percent of the foreign fish catch and 70 percent of the fish products exported from the United States are from Alaskan waters. Alaska is represented on the Northern Pacific Fishery Management Council and the Pacific Marine Fisheries Commission.

The fisheries of the Alaska Region generally are divided into two subregions: Bering Sea/Aleutians and Gulf of Alaska.

In 1984, more than 500 foreign fishing vessels caught nearly three billion pounds of fish and shellfish in the fishery conservation zone off Alaska, of which 2.3 billion pounds were pollock. Of the total foreign catch, Japan took more than two billion pounds. By comparison, before passage of the Magnuson Fishery Conservation and Management Act, 1,400 foreign vessels caught up to 5.7 billion pounds of finfish and shellfish there. In 1984, domestic fishermen sold 979 million pounds of pollock to foreign fishermen in joint ventures, up from 624 million pounds in 1983, and 284 million pounds in 1982.

King and Tanner crab populations dropped substantially from 1981 through 1983, and sharply reduced catches are expected to continue for the next four to five years. Major shrimp populations have been depressed since 1979. As the result of these declines and the continued low levels of the salmon stocks, the Alaska and Northwest fishing fleets have been directing more effort toward catching groundfish, including pollock, Pacific cod, flounders, atka mackerel, and rockfish.

As mentioned in the previous section, chinook salmon stocks are substantially below sustainable yield. Nonetheless, 313,000, chinook salmon were taken in the commercial and recreational fisheries in 1983. Interceptions of Alaska chinook salmon by the Japanese high seas fleet peaked at 380,000, but decreased to 24,000 in 1983. Coho salmon populations appear to be increasing, with a commercial catch of nearly two million salmon in 1983. Interceptions of Bristol Bay sockeye salmon have been cut from 3.5 million in 1976 to 500,000 in 1983. In 1985, more than 23 million Bristol Bay sockeye were caught. Landings of sockeye salmon in other areas of Alaska in 1985 amounted to more than 15 million fish. More than 84 million pink salmon were caught in 1985, leading all other salmon landings. Indeed, the Alaska salmon harvest for 1985 was the largest ever (*National Fisherman,* November 1985).

The greatest potential for increasing the U.S. catch in the U.S. fishery conservation zone lies, according to some fisheries scientists, with the groundfish resources off Alaska. It is thought that these groundfish stocks have a potential yield of more than four billion pounds yearly. Fishermen from Japan, the Soviet Union, Poland, Korea, and West Germany currently take 2.9 billion pounds of this resource.

The principal species of groundfish is Alaskan pollock, which can be processed into seafood substitutes called "surimi." NMFS has estimated an optimum yield of nearly one billion pounds of pollock in the Gulf of Alaska. Pollock stocks in the Bering Sea/Aleutians sub-region are declining, although nearly 2.3 billion pounds were caught, principally by foreign vessels, in 1983. A new analysis of available data indicates that the pollock stock is heavily overfished and that the stock may well collapse (Fletcher 1985).

NMFS has decreased its estimate of the size of the Gulf of Alaska stock of pollock to between 716 million and 1.2 billion pounds, less than half its previous estimate. In addition, NMFS now believes that the stock will continue to decline and has recommended to the North Pacific Fishery Management Council that commercial fishing on pollock be banned in the Gulf of Alaska during 1986 (*National Fisherman,* November 1985).

Other groundfish stocks include cod and flounder, which are both stable in the Gulf of Alaska sub-region with optimum yields estimated at about 130 million pounds and about 75 million pounds respectively. In the Bering Sea/Aleutian sub-region, however, cod is declining while flounder remains stable with an estimated maximum sustainable yield of about 700 to 900 million pounds.

Both halibut and sablefish appear to be increasing in the Gulf of Alaska. Sablefish stocks in the Bering Sea/Aleutian sub-region, however, are substantially below maximum sustainable yield. Rockfish stocks are substantially below maximum sustainable yield in both sub-regions.

In the Bering Sea/Aleutian sub-region, herring stocks are stable with an estimated maximum sustainable yield of about 106 million pounds.

# References

Alverson, Dayton L. 1978. "Commercial fishing," in Howard P. Brokaw, ed., *Wildlife in America*. Government Printing Office, Washington, D.C. pp. 67-85.

Bean, Michael J. 1983. *The Evolution of National Wildlife Law*. Praeger, New York. 449 pp.

Memorandum from Henry R. Beasley, NMFS to Distribution regarding International Fishery Agreements, August 9, 1985.

Bell, F. Howard. 1970. "Management of Pacific halibut," in Norman G. Benson, ed., *A Century of Fisheries in North America, Special Publication No. 7*. American Fisheries Society, Washington, D.C. pp. 209-221.

Brown, Sandra and Ariel E. Lugo. 1981. *Management and Status of U.S. Commercial Fisheries*. Council on Environmental Quality, Washington, D.C. 45 pp.

Buck, Eugene H. 1985. *Federal Agency Programs in Living Aquatic Resources and Aquatic Habitat Protection*. Congressional Research Service, Washington, D.C. 57 pp.

Bricklemyer, Eugene C. and Hans J. Hartmann. 1985. Discard Catch in U.S. Commercial Marine Fisheries: Analysis and Recommendations. Unpublished research proposal. University of Washington, Seattle. 76 pp.

Commission on Marine Science, Engineering and Resources. 1969. *Our Nation and the Sea: A Plan for National Action*. Government Printing Office, Washington, D.C.

Craig, J. and R. Hacker. 1940. "The history and development of the fisheries of the Columbia River." Bureau of Fisheries, U.S. Department of the Interior Bulletin. No. 32. U.S. Department of the Interior, Washington, D.C.

Dasmann, Raymond F. 1968. *Environmental Conservation*. John Wiley Sons, Inc., New York.

Fletcher, R.I. 1985. Estimates of Stock Abundance, Productivity, and Other Measures of Consequence on the Pollock Stock of the S.E. Bering Sea. Great Salt Bay Experimental Station, Damariscotta, Maine. 11 pp.

Testimony of William G. Gordon, Assistant Administrator for Fisheries, NOAA, before the House Subcommittee on Fisheries and Wildlife Conservation and the Environment, February 28, 1984.

Graham, Herbert H. 1970. "Management of the Groundfish Fisheries of the Northwest Atlantic," *in* N.G. Benson ed., *A Century of Fisheries in North America, Special Publication No. 7*. American Fisheries Society. Washington, D.C. pp. 249-261.

Holt, Sidney J. and Lee M. Talbot. 1978. *New Principles for the Conservation of Wild Living Resources*. The Wildlife Society. Washington, D.C. 33 pp.

Testimony of Warren King on behalf of the International Council for Bird Preservation and the Center for Environmental Education before the National Ocean Policy Study, October 9, 1985.

Larkin, P.A. 1970. "Management of Pacific Salmon of North America," *in*

Norman G. Benson, ed., *A Century of Fisheries in North America, Special, Publication No. 7.* American Fisheries Society, Washington, D.C. pp. 223-236.

Lindall, William N., Jr. and Gordon W. Thayer. 1982. "Quantification of National Marine Fisheries Service Habitat Conservation Efforts in the Southeast Region of the United States." *Marine Fisheries Review* 44, no. 12 (December 1982):18-22.

MacLeish, William H. 1985. *Oil and Water: The Struggle of Georges Bank.* The Atlantic Monthly Press, Boston. 304 pp.

Mid-Atlantic Fishery Management Council. 1985. *Striped Bass Fishery Management Plan.* Mid-Atlantic Fishery Management Council, Dover, Delaware. 154 pp.

National Advisory Committee on Oceans and Atmosphere. 1982. *Fisheries for the Future.* NACOA, Washington, D.C. 61 pp.

Memorandum from Kip Robinson and Beverly Carter, Office of Congressional Affairs, NOAA, "List of Legislative Authorities for NOAA," September 1982.

Schaefer, Milner B. 1970. "Management of the American Pacific Tuna Fishery," *in* Norman G. Benson, ed., *A Century of Fisheries in North America, Special Publication No. 7.* American Fisheries Society, Washington, D.C. pp. 237-248.

Stroud, Richard H. 1970. "Future of Fisheries Management in North America," *in* N.G. Benson, ed., *A Century of Fisheries in North America, Special Publication No. 7.* American Fisheries Society, Washington, D.C. pp. 291-308.

Stroud, Richard H. 1978. "Recreational Fishing," *in* Howard P. Brokaw, ed., *Wildlife in America.* Government Printing Office, Washington, D.C. pp. 53-66.

Subcommittee on Aquaculture. 1983. *National Aquaculture Development Plan.* Volume 1. Washington, D.C. 67 pp.

Tiner, Ralph W., Jr. 1984. *Wetlands of the United States, Current Status and Recent Trends.* Government Printing Office, Washington, D.C. 59 pp.

U.S. Comptroller General. 1976. *The U.S. Fishing Industry: Present Condition and Future of Marine Fisheries.* Government Printing Office, Washington, D.C. 107 pp.

U.S. Congress, House, Committee on Merchant Marine and Fisheries, Fishery Conservation and Management Improvement: Report to Accompany H.R. 1533, 99th Congress, 1st Session 1985, H. Rept. 99-165.

U.S. Department of Commerce, Office of Inspector General, Office of Audits. 1985a. *Opportunities for Cost Reductions and Operational Efficiencies in Managing Fishery Resources.* U.S. Department of Commerce. Washington, D.C. 53 pp.

U.S. Department of Commerce, National Oceanic and Atmospheric Administration, National Marine Fisheries Service. 1985b. *Fisheries of the United States 1984.* U.S. Department of Commerce, Washington, D.C. 122 pp.

U.S. Department of Commerce, National Oceanic and Atmospheric Administration, National Marine Fisheries Service. 1985c. *Strategic Plan for National Marine Fisheries Service.* U.S. Department of Commerce. Washington, D.C.

U.S. Department of Commmerce, National Oceanic and Atmospheric Administration, National Marine Fisheries Service. 1985d. *Magnuson Fishery Conservation and Management Act (MFCMA), Operations* Handbook. U.S. Department of Commerce. Washington, D.C. 109 pp. + Appendices.

U.S. Department of Commerce, National Oceanic and Atmospheric Administration, National Marine Fisheries Service. 1984a. *Fishery Statistics of the United States, 1977.* U.S. Department of Commerce. Washington, D.C. 407 pp.

U.S. Department of Commerce, National Oceanic and Atmospheric Administration, National Marine Fisheries Service. 1984b. *Fisheries of the United States, 1983.* U.S. Department of Commerce. Washington, D.C. 122 pp.

U.S. Department of Commerce, National Oceanic and Atmospheric Administration. 1984c. *Budget Estimates: Fiscal Year 1985.* U.S. Department of Commerce, Washington, D.C.

U.S. Department of Commerce, National Oceanic and Atmospheric Administration. 1984d. "Research Facilities and Programs, 1984." Unpublished memorandum. U.S. Department of Commerce, Washington, D.C.

U.S. Department of Commerce, National Oceanic and Atmospheric Administration, National Marine Fisheries Service. 1983a. *Fisheries of the United States 1982.* U.S. Department of Commerce, Washington, D.C. 118 pp.

U.S. Department of Commerce, National Oceanic and Atmospheric Administration, National Marine Fisheries Service. 1983b. *Operational Guidelines— Fishery Management Plan Process.* U.S. Department of Commerce, Washington, D.C. 46 pp. + appendices.

U.S. Department of Commerce, National Oceanic and Atmospheric Administration. 1983c. *Budget Estimates: Fiscal Year 1984.* U.S. Department of Commerce, Washington, D.C.

U.S. Department of Commerce, National Oceanic and Atmospheric Administration, National Marine Fisheries Service. 1983d. *Environmental Assessment of a Program to Reduce the Incidental Take of Sea Turtles by the Commercial Shrimp Fishery in the Southeast United States.* National Marine Fisheries Service, St. Petersburg, Florida. 20 pp.

U.S. Department of Commerce, National Oceanic and Atmospheric Administration. 1982a. *Budget Estimates: Fiscal Year 1983.* U.S. Department of Commerce, Washington, D.C.

U.S. Department of Commerce, National Oceanic and Atmospheric Administration, National Marine Fisheries Service. 1982b. *Background Paper for Proposed Habitat Conservation Policy for National Marine Fisheries Service.* U.S. Department of Commerce, Washington, D.C. 80 pp.

———— 1981a. *Calendar Year 1980 Report on the Implementation of the Magnuson Fishery Conservation and Management Act of 1976.* U.S. Department of Commerce, Washington, D.C.

U.S. Department of Commerce, National Oceanic and Atmospheric Administration. 1981b. *Budget Estimates: Fiscal Year 1982.* U.S. Department of Commerce, Washington, D.C.

U.S. Department of Commerce, National Oceanic and Atmospheric Administration, National Marine Fisheries Service, Marine Recreational Fisheries Task Group. 1981c. *Proposed Policy for NMFS in Marine Recreational Fisheries.* U.S. Department of Commerce, Washington, D.C. 57 pp.

U.S. Department of Commerce, National Oceanic and Atmospheric Administration, National Marine Fisheries Service. 1979. *Fisheries of the United States 1978.* U.S. Department of Commerce, Washington, D.C. 120 pp.

U.S. Department of Commerce. 1978a. *Fisheries of the United States 1977.* U.S. Department of Commerce, Washington, D.C. 113 pp.

U.S. Department of Commerce, National Oceanic and Atmospheric Administration. 1978b. *U.S. Ocean Policy in the 1970s: Status and Issues.* Government Printing Office, Washington, D.C. 328 pp.

Warner, William. 1977. *Distant Water: The Fate of the North Atlantic Fisherman.* Little, Brown and Company, Boston, Massachusetts. 338 pp.

*Michael Weber, a consultant who works part time for the Center for Environmental Education, is a coauthor of* The 1985 Citizen's Guide to the Ocean.

A wildlife biologist prepares to release a radio-tagged bald eagle. The bald eagle is one of a handful of federally listed species that have made a successful comeback.
*U.S. Fish and Wildlife Service*

# The Endangered Species Program

## Michael J. Bean

### Introduction

THE FEDERAL ENDANGERED Species Program is a modest-sized program of the Interior and Commerce departments with the ambitious goal of preventing the avoidable extinction of plants and animals in the United States, other nations, and the sea. It is a program of quite recent vintage: the basic legislation it implements, the federal Endangered Species Act, dates only to 1973; similar, predecessor laws can be traced only to 1966.

Despite its relative newness, the federal Endangered Species Program has helped spawn and helps sustain parallel conservation programs in most states and several territories. In addition, through the program, the United States carries out its obligations under the convention on International Trade in Endangered Species of Wild Fauna and Flora, an international treaty that protects endangered plants and animals by regulating commercial trade in them. That aspect of the program is discussed separately in the International Wildlife Conservation chapter.

Although the Endangered Species Program is chiefly the responsibility of the U.S. Fish and Wildlife Service and the National Marine Fisheries Service, it seeks to affect the way in which all federal agencies do business. It is this influence on the activities of other federal agencies that is simultaneously the source of the program's greatest conservation potential and the source of its greatest controversy.

## Organization and Operations

It has been said that today's unprecendented rate of extinction of species is "the folly our descendants are least likely to forgive us" (Wilson 1982). The reasons are twofold. First, other species represent resources of enormous potential value to human welfare, particularly in the fields of medicine and agriculture. Second, extinction is irreversible. Though forests may be replanted and rivers undammed, living species, once lost, can never be regained. It is the congruence of these two indisputable facts, together with the recognition that wild plants and animals are disappearing faster now than ever before in human history, that fuels concern today with the problem of endangered species.

By the beginning of the 20th century, two examples had driven home the potential for massive human destruction even of widespread and abundant

U.S. Fish and Wildlife Service Endangered Species Program
Table of Organization

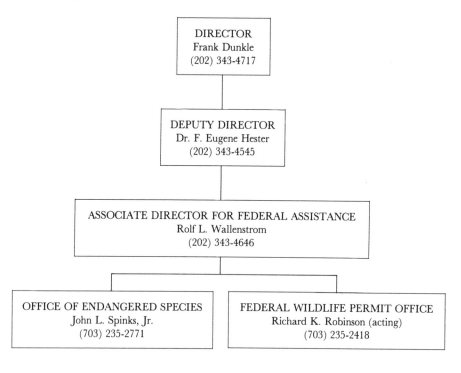

species. The American bison, one of the most numerous large mammals of the North American continent at the outset of the 19th century, had, by the end of the century, been reduced to two small populations—one in the far north of Canada and the other in Yellowstone National Park (Trefethen 1961). Similarly, the passenger pigeon, whose enormous flocks John James Audubon described as blackening the skies in the early 19th century, was, by 1914, entirely extinct.

Two important lessons could be drawn from the experiences of the bison and the passenger pigeon. The alarming lesson was that extinction could come suddenly and dramatically, completely wiping out species that only a few decades earlier had numbered in the millions. The more hopeful lesson, provided by the bison, was that the road to extinction could be reversed. With a remnant wild population in Yellowstone and small captive populations in zoos and private collections, early American conservationists not only averted the complete loss of this magnificent Great-Plains species, but laid the groundwork for its eventual recovery. The basic goals of the federal Endangered Species Program are to prevent further losses such as that of the passenger pigeon and to bring about recoveries such as that of the bison.

***Legal Authority*** The basic legal authority for the federal Endangered Species Program is the Endangered Species Act of 1973 (16 U.S.C.A. 1531 *et seq.*) That federal law completely replaced more limited predecessor laws passed by Congress in 1966 and 1969. The act proclaims its purposes to be "to provide a means whereby the ecosystems upon which endangered species and threatened species depend may be conserved [and] to provide a program for the conservation of such endangered species and threatened species" (16 U.S.C.A. 1531(B)). The principal elements of the conservation program it establishes are:

—the official listing of plants and animals as endangered or threatened;*

—the development of specific plans of action for the recovery of listed species;

—restrictions on the killing, collecting, and sale or purchase of listed species;

—acquisition of habitat for the conservation of listed species;

—assistance to state and foreign governments in carrying out programs for the conservation of listed species; and

—restrictions on actions authorized, funded or carried out by federal agencies that affect listed species.

In addition to the basic authority provided by the Endangered Species

---

* "Endangered" species are those determined to be currently in danger of extinction; "threatened" species are those not currently in such danger, but likely to become so within the foreseeable future. The term "species" is defined in the act to include subspecies and, in the case of vertebrate animals, distinct geographic populations as well.

Act, other laws provide additional authority utilized by the Endangered Species Program. For example, habitat for endangered and threatened species can be acquired pursuant to a variety of other conservation laws. Principal among these is the Land and Water Conservation Fund Act (16 U.S.C.A.4601 *et seq.*), but others include the Fish and Wildlife Coordination Act (16 U.S.C.A. 661 *et seq.*), the Fish and Wildlife Act of 1956 (16 U.S.C.A. 742a *et seq.*), and the Migratory Bird Conservation Act (16 U.S.C.A. 715 *et seq.*). When acquired by the secretary of the Interior, such areas become a part of the National Wildlife Refuge System, where their management is subject to the National Wildlife Refuge System Administration Act (16 U.S.C.A. 668dd *et seq.*). In addition to these specific authorities, Section 7 of the Endangered Species Act (16 U.S.C.A. 1536) directs all federal agencies to use their various legal authorities "in furtherance of the purposes of this Act." In this way, the act endeavors to make endangered species conservation an integral part of the mission of every federal agency.

A final component of the basic legal authority for the program consists of various state laws. One of the purposes of the Endangered Species Act was to stimulate biological conservation initiatives at the state level and thus build a cooperative program among state and federal conservation agencies. Section 6 of the act authorizes the federal government to provide financial assistance to aid in the implementation of state endangered species programs that meet specified standards. Most states have enacted qualifying laws, and these serve as additional legal authorities for the Endangered Species Program.

## Program Administration

The principal responsibility for administration of the Endangered Species Program rests with the secretaries of the Interior and Commerce. In general, the division of responsibility between the two secretaries is as follows: The secretary of Commerce is responsible for marine species and the secretary of the Interior for freshwater and terrestrial species. The two secretaries share responsibility for sea turtles, which spend most of their lives at sea, but come ashore to rest. Seals and sea lions, however, which also divide their time between sea and shore, are the exclusive responsibility of the secretary of Commerce. On the other hand, the walrus, with similar habits, and the sea otter*, which never comes ashore, are the exclusive responsibility of the secretary of the Interior. The reasons for these seemingly arbitrary distinctions are historical rather than biological.

Within their respective spheres of authority, the functions of the two secretaries are quite similar. Each is responsible for deciding which species

---

* The California sea otter is a threatened species; neither the Alaskan sea otter nor the walrus is currently protected by the Endangered Species Act.

should be listed as threatened or endangered*, for enforcing the act's prohibitions against violators, and for reviewing the actions of other federal agencies that may affect listed species. In practice, because the vast majority of listed species always has been under the authority of the secretary of the Interior, the Interior Department share of the program has always received most of the funds and most of the attention.

Responsibility for the actual implementation of the authority conferred on the two secretaries has been delegated to subordinate officials. The duties of the secretary of the Interior are carried out by FWS. Within it, the principal

---

* While the secretary of Commerce may add marine species to the threatened and endangered species lists, he may not remove them from such lists or transfer them from the endangered to the threatened list without the concurrence of the secretary of the Interior. In this single respect, the secretary of Interior exercises a veto authority over the secretary of Commerce. To date, however, the secretary of Interior has never used that authority.

## FWS Regional Office Information

| | Region Address | Region Director/ ES Specialist | Phone |
|---|---|---|---|
| 1 | Lloyd 500 Bldg. Suite 1692 500 N.E. Multonomah St. Portland, Oregon 97332 | Richard J. Myshak/ Wayne White | (503) 231-6118 (503) 231-6131 |
| 2 | P.O. Box 1306 Albuquerque, NM 87103 | Michael J. Spear/ James Johnson | (505) 766-2321 (505) 766-2323 |
| 3 | Federal Bldg. Fort Snelling Twin Cities, Minnesota 55111 | Harvey Nelson/ James N. Engel | (612) 725-3500 (612) 725-3503 |
| 4 | Richard B. Russell Federal Bldg. 75 Spring St., S.W. Atlanta, Georgia 30303 | James W. Pulliam/ Marshall P. Jones | (404) 221-3583 (404) 331-3583 |
| 5 | One Gateway Center Suite 700 Newton Corner, Massachusetts 02158 | Howard Larsen/ Paul Nickerson | (617) 965-5100 (617) 965-5100 |
| 6 | P.O. Box 25486 Denver Federal Center Denver, Colorado 80225 | Galen Buterbaugh/ Barry S. Mulder | (303) 236-7920 (303) 236-7398 |
| 7 | 1011 E. Tudor Road Anchorage, Alaska 99503 | Robert E. Gilmore/ Dennis Money | (907) 786-3542 (907) 786-3435 |

Source: U.S. Fish and Wildlife Service

office responsible for the program is the Office of Endangered Species, under the associate director for Federal Assistance. FWS maintains regional offices in seven major cities. Each office is headed by a regional director and includes one "endangered species specialist." Much of the key work of the Endangered Species Program originates at the regional level, including the initiation of listing proposals, consultation with other federal agencies concerning their actions that may affect listed species, and the development of recovery plans.

The duties of the secretary of Commerce have been delegated to the National Marine Fisheries Service (NMFS), a bureau within the National Oceanic and Atmospheric Administration. The principal office within NMFS for program administration is the Office of Protected Species and Habitats. Five regional offices and four regional fisheries centers carry out much of the agency's program at the field level.

The Department of Agriculture has some limited program responsibilites. Responsibility for enforcing the act with respect to the importation and exportation of terrestrial plants is vested in the secretary of Agriculture, who has delegated that responsibility to the department's Animal and Plant Health Inspection Service, an agency whose principal mission is preventing pests and diseases injurious to agriculture from entering the country.

## Budget and Staff

The figure most often used to quantify the Endangered Species Program budget is the total amount appropriated to FWS for all program activities other than habitat acquisition, plus the amount appropriated for grants to the states pursuant to Section 6 of the act. This figure has increased modestly over the past several years, from about $20 million in FY 1980 to over $30 million in FY 1986.

The above figures actually understate the true size of the program because they omit two of its components. One is the component administrated by NMFS. The reason for this omission is that Congress does not specifically appropriate funds for the latter's share of the Endangered Species Program.

Endangered Species Program Budget
(FWS and State Grants)
(in $000)

| | |
|---|---|
| 1980 | 20,052 |
| 1981 | 22,782 |
| 1982 | 17,769 |
| 1983 | 20,459 |
| 1984 | 22,205 |
| 1985 | 27,065 |
| 1986 | 30,309* |

* based on continuing resolution appropriations passed 12/19/85

Rather, it appropriates funds for functions called "protected species biology and management" that include both the marine mammal and endangered species work of the agency. The omission of Commerce Department figures from the overall Endangered Species Program budget does not distort the latter too severely, for the authorized ceiling on Commerce Department spending under the Endangered Species Act is only $3.5 million.

A more significant omission is the amount appropriated for habitat acquisition. These funds typically are excluded from the program budget totals because they are appropriated pursuant to the Land and Water Conservation Fund Act, rather than the Endangered Species Act. Moreover, they are highly variable, ranging in recent years from less than $2 million (1982) to more than $30 million (1985). Thus, their inclusion in an overall program budget might suggest wilder swings in the program and the number of personnel administering it than is really the case. In fact, the number of full-time equivalent personnel in the Interior Department portion of the program has remained fairly constant at around 400 in recent years.

## Species Recoveries

The ultimate objective of the Endangered Species Program is to bring about the recovery of endangered and threatened species to the point at which they no longer need the protection of the act. To date, this objective has been met for only a small handful of species. In 1985, the southeastern population of the brown pelican was removed from the threatened species list after having recovered from a pesticide-induced population decline. In addition, the Florida population of the American alligator was removed from the endangered list, as were the Texas and Louisiana populations in earlier years. Because alligator populations elsewhere still are endangered, however, the recovered populations are listed as threatened under a special provision of the act that allows such listings when necessary to protect species or populations that are genuinely in danger and that are identical in appearance to the non-endangered population. This simplifies enforcement of the act, which might otherwise be confounded by inability to distinguish endangered from non-endangered specimens.

## New Species Listings

While the pelican and alligator were being taken off the protected lists, another 59 species were added in 1985, the third highest annual total in the act's 13-year history. The increase does not mean that more species actually became endangered in 1985 than in most prior years. Rather, it means that FWS made greater headway in reducing the backlog of species already known to be in need of the act's protection but still awaiting the formality of listing.

Despite this activity, the backlog of candidate species in need of listing is still quite large. Indeed, in an effort to systematize its processing of this backlog, FWS has assigned all candidates to various categories. So-called "category 1" candidates are those for which FWS already has sufficient information to begin the formal listing process. Currently, about 1,000 species are in this category. Even if the relatively rapid listing pace of 1985 continues, nearly two decades would be needed to give protection to all category 1 species.

A cursory review of the species listed in 1985 reveals that with few exceptions, the species are not well known to the general public. They are instead, for the most part, plants, invertebrates, and relatively obscure and geographically limited small vertebrates. The reasons for this are straightforward. The larger and better known species faced with the threat of extinction were among the first species to be protected. What remains are the many lesser-known creatures long neglected in conservation efforts. In addition, suggestions to list species in which there is significant commercial or recreational interest—for example, the spotted owl of old growth forest areas of the Pacific Northwest, the striped bass of the Chesapeake Bay, or some of the seriously declining geese populations of the Pacific Flyway—often have met with vociferous opposition from the interests that could be affected by such listings. As a result, it typically is easier to make rapid progress listing other, less controversial species.

Another trend is evident from last year's additions to the list. No one seriously doubts that the overwhelming majority of species eligible for the act's protection occur outside our borders, and in fact a majority of the currently listed species are foreign. Yet, all but one (the Gulf of California harbor porpoise) of the species added to the endangered and threatened lists in 1985 were U.S. species. This reflects, in part, the recognition that very few activities affecting foreign species—principally international trade—are within the control of the Endangered Species Act. Thus, greater attention to U.S. species, to which the full panoply of protection afforded by the act can be directed, is more likely to produce tangible conservation benefits.

Finally, the 1985 listings include only two species subject to the jurisdiction of the Department of Commerce: the Gulf of California harbor porpoise and the Guadalupe fur seal. These are the first species subject to the Commerce Department's jurisdiction to have been listed since 1979. This reflects both a relative lack of knowledge about the status of most marine creatures and the failure of the Commerce Department to follow the FWS example in undertaking a systematic effort to compile a comprehensive list of potential candidates for future listing.

## Recovery Plans

It bears repeating that the object of the Endangered Species Act is not to get species on the endangered and threatened lists, but rather to get them off. To

Species Added to the Endangered and Threatened Lists in 1985
(through 11/30/85)

| Date | Species | Status |
|------|---------|--------|
| **PLANTS** | | |
| 2/12/85 | San Benito evening primrose | T |
| 3/28/85 | Blue Ridge goldenrod | T |
| 4/19/85 | beautiful goetzea | E |
| 4/26/85 | Rhizome fleabane | E |
| 5/08/85 | large flowered fiddleneck | T |
| 5/08/85 | Carex specuicola | T |
| 5/15/85 | Lakela's mint | E |
| 5/20/85 | Ash Meadows invesia | T |
| | Ash Meadows sunray | T |
| | spring-loving centaury | T |
| | Ash Meadows blazing star | T |
| | Ash Meadows gumplant | T |
| | Ash Meadows niterwort | E |
| 6/27/85 | Mancos Milk-vetch | E |
| 7/18/85 | Ruth's golden aster | E |
| | Miccosukee Gosseberry | E |
| | Florida rockland spurge | E |
| | tiny polygala | E |
| | crenulated lead-plant | E |
| | Small's milkpea | E |
| | Garber's spurge | T |
| 8/10/85 | Lock Lomond coyote-thistle | E |
| 8/13/85 | Vahl's boxwood | E |
| 8/21/85 | Maguire primrose | E |
| | last chance Townsendia | T |
| 9/05/85 | Maguire daisy | E |
| | Short's goldenrod | E |
| 9/18/85 | San Mateo thornmint | E |
| 11/01/85 | fragrant prickly-apple cactus | E |
| | scrub mint | E |
| | longspurred mint | E |
| | slender rush-pea | E |
| 12/20/85 | prickly ash | E |
| **MAMMALS** | | |
| 1/09/85 | Gulf of California harbor porpoise | E |
| 1/30/85 | Fresno kangaroo rat | E |
| 6/06/85 | Alabama beach mouse | E |
| 6/06/85 | Perdido Key beach mouse | E |
| 6/06/85 | Choctawhatchee beach mouse | E |
| 7/01/85 | flying squirrel (fuscus) | E |
| 7/01/85 | flying squirrel (coloratus) | E |
| 12/19/85 | Guadalupe fur seal | T |
| **BIRDS** | | |
| 5/28/85 | interior least tern | E |
| 12/11/85 | piping plover | E—Great lakes region<br>T—elsewhere |

Species Added to the Endangered and Threatened Lists in 1985
(through 11/30/85)—continued

| Date | Species | Status |
|------|---------|--------|
| FISH | | |
| 3/28/85 | Hutton tui club | T |
| 3/28/85 | Foskett speckled dace | T |
| 3/28/85 | Big spring spinedace | T |
| 6/11/85 | Moduc sucker | E |
| 6/12/85 | Niangua darter | T |
| 8/05/85 | Owens tui chub | E |
| | amber darter | E |
| | Conasuaga logperch | E |
| 9/12/85 | White River spinedace | E |
| 9/27/85 | White River springfish | E |
| | Hiko White River springfish | E |
| 9/27/85 | Warner sucker | T |
| INVERTEBRATES | | |
| 5/20/85 | Ash meadows naucorid | T |
| 6/27/85 | Tar River Spiny Mussel | E |

guide that effort, the two services prepare formal, written "recovery plans" for listed species that occur in the United States. The purpose of these plans is to identify actions needed to bring about the species' recovery. In recent years, FWS has made a major commitment to producing these plans. Currently, some 185 plans encompassing 220 listed species have been produced.* In 1985, 18 recovery plans were approved. To date, about 60 percent of the listed U.S. species have such plans, a percentage that has grown greatly since 1981. NMFS has produced only two recovery plans for species under its jurisdiction, one for the Hawaiian monk seal and one for several species of sea turtles.

Recovery plans, though important in identifying the steps needed for species recovery, are like medical prescriptions. The prescription itself is of little value. Rather, it is the buying and taking of the medicine prescribed that is essential to bringing about recovery. No systematic effort yet exists at the federal level to monitor the implementation of recovery plans. FWS has plans to computerize such information, but as yet those plans are unfulfilled.

## Section 6 Cooperative Agreements

Listing actions and promulgation of recovery plans are the principal quantifiable measures of accomplishment in the Endangered Species Program. Another measure is the approval of "cooperative agreements" with state

---

* Some species are lumped together in a single plan, and other widely distributed species, such as the bald eagle, that occur in more than one region of the FWS have multiple plans.

conservation agencies pursuant to Section 6 of the act. As noted at the outset, one of the objectives of the act was to stimulate parallel action by state governments. As an inducement for doing so, Section 6 provides that once a state establishes an endangered species program meeting specified standards, it may enter into a cooperative agreement with the appropriate federal agency and thereby become eligible to receive federal financial assistance for implementing its program. Under Section 6, a state may enter into separate agreements for wildlife and plants. Most states moved relatively quickly to establish wildlife agreements. However, the idea of rare plant conservation was rather novel when the act was passed. As a result, there are still only 21 plant cooperative agreements. In addition, in 1985 NMFS entered into its first marine species conservation agreement with South Carolina, a management program for the short-nosed sturgeon.

## Interagency Consultation

One of the most important provisions of the Endangered Species Act requires all federal agencies to ensure that actions authorized, funded, or carried out by them do not jeopardize the continued existence of any threatened or endangered species. The purpose behind this requirement, embodied in Section 7 of the act, was to influence in a beneficial way the myriad of governmental activities—like dam and highway building—that account for much of the alteration and destruction of wildlife habitat in the United States. The mechanism through which Section 7 works is a process of consultation between FWS or NMFS and the federal agency proposing to authorize or carry out some new action. The most fundamental purpose of that consultation is to determine first whether the planned action may be likely to jeopardize a listed species and, if so, to identify modifications or alterations to the activity that would avoid such jeopardy.

Several important observations can be made about the Section 7 consultation process for fiscal years 1979 through 1984. First, there has been a steady and significant increase in the total number of interagency consultations each year. This probably reflects growing agency compliance with Section 7 procedures and an increased ability on the part of FWS to respond quickly to consultation requests. A second discernible trend is that more of the consultations, on both an absolute and percentage basis, are being handled informally. An "informal" consultation is typically conducted by phone or through one or more meetings. It does not result in a written "biological opinion" from FWS or NMFS, as does a formal consultation. Finally, it is clear that only a minuscule portion of the federal actions that are subject to formal or informal consultation are found likely to cause jeopardy to listed species (about one-quarter of one percent in fiscal year 1984).

Not all of the federal actions that result in jeopardy opinions lead to public-policy convulsions like those produced by the conflict between the en-

## States With Section 6 Cooperative Agreements

| State | Wildlife | Plants |
|---|---|---|
| Alabama | none | none |
| Alaska | X | none |
| Arizona | none | none |
| Arkansas | X | X |
| California | X | X |
| Colorado | X | X |
| Connecticut | X | X |
| Delaware | X | X |
| Florida | X | none |
| Georgia | X | X |
| Hawaii | X | X |
| Idaho | X | none |
| Illinois | X | none |
| Indiana | none | none |
| Iowa | X | none |
| Kansas | X | none |
| Kentucky | none | none |
| Louisiana | none | none |
| Maine | X | X |
| Maryland | X | none |
| Massachusetts | X | none |
| Michigan | X | X |
| Minnesota | X | X |
| Mississippi | X | none |
| Missouri | X | none |
| Montana | X | none |
| Nebraska | X | none |
| Nevada | X | X |
| New Hampshire | X | none |
| New Jersey | X | X |
| New Mexico | X | X |
| New York | X | X |
| North Carolina | X | X |
| North Dakota | X | none |
| Ohio | none | X |
| Oklahoma | X | none |
| Oregon | none | X |
| Pennsylvania | X | none |
| Rhode Island | X | X |
| South Carolina | X | X |
| South Dakota | X | none |
| Tennessee | X | none |
| Texas | none | none |
| Utah | none | none |
| Vermont | none | none |
| Virginia | X | X |
| Washington | X | X |
| West Virginia | X | none |
| Wisconsin | X | none |
| Wyoming | X | none |

Source: U.S. Fish and Wildlife Service

Section 7 Consultations

| Fiscal Year | Total | Informal | Cases in which a finding of jeopardy was made |
|---|---|---|---|
| 1979 | 2,553 | 1,585 | 67 |
| 1980 | 3,081 | 2,374 | 54 |
| 1981 | 4,039 | 3,535 | 29 |
| 1982 | 4,662 | 4,321 | 23 |
| 1983 | 5,588 | 5,305 | 33 |
| 1984 | 8,483 | 8,165 | 23 |

dangered snail darter and the Tennessee Valley Authority's Tellico Dam in the late 1970s. Indeed, though the act was amended in 1978 to provide a process for exempting worthy federal projects from the requirements of Section 7, it was not until October 1985 that the first exemption application was filed since Tellico and the Grey Rocks Dam in Wyoming were considered in early 1979. That application, filed by a barge company, sought exemption from Section 7 so that it might obtain a needed federal permit to establish a barge fleeting site on the lower Ohio River. FWS determined that the proposal was likely to jeopardize the continued existence of an endangered freshwater mussel. The exemption request was withdrawn in January 1986.

# Problems and Issues

Congressional committees held a total of six hearings in 1985 in connection with Congress' reauthorization of the Endangered Species Act. Those hearings served to identify a set of significant problems and issues affecting the Endangered Species Program. Some of these are likely to be resolved by the legislation reauthorizing the act, others are being resolved by administrative or judicial action, and still others remain unresolved.

## Adequacy of Protection for Candidate Species

FWS has compiled an extensive list of plants and animals that it believes warrant being formally proposed for protection under the act. However, until these candidates actually are proposed and listed, they receive no legal protection under the act. Indeed, they may be captured, killed, bought, and sold—even bulldozed out of existence—without any restraint by the Endangered Species Act.

Testimony presented at the 1985 congressional hearings showed that in fact many of these candidate species had declined significantly in numbers or range since being identified as candidates, and several apparently had gone extinct or nearly so before being listed*. These facts showed either that FWS was not adequately informed as to what was happening to its candidate species, or that it was informed but was unable or unwilling to take immediate action to try to stem their loss. To remedy this, Congress probably will direct FWS to monitor the status of candidate species and use its emergency listing authority whenever a significant risk to the well-being of a candidate species arose.

## Uncertainty Over the Act's Application to American Indians

The act prohibits the shooting, capturing, and any other taking of endangered species, subject only to certain narrowly limited exceptions. Apart from a limited exception for Alaskan Natives, the act affords no special treatment to Native Americans. Nonetheless, whether the act's taking prohibitions apply to Indians with treaty-guaranteed hunting and fishing rights is a question that has not yet been resolved authoritatively, though the United States Supreme Court is likely to do so soon. The outcome could significantly affect conservation efforts for a number of endangered and threatened species, including bald eagles and the Florida panther.

Many Indians tribes negotiated formal treaties with the United States in the 18th and 19th centuries by which the Indians typically agreed to cease hostilities, cede large tracts of land to the United States, and reside on unceded lands set apart as Indian reservations. Though there is enormous variety among such treaties, the United States typically agreed to allow the Indians to continue to carry out certain activities, including hunting and fishing, within and sometimes even outside their reservations.

In the last two decades, an enormous quantity of litigation has reached both state and federal courts over the question of whether Indians belonging to tribes with treaty hunting or fishing rights must comply with state hunting and fishing laws. In general, Indian interests have enjoyed great success in persuading the courts that their treaty-established hunting and fishing rights are immune from most forms of *state* regulation. Whether Indians enjoy that same immunity from *federal* conservation regulation has not often been addressed.

In early 1985, the United States Court of Appeals for the Eighth Circuit considered for the first time whether the taking prohibition of the Endangered Species Act applied to Indians. This was in the case of a Yankton Sioux Indian from South Dakota who was accused of killing endangered bald eagles on his reservation. He is one of several Indians arrested in an FWS undercover investigation of illegal trade in eagle and other bird feathers. The court held that treaty hunting rights were not affected by the Endangered Species Act and

* Examples include the Texas Henslow's sparrow, the Tarahamaro frog, the Wyoming toad (apparently already extinct by the time of its listing), the Guam bridled white-eye, the Guam broadbill, the Guam rail (virtually extinct in the wild by the time of its listing), and the large-fruited sand verbena.

that those rights could continue to be exercised without restraint (*United States v. Dion,* 752 F. 2nd 1261).

In response to this decision, the Subcommittee on Fisheries and Wildlife Conservation and the Environment of the House Merchant Marine and Fisheries Committee held a hearing in June 1985 to determine whether to amend the Endangered Species Act so as to make clear that it did apply to Indians as well as non-Indians. Several Indian witnesses testified strongly against any such amendment. They contended that Indian tribes should be allowed to develop and enforce their own conservation programs independent of the Endangered Species Act. They also argued that any amendment might infringe upon their religious practices. Ultimately, the subcommittee agreed not to take any legislative action because of the pendency of the government's petition for Supreme Court review of the Eighth Circuit decision. In October, the Supreme Court agreed that it would review the case.

The Supreme Court's decision, expected by the middle of 1986, probably will affect the conservation prospects of a number of endangered and threatened species in addition to bald eagles. For example, based on the *Dion* decision, a Florida court has dismissed state charges against a Seminole Indian for killing a Florida panther, of which perhaps fewer than 30 still survive in the wild. In addition, FWS has identified several dozen protected species believed to occur on or near Indian reservations. The taking of such species by Indians could undermine seriously the conservation efforts of the Endangered Species Program.

## Illegal Trade in Peregrine Falcons

In general, the act's prohibitions on commercial activities involving threatened and endangered species apply to animals both in the wild and in captivity. However, in 1978, organized falconry interests persuaded Congress to enact a special exemption allowing commercial trade in endangered raptors then in captivity as well as their progeny. In practical effect, the exemption applies only to peregrine falcons, the principal endangered raptor used in falconry. The rationale for this exemption was that allowing the sale of such birds would encourage captive breeding, which would in turn provide a supply of birds that could be reintroduced to the wild.

Although the measure passed easily in 1978, it was not without its critics, who contended that by allowing commercial transactions in captive birds, unscrupulous individuals would be tempted to remove birds from the wild and try to pass them off as captive bred birds. That fear soon proved to be well founded. An FWS undercover investigation, dubbed "Operation Falcon," revealed an extensive black market in peregrines and other birds of prey. At least 71 peregrines were found to have been taken illegally from the wild in the United States. Most subsequently were claimed falsely to be captive-bred birds entitled to the act's special raptor exemption (Leape 1985). Moreover, the belief in 1978 that the exemption would facilitate greatly the production of captive birds for reintroduction to the wild proved to have been overly optimistic. By the end of 1984, only five of 65 private breeders had produced peregrines for release to the wild, and they had released a total of only 16 birds (Leape 1985).

As a result of these developments, in 1985 several conservation organization, led by the National Audubon Society, asked Congress to repeal the 1978 exemption and restore to the peregrine the same protection that the act gives to every other endangered species. Despite the evidence of the abuse of the exemption, falconry interests organized an effective lobbying campaign and dissuaded Congress from modifying it. Meanwhile, FWS is re-examining its implementation regulations to determine whether any modifications would make evasion of the law more difficult. Absent the very serious tightening of those regulations, the act's raptor exemption is likely to remain a significant loophole complicating law enforcement and species recovery efforts.

## Western Water Conflicts

One of the most volatile issues affecting the Endangered Species Program concerns the potential for conflict between the conservation needs of endangered fish in the semi-arid West and the interests of various water users in developing and using the region's scarce water resources. To understand why this issue is so volatile requires an appreciation of the importance of water to the economy of the West and an understanding of some of the unique features of western water law.

In the semi-arid West, unlike most other parts of the country, permanent water supplies are scarce. To get water to dry areas, it often is necessary to divert it from the nearest stream through pipes or ditches. To protect the investments made through such efforts, a system of water law unique to the region came to be developed. Under this "prior appropriation" system, the person who first diverts water and puts it to a beneficial use on his property acquires a legal right to continue doing so. Later "appropriators" can divert water from the stream only to the extent that sufficient water remains after prior appropriators have taken their share. In years of drought, junior water-rights holders might have no water available at all, for the needs of senior rights holders could completely consume the stream's supply.

With this rather simplified description of how the system works, one might properly ask "What about the fish and other creatures that depend upon that same water for their survival?" The short answer is that the prior-appropriation system developed well before anyone cared very much about such matters. Indeed, the thought of leaving water in a stream, rather than diverting it for use elsewhere, was anathema to the whole premise of the system. In its traditional form, Western water law refused to treat so-called "in-stream" uses of water—such as for fish and wildlife conservation—as beneficial uses. And since only beneficial uses, i.e. human uses, are entitled to the law's protection, fish and wildlife are simply out of luck.

The depletion of water from the Colorado River and its major tributaries and the radical alteration of the river's basic character as a result of damming for water storage has brought about the endangerment of three fish species: the Colorado squawfish, the humpback chub, and the bonytail chub. The squawfish, actually a type of minnow, is capable of growing in excess of 100 pounds and often was referred to as the "white salmon" because of its salmon-like spawning migrations. The squawfish and the other two fish have all been reduced greatly in range and numbers. The bonytail chub may, in fact, already be extinct as a breeding species.

In the nearby Platte River, a tributary of the Missouri, dams and water depletion threaten two birds: the endangered whooping crane and the piping plover, a bird recently added to the threatened list. The whooping crane traditionally has used the Platte and its sandbars as a resting place on its migrations between Canada and Texas. As the flow of the Platte has been reduced, the river has narrowed and vegetation is no longer regularly swept from the sandbars during peak spring flows, degrading them as whooper habitat.

Further water diversions in these two river systems could jeopardize the continued existence of one or more of these species. Under Section 7 of the Endangered Species Act, federal agencies may not authorize or carry out any action that results in such jeopardy. Since most of the planned future diversions will require some form of federal approval, such as a right-of-way from the Bureau of Land Management, a dredge and fill permit from the U.S. Army Corps of Engineers, or a dam-building license from the Federal Energy Regulatory Commission, Section 7 could be an obstacle to future damming and water diversion. This, in the eyes of western water-development interests, represents an unconscionable federal interference with the right of the states to allocate the use of water within their borders.

To date, this potential for conflict remains only that. No western water-development project has yet been halted as a result of Section 7. However, the threat is perceived to be sufficiently serious that western water interests initially sought in 1985 to persuade Congress to limit its reauthorization of the Endangered Species Act to a single year so that a long-term solution could be developed and presented to Congress the following year. Congress did not want to limit the reauthorization period, however, and the issue disappeared from the legislative agenda.

At the administrative level, the issue continues to get enormous attention. Throughout most of 1985, FWS coordinated a joint effort among itself, the Bureau of Reclamation, representatives of appropriate states, and both water-development and environmental interests to identify in-stream flow requirements and other measures for the conservation of endangered species in the Upper Colorado River Basin while eliminating as much uncertainty as possible about the location and extent of water development that can occur safely in the basin. A similar effort focused on the Platte River has begun, but has not advanced as far. At year's end, no final agreement had been reached, but many differences had been narrowed, and it appeared possible that a solution capable of assuring the survival of the Colorado River fish might be reached.

## Protection for Threatened Predators

One of the issues that received a great deal of attention in 1985 concerned the act's protection for wolves and grizzly bears, two predators that, in the lower 48 states, are listed as threatened. FWS in 1984 issued regulations permitting the hunting of the Minnesota population of wolves. In early 1985, however, the United States Court of Appeals for the Eighth Circuit ruled that the FWS regulations permitting the hunting of wolves in Minnesota were unlawful (*Sierra Club v. Clark,* 755 F. 2nd 608). The basis for the court's ruling was that, under the Endangered Species Act, the hunting of threatened species may be permitted only when it is necessary to relieve extraordinary population pressures within a given ecosystem. No such situation existed for the wolf in Minnesota, the Court concluded.

As a result of that ruling, attention shifted to the grizzly bear. Since 1975, FWS regulations have permitted the hunting of grizzlies in Montana's so-called "northern ecosystem," an area that includes the Bob Marshall Wilderness south of Glacier National Park. FWS and the Montana Department of Fish, Wildlife, and Parks feared that a similar suit might be brought to end grizzly bear hunting. Defenders of Wildlife, a leading plaintiff in the Minnesota wolf case, threatened just such a suit. In response, the state asked Congress to liberalize the act's restrictions on the hunting of threatened species. When Congress showed no interest in that idea, Montana tightened controls on its bear hunting program and reduced the number of bears that could be hunted. That action averted any lawsuit to close hunting altogether. The future of grizzly hunting in Montana is likely to be determined as a result of a comprehensive study now under way by the state that will produce a bear-management environmental impact statement.

## Establishing a New Population of California Sea Otters

The California sea otter, once thought to have been entirely eliminated as a result of intense exploitation for its fur, manages to survive in a single population along a little more than a hundred miles of California coast. Listed as a threatened species, its recovery is likely to be aided most significantly by establishing one or more new populations physically separate from the existing population. Establishing a new population of otters would reduce the risk that a single catastrophic incident, such as an oil spill, might destroy most or all of the single surviving population.

Planning to carry out a translocation of otters has been under way for several years. After examining a wide range of other options, the site that has emerged as the most likely candidate is San Nicolas Island, one of the outer Channel Islands west of Santa Barbara. Because of the act's rigorous protections, however, establishing a new population of any listed species is likely to stir controversy today. The San Nicolas site caused concern within the oil and gas industry because of its proximity to waters where intensive oil development is ongoing and where further exploration is planned. The industry interposed a number of legal and other objections to any relocation. As a result, FWS, trying to answer the industry's many objections, fell farther and farther behind in its recovery efforts.

Congressional reauthorization of the Endangered Species Act provided an opportunity for intense discussions among government, industry, and environmental interests. Those discussions produced consensus on an amendment to the act that would provide a detailed framework within which to carry out a translocation. This framework guarantees substantial, but not absolute, protection of the experimentally translocated otter population and provides a means for oil and gas interests to obtain a precise explanation of their obligations *vis-a-vis* both the existing and the translocated population before the translocation occurs. Barring further complications, the long-postponed transplant could occur in 1986.

## Legislation

In 1985, Congress considered legislation to reauthorize the Endangered Species Act, but did not complete action on the matter before the end of the first congressional session. The House of Representative passed a bill (H.R. 1027) that would reauthorize the act through FY 1988 and make a few limited amendments to it. In the Senate, the Committee on Environment and Public Works on December 4 reported out a bill (S. 725) that made no substantive amendments. A floor vote in the Senate on this measure will occur sometime in 1986.

How many of the House-passed amendments to the act will survive the conference committee that probably will meet to resolve differences in the House and Senate versions of the reauthorizing legislation is a matter of conjecture. Assuming all House provisions are accepted, the following changes would be made to the act:

(1) The secretaries of Interior and Commerce will be required to "implement a system to monitor effectively" the status of candidate species and to use their emergency listing authority to list such species if a significant threat to their well-being arises. This measure was developed in response to the evidence presented at the congressional hearings that numerous candidates had seriously declined since first being identified as candidates.

(2) The secretary of Commerce will have authority to issue permits authorizing the incidental take of endangered species on the high seas. Currently, the authority to issue permits for the incidental take of endangered species applies only to such takings within the United States or in its territorial waters (i.e. three miles from shore). An extension of this authority to the high seas would allow the secretary of Commerce to regulate the incidental netting of endangered sea turtles by shrimp fishermen fishing more than three miles from ashore. Although such unintended netting technically is illegal, the secretary is without many practical means of enforcing the act. The incidental-take permitting authority could give him greater flexibility to influence fishing practices so as to benefit turtles.

(3) Certain apparent inconsistencies between the Endangered Species Act and the Marine Mammal Protection Act will be harmonized. Occasionally, a federal agency undertakes an action that has been found not to jeopardize the continued existence of a listed species but nevertheless results in the taking of a few individuals. Currently, such takings are exempt from the prohibitions of the Endangered Species Act so long as the agency complies with measures specified by the secretary to minimize the takings. If the species involved is a marine mammal, however, the same takings would be illegal under the Marine Mammal Protection Act. The amendment eliminates this mostly theoretical dilemma by establishing a single set of standards authorizing an exemption from the taking prohibitions of both laws.

(4) Finally, a lengthy and somewhat complex amendment will be added that pertains solely to the experimental establishment of a second population of California sea otters. The amendment, the product of negotiations principally between the Western Oil and Gas Associations and Friends of the Sea Otter, directs the secretary of the Interior to develop and implement a plan for the carrying out of this experiment. Under the plan, the secretary is to designate a "translocation zone" to which otters are to be transferred.

Comparison of Current and Proposed Authorization Ceilings
(House/Senate versions*)
(in $ millions)

| | Current (FY83 thru FY85) | FY86 | Proposed FY87 | FY88 |
|---|---|---|---|---|
| Interior Dept. | 27 | 27/30 | 31 | 35 |
| Commerce Dept. | 3.50 | 3.50/4 | 3.80/5 | 4/5.75 |
| State Grants | 6 | 6 | 9/10 | 12 |
| Agriculture Dept. | 1.85 | 1.85 | 2 | 2.20 |
| Misc. | 0.90 | 0.90 | 0.95/1 | 1 |
| Total | 39.25 | 39.25/42.75 | 46.75/49 | 54.20/55.95 |

* H.R. 1027 as passed by the House and S. 725 as reported by the Senate Committee on Environment and Public Works

Appropriations for Fish and Wildlife Service
Endangered Species Program*
(in $ millions)

| Function | FY85 | FY86 Admin. Request | FY86 Final Appropriation |
|---|---|---|---|
| Listing | 2.967 | 2.924 | 3.225 |
| Law Enforcement | 7.363 | 7.341 | 8.648 |
| Consultation | 2.593 | 2.552 | 2.614 |
| Recovery | 5.985 | 5.869 | 6.884 |
| Research | 4.237 | 4.252 | 4.545 |
| State Grants | 3.920 | 3.920 | 4.393 |
| Totals | 27.065 | 26.858 | 30.309 |

* Includes appropriations made only to the Department of the Interior, U.S. Fish and Wildlife Service

Within that translocation zone, Section 7 of the act (pertaining to federal agency actions) applies in full to non-defense-related federal activities. The exception for defense-related activities was put in the amendment because the likely translocation site, San Nicolas Island, is used for certain practice maneuvers by the Navy. Beyond the translocation zone, the secretary is to specify a "management zone" that will act as a sort of buffer between the translocation zone and the parent populations. Otters found in it are to be returned by FWS, if possible, to the parent or experimental populations. Before the translocation is to begin, prospective federal-permit applicants (i.e., oil companies seeking federal off-shore exploration or development permits) are to be given an opportunity to request the opinion of FWS on whether their proposed actions will be compatible with Section 7 requirements. If they receive FWS approval, oil companies may proceed with their activities without fear of restraint by Section 7 unless significant new information arises that warrants reconsideration of the FWS opinion.

Both the House and the Senate bills would increase significantly authorization ceilings for appropriations to carry out the Endangered Species Program. Conservation organizations made a convincing showing that the program was seriously underfunded, particularly in light of the large backlog of candidate species awaiting listing action. That showing helped boost program-authorization ceilings, though only to a little more than half of what many conservation groups had recommended.

## Legal Developments

In *U.S. v. Dion* (752 F.2d 1261 [8th Cir. 1985]), the Eighth Circuit reviewed the prosecutions of several Indians convicted of taking and selling bald eagles in violation of the Endangered Species Act, the Eagle Protection Act, and the

Migratory Bird Treaty Act. In an undercover operation, FWS agents, posing as traders and collectors, purchased carcasses and portions of protected birds from the Indians. The Indians argued that their tribe's treaties with the United States conferred upon them the right to take and sell bald eagles. FWS contended that any such treaty right had been abrogated by the Endangered Species Act. Sitting *en banc,* the Eighth Circuit held that the Indians' treaties allowed continuation of their traditional activities, including take, on the reservations, but did not permit the sale of bald eagles. Finding no express congressional intent to abrogate the treaty rights in the language or history of the Endangered Species Act, the court held the Indians could not be prosecuted for exercise of those rights. The case was remanded to a panel of the court for determinations of whether the alleged activities were so protected. The U.S. Supreme Court has granted *certiorari.*

In *Enos v. Marsh,* (769 F.2d 1363 [9th Cir. 1985]), the Ninth Circuit refused to enjoin construction of a deep-water harbor on the island of Oahu, Hawaii, and affirmed the district court's grant of summary judgment against all of the plaintiff's claims. Plaintiffs alleged that FWS and the Corps of Engineers violated the Endangered Species Act in failing to protect adequately the 'akoko plant, a species proposed for designation as an endangered species (the 'akoko was officially listed in August, 1984, the same month construction began on the challenged project). The court held that because the 'akoko was only proposed for listing, the Endangered Species Act required only that the Corps "confer" with FWS before taking action that would adversely affect the species. The court found that the Corps had fulfilled this duty. The plaintiffs also alleged that the secretary of the Interior had violated the Endangered Species Act in refusing to designate critical habitat for the 'akoko once it actually was listed as an endangered species. The court held, however, that the secretary had not abused his discretion in refusing to designate where the plant was found in non-native habitat.

In *NWF v. Hodel,* (E.D. Calif.), the Federation sought to enjoin under the Endangered Species Act, migratory bird hunting with lead shot in portions of five states, citing evidence that lead-shot hunting was the leading cause of lead poisoning in wild bald eagles (the eagles are poisoned when they ingest migratory birds carrying lead shot).[*] Under the Migratory Bird Treaty Act, hunting of migratory birds is prohibited unless authorized by the secretary of the Interior. Granting the federation's motion for preliminary injunction, the court held that it had a substantial chance of success on the merits of two Endangered Species Act claims. First, under Endangered Species Act Section 7(a)(1), the court found that the secretary had a duty to use all means necessary to protect an endangered species. Interior had argued that it had discretion to choose the best means of fulfilling this obligation. The court held, however, that it could not uphold the Interior's choice of action here because they failed

---

[*] The bald eagle is classified as endangered in four of the states concerned and threatened in one.

to present a factual basis for their choice. Second, the court found that authorization of lead-shot hunting was an illegal "taking." While the secretary of the Interior could authorize such a taking under Section 10, he was required to specify means to mitigate this action. The court held the secretary had failed to do so. The court enjoined Interior's authorization of the 1985-86 migratory bird hunting season in the disputed areas until a steel-shot requirement was imposed or Interior complied with National Environmental Policy Act and Endangered Species Act.

## Status of the Resource

For most of the nearly 900 species currently listed as threatened or endangered, one cannot establish with much certainty whether the provisions of the act have yet had any effect in halting their decline or bringing about their recovery. Neither FWS nor NMFS has collected sufficient data to determine whether even the approximately 400 listed U.S. species are increasing, declining, or remaining stable. For the much larger number of identified candidates for future listing, even less is known.

In making judgments about the success or failure of the Endangered Species Program, however, one must recognize that recovery of a severely depleted species may take decades and that very little is known about the basic biology and ecological needs of such species. Thus, many species may be expected to continue to decline even after their listing while the government endeavors to pinpoint and reverse the factors causing their decline.

The fact that there have been relatively few complete recoveries like those of the eastern brown pelican and the Florida population of American alligators thus does not necessarily mean that the program is failing to make significant headway toward its goals. Rather, one must recognize that the measure of progress is neither absolutely clear and quantifiable, nor likely to be identical for all species. These general observations are important to keep in mind, if only to help resist the temptation to reach premature judgments about the program as a whole based on success or setbacks involving individual species.

### Recovering Species

While relatively few species have yet recovered to the point at which they no longer need to be listed under the act, several appear to be on the road to recovery. The bald eagle, for example, listed as endangered in 43 states and threatened in five others, has increased steadily throughout most of its range, according to annual midwinter surveys conducted in recent years. The eagle's recovery, however, almost certainly owes more to the banning of the pesticide DDT than to actions taken under the Endangered Species Act. The peregrine falcon, once entirely eliminated from the eastern United States because of

DDT, is being reintroduced successfully there as a result of a major captive-breeding program.

Another endangered species slowly increasing its numbers is the whooping crane. Its recovery to date is the result of an intensive conservation effort that began well before the Endangered Species Act became law. The key element of that program has been the establishment of a second wild flock of birds through foster parenting by related sandhill cranes. Whether this artificially created flock of whoopers will become a breeding flock has yet to be determined.

The snail kite, formally known as the Everglades kite, the Aleutian Canada goose, and the California least tern are other endangered birds whose numbers generally have increased over the past decade. Illustrating the danger of attaching too much importance to numbers, however, is the fact that annual fluctuations in the snail kite population probably owe more to rainfall levels than to conservation efforts.

## Declining Species

In contrast to these apparent success stories, there have been some serious setbacks, two of which in 1985 involved some of the most widely known species that the program has tried to recover: the black-footed ferret and the California condor. Until the accidental discovery of a dead ferret in Wyoming in 1981, many people had believed that the black-footed ferret had become extinct during the previous decade. That discovery, however, set off an intensive effort to locate and then protect the world's only known population of black-footed ferrets in about 8,000 acres of prairie dog towns near Meeteetse, Wyoming.

By 1984, the ferret population near Meeteetse was estimated at 128. Plans were being formulated to initiate a captive-breeding program for future reintroductions into the wild elsewhere. Wyoming, desirous of demonstrating is ability to bring about the recovery of one of the rarest mammals on Earth, wanted to have an appropriate breeding facility built in the state rather than ship ferrets to existing breeding facilities elsewhere. The FWS agreed.

By August 1985, however, preliminary field surveys by researchers connected with Idaho State University showed that ferret numbers apparently had plunged to less than 60. By September 10, field data showed only 31 ferrets. A month later, 14 of these were gone. Recognizing the need to begin capturing ferrets quickly if any were to be available for captive breeding, the state trapped a few animals. One of these was diagnosed as having canine distemper, an incurable and always fatal disease. By the end of November, the Meeteetse colony of ferrets had all but disappeared evidently because of a distemper infection. Seven animals were in captivity. Estimates of the number still in the wild range from three to 10.

From an apparently healthy and sizeable population only a year earlier, the black-footed ferret again virtually disappeared from our midst. Its survival apparently now depends on a tiny captive population or the possibility that yet another long-overlooked population might still exist elsewhere in the wild.

A slower, less dramatic, but no less serious decline has left the California condor also teetering on the brink of extinction. Beginning several years ago, when some 25 to 30 condors were thought to remain in the wild, FWS, together with the California Department of Fish and Game, the National Audubon Society, the Forest Service, and the Bureau of Land Management, began a controversial crash program to capture some of the wild condors and begin a captive-breeding program. Several birds were taken into captivity. Several others were captured, tagged with radio transmitters so that their activities could be monitored, and released.

In 1984, the number of condors in the wild stood at 15, including at least five breeding pairs. By early 1985, six birds could not be located. One was found emaciated and near death. It died shortly thereafter. By September, the total population in the wild stood at only six birds. An additional 21 birds are in captivity, but of these only one, a male, is of breeding age. The survival of this species this appears to be dependent on future captive-breeding efforts, despite decades of efforts to preserve the wild population, it appears to be facing imminent extinction. As 1985 drew to a close, FWS announced plans to try to capture the remaining condors in the wild, thus ending its decades-long effort to preserve a viable wild condor population.

## References

Leape, J.P. 1985. Statement of the National Audubon Society on the Raptor Exemption, H.R. 2767, before the Subcommittee on Fish and Wildlife of the House Committee on Merchant Marine and Fisheries.

Trefethen, J.B. 1961. *Crusade for Wildlife.* Boone and Crockett Club. New York. 377 pp.

Wilson, E.O. 1982. Statement before the Senate Committee on Environment and Public Works Concerning the Reauthorization of the Endangered Species Act.

*Michael J. Bean is chairman of the Environmental Defense Fund's Wildlife Program and author of* The Evolution of National Wildlife Law.

Wetlands, being lost at the rate of a half million acres yearly in the United States, are vital to a variety of wildlife, including the white-tailed deer and Canada geese seen here.

*William J. Jahoda/Photo Researchers*

◆ ———————————————————————— ◆

# Federal Wetlands Protection Programs

## Katherine Barton

## Introduction

WETLANDS ARE AMONG the most productive ecosystems in the world and provide crucial fish and wildlife habitat. Approximately 5,000 species of plants, 190 species of amphibians, and a third of all bird species in the United States occur in wetlands. Approximately two-thirds of the 10 to 12 million waterfowl in the lower 48 states reproduce in the prairie potholes of the Midwest, and millions of ducks winter in the bottomland hardwoods of the south-central states. More than half of the marine sport fish caught in the United States are dependent on wetland estuaries—particularly in the early part of their life cycles—and roughly two-thirds of the major U.S. commercial fish are dependent on estuaries and salt marshes for nursery or spawning grounds. Wetlands also serve a variety of other ecological functions, depending on their type and location, such as improving water quality, facilitating groundwater recharge, stabilizing shorelines, reducing floodwaters, and trapping sediments.

Roughly 99 million acres of wetlands remain in the lower 48 states, an area about the size of California and representing five percent of the land surface in the contiguous United States.* About 94 percent of these are inland,

---

*All data in this discussion is from *Wetlands of the United States: Current Status and Trends,* by the Fish and Wildlife Service, 1984.

freshwater wetlands, more than half of which are forested. The remaining six percent, about five million acres, are saltwater coastal wetlands. In addition, Alaska is estimated to contain about 200 million acres of wetlands. Wetlands include a variety of ecosystems: red-maple swamps and black-spruce bogs in the northern states, salt marshes along the coasts, bottomland-hardwood forests in the Southeast, prairie potholes in the Midwest, playa lakes and cottonwood-willow riparian wetlands in the western states, and wet tundra in Alaska.

Less than 46 percent of the original 215 million acres of wetlands in the lower 48 states remain today, and the losses have been particularly severe in certain important areas. For example, the bottomland-hardwood wetlands of the lower Mississippi have been reduced by 80 percent, California's wetlands by 90 percent, and Iowa's by 95 percent. And in spite of a growing awareness of the important environmental and economic values of wetlands, they continue to be destroyed at the alarming rate of some 450,000 acres per year. According to the U.S. Fish and Wildlife Service (FWS), the vast majority of this loss, 87 percent, is due to the conversion of wetlands to agricultural use. Urban development is responsible for eight percent of the loss and other development for the remaining five percent.

The federal government protects wetlands through acquisition and leasing, primarily to protect waterfowl habitat. Such wetlands largely are managed as part of the National Wildlife Refuge System. However, the vast majority of wetlands is owned by private interests or by other public agencies whose primary purposes are not wetland protection. The federal government controls some destruction of these wetlands by regulating the disposal of dredged and fill material under Section 404 of the Clean Water Act. A third important aspect of the federal wetlands program is the FWS National Wetlands Inventory, which identifies and maps wetlands nationwide and provides scientific support for federal and other wetland-protection efforts. This chapter covers these three elements of the federal wetlands-protection program.*

A number of other federal laws and programs indirectly provide some protection for wetlands. The National Environmental Policy Act (42 U.S.C.A. 4321-4361) requires federal agencies to consider the environmental impacts of their activities, including those affecting wetlands. The Coastal Zone Management Act (16 U.S.C.A. 1451-1464) encourages and funds states to develop coastal management plans that include wetland-protection measures. The Coastal Barrier Resources Act (16 U.S.C.A. 3501 et seq.) eliminates federal insurance and subsidies for development on certain barrier islands, removing some incentives for developing wetlands in these areas. The executive orders on Floodplain Management (E.O. 11988) and Protection of Wetlands (E.O.

---

*A number of states also have acquisition or regulatory programs for wetlands protection, and private groups such as Ducks Unlimited, the Nature Conservancy, and the National Audubon Society have protected substantial wetland acreage. Only federal programs are discussed here.

11990) require federal agencies to take action to eliminate wetlands destruction and to preserve their beneficial values. Federal land protection systems, including the Wild and Scenic Rivers System, the National Wilderness Preservation System, and the National Park System, prevent development of the wetlands included within their boundaries.

On the other hand, a number of federal programs and policies contribute to wetlands destruction. Federal construction of water projects—including dams, channelization projects, ports and harbors, and shoreline stabilization —have caused or contributed to the loss of millions of acres of wetlands. A variety of federal policies or assistance programs encourage the private conversion of wetlands, including tax incentives, agricultural commodity programs, disaster payments, crop insurance, and Farmers Home Administration loans. Congress began to address these inconsistencies by including a provision in the 1985 Farm Bill that denies certain federal subsidies to farmers who convert wetlands to cropland. In addition, several federal studies are under way on the effects of other federal programs on wetlands, and Congress may include some provisions that remove tax incentives for wetlands conversion if it passes a tax reform bill.

# Wetlands Acquisition and Leasing

The federal government has no acquisition program that focuses solely on purchasing wetlands. However, FWS purchases a significant amount of wetlands as part of its effort to protect waterfowl habitat, and the Agricultural Stabilization and Conservation Service of the Department of Agriculture leases certain wetlands, also to protect waterfowl habitat.

## Migratory Bird Conservation Fund

Most federal wetlands acquisition is accomplished under the authorities of the Migratory Bird Conservation Act of 1929 (codified at scattered sections of 16 U.S.C.A. 715), which authorizes federal acquisition of land for migratory waterfowl refuges, and the Migratory Bird Hunting and Conservation Stamp Act of 1934* (16 U.S.C.A. 718 *et seq.*), which, as amended in 1958, authorizes the acquisition of small wetlands and prairie potholes for "waterfowl production areas." The government may acquire full title to such lands, may purchase conservation easements, or may lease them.

Funding for this acquisition comes from the Migratory Bird Conservation Fund, established by the 1934 Stamp Act. That act required all migratory waterfowl hunters aged 16 or over to purchase a federal migratory bird hunting stamp, often called a duck stamp, with all receipts deposited into the fund.

---

*These and related laws are discussed in more detail in the migratory birds chapter.

Migratory Bird Conservation Fund—Appropriations and Acquisition History, FY 1962[1] to FY 1985

| Year | Duck Stamp Receipts | Loan Act Advance | Obligated Funds | Acres Acquired | | |
|---|---|---|---|---|---|---|
| | | | | Easement | Fee | Total |
| 1962 | $ 4,094,874 | — | $ 2,678,858 | 4,968 | 30,579 | 35,565 |
| 1963 | 3,418,638 | $ 7,000,000 | 9,008,961 | 12,774 | 75,807 | 88,581 |
| 1964 | 4,559,564 | 10,000,000 | 8,748,887 | 71,575 | 65,819 | 137,394 |
| 1965 | 4,622,688 | 8,000,000 | 12,018,535 | 177,796 | 76,356 | 254,152 |
| 1966 | 4,684,908 | 7,500,000 | 11,669,999 | 146,031 | 79,556 | 225,587 |
| 1967 | 5,385,069 | 6,000,000 | 9,060,515 | 106,954 | 54,967 | 161,921 |
| 1968 | 5,825,238 | 7,500,000 | 10,466,989 | 87,770 | 65,645 | 153,415 |
| 1969 | 5,562,303 | 7,500,000 | 8,720,734 | 61,354 | 51,577 | 112,931 |
| 1970 | 6,107,280 | 5,800,000 | 9,319,380 | 100,411 | 59,186 | 159,597 |
| 1971 | 7,181,256 | 7,500,000 | 11,749,588 | 60,258 | 72,023 | 132,281 |
| 1972 | 7,351,425 | 7,500,000 | 10,227,624 | 51,349 | 50,927 | 102,276 |
| 1973 | 10,734,313 | 7,100,000 | 7,843,144 | 58,289 | 35,157 | 93,446 |
| 1974 | 10,219,685 | 3,500,000 | 15,561,186 | 57,149 | 35,118 | 92,267 |
| 1975 | 11,019,133 | 1,000,000 | 7,283,502 | 34,072 | 19,886 | 53,958 |
| 1976 | 13,700,270 | 7,500,000 | 14,002,727 | 28,472 | 46,911 | 75,383 |
| 1977 | 10,667,020 | 14,000,000 | 18,577,782 | 36,796 | 38,156 | 74,952 |
| 1978 | 11,144,449 | 10,000,000 | 13,909,035 | 23,216 | 32,580 | 55,796 |
| 1979 | 11,079,528 | 10,000,000 | 16,106,843 | 17,015 | 38,525 | 55,540 |
| 1980 | 16,638,831 | 15,000,000 | 22,725,644 | 16,168 | 66,263 | 82,431 |
| 1981 | 14,916,720 | 1,250,000 | 9,387,646 | 14,320 | 10,029 | 24,349 |
| 1982 | 14,598,651 | 1,200,000 | 11,418,673 | 16,535 | 16,003 | 32,538 |
| 1983 | 14,663,828 | 2,000,000 | 11,550,802 | 9,413 | 16,852 | 26,265 |
| 1984 | 13,789,613 | 7,000,000 | 14,439,201 | 8,312 | 21,477 | 29,789 |
| 1985 | 14,411,748 | 21,266,000 | 29,622,192 | 14,692 | 38,755 | 53,447 |
| 1986 | 14,400,000[2] | 14,910,000[3] | N/A | N/A | N/A | N/A |
| TOTAL | | $190,026,000 | $296,099,447 | 1,215,689 | 1,098,172 | 2,313,861 |

[1] Since passage of the Wetlands Loan Act
[2] Projected receipts
[3] Initial appropriation only. Does not include any supplemental funds or rescissions.
Source: U.S. Department of the Interior, Fish and Wildlife Service, Division of Realty

In addition, in 1961, Congress enacted the Wetlands Loan Act (16 U.S.C.A. 715k-3 to 715k-5) to speed acquisition of waterfowl habitat in the face of accelerated wetland drainage for agriculture. The Loan Act authorized advance appropriations to the Migratory Bird Conservation Fund of $105 million, later increased to $200 million. Duck stamp receipts are automatically available for expenditure without congressional action, but Loan Act money is available only if appropriated by Congress. Much of the land purchased under the fund is upland habitat surrounding wetlands needed for nesting and breeding, but a substantial, although undetermined, amount of wetland acreage is acquired as well.

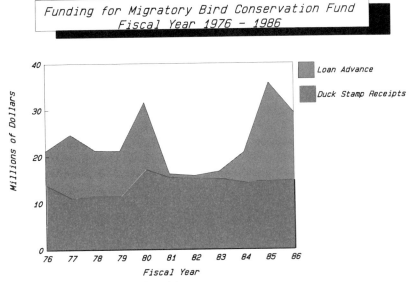

Funding for Migratory Bird Conservation Fund
Fiscal Year 1976 - 1986

1] Duck Stamp receipts estimated; Loan Act
appropriations as of 1/15/86
Source: FWS Realty Office

## Land and Water Conservation Fund

The other major source of funds for acquisition by FWS is the Land and Water Conservation Fund, which is funded primarily by receipts from offshore oil and gas leasing and development. The Land and Water Conservation Fund can be used to acquire a variety of outdoor recreation lands and natural areas, including wetlands, but cannot be used to purchase migratory waterfowl areas authorized for acquisition by the Migratory Bird Conservation Act. The Land and Water Fund is authorized to provide up to $900 million a year, but requires appropriation by Congress. Types of areas purchased under the Land and Water Fund vary from year to year and may or may not include significant amounts of wetland acreage.

## Water Bank

The Water Bank Program was authorized by the Water Bank Act of 1970 (16 U.S.C.A. 1301 *et seq.*). Under the Water Bank Program, landowners or operators agree to protect certain of their wetlands and adjacent uplands in exchange for annual payments by the secretary of Agriculture. The Department of Agriculture may also share the cost of conservation practices on the land. The Water Bank Act authorizes up to $10 million yearly for lease payments, but the money must be appropriated by Congress. Administered by the Agri-

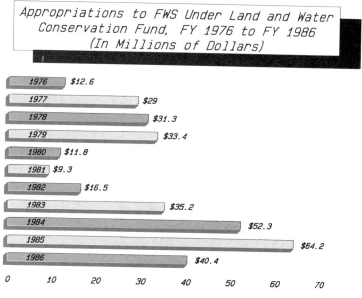

Appropriations to FWS Under Land and Water
Conservation Fund, FY 1976 to FY 1986
(In Millions of Dollars)

| Year | Amount |
|------|--------|
| 1976 | $12.6 |
| 1977 | $29 |
| 1978 | $31.3 |
| 1979 | $33.4 |
| 1980 | $11.8 |
| 1981 | $9.3 |
| 1982 | $16.5 |
| 1983 | $35.2 |
| 1984 | $52.3 |
| 1985 | $64.2 |
| 1986 | $40.4 |

Note: All figures include supplementals and
recissions except FY 1986.
Source: FWS Realty Office

cultural Stabilization and Conservation Service, the Water Bank Program focuses on protecting important waterfowl nesting and breeding areas, primarily in the northern part of the Central Flyway and in the northern and southern parts of the Mississippi Flyway. Like the FWS program for acquiring migratory waterfowl habitat, the Water Bank protects substantial upland habitat in addition to wetlands.

## Acquisition Accomplishments and Trends

The federal government keeps no record of the acres of wetlands in federal ownership, although the Water Bank Program does track the amount of wetlands it has under lease. This discussion assumes that there is a rough correlation between overall FWS acquisition trends in the Fish and Wildlife Service and trends in wetlands acquisition.

In 1985, land acquisition was substantially higher than for the previous four years, when acquisition was unusually low. FWS purchased 79,620 acres under the Migratory Bird Conservation Fund, the highest acquisition level since 1980, and purchased 55,905 acres under the Land and Water Conservation Fund, the most acreage ever acquired by FWS under the fund in a single

Status of Agreements Under the Water Bank Program, FY 1976–1985

| State | Agreements (#) | Wetland Acreage | Adjacent Acreage | Total Acreage | Annual Payment ($) |
|-------|------|------|------|------|------|
| Arkansas | 235 | 22,767 | 19,500 | 42,267 | $ 292,764 |
| California | 102 | 6,696 | 19,988 | 26,684 | 407,590 |
| Louisiana | 224 | 9,508 | 21,272 | 30,780 | 392,740 |
| Maine | 106 | 1,983 | 4,573 | 6,556 | 53,962 |
| Michigan | 120 | 1,409 | 3,580 | 4,989 | 91,123 |
| Minnesota | 1,414 | 20,523 | 58,131 | 78,654 | 1,922,250 |
| Mississippi | 201 | 14,551 | 23,321 | 37,872 | 319,255 |
| Montana | 124 | 3,205 | 15,541 | 18,746 | 301,985 |
| Nebraska | 86 | 2,770 | 4,727 | 7,497 | 170,099 |
| North Dakota | 1,434 | 59,490 | 154,770 | 214,260 | 3,609,591 |
| South Dakota | 878 | 24,657 | 90,293 | 114,950 | 1,756,183 |
| Vermont | 35 | 793 | 1,043 | 1,836 | 16,544 |
| Wisconsin | 454 | 7,857 | 13,029 | 20,886 | 465,130 |
| Total | 5,413 | 176,209 | 433,328 | 605,977 | $9,799,216 |

Source: Agricultural Stabilization and Conservation Service, USDA

year.* FWS also received record high levels of funding for acquisition in FY 1985: the Loan Act was funded at $21,266,000 and the Land and Water Conservation Fund at $64,218,000. Under pressure to reduce the federal deficit, Congress provided slightly lower levels of funding for acquisition in FY 1986: $14,910,000 under the Loan Act and $40,426,000 under the Land and Water Conservation Fund. However, this funding was still substantially higher than the administration's request of $1.5 million for the two combined.

Taking a longer view, however, these acquisition levels are not particularly high. Soon after the Loan Act was authorized in 1962, land acquisition jumped to well in excess of 100,000 acres yearly from 1964 to 1971, with a high of 254,000 acres in 1965. Loan Act acquisitions declined somewhat during the 1970s, but the difference largely was made up by increasing acquisition under the Land and Water Conservation Fund, keeping total acquisition levels at about 100,000 acres per year. Acquisition dropped dramatically from 1981 to 1984 because of cutbacks in funding for land acquisition initiated by the administration.

Compared to FWS acquisition goals, acquisition levels clearly are inadequate. In 1976, FWS determined that an additional 1.94 million acres of waterfowl habitat was necessary to maintain waterfowl populations, and set a goal of acquiring this acreage by the end of FY 1986. Through FY 1985, about 435,000 acres had been acquired—only 22 percent of the target.

Wetland leasing under the Water Bank in 1985 continued at about 1984 levels. Approximately 606,000 acres were under lease in 13 states, including

*Not including a donation of 120,000 acres in 1984.

Fish and Wildlife Service Acquisition and Appropriation History-Land and Water Conservation Fund

| Year | Appropriations | Obligations | Acres Acquired |
|------|----------------|-------------|----------------|
| 1967 | $    147,915 | $    21,116 | 3 |
| 1968 | 1,797,637 | 1,290,573 | 2,561 |
| 1969 | 748,912 | 1,239,476 | 832 |
| 1970 | 1,587,120 | 1,699,170 | 15,031 |
| 1971 | 7,993,100 | 5,070,371 | 4,530 |
| 1972 | 3,488,000 | 4,246,494 | 11,506 |
| 1973 | 4,597,000 | 4,141,817 | 3,017 |
| 1974 | — | 1,515,364 | 2,859 |
| 1975 | 9,494,000 | 2,864,486 | 2,625 |
| 1976 | 12,621,000 | 14,289,735 | 25,054 |
| 1977 | 28,993,000 | 17,028,778 | 27,403 |
| 1978 | 31,285,000 | 22,697,558 | 26,599 |
| 1979 | 33,430,000 | 28,846,496 | 37,842 |
| 1980 | 11,750,000 | 22,867,424 | 21,540 |
| 1981 | 9,303,000 | 27,511,849 | 21,202 |
| 1982 | 16,491,000 | 13,146,842 | 14,101 |
| 1983 | 35,200,000 | 21,606,168 | 18,921 |
| 1984 | 52,297,000 | 26,027,688 | 164,448[1] |
| 1985 | 64,218,000 | 77,907,568 | 79,620 |
| 1986 | 40,426,000[2] | N/A | N/A |

[1] Includes the donation of 120,000 acres at Alligator River, N.C.
[2] Initial appropriation. Does not include any supplementals or rescissions.
Source: U.S. Department of the Interior, Fish and Wildlife Service.

176,000 acres of wetlands. The Water Bank was funded at $8.8 million in 1985, the same level of funding provided since 1982.* At this level of funding, the Agricultural Stabilization and Conservation Service can keep the program at roughly 600,000 acres but cannot expand. Agricultural Stabilization and Conservation Service officials say there is additional demand among landowners to bring new lands into the bank, but that the agency does not have sufficient funding to meet this demand. As the *Audubon Wildlife Report* was going to press, Congress eliminated funding for the Water Bank Program in the 1986 continuing resolution. Agricultural Stabilization and Conservation Service staff say the agency will continue to make payments on agreements entered into prior to FY 1986, but will sign no new agreements and cannot renew those that are expiring.

Wetlands acquisition could be boosted significantly if Congress were to enact and fund the Emergency Wetlands Conservation Act that has been under congressional consideration for the past three years. It could be reduced substantially, however, if the Wetlands Loan Act, scheduled to expire at the

*Congress provided $10 million yearly for the Water Bank in previous years.

end of FY 1986, is not extended or, worse, if repayment of the loan advance is not forgiven, in which case FWS will have to use most duck stamp receipts to pay back the loan.*

# Wetlands Inventory and Related Research

FWS National Wetlands Inventory generates and disseminates scientific information on the characteristics of wetlands and provides topical wetland maps that accurately represent these valuable resources. The inventory does not conduct any wetland protection efforts itself, but the information it provides supports the protection and regulatory efforts of many other parties. This section covers the status of various activities under the National Wetlands Inventory.

## Wetland Inventory and Mapping

The major activity of the National Wetlands Inventory is producing maps of the nation's wetlands. The maps are intended to assist local, state, and federal agencies in identifying wetlands. However, various programs and agencies have differing definitions of what constitutes a wetland, and the FWS maps do not single out subsets of wetlands as defined by these other agencies and programs.† FWS has identified several categories of wetlands to receive top priority for mapping: wetlands in the coastal zone, including that of the Great Lakes; prairie wetlands; playa lakes; and the floodplains of major rivers. These areas total 55 percent of the wetland acreage of the contiguous United States and 32 percent of Alaska. Specific areas within these general categories are selected each year for mapping based on a number of factors, including their importance for fish and wildlife and the ability of mapping to assist regulatory and other protection efforts.

By the end of FY 1985, the inventory had completed mapping for 40 percent of the lower 48 states and 10 percent of Alaska. It had fully completed mapping in eight states—Arizona, Connecticut, Delaware, Hawaii, Massachusetts, New Jersey, Rhode Island, and Vermont. The inventory staff expects to continue mapping at a rate of five percent of the lower 48 states per year and to complete all the high priority areas in the contiguous U.S. and half of those in Alaska by the end of FY 1988. Completed maps are available from the FWS regional wetlands coordinators in each FWS region and from selected state distribution centers (see appendix), or by calling the U.S. Geological Survey at 1-800-USA-MAPS.

---

*These issues are discussed further in the migratory bird chapter.
† The definition of wetlands regulated by section 404 of the Clean Water Act is narrower than the FWS definition of wetlands, as discussed later.

## Other Data Collection Efforts

The National Wetlands Inventory is conducting three other important data-collection efforts. The inventory, in conjunction with the Soil Conservation Service, has developed a list of hydric soils—soils that are saturated by water for significant periods or are frequently flooded for long periods during the growing season—to assist in delineating wetlands. The national list, entitled "Hydric Soils of the United States," as well as lists for each state are available from soil scientists at Soil Conservation Service state offices. The inventory also is developing a list of wetland vascular plants for use in wetland identification. Plants are categorized on the basis of how frequently they occur in wetlands, and data is being developed on their ecology, geographic distribution, and common names. This list is expected to be completed by the end of 1986 and will contain information on 5,400 plant species.*

Finally, the inventory has developed a computerized data base on the attributes and functions of wetlands. The data base consists of an annotated bibliography that pulls together relevant information in the scientific literature. It is intended to help accurately assess wetland values, aid in developing priorities for wetland protection, and assist in identifying the significance of specific wetland losses. By the end of FY 1985, the data base contained approximately 4,000 articles. It is expected to include 7,000 entries when completed.†

## Studies on Federal Incentives for Wetlands Destruction

The Reagan administration and Congress have shown increasing interest in recent years in addressing federal programs and policies that encourage wetlands destruction. For the most part, however, little information exists on the extent to which various federal programs contribute to wetlands loss. To lay the groundwork for future action on this issue, Congress in FY 1985 appropriated $240,000 to the FWS to begin a series of studies on the impacts of federal programs on wetlands and the potential impacts and benefits of revising them.

FWS, through the National Wetlands Inventory, has contracted for three studies with this funding. One study is focusing on the bottomland-hardwood forests of the lower Mississippi alluvial plain—wetlands of high environmental value that are being lost at the rapid rate of 100,000 acres yearly. The programs to be analyzed include flood control and small watershed projects, agricultural assistance, and tax-code provisions. Two additional

*The wetland-plant list will be available from the Fish and Wildlife Service, 9720 Executive Center Drive, The Monroe Building, Suite 101, St. Petersburg, Florida 33702.
† For more information on the wetlands data base, contact the Data Base Administrator, Western Energy and Land-Use Team, U.S. Fish and Wildlife Service, Drake Creekside One, 2627 Redwing Road, Fort Collins, Colorado 80526-2899. Phone: (303) 226-9475.

studies are looking at wetlands in the prairie potholes region, wetlands that provide critical waterfowl habitat but that have been reduced to 25 percent of their original area. These studies are investigating the effects of highway construction, agricultural assistance, and tax-code provisions. An additional study may be undertaken in FY 1986 elsewhere in the country.

Final reports from the contractors on two of the studies—the bottom-land-hardwoods study and one of the studies on the prairie potholes—are scheduled to be completed by early spring 1986. FWS drafts of the studies are scheduled to be completed by summer and to be cleared through the Interior Department by November 1986. Depending on the outcome of these studies, FWS may begin developing a legislative proposal based on the findings of the studies after the Office of Management and Budget has reviewed them.

## Wetlands Assessments and Evaluations

Through the National Wetlands Inventory, FWS is participating in an interagency effort to develop and implement a standard methodology to assess wetland functions and values. Fifteen different federal agencies are involved in the effort, including the Army Corps of Engineers, the Environmental Protection Agency, the Federal Highway Administration, and the National Oceanic and Atmospheric Administration. These federal efforts are coordinated with those at the state level through the Association of State Wetland Managers and the International Association of Fish and Wildlife Agencies. Through an Interagency Coordinating Committee, these agencies are revising a methodology developed by Paul Adamus for the Federal Highway Administration, which will be field tested and revised again as necessary. The assessment system then will be regionalized, and reports on how to apply the assessment will be developed.

Inasmuch as the Adamus system of evaluation is based upon the scientific literature, application of the system has revealed serious gaps in our knowledge of certain wetland functions. Several agencies have adjusted their wetlands research programs to fill these gaps and are coordinating these research activities through the Interagency Coordinating Committee. The National Wetlands Technical Council, a private organization of scientists, also is assisting in these efforts by holding a series of regional workshops designed to reveal state-of-the-art wetland research in the various regions, as well as to uncover regional differences. These workshops, initiated in 1985, are funded by the Donner Foundation and several federal agencies.

Identification of wetland functions is important in determining how to mitigate and compensate for wetland losses. However, when scientists move into the realm of assigning relative values to wetlands—essentially ranking them—many environmental groups become wary of the concept, in part because they believe it is extremely difficult to weigh the varied and complex functions of one wetland against another with different functions and in part because they are concerned that ranking decisions could be misapplied or politicized.

# The 404 Permit Program

## Program Administration

The major federal regulatory program controlling the destruction of wetlands is authorized by Section 404 of the Clean Water Act, which requires the issuance of a permit from the U.S. Army Corps of Engineers for the discharge of dredged or fill material into the waters of the United States, including most wetlands. The 404 permit program has prevented the destruction of hundreds of thousands of acres of wetlands, but vast acreages of wetlands continue to be lost each year—in part because the program does not cover many activities that destroy wetlands* and in part because of the limited way in which the Corps of Engineers has implemented the program.

*Statutory Authority.* The 404 program was established by the Federal Water Pollution Control Act Amendments of 1972 (P.L. 92-500, 86 Stat. 816 [currently codified at 33 U.S.C.A. 1251 *et seq.*]). Although primary authority for implementing the act generally was given to the Environmental Protection Agency (EPA), Congress placed responsibility for issuing Section 404 permits under the Corps of Engineers, since the Corps already operated a permit program for certain activities in navigable waters under Section 10 of the River and Harbor Act (33 U.S.C.A. 403). Congress reaffirmed its support for the 404 program in the Clean Water Act of 1977 (P.L. 95-217, 91 Stat. 1600) and made a number of changes to clarify the program's scope and to stream-line parts of the program.

*Agency Responsibilities.* Although the Corps of Engineers is responsible for issuing Section 404 permits, has extensive authority for determining how the 404 program shall be run. Before issuing a permit, the Corps must consult with EPA as well as with other agencies, as discussed below. EPA sets the environmental standards that projects must meet to receive a permit, as authorized in Section 404(b)(1) of the act, and is responsible for defining activities that may be exempted from the 404 permit requirement under Section 404(f). EPA also is responsible for approval and oversight of state assumption of 404 responsibilities in waters where the Clean Water Act allows the states to take on the program: waters other than tidal waters or those related to navigation and wetlands adjacent to those waters. Finally, EPA has a virtual veto

---

*A 1984 report by the congressional Office of Technology Assessment found that more than 80 percent of wetland losses is due to agricultural conversion, most of which has not been regulated under Section 404.

over Corps permit decisions under Section 404(c), which authorizes EPA to prohibit or restrict the use of an area as a disposal site for dredged or fill material if the discharge will have unacceptable adverse effects on municipal water supplies, shellfish beds and fishery areas, wildlife, or recreational areas.

EPA and the Corps share responsibility over certain other aspects of the program. Although the law does not specify which agency has ultimate responsibility for determining and defining areas that will be considered wetlands regulated by 404, a U.S. Attorney General opinion in 1979 determined that the authority resides with EPA. But because the Corps has a more extensive field structure than does EPA and is responsible for permit issuance, EPA and the Corps have signed a memorandum of understanding on 404 jurisdiction that allows the Corps to make wetland determinations in the field unless EPA has identified an area as a "special case" and wants to make the determination itself. EPA has identified two such special cases where specific controversies over wetland delineations have arisen—the bottomland hardwoods and a bay in California—but has taken little action to enforce the provision in recent years. EPA and the Corps share authority for enforcing the 404 program, with EPA largely responsible for enforcement against unauthorized activities and the Corps largely responsible for permit violations, although in fact most enforcement has been carried out by the Corps.*

Federal and state fish and wildlife agencies also are involved in 404 permit decisions. Under the Fish and Wildlife Coordination Act (16 U.S.C.A. 661 *et seq.*), the Corps of Engineers is required to consult with FWS, the National Marine Fisheries Service, and state fish and wildlife agencies and to give full consideration to their recommendations for preventing or reducing fish and wildlife losses in issuing the permit. Section 404(q) directs the secretary of the Army to enter into agreements with the federal agencies, including EPA, that are responsible for reviewing 404 permit applications to minimize needless paperwork and delays. These agreements have been extremely controversial and recently were revised, as discussed later. Permit review within the FWS is carried out by the 57 Ecological Services field offices, within National Marine Fisheries Service by the 13 Habitat Conservation field offices, and within EPA by the 10 regional offices (listed in the appendices to this book).

The states also have opportunities to influence or prevent issuance of 404 permits. The Corps cannot issue a permit if a state refuses to certify its issuance as provided under Section 401 of the Clean Water Act or if it determines permit issuance would be inconsistent with the state's coastal zone management plan approved under the Coastal Zone Management Act. The Corps also cannot issue a 404 permit if a necessary state or local permit for the activity previously was denied.

---

*Amendments to the Clean Water Act currently pending in Congress would allow the agencies to impose administrative penalties for 404 violations and would specify enforcement responsibilities.

## Permit Issuance

Section 404 permit decisions generally are made by Corps district engineers.* Prior to deciding on a permit, the Corps consults with the appropriate resource agencies and the affected state or states and seeks public comment on the permit application. In determining whether to issue a permit, the Corps uses two basic standards. First, the project must comply with the 404(b)(1) guidelines, which set particularly strict environmental standards for authorizing permits for activities in wetlands. For all aquatic areas, the guidelines authorize the issuance of a 404 permit only if there is no practicable alternative that is less environmentally damaging. For activities in the "special aquatic sites" defined in the guidelines, which include wetlands, the guidelines assume that if the activity is not water-dependent, then a less damaging alternative can be found, unless the applicant demonstrates otherwise. This water-dependency test discourages developers from construction in wetlands and is a key tool for wetlands protection in the 404 program.

If a project complies with the 404(b)(1) guidelines, the Corps then determines if the project is in the public interest by balancing the potential benefits of the activity against its foreseeable detriments. The Corps considers a wide range of factors in the public-interest review, including environmental concerns, recreation, water conservation and quality, energy, mineral and food needs, property ownership, and more. If a project does not comply with the 404(b)(1) guidelines, the permit is supposed to be denied. If it does comply with the guidelines, the permit will be issued unless the Corps finds it would be contrary to the public interest.

## Scope of the Program

Not all dredge and fill activities require the issuance of an individual 404 permit. A number of activities, such as normal farming, ranching, and silvicultural activities, are exempted from the permit requirement under Section 404(f)(1) as long as they are not intended to bring wetlands into a new use that would convert them to upland—as specified in Section 404(f)(2). Federal projects specifically authorized by Congress are exempt from the permit requirement under Section 404(r) as long as information on their impacts that would be required for a 404 permit is included in the project's environmental impact statement and is submitted to Congress prior to authorization or appropriation of funds.

In addition to these exemptions, the Corps can forego review of individual activities by issuing state, regional, or national general permits. Section 404(e) specifies that general permits can be issued for "categories of activities that are similar in nature" and that will cause only minimal individual and cumulative adverse environmental impacts. The Corps has issued 26 nation-

*See the appendix for further information on the permitting process and a list of district offices and other key Corps contacts.

wide permits and many more general permits at the state and regional levels, covering tens of thousands of activities. Some of these permits require notification to the Corps prior to undertaking a discharge, others do not. All general permits specify certain conditions that must be met, and the district or division engineer has authority to require an individual permit if he believes it is necessary. However, activities conducted under general permits often receive minimal monitoring for compliance, and the Corps often does not even know of their occurrence.

The 404 program does not regulate all wetlands, although there is substantial disagreement about exactly what wetlands it does regulate. Two important considerations are made in determining the scope of the program. First, the Corps determines whether a particular wetland is covered by the program or not. The 404 program covers "the waters of the United States," which the courts have interpreted as including all the waters that Congress constitutionally has authority to regulate under its power to regulate interstate commerce (*NRDC v. Calloway*, 392 F. Supp. 685 [D.D.C. 1975]). Wetlands adjacent to interstate rivers and streams and coastal waters clearly are covered by 404.* But wetlands adjacent to intermittent streams and other intrastate waters, and most notably isolated lakes and wetlands such as prairie potholes and playa lakes, are covered only to the extent that their degradation could affect interstate commerce. Just what constitutes such a connection to interstate commerce is currently being debated and may be the subject of a lawsuit in 1986, as discussed later.

If a wetland is covered by 404, then the Corps—or in "special cases," EPA—determines its boundaries. Under 404 regulations, wetlands are defined as "areas that are inundated or saturated by surface or ground water at a frequency and duration sufficient to support, and that under normal circumstances do support, a prevalence of vegetation adapted for life in saturated soil conditions" (33 CFR 323.2[c]). This definition is narrower than that used by FWS for its wetland inventory and generally requires an area to be wetter than does the FWS wetland definition. FWS estimates that slightly less than 99 million acres of wetlands exist in the lower 48 states. The Corps estimates that 64 million acres of wetlands, about two-thirds of the total, are regulated under 404 (Office of Technology Assessment 1984).

The issue of which activities require a 404 permit and what waters are subject to the permit requirement are at the heart of many of the controversies that have dogged the 404 permit program since its inception and are discussed further under Problems and Issues.

## Program Accomplishments and Trends

It is difficult to measure 404 program accomplishments. The Corps keeps track of the number of permits issued and the number denied, but does not

---

*This interpretation of the law was confirmed by a Supreme Court decision in 1985, as discussed in the litigation section.

track the wetland acreage saved by permit denials. In addition, although very few permits actually are denied, many projects are modified, some substantially, to reduce their impacts before a permit is issued. Wetland losses prevented by such project modifications are not tracked. However, in a 1984 report based on Corps data for 1980 and 1981, the Office of Technology Assessment concluded that 404 permit denials or required project modifications reduced the amount of wetlands loss proposed in the original permit applications by half: about 100,000 acres of wetlands conversion originally was proposed and about 50,000 acres of this loss was prevented. (Office of Technology Assessment 1984) The effect of the 404 program, however, is greater than these statistics show, since it also protects wetlands by discouraging individuals from planning activities in wetlands in the first place and by encouraging individuals to plan their projects to minimize wetland impacts even before they apply for a permit.

Lacking data on wetlands losses prevented by the 404 program, this discussion instead covers progress on administering the 404 program, assuming this translates into better wetlands protection on the ground. This section covers aspects of implementation that are relatively uncontroversial; aspects of the 404 program that are highly controversial or considered by environmental groups to be major problems are discussed later under Problems and Issues.

*Permits Issued and Denied.* In FY 1985, the Corps received about 8,500 applications for individual 404 permits, issued about 5,300 permits, and de-

### Section 404 Permits Issued and Denied FY 1974–1985

| Year | Permit Applications[1] Received | Permits Issued | % of Total Issued | Permits Denied | % of Total Denied |
|------|------|------|------|------|------|
| 1974 | 2,878 | 1,883 | 65% | 38 | 1.3% |
| 1975 | 4,353 | 2,958 | 68 | 52 | 1.2 |
| 1976 | 7,734 | 4,625 | 60 | 99 | 1.3 |
| (1976 TQ[2]) | (2,522) | (1,783) | (71) | (16) | (0.6) |
| 1977 | 10,754 | 7,698 | 72 | 91 | 0.8 |
| 1978 | 10,064 | 8,078 | 80 | 146 | 1.5 |
| 1979 | 10,196 | 8,112 | 80 | 182 | 1.8 |
| 1980 | 10,097 | 8,013 | 80 | 253 | 2.5 |
| 1981 | 10,718 | 8,552 | 80 | 291 | 2.7 |
| 1982 | 9,624 | 9,030 | 94 | 324 | 3.4 |
| 1983 | 8,435 | 7,084 | 84 | 373 | 4.4 |
| 1984 | 8,130 | 6,050 | 74 | 351 | 4.3 |
| 1985 | 8,464 | 5,289 | 62 | 365 | 4.3 |

[1] Includes applications for activities that require only a Section 404 permit and that require both a Section 404 and Section 10 permit under the Rivers and Harbors Act.
[2] Covers permit data for the "fifth" quarter added to the 1976 fiscal year when the government switched the start of its fiscal year from July to October.
Source: U.S. Army Corps of Engineers Annual Regulatory Reports

nied 365. Some applications received in 1985 were withdrawn and others still are pending in 1986. In 1985, the Corps denied 4.3 percent of the applications received, roughly the same rate since FY 1983 and slightly higher than in prior years.

Total applications received rose dramatically in the early 1970s as the Corps was directed by a court order to expand the program's jurisdiction. Permit applications have declined since 1981, coinciding with the Corps' move to authorize more activities under general permits. The Corps does not have good data on the numbers of activities subject to 404 that are covered by general permits, but estimates that more than 50,000 activities annually are covered by nationwide permits. The Corps has somewhat better data on activities covered by regional and statewide permits and estimates that they covered about 10,000 to 12,000 dredge-and-fill activities in 1985, roughly double the number of activities covered by such permits in 1982.

The percent of permit denials has increased since the 404 program's inception, although the increase is not substantial. There is no sure reason why the rate has increased, nor is there any data showing the effects of this increase in terms of wetland protection or losses. At any rate, most of the wetlands saved by 404 are due to modifications to projects and other mitigation measures for which the Corps has no nationwide statistics.

*Progress on Fish and Wildlife Mitigation.* Each of the agencies involved in 404 implementation is moving to clarify or improve the procedures for mitigating the adverse environmental impacts, including fish and wildlife impacts, of 404 permit projects.

The most notable action on mitigation in 1985 was the Corps' issuance to the field of regulatory guidance on how to apply fish and wildlife mitigation in the 404 permit process and on the role of FWS in mitigation decisions. The Corps has been criticized for making arbitrary and inconsistent decisions on mitigation at the field level, decisions with which environmentalists and FWS often disagree. In addition, FWS, which is the agency with statutory responsibility for assessing mitigation needs, has been increasingly frustrated at having its mitigation recommendations overruled or ignored by the Corps. The Corps responds that mitigation recommendations from other agencies are sometimes unreasonable in comparison with the resources lost and that the Fish and Wildlife Coordination Act requires the Corps to include only "justifiable" wildlife mitigation measures, meaning the Corps must balance other factors of the public interest in making mitigation decisions. Prior to 1985, however, the Corps had not issued explicit regulatory guidance to the field on how mitigation was to be applied.

The issuance of the mitigation guidance was one of three actions taken by the Corps in early November after several senators had blocked the nomination of Robert Dawson as assistant secretary of the Army for Civil Works, as discussed later. The guidance contains three main elements. It specifies the types of measures the district engineers are to consider in mitigating fish and wildlife losses by reiterating the definition of mitigation contained in the Council on Environmental Quality regulations for implementing the National Environmental Policy Act. Those regulations outline five aspects to be considered in evaluating mitigation needs, which include avoiding losses in the first place, minimizing impacts by modifying the proposed project, repairing or restoring damaged resources, requiring ongoing operations to reduce impacts, and compensating for losses not prevented by other mitigation measures through the acquisition or improvement of other wildlife habitat.

Second, the Corps guidance specifies that failure by the district engineer to give full consideration to FWS mitigation recommendations will constitute "insufficient coordination," one of the criteria under which the Department of the Interior may request that a permit decision be elevated to higher levels. The guidance urges district engineers to cooperate with FWS to avoid the delay caused by such elevations.

Finally, the district engineer is required to document his decision, describing how mitigation measures required in the permit are expected to reduce adverse project impacts and/or compensate for damaged or lost resources. If the district engineer does not accept the mitigation recommendations of the resource agency, he must document the basis for his decision.

The Corps says the mitigation guidance merely brings together existing policies, but the guidance could have a substantive effect. It is the first formal guidance letter on mitigation by the Corps to the field, elevating the importance of mitigation and outlining a unified statement of Corps policy. The effectiveness of the guidance, however, will depend on how it is implemented, and basic disagreements over how mitigation is applied and how much should be required are likely to continue. Even as the mitigation guidance was issued, environmental groups and the resource agencies were lined up against the Corps because of the way in which the Corps accepted mitigation as a justification for issuing a 404 permit for a shopping mall in Attelboro, Massachusetts. This potentially precedent-setting case is discussed below.

Other activity on mitigation is less high-profile. EPA is developing mitigation guidance as part of its overall reformulation of its implementation of the 404 program. FWS is establishing procedures for assessing the success of its mitigation recommendations as part of its ongoing permit-review effort. FWS is developing procedures and a data base and information system for the new effort, targeted for implementation in FY 1987. The National Marine Fisheries Service is completing follow-up studies on wetlands mitigation in Texas and North Carolina and is initiating studies of post-larval fish and shellfish use of 7,200 acres of a marsh-management area in Louisiana.

*Implementation of the Pre-discharge Notification Requirement.* In October 1984, the Corps of Engineers issued new regulations outlining permit requirements for dredge and fill activities in isolated waters—such as lakes and their adjacent wetlands and the prairie potholes—and in waters that are above the headwaters of navigable streams, defined by the Corps as having a mean annual flow of five cubic feet per second or less (49 *Fed. Reg.* 39478-39485 [1984]; Correction at 49 Federal Register 39843 [1984]). The 1984 regulations were issued as part of the settlement agreement in *NWF v. Marsh,* a lawsuit brought by a consortium of environmental groups* against regulations issued by the Corps on July 22, 1982 (47 *Federal Register* 31800-31834). Among other things, those regulations revised two former nationwide permits allowing discharges of dredged or fill material, regardless of size or purpose, to proceed without obtaining an individual 404 permit in isolated waters and headwaters, which include some 13 million acres of wetlands.

As a result of the settlement agreement, Corps regulations now require an individual permit for activities in isolated waters and headwaters that would cause "the loss or substantial modification" of 10 or more acres of waters or wetlands. For activities that will cause the loss or substantial modification of from one to 10 acres, individuals are required to give the Corps of Engineers "pre-discharge notice" and must obtain an individual permit if the project's environmental impacts will be more than minimal. Activities affecting less than one acre or that do not cause the loss or substantial modification of a larger area can proceed under the revised nationwide permit without notification of the Corps as long as specified conditions are met.

Some concern has been expressed that the Corps is not moving aggressively enough to implement this new regulatory scheme for isolated waters and headwaters. The rules require the Corps to seek the views of the resource agencies when it receives pre-discharge notices of activities proposed in areas of particular interest to the agencies. In certain cases, field officers of the resource agencies asked the Corps to forward pre-discharge notices for all waters in a region. The Corps initially refused to do so, arguing that the intent of the settlement agreement was that the resource agencies would identify only discrete waters of particular importance, but agreed to do so after the agencies submitted detailed lists of the waters concerned.

Another concern is that the Corps is not informing the public sufficiently of the need to obtain a permit or to give pre-discharge notice for activities in isolated waters. Although the Corps had issued public notice of the new requirement, in the first seven months after the new regulations were issued only 68 pre-discharge notices were received by the Corps, although the Corps had estimated that 9,000 to 10,000 activities occur annually in isolated waters (U.S. Congress 1985). The Corps says that most of these activities, however, affect less than the one acre needed to trigger notification and that it takes

*This and other aspects of *NWF v. Marsh* and the outcome of the settlement agreement are discussed in more detail in the *Audubon Wildlife Report 1985.*

time for the public to learn of such new requirements. EPA is investigating the possibility of working with the Corps to conduct additional public awareness efforts.

*Wetlands Delineation.* The Corps of Engineers and EPA are working together to develop a methodology for identifying and setting the boundaries of wetlands in the field — based largely on work already done by the Corps— and expect to issue compatible guidance in 1986. This guidance should be particularly helpful in delineating bottomland-hardwood wetlands, where disputes over wetland boundaries have been most severe. EPA and the Corps also expect to resume discussions on revising their memorandum of understanding on jurisdiction, which allocates responsibilities between the agencies for delineating wetlands.

*EPA Upgrading Its 404 Program.* Environmental groups have long criticized EPA for failure to exercise its considerable authority over the 404 permit program. In the past, for example, EPA has conducted only minimal enforcement efforts on 404. In addition, although EPA has authority under Section 404(c) to veto 404 permits, prior to 1983 EPA had initiated a 404(c) action on only one permit.

In 1983, however, when William Ruckelshaus became EPA administrator, the agency identified 404 as a high priority and began a multi-pronged effort to improve its administration of the program. EPA's current focus is on strengthening internal guidance, reformulating and clarifying jurisdictional responsibilities between EPA and the Corps, improving methodologies and the scientific base for the program, and developing strategies for the most effective use of EPA's limited resources. EPA already has stepped up its implementation of the 404 program, but the bulk of the new guidance and strategies are not expected to be fully implemented in the regions until FY 1987. Major EPA efforts include the following:

*404(c) Actions and Advance Identification of Restricted Sites.* Over the past three years, EPA has stepped up its use of its 404(c) veto power. Since 1983, EPA has initiated 404(c) actions on 10 permits, compared to one action in the previous decade. In addition, EPA is moving to implement its authority, implicit in 404(c), to designate high-value areas as off-limits to all or certain discharges of dredged and fill material even prior to any proposed project or permit application. The agency is reviewing its 404(c) regulations to determine if they need to be revised to facilitate advanced identification of restricted sites and in some cases is working cooperatively with the Corps and/or other state and local agencies to identify and agree on high-priority areas to receive such protection. EPA expects to use its 404(c) authority to protect certain wetlands in Grays Harbor, Washington, as the result of a special-area-management planning effort conducted by state, federal, and local agencies. Other efforts to give up-front protection for high-value areas have been initiated in several EPA regions to protect stream corridors in the Midwest, to protect wetlands in the Rainwater Basin in Nebraska, and to identify important wetlands for protection on Chincoteague Island in Virginia.

The Corps also is encouraging special-area-management planning, including advanced 404(c) designation by EPA of high-value areas. In lower-value areas, the Corps might tailor its regulatory program by issuing more general permits or by requiring abbreviated permit processing for activities in lower-value wetlands. The Corps plans to issue guidance to the field on special-area-management planning in 1986.

*Identifying High-Priority Wetlands.* Related to the efforts to identify areas for advance protection, EPA in 1986 asked its regions to identify wetlands that should receive priority for protection. The identification of priority areas is intended to help EPA focus its limited resources most effectively. For example, the intensive efforts necessary to declare a wetland off-limits to dredge-and-fill activities under 404(c) would be focused in the priority areas. A list of priority areas should be completed in 1986.

*Emphasis on Bottomland Hardwoods and Isolated Wetlands.* At the headquarters level, EPA already has begun to focus increased resources on two critical types of wetlands: the bottomland hardwoods of the lower Mississippi alluvial plain and isolated wetlands, such as prairie potholes and playa lakes.

The 404 program has been particularly controversial in the rapidly disappearing bottomland hardwoods, where disagreements over wetland delineations and what types of agricultural activities are regulated by 404 have been most severe and have made 404 protection of the bottomland hardwoods almost meaningless. A 1983 court decision, however, confirmed the acceptability of EPA's methodology for wetlands delineation, which was more expansive than the Corps', and clarified that certain agricultural activities—which are primarily responsible for wetlands loss in bottomland hardwoods—are to be regulated. To ensure that the court's ruling is fully implemented, EPA issued detailed interim policy guidance to its field staff in 1984 on what areas and which activities are subject to a 404 permit. EPA also initiated a series of workshops, concluded in January 1986, to characterize the bottomland-hardwoods ecosystem and to evaluate the impacts on the ecosystem of different activities and management approaches. EPA intends to issue final policy guidance on the bottomland hardwoods in the spring of 1986.

Isolated wetlands are another high-value category of wetlands in which application of the 404 program is controversial and uncertain because of regulatory changes and disagreements over which isolated wetlands are covered by 404. EPA has instructed its regions to place greater emphasis on implementing the 404 program in isolated wetlands and specifically on reviewing the newly required pre-discharge notices for activities affecting one to 10 acres of such wetlands.

*Enforcement.* EPA is moving to improve its enforcement of the 404 program by developing guidance and sample enforcement documents for the regions, conducting special training efforts for regional personnel, and incorporating enforcement goals into EPA's strategic planning and management system, which drives EPA program priorities. EPA also plans to try to renegotiate its memorandum of understanding with the Corps on enforcement responsibilities. The Corps, which has in the past conducted the vast majority of 404 enforcement activities, also recognizes the need to improve its enforcement program and says it is expanding its emphasis on enforcement by reassigning to it resources freed by general permits and other efforts aimed at reducing administrative activities.

*Wetlands Research.* EPA will begin a wetland research program in 1986. The Corps and FWS already conduct substantial wetlands research. The EPA program is intended to supplement these efforts and to focus research specifically in areas that can assist EPA implementation of the program. The program is small, initially funded at less than $1 million yearly, and will focus on three major issues: (1) quantifying the water-quality functions of freshwater wetlands; (2) assessing the cumulative impacts of incremental wetland losses; and (3) determining how mitigation projects can lessen the impact of wetland loss.

## Problems and Issues

The most prominent problems in recent federal wetland-protection efforts have had to do with implementation of the Section 404 permit program. The 404 program has been a battleground between the Corps and environmental groups ever since its inception. Throughout the history of the 404 program, the Army consistently has interpreted and applied the program narrowly, limiting the area the program covers and the activities to which it applies. In response, environmental groups have pressed for and often have won expansion of the program, primarily through court decisions that have overturned the Corps' interpretation of the law. Battles over the program's scope continue, focusing particularly on the application of 404 to isolated wetlands, as discussed below.

In addition, the 404 program was identified in 1981 by the Presidential Task Force on Regulatory Relief as a top priority for reform. In the name of regulatory relief, the Army has sought to issue more general and nationwide permits, to give more authority for the program to the states, to limit the ability of the environmental agencies to influence permit conditions and decisions, and to relax the program's environmental requirements while giving more deference to private property rights. Some of these proposals have been blocked, blunted, or overturned, particularly as a result of a settlement agreement on the environmentalist lawsuit, *NWF v. Marsh,* brought against Corps regulations issued in July 1982. But significant portions of the regulatory relief effort have taken effect or are still in the works. The Corps says the changes made under regulatory relief have allowed it to speedup permit issuance and to target staff and funding to the most important aspects of the program without weakening environmental standards. Environmental groups and the natural resource agencies, however, have objected to aspects of almost all the changes.

The Department of the Army's efforts to restrict the 404 program prompted the Senate Environmental Pollution Subcommittee, under the combined efforts of its chairman, Senator John Chafee (R-RI), and ranking Democrat, Senator John Mitchell (ME)—to hold a series of oversight hearings in 1985 on the program's implementation. In four hearings—held in May, June, July, and September—key department officials, most notably then-Acting Assistant Secretary of the Army for Civil Works Robert Dawson, were questioned on their interpretation and implementation of the law and on progress in resolving problems and disagreements.

In spite of persistent pressure from committee members, the hearings process yielded almost no results until certain committee members succeeded in temporarily holding up Dawson's nomination for the post of assistant secretary of the Army for Civil Works, which oversees the Corps. As a result, in a period of two-and-a half weeks, the Army signed new memoranda of agreement with both the Department of the Interior and EPA (see below), issued a notice to the field on regulation of isolated wetlands, and issued new mitigation guidance, as previously discussed. In spite of continued opposition to Dawson's nomination by a number of senators and almost every national environmental group, including the National Audubon Society and the National Wildlife Federation, Dawson subsequently was confirmed by the Senate in a 60 to 34 vote.

Despite the end-of-the-year flurry of activity within the Corps, most issues addressed in the hearings remain unresolved, and other issues that were relatively quiet or not ripe for action in 1985 are likely to arise in 1986.

*Memoranda of Agreement.* Controversy over the 404(q) memoranda of agreement may have been the event that finally provoked the Senate Environmental Pollution Subcommittee to begin its oversight hearings. These memoranda are signed between the Army and each of the departments responsible for evaluating proposed 404 permits, including EPA, the Department of the Interior for FWS, and the Department of Commerce for the National Marine Fisheries Service. The agreements, required under Section 404 to reduce delays, paperwork, and duplication of effort, outline procedures for the review of permit applications by the resource agencies and for elevating permit decisions to higher levels if the resource agencies disagree with the decisions rendered by the district engineers. Under direction from the Task Force on Regulatory Relief, the memoranda of agreement were revised substantially in 1982 to the point that the resource agencies found them unworkable. After more than two years of unsuccessfully trying to renegotiate Interior's memorandum of agreement, then-Interior Assistant Secretary G. Ray Arnett, in an irate letter to the Army, described the 404 program as "so flawed, it is no longer a useable tool to adequately protect wetlands" (Arnett 1984). This alarming assessment, from a relatively conservative Reagan administration appointee, grabbed substantial attention.

Prior to the regulatory relief revisions, the various agencies operated under memoranda of agreement signed in 1980, which provided for permit decisions to be elevated automatically to the division engineer if one of the resource agencies so requested and allowed permits to be elevated through as many as four levels. Actual elevations occurred infrequently—for example, EPA elevated 11 permits in two years—but it did encourage permit applicants and district engineers to negotiate permit terms with the resource agencies in order to avoid further levels of review and potential delays. The Corps, however, saw this as blackmail—holding a threat over the permit applicant's head to force him to accept mitigation decisions—and objected to the resource agencies' ability to dictate at what level a permit decision would be made.

The 1982 memoranda of agreement made substantial changes. They set tight timetables and procedures for permit review and elevation, making it difficult for the agencies to negotiate disagreements at the district level. They also sharply limited the resource agencies' ability to elevate permits by specifying narrow criteria for which an elevation could be requested and eliminating environmental impacts as a basis for elevation; by giving the Army authority to refuse to elevate the permit if it did not want to do so; and by allowing the permit to be elevated only once, to whatever level the Army determined was appropriate.

The resource agencies soon began protesting the new agreements. With permits less likely to be elevated, the resource agencies said that district engineers and permit applicants paid less heed to agency recommendations. As a result, the number of permit decisions with which the resource agencies disagreed increased, but the agencies generally were unable to elevate the decisions either because of the restrictive criteria for elevation or because the Army refused the elevation request. Furthermore, the resource agencies argued that the new memoranda of agreement did not contribute to regulatory relief, but further complicated the program by resulting in increased numbers of lawsuits against Corps permit decisions and by requiring more involvement in permit processing at top departmental levels. The Corps maintains that its decisions under the 1982 memoranda of agreement were the same as before, only quicker, and says that more permits were denied for environmental reasons after the 1982 memoranda than before.

Efforts to get the Corps to renegotiate the memoranda were unsuccessful until late in the fall of 1985, when Senator Chafee and several other senators put a hold on Dawson's nomination as assistant secretary of the Army. By the beginning of November, both EPA and Interior had signed new agreements, and the Department of Commerce was expected to have a new memoranda of agreement signed early in 1986. The revised memoranda share the same basic provisions:

(1) They provide some additional flexibility in timing and procedures for permit review at the district level, giving more opportunity for differences to be resolved at this early stage.

(2) They provide for informal consultation at the division engineer's level—where many problems were resolved under the 1980 memoranda—and require regular meetings at this level to review program implementation and to resolve problems.

(3) They provide additional criteria under which the resource agencies can request an elevation. EPA can now seek elevation of a permit if EPA disagrees with the Corps over compliance with the 404(b)(1) guidelines; FWS can ask to elevate a permit if FWS recommendations for mitigation are not given full consideration.

(4) The assistant secretary of the Army retains the authority to deny elevation requests, but he must document such denials in writing and must address each of the issues raised by the resource agencies and provide supporting data.

(5) In addition, EPA's new memorandum of agreement provides some additional time between when the Corps notifies EPA that it plans to issue a permit over EPA objections and the actual issuance of a permit in order to allow EPA time to start a 404(c) action.

Officials of all three resource agencies believe the new memoranda of understanding are significant improvements over the 1982 versions. However, all agree that the test will be in the implementation; if the Army wants to deny elevations, it can still do so. And of course under Section 404, the Army still holds the authority—aside from EPA's veto—to issue permits over other agencies' objections.

*Isolated Waters and Interstate Commerce.* Since the enactment of the 404 program, the Army has tried to avoid applying it to many of the nation's waters and particularly to isolated waters and to wetlands that are not connected to large rivers and streams. Isolated wetlands include millions of acres of high-value wetlands, such as prairie potholes, playa lakes, wet meadows, and deep bogs in ancient glacial lakes. Environmental groups and the resource agencies place high priority on protection of many of these wetlands because of their special values, including in many cases their importance as migratory waterfowl habitat. The Army maintains that Section 404 originally was not intended to protect wetlands and resists regulating them in part because it often means regulating the use of land that is in private ownership.

The battle over the scope of the 404 program began in 1974, when the Corps issued regulations applying the 404 program only to those waters it had regulated previously under the Rivers and Harbors Act, which included tidal waters and those that were or could be used for interstate navigation, omitting many small waterways and most wetlands. In 1975, the Army was ordered by a federal court in *NRDC v. Calloway* to expand the program to cover all waters that Congress may regulate constitutionally under its Commerce Clause authority. The Corps began to phase in jurisdiction over these new areas, which included wetlands adjacent to tidal and interstate waters and isolated lakes and wetlands with an interstate-commerce connection.

Unable to win in court, the Army, along with the Department of Agriculture, issued inflammatory press releases warning of the extensive coverage of the expanded program. This prompted attempts to amend the law to eliminate Section 404's application to most wetlands when the law came up for renewal in 1977. These amendments were rejected, confirming the broad application of the 404 permit requirement. At the same time, however, Congress—in an effort to keep the program from becoming overly burdensome—exempted many generally minor activities from the permit requirements, authorized the states to assume 404 responsibilities in certain waters, and added a mechanism to the law—the general permit—with which the Corps could allow activities with minimal environmental effects to proceed without undergoing individual-permit review.

Rules to implement this and other new provisions were issued July 22, 1982, after they were revised to reflect the goals of regulatory relief. Although these rules technically maintained the broad jurisdiction of the 404 program, they revised and expanded a nationwide permit—originally issued prior to the 1977 Clean Water Act amendments—which as revised authorized dredge and fill disposal in all isolated waters and headwaters, regardless of the size or purpose of the activity involved. Environmental groups claimed that the new nationwide permit significantly expanded coverage of the previous permit, which did not extend to natural lakes and adjacent wetlands in excess of 10 acres. Several groups went to court (*NWF v. Marsh*), charging that the permit violated the requirements of Section 404(e), that general permits be issued only for categories of activities that are similar in nature and that have minimal individual or cumulative adverse impacts. The Corps argued that the legislative history shows that Congress approved of the Corps' use of the nationwide permit in headwaters and isolated waters and did not intend to invalidate them with the 404(e) language. These issues, however, were never resolved, since the case was settled out of court in 1984, when regulations implementing the settlement agreement expanded the permit requirements for isolated waters and headwaters. As described earlier, activities that substantially modify more than 10 acres of such waters now require individual permits, and new notification requirements and conditions were added for activities modifying smaller areas.

The continuing debate over which isolated wetlands are covered by 404 now focuses on determining which wetlands have sufficient connection to interstate commerce. This was one of the major topics addressed in the congressional oversight hearings. Senator Mitchell and environmental groups maintain that court decisions repeatedly have found that the federal government has very broad authority under the Commerce Clause. Environmental groups maintain the Army could regulate isolated wetlands as a class, without identifying a specific connection to interstate commerce in each and every case. EPA says that the body of law gives Congress the authority to regulate activities that cumulatively could have a significant effect on interstate commerce even if a particular individual activity would not. The Army, however, says that the court decisions are contradictory, and maintains that it must make determinations on isolated waters on a case-by-case basis and must demonstrate more than a trivial connection to interstate commerce. However, the Corps has issued no clear national guidance to its district offices on how to make such determinations, leaving the interpretation of this complex and controversial question to each of its 36 district engineers. One of the most controversial results of this uneven implementation has been decisions by some district engineers not to regulate certain wetlands that provide waterfowl habitat, although it has long been accepted generally that migratory birds and their habitat may be regulated under the Constitution's Commerce Clause.

The hearings prompted some action by the Corps on the interstate-commerce question, although it is unclear what effect the action will have. Under pressure from Senator Mitchell, Acting Assistant Secretary Dawson said the Army agreed with a list of seven factors presented by EPA as indicating an interstate commerce connection—including the use of an area by migratory birds and endangered species—and that waters that only potentially could be used by migratory birds also were covered by 404. As a result of a commitment made by Dawson at the hearings, the Corps sent an EPA general-counsel memo on interstate commerce to its field staff with a cover letter that described what had occurred at the hearings. The letter, however, gave no direct guidance on how the memo should be applied and implied that it should be applied narrowly. Dawson, however, also agreed to work with EPA and Interior to develop a national policy statement on the connection to interstate commerce for determining 404 jurisdiction.

In the meantime, a case has arisen which shows that the Corps still intends to take a narrow view of the interstate-commerce authority and, true to 404's history, the question ultimately may be decided in court. Just two weeks prior to Dawson's agreement with EPA's interpretation on interstate commerce, the Corps decided not to require a permit for the dredging of a channel that destroyed a 30-acre playa lake in Texas on the grounds that the lake was not covered by 404. Although and FWS study found that the lake, called Pond 12, was used by thousands of birds of some 50 species covered by the Migratory Bird Treaty Act, the Corps said bird use of the pond was too trivial to constitute a connection to interstate commerce. The National Wildlife Federation has indicated that it may sue the Corps over its failure to assert 404 jurisdiction.

### The Attelboro Mall Permit and the Water Dependency Test.    In one of the most controversial 404 permit decisions of 1985, the Corps of Engineers approved a permit for the construction of a shopping mall in Attelboro, Massa-

chusetts, that would destroy 32 acres of wetlands. The case calls into question one of the key aspects of the 404 program, the water-dependency test—specifically how mitigation should be used in applying the test—and what constitutes a practicable alternative under the 404(b)(1) guidelines.

The Sweedens Swamp permit decision is the most recent action in a string of efforts by the Army to weaken the 404(b)(1) guidelines and to eliminate the water-dependency test. In 1982, the Task Force on Regulatory Relief identified the 404(b)(1) guidelines as in need of regulatory reform. At about the same time, the Army tried to weaken the guidelines by arguing that they were advisory in nature rather than regulatory. The Office of Management and Budget said it believed the 404(b)(1) guidelines were meant to be mandatory, but that the current guidelines were too detailed and burdensome on the Corps. The Office of Management and Budget directed EPA and the Corps to revise the guidelines, and EPA initiated this effort by soliciting public comment on needed changes. In 1983, however, EPA Administrator William Ruckelshaus determined that the record did not substantiate the need for changes and refused to revise the guidelines unless and until it was demonstrated that they were causing unnecessary burdens.

Regulatory changes issued and proposed by the Army in 1982 and 1983 raised further questions as to how the Corps intended the guidelines and the water-dependency test to be applied, but these efforts were halted in 1984 when the Corps' regulations, issued as a result of the legal settlement agreement in *NWF v. Marsh,* prohibited the issuance of a 404 permit unless it complied with the 404(b)(1) guidelines.

Bound to abide by the 404(b)(1) guidelines, the Corps, environmentalists believe, is using the Attelboro case to try to reinterpret their meaning. The case began in 1984, when Pyramid Companies applied for a 404 permit to construct a shopping mall on an 80-acre site that included a 50-acre red-maple-swamp wetland called Sweedens Swamp. Pyramid had investigated several other non-wetland sites in the area, but rejected them for various reasons. The New England division engineer planned to deny the permit because the shopping mall was not a water-dependent activity and because a practicable alternative site that did not involve wetlands existed three miles away in North Attelboro. Before the permit was denied, however, the director of Civil Works for the Corps at that time, Major General John Wall, made the unusual request to review the decision in order to "resolve the policy issue of practicable alternatives as applied to non-water dependent activities under the Section 404(b)(1) guidelines and the use of mitigation" to satisfy the practicable alternatives requirement (Letter from Major General John Wall to Commander, New England Division, May 31, 1985). In May 1985, General Wall directed the division engineer to issue the permit with conditions.

The Corps' main justification for issuing the permit was that Pyramid's proposed mitigation measures—which included the construction of 35 to 50 acres of wetlands at another site and enhancement of existing on-site wetlands—would fully compensate for the project's environmental impacts and in fact provide net benefits. If the project had no net environmental impacts, the Corps reasoned that there could be no practicable alternative that would have less environmentally damaging impacts. Thus, the Corps said the project would be in compliance with the water-dependency test.

Environmental groups and EPA challenged the Corps' contention that there would be no environmental impacts, saying that there is no assurance that the new wetlands would be successful or that it would fulfill the functions and values of the existing swamp. But regardless of the success of the mitigation, the groups argued that the Corps had misapplied the water-dependency test and the use of mitigation in making the permit decision. Environmental groups say the test is meant to deter non-water-dependent development in wetlands and that mitigation may be considered only *after* it has been determined that there are no practicable alternatives.

A secondary issue is what constitutes a practicable alternative. Major General Wall maintained that the North Attelboro site was not a practicable alternative to the Pyramid site because it was not available for purchase at the time the permit application was being considered—although it had been available when Pyramid began planning the project — and did not fulfill the project's purposes from the applicant's point of view—even though the site had since been purchased by another mall developer.

Environmental groups argue that such an interpretation is erroneous and would reward speculative investment in wetlands. Pyramid was warned that it might have difficulty getting a 404 permit, but purchased the property anyway since it thought the site had other advantages over the North Attelboro site. The other mall developer, also aware of the 404 difficulties at the South Attelboro site, purchased the North Attelboro site and has subsequently worked out many of the other problems posed by that location. Granting the permit would reward Pyramid for abandoning the upland site and could encourage other developers to follow Pyramid's example, conservationists fear.

Whether and how these issues will be decided is unclear. EPA has initiated a 404(c) action that could lead to a veto of the permit. Pyramid tried unsuccessfully to get a court order to halt EPA from making a 404(c) determination while it negotiated on further mitigation efforts. EPA's final 404(c) decision is expected by March 1985, at which time further lawsuits are likely. In the long run, many believe the Attelboro case could determine how the water-dependency test is to be applied and whether the Corps or EPA has authority to interpret the 404(b)(1) guidelines.

*South Carolina Coastal Wetlands.*   One site-specific area of recent controversy has been South Carolina's coastal wetlands. In April 1985, EPA issued a 404(c) determination prohibiting impoundment of wetlands with dikes at a site in Charleston County, South Carolina. The permit applicant, a private citizen, proposed to impound 900 acres of wetlands for waterfowl hunting and aquaculture. The Corps of Engineers issued the permit over the objections of the federal resource agencies, and the Army refused requests by EPA, NMFS, and FWS to elevate the permit decision. Following a public hearing, EPA issued a 404(c) determination, citing numerous environmental impacts, including loss of spawning, nursery, and forage habitat for fish in the area, which already has suffered substantial cumulative wetlands loss. EPA has initiated another 404(c) action on a similar permit—again issued by the Corps over resource-agency objections—authorizing the impoundment of 550 acres in Georgetown County, South Carolina, for waterfowl hunting and mariculture. However, at the request of the permit applicant, EPA has halted its 404(c) action pending a decision by the South Carolina Supreme Court regarding a state-level permit. A Corps decision on a third similar applications pending.*

***Other Pending 404 Issues.*** A number of 404-related issues saw no action in 1985, but are expected to arise again in 1986. Most of these are related to the regulatory relief effort. They include the following:

- The Corps expects to issue its "consolidated regulations" for the 404 program, which will pull together most regulatory changes into a single package. This will include the issuance of some new regulations, based on proposed regulations issued May 12, 1983, and comments on the interim final regulations issued July 22, 1982. The proposed rules contained a number of regulatory relief initiatives opposed by environmentalists. Some of the issues in those regulations were dealt with in the settlement agreement on *NWF v. Marsh*. The most controversial change—a redefinition of some of the terms used in defining wetlands, which would have eliminated 404 coverage for millions of acres†—will not be included in the final rules since the Corps cannot issue a new definition without EPA approval. However, other aspects of the pending new rules could still be controversial.
- EPA expects to issue its streamlined procedures and requirements for state assumption of the 404 permit program—another effort prompted by the Task Force on Regulatory Relief. The proposed rules, issued in October 1984, were criticized by environmental groups as being too lax and by the Corps as still being too stringent.
- The issue of proposed revisions to the Corps' National Environmental Policy Act regulations, which play an important role in the effectiveness of the 404 program, should heat up again. The Corps proposed changes to those regulations in January 1984 as part of the regulatory relief effort. The changes were criticized heavily by environmental groups and EPA. When

---

*These three cases are known respectively as the Maybank, Reeves, and Mitchell cases after the citizens who filed the permit applications.
† The Corps says there was a technical error in this proposal and that the Corps did not intend the redefinitions to reduce so severely the wetland acreage covered.

it became apparent that the Corps planned to issue final regulations that retained many controversial provisions, EPA referred the matter to the Council on Environmental Quality, saying that the proposed revisions would have an adverse effect on EPA's program to prevent unacceptable discharges under 404. The Corps obtained repeated extensions from the Council on Environmenal Quality throughout 1985 for responding to the EPA charges, but the issue should resume in 1986.

- EPA and the Corps are expected to resolve the question of who should regulate the disposal of solid waste in the nation's waters. EPA has maintained that the Corps should regulate it as fill under Section 404. The Corps has argued that EPA should ultimately regulate it under the nation's solid-waste-disposal law, the Resource Conservation and Recovery Act, and in the interim should regulate it as pollution under Section 402 of the Clean Water Act. Environmentalists say the lack of clear authority has meant that discharges of solid waste, some that have included toxic pollutants, have gone unregulated, and that cleanups have not been enforced. As part of the settlement agreement in *NWF v. Marsh,* EPA and the Corps agreed to resolve the issue by proposing a definition of fill material by May 1984. The agencies missed this deadline, but promised the Senate Environmental Pollution Subcommittee that they would resolve the issue by January 1986.

# Legislation

## The 1985 Farm Bill

The farm bill approved by Congress at the end of 1985 contained outstanding conservation provisions that should yield substantial benefits for soil conservation, fish and wildlife, and wetlands. Entitled the Food Security Act of 1985 (P. L. 99-198), the new law contains four major conservation programs: (1) a long-term conservation reserve; (2) a "sodbusters" provision denying certain federal farm subsidies to farmers who plow highly erodible land; (3) a "swampbusters" provision extending the sodbusters concept to agricultural conversions of wetlands; and (4) a provision in the farm-debt restructure program that allows the federal government to acquire conservation easements on a farmer's land while cancelling part of the farmer's debt.

*Conservation Reserve.* The conservation reserve is the most significant conservation program in the farm bill for soil erosion and fish and wildlife, although its significance is somewhat less for wetlands. The reserve is intended to get highly erodible cropland out of production. It requires 40 to 45 million acres of highly erodible cropland to be converted to permanent cover—trees or grass—by 1990. Farmers voluntarily enter into contracts of 10 to 15 years duration and receive cost-sharing payments for establishing the cover and annual rental payments for keeping the land out of production. FWS estimates that if the program were fully implemented, 11 percent of the nation's cropland would be placed under long-term conservation cover.

The conservation reserve, by decreasing erosion and siltation and reducing the use of pesticides and fertilizers, can help improve wetlands water quality. In addition, the secretary of Agriculture is authorized to include lands in the reserve that are related to off-farm environmental threats. The Agriculture Department could use this authority to reduce agriculture-related water pollution in lands along lakes and streams, areas that could include wetlands.

*Sodbusters and Swampbusters.*  Both these provisions attempt to discourage farmers from conducting certain activities that conflict with federal policy by denying federal subsidies for support of the activities. Both provisions deny eligibility for the following programs: price support payments, farm-storage-facility loans, crop insurance, disaster payments, payments for storage of grain owned by the Commodity Credit Corporation, and Farmers Home Administration mortgage loans if they would be used for purposes that will contribute to excessive erosion.

The sodbusters provision is meant to work in tandem with the conservation reserve to combat soil erosion. While the reserve takes erodible land out of production, the sodbusters provision discourages new erodible land from being brought into production. The new program denies all the federal subsidies listed above to any farm on which highly erodible land is plowed. Erodible lands already in production can be farmed without penalty until 1990, after which the lands must be covered by a conservation plan approved by the soil and water conservation district or the penalties will take effect. The sodbusters provision, although not directly affecting wetlands, could provide some benefits by reducing water pollution from agricultural runoff.

The swampbusters provision denies eligibility for the above federal programs to farmers who convert wetlands to annual crop production. Exempted from this limitation are wetlands on which conversion commenced before enactment of the farm bill and wetlands that were created artificially. Wetlands also can be cropped during normal drought years, and the secretary of Agriculture can authorize an exemption if the individual or cumulative effect of the conversion on the hydrological and biological characteristics of a wetland is minimal. The definition of wetlands covered by the swampbusters provision is similar to that for wetlands under 404. The secretary of Agriculture is required to consult with Interior on identifying wetlands, determining exemptions, and issuing regulations to implement the provision.

FWS estimates that more than five million acres of wetlands in the lower 48 states have high or moderate potential for conversion to cropland. But to what extent the swampbuster provision will discourage wetlands conversions is uncertain. However, agricultural conversion is the major cause of wetlands loss in two critical wetlands regions—the prairie potholes and the lower Mississippi bottomland hardwoods—and the swampbuster provision should help slow the losses in these areas.

The sodbuster and swampbuster provisions should be fairly effective now while commodity prices are low and farmers are dependent on federal subsidies. They could lose their effectiveness, however, if and when commodity prices substantially rise again and subsidies are not so critical.

*Conservation Easements.* This provision, included under Title XIII of the farm bill, amends the Farm and Rural Development Act. It authorizes the Farmers Home Administration to acquire and retain for at least 50 years easements on certain lands for conservation, recreation, and fish and wildlife purposes. Lands are eligible for this provision if they are wetlands, uplands, or highly erodible lands and if they are farmed by a holder of a Farmers Home Administration loan who is unable to repay the loan or if the property is administered by the Department of Agriculture. The easement is purchased by reducing the borrower's loan. The Department of Agriculture is required to consult with the Fish and Wildlife Service in selecting lands unsuitable for easements and formulating their terms, conditions, and enforcement.

Easement areas could be managed in a variety of ways, including as part of the National Wildlife Refuge System or as state wildlife management areas. The impact of this provision on wetlands is unclear, but farmers would be certain to give up their least productive lands first, which would include those that frequently are flooded and could be restored as functioning wetlands. FWS predicts the program could have positive impacts on the prairie potholes, lower Mississippi bottomland hardwoods, the Rainwater Basin and Sandhills in Nebraska, playa lakes, wetlands in the Pacific Northwest, the Upper Mississippi River and adjacent wetlands, and wetlands in the Atlantic Flyway.

## Amendments to the Fish and Wildlife Coordination Act

For the second year in a row, the House of Representatives passed a bill to amend the Fish and Wildlife Coordination Act, the law that requires the involvement of fish and wildlife agencies in federal-water-project decisions, including decisions on Section 404 permits. The bill, H.R. 2704, is nearly identical to H.R. 5755, passed by the House in October 1984. The amendments make only relatively minor changes in the existing law. They generally are supported by environmental groups—with some caveats—as somewhat strengthening the role of the fish and wildlife agencies.

The amendments would require the Corps to transfer funds to FWS and the National Marine Fisheries Service to conduct reviews and prepare fish and wildlife reports on Corps' water projects. This does not, however, include review of 404 permits. This amendment was prompted in part by an Army proposal in 1982 to terminate the transfer of funds, which currently is discretionary. In addition, FWS says the Corps has not always provided the consistent and reliable funding needed for FWS to meet adequately the Coordination Act's consultation requirements.

The amendments also would add language confirming the authority of the resource agencies to undertake certain types of mitigation efforts. Specifically, they would authorize the agencies to enter into long-term agreements regarding fish and wildlife mitigation requirements for large-scale, long-term projects that require multiple permits. They also would recognize the authority of the agencies to recommend off-site mitigation. This provision is intended primarily to boost the concept of mitigation banking, which allows a project operator to protect or enhance habitat off the project site and to use the protected area to provide "credits" against losses caused by future projects. Mitigation banking has caused some concern among fish and wildlife interests, who say that some agreements have not guaranteed long-term protection of mitigation areas and that off-site mitigation is being used to justify impacts on wetlands that could be avoided. The committee report on H.R. 2704 states that mitigation banking should not be used to circumvent existing regulations or policies on development in wetlands areas.

Finally, the amendments require the resource agencies to evaluate the extent to which their mitigation recommendations were incorporated as conditions for water-resource projects and 404 permits, and to evaluate the results and effectiveness of the recommendations. FWS and the National Marine Fisheries Service already are starting up such efforts. In addition, the Corps of Engineers is required to assess the extent to which that permittees or project operators have complied with the required mitigation measures.

The Senate Environmental Pollution Subcommittee expects to take up the bill in late spring or early summer of 1986 and is likely to make a number of changes to the legislation.

## Emergency Wetlands Acquisition

Congress has been working for several years on legislation to provide substantially increased funding—up to $100 million yearly—for wetlands acquisition and conservation. The funds would be raised by tapping the Land and Water Conservation Fund, increasing duck stamp fees, and charging entrance fees at some national wildlife refuges. The bill came close to clearing Congress in 1984, but failed because of opposition to an unrelated amendment attached to the bill which would have authorized a controversial Corps project in North Carolina.

Deliberations on the legislation (H.R. 1203, S. 740) began again in 1985, and the House bill was approved by the Merchant Marine and Fisheries Committee. But pressure to reduce federal spending and constraints on the approval of new spending imposed by the Gramm-Rudman deficit-reduction law have dimmed the prospects for the bill's final passage in the near future.

## Clean Water Act Amendments

In 1985, Congress continued to work on reauthorization of and amendments to the Clean Water Act. The legislation under consideration, H.R. 8 and S. 1128, makes no substantive amendments to the Section 404 permit program. Amendments intended to strengthen enforcement of the Clean Water Act would authorize EPA and/or the Corps—the bills differ on this point—to impose administrative penalties for permit violations in an effort to speed and simplify enforcement of the program. The bills have been passed by both houses, and conferees were scheduled to meet in early 1986 to work out differences between the two bills. Even if Congress completes action on the bill, however, it could be in trouble, since the president has threatened to veto the bill if it includes too much federal spending.

# Legal Developments

The courts have claimed center stage in wetlands law this year, delineating the scope of Corps authority and responsibilities under Section 404. Most important is the Supreme Court's decision in *United States v. Riverside Bayview Homes* (106 S.Ct. 455 [1985]). Reviewing an enforcement action brought by the Corps of Engineers, the Sixth Circuit had ruled that Section 404 must be construed narrowly to avoid unconstitutional "taking" of property rights and should therefore be applied only to wetlands that are "frequently flooded by adjacent streams" (729 F.2nd 391 [6th Cir. 1984]). The Supreme Court unanimously reversed. Stating that "the mere assertion of regulatory jurisdiction" was not enough to constitute a taking, the court held that the Constitution did not compel a cramped construction of the statute. The court found that, in light of the facts found by the district court, the subject wetlands were clearly within Corps regulations. Looking to the statute and its legislative history, the court found that the jurisdiction asserted by the Corps regulations was "reasonable and not in conflict with the expressed intent of Congress." The court's decision sheds new light on the takings issue in environmental regulation and should put to rest oft-heard claims that Section 404 was not intended to regulate wetlands.

The Corps fared less well in an earlier decision from the Court of Claims (*Florida Rock Industries, Inc. v. United States*, (8 Cl. Ct. 160 [1985]). Florida Rock had sought a permit to mine limestone deposits lying beneath the Biscayne Aquifer in Dade County. The Corps denied the permit and Florida Rock sued, claiming that its property had been "taken" in violation of the Constitution. The Court of Claims agreed, finding that the permit denial made profitable mining impossible and that there was no other viable economic use of the property. The government's defenses were numerous and complex, emphasizing that the property still retained some market value and arguing that the government should not have to compensate a landowner when it prohibits activities that cause harm to the public welfare. All defenses were rejected, and the government was held liable. The case is now on appeal.

In *Louisiana Wildlife Federation v. York* (761 F.2nd 1044 5th Circ. [1985]), conservation groups challenged six section 404 permits issued by the Corps allowing the conversion of 5,200 acres of bottomland-hardwood wetlands for soybean farming. Because the area had been designated as a "special aquatic site" and proposed use was not water dependent, the permit applicant was required under the EPA guidelines to show that no practicable alternatives to the proposed developments existed.

The plaintiffs claimed that in granting the permits, the Corps impermissibly confined its analysis of practicable alternatives to only those alternatives that would serve the applicant's objectives and achieve maximum profits. The district court dismissed the complaint. On appeal, the Fifth Circuit affirmed.

The court rejected the plaintiffs' view that the Corps gave impermissible weight to economic considerations, finding that environmental mitigation measures required by the Corps had in fact prevented the applicants from maximizing their profits. The court also found that the EPA guidelines intended the Corps to consider the applicants' proposed use of the wetlands when evaluating alternative sites.

In *United States v. Huebner* (752 F.2nd 1235 7th Circ. [1985]), the Corps sued Wisconsin farmers for conducting various dredge-and-fill activities in their wetlands-cranberry bogs without a permit, in violation of Section 404 and a 1978 consent decree. The farmers claimed that their activities were exempt from the Corps permit process under Section 404(f)(1), which waives the permit requirement for activities such as plowing, seeding, and construction or maintenance of roads and farm ponds.

The district court held the farmers in contempt for violation of the consent decree. The court of appeals affirmed. Reviewing the legislative history of the Clean Water Act, the court concluded that Section 404(f)(1) exemptions were intended by Congress to be narrowly construed to include only activities that have minimal impact upon the integrity of the wetlands and that any conversion of wetlands to farming was explicitly subject to the permit requirement under Section 404(f)(2). The court thus found that the defendants' activities were not within the scope of the exemption and were contrary to the terms of the consent decree.

Finally, the courts upheld EPA's authority to review Corps permit decisions pursuant to Section 404(c). In *Newport Galleria Group v. Deland* (Civil Action No. 85-2747), a shopping mall developer (Pyramid) asked the court to enjoin EPA from initiating proceedings under Section 404(c) in order to review Pyramid's proposed construction of a shopping mall in wetlands area. Pyramid argued that since the Corps had given notice of its intent to issue Pyramid a 404 permit to fill the wetlands area, the EPA proceedings, which acted to suspend the issuance of the permit, were illegal.

Originally, the Corps' district engineer had joined with EPA and FWS in recommending that the permit be denied because of the habitat losses that would occur despite on-site mitigation efforts. The Corps then changed its position, finding that habitat losses would be mitigated adequately and that consideration of alternative sites therefore was unnecessary.

EPA disagreed, suspended the permit under Section 404(c), and announced that it would hold public hearings to determine whether the permit should be vetoed. The court upheld the EPA suspension, finding that EPA was not bound by the Corps' determination that the project was environmentally sound, as such a finding by the court would nullify EPA's statutory veto power. The court also held that the EPA decision to initiate 404(c) proceedings was not a "final agency action," and therefore was not subject to judicial review. The court dismissed the case for lack of jurisdiction. The developer has appealed.

## Status of the Resource

The best available data on the status of wetlands is the status and trends analysis conducted by the FWS National Wetlands Inventory and completed in 1982 (Frayer 1983). This study was covered in some detail in the *Audubon Wildlife Report 1985,* and no significant new information has become available in the past year. A brief summary of the study's findings is given here.

According to the status and trends survey, from the mid-1950s to the mid-1970s, approximately 11 million acres of wetlands were lost, an average annual loss rate of approximately 550,000 acres. At the same time, there was a gain of about 2.3 million acres, primarily because of farm-pond construction. This results in a net loss of about nine million acres over a 20-year period, or an average loss of 458,000 acres yearly. Although some sources have suggested that wetlands loss may have slowed since the mid-1970s, FWS says that no scientific data confirms this claim and assumes wetland losses continue at a rate of 458,000 acres yearly.

Most of the loss during this period was from inland wetlands, which accounted for 97 percent of the reduction. This included losses of six million acres of forested wetlands, 4.7 million acres of inland marshes, and 400,000 acres of shrub wetlands. About 400,000 acres of coastal marshes and mangroves were lost, with coastal wetlands conversion occurring at about 75 percent of the rate of inland conversion. The proportion of wetlands loss also varies considerably from region to region, although there is no consistently good data at the regional or state level. States suffering the heaviest losses during this 20-year period were Alabama, Louisiana, Mississippi, Texas, Arkansas, Florida, Georgia, South Carolina, North Carolina, Minnesota, North Dakota, South Dakota, Nebraska, Michigan, Wisconsin, Illinois, Maryland, New Jersey, and Delaware.

FWS has identified nine problem areas where wetlands are in greatest jeopardy from the standpoint of national interest. These are areas of high resource value that need special attention to stem further serious losses. The nine areas are discussed in some detail in the *Status and Trends* report. Briefly, they include the following areas:

- Forested Wetlands of the Lower Mississippi Alluvial Plain—Particularly important as wintering habitat for millions of migratory birds, these wetlands have been reduced by 80 percent of their original extent.
- Estuarine Wetlands of the Coastal Zones—More than half of these wetlands, important for commercial and recreational fisheries, have been lost, and the rate of loss has increased because of urbanization.
- Louisiana's Coastal Marshes—These marshes, which support Louisiana's multi-million-dollar commercial inshore shrimp fishery, are being lost to a combination of natural and man-induced factors at a rate of 25,000 acres yearly.
- Chesapeake Bay's Submerged Aquatic Beds—The seagrass beds that support the waterfowl and fisheries of the nation's largest estuary have declined dramatically because of runoff and a combination of other factors.
- South Florida's Palustrine Wetlands—Massive channelization in south Florida has disrupted water flows and led to the destruction of more than 100,000 acres of wetlands, threatening Everglades National Park, colonial-wading-bird populations, and south Florida's offshore fishery.
- Prairie Pothole Region Emergent Wetlands—The prairie potholes, the continent's most valuable inland marshes for waterfowl production, have been depleted to about 25 percent their original extent and continue to be destroyed at a rapid rate primarily because of agricultural activities.
- Wetlands of Nebraska's Sandhills and Rainwater Basin—Substantial losses of these wetlands, which provide vital staging areas and roosting habitat for sandhill cranes, have caused serious overcrowding of bird populations. This has caused massive outbreaks of disease and holds the potential for catastrophic losses of sandhill cranes.
- North Carolina's Pocosins—Losses of these evergreen forested and scrub-shrub wetlands, already reduced to less than half their original extent, could damage North Carolina's multi-million-dollar commercial fishery.
- Western Riparian Wetlands—These margins along western lakes and streams, which support a high diversity of fish and wildlife, are classified by FWS as "the most modified land type in the West."

The next status and trends report will cover wetlands trends from 1954 through 1984. It is scheduled for completion in 1989.

## References

Eggert, Thomas. 1985. "Out with the old, in with the new: the Corps' controversial interpretation of the 404(b)(1) Guidelines." *National Wetlands Newsletter,* Vol. 7, No. 5 (Sept.-Oct. 1985): pp. 2-4.

Frayer, W. E. *et al.* 1983. *Status and Trends of Wetlands and Deepwater Habitats in the Coterminous United States, 1950s to 1970s.* Colorado State University. Fort Collins, Colorado.

Letter from G. Ray Arnett, Assistant Secretary of the Interior for Fish and Wildlife and Parks to William R. Gianelli, Assistant Secretary of the Army for Civil Works, June 27, 1983.

Letter from Major General John F. Wall, Director of Civil Works, to Commander, New England Division, May 31, 1985.

U.S. Congress, Office of Technology Assessment. 1984. *Wetlands: Their Use and Regulation.* Government Printing Office. Washington, D.C.

U.S. Congress, Senate, Committee on Environment and Public Works. 1985. *Oversight Hearings on Section 404 of the Clean Water Act,* S. Hrg. 99-278. Government Printing Office. Washington, D.C.

U.S. Congress, Senate. 1985. *Congressional Record,* 99th Cong., 1st Sess.: pp. 11646-16901.

U.S. Department of the Interior, Fish and Wildlife Service. 1984. *Wetlands of the United States: Current Status and Recent Trends.* Government Printing Office. Washington, D.C.

*Katherine Barton, a freelance writer who specializes in conservation issues, is based in Washington D.C.*

The National Wildlife Refuge System, which now includes some 420 refuges, was initially established for the protection of waterfowl, such as these Canada geese.

*Leonard Lee Rue III*

# The National Wildlife Refuge System

## Wendy Smith Lee

## Introduction

THE NATIONAL WILDLIFE Refuge System is a 90-million-acre nationwide network of lands and waters maintained to safeguard wildlife species and their habitats. It is the only extensive system of federally owned lands set aside chiefly for wildlife conservation. The system is administered by the U.S. Fish and Wildlife Service (FWS) and is managed for both wildlife and public use benefits.

The National Wildlife Refuge System is widespread and varied. It extends from Alaska to Florida and from California to Maine, with refuges in every state except West Virginia. The refuge system emphasizes protection of wetlands for migratory waterfowl—more than three-fourths of all refuges were established for this purpose—but hundreds of other species benefit from the system, including more than 220 species of mammals, 250 species of reptiles and amphibians, 200 species of fish, and 600 of the 813 bird species recorded in the United States. Most of the species on the U.S. endangered list have habitat in refuges, which are often a chief factor in the species' continued survival (Riley 1979).

The National Wildlife Refuge System includes the following types of areas:

*National Wildlife Refuges.* Most of the system is made up of units called refuges, defined as areas of land and water that provide public benefits

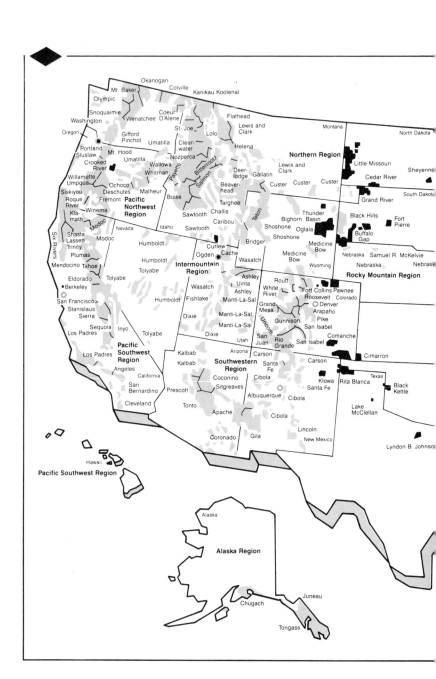

The National Wildlife Refuge System

Areas in the National Wildlife Refuge System, 1984

| Type of Unit | # of units | Reserved From Public Domain[A] | | Acquired by Other Federal Agency[B] | | Devise[C] or Gift | Purchased[D] | | Agreement Easement or Lease[E,F] | Total Acres |
|---|---|---|---|---|---|---|---|---|---|---|
| | | Sole or Primary | Secondary | Sole or Primary | Secondary | | Acres | Cost | | |
| National Wildlife Refuges | 424 | 79,966,599 | 689,927 | 1,243,052 | 840,800 | 1,463,667 | 2,380,065 | 328,320,914 | 1,468,830 | 88,052,940 |
| Waterfowl Production Areas | 149 | 9,504 | | 1,052 | | 408 | 489,918 | 71,910,429 | 1,184,264 | 1,685,146 |
| Total | 573 | 79,976,103 | 689,927 | 1,244,104 | 840,800 | 1,464,075 | 2,869,983 | 400,231,243 | 2,653,094 | 89,738,086 |
| Coordination Areas | 58 | 57,899 | | 188,679 | 58,684 | | 922 | 22,538 | 116,934 | 423,118 |
| Total Refuge System | 631 | 80,034,002 | 689,927 | 1,432,783 | 899,484 | 1,464,075 | 2,870,905 | 400,253,881 | 2,770,028 | 90,161,204 |
| Wildlife Research Centers | 10 | 43 | 14 | 27 | 55 | | 612 | 616,678 | 2,729 | 3,423 |
| Administrative Sites | 33 | | | 277 | 39 | | 10 | 220,826 | 16 | 399 |
| Fish Hatcheries | 81 | 3,696 | 828 | 2,463 | 3,680 | 1,923 | 6,251 | 1,795,975 | 460 | 19,301 |
| Fishery Research Stations | 16 | 5 | 159 | 5 | 351 | 98 | 979 | 721,703 | 31 | 1,628 |
| Total Other | 140 | 3,744 | 1,001 | 2,772 | 4,125 | 2,021 | 7,852 | 3,355,182 | 3,236 | 24,751 |
| Grand Total | 771 | 80,037,746 | 690,928 | 1,435,555 | 903,609 | 1,466,096 | 2,878,757 | 403,609,063 | 2,773,264 | 90,185,955 |

[A] Reserved from public domain-lands in federal ownership that have not been patented out at any time

1. Sole-refuge department has primary jurisdiction
2. Secondary-project by another federal agency, such as the Bureau of Reclamation that may result in a secondary withdrawal for the national Wildlife Refuge System. Might be with the Corps, Coast Guard, DOD, etc. Dam or similar structure may be built and during the permit process etc. Biological/Ecological Services will be apprised of an opportunity for such a secondary withdrawal.

[B] Acquired by other federal agency

1. private lands acquired by another federal agency. Many, for example, were acquired by the Department of Agriculture during the depression when they bought it from farmers who turned their lands over to the govt.

[C] Devise-will, estate, gift, etc.

[D] Agreement—can be a cooperative agreement where the DOI can manage a property along with the Corps or perhaps with the Nature Conservancy or Audubon, or perhaps with the states

[E] Easement-acquire partial right or interest. This can, for example, be in WPA's. The farmer may agree not to drain or burn on his land—this is an easement, or a right which has been purchased by the government to ensure certain uses, or that certain uses not occur. May be a right to various kinds of property uses, flowage easements, etc.

[F] Lease—5-year lease for example. May involve state lands, administrative sites. Do it to save money and not involve federal ownership on it. Also, so as not to remove lands from the tax base. Many states do this because they legally cannot divest certain properties.

through protection of the wildlife for which the federal government has responsibility, particularly migratory birds and endangered species. There are more than 430 refuge units, encompassing 87.8 million acres, 77 million of them in Alaska.* Refuges are staffed and managed by FWS personnel and have a wider range of objectives and benefits than do waterfowl production areas and coordination areas.

*Waterfowl Production Areas.* These are small wetland or prairie pothole areas, generally 40 to 2,000 acres in size. There are currently 152 waterfowl production areas totaling approximately 1.7 million acres, most of which are concentrated in Iowa, Michigan, Minnesota, Montana, Nebraska, North Dakota, South Dakota, Wisconsin, and Wyoming. Waterfowl production areas acquired in Iowa, Michigan, and Wisconsin are managed by the states under cooperative agreements with FWS. All other waterfowl protection areas are managed directly by FWS.

*Coordination Areas.* Coordination areas are federally owned land, usually acquired by the Corps of Engineers or the Bureau of Reclamation as part of a water-resource project, that are managed for wildlife purposes under a cooperative agreement between the purchasing agency, FWS, and the state in which the area is located. There are 58 coordination areas encompassing approximately 423,000 acres. Day-to-day management is conducted by the states under FWS-approved management plans.

## Legislative Authority

### Refuge Establishment

Wildlife refuges have been established by a variety of methods through the years. The first refuges were established by presidential proclamations directing that certain areas of the public domain be set-aside or "withdrawn" for the protection of wildlife. President Theodore Roosevelt pioneered this method of refuge establishment with the designation of the first national wildlife refuge, Florida's Pelican Island, in 1903. Through the years, the authority to create refuges by executive order evolved and was delegated to the secretary of the Interior in 1942, who could establish refuges by issuing numbered public-land orders. This authority was eliminated, however, in 1976 with the passage of the Federal Land Policy and Management Act (43 U.S.C.A. 1701 *et seq.*).

Today, areas are added to the refuge system in one of three ways: the secretary of the Interior can acquire lands for inclusion in the refuge system under various statutory authorities; Congress can pass legislation designating

*Because the Alaska refuges make up such a major portion of the refuge system and because of many special requirements governing their management, Alaska refuges are discussed separately later in this chapter.

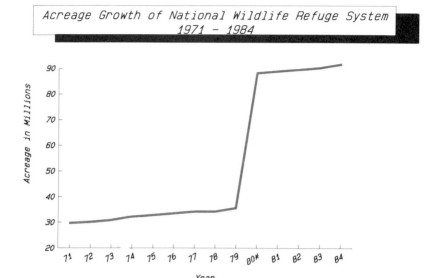

Acreage Growth of National Wildlife Refuge System
1971 – 1984

\* Represents passage of the Alaska National
Interest Lands Conservation Act, which added
54 million acres in Alaska to the refuge system.
Source: FWS, Office of Refuge Management

a specific area as a refuge; and lands donated or transferred to FWS can be established as refuges. Each of these methods is described below.

Eleven different statutes give the secretary of the Interior general authority to establish national wildlife refuges. Chief among these is the Migratory Bird Conservation Act (16 U.S.C.A. 715 *et seq.*), which authorizes the secretary of the Interior to acquire lands as refuges for migratory birds. Such acquisitions are funded by the Migratory Bird Conservation Fund (discussed below), but first must be approved by the governor or the director of the department of fish and game in each state in which land would be acquired. The proposal must then be approved by the Migratory Bird Conservation Commission, composed of the secretary of the Interior as chairman, the secretaries of Transportation and Agriculture, two members of the Senate—currently Senator Thad Cochran (R-MS) and Senator David Pryor (D-AR)—two members of the House of Representatives—currently Congressman Silvio Conte (R-MA) and Congressman John Dingell (D-MI)—and an *ex-officio* representative from the government of each state involved. Among the hundreds of refuges established in this manner are Ruby Lake National Wildlife Refuge in Nevada and Lake Woodruff National Wildlife Refuge in Florida. Additional authority for acquiring migratory waterfowl habitat comes from the Migratory Bird Hunting and Conservation Stamp Act (16 U.S.C.A. 718-718h), which authorizes the acquisition of waterfowl production areas. Acquisition of WPAs also is funded by the Migratory Bird Conservation Fund, but does not require approval by the Migratory Bird Conservation Commission.

The secretary's authority to acquire refuge lands was expanded beyond acquiring habitat for migratory birds by two important laws. The Endangered Species Act (16 U.S.C.A. 1531-1543) authorizes the secretary of the Interior to establish and acquire lands for refuges as part of a program to conserve fish, wildlife, and plants determined to be endangered or threatened with extinction. The Mississippi Sandhill Crane National Wildlife Refuge in Mississippi was established using this authority. In addition, the Fish and Wildlife Act of 1956 (16 U.S.C.A. 742[f]) gives the secretary general authority to take steps necessary for the conservation of fish and wildlife resources, including acquisition by purchase or by exchange of land and water or interests therein. Harbor Island National Wildlife Refuge in Michigan was established under this authority.

More than 30 refuges have come into the system by specific acts of Congress. This method generally is used to establish a refuge for a particular purpose, such as the preservation of a certain species or to specify additional purposes for the refuge's establishment, generally recreational or educational purposes. For example, Congress established the San Francisco Bay National Wildlife Refuge, specifying that recreation and environmental education purposes were co-equal with wildlife conservation.

Other refuges have been established by donation of land to the federal government, under cooperative agreement with other federal agencies, and through interagency land transfers. Such lands can be incorporated into the

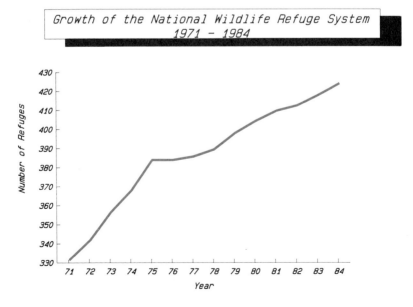

Growth of the National Wildlife Refuge System
1971 – 1984

Source: FWS, Office of Refuge Management

refuge system under the authority of the Endangered Species Act, the National Wildlife Refuge System Administration Act (16 U.S.C.A. 668dd and 668ee), the Fish and Wildlife Coordination Act (16 U.S.C.A. 633), or various other authorities. The Eastern Shore of Virginia National Wildlife Refuge, formerly Cape Charles Air Force Base, is an example of a refuge created out of an interagency transfer of land no longer useful to the original managing agency. Refuges created out of donated land include the 220,000-acre Sevilleta National Wildlife Refuge in New Mexico, donated by the Campbell Family Foundation, and the 120,000-acre Alligator River National Wildlife Refuge in North Carolina, donated by the Prudential Insurance Company.

## Refuge Acquisition: Funding and Priorities

Two sources of funding account for 99 percent of refuge acquisitions. The Migratory Bird Conservation Fund provides the Department of the Interior with moneys for the acquisition of migratory-bird habitat. The fund primarily is made up of revenues from the sale of Migratory Bird Hunting and Conservation Stamps—generally called duck stamps—as provided for under the Migratory Bird Hunting and Conservation Stamp Act of 1934, and from advance appropriations against future duck stamp receipts, up to $200 million, as authorized by the Wetlands Loan Act (16 U.S.C.A. 715k-3 to 715k-5). Duck stamp receipts are available for expenditure without congressional appropriation, but loan act advances are available only to the extent that they are appropriated by Congress.

The other major source of acquisition funding is the Land and Water Conservation Fund, authorized in the Land and Water Conservation Fund Act of 1964 (16 U.S.C.A. 460l-4 to 460l-11), which is used to acquire lands for endangered species protection, interpretation and recreation, and congressionally authorized refuges. The Land and Water Conservation Fund is made up primarily of $1 million in motorboat fuel taxes, proceeds from the sale of surplus federal real property, and a portion of receipts from outer continental shelf oil and gas leasing. The Land and Water Conservation Fund moneys are available only to the extent appropriated by Congress and may not be used to acquire migratory bird habitat authorized under the MBCA.

Funding for refuge land acquisition varies widely depending on the level of congressional appropriations. Duck stamp receipts provide a dependable base level for acquisition, averaging just under $15 million a year since 1980. In years where appropriations under the Wetlands Loan Act and the Land and Water Conservation Fund are low, as in 1981 and 1982, duck stamps account for a significant portion of acquisition dollars. Since 1982, however, Congress generally has provided increasing and substantial appropriations for refuge acquisition, to record highs in FY 1985 of $21.3 million under the Wetlands Loan Act and $64.2 million under the Land and Water Conservation Fund. Under pressure to reduce the federal deficit, Congress in FY 1986 approved $14.9 million under the Loan Act and $40.4 million under the Land and Water Conservation Fund.

Since 1982, the Reagan administration has attempted to place a moratorium on FWS land acquisition. The administration repeatedly has requested only about $1.5 million yearly under the Land and Water Conservation Fund to cover certain mandatory costs and has requested no funds under the Wetlands Loan Act. The one exception was in the FY 1985 budget request, made in the 1984 presidential election year, which sought $57.5 million for land acquisition. With the FY 1986 budget, the administration resumed its proposal for an acquisition moratorium. Congress has repeatedly rejected the moratorium proposal.*

FWS priorities for land acquisition are developed from recommendations made by the managers of the various FWS programs. The most important considerations are the degree of threat to the resource, particularly if the damage is viewed as irreversible; the opportunity to round out an existing refuge unit to optimize its management; and the availability of a willing seller. These variables are analyzed relative to endangered and threatened species considerations and other top-priority wildlife issues. Members of Congress also play a large role in determining priorities by identifying areas that are important to their constituents.

## Organization and Operations

FWS organizes its resource-management activities into eight national programs, each supervised by a program manager. The National Wildlife Refuge System is administered within the Wildlife Resources Program. Various other programs provide technical support to the refuge program upon request by the Division of Refuge Management.

The Division of Refuge Management in Washington D.C. has responsibility for developing overall refuge policy, but specific program guidance, supervision, and oversight is provided at the regional level. The regional directors are responsible for FWS activities within their region and report directly to the FWS director. Each regional staff includes an assistant director for Wildlife Resources and, under him, a refuge supervisor who have line authority for refuges in the region.

Each refuge is run by a refuge manager, who has considerable responsibility over refuge management. With minimal supervision, the refuge manager inventories the refuge resources, maintains a relationship with the public, determines environmental impacts of biological processes and public use, alerts regional and directorate FWS officials to refuge problems, and, most importantly, is responsible for making determinations of compatibility—judging

*For further discussion of acquisition trends, see the chapter on wetlands protection.

Key Contacts in the National Wildlife Refuge System

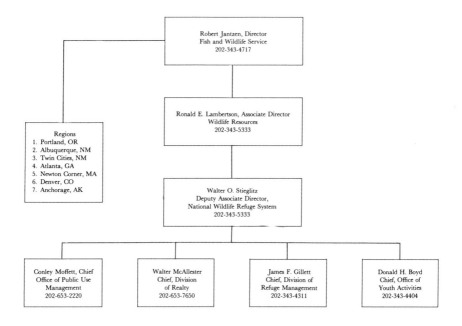

whether proposed economic and recreational uses of the refuges would be detrimental to its wildlife. However, in situations where compatibility decisions are controversial or involve sensitive species or habitats, the region oversees the determination and provides guidance to the refuge manager.

## Refuge Planning and Inventory

Each unit of the refuge system has one or more management plans that guide operations such as public use, habitat management, fire management, and oil and gas leasing. These management plans provide the broad framework for budgeting and short-term planning. More specific descriptions of work to be

Refuge Management Line Authority

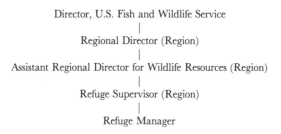

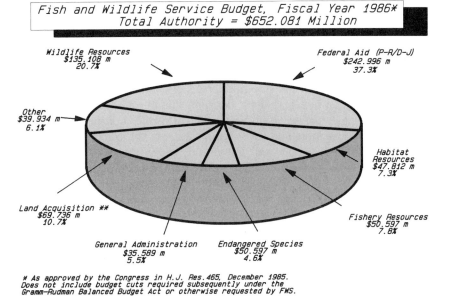

Fish and Wildlife Service Budget, Fiscal Year 1986*
Total Authority = $652.081 Million

Wildlife Resources
$135.108 m
20.7%

Federal Aid (P-R/D-J)
$242.996 m
37.3%

Other
$39.934 m
6.1%

Habitat
Resources
$47.812 m
7.3%

Land Acquisition **
$69.736 m
10.7%

Fishery Resources
$50.597 m
7.8%

General Administration
$35.589 m
5.5%

Endangered Species
$50.597 m
4.6%

* As approved by the Congress in H.J. Res.465, December 1985.
Does not include budget cuts required subsequently under the
Gramm-Rudman Balanced Budget Act or otherwise requested by FWS.
** Includes migratory bird conservation account
Source:  Budget Office, FWS

done at each refuge and funding and personnel requirements are included in annual work plans.

For certain refuges, FWS prepares master plans, documents that generally cover a 10-year to 20-year period and set long-term objectives for land-use management. Regional directors are responsible for determining whether a refuge needs a master plan prepared or revised. Refuges that do not have master plans identify long-term needs and objectives in their management plans.

A comprehensive inventory of the resources on a wildlife refuge is a critical component of the refuge management plan. The quality and extent of the inventory, determined by the refuge manager, vary from refuge to refuge and depend on the availability of money and manpower and the significance of the resource. Refuge managers are to determine which species will be the subject of the most extensive or intensive surveys by considering factors such as long-range and short-range goals, potential future conflicts with development, and the prospect of continued habitat loss and degradation. Top priorities for inventory are species that FWS has a general legal mandate to protect, such as endangered species, or species for the protection of which refuges have been specifically established. FWS officials say that good inventory data generally exists for the larger species, such as big game, and for the rarer species with a high degree of threat. Inventory data is kept at the refuge level and in some cases is computerized, but the data is not collected and centralized elsewhere.

In addition to formal inventories conducted by FWS, additional data comes from observations by local refuge users, bird watchers, and visitors, and from volunteers who donate time to assist in data-gathering operations. Under an administration policy of increasing volunteer contributions to public-land management, and because of funding constraints, FWS has moved to rely more and more on volunteer assistance in the gathering of such data.

Inventories are an integral component of compatibility decisions (discussed below) and all other resource decisions that affect refuge animal populations. The agency has come under harsh criticism for not having sufficient inventories of refuge biota and for not providing more clearly delineated goals to refuge managers. Despite the importance of inventory information, the FWS *Refuge Manual* recommends that refuge managers devote five percent of personnel and funding resources to this effort. FWS says this does not imply that inventory responsibilities are low priority and maintains that the current level of effort is satisfactory.

## Refuge Management

Refuge management falls into two major categories: management of the refuge's wildlife and the habitat on which it depends; and management of refuge uses, both recreational and economic. In addition, a large portion of refuge management is devoted to maintenance, including maintenance of habitat improvements, public-use facilities, and vehicles and equipment used in refuge-management activities. FWS has emphasized and devoted greater resources to its maintenance program in recent years, as discussed later.

## Resource Management

Refuge resources are managed to meet specific refuge purposes as prescribed in enabling legislation and/or to meet objectives set in the refuge management plans. In some cases, FWS may manage for enhancement of a particular species; in other cases, it may manage for diversity. FWS divides resource management efforts into several broad categories, as described below. Management activities to be conducted under each category are described in a management plan.

- Marsh and Water Management. Water and marshland are extremely important to refuges, especially for the production and conservation of waterfowl. On many refuges, FWS uses water-control structures such as dikes, pumps, and impoundments to modify the natural habitat to enhance waterfowl production.
- Grassland Management. Grasses are important as cover for ground-nesting birds, as forage for mammals, and as components in the diversity of habitat necessary to sustain a variety of wildlife species. FWS manipulation of grasslands includes cultivation of grasses as well as grazing and

haying, if they are compatible with wildlife-management objectives. As with other economic uses of the refuges, however, these practices often are controversial, since in many cases conservation groups disagree with the FWS determination that the uses are compatible with sound wildlife management.

- Cropland Management. FWS farms or permits farming on certain refuges in order to supplement natural food sources, provide cover for wildlife, and alleviate wildlife depredations on adjacent private lands. Current data show that 93,000 acres are cultivated on 93 refuges and 15 wetland management districts.
- Fire Management. In addition to preventing and fighting fires on refuges, FWS personnel engage in controlled burning to enhance habitat for wildlife—for example, by thinning out underbrush to allow growth of small edible plants. Prescribed burning is used on 374 refuges.

FWS also does some direct manipulation of wildlife itself. It runs a number of captive-breeding programs to restore endangered species, primarily under the Endangered Species Program. Occasionally, FWS will use hunting and trapping to reduce populations, but for the most part hunting on refuges is done for recreation rather than for wildlife-management purposes.

***Public-Use and Economic-Use Management.*** Although wildlife conservation is almost always the primary purpose of refuge management, two key laws governing refuge administration authorize other uses of the refuges under certain circumstances. The National Wildlife Refuge System Administration Act of 1966, which consolidated the various federal refuges into a single system under FWS jurisdiction, authorized the secretary of the Interior to "permit the use of any areas within the System for any purpose, including but not limited to hunting, fishing, public recreation and accommodations, and access *whenever he determines that such uses are compatible with the major purposes for which such areas were established*" (emphasis added). The Refuge Recreation Act of 1962 (16 U.S.C.A. 460k to 460k-4) authorized the secretary to administer the system for public recreation, but "only to the extent that it is practicable and not inconsistent with the primary objectives for which each particular area is established." In addition, the enabling legislation for specific refuges may authorize or require FWS to allow certain non-wildlife activities on the refuge.

Thus, within these constraints, FWS can permit a variety of recreation and economic uses, including furbearer trapping, logging, grazing, haying, mineral extraction, and oil and other energy exploration and development. Receipts from these activities are used in part to cover FWS administration costs related to these activities. The remainder of the receipts are paid to the counties in which refuge lands are located as compensation for the counties' inability to tax federal refuge lands. However, receipts usually are not sufficient to cover the payments and additional funds must be appropriated. In its early years, the Reagan administration attempted to increase economic uses on refuges, in part to increase receipts to the federal government, but this effort was largely blocked by public and congressional opposition.

*Compatibility Determinations.* Except where otherwise mandated by law, FWS must determine whether a particular use is compatible with refuge resources before permitting it.* Compatibility determinations are normally made by the refuge manager in accordance with guidelines developed by FWS. Under these guidelines, a compatible use is defined as one that "will not materially interfere with or detract from the purpose(s) for which the refuge was established." Compatible uses may support refuge purposes or may have a neutral effect. In making a compatibility determination, the refuge manager must first determine if the use is compatible with refuge purposes strictly on biological grounds. After making such a determination, he must further consider applicable laws, FWS policy, and public opinion.

The analysis begins with the submission of a description of the proposed use, which must include information on the location, timing, and duration of the activity and must specify how the use will be conducted and the reasons for and objectives of the activity.

The refuge manager then assesses the impact of the use on refuge purposes as listed in the document authorizing the refuge's creation. In assessing impacts, the refuge manager must consider direct effects, such as disturbance of wildlife or habitat destruction; indirect effects, for example, if the use will require the diversion of funds or personnel from existing management programs; and long-term impacts. Long-term impacts include effects that are not apparent until long after the activity has ceased. Oil excavation projects, for example, may slightly alter the geologic infrastructure of an area with no immediately discernible effects, but could impair groundwater recharge systems in the long run.

The refuge manager may make certain stipulations on the activity— such as restricting it to certain times of the day or to a smaller area than was proposed originally—to lessen or avoid potential damages that would otherwise make the activity clearly incompatible with refuge purposes. However, FWS does not allow incompatible impacts of activities on refuges to be justified by the provision of compensating mitigation elsewhere. For example, an activity that caused permanent wetland loss on a refuge would not be justified by the creation or enhancement of wetlands elsewhere.

The refuge manager is required to use all available tools when preparing use-impact assessments, including planning documents, research data, refuge inventories, and earlier documented compatibility determinations for a similar

---

*Refuge system units that are administered under cooperative agreement between FWS and another federal agency may be subject to rules made by the other agency that supersede FWS regulations. For example, on lands cooperatively managed by the Bureau of Reclamation and FWS, BuRec can issue rights-of-way based on its own judgment; no compatibility requirement has to be met and FWS objections can be overruled.

use. He is not, however, required to conduct new population studies. In some cases, critics have charged that many refuges lack adequate inventory data, which they believe hinders the refuge manager's ability to make an informed compatibility determination.

Based on the biological review, the refuge manager classifies the use under one of three categories: (1) clearly incompatible, which precludes any use; (2) neutral effect, such as recreational uses in areas set aside for migratory-bird enhancement where the use would not interfere with refuge purposes; and (3) definitely compatible, where the use will enhance or add to the purposes for which the refuge was established. Then the proposal is evaluated on legal and other grounds, including adherence to FWS and Interior Department policies, consistency with overall refuge system objectives, the ability of refuge facilities or funding levels to sustain the use, and public opinion.

Finally, FWS must consider additional issues, most notably certain rights of private parties to use or develop certain resources on the refuges. These include water rights, rights or privileges affected by a treaty or other legally binding agreements, and reserved rights to explore for and develop oil and gas beneath refuge lands. Under what circumstances such rights can be exercised is one of the most hotly debated topics in refuge management, as discussed later.

The refuge manager renders the final compatability decision, except in the following cases, when he must submit his decision to the regional director for review: when the proposal involves opening a refuge to hunting, fishing, or other public use; when an applicant for a special-use permit appeals the refuge manager's denial of such a permit on the basis of incompatibility; whenever other documentation, such as an environmental assessment, must be prepared; and whenever deemed necessary by the regional director or the refuge manager.

Management of public uses of the refuges—particularly for recreational and educational uses—is a significant element of refuge management in some units and is of increasing importance and controversy as FWS seeks to expand public use of the refuges. The general issue of what uses should be permitted within the national wildlife refuges and under what conditions is one of the most frequent sources of controversy over refuge management. A number of examples of such debates are covered in the Current Issues section of this chapter.

## Research

Research is conducted on refuges both to develop a better understanding of ecological relationships on the refuge and to contribute to scientific knowledge in general. Refuges often are considered ideal field locations for research, and many projects conducted on wildlife refuges have yielded important new biological data.

Research projects may be initiated by a variety of sources, including the

FWS wildlife research and development programs, universities, wildlife and fishery co-op units, and refuge staff. Refuge research studies also can take advantage of local educational or naturalist associations who may initiate projects themselves or who may undertake projects at the suggestion of the refuge manager. Research subjects cover a wide spectrum, including management studies, environmental monitoring, and scientific studies of individual species, populations, and ecosystems.

## Wilderness in the Refuge System

With the enactment of the Wilderness Act in 1964 (16 U.S.C.A. 1121-1136), the secretary of the Interior was required to review all roadless areas of at least 5,000 acres in size and all roadless islands of any size in the National Wildlife Refuge System for possible designation as wilderness. The study, completed in 1974, led to the congressional designation of 67 refuge wilderness areas totaling 19.3 million acres as of the end of 1984. An additional 3.4 million acres on 26 refuges have been recommended for wilderness status but have not yet been designated. FWS interprets the Wilderness Act as requiring wilderness review only on refuges in existence at the time of the act's passage and does not review the wilderness potential of refuges established after 1964. The exception is the Alaska refuges, where under specific direction of the 1980 Alaska National Interest Lands Conservation Act (16 U.S.C.A. 3101), FWS is conducting wilderness review of 16 study areas encompassing almost 58 million acres.

Although refuge areas designated as wilderness remain under FWS jurisdiction, the Wilderness Act requires a different standard of management for wilderness than for other refuge areas. The act defines wilderness as an area of undeveloped federal land retaining its primeval character and influence, without permanent improvements or human habitation, which is protected and managed so as to preserve its natural conditions. To achieve this goal, Section 4 of the act prohibits numerous activities in wilderness, including commercial enterprise; permanent roads, except as necessary to meet minimum administration requirements; temporary roads; use of motor vehicles, motorized equipment, and motorboats, or other forms of mechanical transport (except for snowmobiles in Alaskan wilderness); landing of aircraft; and structures or installations. The act makes no specific mention of wildlife and does not specify what types of habitat or wildlife management may or may not be allowed. FWS allows such activities if they do not damage the wilderness character of an area, a determination made on a case-by-case basis by the refuge managers.

## Budget

Operation of the National Wildlife Refuge System is funded primarily as part of the Wildlife Resources Program, although other FWS programs also pro-

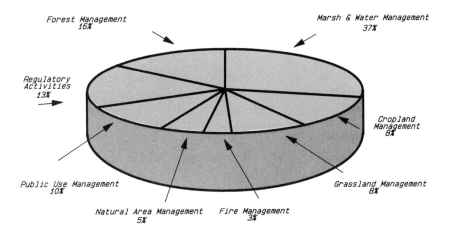

Distribution of National Wildlife Refuge Operation Funds
(Exclusilve of Alaska)

Forest Management
16%

Marsh & Water Management
37%

Regulatory
Activities
13%

Cropland
Management
8%

Public Use Management
10%

Grassland Management
8%

Natural Area Management
5%

Fire Management
3%

vide a small amount of funds. For example, the Fishery Resources and Endangered Species Programs together provided $2.8 million for refuge operations in 1985.

Refuge operations and maintenance accounts for a substantial portion of FWS budget. In FY 1986, Congress appropriated $381.53 million to FWS, with $105.63 million, nearly 30 percent of the total, allocated to refuges. Most of the funding, $71.43 million or 68 percent of total refuge funding, is for operations, with the remaining 32 percent allocated to maintenance.

The refuge budget for FY 1986 represents a 43 percent increase in funding since FY 1983—the first year that FWS accounted for refuge funds in a separate budget line item—compared to a 16 percent increase in total FWS appropriations during the same time period. Most of the increase in refuge spending has come in the maintenance portion of the budget, which has nearly tripled since 1983 as a result of the administration's increased emphasis on

Funding for Refuge Operations and Maintenance, FY 1983–1986

| Year | Appropriations in millions of dollars | | |
|---|---|---|---|
| | Operations | Maintenance | Total |
| 1983 | $62.2 m | $11.6 m | $ 73.8 m |
| 1984 | 63.5 | 26.8 m | 90.3 |
| 1985 | 67.8 | 32.9 m | 100.7 |
| 1986 | 71.4 | 34.2 m | 105.63 |
| Percent Change from 1983–86 | +15% | +195% | +43% |

maintenance. Funding for refuge operations increased 15 percent during the same period.

Another important aspect of refuge funding is the land-acquisition budget. This was discussed earlier under Refuge Acquisition.

# Current Program Trends

For the most part, the refuge program in 1985 continued initiatives begun in previous years. These include improving maintenance of refuge facilities and equipment, promoting increased public use of refuges for recreational and educational purposes, and making increased use of volunteers to carry out refuge work—all efforts strongly promoted by the Reagan administration. FWS also has nearly completed a new system for identifying refuge land-acquisition priorities.

## Increased Public Use

In FY 1985, FWS continued its emphasis on encouraging increased public use of refuges in an effort to change what it believes is its antiquated image of keeping people away from refuges in order to maintain refuge integrity. FWS says the future of the refuge system lies in part in maintaining and increasing public support, through direct participation and enjoyment, to help keep the refuge system a vital and energetic priority. Thus, current FWS policy is to expand public use of the system to the extent practicable, so long as it is compatible with refuge purposes.

FWS says that "one of the best approaches to protecting wildlife resources is through increased public awareness" (Department of the Interior 1985a). To further this goal in FY 1985, FWS received an increase from Congress of nearly $500,000 to enhance public-use programs by providing training for managers and public-use specialists and by placing or upgrading exhibits in visitor stations. This funding was cut back to $287,000 in FY 1986, and these funds will be used generally to support public-use programs on the refuges.

As part of this policy of maximizing public use, FWS is moving to open all refuges to hunting and fishing wherever compatible with refuge purposes. In 1984, FWS initiated new hunting programs on 13 refuges and new fishing programs on three refuges and expanded existing hunting programs to provide for longer hunting seasons and more acreage and more species available to hunting. During 1985, another 15 new hunting programs were initiated on seven refuges. As of October 31, 1985, 255 refuges—60 percent of the total— were open to hunting, and 197 refuges—47 percent of the total—were open to fishing. The emphasis on permitting hunting in refuges is controversial and is discussed in more detail under Current Issues.

National Wildlife Refuge System Public Uses (Visits)

| Activity | FY 1982 | FY 1983 | FY 1984 | FY 1985* | FY 1986* |
|---|---|---|---|---|---|
| Interpretation | 5,638,000 | 5,564,000 | 6,034,000 | 6,200,000 | 6,710,000 |
| Education | 131,000 | 129,000 | 239,000 | 240,000 | 260,000 |
| Hunting | 1,087,000 | 1,120,000 | 1,152,000 | 1,300,000 | 1,300,000 |
| Fishing | 4,999,000 | 4,598,000 | 4,657,000 | 5,000,000 | 5,200,000 |
| Other Consumptive Wildlife Recreation | 724,000 | 772,000 | 777,000 | 800,000 | 850,000 |
| Wildlife Observation | 13,809,000 | 12,416,000 | 14,066,000 | 14,200,000 | 14,400,000 |
| Non-Wildlife Oriented Recreation (camping, ORVs, etc.) | 4,051,000 | 3,540,000 | 2,992,000 | 3,000,000 | 3,200,000 |
| Totals | 30,439,000 | 28,139,000 | 29,917,000 | 30,740,000 | 31,920,000 |

*Estimated figures for this FY
NOTE: These projections are based on the number of refuges currently open to hunting. This figure will increase significantly as more refuges are opened.
Source: U.S. Fish and Wildlife Service

## Accelerated Refuge Maintenance and Management Program

1985 marked the second year of a major initiative to improve maintenance on refuges—the Accelerated Maintenance and Management Program—but the effort already is falling short of its ambitious goals. The Accelerated Refuge Maintenance and Management Program, the counterpart of a similar new program in the national park system, was developed to rehabilitate and modernize refuge facilities and equipment that had been allowed to deteriorate. FWS estimates that prior to 1984, roughly $6 million a year was spent on the upkeep of refuge facilities, including water-management facilities, dikes, dams, roads, bridges, and vehicles—far below the roughly $60 million FWS estimates is necessary to protect its more than $2 billion investment in these facilities. In 1984, FWS embarked on an ambitious five-year effort to increase annual maintenance funding by $8 billion a year, with the goal of establishing a permanent maintenance fund of $60 million a year by FY 1989.

The maintenance budget has risen substantially over the past three fiscal years, but the Accelerated Refuge Maintenance and Management Program is still significantly short of its goals. The Accelerated Refuge Maintenance and Management Program was funded at $14.6 million in 1984, but was increased to only $15.9 million in FY 1985 and $18.9 million in FY 1986 (before Gramm-Rudman cuts)—far below the target level of a yearly $8 million increase. FWS staff say the Accelerted Refuge Maintenance and Management Program is still a high priority, but that it will take more time than anticipated to build funding to sufficient levels.

The Accelerated Refuge Maintenance and Management funds are allocated to refuges under priorities determined by the FWS director. Maintenance activities related to health and safety, such as the upkeep of sewage-treatment plants, domestic water-supply systems, and road and vehicle maintenance, currently are the top priorities for Accelerated Refuge Maintenance and Management funding. FWS stresses, however, that the Accelerated Refuge Maintenance and Management Program, though concentrating on physical facilities, will have an enormous impact on habitat and wildlife. And while refuge maintenance has received the sharpest increase in the refuge budget, Congress at the same time has provided additional funds in the operations portion of the budget—$5 million in both FY 1984 and FY 1985—specifically to address resource problems as well.

## Increased Use of Volunteers

Volunteers on national wildlife refuges are one of the fastest growing components of public use. Volunteers provided 527,150 hours of work worth $3.6 million in 1984, a tripling of the volunteer effort over 1982 levels. Complete figures are not available for FY 1985, but FWS estimates that volunteer assistance continued at about 1984 levels.

The increased use of volunteers has a number of benefits. Volunteers accomplish valuable work, such as improving educational programs and visitor facilities, collecting data, and conducting population surveys and counts. As discussed earlier, many refuge managers include volunteers in management planning and rely on them to help in censusing. The use of volunteers also helps build a more informed and committed constituency for the wildlife refuge system. FWS hopes to continue to increase its use of volunteers, saying there is much additional assistance they could provide.

## The Land Acquisition Priority System

In 1983, the Department of the Interior directed FWS to develop a standardized procedure for evaluating and ranking proposed acquisitions. With the likely prospect of tight acquisition budgets ahead, such a standardized procedure is meant to help ensure that FWS spends its funds on top priority areas. It also will help the Service justify the need for such funds.

In response to the departmental directive, FWS has developed the Land Acquisition Priority System, a computer matrix that classifies, evaluates, and ranks each proposed acquisition based on its value as one of four types of habitat: habitat for endangered species, habitat for migratory birds, general wildlife habitat of national significance, and wetlands of national significance. The considerations used in evaluating land parcels in each of these four categories are described below.

*Endangered Species.* Under this category, a potential acquisition area is ranked according to its value to the endangered and/or threatened species that use it. FWS will acquire areas for endangered or threatened species only if their acquisition is part of a recovery plan. In evaluating a particular parcel, FWS considers the following:

1. Habitat value
   a. will acquisition prevent a species from becoming extinct
   b. will acquisition enhance the probability of that species' recovery
   c. will *not* acquiring the area prevent recovery
2. Species values
   a. what is the level of threat to the species; is extinction probable or immediate
   b. what is the potential for recovery: are threats to the species well understood and easily alleviated; are the species' biological and ecological limiting factors well understood; is intensive management necessary
   c. is there more than one threatened or endangered species on the site

*Migratory Birds.* Acquisitions under this category are those that will benefit migratory bird species and populations of greatest interest that are being limited or negatively affected by habitat problems. Species for which these lands may be acquired have important ecological, aesthetic, or sport-hunting values, but none are threatened or endangered species. Sites are ranked on the following factors:

1. Habitat value
   a. is loss or degradation of a seasonal habitat (breeding, wintering, migrating, or molting) a contributing factor to a diminishing population and, if so, is it the primary factor, an important factor, or one of many factors
2. Species value
   a. what is the trend of the species or population, i.e., the long-term indicator of population health or numbers
   b. what is the status of the species or population

*Nationally Significant Wildlife Habitats.* Sites can be considered for acquisition under this category *only* if they contain a one-of-a-kind concentration or variety of wildlife and/or plant species. Sites are evaluated on the following factors:

1. Contribution to FWS goals
   a. is the site significantly different from others that already are protected
   b. does the area fall within the purview of a state natural heritage program or the National Park Service National Landmark Inventory
2. Habitat value
   a. does the area contain wildlife habitat that is declining in quality
   b. does the area contain a highly vulnerable wildlife community
   c. is loss of habitat quality and/or quantity likely to occur in the near future, and how immediate is the danger

3. Public use value
    a. is the area readily accessible to large numbers of people

*Nationally Significant Wetlands.* FWS considers all wetlands to be valuable, and any wetland may be eligible for acquisition. Wetland-site rankings are based on the following considerations:

1. the contribution the wetland makes to wildlife, including endangered and threatened species, migratory birds, and resident species;
2. the threat of loss, both of the particular site and of the type of wetland it represents;
3. the contribution it makes to various wetland functions, including quality and quantity of surface and ground water, flood control, and commercial and sport fisheries.

The Land Acquisition Priority System has been released as a final draft and should be implemented by mid-1986. However, because of the lead time required in developing agency budget requests, the system first will be used to help formulate land-acquisition priorities in the FY 1988 budget, to be submitted to Congress in February 1987.

## Biological Monitoring

FWS, in its commitment to the study and resolution of key resource problems, places particular emphasis on water quality, waste disposal, and noxious-weed control. FWS says it is emphasizing the need to increase biological investigations to ascertain whether present management practices are the most desirable and says it will continue to conduct baseline assessments of various contaminants and the effects of energy and mining exploration on refuge systems. In 1985, FWS added to the *Refuge Manual* new guidance on biological monitoring, emphasizing the importance of basic science and describing record-keeping methodologies and other related subjects. However, no increased funds or personnel have been devoted for this purpose and no specific directives for increased biological monitoring have been made to refuge managers.

## Current Issues

A number of problems currently affect refuge management. These include off-site threats to various refuges, FWS refuge-management actions seen by critics as detrimental to wildlife, and lack of funding for management activities authorized by statute. Many of the controversies stem from the broad discretion given to the secretary of the Interior by the Refuge Administration Act to allow various refuge uses that may conflict with wildlife conservation. A sample of recent conflicts is discussed here.

## Increased Hunting on Refuges

FWS emphasis on increasing public use of the refuges has been controversial from the start. Conservation groups have charged that heavy public use is often incompatible with wildlife and wilderness objectives. Pointing to the overcrowding currently creating resource problems in a number of national parks, these groups say that FWS should increase such use only after careful study and planning to ensure that use does not exceed refuge carrying capacity.

But by far the most controversial non-commercial use of refuges is hunting. In addition to concerns about the impacts on the wildlife resources, the promotion of more hunting on refuges is protested by other types of recreationists who consider hunting incompatible with their activities and by those who are philosophically opposed to hunting.

Hunting on refuges has increased in fits and starts through the system's history. Before 1949, hunting was allowed primarily on refuges where it had been a traditional activity before the refuge was incorporated into the system, but was prohibited on migratory-bird refuges, which were considered to be "inviolate sanctuaries" under the Migratory Bird Conservation Act. In 1949, an act of Congress that raised the price of duck stamps also authorized the secretary of the Interior to allow hunting on 25 percent of each area acquired with duck-stamp receipts. Various other laws further expanded the secretary's authority to allow hunting. Today, the secretary of the Interior can authorize hunting of resident species on all refuges, as long as it is compatible with refuge purposes, and can authorize migratory waterfowl hunting on 40 percent of any given refuge, although this restriction can be waived if the secretary finds it would be beneficial to the species.

As described earlier, FWS has rapidly expanded hunting opportunities on wildlife refuges in recent years. In 1984, in order to standardize procedures for increasing visitor use, FWS issued to field staff a document entitled "Public Use Requirements." The document, which reiterates FWS policy on hunting on refuges, directs refuge managers to "provide a quality hunting program with sound resource management" and to "investigate ways to increase hunting opportunities, if practical, that conform to Service policy" (8 Refuge Manual 5.1). FWS says the concept of a refuge as a total sanctuary is outdated and firmly stands behind a goal of creating a hunting program on every refuge where it is legally and biologically appropriate and justifiable.

The Buenos Aires National Wildlife Refuge in Arizona illustrates the type of controversy that can arise from the expansion of hunting on the refuge system. The refuge was acquired in late February 1985 for the protection of the masked bobwhite quail, a federally listed endangered species. FWS plans to reintroduce the quail on a 50,000-acre area within the refuge, approximately 42 percent of total refuge acreage.

In May 1985, FWS proposed to open Buenos Aires to hunting in order to allow the continuance of hunting activities that occurred prior to refuge designation. Although the bobwhite reintroduction area would be closed to hunting, opponents of the proposal charged that the hunting program—which allowed hunters to use a limited number of hunting dogs and lead shot— would impair the reintroduction plan severely. FWS says that hunter education, posting of the closed area, law enforcement, and population monitoring will reduce the likelihood of any adverse impacts from hunting and has allowed hunting on the refuge to proceed.

In addition to opening new areas to hunting, in 1984 FWS revised its approach to hunting regulation, provoking further controversy and a lawsuit. Prior to 1984, FWS regions annually issued regulations for each refuge open to hunting. These regulations generally adopted state hunting regulations, with modifications as necessary to ensure that FWS meets its management responsibilities. In 1984, FWS replaced the refuge-by-refuge approach with a single, codified set of refuge hunting regulations, with variations for individual refuges as needed. The code regulations remain in effect on each refuge until amended by subsequent notices in the *Federal Register*. Thus, although FWS says the refuges still review their hunting regulations each year, the consolidated regulations remove the process which had helped ensure consistent, regular annual review reissuance. As in the past, this consolidated approach relies heavily on state regulations, with modifications as necessary.

The codification of the hunting regulations prompted the Humane Society of the United States to sue FWS (*Humane Society of the United States v. Hodel*). The suit notes the rapid increase of refuges opened to hunting during 1984 alone and seeks an injunction against the implementation of the hunting regulations on the following grounds:

- that the full impact of the regulations has not been studied. The Humane Society also contends no adequate opportunity was given for study and comment on the proposed regulations;
- that the intent of codifying the hunting regulations is to circumvent the annual study and justification process that previously was required;
- that funds and manpower have been diverted illegally to managing these new hunting programs;
- that positive compatibility determinations were made hastily and inadequately;
- that, historically, hunting has been permitted in refuges only under very narrow circumstances and that FWS has violated stipulations of the Refuge Recreation Act, which prohibits recreational use until the secretary determines that it will not interfere with the primary purposes for which the refuge was established; and
- that FWS has delegated administrative authority to the states unlawfully by transferring to them responsibility for overseeing hunting activities.

The case is still in litigation, with oral arguments scheduled to begin in spring 1986.

## Trapping/Steel-Jaw Traps

Trapping continues to be a controversial practice on national wildlife refuges, mainly because of concerns that trapping is inhumane. FWS regards trapping, currently allowed on 115 refuges, as an effective tool for wildlife population management and a legitimate recreational and economic activity. Trapping programs are instituted to meet the following goals:

- to minimize damage by furbearers to physical facilities;
- to expedite the attainment of goals for migratory and nonmigratory birds, mammals, and endangered species by trapping species that depredate on them;
- to minimize high population densities of certain species that have the potential to transmit contagious diseases;
- to provide educational and recreational opportunities.

Trapping programs are governed by state fish and game regulations and permit requirements. In addition, trapping on wildlife refuges requires a federal permit and usually is conducted under a trapping plan, except on waterfowl production areas that are open to public trapping simply in accordance with state regulations.

Opponents of trapping charge that it is inhumane because the most widely used trap, the steel-jaw leghold trap, causes excruciating pain to the animal it ensnares. FWS acknowledges this objection, but contends that leghold traps are the only traps that can withstand variations in environmental conditions and that are available in the full range of sizes needed to accommodate most furbearers. Animal welfare proponents say that a wide variety of humane traps are available—such as the leg snare, the easy-on-'em snare, and the box trap—all of which they say have proven reliability for a single target species. Since most trappers pursue only one or two species at a time, opponents of steel-jaw traps say trappers do not need a single trap that is effective for all furbearer species.

In response to the animal welfare movement's demand for more humane trapping regulations, FWS is testing leg snares and other similar traps, such as Conibear traps, but says it has not found any model which can be used as widely, irrespective of the species involved, as the steel-jaw leghold trap.

## Oil and Gas Exploration and the D'Arbonne National Wildlife Refuge

A potentially precedent-setting lawsuit regarding oil and gas drilling on the D'Arbonne National Wildlife Refuge in Louisiana may ultimately determine how much control FWS has over oil and gas activities on much of its lands. In the D'Arbonne case, the government has asked the court to determine specifically whether FWS can require a special-use permit for the development of subsurface resources that underlie federal refuges but are owned by private interests. Such rights occur on refuges where the federal government purchased overlying land from private parties, but did not purchase the underlying mineral rights. According to FWS estimates, the majority of oil and gas activities on refuges occur where there are such private rights: in 48 of the 67 refuges units in the lower 48 states that have oil and gas activities, the activities occur where there are reserved or excepted subsurface rights. FWS estimates that parties other than FWS hold the rights to oil and gas underlying 1.6 million acres of the refuge system, to coal under 1.2 million acres, and to other mineral resources under 1.7 million acres.*

The D'Arbonne controversy erupted in 1984 over FWS supervision of oil and gas drilling by a private firm that holds rights to oil and gas underlying the refuge. About 145 gas wells exist on the refuge, most of them drilled before D'Arbonne was acquired by FWS in 1977. The current dispute began when the firm, TerrOnne Corporation, entered the refuge and began drilling operations without an FWS permit. The company planned to drill 58 new wells on the 17,000-acre refuge.

The Department of the Interior historically has taken the position that a use associated with a reserved right, such as oil, gas, and mineral exploration, overrides any test of compatibility, since the holder of the reserved right must, by law, be afforded reasonable access to those rights. The prohibition of such rights, according to Interior's legal interpretation, would constitute an illegal taking of an individual's property. Furthermore, FWS provides little guidance to refuge managers on how to cope with inevitable conflicts from such mineral development. For these reasons, the refuge manager at D'Arbonne thought he had no authority over the TerrOnne operation and did not require a permit for the drilling.

The local Sierra Club chapter, however, sought a court order to stop the drilling on the grounds that FWS had failed to issue a permit and had not done an environmental analysis of the drilling activity. This helped prompt FWS to obtain a biological opinion from its endangered species staff on the effects of the drilling on the red-cockaded woodpecker, an endangered species that inhabits D'Arbonne. The opinion found that the drilling would drive the woodpeckers from the refuge. In addition, the suit caused FWS to seek an opinion on its permitting authority from the Interior Department's solicitor's office, which determined that FWS could indeed require a permit. TerrOnne, however, initially refused to agree to a permit that required some conditions for environmental protection, and a district court denied an FWS request for a preliminary injunction to stop the drilling. After further negotiations with TerrOnne, FWS issued a "compromise" permit that contained some conditions to protect the woodpecker, but also contained many loopholes.

---

*Some of these areas overlap, so that the total acreage in reserved or excepted rights is less than the total of these three figures; in addition, these acreage figures include areas where the mineral rights were reserved, but the mineral resources are insignificant and unlikely to be developed.

The Sierra Club, joined by the Sierra Club Legal Defense Fund and Defenders of Wildlife, pressed its suit and sought to block drilling under the compromise permit, charging that FWS did not comply with the National Environmental Policy Act, that the drilling would destroy red-cockaded woodpecker habitat, that the destruction represented a taking of wildlife prohibited by the Endangered Species Act, and that FWS did not properly follow mandates under existing authorities to protect the refuge.

The district court denied the environmentalists' request for an injunction, but delayed ruling on the substantive issues in the case. As a result of the suit, however, FWS agreed to conduct an environmental analysis of the drilling project. In 1985, FWS issued a draft environmental assessment that included recommendations for additional requirements for the drilling permit, including a spacing requirement of one well per 40 acres in certain parts of the refuge. FWS planned to incorporate these new conditions into TerrOnne's drilling permit. However, TerrOnne, which continued to drill throughout the entire period, indicated it would refuse to accept the revised permit terms, and FWS backed off the proposal, believing it had no leverage to force the company to do so.

In October 1985, the Sierra Club Legal Defense Fund sought final judgment on its suit against drilling in D'Arbonne and again asked for a temporary injunction to halt environmental damages from the operation. According to a Sierra Club Legal Defense Fund attorney, the federal government has all the legal power it needs under the property clause of the Constitution to protect the lands it manages from activities that would adversely affect them or their resident wildlife. In the meantime, Interior has asked the court to rule on the basic question of whether it can require a special-use permit for drilling on the refuge, since without clarification of this point FWS believes TerrOnne will continue to refuse to abide by stricter permit terms. The Sierra Club Legal Defense Fund's request for a temporary injunction was denied, and the judge has said he will rule on Interior's suit, regarding its authority to require a permit, before considering the issues brought by environmentalists.

In the meantime, a similar case has arisen on Ouachita NWR, also in Louisiana. In this instance, the federal government has brought suit against the IMC Corporation for initiating natural-gas drilling on the Upper Ouachita without an FWS special-use permit. The Sierra Club, Defenders of Wildlife, and the Baton Rouge Audubon Society, all represented by the Sierra Club Legal Defense Fund, have filed a motion to intervene on the government's behalf. The court, presided over by the same judge now hearing the D'Arbonne case, denied a preliminary injunction to halt the drilling, and the case is pending.

In part as a result of the D'Arbonne situation, on May 20, 1985, FWS issued a notice of intent to review its existing regulations (50 Code of Federal Regulations 29.32) governing the exercise of reserved or excepted mineral rights on the National Wildlife Refuge System. FWS is seeking public comment on how the regulations might be revised and is considering such issues as whether it should be required to issue permits, approval of a plan of operations prior to the drilling, and for a performance bond to ensure compliance with permit terms. FWS has not yet proposed any actual regulatory changes because the agency has decided to complete an environmental impact statement on the proposed rule changes in the context of a larger environmental impact statement, still in the planning stages, on all refuge-system operations. In addition, Interior is first reviewing a number of legal issues, including whether revised regulations would apply retroactively to mineral rights transferred prior to promulgation of the new rules. And, of course, the court's decision in the D'Arbonne case may well influence the content of any changes in the regulations.

## Predator Control and Grazing on Malheur National Wildlife Refuge

Recent debate surrounding management of Malheur National Wildlife Refuge in Oregon illustrates the type of debate that can arise over two often controversial activities on national wildlife refuges—livestock grazing and predator control—activities that conservation organizations often believe are not compatible with refuge purposes.

Malheur National Wildlife Refuge encompasses 184,000 acres of shallow marsh, small ponds, irrigated meadows, alkaline lakes, and grass and sagebrush uplands. Malheur is an important spring and fall gathering point for Pacific Flyway waterfowl and is considered one of the best birdwatching spots in the Pacific Northwest. In addition, Malheur is the single most important nesting area for the Central Valley population of greater sandhill cranes, considered by FWS to be a "sensitive" species in the region.

After the establishment of Malheur National Wildlife Refuge, FWS allowed cattle grazing, a traditional use in the area, to continue but restricted grazing to fewer than 40,000 animal unit months a year.* During the 1940s, however, the grazing program began a rapid acceleration. By 1972, the amount of acreage open to grazing had tripled. By 1975, Malheur accounted for approximately 28 percent of all grazing in the entire wildlife refuge system. The upsurge in grazing corresponded with a drop of more than 40 percent of duck nesting success on the refuge. Total waterfowl production declined from 151,000 ducklings and goslings in 1948 to 13,300 in 1973, more than a 90-percent drop.

Intensive grazing and trampling by cattle of nesting cover also was causing native plant cover to be replaced by patches of thistle or invaders, which

*An animal unit month is a standard grazing unit equal to the forage consumed in a month by one cow.

FWS then had to control with herbicides. Grazing fences destroyed or divided many nesting territories, feeding grounds, and roosting sites and were responsible for many deaths of birds and deer from entanglement. In addition, haying operations on the refuge required intensive irrigation, which directly threatened nests of both waterfowl and sandhill cranes. By the mid-1970s, visitors to Malheur began to complain about the cattle, the overgrazed habitat, and the greatly reduced bird counts.

In response to these problems, the refuge manager at Malheur began an effort to reduce livestock grazing and to improve sandhill crane habitat. By 1982, cattle grazing was reduced to 22 percent of the 1973 level, and many fences had been dismantled and lowered.

In spite of these efforts, sandhill crane populations continued to decline, from an estimated 236 pairs in 1971 to 186 pairs in 1985. The cause of this decline, however, is currently debated. Unusual climatic conditions have caused heavy flooding on the refuge in recent years, which not only has inundated some crane nesting areas but has prompted the granting of emergency grazing and haying permits for nonflooded areas on the refuge to neighboring ranchers whose lands were flooded and could not be grazed. Moreover, sedimentation and pesticide use from upstream logging operations have caused water quality in the refuge to decline.

FWS, however, says the decline also corresponds with the reduction of coyote control on the refuge, which began in the early 1970s, and maintains that predation is the major cause of the crane's recent decline. An interagency environmental assessment was prepared to study the initiation of a predator control program to offset crane losses, and FWS proposed a program targeted primarily against coyotes, raccoons, and ravens that would involve aerial gunning, trapping, and denning of coyotes and injections of the selective toxicant DRC-1339 into chicken eggs placed in areas to resemble crane nests.

The proposed predator control program has been criticized on a number of grounds. Critics charge that FWS did not consider adequately the effects on the cranes of flooding and water quality problems, which the critics contend are the primary cause of the decline. They also criticize the environmental assessment's lack of provisions to reduce grazing and haying—still components of management—activities that the critics believe cannot be justified on the refuge while there is still a possibility that they might contribute to the reduction in crane nesting success. Finally, they criticize the intended methods of predator control, arguing that the methods could affect endangered and threatened wildlife on the refuge, including the American peregrine falcon and the northern bald eagle. The environmental assessment did not study the possible effects of the predator control program on nontarget species, usually a consideration in such programs.

In spite of these concerns, FWS approved the predator control program early in 1986, and shooting of coyotes is scheduled to begin in late winter.

## Changes to Predator Control Policy

In general, predator control has not been utilized extensively on national wildlife refuges. However, with the increased emphasis on migratory-waterfowl production under the Reagan administration, and under pressure from waterfowl hunters to increase migratory bird numbers, the Interior Department appears to be moving to accelerate predator control on refuges where it might benefit waterfowl populations. A 1983 memo from department officials directed FWS to stress the "controlled removal of mammalian, avian, or reptilian predators which are present on areas within the refuge system where the primary objective is the production of waterfowl and where these predators are significantly limiting waterfowl production" (Memo from Robert E. Putz 1983). To accomplish this goal, Interior anticipates "that a moderate amount of reprogramming of funds may be required."

In June 1985, FWS issued to the field, as part of the *Refuge Manual*, a revised policy on predator management. The revised manual states that it is FWS policy "to aggressively implement predator management in those circumstances where a determination has been made that waterfowl production objectives are being compromised on Service lands due to predation" (7 *Refuge Manual* 3 Exhibit 2). It specified, however, that the policy "is not directed at range-wide reduction of predator populations." The transmittal letter accompanying the new policy said it is an interim policy statement, to be followed in the future with a revision of waterfowl management policy and other manual chapters dealing with predator management.

FWS considers predator control justifiable when used to meet the objectives of providing the optimum opportunity for people to use and enjoy waterfowl and has proposed control programs for a number of migratory-waterfowl areas. However, FWS says that no new refuge predator control programs have been implemented as a result of the new directive.

## Contaminants and the Kesterson National Wildlife Refuge

In 1985, the issue of toxic contaminants on national wildlife refuges, which traditionally has received little attention from the federal government, suddenly became a sensitive topic at FWS and in the entire Department of the Interior. An announcement in March 1985 by the Interior Department that it would shut off the flow of irrigation water into Kesterson National Wildlife Refuge in California, where selenium-laden waters were killing waterfowl, and new evidence that the selenium problem may extend far beyond this single refuge, spawned scientific studies, intense monitoring of the issue in Congress, and charges that the federal government has concealed information and has forced a new look at the impacts of agricultural drainage systems. Most importantly, it has focused attention on the presence of toxics on national wildlife refuges in general, a critical issue that demands immediate scrutiny.

Until the incident at Kesterson, little was known about toxic contamination on refuges. Beginning in 1967, each FWS region had a contaminant specialist who routinely studied the use and impacts of pesticides on refuge lands, but no comprehensive survey of toxic contaminants was initiated until after the 1980 enactment of the Superfund law (the Comprehensive Environmental Response, Compensation, and Liability Act, P.L. 96-510, 94 Stat. 2767, codified at scattered sections of 26 and 43 U.S.C.A.), which directed every refuge to report hazardous wastes, either buried or otherwise disposed, on its lands. Data submitted by land managers on refuges, FWS hatcheries, and research areas were compiled, and contaminated sites were recorded on a "Resource Contamination" list. At about the same time, an unrelated refuge-wide survey in 1983, now known as "Fish and Wildlife Service Resource Problems," reported toxic chemicals causing water-quality problems at 121 refuges and other FWS sites.

Based on data from these surveys, FWS identified in each region the five refuges most critically threatened by toxic contaminants. For each of these refuges, the regions prepared a remedial study to determine the extent of the problem, and developed a clean-up plan and a contract development strategy for conducting the clean-up. There have been some limited efforts to remove certain hazardous wastes from the refuges—primarily the removal by the Department of Defense of ammunition and containers located on FWS lands since World War II. But no comprehensive clean-up effort has begun on any of the sites on the Resource Contamination list. Funds for such clean-ups will have to be appropriated by Congress, since the Environmental Protection Agency plans to use the clean-up moneys in the Superfund primarily for sites that pose threats to human health.

Kesterson, a sanctuary for many species of migratory waterfowl and other birds, lies at the end of one of the Bureau of Reclamation's most elaborate irrigation drainage systems. The U.S. Geological Survey and the Bureau of Reclamation have known for years that selenium, a naturally occurring mineral in the rocks of the San Joaquin Valley, was accumulating in increasing amounts in the refuge, but the matter did not come to the public's attention until FWS linked widespread deaths and deformities in refuge birds to the high concentration of selenium in refuge waters—up to 4,200 parts per billion.* The Environmental Protection Agency recognizes 10 parts per billion as the level safe for drinking water.

Under pressure from the state of California, which declared the reservoirs at the refuge as hazardous waste sites; the local water district, which was concerned about the potential threat to Los Angeles' drinking water; and from conservationists who charged that the killing of birds by selenium constituted a "taking" under the Migratory Bird Treaty Act, the Department of the Interior announced in March 1985 that it was phasing out the flow of irriga-

*See *Audubon Wildlife Report 1985* for further background on Kesterson.

## Master List of Service Lands with Contaminant Studies

| Name | Chemical Studies* | Results |
|------|-------------------|---------|
| *Region 1* | | |
| Umatilla NWR, WA | OCs, especially heptachlor in birds and on seed grain | WA and OR state restrictions on heptachlor use |
| McNary NWR, WA | Same as above, used as control | Indicates no problem |
| Snake River Islands NWR, ID | Same as above | Indicates no problem |
| †Kesterson NWR, CA | TMs, especially selenium | High Levels of Se and other TMs—major impact on F&W |
| Deer Flat NWR, ID | OCs in fish | Indicates no problem |
| Columbia NWR, ID | OCs in fish | Indicates no problem |
| Ruby Lake NWR, NV | OCs in herons | High levels found in herons but appear to be coming from south of the border |
| San Francisco NWR, CA | OCs and TMs in ducks | Found high levels of Mercury, selenium and cadmium |
| †Kalmath Basin NWR, CA | OCs and lead in eagles | Found high levels of lead; Coop. Res. unit wants to continue study. |
| †Grays Lake NWR, ID | Special Cong. appropriation for water quality monitoring | None yet |
| †Malheur NWR, ID | USGS looking at water quality | None yet |
| †Hawaiian Island NWR, HA | OCs in fish and endangered birds | High levels of pesticide found |
| *Region 2* | | |
| †Aransas NWR, TX | Oil & Gas Dev., polynuclear aromatic hydrocarbons (PAHs) | Preliminary results suggest further study |
| †Wichita Mtns. NWR, OK | TMs from past mining activities | Same as above |
| †Santa Ana NWR, TX | OC scans, intensive agricultural development | None yet |
| †Lower Rio Grande NWR, TX | Same as above | None yet |
| †Laguna Atascosa NWR, TX | Same as above | None yet |
| †Anahuac NWR, TX | Broad organic scan—part of Galveston Bay study | None yet |
| *Region 3* | | |
| †Crab Orchard NWR, IL | PCBs and lead from DOD contractor activities | High levels of PCBs found in soil and in fish |

† Refers to studies planned in FY85
*OCs = Organochlorines, TMs = Trace Metals
[1] BOD = Biological Oxygen Demand
[2] SS = Suspended Solids

442

| Name | Chemical Studies* | Results |
|------|-------------------|---------|
| †Tamarac NWR, IL | Identity of Xs solvents stored on refuge | Meeting RCRA requirements for removal of solvents |
| Muskaw NWR, IN | TMs in fish | Indicates no problem |
| Ottawa NWR, IA | Radiological tests down wind from nuclear power plant | Indicates no problem |
| Upper Miss. NWR Savanna District, IL | Lead levels near battery mfg. plant | Indicates no problem |
| Swan Lake NWR, ND | Pesticide levels in fish from run off into Swan Lake | Indicates no problem |
| †De Sota NWR, IA | TMs from the use of sludge as a soil conditioner | None yet |
| *Region 4* | | |
| Loxahatchee NWR, FL | OCs and TMs in fish | Some indication of TMs and lindane. Further study required |
| Yazoo NWR, MS | Same as above | Some indication of DDT and toxaphene. Further study required. |
| Matthews Brake NWR, MS | Same as above | Indicates no problem |
| Morgan Brake NWR, MS | Same as above | Indicates no problem |
| †Wheeler NWR, AL | OCs in fish and waterfowl | Very high levels of DDT found in fish. Consent decree with Olin Corp. for remedial action |
| Big lake NWR, AL | OCs and TMs in fish | Indicates no problem |
| Reelfoot NWR, TN | Same as above | Indicates no problem |
| †Mattamuskeet MWR, NC | Same as above | Some indication of mercury and lead. Further study required. |
| †Tensas NWR, MS | Same as above | Some indication of DDT and toxaphene. Further study required. |
| Savannah NWR, GA | Same as above | Indicates no problem |
| †Lacassine NWR, AL | Same, dependent on NWR support | None yet |
| †Tennessee NWR, TN | Same as above | None yet |
| †Wapanoca NWR, AR | Same as above | None yet |
| †White River NWR, AR | Same as above | None yet |
| †Meritt Island NWR, FL | Same as above | None yet |
| *Region 5* | | |
| †Tinicum Nat'l Env, Ctr., PA | PCBs in turtles, other studies by EPA not released | Indication of PCBs, further studies warranted |

† Refers to studies planned in FY85
*OCs = Organochlorines, TMs = Trace Metals
[1] BOD = Biological Oxygen Demand
[2] SS = Suspended Solids

| Name | Chemical Studies* | Results |
|------|-------------------|---------|
| *Region 5 continued* | | |
| Fisherman's Island, NWR, VA | DDT/DDE in small mammals | Indicates no problem |
| †Erie NWR, PA | Plan to sample for endrin + 2-4-5 T in water supply | None yet |
| Great Swamp NWR, NJ | EPA has taken samples of asbestos covered paths | None yet |
| *Region 6* | | |
| Benton Lake NWR, MT | OCs in sediment | Indicates no problem |
| Medicene Lake NWR, MT | OCs & TMs in sediment | Indicates no problem |
| Des Lacs NWR, ND | OCs & TMs in sediment | Indicates no problem |
| J. Clark Salyer NWR, ND | OCs & TMs in sediment | Indicates no problem |
| Audubon NWR, ND | OCs & TMs in sediment | Indicates no problem |
| Coal Creek WPA, ND | TMs in sediments | Indicates no problem |
| Jamestown WPA, ND | OCs & TMs in sediment | Indicates no problem |
| Arrowwood NWR, ND | OCs in fish, OCs & TMs in sediment | Indicates no problem |
| Sand Lake NWR, SD | OCs in fish, OCs & TMs in sediment | Indicates no problem |
| Madison & Wise WPA, SD | OCs & TMs in sediment | Indicates no problem |
| †Lake Andes NWR, SD | OCs in fish, OCs & TMs in sediment | Found arsenic levels of concern, continuing to study. |
| Union Slough NWR, ID | OCs in fish, OCs & TMs in sediment | Indicates no problem |
| Bear River NWR, ID | OCs in sediment | Indicates no problem |
| Arapaho NWR, CO | OCs in fish | Indicates no problem |
| Monte Vista NWR, CO | OCs in fish | Found DDE at low levels, No indication of any problem |
| Alamosa NWR, CO | OCs in fish | Same as above |
| Hutton Lake NWR, WY | OCs in fish | Indicates no problem |
| Hastings WPA, NE | OCs & TMs in sediment | Indicates no problem |
| Flint Hill NWR, KS | OCs in fish | Indicates no problem |
| †Rainwater Basin WMD, NE | Volative hydrocarbons in drinking water | None yet |
| †Juhl WPD ND | OC scan—pesticides leaching from "empty" containers in dumpsite. | Low levels—not of concern |

† Refers to studies planned in FY85
*OCs = Organochlorines, TMs = Trace Metals
[1] BOD = Biological Oxygen Demand
[2] SS = Suspended Solids

| Name | Chemical Studies* | Results |
|------|-------------------|---------|
| †CM Russell NWR, MT | Arsenic migrating from buried As treated grain | None yet |
| *Region 7* | | |
| †Yukon Delta NWR, AK | Arsenic and mercury in birds | Levels suggest further study required |
| †Innoko NWR, VK | TMs in fish due to effects from placer mines | Same as above |
| †Kodiak NWR, AK | BOD,[1] SS[2] in water due to effects from sea food processor | Same as above |
| †Kenai NWR, AK | 1) Hydrocarbons, OCs & TMs due to oil and gas development | Same as above |
| | 2) Effects from human contamination | Same as above |
| †Alaska Pennisula NWR, AK | Base line TM sampling before mine development | None yet |
| †Knuti NWR, AK | | None yet |
| †Nowitna NWR, AK | TMs in fish from placer mining | None yet |
| †Togiak NWR, AK | —dependent on WR support | None yet |
| †Yukon Flats NWR, AK | | |

† Refers to studies planned in FY85
*OCs = Organochlorines, TMs = Trace Metals
[1] BOD = Biological Oxygen Demand
[2] SS = Suspended Solids

tion waters into the refuge. Interior has requested $12.6 million for studies and investigations that will allow FWS, the Geological Survey, and the Bureau of Reclamation to determine how best to meet state and federal laws applying to the Kesterson situation.

Shortly after the Kesterson issue became public, Congressman Sidney Yates (D-IL), chairman of the subcommittee that oversees Interior Department appropriations, requested that the U.S. Geological Survey develop a strategy to define the quality of the nation's surface and groundwater resources. In June 1985, the Geological Survey submitted a concept outline for the effort. Congressman Yates added $5 million to the Geological Survey budget for FY 1985 to initiate and develop the program, now called the National Water Quality Assessment Program, and the Interior Department established a task force to coordinate review and policy aspects of the program among the various federal and state agencies involved.

Controversy over selenium contamination expanded beyond Kesterson later in 1985 when the *Sacramento Bee* published a series of articles on selenium contamination which contended that Interior Department officials had suppressed efforts to mount a major search for selenium in irrigation drainage flows throughout the West out of fears that the discovery of further problems would lead to lawsuits and huge clean-up costs. The *Bee* alleged that Interior's Assistant Secretary of Water and Science Robert Broadbent had received in April 1985 a plan to prepare a study of other federal water projects with problems similar to or potentially as catastrophic as that of Kesterson. This study, requested by Interior Secretary Donald Hodel, was to be conducted by U.S. Geological Survey and FWS scientists and Bureau of Reclamation officials. However, according to the *Bee*, Broadbent "killed it because the solicitor said it would raise serious questions about legal liabilities wherever . . . selenium was found" (*Sacramento Bee*, Sept. 10, 1985). In addition, the *Bee* claimed to have evidence that selenium levels are at the danger level in Bureau of Reclamation irrigation drains affecting waterfowl refuges in Idaho, Montana, South Dakota, Utah, New Mexico, and Arizona, with less serious build-ups in refuges in eight other states. The *Bee* also reported that livestock had been contaminated in at least five western states.

The Interior Department denied stalling study of the selenium problem, and the department officially was cleared in a report by Interior's inspector general, which concluded that none of the "cover-up" accusations could be verified. However, in response to the *Bee's* reports of the widespread nature of the selenium problem, Congress has directed Interior to conduct field studies on selenium contamination in the West, and Yates' Interior Appropriations Subcommittee has requested quarterly reports on the department's progress.

This new emphasis on toxics in wildlife refuges portends a major shift in departmental priorities that could strain Interior's financial and professional resources. FWS currently is initiating several efforts to address the problem. FWS is attempting to make up for its historical lack of routine toxic monitoring by developing more comprehensive bio-monitoring programs. These programs will be managed by the FWS Resource Contamination Division, with laboratory support to come from the Patuxent Analytical Control Facility in Beltsville, Maryland, now under construction. Technologies are being developed to assess contaminant impacts. FWS also will study the investigation and apprehension of parties suspected of violating federal fish and wildlife laws and regulations. Most probably, this will be used to assign culpability and receive remuneration for clean-up costs.

The long-term costs to address the toxics problem could be high. Clean-up costs, many of which will not be covered by nongovernmental parties, could be massive—estimates for cleaning up Kesterson have been as high as $195 million. In addition, the paucity of knowledge about selenium reflects a basic lack of understanding of many substances that are toxic within a certain range, but are safe and even necessary at certain levels. Lethal-dose levels and tolerance ranges have yet to be calculated for many of these, and the time and expense to do so will be substantial. Altogether, the task of identifying and resolving toxic problems on the national wildlife refuge system could overtake many other departmental and federal land priorities.

## Contaminants at Wheeler National Wildlife Refuge

One refuge with a long-standing contaminant problem, the Wheeler National Wildlife Refuge in Alabama, finally is scheduled for clean-up. The refuge was created in 1938 as an overlay project on Tennessee Valley Authority's Wheeler Reservoir. It was established to provide a bed for and buffer strip around the reservoir and as a breeding ground for migratory birds and other wildlife. The refuge hosts one of the southernmost concentrations of Canada geese, as well as Alabama's largest population of wintering ducks. The refuge also provides a wide variety of public-use opportunities, including hunting, fishing, wildlife trails, an interpretive center, and environmental education classes, attracting some 600,000 visitors yearly.

From the early 1950s until 1970, Olin Corporation produced DDT on the Redstone Arsenal near the Wheeler Refuge. Discharges from the site have seriously contaminated the Huntsville Spring Branch of Indian Creek, which flows through Wheeler before it joins the Tennessee River. The creek's sediments are laden with DDT and associated metabolites, and samples of fish from the creek show bioaccumulations of the contaminants at levels hazardous to human health. FWS now is collecting and analyzing blackbird and mallard eggs and fledglings to determine their level of accumulation. Other migratory-bird species, particularly herons and egrets, will be analyzed in 1986.

Under a consent decree with the Environmental Protection Agency and other agencies, Olin has agreed to mitigate the environmental damage. The company will bury an estimated 323 tons of contaminated material under fill dirt and will encompass the site with earthen dams and a channel to divert creek waters. Additionally, 1.6 miles of streambed will be buried to secure the contaminated sediments in place. These remedial actions are scheduled to begin in 1986.

## Chincoteague National Wildlife Refuge and Conflicts with Development

Chincoteague National Wildlife Refuge encompasses about 10,000 acres located primarily on the Virginia portion of Assateague Island, which represents one of the last major undeveloped barrier island ecosystems on the Atlantic seaboard. In 1965, Chincoteague became part of the Assateague Island National Seashore, but continued to be administered as a national wildlife refuge.

Chincoteague provides principal wintering and nesting habitat for more than 275 bird species and is one of the largest concentration points for greater snow geese and migrating peregrine falcons. It forms a major component of a protected wildlife habitat complex stretching from Bombay Hook, Delaware, to Cape Charles, Virginia, and provides habitat for several endangered and threatened species.

At the same time, Chincoteague's proximity to a number of large cities and the attractiveness of its beach frontage to recreationists draws 1.5 million visitors a year, making Chincoteague the second most highly visited refuge in the United States. This intensive use has encouraged certain local politicians and businessmen to attempt to transform the town of Chincoteague—which lies at the entrance to the refuge—into a major beach resort. To further this goal, these interests are seeking to increase public access to the beach by pressuring FWS to reconstruct a road, recently washed out in a storm, that runs behind the dunes, and to create additional parking.

FWS has resisted these efforts, citing numerous environmental impacts. Because Assateague is a barrier island, its contours are constantly changing, and experts predict that the proposed roads and parking lots would be completely submerged by the year 2000. In addition, the magnitude of public use already has forced FWS to set limits on the number of people permitted at any one time on the refuge beach, and counts of birds stopping over at the refuge are down. Moreover, fears for nesting colonial birds, such as the piping plover—recently listed as a threatened species—have firmed the resolve of FWS and conservationists to keep vehicles off the refuge beach, particularly during shorebird nesting season, which extends from April 1 to August 1.

FWS is preparing a master plan for the refuge, scheduled for release in 1986. Conservationists have made a number of suggestions for alternative methods of dealing with public use, such as using a shuttle system to carry visitors into the refuge, and the Department of the Interior is considering the use of entrance fees to limit use. Business interests and the mayor, however, have said they are frustrated with FWS and want the popular refuge removed from FWS control. Congressman Herbert Bateman (R-VA) has promised to introduce legislation to transfer the refuge beach to the National Park Service, which is seen as more sympathetic to recreation use, if the FWS master plan fails to accommodate recreational needs.

## Alaska Refuges

The vast majority of refuge system lands—77 million acres or 85 percent of the total—are in Alaska. For a number of reasons—including special provisions governing their management, Alaska Native cultural traditions, pressures for additional oil and gas development, "states rights" interests in the management of fish and game, and the size and ecological vulnerability of these areas — the Alaska refuges often pose different and sometimes more difficult management problems than refuges elsewhere in the United States.

For most of its history, Alaska largely has been open for exploitation. Russian explorers who settled the coastal area in the mid-1700s rapidly reduced fur seal and sea otter populations in their zeal for furs. In 1867, because of the declining fur trade and depressed economic conditions, Alaska was sold to the United States. U.S. policy generally perpetuated the indiscriminate taking of furbearers, and salmon fishing, whaling, and walrus hunting flourished.

However, the need for special conservation measures to protect at least some of Alaska's resources quickly became apparent. In the early 1890s, President Benjamin Harrison reserved Afognak Island to protect the salmon fishery and other wildlife. Alaska's pristine and unique beauty was acknowledged when 21 million acres of the Tongass and Chugach forests were made part of the National Forest System. By 1913, approximately eight million acres of coastal islands and the Aleutian chain had been added to the refuge system. By 1950, 57 million acres of public land in Alaska had been set aside by the federal government for other, nonconservation purposes, bringing the total amount of federally reserved lands to 94 million acres.

Statehood was granted to Alaska in 1959, and the new state was entitled to select for state ownership 104 million acres of unappropriated federal land in Alaska. In 1971, the Alaska Native Claims Settlement Act (43 U.S.C.A. 1601 *et seq.*) acknowledged Native claims to Alaska lands and resources based on historical use and occupancy. The act established 12 Native Regional Corporations and more than 210 Native Village Corporations to oversee the selection of 44 million acres of public lands. ANCSA also set the stage for the preservation of large areas of federal lands in Alaska by requiring the Department of the Interior to withdraw appropriate federal lands "in the national interest" and to make recommendations to Congress on how those lands should be apportioned among the national conservation systems, including national wildlife refuges, parks, preserves, and forests; the wild and scenic rivers system; national recreation areas; and national conservation areas under the Bureau of Land Management.

In 1980, the decade-long debate over conservation of these lands was resolved officially in the Alaska National Interest Lands Conservation Act (16 U.S.C.A. 3101 *et seq.*), which set aside approximately 105 million acres of federal land in the various conservation units. This included the addition of about 54 million acres to the National Wildlife Refuge System, which, when combined with the 13 million acres of previously designated refuges, brought the total refuge acreage in Alaska to its present 77 million acres.

*Alaska Refuge Management.* The Alaska National Interest Lands Conservation Act contains a number of special provisions for the management of refuges in Alaska, in part to meet the unique management needs in the state and in part to avoid many of the problems that have plagued refuge management in the lower 48 states. One key concept applying to all the conservation units designated in the bill was to include entire ecosystems within the conservation areas to help maintain their ecological integrity. As stated in congressional legislative history:

## Acreages of National Wildlife Refuges in Alaska

| National Wildlife Refuge | Established Before 1971 | New Unit or Additions of 1980* | Total Acres |
|---|---|---|---|
| Alaska Manome NWR includes: | | | |
| Aleutian Islands NWR | 2.720.225 | | |
| Bering Sea NWR | 81.340 | | |
| Bogoslof NWR | 175 | | |
| Chamisso NWR | 455 | | |
| Forrester Island NWR | 2.832 | | |
| Hazy Islands NWR | 32 | | |
| Pribilof NWR | 173 | | |
| St. Lazaria NWR | 65 | | |
| Semidi NWR | 251.930 | | |
| Simeonof NWR | 26.046 | | |
| Tuxedni NWR | 5.683 | | |
| | 3.088.956 | 460.000 | 3.548.956 |
| Alaska Pennisula NWR | | 3.500.000 | 3.500.000 |
| Arctic NWR includes: | | | |
| William O. Douglas Arctic NWR | 8.894.624 | 9.160.000 | 18.054.624(+)(−) |
| Becharof NWR | | 1.200.000 | 1.200.000 |
| Innoko NWR | | 3.850.000 | 3.850.000 |
| Izembek NWR | 320.893 | | 320.893 |
| Kanun NWR | | 1.430.000 | 1.430.000 |
| Kenai NWR includes: | | | |
| Kenai Nat'l Moose Range | 1.730.000 | 240.00 | 1.970.000 |
| Kodiak NWR includes: | | | |
| Kodiak NWR | 1.815.000 | 50.000 | 1.865.000 |
| Koyukuk NWR | | 3.550.000 | 3.550.000 |
| Nowitna NWR | | 1.560.000 | 1.560.000 |
| Seiawik NWR | | 2.150.000 | 2.150.000 |
| Tetin NWR | | 700.000 | 700.000 |
| Togiak NWR includes: | | | |
| Cape Newenham NWR | 265.000 | 3.840.000 | 4.105.000 |
| Yukon Delta NWR includes: | | | |
| Clarence Rhode NWR | 2.887.026 | | |
| Hazen Bay NWR | 6.800 | | |
| Nunivak NWR | 3.330.632 | | |
| | 6.224.458 | 13.400.000 | 19.624.458 |
| Yukon Flats NWR | | 8.630.000 | 8.630.000 |
| | 22.338.931 | 53.720.000 | 77.058.931(+)(−) |

*National Wildlife Refuges established by the Alaska National Interest Lands Conservation Act. Acreages are approximate pending clarification of land status and relinquishment of State selections of 1978.

The action in this committee in designating these new Alaskan National Wildlife Refuges carries on a major principle in land conservation—that certain public lands could and should be dedicated and managed as key ecological components of wildlife habitat for wildlife utilization for the ultimate public benefit. It is fitting that, in a state as vast as Alaska, these units will assure to the greatest extent possible, the protection of the ecological units and processes that support entire habitats for Alaska's diverse fish and wildlife resources (S. Rep. No. 96-413).

In contrast to refuges elsewhere in the United States, which have no specific statutory planning requirements, the Alaska Lands Act (Section 304(g)) requires that a "comprehensive conservation plan" be prepared for each of the 16 Alaska refuges. These plans are to designate areas within the refuge according to their resources and values, specify programs for conserving fish and wildlife, and specify uses that are compatible with refuge purposes, including recreational, educational, and research activities. The act specifically requires FWS to base these plans on a preliminary study that inventories refuge resources and characteristics, identifies unique refuge values, designates areas within the refuge that are suitable for visitor facilities, lists requirements for access, and assesses the impacts and benefits of alternative management strategies and public uses. FWS is required to present several different management alternatives and seek public comment before deciding on the final plan.

The Alaska National Interest Lands Conservation Act required FWS to complete five of the 16 refuge plans by 1983 and the remaining 11 plans by 1987. By the end of FY 1985, plans had been completed for only four refuges: Kenai, Izembek, Becharof, and Alaska Peninsula.

Section 801 of the Lands Act provides for continued subsistence use of Alaska refuges. The act permits the nonwasteful taking of fish and wildlife by Native and non-Native rural residents on refuge lands for consumptive (non-sport) purposes, insofar as this is consistent with "the conservation of healthy populations of fish and wildlife." This contrasts with refuges in the lower 48, where hunting and fishing are recreational activities permitted only if compatible with the purposes for which a refuge was established. In cases where consumptive use must be restricted, subsistence use is the first priority. The Alaska Lands Act requires the establishment of an administrative structure to enable rural residents to have a role in the management of fish, wildlife, and subsistence uses on Alaska's public lands. It also requires FWS to monitor various wildlife populations, subsistence resources, and sport uses of wildlife to ensure the viability of all resources upon which subsistence depends. In most cases, Natives have shown a willingness to work with biologists to modify uses where necessary (National Audubon Society 1981).

Section 1008 of the act specifically requires Interior to complete appropriate studies of refuge lands to assist in making compatibility determinations for proposed oil and gas exploration and recovery operations. The studies must review both the area's potential for oil and gas discovery as well as the "environmental characteristics and wildlife resources which would be affected by the exploration. . . ." The secretary may approve leasing only when the plan demonstrates that the leasing activity will conform with requirements for the protection and use of the land for the purposes for which it is being managed. If significant environmental or economic changes occur during the life of the leasing operation, the secretary is required to suspend operations for up to five years, provided that he makes the following determinations: that the damage will be immediate and irreparable; that the threat will not disappear; and that the advantages of cancellation outweigh the advantages of continuing the lease.

The Alaska Lands Act also includes special provisions for the Arctic National Wildlife Refuge, an area that the oil industry says could hold important oil reserves. Sections 1002 through 1006 require the Interior Department to prepare a special "Coastal Plain Resources Assessment" for the Arctic refuge, scheduled to be completed and submitted to Congress by September 1986. Interior is required to conduct a baseline inventory of all the fish and wildlife resources on the refuge's coastal plain and an assessment of the impacts of human activities, including oil and gas exploration, on the resources as well as on Native activities and culture. Oil and gas production is prohibited unless specifically authorized by an act of Congress. In addition, the secretary of the Interior also is required to review lands on the Arctic coastal plain for possible wilderness designation, which would preclude commodity uses such as oil, gas, and mineral development and would ensure the highest possible protection for fish and wildlife populations and habitats in their natural diversity.

Section 1302 of the Alaska Land Act outlines the secretary of the Interior's authority to make land exchanges to aid the completion of land acquisition within the boundaries of conservation-system units, including national wildlife refuges. Limitations on this authority were clarified in a 1984 court decision on a case brought by the National Audubon Society and other conservation organizations against an exchange involving St. Matthew Island, a national wildlife refuge and wilderness area in the Bering Sea.*

*Current Program Emphasis.* Most of the refuge program in Alaska is directed toward meeting mandates of the Alaska Lands Act. Data gathering is continuing for all 16 units for use in the comprehensive conservation plans, which FWS expects to complete by the mandated 1987 deadline. Wilderness review for all Alaska refuge lands is ongoing and is scheduled to coincide with submission of the final plans. In addition, FWS now is preparing management plans—which detail the procedures for meeting responsibilities for subsistence,

*See the *Audubon Wildlife Report 1985* for further discussion.

transportation and utility systems, access, and ascertaining compatibility—and will begin implementation of priority projects identified in the completed comprehensive conservation plans.

FWS also is conducting a number of activities related to oil and gas. It is moving to complete the Arctic refuge coastal-plain study, and other refuges are being evaluated as part of the comprehensive planning process to identify areas where FWS may allow oil and gas development. Habitat studies are being initiated on the Yukon Flats National Wildlife Refuge and the Yukon Delta National Wildlife Refuge to assist in making decisions on oil and gas leasing on these refuges, where industry already has made 730 lease offers.

*Problems and Issues.* The management of Alaska refuges has posed new and difficult challenges for a number of reasons. The remoteness and inaccessibility of many of the refuges create numerous problems: they are hard to patrol, making law enforcement difficult; living conditions are sometimes inadequate for refuge managers; and there is frequent turnover in refuge personnel. The sheer size of the acreage added to the refuge system by the Alaska Lands Act has taxed FWS' limited financial and personnel resources and has hampered reasonable progress on baseline inventories. The funding situation is aggravated by the high cost of living in Alaska and a rapid inflation rate with which appropriations have not kept pace. The requirement to provide for subsistence use has placed an entirely new perspective on refuge management by involving cultural and historical considerations in management planning. And the lack of information on tundra ecosystems and the impacts of development on it makes it difficult to predict the environmental effects of economic uses, particularly oil and gas exploration and recovery. This inability to predict impacts seems to have caused a certain degree of nonchalance on the part of those making compatibility determinations. More specific problems and issues are discussed below.

The other major problem challenging the sound management of Alaska refuges is the strong pressure for development of oil and gas and other commodity resources. This pressure comes from two important sources: the Alaska Land Use Council—a council established by the Alaska Lands Act to oversee and make recommendations on the law's implementation—and the Department of the Interior. Environmentalists say this development bias is causing FWS to amend refuge plans to accommodate resource development and to fail to recommend lands that are suitable for inclusion in the National Wilderness Preservation System.

*Budget.* The Alaska refuges account for 85 percent of the acreage in the National Wildlife Refuge System, but receive slightly less than 10 percent of the funding. In FY 1986, for example, Congress appropriated $11.533 million for Alaska refuges—out of a total refuge and operation and maintenance budget of $105.634 million—which must cover the preparation of comprehensive conservation plans for all 16 units, study of the Alaska refuges for possible wilderness designation, working with local entities to address subsistence provisions and assess the anticipated and actual effects of all land-use decisions on subsistence harvest of migratory birds, and evaluation of all Alaska refuges to determine areas in which FWS may permit oil and gas exploration and development.

About $1 million, nearly 10 percent of funding for Alaska refuges, is appropriated to conduct the baseline assessments of oil and gas, biological, and wilderness resources on the coastal plain of the Arctic National Wildlife Refuge and to determine the effects that oil and gas exploration and development would have on the resources. This development-oriented task consumes more than 90 percent of total funding for the Arctic refuge, while conservationists charge that other vitally important refuge issues are being addressed inadequately.

FWS has noted the low funding for Alaska refuges in comparison to other conservation system units and blames it on its own public image. In a July 1984 Alaska planning document, FWS compared funding for the Chugach National Forest, Denali National Park, and Kenai National Wildlife Refuge, saying: "The differences in budget and management . . . reflect the respective agencies' national images; the U.S. Forest Service and the National Park Service have high recognition, the FWS has little recognition. In Alaska alone the budget of the six-million-acre Chugach National Forest is nearly equal to the entire budget of all 16 refuges totalling nearly 80 million acres. The disparities experienced by Kenai Refuge when compared to Chugach National Forest and Denali National Park are probably symptomatic of the FWS's low-key status" (Department of the Interior 1984).

*Alaska Refuge Planning.* Alaska refuge planning is proceeding more slowly than scheduled. Although five plans were due by 1983, only four had been completed by 1985. In addition, the four completed plans have been roundly criticized by conservation groups, sportsmen, and private citizens for a variety of reasons. Among their complaints are the following:

- Habitat studies and baseline wildlife population inventories used in making compatibility determinations are deficient. Critics say this lack of information has made it virtually impossible to weigh proposed alternatives. For example, the plan for Kenai National Wildlife Refuge states, "Human uses and development have been allowed on the refuge with neither the knowledge of the effects nor monitoring to determine the impact" (Department of the Interior 1985, pp. 1-7). Uses are justified on the basis of the "best available data," a term open to interpretation.
- FWS, through a memorandum of understanding, has delegated authority to the state of Alaska for management of wildlife populations, habitat, and

public use. The Alaska Department of Fish and Game is responsible for managing wildlife for consumptive use and local benefit. Critics say that this objective is at cross-purposes with the broader refuge goals of protecting natural diversity and conserving wildlife for public benefit in the national interest, and maintain that wildlife will suffer with the federal abdication of responsibility.

- Decisions to expand public uses, based on determinations that the use will have no significant impact, are inadequately documented. Maps and data provided in the plans, for example, frequently have no information on migratory-bird breeding cycles, nesting habitat preference, or seasonal ranges. Yet motor and aerial access routes are proposed into freshwater lake areas that probably serve as sites for some portion of migratory-bird life cycles.

- The plans favor economic activities, most notably oil and gas exploration. Critics of the Alaska Peninsula National Wildlife Refuge plan charge that the preferred alternative "seems premised on the inference that [oil and gas development] are integral to refuge management and should be accommodated wherever possible" (Department of the Interior 1985b). The draft plan did not address the requirements of the Alaska National Interest Lands Conservation Act for extensive preliminary studies and consultations, followed by a national interest determination, before allowing energy development.

- The plans continue to emphasize management of favored game species, such as moose, rather than pursuing the principal refuge objective of conserving fish and wildlife populations and habitats in their natural diversity.

- Wilderness suitability reviews and recommendations are inadequate. The plan for the Yukon Flats National Wildlife Refuge, for example, fails to make a comprehensive suitability finding, fails to discuss wilderness values, and fails to make wilderness recommendations.

# Legislation

## Extension of Acquisition Authority

In 1985, Congress extended the authority for acquiring land at four existing units of the refuge system: Bogue Chitto, Bon Secour, and Tensas River national wildlife refuges and the Tinicum National Education Center. The new law, P.L. 99-191, extended the time period for acquiring lands in these refuges—pre-existing authority expired at the end of September 1985—and in some cases authorized additional funds to allow acquisition to be completed. These refuges contain some of the most valuable bottomland-hardwood stands in the United States and are key tracts within areas that are being drained rapidly for development.

## Cape Charles Training Center

Congress also passed legislation (H.R. 1440) to authorize a National Fish and Wildlife Service Training Center at the newly created Eastern Shore of Virginia National Wildlife Refuge in Cape Charles, Virginia, but the bill was vetoed by the president. The training center would have consolidated several programs that now are dispersed throughout the United States and would have provided a modernized and expanded facility. The legislation, sponsored by Congressman Herbert Bateman (R-VA) in the House and Senator Paul Trible (R-VA) in the Senate, would have authorized $7 million for initial construction of the center. The Department of the Interior was authorized to lease the facilities and collect fees to offset operating costs.

Conservation groups solidly supported the legislation, and many testified before Congress that they intended to use the training center and were willing to help support it financially. The Reagan administration, however, opposed the training center from the outset, contending that it was not needed, that it duplicated existing operations unnecessarily, and that the expense could not be justified.

## Florida Panther National Wildlife Refuge

The only other legislation dealing with refuges was S. 897, a bill proposed by Senator Paula Hawkins (R-FL) that would establish the Florida Panther National Wildlife Refuge. The Senate Environment and Public Works Committee approved and reported the bill out of committee at the end of the 1985 congressional session.

# Legal Development

No major legal developments concerning national wildlife refuges occurred in 1985.

# Status of the Resource

FWS does not have the capability to compile and analyze comprehensive information on the condition of the lands, wildlife, and facilities that the National Wildlife Refuge System contains. It is therefore impossible to assess the status of the resources in the system as a whole. The refuge managers prepare yearly narrative reports that provide what is probably the most detailed information available. However, the level of detail in refuge reports varies widely among all the field stations. No standardized guidelines exist for reporting requirements on the amount of data that should be researched and docu-

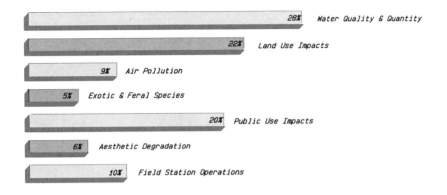

**Percent of Reported Resource Problems by Category**

- 28% Water Quality & Quantity
- 22% Land Use Impacts
- 9% Air Pollution
- 5% Exotic & Feral Species
- 20% Public Use Impacts
- 6% Aesthetic Degradation
- 10% Field Station Operations

Source: Fish and Wildlife Resource Problems
U.S. Fish and Wildlife Service, 1983

mented, or for the level of detail. Nor has any effort ever been made to consolidate this data into a useable format, although FWS is now considering the development of a system to compile existing refuge data and make it available for exchange and use by all refuge managers.

In 1982, FWS initiated a study to identify resource problems on all field stations, including national wildlife refuges, national fish hatcheries, and research facilities. Answering a detailed questionnaire, field-station managers and other personnel identified threats to the lands and species that they manage.* The terms threat, conflict, problem, and resource problem were used more or less interchangeably to refer to what the questionnaire defines as "those pollutants, land use, public uses, exotic species, individual development projects, etc., that are currently causing or have the potential to cause significant damage to Service-managed natural resources or physical facilities, or to those phenomena which seriously degrade important Service-managed values or visitor experiences."

The survey results were published in July 1983, in a document entitled "Fish and Wildlife Service Resource Problems." The report identifies 65 problems grouped into seven categories: Water Quality and Quantity, Land Use, Air Pollution, Exotic and Feral Species, Public Use, Aesthetic Degradation, and Field Station Operations. All 65 problems were found to affect some

---

*A total of 473 field stations were surveyed: 373 of the then 410 refuges, 89 hatcheries, and 11 research facilities.

## Resource Problems Reported by Units of the National Wildlife Refuge System

| Resource Affected | TYPE* | RF** | FH** | RES** | Total | % Stations Reporting |
|---|---|---|---|---|---|---|
| 1. Water Quality | BIO | 288 | 71 | 6 | 365 | 77 |
| 2. General Scene (public, etc.) | AES | 306 | 37 | 6 | 349 | 74 |
| 3. Waterfowl | BIO | 318 | 0 | 3 | 321 | 68 |
| 4. Health/Safety (public-employee) | OPS | 241 | 69 | 7 | 317 | 67 |
| 5. Other Migratory Birds | BIO | 313 | 0 | 2 | 315 | 67 |
| 6. Wetland Communities/Habitats | BIO | 294 | 1 | 3 | 298 | 63 |
| 7. Building & Utility Systems | OPS | 184 | 63 | 6 | 253 | 54 |
| 8. Large Mammals | BIO | 242 | 4 | 3 | 249 | 53 |
| 9. Habitat Protection Facilities | OPS | 222 | 19 | 1 | 242 | 51 |
| 10. Fish | BIO | 165 | 65 | 4 | 234 | 50 |
| 11. Outdoor Experience | AES | 220 | 12 | 0 | 232 | 49 |
| 12. Air Quality & Visibility | PHY | 225 | 4 | 2 | 231 | 49 |
| 13. Water Supply | PHY | 154 | 68 | 5 | 227 | 48 |
| 14. Plants (land & water) | BIO | 221 | 0 | 2 | 223 | 47 |
| 15. Vehicles & Heavy Equipment | OPS | 161 | 51 | 3 | 215 | 46 |
| 16. Invertebrates (land & water) | BIO | 197 | 6 | 4 | 207 | 44 |
| 17. Small Mammals | BIO | 202 | 2 | 2 | 206 | 44 |
| 18. Public Use Facilities | OPS | 196 | 7 | 1 | 204 | 43 |
| 19. Water Management Facilities | OPS | 166 | 35 | 1 | 202 | 43 |
| 20. Non-Migratory Birds | BIO | 183 | 1 | 1 | 185 | 39 |
| 21. Grassland Communities/Habitats | BIO | 173 | 1 | 1 | 175 | 37 |
| 22. Forest Communities/Habitats | BIO | 160 | 2 | 4 | 166 | 35 |
| 23. Roads & Trails | OPS | 160 | 3 | 1 | 164 | 35 |
| 24. Endangered/Threatened Species | BIO | 154 | 0 | 2 | 156 | 33 |
| 25. Wildlife Observation | AES | 122 | 10 | 1 | 133 | 28 |
| 26. Soils | PHY | 129 | 1 | 0 | 130 | 28 |
| 27. Other-Operational | OPS | 122 | 2 | 5 | 129 | 27 |

*TYPE: BIO—Biological
OPS—Operational
PHY—Physical
AES—Aesthetic
CUL—Cultural
**Field Stations: RF—National Wildlife Refuge
FH—National Fish Hatchery
RES—National Fish or Wildlife Research Center

Resource Problems Reported by Units of the National Wildlife Refuge System (continued)

| Resource Affected | TYPE* | RF** | FH** | RES** | Total | % Stations Reporting |
|---|---|---|---|---|---|---|
| | | | Number of Field Stations | | | |
| 28. Wilderness (natural scene) | AES | 111 | 7 | 0 | 118 | 25 |
| 29. Odor | AES | 94 | 9 | 2 | 105 | 22 |
| 30. Other-Biological | BIO | 74 | 1 | 1 | 76 | 16 |
| 31. Sites (historic, archeological) | CUL | 69 | 0 | 2 | 71 | 15 |
| 22. Amphibians & Reptiles | BIO | 59 | 1 | 1 | 61 | 13 |
| 33. Beach/Dunes | PHY | 60 | 0 | 1 | 61 | 13 |
| 34. Scientific Equipment | OPS | 23 | 29 | 4 | 56 | 12 |
| 35. Plankton/Microbiota | BIO | 53 | 1 | 0 | 54 | 11 |
| 36. Landscapes (historic) | AES | 29 | 0 | 1 | 30 | 6 |
| 37. Structures (historic, archeological) | AES | 25 | 1 | 0 | 26 | 6 |
| 38. Other Physical | PHY | 23 | 0 | 1 | 24 | 5 |
| 39. Other-Aesthetic | AES | 21 | 0 | 0 | 21 | 4 |
| 40. Desert Communities/ Habitats | BIO | 19 | 0 | 0 | 19 | 4 |
| 41. Geological Features (unique) | PHY | 13 | 0 | 0 | 13 | 3 |
| 42. Tropical Communities/ Habitats | BIO | 12 | 0 | 0 | 12 | 3 |
| 43. Tundra Communities/ Habitats | BIO | 12 | 0 | 0 | 12 | 3 |
| 44. Minerals | PHY | 8 | 0 | 0 | 8 | 2 |
| 45. Other-Cultural | CUL | 5 | 0 | 0 | 5 | 1 |

*TYPE: BIO—Biological
      OPS—Operational
      PHY—Physical
      AES—Aesthetic
      CUL—Cultural
**Field Stations: RF—National Wildlife Refuge
      FH—National Fish Hatchery
      RES—National Fish or Wildlife Research Center

refuges, 55 of them to affect some hatcheries, and 47 to affect some research stations.

FWS regional offices were instructed to prepare strategies by January 1984 for addressing the problems occurring in their regions. The Accelerated Refuge Maintenance and Management program was developed in part to help alleviate problems stemming from inadequate maintenance of refuge facilities and equipment, the third-most-frequently reported problem. However, although some 50 percent of the reported problems pertained to biological and environmental matters, FWS has taken no significant initiative toward solving the problems. However, certain individual refuge plans have included corrective actions for problems identified in the survey. For example, the 1984 plan for Sabine National Wildlife Refuge identified chemical and thermal pollutants from industrial sources and alligator poaching among refuge research problems. Management strategies ultimately were developed for extensive water quality testing and intensification of law-enforcement efforts to prevent illegal hunting.

Substantial information needs still exist in both the maintenance and resource arenas: FWS still needs a maintenance management system that compiles information on the condition of refuge facilities as well as a clear set of standards and priorities for inventorying refuge resources.

# References

Harris, Tom. 1985. "U.S. Government Quashes Efforts to Probe Selenium." *Sacramento Bee,* September 5, 1985.

Memo from Robert E. Putz, Assistant Deputy Director, U.S. Department of the Interior, to Directors of Fish and Wildlife Service Regions 1-7, April 23, 1983.

National Audubon Society. 1981. "Wildlife refuges: what future for Alaska?" in *Proceedings of the National Audubon Society Alaska Regional Conference,* May 7-10, 1981, Anchorage, Alaska. National Audubon Society. Washington, D.C.

Riley, Laura and William. 1979. *Guide to the National Wildlife Refuges.* Anchor Books. Garden City, New York.

U.S. Department of the Interior, Fish and Wildlife Service. 1985a. *U.S. Department of the Interior Budget Justifications, FY 1986: Fish and Wildlife Service.* USDI. Washington, D.C.

U.S. Department of the Interior, Fish and Wildlife Service. 1985b. *The Kenai National Wildlife Refuge: Comprehensive Conservation Plan/Environmental Impact Statement/Wilderness Review—Final.* USDI. Washington, D.C.

U.S. Department of the Interior, Fish and Wildlife Service. 1985c. *Alaska Peninsula National Wildlife Refuge: Comprehensive Conservation Plan/Environmental Impact Statement/Wilderness Review—Final.* USDI. Washington, D.C.

U.S. Department of the Interior, Office of Budget. 1984. *Welcome to Alaska, Kris Marcie.* USDI. Washington, D.C.

*Wendy Lee Smith is a Washington D.C. freelance writer.*

A National Park Service guide leads visitors through Redwood National Park. The parks have proved vital to the survival in the lower 48 states of species such as the wolf and grizzly.

*National Park Service*

# Wildlife and the National Park Service

## Chris Elfring

## Introduction

T HE NATIONAL PARKS play a clear and critical role in preserving the nation's wildlife heritage. When Congress established the National Park Service in 1916, it declared that one of the goals of the park system was "to conserve the wildlife therein." While the 337 units now in the system vary tremendously in character and include historic, recreational, and cultural sites, the parks set aside for their spectacular natural environments are particularly important for wildlife because they provide irreplaceable natural habitat. In fact, the survival of certain wildlife species, such as the grizzly bear in the lower 48 states, can be attributed directly to the existence of the national parks.

In the years that have elapsed since the nation's first national park, Yellowstone, was established in 1872, the Park Service has evolved in its understanding of both nature and its own mission. Originally, the Service protected "things" like grand scenery and unique landforms. When the early parks were established, little or no awareness was shown of the need to preserve complete ecosystems. Today, the Park Service more often tries to take an ecosystem approach to resource management—planning and carrying out activities designed to keep ecosystems and their natural processes functioning in perpetuity. Wildlife is considered a key element of park ecosystems, but the Service rarely manages exclusively for wildlife. Instead, it attempts to integrate wildlife considerations into its other management activities.

Although natural-resource management is an essential part of the Park Service's mandate, its enabling legislation also identifies the enjoyment of parks by people as a primary concern. Thus, the modern Park Service has a strong visitor-use orientation. It can at times be inherently difficult, and sometimes contradictory, to manage for both people and natural resources.

It is increasingly clear that park natural resources are subject to a complex array of influences, both internal and external to the parks, that threaten their long-term preservation. Wildlife, perhaps more than other park resources, is highly susceptible to threats emanating from activities on land adjacent to the parks. The reason is simple: Wildlife does not recognize boundaries contrived by people, and habitat outside the parks often is critical to its survival.

# Legislative Authority

The evolution of wildlife policy in the national parks can be traced from 1872, when Yellowstone National Park was established. This first national park was dedicated as a "pleasuring ground for the benefit and enjoyment of people" for all time. In actual practice, however, Yellowstone's first superintendent lacked both staff and salary for park management, and park wildlife often was killed by hunters.

Eventually recognizing the need to protect and manage the parks it was creating, Congress in 1916 passed the National Park System Organic Act (16 U.S.C.A. 1,2-3). This law created the National Park Service and set the basic purpose of the parks that still guides their management today. "The fundamental purpose of said parks," reads the act, is "to conserve the scenery and the natural and historic objects and the *wildlife therein* and to provide for the enjoyment of the same in such manner and by such means as will leave them unimpaired for the enjoyment of future generations" (emphasis added). With the passage of the Organic Act, Congress was no longer just setting aside areas of spectacular scenery and scientific curiosities. Now it also was requiring the protection of park resources, including wildlife.

## Management Philosophy

The National Park Service is responsible for protecting all the resources in the national parks and for assuring that people can enjoy these resources. The service rarely manages exclusively for wildlife. Instead, it attempts to integrate wildlife considerations into its other activities. Overall, today's Park Service tries to take an ecosystem approach to resource management—planning and carrying out activities designed to keep ecosystems and their natural processes functioning in perpetuity.

Regarding wildlife in the parks, the Park Service's Management Policies (Department of the Interior 1978) states:

> The Service will perpetuate the native animal life of the parks for the essential role in the natural ecosystems. Such management, conformable with the general and specific provisions of law and consistent with the following provisions, will strive to maintain the natural abundance, behavior, diversity, and ecological integrity of native animals in natural portions of parks as part of the park ecosystem.

Under Park Service law, policy, and regulations, native animal life in the national parks is protected from hunting, removal, destruction, harassment, or other harm caused by human actions, with the following exceptions:

1. Hunting, and in some cases trapping, may be allowed where specifically permitted by law. To date, Congress has authorized hunting in 52 units managed by the park service. These primarily are national recreation areas, national seashores, and national preserves. Trapping also is allowed in 26 of these units.
2. Sport fishing is allowed unless specifically prohibited.
3. Park Service officials may use necessary control measures for specific populations of wildlife where required for the maintenance of a healthy park ecosystem.
4. Animals may be removed or controlled where necessary for human health and safety.

It is National Park Service policy to rely to the greatest extent possible on natural processes to regulate populations of native species. Nonnative species are not to be allowed to displace native species if the displacement can be prevented by management. When control is deemed necessary, trapping and removal are the activities of choice, but killing is not prohibited if alternative methods are unavailable. The need for and results of any such wildlife management activity is documented and evaluated with research.

Wildlife management within the national parks is the responsibility of the National Park Service unless specifically stated otherwise in law. Most of the parks that allow hunting, fishing, or trapping have enabling legislation that specifies that these activities will be regulated by state law. Even in cases where the federal government has legal jurisdiction over these activities, the Park Service generally manages wildlife according to state regulations unless the Service determines that more restrictive rules are needed. The Park Service stresses the importance of cooperation between state and federal authorities, but overall the Park Service has the final say in wildlife management decisions.

# Organization and Operations

## Agency Structure

The National Park System now includes 337 areas in 49 states, the District of Columbia, Puerto Rico, Guam, the Trust Territories, and the Virgin Islands. Parks range in size and character from the immense roadless wilderness of Gates of the Arctic National Park in Alaska to Federal Hall National Memorial in Manhattan. Overall, the Service is responsible for 74.8 million acres of federal land (including 52.1 million in Alaska), an area larger than Arizona. An additional 4.6 million acres within the National Park System boundaries are owned by private individuals or other public entities. Visitation was projected to reach 256.8 million in 1985 (Department of the Interior 1985).

The National Park Service, a bureau within the Department of the Interior, is headed by a director and deputy director. The Service has a headquarters staff in Washington, D.C., and the following field units:

- 10 regional offices responsible for designated geographic areas;
- 337 parks, monuments, historic sites, recreation sites, etc., located within the 10 regions;
- a Denver Service Center responsible for providing technical assistance in park planning and developments;
- a Harpers Ferry Center that helps prepare interpretive plans and media presentations;
- training centers at Grand Canyon National Park, Arizona, and Harpers Ferry, West Virginia; and
- three archaeological centers that support archaeology in the parks.

The headquarters staff report to the director and are responsible for developing policies, programs, and regulations, and for coordination with Congress, the Office of Management and Budget, other agencies, and the public. The associate director for Natural Resources, Richard Briceland, has the most important responsibilities relating to wildlife. He overseas activities relating to the natural, social, and physical sciences in the parks, as well as natural-resource management. This includes the inventory, monitoring, and preservation of natural resources. The associate director supervises five divisions: Air Quality; Water Resources; Special Science Projects; Energy, Mining, and Minerals; and Biological Resources, and one separate field unit for Geographic Information Systems.

The Biological Resources Division has official responsibility for natural history, natural science, and natural resources activities in the National Park System, including wildlife management. In practice, however, the division's responsibilities are not as broad as they appear. The division is responsible for setting general policy and reviewing programs related to exotic species, endangered species, aquatic and terrestrial resources, research proposals and con-

# National Park Service Organization Headquarters

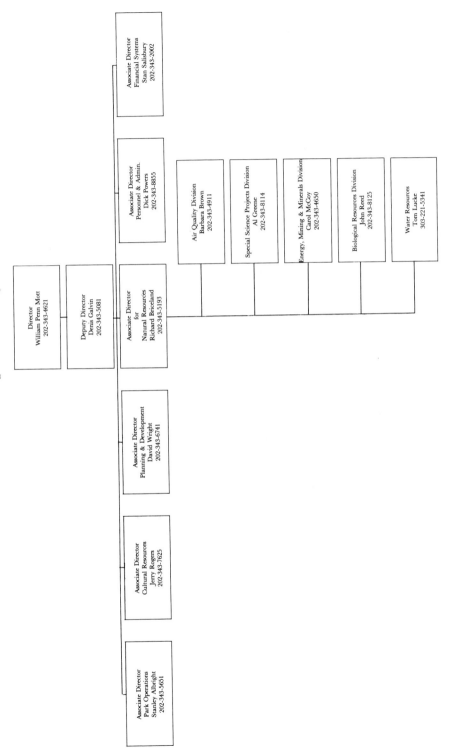

Director
William Penn Mott
202-343-4621

Deputy Director
Denis Galvin
202-343-5081

Associate Director
Park Operations
Stanley Albright
202-343-5651

Associate Director
Cultural Resources
Jerry Rogers
202-343-7625

Associate Director
Planning & Development
David Wright
202-343-6741

Associate Director
for
Natural Resources
Richard Briceland
202-343-5193

Associate Director
Personnel & Admin.
Dick Powers
202-343-8855

Associate Director
Financial Systems
Stan Salisbury
202-343-2002

Air Quality Division
Barbara Brown
202-343-4911

Special Science Projects Division
Al Greene
202-343-8114

Energy, Mining & Minerals Division
Carol McCoy
202-343-4650

Biological Resources Division
John Reed
202-343-8125

Water Resources
Tom Lucke
303-221-5341

tracts, research permits, resource monitoring, and publications. But most wildlife management activities are designed and conducted by field staff.

The next level of management in the National Park Service is the region. A region includes all the parks within one or more states and territories (see appendix). The regional director supervises all the park superintendents within the region and is the principal local representative of the Service. The regional director approves all programs, plans, and activities in accordance with Park Service policy. Each region has a chief scientist who oversees research, including wildlife research, throughout the region, and a resource management specialist who oversees park natural-resource management, including wildlife management.

The basic management unit of the National Park System is the park. Natural-resource-management activities, including wildlife activities, generally are planned and carried out at the park level. Each park is headed by a superintendent who is responsible for day-to-day management. Depending on the size and complexity of the park, there may be an assistant superintendent and various staff members trained in administration, protection (law enforcement), interpretation, resource management, and maintenance. Some parks also are staffed with biologists, ecologists, landscape architects, or other specialized personnel, some of whom may have special responsibilities for wildlife.

## Planning

Planning has a long history in the National Park Service and is considered a crucial step in fulfilling the agency's mission. Planning gives specific guidance on park preservation, use, and development and is done to assure that the purpose for which each park was created is achieved.

National Park Service Units With One or More Natural Resource Specialists*

| Region | Natural Resource Specialist(s) Present in Regional Office | Number of Parks w/Specialist(s) |
|---|---|---|
| Alaska | Yes | 3 |
| Mid-Atlantic | Yes | 6 |
| Midwest | Yes | 13 |
| National Capital | Yes | 4 |
| North Atlantic | Yes | 5 |
| Pacific Northwest | Yes | 3 |
| Rocky Mountain | No | 14 |
| Southeast | Yes | 8 |
| Southwest | Yes | 10 |
| Western | Yes | 18 |

* A natural resource specialist is a staff member assigned to resource management 91 to 100 percent of the time. These specialists include biologists, ecologists, landscape architects and other personnel with special responsibilities.

Source: NPS, Division of Biological Resources, 1985

Planning is initiated at the park level and begins with the identification of important issues, problems, and objectives (Department of the Interior 1982). The first step in the planning process is a document called a statement for management. The statement attempts to provide an up-to-date inventory of the park's condition and an analysis of its problems. The statement does not prescribe solutions. It is a baseline assessment of the park's status and needs. This document sets broad management objectives.

The park uses this information to prepare its most important document, the general management plan. This plan sets forth a park's basic management philosophy and goals. It provides general strategies to resolve problems and achieve the broad management objectives outlined in the statement for management. Resources management, visitor use, and all aspects of park operations are addressed. These plans are prepared with public involvement, providing an important opportunity for public participation in basic park-management decisions.

General management plans are required by law for all units of the National Park System. Of 337 units, 276 have approved plans and 61 are without plans. The Park Service, however, may never prepare plans for some very small units, such as Federal Hall National Monument in New York. The Service expects each plan to have a useful life of 10 to 20 years, depending on circumstances. Plans can be updated as needed.

The Park Service also prepares specific action plans that contain detailed information for field activities. For instance, a park might have a fire-management plan or a bear-management plan. One such plan, called a resource-management plan, delineates management activities needed to deal with particular resource problems within a park. These resource-management plans describe the principal projects needed to protect, preserve, and perpetuate an individual park's natural and cultural resources. They may discuss the impacts of development, plan measures to mitigate such impacts, or describe site-specific management actions to deal with a resource problem. Priority for implementing the projects listed in the plan normally is based on the significance of the resource. No research can be funded unless it first is identified in a plan, but being listed in no way assures funding.

Wildlife-related activities are one of many types of projects included in the plans. For instance, Yellowstone's plan calls for more detailed study of the impact on the grizzly bear of the Fishing Bridge Village visitor facilities, being built at an area used seasonally by grizzlies. Other wildlife activities might include projects to address overpopulation of native species such as elk or bison; wildlife disease occurrences such as rabies, brucellosis, and encephalitis; restoration of extirpated species; removal of exotic species; and wildlife monitoring. As of 1983, 246 park units had resource-management plans.*

* A current count is not available because in 1983 the Biological Resources Division in Washington, D.C., stopped reviewing all plans. The plans now are reviewed only at the regional offices, and more recent plans are not logged at National Park Service headquarters. Service officials estimate, however, that about 280 units probably now have resource-management plans.

Despite this extensive planning process, some critics argue that the Park Service continues to be shortsighted in its management of park resources. In addition, the Service has been criticized for its lack of national planning. Although some early efforts were made at planning on the regional level, almost all planning to date has been park oriented. As one critic explained:

> The National Park Service has no systemwide, long-range planning process to assess resource needs, develop programs, and implement programs over time. As a result, the Service often finds itself reacting to crises, rather than anticipating needs (Shands 1983).

While it will continue to be essential to conduct site-specific planning to meet the specific needs of each park unit, national planning would benefit the overall administration of the park system, particularly when it comes to securing funds, personnel, and support for National Park Service objectives. It would enable the 337 units to function as a coordinated system and help improve long-range planning.

## Budgeting

Formulation of the budget is a complex process involving interactions between park superintendents, regional directors, the director of the National Park Service, the secretary of the Interior, the Office of Management and Budget, and both houses of Congress. In general, budget needs are identified in the parks, but budget planning is guided and ultimately controlled at the national level.

It is not possible to track specific wildlife-related expenditures in the National Park Service budget because few activities are focused exclusively on wildlife and because of the great variety of park management activities that can directly and indirectly affect wildlife. Also, it is difficult to determine how much time and resources are devoted to wildlife because park personnel typically have many and varied duties and cannot account precisely for all wildlife-related activities. The Service maintains that its ecosystem-management approach integrates wildlife concerns into all its management activities.

Although wildlife funds cannot be tracked specifically, most funds allocated for direct wildlife-related activities are contained within the park operations account under the subheading "natural resources management." Natural-resources-management funds have remained a relatively constant—though small—percentage of the budget over the past five years, generally four to five percent. However, a review of funding trends can be misleading because the definition of what constitutes resource management can change from year to year, and some critics claim that essentially unrelated items are sometimes included under this category. This would make resource-management activities appear to constitute a larger share of the budget than they really do.

National Park Service Budget FY 1982–1986 (in $000s)

| FY | Total Funds* | Congressional Appropriation | | President's Request Natural Resources Management | Natural Resources as a percent of total Funds Appropriated |
|---|---|---|---|---|---|
| | | Operating Budget | Natural Resources Management | | |
| 1982 | $ 803,036 | $538,347 | $39,239 | —** | 4.8 |
| 1983 | 1,123,769 | 619,670 | 48,468 | 48,468 | 4.3 |
| 1984 | 954,919 | 629,309 | 48,906 | 48,156 | 5.1 |
| 1985 | 964,098 | 628,498 | 50,916 | 51,955 | 5.3 |
| 1986 | 905,643 | 627,763 | 52,986 | 50,797 | 5.8 |

*The Natioanl Park Service budget is the amount appropriated for normal operating expenses. The total National Park Service budget also includes funds authorized for specific land acquisition programs or construction, which can vary greatly from year to year. For instance, funds for National Trust for Historic Preservation and the Kennedy Center are included. The increase in 1983 reflects funds authorized for the Park Restoration and Improvement Program.
**Amounts requested prior to 1983 are not available.
Source: National Park Service Budget Office, 1986.

For FY 1986, Congress appointed a total of $905,643,000 for the National Park Service. This is down slightly from the previous year. Of this sum, Congress appropriated $627,763,000 for operation of the National Park System, a compromise between the $628,996,000 proposed by the House and $619,548,000 proposed by the Senate. The operating budget is the money appropriated for normal operating expenses in the national park system. The total appropriation includes funds authorized for specific land acquisition, construction, special programs, and the Kennedy Center for the Performing Arts.

## Research

Research is one component of the broader activity called resource management. In 1985, research and development funding was $15 million, only 1.5 percent of the total Park Service budget. About 150 Park Service research scientists work on natural-resource problems in the parks. Each region has a chief scientist responsible for overseeing research in his region.

National Park Service headquarters does not maintain a separate research division because research is considered an integral part of natural-resource management. Research policy and program oversight relating to wildlife is primarily the responsibility of the Biological Resources Division and the special Science Projects Division.

The types of projects conducted by the Park Service vary considerably. They have included air-quality and water-quality monitoring; ecological base-line data surveys; impacts of and methods to control exotic species; ani-

National Park Service Research and Development Funding* FY 1982–1986

| FY | Funds Appropriated |
|---|---|
| 1982 | $11,203,000 |
| 1983 | 13,746,000 |
| 1984 | 14,000,000 |
| 1985 | 15,000,000 |
| 1986 | 15,500,000 |

*These are funds devoted specifically to national-park research projects, including money for college and university research, technical assistance, and other hands-on research. It does not include salaries for the regional chief scientist or Washington office staff.
Source: National Park Service Office, 1986.

mal and plant surveys; studies on the ecology, management, or restoration of threatened or endangered species; the role of fire in maintaining natural ecosystems; human impacts on backcountry resources; hydrologic studies; and more.

The Park Service also gets important research information from its cooperative park study units. The Service has cooperative agreements with 21 universities and other institutions to facilitate research and provide technical assistance to the parks (see appendix). Under the agreements, a Park Service scientist may be stationed at the unit, thus gaining improved access to current information and expertise. The Park Service scientist also acts as a liason to enlist faculty and graduate students to conduct research needed by the parks. Some examples of cooperative park study units research related to wildlife include "Status of the River Otter (*Lutra canadensis*) at Acadia National Park," "Ecology and Management of Colonially Nesting Waterbirds at Selected Atlantic Coast National Parks," and "White-Tailed Deer Management Study at Fire Island National Seashore."

The relatively new cooperative park study unit at Rutgers University is unique in that it is an inter-regional effort focused on Atlantic and Gulf Coast barrier island national parks. The three regions involved are the North Atlantic, Mid-Atlantic, and Southeast.

Research in the parks also is contracted directly with universities. In addition, other federal agencies, state agencies, private organizations, and private researchers play significant roles in funding and conducting research in the parks.

# Current Program Trends

## The New Director and his 12-Point Plan

An important change within the Park Service in 1985 was the appointment of William Penn Mott, Jr., as director. Mott's selection was greeted enthusiastically by the conservation community. Mott began his Park Service career in 1933, and he worked many years for city parks in California. He went on to become director of the California State Department of Parks and Recreation under Governor Ronald Reagan, and during his tenure the size of the state system doubled.

Director Mott's first action was to call together Park Service personnel and representatives of more than 40 conservation organizations for a meeting in Yellowstone. He used the opportunity to foster a feeling of unity of purpose among park proponents and to present a 12-point plan (Department of the Interior 1985) for the National Park Service. While some critics argue that there is nothing new in the plan and that, in fact, it is articulating points long discussed and actually mandated by the 1916 Organic Act, other experts say that "while the words may not be new, the top-level commitment is." Mott's 12 objectives for the Service include:

1. Develop a long-range strategy to better protect natural, cultural, and recreational resources.
2. Pursue a creative, expanded land-protection initiative.
3. Stimulate and increase interpretative and visitor-service activities for greater public impact.
4. Effectively share with the public an understanding of critical resource issues.
5. Increase public understanding of the role and function of the National Park Service.
6. Expand the role and involvement of citizens and citizen groups at all levels in the National Park Service.
7. Seek a better balance between visitor use and resource management.
8. Enhance the Service's ability to meet the diverse uses that the public expects in national parks.
9. Expand career opportunities for all employees.
10. Plan, design, and maintain appropriate park facilities.
11. Develop a team relationship between concessionaires and the National Park Service.
12. Foster and encourage more creativity, efficiency, and effectiveness in the management and administration of the National Park Service.

The 12 point objectives admittedly are general. Further efforts to implement the policies through actual programs and initiatives will require considerable effort. To begin, Mott has assigned one objective to each regional director and asked them to recommend concrete steps to achieve the objectives Service-wide. The action plan detailing this work will be completed in early 1986.

## Land Acquisition

In 1985, the National Park Service increased its number of units by three, up to 337. The new units are the Potomac Heritage and the Natchez Trace national scenic trails and the Missouri National Recreation River. Fort Benton

Congressional Appropriations for Land Acquisition by the National Park Service

| 1982 | 123.2 million |
|------|---------------|
| 1983 | 116.5 million |
| 1984 | 122.5 million |
| 1985 | 125.7 million |
| 1986 | 98.4 million |

was transferred to the Bureau of Land Management. The changes do not add significant acreage to the national park system because they reflect a change in accounting more than acquisition of new land.

During 1985, the Park Service acquired about 29,170,000 acres of new land. The land was acquired in 714 tracts in about 35 park units. Many of the parcels were purchased as part of efforts to relocate and protect parts of the Appalachian Trail. Other tracts were purchased to be included in Santa Monica Mountains National Recreation Area, Rocky Mountain National Park, Cuyahoga Valley National Recreation Area, Voyageurs National Park, and Point Reyes National Seashore.

Congress appropriated $98.4 million to the National Park Service for land acquisition in FY 1986. Of this, $50 million is for assistance to the states in acquiring park land under the Land and Water Conservation Fund. About $7 million of the remaining federal share will be used for the Appalachian Trail. Other federal funds will be used to acquire land in 14 park units. About $3 million is authorized for the purchase of inholdings.

## Accomplishments

The National Park Service manages 74.8 million acres, an area larger than Arizona. The system includes 337 units in 49 states and the District of Columbia. Parks vary tremendously in size and character, including natural, cultural, and recreational areas. Visitation is projected to reach 256.8 million in 1985, of which more than 16 million visitors are expected to stay overnight. Managing a system of such diversity is an accomplishment of notable merit.

To protect and preserve the parks requires a combination of professional resource management and people management. Part of people management is establishing a constituency of visitors who care about the parks, and this the Park Service does well. Park Service employees are dedicated and well respected. Their contributions to maintaining the quality of the parks are essential. In particular, interpretative programs conducted by park rangers help visitors appreciate and understand the priceless resources that the Service manages. In addition, unpaid volunteers are increasingly essential to operations in many parks.

The Service has made strides in resource management, and a number of programs exist for planning, research, monitoring, and corrective actions.

Most parks now have Resource Management Plans to describe resource problems and discuss management options. The Park Service's air-quality program, which protects air quality in 48 national parks designated as Class I airsheds, is particularly well regarded.*

Similarly, the Service's participation in the Interagency Fire Center in Boise, Idaho, and the Interagency Grizzly Bear Committee merit attention. One other program of note is the Natural Resource Specialist Trainee Program.

*The Natural Resource Specialist Trainee Program.* This program was initiated in 1982 as a response to the *State of the Parks* report (Department of the Interior 1980), a report requested by Congress on problems facing the park system. The program is an attempt to train highly qualified specialists for natural-resources-management positions in the parks. (Currently, less than one percent of the Service's permanent work force is involved with natural-resource management full-time.) The program provides funds for selected trainees to participate in a 22-month program of field training and classroom work in resource management. At the completion of the program, each participant is assigned to a permanent position in the field as a resource-management specialist. The program is funded and managed by the Washington office and received just under $1 million yearly. Future funding is in question.

To date, one class has been graduated from the program (32 people in the 1983-1984 class), and a second class is enrolled now (23 people in the 1985-86 class). The second class of trainees is receiving more formal preparation than the first class—more classroom work, more supervised field work, and more individual guidance. Their program includes 30 weeks of classroom work, with courses on microcomputer use, vegetation and wildlife management, mining and minerals, air quality, and other topics. Each trainee is assigned to a training location where he or she participates in day-to-day management activities under the guidance of an experienced resource manager. There is also a regional coordinator and an overall coordinator at the Washington office to help ensure program quality.

To gain practical experience, the trainees are required, as part of the program, to design and implement an individual project at their training park. Wildlife oriented projects include:

- Preparation of the Approved Management Plan for the Reintroduction of Bighorn Sheep to the Great Western Divide, Sequoia, and Kings Canyon national parks.
- The Vertebrate Faunal Inventory of Saint-Gaudens National Historic Site.
- The Spotted Owl Suitable Habitat Evaluation, Mount Rainier.

* Class I airsheds were designated by the Clean Air Act of 1977 and include all national parks greater than 6,000 acres that existed at that time. Air quality in these areas is strictly protected.

- Baseline Data Collection and Design of Monitoring Program for Protection of State Endangered Species, Indiana Dunes National Lakeshore.

Competition to enter the class was keen, and the Service selected trainees who already had a natural-science background and some experience working in a natural-resource field. The program is designed to be an intensive introduction to field-level resource management. Its goal is to place experienced natural-resource managers in as many parks as is practical and thus make resource management a more active part of the Park Service. However, the future of the National Resources Management Trainee Program is in question. Plans for the 1987-88 class are less ambitious than those for earlier classes because of a reallocation of funds.

## Wildlife Management

Wildlife is a key elements in park ecosystems, but the National Park Service rarely manages exclusively for wildlife. Instead, it attempts to integrate wildlife considerations into its other management activities. But because wildlife is such an important and highly visible park resource, park managers are eager to undertake activities to benefit wildlife. Many of the projects are small, have limited budgets, and inevitably stretch over a number of years. The following is a sample of some significant wildlife-related activities ongoing during 1985.

*Herpetofauna Restoration at Jamaica Bay.* The Jamaica Bay Wildlife Refuge is part of Gateway National Recreation Area—more than 9,000 acres of saltwater bay, marshes, and upland habitats scattered among 25 islands in southern Brooklyn and Queens in New York City. While the area and the refuge have been managed by the National Park Service over the years to benefit the 320 species of birds that have been recorded there, there is a contrasting scarcity of other wildlife, particularly amphibians and reptiles (herpetofauna). Park managers saw a unique opportunity: a chance to restore a representative natural community within the highly urbanized and populated New York metropolitan area.

Efforts to inventory the refuge's herpetofauna populations began in 1979. Next came a program of habitat improvements—management to provide food, water, cover, and other requirements for species that originally would have been present at the site. Small freshwater ponds were created, largely using volunteer labor, and aquatic plants and suitable cover were added.

The staff began introducing regionally native species. They began simply, choosing three species. Spring peepers, northern brown snakes, and eastern box turtles were collected locally from areas with large populations or populations already faced with extirpation and released in the refuge. By 1985, nine species were being released, including the black racer snake, red-backed salamander, painted turtle, snapping turtle, milk snake, green snake, hognose snake, and green frog. The program began its first introduction of mammals with the release of 26 chipmunks. In addition, the refuge now has 14 nest boxes for barn owls; seven show signs of owl activity.

Any program to enhance an animal community will progress slowly, over the course of years. Staff hope their efforts will continue to be successful in establishing a balanced, self-perpetuating animal community that is representative of pre-urban New York. As urban growth continues, the park may someday be one of the only places left in New York City where visitors can observe native wildlife.

*Oryx at White Sands National Monument.* The oryx is a large (ranging up to 400 pounds) African antelope, an exotic released as a game animal in the late 1960s and early 1970s. Today, more than 800 of them range freely in New Mexico, where they have become a significant problem in White Sands National Monument. These grazers can severely damage the limited vegetation of the dunes, which is key to maintaining the dune ecosystem.

In a successful attempt to manage the oryx by non-lethel means, park managers at White Sands built a 19-mile fence bounding the south and west sides of the park, fencing out more than 60 animals. Though some oryx still drift in from the north and a few remain in the park from before the fencing, Park Service personnel are optimistic that the technique will work and the remaining animals will disperse. The fence itself was designed to accommodate the needs of native wildlife. It is a smooth-wire fence to prevent harming animals that might run into it, and it is designed so that native pronghorn, smaller than the oryx, can come and go under the bottom strand.

*Peregrine Falcon Program.* For 10 years, the National Park Service has been involved in efforts to restore populations of peregrine falcons to their native range, and these efforts are one of the most encouraging wildlife-management successes on Park Service land. Working closely with the Peregrine Fund, a private organization dedicated to the protection and restoration of birds of prey, Park Service staff have helped bring about a substantial recovery in peregrine populations in a number of western parks. Peregrines have been released in Grand Teton, Rocky Mountain, Dinosaur,* Canyonlands, and Capitol Reef national parks. In the East, Acadia National Park has had young birds reared and released on its cliffs.

Much of the best peregrine habitat is in the Rocky Mountain Region, particularly the canyon parks. The Rocky Mountain Region conducted two types of peregrine activity in 1985. First, the region contracted with the Peregrine Fund to conduct the first comprehensive peregrine-population survey. Far greater populations were discovered in some areas than had ever been

---

* No peregrines were released in Dinosaur this year because of pesticide spraying in the area.

known. Fourteen pairs of birds were located in Zion National Park, giving the park the greatest concentration of peregrines outside of Alaska. The region estimates that they had about 130 peregrines during the 1985 season.

Second, the region continued its program to restore populations levels by introducing young birds to suitable habitats. Using two hack sites at Rocky Mountain, two at Grand Teton, and one at Yellowstone, 25 young birds were hacked (for a full description of hacking and peregrine management, see this volume's chapter on the peregrine). Much of the work involved in collecting eggs and hacking the young birds is done by volunteers. Surveys show that peregrines released in previous years are beginning to return to the areas around the parks, and staff hope eventually to establish a population capable of sustaining itself without human interference. The Park Service plans to have the Peregrine Fund conduct a follow-up survey in 1987 to determine the effects of the ongoing program.

***Combating Exotic Rodents at Channel Islands.*** Park managers at Channel Islands National Park in California noticed that the native deer mouse (*Peromyscus maniculatus*) had disappeared on the smallest island of the Channel Island group, East Anacapa. The cause: Rats that reached the island, 15 miles off the coast, by boat, perhaps stowed away with supplies destined for Coast Guard personnel who had lived on the islands for 50 years. Because the more aggressive rats thrived on the same food and habitat as the mice, and even preyed on the smaller rodents, they had outcompeted the native population. It was a small, but classic, example of the problem caused by exotic intruders.

After research to verify that the native mice were indeed gone, park managers undertook a lethal control program to control the rats and restore the native mice. Through carefully timed trapping over a period of months, conducted primarily by volunteers, they caught 500 rats on the 90-acre island. Park managers still are trapping a few remaining animals. They hope to use the information they have gained through this combined research/management activity to help combat rats on two other islands where the situation is more complex. They hope to obtain funds to study management where rats are mixed with populations of mice and foxes, and where trapping might be dangerous to the native animals. Park staff now are waiting to see if native mice from nearby Middle Anacapa, connected to East Anacapa at low tide, will recolonize the island.

# Current Issues

The Park Service mission is a complicated one, and problems in the parks are inevitable. Problems emanate from both internal and external sources and affect natural resources in all the parks, regardless of size, use, or location. In particular, wildlife in the nation's parks are increasingly threatened by human development, habitat loss, and other external pressures. Without strengthened commitment in the future, it may become increasingly difficult for the parks to serve their fundamental purpose of protecting the scenic, natural, and historic resources of the parks and "wildlife therein." As the parks face increasing visitation pressures within their borders and development pressures outside, the Park Service's limited commitment of staff and funding for natural-resource management, including wildlife, will become especially troublesome and is likely to lead to increasingly visible problems in the future.

In 1980, responding to a request from Congress, the Park Service issued its *State of the Parks Report* (Department of the Interior 1980). Though now outdated, the findings of this report still are valid in documenting the breadth and depth of the problems facing the parks. The report cataloged 73 types of threats, including pollutants, visitor activities, exotic species, and industrial development projects, that park staff perceived to have the potential to cause damage to park resources.

The report noted that parks set aside primarily to protect natural areas, which include the parks most valuable for wildlife, are especially hard hit with problems. The 63 national parks greater than 30,000 acres reported twice as many threats as the Service-wide norm. This frequency of threats may be due partly to the fact that the larger parks have more professionally trained staff who are more capable of recognizing threats. The parks that are also part of the Biosphere Reserve network, internationally recognized for their scientific importance through the United Nation's Man and the Biosphere program reported an average number of threats three times greater than the norm. This is particularly disturbing because the Biosphere Reserve, parks are considered global benchmarks of ecological health and outstanding examples of the world's ecosystems and biological diversity.

More than 50 percent of the potential problems emanated from sources outside the parks. Industrial and commercial development, air pollution, urban encroachment, and roads were the most frequently cited external threats. The most frequently perceived internal problems were associated with heavy visitor use, utility access corridors, vehicle noise, soil erosion, and the proliferation of exotic plants and animals. The report found that scenic resources were threatened in more than 60 percent of the parks; air quality in more than 45 percent; and mammal, plant, and freshwater resources in more than 40 percent. A disturbing 75 percent of the problems were cited as inadequately documented and in need of research.

Problems specifically affecting wildlife included direct problems such as hunting and poaching, competition from exotic species, harassment, and habitat destruction. Other problems indirectly harming wildlife included air pollution, development of lands adjacent to parks, and some visitor use. Some of the major issues facing the Park Service are discussed here. Also, see the *Audubon Wildlife Report 1985* for a broader discussion of park threats. Some of the material contained here is an abridgement of information contained in the 1985 volume.

## Pressures from Adjacent Lands

The national parks suffer a variety of pressures emanating from adjacent lands. These range from observable habitat destruction caused by various types of land-use development to more insidious problems such as air pollution, groundwater depletion, and acid rain. Problems caused by outside sources often are complex and frequently are more difficult to deal with than internal problems because the Park Service has no authority to control them.

The types of adjacent-land pressures of concern to the parks include residential, commercial, industrial, and road development; grazing; logging; agriculture; energy extraction and production; mining; recreation; and many others. The extent and rapid expansion of these externally-caused problems has introduced new economic, legal, and technical issues into park management.

As the nation's human population has grown, the public lands adjacent to the parks have become increasingly subject to a variety of uses. When management activities on land surrounding a national park differ greatly from the management inside, the park may become an ecological island. The natural ebb and flow of wildlife into and out of the park can be disturbed. Habitat outside the park that is vital to park species—for example, winter range for migrating species—can be lost.

Elk populations in Rocky Mountain National Park illustrate this dilemma. While the park provides excellent summer range, conflicts arise when the animals move out of the park in search of winter forage. More and more, they have been creating problems in the town of Estes Park, Colorado.

The most recent and graphic example involves Yellowstone's buffalo. In December 1985, Montana allowed its first legal buffalo hunt in 25 years. The hunt was authorized by the Montana legislature as an effort to control bison that wander beyond the park onto private ranches as the winter deepens. Ranchers fear the animals because they can transmit brucellosis, a cattle disease. Three bison have been shot outside the park so far, and others will be hunted if they leave the park boundaries (*The Washington Post,* December 31, 1985).

Conflicts between people and wildlife will only increase as human activities occur closer to the parks. Examples of such conflicts can be found in both Shenandoah National Park in Virginia and Great Smoky Mountain National Park in North Carolina/Tennessee, where the parks are losing black bears to poaching, road kills, and loss of habitat as the land around the parks is developed.

Predator control on adjacent lands also is a continuing issue. Near Carlsbad Caverns in New Mexico, ranchers have claimed that mountain lions kill their livestock and then retreat into the park. The ranchers have argued that the lions should be followed into the park and killed to prevent future depredations. When the Department of the Interior in 1983 announced plans to allow the killing of lions in the park, Defenders of Wildlife and the Sierra Club sought an injection to prevent it. Interior subsequently dropped the plan.

Similar management dilemmas can be seen in parks with extensive prairie dog populations, such as Wind Cave and Badlands in South Dakota, Fort Larned in Kansas, Curecanti in Colorado, and Devil's Tower in Wyoming. Prairie dogs are native species in these parks, but few predators remain to keep their populations in check. Because prairie dogs can compete with other native wildlife for range and food and can cause human-health problems, parks sometimes act to manage overabundant populations. In some areas, the pesticide Sevin is dusted into prairie dog holes to control fleas and thus prevent the spread of plague.

In other areas, poisons are used to reduce populations. In Badlands, for instance, a court has ordered the park to maintain free of prairie dogs a one-mile buffer along its boundary. The order resulted from complaints filed by local ranchers who felt the park's prairie dogs were deteriorating their range. The park uses a theoretically species-specific poisoning method. A two-percent application of zinc phosphide incorporated in rolled oats is placed near known prairie dog holes in the fall, after grain-feeding birds are gone. However, this method remains controversial as some conservationists fear harm to nontarget species, including the very rare black-footed ferret.

Privately owned land remaining within park boundaries can be the source of wildlife-people conflicts.* For example, within the boundaries of Rocky Mountain National Park is a ski resort, Ski Estes Park. Ski Estes is a small, family-oriented resort, but its managers (the Estes Valley Recreation and Park District, part of the town government) have unveiled controversial plans to expand the area two fold. The expansion would cut trees, thus eliminating wildlife habitat and food, and draw significant water from a nearby stream for snowmaking, which in turn would affect habitat of the threatened greenback cutthroat trout (National Parks and Conservation Association 1985a).

Many conservation groups, half the population of the town of Estes Park, and the park itself all oppose the growth. Further, the expansion contradicts the park's master plan. The master plan states that the facilities at Ski Estes should be controlled strictly to reduce aesthetic and environmental impacts and that they actually should be phased out and the area reforested when alternative facilities become available outside the park.

Other examples of adjacent-lands problems in the National Park System include:

- Dinosaur National Monument in Colorado and Utah, where cricket-control programs using the pesticide Sevin are being conducted by the federal

---

* The National Park Service definition of "in-holdings" includes only privately owned land surrounded by service land before 1959. The service does not use the term simply to refer to any privately owned land within park boundaries.

Animal and Plant Health Inspection Service (APHIS) on adjacent lands. This may interfere with the breeding success of the park's peregrine falcons or disturb the populations in other ways. FWS had recommended that APHIS stop spraying within 10 miles of known peregrine nests or hacking sites, but APHIS conducted the program disregarding the recommendation.* Thus, in 1985, the Park Service decided not to release any young peregrines in Dinosaur. The National Parks and Conservation Association and the Sierra Club have filed suit to stop the spraying program.

- Glacier National Park in Montana, where minerals extraction, timber harvesting, road construction, and oil and gas leasing on U.S. Forest Service lands adjacent to the park are degrading grizzly bear migration corridors, elk calving grounds, and spring feeding grounds for moose.
- Sleeping Bear Dunes National Lakeshore in Michigan, where local authorities hold title to 42 miles of roads on North Island, a recently acquired part of the park, and are threatening to harvest timber along their right-of-way unless they receive compensation for the highway funds they lost when the Park Service acquired the island. Logging would alter the character of the island and damage wildlife habitat and food supplies.
- Canyonlands National Park in Utah, where the Department of Energy has been considering a site in Davis Canyon, less than one mile from the eastern boundary of the park, for a proposed high-level nuclear-waste dump. This would create a small town where none now exists and would route hazardous materials near the park. Although the Davis Canyon site next to Canyonlands was not listed as on the Department of Energy's top three sites in the first round of selection conducted this year, the park is still in jeopardy because the Department of Energy is changing its ranking procedures and could select the site for further testing. Testing would include drilling 47 deep boreholes adjacent to the park, and digging two large shafts 3,000 feet deep and 25 feet wide, plus the development of accompanying buildings and roads (National Parks and Conservation Association 1985b).
- Everglades National Park in Florida, where diversion of natural freshwater flows by Army Corps of Engineers projects and overfishing by commercial operators supposedly regulated by the National Marine Fisheries Service have affected the environment so seriously that wading-bird populations have declined 90 percent since the park was established.
- Yellowstone National Park in Montana and Wyoming, where geothermal development, oil and gas leasing, and development on adjacent lands are threatening or destroying vital habitat for the threatened grizzly bear population and increasing the number of conflicts between bears and people.

* After similar spraying in 1985, six endangered peregrines disappeared. Critics have suggested that an integrated pest management strategy using bran treated with disease organisms that affect only the problem crickets offers a viable, environmentally acceptable alternative method to control the insect outbreak.

Ongoing debates over Yellowstone are particularly heated and illustrative of the complexity of adjacent-land pressures, even when the management activities are occurring inside the park. One controversial dispute involves the park service's long-term plan to shift tourists away from Fishing Bridge, an environmentally sensitive area. The Park Service wants to close the Fishing Bridge campground and facilities and use new ones recently established at Grant Village 25 miles away. They planned this change because Fishing Bridge is an area where the park's threatened grizzly bears fish and forage along the shores of Yellowstone Lake. The staff considers it dangerous to concentrate people so near prime bear habitat, where their presence would be detrimental to the bears. Yellowstone's grizzly population has declined to an estimated 200 bears, and the bear is now Yellowstone's highest priority management issue.

The building of Grant Village originally was intended to be contingent upon the closing of the Fishing Bridge facilities, and the closing was scheduled for summer 1985 in the park's 1974 master plan. However, the closing was blocked by Wyoming businessmen and members of Wyoming's congressional delegation—Senators Alan Simpson (R) and Malcolm Wallop (R) and Representative Richard Cheney (R). Concerned local residents feared that the change would divert significant tourist revenues away from the park gateway town of Cody. Through their congressional delegation, they pressured the Park Service into spending two more years studying the impact of the relocation, including the effects on business in Cody. In the meantime, the new facilities at Grant Village and the old facilities at Fishing Bridge are both open, and critics charge that the park submitted to political pressure that was intended all along to create two large, permanent tourist developments in the park. Further, some people argue that the new Grant Village facilities also infringe on sensitive bear habitat. "It is a tangled web, to the say the least," one Yellowstone official explained (*The New York Times*, August 5, 1985).

Activities on adjacent lands often have subtle effects on wildlife. For example, groundwater depletion in Everglades National Park is destroying habitat and changing the complex ecosystem's character. Elsewhere, small changes in lake or stream acidity caused by acid precipitation can inhibit reproduction in fish, and higher levels can impair body organs, alter growth rates, and decrease resistance to environmental stresses. Frogs and salamanders may be affected similarly. The loss of such species can then affect other wildlife through the food chain. The elimination of fish from a lake, for instance, would reduce lake use by loons, mergansers, or other species dependent upon fish for food.

A recent study by the World Resources Institute (Roth *et al* 1985) identified acid precipitation as a problem in Yosemite, Sequoia, Mount Rainier, North Cascades, and Rocky Mountain national parks. Other parks, including Yellowstone, Kings Canyon, Devils Postpile, Olympic, Crater Lake, and Glacier also were found to be sensitive to acid rain damage, and still other parks are being investigated for potential problems.

All the national parks will become more stressed as incompatible adjacent-land uses continue. Because the viability of an important park resource—wildlife—often is dependent upon habitat outside the parks, the future is likely to bring this issue increasingly into the limelight. Yet the National Park Service has limited authority and methods to deal with the problems caused by incompatible adjacent-land uses, whether the use takes place on private lands or on lands owned by other federal agencies such as the Forest Service or Bureau of Land Management.

## Exotic Species

One of the most difficult issues for park managers, and one with profound impacts on park wildlife, is the introduction into park ecosystems of non-indigenous or "exotic" species, which are nonnative species that occur in a given place or region as a result of direct or indirect, deliberate or accidental, introduction of the species by humans. In the 1980 *State of the Parks* report, more than 300 park units reported a total of 602 problems related to exotic species. Because of the seriousness of these problems, this natural-resource-management issue has received considerable attention and funds in recent years, but in far too many cases the Park Service has been unable to eradicate the harmful species or to remedy problems caused by the species.

The most common problems caused by exotic animals concern habitat destruction and competition for resources. Some exotic species have become so firmly established and are so destructive of the local ecosystem that populations of native species have been reduced or even extirpated. Exotics can change normal ecological processes, such as nutrient and energy cycling; modify predator-prey and herbivore-plant relationships; and affect soil building and erosion. Because exotic species have few, if any, predators and parasites in their new environments, their long-term population growth can be explosive.

Exotic species problems are varied and widespread and involve both plants and animals. Examples of some animal problems include wild boars in Great Smoky Mountain, Haleakala, and Hawaii Volcanoes national parks; mountain goats in Olympic National Park; Barbary sheep in Carlsbad Caverns and Guadalupe Mountains national parks; and feral burros in a number of western parks. Exotic fish introduced in earlier years to improve sport fishing also pose problems. European brown trout and western rainbow trout outcompete native Appalachian brook trout in the Great Smokies. Conversely, introduced eastern brook trout are causing similar problems in western parks such as Yellowstone, Sequoia, and Kings Canyon.

***Wild Boars at Great Smoky Mountains:*** European wild boars were introduced into a private hunting preserve in Tennessee in 1912. Some boars escaped the preserve and, in an ecosystem lacking natural checks and balances, multiplied and extended their range. The boars now inhabit three-quarters of Great Smoky National Park and have been causing serious problems, primarily destruction of forest-floor plants and related animal communities. In the most damaged sites, the voracious boars have reduced herbaceous ground cover by as much as 98 percent. Their rooting disturbs wildflowers: one threatened species (the small-whorled pogonia) and eight "sensitive" species could be affected. They also eat native small animals and can radically change the upper soil structure, affecting small mammals such as voles and shrews. The hogs also compete with native black bears, white-tailed deer, gray squirrel, and wild turkey for fruits, nuts and acorns. Two endemic species—a salamander and a snail—are threatened because of the wild boars.

Management is extremely difficult, in part because the animals are elusive and in part because of strong local sentiment regarding the issue. Only one percent of North Carolina's sportsmen hunt boars, but they are a vocal minority and have brought great political pressure to the debate. They would prefer to be allowed to hunt in the national park, and are opposed to the use of lethal control by the FWS. Since hunting is not allowed in the park, park personnel have been live-trapping the boars and transferring them to the Forest Service to stock national forests where boar hunting is permitted.* Since the stocking program began in 1962, 25,000 acres of national forest have been stocked. The native flora and fauna of these forests are now being disturbed by the introduced animals.

In a recent renewal of the controversy, hunters pressured the forest supervisor of Nantahala National Forest to allow 9,000 acres of the forest, not now populated with wild boars, to be stocked. This would open an entirely new range to the boars and their destructive behavior. Environmental groups appealed, and in the summer of 1985 the regional forester overturned the supervisor's decision. That decision is now being appealed.

*Mountain Goats at Olympic:* Mountain goats, while native to the eastern side of Washington's Cascade Range, were introduced into the Olympic Mountains of western Washington around 1925. Now numbering more than 1,100 animals, the goats cause problems because they reduce plant cover, shift the relative abundance of different species of plants, and cause severe soil erosion in fragile alpine areas. Goats eat at least three rare plant species endemic to the Olympic Range and eventually could cause their extinction. The Park Service is studying the response of native vegetation and soil systems to the goats and is testing several goat removal and sterilization techniques.

*Feral Burros in Grand Canyon, Death Valley, and Bandelier:* Burros were left in these areas by miners and prospectors in the late 1800s. As the numbers of burros grew, these animals became a major threat to park resources. Large populations destroyed vegetation, caused severe erosion, dam-

* The park service also kills some boars.

aged prehistoric sites, and competed with native species such as bighorn sheep and mule deer. For many years, populations were kept in check by routine shooting. However, park managers, anticipating public pressure, stopped that procedure.

Without some form of control, the burro populations grew quickly, as did a variety of environmental problems associated with them (see the *Audubon Wildlife Report 1985* for details). In Grand Canyon, live capture and removal proved costly, but with the help of burro protection groups essentially all the burros have been eliminated from the park. Similarly, essentially all of the burros have been removed from Death Valley.* Continued monitoring and maintenance of the burro populations will be necessary to keep the animals from getting out of control again.

***Eastern Brook Trout in Yellowstone:*** The summer of 1985 saw park managers in Yellowstone taking swift action against an exotic fish. During a routine wildlife census, staff discovered Eastern brook trout inhabiting a stream near Yellowstone Lake. The discovery was particularly troublesome because the replacement of the native cutthroat trout by the eastern brook trout could have disrupted nature's intricate food chain, with dangerous consequences for nonaquatic Yellowstone animals. Cutthroat trout swim upstream to spawn from May to July and are the main summer food for many animals, including osprey, pelicans, black bear, bald eagles, and grizzly bears. Eastern brook trout do not spawn until October or November; if they were to outcompete the cutthroats, many land animals would be deprived of their chief summertime food.

Acting quickly to prevent spread of the species, park managers distributed a fish toxicant into the creek, killing 80,000 fish, exotic and native alike. Native cutthroat trout will migrate back into the creek and repopulate it next year. The Park Service is attempting to determine who released the exotic species in the creek; they suspect it was a fisherman who favored brook trout and did not think through the implications of his actions. "It was probably innocent," said a biologist involved, "but it broke the main rule of a national park: leave everything the way nature made it" (*The Washington Post*, September 14, 1985).

## Exotic Plant Species

An equally pressing issue in many parks is the problem created by the introduction of nonnative plants. Like exotic animals, exotic plants can replace native flora and alter park ecosystems. Exotic plants tend to lower the level of diversity in an ecosystem, which can interrupt the food chain, harm birds and insects, and change animal population dynamics.

* As of December 31, 1985.

For example, African ice plants have taken over eroded areas in Channel Islands National Park in California, where they effectively outcompete rare native species. Tamarisk, native to the Mediterranean, has invaded springs and waterways in several desert parks. The plant's deep roots lower the water table and eliminate surface water essential to native wildlife.

Hawaii Volcanoes National Park has serious problems with exotic plant species, especially with those that disrupt the natural diversity in the rain forests. Lantana (*Lantana camara*), guava (*Psidium guajava; Psidium cattleianum*), and Christmans berry (*Shinus terebinthifolius*) are significant problems in Hawaii. These exotics are aggressive and spread easily. They tend to establish monotypic (all of one kind) stands of vegetation, excluding native species. This disrupts food sources and the overall habitat for wildlife.

Perhaps some of the most serious problems with exotic plants are visible in Everglades National Park in Florida. Exotics have significantly altered the character of Everglades. Australian pine (*Causarina*), introduced as a windbreak and now common throughout Florida, can change the deposition of sand on beaches. This can reduce nesting sites for the American crocodile and sea turtles. Another troublesome exotic, *Melaleuca,* was aerially seeded in 1936 in an attempt to help "dry up" the flooded potholes of the Everglades, with the hope of reducing mosquitos. *Melaleuca* is now prolific in the park. Stands of this exotic are so dense that deer will not enter to find shelter or food, and most food plants are gone. Further, the plant is indeed doing its intended job— drying up areas formerly covered by water, to the detriment of other plants, fish, and wildlife. In the future, it may prove to be a major factor in destroying habitat for the endangered Everglades kite (Courtenay 1978). A third exotic, Brazilian pepper, also is widespread and prevents native species from occupying certain areas. Any change in plant species affects food resources and thus affects wildlife in the park.

Management is difficult. For now, the park relies primarily on pulling out small plants or using herbicides on larger specimens, but efforts are small compared to the size of the problem. Further, management always will remain difficult because the park is surrounded by lands where these exotics are common and the likelihood of reintroduction is high.

The problems associated with exotic plant and animal species will continue to challenge park managers. The most visible success so far has been the removal of feral burros. On the whole, however, removal of exotics is tedious, expensive, and sometimes impossible. Shooting, perhaps the most effective and economical technique for larger animals, generally arouses tremendous controversy from humane groups. Eradication of exotic plant species, while less controversial, can be even more difficult because of the immensity of the task. In general, much remains to be learned about the effects of exotic species and about ways to control their populations to prevent irreversible damage to park ecosystems and native wildlife. One of the most promising techniques is biological control—the use of one organism to prevent population outbreaks of another.

## Low Priority for Natural Resource Management

The National Park Service has a dual mandate: to protect park resources and to provide for the public's enjoyment of them. Historically, emphasis within the agency has shifted between the two objectives, more often focusing on visitor enjoyment. A strong and consistent commitment to resource protection, however, is essential if the Park Service is to maintain the values for which the parks were set aside. The diversity and complexity of the many problems currently facing the parks should serve to emphasize the need for an expanded program to protect and preserve park resources.

Many factors contribute to the low priority given natural-resource management in the Park Service. Lack of funds, competing demands, conflicting visions of the Park Service mission, political influences, and bureaucratic inertia all have played a part. Meanwhile, the parks suffer from this lack of commitment to natural-resource management. Only about four percent of the total permanent staff, or about 300 people, specialize in natural-resource management. Only 20 percent of the parks have basic inventories of their natural resources. The *State of the Parks* report (Department of the Interior 1980) said that 75 percent of the threats identified were inadequately documented with research. Accurate baseline data are essential to monitor any future changes in the resources and to know if they are caused by some human influence or if the variability is natural. Further, such data are needed to identify management priorities, support difficult or controversial decisions, and to direct the allocation of scarce funds effectively.

Some steps have been taken to improve the management of park resources. These include renewed enthusiasm for preparing Resource Management Plans for all park units, the identification and funding of some natural-resource preservation problems, and the establishment of the Natural Resource Management Specialist Trainee Program. In addition, week-long courses in natural-resource management and related issues such as air and water quality, integrated pest management, etc., have been developed for park superintendents, mid-level managers, and resource specialists.

Director Mott's 12-point plan identifies a number of constructive ideas for better protecting park resources. Though not necessarily new, his plan is at least a vigorous return to the sense of stewardship so essential to the park service mission. If actions follow words, perhaps the future will see a return to high-priority attention for natural-resource management in the national parks.

# Legislation

The 98th Congress (1983-1984) considered five bills relating to wildlife in the national parks, but none were enacted (for more details, see the *Audubon Wildlife Report 1985*):

- The Park Protection and Resources Management Act (H.R. 2379), which was introduced by Representative John Seiberling (D-OH) and passed the House in both the 97th and 98th Congresses, was a response to the 1980 *State of the Parks* report. It required increased National Park Service efforts to address natural and cultural resource problems, including those on adjacent lands. The bill was never taken up by the Senate.
- The Wildlife and the National Parks Act of 1984 (Amendment No. 2807 to S. 978, introduced by Senator John Chafee [R-RI]), was developed to protect fish and wildlife in the National Park System from detrimental, federally supported activities occurring both within and outside park boundaries. The bill was not reported by the Senate Environment and Public Works Committee.
- The Alaska Sport Hunting bill (S.49), introduced by Senator Ted Stevens (R-AK), would have redesignated 12 million acres, later amended to 4.9 million acres, of national park land in Alaska as National Park Preserves, thus opening the lands to sport hunting. Although reported from committee, the bill never was called up for floor vote.
- H. R. 4962, an omnibus bill to allow trapping in 11 national park units where it is not now specifically authorized, was never reported.
- H. R. 2122, a bill authorizing trapping in the Ozarks National Scenic Riverways, also was never reported.

The 99th Congress (1985-1986) devoted little attention to national park issues during its first session. The National Park Protection Act and the Alaska Sport Hunting Act have not been reintroduced, and it is unlikely that they will reappear. Trapping in the parks remained an issue, as did general protection of park resources. In addition, the House Interior and Insular Affairs Committee reported legislation to create a new Great Basin National Park.

## Trapping in National Parks

While sponsors of the omnibus trapping bill did not reintroduce that broad legislation intended to open more park units to trapping, three specific trapping bills have been introduced. Each of these measures would allow trapping in a particular area that had been included in the omnibus bill: H.R. 103, Trapping in the Ozarks National Scenic Riverways (Representative Bill Emerson [R-MO]); H.R. 2490, Trapping in Pictured Rocks National Lakeshore (Representative Robert Davis [R-MI]); and H.R. 2772, Trapping in the New River Gorge National Riverway (Representative Alan Mollohan [D-WV]). The sponsors contend that their units' enabling legislation intended trapping to be included when it specified that hunting and fishing would be allowed as applicable under state laws. All three bills were referred to the House Subcommittee on National Parks, but received no action in 1985.

On another front, the National Rifle Association has filed suit to overturn existing Park Service rules that disallow trapping in the National Park System unless specifically authorized in a unit's enabling legislation. While the suit is pending, the Park Service rules have been amended to allow trapping to continue in four parks until January 15, 1987, or until the lawsuit is concluded, whichever occurs first. The following park areas are affected: Buffalo National River, Arkansas; Ozark National Scenic Riverways, Missouri; Saint Croix National Scenic Riverway, Wisconsin/Minnesota; and Delaware Water Gap National Recreation Area, Pennsylvania/New Jersey.

In November 1985, H.R. 3804 was introduced by Representative Glenn Anderson (D-CA). This bill is intended to control trapping within the National Park System and some other public lands. It specifically states that trapping is not permitted in units of the National Park System except where specifically authorized by law or when carried out by park personnel for wildlife management purposes. The bill is an attempt to clarify the long-standing controversy over trapping in parks where it is not specifically authorized in the enabling legislation and to state clearly that such activities are not within the purpose of the park system. The bill was referred jointly to the committees on Interior and Insular Affairs, Agriculture, and Ways and Means.

## S. 1839 Environmental Zone Deductions

S. 1839 would amend the tax code so that certain tax deductions and credits would not be allowed for expenditures within an "environmental zone," defined to mean designated natural areas of ecological significance. As Senator John Chafee (R-RI), the bill's sponsor, explained, "It seems only logical that we should not allow tax incentives to encourage unwanted development in areas we are seeking to protect through other nontax legislation. . . . [The bill is] saying to would-be developers, proceed if you wish, but you will get no encouragement from the Federal Government in the way of tax breaks." (*Congressional Record* 1985)

The term "environmental zones," includes areas already identified as important natural areas either by Congress or, pursuant to other laws, by the secretaries of the Interior or Agriculture. This includes lands designated for addition to the National Park, Forest, or Wild Scenic River systems. It also includes critical habitat designated under the Endangered Species Act, units identified as part of the Coastal Barrier Resources System, and national natural landmarks designated under the Historic Sites, Buildings, and Antiquities Act.*

---

* The National Natural Landmark program is administered by the National Park Service, but landmark registration is voluntary and does not change ownership or require specific protective measures. The program attempts to help preserve a variety of significant natural areas that, when considered together, illustrate the diversity of the country's natural history.

Examples of the incentives that would be unavailable to those seeking to develop environmental zones covered by the bill include the investment tax credit, accelerated depreciation, percentage depletion, immediate expensing of intangible drilling costs, special treatment for land-clearing expenditures or soil- and water-conservation expenditures, and capital-gains treatment for timber, coal, or iron ore operations. Hearings are planned for 1986, but not scheduled. The bill was referred to the Committee on Finance.

## Great Basin National Park

A measure that would create the first new major U.S. national park in nearly 15 years was approved by the House Interior Committee on November 6, 1985, as an amendment to the Nevada Wilderness bill (H.R. 3302). The designated area would preserve 174,000 acres of the Great Basin in Nevada, including a number of cave formations, habitat for a rare species of cutthroat trout, a unique rock glacier, and two groves of ancient bristlecone pines—some of the world's oldest living organisms. Lehman Cave National Monument would be incorporated into the new park. Most of the land that would be incorporated into the park already is owned by the federal government.

The Great Basin Park originally was proposed some 30 years ago, and its establishment is supported by Director Mott and the National Park Service. Representative Bruce Vento (D-MN), chair of the House Interior Committee's Subcommittee on National Parks, authored the amendment. However, Nevada legislators led by Representative Barbara Vucanovich (R-NV) oppose the inclusion of the Great Basin Park proposal in the wilderness bill and want to see it addressed in a separate bill. Local business stands to benefit from the park, but hunters and mining and grazing interests oppose it. Under current Forest Service management, these activities are allowed. The strength of the opposition is limited, however. Only five percent of the county's deer take comes from the park, only 10 small-to-midsized mine claims are owned, and fewer than 600 cattle are grazed there (National Parks and Conservation Association 1986). The bill has not been introduced in the Senate, but hearings are planned in 1986.

## Nassau River Valley Ecological Preserve

H.R. 2483, proposed by Representative Charles Bennet (D-FL), would add a "national ecological preserve" to the National Park System. The proposed preserve would protect 80,000 acres of estuarine wetlands and several historical sites in Northern Florida. As a preserve, the area would be regulated less strictly than a park, and H.R. 2483 would allow hunting, fishing, and trapping to continue in the area except where such activities threaten public safety or enjoyment of the preserve. Support for the bill is limited and no companion legislation has been introduced in the Senate.

## Legal Developments

Two court actions in 1985 successfully challenged threats to the parks. In *Northern Alaska Environmental Center v. Hodel,* (Civ. No. J85-009)(D. Alaska, July 24, 1985), conservation groups sought to stop mining operations in the national parks of Alaska. The court found that the National Park Service had violated its own regulations by failing to require permits for access to the mining inholdings and that the National Environmental Policy Act required the Service to prepared environmental analyses before issuing the access permits or approving the plans of operation at each mine, a duty the service had not fulfilled. The court granted the plaintiffs' motion for a preliminary injunction.

In a controversy arising from the peculiar history of Voyageurs National Park, conservationists challenged Park Service approval of a state wildlife-management plan that allowed trapping on state lands within the park (*Voyageurs National Park Association v. Arnett,* 609 F.Supp. [D. Minn. 1985]). The lands involved, originally included as part of the park, had been ceded back to the state on the condition that the state would develop a wildlife management plan. The state plan proposed to allow duck hunting and trapping on the ceded lands, and the Park Service approved. Challenging this decision, the conservationists argued that, while Congress intended to allow duck hunting on the ceded lands, it had not intended to allow any other form of hunting. The district court agreed, finding that trapping would be inconsistent with the congressional mandate that the ceded lands be managed "to preserve the natural resources of the area so as to complement to the fullest extent possible the purposes for which the park was established."

## Status of the Resource

The National Park Service does not have a comprehensive, coordinated system to inventory or monitor the types, numbers, or status of wildlife populations in national park units. Some data are available in individual parks, either in resource-management plans or from staff, but this information is not aggregated at the national level.

Despite recent efforts to prepare resource-management plans for all parks, few parks actually have complete inventories of their wildlife. Yet adequate knowledge of the identity and status of such resources and how they function within ecosystems is a prerequisite to their wise stewardship. At the park level, adequate knowledge about wildlife and other natural resources is key to producing good general-management plans and resource-management plans that document threats to the resources and implement appropriate management actions. Similarly, such basic information is critical for national planning. Although the resource-management plan process has helped to provide better information on a park-by-park basis, it does not help in assessing overall status and trends nationally. With tight budgets, the likelihood of funding such synthesis efforts in the future is minimal.

Approximately half of the species of animals listed as threatened or endangered in this country occur in units of the National Park System. Yet the Service does not have an inventory of all the endangered or threatened species that live in the parks. This limits the agency's ability to comprehensively protect these species, especially some of the lesser-known ones.

Only the Southeast and the Southwest regions maintain current, comprehensive lists of the threatened and endangered species occurring in their parks. The Southeast Region, in particular, has developed a useful format designed to be easily updated as additional information is collected.

The National Park Service's Geographic Information Systems field unit, located at the Denver Service Center, conducts some useful monitoring activities. The Remote Sensing Program, for instance, uses satellites and aerial photography to collect data on land use and to document changes around park borders. These techniques are not directly useful in monitoring wildlife because they cannot register small-scale differences. However, they are useful in monitoring vegetative changes. In the late 1970s, for example, satellite data on the perimeter of Olympic National Park discovered some trespass clearcuts.

Another program, Digital Cartography, works to compile and synthesize a variety of map data, such as geologic and vegetation maps, for national park units. Computer technology allows the staff to produce various composite maps and do many more analyses than previously possible. The content of computerized data bases, compiled for 20 parks, varies from park to park depending on the type of park and the amount of funding.

The National Park Service has developed another data base, NPFLORA. This growing compilation of information on vascular plants in the parks is a review of existing literature and an update of plant nomenclature, not a field inventory of park flora. About 85 parks are represented, and about 30 parks are to be added yearly during the next several years. Some interest has been expressed in creating a similar data base for animals, NPFAUNA, but his data base will not be considered until the plant system is complete.

One problem that arises from the lack of national data on wildlife status and trends is the difficulty of determining the priority of various wildlife-related activities during planning at the regional or national levels. Without baseline data, no means exist to make comparisons from year to year or to chart long-term progress. Thus, changing attitudes, more than actual need, can sometimes play too large a role in determining wildlife-management priorities and funding.

# References

Congressional Record. November 7, 1985. S 15118.

Courtenay, W.R., Jr. 1978. "The Introduction of Exotic Organisms," *in* H. Brokaw ed., *Wildlife and America.* Council on Environmental Quality.

Gregory, G. 1982. "State of the Parks 1980: Problems and Plans," in *National Parks in Crisis.* National Parks and Conservation Association. Washington, D.C.

*National Parks.* 1985. "Canyonlands Not off Hook as Nuke Dump Target." National Parks and Conservation Association. March/April.

*National Parks.* 1985. "Ski Area Expansion Planned for Rocky Mountain Park." National Parks and Conservation Association. September/October.

*National Parks.* 1986. "Nevada Great Basin Discussed at Hearing." National Parks and Conservation Association. January/February.

The New York Times. 1985. "Conservation and Tourist Interests at Odds in Dispute at Yellowstone." August 5.

Roth, P., et al. 1985. *The American West's Acid Rain Test.* World Resources Institute, Research Report #1.

Shands, W.E. 1983. Testimony before the Subcommittee on Public Lands and National Parks of the Committee on Interior and Insular Affairs, U.S. House of Representatives, April 7, 1983. The Conservation Foundation.

U.S. Department of the Interior, National Park Service. 1978. *Management Policies.*

U.S. Department of the Interior, National Park Service, Office of Science and Technology. 1980. *State of the Parks—1980*

U.S. Department of the Interior, National Park Service. 1982. *Planning Process Guidelines.*

U.S. Department of the Interior, National Park Service. 1985. *The 12 Point Plan: The Challenge.*

U.S. Department of the Interior, National Park Service, Office of Public Affairs. 1985. Personal Communication. December.

*Chris Elfring is a freelance editor and writer in Washington D.C.*

.

Bureau of Land Management holdings, some 300 million acres primarily in the West and Alaska, include habitat essential to wildlife, such as this pronghorn.
*Bureau of Land Management*

# Wildlife and the Bureau of Land Management

## Katherine Barton

## Introduction

T HE BUREAU OF Land Management (BLM) manages more land than any other federal agency. It oversees more than 300 million acres, generally referred to as the public lands, which constitute approximately one-eighth of the land in the United States and 60 percent of the land under federal jurisdiction. BLM also has jurisdiction over mineral resources that underlie an additional 300 million acres of land administered by other federal agencies or in private ownership.

The public lands provide extensive and valuable fish and wildlife habitat. These lands support one of every five big-game animals in the United States, including most of the caribou, brown bears, grizzly bears, desert bighorn sheep, moose, mule deer, and pronghorns. They also provide habitat for numerous small game and nongame wildlife, including 109 federally listed endangered and threatened species of plants and animals and hundreds of species under consideration for future listing. The bureau manages substantial aquatic and riparian areas, including 16.3 million acres of wetlands, 15.4 million acres of riparian habitat, 4.0 million surface acres of lakes and reservoirs, and 84,800 miles of perennial streams, much of which support trout, salmon, and other sport fish.

Fish and wildlife are just one of many natural resources managed by BLM. The major law covering the management of the public lands, the Federal Land Policy and Management Act, requires BLM to manage for multiple use. In addition to fish and wildlife habitat, BLM manages the public lands for the development of energy resources such as coal, oil, and gas, hardrock mining, timber production, livestock grazing, rights-of-way, recreation, protection of cultural resources and natural scenic and scientific values, and the provision of range for wild horses and burros. Thus, the management of wildlife habitat on the public lands is a balancing act, a matter of trade-offs among competing uses. As a result, how the agency administers non-wildlife uses such as livestock grazing and mineral development can have as much or greater impact on wildlife than its specific efforts directed at habitat protection.

In spite of its extensive responsibilities, BLM is a relatively small agency in funding and personnel and has never had the capability to manage its lands intensively. In addition, BLM's largest and most powerful constituency traditionally has been the livestock industry, so that livestock grazing has been the predominant use of the public lands while noncommodity uses have been largely neglected. After the passage of the Federal Land Policy and Management Act in 1976 the Carter administration sharply increased funding and personnel for multiple-use management of these lands, beginning a move toward more balance and increased attention to wildlife and other conservation efforts. But over the past five years, under the Reagan administration, the agency has moved back toward giving priority to commodity uses, particularly energy and mineral development, while reducing wildlife-habitat management and other conservation programs.

In 1985, Congress provided a modest boost in funding for wildlife-habitat management, which allowed the program to step up some of its efforts, particularly for threatened and endangered species, and to undertake some new initiatives. The agency began to develop a new policy for protection of riparian zones, one of the key concerns of conservation organizations. However, conservationists criticized an early draft of the policy as being too weak, and a federal court ordered BLM to halt a program that gave certain livestock operators control over grazing-management decisions. Overall, the trend in favor of commodity interests and against resource-conservation programs continued. The one item that held significant potential for making a change in this pattern—a comprehensive range-improvement bill tied to reauthorization of the grazing-fee formula—never got off the ground.

# Organization and Operations

## Land Base and Uses

BLM manages land in 28 states, but the vast majority of the public lands are in the West and Alaska. Of the 176,266,000 acres of public-domain lands in the lower 48 states, 175,834,000 acres are in the states referred to as the "11 western states:" Arizona, California, Colorado, Idaho, Montana, Nevada, New Mexico, Oregon, Utah, Washington, and Wyoming. BLM lands account for about half of the total acreage in these states, ranging from less than one percent in Washington to 70 percent in Nevada. Approximately 124 million acres of public lands are in Alaska, about 34 percent of the state's acreage. Management of the public lands often is a critical factor in the health of fish and wildlife populations in these states.

Approximately 170 million acres or 97 percent of the public lands in the lower 48 states are classified rangeland. The principal economic use of these lands—at least in terms of acreage—is livestock grazing, which is authorized on 170 million acres. The public lands account for about three percent of the forage consumed by livestock in the United States; about four percent of the nation's beef cattle and 28 percent of the sheep depend on the public lands for all or part of their yearly forage requirement (Clarke 1985, U.S. GAO, 1982). The other five million acres of BLM land in the lower 48 are classified as commercial forest land and produced 1.2 billion board feet of timber in 1984. More than 90 percent of the timber production on BLM lands comes from about two million acres in western Oregon that the agency describes as "some of the most productive forests in the world." Most of these lands originally were a railroad grant that was returned to the federal government. They are called the Oregon and California Grant Lands. In addition, most BLM lands are open to energy and mineral development, including oil and gas, coal, and geothermal leasing and hardrock mining.

BLM lands are essentially leftovers from public domain lands that were not specifically reserved for some public purpose, such as the national parks, forests, or refuges, or were not given away or sold to state or private interests through a variety of land-grant and homesteading laws in the 1800s and early 1900s. Thus, these lands tend to be intermingled with scattered parcels of state, private, and sometimes federal lands, often posing difficult management problems. BLM lands frequently are more arid and less productive than nearby nonfederal lands that were more attractive to western settlers and land speculators or than national forest lands that were specifically set aside to protect timber and watershed values.

## Legal Authority

BLM's current mandate to protect the public lands for the public good and to manage them for multiple use is very recent. Throughout most of the nation's history, it was the federal government's policy to dispose of these lands. For many years, the Department of the Interior had little or no authority or funding for managing the public lands and their use was largely uncontrolled. By the late 1800s, many of these lands were badly overgrazed, causing serious damage to the condition of the range. Furthermore, while federal management of the national parks and national forests was authorized in the late 1800s, the political strength of the livestock industry and the reluctance of many westerners to allow federal control of additional lands prevented the Interior Department from gaining any management authority over the public domain until 1934, when the Taylor Grazing Act (43 U.S.C.A. 315) authorized the federal government to control grazing through a permit program. Even then the Grazing Service, the precursor to BLM, was unable politically to require significant grazing reductions or to charge adequate grazing fees. The Grazing Service was all but eliminated in the congressional struggle over these issues.

BLM was established in 1946 as a replacement for the Grazing Service. Although the agency had no specific congressional authority to do so, it began to move toward managing its lands for multiple use during the 1950s. By 1961, the bureau had hired its first wildlife biologist, and in 1964 BLM was given authority, although temporary, to manage its lands for multiple use under the Classification and Multiple-Use Act (P.L. 88-607, 78 Stat. 986 [terminated December 20, 1970]).

With the environmental movement of the 1970s, pressure grew for more conservation-oriented management of BLM lands. In 1974, a district court ruled in favor of environmentalists on a lawsuit brought by the Natural Resources Defense Council (*NRDC v. Morton*) and ordered BLM to prepare environmental impact statements on the grazing program at the local level. In 1976, just a decade ago, Congress passed the first comprehensive law for the management of BLM lands. For the first time, Congress declared it was federal policy to retain most of the public domain and gave BLM a permanent mandate to manage its lands for multiple use, specifically including fish and wildlife habitat. This law, the Federal Land Policy and Management Act, is the major law that guides management of the public lands today.

The Federal Land Policy and Management Act (often called by its acronym, pronounced "flip-ma") is a long and complex law.* Briefly, in addition to ts multiple-use mandate, the act directs BLM to undertake the following efforts of importance to wildlife:

- to manage its lands according to comprehensive land-use plans developed with public participation;
- to prepare and maintain an inventory of the public lands and their resource values;
- to give priority to designating and protecting Areas of Critical Environment a Concern in order to protect fish and wildlife resources and other values;
- to conduct a wilderness review of its roadless areas, with recommendations due by 1991; and
- to allocate 50 percent of grazing-fee receipts to range improvements, including improvements for fish and wildlife habitat.

* The Federal Land Policy and Management Act is covered in more detail in the *Audubon Wildlife Report 1985*.

BLM has several other important authorities in addition to the Federal Land Policy and Management Act. The Public Rangelands Improvement Act of 1978 (43 U.S.C.A. 1701 *et seq.*) addressed continuing concerns about the poor condition of the range and authorized $365 million over a 20-year period for range improvements, although no funds have ever been appropriated. In practice, the more significant provision of this law was the congressional establishment of a grazing fee formula that has caused grazing fees to drop steadily since 1980. The Wild Free-Roaming Horses and Burros Act of 1971 (16 U.S.C.A. 1331 *et seq.*) directs BLM to protect and manage wild horses and burros on certain areas of the public lands. The Oregon and California Grant Lands Act of 1937 (43 U.S.C.A. 1181 *et seq.*) provides for the management of the Oregon and California Grant Lands, a law that BLM interprets as giving priority to timber production.

Finally, BLM must comply with a variety of other laws that relate to its activities. For fish and wildlife, these include the Migratory Bird Conservation Act of 1929 (codified at scattered sections of 16 U.S.C.A. 715), the Sikes Act Extension of 1974 (16 U.S.C.A. 670g-670o), the Endangered Species Act of 1973 (16 U.S.C.A. 1531 *et seq.*), and the executive orders on Floodplain Management (E.O. 11988) and Wetlands Protection (E.O. 11990).

## Organization

BLM is an agency within the Department of the Interior, supervised by the assistant secretary for Land and Minerals Management, who also oversees three other agencies with mineral responsibilities: the Bureau of Mines, the Minerals Management Service, and the Office of Surface Mining. BLM is headed by a director who is a political appointee. He is assisted in Washington by three deputy directors, who in turn are supported by six assistant directors. The Division of Wildlife is under the assistant director for Renewable Resources, who also oversees the divisions of Rangeland Resources, Forestry, and Wild Horses and Burros.

BLM is highly decentralized, with major decisions over land management made by the field staff. BLM has 12 state offices: one in Alaska, one in Virginia to carry out BLM responsibilities east of Kansas City, and one in each of the 11 western states except Washington. Each office is headed by a state director, who is assisted by the state office staff. Each state office has one or two wildlife biologists. The area within the jurisdiction of each state office is divided into districts. There are 55 district offices, each headed by a district manager. Districts are further divided into resource areas, the basic field component of BLM, each headed by an area manager responsible for day-to-day management activities and on-the-ground implementation of BLM programs. BLM does not have a wildlife biologist in each of its 154 resource areas, although some areas have more than one.

# Key Offices Involved in
# BLM Fish and Wildlife Management*

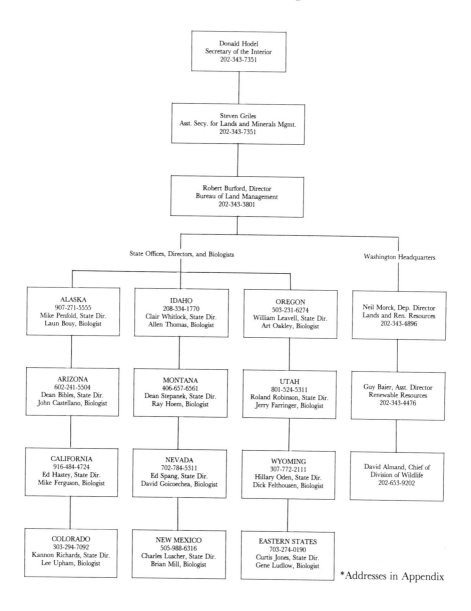

Donald Hodel
Secretary of the Interior
202-343-7351

Steven Griles
Asst. Secy. for Lands and Minerals Mgmt.
202-343-7351

Robert Burford, Director
Bureau of Land Management
202-343-3801

State Offices, Directors, and Biologists

Washington Headquarters

ALASKA
907-271-5555
Mike Penfold, State Dir.
Laun Bouy, Biologist

IDAHO
208-334-1770
Clair Whitlock, State Dir.
Allen Thomas, Biologist

OREGON
503-231-6274
William Leavell, State Dir.
Art Oakley, Biologist

Neil Morck, Dep. Director
Lands and Ren. Resources
202-343-4896

ARIZONA
602-241-5504
Dean Bibles, State Dir.
John Castellano, Biologist

MONTANA
406-657-6561
Dean Stepanek, State Dir.
Ray Hoem, Biologist

UTAH
801-524-5311
Roland Robinson, State Dir.
Jerry Farringer, Biologist

Guy Baier, Asst. Director
Renewable Resources
202-343-4476

CALIFORNIA
916-484-4724
Ed Hastey, State Dir.
Mike Ferguson, Biologist

NEVADA
702-784-5311
Ed Spang, State Dir.
David Goicoechea, Biologist

WYOMING
307-772-2111
Hillary Oden, State Dir.
Dick Felthousen, Biologist

David Almand, Chief of
Division of Wildlife
202-653-9202

COLORADO
303-294-7092
Kannon Richards, State Dir.
Lee Upham, Biologist

NEW MEXICO
505-988-6316
Charles Luscher, State Dir.
Brian Mill, Biologist

EASTERN STATES
703-274-0190
Curtis Jones, State Dir.
Gene Ludlow, Biologist

*Addresses in Appendix

## Land-Use Planning

The major decisions regarding public-land management, including decisions affecting wildlife, are made within BLM's planning process. The key documents in this system are the land-use plans prepared for each resource area, which are supposed to address multiple-use conflicts, allocate resources, and select appropriate uses and levels of use for the area. Activities identified in these plans, such as the need for a concerted habitat-management effort at a certain site, may be further described in supplementary plans called activity plans. The most important of all BLM activity plans to wildlife are the allotment management plans, which specify how livestock grazing will be conducted. (Wildlife Management Institute 1981, p. 13) Also important are habitat-management plans, prepared for specific wildlife-management efforts.

BLM resource areas currently operate under two different types of land-use plans. Prior to the Federal Land Policy and Management Act planning process, BLM prepared Management Framework Plans. These earlier plans were developed with less public involvement than is used for the Federal Land Policy and Management Act plans and without considering a variety of fully developed alternatives. Most resource areas are still operating under these plans, some of which are quite old. Plans prepared pursuant to the Federal Land Policy and Management Act's more comprehensive requirements are called Resource Management Plans. The management act requires that all activities on BLM lands must be consistent with the land-use plans or the plans must be amended or revised as necessary to accommodate the proposed action. Sixteen Resource Management Plans had been approved by the end of FY 1985.

The Federal Land Policy and Management Act requires extensive public participation in the land-use planning process, and BLM provides opportunities for public involvement at various points. Two are critical points: the scoping stage, when BLM identifies specific issues to be addressed in the plan; and the release of the draft plan and draft environmental impact statement for public comment. In addition, citizens who have participated in the planning process can protest elements of the final plan when it is proposed by the state director.*

## Wildlife Habitat Management

In theory, BLM manages fish and wildlife habitat as opposed to species. Through a variety of cooperative agreements, BLM technically leaves responsibility for management of resident species of fish and wildlife to the states. In practice, however, BLM and the states generally work closely together to accomplish the work they agree needs to be done.

---

* BLM's 22-page pamphlet called "BLM Planning: A Guide to Resource Management Planning on the Public Lands" provides details on participation in the land-use planning process.

The major activities of the BLM wildlife program are to conduct the inventories and monitoring necessary to make planning decisions, to carry out BLM responsibilities for the protection and recovery of federally listed threatened and endangered species, and to carry out habitat maintenance and improvement projects. Wildlife field staff also work to assess and mitigate the impacts on wildlife of other activities on BLM lands, such as livestock grazing and development of energy resources and other minerals. Such efforts technically are not part of the wildlife program since the cost of this work is paid for from the budgets of the activity in question. Nevertheless, such assessment and mitigation work consumes a large portion of the limited wildlife staff's time and means that biologists are not available for other wildlife-program work.

As funding and personnel for the wildlife program have been reduced and the rate of development activities has increased, the wildlife program has been seriously strained. Its efforts now focus on meeting its legal mandate to protect an increasing number of species listed as threatened and endangered on the one hand and trying to keep up with the work load demanded by planning and development activities on the other. This leaves little opportunity for direct habitat maintenance and improvement work on the bulk of the public lands.

## Budget and Personnel

Although BLM manages more land than any other federal agency, it has a relatively small budget and low levels of personnel. In FY 1986, Congress appropriated $574 million for BLM*, and the agency was staffed at a level of roughly 10,000 full-time equivalents, the federal government's measure of employment. In comparison, the Forest Service was funded at nearly $1.5 billion and was staffed at about 32,000 full-time equivalents, and the National Park Service was funded at $886 million with about 16,000 full-time equivalents.

Of the $574 million appropriated to BLM in 1986, about $118 million, or 20 percent, was allocated to renewable resources management, which includes management of range, recreation, forest, fish and wildlife habitat, fire, and soil, water, and air. About 40 percent of this was for range management, which includes wild horses and burros. Other programs receiving substantial

* This and subsequent numbers do not include permanent appropriations and trust funds.

### BLM Wildlife-Related Scientists, FY 1985

| | |
|---|---|
| Wildlife biologists: | 219 |
| Wildlife/fishery biologists: | 3 |
| Fishery biologists | 32 |
| Botanists | 10 |
| Other Specialists | 16 |
| TOTAL | 280 |

funding are energy and minerals, funded at $84 million and accounting for 15 percent of the total BLM budget, and payments to local governments in lieu of taxes, funded at $104 million or 18 percent of the total.

Congress appropriated $16 million for wildlife-habitat management in FY 1986, about three percent of total BLM appropriations. As it has for the past four years, Congress provided the program with a substantial boost over the administration's request of $13.8 million. After operating at depressed levels of funding for the past four years, the wildlife-habitat-management program was restored to roughly its 1981 funding level. Nevertheless, accounting for inflation, the program has still suffered a 20-percent cut in spending power. Furthermore, habitat-management funding for 1986—like funding for other programs—is expected to be reduced by budget cuts under the Gramm-Rudman deficit-reduction legislation. The administration expects the program to be cut to $15.3 million.

Out of the funds in the habitat-management budget, BLM expects to spend $3.8 million, nearly 25 percent, on endangered and threatened species efforts. This is about the same level of funding as provided in FY 1985 and maintains the program's recent emphasis on endangered species protection. Funding for this effort has increased from $1.65 million in FY 1983, the first year this funding appeared separately in the budget, to $2.65 million in FY 1984 and roughly $3.9 million in FY 1985 and 1986.

Personnel levels for the wildlife-habitat management program continue at a low level. Congress rejected administration proposals to further reduce wildlife-habitat management personnel to 274 full-time equivalents in 1986, specifically directing BLM to maintain the 1985 level of 295 full-time equivalents. However, staff for the program have declined 18 percent from the 1982 level of 360 full-time equivalents. Wildlife personnel have declined even more sharply since 1981, but an accurate measure of the magnitude of that decline is difficult since BLM used a different measure of personnel levels prior to 1982.

BLM Wildlife Habitat Management Appropriations
FY 1981-86

| Year | Budget Request | Congressional Appropriation | Appropriation in 1980 Constant Dollars |
|------|----------------|-----------------------------|----------------------------------------|
| 1981* | — | $16.017 | $16.017 |
| 1982* | $12.594 | 14.918 | 13.917 |
| 1983 | 13.642 | 15.160 | 13.608 |
| 1984 | 10.515 | 13.515 | 11.686 |
| 1985 | 11.705 | 15.783 | 13.160 |
| 1986 | 13.801 | 16.054 | 12.822 (estimated) |

*Prior to 1983, BLM included general administration costs in the program accounts. The 1981 and 1982 appropriations and the 1982 budget request shown here have been recalculated to remove general administration costs for accurate comparison. No similar figure is available for the 1981 request.

Although Congress repeatedly has restored some of the cuts requested by the administration in the wildlife-habitat management program, it generally has followed the administration's emphasis on revenue-producing commodity programs at the expense of renewable-resource programs. From 1981 to 1986, Congress has increased funding for the timber-producing Oregon and California Grant Lands by 29 percent (three percent in constant dollars) and has boosted funding for energy and minerals development by 58 percent (26 percent in constant dollars)—although some of this latter increase is due to the transfer of new minerals responsibilities to BLM from the Minerals Management Service.

During the same time period, in addition to the 20-percent decline in spending power in the wildlife-habitat management program, Congress cut funding for soil, water, and air management by nine percent (27 percent in constant dollars) and for grazing management by 15 percent (32 percent in constant dollars). This decline in grazing management funding comes at a time when wildlife conservationists are increasingly concerned about the impacts of livestock grazing on riparian areas, a problem that in part will require carefully crafted and monitored grazing systems and intensive grazing management to solve. Funding for range improvements also has declined—by 24 percent (39 percent in constant dollars)—due to the decline in grazing fees, although the Federal Land Policy and Management Act requirement that these funds not fall below $10 million a year has kept appropriations steady since 1984. In sum, renewable resources programs remain low priority in the BLM management scheme.

# Current Program Trends

## General Accomplishments

Because BLM is highly decentralized, it is difficult to track wildlife-program accomplishments. The state offices are required to give only minimal reports

FY 1985 Wildlife Program Accomplishments

| | |
|---|---|
| Acres Inventoried: | 14.5 million acres[1] |
| Habitat Mgmt. Plans Prepared or Revised: | 67 |
| HMP's and Other Plans Monitored: | 750[2] |
| Habitat Development Projects: | 570[3] |
| Habitat projects Maintained: | 1,100 |
| T/E Acres Inventoried | 3.8 million |
| Plans Monitored for T/E | 200 |
| T/E Plans Implemented | 81[4] |

[1] Estimate, complete data of actual accomplishments not available.
[2] Does not include recreation plans or endangered species plans.
[3] Includes projects such as waterhole developments and fences.
[4] Includes recovery plans and other activity plans for threatened and endangered species

on accomplishments to BLM headquarters, and the types of information they are required to send to Washington was revised in 1985, making trends difficult to discern. In addition, some of the data reported may be inconsistent from state to state—for example, although each stae is required to report acres of habitat inventoried, the quality of the inventory may vary sharply. And while the data give a quantitative accounting of workload and accomplishments, they give no picture of the quality of the work done or of its benefits for wildlife.

## Endangered and Threatened Species

BLM's responsibilities relating to threatened and endangered species continue to grow. At the end of FY 1985, BLM had some management responsibility for 109 listed species—70 animal species and 39 plant species—located on public lands managed by BLM or private lands where BLM manages federal subsurface mineral rights. The number of listed species affected by BLM management has grown rapidly in recent years, and this number should continue to grow significantly: 16 animal species and 11 plant species on BLM lands have been proposed for listing under the Endangered Species Act, and 170 animal species and more than 600 plant species on the public lands are candidates for listing. Candidate species are those for which existing information indicates that listing may be appropriate, but for which listing has not been proposed formally either because the species are in a lower listing priority than other species or because additional information needs to be collected.

Over the past several years, BLM has given priority to areas where threats are most severe or the need most significant. This has resulted in the allocation of increasing proportions of the BLM wildlife budget to endangered species management, allowing the agency to accelerate this program. As of the end of FY 1985, 57 recovery plans had been prepared for species on BLM lands, an increase of 13 plans over 1984 levels. BLM was implementing at least a portion of its responsibilities for 44 of the plans. In FY 1986, BLM expects to assist the U.S. Fish and Wildlife Service (FWS), the lead agency on implementing the Endangered Species Act, in preparing another 15 recovery plans.

BLM also began work to strengthen some of its endangered and threatened species policies in 1985, efforts expected to come to fruition in 1986. In one of these efforts, BLM is developing a policy that will require some positive efforts to recover candidate species, with the ultimate goal of preventing the need to list them. Currently, BLM attempts to ensure that land-use decisions do not cause further deterioration of candidate species' habitat, but does not have a policy of trying to improve that habitat. In a separate effort, BLM is working on regulations for the protection of endangered, threatened, and other plants on the public lands.

*Desert Tortoise.* One species of particular recent interest on the public lands is the desert tortoise. The Utah population of the tortoise has been listed as threatened under the federal Endangered Species Act, and a number of studies have indicated that desert tortoise populations in Arizona, California, and Nevada are being affected seriously by livestock grazing, off-road vehicle use, and oil and gas exploration. In 1984, the Desert Tortoise Council petitioned FWS to add all desert tortoise populations to the federal endangered species list. In the fall of 1985, FWS determined that listing of the tortoise was warranted but precluded at the current time by other listing priorities. Under the requirements of the act, FWS must re-evaluate the need for listing the tortoise every 12 months. In the meanwhile, additional data on the tortoise is being gathered. One possibility would be to list the populations for which FWS has more complete information, while continuing studies on others.

*Desert Bighorn Sheep.* In FY 1985, Congress provided BLM a $294,000 challenge grant—which the agency was to use to encourage matching contributions from private sources—for efforts to recover the desert bighorn sheep. Eighty percent of the desert bighorn sheep in the United States occur on federal lands—most of which are managed by BLM—in Arizona, Nevada, New Mexico, California, and Utah, but current studies show that a number of sheep populations have been extirpated from their ranges, and others are declining. BLM obtained an estimated $305,000 in contributions—exceeding the required match—primarily in volunteer labor from local conservation groups. With this funding and assistance, BLM reintroduced desert bighorns into four new areas in Arizona, constructed 14 water facilities, conducted two habitat-monitoring and population-monitoring projects and one lamb-mortality study, and completed surveys and designs for four future projects. Congress provided another $300,000 challenge grant ($289,000 after Gramm-Rudman cuts) to continue the program in FY 1986, and BLM expects to get at least the same level of private contributions as in 1985.

## Habitat Management Plans

With funding for wildlife habitat management becoming increasingly tight, BLM in 1985 directed its state offices to evaluate habitat management plans on the public lands to ensure that they focus on high-priority species and that they support current program objectives and initiatives. The review identified the types of species or habitats the plans were primarily intended to benefit; whether the plans were up-to-date, needed revision, or should be eliminated; and the plans' implementation status. In the statistics and chart below, completed plans are those for which 90 percent of needed funding has been obligated and which are essentially in a maintenance and monitoring phase;

implemented plans are those for which funds have been obligated; and new plans are those that have not yet been funded.

The review showed that of the 401 total habitat management plans, 109 have been completed, 212 have been implemented to some degree, and 80 are new, unfunded plans. The states determined that the vast majority of plans were up-to-date, but recommended revisions for 77 plans, or 19 percent of the total, and proposed the elimination of 12 plans. The largest number of plans—176 plans, or 44 percent of the total—address terrestrial habitats not related to endangered or other special-status species. The 79 plans for listed, proposed, and candidate species accounted for the second largest group. A roughly equal number of plans address sensitive species, riparian and wetland habitats, and aquatic and fisheries habitats.

Based on the results of the Habitat Management Plan evaluation, the state offices are to focus future habitat-management-plan efforts so as to bring the program in line with current priorities. First, the state offices are to emphasize the completion of plan implementation and ensure the maintenance of completed plans before preparing new ones. Plans that are not producing wildlife benefits are to be dropped. When new plans are developed, they are to address priority species and habitats as follows: within the endangered species program, the top priority is to develop plans for listed species over proposed or candidate species; for nonendangered species, the top priority is to address riparian and aquatic habitats, with terrestrial habitat—which has received the most attention in the past—the lowest priority.

## Status of Habitat Management Plans, FY 1985

| Category | New | Implemented | Completed | Total | Need Revision | Proposed for Elimination |
|---|---|---|---|---|---|---|
| Listed T/E Species | 16 | 24 | 16 | 56 | 6 | 2 |
| Proposed and Candidate Species | 7 | 14 | 2 | 23 | 3 | 0 |
| Sensitive Species | 14 | 18 | 11 | 43 | 13 | 1 |
| Riparian/ Wetlands Habitat | 7 | 33 | 15 | 55 | 6 | 0 |
| Aquatic/Fisheries Habitat | 12 | 28 | 8 | 48 | 7 | 1 |
| Terrestrial Habitat | 24 | 95 | 57 | 176 | 42 | 8 |
| TOTAL | 80 | 212 | 109 | 401 | 77 | 12 |

Source: Bureau of Land Management

## Nonfederal Contributions

Under the Reagan administration, BLM, like other federal natural-resource agencies, has worked to supplement its wildlife program with donated funds and labor from states, conservation groups, and other private interests. In 1983 and 1984, BLM estimated the value of these donations at about $1.5 million, most of this coming in volunteer labor. Complete figures for 1985 are not available, but BLM officials estimate nonfederal contributions remained at about the same level.

The move to emphasize nonfederal contributions to the wildlife program has been somewhat controversial. While such contributions can provide a valuable supplement to the program, conservationists have charged that the administration is using them to try to cut the federal program, a charge supported in part by the low funding requests consistently made by the administration for the BLM wildlife program. Furthermore, as BLM tries to extend its limited resources by taking advantage of donated funds and help, the danger exists that the volunteer efforts will begin to drive BLM wildlife-program priorities. For example, while BLM is moving to emphasize species and habitats in serious trouble—such as endangered species and riparian areas—state fish and game departments and portions of the public are most interested in offering assistance for the enhancement of popular, but not particularly jeopardized, big-game species, which BLM is trying to de-emphasize.

## Research and Development

Only a very small portion of BLM's wildlife budget is spent on research. In FY 1985, 2.8 percent of appropriated funds, about $440,000, was spent on research.* This funded about 25 ongoing major research and development efforts and an unknown number of small projects that BLM does not track. Most of the projects address endangered species, raptors, bighorn sheep, or riparian and aquatic systems. Using these funds, BLM started up its aquatic and riparian data-base system in FY 1985, which will allow the agency to compile inventory and monitoring data on these critical systems from all public lands. Priorities for future research include endangered and threatened species and riparian and wetlands habitats.

## Riparian Policy

Over the past two years, conservation organizations have worked to focus public and congressional attention on the seriously degraded riparian areas of the public lands. These areas—which include streams and lakes and their associated wetlands and adjacent vegetation—are the lifeblood of the desert

---

* By comparison, the Forest Service was appropriated $9.11 million for fish, wildlife, and range research in 1985.

for fish and wildlife, providing cover, food, nesting habitat, water, and shade for a rich diversity of species. They also provide popular recreation and scenic areas, and their health and stability is key to maintaining water quality and watershed characteristics. Many of the riparian areas on BLM lands, as well as on Forest Service lands, have been damaged seriously, primarily by livestock grazing but also by road construction, mining operations, dams, and recreational use.

In 1985, in reponse to growing public concern about riparian area protection—and perhaps, more importantly, because of the prospect of new legislation requiring BLM to give special emphasis to key riparian areas (discussed later)—BLM began developing an agency-wide riparian-area management policy. Although conservationists supported the effort, they criticized early drafts of the policy as being weaker than exisiting BLM policy on riparian areas included in the BLM manual. BLM said the policy in the manual is solely a fish and wildlife policy and that the new policy would apply to all aspects of BLM operations and address other values of riparian areas, such as vegetation and soil and water management.

Although the current policy may be stronger, the fact is that it is not being implemented. The new policy could have broader acceptance and be given higher priority for implementation. For example, the new policy is being developed under the lead of the Range Management Division, which oversees livestock grazing, the activity most responsible for riparian-area degradation. By specifically including other values of riparian areas in the protection policy, it is expected that programs other than the wildlife-habitat management program would allocate funds for the policy's implementation and actively move to carry out its requirements.

The policy was nearly ready for release at the end of 1985, but conservationists were concerned that the failure of Congress to move on a range bill, and the unlikely prospect that deliberations on such a bill would continue in 1986, would mean BLM, thinking that pressure to address riparian-area protection had diminished, would indefinitely stall the policy's issuance.

## Current Issues

Although BLM manages more land than any other agency, it is probably the weakest natural-resource bureau in the federal government. BLM is seriously underfunded and understaffed. Politically, it has long been dominated by the livestock industry, which has had strong backers in Congress. Until relatively recently, it received little attention or support from the public or from conservation organizations.

Much of this is due to historical circumstances. BLM manages lands that nobody wanted when they were available at little or no cost, and it has taken many years for the public to become aware of the many important values of these lands. Historically, the government's ultimate goal was to dispose of these lands, and there is still strong sentiment in the West against government intervention in their management and use. The lands were overgrazed seriously before the government began to regulate their use, and 50 years later BLM still has not been able to reduce livestock numbers to the capacity of the range.

In the 1970s, it appeared that the management of BLM lands was turning dramatically toward conservation. Under a 1974 court order, BLM began preparing a series of environmental impact statements on its grazing program, and in 1976 the Federal Land Policy and Management Act clearly mandated multiple-use management of BLM lands, directing that the agency move to prevent further degradation and improve their condition. The Carter administration moved aggressively to implement the law, appointing a pro-conservation director—Frank Gregg, a former executive director of the Izaak Walton League of America. The administration sought and received accelerated funding and personnel for the agency, particularly for noncommercial programs including fish and wildlife, and attempted to increase emphasis on recreation, wilderness protection, and the like.

This new emphasis, however, was short-lived. President Reagan and his first Interior secretary, James Watt, were self-proclaimed "sagebrush rebels," dedicated to reducing the government's role in managing the public lands. BLM's new director, Robert Burford, is a livestock operator, holder of a BLM grazing permit, and an advocate of less government interference in range management. From 1981 to 1985, BLM has suffered more severe funding and personnel cuts than any other natural-resource agency, with the cuts made primarily in renewable-resource management, including wildlife-habitat management. The agency has emphasized production and development of livestock and energy and mineral resources and has taken a number of moves to return more control over grazing management to livestock operators.

Almost all of the current problems and issues discussed below are part of this general trend to restrict conservation efforts and relinquish agency control of land-management decisions. Some believe that efforts to weaken the agency are reaching a critical point. In a 1985 study of six federal natural-resource agencies published by the State University of New York, two researchers summed up BLM's current situation as follows:

"Clearly the BLM faces an uncertain future. Perhaps more than any other agency the BLM has undergone rapid changes to its mission and priorities; it has been the agency most affected by the Reagan-Watt policies. . . . Indeed, it appears as though the Bureau were targeted for elimination. If it is to emerge as a countervailing power to the various interests now descending on the public domain, the agency will need a considerable boost in the basic agency resources of manpower, money, and expertise. To date, the agency's potential remains woefully underutilized and its future is in doubt." (Clarke 1985)

## Grazing Fee Reauthorization and Range Legislation

With the grazing-fee formula and the grazing advisory boards scheduled to expire at the end of 1985, wildlife conservationists hoped that Congress would pass legislation raising the fees and requiring improvements in rangeland management. Throughout 1985, the key players on the Senate Committee on Energy and Natural Resources and the House Committee on Interior and Insular Affairs worked to develop a compromise range bill but failed to reach agreement before the end of the year. Although drafts of potential legislation were circulated for public comment, no bill was ever introduced in Congress, and the grazing-fee formula was not reauthorized.

Grazing fees have been controversial since the beginning of the federal grazing program, but the western livestock industry has succeeded in keeping the fees low. In 1969, after decades of charging low fees, the federal government embarked on an effort to gradually raise fees to fair market value, but the increase was slowed by several moratoria on fee increases. With the passage of the Federal Land Policy and Management Act in 1976, Congress declared that the federal government should receive fair market value for the use of the public lands, but did not extend this policy to grazing fees. Instead, Congress froze grazing fees at current levels and ordered a study to devise an appropriate fee formula.

In 1978, Congress adopted a fee formula in the Public Rangelands Improvement Act that was based not on fair market value, but on the livestock operator's ability to pay. Under that formula, the fees rose to a high of $2.36 per animal unit month (AUM) in 1980 and have dropped steadily ever since to $1.35 per AUM in 1985. According to a draft government report on grazing fees, in 1983 the appraised market value of grazing on the public lands ranged from $4.05 to $8.85 per AUM. The actual fee charged that year was $1.40.

Western livestock interests want to keep the current fee formula, citing the bad financial shape of the western livestock industry and arguing that the costs of grazing are higher on public lands than on private lands. Those concerned about federal spending object to the low fees, saying they unfairly subsidize a very small element of the livestock industry—the public lands support only four percent of the nation's beef cattle (U.S. Government Accounting Office 1982, p.5)—and that the fees charged by the government cover only about half the costs of running the program. In 1983, the grazing program cost the taxpayers $34.7 million. Conservationists generally believe the fees should be increased, in part because they believe the low fees encourage overgrazing and in part because higher fees could provide additional funds for improving the condition of the range, including wildlife habitat.

With the grazing fee dropping over the past five years, increasing pressure to reduce federal spending, and conservationists angry over BLM's bias against resource protection and refusal to make grazing reductions, the stage was set for a massive battle over the grazing fee formula, scheduled to expire December 31, 1985. In an effort to head off such a battle, the Congressional Research Service convened a series of workshops in the fall of 1984, intended to get western livestock interests and conservationists to negotiate a compromise range bill for introduction and easy passage in 1985.

In May 1985, the key congressional leaders on public lands issues—Representatives Morris Udall (D-AZ) and John Seiberling (D-OH) and Senators James McClure (R-ID) and Malcolm Wallop (R-WY)—issued a draft bill for public comment that they said reflected the ideas and compromises advanced at the workshops. The legislation contained the following major elements:

- it continued the Public Rangelands Improvement Act grazing-fee formula indefinitely, without an expiration date;
- it extended the grazing advisory boards indefinitely, but required the boards to include two members representing wildlife interests;
- it required BLM and the Forest Service to designate key riparian areas to receive special management emphasis and increased funding;
- it authorized BLM and the Forest Service to designate areas as unsuitable for livestock grazing; and
- it required that a portion of grazing-fee receipts be allocated to fund riparian area and other wildlife habitat improvements.

Conservationists were aghast at the contents of the bill. They charged that the western livestock industry got everything it wanted—no increase in the grazing-fee formula and continuance of the district advisory boards—while the portions of the draft bill intended to address conservationist concerns were "a lot of words adding up to nothing" (*Land Letter* 1985). A top priority for wildlife conservationists was a program to restore and protect riparian areas, which have been degraded seriously by livestock grazing and other uses, but they charged that the riparian area program in the draft bill was totally permissive and mandated no real action. Likewise, they said the provision to declare areas unsuitable for livestock grazing lacked teeth and would accomplish little. And while wildlife conservationists would like to see a portion of the grazing-fee receipts allocated to habitat improvement, the manner in which the draft bill did so would have required additional appropriations—that is, new federal spending—a proposal unlikely to win congressional approval.

The western livestock industry, represented primarily by the National Cattlemen's Association, had some minor problems with the conservation portions of the bill but otherwise supported it.

With conservationists refusing to support the May draft, negotiations continued among the congressional leaders throughout the rest of the year in order to develop an acceptable compromise, but they failed to do so. The failure to enact a new grazing-fee formula means the task of establishing fee levels reverts to the administration. The pressure for deficit reduction could encourage the administration to raise the fees, although there will also be pressure from the western livestock industry and western republican senators up for ré-election in 1986 to keep the fees low. Congress, of course, could step in and enact a fee formula at any time.

With the expiration of the Public Rangeland Improvement Act grazing-fee formula, the pressure for a range bill seems likely to wane. Prospects were further dimmed at the end of 1985 when Representative Seiberling, the conservationists' chief advocate on the range legislation, announced he planned to retire at the end of 1986.

## Resource Management Planning

The Federal Land Policy and Management Act requires BLM to make key decisions about managing the public lands in the context of comprehensive land-use plans, which BLM calls Resource Management Plans. Nearly a decade after passage of the Federal Land Policy and Management Act, little progress has been made toward this goal for two major reasons: BLM has proceeded slowly in preparing Resource Management Plans and the few plans that have been completed are for the most part broad, general documents that fail to make critical management decisions. Two events in 1985 indicate that there may be some progress in the near future on both these issues.

The development of Resource Management Plans for BLM resource areas is proceeding slowly. The first plan—for the Glenwood Springs resource area in Colorado—was approved in January 1984, nearly eight years after the law's enactment. Four additional plans were approved in FY 1984, and 11 were approved in FY 1985, for a total of 16 plans completed by the beginning of FY 1986.

An additional 42 plans were in some stage of development at the end of the fiscal year: 17 final plans had been proposed by state directors but were undergoing appeals, 10 plans had been issued in draft form for public comment, and 15 additional plans were under way but had not reached draft stage by the end of FY 1985. Thus, a total of 58 plans were completed or under way at the end of 1985. It is unclear what proportion this is of the total number of Resource Management Plans that would be needed to cover all of the public lands. BLM manages 154 resource areas, but planning areas do not always coincide with resource-area boundaries, and a number of plans cover more than one resource area.

BLM had scheduled to start work on 11 new plans in 1986, but budget cuts anticipated to meet 1986 deficit-reduction goals under the Gramm-Rudman legislation were expected to force the agency to initiate fewer plans.

In the meantime, most resource areas continue to be managed under the older Management Framework Plans, which environmental groups have criticized as seriously inadequate planning documents. Unlike the Resource Man-

Status of Resource Management Plans
as of October 1, 1985

| Plans Under Way | Plans Released in Draft | Proposed Plans | Approved Plans |
|---|---|---|---|
| 1. Little Snake, CO | 1. Central Yukon, AK | 1. Steese, AK | 1. Aturas, CA |
| 2. San Luis, CO | 2. Grand Junction, CO | 2. White Mountains, AK | 2. Coast/Valley, CA |
| 3. Uncompaghre, CO | 3. Lemhi, ID | 3. Lower Gila South, AZ | 3. Hollister, CA |
| 4. Cascade, ID | 4. Egan, NV | 4. Yuma, AZ | 4. Glenwood Springs, CO |
| 5. West Hi-line, MT | 5. Elko, NV | 5. Northwest, CO | 5. Kremmling, CO |
| 6. Carlsbad, NM | 6. Shoshone-Eureka, NV | 6. Piceance Basin, CO | 6. Cassia, ID |
| 7. Farmington, NM | 7. Esmeralda-Southern Nye, NV | 7. San Juan/San Miguel, CO | 7. Monument, ID |
| 8. Taos, NM | 8. South Dakota | 8. Jarbidge, ID | 8. Billings, MT |
| 9. North Dakota | 9. Box Elder, VT | 9. Medicine Lodge, ID | 9. Headwaters, MT |
| 10. Baker, OR | 10. Kemmerer, WY | 10. Garnet, MT | 10. Powder River, MT |
| 11. House Range, VT | | 11. Walker, NV | 11. Lahontan, NV |
| 12. San Juan, VT | | 12. Rio Puerco, NM | 12. Wells, NV |
| 13. Warm Springs, VT | | 13. White Sands, NM | 13. John Day, OR |
| 14. Lander, WY | | 14. Spokane, OR | 14. Bookcliffs, VT |
| 15. Pinedale, WY | | 15. Two Rivers, OR | 15. Grand, VT |
| | | 16. Cedar/Beaver/ Garfield/ Antimony, UT | 16. Platte River, WY |
| | | 17. Buffalo, WY | |

agement Plans, the preparation of Management Framework Plans completed prior to the planning requirements of the Federal Land Policy and Management Act included public participation only after major aspects of the plans had been completed and failed to integrate environmental analysis of the effects of the proposed plan and potential alternatives into the planning process. The General Accounting Office, in an analysis of differences between the two types of plans, found that a Management Framework Plan is not "the comprehensive multiple-resource plan" that a Resource Management Plan is (U.S. General Accounting Office 1980). BLM relies heavily on plan amendments to make necessary changes to these plans, rather than revising them by preparing the newer Resource Management Plans. In fact, BLM currently does not have a schedule for preparing Resource Management Plans for all resource areas, and some areas may continue to be managed indefinitely under the older plans.

A federal court action in late 1985, however, could eventually force BLM to step up its development of Resource Management Plans. In December 1985, the U.S. District Court for the District of Columbia issued a preliminary injunction revoking actions taken by BLM since 1981 to remove protective classifications on 161 million acres of public land (*National Wildlife Federation v. Burford*, Civil Action No. 85-2238). In issuing the injunction, the judge found that the plaintiffs, the National Wildlife Federation, were likely to win their suit partly on the grounds that BLM had terminated the classifications without considering them in the context of a Resource Management Plan, as required by the Federal Land Policy and Management Act. The judge said the older Management Framework Plans are not substitutes for Resource Management Plans and that Congress intended BLM to continue using Management Framework Plans only temporarily after the passage of the Federal Land Policy and Management Act. If the court's final decision on the case affirms this point of view, it will clearly stir up the planning process. A favorable ruling would almost certainly mean that BLM will have to prepare Resource Management Plan before reclassifying significant acreage and is likely to indicate that Resource Managment Plans are necessary before BLM makes other significant land-use decisions as well. The suit is discussed later in more detail.

The Resource Management Plans issued so far, however, also have been criticized for a number of reasons. Environmentalists charge that the plans are vague and fail to make the type of specific management decisions envisioned by the Federal Land Policy and Management Act. The plans also lack consistency in content and quality and often are not comprehensive, addressing only a few selected aspects of land management. Planning guidance in BLM regulations (43 CFR 1600) and the BLM planning manual is fairly general.

To address some of these problems, BLM is developing "supplemental program guidance" to define the types of decisions and determinations to be made in the plans, specify analyses and information required in plan development, and outline additional consultation requirements not included in other guidance. It does not, however, establish a consistent format for the plans. The guidance should help insure that important land-management decisions actually are made in the planning process, and should give public participants in the planning process a concrete description of items to be covered in the plan, which they can use to pressure BLM to make key determinations in the plans.

The supplemental program guidance is being developed and issued in two phases. Guidance on topics covered in the first phase was issued in December 1985 and included the following items: all of the renewable-resource programs, including fish and wildlife habitat management, forestry management, livestock grazing management, and wild horse and burro management; lands; rights-of-way; non-energy leasable minerals; acquisition; fire management;

and plan-documentation requirements. Copies of the guidance are available from BLM. For fish and wildlife, the guidance requires the plans to make the following types of determinations. They must select priority species and establish objectives for maintaining, improving, and expanding their populations and habitat. They must identify areas for which habitat management plans are to be prepared and for designation as areas of critical environment concern. They must include management prescriptions on other uses to protect fish and wildlife, establish habitat-monitoring objectives, and identify at what level of habitat degradation management activities must be modified. Finally, the plans are to include positive conservation measures for species that are listed, proposed for listing, or are candidates for listing as endangered or threatened species.

Program guidance for the remaining topics was issued in draft form at the end of 1985 for a 45-day public-comment period. This second phase covered air resources; soil and water resources; vegetation; visual resources; cultural resources; natural history; recreation; wilderness; coal; fluid minerals (oil and gas); locatable minerals; mineral materials; engineering; and social and economic factors. Guidance on these items should be issued in final form during 1986.

## Low Priority for Areas of Environmental Concern

The Federal Land Policy and Management Act gave BLM a potentially important tool for the protection of fish and wildlife as well as other resources by establishing a new category of areas to receive special management attention, called areas of critical environmental concern. The act directed BLM to give priority to identifying potential areas of critical environmental concern in its inventory of the public lands and to give priority to designating and protecting such areas in the development and revision of land-use plans. BLM has not followed the Federal Land Policy and Management Act mandate to give priority to areas of critical environmental concern, and only a small portion of BLM acreage has been placed in this designation to date.

Areas of critical environmental concern are defined in the Federal Land Policy and Management Act as "areas within the public lands where special management attention is required . . . to protect and prevent irreparable damage to important historic, cultural, or scenic values, fish and wildlife resources, or other natural systems or processes, or to protect life and safety from natural hazards." The areas are an administrative designation, made in the land-use planning process and approved by the appropriate BLM state director. The designation does not automatically impose any particular restrictions on the designated area. Activities and uses considered compatible or incompatible with the protection of resources within areas of critical environmental concern resources are outlined in the land-use plan, and further management prescriptions may be included in an activity plan detailing how the area is to be managed. Once an area of critical environmental concern is designated, any action that would be incompatible with objectives set forth in the land-use plan can occur only if the plan is revised or amended to allow it.

In FY 1985, BLM designated 17 new areas of critical environmental concern in three states—eight in California, seven in Colorado, and two in Oregon—totalling 241,841 acres. Twelve of these were designated at least in part to protect fish and wildlife or other ecological values. With the addition of these new areas, 200 areas of critical environmental concern had been designated on BLM lands by the end of FY 1985. They covered 1.75 million acres, less than one percent of the total acreage managed by BLM. About half of the areas were designated at least in part to protect fish and wildlife.

BLM's use of the areas of critical environmental concern designation varies widely from state to state, and the overall figures give a more positive picture of progress in designations than is the case. Of the 200 designated areas, 151 are located in just two states—California and Oregon—and account for more than 60 percent of all acreage included in areas of critical environmental concern acreage. In the remaining states, which contain 270 million acres of public lands, only 49 areas have been designated, covering 746,000 acres. Very few land-use plans designate any areas at all: of the 11 Resource Management Plans approved in FY 1985, only one—for the Kremmling resource area—designated any areas of critical environmental concern. The failure to designate areas of critical environmental concern is one of the most frequent reasons for conservationist protests on land-use plans.

There appear to be several interrelated reasons for the failure to designate areas of critical environmental concern. One problem is confusion over when to use one of BLM's internal "natural area" designations and when to use the areas of critical environmental concern designation. Unlike areas of critical environmental concern, the various natural area designations—such as research natural areas, outstanding natural areas, and primitive areas—are not authorized by law and their protection is not required legally. Thus in some cases, BLM field staff reportedly will choose one of these unofficial designations out of concern that designation of an area of critical environmental concern will limit their management flexibility. BLM's Recreation Division, which handles staff work in Washington on areas of critical environmental concern, has suggested that BLM adopt a policy of using the designation as an umbrella to provide a basis in law for protection of all the natural areas, but this idea has made no progress at higher BLM levels.

A larger problem, however, is the failure of high-level BLM officials to direct the field to give priority to designation of areas of critical environmental concern. BLM field staff frequently face stiff pressure from development-oriented users of BLM land not to use the designation, which often is perceived as likely to foreclose development of these lands. With no encouragement from within the agency to resist this pressure, proposed areas of critical environmental concern repeatedly have been dropped during the planning process. More-

Areas of Critical Environmental Concern, October 1, 1985

| State | ACECS added in FY85 | | Total Wildlife ACECS[1] | | Total Plant ACECS[2] | | Total ACECS | | Percent Acreage in ACEC to Total BLM Acreage in State |
|---|---|---|---|---|---|---|---|---|---|
| | # | Acres | # | Acres | # | Acres | # | Acres | |
| Alaska | 0 | 0 | 0 | 0 | 0 | 0 | 0 | 0 | 0 |
| Arizona | 0 | 0 | 0 | 0 | 0 | 0 | 0 | 0 | 0 |
| California | 8 | 75,036 | 30 | 419,926 | 12 | 37,815 | 87 | 766,026 | 4.5% |
| Colorado | 7 | 165,475 | 2 | 1,190 | 4 | 8,835 | 12 | 186,802 | 2.2% |
| Idaho | 0 | 0 | 4 | 196,345 | 0 | 0 | 5 | 228,345 | 1.9% |
| Montana | 0 | 0 | 1 | 12,048 | 0 | 0 | 1 | 12,048 | 0.1% |
| Nevada | 0 | 0 | 1 | 307 | 2 | 100 | 4 | 1,479 | negligible |
| New Mexico | 0 | 0 | 4 | 6,697 | 1 | 2,468 | 7 | 19,392 | 0.1% |
| Oregon | 2 | 1,330 | 19 | 101,163 | 36 | 50,610 | 64 | 240,061 | 1.5% |
| Utah | 0 | 0 | 2 | 12,392 | 2 | 6,400 | 7 | 89,231 | 0.4% |
| Wyoming | 0 | 0 | 9 | 131,949 | 2 | 1,196 | 13 | 208,385 | 1.1% |
| Eastern States | 0 | 0 | 0 | 0 | 0 | 0 | 0 | 0 | 0 |
| TOTAL | 17 | 241,841 | 72 | 882,017 | 59 | 107,424 | 200 | 1,751,769 | 0.6% |

[1]Includes all ACECS that list wildlife as a value. If an area has both wildlife and plant values, it is listed only under wildlife.
[2]Includes areas that have botanical or ecosystem values but that do not have wildlife values.
Source: Department of the Interior

over, there are repeated reports of high-level Interior Department and BLM officials giving oral instructions to field staff *not* to designate such areas. In this climate, the areas of critical environmental concern program is making little progress.

## Northern Spotted Owl/Oregon and California Grant Lands

The northern spotted owl is native to the coniferous old-growth forests of the Pacific Northwest. Its range, which extends from central California to just north of the Canadian border, overlaps the most economically valuable timber stands in the nation. Most of its remaining habitat lies within the national forest system, but some is on public land in western Oregon, primarily the Oregon and California Grant Lands. The spotted owl is classified as a "sensitive" species by the Forest Service and is listed as a threatened species under Oregon state law. The Fish and Wildlife Service estimates that almost all the old-growth timber stands within the spotted owl's range will be harvested within the next five to 20 years if present management objectives are not changed (U.S. Department of the Interior, 1982, p. 22).

In 1979, a federal-state interagency task force developed an Interagency Spotted Owl Management Plan, under which BLM agreed to protect 300 acres and later 1,000 acres of old-growth habitat for each of 90 pairs of spotted owls on BLM land in western Oregon. In 1982, however, BLM announced that its agreement to adhere to the Spotted Owl Management Plan had been only an interim measure to be used until timber-management decisions were reached through the planning process. BLM prohibited land-use plans from preserving habitat for state-listed species within areas classified as commercial forest. The first draft plan issued under the Reagan administration included no old-growth set-asides for wildlife, even though under the Interagency Spotted Owl Management Plan BLM was supposed to maintain 16 pairs of owls in the area covered by this plan.

After a storm of public protests, threats by environmental groups to pursue federal listing for the spotted owl as a threatened species, and the refusal of the state of Oregon to find the plan consistent with its federally approved coastal zone management plan,* BLM signed an agreement with the state to maintain 90 pairs of spotted owls for five years on its lands in western Oregon. The agreement will be reviewed in 1988 in light of any new information about the spotted owl to determine what continued actions are necessary for its protection.

In FY 1985, the Oregon Department of Fish and Wildlife began a review of the 90 areas identified by BLM for the temporary protection of the 90

---

* Section 307(c)(1) of the Coastal Zone Management Act requires the federal government to ensure that activities funded or supported by it are consistent, to the maximum extent practicable, with approved state coastal zone management plans.

pairs of owls to determine if the areas could support the owls adequately. The department found that BLM needed to protect a minimum of 130 areas in order to provide habitat for the 90 pairs of owls because BLM landholdings in western Oregon are interspersed with private and other federal lands and much of the remaining old-growth forest is in small, fragmented patches. The Department of Fish and Wildlife identified an additional 55 potential sites for spotted owl protection, giving BLM 145 areas from which to select the recommended 130 sites. BLM is reviewing the department's recommendations, and negotiations on which areas to protect are expected to be concluded in FY 1986.

In the meantime, the more significant actions on spotted owl management are taking place in the Forest Service's land-management planning process. As a result of appeals by environmental groups, the Forest Service is revising its planning guide for the Pacific Northwest region and is preparing a supplemental environmental impact statement on the plan's effects on the spotted owl. Environmental groups have requested BLM and the service to do a joint impact statement, but BLM failed to respond to the request. Early indications from new data covered in the environmental review are that the 1,000-acre old-growth set-asides for each owl site are far from adequate, particularly in the northern end of its range, and that substantial changes may have to be made in Forest Service timber-harvest plans in the region.*

## Lawsuit to Reinstate Protective Withdrawals and Classifications

On December 4, 1985, the United States District Court for the District of Columbia granted a preliminary injunction halting mining and certain other activities on 170 million acres of public land that the Department of the Interior had opened to new development uses over the previous four years. The injunction was in response to a suit brought by the National Wildlife Federation in May 1985 charging that the department's removal of various restrictions on the use of these lands violated certain provisions of the Federal Land Policy and Management Act and the National Environmental Policy Act. According to the National Wildlife Federation, as of mid-1985 BLM had opened approximately 13 million acres of previously protected land to the staking and development of mining claims under the 1872 Mining Law, six million acres to oil and gas leasing, and more than 100 million acres to sale and land exchanges. BLM was considering removal of similar restrictions on an additional 50 million acres.

At issue are a variety of actions taken by the Department of the Interior over the past 70 years to protect the public lands from certain uses. Prior to the passage of the Federal Land Policy and Management Act, which generally directed BLM to retain the public lands and authorized their protection and

* See the Forest Service "Current Issues" section for further discussion.

management, the federal government protected certain areas from private settlement and development by two methods: either by classifying them for particular uses, primarily under the authority of the Classification and Multiple-Use Act; or by formally "withdrawing" them from the operation of certain laws permitting the sale, settlement, mining, and other uses of the public lands.

When the Federal Land Policy and Management Act was enacted, Congress specified that all existing withdrawals, classifications, or other reservations were to remain in effect until they were modified under the provisions of the act or other applicable law. With regard to withdrawals, the Federal Land Policy and Management Act authorized the secretary of the Interior to make, modify, extend, or revoke withdrawals, but only in accordance with certain limitations and requirements outlined in the act. The act also set up a special procedure for the review of certain withdrawals on various public lands in the 11 western states, directing the secretary of the Interior to complete the review by 1991 and to make recommendations to Congress as to whether and for how long such withdrawals should be continued. With regard to classifications, the Federal Land Policy and Management Act specified that the secretary of the Interior may modify or terminate classifications of public land as long as they are consistent with land-use plans developed under the Federal Land Policy and Managment Act Section 202 planning process.

According to the National Wildlife Federation, the Interior Department originally was scheduled to complete the review of existing withdrawals and classification orders by the end of 1991. In 1981, however, Secretary of the Interior James Watt accelerated the review of classification orders because of "continuing emphasis upon elimination of public land 'lock-ups'," and directed BLM to complete most of the classification review by October 1984. BLM came close to meeting this goal: by mid-1985, BLM had completed review of 167.7 million acres of classified areas. It had terminated classification orders on 160.8 million of these acres and had set aside seven million acres for deferred review under detailed planning procedures. BLM has moved somewhat less rapidly on withdrawal review. Of 51.9 million acres of withdrawals, BLM had revoked withdrawals on 19.9 million acres by mid-1985 and had submitted recommendations on 17.5 million acres for presidential review, but these were returned to BLM for further study. Recommendations on another 14.5 million acres were under review at the secretary's level, and the remainder were still under review by BLM.

In spite of the magnitude of the acreage involved, it was some time before BLM's revocation of the classifications and withdrawal drew any public attention because of BLM's piecemeal and low-profile approach to the effort. Although BLM published notices of such revocations in the *Federal Register,* there was no opportunity for public comment. The National Wildlife Federation called the notices "opaque," saying they often provided insufficient information for the public to understand their effect. In contacting various fish and game departments in the 11 western states for information on the withdrawal and classification review, the federation discovered that the departments often were unaware that such a review was even under way.

The federation challenged BLM's withdrawal-review program on eight counts. The federation charged that the program violated the National Environmental Policy Act by failing to prepare an environmental impact statement analyzing the cumulative environmental impact of removing restrictions on 170 million acres of land or more. It also claimed that BLM violated various provisions of the Federal Land Policy and Management Act by failing to prepare Resource Management Plans prior to revoking the classifications and withdrawals, by not providing for public participation in determining whether to remove such restrictions, and by failing to make recommendations to the president and Congress prior to revoking withdrawals in the 11 western states.

In deciding to grant the injunction, the court found that the National Wildlife Federation was likely to win its suit on at least two points. First, the court agreed that Interior improperly terminated land classifications without preparing Resource Management Plans. The department had argued that the Management Framework Plans prepared prior to the planning requirements of the Federal Land Policy and Management Act provide an adequate basis for considering classifications, but in a finding that could affect BLM's current approach to land management planning, the court found that Management Framework Plans do not satisfy the management act's comprehensive planning requirements.* The court did not agree with the federation that withdrawal revocations also must be considered in the context of Resource Management Plans but did agree that the Federal Land Policy and Management Act required public participation in such decisions, which Interior had not allowed. In addition, the court said that the failure to issue an injunction would allow the initiation of mining and other activities that could permanently destroy wildlife habitat, air and water quality, natural beauty, and other environmental values.

The injunction prohibits Interior from modifying or terminating any withdrawal or classification that was in effect on January 1, 1981, or from taking any action inconsistent with the lands restored protective status.

## BLM Wilderness Study and Management

Controversy surrounding BLM's wilderness study continued and escalated in 1985. Critics continued to voice two major concerns: that wilderness study areas are not being protected adequately to preserve their wilderness characteristics and that the study and resulting BLM recommendations are biased against wilderness.

BLM is directed by the Federal Land Policy and Management Act to

---

* Discussed previously under "Resource Management Planning."

conduct wilderness studies on roadless areas of 5,000 acres or more and on roadless "islands" of the public lands that are identified as having wilderness characteristics. The secretary of the Interior is required to make wilderness recommendations to the president by 1991, and the president is required to send his recommendations to Congress within two years of receiving recommendations from the secretary. The Federal Land Policy and Management Act also requires an accelerated review of areas that were classified as primitive or natural areas prior to November 1, 1975, called "instant study areas." BLM can consider wilderness designation for other areas during the land-use planning process.

All of the wilderness study areas are to be managed during the study so as not to impair their suitability for wilderness designation, except that the Federal Land Policy and Management Act authorizes the continuance of certain grazing and mining activities that existed at the time of the act's passage. Once Congress designates an area as wilderness, it is to be managed according to the provisions of the 1964 Wilderness Act. Although no specific requirements exist regarding wildlife conservation in wilderness areas, wilderness designation can provide some additional protection for fish and wildlife since the areas are to be managed to ensure that they remain in their natural state and to prevent degradation of their resource values. With the rapid development of non-wilderness areas on the public lands, many important species that need wild, roadless habitat—such as the desert bighorn sheep—may eventually survive only in designated wilderness.

In response to complaints from national environmental groups and local wilderness organizations about BLM's wilderness study, the House Public Lands Subcommittee, chaired by Representative John Seiberling (D-OH), held a series of oversight hearings on the study, including two sets of hearings in 1985. The major complaint has been that BLM is not adequately protecting potential wilderness areas during the study process. According to numerous environmental witnesses at the hearings, BLM has authorized activities such as expanded and intensified grazing, off-road vehicle use, road construction, and mineral development where there are no valid existing rights, activities that could damage the wilderness characteristics of the study areas and jeopardize their potential for eventual wilderness designation. In addition, numerous unauthorized activities are reported in the study areas, including road construction and illegal mining and woodcutting, which BLM apparently is unaware of or unable to control.

Under pressure from continued congressional scrutiny, Interior Secretary Donald Hodel announced in July a number of steps taken to address criticisms of BLM management of wilderness study areas. BLM now has adopted a policy of requesting public comments on activities proposed for wilderness study areas 30 days prior to the activities' authorization. BLM also has instructed its field officials to conduct monthly surveys of wilderness study areas during the portion of the year when the area is accessible to the public—

an effort meant to reduce unauthorized activities. BLM state offices have been directed to track all authorized activities and report them to Washington for central tracking when and if so requested. Finally, Hodel said that BLM had reinforced instructions to the field offices "to be extremely cautious" in approving activities in wilderness study areas.

Hodel also addressed the issue of allowing increases in grazing in wilderness study areas, but made no policy changes. Hodel said that the Interior Department's Solicitor's Office had concluded that BLM could allow the increases as long as they do not adversely affect wilderness quality, even though the Federal Land Policy and Management Act states that grazing in wilderness study areas can occur only "in the manner and degree in which it was being conducted" at the time of the act's passage. Hodel said BLM had issued explicit guidance to all state directors prescribing criteria to be used in evaluating potential grazing increases in wilderness areas.

In spite of these changes, wilderness advocates still are concerned about study-area management, pointing out that BLM does not have to follow the public comments it receives on proposed activities, that the agency interprets its non-impairment policy too loosely, and that it does not consider adequately the cumulative impacts of activities in wilderness study areas. The House version of the FY 1986 appropriations bill for the Department of the Interior and related agencies (H.R. 3011) included two measures intended to address study-area management concerns. It proposed to cut $1 million from the administration request for wilderness studies, charging that the studies were deficient because they are being rushed, and to add $1.5 million for wilderness study area management. It also included language prohibiting BLM from authorizing increases in study-area grazing above 1976 levels. The final appropriations bill, however, maintained the administration's requested funding for wilderness studies, boosted funding for the management of designated wilderness and wilderness study areas by only $750,000, and included no language restricting grazing.

The other major concern of wilderness advocates is the adequacy of the wilderness study itself. BLM has identified for wilderness study approximately 25 million acres in almost 900 separate tracts. As of October 10, 1985, BLM had completed draft environmental impact statements for, and made preliminary recommendations on, about 19 million acres. The agency recommended 7.26 million acres, 38 percent of the acres studied so far, as suitable for wilderness designation and the remaining 11.64 million acres, more than 60 percent, as unsuitable. BLM expects to complete most of the studies by 1987, although some will not be completed until 1990. Before the secretary of the Interior recommends an area to the president for wilderness designation, the area must be surveyed for mineral potential by the U.S. Geologic Survey. BLM expects to meet the Federal Land Policy and Management Act deadline for transmitting the last of its wilderness recommendations to the president by 1991.

Wilderness supporters charge that BLM's initial inventory, which identified areas to receive further wilderness study, was inadequate and that other areas in addition to the 25 million acres selected should be reviewed for wilderness potential. They also charge that the studies themselves have been inadequate and that BLM is recommending insufficient acreage as suitable for wilderness. In Utah, for example, wilderness advocates support the designation of approximately five million acres of wilderness, but BLM has studied only about three million acres and is expected to recommend only one million. These issues could come back to haunt BLM. Both wilderness groups and Representative Seiberling have compared the BLM wilderness study to the Forest Service's Roadless Area Review and Evaluation process, which because of controversy went through two entire cycles, was challenged legally at both stages, and still is not finally settled some 15 years after its initiation.

In the meantime, the accelerated instant-study-area review mandated by the Federal Land Policy and Management Act is almost complete. In April 1985, the President recommended to Congress the designation of four new BLM wilderness areas covering approximately 382,000 acres. These are: Great Rift, Idaho, 322,450 acres; Humbug Spires, Montana, 8,791 acres; Powderhorn, Colorado, 43,311 acres; and Scab Creek, Wyoming, 7,636 acres. Another 26 areas totalling 102,000 acres were recommended for nonwilderness. Two instant study areas are still under BLM review; the study of 15 other areas has been combined with the study of larger contiguous roadless areas, and the remaining areas have either been designated, released, or transferred to other agencies by Congress.

One controversy surrounding the wilderness study was resolved this year. In 1982, Interior Secretary James Watt deleted 1.6 million acres of roadless areas from wilderness study on the grounds that they were too small or that the federal government did not hold the underlying mineral rights.* In a decision issued on April 18, 1985, the U.S. District Court for the Eastern District of California held that the Federal Land Policy and Management Act did require the study of lands where the government did not own the mineral rights and that although the act did not require the study of areas smaller than 5,000 acres, Watt had followed improper procedures in deleting them from the study. As a result of this suit, the Department of the Interior has agreed to restore all the areas to wilderness study.

There was also a slight flare-up over regulations BLM issued in 1985 regarding management of designated wilderness. BLM currently has 23 designated wilderness areas totalling 368,739 acres in nine states. On February 25, 1985, the Department of the Interior issued final regulations governing management of these wilderness areas (50 *Fed. Reg.* 7704, 1985). The rules were relatively uncontroversial, except for a provision setting forth the requirements for allowing mining in wilderness areas. Wilderness advocates protested that the regulations did not require mining-claim holders to show that they had

---

* See *Audubon Wildlife Report 1985* for details.

found a "valuable mineral deposit," as BLM traditionally has required. Not only would this have weakened the standard for mining in BLM wilderness, but sources report that BLM hoped to use the revised language as a precedent to pressure the Forest Service into revising its mining policy, too. Current Forest Service policy requires the discovery of a valuable mineral deposit before mining in its 32 million acres of wilderness. Due to public pressure and the threat of a lawsuit, the provision was withdrawn from the regulations and subsequently was reproposed in August in a version that maintained current standards for mining in wilderness (50 *Federal Register* 31734, 1985). The rule was expected to be issued in final form without significant changes.

## BLM/Forest Service Land Swap

In January 1985, the administration proposed an exchange of 35 million acres between the Forest Service and the BLM. The basic goal of the exchange was to consolidate intermingled lands into larger blocks managed by one agency, with the Forest Service focusing on forest management and the BLM on range management.

The exchange proposal was described in more detail in a series of implementation guides issued for public comment in June 1985. The administration proposed to transfer approximately 18.3 million acres from BLM to the Forest Service and 16 million acres from the Forest Service to BLM, for a net gain of 2.3 million acres to the National Forest System. The consolidation of the lands into larger management units was expected to allow the government to reduce the number of towns in which both agencies have offices from 71 to 22. Personnel would be reduced by up to 800 positions overall. The exchange was expected to save $69 million to $77 million over the first five years and $27 million to $32 million each year thereafter.

In addition to exchanging the lands, the administration proposed some changes in land management. The most significant proposal was to give the Forest Service sole authority over the administration of energy and mineral activities on National Forest System land. Currently, BLM administers almost all mineral activities on all federal lands, including the National Forest System, although the Forest Service generally is responsible for conducting environmental studies and making recommendations on whether and how mineral activities should be conducted on lands under its jurisdiction. The administration's goal was to provide one-stop service for mineral operators, but the proposal also has received support from conservationists who believe the Forest Service is more conservation oriented than BLM.

Because the Forest Service and BLM manage their lands largely under different authorities, some questions and controversies have arisen over how the exchanged lands would be managed. For example, BLM has general authority under the Federal Land Policy and Management Act to sell its lands, while the Forest Service has only limited authority to sell small parcels from the National Forest System. Thus, national forest areas currently off limits to sale would be eligible for disposal if transferred to BLM. Conversely, BLM lands transferred to the Forest Service would be expected to become ineligible for sale. However, the administration has proposed that such lands remain available for disposal at least temporarily. A similar situation exists with wilderness study areas. Areas being studied for potential wilderness designation by BLM must be protected for their wilderness values until they are released to development by Congress. If transferred to the Forest Service, however, these lands could be released administratively, without congressional action or approval.

Although conservationists believe that some land exchanges between the two agencies could improve management and efficiency, some groups say they should be evaluated on a case-by-case basis and have objected to the massive approach proposed by the administration. In addition, conservationists, particularly at the local level, have opposed the exchange of a number of specific areas included in the proposal. Most of these complaints are about the transfer to BLM of lands currently under Forest Service management. Conservationists are concerned that areas transferred to BLM could be sold, that BLM will take a less conservation-minded approach to managing these lands, and that BLM lacks the funds and personnel to properly manage areas requiring intensive management.

Many other affected interests also oppose or are unenthusiastic about the land-swap proposal. Ranchers, miners, and other commodity interests are worried about some lands currently under BLM management being transferred to what they view as more restrictive Forest Service management.

The land exchange and the various proposed policy changes can be made only through legislation passed by Congress. Most congressional members have been noncommittal about the proposal while waiting for the administration to develop a specific legislative package. In the interim, however, Congress has prohibited the agencies from reducing personnel, closing field offices, or undertaking other actions to gear up for the exchange prior to the enactment of legislation implementing it. This prohibition currently extends through FY 1986 and was made in amendments to the FY 1985 Supplemental Appropriations Act (Pub. L. 99-88) and the FY 1986 continuing resolution (Pub. L. 99-190).

In the meantime, the administration has been working to revise the exchange proposal based on public comments. The administration is expected to submit proposed legislation to Congress in early 1986 outlining a scaled-down version of the land exchange.

## Range Monitoring/Grazing Modifications

BLM is supposed to monitor the condition of various resources to determine if management objectives are being met and to determine whether management needs to be altered or resources improved. For example, the agency monitors habitat conditions where habitat management plans are being implemented to determine if they are achieving their goals; monitors wild horse and burro range condition to determine if populations are too high; and monitors forage conditions on grazing allotments to determine whether current management is appropriate or needs to be changed.

Monitoring has taken on added importance because of recent changes in BLM policy. As BLM began completing its grazing environmental impact statements in the late 1970s, some of its conclusions regarding necessary changes in livestock reductions management were challenged by livestock interests on the grounds that the data were inadequate to support the adjustments. In 1982, BLM reversed its policy of adjusting livestock use based on data used in the grazing impact statements and ordered that the data be supported by the results of monitoring studies before making decisions on how to allocate forage among livestock, wildlife, and horses and burros. This policy was codified and clarified in 1984 revisions to BLM's grazing regulations, which specify that in the absence of acceptable data, grazing-allotment decisions will be delayed up to five years while monitoring data are collected. Once decisions on grazing adjustments are made, the adjustments can be phased in over a five-year period. This means that reductions in the number of livestock or changes in grazing systems may not be implemented for 10 years: five years of monitoring and five of implementation.

Conservationists generally oppose this delay in making grazing adjustments. They believe that BLM has years of data showing that range condition overwhelmingly is in unsatisfactory condition and that much of the cause of the damage is overgrazing by livestock. In addition, however, there is increasing concern that BLM is not conducting monitoring studies of sufficient quantity or quality to meet its goal of having the necessary data to support grazing adjustments within five years. This concern has increased as BLM funding and personnel continually have been reduced over the past several years. These funding cuts have been particularly serious for the wildlife habitat management program, which was short on personnel even before the reductions, and could mean that the monitoring data to support grazing adjustments that meet fish and wildlife habitat needs will not be developed in many areas. Conservationists are concerned that without strong supporting data, BLM may again succumb to pressure to delay grazing decisions or that, if it does pursue grazing reductions, its actions may be challenged by Congress or in the courts.

No agency-wide prescription exists for monitoring requirements. The individual state and district offices are responsible for detailing how monitoring is to be accomplished, and the procedures for and adequacy of monitoring among resource areas vary widely. There is no agency-wide compilation of what is being accomplished in monitoring, nor does BLM headquarters even know whether adequate monitoring is being conducted to support the management decisions the agency needs to make.

In 1985, BLM's state office in Utah completed a special evaluation report on rangeland monitoring throughout BLM's lands in the state. Experts familiar with BLM monitoring efforts say the findings in the report generally reflect the problems of the monitoring program as a whole. Monitoring is a high priority in the Utah BLM program, and the report states that the general health of the range-monitoring program in Utah is relatively good. However, it outlines a number of problems in the program, some of which the report says could mean that the agency will not have sufficient data on which to base management decisions in the future. These include:

- Lack of specific management objectives in land-use plans and activity plans, resulting in situations where the monitoring being done is too general or is not directed toward the types of management decisions that need to be made for the area.

- Inadequate monitoring plans, including failure of monitoring plans to integrate wildlife, range, and other resource objectives, to explain methodologies for conducting monitoring studies, or to outline responsibilities for carrying out the studies. This results in an inefficient monitoring program—a serious problem considering the agency's limited resources. The failure to integrate wildlife objectives may mean that wildlife monitoring does not get done simply because of a lack of manpower and that monitoring studies may answer questions only about livestock-grazing needs. Failure to outline responsibilities means that some studies fall through the cracks.

- Inadequacies in the monitoring studies themselves, including failure to conduct all necessary types of studies on all allotments and inadequate documentation of the results of monitoring studies. These are serious deficiencies that the report says mean there will not be enough data upon which to base management decisions.

- Numerous problems in the analysis and evaluation of monitoring studies, including failure to evaluate formally the results of various studies conducted on grazing allotments at the end of a grazing cycle and failure to summarize and analyze information from rangeland monitoring studies at the end of each field session. The study found a general lack of confidence among BLM staff that the monitoring data being gathered can or will be used by managers to make resource-management decisions.

BLM is taking some initial steps toward improving its monitoring program. The Utah office is proceeding with efforts to implement recommendations made in its evaluation and has sent directly to the district managers specific findings and suggestions for each resource area. At the headquarters level, BLM plans to conduct in 1986 a special evaluation of on-the-ground monitoring studies. The Wildlife Division will take the lead in the evaluation, with joint participation from the Range, Forestry, and Wild Horse and Burros divisions. The bureau will look into how monitoring efforts are organized throughout the agency's hierarchy and will review guidance established at the state and district levels. It will also survey efforts to coordinate with other interests in the development of monitoring studies. The general goal of the review is to determine if monitoring data are providing the information needed to make informed management decisions. The evaluation is targeted for completion in FY 1986; implementation of its conclusions is targeted to begin at the state level in FY 1987.

## Wild Horses and Burros

Controversy over the management of wild horses and burros continued in 1985 and is not likely to end any time soon. These animals are not native to the West—horses were first brought to the New World from Spain—and many scientific studies indicate that they may compete with native wildlife, the most serious example being competition between burros and desert bighorn sheep. BLM sees these animals largely as a management problem, blaming them for range deterioration in some areas. However, wild horses have roamed the West for several hundred years in some areas, and much of the public believes the horses should be protected as living symbols of American history. In addition, because these animals were for years brutally captured and killed for sale as pet food, strong sentiment exists for assuring that they are treated humanely.

Wild horses and burros are protected on the public lands by the Wild Free-Roaming Horses and Burros Act of 1971 (16 U.S.C.A. 1331 *et seq.*).* The act generally protects the animals from capture, harassment, branding, or killing, but allows BLM to remove "excess" animals where overpopulations occur. Old or sick captured animals are to be destroyed as humanely as possible. Healthy animals must be put up for adoption by private individuals, but may be destroyed if no adoption demand exists. However, BLM has had a moratorium on destroying healthy but unadopted horses and burros since 1982.

For more than a decade, BLM has had an aggressive horse and burro removal program. Shortly after the protection of the animals by the 1971 Horses and Burros Act, BLM estimated that populations began to increase rapidly, from an estimated 25,400 animals in 1971 to 64,000 by 1980.† The effects of the capture program began to force populations back down in the early 1980s. In 1982, however, BLM sharply raised adoption fees, and this increased cost, perhaps combined with the economic recession, caused a sudden drop in the adoption of the captured animals. BLM had to divert funds from the capture effort to feeding and caring for unadopted animals in its

---

* The Wild Free-Roaming Horses and Burros Act applies to the National Forest System as well, but 98 percent of the animals are located on BLM lands.
† BLM's original population estimates, its estimates of the rate of population increases, and assumptions about damage done to the public lands by these animals were all questioned in a National Academy of Sciences study in 1982. See the *Audubon Wildlife Report 1985* for further discussion.

corrals, and horse and burro populations on the public lands began increasing again.

Congress, prompted chiefly by Senator James McClure (R-ID), responded by accelerating funding for the wild horse and burro program, boosting it from $5.77 million in FY 1984 to $17.239 million in FY 1985, a higher level of funding than provided for BLM's entire wildlife program. This allowed BLM to remove almost 19,000 animals from the public lands, reducing populations to an estimated 50,400 at the end of FY 1985, the lowest level since the removals began. However, this meant that BLM had record high levels of animals in its corrals, estimated to be about 9,000 animals at the end of FY 1985. BLM says it costs as much as $2 a day to maintain each animal.

Due to the growing number of horses and burros in the government's care, the House of Representatives, in its FY 1986 appropriations bill for the Department of the Interior, eliminated all funding for the removal of horses and burros from the public lands and prohibited any further removals until all animals previously captured had been adopted. The Senate, however, prevailed. The horse and burro program received $16.964 million in FY 1986—almost the same as 1985—and no language restricting the program was included.

The increasing number of wild horses and burros in the government's corrals is likely to increase support for an administration-backed proposal to authorize the government to sell unadopted animals for commercial purposes. Legislation giving the government such sales authority cleared the Senate Energy and Natural Resources Committee in 1983, but Congress took no further action on it. Sales authority also was included in the draft range bill circulated in May 1985 (discussed earlier), but negotiations on that legislation failed and no bill was ever introduced. Further action is uncertain, but since the sale of horses and burros would help recover the costs of the adoption program, sales authority could look more attractive as Congress tries to find ways to reduce the federal deficit.

In the meantime, BLM is sponsoring research, with funds provided by Congress in FY 1985, into other mechanisms for controlling horse and burro populations. One study is looking into wild horse genetics, to determine the parentage of wild horses—in particular to determine if the dominant stallion in a herd is the primary parent. A second study is looking into the possibility of vasectomizing stallions and giving long-term doses of contraceptives to mares.

# Legislation

## Military Lands Withdrawal Act of 1985

In 1985, the House Public Lands Subcommittee began considering a bill that would withdraw more than seven million acres of public lands for military purposes. The bill, H.R. 1790 sponsored by Representative Beverly Byron (R-

MD), covers six areas in Arizona, New Mexico, Nevada, and Alaska, involving parcels from 21,000 acres to 2.9 million acres. Many of the areas were withdrawn previously for military uses, but the withdrawals have expired and need to be renewed. Two of the proposed withdrawals contain lands in national wildlife refuges in Arizona and Nevada and are of particular concern to conservationists.

At hearings before the House Public Lands Subcommittee on November 14, 1985, the Wilderness Society urged the committee to require additional surveys and the preparation of statewide or regional environmental impact statements on the proposal. The Wilderness Society charged that many of the environmental assessments prepared by the military on the withdrawals are outdated, fail to cover activities proposed for the withdrawn areas, and fail to take a comprehensive look at the need for and impacts of military withdrawals on a statewide or regional scale. For example, the Wilderness Society says the environmental assessment for an area in Nevada called Bravo 20 assumed there would be no changes in the use of the land. In the meantime, however, the Navy has proposed to establish a 5,600-square-mile supersonic operations area that will require substantial construction of new roads, power lines, and other facilities.

The Public Lands Subcommittee tentatively plans to hold hearings on each of the areas in the bill in FY 1986, although this approach could change. Some sources suggest that Congress may deal with the withdrawals on a case-by-case basis. In fact, during the 98th Congress the administration did introduce separate bills for each withdrawal and it is unclear why they chose an omnibus approach this time around. The bill also has been referred to the Armed Services Committee, which has taken no action on it so far.

# Legal Development

## Cooperative Management Agreements and Revised Grazing Rules

On August 30, 1985, Judge Raul A. Ramirez of the U.S. District Court for the Eastern District of California overturned several provisions of BLM's 1983 grazing regulations. The ruling came on a suit filed against the Department of the Interior by the Natural Resources Defense Council and four other conservation groups,* who charged that the grazing regulations would seriously impair BLM's ability "to curb the improper and excessive livestock use that has destroyed wildlife habitat, accelerated soil erosion and desertification, and caused the deterioration of the recreational and scenic values of the public lands." Most significant, the court overturned BLM's cooperative management agreement program, which essentially allowed certain ranchers to manage livestock grazing on the public lands as they saw fit. The court found that

---

* Sierra Club, Wilderness Society, Defenders of Wildlife, and the Animal Defense Council.

the Cooperative Management Agreement regulations "violate the spirit and the letter of federal laws which are intended to preserve and improve the ravaged public commons" (*NRDC v. Hodel*, No. Civ. S-84-616RAR).

*Cooperative Management Agreements.* BLM began implementing the Cooperative Management Agreement Program in 1983 and codified it in the 1984 rules. Prior to the program, BLM controlled grazing by issuing permits or leases that specified the allowable numbers of livestock and seasons of use or by preparing more detailed allotment management plans specifying grazing system and range improvements to be implemented. BLM said the new program was intended to reward good stewardship and to encourage private investment in range improvements by allowing livestock operators who demonstrated exemplary rangeland management practices "to manage livestock grazing on the allotment as they determine appropriate" (48 *Federal Register* 21823, 1983). The regulations required the cooperative management agreements to establish "the responsibilities and performance standards" of the cooperating parties but did not require them to specify grazing limitations. The agreements were required to be issued for a term of 10 years and their termination was authorized only if the permittee violated the agreement's terms or conditions or transferred the agreement without BLM authorization.

The court agreed with the plaintiffs that the cooperative management agreements program was a "naked violation" of the Interior Department's duties under the Taylor Grazing Act, The Federal Land Policy and Management Act, and the Public Rangelands Improvement Act. The court found that under the Federal Land Policy and Management Act the secretary can authorize livestock grazing only through permits or leases that specify the number of animals to be grazed and the seasons of use or through allotment management plans that prescribe in more detail how livestock operations will be conducted, also including livestock numbers and seasons of use. The court held that the new regulations were "intended to and did create and authorize a new regulatory form not authorized by statute," and noted that examples of cooperative management agreements presented by both the defendants and plaintiffs contained no grazing specifications.

The court also held that the requirement that the agreements extend for 10 years, with cancellation authorized only under certain limited circumstances, fell far short of the Federal Land Policy and Management Act standards, which require that BLM be able to re-examine the condition of the range at any time and, if necessary, readjust prescriptions for livestock grazing. The court also called BLM's environmental assessment on the cooperative management agreement program "essentially a policy justification for the new program with little space devoted to consideration of the threatened environmental impacts which might result therefrom" and held that the bureau had violated the National Environmental Policy Act by failing to prepare a full environmental impact statement.

In summary, the court said, "The apparent goal and inevitable result of the cooperative management agreement program is to allow ranchers, for a term of at least 10 years, to rule the range as they see fit with little or no governmental interference." In contrast, the court said that Congress precluded entrusting such management to livestock operators "apparently because after years of rancher dominance of range decisions, it found substantial evidence of rangeland deterioration."

***Dilution of Allotment Management Plans.*** The Natural Resources Defense Council also prevailed on its charge that BLM had illegally diluted requirements regarding allotment management plans. Prior to the regulatory revisions, BLM required grazing allotment management plans to "prescribe" a system of grazing on an allotment and to contain "mandatory terms and conditions," including limitations on the numbers of livestock and seasons of use. The revised regulations required only that allotment management plans "describe" the livestock grazing practices necessary to meet specific multiple-use management objectives. In its *Federal Register* notice on the proposed regulations, BLM described this change as merely "eliminating redundancy." The court found, however, that the rules allowed BLM to omit prescriptions regarding livestock numbers, seasons of use, and provisions authorizing cancellation, suspension, and modification of permits and therefore constituted a basic policy change. The court nullified the regulations on procedural grounds, saying that BLM's description of the new regulations was "patently misleading" and violated the Administrative Procedure Act's requirements that the public be given adequate notice of and an opportunity to respond to proposed regulatory changes. In a footnote to the decision, however, the judge said that even if the provision had not been invalidated on procedural grounds, it would not have met the Federal Land Policy and Management Act requirements that BLM include specific seasons, numbers, and cancellation provisions in all grazing permits.

***Dilution of Land-Use Plans.*** A third issue decided in favor of conservationists was BLM's dilution of the role of land-use plans in making grazing decisions. Prior to the 1984 changes, the grazing regulations required BLM officers to modify, suspend, or cancel grazing permits if they were inconsistent with the governing land-use plan. The revised regulations specified that BLM officers "*may modify* the terms and conditions of the permit or lease *if monitoring data show that present grazing use is not meeting the land use plan or management objectives*" (emphasis added). This change eliminated BLM's authority to cancel permits, made the authority to modify permits discretionary and authorized modification only if monitoring data show there is an inconsistency. The court noted that this was a substantive and controversial change and that BLM's failure to explain the reason for the change, to respond to extensive public criticism of the proposal, or to address at all the elimination of cancellation authority or the requirement for supporting monitoring data in its *Federal Register* notice violated the Administrative Procedure Act. Although this ruling, too, was based purely on procedural grounds, the opinion of the court made it clear that BLM's effort to weaken land-use plans was contrary to substantive statutory requirements.

*Penalties for Violators and Supplemental Feeding.* The court invalidated two additional provisions on procedural grounds. One was the deletion of provisions authorizing penalties for livestock operators who had been convicted of violating federal or state environmental laws, including those related to air, water, wildlife, plant, fish, and wild horse and burro protection and the use of chemical toxicants. The other was a provision allowing ranchers to use supplemental-feeding techniques on their allotments without prior BLM authorization. Both provisions were criticized heavily in public comments. Even BLM's state director for Montana warned that allowing permittees to engage in supplemental feeding without prior BLM approval would result in the use of hay containing noxious weeds or poisonous plants, the feeding of livestock in riparian areas or crucial-habitat areas, and a number of other problems. The court ruled that BLM had violated the Administrative Procedure Act by failing to respond adequately to critical comments on both proposals and that it had violated the National Environmental Policy Act by failing to prepare an environmental impact statement on the supplemental-feeding provision.

*Definition of Affected Interests.* The one count on which the court ruled in favor of BLM involved a provision that could limit public participation in grazing decisions. Prior to the 1984 regulatory amendments, BLM's grazing regulations defined "affected interests" who may participate in the grazing decision-making process as anyone who has expressed in writing an interest in livestock grazing on particular allotments. The new regulation redefined affected interests to include only individuals or organizations that have expressed their interest in writing *and* have been determined by BLM to be actually affected by a proposed action.

The plaintiffs argued that the rule should be overturned on procedural and substantive grounds. The court ruled that BLM had followed proper procedures in issuing the rule. On the substantive issue, the court noted that "the new definition obviously reflects a new reluctance on the part of the Secretary with respect to public participation." However, it found there was no evidence that BLM officers actually had abused the discretion granted by this regulation to exclude members of the public from participation and said that it would be premature to rule on the issue unless and until BLM actually did use the rule to impermissibly prevent public participation in livestock-management decision-making.

BLM has decided not to appeal the court's decision. The Washington headquarters has instructed the field to discontinue all cooperative management agreements and to halt all work on any new agreements. In the other cases where the court ruled against BLM regulations, the agency has reverted to operating under the previous 1983 rules. BLM may propose new regulations in the future to replace them that the court struck down on procedural grounds alone.

## Fencing of Public Lands

BLM gained new power to protect wildlife on public lands in a recent decision by the U.S. District Court in Wyoming. In *Bergen v. Lawrence*, (620 F. Supp. 1414 [D.Wyo 1985]), the U.S. Attorney and the National Wildlife Federation challenged a rancher's attempt to fence pronghorns off of their critical habitat, alleging that the fence violated the Unlawful Inclosures Act. The rancher ran cattle during the summer near Rawlins, Wyoming, in an area known as Red Rim, a 22,000-acre parcel which, because of its topography, is blown free of snow by winter winds, allowing pronghorns to forage when surrounding areas remain snow covered. The area is a checkerboard of public and private ownership. The rancher constructed a 28-mile fence around Red Rim, gerrymandering the fence so that it was entirely on privately owned squares of the checkerboard, except where crossing at the corners of public and private squares. As a result, BLM acreage was enclosed in an antelope-proof fence. The rancher alleged that as the fence was on private land, he was not subject to BLM regulations requiring that fences be designed to allow wildlife passage. BLM contended that as the fence enclosed public lands and did not meet BLM regulations, it violated the Unlawful Inclosures Act. Evidence presented showed that as the fence stood, it might decimate the 2,000 pronghorns that have long depended on the Red Rim area for winter feeding. Invoking *Canfield v. United States* (167 U.S. 518), an 1897 Supreme Court decision under the Unlawful Inclosures Act, the court held that the rancher could not use the fence to block wildlife access to public lands and noted that BLM had the authority to prevent this fence construction. The court therefore ordered the rancher to remove the fence or change it to conform to BLM regulations.

# Status of the Resource

No reliable information exists on the biological status of wildlife on the public lands or on the adequacy of wildlife habitat. BLM does not maintain population estimates for wildlife species. The state fish and game agencies prepare population estimates every five years for 11 big-game animals, which are reported in the Department of the Interior's *Public Land Statistics,* but BLM wildlife officials say these numbers are not reliable enough to be used to show population trends. BLM's informal assessment is that the big-game populations, with the exception of the desert bighorn sheep, are in pretty good shape. Even less is known about the status of small game and nongame animals, except for those whose populations already have reached dangerously low levels.

In spite of the lack of reliable data, it is clear that today's wildlife populations in the West are far below the levels that existed prior to extensive human settlement. According to one highly speculative estimate, there may have been 20 to 30 million big-game animals in the 11 western states in the pre-Columbian era. As of 1975, overall populations of big-game animals were at about 15 to 20 percent of this level, and climax species—bison, pronghorns, and bighorn sheep—were at less than five percent of their estimated pre-settlement numbers (Wagner 1978).

Although there is no comprehensive information on the status of fish and wildlife habitat on the public lands, several studies have been done over the years on general range condition. They have consistently found that the majority of the range is in unsatisfactory condition. Two recent reports show that the range remains in a deteriorated state. In 1984, BLM released a report declaring that 60 percent of the range is in unsatisfactory condition—that is, producing at less than 50 percent of its ecological potential (Department of the Interior 1984). However, because the condition of 70 million acres in the study was based not on range-inventory data but on "professional knowledge and judgment," many considered the validity of the estimate to be questionable.

A subsequent report by the National Wildlife Federation and the Natural Resources Defense Council, based on published data from BLM environmental impact statements and land-use plans, indicated that the BLM estimate may have been overly optimistic (Wald 1985). Of the 118 million acres for which published data were available, the report found that 84 million acres, or 71 percent of the acreage, was in unsatisfactory condition. The Natural Resource Defense Council and the National Wildlife Federation say the main reasons for this deteriorated condition are mismanagement of livestock grazing and insufficient funding for range-management and range-improvement programs. They also predicted that significant improvements in existing

Comparative Percentages of the Public Rangelands in Excellent, Good, Fair, and Poor Condition, 1936-1985

| Year | Excellent | Good | Percent by Condition Class | |
| | | | Fair | Poor or Bad |
|---|---|---|---|---|
| 1936[a] | 1.5 | 14.3 | 47.9 | 36.3 |
| 1966[b] | 2.2 | 16.7 | 51.6 | 29.5 |
| 1975[c] | 2.0 | 15.0 | 50.0 | 33.0 |
| 1984[d] | 5.0 | 31.0 | 42.0 | 18.0 |
| 1985[e] | 1.9 | 27.1 | 42.0 | 29.0 |

Sources:
[a] Data adapted from *The Western Range,* Senate Document 199, 75th Congress, 2nd Session.
[b] *The Forage Resource,* Pacific Consultants (1969).
[c] *Range Condition Report,* Department of the Interior (1975).
[d] Aggregation by BLM of all baseline records maintained at each of the resource areas within BLM. Data on 98 million acres from range inventories conducted for grazing impact statements; condition rating for 70 million acres based on professional knowledge and judgment.
[e] *Our Ailing Public Rangelands: Condition Report - 1985,* National Wildlife Federation and Natural Resources Defense Council (1985).
Table Compiled from: *50 Years of Public Land Management,* BLM, 1984; and *Our Ailing Public Rangelands,* NWF, 1985.

conditions are unlikely to occur because of declining grazing-fee receipts and budget cuts in range-management programs.

A number of problems, however, prevent correlating this range-condition data with the condition of wildlife habitat. A determination that an area is in unsatisfactory condition does not indicate what it is satisfactory for: for livestock or for wildlife or for what species of wildlife? In addition, general range condition figures do not address the most significant habitat areas that are the critical factor in determining wildlife populations, such as riparian areas, wintering habitat, and nesting grounds. In summary, very little reliable data exists on wildlife in the agency that manages more habitat in the United States than any other federal agency.

# References

Clark, J.N. and D. McCool. 1985. *Staking Out the Terrain: Power Differentials Among Natural Resource Management Agencies.* State University of New York Press, Albany.

National Research Council, Board on Agriculture and Renewable Resources, Committee on Wild and Free-Roaming Horses and Burros. 1982. *Wild and Free-Roaming Horses and Burros, Final Report.* National Academy Press, Washington, D.C.

Reffalt, W.C. 1985. "Statement of William C. Reffalt, Representing the Wilderness Society, Before the Public Lands Subcommittee of the House Interior Committee, November 14, 1985, on H.R. 1790, the 'Military Withdrawal Act of 1985.'" Congressional testimony. The Wilderness Society, Washington, D.C.

U.S. Department of Agriculture, Forest Service, and U.S. Department of the Interior, Bureau of Land Management. 1985. *1985 Grazing Fee Review and Evaluation, Draft Report.* U.S. Department of Agriculture and U.S. Department of the Interior, Washington, D.C.

U.S. Department of the Interior, Bureau of Land Management. 1984. *50 Years of Public Land Management.* U.S. Department of the Interior, Washington, D.C.

U.S. Department of the Interior, Fish and Wildlife Service. 1982. *The Northern Spotted Owl: A Status Review.* U.S. Department of the Interior, Washington, D.C.

U.S. General Accounting Office. 1982. *Public Rangeland Improvement—A Slow, Costly Process in Need of Alternate Funding.* Government Printing Office. Washington, D.C.

U.S. General Accounting Office. 1980. *Changes in Public Land Management Required to Achieve Congressional Expectations.* Government Printing Office, Washington, D.C.

Wagner, F.H. 1978. "Livestock Grazing and the Livestock Industry," in Howard Brokaw, ed., Council on Environmental Quality, *Wildlife and America: Contributions to an Understanding of American Wildlife and its Conservation.* Government Printing Office, Washington, D.C.

Wald, J. and D. Alberswerth. 1985. *Our Ailing Public Rangelands: Condition Report—1985.* National Wildlife Federation and Natural Resources Defense Council, Washington, D.C.

Wildlife Management Institute. 1981. *Evaluation of Bureau of L and Management Program Interactions with Rangeland Management.* Wildlife Management Institute, Washington, D.C.

*Katherine Barton, a freelance writer who specializes in conservation issues, is based in Washington D.C.*

Spotted cats, such as this African leopard, were among the first animals to benefit from international treaties for the protection of wildlife jeopardized by trade.

*Leonard Lee Rue III*

# International Wildlife Conservation

## Michael J. Bean

## Introduction

MANY SPECIES, INCLUDING most of our familiar songbirds and even some butterflies, migrate vast distances. In the course of their migrations they pass over the same mountain ranges, river courses, and forests that their ancestors for countless generations traversed, unaware of the political boundaries by which man has divided up the Earth. Yet, because of those political boundaries, the conservation and even the ultimate survival of many migratory species lie beyond the exclusive control of any one nation. The draining of wetlands in the Canadian prairie, where many waterfowl species breed, could spell disaster for "our" autumn flocks of ducks and geese just as surely as accelerating deforestation and destruction of aquatic areas in Central and tropical South America could doom many of "our" familiar spring songbirds. Looked at from the perspective of our neighbors, overhunting of waterfowl in the United States could undermine Canada's efforts to protect "its" goose and duck breeding populations, while the fragmentation of North American forests may be contributing to the decline of Latin America's songbird populations.

The lesson to be drawn from these examples and from many others like them is that migratory species are neither "ours" nor "theirs," but a shared resource. Since one nation, through its action or inaction, can frustrate the conservation objectives of other nations, international cooperation is essential to the conservation of such species. That lesson is even more evident with respect to wildlife outside the political jurisdiction of any nation, such as the whales, fish, and other creatures of the high seas. Without international cooperation for the conservation of these species they become a free good, part of the "global commons." Because the rewards of restraint by one nation will only be reaped by others less concerned with the long-term consequences of their actions, not even enlightened self-interest significantly restrains a nation's appetite to harvest such free goods or pollute the marine environment. This "tragedy of the commons," as Garrett Hardin described it nearly 20 years ago (Hardin 1968), makes international cooperation for conservation not just desirable, but a practical necessity.

The principles underlying the need for international cooperation in the conservation of migratory and high-seas species are clear enough and have been recognized for many decades. More recently, a new notion has evolved about the conservation of the world's wildlife. All of human welfare and human life is linked to the preservation of our fellow beings. The loss of species in some seemingly remote corner of the Earth, whether migratory or entirely endemic, potentially affects us all. From such species may come discoveries useful to science, medicine, and agriculture, and thus to human welfare itself. With the loss of such species, not only are the diversity and beauty of nature diminished, but so too is the potential for human advancement. In this view, the living resources of the world are part of the common heritage of mankind, and cooperative international action to protect that heritage is imperative.

## The Special Setting for International Cooperation

Fundamental to the success of international conservation efforts is an understanding of the unique, and occasionally arcane, principles of international law.

In the U.S. domestic arena, the rights and duties of citizens are reasonably clear cut and developed in a familiar lawmaking process. Laws are made by the legislative branch of government, enforced by the executive branch, and interpreted by the judicial branch.

No comparable international authorities govern relations among nations. International law emanates from a variety of sources, including custom, executive agreements or other informal arrangements, and formal treaties. For example, the principle of freedom of the seas and the concomitant right of nations to harvest freely the living resources of the sea developed as customary law over the centuries and are now reflected in various formal treaties.

Ultimately, the willingness of nations to accept and abide by their customs or formal agreements determines the success of international conservation efforts. Although international tribunals similar to American courts do exist to provide legal interpretations of international law, they are infrequently used and of far less importance than their domestic counterparts. Furthermore, much of the international conservation work of the various agencies of the United States arises opportunistically from international educational, scientific, and cultural undertakings, rather than from any narrowly defined category of conservation law. In sum, the foundation upon which much of international conservation is built is inherently less stable and predictable than that upon which purely domestic conservation programs rest.

A final point worth noting is the often close relationship between international conservation diplomacy and domestic politics. No less than in other areas of foreign affairs, the two are often inextricably linked. International conservation agreements have been used to further domestic political ends, just as domestic political considerations sometimes impose constraints upon international conservation initiatives.

This chapter focuses principally upon a few of the more important programs that involve the United States. It is a selective sample that illustrates the range of problems and issues that currently confront wildlife policymakers in the United States. Because it is selective, however, there is much more that might be treated in a more comprehensive survey of the subject, and very much more if one were to examine the many international conservation initiatives of the other nations of the world. Some subjects of international law also are covered in other chapters, notably the chapters on marine mammals, migratory birds, and the National Marine Fisheries Service. See also the appropriate chapter in the *Audubon Wildlife Report 1985.*

# History and Legislative Authority

Although wildlife conservation itself has a long history, international cooperation for conservation is much more recent. The first wildlife conservation initiatives originated at least as far back as ancient Egypt, but the first international conservation efforts, other than for ocean fisheries, date only from the latter years of the 19th century.

United States involvement in international wildlife conservation is even more recent. Not until 1911, when the United States, Russia, Japan, and Great Britain negotiated a Treaty for the Preservation and Protection of Fur Seals (37 Stat. 1542, T.S. No. 564),* did the United States expand its international conservation horizon beyond fishery agreements (Bean 1983). For some decades earlier, the four nations had been engaged in commercial hunting of northern fur seals in the North Pacific. The seals were killed on island rookeries then under the jurisdiction of Japan, Russia, and the United States. Pelagic sealing, the hunting of seals migrating by the sea to the rookeries, also was widespread. Although the difficulty of retrieving killed and wounded seals

---

*The 1911 treaty was terminated after Japan's withdrawal in 1941. It was replaced in 1957 by an Interim Convention on Conservation of North Pacific Fur Seals, 8 U.S.T. 2283, T.I.A.S. No. 3948, 314 U.N.T.S. 105. The Interim Convention, which was to have been in effect only six years, has been extended on three occasions by further protocols and is currently being considered for fourth extension.

made pelagic sealing inefficient and highly wasteful, the practice enabled each country to kill seals otherwise destined for rookeries belonging to the other nations. Indeed, for Great Britain, which claimed none of the island rookeries, pelagic sealing was the only means of participating in the lucrative seal hunt.

When the unregulated hunting and wasteful pelagic sealing caused serious declines in the seal populations, the United States took the lead in an effort to secure mutual restraint. An informal agreement between the United States and Great Britain in 1891 sought to limit the take by each nation and expedite a resolution of Britain's avowed right to engage in sealing in waters claimed by the United States. Without the participation of all the sealing nations, however, hunting limitations offered no guarantee of effective seal conservation. A full 20 years elapsed before that participation was ensured by the signing of the 1911 treaty, which outlawed pelagic sealing and provided a mechanism for limiting the annual hunting of seals to levels that could be indefinitely sustained. Thus was born the first formal international conservation treaty to which the United States was a party.

Other international agreements soon followed. A 1916 treaty with Great Britain, on behalf of Canada, was the first of four bilateral agreements that the United States has negotiated for the conservation of migratory birds. A 1923 agreement with Canada to protect the Pacific halibut fishery was the first of literally dozens of bilateral and multilateral commercial fishery agreements. Whale conservation took its first halting steps with the conclusion in 1931 of a Convention for the Regulation of Whaling (49 Stat. 3079, T.S. No. 880), predecessor to today's International Convention for the Regulation of Whaling (62 Stat. 1716, T.I.A.S. No. 1849) under which nearly all commercial whaling has been halted. Later, the United States spearheaded efforts to focus attention on the common conservation problems of the nations of the New World, concluding in 1940 the Convention on Nature Protection and Wildlife Preservation in the Western Hemisphere (56 Stat., T.S. No. 981).

By the 1970s, the focus had expanded still further to encompass global problems and efforts to encourage coordinated action to address those problems. The 1973 Convention on International Trade in Endangered Species of Wild Fauna and Flora (CITES) (27 U.S.T. 1087, T.I.A.S. No. 8249), uniting nearly 90 nations in a common effort to stem the loss of species from inadequately regulated commercial trade, is the most important of those efforts.

# Organization and Operations

## The Treaty-making Process

The impetus for negotiating a treaty can come from a variety of different sources, including government agencies responsible for conservation, other nations, and even nongovernmental interest groups. However, since international treaties embody the formal undertakings and obligations to which the United

States pledges to adhere, the Department of State, as the government's representative on all foreign affairs matters, is responsible for treaty negotiation and supervision. On environmental matters generally, the responsible office within the State Department is the Division of Environmental Affairs within the Bureau of Oceans and International Environmental and Scientific Affairs. A deputy office director and an international wildlife and conservation officer handle most wildlife related issues for the division.

The negotiating process ends with the formal signing of a treaty text. Signing the text of a treaty does not obligate the United States to adhere to it, however. First, the treaty must be ratified. Ratification requires that two-thirds of the members of the U.S. Senate approve the treaty. The key Senate committee in the ratification process is the Foreign Relations Committee, which is in its key position not because of any particular expertise in matters of conservation, but because of its primary jurisdiction over all matters involving foreign affairs.

Once ratified, a treaty becomes binding upon the United States and, under the Supremacy Clause of the Constitution, part of the supreme law of the land. Whether its provisions also bind citizens of the United States, as distinct from the government itself, depends upon whether it is self-executing or requires the enactment of new, implementing legislation. Most treaties are not self-executing, and most of the conservation treaties examined in this chapter have in fact been implemented domestically by federal legislation.

Enactment of implementing legislation brings a new set of congressional players onto the scene. The principal House committee with jurisdiction over wildlife conservation matters is the Committee on Merchant Marine and Fisheries, particularly its Subcommittee on Fisheries and Wildlife Conservation and the Environment. In the Senate, committee jurisdiction is divided, depending upon whether the subject matter concerns marine or non-marine wildlife. Jurisdiction over marine wildlife matters is vested in the Committee on Commerce, Science, and Transportation. Jurisdiction over non-marine wildlife matters is vested in the Committee on Environment and Public Works. Proposed legislation to implement new wildlife conservation treaties originates and is largely shaped in these committees. They, and to a lesser extent the Senate Foreign Relations Committee and House Committee on Foreign Affairs, also oversee the implementation of conservation programs established to carry out the treaties and their implementing legislation.

## Agencies and Programs

At least a dozen different federal offices and agencies are engaged to some degree in international conservation activities. To varying degrees, these activities are monitored and facilitated by the State Department, particularly by the Office of Food and Natural Resources within the Bureau of Oceans and International Environmental and Scientific Affairs. The department does not itself have any special wildlife conservation expertise. However, as part of its

Key State Department Offices Having International Conservation Responsibilities

Secretary of State
George P. Schultz

Assistant Secretary for Oceans and International
Environmental and Scientific Affairs
John D. Negroponte
(202) 632-1554

Deputy Assistant Secretary for Environment, Health and
Natural Resources
Mary Rose Hughes
(202) 632-7904

Director, Office of Food and Natural Resources
Bill L. Long
(202) 632-2418

Deputy Director, International Wildlife Conservation Officer
George A. Furness
(202) 632-3367

general duty to represent the government in all matters of foreign affairs, the department functions as a liaison with international organizations, foreign governments, and U.S. missions abroad. For example, the department is represented regularly at CITES meetings and at meetings of it various CITES committees. It also monitors CITES financial matters and processes the U.S. contribution to the special trust fund that finances CITES activities.

*Agencies of the Interior Department* The key federal agency with substantive wildlife conservation responsibilities is the Department of the Interior and, within it, the U.S. Fish and Wildlife Service (FWS). The FWS Office of International Affairs is charged with most of the agency's international responsibilities. It is a tiny office assigned to the Office of the Deputy Director and has only six professionals on its staff. The bulk of the office's activities are focused on implementing the Convention on Nature Protection and Wildlife Preservation in the Western Hemisphere.

The office also carries out conservation activities under a Special Foreign Currency Program, principally using monies accrued under the Agricultural Trade Development and Assistance Act of 1954, or, as it is more commonly known, Public Law 480 (7 U.S.C.A. 1691). The latter is a statutory program under which the United States allows certain foreign countries to purchase American agricultural products with their own currencies rather than with U.S. dollars. The United States promises to spend those currencies in the countries of origin as way of bolstering their economic development. Among the agencies that have used these currencies to aid conservation activities abroad are the National Park Service, the Smithsonian Institution, and FWS.

Key Interior Department Offices Having International Conservation
Responsibilities

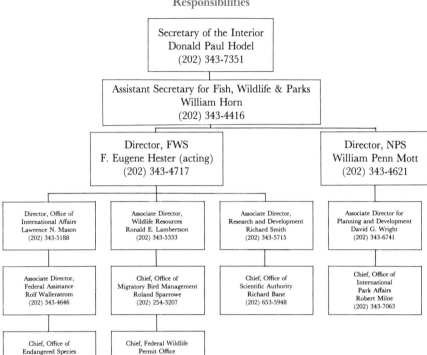

Authority for FWS activities is found in Section 8 of the Endangered Species
Act of 1973, which authorizes the use of such "excess currencies" for aiding the
endangered species conservation programs of foreign governments. With such
funds the Office of International Affairs since 1977 has supported species surveys, wildlife management research, preparation of educational materials,
wetlands surveys, and training of wildlife managers, primarily in India, Paki-
stan, and Egypt.

A third major area of activity for the Office of International Affairs
concerns a 1972 executive agreement on environmental protection between
the United States and the Soviet Union. The office carries out or coordinates
with other federal agencies a variety of activities under this agreement. Most of
those activities involve the exchange of scientists between the two nations for
research on topics such as endangered species, biosphere reserves, and so on. A
similar cooperative effort with the People's Republic of China currently is
being developed.

Other FWS offices also have important international conservation responsibilities. The Office of Migratory Bird Management carries out cooperative bird censuses in Canada and Mexico; provides assistance in the

Special Foreign Currency Program Obligations in $000's

| Fiscal Year | Pakistan | India | Egypt | Total |
|---|---|---|---|---|
| 1981 | 6.9 | 515.7 | 16.7 | 539.3 |
| 1982 | 4.2 | 309.7 | 10.4 | 324.3 |
| 1983 | 17.6 | 1022.7 | 57.2 | 1097.5 |
| 1984 | 30.5 | 88.6 | 6.8 | 125.9 |
| 1985* | 150.0 | 1660.0 | 150.0 | 1960.0 |

*projected figures
Source: U.S. Fish and Wildlife Service

management of raptors to countries in Latin America, Europe, and the Pacific region; and, in cooperation with the Office of International Affairs, supports studies of North American breeding birds in their Latin American winter ranges. The Office of Endangered Species confers with foreign authorities concerning the status of foreign species being considered for listing under the U.S. Endangered Species Act. Enforcement of the Endangered Species act, CITES, and the Lacey Act pertaining to international trade are the responsibility of the FWS Division of Law Enforcement and the Justice Department's Wildlife and Marine Resources Section of the Division of Lands and Natural Resources. The Federal Wildlife Permit Office and the Office of Scientific Authority function, respectively, as the management and scientific authorities for the United States under CITES. Their roles under that treaty are described in detail later in this chapter. The FWS Research and Development offices carry out a broad wildlife research program, including studies that pertain to foreign species and habitats. The Patuxent Wildlife Research Center conducts most of this research and, with the Office of International Affairs, operates a literature distribution service for foreign biologists.

Another Interior agency with important international responsibilities is the National Park Service. Its Office of International Parks Affairs is a small office of less than 10 people responsible to the Service's assistant director for Planning and Development. Like its counterpart in FWS, it participates in the Special Currency Program authorized by the Endangered Species Act and carries out other activities related to the implementation of the Western Hemisphere Convention. In addition, it plays a major role in providing training and study opportunities for park professionals from other countries. It has provided training for professionals from most of the 120 nations that maintain national park systems and has supported regional training centers such as the College of African Wildlife Management in Tanzania (for English-speaking African countries) and in Cameroon (for French-speaking countries).

*Other Agencies*   Agencies outside the Interior Department also contribute to international wildlife conservation programs. The Department of Commerce, through its National Marine Fisheries Service (NMFS, pronounced "nymphs"), is responsible for the implementation and enforcement of the Endangered Species Act with respect to marine species. Thus, its responsibilities parallel those of the Office of Endangered Species and the Division of Law Enforcement in FWS. NMFS also is the key agency responsible for U.S. participation in the International Whaling Commission, the North Pacific Fur Seal Commission, the Convention for the Conservation of Antarctic Marine Living Resources, and a host of commercial fishing treaties. Some fishery treaties provide a framework for addressing conservation problems broader than the original fishing concerns that brought them into being. The Inter-American Tropical Tuna Commission, for example, through the persistence of U.S. efforts, monitors the incidental drowning of porpoises by various of the national fleets fishing for tuna in the eastern tropical Pacific Ocean.

Providing assistance for the development of Third World countries is another facet of governmental activity with great importance for wildlife conservation. Most of the assistance provided by the United States is given either unilaterally through the Agency for International Development, an arm of the State Department, or through multilateral lending institutions like the World Bank and the Inter-American Development Bank. U.S. foreign assistance programs recently have been more closely scrutinized for their environmental effects. In 1983, Congress amended Title VII of the Foreign Assistance Act of 1961 to make the conservation of wildlife and wildlife habitat for the first time "an important objective of U.S. development assistance" (Pub.L. No. 98-164, Title 7). That amendment also directed the administrator of the Agency for International Development, in cooperation with other federal agency heads, to develop a United States strategy for conserving biological diversity in developing countries and further directed the secretaries of State and Interior to develop recommendations to improve their capabilities relating to the conservation of international wildlife resources. Reports prepared in response to these two directives provide a very useful summary of existing international conservation activities and of opportunities to link conservation more effectively with development assistance in the future (Agency for International Development, 1985; U.S. Dept of State 1984).

Some of the activities of the Agency for International Development having most significance for international conservation include preparing for more than 30 developing countries environmental profiles that identify major environmental and natural resource problems and needs, drawing up guidelines for projects involving the clearing of forests in the Amazon basin, and providing assistance for the setting aside of nature reserves. The agency also cooperates with some of the international projects administered by FWS and the Park Service.

The United States is not able to dictate what types of development activities multilateral lending institutions will or will not support, but because of its position as a major financial contributor, the United States can significantly influence bank decision making. United States interests in the multilateral lending institutions to which it belongs are represented by the Treasury Department. In recent years, under pressure from the Subcommittee on International Development Institutions and Finance of the House Committee on Banking, Finance, and Urban Affairs, the Treasury Department and other agencies have begun a closer examination and evaluation of the environmental policies and procedures of the lending banks.

In conclusion, it is clear that international wildlife conservation is an activity whose many participants play many roles. No single agency or program provides overall direction or guidance for U.S. international conservation efforts. Nevertheless, certain major programs, because of their scope, magnitude, or history, have achieved a special prominence. The following sections cover the most important of these: migratory birds, the Western Hemisphere Convention, and the regulation of wildlife trade under CITES.

## Migratory Bird Treaties

*Introduction* Political boundaries rarely correspond with ecological boundaries, and nowhere is this more true than with respect to migratory birds. Where neighboring nations are on reasonably friendly terms, as the United States historically has been with its immediate neighbors, joint action for the conservation of migratory birds and other shared resources is feasible. In fact, the United States has entered into a great variety of bilateral treaties and other less formal agreements with Canada and Mexico. These include treaties relating not only to migratory birds, but also to the pollution of the Great Lakes and the regulation of ocean and anadromous fisheries, among others. More recently, the United States and Canada have been struggling to develop a mutually satisfactory framework for cooperation in the conservation of the migratory Porcupine caribou herd and the more intractable problem of controlling acid rain. From that great variety of potential subjects, this section focuses on our international migratory bird program and the four bilateral treaties it implements. That choice is based upon the special historical significance of the original 1916 treaty with Canada and the importance of the migratory bird conservation effort as an illustration of what international cooperation can accomplish.

*History and Legislative Authority* By the latter years of the 19th Century, a nascent conservation movement was alarmed by the dramatic decline of many U.S. wildlife species, in particular many once-abundant migratory birds. The passenger pigeon, whose enormous flocks had blackened the skies for miles only a few decades earlier, was disappearing rapidly and clearly headed for extinction. The majestic plume birds of the Southeast were being decimated to supply the millinery trade of the young nation's urban centers. Elsewhere, market hunters killed enormous numbers of waterfowl and other game birds to supply the restaurants and food markets of the day. In the

Midwest, spring hunting took a huge toll of birds migrating to the breeding grounds.

The responsibility and authority for protecting wildlife was at that time lodged almost exclusively in the individual states. Yet, because many of the birds suffering from overexploitation were migratory, no single state could take effective action to arrest their decline. The balkanization of legal authority thus produced another example of the familiar tragedy of the commons whereby stringent measures imposed by one state to regulate bird hunting would result in sacrifice by its citizens without any compensating benefit unless other states also imposed significant restrictions. In this situation, a few of the early conservationists in private organizations and in the federal government recognized the need for national action to avert the developing wildlife tragedy. In 1913, Congress declared, as part of its annual appropriations bill for the Department of Agriculture (which then housed the Bureau of Biological Survey, predecessor of today's FWS), that all migratory birds were "within the custody and protection of the government of the United States" and prohibited their killing except in accordance with federal regulations (37 Stat. 828, repealed in 1918).

The 1913 law was short-lived. It was challenged immediately in two separate lawsuits by parties asserting that the federal government had unlawfully usurped a conservation authority that belonged exclusively to the states. Lower federal courts agreed in other cases.* One of those cases was appealed to the Supreme Court and argued there. While the court was still deliberating the legal issues, private conservationists and federal officials in the Agriculture Department, fearful of an adverse ruling, collaborated on a strategy to bolster the government's position (Hawkins 1984). If the United States were to negotiate a formal bird conservation treaty with Canada, they reasoned, congressional authority to enact a law that protected birds by implementing the treaty would be legally secure because of the constitutional provision making treaties part of the supreme law of the land. They persuaded Congress and the State Department to go along with this strategy, and in 1916 the United States and Great Britain, on behalf of Canada, formally concluded the Convention for the Protection of Migratory Birds (Stat. 1702, T.S. No. 628). Among its most important provisions was a ban on spring and summer hunting of all migratory birds, including waterfowl. Two years later, Congress passed the Migratory Bird Treaty Act (16 U.S.C.A. 703-711) to implement the convention.

Because of these intervening events, the Supreme Court dismissed the challenges to the 1913 law without ever ruling on them. It was soon faced with a challenge to the new Migratory Bird Treaty Act, however. This was brought by the state of Missouri, which had resisted the federal measure because of the

---

*United States v. Shauver, 214 F. 154 (E.D.Ark 1914), appeal dismissed, 248 U.S. 594 (1919); United States v. McCullagh, 221 F. 288 (D. Kan 1915).

popularity of spring waterfowl hunting within the state. The case was precipitated when Missouri's attorney general and four hunting companions with 68 birds taken out of season were arrested by a conscientious United States game warden, Ray Holland (Vose 1984). The Supreme Court's 1920 decision in *Missouri v. Holland* (252 U.S. 416 (1920)) was a landmark not only for conservation but for the development of constitutional law itself. It has been referred to as "perhaps the most famous and most discussed case in the constitutional law of foreign affairs" (Henkin 1972). Justice Oliver Wendell Holmes, one of the most respected jurists in the court's history, wrote the majority opinion in which he reasoned that:

> [b]ut for the treaty and the statute there soon might be no birds for any powers to deal with. We see nothing in the Constitution that compels the Government to sit by while a food supply is cut off and the protectors of our forests and our crops are destroyed. It is not sufficient to rely upon the States. The reliance is vain . . . (252 U.S. at 435 [1920]).

The 1916 Convention for the Protection of Migratory Birds was thus a successful gambit aimed as much at settling a divisive domestic political dispute between the state and federal governments as at establishing a new program of international cooperation. In time, however, it was to become the cornerstone of a true international effort to bring about the conservation of migratory birds and the model upon which subsequent agreements with three other nations would be based.

The first of those agreements was with Mexico. As early as 1926, the chief of the Bureau of Biological Survey noted in his annual report the desirability of negotiating bird protection treaties with Latin American nations so as to encompass more of the winter range of many of the species covered by the Canadian agreement, as well as to extend protection to other migratory species not protected by the 1916 treaty (Lamberston undated). Ten years later, on the final day of the first North American Wildlife Conference, called by President Franklin Roosevelt, a convention between the United States of America and the United Mexican States for the protection of Migratory Birds and Game Animals was concluded (50 Stat. 1311, T.S. No. 913). Like the earlier Canadian treaty it prohibited spring and summer hunting, though the closed season dates do not correspond precisely between the two treaties. A new feature of the Mexican treaty was a directive to establish refuge zones in which all bird hunting was to be prohibited. In addition, the Mexican treaty gave limited protection to game mammals by prohibiting cross-border shipments of them without appropriate permits.

The next major international migratory bird initiative came in the 1970s, when the United States concluded two new treaties with Japan and the Soviet Union. The Japanese treaty was signed in 1972. In that same year, reflecting the spirit of detente then prevailing, the United States and the Soviet Union entered into the Agreement on Cooperation in the Field of Environmental Protection (23 U.S.T. 845, T.I.A.S. No. 7345). That agreement was not a formal treaty submitted to the Senate for its approval and ratification. Rather, it was a less formal executive agreement, an example of the variety of ways that nations can embody their mutual understandings. It pledged cooperation, principally through exchange of scientists and scientific information, on a wide variety of environmental topics, among them "preservation of nature and the organization of preserves." The first major result of that cooperation was the conclusion in 1976 of the Convention Concerning Conservation of Migratory Birds and Their Environment (29 U.S.T. 4647, T.I.A.S. No. 9073).

The Japanese and Soviet treaties are in general quite similar, though minor differences do distinguish them. Most importantly, both broaden the focus of concern from merely controlling the hunting of birds to protecting their habitat. The habitat-protection provisions of the Japanese treaty are fairly general, requiring the two nations to "endeavor to take appropriate measures to preserve and enhance the environment" of protected birds, particularly with respect to stemming pollution of the seas and the introduction of exotic plants and animals to unique island environments. The provisions of the Soviet treaty are somewhat more detailed. For example, it provides for the establishment of a mutual warning system whereby each nation is to alert the other of pending major environmental disturbances and to cooperate in the rehabilitation of damaged areas. The Soviet treaty also directs the two nations to identify "areas of breeding, wintering, feeding, and moulting which are of special importance in the conservation of migratory birds within the areas under its jurisdiction" and to protect the ecosystems in such areas against detrimental alteration. Though an initial list of such areas was to be developed within a year after the treaty entered into force, neither party has yet done so.

The Migratory Bird Treaty Act implements all four treaties. It authorizes the secretary of the Interior to determine when, how, and to what extent migratory birds may be taken consistent with the treaties it implements and prohibits anyone from taking such birds except in accordance with the secretary's regulations. Following ratification of the Japanese and Soviet treaties, FWS considered asking Congress to enact new legislation specifically implementing the habitat-protection provisions of those treaties, but ultimately declined to do so. Thus, the habitat-protection provisions of these treaties are not specifically implemented by the Treaty Act or any other legislation. However, specific implementing legislation probably is not necessary in order for the United States to designate areas of special importance to migratory birds or set up a mutual warning system.

*Organization and Operations* Joint waterfowl breeding ground surveys by the United States and Canada and, to a lesser extent, by Mexico are the major activity of the international bird conservation program. Survey results show how the breeding populations of various migratory species vary from year to year, and this information, in turn, is used to prescribe annual hunting regulations.

FWS and its Canadian counterpart began aerial surveys of waterfowl breeding grounds in the United States and Canada in 1947, the year the Dominion Wildlife Service, later renamed the Canadian Wildlife Service, was established. They began supplementing these with on-the-ground data collection in 1955. These surveys are now fairly routine and conducted with the cooperation of the various state and provincial wildlife agencies. FWS also carries out more limited surveys of winter waterfowl populations in Mexico. These began in 1948 and, since 1959, usually have included Mexican participants. These surveys initially required rather formal arrangements through the Department of State and the Mexican Consulate. Indeed, at one point the Mexican military joined the FWS survey crews, apparently because of suspicions about their true purpose (Smith 1984). In 1977, a more informal approval mechanism was agreed to by the Mexican government, and the surveys have since been easier to conduct.

Within FWS, the Office of Migratory Bird Management oversees the breeding-population surveys. Although these surveys are supposed to determine overall take levels and ultimately the regulations that will meet those levels, none of the treaties specifies a desired population or take or any formal means of allocating national shares of the available migratory bird kill. In fact, the United States takes the lion's share of the North American kill, each year killing about 17 million waterfowl, compared to approximately four million in Canada. The treaties do not require parity or any other particular allocation of birds among the participating countries, and serious disputes over that issue seem not to have arisen.

The Office of Migratory Bird Management also is responsible for overseeing the preparation of a new North American Waterfowl Plan that will be implemented jointly by the United States and Canada. The plan, which does not include Mexico, sets forth a common strategy for setting habitat-protection goals, breeding-population objectives for various populations of geese and ducks, and other management goals for conserving waterfowl at desired levels. A draft of the plan is expected to be released for public review and comment by the end of 1985 and a final plan adopted in the spring of 1986. A preliminary draft of the plan was circulated to state wildlife agencies and a very limited number of conservation organizations earlier in 1985. The preliminary draft generated some controversy because of its provision for joint action, possibly including kill reductions, if waterfowl populations declined to certain predetermined levels. The plan was especially controversial because its proposal coincided with an FWS announcement of a separate proposal to reduce the waterfowl kill in the light of current population declines. The draft plan probably will be modified as a result of the controversy.

In addition to the waterfowl surveys, FWS carries out other bird-related international activities. Many of these activities are conducted under the auspices of a U.S.-Mexico Joint Committee on Wildlife Conservation, which was established in 1975 and meets annually to review progress on a variety of joint projects relating not only to migratory birds but to endangered species, wildlife research, wildlife introduction, law enforcement, training and education, and other topics. Each committee project has two leaders, one from Mexico and the other from the United States. Recent migratory bird projects have focused on surveying, with National Audubon Society participation, Mexico's raptor and nongame waterbird populations; intensive habitat and population dynamics research on white-winged doves; and various joint recovery activities pertaining to endangered birds, among them the masked bobwhite quail, peregrine falcon, bald eagle, and Yuma clapper rail. State government personnel and even private conservation organizations frequently participate in the joint committee's various projects.

Activities similar to those carried out with Mexico are conducted with Japan under the auspices of either the migratory bird treaty or the 1975 Agreement on Cooperation in the Field of Environmental Protection (T.I.A.S. No. 8175). Like the similar Soviet agreement discussed earlier, this is not a formal treaty but has nonetheless provided a useful umbrella for a wide range of discussions and actions relating to the environment. Among them are the periodic meetings of a U.S.-Japan Natural Resources Panel, which has established a Wildlife Protection Project. One of the most significant migratory bird issues to be addressed recently as part of that project is the incidental capture and drowning of large numbers of seabirds in the drift nets employed by Japanese fishermen catching salmon off the coast of Alaska. As a result of discussions in that and other meetings, Japan agreed to the collection of seabird mortality data by United States observers stationed abroad its fishing vessels. The National Marine Fisheries Service of the Commerce Department is an integral participant in this effort because its observers, aboard the Japanese vessels in the first place because of U.S. laws relating to marine mammal protection, function in the dual capacity of marine mammal and seabird observers.

# Current Issues

## Amending the Treaties to Allow Subsistence Taking

One of the most contentious issues of recent years concerns the failure of the federal government to enforce the Canadian treaty and the Migratory Bird Treaty Act against certain Alaskan natives engaged in the illegal taking of migratory birds and their eggs. The history of this controversy goes back almost as far as that of the treaty itself and, like the history of the treaty, reveals the very close connection between domestic political concerns and international initiatives.

As originally drafted in 1916, the treaty with Canada exempted certain native inhabitants of the two nations from some closed-season requirements. Specifically, it authorized Eskimos and Indians to take auks, auklets, guillemots, murres, puffins, and their eggs for food or clothing at any time of the year. In addition, it authorized Indians to take scoters for food only. Why these particular birds were singled out is a mystery. Other species, including mallards, pintails, eiders, geese, and swans, apparently were of greater importance to many Alaskan and Canadian natives. Indeed, for natives not living in coastal areas, the special exceptions were of no practical value because the excepted birds were unavailable to them.

Apparently in recognizing that the treaty's special subsistence exceptions for natives did not match their needs, the federal government very early on adopted a policy of disregarding the treaty. As early as 1925, the secretary of Agriculture issued a regulation for the Alaskan Territory authorizing virtually anyone there to take birds "at any time . . . when in absolute need of food and other food is not available."* This regulation continued in effect until Alaskan statehood in 1958. From that date forward, except for the limited subsistence provisions of the treaty itself, all Alaskans were prohibited from taking birds other than in the fall and winter hunting seasons.

Soon after early post-statehood efforts to begin enforcing the Migratory Bird Treaty Act against spring subsistence hunters met with widespread opposition from the hunters, FWS adopted a policy of deliberate nonenforcement. That policy had both a social and a practical component. From a social point of view, it enables traditional subsistence hunters to carry on important customs and to have access to one of the first available sources of fresh protein after the harsh Alaskan winter. From a practical viewpoint, it made unnecessary the policing of the vast and remote areas in which spring subsistence hunting is carried out. FWS estimated in 1980 that effective law enforcement in the most important subsistence areas would require more than a tenfold increase in its Alaskan migratory bird law enforcement budget, from slightly more than $100,000 that year to $1.6 million (U.S. Fish and Wildlife Service 1980).

In addition to the social and practical considerations, the policy potentially had major biological consequences. The very foundation of the migratory bird management program rests in part on the belief that careful monitoring and regulation of hunting is essential to meet desired management objectives. Yet, because spring hunting is in fact illegal, those engaged in it are unlikely to volunteer much quantifiable information about their activities, making even monitoring of the take difficult. Alaska, moreover, provides breeding grounds for 15 to 20 percent of the entire North American waterfowl population. For certain species Alaska is even more critically important, accounting for more than half the entire continental population of 15 waterfowl species.

Many of these species have declined dramatically in recent years, although the extent to which spring subsistence hunting has contributed to those

*Regulation No. 8 of the 1925 Alaska Game Law, quoted in U.S. Fish and Wildlife Service, 1980.

Relationship of Alaskan Waterfowl Populations to Continental Populations

| Species | Alaskan population | % of continental population |
|---|---|---|
| Whooper swan | 300 | 100 |
| Trumpter swan | 4,500 | 82 |
| Whistling Swan | 74,000 | 55 |
| ALL SWANS | 78,000 | 56 |
| Emperor goose | 175,000 | 100 |
| Cackling Canada goose | 150,000 | 100 |
| Lesser Canada goose | 250,000 | 100 |
| Dusky Canada goose | 35,000 | 100 |
| Aleutian Canada goose | 1,600 | 100 |
| Black brant | 150,000 | 100 |
| Vancouver Canada goose | 80,000 | 92 |
| Lesser Canada goose | 250,000 | 64 |
| White-fronted goose | 250,000 | 60 |
| ALL GEESE | 1,416,600 | 56 |
| Aleutian green-winged tail | 10,000 | 100 |
| Steller's eider | 200,000 | 100 |
| Greater scaup | 550,000 | 73 |

Source: U.S. Fish and Wildlife Service, 1980.

declines is unknown. FWS has carefully refrained from drawing any firm conclusions with respect to this matter (U.S. Fish and Wildlife Service 1980). Overall, Alaska subsistence hunters are believed to take more than a quarter million birds yearly and perhaps an additional 50,000 eggs. In Canada, where nonenforcement of the treaty's closed seasons against subsistence hunters also prevails, a million birds are believed to be taken yearly. Although small in relation to an estimated overall annual kill in North America of more than 20 million birds, the subsistence harvest is concentrated in several areas of major importance to a few waterfowl species. For example, about half the total Alaskan subsistence harvest occurs in the Yukon-Kuskokwim Delta area, where virtually the entire Pacific Flyway population of the white-fronted goose breeds. That population has declined by nearly half since 1962, to about 70,000 birds.

By the mid-1970s, the decline in many Alaskan waterfowl breeding populations and the belief that unregulated spring subsistence hunting may have contributed to that decline caused FWS to re-evaluate its policy. Three basic choices presented themselves: continue the existing policy of nonenforcement, reverse that policy and crack down on subsistence hunters hunting illegally, or try to change the law to make it accommodate the reality of continued subsistence hunting while gaining a measure of control over that hunting. FWS clearly signalled its choice of the third alternative in the 1976 Soviet agreement, which contained a special exception from its taking prohibitions for the "nutritional and other essential needs" of the indigenous inhabitants of Alaska and certain areas in the Soviet Union. When Congress amended the Migratory Bird Treaty Act in 1978 to implement the new Soviet treaty, it indicated through legislative history its desire that the previous treaties be renegotiated and amended so as to conform on this point with the new treaty.

In January 1979, the United States and Canada signed a protocol, or amendment, to the 1916 treaty intended to legitimize the ongoing subsistence harvest and bring it under regulation.* Although the protocol cannot be implemented until it is approved by the Senate, it quickly ran into a buzz saw of domestic oppostion principally from recreational hunting interests and state wildlife management agencies in the Pacific Flyway. The most significant underlying concern was that once the ongoing subsistence take was legitimized, it might be given priority over recreational hunting in the event of a need to reduce overall take. Other concerns stemmed from the uncertain breadth of the "other essential needs" sanctioned in the protocol and from the fact that, for the United States at least, the special provision was not intended to be limited to aborginal Alaskans, but was to include any Alaska resident who could demonstrate a subsistence need to take migratory birds out of season. In September 1979, the International Association of Fish and Wildlife Agencies, representing both state and provincial fish and game conservation agencies, adopted a resolution expressing its opposition "to ratification of the protocol by either the United States or Canada until it is clarified which peoples will qualify for subsistence taking of waterfowl and their eggs, what this utilization is estimated to be by species, and how regulations are to be enforced" (International Association of Fish and Wildlife Agencies 1979).

Because of the domestic political opposition, Interior Secretary James Watt asked the Senate to put off indefinitely its consideration of the protocol. For a time FWS considered renegotiating the protocol, but apparently has abandoned the idea. Instead, it is now at work on a comprehensive statement that shows clearly how it interprets and intends to implement the protocol. This statement is planned to be incorporated in an exchange of diplomatic notes between the United States and Canada and then submitted to the Senate along with the protocol. FWS hopes through this statement to allay the concerns of those who have expressed reservations about the less than precise terms of the protocol and pave the way for Senate ratification, possibly in 1986.

Complicating all of the above, however, is a lawsuit now pending in Alaska in which sport-hunting interests are endeavoring to force FWS to begin enforcing the existing law against subsistence hunters (*Alaska Fish and Wildlife Federation and Outdoor Council, Inc. v. Jantzen*, Civ. no. J84-013 [D. Alaska]). The judge in that case has put off any ruling until he receives state and federal reports on the waterfowl problem. The delay also gives FWS more time to

---

*The text of the protocol is in FWS 1980.

Estimated average annual subsistence harvest of migratory birds of the major rural regions of Alaska where they provide a significant source of food during spring and summer, late 1960's–early 1970's.[1]

| Area | Ducks | Geese | Swans | Cranes | Snowy Owls | Seabirds | Eggs |
|------|-------|-------|-------|--------|------------|----------|------|
| Chukchi-Imuruk (Seward Peninsula & King Island) | 16,400 | 3,670 | — | 125 | 30 | 1,500 | 7,800 |
| Iliamna | 15,000 | 5,000 | | | | | |
| Koyukuk | 10,830 | 4,800 | | 8 | | | |
| Noatak & Selawik | 17,720 | 3,650 | — | 37 | 225 | 220 | (3,000) |
| Togiak | 6,000 | 2,000 | 100 | 100 | — | — | |
| Yukon Delta [3] | 38,000 | 83,000 | 5,600 | 1,030 | | | 39,800 |
| Yukon Flats | 10,950 | 2,800 | | | 5 | | |
| North Slope [4] | 11,000 | 200 | | | | | |
| | 125,900 | 105,120 | 5,700 | 1,300 | 260 | 1,720 | 50,600 |

[1] Principal Source: U.S.D.I., 1974
[2] Harvests for Buckland, Deering, and Kotzebue have been deleted here as they are already included with the Noatak and Selavik figures.
[3] Yukon-Kuskokwim Delta data from Klein (1966).
[4] Harvest estimates are for Barrow and Kaktovik only. Barrow projected harvest based on information contained in Johnson (1971) and Timson (1975).
Source: Fish and Wildlife Service, 1980, p. 40

negotiate voluntary waterfowl management agreements with some of the native interests, such as limiting subsistence hunting of certain key species. The first such voluntary agreement, the so-called "Hooper Bay agreement," was negotiated in 1983 and has been subsumed in a later, more comprehensive agreement known as the Yukon-Kuskokwim Delta Management Agreement. Under it, FWS and native interests have agreed to cooperate in carrying out certain research, including studies of the magnitude of subsistence use, law enforcement, and other matters. The natives also have agreed to refrain from taking the most critically threatened species.

Even assuming the Canadian protocol eventually is ratified, it will not necessarily end the matter. Following the signing of the protocol, Interior sought to initiate negotiations leading to the conclusion of similar protocols for the Mexican and Japanese treaties. This was thought necessary because many of the birds taken by Alaskan subsistence hunters are protected not just by the Canadian treaty but also by the Mexican and Japanese treaties. The Mexican treaty is particularly troublesome, for it contains no subsistence exception at all, not even one as limited as that found in the 1916 treaty. Thus, it could stymie efforts to permit subsistence hunting under the Canadian treaty. Yet

Mexico turned aside initial informal overtures to negotiate a protocol apparently because of its concerns that its own large indigenous population would be stirred to seek special privledges if the treaty were re-opened. The Japanese treaty is less of a problem because it contains a subsistence provision very similar to that of the Soviet treaty (the Japanese treaty authorizes taking by Eskimos and certain others for their own "food and clothing;" the Soviet treaty's similar provision authorizes taking for "nutritional and other essential needs"). Nevertheless, because of strained relations over whaling and fishery disputes, the Japanese have shown no interest in re-opening their treaty to solve a problem that does not greatly affect them. Thus, the controversy over subsistence hunting by Alaskan natives may continue.

## Acceding to the Ramsar Convention

Another recurrent issue of particular interest to the international migratory bird program is whether the United States should join the 1971 Convention on Wetlands of International Importance Especially as Waterfowl Habitat (11 I.L.M 963). That convention, negotiated in the Iranian city of Ramsar, is commonly referred to as the "Ramsar Convention." The question of whether or not to accede has come up periodically since the treaty's initial negotiation and has only very recently been resolved in favor of accession. The treaty is expected to be submitted to the Senate for approval in late 1985 or 1986.

The impetus for the Ramsar Convention came principally from a non-governmental organization, the London-based International Waterfowl Research Bureau. Though it sought to stimulate a global cooperative program for the protection of wetlands, nearly half of the 40 member nations are from Europe. Nations that join the convention undertake principally to designate within their jurisdictions areas suitable for inclusion on a list of internationally important wetlands in order to better protect the sites. The nations also agree to warn the International Union for the Conservation of Nature and Natural Resources of any actual or anticipated threats to the ecological integrity of listed areas. The union, which performs a variety of administrative functions under the treaty, is to transmit the warnings to all other parties. A variety of other provisions relate more generally to the encouragement of wetlands research, the training of management personnel, and the coordination of policies relating to the conservation of wetlands and their associated biota.

The initial reluctance of the United States to join the Ramsar Convention apparently stemmed from the view that the United States already had enough major programs to conserve wetlands and waterfowl. The official view was that the treaty was perhaps a good idea for the rest of the world, but unnecessary for the United States. In addition, the generality of the treaty's goal, to "promote the conservation" of listed areas and take other actions, gave rise to at least some anxiety, particularly among state agencies, as to the precise nature of the commitments that the United States would be undertaking if it joined the treaty. Many private conservation organizations, on the other hand, believed the treaty's lack of substantive criteria for protection of listed areas made it likely to be ineffective.

A decade of actual experience since the treaty entered into force in 1975 has now produced a much more hospitable official view concerning participation by the United States. Not a single member nation has interpreted the treaty in a way that would serve as a basis for restricting state wildlife management authority. Moreover, the treaty has helped to strengthen wetland protection: Some 300 different wetland sites containing more than 300 million acres have been designated by the convention parties. Twenty-five million of those acres have been designated by Canada since it joined the convention in 1981. For many countries the fact of designation, though it imposes no clear legal duty to prevent adverse developments, has been politically very useful in trying to prevent or ameliorate damage to listed areas. It also has helped to stimulate acquisition of or protection for areas that were added to the list before any protective measures were applied to them.

The parties to the Ramsar Convention have met from time to time to assess its implementation. Participation in the convention and its periodic meetings provides an opportunity to help influence the conservation and management of important wetland areas outside our borders and, potentially, to secure better coordination of conservation activities with nations with which we do not have bilateral treaties. Membership in the convention probably is not essential to any of that, but it does at least provide a legitimizing legal umbrella for conservation activities that otherwise might rest on a more nebulous basis. Recognition of these factors has led the United States to reassess its views and, on September 13, 1985, finally sign the treaty in Paris. Several national wildlife refuge areas are being considered for initial designation, and Delaware and New Jersey have expressed interest in securing designations for wetlands areas within their jurisdictions.

## The Western Hemisphere Convention

*History and Legislative Authority*   Efforts to address common wildlife conservation problems on a regional basis began as early as 1900, when six European colonial powers concluded the Convention for the Preservation of Wild Animals, Birds, and Fish in Africa (94 B.S.F.P. 715). Then, in 1902, 12 European nations joined together in the convention for the protection of Birds Useful to Agriculture (102 B.S.F.P. 969). A later and somewhat broadened African convention superceded the 1900 treaty in 1933 (172 L.N.T.S. 241).

These stirrings abroad were of keen interest to a small band of internationalists in the American conservation movement. Foremost among them was Harvard zoologist Harold Coolidge, who in 1930 was instrumental in the founding of the American Committee for International Wildlife Protection. Comprised of representatives of some of the leading American conservation organizations of the time, the committee promoted cooperation with foreign governments and international institutions for conservation. One of its objectives was the conclusion of a nature protection agreement among Western Hemisphere countries.

The opportunity came in 1938, at the Eighth International Conference of American States in Lima, Peru. One of the recommendations of that conference was that the Pan American Union, predecessor of today's Organization of American States, appoint a committee of experts to study the problems of nature and wildlife in the Western Hemisphere and draft a convention to address these problems. The committee produced what became in 1940 the Convention on Nature Protection and Wildlife Conservation in the Western Hemisphere. The treaty calls for the enactment of domestic wildlife conservation laws, control on international wildlife trade, cooperation in scientific research and other endeavors related to the convention's purposes, and the establishment of national parks, strict wilderness reserves, nature monuments, and other protected areas. Eighteen Western Hemisphere nations are now parties.* Although many of the steps called for by the convention, including the establishment of national parks and the enactment of wildlife conservation laws, were undertaken in the United States, it was not until enactment of the Endangered Species Act of 1973 (16 U.S.C.A. 1531-1546) that the convention was mentioned in any domestic legislation. The act directed the president to designate which federal agencies would act on the government's behalf in Western Hemisphere Convention matters. Three years later, by executive order, President Gerald Ford designated the secretary of Interior to carry out these duties (Exec. Order 11911, April 13, 1976).

*Organization and Operations* Within the Department of the Interior, the Office of International Park Affairs of the National Park Service and the FWS Office of International Affairs share responsibilities for Western Hemisphere Convention implementation. Both offices, following the 1976 executive order, moved swiftly to stimulate greater attention to the conservation problems of the hemisphere and to the convention as a framework for addressing them. The offices organized from 1977 to 1979 a series of technical meetings on marine mammals, migratory wildlife, terrestrial ecosystems, education and training, and conservation law. Among the key institutional recommendations to emerge from those meetings was that the Organization of American States should assume an active administrative role as true secretariat for the convention and that the parties to the convention meet biennially to review implementation of it. However, the arrival of the Reagan administration ended any official efforts to push those recommendations further.

---

*They are Argentina, Brazil, Chile, Costa Rica, Dominican Republic, Ecuador, El Salvador, Guatemala, Haiti, Mexico, Nicaragua, Panama, Paraguay, Peru, Trinidad and Tobago, Uruguay, United States of America, and Venezuela. In addition, Bolivia, Columbia, and Cuba are signatories but not yet parties.

Moneys Appropriated for Use of Fish and Wildlife Service's
Office of International Activities

| Fiscal Year | Salary and Overhead | Special W. Hemisphere Appropriation |
|---|---|---|
| 1981 | $324,000 | n.a. |
| 1982 | $337,000 | n.a. |
| 1983 | $398,000 | $150,000 |
| 1984 | $451,000 | $150,000 |
| 1985 | $427,000 | $141,000 |

Note: does not include monies identified in Special Foreign Currency Program Obligations Table.
Source: U.S. Fish and Wildlife Service

In 1982, however, the efforts of the World Wildlife Fund-U.S. and other conservation organizations led Congress to examine the convention more closely than ever before. Finding in that agreement the potential for significant hemispheric cooperative actions on key conservation issues, Congress, in its 1982 amendments to the Endangered species Act, codified the executive order making the secretary of the Interior responsible for implementing the convention and directed him to give particular attention in his implementation efforts to three needs (16 U.S.C.A. 1537[e]). These were to develop personnel resources, to implement cooperative measures to ensure that migratory birds do not become endangered or threatened, and to bolster the conservation of wild plants. Even more significantly, Congress for the first time authorized a specific appropriation of funds for implementation of the convention. Because these changes were enacted as amendments to the Endangered Species Act, the act has become the legislative vehicle for reviewing the convention.

With the aid of the moneys specifically appropriated, the Interior Department is carrying out an active program of technical assistance, joint research, training, and information exchange with most of the Latin American nations. For example, for the past five years it has conducted a Spanish language annual workshop on the management of wildlife refuges and for the past three years a similar workshop on the management and conservation of migratory birds. It has helped in the mapping of significant plant communities in Latin America and the development of a plant-protection action plan for the region. In fiscal year 1985, FWS is supporting some 23 different projects under the rubric of the Western Hemisphere Convention. Most of these are quite low in cost, the most expensive being only $60,000. The parallel office in the National Park Service carries out training programs and regional studies relating to park and wildlife matters.

*Current Concerns* Although the 1982 amendments to the Endangered Species Act authorized the appropriation of very modest funding for implementation of the Western Hemisphere Convention, getting money appropriated for that purpose has not been easy. Successful conservation of the natural resource base in Latin America is likely to be a prerequisite for sustainable economic development there. The Western Hemisphere Convention offers a framework for integrating conservation into economic development, assuring the long-term success of that development.

Despite the Reagan administration's proclaimed goals of encouraging economic progress in Latin America and the Caribbean, it has not sought to have money appropriated to implement the convention. The moneys actually appropriated since 1982 have come not in response to administration requests but to appeals from nongovernmental conservation organizations. Each year those appeals are renewed in the hope that the Congressional appropriations committees will recognize the value of the work being done under the convention.

The modest amounts appropriated have supported only the FWS activities. National Park Service convention activities have an even more tenuous economic lifeline. A line item in the Service's annual park management and operations appropriation covers the salaries and basic overhead for the staff of its Office of International Affairs. All other expenses, including travel, must be raised by the office by "contracting" with other federal agencies, such as the Agency for International Development, the Peace Corps, and others, for reimbursement of the Park Service's costs of participating in the other agencies' conservation projects. Sometimes even nongovernmental organizations provide the funds that allow Service personnel to participate in international conservation projects. Being dependent on others for much of its support, the Park Service is hobbled in its ability to plan activities even a year in advance.

Putting funding for the implementation of the Western Hemisphere Convention on a stronger footing, more commensurate with the magnitude of both the problems and opportunities that exist, is thus an issue of continuing concern. A longer range issue concerns the need for more support and for funding from more sources. As noted previously, two ideas that have been advanced are to designate a permanent convention secretariet charged with stimulating the parties to perform their convention responsibilities, and to hold regular meetings of the parties. These measures could be effected by amending the convention, an idea discussed in late 1970s. Although an amendment may not be necessary to accomplish these purposes, some sort of action-forcing mechanism clearly seems necessary to elevate the convention and its potential importance for international conservation to a position of greater visibility in the eyes of policymakers.

## The Convention on International Trade in Endangered Species of Wild Fauna and Flora

*History and Legislative Authority*  On a single day in London in 1898, the bustling markets for wild animal products reportedly sold more than half-million bird skins, among them more than 100,000 hummingbird skins and some 200,000 bundles of Indian parrots marketed for decorative purposes. Such large-scale plunder of birds and other wildlife alarmed early conservationists, among them Paul Sarasin, a Swiss whose call in 1911 for restrictions on the booming trade, though a prescient warning of the dangers that lay ahead, went unheeded.

By 1940, when the Western Hemisphere Convention was negotiated, the threat that unregulated international trade posed to conservation was more widely recognized. Article IX of that treaty pledged the signatory nations to "control and regulate the importation, exportation and transit of protected flora and fauna" by means of a system of permits. Like much of the rest of that treaty, however, most of the parties ignored this provision.

Support for an effective, comprehensive system of controls grew as the trade in wild animal products burgeoned in the period of prosperity following World War II. In 1963, the General Assembly of the International Union for the Conservation of Nature and Natural Resources issued a call for "an international convention on regulation of export, transit and import of rare or threatened wildlife species or their skins or trophies." For a decade, the union took a leading role in the effort to translate this recommendation into reality, including preparing and widely circulating a draft of the sort of treaty it believed was necessary. The union's efforts gained momentum as individual governments added their support for the idea.

As part of the Endangered Species Conservation Act of 1969, Congress directed the secretaries of State and Interior to "seek the convening of an international ministerial meeting" within two years for the purpose of concluding "a binding international convention on the conservation of endangered species." In February and March 1973, representatives from 87 nations attended in Washington the meeting for which Congress had called. There they negotiated and signed the Convention on International Trade in Endangered Species of Wild Fauna and Flora. The United States was the first nation to ratify the new treaty and by the end of the year had passed the Endangered Species Act of 1973 to implement it. In June 1975, when the tenth signatory nation had ratified it, the treaty came into force. In the United States the convention is commonly referred to by its abbreviated acronym, CITES. In much of the rest of the world it is known simply as the Washington Convention.

***Organization and Operations*** It is not the purpose of CITES to eliminate trade in wild animals or plants. Rather, its purpose is to prevent international trade from being a factor contributing to the endangerment of any species. To achieve this, it establishes a system of trade controls that vary in their restrictiveness, depending upon the degree of jeopardy each species faces.

The trade controls imposed by CITES apply only to species listed on one of three treaty appendices. Species may be added to or removed from appendices I and II by a two-thirds majority of the member countries at their biennial meetings. Species placed on Appendix I receive the most protection. They cannot be imported or exported for primarily commercial purposes. To be traded for other purposes, a specimen of an Appendix I species must be accompanied by an export permit from the country of export and an import permit from the importing country.

Appendix II species, which comprise the vast majority of all CITES-protected species, can be traded for both commercial and noncommercial purposes. However, they must be accompanied by an export permit, which may be issued only upon finding that the export of the specimens concerned will not be detrimental to the survival of the species. This requirement allows countries to control trade in Appendix II species.

Unlike the prior two appendices, member countries may unilaterally place on Appendix III any species that are protected within their borders. The purpose of Appendix III is to obtain international cooperation in the enforcement of national conservation laws. Countries importing specimens of an Appendix III species from the country responsible for placing it on the appendix must insist upon presentation of a permit showing that the specimen was lawfully acquired and exported from that country. To date, Appendix III has been very little used.

When CITES was negotiated, a relatively small number of species was included in the original appendices I and II. Since then the appendices have grown dramatically as a result of additions made by the parties at their biennial meetings. Five such meetings have been held since the treaty came into force, the most recent at Buenos Aires, Argentina, in April and May 1985. Amendments to the appendices are made by a two-thirds majority of participating parties.

The meetings of the parties also are forums for discussion of treaty implementation. In an effort to secure reasonable uniformity in treaty interpretation and implementation, the parties have developed the practice of debating and passing resolutions setting forth how they agree to carry out certain treaty provisions. Though these resolutions may not be technically binding, they are taken quite seriously and often debated with great intensity.

Since the meetings are the principal forums in which the most basic decisions are made, considerable energy is spent preparing for them. In the United States, the process begins more than six months in advance. FWS solicits public views to supplement its ongoing review of what changes in the appendices may be warranted and what implementation subjects should be added to the forthcoming meeting's agenda. Four to five months before the meeting, the appendices revisions and agenda topics suggested by all the parties are made known. FWS then begins a formal process of developing a tentative position on each of these matters. Shortly before the meeting, the process culminates with publication in the *Federal Register* of tentative U.S. positions. This degree of public involvement is unusual in the realm of international diplomacy, where secrecy and confidentiality more often are the norm.

The meetings themselves also are unusual. Unlike most other international treaties, CITES explicitly authorizes participation by international and qualified national nongovernmental organizations. They participate as nonvoting observers, but participate actively, joining in the debates and serving on committees, occasionally even chairing them. Though conservation organizations are included, the ranks of the nongovernmental observers comprise many representatives of affected industries, humane organizations, and others.

As membership in CITES has grown to 89 countries, the meetings have become ever larger affairs. Fewer than 200 delegates and observers attended the 1979 meeting in Costa Rica. Six years later some 450 attended in Buenos Aires. The considerable task of organizing and running these meetings devolves on the CITES Secretariat, which also is responsible for the basic administration of the treaty between meetings. A secretary general, three principal lieutenants, and several clerical personnel comprise the Secretariat at its Swiss headquaters. Until 1984, the Secretariat was directly connected with the International Union for Conservation of Nature and Natural Resource and housed in its home office. It has since severed its formal union administrative connection and now functions as part of the United Nations Environment Program. The union continues in an important advisory role to the Secretariat, however.

*Staff and Budget*   While the meetings are the main forums for the most basic decision making, the day-to-day business of the treaty is carried out by the parties themselves. Each party is required by the treaty to establish a "scientific authority" and a "management authority" for implementing the treaty. In the United States, FWS performs both roles. The Federal Wildlife Permit Office functions as the management authority and the Office of the Scientific Authority as the scientific authority. Both are small offices under the associate director for federal assistance. The Office of the Scientific Authority has a staff of only five and an annual budget of less than a quarter-million dollars. The Federal Wildlife Permit Office handles its CITES responsibilities as well as permit responsibilities under all federal wildlife laws with a staff of about two dozen and an annual budget of around $800,000.

Before any specimen of an Appendix I or II species is exported, the Scientific Authority must find that its export will not be detrimental to the survival of the species. The Management Authority, which issues the required permits, must make certain other findings, among them that the specimen was lawfully acquired and will be shipped so as to minimize risk of injury. With

**Moneys Appropriated for Activities of the Federal Wildlife Permit Office (in thousands)**

| 1981 | 1982 | 1983 | 1984 | 1985 |
|------|------|------|------|------|
| $662 | $675 | $619 | $627 | $825 |

Source: U.S. Fish and Wildlife Service

respect to imports, permits are required only for Appendix I species. Prior to issuing these, the Management Authority must find that the imported specimens will not be used for primarily commercial purposes and the Scientific Authority that living specimens will be suitably housed and cared for.

*Current Concerns*  With 89 member nations, including nearly all major wildlife trading nations, CITES has in a single decade almost certainly become the most ambitious effort ever at international cooperation for conservation. Yet, it has throughout its short history struggled with a series of contentious disputes that continue to divide the governments that adhere to it. Most of these trace back to a fundamentally different conception of how to administer the convention most effectively. One camp gives primacy to consideration of law enforcement, the other to scientific considerations.

Illustrative of the basic split in outlook among the parties is the continuing dispute over the listing on the appendices of related groups of animals or plants, usually at the family level, rather than individual species. Such listings, in the view of proponents, facilitate law enforcement efforts because most customs inspectors, particularly those in less developed nations, are insufficiently trained and lack the resources necessary to make the more sophisticated identifications of required specimens listed at the species level. In addition, the listing of larger taxa enables authorities to monitor trade in groups of related species in which trade patterns may change suddenly. For example, the CITES parties in 1977 voted to include on Appendix II all wild members of the cat family not already on Appendix I. This was done because the earlier listing on Appendix I of most of the large spotted cats was believed to have caused a dramatic shift in trade pressure to many of the smaller cats that had not previously been particularly prominent in international trade.

Group listings, however, have sparked serious controversy. For example, the listing of all wild cats on Appendix II obligated the United States to regulate the export of bobcats, a widespread U.S. species trapped primarily for pelt sales abroad. At the time, the functions of the U.S. Scientific Authority were assigned to the Endangered Species Scientific Authority, an independent agency under the Office of the Secretary of the Interior. In order to authorize the export of bobcats, the Endangered Species Scientific Authority had to find that export would not be detrimental to the survival of the species. In carrying out this duty, the authority startled trapping interests and state fish and wildlife agencies by announcing that it would be unable to make such a finding without more detailed data on the status of the species in each of the states. Without the data, the authority said, it would effectively prohibit further exports.

What rankled state fish and game interests was their belief that the survival of the bobcat in at least most states was unquestionably secure and that the additional data gathering requirements unnecessary. Though the Endangered Species Scientific Authority would eventually authorize bobcat exports from 34 states, the pressure from state agencies to rein in the independent agency was so great that in 1979 Congress replaced it with a new scientific authority, called the International Convention Advisory Commission. Meanwhile, Defenders of Wildlife, a private conservation organization, filed a legal challenge against the approval of bobcat exports and against the data requirement guidelines upon which the approval had been based. In 1981, in *Defenders of Wildlife v. Endangered Species Scientific Authority*, a federal court of appeals agreed with Defenders' position (659 F. 2nd 168 [D.C.Cir], *cert. denied*, 454 U.S. 963 [1981]). The major deficiency, in the court's view, was that the scientific authority had not required a "reliable estimate" of bobcat numbers prior to authorizing export. Instead, it had accepted data indicating general population trends, which the court deemed insufficient.

The court decision set off another congressional battle over the implementation of CITES and led to development of a new scientific authority. In 1982, Congress effectively reversed the appellate court's decision and made the secretary of the Interior both the management and scientific authority for the United States, with the requirement that both functions be carried out through FWS (16 U.S.C.A 1537A).

Though the battle over bobcats subsided, the larger question of the wisdom of the original CITES decision to group-list wild felines remained. The new policy took hold when the new Reagan administration, upon taking office, quickly reversed a tentative U.S. position supporting the proposed listing of nearly all psittacine birds on Appendix I at the 1981 CITES meeting. Henceforth, the United States would oppose mass listings of large taxonomic groups. It would instead insist that the listing of each species be considered on its own scientific merits, with considerations of enforcement difficulties secondary. There was other fallout from the long and bitter bobcat controversy: The resulting skepticism of state fish and game interests toward new international treaties was a major factor in the U.S. decision not to join the Convention on the Conservation of Migratory Species of Wild Animals. Called the "Bonn Convention," this treaty was negotiated in 1979 and was designed to foster the development of subsidiary treaties for the protection of migratory species shared by the various nations.

***Farming and Ranching*** Another important policy dispute arises when one or more national populations of an otherwise highly endangered Appendix I species are relatively healthy. The debate over whether to allow international trade in specimens from the healthy populations pits international enforcement considerations against national management desires. Because enforcement personnel cannot distinguish between products from healthy populations and products from jeopardized populations, trade in specimens from stable populations seriously hampers protection of jeopardized populations. However, protecting healthy populations often flies in the face of national management goals. Consequently, some countries have sought to find a way around the tight Appendix I strictures against commercial trade. One of the means of doing so is through "ranching." Although CITES generally prohibits commercial trade in Appendix I species, it contains a number of exceptions to this prohibition, one of which is for specimens that have been bred in captivity. However, the CITES parties in 1979 adopted an interpretive resolution narrowly limiting this exception to breeding enterprises that have demonstrated their complete independence from wild sources of animals by producing at least two generations in captivity.* At the time, Surinam was beginning a new program to collect wild-laid green sea turtle eggs, hatch them and raise the young turtles to a substantial size, then slaughter them and sell their products in international commerce. The Surinamese authorities had no intention of trying to breed turtles in captivity, but believed their program would benefit the conservation of sea turtles in Surinam by generating income that could be used for protecting nesting beaches and other conservation purposes. Unable to qualify under the bred-in-captivity exception, the Surinamese plan was barred by the Appendix I trade prohibition.

At the next CITES meeting in 1981, the parties passed a new resolution in response to the Surinam situation.** That resolution purported to establish new criteria for considering the transfer of particular national populations of Appendix I species to appendix II so that ranching operations could be freed from the otherwise absolute prohibition of commercial trade in Appendix I species. Since then, a series of proposals has been put forth for various sea turtle and crocodile ranching schemes. These have often been quite controversial. Proponents have emphasized the opportunity such schemes provide for obtaining some tangible value from managing rare wildlife populations. Opponents emphasize the difficulty of law enforcement when trade in a species from one or a few countries is authorized and trade in the same species from other countries is banned. To date, neither the Surinamese nor any other sea-turtle-ranching proposal has been approved, though a few crocodile-ranching proposals have been accepted.

The debate over the various ranching proposals is but one part of a larger and longer debate over the criteria that should be used when considering proposals to transfer species to less protected status. At the first CITES meeting in Berne, Switzerland, in 1976, the parties agreed upon a set of criteria that would guide future additions to or removals from the appendices. Those "Berne criteria" were intended to standardize the data requirements for future revisions of the appendices. They have, however, been the source of continuing controversy, both because they often appear not to be rigorously followed in particular decisions and because, in the views of some, they make it too difficult to remove protection from a species that either did not need such stringent protection at the time it was added to the appendices or is believed to have since recovered.

---

*The resolution is contained in Conference Document 2.12.
**The resolution is contained in Conference Document 3.15.

Overshadowing all of these disputes, however, is a concern for how much CITES is in fact accomplishing. CITES has been called "perhaps the most successful of all international treaties concerned with the conservation of wildlife" (Lyster 1985). In the view of most observers, however, that judgement is probably premature. Certainly the trade in wild plants and animals remains a big and lucrative business. For example, the large volume of orchids imported into the United States grew by 50 percent from 1981 through 1984. In the United States, still the largest consumer of most wild plant and animal products, the annual declared value of imported wildlife exceeded $760 million in 1982 (World Wildlife Fund undated). The volume of illegal trade is nearly impossible to quantify, but has been estimated at up to a quarter of the legal trade. The South American nations are the major suppliers of the world trade in wildlife, accounting for more than a third. Some 30 percent of that is believed to be illegal (World Wildlife Fund).

What figures like these do not reveal is what trade levels would have been without CITES. Nor do they shed light on how CITES has affected the survival prospects of particular species. For some animals, such as large spotted cats once popular for their furs, commercial trade is believed to have been substantially reduced since CITES was negotiated, though most may still be seriously jeopardized by habitat destruction and other factors. Other species, such as the African elephant and the rhinoceros, are known to have continued dramatic declines despite CITES because of the extraordinary prices their ivory and horn fetch on the world market. For most species, however, we simply do not have a very good idea what difference CITES has yet made or whether it will ultimately make any difference at all. Success under CITES, however, should not be equated with an end to all commercial wildlife trade. It is not the object of CITES to prevent trade, but rather to ensure that trade shall cease to be, and never become again, a contributor to the extinction of any species.

*Legislation*   In general, the international programs discussed here are not subject to frequent, regular oversight by Congress. Indeed, in the 1985 congressional deliberations over the reauthorization of the Endangered Species Act, which implements both CITES and the Western Hemisphere Convention, neither of those international programs was examined at all.

One potentially significant legislative development in 1985 was the sudden interest shown by the Subcommittee on Public Lands of the House Committee on Interior and Insular Affairs in international conservation matters. Subcommittee Chairman John Seiberling (D-Ohio) had in the preceding year represented the United States at an interparlimentary conference on the environment in Nairobi, from which a series of recommendations on deforestation, desertification, wildlife protection, and other issues had been made. In October 1985, Representative Seiberling's subcommittee held an oversight hearing to examine the international conservation programs of the Interior Department, U.S. Forest Service, Agency for International Developement, and State Department Office of Food and Natural Resources. He wanted to examine the extent to which conference recommendations were being pursued by these agencies and to encourage them to give greater attention to the recommendations. Much of his interest focused on the Western Hemisphere Convention as a vehicle for addressing the major environmental problems of the United States and its Latin American neighbors.

Although no proposed legislation has yet emerged from the Seiberling hearings, the chairman did promise to hold further hearings in 1986, thus creating some pressure for the agencies to show further progress in the implementation of their international conservation programs. Also in 1986, the Senate is expected to be asked to give its advice and consent to the ratification of the Ramsar Treaty and very likely to the subsistence hunting protocol of the Canadian migratory bird treaty.

## Legal Developments

Litigation involving treaties and the implementation of international conservation programs is very rare. Indeed, the Western Hemisphere Convention has never been the subject of any litigation in its entire 45 year history. CITES, too, has not often been the subject of much litigation. The last major litigation under CITES was *Defenders of Wildlife v. Endangered Species Scientific Authority,* discussed earlier in this chapter.

Currently, the most significant litigation relating to the international conservation programs described in this chapter is *Alaska Fish and Wildlife Federation and Outdoor Council, Inc. v. Jantzen.* In it the plaintiff has challenged the Interior Department's policy of not enforcing the Migratory Bird Treaty Act against native subsistence hunters in Alaska. To date, no rulings have been issued in this case. Details of the case were discussed above.

## Status of the Resource

Of the international conservation programs described in this chapter, only the migratory bird programs provide a reasonably reliable means of monitoring the status of the wildlife resources it is intended to conserve. But even in this case only a small portion of the resource—waterfowl—is carefully monitored. For most nongame migratory birds, which includes the great majority of species protected by the various migratory bird treaties, no comparable monitoring effort has been undertaken, and sure conclusions about their status are unavailable. The overall North American breeding population of migratory waterfowl has remained fairly constant over the past three decades, although it currently is at a low point apparently because of a drought in the Canadian breeding areas. Within the overall population, more marked changes have occurred in the abundance of particular species. In addition to certain of the Pacific Flyway geese, whose decline was mentioned earlier in this chapter, the black duck has suffered a prolonged decline. The Mexican duck, which was never particularly abundant in the United States, apparently has disappeared altogether from this country in recent years as a result of hybridization with the growing mallard population. It now exists only in Mexico. For more details see the chapter on migratory birds.

As mentioned above, little is known about the effect that the CITES treaty has had on the species it protects. Indeed, even documenting the effect that CITES has had on international trade levels is difficult. Although each CITES party is required to prepare an annual report documenting the volume of trade in each of the protected species, many countries have failed to prepare reports or are years behind in preparation. Moreover, the reports have often revealed major discrepancies, such as an exporting country reporting a substantially different volume of exports to an importing country than the latter reports as having imported from the former country. Difficulties of this sort have made conclusions about the effect of CITES on the status of the resources it seeks to protect quite speculative.

In addition to the reporting requirements of the treaty itself, the CITES parties have sought to force a periodic re-evaluation of the status of protected species through a 10-year review of the appendices. The object of this procedure, agreed to by the parties at the 1981 meeting in New Delhi, was to examine at each meeting the status of the species that had been placed on the treaty's appendices 10 years earlier. To date, the United States and only a few other countries appear to have made a serious commitment to this effort. As a result, for many CITES protected species not much more is known about their status now than at the time they first received the treaty's protection.

# References

Agency for International Development. 1985. *U.S. Strategy on the Conservation of Biological Diversity: An Interagency Task Force Report to Congress.* 54 pp.

Bean, M. 1983. *The Evolution of National Wildlife Law.* Praeger. New York. 449 pp.

Boucher, N. 1983. "The wildlife trade." *Atlantic* (March 1983). p. 11.

Hardin, G. 1968. "The tragedy of the Commons." *Science* 162:1,243

Hawkins, A. 1984. "Crisis along the flyways: the United States response," *in* Hawkins *et al* eds., *Flyways: Pioneering Waterfowl Management in North America.* Government Printing Office, Washington, D.C.

Henkin, L. 1972. Foreign Affairs and the Constitution, as cited in Vose, "State against nation: The conservation case of *Missouri v. Holland.*" *Prologue* 16:4 (1984) at 233.

International Association of Fish and Wildlife Agencies. 1979. *Proceedings of the 1979 Meeting.* Washington, D.C.

Lambertson, R. (undated). Memorandum to the Director of the Fish and Wildlife Service *re* Migratory Birds Protected Under the Migratory Bird Treaty Act. 16 pp.

Lyster, S. 1985. *International Wildlife Law.* Grotius Publications. Cambridge U.K. 470 pp

Smith, R. 1984. "From Tundra to Tropics," *in* Hawkins *et al, Flyways: Pioneering Waterfowl Management in North America.* Government Printing Office. Washington, D.C.

U.S. Department of State. 1984. *Conserving International Wildlife Resources: The United States Response.* 72 pp.

U.S. Fish and Wildlife Service. 1980. *Final Environmental Assessment: Subsistence Hunting of Migratory Birds in Alaska and Canada.* Washington, D.C.

Vose, C. 1984. "State against nation: the conservation case of *Missouri v. Holland,*" *Prologue* 16:4 (1984) at 233.

World Wildlife fund. (undated). News Release: New Efforts to Halt Illegal Wildlife Trade Announced. Washington D.C. 2 pp.

*Michael J. Bean is chairman of the Environmental Defense Fund's Wildlife Program and author of* The Evolution of National Wildlife Law.

# PART 3

# Conservation
and the States

A biologist from the Montana Department of Fish and Game prepares to fling a paint-filled globe from a helicopter to mark a moose for study.

*Jack Fields/Photo Researchers*

# State Wildlife Conservation: An Overview

## William J. Chandler

## Introduction

Laws FOR THE conservation of fish and wildlife were developed first by the American colonies. The basic purpose of the laws was to protect certain game species, such as deer, from overhunting and thus maintain populations of game for food. The use of wildlife for food carried over into the early years of the 20th century, at which time sport hunting and fishing became the dominant uses.

Massachusetts established the first fish and wildlife agency in 1865. By 1880, all the states had enacted fish and wildlife protection laws of one kind or another, and most employed game wardens. By 1923, all had fully established fish and wildlife programs (Gottschalk 1978). At that time, state management efforts were devoted principally to enforcing game laws, establishing wildlife refuges, propagating fish and game animals for stocking purposes, and suppressing species of animals that killed livestock or damaged crops.

### The Professionalization of State Wildlife Agencies

The next phase of state-agency development began in 1937, when the Congress passed the Pittman-Robertson Act (16 U.S.C.A. 669 *et seq.*). This law established a program of federal financial grants to state fish and wildlife agencies to help restore depleted wildlife populations. States that qualified for participation were authorized to use their money for a wide variety of activities, including land acquisition, habitat management, and biological research. The Pittman-Robertson program provided a sustained source of federal money to poorly financed state wildlife agencies, which in turn enabled the agencies to hire biologists and other professionals needed to augment their programs. A similar federal assistance program, the Dingell-Johnson Act (16 U.S.C.A. 777 *et seq.*), was created in 1950 to improve state sport-fishery management.

Under both the Pittman-Robertson and Dingell-Johnson acts, the states have invested their financial and professional resources almost entirely on the management of game wildlife and sport fish. While some activities conducted on behalf of these species have benefited some nongame species, including those threatened or endangered with extinction, these benefits for the most part have been incidental to other objectives.

Public concern for the plight of endangered animals, and a related concern for the protection of entire ecological systems, has led to a new phase of wildlife-agency evolution. Most states have established some kind of program for the protection of endangered species and nongame wildlife. By 1968, 24 state agencies were monitoring or had studied the population status of one or more seriously had jeopardized species. Twenty-six states had preserved habitat for endangered species, and 15 maintained refuges for nongame wildlife (Wildlife Management Institute 1968). Further progress has been made since the passage of the federal Endangered Species Act in 1973, which greatly accelerated state efforts to conserve the full array of biological resources by providing matching grants for endangered species conservation. Forty-five states and territories have signed cooperative agreements with the Fish and Wildlife Service (FWS) to conserve endangered animals and 22 to conserve plants.

Another federal statute, the Fish and Wildlife Conservation Act (or Nongame Act) was passed in 1980 to promote the conservation of nonhunted, nonendangered species. This statute authorizes matching federal financial assistance to the states for the preparation of nongame conservation plans and the execution of individual nongame projects. However, no funds to implement the program ever have been requested by FWS or appropriated by Congress.

Despite lack of federal assistance, the states have forged ahead on their own to add nongame components to their fish and wildlife programs. While a few states initiated some form of nongame conservation effort before the 1970s, it was in that decade that most moved to add nongame programs to their scope of activities. In FY 1985, 44 states provided some kind of funding for nongame or endangered species. The majority of these programs were financed with special funds derived from voluntary donations or special fees.

The addition of endangered species protection and nongame conservation to wildlife agency agendas is impelling state agencies to change their identity from one of game managers for sportsmen to ecological managers of all biological resources. This process is just under way.

While the regulation of hunting and fishing will continue to be an important agency function, a much larger task confronts each wildlife agency in the 1980s: how to obtain and allocate adequate resources to ensure that each state's biological heritage is conserved and maintained in the face of accelerating development pressure. Most state fish and wildlife agencies still focus the bulk of their efforts on game species and have a long way to go before they can legitimately consider themselves stewards of the states' biological diversity.

## State Authority for Fish and Wildlife Management

### Constitutional Basis

The states manage fish and wildlife under the authorities granted them by the Constitution. But since the Constitution nowhere specially addresses the subject of wildlife, the federal courts have played a key role in delineating the wildlife-management powers of the states and the federal government. While the U.S. Supreme Court has recognized the right of states to regulate the use of wildlife (*Geer v. Connecticut,* 16 U.S. 519 [1896] ), it also has made clear that the states do not hold that right "exclusive of paramount powers" (*Missouri v. Holland,* 252 U.S. 416 [1920] ). Over the years, the court has upheld federal wildlife statutes on the basis of the federal government's paramount constitutional powers to make treaties with foreign nations, to protect federal property, and to regulate interstate commerce.

In practice, though, the management of fish and wildlife is not neatly divided into distinct areas of federal and state responsibility. A number of federal statutes establish cooperative wildlife programs in which the states' right to regulate wildlife is recognized clearly and depended upon to achieve management goals. Even wildlife on federal lands is managed, in most cases, under state game and fish regulations to prevail, either because directed to do so by statute or because this is the most sensible and efficient approach. Even in cases where the federal government clearly has pre-empted state authority, such as in the management of migratory birds, the states are relied on for advice and assistance in achieving conservation objectives.

In sum, the states have the constitutionally established right to regulate fish and wildlife and their use for the benefit of the public and to preserve those resources as a public trust. This right often is referred to as the "right to manage fish and resident wildlife." A state's powers to regulate its fish and wildlife are comprehensive and complete, except in cases where the federal government has exercised paramount constitutional powers.*

* For an in-depth discussion of federal and state wildlife law, see Michael J. Bean's *The Evolution of National Wildlife Law* (1983).

## Specific State Authorities

While the states theoretically have the constitutional power to protect and regulate all fish and wildlife in the broadest possible biological meaning of those terms, the "biological jurisdiction" of state wildlife agencies varies from state to state depending on state legislation. All state wildlife agencies have the authority to regulate the management and take of game animals and fish. Many, but not all, agencies have responsibility for controlling the depredations of predators. (In some states, predator control is the responsibility of the state agricultural agency or local governments.) Forty-five states and territories have endangered species programs for wildlife, but state law may limit the types of species for which conservation action may be taken. Many states, for example, do not have endangered species programs for invertebrates.

Forty-six states have nongame programs, but again the scope of the programs may be limited. Nongame generally is defined to mean any native, wild vertebrate not ordinarily taken for sport, fur, food, or commercial purposes, but only 23 state nongame programs have authority over invertebrates, and only 11 for plants.

Finally, all state agencies have the authority to acquire and manage habitat for species within the scope of their jurisdiction. While most of the areas acquired and managed by the states have been for game and sport-fish purposes, the same areas provide incidental benefits to nongame species as well. In addition, most states now have the authority to acquire or manage lands specifically for nongame and endangered species.

# Organization and Operations

Initially, most state fish and wildlife agencies were constituted as separate, independent commissions within state government. Over time, a number of these agencies have been merged into natural-resource agencies or conservation departments. Today, about half the agencies have retained their status as separate departments.* The trend of consolidation is likely to continue as state governments seek the most efficient way to administer natural resources.

## Agency Functions

Whether an independent agency or a subordinate division of a larger natural-resources department, the typical state fish and wildlife agency undertakes several key functions. These include:

• Financing its operations with a combination of license fees, federal grants, general appropriations, and other revenue.

* Of the independent units, a few are combined wildlife and parks departments.

- Developing short-term and long-term plans to guide resource-management efforts.
- Conducting surveys and research to determine the existence, distribution, and population status of fish and wildlife and developing techniques and strategies for their conservation and management.
- Managing game, nongame, and endangered species, usually as individual populations.
- Conserving fish and wildlife habitat through acquisition or lease and making these areas accessible to the public.
- Conducting education and information programs to promote wildlife conservation and to inform citizens of state laws, regulations, and programs. In addition, all states conduct hunter-education programs to train hunters in firearms safety and hunting ethics.
- Enforcing fish and game laws and regulations.
- Consulting with public development agencies and private developers on the biological impacts of their projects and advising them on how to minimize resource damage.

## Financing

In a survey of state fish and wildlife agencies budgets for fiscal years 1978 or 1979, the states reported aggregate expenditures of $602.8 million for their fish and wildlife programs.* Of this amount, 58.3 percent came from hunting-and fishing-license revenues, 17.8 percent from federal assistance (principally under the Pittman-Robertson and Dingell-Johnson acts†), 8.7 percent from special and other sources, and 1.4 percent from interest income (Wildlife Legislative Fund of America 1980).

License revenues are still the backbone of state wildlife programs, but prices charged for licenses have not risen as much as inflation in recent years (Anderson *et al* 1985). There has been concern expressed for a number of years however, that fee increases alone, even if politically feasible, cannot provide the revenue state fish and wildlife agencies need to do their jobs competently.

Some states have attacked their financing problems with creativity and success, as these examples show:

- Missouri approved a special one-eighth percent increase in its sales tax to pay for its wildlife and forestry programs. The tax brings in some $30 million yearly.
- Washington uses receipts from the sale of personalized license plates to pay for its nongame program.

* According to Morse (1984), total agency expenditures exceeded $889 million in 1984 (based on data from 49 states).
† In addition to Pittman-Robertson and Dingell-Johnson funds, the states received money from more than 20 other federal sources.

| State | Total Revenue | License Fees | Federal Payments | General Taxation |
|---|---|---|---|---|
| X ALABAMA | 6,455,844 | 4,139,637 | 1,451,107 | 400,000 |
| X ALASKA | 31,068,835 | 4,895,635 | 6,576,700 | 19,141,400 |
| ARIZONA | 8,099,900 | 4,698,800 | 2,161,200 | — |
| ARKANSAS | 10,925,489 | 8,299,486 | 1,925,255 | — |
| CALIFORNIA | 38,944,229 | 25,942,766 | 6,954,985 | 4,000,000 |
| COLORADO | 26,011,956 | 20,564,485 | 2,451,356 | 117,582 |
| X CONNECTICUT | 1,170,000 | 500,000 | 595,000 | — |
| DELAWARE | 1,714,004 | 338,062 | 737,880 | 338,062 |
| X FLORIDA | 14,628,767 | 7,735,370 | 2,417,167 | 4,476,230 |
| GEORGIA | 12,502,935 | 4,850,198 | 2,502,417 | 4,894,266 |
| HAWAII | 1,857,352 | 133,702 | 339,545 | 1,384,105 |
| X IDAHO | 9,644,861 | 6,093,627 | 3,332,376 | — |
| ILLINOIS | 8,382,000 | 4,663,000 | 2,300,000 | — |
| INDIANA | 8,796,876 | 4,464,481 | 2,452,663 | 312,139 |
| IOWA | 9,484,000 | 7,700,000 | 1,350,000 | — |
| KANSAS | 6,632,599 | 3,949,327 | 2,349,650 | — |
| X KENTUCKY | 7,262,043 | 5,395,403 | 1,302,877 | — |
| X LOUISIANA | 16,020,085 | 4,279,898 | 2,399,379 | (Begins 1980) |
| X MAINE | 6,953,507 | 4,971,758 | 748,869 | 6,954 |
| MARYLAND | 3,758,419 | 2,953,027 | 736,546 | 52,379 |
| MASSACHUSETTS | 3,550,000 | 2,500,000 | 750,000 | — |
| X MICHIGAN | 23,615,691 | 17,595,893 | 1,969,500 | — |
| MINNESOTA | 25,198,000 | 14,000,000 | 4,360,000 | 6,500,000 |
| MISSISSIPPI | 8,400,344 | 5,015,695 | 2,193,464 | 72,295 |
| MISSOURI | 46,730,364 | 10,171,530 | 3,075,788 | — |
| MONTANA | 10,883,730 | 7,983,969 | 2,629,961 | — |
| NEBRASKA | 7,877,667 | 5,053,159 | 1,560,424 | 503,519 |
| NEVADA | 6,819,816 | 4,336,348 | 1,973,358 | 104,681 |
| NEW HAMPSHIRE | 3,750,730 | 2,542,062 | 679,370 | — |
| X NEW JERSEY | 5,084,976 | 3,796,532 | 756,799 | — |
| X NEW MEXICO | 5,736,889 | 4,154,254 | 1,367,947 | — |
| NEW YORK | 14,897,258 | 12,511,700 | 1,339,202 | — |
| X NORTH CAROLINA | 9,894,681 | 6,560,183 | 2,179,344 | — |
| NORTH DAKOTA | 4,524,654 | 2,500,000 | 1,599,654 | — |
| OHIO | 11,431,272 | 9,377,091 | 1,086,868 | — |
| OKLAHOMA | 9,424,588 | 6,565,627 | 1,878,618 | — |
| X OREGON | 21,586,927 | 13,982,391 | 5,771,139 | — |
| PENNSYLVANIA | 25,321,214 | 14,385,658 | 4,539,414 | — |
| RHODE ISLAND | 1,547,000 | 290,000 | 624,000 | 601,000 |
| SOUTH CAROLINA | 17,720,782 | 3,360,459 | 2,731,227 | 7,957,530 |
| X SOUTH DAKOTA | 4,449,436 | 2,586,279 | 1,261,697 | — |
| TENNESSEE | 9,881,487 | 7,175,223 | 2,254,961 | — |
| X TEXAS | 19,327,060 | 13,114,313 | 3,606,052 | — |
| UTAH | 9,800,000 | 6,500,000 | 1,400,000 | 1,600,000 |
| VERMONT | 2,877,314 | 2,427,314 | 425,000 | — |
| VIRGINIA | 7,790,006 | 6,491,823 | 870,463 | — |
| X WASHINGTON | 18,058,715 | 10,634,263 | 4,997,004 | — |
| X WEST VIRGINIA | 5,946,283 | 4,138,222 | 929,145 | 187,584 |
| X WISCONSIN | 19,826,260 | 16,648,400 | 2,135,860 | — |
| X WYOMING | 10,609,473 | 8,381,774 | 1,112,328 | — |
| Total | 602,876,318 | 351,618,824 | 107,143,559 | 52,649,726 |
| Percentage of Total | | 58.3% | 17.8% | 8.7% |

"X" indicates figures are for 1978 fiscal year; others are for 1979.

Source: The Wildlife conservation Fund of America (1980) Reprinted with permission

| | | Percent of Total | | | | |
|---|---|---|---|---|---|---|
| Interest Income | Special & Other | License Fees | Federal Payments | General Taxation | Interest Income | Special & Other |
| — | 465,100 | 64.1 | 22.5 | 6.2 | — | 7.2 |
| — | 455,100 | 15.7 | 21.2 | 61.6 | — | 1.5 |
| 307,800 | 932,100 | 58.0 | 26.7 | — | 3.8 | 11.5 |
| — | 1,632,848 | 76.0 | 17.6 | — | — | 6.4 |
| 350,000 | 1,696,478 | 66.7 | 17.9 | 10.3 | .9 | 4.3 |
| 835,621 | 2,049,912 | 79.1 | 9.4 | .5 | 3.2 | 7.8 |
| — | 75,000 | 42.7 | 50.9 | — | — | 6.4 |
| — | 300,000 | 19.7 | 43.1 | 19.7 | — | 17.5 |
| — | — | 52.9 | 16.5 | 30.6 | — | — |
| — | 256,054 | 38.8 | 20.0 | 39.1 | — | 2.1 |
| — | — | 7.2 | 18.3 | 74.5 | — | — |
| — | 218,858 | 63.2 | 34.6 | — | — | 2.2 |
| — | 1,419,000 | 55.6 | 27.5 | — | — | 16.9 |
| — | 1,567,593 | 50.8 | 27.9 | 3.5 | — | 17.8 |
| 80,000 | 354,000 | 81.2 | 14.2 | — | .8 | 3.7 |
| — | 333,622 | 59.5 | 35.5 | — | — | 5.0 |
| — | 563,763 | 74.3 | 18.0 | — | — | 7.7 |
| — | 9,340,808 | 26.7 | 15.0 | — | — | 58.3 |
| — | 1,225,926 | 71.5 | 10.8 | .1 | — | 17.6 |
| — | 16,467 | 78.6 | 19.6 | 1.4 | — | .4 |
| — | 300,000 | 70.4 | 21.1 | — | — | 8.5 |
| 410,380 | 3,639,918 | 74.5 | 8.4 | — | 1.7 | 15.4 |
| — | 338,000 | 55.6 | 17.3 | 25.8 | — | 1.3 |
| 118,558 | 1,000,332 | 59.7 | 26.1 | .9 | 1.4 | 11.9 |
| 792,409 | 32,690,637 | 21.8 | 6.6 | — | 1.7 | 69.9 |
| — | 269,800 | 73.3 | 24.2 | — | — | 2.5 |
| 208,725 | 551,840 | 64.2 | 19.8 | 6.4 | 2.6 | 7.0 |
| 180,600 | 224,829 | 63.6 | 28.9 | 1.5 | 2.7 | 3.3 |
| — | 529,298 | 67.8 | 18.1 | — | — | 14.1 |
| — | 531,645 | 74.7 | 14.9 | — | — | 10.4 |
| — | 214,688 | 72.4 | 23.8 | — | — | 3.8 |
| 428,592 | 617,764 | 84.0 | 9.0 | — | 2.9 | 4.1 |
| — | 1,155,154 | 66.3 | 22.0 | — | — | 11.7 |
| 325,000 | 100,000 | 55.3 | 35.3 | — | 7.2 | 2.2 |
| (Begins 1979) | 967,313 | 82.0 | 9.5 | — | — | 8.5 |
| 427,252 | 553,091 | 69.7 | 20.2 | — | 4.5 | 5.8 |
| — | 1,833,397 | 64.8 | 26.7 | — | — | 8.5 |
| 1,893,317 | 4,502,825 | 56.8 | 17.9 | — | 7.5 | 17.8 |
| — | 32,000 | 18.7 | 40.3 | 38.9 | — | 2.1 |
| — | 3,401,566 | 20.5 | 15.4 | 44.9 | — | 19.2 |
| 137,941 | 463,519 | 58.1 | 28.4 | — | 3.1 | 10.4 |
| (Begins 1979) | 451,303 | 72.6 | 22.8 | — | — | 4.6 |
| — | 2,606,695 | 67.9 | 18.6 | — | — | 13.5 |
| — | 300,000 | 66.3 | 14.3 | 16.3 | — | 3.1 |
| — | 25,000 | 84.3 | 14.8 | — | — | .9 |
| — | 427,720 | 83.3 | 11.2 | — | — | 5.5 |
| 220,189 | 2,207,259 | 58.9 | 27.7 | — | 1.2 | 12.2 |
| 184,447 | 506,885 | 69.6 | 15.6 | 3.2 | 3.1 | 8.5 |
| 533,500 | 508,500 | 84.0 | 10.8 | — | 2.7 | 2.5 |
| 676,180 | 439,191 | 79.0 | 10.5 | — | 6.4 | 4.1 |
| 8,110,511 | 83,353,698 | | | | | |
| 1.4% | 13.8% | | | | | |

- Thirty-one states have added "check-off" boxes to state income-tax returns to encourage taxpayers to donate refund money for nongame management.
- Several state wildlife agencies, such as Louisiana's, obtain revenue from severance taxes on natural resources (oysters, oyster/shells, shrimp, fur, gravel).
- Indiana uses a one-cent tax on cigarettes to generate about $1 million annually.

If other states emulated these examples, wildlife agency revenues could be augmented substantially in some cases.

## Research

Every state fish and wildlife agency funds fish and wildlife surveys and research. Most of the state money for these projects is matched with Pittman-Robertson or Dingell-Johnson funds. In addition, a number of states receive federal financial assistance for research under other federal laws, such as the Endangered Species Act and the Anadromous Fish Conservation Act.

In an evaluation of Pittman-Robertson-funded research in 1981, Sousa (1982a) determined that 61.3 percent of the moneys allocated to all states was used for various types of wildlife studies (e.g., hunter-take surveys, population surveys, food habits), 27.8 percent was for environmental surveys/habitat studies, and 10.3 percent for planning and user studies. The most frequently conducted studies were hunter-take surveys (25.8 percent of all research expenditures), population surveys (17.3 percent), and environmental surveys (17.9 percent). Relatively few funds were devoted to study the effects of pollution on wildlife, degradation of wildlife habitat, or habitat studies. Sousa also categorized research expenditures by species group. He found that the overwhelming majority of funds went to game mammals and birds. Only 2.2 percent of all funds were expended on nongame or endangered wildlife and raptors.

A similar review of research expenditures for fish studies under the Dingell-Johnson Act by Sousa (1982b) showed that 25.6 percent of all research funds in 1981 went for environmental surveys, 19.4 percent for fish-take surveys, 11.7 percent for population surveys, 7.2 percent for life-history studies, and 7 percent for management techniques. Very little money was spent for pollution, water quality or quantity, or stream-improvement and lake-improvement research. When broken down by species group, those receiving the most funds were salmonids, 24.9 percent; bass 13.5 percent; warm-water fish, 13.3 percent; freshwater fish 10.3 percent; and marine fish 6.2 percent.

## Planning

Although most state fish and wildlife agencies engage in some form of planning to guide their work, 27 states and territories do not have a formal planning process as part of their administrative procedures, according to FWS officials in the Division of Federal Aid. The Pittman-Robertson and Dingell-Johnson acts both were amended in 1970 to promote the adoption of a formal planning process by state wildlife agencies. The amendments authorized the provision of federal assistance to states that prepare comprehensive fish and wildlife management plans. In addition, the Fish and Wildlife Conservation Act of 1980 calls for the preparation of conservation plans for both game and nongame fish and wildlife.

Based on these authorities, FWS provides matching federal assistance to states that prepare "comprehensive" or "modular" fish and wildlife plans. A comprehensive plan is one that covers the agency's entire mission and scope of effort and establishes conservation objectives for all species for which the agency has authority. A modular plan covers one portion of the states program (e.g. big game, warm-water fish, nongame, etc.)

According to FWS, 27 states and territories have initiated or completed either comprehensive plans or one or more modular plans, but another 27 agencies have not set up a formal planning effort. Only Colorado, Tennessee, Kansas, and Wyoming have had their comprehensive plans approved and funded by FWS. New Mexico and Washington have completed comprehensive plans but have not sought federal funding for them, and Florida, Illinois, Indiana, Minnesota, Montana, and West Virginia are developing comprehensive plans either independently or with federal assistance.

Only Maryland, Maine, and Wisconsin have had a modular plan approved by FWS. California, Idaho, and Missouri also have completed modular plans, but have not requested federal financial assistance for them. Another 10 states are preparing modular plans.

According to FWS officials, several reasons explain why many states have failed to adopt planning. These include inertia, outright hostility to planning because of a failure to appreciate its merits, the failure of universities to teach planning in their wildlife management schools, and a fear that planning will require a change in the game and sport-fish orientation of some agencies. In sum, state planning efforts have fallen far short of the mark set by Congress 16 years ago. (See the federal aid chapter for further details on the status of state planning efforts.)

## Species Management

All agencies undertake a variety of actions designed to maintain or increase populations of fish and wildlife species important to the public. Agencies conduct routine annual surveys to determine population levels and trends of game animals, waterfowl, and upland game birds principally for the purpose of setting hunting regulations and sustaining populations at desired levels. Fish populations in various water bodies also are sampled periodically to determine productivity and numbers. Both fish and wildlife populations are managed on the basis of discrete geographical units designed to reflect the natural ecological boundaries of different populations.

The annual establishment of hunting regulations is a key agency activity. The process that occurs in Virginia is typical of that in most states. After the close of the hunting season, the Virginia Game and Inland Fish Commission holds a series of regional meetings in which it reviews hunter-take data, population-status reports, and other biological studies. The next step is to draw up a draft plan that sets season opening and closing dates, bag limits, and other regulations relevant to hunting. A two-day public hearing is held on the plan in March. On the first day, the agency's biologists present their findings and recommendations, and public comment is received. On the second day, the commission votes on the plan.

The commission-approved regulations are then advertised, and a 60-day period ensues during which any further considerations may be brought forward. At the end of the period, the commission meets again to give final approval to the proposal. At this time, the commission has the power to make the proposed regulations less restrictive, but not more restrictive.

The process for establishing fishing regulations follows a similar process. A draft of the proposed regulations is prepared in August and advertised. The regulations are reviewed again in November, at which time the commission approves them. The regulations take effect the following January. Public participation in the fish-regulations process is not nearly as great or as intense as that for hunting regulations.

## Habitat Acquisition

All state agencies have authority to acquire and manage habitat for fish and wildlife, and all of them maintain areas for public hunting and fishing. Some states also lease lands from private owners or sign cooperative agreements that provide for public use of privately owned lands for hunting and fishing.

No federal, state, or private agency annuallly compiles information on the amount and type of habitat owned, leased, or otherwise controlled by state fish and wildlife agencies. However, the FWS Division of Federal Aid does keep records of land that states have acquired using Pittman-Robertson and Dingell-Johnson funds. Between 1938 and 1984, the states collectively acquired 4,098,133 acres at a cost of $284.3 million.

The Division of Federal Aid also keeps records on state wildlife management areas and refuges acquired, developed, or managed by the states. As of September 30, 1984, state hunting acreage totaled 37,670,355 million acres, and refuge acreage 562,503 for a total of 38,232,858 million acres under state management (see the federal aid chapter for further details).

## Information and Education

The typical state wildlife agency has an Information and Education division whose function is to publicize agency actions and accomplishments, promote awareness and understanding of the state's fish and wildlife resources, and explain state wildlife laws and regulations. A typical division prepares materials for radio and television and may sponsor shows of its own; publishes a state wildlife magazine; issues news releases; prepares exhibits on wildlife and wildlife problems; and conducts youth and adult education programs. In some states, the division also may have wildlife extension specialists who demonstrate fish and wildlife management practices to private landowners.

All states now have hunter-education programs whose purpose is to train hunters in firearms safety, wildlife identification, and hunter ethics. In 26 states, this program is run by an information and education unit. In 20 others, the law-enforcement division supervises the program, and in the remaining four, the work is performed by another department or division.

## Law Enforcement

In the majority of states, the fish and wildlife agency has a law-enforcement division responsible for securing compliance with state laws and regulations. However, in states where the wildlife agency has been merged into a larger natural resources or conservation department, a law-enforcement division may enforce all laws within the department's jurisdiction. In two states, Oregon and Alaska, wildlife-law enforcement is assigned to the state police department.

Law enforcement constitutes a substantial portion of state agency budgets and staff. In 1984, the states collectively spent 29.7 percent of their total budgets on law enforcement and allocated 32.5 percent of their total staff to this activity (Morse 1984).

The key activity performed by the law-enforcement division is field patrol. Uniformed, armed conservation officers are assigned to districts where they seek to deter violations and arrest those who break the law. In many states, the conservation officer also is responsible for enforcing a variety of other outdoor recreation laws, such as those relating to boating and snowmobiling. (See the chapter on state law enforcement for more details.)

## Consultation

All state fish and wildlife agencies provide technical advice to a variety of other state and federal agencies and to private landowners. In many cases the agency maintains cooperative planning and management programs with those entities as well.

The average fish and wildlife agency is asked to review hundreds of development proposals each year and to comment on their impact on fish and wildlife. According to the Wildlife Management Institute (1977), many states do not have the capability to assess competently the many land and water development proposals sent to them each year.

# References

Anderson, Mark W., S.D. Reiling and G.K. Criner. 1985. "Consumer demand theory and wildlife agency revenue structure." *Wildlife Society Bulletin* 13:375, 1985.

Bean, Michael J. 1983. *The Evolution of National Wildlife Law*. Praeger Publishers. New York. 449 pp.

Gottschalk, John S. 1978. "The State-Federal Partnership in Wildlife Conservation," in Howard P. Brokaw, ed., *Wildlife and America*, U.S. Government Printing Office. Washington, D.C.

Morse, William B. 1984. *Wildlife Law Enforcement, 1984*. Wildlife Management Institute. Washington, D.C.

Sousa, Robert J. 1982a. "A National Overview of Wildlife Management Investigations Funded by the Pittman-Robertson (P-R) Program." *Wildlife Society Bulletin*, Vol. 10, No. 3, 1982: 254.

————. 1982b. "A National Overview of Fishery Research Funded by the Dingell-Johnson Program." *Fisheries*, Vol. 7, No. 1 (January-February 1982): p. 3.

The Wildlife Conservation Fund of America. 1980. *Fish and Wildlife Agency Funding*. The Wildlife Conservation Fund of America. Columbus, Ohio.

Wildlife Management Institute. 1968. *Organization, Authority and Programs of State and Wildlife Agencies*. Washington Management Institute. Washington, D.C.

Wildlife Management Institute, 1977. *Organization, Authority and Programs of State Fish and Wildlife Agencies*. Wildlife Management Institute, Washington, D.C.

*William J. Chandler is president of W. J. Chandler Associates, a Washington D.C. environmental policy and government relations consulting firm, and publisher of* Land Letter, *a newsletter for natural-resources professionals.*

A law officer from the Missouri Department of Conservation inspects a hunter's license. Law enforcement constitutes a major portion of state wildlife budgets and personnel.

*Jim Rathert/ Missouri Department of Conservation*

# State Wildlife Law Enforcement

## William J. Chandler

### Introduction

T HE ENFORCEMENT OF colonial laws that protected game spe-
cies was the first form of wildlife management in the United States.* Initially,
these early laws "were enforced by local peace officers, but later special officers
known as wardens or protectors were given the job. The earliest of these
special officers were the deer wardens of Massachusetts in 1739 and New
Hampshire in 1764" (Bavin 1978, p. 350).

Even with the emergence of the fish and wildlife profession in the early
1900s, enforcement of game laws remained the major activity conducted by
state wildlife officers. Eventually, however, state wildlife agencies, with federal
assistance under the Pittman-Robertson Act, added research, biological management, habitat acquisition, and other modern-day management activities to
their programs, and law enforcement became one of several complementary
management functions.

Today, the enforcement of wildlife laws in most states still is the responsibility of the state wildlife agency. The primary purpose of law enforcement is

* The author would like to acknowledge his reliance on the work of William B. Morse, Western
Representative, Wildlife Management Institute, in preparing this chapter. Morse has for years
conducted periodic surveys of state law enforcement programs. This chapter relies heavily on
Morse's findings and uses charts and data prepared by him.

593

to ensure that wildlife resources "are not significantly affected by unlawful activities"* (Brantly 1984, p. 12.).

To deter unlawful acts, enforcement programs rely heavily on field patrol by uniformed officers:

> . . . Patrol is the heart of the law enforcement process. During patrol, officers move about their areas by foot, automobile, boat or airplane to observe, question, or simply converse. Conversations often yield information on illegal wildlife activities. On patrol, officers can be seen and recognized in their assigned areas and thus create the belief that they may be anywhere at any time and that violators are likely to be apprehended (Bavin 1978, p. 351).

The deterence of unlawful acts and the apprehension of violators is a mammoth, never-ending task, given the number of laws and regulations to be enforced, the vast areas to be covered by individual conservation officers, the number of hunters and fishermen afield, and the fact that crimes against wildlife usually are committed in secret and involve no human victims. In 1984, 40 states reported 381,496 arrests by their wildlife agencies, of which 69.7 percent were violations of fish and game laws. Only 1.9 percent of all arrests were for violations of laws pertaining to nongame or endangered species (Morse 1984).

Law-enforcement activities constitute a significant proportion of all wildlife-agency activities and make up a substantial part of agency budgets. In 1984, conservation officers constituted 32.5 percent of all state fish and wildlife employees, and law-enforcement operating budgets averaged 29.7 percent of all agency expenditures (Morse 1984).

## Organization and Operations

States organize their law-enforcement activity in three basic ways. Wildlife-law enforcement may be performed by a division of the wildlife agency itself, by a law-enforcement unit of the state natural resource or conservation agency, or by the state police department.

In states where there is a division of law enforcement within the wildlife agency, the law-enforcement chief usually reports directly to the agency director. The organization of the Virginia Commission of Game and Inland Fisheries, shown in the accompanying chart, is typical of this arrangement.

Over the past 20 years, there has been a trend to consolidate all state

---

* Brantly's definition of law enforcement appears to be the one that most accurately reflects state law enforcement philosophy today. However, Black (1984, p. 10) offers a different definition that focuses on the equitable distribution of fishing and hunting opportunities among sportsmen: "Conservation law enforcement is a function of game and fisheries management which enforces laws and regulations that allow for the legal harvest of certain species of animals and fish by the licensed public, and this harvest should be distributed among the licensees in an equitably practical manner."

natural-resource-management activities into one cabinet-level department or commission. Where such agencies have been created, wildlife-law enforcement may be one of several enforcement functions assigned to a department enforcement division. For example, in Wisconsin, the Department of Natural Resources has responsibility for fish and wildlife, forests and parks, control of air and water pollution, and water-resource management, among other duties. At the divisional level, fish and wildlife management activities are handled by the Division of Resource Management. The enforcement of all agency laws, including wildlife laws, is the responsibility of the Division of Enforcement.

In two states, the enforcement of fish and wildlife laws has been assigned to the state police department. In Alaska, conservation officers are members of the Department of Public Safety; in Oregon, wildlife-law enforcement is the responsibility of the state police.

At the field level, law-enforcement duties usually are carried out by uniformed conservation officers assigned to specific geographic areas either individually or as members of an enforcement team. Occasionally, the officers may be withdrawn from their areas to work on special enforcement problems elsewhere.

## Expenditure of Time

How conservation officers spend their time varies from state to state. In states such as Colorado, Montana, and New Mexico, the officer works on wildlife management, hunter education, education and public relations projects as well as law enforcement.* In many states, the conservation officer also may be responsible for enforcing other natural resource or recreation laws, such as those pertaining to snowmobiling, boating, litter, pollution, vandalism, and trespass.

State estimates indicate that the largest blocks of a conservation officer's time are allocated, in decreasing amounts, to fish- and game-law enforcement, biological management, hunter and public education, and boating safety. Very few states report the expenditure of significant amounts of time on enforcing laws relating to endangered species or nongame wildlife, pollution, forest and parks use, litter, or outdoor-recreational-vehicle use.

## Staff and Budget

Law enforcement constitutes a significant portion of all state wildlife management activities. In 1984, about a third of all state fish and wildlife personnel were involved in law enforcement, and almost 30 percent of all fish and wildlife agency expenditures were enforcement related.

---

* According to the Colorado Division of Wildlife, field officers spend about 25 percent of their time on enforcement matters.

596

Virginia Commission of Game and Inland Fisheries

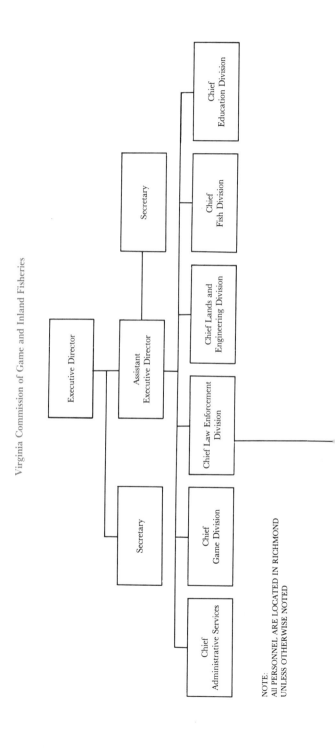

NOTE:
All PERSONNEL ARE LOCATED IN RICHMOND
UNLESS OTHERWISE NOTED

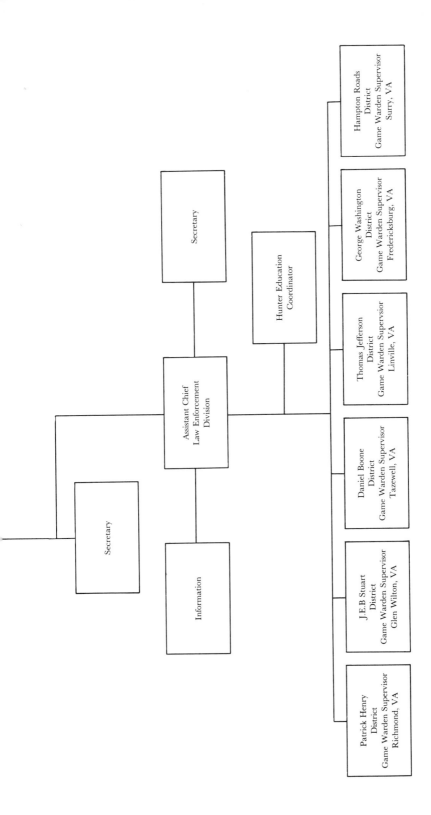

Secretary

Assistant Chief
Law Enforcement
Division

Secretary

Information

Hunter Education
Coordinator

Patrick Henry
District
Game Warden Supervisor
Richmond, VA

J.E.B Stuart
District
Game Warden Supervisor
Glen Wilton, VA

Daniel Boone
District
Game Warden Supervisor
Tazewell, VA

Thomas Jefferson
District
Game Warden Supervisor
Linville, VA

George Washington
District
Game Warden Supervisor
Fredericksburg, VA

Hampton Roads
District
Game Warden Supervisor
Surry, VA

State Estimates of How the Conservation Officer Allocates Time, 1984

| | Game Enf. % | Non-Game Enf. | End-dngrd Species | Fish Enf. | Total Fish & WL Enf. | Game Mgt. | Fish Mgt. | Hunter Sfty. | Edu. & PR | Pollution Enf. | Forest Enf. | Parks Enf. | Litter | ORV & Snow-Mobiles | Boating |
|---|---|---|---|---|---|---|---|---|---|---|---|---|---|---|---|
| **West** | | | | | | | | | | | | | | | |
| Alaska* | 38 | 3 | — | 51 | 92 | TR | TR | TR | 2 | TR | — | — | TR | TR | TR |
| Arizona | — | 2 | 1 | — | 50⁽¹⁾ | 15 | 15 | 1 | 15 | 1 | — | — | — | — | — |
| California | 18 | 2 | 1 | 22 | 43 | — | — | 1 | 1 | 2 | — | — | .5 | .3 | — |
| Colorado | — | — | — | — | — | — | — | — | — | — | — | — | — | — | — |
| Hawaii* | 12 | 2 | TR | 23 | 37 | — | — | — | .2 | — | 8.5 | 15 | — | 1 | 0 |
| Idaho | 24 | 4 | 2 | 25 | 55 | 22 | 7 | 5 | 4 | 1 | 1 | .5 | .5 | 1 | 7 |
| Montana | 21 | 1 | 1 | 22 | 45 | 2 | 3 | 1 | 2 | TR | — | 12 | 1 | 4 | — |
| Nevada | — | — | — | — | 66 | 8 | 5 | 2 | 5 | 1 | — | — | 2 | — | 25 |
| New Mexico | 25 | 1 | 1 | 25 | 52 | 1 | 1 | 5 | 5 | 1 | — | — | 3 | 7 | — |
| Oregon | 45 | 2 | 1 | 43 | 91 | 20 | 10 | 4 | 2 | 4 | — | — | — | — | 1.2 |
| Utah* | — | — | — | — | 55 | 12 | 12 | 1 | 10 | — | — | — | 1 | — | 1 |
| Wash. (Game) | 27 | 2 | 1 | 27 | 57 | — | — | — | — | — | — | — | 1 | — | 5 |
| Wash. (Fish) | 10 | — | — | 90 | 100 | — | — | — | — | — | — | — | — | — | — |
| Wyoming | 10 | 5 | 5 | 10 | 30 | 30 | — | 5 | 10 | — | — | — | 5 | — | — |
| *Based on Studies | (1) All Law Enforcement | | | | | | | | | | | | | | |
| **Midwest** | | | | | | | | | | | | | | | |
| Illinois* | 21.2 | — | .01 | 15.1 | 36.3 | — | — | 3.2 | 4.7 | — | .1 | 5 | — | .3 | 3.5 |
| Indiana | 50 | 3 | — | — | 44 | — | — | — | 24 | 5 | — | — | — | — | 24 |
| Iowa | 17 | 3 | — | 15 | 35 | 3 | 3 | 2 | 12.7 | — | — | — | — | 3 | 11.5 |
| Kansas | 25 | 2 | 2 | 25 | 54 | — | 3 | 1 | 17 | 2 | — | — | .5 | .5 | 12 |
| Michigan* | 23.3 | 2.6 | .1 | 24.2 | 63.6 | 11 | — | 2.5 | — | 4.5 | 7.5 | .3 | — | 3.7 | 10.2 |
| Minnesota* | 22 | .3 | — | 24 | 47.3 | — | 3 | 3 | 6.6 | .1 | TR | .3 | .2 | 1.5 | 2.6 |
| Missouri | — | — | — | — | 50 | 3 | 3 | — | — | — | — | — | — | — | — |
| Nebraska | 22 | 2 | 1 | 25 | 50 | 3 | — | 1 | 11 | — | — | 24 | — | 1 | 7 |
| No. Dakota | — | — | — | — | 75 | — | — | 5 | 6 | — | — | — | — | 2 | 5 |
| Ohio | — | — | — | — | 70 | 10 | 5 | — | — | — | — | — | — | — | — |
| So. Dakota | 15 | 10 | .5 | 12 | 37.5 | — | — | 2 | 15 | .5 | .5 | 3 | 3 | 4 | 6 |
| Wisconsin* | 25.3 | — | — | 16 | 41.3 | — | — | 2 | 3 | .09 | — | 1 | .05 | 2.5 | 8.3 |

## Northeast

| | | | | | | | | | | | | | | |
|---|---|---|---|---|---|---|---|---|---|---|---|---|---|---|
| Connecticut | 35 | 2 | 35 | 70 | 1 | 1 | — | 2 | — | — | 1 | — | 1 | 20 |
| Delaware | — | — | — | — | — | — | — | — | — | — | — | — | — | — |
| Maine* | 26.6 | .4 | 19.2 | 70.5[1] | .01 | 3.6 | .1 | 1.6 | .1 | — | 5 | .2 | 1.7 | 19 |
| Mass. | 39 | 3 | 35 | 81 | 5 | — | 5 | 3 | 2 | 1 | — | 1 | 2 | 2 |
| New Hamp. | — | 1 | — | 62 | 5 | 2 | 1 | 2 | 1 | — | — | 1 | 8 | 0 |
| New Jersey | 43 | 1 | 33 | 78 | 1 | 1 | 6 | — | 5 | — | — | 1 | 3 | — |
| New York | — | — | — | — | — | — | — | — | — | — | — | — | — | — |
| Penn. (Game) | 65 | 2 | 1 | 69 | 3 | — | 5 | 6 | — | — | — | 1 | — | 14 |
| Penn. (Fish)* | 2 | — | 33 | 35.2 | — | 4.5 | — | 8 | 4.5 | — | — | — | — | — |
| Rhode Island | — | — | — | — | — | — | — | — | — | — | — | — | — | — |
| Vermont | 45 | 2 | 40 | 90 | — | — | — | — | — | — | — | — | — | — |
| W. Virginia* | 42 | — | 12.8 | 54.8 | — | — | 4 | — | 1.3 | .9 | 14 | 5 | — | 2.9 |

*Based on Studies    (1) Includes General Patrol

## Southeast

| | | | | | | | | | | | | | | |
|---|---|---|---|---|---|---|---|---|---|---|---|---|---|---|
| Alabama | 35 | 2 | 5 | 35 | 80 | 2 | 2 | 1 | 7 | 2 | — | 1 | — | 5 |
| Arkansas | — | — | — | — | — | — | — | — | — | — | — | — | — | — |
| Florida | 23.7 | 4.8 | .6 | 42 | 71.1 | 4.8 | 4.8 | 1 | 4 | 1 | — | 1 | — | 8 |
| Georgia | 19 | 1 | .5 | 54 | 75.5 | .5 | 5 | 2 | .5 | — | .5 | 1 | — | 20 |
| Kentucky | 30 | 5 | 5 | 30 | 70 | 10 | 10 | 3 | 6 | — | — | — | — | — |
| Louisiana | 20 | 20 | 2 | 20 | 62 | — | — | 5 | 8 | — | — | — | — | 20 |
| Maryland | 35 | 1 | 5 | 15 | 50 | — | — | 2.4 | 13 | 1 | — | — | — | 50 |
| Mississippi | 45 | 1 | 4 | 20 | 70 | 3 | 2 | 2 | 7 | — | — | 5 | — | 11 |
| No. Carolina | 33 | 5 | 2 | 35 | 75 | 2 | 2 | 5 | 4 | TR | — | TR | — | 10 |
| Oklahoma | 25 | 5 | 5 | 30 | 65 | 3.5 | 1.5 | 5 | 25 | — | — | — | — | — |
| So. Carolina | 30 | 3 | 3 | 25 | 61 | 0 | 0 | — | — | — | 10 | — | 3 | 25 |
| Tennessee* | 36 | — | — | 17 | 53 | 4 | 2 | 3 | — | 1 | — | 1 | — | 8 |
| Texas | 40 | 1 | 1 | 16 | 58 | 2 | 2 | 1 | 7 | 1 | — | 1 | — | 16 |
| Virginia* | 38 | — | — | 21 | 59 | 3 | 1 | 3 | 8 | — | — | — | — | 6 |

*Based on Studies    Source: Morse (1984), Wildlife Management Institute

Allocation of Fish & Wildlife Agency Staff and Budget to Law Enforcement By Region and State 1984

| West | Percent of Staff Enforcement | Percent of Budget for Enforcement |
|---|---|---|
| Alaska | 11.5 | 16.4 |
| Arizona | 25.6 | 19.8 |
| California | 25.0 | 30.7 |
| Colorado | 27.3 | — |
| Hawaii[1] | 54.8 | 34.8 |
| Idaho | 29.1 | 24.5 |
| Montana | 26.6 | — |
| Nevada | 17.8 | 16.3 |
| New Mexico | 28.9 | 28.9 |
| Oregon | 14.2 | 14.7 |
| Utah | 24.6 | 21.2 |
| Wash. (Game) | 19.3 | 25.2 |
| Wash. (Fish) | 9.6 | 10.4 |
| Wyoming | 27.2 | 34.5 |
| Average | 19.4 | 20.2 |

| Midwest | | |
|---|---|---|
| Illinois | 40.6 | 40.3 |
| Indiana | 48.9 | 61.4 |
| Iowa | 15.5 | 25.9 |
| Kansas | 25.9 | 22.8 |
| Michigan | 34.3 | 40.3 |
| Minnesota | 34.7 | 30.0 |
| Missouri | 14.1 | 11.9 |
| Nebraska | 29.6 | 36.5 |
| North Dakota | 28.4 | 25.6 |
| Ohio | 35.9 | 24.5 |
| South Dakota | 40.0 | 32.4 |
| Wisconsin | 29.2 | 33.1 |
| Average | 28.8 | 29.9 |

| Northeast | | |
|---|---|---|
| Connecticut | 43.2 | 46.3 |
| Delaware | 28.0 | 36.2 |
| Maine | 41.1 | 48.6 |
| Mass. | 34.3 | 26.8 |
| New Hampshire | 31.7 | 35.8 |
| New Jersey | 15.4 | 24.0 |
| New York | 43.0 | 31.4 |
| Penn. (Game) | 23.5 | 23.4 |
| Penn. (Fish) | 23.5 | 23.3 |
| Rhode Island | 60.7 | 46.2 |
| Vermont | 54.3 | 45.7 |
| W. Virginia | 40.1 | 37.7 |
| Average | 29.8 | 31.1 |

[1] More than 99%

Allocation of Fish & Wildlife Agency Staff and Budget to Law Enforcement By Region and State 1984—Continued

| West | Percent of Staff Enforcement | Percent of Budget for Enforcement |
|---|---|---|
| Alabama | 57.6 | 50.0 |
| Arkansas | 35.7 | 30.6 |
| Florida | 39.1 | 47.0 |
| Georgia | 50.5 | 49.4 |
| Kentucky | 44.4 | 37.5 |
| Louisiana | 54.3 | 26.5 |
| Maryland | 34.8 | — |
| Mississippi | 67.7 | 50.4 |
| No. Carolina | 49.5 | 45.0 |
| Oklahoma | — | — |
| So. Carolina | 34.2 | 32.3 |
| Tennessee | 41.5 | 40.1 |
| Texas | 47.8 | 58.9 |
| Virginia | 44.8 | 36.7 |
| Average | 47.6 | 40.9 |

*Includes Marine     Source: Morse (1984), Wildlife Management Institute

The emphasis on enforcement varies from state to state, and from region to region. Southeastern states allocated an average 47.6 percent of their staff and 40.9 percent of their wildlife budgets to enforcement in 1984. At the other end of the scale, western states allocated 19.4 percent of their personnel and 20.2 percent of their budget to enforcement. According to one state official, this variation may be related to several factors. In states east of the Mississippi, a greater need exists to monitor and regulate human activities because of the higher population densities, greater number of sportsmen afield, and relatively fewer acres accessible for hunting and fishing. In western states, there appears to be less emphasis on enforcement and more on other wildlife-management activities because most game populations are in pretty good shape, fewer people use the resource, much of the wildlife resource resides on federal lands, and more opportunity exists for finding good hunting and fishing areas.

Since 1976, only a slight growth has occurred nationwide in law-enforcement staff and budget allocations relative to all fish and wildlife agency personnel and expenditures. Total enforcement personnel increased from 6,500 in 1976 (30.2 percent of all employees) to 7,180 in 1984 (32.5 percent). Combined state enforcement budgets increased 120 percent, from $125.2 million in 1976 (27.7 percent of all wildlife expenditures) to $275.5 million in 1984 (29.7 percent) (Morse 1976 and 1984).

State estimates of expected future growth in law-enforcement personnel confirm the rather static position of enforcement in overall wildlife management efforts. For 1985 and 1986, the states predict a combined law-enforcement staff increase of 131 persons, a 1.8 percent increase from the current level. Budget growth likewise is expected to be minimal with any increases attributable mainly to inflation (Morse 1984).

**Basic Information on State Conservation Officers, 1984**

| | No. Empl. in Dept. | No. C.O. | No. CO. Supervisors | 2-yr Expansion | 2-yr Replacement | CO w/WL Degree | CO w/ Other Degree | Min. Education | Res. Rqmt. Months | No. CO. with Police Cert. | No. CO w/Spec. Training |
|---|---|---|---|---|---|---|---|---|---|---|---|
| **West** | | | | | | | | | | | |
| Alaska | 983 | 104[1] | 9 | 0 | 10 | 37 (Est) | 63 (Est) | HS | 0 | 12 (Est) | 20 |
| Arizona | 355 | 78 | 13 | — | — | 101 | 1 | BS-WL | 0 | — | 37 |
| California | 1,382 | 333 | 12 | 0 | 30 | — | — | 2 yr. Coll. | 0 | 5 | 12 |
| Colorado | 527 | 136 | 8 | 3 | 12 | 107 | 0 | BS-WL | 0 | 24 | — |
| Hawaii | 124 | 62 | 6 | — | — | 0 | 9 | HS | 0 | 5 | — |
| Idaho | 316 | 83 | 9 | 0 | — | 86 | 2 | BS | 0 | 5 | 0 |
| Montana | 346 | 80 | 12 | 0 | 2 | 38 | 15 | BS | 12 | 1 | 0 |
| Nevada | 152 | 27 | 6 | — | 3 | 22 | 2 | BS-WL | 6 | 5 | — |
| New Mexico | 218 | 50 | 13 | 0 | 10 | 33 | 5 | BS | 0 | 8 | 8 |
| Oregon | 901 | 120 | 8 | 0 | 2 | 21 | 10 | HS | 0 | 1 | 4 |
| Utah | 289 | 64 | 7 | 1 | 6 | 61 | 2 | BS | 0 | | 9 |
| Wash. (Game) | 517 | 90 | 10 | 6 | 4 | — | — | 2 yr. Coll. | 0 | | 0 |
| Wash. (Fish) | 551 | 49 | 2 | 5 | 3 | — | — | 2 yr. Coll. | 0 | 6 | — |
| Wyoming | 320 | 75 | 12 | 1 | 2 | 54 | 4 | BS | 0 | 6 | — |
| Total | 6,981 | 1,351 | 127 | 16 | 84 | 560 | 113[2] | BS-8 2 yr. C.-3 HS-3 | 2 | 78 | 90 |

[1]Also 50 Seasonal Employees
[2]8 (partial) of these are in Criminal Justice

| **Midwest** | | | | | | | | | | | |
|---|---|---|---|---|---|---|---|---|---|---|---|
| Illinois | 305 | 124 | 12 | 0 | 15 | — | 47 | 2 yr. Coll. | 0 | 20 | 2 |
| Indiana | 386 | 189 | 8 | 0 | 10 | 4 | 25 | 2 yr. Coll. | 0 | 9 | 125 |
| Iowa | 524 | 81 | 8 | 0 | 5 | 28 | 28 | HS | 0 | 3 | 75 |
| Kansas | 270 | 70 | 9 | 6 | 15 | 17 | 2 | HS | 0 | — | 10 |
| Michigan | 638 | 219 | 10 | 0 | 10 | 14 | 88 | HS | 12 | 30 | 13 |

|  |  |  |  |  |  |  |  | Degree |  |  |  |
|---|---|---|---|---|---|---|---|---|---|---|---|
| Minnesota | 510 | 177 | 8 | 4 | 30 | — | — | HS | 0 | — | 10 |
| Missouri | 1,032 | 145 | 14 | — | 15 | 73 | 29 | BS | 0 | 47 | 9 |
| Nebraska | 196 | 58 | 6 | 2 | 5 | 6 | 16 | HS | 0 | 13 | — |
| North Dakota | 102 | 29 | 1 | 0 | 0 | 0 | 15 | BS | 0 | 7 | — |
| Ohio | 509 | 183 | 8 | 0 | 15 | — | — | HS | 0 | — | 44 |
| South Dakota | 180 | 72 | 6 | 1 | — | 52 | 6 | BS-WL | 0 | 6 | — |
| Wisconsin | 622 | 172 | 16 | 3 | 18 | — | — | None | 0 | — | — |
| Total | 5,274 | 1,519 | 106 | 16 | 138 | 194 | 256[1] | BS-3 / 2 yr. C-2 / HS-6 | 1 | 135 | 288 |

[1]39 of these are Criminal Justice Degrees
Source: Morse (1984), Wildlife Management Institute

### Northeast

|  |  |  |  |  |  |  |  | Degree |  |  |  |
|---|---|---|---|---|---|---|---|---|---|---|---|
| Connecticut | 132 | 51 | 6 | 6 | 4 | — | — | BS | 0 | — | 5 |
| Delaware | 100 | 24 | 4 | 0 | 0 | 0 | 4 | 2 yr. Coll. | 0 | 3 | — |
| Maine | 292 | 113 | 7 | — | 8 | 7 | 17 | HS | 0 | 8 | 2 |
| Mass. | 210 | 67 | 5 | 3 | 10 | — | 3 | HS | 0 | — | 4 |
| New Hampshire | 139 | 41 | 3 | 6 | 1 | 8 | 5 | HS | 0 | 2 | 0 |
| New Jersey | 356 | 50 | 5 | 6 | 8 | 40 | 0 | BS | 0 | 2 | 3 |
| New York | 693 | 280 | 18 | 0 | 8 | — | — | 2 yr. Coll. | 0 | 298 | 35 |
| Penn. (Game) | 710 | 150 | 17 | 0 | 25 | — | 10 | HS | 0 | — | 44 |
| Penn. (Fish) | 429 | 86 | 15 | 2 | 8 | 1 | 2 | HS | 6 | 4 | — |
| Rhode Island | 61 | 30 | 7 | 4 | 4 | 5 | 2 | HS | 0 | 0 | 23 |
| Vermont | 92 | 48 | 2 | 0 | 3 | 6 | 15 | HS | 0 | 2 | 0 |
| W. Virginia | 309 | 109 | 15 | — | — | — | — | BS | 0 | — | 6 |
| Total | 3,523 | 1,049 | 104 | 24 | 79 | 67 | 58 | BS-3 / 2-2 yr. C. / HS-7 | 1 | 319 | 122 |

Basic Information on State Conservation Officers, 1984—Continued

| West | No. Empl. in Dept. | No. C.O. | No. CO Super-visors | 2-yr Expan-sion | 2-yr Replace-ment | CO w/WL Degree | CO w/ Other Degree | Min. Education | Res. Rqmt. Months | No. CO. with Police Cert. | No. CO w/Spec. Training |
|---|---|---|---|---|---|---|---|---|---|---|---|
| Alabama | 255 | 145 | 2 | 0 | 12 | 3 | 15 | HS | 0 | 110 | — |
| Arkansas | 384 | 135 | 2 | 25 | 10 | — | — | HS | 0 | 137 | 4 |
| Florida | 762 | 288 | 10 | — | 28 (1) | 16 | 76 | HS | 0 | 313 | 32 |
| Georgia | 477 | 236 | 5 | 0 | 25 | 1 | 45 | HS | 0 | 236 | 6 |
| Kentucky | 279 | 122 | 2 | 5 | 12 | 2 | 14 | HS | 0 | — | 0 |
| Louisiana | 471 | 241 | 15 | 0 | 80 | 5-apprx. | 30 | None | 0 | 241 | 2 |
| Maryland | 594 | 190 | 13 | 6 | 25 | 2 | 16 | HS | 0 | 203 | 13 |
| Mississippi | 313 | 194 | 18 | 10 | 6 | 0 | 43 | HS | 0 | 194 | 4 |
| No. Carolina | 428 | 207 | 5 | 0 | 20 | 1 | 13 | HS | 12 | 60 | 4 |
| Oklahoma | — | 106 | 2 | 0 | 9 | 15 | 5 | HS | 12 | 108 | 9 |
| So. Carolina | 655 | 200 | 24 | 0 | 25 | 5 | 30 | HS | 6 | 224 | — |
| Tennessee | 441 | 158 | 25 | 0 | 15 | —(2) | — | BS-WL | 0 | — | 29 |
| Texas | 935 | 428 | 19 | 29 | 25 | — | — | HS | 12 | — | 0 |
| Virginia | 315 | 120 | 21 | 0 | 0 | 1 | 26 | HS | 0 | — | 0 |
| Total | 5,933 | 2,770 | 163 | 75 | 289 | 51 | 311 (3) | BS-1 HS-12 None-1 | 4 Res-(2) | 713 | 100 |

(1) 10% Turn over a year
(2) In 1980 reported 50
(3) 87 of these criminal justice

## Law Enforcement Personnel as a Percentage of All Fish and Wildlife Employees

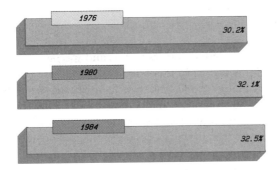

1976  30.2%
1980  32.1%
1984  32.5%

## Expenditures for State Law Enforcement as a Percentage of all Fish and Wildlife Expenditures

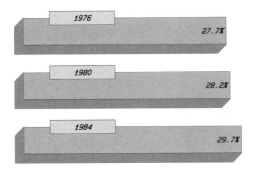

1976  27.7%
1980  28.2%
1984  29.7%

## Personnel Qualification, Selection, and Training

Most state law enforcement staffs have enhanced their professionalism over the past eight years by increasing their qualification, selection, and training standards. All states hire conservation officers under a competitive civil service or merit system or through a department exam or screening process. This contrasts with the political patronage employment system that dominated in many states from the turn of the century through the 1960s.

Sixteen states require new applicants to have college degrees. Forty-two states have no residence requirement for applicants, so they can seek new recruits nationwide basis. Most states conduct affirmative action programs to hire minorities. In 1984, minorities constituted about five percent of all state enforcement personnel, an increase of 1.4 percent since 1980 (Morse 1984).

Training of officers includes basic, refresher, and special training courses. Forty-one states require new officers to attend a police academy, nine have a wildlife department training center, and two have shorter training periods combined with on-the-job experience under supervision. This contrasts with the situation in 1976, when only 21 states required police-academy training, and 21 had departmental schools or on-the-job training. The number of law-enforcement personnel with professional police certificates has increased from 2,767 in 1976 (42.5 percent of all officers) to 5,163 in 1983 (71.8 percent) (Morse 1976 and 1984).

Forty-five states conduct annual in-service training programs for their officers. These programs cover a variety of subjects, including:

- Review of existing and new laws.
- Stress-management techniques.
- Proper arrest methods and procedures and their relation to the judicial process.
- Officer safety, including proper use and control of firearms, disarming assailants, and self-defense techniques.
- Avoidance of civil liability suits.

Since 1978, the Division of Law Enforcement of the U.S. Fish and Wildlife Service has provided undercover training to federal, state, and foreign conservation officers at Glynco, Georgia. A total of 317 officers, including individuals from 49 states and three territories, have been trained at the facility. Currently, training consists of a one-week course in which conservation officers are taught how to identify the legal, operational, physical and mental requirements of undercover work and to obtain expertise in the use of special equipment. FWS is developing a two-week course for 1987 which will incorporate practical exercises.

## Allocation of Resources

The most significant decision in an effective law-enforcement program is the allocation of officer time. Enforcement policies must be selective because it is impossible to prevent all violations of all laws or to catch all law-breakers. Selective enforcement policies are those

> . . . which give guidance to individual officers so that they may make conscious decisions to enforce the law against certain parties, or in certain places, or at certain times, or against certain types of violations. Such policies should take the form of a scheme of priorities with respect to the laws under their jurisdiction and the relation of these priorities to the other services which conservation officers must perform. These enforcement priorities may result in nearly full enforcement of some laws, partial enforcement of others, and practically no enforcement of still another (Bavin 1978, p. 359-60).

To establish enforcement priorities, Bavin identifies five criteria:

> . . . First, the effect of the offense on the resource in terms of both species and quantity of wildlife involved. In some situations a species of less importance because of abundance may warrant enforcement effort because of its similarity to a less abundant species. For example, enforcement effort to control illegal shooting of hawks is important because the same violators may also be killing Bald Eagles. Second is the effect of commercialization and market hunting. These practices have a consistent and increasing effect on the animal population and a devastating effect on enforcement morale. Third, the intent of the offender should be considered so that priority is given to those individuals who purposely violate conservation laws. Fourth, the attitude of the prosecutor and the court must be considered in establishing priorities because they reflect public opinion. Finally, priority should be given to those offenders whose apprehension is necessary to maintain respect for the enforcement arm. That is, habitual violators may need special attention lest the public assume that some individuals are above the law.

> In addition to the above criteria for establishing enforcement priorities, it may be necessary to focus attention on special problems, such as license cases or flagrant noncompliance in specific areas, even though they might not otherwise come within the ambit of the priority scheme. (1978 p. 360).

Ideally, the establishment of enforcement priorities should be made through a comprehensive planning process that carefully weighs resource needs and identifies problems, objectives, and strategies. Yet many states operate without a comprehensive enforcement plan. In these states it is impossible to integrate enforcement objectives with department resource-management objectives (Morse 1984).

States may receive federal grant assistance under the Pittman-Robertson and Dingell-Johnson acts for preparing comprehensive fish and wildlife plans. A comprehensive plan focuses on achieving resource objectives and may include the identification of law-enforcement actions that would help meet those objectives.* However, a state cannot receive assistance under the Pittman-Robertson or Dingell-Johnson programs for developing specific law-enforcement plans.

---

* As of the end of 1985, only Tennessee, Wyoming, Kansas, and Colorado had developed comprehensive plans. See the Federal Aid chapter for a summary of state planning efforts.

Morse (1984) cites Colorado as a state with a good enforcement plan. The plan is directed toward these objectives:

1. Reducing the illegal take of wildlife.
2. Reducing the numbers of hunters and fishermen operating without licenses.
3. Reducing the number of resident licenses sold to nonresidents.
4. Decreasing the number of wildlife-law violations committed unintentionally by uninformed persons.
5. Establishing standards of law-enforcement knowledge and a training program for existing staff to ensure these standards are met.
6. Analyzing and recommending changes in complex and outdated statutes and regulations.
7. Increasing the statewide rate of convictions for wildlife violations from 65 to 90 percent.
8. Conducting psychological research to determine why wildlife users violate laws.
9. Conducting research to adequately measure the effectiveness of the law-enforcement effort (Colorado Department of Natural Resources, undated).

## Research

Relatively little research on wildlife-law enforcement is conducted by the states or the federal government. Only 17 full-time personnel were assigned to research by all states in 1984, and just seven university research projects were under way (Morse 1984).

Most current research is oriented toward improving law-enforcement operations. A few studies have been conducted to estimate compliance with wildlife laws, to quantify the illegal take of big-game animals, and to characterize violators. Even fewer studies have attempted to measure the effectiveness of law-enforcement programs in deterring violations or in determining the exact relationship between specific law-enforcement activities and their affect on the biological health of fish and wildlife populations.

This lack of research activity is attributed to several factors, including disinterest on the part of fish and wildlife professionals; other, more pressing, budget priorities; and the prohibition of federal financial assistance for law-enforcement activities under the Pittman-Robertson and Dingell-Johnson programs.*

Another major factor limiting research is the sheer difficulty in obtaining the basic data needed to test hypotheses. Wildlife crimes, because they take place in sparsely inhabited areas, are unlikely to be observed. Even if a violation is observed by hunters or other individuals, it usually is not reported, since there is no human victim.

---

* Some state wildlife agency officials would like to see these laws amended to allow states to obtain matching funds for law-enforcement activities.

Despite these obstacles, some wildlife professionals believe that more research needs to be done:

> . . . To improve efficiency and effectiveness, some portion of the enforcement budget should be devoted to enforcement research. Not only is work needed in defining measurable objectives and improving techniques and procedures for apprehending violators and gaining compliance, but attention must be given to the effects of noncompliance in the wildlife resource. In making analyses of wildlife law enforcement activities, however, researchers should be extremely careful to distinguish between cause and effect (Bavin 1978, p. 359).

## Wildlife Violations

According to Sigler (1980 pp. 121-132) there are nine major types of wildlife-law violations which cover most citations and arrests made by conservation officers:

- *Taking or attempting to take game wildlife or fish out of season.* Such violations result when species are killed during closed season or outside of prescribed hunting hours.
- *Taking or attempting to take wildlife in an illegal place.* In most states, it is against the law to seek fish or game in closed areas, refuges, or on private property posted against hunting and fishing.
- *Improper license.* This violation occurs if a person hunts or fishes without a license, uses a license issued to someone else, fails to properly display a license, or uses a resident license when a nonresident license is required.*
- *Illegal method.* Most states have laws that establish proper and improper methods and equipment for taking fish and wildlife. In most states it is against the law to hunt deer with a spotlight or with a .22-caliber rifle, to use a shotgun that holds more than three shells when hunting ducks or geese, to use fishing gear with too many hooks, and so forth.
- *Illegal possession.* Once fish have been caught or wildlife killed, they become the possession of the sportsman. Most states have laws that prohibit the possession of fish or wildlife or their parts at certain times of the year or that limit the number of animals that may be taken per day, season, or year and that may be possessed at any one time.
- *Illegal procedure.* The most common proceduralviolation is failure to properly tag big-game animals. In most states, tags are used to identify the hunter who killed the animal and must remain attached to the animal during transit and storage.
- *Illegal importation or exportation of protected species.* Most states have laws regu-

---

* Failure to purchase a license or the purchase of a resident license when a more expensive nonresident license is required are practices which deprive states of millions of dollars in revenue each year. The Colorado Division of Wildlife estimates that it loses approximately $2.5 million yearly because of license violations.

Arrests and Convictions, State Conservation Officers, 1984

| | Arrests per C.O. | Percent Convictions | Arrests per Thousand Licenses | Hunters & Anglers per C.O. | Average Patrol Dist. sq. mi. | Percent of Staff Enforcement | Percent of Budget for Enforcement |
|---|---|---|---|---|---|---|---|
| **West** | | | | | | | |
| Alaska | 29 | — | 9.3 | 3,155 | — | 11.5 | 16.4 |
| Arizona | 70 | 92 | 8.1 | 7,337 | 924 | 25.6 | 19.8 |
| California | 88 | 92 | 9.7 | 9,068 | 433 | 25.0 | 30.7 |
| Colorado | 43 | — | 5.4 | 8,024 | 744 | 27.3 | — |
| Hawaii[1] | 10 | — | 30.9 | 318 | — | 54.8 | 34.8 |
| Idaho | 49 | 90 | 6.2 | 7,925 | 992 | 29.1 | 24.5 |
| Montana | 42 | 98 | 5.9 | 7,137 | 1,829 | 26.6 | — |
| Nevada | 80 | 97 | 8.7 | 9,270 | 4,094 | 17.8 | 16.3 |
| New Mexico | 62 | 90 | 7.7 | 8,059 | 2,433 | 28.9 | 28.9 |
| Oregon | 90 | — | 9.9 | 9,139 | 799 | 14.2 | 14.7 |
| Utah | 70 | 97 | 6.6 | 7,528 | 1,327 | 24.6 | 21.2 |
| Wash. (Game) | 94 | 93 | 9.2 | 8,820 | 756 | 19.3 | 25.2 |
| Wash. (Fish) | 56 | 97 | — | — | — | 9.6 | 10.4 |
| Wyoming | 41 | 95 | 6.8 | 6,012 | 1,013 | 27.2 | 34.5 |
| Average | 64.07 | 93.02 | 8.27 | 7,747 | 930.7[2] | 19.4 | 20.2 |
| **Midwest** | | | | | | | |
| Illinois | 73 | — | 7.3 | 10,037 | 455 | 40.6 | 40.3 |
| Indiana | 58 | — | 10.5 | 5,543 | 192 | 48.9 | 61.4 |
| Iowa | 86 | 96 | 8.9 | 6,053 | 654 | 15.5 | 25.9 |
| Kansas | 61 | 99 | 7.4 | 8,191 | 1,175 | 25.9 | 22.8 |
| Michigan | 110 | 94 | 9.6 | 11,536 | 247 | 34.3 | 40.3 |
| Minnesota | 60 | 98 | 4.8 | 12,545 | 473 | 34.7 | 30.0 |
| Missouri | 51 | 97 | 5.2 | 9,766 | 477 | 14.1 | 11.9 |

[1] Excludes 4,905 Parking Citations
[2] Excludes Alaska and Hawaii

| | | | | | | |
|---|---|---|---|---|---|---|
| Nebraska | 92 | 97 | 12.5 | 7,361 | 1,310 | 29.6 | 36.5 |
| North Dakota | 33 | 96 | 3.5 | 9,450 | 2,414 | 28.4 | 25.6 |
| Ohio | 54 | 98 | 6.2 | 8,807 | 224 | 35.9 | 24.5 |
| South Dakota | 24 | 97 | 4.7 | 5,060 | 1,070 | 40.0 | 32.4 |
| Wisconsin | 109 | 94 | 8.3 | 13,141 | 318 | 29.2 | 33.1 |
| Average | 72.4 | 96.0 | 7.45 | 9,716 | 496.2 | 28.8 | 29.9 |

Source: Morse (1984), Wildlife Management Institute

**Northeast**

| | | | | | | |
|---|---|---|---|---|---|---|
| Connecticut | 70 | — | 11.8 | 5,943 | 98 | 43.2 | 46.3 |
| Delaware | 38 | — | 20.5 | 1,831 | 81 | 28.0 | 36.2 |
| Maine | 40 | 95 | 9.5 | 4,174 | 263 | 41.1 | 48.6 |
| Mass. | — | — | — | 4,668 | 116 | 34.3 | 26.8 |
| New Hampshire | 29 | 98 | 5.2 | 5,557 | 244 | 31.7 | 35.8 |
| New Jersey | 58 | 96 | 8.6 | 6,717 | 157 | 15.4 | 24.0 |
| New York | 52 | 92 | 8.2 | 6,290 | 177 | 43.0 | 31.4 |
| Penn. (Game) | 81 | 97 | 9.2 | 8,749 | 302 | 23.5 | 23.4 |
| Penn. (Fish) | 148 | 99 | 11.6 | 12,708 | 527 | 23.5 | 23.3 |
| Rhode Island | 35 | 99[1] | 24.7 | 1,412 | 40 | 60.7 | 46.2 |
| Vermont | 30 | 88 | 5.2 | 5,790 | 188 | 54.3 | 45.7 |
| W. Virginia | 86 | — | 14.8 | 5,779 | 222 | 40.1 | 37.7 |
| Average | 61.2 | 97.7 | 9.88 | 6,494 | 183 | 29.8 | 31.1 |

[1] More than 99%

Arrests and Convictions, State Conservation Officers, 1984—Continued

| Southeast | Arrests per C.O. | Percent Convictions | Arrests per Thousand Licenses | Hunters & Anglers per C.O. | Average Patrol Dist. sq. mi. | Percent of Staff Enforcement | Percent of Budget for Enforcement |
|---|---|---|---|---|---|---|---|
| Alabama | 90 | 95 | 14.6 | 6,158 | 356 | 57.6 | 50.0 |
| Arkansas | 41 | 97 | 5.7 | 7,176 | 393 | 35.7 | 30.6 |
| Florida | 81 | 94 | 24.8 | 3,258 | 201 | 39.1 | 47.0 |
| Georgia | 62 | — | 14.5 | 4,283 | 249 | 50.5 | 49.4 |
| Kentucky | 62 | 66 | 7.9 | 7,818 | 331 | 44.4 | 37.5 |
| Louisiana | 112 | — | 29.6 | 3,784 | 210 | 54.3 | 26.5 |
| Maryland | 45 | — | 28.4 | 1,568* | 58* | 34.8 | — |
| Mississippi | 65 | 80 | 18.1 | 3,567 | 195 | 67.7 | 50.4 |
| No. Carolina | 63 | 93 | 16.1 | 3,930 | 255 | 49.5 | 45.0 |
| Oklahoma | 61 | — | 7.0 | 8,740 | 658 | — | — |
| So. Carolina | 59 | 95 | 19.0 | 3,093 | 155 | 34.2 | 32.3 |
| Tennessee | 35 | — | 4.3 | 8,283 | 266 | 41.5 | 40.1 |
| Texas | 115 | 95 | 17.0 | 6,825 | 616 | 47.8 | 58.9 |
| Virginia | 148 | 81 | 17.1 | 7,007 | 340 | 44.8 | 36.7 |
| Average | 78.7 | 93 | 15.7 | 5,160 | 311 | 47.6 | 40.9 |

*Includes Marine

Source: Morse (1984), Wildlife Management Institute

Percent of Arrests by Category, Regional Summary 1984*

| Area | Number of States Reporting: | Percent of Arrests by Category | | | | | | | | |
|---|---|---|---|---|---|---|---|---|---|---|
| | | Game | Non-Game | Fish | Boating | Forest | Litter | Pollution | Parks | Other |
| West | 11 | 26 | 1.0 | 61 | 5 | TR | 1.3 | 0.4 | 0.3 | 5 |
| Midwest | 11 | 29 | 0.5 | 33 | 13 | 0.7 | 1.2 | 0.4 | 9 | 13 |
| Northeast | 10 | 39 | 0.6 | 30 | 12 | 0.6 | 4 | 1.8 | 2 | 10 |
| Southeast | 8 | 30 | 0.8 | 40 | 24 | — | 0.7 | 0.5 | — | 4 |
| Total | 40 | 30.7 | 0.6 | 40.7 | 15.6 | 0.28 | 1.4 | 0.3 | 2.7 | 7.4 |
| (1980) | 41 | 31.4 | 1.9 | 38.3 | 12.3 | 0.2 | 2.1 | 0.29 | — | 12.9 |

*Based on 381,496 arrests
Source: Morse (1984), Wildlife Management Institute

lating the transportation of fish and wildlife, in whole or in part, across state lines. In some cases, the importation or exportation of certain species may be prohibited totally. For example, Oklahoma prohibits the transportation, for sale outside the state, of minnows caught in Oklahoma. Idaho in some cases prohibits the transport of any animal or part thereof outside the state unless the taking of the animal first has been reported to state officials.

- *Illegal taking or possession of protected species.* Federal law prohibits the taking of some 300 animals listed as endangered or threatened under the Endangered Species Act. State laws also prohibit the taking of federally listed species or state listed species that are rare, endangered, or otherwise of significance.
- *Offering for sale wildlife species in violation of federal or state law.* Most states prohibit the offering for sale of animals killed out of season or otherwise illegally taken. This provision is aimed at prosecuting those who take large amounts of game for commercial purposes.

## Arrests and Violations

The deterrence of violations and the apprehension of lawbreakers are the two broad goals of every state wildlife-law enforcement program. The national

Incidence of Certain Fish and Wildlife Violations in Colorado and Virginia

| Type of Violation | Number (Percent of Total Violations of All Types Cited by the Agency) | |
|---|---|---|
| Hunting and Trapping | Colorado* Total Violations = 6,484 | Virginia** Total Violations = 12,981 |
| Without license | 343 (5.3%) | 396 (3/1%) |
| Illegal possession | 727 (11.2%) | U |
| On private property (trespass) | 304 (4.7%) | 955 (7.4%) |
| On closed area or after hours | 137 (2.1%) | 65 (0.5%) |
| Out of season | 87 (1.3%) | 352 (2.7%) |
| Illegal method/weapon | 208 (3.2%) | 844 (6.5%) |
| Failure to tag or sex | 339 (5.2%) | 231 (1.8%) |
| Fishing | | |
| Without license | 1,553 (24.0%) | 4,043 (31.0%) |
| Illegal possession | 242 (3.7%) | 25 (2.5%) |
| On private property (trespass) | 27 (.4%) | 737 (5.7%) |
| Illegal method (unlawful device, unattended pole, 2 poles, wrong bait or lure, etc.) | 471 (7.3%) | 43 (0.3%) |
| On closed area | 56 (.9%) | U |

U Undeterminable from report format.
 * 1984 Annual Report, Colorado Division of Wildlife Law Enforcement.
** 1985 Annual Report, Law Enforcement Division, Virginia Commission of Game and Inland Fisheries.

average for the number of arrests made by a conservation officer increased 14 percent from 62.5 arrests per thousand licenses in 1980 to 71.5 arrests per thousand licenses in 1984, while the number of licensed hunters and anglers per officer dropped from 7,039 to 6,926 (-1.6 percent). Morse (1984) attributes this increase in arrests to a combination of factors, including increased enforcement effort, broader enforcement authorities, and a national upward trend in crime, but does not distinguish the relative weight of any one factor. Another reason for the increase, according to one state wildlife official, is that wildlife administrators expect and demand better police work from their highly trained personnel.

Violation of game laws constituted 30.7 percent of total arrests made in 1984, and fishery violations, 40.7 percent. Boating-law violations comprised 15.6 percent of all arrests, and park-law violations, 2.7 percent. Nongame violations comprised just 0.6 percent of all arrests; forest law violations, 0.28 percent; and pollution violations, 0.29 percent.

The types and frequencies of fish and wildlife violations cited by state law-enforcement officers varies from state to state, depending largely on enforcement priorities. Based on a review of statistics supplied by Colorado and Virginia, the most frequently cited violations include hunting or fishing without a license, illegal possession of wildlife, illegal methods of take and illegal procedure.

## Commercialization of Wildlife

Notably absent from these violation records are those related to the illegal import, export, or sale of species for profit. Many enforcement professionals believe that the illegal taking of wildlife for commercial purposes is on the rise. The lack of state-reported violations in this area is due to several factors. First, it is not always possible to determine if someone arrested for illegal possession actually intended to sell the wildlife. Second, import and export violations and actual illegal sales are hard to discover. To prove such cases would require considerable effort and cost, almost always requiring undercover work. Most states have been unwilling to divert resources from their standard enforcement practices to establish permanent undercover units. However, this attitude is changing. Some states have had permanent undercover units for years, and others are moving in that direction.*

There are few statistics or even good estimates of the numbers of wildlife taken illegally for commercial sale. FWS law-enforcement officials, however, believe that illegal taking of wildlife has increased. This belief is based on several considerations. First, the commercial value of certain wildlife species is known to have increased tremendously, and opportunity for profit stongly

---

* States with permanent undercover units include Michigan, Illinois, Missouri, Utah, California, Florida, New York, South Carolina, Louisiana, Maine, Wisconsin, Minnesota, Texas, Indiana, and Virginia.

induces some individuals to break wildlife laws. Some examples of wildlife values cited by Germani (1985, p.l):

- Big-game trophy collectors pay thousands of dollars for a "guaranteed hunt," in which guides take them on unlicensed, out-of-season hunts;
- Buyers for the Asian medicinal market pay as much as $5,000 for a black bear carcass and $60 to $70 a pound for elk antlers in velvet, the soft fur that covers growing antlers (a rack of antlers weighs 15 pounds);
- Wealthy Arabs have paid up to $100,000 for a live white gyrfalcon for sporting use;
- One bighorn sheep carcass was sold three times - first for $350, then $1,200, and finally $6,000;
- one hunter paid $33,000 for a license to hunt bighorn sheep in Utah.

According to a New Hampshire law-enforcement official, a fisher skin can be sold for $200 or more to fur dealers.

Second, there has been a large increase in the amount and value of wildlife and wildlife products in *legal* commercial trade. The declared world-wide value of wildlife and wildlife products in 1982 exceeded $760 million (World Wildlife Fund). Such increases usually mean a significant rise in black marketeering as well. Estimates of illegal trade range as high as one quarter the value of the legal commerce in wildlife.

Finally, FWS, in cooperation with state law-enforcement officers, has uncovered significant, commercially related violations of both federal and state wildlife laws in recent years. Some examples of major federal-state investigations:

- *Operation Gillnet,* an 18-month covert investigation concluded in 1982, that documented the illegal catch and sale of Great Lakes fish. The investigation showed that approximately 60,000 pounds of fish, especially lake trout, were taken illegally each year and resold in Wisconsin, Michigan, Illinois, Indiana, and Tennessee. Ninety individuals have been convicted as of September 1985 and fines in excess of $120,000 levied.
- *Operation Trophy Kill,* a three-year investigation that focused on illegal poaching and smuggling of native and foreign species of wildlife. Violations included illegal smuggling of endangered species skins and the interstate shipment of illegally taken U.S. wildlife such as bighorn sheep, mountain goats, elk, lynx, mule deer, black bear, antelope, mountain lion, and bobcat. Also uncovered were violations of federal migratory bird laws. Forty-six individuals have been convicted. Collective sentences include 51 years in jail and $120,138 in fines. One defendant received a 23-year jail sentence and must serve 15 of those years—the longest jail term ever rendered for any wildlife violation in the United States.
- *East-Coast Poaching,* an investigation that led to 130 arrests for the illegal taking of deer and other species and their illegal shipment in interstate commerce for commercial purposes. One phase of the operation uncovered

an illegal market in striped bass taken from the Chesapeake Bay or its tributary waters and their illegal sale to fish markets and buyers in Pennsylvania, New York, Maryland, Virginia, and Washington, D.C. So far, 108 individuals have been convicted and fines totaling $344,917 levied.

- *Midwest Fur Poaching,* a two-year covert operation involving the illegal transport and sale of fisher, bobcat, lynx, and other skins. The investigation took place principally in the states of Michigan, Minnesota, and Wisconsin, but traced illegal fur shipments to other states such as New Hampshire, New York and Pennsylvania. Completed in 1985, the operation could result in charges being filed against nearly 300 individuals.

- *Operation Falcon,* a covert investigation of illegal activity involving raptors, was initiated in 1981 and ended in 1984. Of the 63 individuals charged in the United States so far, 52 have been convicted and eight (all foreign nationals) are fugitives. The collective sentences imposed to date are $269,225 in fines, two years in jail, more than 55 years probation, and more than 1,200 hours of community service. Most of the violations fall into three categories: (1) illegal taking of birds from the wild, and the illegal possession, transportation, sale, or purchase of the birds; (2) the manipulation of federal bird bands and the falsification of records to conceal or thwart detection of birds unlawfully taken from the wild or otherwise unlawfully acquired (in some cases by claiming the birds were captive-bred when in fact they were taken from the wild); and (3) the smuggling of birds into, or their illegal export out of, the United States for profit. (Interior 1985).

## Fines

Seventeen states reported collecting fines totaling $8,978,549 in 1984, of which 79.3 percent were derived from various fish and wildlife infractions. Only nine state wildlife agencies receive a portion or all of the fines collected. In other states, fine revenues are returned either to the state general fund or are dedicated to other uses such as courts, schools, and libraries. Based on the average of $528,150 in fines collected in each of the 17 states, a substantial amount of fish and wildlife related revenue is being lost by wildlife agencies that are not authorized to keep fine receipts.

## Operation Game Thief

In an attempt to discover fish and wildlife violations that otherwise would go unreported, many fish and wildlife agencies have established "hotlines" for the purpose of receiving anonymous information on poachers. These programs, modeled after the "operation game thief" program initiated by New Mexico in 1977, have been especially helpful in uncovering poaching violations.*

---

* Poaching is the taking of fish or wildlife by illegal means, during closed season, or in excess of legal limits.

Studies conducted by several states have indicated that the numbers of game animals of certain species killed out of season equals or exceeds the number killed in season. For example, New Mexico's best estimate on out-of-season deer kills in 1975-76 was about 34,000, which approximates the annual legal take (Pursley 1977).* Such estimates are indicative of the large number of scofflaws afield.

One way to detect poaching violations is by providing incentives for observers or associates of the wildlife criminal to report the crime anonymously. New Mexico offers a standard minimum reward for information leading to arrest and convictions, of $150 for fish and small game violations and a maximum reward of $750 for big horn sheep poaching reports as the necessary inducement to make the hotline work.†

New Mexico officials say that 85 to 90 percent of all calls received reveal crimes that otherwise would have remained undetected. Of the total 965 infractions reported to date involving wildlife, the overwhelming number were

* The New Mexico deer season lasts two weeks; during the remaining 50 weeks, deer hunting is illegal. This estimate was based on a poacher simulation experiment conducted by the wildlife agency.
† Larger rewards may be paid for particularly flagrant violations.

### New Mexico Operation Game Thief Statistics June 1, 1977 Through July 31, 1985

| | | |
|---|---|---|
| *Reward Data* | | |
| | Rewards Paid | $77,825 |
| *Case Data* | | |
| | Total Calls | 1127 |
| | Cases Solved | 459 (40%) |
| | Citations or Arrests | 748 |
| | Conviction Rate | 98.1% |
| *Animals Involved* | | |
| | Antelope | 55 |
| | Bear | 12 |
| | Bighorn Sheep | 3 |
| | Bird (other than raptor & turkey) | 91 |
| | Bobcat | 3 |
| | Cougar | 8 |
| | Deer | 220 |
| | Elk | 90 |
| | Fish (approx.) | 442 |
| | Furbearer (other than bobcat) | 11 |
| | Turkey | 5 |
| | Raptor | 23 |
| | Reptile | 1 |
| | Miscellaneous | 1 |
| | Total | 965 |

Source: New Mexico Department of Game and Fish

fish violations (442) and deer poaching (220). Other frequent violations included those involving birds (91), elk (90), and raptors (23).

After eight years of operation, New Mexico rates its program highly successful for these reasons:

- It has substantially increased the apprehension of violators. Out of 1,127 calls received, 748 citations or arrests were made and 459 cases (40 percent) solved, and a conviction rate of 98.1 percent. Total rewards paid were $77,825, an average of $169 per solved case.
- It has instilled fear of apprehension among poachers and hence has value as a deterrent.
- It has increased respect for the wildlife agency among its wildlife-user constituency.

## Other State Poacher Reporting Programs

The Operation Game Thief concept has spread to 42 other states. Of the 43 existing programs, 32 offer rewards and 11 do not. Of the seven states without programs, five indicate an interest in commencing a poacher reporting program in the future (Breedlove 1985).

An analysis conducted by the Illinois Department of Conservation on the effectiveness of reward programs versus nonreward programs in 37 states shows that the average number of hotline-generated arrests in reward states is 152. In nonreward states, the average is 86. These results indicate that states that adopt a reward system could increase the number of hotline-generated arrests by as much as 76.7 percent (Breedlove 1985).

In the survey, 24 states with comparable data reported paying a total of $643,256 in rewards since the inception of their programs. The average annual amount of rewards paid per state was $8,121.*

All 32 states with reward systems were asked how offering a reward affected their poacher-reporting program. Twenty-five (78.1 percent) said it increased the quantity of calls received, 20 (62.5 percent) said it improved the quality of information received, and 17 (53.1 percent) said it increased the number of arrests made.†

The major problems associated with poacher-reporting programs are financing the reward payments and use of the hotline by the public to obtain

---

* A few private conservation organizations pay rewards for information leading to the conviction of those who illegally take certain species. The National Audubon Society pays rewards for information leading to the arrest and conviction of those who poach grizzly bear, whooping crane, California condor, woodland caribou, grey wolf, and bald eagle. The National Wildlife Federation also pays a reward for bald eagle-poaching information.

† Generally, only those states that started with a nonreward system and later moved to a reward system could offer objective opinions on arrest increases.

## State Poacher-Reporting Programs

| | Has Program | | No Program |
|---|---|---|---|
| | Rewards | No Rewards | |
| Alabama | | x | |
| Alaska | x | | |
| Arizona | x | | |
| Arkansas | x | | |
| California | x | | |
| Colorado | x | | |
| Connecticut | x | | |
| Delaware | x | | |
| Florida | x | | |
| Georgia | x | | |
| Hawaii | x | | |
| Idaho | x | | |
| Illinois | | x[a] | |
| Indiana | x | | |
| Iowa | x | | |
| Kansas | | x | |
| Kentucky | | x | |
| Louisiana | x | | |
| Maine | | x[a] | |
| Maryland | x | | |
| Massachusetts | x | | |
| Michigan | x | | |
| Minnesota | x | | |
| Mississippi | | | x[b] |
| Missouri | x | | |
| Montana | x | | |
| Nebraska | x | | |
| Nevada | x | | |
| New Hampshire | | | x |
| New Jersey | x | | |
| New Mexico | x | | |
| New York | | | x[b] |
| North Carolina | | x | |
| North Dakota | x | | |
| Ohio | x | | |
| Oklahoma | x | | |
| Oregon | | x[a] | |
| Pennsylvania | | x | |
| Rhode Island | | x | |
| South Carolina | x | | |
| South Dakota | x | | |
| Tennessee | | | x[b] |
| Texas | x | | |
| Utah | x | | |
| Vermont | | | x[b] |
| Virginia | | | x[b] |
| Washington | | x | |
| West Virginia | | | x |
| Wisconsin | | x | |
| Wyoming | x | | |

a = States interested in adding rewards to program.
b = States interested in initiating a program
Source: Breedlove (1985)

Assault Rate on State and Province Conservation Officers

|  | Number of Officers Surveyed | Assault Rate |
|---|---|---|
| 1981 | 6,516 | 2.22% |
| 1982 | 6,579 | 2.38% |
| 1983 | 6,122 | 2.70% |

Source: *The International Game Warden,* Summer, 1984.

general information. All of the 10 states experiencing problems with reward funding rely on voluntary private donations, in contrast to more secure sources of funding such as general-fund appropriations, license fees, fines, and other dedicated sources.

## Assaults

In issuing a citation or making an arrest, a conservation officer frequently must confront armed individuals in isolated areas. A survey of assaults in 1981, 1982, and 1983 conducted by the International Association of Fish and Wildlife Agencies showed that assailants who attacked conservation officers had weapons in 30 percent of all assaults. While studies indicate that police officers who are not wildlife-law enforcement personnel are eight times more likely to be assaulted, a conservation officer in the United States or Canada faces a weapon about twice as often when an assault occurs (Anonymus 1984).

A study of assaults on U.S. conservation officers conducted by Morse (1982) showed a national annual average of 2.9 assaults per 100 officers in three different years. Morse found a higher incidence of assaults in 10 western and midwestern states that gave officers the option of wearing a sidearm than he did in other states in those regions which required the wearing of firearms. In the West, the overall rates of assault for the three study years were 6.5 per 100 officers in optional-side arm states and 1.7 in mandatory-sidearm states. In the Midwest, the assault rate was 5.7 per 100 officers in optional states and 2.9 in mandatory states. Morse concluded that states with optional policies should drop them in favor of mandatory sidearm use.

Assault Rates per 100 Conservation Officers by Region in the United States

| Year | West | Midwest | Northeast | Southeast | Total |
|---|---|---|---|---|---|
| 1971 | 4.1 | 4 | 1.6 | 2.7 | 3.1 |
| 1975 | 2.2 | 3.9 | 2.5 | 2 | 2.6 |
| 1979 | 3.8 | 3.4 | 3.9 | 2.4 | 3.1 |
| Total | 3.3 | 3.8 | 2.6 | 2.3 | 2.9 |
| No. Officers | 3,592 | 3,883 | 2,873 | 6,890 | 17,238 |
| Assaults | 119 | 146 | 74 | 161 | 500 |

Source: Morse (1982), Wildlife Management Institute

## Officers Killed in Line of Duty

During the period October 21, 1984 to November 15, 1985, four state conservation officers were killed by assailants in the United States.

- In October, 1984, a man came to the home of Mississippi officer Jimmie Woods at 10 p.m. as Woods and his family prepared for bed. The man asked Woods to come out and talk with him. When Woods did so, he was killed from ambush with a shotgun. Woods' young daughter was looking out the window and recognized the assailant, as did Woods, and he was apprehended quickly.
- In November, 1984, Washington conservation officer Terry Hoffer and another officer were patrolling a timber-company road when they flagged down an approaching auto to check it. The auto stopped beyond the warden's car and as one officer got out, a shot rang out and Hoffer slumped at the wheel, dead. The car left the scene. Evidence later proved that the occupants were carrying a loaded rifle in violation of Washington state law and were hurriedly attempting to unload it before the warden could approach them. It went off in the process, accidentally killing Hoffer.
- In December, 1984, Florida officer Peggy Parks stopped a van to check it in an area where complaints had been received. She found a loaded pistol under the driver's feet. As she went to her radio to check out the driver, he attacked, knocked her to the ground, and killed her. The suspect was apprehended after someone came forward with information. The murderer was a paroled convict who would probably have lost parole had Parks been able to arrest him for carrying a loaded pistol.
- In January, 1985, school teacher Jim Vince of Alabama, who also served as a deputy warden for the Alabama Division of Game and Fish, was called by another Alabama warden to go check a report of illegal night hunters. They entered the field where the hunters were. When Vince called out to them that he was an officer, a hunter fired at him point blank with a shotgun and killed him. The hunters fled, but the shooter was later apprehended (Hastings 1985).

# Current Issues

## Public Indifference

The enforcement of laws regulating the take, possession, and sale of fish and wildlife has been an uphill struggle at both the state and federal level since the first such laws were passed. While this situation has improved gradually, the FWS chief of Law Enforcement in 1978 cited public apathy as a major problem. Such apathy, he said, is manifested by the enactment of poorly crafted and weak wildlife laws, inadequate budgets for state and federal conservation agencies, failure of hunters and fishermen to report observed violations, and light fines and sentences imposed by the courts for wildlife violations (Bavin 1978).

Exactly how bad the "indifference factor" is today is unclear. No attempt has been made to survey or otherwise assess the problem in systematic fashion either by FWS, the International Association of Fish and Wildlife Agencies, individual states, or university researchers. However, some wildlife professionals believe that at least in some states, apathy has diminished. With the increased attention given by the media to environmental matters—a trend that began with Earth Day in 1970—advances in wildlife protection have been made. These include:

- The creation of poacher hotlines in 43 states. A hotline, by guaranteeing anonymity to callers, can encourage citizens to report more wildlife crimes.
- The strengthening of state penalties for wildlife infractions. Tennessee and other states, for example, automatically revoke hunting privileges for certain infractions.
- Larger fines. In 1985, South Dakota enacted the following penalties for poachers: $10,000 for mountain goat and big horn sheep; $5,000 for elk and buffalo; $1,000 for deer and antelope (Wildlife Management Institute 1985).
- The reform of the federal Lacey Act in 1981. These reforms included expansion of the law's coverage to all wild animals and certain plants, making interstate trafficking in wildlife specimens "possessed" in violation to state or foreign law a crime, and increasing the maximum criminal fine assessed from $10,000 to $20,000 and the maximum jail sentence from one to five years. In addition, the act provides for a potential maximum civil penalty of $10,000.
- Tougher sentences. A poacher recently convicted in Montana by a federal court was sentenced to serve 15 years in jail.

Some states systematically are attacking the indifference problem. For example, the Colorado Division of Wildlife made recommendations to the state legislature for the simplification and updating of state fish and wildlife laws and simplified and rewrote its departmental regulations. In addition, the division launched an initiative to increase its rate of court convictions statewide from 65 to 90 percent. Many states actively publicize their wildlife-law enforcement efforts to gain public understanding and support.

## Dilution of Enforcement Programs

The primary mission of law enforcement is the protection of fish and wildlife resources, and the primary method for achieving this mission is the conduct of field patrols by uniformed conservation officers. Over the years, however, many other responsibilities have been assigned to state wildlife-enforcement

Types of Laws Enforced by Conservation Officers, 1984
Number of States with Authority

| Area | No. States | Fish | Game | Non-Game | Boat | For-est | Pollu-tion | Parks | Lit-ter | Vdl-ism | Snow-Mbl. | Off Road Vhcl. | Gun | Tres-pass | General Peace Officer Powers |
|------|-----------|------|------|----------|------|---------|------------|-------|---------|---------|-----------|----------------|-----|-----------|------------------------------|
| West | (14) | 14 | 14 | 13 | 8 | 5 | 10 | 5 | 13 | 9 | 6 | 9 | 10 | 10 | 8[2] |
| Midwest | (12) | 12 | 12 | 12 | 12 | 11 | 12 | 9 | 12 | 11 | 10 | 11 | 10 | 11 | 10[1] |
| Northeast | (12) | 12 | 12 | 12 | 12 | 11 | 12 | 9 | 12 | 11 | 10 | 10 | 11 | 11 | 9 |
| Southeast | (14) | 14 | 14 | 14 | 13 | 7 | 10 | 8 | 13 | 9 | 1 | 6 | 8 | 13 | 8 |
| Nationwide | (52) | 52 | 52 | 51 | 45 | 34 | 44 | 31 | 50 | 40 | 27 | 36 | 39 | 45 | 33 |
| 1980 | (47) | (48) | (48) | (48) | (43) | (27) | (40) | (27) | (47) | (38) | (24) | (29) | (35) | (39) | (29) |

[1] 3 of these have Peace Officer powers only under restricted conditions
[2] 1 of these emergency only
Source: Morse (1984), Wildlife Management Institute

624

programs. These include the enforcement of a variety of outdoor recreation and other natural-resource laws, the provision of public services unrelated to wildlife-law infractions, and the maintenance of law and order in general in accordance with the general police powers possessed by most state conservation officers.

In 1984, Morse found that a majority of fish and wildlife agencies have the authority to enforce boating, forest, pollution, parks, litter, vandalism, snowmobile, off-road vehicle, gun, and trespass laws. The estimated time spent enforcing these laws varies greatly from state to state.

According to Robert Brantly, executive director of Florida's Game and Fresh Water Fish Commission, state conservation officers spend a "high percentage" of time on public services that are not directly related to wildlife law enforcement. As examples of such services, Brantly cites the following:

- nuisance wildlife, from ducks eating golf greens to owls in the attic to alligators in the swimming pool;
- trespass, more often than not, unrelated to wildlife violations;
- policing of campsites, boat ramps, and other outdoor-use areas, a necessary function but not related to wildlife violations;
- requests for information on laws, public-use areas, wildlife biology, and a myriad of other subjects;
- speaking engagements before sportsmen's, civic, and other groups;
- settling of disputes among outdoor users in campgrounds and other areas some of which carry potential for violence;
- search and rescue, assistance to stranded sportsmen, recovery of lost or stolen property (Brantly 1984).

The danger in expanding the duties of the conservation officer beyond his traditional wildlife duties is that wildlife-resource protection could suffer unless the wildlife agency receives sufficient funding to execute adequately all of its responsibilities.

In 1975, states law-enforcement supervisors identified expanding work loads and insufficient budgets as their primary problem (Bavin 1978). While no comparable survey has been conducted recently, knowledgeable state officials believe that some states still are plagued by this problem. The Michigan law-enforcement staff, for example, has decreased from 255 field personnel in 1955 to 138 in 1985. Yet outdoor-recreation activity is estimated to have doubled in the state during this same period, according to a Michigan Natural Resource Department official.

## Planning and Record Keeping

Morse (1984) says that only a few states have comprehensive plans to guide their enforcement programs and that most states do not have good record-keeping systems. The lack of both of these important management tools reduces program efficiency and public support.

An enforcement plan is essential to ensure the proper allocation of enforcement activities to objectively identified protection priorities and to establish methods for measuring results. Computerized data-management systems are needed for two reasons. They enhance efficiency overall, provide the capability for evaluating the effectiveness of state law-enforcement efforts, and enable the states to track repeat offenders more easily. Equally important, a nationally standardized data system would allow states to share information needed in the pursuit of wildlife criminals operating in several states and would enable individual states to compare their enforcement achievements with those of others.

Morse notes that with wildlife law-enforcement programs spending $275 million yearly, it is time for state wildlife agencies to manage their enforcement activities with modern technology and management concepts. As yet, however, there appears to be no great movement in that direction.

## Commercialization of Wildlife

The illegal taking of fish and wildlife for commercial purposes has been a continuing problem ever since game protection laws were passed. In New Hampshire, for instance, deer meat fetches $1.50 to $4.00 per pound, a snowshoe hare $5 apiece, and moose meat up to $4.50 per pound. Even raccoons are being sold for the pot at $5 apiece. In addition, fur-bearing animals are being trapped illegally and their pelts sold to commercial fur dealers, hunting guides are helping clients bag big-game animals out of season, and rare species—many of them threatened or endangered—are being collected and sold because of their rarity or other value.

While all state wildlife agencies know that wildlife is being taken illegally for commercial purposes, few have a good understanding of the degree of commercial activity in their state or of its overall effect on state wildlife populations.* Furthermore, statistics on commercial violations are not aggregated and disseminated routinely by either FWS or state-wildlife-agency associations. Thus, state law-enforcement directors have no easy way of learning what types of violations may be occurring in other states or the value of the wildlife species involved. If such information were available, it could serve as a warning that the same species in their states also could be at risk.

Generally, most states have relied upon the FWS Division of Law Enforcement to pursue criminals engaging in the interstate trafficking of wildlife taken, transported, sold, or possessed in violation of state law. However, this

* In some states, wildlife officials believe that the illegal taking of wildlife for commercial purposes is not that significant a problem, especially for big-game species. In New Mexico, for example, "buddy hunting"—the practice of a skilled hunter exceeding his legal bag limit by killing animals for other individuals who have taken out licenses but do not actually hunt—is thought to have a much greater impact on species such as deer than does poaching for commercial reasons.

ignores the fact that many more commercial crimes are being committed than FWS can police adequately. According to FWS officials, the Division of Law Enforcement annually receives many more requests from states for assistance on wildlife violations than it can possibly fulfill.

Given what is known about commercial wildlife activity, said a federal official, all state law-enforcement programs could benefit by having under-cover-operations teams. Many states would like to establish undercover units, but have been unable to do so. In some instances, according to one state official, the state legislature is reluctant to authorize undercover operations for wildlife crimes because undercover work is viewed as giving an unfair, un-sportsmanlike advantage to the conservation officer. This attitude may coexist with the Depression-bred belief that poachers only take wildlife to eat or sup-port their families. Even in states that have undercover units, the enforcement agency may have to be careful as to how or who they investigate, in some cases ignoring infractions by people with political clout.

In other states the problem may be funding, lack of training in under-cover operations, or lack of interest or commitment in undercover work by wildlife-agency personnel. Undercover operations require extensive commit-ments of time, personnel and funding. Two to three years of work may be required to conclude investigations successfully that involve at most relatively few individuals. On the other hand, the impact of commercial violators may be great. Furthermore, an attitude of permissiveness toward commercial viola-tors breeds contempt of the law on the part of recreational hunters and fisher-men.

## Wildlife Forsenics

Wildlife forensics—the study of evidence to establish wildlife crimes—is still in its infancy (Sigler 1980). Although a significant amount of research has been done in this area, state wildlife forsenic work is at least 10 years behind that of police forensic laboratories, according to one federal official.* Some wildlife crimes are going unprosecuted because of the lack of techniques to identify conclusively wildlife parts or products.

Few wildlife agencies have their own forensics staff or laboratories.† Most rely on state police labs for analyses of evidence, but this can pose problems. Work on wildlife crimes is often the last priority of state labs. Fur-thermore, police labs may not have the staff with the specialized knowledge and skills required to analyze and identify wildlife parts and products.

* An excellent source of information on wildlife forensics is the "Blue Book," a publication of the Midwest Game and Fish Law Enforcement Officers. The book contains some 50 descriptions of forensic lab and field techniques, such as how to determine time of death in deer and waterfowl.
† States that have a full-time forensics staff or lab include California, Montana, Wyoming, Ne-braska, Alaska, and Missouri.

# References

Anonymous. "Will You Be Assaulted?" *The International Game Warden,* Summer 1984. p. 10.

Bavin, C.R. 1978. "Wildlife Law Enforcement," in *Wildlife and America.* U.S. Government Printing Office. Washington, D.C. p. 350.

Black, S.K. 1984. "Are We Overregulating the Sportsman?" *The International Game Warden,* Fall, 1984:1.

Brantly, R. 1984. "Law Enforcement: How Much is Enough?" *The International Game Warden,* Summer, 1984:12.

Breedlove, J. 1985. "Nationwide Poacher Reporting Program Survey, Analysis and Results." Department of Conservation, Division of Law Enforcement. Springfield, Illinois.

Colorado Department of Natural Resources, Division of Wildlife. 1984. Law Enforcement Annual Report. Denver, Colorado.

———. Undated. Law Enforcement Plan, 1981-1984. Denver, Colorado.

Germani, C. 1985. "Trapping Poachers Who Prey on Endangered Wildlife." *Endangered Species Technical Bulletin Reprint* 2:10 (August 1985): p. 1.

Hastings, D.L., Jr. 1985. Personal communication.

Morse, W.B. 1976. "Wildlife Law Enforcement, 1976." Unpublished manuscript. Wildlife Management Institute, Washington, D.C.

———. 1980. "Wildlife Law Enforcement, 1980." Unpublished manuscript. Wildlife Management Institute. Washington, D.C.

———. 1982. "Sidearms Policy and Assaults on Wildlife law enforcement officer." Unpublished manuscript. Wildlife Management Institute. Washington, D.C.

———. 1984. "Wildlife Law Enforcement, 1984." Unpublished manuscript. Wildlife Management Institute. Washington, D.C.

Pursley, D. 1977. "Minus X: The Poaching Factor." *New Mexico Wildlife.* March-April, 1977: p. 2

Sigler, W.F. 1980. *Wildlife Law Enforcement.* William C. Brown Company. Dubuque, Iowa. 430 pp.

U.S. Department of the Interior, Fish and Wildlife Service, Division of Law Enforcement. 1985. Personal communication.

Virginia Commission of Game and Inland Fisheries. 1985. "Annual Report, Law Enforcement Division." Richmond, Virginia.

Wildlife Management Institute. 1985. "South Dakota Gets Poacher's Attention." *Outdoor News Bulletin,* October 18, 1985.

World Wildlife Fund. Undated. News release: "New Efforts to Halt Wildlife Trade Announced."

*William J. Chandler is president of W. J. Chandler Associates, a Washington D.C. environmental policy and government relations consulting firm, and publisher of* Land Letter, *a newsletter for natural-resources professionals.*

An Oklahoma Department of Wildlife Conservation biologist builds an osprey
nesting-platform as part of the state's nongame program, funded by a state income
tax checkoff.

*Oklahoma Department of Wildlife Conservation*

# State Nongame Wildlife Programs

## Susan Cerulean
## and
## Whit Fosburgh

## Introduction

STATE FISH AND wildlife agencies traditionally have focused on species of economic or sport value, such as big game, small game, waterfowl, upland game birds, and furbearers. But as species and habitats began to disappear by the early 1900s, the realization grew that each organism is a part of a greater whole—of an interrelated web of soil, water, and vegetation.

Management and legislative emphasis slowly began to shift toward wildlife habitat protection in the early 1900s. In the 1930s, the first American Game Policy, formulated at the Wildlife Management Institute's 17th American Game Conference, formally acknowledged the need to protect habitat. Though primarily concerned with game species, it recognized that all wild creatures had social value and that the public interest favored the whole spectrum of the wild kingdom. Aldo Leopold spearheaded a movement toward more holistic wildlife management when he said, "The public, not the sportsman, owns the game. The public (and the sportsman) ought to be just as interested in conserving nongame species, forests, fish and other wildlife as in conserving game. In the long run, lop-sided programs dealing with game only, songbirds only, forests only, or fish only, will fail because they cost too much, use up too much energy in friction, and lack sufficient volume of support" (Wilson 1984).

The states have been slow to move away from this traditional interest in serving sportsmen, even though nongame species make up 80 to 90 percent of the nation's wildlife. Because of the states' failure to broaden the spectrum of their wildlife management objectives, the federal government has had to assume wider conservation responsibilities. This began early. In 1918, the federal government took control of the migratory bird management. Much more recently, the federal government has assumed management responsibility for marine mammals and endangered species (see the chapters in this volume on these subjects for a full account; see also the *Audubon Wildlife Report 1985*).

In the early 1970s, conservationists began to urge federal involvement in state nongame management. In 1973, the Committee on American Game Policy, led by wildlife biologist Durward Allen, clearly outlined the need to broaden the approach of traditional game regulation and management and made plain that the greatest value of the wildlife resource is its "nonconsumptive" use.

The Wildlife Management Institute issued a report in 1975 calling for a national act that would help fund state nongame programs. The recommendation became reality in 1980 when Congress passed the Fish and Wildlife Conservation Act (16 U.S.C.A. 2901 *et seq.*). The act authorized the annual appropriation of up to $5 million, to be distributed to the states as matching funds, but to date no money has been appropriated.

Meanwhile, the states began showing more initiative in launching programs that covered the full spectrum of wildlife. In 1977, the Colorado legislature established a check-off on the state's income tax returns through which residents could voluntarily support nongame wildlife management.* The check-off is now used by 31 states. The Pittman-Robertson Act (16 U.S.C.A. 669 *et seq.*) also provides funds that can be used for state nongame management, but these funds still are used primarily for game species.

Public interest in these progams is reflected by the fact that since 1967, 44 states have initiated programs to conserve and manage nongame species. (Missouri's program began in 1937, and Hawaii's in 1928). Activities include inventory, public education, research, management, planning and special programs for urban wildlife. Ninety-three million Americans (55 percent of the population 16 and older in 1980) actively participate in some form of nonconsumptive use of wildlife (Shaw and Mangun 1984). In a national survey, Kellert (1979, 1980a, 1980b) found that Americans consider wildlife an important part of their heritage.†

---

* Under the check-off system, state income tax forms provide a line where taxpayers can check off or write in the amount they wish to contribute to the state's nongame program. If a refund is due, the amount indicated will be subtracted from the total refund and funneled to the nongame fund.
† Kellert also found that more than 27 percent of the population more than nine years old took trips for the primary purpose of observing wildlife, 25 percent birdwatched, 78 percent viewed at least one wildlife-related television program, and 35 percent read books on wildlife. Dick and Hendee (1984) found that more than 90 percent of persons interviewed to determine human responses to encounters in urban parks said that wildlife encounters enhanced their visits to the parks.

But problems still hamper even the most well established programs. Few states have ongoing and reliable funding mechanisms. Nongame check-offs are being challenged by competing interests. Federal funds are becoming increasingly scarce. Many states have very fragmented wildlifemanagement programs, where game and nongame actually compete against each other. And finally, public knowledge of nongame wildlife remains limited. Consequently, demand for broader management has not yet been strong enough in many states to give nongame programs little more than token recognition within the wildlife agencies.

## Organization and Operations

The states have primary authority under the Constitution to regulate resident wildlife species. This regulation generally is accomplished through a state fish and wildlife agency or through a fish and wildlife division within a larger conservation agency. Nongame wildlife activities, usually placed within the state wildlife agency, are organized either as separate programs or are integrated with the game program.* Some states, including California, Missouri, Illinois, and Colorado, do not administratively separate nongame activities from other wildlife programs. Wildlife agencies in these states assume responsibility for the state's biological diversity as a whole, including game, nongame, and habitat. Often a natural history division of the agency performs a coordinating function for nongame wildlife and acts as a repository for data.

### Definition of Nongame

Each state defines "nongame wildlife" slightly differently in its statutes. Generally, any native, wild vertebrate animal not ordinarily taken for sport, fur, food and/or commercial purposes is considered nongame. The inclusion of invertebrates, plants and plant communities, and endangered species in the definition of nongame varies, however, from state to state. Several western states specifically exclude predators from their definition of nongame.

Of 38 state nongame programs that responded to a 1984 survey by Mashburn, 23 had statutory authority to conserve invertebrate species. With the exception of Illinois, however, no state has developed a thorough, systematic approach to invertebrate conservation. Seventeen have developed programs to address the needs of at least some invertebrate species. However, most of these efforts are minimal, probably because of the immensity of the task and the lack of public interest. The invertebrate taxonomic groups most frequently inventoried by nongame programs are mollusks and crustaceans.

---

* A similar split of authority often occurs over species of nongame wildlife and the management of the habitats upon which they depend. Authority to manage plants and plant communities often is vested in an entirely separate agency.

At least four states support work with butterflies, particularly federally threatened and endangered species. Nongame programs that include invertebrates commonly provide comments to the U.S. Fish and Wildlife Service (FWS) on species status, maintain contact with The Nature Conservancy Heritage Program staff, and occasionally make contracts with universities for survey work.

While 21 states have Section 6 agreements with FWS covering endangered plant species, only 11 nongame programs have management authority within their states for individual plant species. Very few programs protect or manage plant species other than those with threatened or endangered federal status. In at least 10 states, no agency has statutory authority for plant protection and management. In these states, often the only work that directly supports plant management is performed in university research programs.

## Program Goals

Preservation of wildlife diversity and abundance is claimed as a primary goal by nearly every state nongame program. State programs vary widely in the objectives and strategies they develop to work toward this comprehensive goal. Most programs use similar functional elements to achieve their ends, including research, inventory, education and information, habitat and species management, urban wildlife programs, land acquisition, wildlife rehabilitation, direct or indirect involvement with the state's endangered species program, and law enforcement.

## Functional Elements of State Nongame Programs

*Inventory:* Comprehensive inventory—finding out how many organisms of what kind live where—and subsequent periodic monitoring are probably the most important tasks of nongame programs. Inventories provide baseline data that enable biologists to identify research gaps, set objectives, and monitor progress toward objectives. Specifically, state nongame programs use inventories to ascertain species distribution and population abundance, habitat distribution and quality, species-habitat relationships, and rates of change in species and habitats. This information provides the basis for objective analysis of nongame status, management needs, and land-use decisions, and early recognition of species or communities in trouble.

The Illinois Natural History Survey is the premier of inventories. This 127-year-old program has financed statewide surveys of 20 taxonomic groups (mostly orders, classes, or families), including all classes of vertebrates, various

---

* Heritage programs are generally started by The Nature Conservancy, with the understanding that the program eventually will be taken over by the state. The program is essentially an inventory process; a data storage and retrieval system which enables the possessor to identify top conservation priority needs, including unique ecosystems, or rare and endangered species. The program is useful in impact analysis and guiding development away from sensitive ecological areas. Forty-two states have Nature Conservancy-developed heritage programs.

groups of insects, and other invertebrates. Because of its longevity, the survey has begun to repeat inventories on certain groups and document historical changes in distribution and abundance. Often it has identified the environmental factors that have led to adverse changes (Page 1984).

Most state nongame wildlife programs are much younger and less well endowed than the Illinois survey and therefore currently place their most intensive emphasis on endangered and threatened species and species of special concern. In particular, the minimally funded programs with only one or two biologists, as in Connecticut, Maine, Rhode Island, and North Dakota, have been able to inventory only the most seriously jeopardized species in their states.

In better established state programs with higher funding levels, avifauna often receive the most inventory attention, after species of special concern. Individual bird species occasionally are inventoried, while other efforts are directed toward wading bird rookeries, colonial nesting birds, shorebird concentrations, and raptors. A number of nongame programs assume some responsibility for developing a state breeding bird atlas, and several are involved in nest record card programs, both of which rely heavily on citizen volunteers. Many nongame program directors emphasize the importance of bird inventories because, in addition to their ecological significance, they have high visibility and public support.

Surveys and monitoring of mammals, reptiles, amphibians, and fish within the state nongame program still are performed infrequently. A few well-funded programs (Oregon, California, New Mexico, Texas, Missouri, Minnesota, Illinois, and Colorado) have done extensive work on these animals, especially the vertebrates. Invertebrate surveys, where conducted, primarily investigate crustaceans and mollusks.

Individual plant inventories sponsored by nongame programs are almost solely limited to status surveys of organisms proposed for federal listing as endangered or threatened species. Several states perform organized surveys of wildlife habitat, most often endangered plant communities or riparian and wetland habitats, as part of their nongame programs.

***Research.*** A number of states have developed research programs to support their nongame management and conservation activities. Twenty-four of 25 state nongame programs responding to a 1984 survey funded nongame and endangered species investigations during 1984-85. On the average, these states dedicated 25 percent of their research budgets to nongame wildlife and endangered species. Six states spent less than $10,000, 10 spent between $10,000 and $50,000, and five states allocated between $50,000 and $100,000. New York, Oregon, Virginia, and Washington spent between $150,000 and $200,000 on nongame research (Mashburn 1984). Florida's new nongame wildlife program has been directed by its advisory council to spend $600,000 annually of its $1.6 million budget on nongame research and grants.

State nongame research may be conducted by in-house staff or contracted to an outside entity, usually a university. Agencies responding to a 1984 survey generally stated that research is comparable in quality and more cost effective when performed outside the agency, provided that limited and specific objectives are agreed upon by both parties (Mashburn 1984).

Little data is available to compare total research expenditures on game and nongame at the national level. However, an overview by Stansell (1981) indicates that in the southeastern United States, the majority of endangered and nongame wildlife species receive little notice from the wildlife management research community. Less than 15 percent of all wildlife papers published in the Proceedings of the Southeastern Association of Fish and Wildlife Agencies for the past decade concerned nongame or endangered wildlife. Most of these papers covered only a few species, such as the American alligator, red-cockaded woodpecker, and loggerhead turtle. Endangered species, particularly birds and herptiles, received the majority of nongame research funds. Nongame birds are the next most studied, whereas nongame fishes, nonendangered herptiles, and mammals are decidedly neglected. Stansell (1981) also documented that state agencies lag behind universities and the federal government in addressing nongame management and research.

*Management.* The management of nongame wildlife presents a formidable challenge to wildlife agencies. Classic game management is based on an autecological approach that assures the prosperity of only one, or at most a few, species. A holistic or ecosystem approach is required to maintain a full complement of both game and nongame species, simply because there are far too many vertebrate species to allow for individual management. The management focus for a nongame wildlife program must shift to habitats or plant communities to protect the full spectrum of native fauna and flora.* Land acquisition, on-the-ground habitat manipulation, and reintroduction of extirpated species are some of the types of management that states employ to help nongame.

Protecting wildlife habitat by the outright purchase of land is the best possible insurance for wildlife perpetuation. According to a study by Carothers (1984), 16 states specifically acquired land for nongame projects. The average amount of land acquired per state was 9,093 acres. Western states acquired more land (nearly 20,000 acres total) than did states in any other region. Midwestern states reported the least amount of land acquisition (413 acres). However, habitat is being lost rapidly. Wetlands alone are disappearing at the rate of nearly a half-million acres yearly. Moreover, most state nongame programs are still so limited in funds that fee acquisition is not a realistic expecta-

---

* For example, the historical management of forests for wildlife has emphasized the creation of openings and a maximum of edge habitats to enhance productivity of plants and insects and thus of higher order game animals. Certain nongame species also thrive on edge habitats and forest openings. However, obligate forest-interior species of birds are decreasing in parts of North America where extensive forests are being replaced by isolated woodlands (Robbins 1984).

tion, except in the case of small acreage tracts that are of special nongame interest, such as a bat maternity cave.*

Simply protecting habitats and rendering them as natural as possible, thereby protecting as many species as possible, is a first step recommended by the Illinois Natural History Survey (Page 1984), The Nature Conservancy, and others. However, nongame biologists need research information to determine what constitutes a "natural" community and exactly what habitat manipulations should be performed to maintain it. This type of information is scarce.

*Education and Information.* Thirty-five states have educational programs dealing specifically with nongame species; 37 have programs focusing on endangered species (Carothers 1984). Distribution of literature to the public, presentations to organizations, and direct contact with individuals are the most important methods used. Teacher workshops were cited least often, but still viewed as important. Project WILD, a supplementary environmental education program emphasizing wildlife, is promoted by most state nongame programs to teach elementary and secondary school students.

In states with nongame tax return check-offs and other voluntary funding mechanisms, information and education staff spend a good deal of time in program promotion. Carothers (1984) found that 31 states use the media to promote their nongame programs, primarily television, newspapers, radio, and literature. Announcements appear as both community service announcements and paid advertisements. These states indicated that direct mail was the least effective way to reach, educate, and inform the public.

*Urban Wildlife.* State urban wildlife programs generally have two goals: (1) to improve city and suburban residents' understanding of and interaction with wildlife; and (2) to enhance and preserve the habitat of certain species that populate urban areas.† Species commonly thought of as game species, such as deer and squirrels, are considered nongame when in an urban environment. Fourteen states currently have urban wildlife programs within their nongame programs. But with the exception of a few states, such as New York and Missouri, urban wildlife programs tend to be very small and poorly funded. A survey conducted in 1983 found that even among states with established urban programs, funding usually comprises less than one percent of the state's total fish and wildlife budget (Lowell and Leedy 1984).

* Nongame programs can help other state land acquisition programs by providing inventory information about species and habitats on lands considered for purchase.

† Nearly 75 percent of all Americans lived in metropolitan areas in 1980 (U.S. Bureau of Census, 1980) and the attitudes, interests and concerns of the urban public are a dominant influence in American society (Lowell and Leedy 1984, Kellert 1979, Applegate 1973). Urban residents have a strong interest in wildlife. In 1980, a national survey found that 35 percent of all big-city residents and more than 50 percent of all small-city residents engaged in primary nonconsumptive wildlife-related recreation, such as observation, photography, and feeding. Overall, more than two-thirds of the participants in nonconsumptive wildlife-related recreation were urban residents (U.S. Fish and Wildlife Service 1982).

The Missouri Department of Conservation has developed an excellent prototype for urban wildlife programs. Its overall purpose is to heighten awareness, understanding, and appreciation for wildlife and habitat. Three primary objectives are to provide information regarding natural history topics to the general public; to assist landowners, both public and private, with habitat management; and to acquire significant habitats in or around metropolitan areas.

*Planning and Evaluation.* The federal Fish and Wildlife Coordination Act of 1980, also known as the Nongame Act, requires the states to prepare a comprehensive plan to qualify for federal funds for nongame species management.* FWS has sponsored the development of several model state plans to assist the states in qualifying for federal funds should they ever come available. Twelve states currently have a completed comprehensive plan or a modular nongame plan.

Minnesota's nongame planning effort is probably the most elaborate. The plan, currently being drafted, will include a summary of the current and prospective conditions of nongame species and their habitats; an analysis of the major issues involved in nongame resource management; and a determination of program goals and management actions for each issue.

Provision for public participation in the planning process is a special need of nongame programs. Public donations through check-offs and other voluntary mechanisms still provide the funding base for most nongame programs. In addition, the public represents a wildlife constituency new to most game and sport-fish oriented agencies. They potentially include wildlife rehabilitators, birdwatchers, schoolteachers, naturalists, sportsmen, and conservationists. Many nongame programs are directed in part by technical or citizens advisory boards to ensure public input. Since state funding mechanisms were established, however, there has not been a reciprocal commitment to nongame by the federal government (Jahn 1983). Instead, resource administrators have been forced by inflation and expanding legal responsibilities to spread their funding, research, and management efforts wider and thinner. Periodic license-fee increases have been inadequate to meet increasing public and legal demands for wildlife management.

# Funding

The states have developed a variety of funding sources to support their nongame programs. Voluntary income tax check-off systems, state sales taxes,

---

* Comprehensive planning can help young nongame programs address a particularly complex set of problems, including new funding mechanisms, complicated interlagency and intra-agency coordination, legal mandates to address many species, inadequate species and habitat data and management techniques, and new constituencies for traditionally game-oriented agencies

sales of personalized auto tags, a special tax on car registrations, and the establishment of endowment funds are the most common and successful means of funding state programs.

In FY 1985, 45 states allocated funds for nongame and endangered wildlife programs. Five states expended $1 million dollars: or more California ($9.3 million), Missouri ($2.5 million) Florida ($1.3 million—nongame only), Colorado ($1.2 million) and New York ($1 million). Twenty-three states spent $100,000 to $500,000 on nongame and endangered wildlife programs. Three states spent less than $50,000 (North Dakota, Rhode Island, and Delaware), and only Louisiana*, Mississippi, New Hampshire, and South Dakota spent no funds.

Thirty-one states currently have wildlife and wildlife-related income tax check-off programs. Taxpayers in these states donated some $8.96 million when they filed their 1983 state income tax returns. This figure represented a significant increase over the 1982 tax year, when a total of $6.525 million was raised in 20 states (McCance 1985), but is a slight decrease in the average amount of money raised per state.

Check-offs first appeared on tax forms in 1978 in Colorado. Oregon followed in 1980, and then Kansas, Kentucky, Utah, and Minnesota in 1981. Seven more states followed suit in 1982. In some states, the expenditure of nongame check-off funds is not limited to nongame programs. Delaware and Kentucky share revenues with administratively separate natural-areas programs, and Arkansas allocated funds to the best proposals from nongame, natural-areas, and parks programs. New York allows the use of funds for all forms of wildlife management, including game management.

In 1974, citizens of Washington decided by referendum to fund the state's nongame program through the voluntary purchase of personalized automobile license tags. The sale of auto tags raised $523,000 in 1983 and is projected to bring in more than $690,000 by 1987. California and Oregon also have raised money this way.

Illinois and Indiana are developing endowment funds that will accumulate money from existing sources, such as the check-off or general appropriation, until the fund reaches a certain level, at which time the program can be financed by interest from the endowment funds. North Carolina and Wisconsin also are considering endowment-fund development.

In 1976, voters in Missouri approved an initiative to raise the state sales tax by one-eighth of one percent. In 1984 alone, this source raised $48 million, which is used for a variety of projects within the Department of Conservation, including nongame. Washington state currently is considering a similar tax.

* In 1981, the Louisiana legislature passed a check-off that appeared on 1983 tax forms and raised $75,000 for the nongame program. Unfortunately, the legislature had not authorized the use of these funds by the nongame program. New wording has been passed by the legislature allowing the expenditure of these funds, and the state hopes to have a working nongame program by 1986-87.

1983 Tax Year Results

| | Check-off First Tax Year | Program Type | Number of Check-offs | # in 1000s Eligible | #Nongame Donors in 1000s | Participation Percentage | Average Donation | Nongame Income ($1000s) | Donation Rate $ |
|---|---|---|---|---|---|---|---|---|---|
| Alabama | 82 | R | 4 | 825.0 | 14.6 | 1.8 | 3.82 | 55.8 | .068 |
| Arizona | 82 | A | 2 | 1200.0 | 43.8 | 3.7 | 5.60 | 245.2 | .204 |
| Arkansas | 83 | A | 2 | 789.2 | 3.6 | 0.5 | 7.69 | 27.6 | .035 |
| California | 83 | A | 4 | 11000.0 | 109.2 | 1.0 | 4.68 | 511.0 | .046 |
| Colorado | 77 | R | 3 | 968.4 | 81.9 | 8.5 | 5.47 | 447.7 | .462 |
| Delaware | 83 | A | 1 | 286.7 | 9.4 | 3.3 | 8.98 | 84.8 | .296 |
| Idaho | 81 | A | 3 | 356.4 | 19.9 | 5.6 | 4.46 | 88.6 | .249 |
| Illinois | 83 | R | 3 | 2600.0 | 36.4 | 1.4 | 7.15 | 260.3 | .100 |
| Indiana | 82 | R | 1 | 1434.0 | 50.2 | 3.5 | 5.01 | 251.3 | .175 |
| Iowa | 82 | R | 1 | 600.0 | 40.0 | 6.7 | 5.50 | 220.0 | .367 |
| Kansas | 80 | A | 1 | 1306.2 | 20.5 | 1.6 | 6.62 | 135.9 | .104 |
| Kentucky | 80 | R | 1 | 850.5 | 11.3 | 1.3 | 7.99 | 90.4 | .106 |
| Louisiana + | 81 | | 1(?) | | | | | | |
| Maine | 83 | A | 1 | 460.0 | 24.5 | 5.3 | 4.54 | 111.0 | .241 |
| Massachusetts | 83 | R | 2 | 1849.0 | 101.7 | 5.5 | 3.75 | 381.3 | .206 |
| Michigan | 83 | A | 2 | 3934.0 | 79.7 | 2.0 | 3.36 | 267.9 | .068 |
| Minnesota | 80 | A | 1 | 1717.2 | 192.0 | 11.2 | 3.35 | 643.5 | .375 |
| Montana | 83 | R | 1 | 175.0 | 6.6 | 3.8 | 5.34 | 35.4 | .202 |
| New Jersey | 81 | A | 1 | 3000.0 | 109.0 | 3.6 | 4.27 | 465.8 | .155 |
| New Mexico | 81 | R | 1 | 460.0 | 30.6 | 6.7 | 8.32 | 255.1 | .555 |
| New York | 82 | A | 1 | 6800.0 | 345.4 | 5.1 | 4.93 | 1701.1 | .250 |
| N. Carolina | 83 | R | 1 | 1890.4 | 28.4 | 1.5 | 8.06 | 228.9 | .121 |
| Ohio | 83 | R | 2 | 2640.8 | 132.6 | 5.0 | 3.68 | 488.2 | .185 |
| Oklahoma | 82 | R | 1 | 703.9 | 28.5 | 4.0 | 6.16 | 175.6 | .249 |
| Oregon | 79 | R | 2 | 657.2 | 49.6 | 7.5 | 4.72 | 234.0 | .356 |
| Pennsylvania | 82 | R | 1 | 1508.0 | 107.1 | 7.1 | 3.69 | 395.8 | .263 |
| S. Carolina | 81 | A | 1 | 1211.2 | 33.1 | 2.7 | 4.81 | 158.9 | .131 |

| | | Program Type | No. of Check-offs | | | | | | |
|---|---|---|---|---|---|---|---|---|---|
| Utah | 80 | R | 1 | 308.2 | 33.7 | 10.9 | 4.88 | 164.2 | .533 |
| Virginia | 81 | R | 3 | 1750.0 | 56.3 | 3.2 | 7.92 | 446.2 | .255 |
| West VA* | 81 | R | 2 | 460.0 | 18.0 | 3.9 | 5.47 | 98.5 | .214 |
| Wisconsin | 83 | A | 1 | 2967.2 | 46.7 | 1.6 | 6.24 | 291.7 | .164 |
| TOTALS | 31 | | 51 | 54708.5 | 1864.3 | 3.4 | 4.81 | 8961.7 | .164 |
| MEDIAN | — | | — | 1084.2 | 35.1 | 3.7 | 4.97 | 231.5 | .203 |
| AVERAGE | — | | — | 1823.6 | 62.1 | 4.3 | 5.54 | 298.7 | .222 |

1. Program Type: A = All tax returns eligible to donate via the tax return.
   R = Refunds only are eligible to donate via the tax return.

2. Number of Check-offs: Number of taxpayers eligible to donate to the nongame check-off via the tax forms

2. Number of Check-offs: Number of separate check-offs which allow taxpayers to donate their money.

3. Number (in 1000s) Eligible: Number of taxpayers eligible to donate to the nongame check-off via the tax forms

4. Nongame Income ($1000s): Income obtained via the tax collection agency that has been donated to the check-off that includes the nongame program. This excludes funds donated directly to the nongame program and includes money that may not be available for nongame wildlife management. (DE & KY share income with natural area programs administered by another agency.)

5. Totals: Columns for participation percentage, average donation and donation rate are used to provide national averages.

6. Median: Average of the two middle numbers.

7. Average: Unweighted average of each column.

+ Louisiana data unavailable

*WV data current through June 84

| State | Check-off | Endow-ment Fund | General Fund | Dona-tion | ESA | PR-DJ | Other (Type) | (amount) | Total |
|---|---|---|---|---|---|---|---|---|---|
| ALABAMA | 55.8 | NA | NA | NA | NA | 7.0 | NA | NA | 62.8 |
| ALASKA | NA | NA | NA | NA | NA | NA | NA | NA | NA |
| ARIZONA | 290.0 | NA | NA | NA | 70.0 | 47.0 | License Sales | 56.0 | 463.0 |
| ARKANSAS | 27.0 | NA | 15.0 | NA | 60.0 | 62.0 | NA | NA | 164.0 |
| CALIFORNIA | 500.0* | NA | 6,000.0* | 205.0* | Together 1,500.0 | | Per. Lic. Plates | 1,100.0 | 9,305.0 |
| COLORADO | 691.6 | NA | NA | NA | 119.0 | 393.5 | 1984-85 Carryover | 7.5 | 1,211.6 |
| CONNECTICUT | NA | NA | 60.0 | NA | NA | NA | NA | NA | 60.0 |
| DELAWARE | 40.0 | NA | NA | NA | 10.0 | NA | License Sales, Land Rental | 5.0 | 45.0 |
| FLORIDA | NA | NA | NA | NA | 203.0 | NA | Auto Registra-tion | 1,300.0 | 1,503.0* |
| GEORGIA | NA | NA | NA | NA | 105.0 | 15.0 | NA | NA | 120.0 |
| HAWAII | NA | NA | NA | NA | NA | NA | NA | NA | NA |
| IDAHO | 91.8 | NA | NA | NA | 116.0 | NA | NA | NA | 207.8 |
| ILLINOIS | 390.0 | NA | 1,393.0 | NA | 17.0 | NA | NA | NA | 1,800.0 |
| INDIANA | 156.0 | NA | NA | NA | NA | NA | NA | NA | 156.0 |
| IOWA | 126.0 | NA | NA | NA | NA | NA | NA | NA | 126.0 |
| KANSAS | 150.0 | NA | NA | NA | NA | NA | License Sales | 35.0 | 185.0 |
| KENTUCKY | 74.1 | NA | NA | NA | NA | 35.0 | NA | NA | 109.1 |
| LOUISIANA | 75.0 | NA | NA | NA | NA | NA | NA | NA | 75.0 |
| MAINE | 110.0 | NA | NA | NA | 40.0 | NA | NA | NA | 150.0 |
| MARYLAND | NA | NA | NA | NA | 25.0 | 60.0 | License Sales; Sale of NG Stamp | 44.0 | 129.0 |
| MASSACHU-SETTS | 285.5 | NA | NA | 14.0 | 7.5 | NA | NA | NA | 307.0 |
| MICHIGAN | 400.0 | NA | NA | NA | 170.0 | NA | T-shirt, Patch, Print Sale Proceeds | 30.0 | 600.0 |
| MINNESOTA | 664.0 | NA | NA | 5.0 | 15.0 | NA | NA | NA | 684.0 |
| MISSISSIPPI | NA | NA | NA | NA | NA | NA | NA | NA | NA |
| MISSOURI | NA | NA | NA | NA | 22.0 | NA | Sales Tax | NA | 2,500.0 |
| MONTANA | 36.0 | NA | NA | NA | 139.5 | 17.0 | NA | NA | 192.5 |
| NEBRASKA | 112.5 | NA | 154.0 | NA | 10.0 | NA | NA | NA | 276.5 |

| State | Check-off | Endow-ment Fund | General Fund | Dona-tion | ESA | PR-DJ | Other (Type) | (amount) | Total |
|---|---|---|---|---|---|---|---|---|---|
| NEVADA | NA | NA | 58.0 | NA | 18.0 | 144.3 | NA | NA | 220.3 |
| NEW HAMPSHIRE | NA | NA | NA | NA | NA | NA | NA | NA | NA |
| NEW JERSEY | 415.0 | NA | NA | NA | 5.0 | NA | NA | NA | 420.0 |
| NEW MEXICO | 236.5 | NA | 76.2 | NA | 92.8 | 228.6 | NA | NA | 634.1 |
| NEW YORK | 700.0 | NA | NA | NA | 30.0 | 140.0 | License Sales | 130.0 | 1,000.0 |
| NORTH CAROLINA | 260.0 | NA | NA | NA | 40.0 | NA | NA | NA | 300.0 |
| NORTH DAKOTA | NA | NA | NA | NA | NA | 10.0 | License Sales | 30.0 | 40.0 |
| OHIO | 486.5 | NA | NA | NA | NA | NA | NA | NA | 486.5 |
| OKLAHOMA | 151.4 | NA | NA | NA | NA | NA | NA | NA | 151.4 |
| OREGON | 284.0 | NA | NA | NA | NA | NA | License Sales | 300.0 | 584.0 |
| PENNSYLVANIA | 395.8 | NA | NA | NA | NA | NA | NA | NA | NA |
| RHODE ISLAND | NA | NA | 4.0 | 6.5 | 1.6 | 31.0 | NA | NA | 43.1 |
| SOUTH CAROLINA | 248.0 | NA | 339.4 | NA | 120.0 | NA | NA | NA | 707.4* |
| SOUTH DAKOTA | NA | NA | NA | NA | NA | NA | NA | NA | NA |
| TENNESSEE | NA | NA | 100.0 | 12.5 | 23.5 | NA | License Sales | 114.0 | 250.0 |
| TEXAS | NA | NA | 173.0 | NA | NA | NA | NA | NA | 173.0 |
| UTAH | 200.0 | NA | 300.0 | NA | 200.0 | NA | NA | NA | 700.0 |
| VERMONT | NA | NA | NA | NA | NA | NA | NA | NA | NA |

NOTES                                                          (continued next page)

NA—Information not Available

*SC—South Carolina total includes Heritage Program

*Cal—C-O includes License sales.

   GF includes Law Enforcement for non-game WL and environmental profit review.

   PLP includes Natural Heritage program (approx 750.0)

   Don includes Donations, decal sales, and $ from use of Heritage data base.

*FLA—Nongame Budget is 1,300 million. Endangered species has separate budget.

NA = Information not available

Arizona = ESA money comes under Sec. 4 of the ESA.

California = Check-off figure includes money from license sales

   = Monies from the general fund are also used for law enforcement for nongame species and for environmental project review.

   = Donation includes direct donations, decal sales, and money derived from allowing others access to the Heritage data base.

   = PLP monies also support the Natural Heritage Program, which has an estimated operating budget of $750,000.

Florida = 1,300,000 is the operating budget for the Florida nongame program. ESA money goes to the endangered species program.

South Carolina = total includes Heritage Program.

Virginia = Numbers are for FY1984-85. PR money includes ESA.

All numbers are bases on a state by state telephone survey. Most numbers are approximations.

FY—1985-86 Nongame and Endangered Species Budgets ($1000)—continued .

| State | Check-off | Endow-ment Fund | General Fund | Dona-tion | ESA | PR-DJ | Other (Type) | (amount) | Total |
|---|---|---|---|---|---|---|---|---|---|
| VIRGINIA | 480.0 | NA | NA | NA | NA | 228.2* | NA | NA | 702.2 |
| WASHINGTON | NA | NA | NA | NA | 40.0 | NA | Person-alized License Plates | 700.0 | 740.0 |
| WEST VIRGINIA | 78.0 | NA | NA | 1.7 | 35.0 | NA | NA | NA | 114.7 |
| WISCONSIN | 291.7 | NA | NA | NA | NA | NA | NA | NA | NA |
| WYOMING | NA | NA | NA | NA | 45.0 | NA | License Sales | 626.3 | 671.3 |

Maryland and Texas are attempting to raise funds for their nongame programs through the sale of nongame wildlife prints and stamps, modeled after the federal duck stamp. No results have been reported from Texas yet, but in its first year in Maryland (1984), the stamp raised only about $4,000, largely because of a lack of publicity.

Florida finances its program with a tax on vehicles registered in that state for the first time. With more than 5,000 people moving to Florida each week, the first year's receipts have generated nearly $20,000 more per month than anticipated. The first 10 months already have yielded in excess of $1.9 million. Florida also has added a provision for voluntary contributions to the Nongame Wildlife Trust Fund by encouraging all residents to add $1 to their fee when they renew their annual vehicle registrations.

# State Profiles

This section looks at the nongame programs of three states—Colorado, Florida, and New York. These successful nongame programs represent different appoaches to different challenges. Colorado was the first state with a tax check-off and is now attempting to integrate its program into a new management scheme that combines game and nongame. Florida's nongame program is among the nation's newest, but is also the fastest growing. New York receives more money from its check-off program than any other state, but authority for the different aspects of nongame management is dispersed throughout different divisions.

## Colorado

The rise of state nongame wildlife management in the past decade began in 1977 when the Colorado legislature passed the first tax check-off for wildlife.

Today, Colorado continues to be an innovator in nongame management. While the successes and public support of the Colorado nongame program have been great since its inception, in 1984 the state shifted the structure of its wildlife and fisheries management program to encompass all wildlife, aiming for an approach in which ecosystems are managed without favoring one species over another. While wildlife experts agree that this approach is ecologically superior, some have questioned whether in practice nongame species will receive the same attention that they have received over the past decade. A more important concern for Colorado's wildlife managers is funding, which remains separate for game and nongame and, in the case of nongame, has declined in recent years. Officials see this trend continuing as federal dollars become scarcer because of the drive to reduce the budget deficit.

Colorado officially began its nongame program in 1972, when the state legislature appropriated enough money to hire one biologist specifically for nongame species. The following year, spurred by the passage of the federal Endangered Species Act, the state passed its own Nongame, Endangered and Threatened Species Conservation Act. The legislature used this authority to allocate $86,000 to hire a full-time mammalogist and ornitholigist in 1974. The first major endeavor undertaken by the staff was a survey of Colorado's wildlife and fishes.

In 1977, the program took a giant step forward. Insufficient funding was limiting the program to survey work on a few endangered species, such as the peregrine falcon, for which the state could receive federal dollars. A nongame advisory council, made up of local conservationists, put forward the proposal that a check-off be included on the state income tax return form, and that all donations would go to the nongame program. The check-off allows residents to donate any amount they choose, either from their refund or from the total tax bill.

The check-off proved an immediate success. In 1978, the first year it appeared on Colorado's tax form, residents donated $350,000. The amount increased to $501,405 the next year, $647,200 in 1980, and reached a high of $740,700 in 1981. The amount then declined to $692,000 in 1982, and in 1983 the sum was $552,449. In 1984, the program raised $458,758, and in 1985, $397,533. In total, the check-off has raised more than $4 million.

The 1985-86 budget for Colorado's nongame program is approximately $1.2 million. Of this, about $690,000 is from the state's nongame cash fund, which is derived from check-off revenues; $119,000 is provided by the federal government under Section 6 of the Endangered Species Act; and the remaining $393,000 is provided from the state's allocation under the Dingell-Johnson Act and the Pittman-Robertson Act.

States which derive a substantial portion of their nongame funding from public donation, such as the check-off, must carefully balance their projects between those with high visibility and public interest, which are more likely to generate continued public support and financial backing, and other less glamorous projects that may be more important ecologically.

| State | Non-game Program | Year Initia-ted | Funding Source (Year Initiated) | T & E Species | T & E Plants | Urban Wildlife | Heritage Prog. or Equiv-alent | Comprehen-sive/ Modu-lar NF Plan | Notes |
|---|---|---|---|---|---|---|---|---|---|
| ALABAMA | yes | 1982 | Check-off (1982) | no | no | no | yes | no | |
| ALASKA | yes | 1981 | General Funds | yes | no | no | no | no | |
| ARIZONA | yes | 1967 | Checkoff (1982) | yes | UR | no | yes | Dev. | |
| ARKANSAS | yes | 1977 | Checkoff (1983), ESA | yes | UR | yes | yes | no | |
| CALIFORNIA | yes | 1968 | C-O (1983), PLPs, ESA | yes | yes | no | yes | yes | |
| COLORADO | yes | 1972 | C-O (1977) | yes | yes | yes | yes | yes | |
| CONNECTICUT | yes | 1973 | GF | yes | yes | no | yes | Dev. | |
| DELAWARE | yes | 1977 | C-O (1983) | yes | yes | yes | yes | Dev. | |
| FLORIDA | yes | 1983 | Auto Reg (1983) | yes | no | yes | yes | Dev. | |
| GEORGIA | yes | 1974 | ESA; PR; CO (1979) | yes | yes | no | yes | no | |
| HAWAII | yes | 1928 | License Fees | yes | yes | | no | no | |
| IDAHO | yes | 1982 | C-O (1981) | yes | no | no | yes | yes | |
| ILLINOIS | yes | 1972 | C-O (83); E-F | yes | no | no | yes | Dev. | |
| INDIANA | yes | 1973 | C-O (1982) | UR | no | no | yes | Dev. | |
| IOWA | yes | 1976 | C-O (82); | yes | UR | yes | yes | no | |
| KANSAS | yes | 1975 | C-O ('80); | yes | no | yes | no | yes | |
| KENTUCKY | yes | 1980 | C-O ('80) | yes | UR | no | yes | no | |
| LOUISIANA | no | — | C-O (1981) | no | no | no | yes | no | |
| MAINE | yes | 1975 | C-O (1983) | yes | yes | no | yes | yes | |
| MARYLAND | yes | 1973 | License Fees; PR; ESA | yes | no | yes | yes | yes | |

| State | Non-game Pro-gram | Year Initia-ted | Funding Source (Year Initiated) | T & E Species | T & E Plants | Urban Wildlife | Heritage Prog. or Equiv-alent | Comprehen-sive/ Modu-lar NF Plan | Notes |
|---|---|---|---|---|---|---|---|---|---|
| MASSACHU-SETTS | yes | 1977 | C-O (1983) | yes | UR | no | yes | no | |
| MICHIGAN | yes | 1978 | C-O (1983) | yes | yes | no | yes | Dev. | |
| MINNESOTA | yes | 1977 | C-O (1980) | yes | yes | no | yes | no | |
| MISSISSIPPI | no | — | C-O (1985) | yes | UR | no | yes | no | |
| MISSOURI | yes | 1937 | Sales Tax; | yes | no | yes | yes | yes | |
| MONTANA | yes | 1974 | C-O (1983) | yes | no | no | yes | yes | |
| NEBRASKA | yes | 1971 | C-O (1984) | yes | no | yes | no | no | |
| NEVADA | yes | 1973 | PR; GF; ESA | yes | yes | no | no | Dev. | |
| NEW HAMPSHIRE | no | — | — | yes | no | no | yes | no | |
| NEW JERSEY | yes | 1973 | C-O (1981) | yes | yes | no | yes | Dev. | |
| NEW MEXICO | yes | 1974 | C-O (1981) | yes | yes | no | yes | yes | |
| NEW YORK | yes | ? | C-O (1982) | yes | yes | yes | yes | no | |
| NORTH CAROLINA | yes | 1983 | C-O (1983); ESA | yes | yes | yes | yes | no | |
| NORTH DAKOTA | yes | 1975 | License Fees; | yes | no | no | yes | no | |
| OHIO | Yes | 1974 | C-O (1983); | UR | yes | yes | yes | no | |
| OKLAHOMA | yes | 1983 | C-O (1982) | UR | no | no | yes | no | |
| OREGON | yes | 1971 | License Sales; C-O (79) | no | yes | no | yes | Dev. | |
| PENNSYLVANIA | yes | | C-O (1982) | yes | no* | | yes | no | |
| RHODE ISLAND | yes | 1973 | PR; Don; GF | yes | yes | no | yes | no | |

| State | Non-game Program | Year Initiated | Funding Source (Year Initiated) | T & E Species | T & E Plants | Urban Wildlife | Heritage Prog. or Equivalent | Comprehensive/Modular NF Plan | Notes |
|---|---|---|---|---|---|---|---|---|---|
| SOUTH CAROLINA | yes | 1976 | C-O (81) | yes | yes | no | yes | no | |
| SOUTH DAKOTA | no | — | — | yes | UR | no | yes | no | |
| TENNESSEE | yes | 1970 | GF, License Sales | yes | UR | yes | yes | Dev. | |
| TEXAS | yes | 1970 | General Fund | no | no | no | yes | no | |
| UTAH | yes | 1975 | C-O (1980) | yes | no | yes | yes | no | |
| VERMONT | no | — | — | no | no | no | yes | no | |
| VIRGINIA | yes | 1982 | C-O (1981) | yes | yes | no | yes | no | |
| WASHINGTON | yes | 1971 | Personalized License Plates ('73) | yes | yes | yes | yes | yes | |
| WEST VIRGINIA | yes | 1981 | C-O (1981) | yes | no | no | yes | Dev. | |
| WISCONSIN | yes | 1978 | C-O (1983); EF | yes | yes | | yes | yes | |
| WYOMING | yes | 1977 | License Fees | yes | no | no | yes | yes | |

NOTES
UR—Under Review
Dev.—Comprehensive or Modular nongame plan currently being developed.
PLP—Personalized license plate sale receipts
GF—General Fund
C-O—Check-off
EF—Endowment Fund
PR—Pitman-Robertson Federal Aid
DJ—Dingell-Johnson Federal Aid
ESA—Sec. 6 Funding from Engandgered Species Act
Funding Sources:
    C-O = check-off
    PLP = sale of personalized license plates
    ESA = funds from Section 6 of the Endangered Species Act

Colorado is no exception. Among the highly publicized projects under-way is the reintroduction of river otters. The river otter was thought to have been extirpated from Colorado in the 1920s as a result of water pollution from mining activities and over-trapping. One of the first projects to be undertaken by the fledgling nongame program in the late 1970s was an ambitious plan to reintroduce the otter to many of the remote rivers in the state. The project was described in various articles in the Colorado Division of Wildlife's magazine, *Colorado Outdoors*, and in local newspapers. Work under the nongame program also permitted the delisting of the white pelican in 1985, a species previously state listed as threatened. Breeding pairs of white pelicans have increased from only 260 a decade ago to some 1,000 today. Also, more peregrine falcons are breeding in Colorado than at any time since the species declined in the 1960s from exposure to DDT. In 1972, no peregrines were breeding in Colorado. In 1985, 13 pairs nested. Work on the threatened greenback cutthroat trout may result in its delisting in five to seven years.

The biological successes and public acceptance of nongame projects such as the river otter reintroduction have allowed biologists to pursue other less glamorous projects. One is preserving the threatened wood frog; another is a cooperative effort with FWS to stem the decline of Colorado River fishes such as the Colorado squawfish and the humpback chub.

By the early 1980s, there was a growing realization within the Colorado Division of Wildlife that the structural organization of the department was artificial at best. Game and nongame were separate programs, with separate personnel, locations, and responsibilities. But clearly a game-nongame distinc-tion does not exist in the wild. A wetland created specifically for ducks and geese also may be used by great blue herons. Though the sage grouse is a game species, it is becoming increasingly popular with nonconsumptive users who enjoy observing the bird's elaborate courtship displays. In fact, several wildlife projects in Colorado that are funded by nongame and game dollars are aimed at benefiting a variety of species. In 1982, the division acquired several hundred acres of valuable marsh habitat in the south-central portion of the state. This parcel of land, bought with check-off and game-cash funds, benefits not only nesting shorebirds, such as herons and ibises, but also pro-

GF = state general fund appropriation
License fees = revenues generated from the sale of hunting and fishing licenses
PR = Pittman-Robertson federal aid.
Don = direct donation (does not include check-off money)
Sales Tax = in Missouri, 1/8 of one percent of the sales tax goes to conservation programs
Threatened and Endangered Wildlife and Plants:
Yes = State has a Sec. 6 agreement with FWS
No = State does NOT have Sec. 6 agreement.
UR = Sec. 6 agreement currently under review within the FWS
Comprehensive or Modular Nongame Plan
Yes = Comprehensive Plan or modular nongame plan completed and approved by the FWS
Dev = Plan currently being developed by the state.

vides an area for duck hunting. Currently, game and nongame funds are being used to conserve wildlife-rich riparian ecosystems.

In 1984, James Ruch was hired as director of the Division of Wildlife, and his first task was to reorganize the division. The nongame and game programs were replaced by aquatic and terrestrial programs, within which there are aquatic and terrestrial nongame supervisors who oversee operations statewide. At the field level, there is no delineation between game and nongame personnel. There was no reduction in personnel, merely shifts of responsibility within the division. Initially, many nongame supporters feared that nongame would be swallowed up and dominated by game interests, a fear that is prevalent in most states. But Colorado officials claimed that the new organization would allow a more effective and efficient use of personnel and dollars. However, the funding mechanisms for nongame remained separate, allowing the public to donate specifically to nongame.

Nonetheless, the biggest problem facing nongame in Colorado today is funding. The legislation that authorizes the use of license-sale proceeds for game-species management also prohibits the use of any of these funds for nongame management. Moreover, the decline in check-off monies from $747,000 in 1981 to $398,000 in 1985, is a direct result of two competing check-offs that appeared during these years, one for victims of domestic abuse, the other supporting the U.S. Olympic team. The nongame check-off, while receiving fewer dollars each year, still funds more than 50 percent of the nongame program. This funding source, however, will expire January 1, 1988, if not reauthorized by the Colorado legislature. In addition, there is a very real possibility that Section 6 funds will be reduced greatly, and possibly halted altogether, because of the passage of the Gramm-Rudman-Hollings deficit reduction bill and because of Reagan-administration attempts to cut all funding from the program. Though Pittman-Robertson and Dingell-Johnson funds are derived from a federal excise tax, and thus theoretically exempt from the budget cuts, many fear that the Office of Management and Budget will try to impound these funds. New funding sources for nongame work currently are being explored, but no new avenues have been tested.

## Florida

Prior to 1983, Florida had no formal nongame wildlife program, but in less than three years the state's annual nongame budget has grown to exceed $1.3 million, showing what innovation can do in the absence of traditional funding sources. The challenge for Florida now is to put the dollars into a cohesive program, that will keep pace with rapidly expanding population and development pressures.

In 1983, in response to an appeal by conservationists and state biologists, the Florida legislature passed the Nongame Wildlife Act and created the state's Nongame Wildlife Advisory Council. In the absence of a state income tax, no check-off could be used as a funding mechanism, so an alternative had to be found. Both California and Washington have generated significant revenues through the sale of pensonalized license plates, but Florida opted to try a slightly different approach. Since more than 5,000 people enter Florida each week to become residents, a $4 increase was established on the tax for registering cars in Florida that previously were registered in another state. The proceeds of this tax go to the nongame program. The tax was seen as noncontroversial, and it related logically to the harm done to wildlife by habitat loss due to rapid development. In addition, the registration form allows any resident to voluntarily contribute an extra $1 to the Nongame Wildlife Trust Fund.

The fee began in October 1984 and was an immediate success. In the first 10 months of the tax, nearly $2 million was raised. The trust fund now has $1.5 million in it, 96 percent of it from the registration fee.

One of the first projects undertaken by the nongame program was to fund research studies to develop management information and techniques for nongame species. This work was conducted by Game and Fresh Water Fish Commission biologists and by outside contractors. Through FY 1985, 20 research projects have been funded, and several more are scheduled for the upcoming year. Projects include books on the natural ecosystems of Florida and Florida's birds; guides to the state's mammals and butterflies; studies on the Schaus' swallowtail butterfly, marine turtles, cavity-nesting birds, the diamondback rattlesnake, gopher tortoise, sailfin mollie, red-headed woodpecker, wading birds, and the bald eagle; development of a nongame wildlife habitat management demonstration area; and investigations of Florida's scrub and carnivorous plant communities. The program spent $285,000 on these research projects in FY 1985 and in the future plans to increase this amount to $600,000 yearly.

Other aspects of the Florida nongame program include establishment of a comprehensive survey and monitoring system for nongame wildlife and expanding the urban wildlife program. A nongame and endangered species newsletter, *The Skimmer,* currently is circulated to approximately 7,000 people, and posters, coloring books, news releases, and Project WILD are all used to educate and inform the public about nongame wildlife.

The nine-member Nongame Wildlife Advisory Council, appointed by the governor, recommended the current organization of the nongame program. In addition, the council sets priorities and long-term and short-term goals for the program.

Nongame personnel are housed in three divisions of the Game and Fresh Water Fish Commission: the Division of Wildlife; the Office of Environmental Services, which is responsible for habitat preservation; and the Office of Information. More than that of any other state, Florida's nongame program is in a phase of tremendous growth. During FY 1985, the program added 15 new staff positions, bringing the staff total to 21. Of these 21, 11 are located in regional offices and the remaining 10 in the central office in Tallahassee.

Unlike the Colorado program, funding the Florida nongame program does not have a problem. The auto registration fee is an abundant and stable funding source. Instead, the challenge is the effectiveness of the dollars. The task faced by nongame personnel is enormous. Some 1,200 species can be found in the state, each affected to some degree by rapid development. Nongame personnel are seeking the public involvement necessary to ease the inevitable conflicts that will occur with development interests.

## New York

New York's nongame program began in 1976 when the state's first endangered species unit was formed. In 1982, the state legislature passed the "Return A Gift To Wildlife" tax contribution program to fund all fish and wildlife management. For the 1983 tax year, the program raised some $1.7 million (Minnesota's check-off raised the second greatest amount of any state, $644,000). But despite its relatively large financial base, the New York program must combat public attitudes that long have been very game oriented. Moreover, the program has limited concern for plants and invertebrates, which are managed primarily by other agencies within the state.

In New York's Department of Environmental Conservation, the nongame program is located within the Division of Wildlife. The Division's Wildlife Species Section has five program areas: big game, upland game and waterfowl, furbearers, endangered species, and nongame. The endangered species program employs five biologists in its central office in Delmar, New York, and the nongame program employs two people there plus one additional endangered species technician located on Long Island. Both programs employ additional seasonal personnel. Field personnel do both game and nongame work.

Public input is sought in determining projects for which check-off revenues should be used. Some 110 projects were reviewed in 1985 by a citizens' advisory council and a departmental review committee, from which 39 were chosen for funding. Projects solely funded by the check-off are separate from the regular endangered species and nongame budgets. The following is a partial list of projects funded solely through the check-off:

peregrine falcon restoration
colonial waterbird management
common loon study
harbor heron project
breeding bird atlas surveys
breeding bird atlas publication
marine-wildlife strandings program

tern warden program
tern and plover survey
hawk banding station
natural heritage program
urban ranger training
eagle education tour

Approximately $1 million was spent in FY 1985 on nongame and endangered species in New York. Of this, $450,000 comes solely from the contributions for approved nongame projects. In addition to these projects, the contribution program partially funds the operations and budgeted projects of the endangered species and nongame programs. The endangered species and nongame programs have a combined budget of about $550,000, of which $250,000 comes from contribution revenues, $140,000 from Pittman-Robertson federal aid funds, $130,000 from the state's regular conservation fund (made up of the proceeds from hunting-license sales), and the final $30,000 from Section 6, Endangered Species Act federal funds.

Unlike those of many other states, the program in New York supports both the game and nongame projects, as does the regular conservation fund. The state is beginning to increase its efforts to promote the nongame program. Paid radio spots promoting the contributions program have been aired on several stations. The Department of Environmental Conservation official publication, *The Conservationist,* has put special emphasis on the program. Certain projects, such as a bluebird nest box program and the loon project, have been publicized widely and have generated stong public support. While popular projects have helped to publicize the nongame program, some conservationists fear that other, more important projects are not receiving the needed support. For several years, a proposal has been submitted for a statewide reptile, amphibian, and mammal survey, but the project has yet to be funded.

Invertebrates and plants represent another problem. Although the nongame program has the authority necessary for managing invertebrates and plants, these programs lie mostly in other departments. Plants are primarily the responsibility of the Division of Lands and Forests and the Natural Heritage Program, although some endangered plant work is done through the endangered species program. Invertebrates traditionally have been the responsibility of the New York State Museum, but generally the museum's work has focused on taxonomic collection. Some work is being done by the endangered species program on endangered butterflies and on the Chittenango ovate amber snail. Such organizational separation makes effective management difficult. At present, no major organizational changes are planned.

## Current Issues

### Funding

At both the state and federal levels, nongame wildlife programs are grossly underfunded. With little hope at present of federal funding for the Fish and Wildlife Conservation Act, shrinking Section 6 funds, and attacks on Pittman-Robertson and Dingell-Johnson funds under the Reagan administration, nongame wildlife program administrators need to continue the search for recurrent, equitable, and stable sources of funds.

Income tax check-off programs now are threatened by their own success. By 1983, 21 check-offs, in addition to nongame programs, had been added to state tax forms. The rapid growth in the number of competing check-offs is considerable cause for concern to nongame wildlife program administrators. On the 1984 tax forms, three states added alternative check-offs for the first time, and other states have approved additional check-offs (McCance 1985). Additional check-offs added to tax forms are having significant and negative impacts on nongame contributions. In a 1985 study, Harpman and Reuler postulated that an additional check-off on a state's tax form will result in a 70 percent decline in the average donation to the nongame program. For example, Oregon revenues dropped from $360,000 in 1981 to $220,000 by 1983, almost a 40 percent decline in two years, as two new check-offs appeared on the state's tax forms. Harpman and Reuler suggest that although the check-off vehicle has been quite successful in the short run, it cannot be counted on as an ideal mechanism for stable, long-term funding of nongame wildlife programs because of competing causes, inequitability, and economic inefficiency.

## Adequacy of Goals and Objectives

Nongame wildlife programs usually cite preservation of wildlife diversity and abundance as their primary goal. Two pitfalls commonly encountered by these programs are:

(a) Too much emphasis on "glamour" species. This is a real danger involved in a close relationship between endangered species and nongame programs. Endangered species often are higher profile, glamour species. They also require enormously expensive rescue attempts that can devour a joint program budget. This problem underscores the need to have an effective nongame program that will properly manage all species and prevent them from becoming threatened. Some states have been criticized for spending their time and money on other nonendangered glamour species, as bluebirds. But nongame managers are quick to respond that such projects are necessary to keep the nongame program noticed and the public interested. Most programs are dependent on public donations for their funding, and "glamour" projects bring in far more than they cost.

(b) Closely related to the problems mentioned above, research and inventory are not exciting programs in the mind of the public, but both are essential for an effective nongame program. Both are done over long periods of time and require a substantial financial commitment. Without sufficient funds for research and inventory, a nongame wildlife program cannot make informed decisions regarding management priorities and resource allocations.

## Integration of Game and Nongame Conservation

The most far-sighted wildlife administrators view nongame programs as an opportunity finally to develop comprehensive conservation measures for all wildlife. If this is to come to pass, wildlife habitat needs far more consideration than it currently receives. Wildlife-habitat inventory and management should in fact be the basis of a comprehensive wildlife-protection program. Ideally, game and nongame wildlife will receive even-handed consideration, and their management will be integrated into one habitat-based program.

Although integration is the ideal, in practice the goals of nongame wildlife and traditional game-management programs at times conflict. For example, many southeastern states have managed intensively for popular but nonnative feral hog populations. Although the species is of domestic origin, it has assumed an important status among many hunters, and game agencies have responded with wild hog management programs. However, nongame biologists and other ecologists have shown the devastating impacts of hogs on ground-nesting bird populations, the soil substrate, and many species of rare and endangered plants.

# References

Applegate, J.E. 1978. "Wildlife management—1980 and beyond—what and for whom?" *Proceedings of the International Association of Fish and Wildlife Agencies* 68:27-36.

Bean, M.J. 1977. *The Evolution of National Wildlife Law.* Council on Environmental Quality. U.S. Government Printing Office. Washington, D.C.

Carothers, K. 1984. M.S. thesis in preparation.

Dick, R.E. and J.C. Hendee. 1984. Human responses to encounters with wildlife in urban parks. Unpublished manuscript.

Galli, J. 1984. "Planning for the management of nongame wildlife in Minnesota," in *Proceedings of the Workshop on Management of Nongame Species and Ecological Communities. Lexington, Kentucky.*

Harpman, D.A. and Reuler, C.F. 1985. "Economic aspects of the nongame checkoff." *Nongame Newsletter* 3:5.

Jahn, L.R. 1983. Philosophy of nongame fish and wildlife management. Presented at the workshop on a nongame fish and wildlife program for Florida, November 16-17. Tallahassee, Florida.

Kasowski, K. 1986. "Backing off the check-off." *Outdoor America* 51, No. 1 (Winter 1986).

Kellert, S.R. 1979. *Public Attitudes Toward Critical Wildlife and Natural Habitat Issues. Phase I.* Department of the Interior. U.S. Fish and Wildlife Service. Washington, D.C.

Kellert, S.R. 1980a. *Activities of the American Public Relating to Animals. Phase II.* Department of the Interior. U.S. Fish and Wildlife Service, Washington, D.C.

Kellert, S.R. 1980. *Knowledge, Affection and Basic Attitudes Toward Animals in American Society. Phase III.* Department of the Interior. U.S. Fish and Wildlife Service. Washington, D.C.

Lyons, J.R. and D.L. Leedy. 1984. The status of urban wildlife programs. Presented at 49th North American Wildlife and Natural Resources Conference, March 23-28. Boston, Massachusetts.

McCance B. 1985. "Nongame checkoffs raise $9 million in 1984." *Nongame Newletter* 3:5.

McConnell, C.A. 1984. "The national status of nongame programs," in *Proceedings of the Workshop on Management of Nongame Species and Ecological Communities*. Lexington, Kentucky.

Mashburn, S.I. 1984. Florida's nongame wildlife program: inventory, monitoring and project research. A report to the Nature Conservancy. Tallahassee, Florida.

Murphy, J.R. 1978. "Management considerations for some western hawks." *Transactions of the 43rd North American Wildlife and Natural Resource Conference.*

Page, L. 1984. "Research applicable to the management of nongame species: examples from the Illinois Natural History Survey," in *Proceedings of the Workshop on Management of Nongame Species and Ecological Communities*. Lexington, Kentucky.

Robbins, C.S. 1984. "Management to conserve forest ecosystems," in *Proceedings of the Workshop on Management of Nongame Species and Ecological Communities*. Lexington, Kentucky.

Scott, J. 1984. "A bright future for nongame wildlife." *Colorado Outdoors* 33, No. 2 (March-April, 1984).

Stansell, K.B. 1981. "An overview of nongame and endangered species management research in the southeast," *in* R.R. Odum and J.W. Guthrie eds., *Proceedings of the Nongame and Endangered Wildlife Symposium*. Athens, Georgia.

Train, R.E. 1978. "Who owns America's wildlife?" *in* H.P. Brokaw ed., *Wildlife and America*. Council on Environmental Quality. U.S. Government Printing Office. Washington, D.C.

U.S. Department of the Interior, Fish and Wildlife Service and U.S. Department of Commerce, Bureau of the Census. 1982. *1980 National Survey of Fishing, Hunting, and Wildlife-Associated Recreation*. U.S. Government Printing Office. Washington, D.C.

Wildlife Management Institute. 1975. Current investments, projected needs and potential new sources of income for nongame fish and wildlife programs in the United States. Washington, D.C.

Wilson, J.H. 1984. "Nongame conservation: a state responsibility," in *Proceedings of the Workshop on Management of Nongame Species and Ecological Communities*. Lexington, Kentucky.

Zwank, P.J. 1984. "The role of the U.S. Fish and Wildlife Service in Nongame Management," in *Proceedings of the Workshop on Managment of Nongame Species and Ecological Communities*. Lexington, Kentucky.

*Susan Mashburn Cerulean, a biologist who works for the Florida Fresh Water Fish and Game Department as planner of the state nongame program, organized the initial effort to create the nongame program and wrote Florida's Nongame Wildlife Act of 1983 while working for Florida Defenders of the Environment.*

*Whit Fosburgh is on the National Audubon Society's Washington D.C. staff.*

# PART 4

# Wildlife Report

A whooping crane forages at Aransas National Wildlife Refuge, the Texas wintering ground for the cranes, which now number some 170 birds in two flocks.

*Philip Boyer/Photo Researchers*

# The Whooping Crane

## James C. Lewis

U.S. Fish and Wildlife Service

## Species Description and Natural History

WHOOPING CRANES (*Grus americana*), the tallest birds in North America, stand as much as five feet high and have a seven-foot wing span. Their common name comes from the sound of their call. Males weigh as much as 16 pounds and females 14 pounds.

The chick's down is a cinnamon or sayal brown along the crown, neck, and back, and a lighter cinnamon below. At hatching the chick's bill is flesh-pink and the legs pinkish or gray-brown (Erickson and Derrickson 1981). By four to five weeks of age, the down is being replaced with a reddish cinnamon or rusty brown plumage that subsequently is replaced by white feathers. By the time it fledges at the age of three months, the young chick (colt) has a mottled appearance due to the mixture of white and rusty brown feathers. The young bird is predominantly white by its first spring.

Yearlings are similar to adults by their second summer and have the characteristic dark crown. By then the typical feathers are absent from the crown, cheeks, and lores and only scattered black bristlelike feathers remain over granulated skin that is crimson or scarlet. A wedge-shaped patch of black feathers covers the nape just behind the crown. The adult bill is olive-gray to light yellow, and the legs and feet are gray-black. Adult plumage is snowy white, except for the black wing tips, which include the primaries and their

659

greater coverts, and the back of the nape. The black feathers are visible only when the wings are extended.

## Range and Migration

Whooping cranes exist in two wild populations and in captivity at three locations. The only self-sustaining wild flock, comprised of 96 birds in winter, 1986, nests in Wood Buffalo National Park and winters on the central Gulf Coast of Texas at Aransas National Wildlife Refuge, Matagorda Island, and adjacent areas. The second wild group, the Rocky Mountain population, which numbers 30 to 35 birds, was started as an experiment in 1975 in an effort to accelerate recovery and ensure survival of the species in the wild if a natural or environmental catastrophe extirpated the Wood Buffalo National Park/Aransas National Wildlife Refuge population.

This second flock was started at Grays Lake National Wildlife Refuge, a 22,000-acre high-altitude marsh near Wayan in southeastern Idaho. The site was selected because it is in the historical whooping crane nesting range, contains ideal crane habitat, and supports the densest nesting population of sandhill cranes in the United States. Moreover, sandhill crane nesting success is high there, and the nesting chronology is similar to that of the whooper's nesting ground at Wood Buffalo National Park, Canada (Drewien and Bizeau 1977).

The 2,600-mile migration route of the Wood Buffalo/Aransas population extends south-southeastward across Alberta, Saskatchewan, the northeast corner of Montana, the Dakotas, Nebraska, Kansas, Oklahoma, and east-central Texas. The southward migration begins in late September and continues into mid-November. The birds migrate as singles, family groups, or small flocks. They do not migrate simultaneously and it requires six to eight weeks before the entire population arrives on the Texas Coast. The first migrants are the nonbreeders and unsuccessful breeders. Family groups migrate later.

Whooping cranes often spend two to four weeks in southern Saskatchewan, feeding in grain fields before continuing their journey. Flight altitudes average 1,000 to 2,000 feet, but whooping cranes have been observed up to 6,500 feet (Stehn 1985). One radio-tagged young and its parents, followed in their southward migration, traveled 2,403 miles in 31 days, moving southward in 17 days and resting 14 days. Their flight speeds averaged 29 miles per hour.

Individual birds or flocks require several weeks to more than a month to complete migration. One day of migration by a group or individual bird may involve flying 100 to 500 miles at airspeeds of 20 to 44 miles per hour, resting overnight, and feeding before another similar movement. In other instances, a flock may stay at one site a week or more before continuing migration.

The Wood Buffalo/Aransas population winters in the estuarine marshes, shallow bays, and tidal flats of the Texas Gulf Coast. Typical vegetation includes salt grass, saltwort, glasswort, sea oxeye, and cordgrass (Walkinshaw 1973).

Spring migration begins in late-March or early April and most birds are at the nesting grounds by mid-May. Adult pairs begin arriving in late April, and they use the same nesting territory they occupied in previous years. Young of the previous year apparently separate from the parents after arrival at the nesting grounds (Kuyt pers. comm.). Nonbreeders arrive at least a week after the breeders and spend the summer associating with one another between the Sass and Klewi rivers in Wood Buffalo National Park (Kuyt 1979).

The Rocky Mountain population migrates about 750 miles from its summering grounds in southern Idaho and western Wyoming southeasterly across northeastern Utah and Colorado and into the Rio Grande Valley of New Mexico (Drewien and Bizeau 1974, 1981). Most of this flock winters in the Valley between 10 and 100 miles south of Albuquerque, but a few birds continue into Chihuahua, Mexico. Southward migration begins in mid-September, and birds begin arriving in the Rio Grande Valley in early November.

The principal winter area for the Rocky Mountain population is the 57,000-acre Bosque del Apache National Wildlife Refuge, located about 100 miles south of Albuquerque, New Mexico. Crane habitat there is within the bottomlands of the Rio Grande, including 1,300 acres of wetland and 1,500 acres of agricultural crops, principally corn but including wheat, milo, and alfalfa.

The Rocky Mountain population spends two to four weeks each fall and spring in the San Luis Valley of south-central Colorado. During this interval they rest and feed in favored habitats before completing the remainder of their migration. Northward migration from New Mexico begins in early February and terminates at the summer grounds in early May.

## Breeding

The Canadian nesting grounds are large, shallow marsh complexes intermixed with boreal forest (Allen 1956, Novakowski 1966). Ponds, lakes, and bogs form a patchwork within the marshes. Vegetation includes pine, white spruce, birch, trembling aspen, and balsam poplar on the ridges, and swamp birch, willow, alder, bog shrubs, and aquatic plants in wetter sites.

Whooping cranes, with a lifespan in the wild estimated at 22 to 24 years (Binkley and Miller 1980, Kuyt and Goossen 1986) and in captivity at 35 to 40 years, are monogamous, pairing for life. However, they do remate following the death of a mate.

Sexual maturity in some males has been reached at age three to four years, but as an average the first fertile eggs are produced at age 5.4 years (Kuyt and Goossen 1986). Birds appear to select their mates on the wintering grounds, (Bishop 1984) during the time when flocks of subadult or unmated adults associate together, or enroute to the nesting ground. Dancing behavior is most characteristic of courtship activities in winter and spring, but may be seen at any time of the year. During the dance, male and female face one another, leaping and bowing, wings outspread, in one of nature's graceful, beautiful ballets.

The mated pairs returning to Canada use the same nesting territory each year. Fidelity to a nest site where they have nested successfully before helps to ensure that each pair will have an adequate food supply and nesting and escape cover. A pair constructs a new nest each year, but usually locates it near the nest used the previous year. A nesting area repeatedly used by a pair over several years is called a "composite nesting area." These range in size from 0.4 to 18 square miles (Kuyt 1981a).

The composite nesting area includes the area used by the pair from initiation of nesting until the fledging of the young. Nests are constructed of bulrush, less often of sedges, and rarely cattail, found adjacent to the nest site. Nest sites are marshes, sloughs, or lake margins. Nests vary in size. One large nest was five feet by seven feet across and five to six inches high (Walkinshaw 1973). Nests usually are constructed in shallow water (10 inches, Kuyt 1981a). Whooping cranes typically lay two eggs, light-brown or olive buff with purplish-brown blotches. A single egg is uncommon, and three eggs are rare. Eggs measure about 2.5 inches by four inches. The pair will renest if the first clutch is destroyed before mid-incubation (Kuyt pers. comm.).

The pair shares incubation and chick-rearing duties, but females tend to incubate at night and take the primary role in feeding and caring for young. Incubation begins in late April or early May and requires 29 to 31 days.

Although two eggs are produced, pairs infrequently fledge two chicks. Several theories have been proposed to explain this phenomenon. Novakowski (1966) suggested that although two fertile eggs are laid, usually only one is hatched. A second theory is that the oldest chick attacks and kills the younger in the first days after hatching when the size differential between the rapidly growing young is substantial. A third hypothesis is that the older chick competes with the younger for food from the parents and the smaller chick becomes the more vulnerable to predators, disease, or malnutrition. According to the third hypothesis, pairs would fledge both chicks only in years when environmental conditions are optimum, food is abundant so both chicks get an adequate amount, and water depths are sufficient to minimize predation.

Incubation begins with the laying of the first egg. Consequently, the second egg, laid about a day later, hatches proportionately later. Hatching success has averaged 79 percent (Kuyt 1981b). The precocial chicks leave the nest and follow the parents within a few hours after hatching. Parents and young remain near the nest site for the first few days. Gradually, as the chicks become stronger, parents and chicks move greater distances daily. Chicks are brooded by the parents at night and during bad weather. Daily movements average a half mile in the first three weeks of life.

Most chick mortality occurs in the first two weeks of life, and those alive at the end of July have a strong likelihood of surviving the migration flight to Texas. Chick survival is lower during drought years when feeding conditions are not optimum and the flightless chicks are more accessible to terrestrial predators, such as wolves. Young can fly when 80 to 90 days old.

## Diet

Cranes are omnivorous. Summer foods include frogs, minnows, berries, and large nymphal or larval forms of insects. In winter, cranes at Aransas also feed on acorns, insects, berries, and occasionally grains, but major winter foods are found in estuarine habitats and include blue crabs, clams, marine worms, amphibians, crayfish, fish, snails, insects, and sedge tubers.

The Rocky Mountain population probably has a summer diet very similar to the population in Canada, feeding on amphibans, reptiles, insects, crayfish, mollusks, fish, and vegetation. Feeding behavior, and the more terrestrial habitat use of this population, are learned from the foster-parent sandhill cranes. During migration and on the winter grounds, a large part of the whoopers diet is the corn, barley, and wheat left on the ground after grainfields are mechanically harvested.

## Roosting

Whooping cranes generally stand (roost) overnight in shallow water about five to eight inches deep. During migration, most roosts in the Great Plains are on wetlands of less than 2.5 acres located within 0.6 mile of a suitable feeding site (Howe 1986). Water roosts provide nighttime security from nocturnal predators such as coyotes.

## Territoriality

Whooping cranes on the nesting ground defend territories of 0.4 to 18 square miles. Paired birds and families at Aransas National Wildlife Refuge also defend a winter territory. These average 289 acres (Stehn and Johnson 1986). On the winter grounds in the vicinity of Aransas refuge, the cranes use 37 percent of the available marshland. At Wood Buffalo National Park, the whooping cranes nest within 1,467 square miles (8.5 percent) (Kuyt and Goossen 1986) of the 17,300 square-mile park (Allen 1956). Thus, ample nesting and winter habitat seems available for expansion of the Wood Buffalo/Aransas crane population in the foreseeable future.

Whooping cranes in the Rocky Mountain population also defend a territory on their summer grounds. Several adult males have established territories at Grays Lake National Wildlife Refuge and displaced sandhill cranes from these areas. In 1984 and 1985, whoopers exhibiting pairing behavior at Grays Lake National Wildlife Refuge also defended a territory. Sandhill cranes do not defend a winter territory and are more gregarious in their winter behavior than are whooping cranes in Texas. We do not know if successful whooping crane pairs will establish and defend winter territories in New Mexico like their counterparts in Texas. The New Mexico whooping cranes may mimic the more gregarious behavior of their foster parents.

## Significance of the Species

There are many reasons for protecting endangered species, and all apply to the whooping crane. To individuals interested in birds, the whooper's beauty, uniqueness, and existence are sufficient justification for preservation efforts. Among persons of Jewish, Christian, and some other faiths, being a good steward of the things God created, of our natural resources, includes conservation and protection of all organisms. Scientists point out that stable ecosystems are those with a wide diversity of species. Species diversity, then, is an ecologically sound goal. Every species probably is of some value to those neighboring species that share its environment, even if mankind is unable to clearly identify that value.

The whooping crane is one of the endangered species that has a known significant economic value. Only recently have economists developed techniques to measure the value of unique natural resources that have significant nonmarket values. J.R. Stoll and his student, L.A. Johnson (Johnson 1983), used contingent evaluation, in which values are based on individuals willingness-to-pay in a hypothetical situation, as one such technique. The economic valuation includes, then, assessing both the market and nonmarket benefits accruing to each person.

The whooping crane's value was estimated through a mail survey of Texas and out-of-state metropolitan residents and a survey of visitors to Aransas National Wildlife Refuge. "Results showed a mean use value of $4.47 and a combined option price and existence value of $16.33 for visitors to the refuge. The mail surveys produced responses of $7.84 for Texas residents and $7.13 for residents of other states. Estimates on the value of the whooping crane in the United States had upper and lower bounds of $573 million and $1.58 billion" (Johnson 1983). Option value is the amount a potential resource user would be willing to pay to ensure a future opportunity to use (view) the cranes. Existence value is the altruistic willingness of an individual to pay to ensure that the resource continues to exist for use by others or for the intrinsic right of the resource to exist.

Wild whooping cranes are observed most readily at two sites in North America—at Aransas National Wildlife Refuge near Rockport, Texas, and at Bosque del Apache National Wildife Refuge near San Antonio, New Mexico. Whooping cranes are present from November to early April at Aransas and from November to early February at Bosque del Apache. These are the months when public visitation to these refuges is high, and most visitors say they came primarily to see whooping cranes. Annual visitation at Aransas in 1984 was 67,000 people and at Bosque del Apache 77,300. Aransas visitation included some 1,000 visitors from 33 foreign countries. The foreign visitors are primarily avid birders who wish to add whooping cranes to the list of birds they have seen.

At Aransas, visitors can drive along a tour route, and whooping cranes usually are visible from a viewing tower accessible even to the handicapped. Greater numbers of whooping cranes can be viewed from the Intracoastal Waterway, and daily commercial boat trips are available from the Rockport, Texas, area to view these whooping cranes. At Bosque del Apache the cranes are viewed by the public along a 15-mile tour route. These birds usually are seen feeding in refuge grainfields, but occasionally at impoundments where they roost and feed early and late in the day.

Whooping crane nesting grounds are isolated and free of the contaminants that characterize environments altered by man. At Aransas, however, the cranes are valuable as an indicator of environmental conditions. In the aquatic habitats at Aransas, the whoopers eat animals, such as blue crabs, crayfish, and clams, that filter out and accumulate contaminants from the water and sediment they ingest. These contaminants become more concentrated in the whoopers' tissues because the cranes are at the top of the food chain. This type of bio-accumulation means the whoopers act as sentinels for environmental contaminants. They could be the first organisms to show the detrimental effects of contaminants along the Gulf Intracoastal Waterway, used daily by barges hauling a variety of chemicals potentially fatal to aquatic wildlife.

## Historical Perspective

Cranes as a group appeared in the Eocene epoch, 40 to 60 million years ago (Walkinshaw 1973). The whooping crane first appeared in fossil records from the early Pleistocene (Allen 1952) and probably was most abundant during that two-million-year epoch. They once occurred from the Arctic Sea to the high plateau of central Mexico, and from Utah east to New Jersey, South Carolina, and Florida (Allen 1952, Nesbitt 1981). In the 19th century, the principal breeding range extended from central Illinois northwest through northern Iowa, western Minnesota, northeastern North Dakota, southern Manitoba, and Saskatchewan to the vicinity of Edmonton, Alberta. A nonmigratory breeding population still existed in southwestern Louisiana in the early 1900s (Allen 1952).

Allen (1952) described several historical migration routes. One of the most important led from the principal nesting grounds in Iowa, Illinois, Minnesota, North Dakota, and Manitoba to coastal Louisiana. Another went from Texas and the Rio Grande Delta region of Mexico northward to nesting grounds in North Dakota and the Canadian Provinces. A minor migration route, last used before 1857, crossed the Appalachians to the Atlantic Coast. These birds apparently nested in the Hudson Bay area of Canada. A route through west Texas into Mexico probably followed the route still used by sandhill cranes. These whooping cranes wintered in the interior tablelands of western Texas and the high plateau of central Mexico.

The only migration routes in existence today are those described earlier from Northwest Territories, Canada, to the central Gulf Coast of Texas and from the northern Rocky Mountains to New Mexico. The tall-grass prairies of southwestern Louisiana were thought by Allen (1952) to be the whooping crane's principal historical wintering range. Similar prairies also occurred along the Texas Gulf Coast and in northeastern Mexico near the Rio Grande Delta.

The crane disappeared from its principal breeding range in the United States by the 1890s (Whooping Crane Recovery Team 1986). The last known nesting by the nonmigratory flock in Louisiana occurred in 1939. This flock was reduced from 13 to six birds following a severe storm in 1940, and the last surviving member was captured in 1948. The last known nesting in southern Canada was at Muddy Lake, Saskatchewan, in 1922. The only breeding population to survive was that in Northwest Territories, at Wood Buffalo National Park, principally along headwaters of the Sass and Klewi Rivers. This site is so isolated that it was not discovered until 1954, following nine years of intensive searching.

Through use of two independent techniques of population estimation, Banks (1978) derived estimates of 500 to 700 whooping cranes in 1870. By 1941, the migratory population contained only 16 individuals. The whooping crane population decline in the 19th and early 20th century was a consequence of hunting and specimen collection, human disturbance, and conversion of the primary nesting habitat to hay, pastureland, and grain production.

Allen (1952) tabulated data on 389 whooping cranes that died between 1722 and 1948. The heaviest losses occurred between 1880 and 1919. Most of these known losses were birds shot by hunters or specimen collectors. Hahn (1963) reported 309 mounts and nine skeletons in museums throughout the world. Many such specimens lacked data that presumably would be recorded by museum collectors, suggesting the specimens were more frequently collected by nonprofessionals and later donated to museums.

Shooting of this large, white bird undoubtedly did not cease immediately after the Migratory Bird Treaty Act between the United States and Great

Britain (Canada) was signed in 1916. This act protected whooping cranes and other migratory birds. The decline in reported kill was gradual (Allen 1952) as state and federal enforcement became more effective and as education efforts made the public more aware of the whooping crane's precarious population status. The known losses to shooting declined sharply at the turn of the 20th century. The last known loss to shooting was an adult female mistaken for a snow goose near Aransas National Wildlife Refuge in January 1968. A sub-adult male, that died of other causes in New Mexico in 1984, had three shotgun pellets in his body. Such evidence of continued shooting at these birds is uncommon, suggesting it happens infrequently.

Habitat destruction is another major factor thought to have caused the whooping crane's population decline. The conversion of prairie and associated wetlands to agricultural activities in the 1800s in the United States, and slightly later in Canada's prairie provinces, eliminated the principal breeding habitat. Drainage of wetlands, burning of nesting cover, fencing, and conversion of prairie to croplands eliminated sites for feeding, nesting, and roosting. Grazing by livestock eliminated habitat for insects used as food, destroyed nesting cover, and may have diminished some plant species used as crane foods. Trampling by livestock may have destroyed nests and nesting cover, eggs, and chicks, as has occurred in sandhill crane nesting habitat in Idaho. Trampling and fouling of shallow waters may have diminished the numbers of aquatic foods used by whooping cranes. Settlement of the whoopers' primary nesting areas by man assured the drastic population decline.

Agricultural activities, along with other disturbances related to man's presence, sounded the species' death knell across much of the breeding habitat. The isolation of the Wood Buffalo National Park breeding site, and the fact that it remained unknown until 1954, is probably the most important factor that permitted the species to survive. A large white bird on a marsh or prairie is quite visible. As people settled in the primary nesting areas, the birds probably found it progressively more difficult to feed, court, or nest without being disturbed by approaching humans. For the wary whooping crane, which seems to prefer solitude and isolation from man, such disturbances probably led to abandonment of some nesting areas.

Several key events helped halt the whooper's sharp population decline and started its recovery. The Migratory Bird Treaty Act of 1916 already has been mentioned. Wood Buffalo National Park was established by the Canadian government in 1922 for preservation of wood bison. This park assured protection of the only island of nesting habitat that survived to the mid-20th century. After the nesting whooping cranes were discovered in 1954, access, economic exploitation, and aerial activity in that portion of the park were restricted further.

In 1937, Aransas National Wildlife Refuge was established to protect the whooping crane and other wildlife of coastal Texas. This action protected the principal remaining winter-use area of the Wood Buffalo flock. Annual winter aerial surveys by the U.S. Fish and Wildlife Service (FWS), begun in the winter of 1938-39, documented the precarious status of the species. The National Audubon Society, Canadian Wildlife Service, and FWS began a cooperative project to publicize the birds' plight and initiate a study of these birds. The extensive publicity campaign provided a much needed new element of protection along the migration route as the public became aware of the bird's identity and status.

Robert Allen became leader of the cooperative research project in 1946, and his work culminated in his informative monograph on the species in 1952 and his later description of the nesting grounds (Allen 1956). Allen's (1952) monograph described the bird's natural history and stimulated further public interest in preservation efforts.

The establishment of other national wildlife refuges and state management areas in the United States, although not done primarily for whooping cranes, provided protected stopping areas along the migration pathway. Foremost among these are Washita National Wildlife Refuge (established in 1961) and Salt Plains National Wildlife Refuge (1930) in Oklahoma, and Quivira National Wildlife Refuge (1955), Kirwin National Wildlife Refuge (1956), and Cheyenne Bottoms State Waterfowl Management Area in Kansas.

The Endangered Species Act, passed by Congress in 1973, added to the degree of protection already given to whooping cranes. In 1978 the Fish and Wildlife Service, functioning within Section 7 of the Endangered Species Act, declared critical habitat for whooping cranes in Colorado, Idaho, Kansas, Nebraska, New Mexico, Oklahoma, and Texas. Critical habitat is defined as an air, land, or water area which, if destroyed or degraded, would appreciably decrease the likelihood of survival and recovery of a listed species or a segment of its population. This critical habitat designation means that actions authorized, funded, or carried out by the federal government must not jeopardize the species or destroy or modify its habitat.

The critical habitat involved the principal areas used by the Rocky Mountain and Wood Buffalo/Aransas populations in the United States in winter, summer, and during migration. The specific areas are Aransas, Alamosa/Monte Vista, Grays Lake, Kirwin, Quivira, Bosque del Apache, and Salt Plains national wildlife refuges, Cheyenne Bottoms State Waterfowl Management Area, and the Platte River bottomlands between Lexington and Denman, Nebraska. Without such protection it is very likely most of the Platte River water would be diverted for upstream irrigation uses, leaving the riverbed almost dry and choked with vegetation in the area previously used by cranes. Critical habitat also includes the Gulf Intracoastal Waterway and allows closer regulation of dredging and other activities that could harm the cranes wintering area.

As noted previously, whooping cranes normally lay two eggs but seldom are successful in raising more than one chick. Ray Erickson, of the Patuxent Center, postulated that one egg might be removed from each two-egg clutch with little effect on the well-being of the wild population. Scientists in the Canadian Wildlife Service came to a similar conclusion. Efforts to develop a captive flock began at the FWS Patuxent Research Center in Laurel, Maryland, in 1967.

From 1967 to 1974, 50 wild whooping crane eggs were transferred from Canada to Patuxent (Whooping Crane Recovery Team 1986). Chicks raised from these eggs formed the nucleus of the captive flock that is still maintained at Patuxent. A few eggs have been transferred from Canada since 1974, and two wild birds, flightless after collisions with powerlines, also joined the flock. In fall 1985, the captive flock contained 38 whooping cranes, including seven chicks.

The complexity of captive whooping crane production has made development of the Patuxent flock a long-term operation. First, it was necessary to start with eggs because wild-captured birds do not adjust well to captivity. Starting with eggs meant waiting five to six years for sexual maturity, which was further delayed by conditions of captivity. After the first eggs were hatched there were problems formulating adequate diets for the chicks, preventing parasite and disease infections, providing water and space, controlling light and temperature, preventing access by predators, and developing suitable animal husbandry techniques. Many of the husbandry techniques developed earlier for sandhill cranes were inadequate for the more fragile whooping cranes.

The problems mentioned have been solved to a large degree, but, until they were solved, they contributed to losses of eggs, chicks, or adults or to behavioral abnormalities. The biggest single disease loss was the eastern equine encephalitis outbreak in fall 1984. Seven adult and subadult birds died including several of the best breeders. Present emphasis at Patuxent is to rebuild the captive flock in order to replace the encephalitis losses and to build numbers sufficient to allow development of a second captive flock.

In 1974, a proposal to attempt to establish a second wild flock was accepted by the United States and Canada. The plan called for placing whooper eggs in the nests of sandhill cranes. Studies at Grays Lake in the early 1970s, by Rod Drewien of the University of Idaho, indicated that sandhill crane pairs could potentially be foster parents of whooping crane chicks, because sandhill crane pairs readily accepted and incubated eggs from other sandhill cranes when they were substituted for their own eggs. Whooping crane eggs are similar in size and appearance to sandhill crane eggs. Egg transfer from Canada to Idaho began in 1975 and still continues. Two hundred and fifty whooping crane eggs, transferred from Canada and Patuxent Wildlife Research Center have been placed in sandhill crane nests. The Patuxent flock has also contributed eggs to develop the Rocky Mountain wild population. A single whooping crane egg was substituted for the sandhill crane eggs in each nest. As a consequence of this egg transfer, the Rocky Mountain whooping crane population now contains about 30 to 35 birds.

Another activity authorized under the Endangered Species Act was establishment of a recovery team. The six-to-seven-member team is made up of crane experts representing state, federal, university, and private groups. One member is an employee of the Canadian Wildlife Service. Appointed in 1975, their primary objective was to prepare a comprehensive plan for recovery of the species. The first comprehensive plan was published in 1980 and a revised version will be published in 1986. The plan describes recovery objectives, outlines steps to attain these objectives, and discusses schedules and budgets.

Canada and the United States have been working cooperatively to recover the whooping cranes since the 1940s. In 1985, directors of the Canadian Wildlife Service and FWS formalized their cooperative protection efforts by signing a memorandum of understanding. The memorandum details the role of each nation and designates a single individual in each agency as a contact point to ensure coordination and information exchange.

The above described actions, functioning together, have made possible the whooping crane's promising recovery to date.

## Current Trends

In late 1985 the world's whooping crane population, limited only to North America, was about 170 birds, an 11-fold increase from the 15 individuals at Aransas in 1941. The flock's recovery has been slow, but the pace has accelerated in recent years. The flock increased by 10 birds in the five years following 1941, but in the subsequent 12 years showed no net gain. From 1957, it took 13 years for the population of 26 to double. Since 1967, when the transfer of eggs began to build the captive flock and later the Rocky Mountain population, the population has almost tripled (Whooping Crane Recovery Team 1986). Mark Boyce (1986) studied patterns in whooping crane population growth and detected a 10-year periodicity in crane abundance. The precise reasons for these cycles are unknown.

The number of young produced in Canada and making a successful trip to Texas reached a record of 15 birds in 1984 and 16 in 1985. This increase over the previous high of 12 in 1976, and 10 or less on all previous occasions was due to record numbers of breeding pairs (29 in 1984, 28 in 1985) and excellent habitat conditions on the nesting grounds. Water levels were high in 1984 and 1985. Such levels apparently diminish losses of eggs and chicks that would otherwise occur because of terrestrial predators. Associated with the high water level were abundant foods for the chicks. In 1985, the above-average weights of the chicks when captured for banding indicated the good feeding conditions they had experienced.

Drought at Grays Lake, predation on eggs and chicks, and problems associated with incubation temperatures during egg transfer limited survival during the early years of transfer. Improvement in incubation techniques, predator control (Drewien *et al* 1985), and increasing water levels led to higher annual hatching and fledging success from the transferred eggs.

Although all the chicks have been reared at Grays Lake National Wildlife Refuge, as subadults they often wander hundreds of miles from the refuge in subsequent summers. These cranes now summer over parts of Colorado, southern Idaho, northern Utah, western Wyoming, and southwestern Montana. To date, no members of the northern Rocky Mountain population have produced eggs. Most of the birds are not yet old enough. Among the sexually mature birds the sex ratio is unbalanced in favor of males. Also the sexually mature birds are widely distributed on the winter grounds, making it more difficult for them to find a mate. A few of the Rocky Mountain birds have manifested pairing behavior, but this has not yet progressed to egg production.

The Rocky Mountain population would not exist were it not for the intensive management associated with the recovery effort. Most crane pairs at Wood Buffalo would continue to fledge a single chick despite having a clutch of two eggs. The western flock represents one way in which recovery of the species has been accelerated.

## Management

Management activities are made up of actions dealing directly with the bird and actions primarily involving the bird's habitat. The egg transfer from Canada, and from the captive flock in Maryland, to Grays Lake National Wildlife Refuge is an example of direct management that also involves research activities. Maintenance of the captive flock at Patuxent also is a management activity containing many research aspects. One management aspect of the captive-propagation program is the effort to ensure that all parent stock in the Wood Buffalo flock are represented by progeny in the captive flock. In this manner, genetic diversity is maintained to minimize the chance for inbreeding problems.

A management activity in which National Audubon Society members have actively participated with government agencies is the Whooping Crane Network, a twice-annual monitoring of whooping crane movements during migration. Sightings of whooping cranes are reported to the Grand Island, Nebraska, FWS office, where permanent records are maintained.

In 1985, 13 state wildlife agencies and the three FWS regional offices whose areas encompass the crane's migration pathways participated in a cooperative plan for whooping crane protection during migration. When whooping cranes were sighted, the location was checked to ensure that the birds were healthy and safe. This is an ongoing program to protect the birds from hazards such as disease outbreaks, contaminant spills, or accidental shooting. For example, the Rainwater Basin of Nebraska historically has been a migration stopover point for whooping cranes. In the past decade, portions of the basin have had a chronic problem with avian cholera, a disease that has killed thousands of geese and ducks. Whenever whooping cranes are seen in the chronic disease problem areas, they are frightened away to diminish the likelihood that they will contract avian cholera. The plan also is designed to expedite recovery and treatment of any birds found sick or injured. Another part of the cooperative state-federal effort is a conservation education program designed to inform and alert the public just before and during crane migration.

The primary known cause of death of fledged whooping cranes is collision with powerlines. Of 14 that have hit lines since 1956, 10 were killed, two were badly injured and had to be retained in captivity, and two recovered in the wild. FWS, under the auspices of the Endangered Species Act, works with utility companies that have proposed construction of new powerlines. In wetland and cropland where whooping cranes might occur, the utility companies are encouraged to mark the lines with bright aircraft marker balls or other devices that make the lines more visible to birds, thereby diminishing the likelihood of line collisions.

Habitat is managed in several other ways. At the Lillian Annette Rowe National Audubon Sanctuary near Gibbon, Nebraska, grasslands along the river are control-burned or cut for hay to reduce vegetation height and improve insect populations (Strom 1986). These activities make the fields suitable for use by whooping cranes. The river channel is cleared of encroaching willows and cottonwoods by mechanical methods and prescribed burning of small islands. Such woody-vegetation control makes the river channel suitable for roosting by whooping cranes. In fall 1985, whooping cranes roosted at such a site on the Rowe Sanctuary.

Whooping cranes will not use tall, rank grasslands. At Aransas National Wildlife Refuge, height and density of grass in upland fields and savannah are managed by controlled grazing and prescribed burning. Whooping cranes drink at freshwater ponds on Aransas whenever salinity levels become 23 to 24 parts per thousand or more along the Gulf Intracoastal Waterway. These ponds were constructed for the cranes, and aquatic-plant growth in them is minimized so the sites will continue to be attractive to whooping cranes.

Crops are planted for waterfowl and cranes at many refuges and state management areas. Chufa has been planted because cranes eat the tubers. Corn is planted and knocked down or mechanically harvested. Corn provides the major food of whooping cranes at Bosque del Apache and helps attract the birds to the refuge, where they receive greater protection. At the Alamosa/Monte Vista National Wildlife Refuge in Colorado, barley, wheat, and field peas are planted for use by sandhill and whooping cranes (Kauffeld 1982).

Water management to benefit cranes is practiced at refuges such as those in Colorado (Kauffeld 1982) and New Mexico. Water is pumped into or from impoundments to provide suitable roosting-feeding sites and to diminish the likelihood of disease problems such as botulism and fowl cholera (Kauffeld 1986).

# Prognosis

The Whooping Crane Recovery Plan, as revised in 1985, states that the recovery goal is to move the whooping crane from the endangered to the threatened category by managing and protecting the populations from present and future threats and by ensuring the maintenance of self-sustaining populations in the species' natural habitat (Whooping Crane Recovery Team 1986). The prerequisite for downlisting to the threatened category is a population level of 40 pairs at Wood Buffalo National Park and 25 nesting pairs at each of two other wild population sites in North America. These are realistic goals, but will require several decades of management at the same intensity that has existed for the past 20 years.

In 1985, 28 pairs nested at Wood Buffalo National Park. We can expect to achieve the level of 40 nesting pairs before 1995. The Grays Lake population is expected to have its first successful nesting in the next two to three years. Attaining the 25 nesting-pair goal at Grays Lake is much more difficult to predict because it depends in part on the numbers of eggs available for transfer from Canada and the captive flock. Twenty five nesting pairs can be expected from a total population of 100. Growth of the Grays Lake population to that level might be attained between 1995 and 2000. Development of a flock in eastern North America will depend on the same variables as the development of the Grays Lake flock. Cross-fostering, and possibly the release of young pen-reared whooping cranes, may begin at an eastern site as early as 1990. Development of that flock to 25 pairs might occur as early as 2015 because of increasing numbers of eggs and young available from Canada and from captivity.

By the year 2000 it may be possible to set a revised recovery goal of removing the whooping crane from the threatened category. One possible goal, and a realistic one, would be to attain the population levels of 500 to 700 birds that probably existed in 1870 (Banks 1978). If no unexpected setbacks occur, in the mid-21st century most major zoos may have whooping cranes on display. The combination of three self-sustaining wild populations and captive flocks at several sites will ensure the security of whooping cranes as a species.

# Recommendations

The revised recovery plan (Whooping Crane Recovery Team 1986) outlines the steps for downlisting the species from endangered to threatened status. Federal and state conservation agency roles are described along with budgeting and schedules. The key goals of the plan are development of three self-sustaining wild populations, with the Wood Buffalo/Aransas population containing 40 nesting pairs and each of the other two populations containing 25 nesting pairs. The numbers of nesting pairs are minimum goals and are not meant to imply that recovery efforts would stop when those numbers are attained. The figure of 25 nesting pairs is based on the smallest number of isolated breeding individuals, called by geneticists the minimum viable population, necessary to prevent inbreeding over the short term (Samson 1983). FWS and the Canadian Wildlife Service support the general recommendations and approach described in the recovery plan.

Attaining these goals will require continuing the present level of funding and staff commitment of federal and state agencies and private organizations, such as the National Audubon Society, as well as whole-hearted public support. One of the weak links in recovery is the existence of a single captive flock where we have, so to speak, all our captive eggs in one basket. The eastern equine encephalitis outbreak at Patuxent in 1984 illustrated the potential consequences of having a single captive flock. A serious disease outbreak could destroy all the captive flock, jeopardizing the entire recovery program. Attaining the time schedule described in the prognosis section is dependent on a captive flock that actively contributes eggs and young for establishing the second and third wild flocks.

A more secure situation, with greater assurance of recovery of the species, will require establishing a second captive flock at a site comparable in facilities and staff to that in existence at Patuxent. Such a facility probably will have an initial cost of $1,000,000 to $2,000,000 and annual costs of some $200,000. These rough estimates include costs for land purchase, pens, buildings, and salaries for a qualified professional staff. Costs will vary depending on whether the facility is developed separately or is affiliated with an existing zoo or zoological park where space and some facilities and staff already exist. With today's declining state and federal conservation budgets, the development of a second captive flock is very likely to require involvement and support by private groups and the public.

# References

Allen, R.P. 1952. *The Whooping Crane.* Research Report 3. National Audubon Society, New York. 246 pp.

Allen, R.P. 1956. *A Report on the Whooping Crane's Northern Breeding Grounds.* National Audubon Society, New York. 60 pp.

Banks, R.C. 1978. The size of the early whooping crane populations. Unpublished report. U.S. Fish and Wildlife Service files. 10 pp.

Binkley, C.S., and R.S. Miller. 1980. "Survivorship of the whooping crane, *Grus americana.*" *Ecology* 61:434-437.

Bishop, M.A. 1984. The Dynamics of Subadult flocks of Whooping Cranes Wintering in Texas, 1978-79 through 1982-83. M.S. Thesis. Texas A & M University. College Station, Texas. 128 pp.

Drewien, R.C. and E.G. Bizeau. 1974. "Status and distribution of greater sandhill cranes in the Rocky Mountains." *Journal of Wildlife Management* 38:720-742.

Drewien, R.C. and E.G. Bizeau. 1977. "Cross-fostering whooping cranes to sandhill crane foster parents," *in* S.A. Temple ed., *Endangered Birds: Management Techniques for Preserving Threatened Species.* The University of Wisconsin Press. Madison, Wisconsin. pp. 201-222.

Drewien, R.C. and E.G. Bizeau. 1981. "Use of radiotelemetry to study movements of juvenile whooping cranes," *in* J.C. Lewis and H. Masatomi eds., *Crane Research Around the World.* International Crane Foundation. Baraboo, Wisconsin. pp. 130-134.

Drewien, R.C., S.H. Bouffard, D.D. Call, and R.A. Wonacott. 1985. "The whooping crane cross-fostering experiment: the role of animal damage control." Presented at Second Eastern Wildlife Damage Control Conference. Raleigh, North Carolina.

Erickson, R.C. and S.R. Derrickson. 1981. "The whooping crane," *in* J.C. Lewis and H. Masotomi eds., *Crane Research Around the World.* International Crane Foundation. Baraboo, Wisconsin. pp. 104-118.

Howe, M.A. 1986. "Habitat use by migrating whooping cranes in the Aransas-Wood Buffalo corridor," at press *in* J.C. Lewis ed., *Proceedings 1985 Crane Workshop.* Platte River Whooping Crane Trust, Grand Island, Nebraska.

Johnson, L.A. 1983. The value of the whooping crane: an application of valuation techniques for nonmarket resources. Texas A & M Undergraduate Fellows Program. 68 pp.

Kauffeld, J.D. 1982. "Management of migratory crane habitat on Alamosa and Monte Vista National Wildlife Refuges," *in* J.C. Lewis ed., *Proceedings 1981 Crane Workshop.* National Audubon Society. Tavernier, Florida. pp. 117-121.

Kauffeld, J.D. 1986. "An avian cholera epizotic among sandhill cranes in Colorado," At press *in* J.C. Lewis ed., *Proceedings 1985 Crane Workshop.* Platte River Whooping Crane Trust, Grand Island, Nebraska.

Kuyt, E. 1979. "Banding of juvenile whooping cranes and discovery of the summer habitat used by nonbreeders," *in* J.C. Lewis ed., *Proceedings 1978 Crane Workshop.* Colorado State University Printing Service. Ft. Collins, Colorado. pp. 109-111.

Kuyt, E. 1981a. "Population status, nest site fidelity, and breeding habitat of whooping cranes," *in* J.C. Lewis and H. Masatomi eds., *Crane Research Around the World.* International Crane Foundation. Baraboo, Wisconsin. pp. 119-125.

Kuyt, E. 1981b. "Clutch size, hatching success, and survival of whooping crane chicks. Wood Buffalo National Park, Canada," *in* J.C. Lewis and H. Masatomi eds., *Crane Research Around the World.* International Crane Foundation. Baraboo, Wisconsin. pp. 126-129.

Kuyt, E. and J.P. Goossen. 1986. "Survival, age composition, sex ratio, and age at first breeding of whooping cranes in Wood Buffalo National Park, Canada," At press *in* J.C. Lewis ed., *Proceedings 1985 Crane Workshop.* Platte River Whooping Crane Trust, Grand Island, Nebraska.

Novokowksi, N.S. 1966. *Whooping Crane Population Dynamics on the Nesting Grounds, Wood Buffalo National Park, Northwest Territories, Canada.* Canadian Wildlife Service, Research Report Series 1. 20 pp.

Samson, F.B. 1983. "Minimum viable population—a review." *Natural Areas Journal* 3:15-23.

Stehn, T.V. 1985. "Tailing the whoopers." *Texas Parks and Wildlife* 43(3): 18-21.

Stehn, T.V. and E.F.Johnson. 1986. "Distribution of winter territories of whooping cranes on the Texas coast," At press *in* J.C. Lewis ed., *Proceedings 1985 Crane Workshop.* Platte River Whooping Crane Trust, Grand Island, Nebraska.

Strom, K.J. 1986. "Lillian Annette Rowe—managing migratory crane habitat on the Platte River, Nebraska," At press *in* J.C. Lewis ed., *Proceedings 1985 Crane Workshop.* Platte River Whooping Crane Trust, Grand Island, Nebraska.

Walkinshaw, L.H. 1973. *Cranes of the World.* Winchester Press. New York. 370 pp.

Whooping Crane Recovery Team. 1986. *Whooping Crane Recovery Plan.* U.S. Fish and Wildlife Service. Albuquerque, New Mexico. 200 pp.

*James C. Lewis, stationed with the Region 2 Office of Endangered Species in Albuquerque, New Mexico, is the Fish and Wildlife Service's national whooping crane coordinator. He started his crane studies in 1967 with research on sandhill cranes.*

Loon numbers may be declining in some areas. Potential threats to loons include pollution, lake acidification, and entrapment in fishing gear.

*Peter Roberts*

# Common Loon

## Judith W. McIntyre
Utica College of Syracuse University

## Species Description and Natural History

THE FIVE SPECIES of loons all belong to the genus *Gavia,* the family *Gaviidae,* and the order *Gaviiformes.* Common loons (*Gavia immer*) vary in size within their range, but no subspecies are recognized (American Ornithologists' Union 1983). They are the only gaviids that are entirely Nearctic, that is found only in the northern part of the Western Hemisphere.

The adult commmon loon, with its striking black and white feathers, bright red eyes and eerie wail or laughing tremolo, is familiar to all who frequent the northern lake country. Only adults are black and white and then only during the breeding season. The rest of the year they have gray back feathers, white breast and belly plumage, and brown eyes, all similar to the plumage of juvenile loons.

Loons have a partial molt into winter plumage in fall but do not lose their flight feathers. During February and early March, while on the wintering rounds, they molt into the black and white summer feathers. At that time they replace flight feathers and are flightless for nearly a month (Woolfenden 1967). Juveniles molt later, generally early in the summer, and for the first two or three years do not acquire adult breeding plumage.

Weight of adult loons varies geographically between six and 14 pounds. Loons from Minnesota and North Dakota, the south-central part of the breeding range, are smallest, while those at the eastern and western periphery are largest (Rand 1947, Anderson *et al* 1970). Body length is from 24 to 36 inches and wing span from four to five feet. Males generally are larger than females, but there is considerable overlap when a range of specimens is examined. The male is larger than the female within mated pairs both in overall size and in some structures of the digestive tract, leading Barr (1973) to suggest that there may be some partitioning of food resources between the two.

## Foods

Loons are visual predators, primarily fish-eaters. They find prey by dipping their heads beneath the surface of the water, then diving, turning, and pursuing to grasp prey with their bills (Barr 1963). Their primary food is yellow perch (*Perca flavescens*), more easily captured than many other prey species because of its zig-zag swimming behavior (Barr 1973). Loons will take salmonids and whitefish—species with small, smooth scales and no spines—if they can capture them. When these fast-swimming fish are impaired in experimental trials to make capture easier, they are preferred over species with wider bodies, spines, and/or coarse scales (Barr 19873). Under natural conditions, however, the speed of most salmonids requires loons to use more energy than that needed to capture slower or more erratic fish.

## Locomotion

Loons are swift fliers and migrate at about 75 miles per hour (Kerlinger 1982). They have a rapid wing beat of 260 to 265 beats per minute. Although excellent fliers and diving-swimmers, they move poorly on land. Their legs are set far to the rear of their bodies, and they take off only from water, running along the surface for a considerable distance before becoming airborne. They go on land only to copulate and nest.

## Breeding

The breeding range extends all across the northern portion of North America (McIntyre in press). The southernmost record is from the southwest corner of Michigan. Small populations occur in Washington state, Idaho, and Montana and in Wyoming between Yellowstone National Park and the Tetons. Least is known about the western populations. The most western, Alaska's, is uncounted but large.

Nests, made of whatever vegetation is handy, are built at the water's edge, usually in a sheltered and hidden island site. If islands are not available, loons nest on hummock, logs, muskrat houses, or shoreline (McIntyre 1975, Sutcliffe 1980, Alvo 1981, Yonge 1981). Most clutches have two eggs laid two days apart. Incubation begins before the laying of the second egg, and the eggs hatch within 24 hours of each other. Incubation lasts an average of 26 days

(Yonge 1981) but may extend as long as 31. If a clutch is lost, loons may re-nest, but will not do so following loss of chicks.

Both sexes share in all phases of parental care, beginning with nest building and incubation and including feeding and defending. (McIntyre 1975). They also carry the chicks on their backs during the first two weeks out of the nest. Young are called off the nest as soon as they are dry and are taken to a quiet, protected, shallow location, the nursery (McIntyre 1983). Chicks are fed small whole fish, crayfish, and other small invertebrates (Barr 1973, Parker 1985, Dulin 1986). They are incapable of supplying sufficient food for themselves until they are more than eight weeks old (Barr 1983). Small chicks are vulnerable to many underwater predators, especially snapping turtles (*Chelydra serpentina*) and large pike (*Esox lucius*). Should they wander away from the parents and into another loon's territory, they may be killed by the resident loon (Yonge 1981).

Chicks hatch with black downy upperparts and white downy bellies. They molt into a second, gray-brown downy plumage at about 10 days and begin to acquire juvenile contour feathers at four weeks. They have completed the juvenal molt and are able to fly at 11 weeks (Barr 1973, McIntyre 1975).

Young stay in the parental territory until migration if sufficient food is available. Adults leave to fish for themselves on adjacent lakes if their territories have a marginal food supply. When young can fly, they too leave these depauperate lakes and establish permanent feeding sites on nearby lakes until migration (McIntyre 1975). Good territories have an abundance of food, clear water, at least two nest sites, and a quiet nursery location. They average between 50 and 200 acres, depending on whether a pair holds an entire small lake or shares a larger one with other loons (McIntyre in press).

## Migration

Young and adults generally migrate separately, although the pattern varies among individuals. Loons stage for fall migration from September through October (McIntyre and Barr 1983), aggregating on specific large lakes. Loons move in groups of 15 to 25 individuals, although some birds remain solitary or in groups of two or three.

Migratory routes indicate a funneling through the Great Lakes during both fall and spring migration. Loons spend time on the Great Lakes in the fall, with large concentrations on Lake Michigan and on Lake Huron's Georgian Bay. The destination of any one population is incompletely known. The best data are for Minnesota breeders. They spend time in the fall on Mille Lacs Lake in central Minnesota, move to Lake Michigan, and from there go to Florida's Gulf Coast. It appears that birds from the central Canadian portion of the range move through Lake Huron and winter off the Atlantic Coast, while Pacific Coast winter residents probably breed west of the Rocky Mountains.

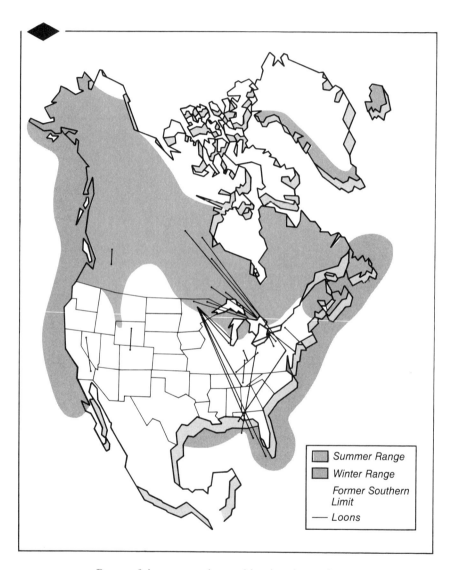

Range of the common loon, with migration pathways

The annual cycle can be summarized as: late fall or early winter to the coastal wintering grounds, molt from late January through early March, beginning of northward migration in April (some as early as late March) following open water, arrival at breeding grounds from April to May, nesting from mid- or late May to early July, chick-rearing period for the next three months, molt of adults beginning late summer, movement to staging grounds in late September or early October, and migration to the wintering grounds just before the lakes become iced over, the birds going first to the Great Lakes (central population) or directly to the coast (eastern population).

## Significance of the Species

Common loons are the symbol of northern wilderness. They evoke images of cool, blue water and pristine wild sectors. They have been described as ". . . putting the stamp of genuineness on a North Country setting like "Sterling" does on silver . . . " (Breckenridge 1949) and as characterizing the true spirit of the wilderness (Olson and Marshall 1952).

Loons hold a special place in Native American tradition. The term "loon-hearted" is used to mean brave, much as the English term "lion-hearted" does (Cooke 1884), and the Ojibway word for loon, "mang", has connotations of proud and handsome (R. Gawboy, pers. comm.).

Loons have little economic value. They are not a game species, although some Native Americans do hunt them. Loons will take game fish when they can, but their diet is composed primarily of nongame species. Loons are at the top of the aquatic freshwater food chain for six to seven months each year, and if their take, estimated at half a ton per family per breeding season (Barr 1973), should be either increased or lost, fish populations might be affected.

Loons are indicators of the quality of northern wilderness country (Titus and Van Druff 1981). What is the worth to a wilderness camper of the sound of a loon call echoing across a moonlit lake? It may not be measurable but if, as Leopold (1933) stated some 50 years ago, it is true that wildlife must be managed as much for man's sake as for wildlife's, then loon conservation is vital to preservation of the tangible evidence of wilderness.

It is hoped that loons may be used as indicators for heavy metal pollution. Loons are susceptible to heavy metal accumulations in body tissue, especially to mercury, and recent studies are seeking to discover if loon feathers can be used to provide an early warning for heavy metal contamination of our water resources.

## Historical Perspective

The breeding range of common loons has shrunk during the past century. It is unknown how much of this has occurred recently and how much is only now becoming visible though caused by events at the turn of the century or earlier.

Breeding range formerly included northern Pennsylvania, Indiana, Illinois, Iowa, and California, all without breeding pairs now (McIntyre in press). Connecticut also had nesting loons, and although summering loons have been reported there recently, no breeding records have been confirmed.

Historical records have been collected for two states, New York and New Hampshire. Declines in New Hampshire are estimated at 53 percent (Sutcliffe 1978), while in New York a decline exceeding 35 percent has occurred since the turn of the century (McIntyre 1979). Much of the New York loss occurred during the 19th century following early settling of the state and heavy boat traffic on the larger lakes. Hunting during spring migration decimated populations.

Brewster (1924), writing about Lake Umbagog on the Maine-New Hampshire border, tells of hunters lining the decks of lake steamers and trying to shoot loons before they could dive. By 1920, few loons were left there. Spring shoots also were popular on the coast, and hunters lined the sides of Buzzards and Manomet bays in Massachusetts to try to hit migrating loons in flight (Forbush 1912). It is tragic that these shootings, not for food or survival but for "fun", erradicated large numbers of loons, extensively reducing populations throughout the East. Present population status in the Northeast continues to bear the scars of this massacre.

## Current Trends

The return of loons to Massachusetts is the most exciting find of the decade for loon biologists. Common loons formerly nested there, and Thoreau mentioned their presence in several of his writings. For nearly a century no confirmed nesting occured. Then, in 1975, a nest was discovered on the Quabbin Reservoir (Clarke 1975). By 1984, six pairs were nesting on the Quabbin and one on the Washusett Reservoir (Lyons and Ehrhardt 1984).

Intensive loon management in New Hampshire has raised productivity from 51 fledged young in 1976 to 77 in 1985 and permitted the adult population to increase from 214 in 1976 to 334 in 1985 (Report of the New Hampshire Loon Preservation Committee 1985). By 1985, 100 adults were summering, although not breeding, in New Hampshire, a sign that there may be more loons than habitat and an indication of a healthy population.

Productivity in New York is higher than it is in areas with denser populations. In the heart of loon range it is considered normal for the average pair to produce a single young offspring every other year, a yearly average of 0.5 fledged young per territorial pair (Titus and Van Druff 1981, Yonge 1981). New York's loons fledge nearly 0.8 young per pair per year (Trivelpiece et al 1979).

Several factors, all man-related, caused declines in the past and are considered to contribute to present problems. The first recognized threat was

Estimated numbers of Common Loon in populations across the northern tier of the contiguous United States.

| State | Number of Adults* |
|---|---|
| Maine | 7,000 |
| New Hampshire | 350 |
| Vermont | 54 |
| New York | 300-400 |
| Massachusetts | 14 |
| Michigan | 600-700 |
| Wisconsin | 2,200 |
| Minnesota | 10,000 |
| North Dakota | unknown |
| Montana | 70-100 |
| Idaho | incompletely known (16 counted during 1985) |
| Wyoming | unknown |
| Washington | 4 |

* Numbers quoted are taken from annual survey reports.

oil pollution in marine waters. Waterbird oiling was reported 50 years ago (Hadley 1930). Periodic spills, both on coastal waters and those further inland pose serious threats.

Some, but not all, environmental pollutants have proved hazardous to loons. Testing of chlorinated hydrocarbon residues in loon tissue has shown relatively low levels in general (Fay and Youatt 1967, Frank *et al* 1983). Loons do accumulate heavy mercury loads. A 1983 die-off along the Gulf Coast from Florida to Alabama involved some 3,000 common loons and led to extensive laboratory testing. High mercury levels in the loon's tissues suggested that mercury may have contributed to the birds' emaciated condition (Strond and Lange 1983). Dead loons weighed only one to three pounds, far below the normal weight of eight to 10 pounds (Stroud and Lange 1983). A Canadian study reported high levels in loons from lakes known to be contaminated with mercury, while loons from lakes free from industrial pollution had relatively low levels (Frank *et al* 1983).

The problem of acid rain should immediately raise the question of its implication for loons. For example, acid-related declines in fish populations should mean a loss of food for loons, and lowered loon productivity on acidified lakes should be expected. Two recent graduate studies provided different answers for this prediction. Parker (1985) discovered that loons on acidified Adirondack lakes continued to breed, fed large numbers of aquatic insects and newts to their young, and were reproductively successful although they had to spend more time in feeding activities. Alvo (1985) worked on lakes ranging from high to low alkalinity near Sudbury, Ontario, and reported significantly lower breeding success on low alkalinity lakes than on those ranked high. He found that loons used lakes in all classes for nesting and successfully hatched young, but that the survival rate was lower on acidified lakes. Mortalities occurred at the time when parental feeding would normally shift from a variety of food items (including vegetation and aquatic insects) to a diet primarily composed of fish.

Shindler et al (1985) artificially acidified a lake over an eight-year period and then carefully monitored changes in the entire ecosystem. They found an initial increase in the biomass of phytoplankton and invertebrates due to a reduction in competition subsequent to the demise of acid-sensitive species. Sadly, they also found that environmental stresses caused by acidification are irreversible and occur earlier in the process than previously recognized, leading first to loss of fish production and eventually to a loss of fish.

The Sudbury environs have been subjected to acidifying emissions since mining began in 1888. By comparison, Adirondack lakes have been acidified recently. Are Alvo's loons providing a warning that acid lakes, including those which Parker studies, cannot continue to provide suitable loon habitat? Both studies show that adult loons continue to use unsuitable habitat whether they are successful or not at rearing young. Will fidelity to traditional sites sound a death knell for loon populations in areas where acid rain is causing the most severe damage?

Acidification may carry an even more insidious threat: Increased acidity accelerates the rate at which mercury is freed from the substrate to enter the water, where it can more readily enter into the loon's food chain. The full effects of acidification would lie unrecognized until loons suffered permanent neurological damage by amassing a heavy mercury load. Stroud and Lange's (1983) reports of mercury loading in the tissues of loons killed during the 1983 Gulf die-off may be a sign that loons are increasingly susceptible to mercury pollution while in their summer range, but that until they are subjected to periodic stresses on the winter range the effects are not apparent.

Direct competition exists between man and loon for the same lakes. Loons prefer large lakes with clear water, an abundance of fish, islands for nesting, and quiet bays in which to raise young. Man also likes lakes with an abundance of fish, crystal clear water, islands for camping, and bays for retreat from rough water. Thus human recreational pursuits and loon reproductive needs clash. Fishermen who stop their boats near islands and over shoals can cause problems. During intrusions near nest sites, incubating loons slip off nests, swim underwater, and emerge at a distance. This leaves the nests open to predation, chiefly by ravens (*Corvus corax*), crows (*Corvus brachyrhynchos*), gulls (*Larus* sp.), raccoons (*Procyon lotor*), foxes (*Vulpes vulpes*), and skunks (*Mephitis mephitis*), depending on geographical location and abundance of the predator species (McIntyre in press).

Some loon nesting habitat has been destroyed by shoreline development. The most damaging is on islands which traditionally have been used for nests. Loons continue to nest in the same locations, frequently before arrival of human summer visitors. If people use their summer homes over Memorial Day, loons may encounter sufficient disturbance to desert their nests. The interval between nest loss and renesting is nearly two weeks (Yonge 1981). If they do renest, they have completed about three weeks of incubation when the next big weekend comes, the Fourth of July, bringing another influx of summer residents and campers. If the loons lose this nest they do not renest. Both cottage residents and campers on islands have been causal agents in nest loss.

Commercial fishing also has taken its toll. During heavy early spring seas, loons frequently are taken in nets off the Atlantic Coast (McIntyre 1978). Large numbers also are killed during spring in northern Canadian waters. At a single site on Great Slave Lake during the last half of May and first half of June in 1960 and 1961, the most recent for which figures are available, a total of 5,662 loons (all species) died in gill nets (Vermeer 1973). Great Lakes commercial fishing operations recently have been recognized as contributing to heavy, though as yet unquantified, losses thoughout the spring and summer. Lake Michigan, Lake Superior, and Georgian Bay in Lake Huron are locations of primary concerns.

From time to time major die-offs occur in Lake Michigan, linked to Type E botulism from alewives (*Alosa pseudoharengus*). Loons by the thousands have died during those outbreaks (Brand *et al* 1983).

Loons are taken for food by several groups of Native Americans. In northern Quebec 2,500 to 6,500 loons are taken yearly, mostly in spring. This figure is thought to be too high to be sustained by the present population of 12,000 pairs (Desgranges and Laportte 1979). The recently initiated FWS (U.S. Fish and Wildlife Service) educational program in Alaska seeking goose conservation by native peoples may pose a threat to other waterbirds. Natives do take loons, among other species, so pressure to lower the goose kill may possibly force an increase in loon take.

## Management

Some loon management has been accomplished by both private conservation groups and state agencies. Both FWS personnel and biologists on national forests have cooperated in loon conservation efforts.

An outstanding example of loon management has been conducted by New Hampshire's Audubon Society (Wood 1979). Following surveys from 1971 to 1975 by a lake association on a New Hampshire lake, the New Hampshire Audubon Society formed the Loon Preservation Committee. This active group has not only continued to survey lakes throughout the state, providing a running record of populations and historical data, but has added a strong public education program, including a newsletter, speaking engagements, and a summer staff of biologists. These Loon Rangers meet with lake residents to offer information on loon protection, encouraging residents to become actively involved in loon conservation. They post warning signs in nesting areas and physically guard loon families. One of the committee's great successes has been the construction and placement of artificial nesting platforms (Sutcliffe 1979). These structures, first used for behavioral studies (McIntyre and Mathisen 1977) and now modified as a management tool, are placed on lakes that lack natural islands. They move up and down with fluctuating water levels to eliminate nest wash-outs and promote nesting in locations offering maximum safety. Artificial islands also are being used successfully in Vermont and Massachusetts.

Loon groups or associations currently are active in 10 states. Some have been initiated by state conservation agencies, others by individuals or conservation groups. State and private programs are cooperative.

Some habitat restoration is possible, but many conservationists believe successful management is people management, or public education. Most loon programs include a large educational component. Speakers are available in every state, and a National-Audubon-sponsored film, *Legacy for a Loon,* is available for showing or purchase. A slide program aimed at grade school children was released in the fall of 1985 (McIntyre 1985).

The primary contribution made by the public to loon conservation has been a willingness to volunteer as loon watchers. These participants monitor loons during summer and submit reports in fall covering loon presence or absence, productivity, and disturbance factors. Three states, Vermont, New Hampshire, and Maine, have added a one-day, statewide survey that has elicited media response and focused public attention on common loons. In Maine, aerial and ground surveys are combined, and the governor has proclaimed an annual Loon Day. For contacts in each state write to:

North American Loon Fund
Main Street
Meredith, New Hampshire 03253

State programs include both surveys and public education. A Minnesota educational program will reach every elementary schools in the state by the end of 1986. Minnesota's banding program, the most extensive, has doubled the total number of loons ever banded. This has increased knowledge of loon movements and lent support to earlier evidence that adults do return to the same territory year after year (McIntyre 1974).

Loons enjoy special status in some states. In New York they are ranked as a species of special concern, and in Wisconsin they are on the Watch List. New Hampshire loons are state listed as threatened, and state endangered species status has just been given to Vermont loons. In Minnesota, where the population is healthy, the loon as the state bird has enjoyed a different kind of special status for the past 25 years as the state bird. Loon programs have benefited by inclusion in the tax check-off projects which have been launched by several states. Funding has permitted extensive surveys and public education, and the write-off programs have finally provided a mechanism for state funding of non-game research.

## Prognosis

Data on the status of the common loon does not begin to approach that of some species for which reliable numbers can be counted, watched, recorded, and reported. In addition to numbers in the contiguous states, Quebec has 35,000 common loons, thousands more summer across Ontario, Manitoba, Saskatchewan, Alberta, and British Columbia, and Alaska has thousands more. Yet the southern limit of the breeding range has been shifting northward. We do not know if populations also have shrunk inward from the north. With oil operations proliferating along the northern extent of common loon range, the possibility of a recession there should be investigated.

Hunting loons for food by Native Americans may pose a threat. In the future, northern wildlife may decline as Native Americans seek to feed increasing populations.

Mercury pollution, lake acidification, and commercial fishing entrapment are of immediate concern. If release of methylmercury to the aquatic community continues, loon demise is inevitable, but it may be years before the full impact is recognized. Mortality from commercial fishing, on the other hand, is immediately apparent. If solutions can be quickly found and implemented, hope remains for retaining loons on the Great Lakes. The major problem lies with funnel traps, into which loons swim and cannot escape. Without a check on this loss, either Michigan's breeding population will be decimated or more northern populations will decline.

Recreational use, which competes with loons, continues to increase. However, loons seem to be adapting to human intrusion. On remote lakes, with rare human intrusion, loons stay on their nests until humans get close, then flush and never sit tight (Titus and Van Druff 1981). By contrast, birds occupying the same territories year after year on more heavily used lakes are sitting tighter in the presence of boating traffic. Some loons that used to leave their nests at the approach of any human intrusion now sit until it has passed, and productivity has increased (New Hampshire Report 1984, pers. obs.). However, Jim Titus, who called human-habituated loons "stickers" (Titus and Van Druff 1981), found that although stickers were residents on lakes with heavy human intrusion, not all loons on those lakes stayed on their nests when approached. Some slipped off before humans got close and quietly emerged at a distance.

Conversely, Smith (1981) found that loons on canoe routes in Alaska flushed and defended closer to her canoe than did loons on control lakes (non-canoe routes). She concluded they were more protective of nests and chicks when continually confronted with humans. Although the results of these two studies appear to offer opposite conclusions, both support the premise that loons can change their behavior in response to human disturbance. Their behavioral plasticity is a hopeful sign for their future in the continuing competition between man and loon.

## Recommendations

Many researchers have made recommendations for common loon management during the past decade and in general their suggestions have been similar and directed to the breeding season (Barr 1973, Sutcliffe 1980, Smith 1981, Titus and Van Druff 1981, Yonge 1981, Parker 1985). They include:

1. Preservation of nesting habitat by curtailing human recreational use and/or restricting numbers of visitors to wilderness areas, limitation of boat engine size, limitation of human activity near nesting sites during May and June and designation of specific campsites beyond the disturbance distance of nesting loons.
2. Construction of artifical islands on lakes that lack natural islands, have a history of low reproductive success, or have fluctuating water levels.
3. Continued monitoring of populations to assess loon status and to verify that loons truly are adapting to human disturbances.
4. Public education, including direct contact with lake owners, posting signs and information at marinas and other lake access points, posting nesting areas, sensitivity briefings for all visitors to wildlife areas, and direct contact through lectures and other forms of program presentations.
5. Research on chick growth and survival comparing acidified and nonacidified lakes. Some lake restoration or restocking (in general this approach was given low priority).

Following the 1979 loon conference, a comprehensive five-year plan for the maintenance and/or restoration of stable breeding populations was written (Plunkett 1979). Emphasis was on states east of Minnesota. Research suggestions included studies on the breeding range, migratory routes, and wintering grounds; improved banding and marking techniques; and management plans restricted to needs on the breeding grounds, with emphasis on habitat protection and public education. The final suggestion was to formulate a coordinating mechanism for all research and management, largely met with the founding of the North American Loon Fund later in 1979. Included on its board are representatives from government agencies, conservation groups, and universities.

Based on these suggestions, recent concerns, and an urgent need to look at a broader perspective, I offer several specific recommendations.

1. *Winter.* Where are loons? Do specific breeding populations winter in discrete areas? What are the ecological needs of wintering loons? What is their social structure? What is the relationship between adults and juveniles? How hazardous to wintering loons are oil spills, commercial fishing conflicts, environmental contaminants, and weather factors? What routes do loons use between wintering and breeding grounds? Research should be started at once to address these questions and, in addition, a coastal winter watch should be implemented.

2. *Juveniles.* Studies should be initiated immediately to find out what young loons do between fledging and their return to northern lakes. Their ecological needs are unknown, as are their migratory routes, wintering grounds, movements for the two or more years they are juveniles, social relationships, age at which they first acquire alternate plumage, and age at first breeding.

3. *Breeding ecology.* Numerous field studies have been conducted in recent years, but little experimental research. Other than Barr's (1973) work, no studies have compared captive and wild-raised birds. Energy requirements are unknown for both adults and young.

4. *Populations.* State surveys must be continued. Only with long-term studies of this kind will it be possible to determine population stability. Surveys now beginning in western states must be encouraged, and surveys should be started in North Dakota and Alaska.

5. *Environmental Contaminants.* Mercury has been implicated in recent loon mortalities and in reduced productivity. Studies analyzing mercury levels in recently molted feathers should be supported in hopes of locating the sources of mercury pollution. Studies should be undertaken to determine biological consequences of heavy metal toxification on loons.

6. *Techniques.* Development of capture methods is essential. Unless loons can be banded and marked, information on movements, relationships, and demography cannot be expanded. At present, the only feasible capture method is night-lighting, and it is restricted to loons on shallow lakes.

7. *Management.* Protection of breeding habitat must be continued. Artificial islands should be placed where water levels fluctuate and on lakes where nesting success has been marginal, but should be avoided where loons already are nesting successfully. Plans may be secured through the North American Loon Fund. Immediate action must be taken concerning Great Lakes commercial fishing mortalities. Fish traps open at the top so loons can escape, combined with more frequent monitoring of traps, would benefit the loons, but a workable program developed between both commercial fishermen and government agencies must be initiated.

8. *Public Education.* Posting nest and nursery sites may work in some places, but in others would serve only to draw attention and may do more harm than good. In most places the critical period is from mid-May to mid-July. After

young are three weeks old, mortality is low, and most normal recreational activities can be resumed without interfering with reproductive success.

This type of information in the form of public education programs is the best form of common loon management. Most human-related loon problems stem from ignorance, not intent. Informational brochures, press releases, person-to-person contact with lake residents, and the presentation of loon programs, beginning with school children, are among the best and most effective methods.

The value of this component in loon conservation cannot be overemphasized. With it, barring a major environmental disaster, we can hope to see the revival of a stable breeding population of common loons across the northern tier of the contiguous United States and assure that the population to the north will remain healthy. If we value our wild treasures, then we must act to protect the visual and vocal symbol of our northern wilderness.

# References

Alvo, R. 1981 "Marsh nesting of common loons (*Gavia immer*)." *Canadian Field Naturalist* 95:357.

———— 1985. The breeding success of common loons in relation to lake acidity. Master's thesis. Trent University. Peterborough, Ontario.

American Ornithologists' Union. 1983. *Check-List of North American Birds*, sixth ed. American Ornithologists' Union, Washington, D.C.

Anderson, D.W., H.G. Lumsden, and J.J. Hickey. 1970. "Geographical variation in the eggshells of the common loon." *Canadian Field Naturalist* 84:351-356.

Barr, J.F. 1973. "Feeding biology of the common loon (*Gavia immer*) in oligotrophic lakes of the Canadian Shield." Unpublished Ph.D thesis, University of Guelph, Ontario.

Breckenridge, W.J. 1949. Birds of the Canadian Border Lakes. Presentation to the Quetico-Superior Committee, Chicago, Illinois.

Brewster, W. 1924. "The loon on Lake Umbagog." *Bird-lore* 26:309-315.

Bystrak, D., ed. 1974. *Wintering Areas of Bird Species Potentially Hazardous to Aircraft*. National Audubon Society. New York, New York.

Clark, R.A. 1975. "Common loons nest again in Massachusetts." *Bird News of Western Massachusetts* 15:65-67.

Cooke, W.W. 1884. "Bird nomenclature of the Chippewa Indians." *Auk* 1:242-250.

Desgranges, J.L. and P. Laporte. 1979. *Preliminary Considerations on the Status of Loons* (Gaviidae) *in Quebec*. Report to Joint Committee of the James Bay and Northern Quebec Agreement. Canadian Wildlife Service, Ottawa.

Dulin, G.S. 1986. Pre-fledging feeding behavior and sibling rivalry in common loons. Master's thesis, Central Michigan University, Mount Pleasant.

Fay, L.D. and W.G. Youatt. 1967. Residues of chlorinated hydrocarbon insecticides in loons, grebes, a gull, and a sample of alewives from Lake Michigan. Michigan Department of Conservation R & D Report No. 109.

Forbush, E.H. 1912. *A history of the Game Birds, Waterfowl and Shore Birds of Massachusetts and Adjacent States.* Massachusetts State Board of Agriculture. pp. 49-58.

Frank, R., H. Lumsden, J.F. Barr and H.E. Braun. 1983. Residues of organichlorine insecticides, industrial chemicals and mercury in eggs and in tissue taken from healthy and emaciated common loons, Ontario, Canada, 1968-1980. *Archives of Environmental Contaminants and Toxicology* 12:641-654.

Hadley, A.H. 1930. "Oil pollution and sea-bird fatalities." *Bird-lore* 32:241-243.

Kerlinger, P. 1982. "The migration of common loons through eastern New York." *Condor* 84:97-100.

Leopold, A. 1933. *Game Management.* Charles Scribner's Sons, New York, New York.

Lyons, P.J. and E. Ehrhardt. 1984. The conservation and management of the common loon in Massachusetts. Final Report 1984.

McIntyre, J.W. 1974. "Territorial affinity of a common loon." *Bird Banding* 45:178.

———— 1975. "Biology and behavior of the common loon (*Gavia immer*) with reference to its adaptability in a man-altered environment." Unpublished Ph.D thesis, University of Minnesota, Minneapolis.

———— 1978. "Wintering behavior of common loons." *Auk* 95:396-403.

———— 1979. "Status of common loons in New York from a historical perspective," in S.A. Sutcliffe ed., *The Common Loon, Proceedings of the Second North American Conference on Common Loon Research and Management.* National Audubon Society. New York, New York. pp. 117-121.

———— 1983. "Nurseries: a consideration of habitat requirements during the early chick-rearing period in common loons." *Journal of Field Ornithology* 54:247-253.

———— Hello, I'm A Loon! Slide-tape program for children. Oikos Research Foundation, Utica College, New York.

———— *The Common Loon.* University of Minnesota Press. Minneapolis, Minnesota. In press.

———— and J.F. Barr. 1983. "Pre-migratory behavior of common loons on the autumn staging grounds." *Wilson Bulletin* 95:121-125.

———— and J. Mathisen. 1977. "Artificial islands as nest sites for common loons." *Journal of Wildlife Management* 41:317-319.

Olson, S.T. and W.H. Marshall. 1952. *The Common Loon in Minnesota.* University of Minnesota Press, Occasional Papers no. 5, Minnesota Museum of Natural History.

Parker, K. 1985. "Foraging and reproduction of the common loon (*Gavia immer*) on acidified lakes in the Adirondack Park, New York." Master's thesis, SUNY College of Environmental Science and Forestry, Syracuse, New York.

Plunkett, R.L. 1979. "Major elements of a five-year comprehensive plan of research and management for the Great Lakes and northeastern United States populations of the common loon (*Gavia immer*)," *in* ed. S.A. Sutcliffe. *The Common Loon, Proceedings of the Second North American Conference on Common Loon Research and Management.* National Audubon Society. New York, New York. pp. 154-162.

Rand, A.L. 1947. "Geographical variation in the loon *Gavia immer.*" *Canadian Field Naturalist* 61: 193-195.

Schindler, D.W., K.H. Mills, D.F. Malley, O.L. Findlay, J.A. Shearer, I.J. Davis, M.A. Turner, G.A. Lindsey and D.R. Cruikshank. 1985. "Long-term ecosystem stress: the effects of years of experimental acidification on a small lake." *Science* 228:1395-1401

Smith, E.L. 1981. "Effects of canoeing on common loon production and survival on the Kenai National Wildlife Refuge, Alaska." Master's thesis, Colorado State University, Fort Collins, Colorado.

Stroud, R.K. and R.E. Lange. 1983. *Common Loon Die-off Winter and Spring of 1983.* Information summary report, National Wildlife Health Labratory. U.S. Fish and Wildlife Service. Madison, Wisconsin.

Sutcliffe, S.A. 1978. "Changes in status and factors affecting common loon populations in New Hampshire." *Transactions of the Northeast Section Wildlife Society 35th Northeast Fish and Wildlife Conference:* 219-224.

———— 1979. "Artificial common loon nesting site construction, placement and utilization in New Hampshire," *in* S.A. Sutcliffe ed., *The Common Loon, Proceedings of the Second North American Conference on Common Loon Research and Management.* National Audubon Society. pp. 147-152.

———— 1980. "Aspects of the nesting ecology of common loons in New Hampshire." Unpublished master's thesis, University of New Hampshire.

Titus, J. and L. Van Druff. 1981. "Response of the common loon to recreational pressure in the Boundary Waters Canoe Area, northeastern Minnesota." *Wildlife Monograph* No. 79.

Trivelpiece, W., S. Brown, A. Hicks, R. Fekete, and N.J. Volkman. 1979. "An analysis of the distribution and reproductive success of the common loon in the Adirondack Park, New York," *in* S.A. Sutlcliffe ed., *The Common Loon, Proceedings of the Second North American Conference on Common Loon Research and Management.* National Audubon Society. pp. 117-121.

Vermeer, K. 1973. "Some aspects of the breeding and mortality of common loons in east-central Alberta." *Canadian Field Naturalist* 87:403-408.

Woolfenden, G.E. 1972. "Selection for the delayed simultaneous wing molt in loons (*Gaviidae*)." *Wilson Bulletin* 79:416-420.

Wood, R.L. 1979. "Management of breeding loon populations in New Hampshire," *in* S.A. Sutcliffe ed., *The Common Loon, Proceedings of the Second North*

*American Conference on Common Loon Research and Management.* National Audubon Society. pp. 141-146.

Yonge, K.S. 1981. "The breeding cycle and annual production of the common loon (*Gavia immer*) in the boreal forest region." Master's thesis, University of Manitoba, Winnipeg.

*Judy McIntyre, an associate professor of biology at the Utica College of Syracuse University, is on the board of the North American Loon Fund and is founder of Oikos, a nonprofit group devoted to scientific research and public education. She has studied loons for 19 years.*

An Atlantic salmon leaps from the rapids. Once abundant in New England streams, the species has been decimated by overfishing and blockage of spawning streams by water projects.

*T. Davidson/ Photo Researchers*

# Atlantic Salmon

## Lawrence W. Stolte

U.S. Fish and Wildlife Service

## Species Description and Natural History

THE ATLANTIC SALMON (*Salmo salar*) is an anadromous species, living as an adult in the sea but breeding in freshwater rivers and small streams, where the eggs are laid and hatched. While in the sea, Atlantic salmon are silvery on their sides, silvery white underneath, and brown, green, or blue on their backs. For a short time after they enter rivers and streams to breed, salmon remain quite silvery and often are referred to as "fresh and bright fish." They gradually lose the silvery color and become darker, taking on a bronze and brown coloration as spawning approaches.

Individual salmon have been recorded weighing as much as 79 to 100 pounds (Sedgwick 1982, MacCrimmon and Gots 1979, Scott and Crossman 1973, Kendall 1935, and Yerrell 1836). Specimens this large undoubtedly were older salmon that had spawned a number of times and returned to the sea after each spawning.

### Range and Diet

The Atlantic salmon's range extends from Portugal to the Arctic Circle in the eastern Atlantic, includes Iceland and southern Greenland, and encompasses the Ungava region of northern Quebec southward to the Connecticut River of New England in the western Atlantic. Salmon from both the eastern and western Atlantic live in the vast feeding grounds off Greenland. Salmon of the eastern Atlantic also feed in the Baltic, in areas near the Faroe Islands, and elsewhere in the eastern Atlantic. Food items principally consist of fishes such as herring, capelin, and sand eels. Large zooplankton such as euphausiids and amphipods also are important in the salmon diet. Salmon are themselves preyed upon by seals, sharks, pollock, tuna, skates, halibut, cod, striped bass, blue fish, and other predators (Scott and Crossman 1973, Mills 1971, Piggins 1959). Man, too, is a significant predator.

## Anadromy and Homing

Atlantic salmon hatch and remain in freshwater for one or more years, then descend to the sea to feed and grow for at least a year before returning to freshwater to reproduce. After breeding, they return to the sea. It is the salmon's anadromy, its dependence on both freshwater and marine environments, that complicates the life cycle of the salmon and has led to a rather long list of terms specific to various stages in the species' life history.

One of the most puzzling of all aspects of the salmon's life history is its homing instinct. That salmon return to their parent stream has been known for several hundred years. The importance of stream odors in the orientation of fish also has been well demonstrated (Hasler 1954, Hasler and Wisby 1951). Research indicates that in salmon the smell of the parent stream is imprinted during a short period before the young descend to the sea (Carlin 1969). Thus, as breeding salmon approach the coastal areas from the open ocean, they probably locate their parent streams by smell. But how the salmon navigate in the ocean, far from their parent streams, still remains a mystery.

Atlantic salmon may leave the sea to spawn in their parent stream during any month of the year (Mills 1971). After entering fresh water, adult salmon cease to feed. They will not eat again until they re-enter the sea some six months to a year later.

Returning salmon usually are between three and six years old, but individuals up to 11 have been reported (Power 1969). Returning salmon in New England range in age from two to at least six, with four the predominate age. Salmon that return after one year at sea (grilse) weigh between two and six pounds. Those returning after two years weigh between six and 15 pounds, while those returning after three years may exceed 20 pounds. Of course, older individuals and repeat spawners probably weigh even more. Salmon enter rivers in New England from April through October, with peak activity occurring in May, June, and July. Throughout its range the Atlantic salmon spawns during the fall and early winter months. In New England, spawning typically occurs in late October through November.

With the onset of spawning the head of the male salmon elongates and the lower jaw enlarges, curving up at the tip to form what is called a "kype." This characteristic easily identifies the male, but its exact biological function is not yet clear.

The female chooses the nest site, usually a gravel-bottom riffle area above or below a pool, and with her strong caudal fin excavates a pit into which the eggs are deposited. More than one male usually participates with a single female in fertilizing the eggs. This process is repeated again and again until all or nearly all of the female's eggs have been deposited. The series of pits into which the eggs have been deposited and covered with gravel is called a "redd." The female deposits roughly 700 eggs per pound of body weight, from 2,000 to more than 15,000 eggs (Mills 1971). The adult fish after spawning are called "kelts" and may return to the sea immediately or during the following spring, as is more typical in New England. Only a small percentage of the kelts, primarily females, will reach the sea and return in later years as repeat spawners.

The salmon eggs that are deposited in the redd normally hatch in late March and April, depending on water temperature. Water temperatures below 50 degrees are desirable for normal egg development, and temperatures in the low 40s are considered optimum (Peterson *et al* 1977). The "alevins," as the newly hatched salmon are called, remain buried in the gravel until the yoke sac has been absorbed. Actual emergence of the alevins, now called "fry," from the gravel occurs from March through June. The fry disperse from the redd site and rapidly assume the coloring of the life stage referred to as "parr." These young salmon have eight to 11 narrow, vertical, pigmented bands on their sides (parr marks) with a single red spot between each band. The parr, basically stream-bottom dwellers, are strongly territorial during stream residency, which may last up to eight years (Power 1969, Saunders and Gee 1964, Keenleyside and Yamomoto 1962, Kalleberg 1958). In New England rivers, parr remain in freshwater from one to three years, with two years predominating.

At a size of five to eight inches the parr undergo physiological and morphometric transformations that prepare them for migration to the sea and the transition from a stream-bottom animal to a free-roaming ocean fish. This transformation is known as "smoltification," and in the migratory stage, which normally occurs during the spring, the parr are more properly called "smolts." After entering the sea the smolts, now referred to as "post-smolts," migrate to thedistant oceanic feeding grounds. Salmon originating from New England rivers will be found in the Greenland waters and along the Labrador and Newfoundland coasts.

During their freshwater residency, young salmon are opportunistic feeders, preying on the most abundant food items. Aquatic insect larvae and nymphs (chironomids, mayflies, caddis flies, black flies, and stone flies) are the principal food items. However, terrestrial insects are eaten and probably are an important part of the diet during certain periods of the year. The young salmon's life is not without its perils, for it falls prey to a number of creatures, including kingfishers, American mergansers, eels, various trout species, pike, and pickerel (MacCrimmon 1954, White 1957 and 1933).

## Freshwater Habitat

The size of Atlantic salmon populations, especially in New England rivers, is governed to a large degree by the quality, quantity, and accessibility of the spawning and nursery habitats. Good spawning habitat includes beds of stones measuring one-half to four inches in diameter. These gravel beds promote the movement of clean, well-oxygenated water through the redd (Peterson 1978, Warner 1963), which is critical since salmon eggs may be deposited as deep as 12 inches (Warner 1963). Spawning habitat should be well dispersed throughout the nursery habitat.

Salmon nursery habitat typically is composed of shallow riffle areas interspersed with deeper riffles and pools. The substrate pebbles, ranging from one-half to greater than nine inches in diameter, afford adequate cover for the juvenile salmon (Knight 1981, Symons and Heland 1978). Clean, well-oxygenated water is a necessity. The young salmon also require relatively warm water for growth. They grow very slowly at temperatures below 45 degrees (Symons 1979) and experience optimal growth in streams with daily peaks of 72 to 77 degrees (Elson 1975).

Returning adult salmon must have access to the spawning grounds. An open, unobstructed river is ideal. Where obstructions, such as impassible dams, occur, fish passage facilities must be provided. The distance traveled upriver ranges from 10 to 600 miles. Once in the river, adult salmon making long migrations require adequate resting and holding pools, up to 12 feet deep, for temporary refuge from the swift current. After two to three weeks rest, the salmon swim another 30 to 50 miles before resting again. Resting sites usually lack the cover and temperature regime of the holding pools. Holding pools normally are located near the spawning grounds and have the cover, depth, temperature regime, and water velocities preferred by adult salmon. The pools should have a gravel substrate with cover provided by large boulders, logs, or ledge outcroppings. Minimum water depth should exceed six feet and water velocities should be less than one and a half feet per second (Frenette *et al* 1972). Water temperature in the holding areas are considered optimum at 50 to 54 degrees. Undisturbed salmon can withstand temperatures of 60 degrees and daily highs of 77 degrees, providing the water cools to 68 degrees or less at night (Elson 1975).

# Significance of the Species

## Worldwide

The Atlantic salmon provides both commercial and sport fishing to the people of Europe and the western Atlantic. In addition, native Greenlanders rely on their annual salmon catches both commercially and as a part of their cultural traditions. More recently, Native Americans in New Brunswick and Quebec are expressing an interest in salmon fishing. A decade ago these peoples did not intensively fish for salmon, but subsistence fishing of salmon in the lower St. John's River has been intensifying. This is partly a response to court rulings that have strengthened Indian fishing rights in the Northwest Pacific. Maine's Penobscot Indians also may initiate more intensive salmon fishing.

Canada alone has an estimated 6,000 licensed commercial fishermen who yearly take more than 600,000 salmon with a landed value that exceeds $7 million (Department of Fisheries and Oceans 1983 and 1982). The recreational value of the species is even more staggering. The eastern Canadian recreational fishery, with approximately 70,000 anglers, takes roughly 100,000 fish yearly, adding between $27 million and $42 million to the economy (Department of Fisheries and Oceans 1983 and 1982).

## New England

Commercial fishing for Atlantic salmon is not permitted in New England because the resource is limited. However, the recreational fishery on the principal salmon river in Maine, the Penobscot, takes between a few hundred fish to as many as 2,000 annually. The value of this fishery to the state's economy has been estimated at greater than $1 million yearly.

At the present time, the real value of the Atlantic salmon to the New England region probably lies in less tangible areas. Each year thousands of people visit salmon hatcheries and fish passage facilities. A good case could be made that public interest in this species transcends the fish's value as a sport or even a commercial product. The Atlantic salmon has become a symbol for cleaner rivers and a rallying cry for repair of past damages. It represents a part of the New England heritage lost nearly a century ago. The return of the Atlantic salmon to the rivers of New England sends out a strong signal that the environment is improving.

The Atlantic salmon continues to have an impact on river development worldwide, particularly the construction of new hydroelectric dams. The building of dams and perpetuation of the salmon resource are not compatible but at times must coexist, in some cases with very expensive mitigative measures. Mitigation usually is in the form of fish passage facilities, but may even include the construction of new salmon hatcheries. In New England, Atlantic salmon rivers presently are under heavy hydroelectric development pressure, and in some cases this pressure is being actively opposed by sport fishing and public interests as well as governmental agencies.

# Historical Perspective

## Worldwide

In the eastern Atlantic, salmon populated literally hundreds and hundreds of rivers. Southward from Iceland, where they inhabited more than 60 rivers, their range extended from the Pechora River of the Barents Sea to the Souro River of northern Portugal and the Bay of Biscay (MacCrimmon and Gots 1979). Countries that contained native salmon populations included Belgium, Czechoslovakia, Denmark, Finland, France, Germany, Iceland, Ireland, Luxembourg, the Netherlands, Norway, Poland, Portugal, Spain, Sweden, Switzerland, England, Wales, Scotland, Northern Ireland, and the Union of the Soviet Socialist Republics. Salmon also inhabited rivers in southern Greenland and were found in the western Atlantic in northern Quebec, Labrador, Newfoundland, the maritime providences of Canada, virtually every river of New England, and possibly the Hudson River of New York. The size of the salmon resource historically is unknown but surely was extremely large.

Over the past several hundred years, man's activities have served to reduce the salmon resource significantly. Water pollution, the building of impassible dams, overfishing, declining populations, and stream acidification have all served to limit the resource (Watt *et al* 1983, Overrein 1980, MacCrimmon and Gots 1979, Netboy 1968). Managers have attempted to compensate for the severe impacts by constructing fish-passage facilities at dams, by limiting commercial and even sport harvests, and by developing significant artificial-propagation programs.

## New England

Historically, some 300,000 salmon may have spawned in the rivers of New England and possibly the Hudson. Rivers such as the Penobscot, Kennebec, and Androscoggin in Maine, as well as the Merrimack and Connecticut in southern New England, were significant salmon producers. For a time following the colonization of the New England region, the Atlantic salmon continued to thrive. By the early 1880s, however, the salmon resource had been reduced severely by the construction of dams, overfishing, water pollution, and ignorance of salmon biology. Continued river development and commercial-fishing pressure reduced the population further, until by 1865 the salmon runs of southern New England had been eliminated and commercial fishing was profitable only in eastern Maine. The decline and decimation of the New England Atlantic salmon populations have been well documented by a number of authors (Beland 1984, Stolte 1981, MacCrimmon and Gots 1979, Netboy 1968, Kendall 1935).

# Current Trends

## Worldwide

The status of the Atlantic salmon in the world today is a stark reminder of man's past actions. Salmon do not now enter the rivers of Belgium, Czechoslovakia, East and West Germany, Luxembourg, the Netherlands, and Switzerland. Populations have been severely limited or reduced in Spain, Portugal, France, Poland, Finland, Sweden, Norway, and Denmark. Some Canadian rivers have witnessed declining salmon populations, and a number of rivers in Nova Scotia are entirely devoid of salmon.

In the United States, only seven rivers, all in Maine, support healthy native populations. This small salmon resource may number between 1,000 and 3,000 fish in any one year. Salmon populations that presently enter rivers such as the St. Croix, Union, Penobscot, Merrimack, Pawcatuck, and Connecticut result principally from restoration programs relying on artificial salmon propagation. Salmon populations in these rivers seldom have salmon returns much greater than 4,000 to 7,000 individuals collectively.

Although the data still are being quantified and drawn together by such groups as the North Atlantic Salmon Conservation Organization (see below), it is clear that salmon populations have decreased throughout the Atlantic in the last decade. Declining commercial catches as well as the number of salmon returning to home rivers indicate this trend. Many biologists believe the species is now in serious trouble.

Factors that are playing a role in this decline are numerous and in some cases little understood. Excessive commercial-fishing take, sport fishing mortalities, hydroelectric development, water pollution, water withdrawals from parent rivers, stream acidification, and poaching of salmon in freshwater are all contributing to the plight of the Atlantic salmon.

## New England

Growth of the salmon resource in New England is limited principally by the ocean commercial fishery, the availability of suitable spawning and nursery habitat to returning salmon, and the size of the artificial-propagation program. The third factor is important simply because the salmon resource of New England is primarily a product of restoration activities.

The impact of the ocean commercial fishery has been explored with extensive smolt-tagging experiments (more than 1,000,000 smolts have been tagged since 1966). These have shown that salmon of United States origin are caught in the Greenland commercial fishery and taken during migration by Canadian fishermen, principally in the Labrador and Newfoundland coastal reaches (Baum 1984). Nearly 60 percent of the tags recovered from commercial fishermen have come from the Greenland area, with about 40 percent coming from the Newfoundland-Labrador areas. Researchers presently estimate that for every salmon that returns to the rivers of New England, one to five are caught in the ocean fishery (Boreman *et al* 1984).

Accessibility of spawning and nursery habitat to returning salmon also limits the growth of the salmon resource in New England. Although this is not a factor in relation to the seven small rivers in Maine that presently contain healthy native runs, it is extremely important in those rivers in which salmon-restoration efforts are under way. Of the six major rivers in which restoration presently is occurring, less than 50 percent of the spawning and nursery habitat is available to returning salmon (Oatis *et al* 1985, Beland 1984, Stolte 1982). At least 29 dams, lacking fish-passage facilities, block salmon access to upriver areas.

The fact that the rivers under restoration, with the exception of the Penobscot, have no native (wild) Atlantic Salmon populations places an extreme importance on the artificial-propagation program. During the past decade, roughly 6,600,000 salmon smolts and 5,500,000 fry and/or parr have been released. The trend in the propagation program is upward. Adult salmon returns to these rivers, although fluctuating annually, generally have increased.

# Management

## Worldwide

Management of the Atlantic salmon consists of activities in six basic areas: 1) regulation to protect the species, 2) restoration, maintenance, and artificial propagation, 3) fish-passage construction, 4) assessment of the impacts of river development, particularly hydro development, on salmon, 5) research (genetic, life history, fish culture, etc.), and 6) routine population assessments.

Probably one of the more significant measures yet taken in the face of declining Atlantic salmon populations was the ratification in 1983 of an international treaty, the Convention for the Conservation of Salmon in the North Atlantic. The convention established the North Atlantic Salmon Conservation Organization, which is composed of three commissions. The North American Commission includes the United States and Canada; the West Greenland Commission includes the United States, Canada, Denmark (representing Greenland), and the European Economic Community; and the membership of the Northeast Atlantic Commission includes Denmark (representing the Faroe Islands and Greenland), the European Economic Community, Finland, Iceland, Norway, and Sweden.

The three commissions presently are involved in studying the status of the salmon populations within their respective areas and in considering appropriate regulatory measures. In 1984, the three commissions agreed upon a catch quota of nearly 300 metric tons less than the quota that previously existed in the West Greenland area. However, the reduction was of no real consequence, since the actual catch was far less than the allowable quota.

Outside the realm of the organization, both Canada and the United States have instituted rather strong conservation measures. Faced with declining salmon resources, Canada has enacted a number of significant conserva-

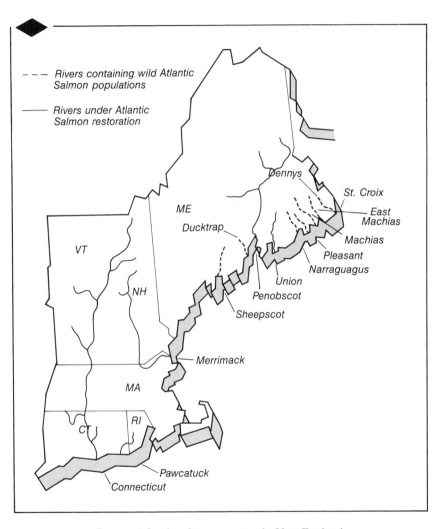

Present Atlantic salmon program in New England

tion measures. Delayed openings for commercial salmon fishing seasons as well as shorter seasons may help provide for stronger spawning populations. Even the recreational salmon fisherman has been forced to accept restrictions in seasonal and daily creel limits. In some cases only grilse may be killed.

In New England, the limited salmon resource has prompted Maine to restrict the seasonal limit for the recreational angler. Elsewhere in New England, recreational anglers must return caught salmon to the river. Only no-kill fishing is permitted. The present angling restrictions have been well received by sportsmen and by conservation organizations such as Trout Unlimited, the Atlantic Salmon Federation, Salmon Unlimited, Restoration of Atlantic Salmon in America, Inc., Connecticut River Salmon Association, various river watershed councils, and others. Some of these organizations desire even more restrictive measures.

## Management Complexities in New England

Management of the Atlantic salmon in New England is complex. Each of the six New England states is an active participant in the Atlantic salmon program. These states are involved with three federal agencies — the U.S. Fish and Wildlife Service (FWS), the National Marine Fisheries Service, and the United States Forest Service—in four unique cooperative efforts. The four cooperative efforts encompass 1) the rivers of Maine, 2) the Merrimack River (New Hampshire and Massachusetts), 3) the Pawcatuck River (Rhode Island), and 4) the Connecticut River (Connecticut, Massachusetts, New Hampshire, and Vermont). The program seeks to restore populations to selected rivers that historically supported this species.

The restoration efforts on the principal rivers are guided by formal plans with long-term objectives. The programs for the Connecticut, Pawcatuck, and Merrimack rivers operate within the framework of strategic plans (Oatis *et al* 1985, Stolte 1982, and Guthrie *et al* 1981). In Maine, a comprehensive strategic plan encompasses the entire state, with the various river systems addressed by individual river management reports (Beland 1984, Baum 1983, Dube 1983, Baum 1982a and 1982b, Baum and Jordan 1982, Beland *et al* 1982, Fletcher *et al* 1982, Fletcher and Melster 1982).

The four restoration programs, with the exception of those encompassing the Connecticut and Pawcatuck rivers, are guided by interagency committees. The interagency committees have no regulatory powers within their respective rivers, since this authority is reserved for the state fishery agencies. The restoration program for the Connecticut River, in contrast, is guided by a federal interstate compact which established a federal interstate commission that does have regulatory powers. The program for the Pawcatuck River is an extremely informal arrangement between FWS and the Rhode Island Department of Environmental Management. The Department of Environmental Management has the sole regulatory responsibility.

Administration of Atlantic Salmon Restoration Programs in New England

| Agencies | Rivers Included |
|---|---|
| Connecticut Department of Environment Protection | |
| Massachusetts Division of Fisheries and Wildlife | |
| New Hampshire Fish and Game Department | Connecticut River |
| Vermont Fish and Game Department | |
| National Marine Fisheries Service | |
| United States Fish and Wildlife Service | |
| Rhode Island Division of Fisheries and Wildlife | Pawcatuck River |
| United States Fish and Wildlife Service | |
| Massachusetts Division of Fisheries and Wildlife | |
| Massacusetts Division of Marine Fisheries | |
| New Hampshire Fish and Game Department | Merrimack River |
| National Marine Fisheries Service | |
| United States Forest Service | |
| United States Fish and Wildlife Service | |
| Maine Atlantic Sea-Run Salmon Commission | |
| Maine Department of Inland Fisheries and Wildlife | Rivers in Maine |
| Maine Department of Marine Resources | |
| United States Fish and Wildlife Service | |

Each of the cooperating agencies has committed funds and manpower to the salmon restoration program. FWS is carrying the greatest commitment of resources because of the interstate and international dimensions of salmon restoration. This is especially true in the areas of artificial propagation and research. FWS presently operates five Atlantic salmon hatcheries and produces greater than 70 percent of the entire smolt and fry production used in the restoration program. This federal agency also is conducting significant research in the areas of salmon genetics, salmon diseases and their control, hatchery diets, and stream acidification.

The fact that the rivers in which salmon restoration is under way contained virtually no salmon around which populations could be developed makes the operation of the artificial propagation program an important concern. Salmon eggs for the program in the past have been obtained from populations that spawn far from the rivers under restoration, a situation that did not provide significant success in the form of returning adult salmon and is not likely to do so (Ritter 1975). Thus, the importance of the few salmon that presently enter the rivers cannot be overstated. Genetic research should help in the development of salmon strains more likely to return to artificially stocked parent streams.

Work now is under way by all participating fisheries agencies to ensure that the salmon which return to the rivers eventually will have access to the spawning and nursery habitats. Negotiation with hydroelectric-dam owners about construction of fish-passage facilities at impassible dams is a continuous process.

Atlantic Salmon Smolt Stocking and Adult Return Records
for New England (1970-1984).

| Year | Number of Atlantic salmon smolts released into New England rivers | Number of Atlantic salmon returning from the ocean to New England rivers |
|---|---|---|
| 1970 | 100,000 | 790 |
| 1971 | 116,000 | 670 |
| 1972 | 141,000 | 1,180 |
| 1973 | 198,000 | 960 |
| 1974 | 215,000 | 1,370 |
| 1975 | 251,000 | 2,190 |
| 1976 | 369,000 | 1,490 |
| 1977 | 406,000 | 1,950 |
| 1978 | 476,000 | 4,090 |
| 1979 | 580,000 | 1,970 |
| 1980 | 773,000 | 5,920 |
| 1981 | 443,000 | 6,270 |
| 1982 | 698,000 | 5,600 |
| 1983 | 861,000 | 2,160 |
| 1984 | 1,277,000 | 3,400 |

Of significant importance to the restoration program is the investigation presently being conducted on potential impacts of proposed new hydroelectric dams. Major rivers, such as the Penobscot, Merrimack, and Connecticut, are facing new hydroelectric-dam development. Impact analyses have led a number of state and federal agencies to oppose development in certain areas.

# Prognosis

## Worldwide

What the future holds for Atlantic salmon worldwide is open to great speculation. However, concern for this species is as strong today as it was in the past, and hope remains that the international salmon treaty organization will provide positive results. The relatively large artificial-propagation program for salmon in various European and Scandinavian countries, Canada, and the United States, coupled with a significant reduction in the ocean commercial fishery, would be extremely beneficial to the Atlantic salmon.

## New England

In New England, the prospect for the Atlantic salmon resource is bright in spite of the problems. This optimistic outlook is prompted by the growing artificial-propagation program, and the progress being made in providing for upstream fish passage at impassible dams.

By 1990, the Atlantic salmon hatchery program will be providing roughly 5,000,000 fry and 1,400,000 smolts yearly for release into selected New England rivers. This kind of stocking program is expected to generate major increases in the size of the salmon resource during the next 25 years. For example, the salmon population is expected to double its present size of 4,000 to 7,000 individuals by 1990. By 1997, a second doubling in size is expected, with gradual increases occurring thereafter. A total of nearly 42,000 salmon is expected to enter at least 14 rivers by 2010. The rivers individually are expected to realize between 40 percent and 100 percent of full salmon restoration. This is a far cry above the present restoration achievement level of less than five percent in any one river system.

These predictions are based to some degree on an anticipated reduction in the ocean commercial take and, more importantly, on the construction of nearly 30 upstream fish-passage facilities. Progress made to date at impassible dams on two large southern New England rivers, the Connecticut and Merrimack, indicate that fish-passage requirements for Atlantic salmon in New England can be met.

Although the restoration-program cooperators are very optimisitic about the future of the Atlantic salmon, some individuals and organizations question the value of the program. This attitude is a response to the Atlantic salmon's impact on river development, notably hydro. If the program were to be curtailed (elimination of federal activities, for example), the Atlantic salmon resource would likely move toward near extinction in New England some time in the future. Total elimination of all federal and state activities would hasten the entire extirpation of the salmon resource.

The optimistic viewpoint toward resource restoration is the one most likely to be realized in the future. The following words of Tom Pero (1977) can best summarize the Atlantic salmon's future in New England:

> Successfully restoring Atlantic salmon to the rivers of home will mean that for one of the few times in the history of civilization, a people will have revived a species its ancestors recklessly abused and exterminated. Restoring the salmon will not be easy. It will take enormous accounts of money, hard work and commitment. Mostly, it will take commitment. Only this will bring the salmon back. We will win, we will lose, we will compromise. But in the end, the salmon will win. And New England will be a better place.

## Recommendations

Although the survival of the Atlantic salmon as a species is probably not in serious jeopardy, the actual strength of the resource worldwide has been debilitated. In many rivers and countries, Atlantic-salmon populations have declined or have been eliminated completely. To reverse the present trend, the salmon-producing as well as salmon-catching countries will have to devise ways in which the ocean commercial fishing industry can allow for the return of adequate numbers of salmon to their parent streams in order to maintain population growth in concert with the freshwater habitat.

In addition to the needed ocean commercial fishery controls there are a number of areas in which actions need to be maintained:

1. In those rivers in which sport fishing for salmon is important, management may be required to implement programs designed to maintain fishing opportunity but minimize the actual kill. This probably will be extremely important in New England.
2. The present artificial-propagation program will have to be maintained. In New England this program may need to expand to meet future production requirements.
3. In New England, existing impassible dams on important salmon rivers will require fish-passage facilities.
4. River development, especially hydro, must be assessed thoroughly in relation to impacts on salmon populations. In New England it will be necessary in some rivers to limit hydro development if restoration of Atlantic salmon is to remain a serious objective.
5. Research in areas such as fish culture (diets, disease prevention, rearing techniques, genetics), population assessments in freshwater, marine migrations, ocean fisheries, and stream acidification must be maintained.

# References

Baum, E. 1984. History and Description of the USA Atlantic Salmon Tagging Program. Unpublished manuscript. Marine Atlantic Sea-Run Salmon Commission. Bangor, Maine. 13 pp.

———— 1983. *The Penobscot River: An Atlantic Salmon River Management Report.* Maine Atlantic Sea-Run Salmon Commission, Bangor, Maine. 67 pp.

———— 1982a. *The Saint John River Watershed: An Atlantic Salmon River Management Report.* Maine Atlantic Sea-Run Salmon Commission, Bangor, Maine. pp. 1-60.

———— 1982b. *The Union River: An Atlantic Salmon River Management Report.* Maine Atlantic Sea-Run Salmon Commission, Bangor, Maine. pp. 1-31.

Baum E. and R. Jordan. 1982. *The Narraguagus and the Pleasant Rivers: Salmon River Management Report.* Maine Atlantic Sea-Run Salmon Commission, Bangor, Maine. pp. 1-69.

Beland, K. 1984. *A Strategic Plan for Management of Atlantic Salmon in the State of Maine.* Maine Atlantic Sea-Run Salmon Commission, Bangor, Maine.

Beland, K., J. Fletcher, and A. Meister. 1982. *The Dennys River: An Atlantic Salmon River Management report.* Maine Atlantic Sea-Run Salmon Commission, Bangor, Maine. pp. 1-40.

Boreman, J., A.M.T. Lange, and V.C. Anthony. 1984. Estimates of harvest of USA Atlantic salmon in non-USA fisheries. ICES. Working Paper 5/84.

Carlin, B. 1969. *The Migration of Salmon.* Swedish Salmon Research Institute. Report LFI Medd. 4/1969.

Couch, J. 1965. *The History of the Fishes of the British Islands. Vol. IV.* Groombridge and Sons, London. pp. 216-218.

Department of Fisheries and Oceans. 1983. *1984 Atlantic Salmon Management Plan.* Information leaflet. I-HQ-84-07E. Ottawa, Canada.

———— 1982. *Management of the Atlantic Salmon in the Late 1980s.* A discussion paper, DFO/620. 7/1982. Ottawa, Canada.

Dube, N. 1983. *The Saco River: An Atlantic Salmon River Management Report.* Maine Atlantic Sea-Run Commission, Bangor, Maine. pp. 1-29.

Elson, P.F. 1975. *Atlantic Salmon Rivers, Smolt Production and Optimal Spawning: An Overview of Natural Production.* I.A.S.F. Special Publication 6, New England Atlantic Salmon Conference. pp. 96-119.

Fletcher, J., R. Jordan, and K. Beland. 1982. *The Machias and East Machias Rivers: An Atlantic Salmon River Management Report.* Maine Atlantic Sea-Run Salmon Commission, Bangor, Maine. pp. 1-68.

Fletcher, J. and A. Meister. 1982. *The St. Croix River: An Atlantic Salmon River Management Report.* Maine Atlantic Sea-Run Salmon Commission, Bangor, Maine. pp. 1-42.

Frenette, M., C. Rae, and B. Tetreault. 1972. *The Creation of Artificial Salmon Pools.* Department of Civil Engineering, Laval University, Quebec, Canada. pp. 17-24.

Guthrie, R.C., J. Stolgitis, and W.L. Bridges. 1983. *Pawcatuck River Watershed—Fisheries Management Survey.* Fisheries Report No. 1. Rhode Island Division of Fish and Wildlife. Providence, Rhode Island. 61 pp.

Hasler, A.D. 1954. "Odor perception and orientation in fishes," *Journal of Fisheries Resources Board of Canada,* II. pp. 107-129.

Hasler, A.D. and W.J. Wisby. 1951. "Discrimination of stream odors by fishes and its relation to parent stream behavior." *American Naturalist* 85:223-238.

Kallebert, H. 1958. "Observations in a stream tank of territoriality and competition in juvenile salmon and trout (*Salmo salar* L. and *S. trutta* L.)." Report of the Institute of Freshwater Research Drottningholm 39:55-98.

Keenleyside, M.H.A. and Yamamoto, F.T. 1962. "Territorial behaviour of juvenile Atlantic salmon (*Salmo salar* L.)." *Behaviour* 19(I):139-169.

Kendall, W.C. 1935. The Fishes of New England. The salmon family. Part 2—The Salmons. *Memoirs of the Boston Society of Natural History* vol. 9, no. 1. 166 pp.

Knight, A.E. 1981. Unpublished data. Mad River, New Hampshire Fish and Wildlife Service. Laconia, New Hampshire.

MacCrimmon, H.R. 1954. "Stream studies on planted Atlantic salmon," *Journal of Fisheries Resources Board Canada* 11(4):362-403.

MacCrimmon, H.R. and B.L. Gots. 1979. "World distribution of Atlantic salmon, *Salmo salar.*" *Journal of the Fisheries Resource Board of Canada* 36:422-457.

Mills, D. 1971. *Salmon and Trout: A Resource, Its Ecology, Conservation and Management.* St. Martin's Press, New York. 351 pp.

Netboy, Anthony. 1974. *The Salmon—Their Fight for Survival.* Houghton Mifflin Company, Boston, Massachusetts. 613 pp.

―――― 1968. *The Atlantic Salmon—A Vanishing Species.* Houghton Mifflin Company, Boston, Massachusetts. 457 pp.

Oatis, P., S. Henry, R. Iwanowicz, J. Greenwood, J. Cookson, J. Lanier, D. Kimball, B. Rizzo, and L. Stolte. 1985. *Restoration of Atlantic Salmon to the Merrimack River.* 1985 through 1999. A Planning Document of the Merrimack River. Policy and Technical Committees. U.S. Fish and Wildlife Service, Fisheries Assistance. Concord, New Hampshire. 24 pp.

Olafsen, E. 1774. Des Vice-Lavmands Eggert Olafsens und des Land-physici Biarne Povelsens Reise durch Island, veranstaltet von der Koniglischen Societat der Wissenshaften in Kopenhagen und beschrieben von bemeldten Eggert Olafsen. Aus dem Danischen ubersetzt. Mit 25 Kupfertafeln und einer neuen Charte uber Island versehen, Kopenhagen und Leipzig, 1: 14 not numb. + 1-328, 25 pl., map.

Overrien, L., H. Seip, and A. Tollan. 1980. *Acid Precipitation - Effects on Forest and Fish.* Research report FR 19, Acid Precipitation - Effects on Forest and Fish Projects, Aas, Norway.

Pero, T. 1977. "Atlantic salmon—Part II," *New England Outdoors* 3(4):38-40. (April).

Peterson, R.H. 1978. *Physical Characteristics of Atlantic Salmon Spawning Gravel in Some New Brunswick Streams.* Fisheries and Marine Service Technical Report 785. 28 pp.

Peterson, R.H., H.C.E. Spinney, and A. Sreedharan. 1977. "Development of Atlantic salmon (*Salmo salar*) eggs and alevins under varied temperature regimes." *Journal of the Fisheries Resource Board of Canada* 34:31-34.

Piggins, D.J. 1959. "Investigations of predators of salmon smolts and parr." Report and Statement of Accounts, the Salmon Research Trust for Ireland Incorporated, Appendix I. 12 pp.

Power, G. 1969. "The salmon of Ungava Bay." *Arctic Institute North American Technical Paper* 22. 72 pp.

Ritter, J.A. 1975. "Lower ocean survival rates for hatchery-reared Atlantic salmon (*Salmo salar*) stocks released in rivers other than their native streams." ICES, C.M. 1975/M. 26. Anadromous and Catadromous Fish Committee. 10 pp.

Saunders, R.L. and J.H. Gee. 1964. "Movements of young Atlantic salmon in a small stream." *Journal of the Fisheries Resource Board of Canada* 21(I):27-36.

Scott, W.B. and E.J. Crossman. 1973. "Freshwater fishes of Canada." *Fisheries Resource Board of Canada Bulletin* 184. Ottawa, Canada. 966 pp.

Sedgwick, S.D. 1982. *The Salmon Handbook.* Robert Hartnoll Ltd., Cornwall, Great Britain. 242 pp.

Smitt, F.A. 1882. "Schematisk framstallning af de i Riksmuseum befintliga laxartade fiskarnes slagtskapforhallanden." *Ofvers. Kongl. Vet.-Akad. Forhandl.* (Stockholm) 39(8):31-40. [S. brevipes (Archangels lax), p. 32].

Stolte, L.W. 1982. *A Strategic Plan for the Restoration of Atlantic Salmon to the Connecticut River Basin* (revised September 1982). U.S. Fish and Wildlife Service, Fisheries Assistance. Laconia, New Hampshire. 84 pp.

———— 1981. *The Forgotton Salmon of the Merrimack.* U.S. Government Printing Office. Washington, D.C. 236 pp.

Symons, P.E.K. 1979. "Estimated escapement of Atlantic salmon (*Salmo salar*) for maximum smolt production in rivers of different productivity." *Journal of the Fisheries Resources Board of Canada* 35:175-183.

Symons, P.E.K. and M. Heland. 1978. "Stream habitats and behavioral interactions of underyearling and yearling Atlantic salmon (*Salmo salar*)." *Journal of the Fisheries Resources Board of Canada* 35:175-183.

Warner, K. 1963. "Natural spawning success of landlocked salmon (*Salmo salar*)." *Transactions of the American Fisheries Society* 92(2):161-164.

Watt, W., C. Scott, and W. White. 1983. "Evidence of acidification of some Nova Scotian rivers and its impact on Atlantic Salmon, *Salmo salar.*" *Canadian Journal of Fishes and Aquatic Science* 40:462-473.

White, H.C. 1957. "Food and natural history of mergansers on salmon waters in the Maritime Provinces of Canada." *Fisheries Resource Board of Canada Bulletin* 116. 63 pp.

White, H.C. 1933. "Salmon fry in still water." Biology Board of Canada *Progr. Rep. Atl.* 7:6-8.

Yarrell, W. 1836. *A History of British Fishes. Vol. 2.* John Van Voorst, London. 472 pp. + 72 page supplement.

*Lawrence W. Stolte is a fisheries biologist in the Ecological Services division of the Fish and Wildlife Service's Concord, New Hampshire, office.*

A fisherman in the Northwest Pacific sorts his catch into different price categories. Chinook salmon are among the species sought by commercial and recreational fishermen.

*Zoltan Gaal/Photo Researchers*

◆ ────────────────────────────── ◆

# Chinook Salmon of the Columbia River Basin

## Lloyd A. Phinney

Washington State Department of Fisheries

T HE COLUMBIA RIVER basin encompasses some 259,000 square miles of Washington, Oregon, Idaho, Montana, Wyoming, Nevada, and British Columbia. From its headwaters in southeastern British Columbia the river courses approximately 1,250 miles to its confluence with the Pacific Ocean. Along its route it picks up the flow of at least 150 tributary streams. The largest of these is the Snake River, which itself exceeds 1,000 miles in length and drains the majority of the state of Idaho, much of eastern Oregon, and southeastern Washington. The average flow of the Columbia River is exceeded in North America only by that of the Mackenzie, Saint Lawrence, and Mississippi rivers (Netboy 1974). The aquatic resources of the Columbia basin are a major asset in the economic and social well-being of the Pacific Northwest.

## Species Description and Natural History

Many species of the family Salmonidae reside in the Columbia River basin. The family includes the Pacific salmon (*Oncorhynchus* spp.), trout (*Salmo* spp.), char (*Salvelinus* spp.), grayling (*Thymallus arcticus*), and the whitefishes (*Prospopium* spp.) (Wydoski and Whitney 1979). Of these, the chinook salmon (*O. tshawytscha*) is perhaps the most economically, culturally, and politically important.

715

## Range

Chinook salmon are found in the eastern Pacific from the Ventura River in southern California to Point Hope, Alaska. They also occur in the western Pacific from Hokkaido, Japan, north to the Anadyr River in Russia (Wydoski and Whitney 1979). Chinook have been transplanted to a number of areas. The most noted successes are the populations presently established in the Great Lakes and New Zealand (Netboy 1980). Nowhere did the chinook's historical abundance exceed that of the Columbia River in its pristine condition. Despite severe environmental degradation, it remains the world's largest single producer of this important salmon species.

Chinook originally were found almost in the very headwaters of the Columbia River at the outlet of Lake Windermere in Canada, some 1,200 miles from the Pacific Ocean. They migrated up the Snake River as far as Shoshone Falls in south-central Idaho, roughly 1,000 miles. Virtually all accessible tributaries were used by this species (Fulton 1968). Production today still exists in virtually all accessible tributaries. Unfortunately, as the following discussion will show, the number and miles of accessible tributaries and main stems has been reduced drastically.

## Chinook Runs of the Columbia

The Columbia River supports three runs of chinook. The runs are defined by the timing of their entry into the river (Mason 1965). Spring chinook enter from January through May, followed by summer chinook in June and July. Fall chinook continue entering as late as November. Each run is composed of a number of stocks which may overlap in their entry and upstream migration, but separate as they approach their streams of origin. In this discussion, the definition of stock follows that of the Northwest Power Planning Council:

> Stock—The fish spawning in a particular stream during a particular season which to a substantial degree do not interbreed with any group spawning in a different stream or at a different time (Northwest Power Planning Council 1984).

Any particular stream may have more than one salmon run. Spawning of the two or more runs is usually well separated both temporally and spacially. In general, where spring and summer (or fall) chinook coexist in the same stream, the summer fish spawn later and in lower reaches of the tributary with minimal overlap.

## Homing

The homing instinct of Pacific salmon and steelhead is marveled at but little understood. Hasler (1966) supports celestial navigation as the guide for salmon returning to the river mouth. Others, however, suggest that homing is aided by electrical voltages in the ocean currents (Royce *et al* 1968). Regardless of the mechanism, salmon and steelhead do return generally to their river and tributary of origin to spawn. It is doubtful, however, that this instinct returns them to precisely the riffle from which they hatched.

## Spawning

All members of the genus *Oncorhynchus* are gravel-nest builders. Chinook typically spawn in flowing water in depths of nine to 42 inches. Spawning nests, known as "redds", frequently are located at the head of a riffle in the tailout of a pool, where water velocities are one and a half to three feet per second. This location provides the proper depth, velocity and, perhaps most importantly, flow of well-oxgenated water. The female constructs the redd by rolling over on her side and violently flexing her tail against the gravel bed. This motion creates currents that lift the gravel into the flow of the stream, which in turn deposits the material downstream. This activity continues until an excavation about a foot deep has been made. At the proper time, the female lies low in the nest and extrudes a portion of her eggs. These are immediately fertilized by attending males. The eggs settle into the interstices of the redd. The female then moves slightly upstream and begins the redd-building process over again. Gravel is then flushed downstream to cover the previously deposited eggs and a new cavity is created. The egg deposition is repeated until all of the eggs have been deposited.

Once completed, the average redd size for summer and fall chinook in the Columbia River is slightly greater than six square yards. Spring chinook—generally smaller fish—make redds that average about four square yards. The female frequently remains on the redd until overtaken by death. The attending males retreat to find another spawning female. Burner (1951) provides an excellent account of the salmon spawning.

The fall chinook that use the free-flowing Hanford Reach of the Columbia River between the head of the McNary Pool and Priest Rapids Dam may spawn in much deeper water than indicated above. These fish have been found spawning in the river at depths exceeding 35 feet (Chapman *et al* 1984). Bauersfeld (1978) found that the redd size in this reach of the Columbia was much larger than that reported by Burner. An average completed redd covered 12.2 square yards. Some redds measured more than 45 square yards.

## Age

Age at time of spawning varies markedly from year to year and from stock to stock. A typical spawning run contains individuals ranging in age from two to five years, with an occasional older fish. For example, fall chinook returning to the lower Columbia River hatcheries below Bonneville Dam from 1970 through 1984 showed an average age distribution of five percent, 37.4 percent,

50.5 percent, and 7.2 percent for ages two through five years respectively. Fall chinook returns to the Bonneville Pool hatcheries in this same period showed a distribution of seven percent, 56.2 percent, 35.2 percent, and 1.6 percent for these same ages respectively. Six-year-old spring chinook are present in some areas but usually comprise less than one percent of the population (Howell *et al* 1985).

## Size

Size varies with run, stock, and age. Comparative weights of spring and fall chinook at the end of their second, third and fourth winters were: 2.8, five, and nine pounds versus 11.5, 14.6, and 18.6 pounds respectively. Fall chinook have spent nearly one year more in the ocean than spring chinook of the same age. This difference in ocean residence accounts for most of the difference in size (Van Hyning 1973). Size at maturity, as measured by the average weight of fish caught by the commercial gill net fishery, varies from year to year. The average weight of spring chinook in the May fishery ranged yearly from 12.9 to 27.6 pounds, while the August catch of fall chinook ranged from 20.6 to 28.2 pounds. Average weight of summer chinook was as high as 32.6 pounds (Pulford 1964).

## Sex Ratio

Sex ratio varies with the age of the fish. Two-year-old spawners are found in fall chinook populations and are almost exclusively precociously mature males. In the Hanford Reach of the Columbia River, three-year-old fish are predominantly males, while the older age classes are dominated by females. In the Willamette spring chinook run, the older age classes are divided almost equally between the sexes, while older fish in the Yakima spring chinook run are primarily females (Howell *et al* 1985).

Sex ratios of naturally spawning fish often are difficult to estimate. As noted above, the females often remain on the redd until death, while the males move off in search of another female or drift slowly downstream to die. Consequently, the sex ratio of carcasses examined along the stream may not reflect the sex ratio of fish on the spawning grounds. Males usually outnumber females on the natural spawning grounds and in the hatchery returns.

## Fecundity

Chinook fecundity usually is estimated at about 5,000 eggs per female (e.g. Wydoski and Whitney 1979). Fecundity is directly proportional to the size of the fish at maturity and differs from stock to stock (Galbreath and Ridenhour 1964). For example, the fecundity of fall chinook at Kalama and Cowlitz hatcheries in the lower Columbia basin from 1978 through 1982 averaged

4,574 and 4,346 eggs respectively, while the fecundity during that same period at other Washington facilities averaged 4,738. Fecundity may vary widely from year to year within the same stock of fish. Klickitat Hatchery spring chinook fecundity ranged from 3,737 to 5,009 eggs annually during the same time period, while the spring chinook in the Warm Springs River in the Deschutes River sub-basin averaged less than 3,500 eggs per female (Howell *et al* 1985).

## Spawning Period

Spawning extends from early August into early December, but is much more condensed for individual stocks and runs. Spring chinook typically begin to spawn in early August and have completed spawning by late September. Snake River summer chinook spawn from late August to mid-September (Howell *et al* 1985), while little spawning activity occurs in upper Columbia summer chinook until late September and extends into early November (Meekin 1967). Hanford Reach fall chinook spawning activity extends from mid-October into early December (Woodin pers. comm.).

## Egg Incubation and Fry Emergence

Eggs incubate within the redd through fall and winter. Shelton (1955) experimented with fall chinook eggs in simulated spawning beds. Eggs deposited in late September had completed hatching by January 6. The newly hatched fish, called "alevins," remain buried in the gravel as long as their yolk sacs remain. Emergence from the gravel commenced on February 2. Emergence continued until May 18, with 50 percent of the fry out of the gravel by April 7. Five spring chinook redds that completed hatching in late September in the Yakima River showed mean emergence dates ranging for early April to mid-May and survival rates from 13 to 30.6 percent (Wasserman *et al* 1985). Length of time hatching and emergence is dependent upon water temperature (Shelton 1955, Wasserman *et al* 1985). Survival within the redd varies with depth, gravel size, siltation, and water velocity through the redd. All of these factors control the amount of oxygen available to the eggs and alevins (Shelton and Pollock 1966).

## Freshwater Residence and Downstream Migration

Chinook exhibit two distinct types of freshwater residence. Some fish remain in the tributary streams until the second spring after their emergence from the gravel. These fish begin smolt migration as yearlings. Yearling chinook smolt move seaward in a relatively short time extending from early April through June as measured at McNary Dam, though 80 percent of the migration usually is completed by mid-May (Delarm *et al* 1984).

Yearling chinook are present in the estuary from late March through June, with peak abundance occurring in late May (Dawley *et al* 1984). These include fish of lower Columbia basin origin, many of which are hatchery-produced fish released in March and April. Summer chinook of Snake River sub-basin origin, and virtually all spring chinook regardless of source, are yearling migrants. Some fall chinook of hatchery origin are released as yearlings.

Other chinook remain in freshwater only for a few weeks or months and migrate, as sub-yearlings or zero-aged smolts, from late April (as recently emerged fry) through at least September at McNary Dam (Delarm *et al* 1984). These fish are primarily the result of natural-spawning fall chinook in the Hanford Reach, naturally produced summer chinook from the upper Columbia River tributaries, and releases of summer and fall chinook from hatcheries at Wells and Priest Rapids Dams. These fish move downstream in a more leisurely manner than the yearling migrants and grow rapidly as they move. They are captured in the estuary beginning in early March and are present throughout the summer and early fall months. This population also receives a significant contribution from releases from lower river hatcheries (Dawley *et al* 1984). Almost all naturally produced fall chinook and the summer chinook of the upper Columbia River exhibit a sub-yearling migration.

## Ocean Distribution

Chinook salmon have a wide distribution within the Pacific Ocean. They are found from central California northward along the coast to the Gulf of Alaska, around the eastern Aleutian Islands, most of the Bering Sea, and in western Pacific waters from the Kamchatka Peninsula to the central Aleutian Islands. Extensive tagging of chinook in the North Pacific revealed Columbia River

Examples of distribution of total catch of certain Columbia River chinook stock expressed as percent of total catch (modified from Buckman et al., 1984 and Howell et al., 1985).

| Stock | Upper Columbia summer chinook | Upper Columbia fall chinook | Bonneville Pool fall chinook | Upper Columbia spring chinook | Cowlitz River spring chinook |
|---|---|---|---|---|---|
| Brood year | 1974-77 | 1974-77 | 1971-72 | 1974, 1976 | 1976 |
| Area of catch | | | | | |
| Alaska | 32.9 | 32.7 | 0.2 | 0.0 | 1.5 |
| Northern B.C. | 28.6 | 25.6 | 1.9 | 0.0 | 7.3 |
| Southern B.C. | 31.5 | 24.9 | 28.3 | 37.6 | 22.9 |
| Washington | 6.6 | 5.4 | 44.38 | 0.0 | 33.3 |
| Oregon | 0.4 | 0.4 | 5.3 | 0.0 | 2.8 |
| California | 0.0 | 0.0 | 0.1 | 0.0 | 0.1 |
| Columbia River | 0.0 | 10.6 | 19.8 | 61.4 | 32.1 |

fish as far west as Adak island (Major *et al* 1978). Most Columbia River chinook, however, appear to be confined to the waters off southeast Alaska, Canada, Washington, and northern Oregon.

The ocean distribution of Columbia River chinook varies widely between stocks and to a lesser degree from brood to brood. This distribution is best depicted by catch patterns, though it must be recognized that fish are not subject to catch at younger age classes and that changes in regulations will affect the apparent distribution.

## Artificial Production

Artificial production of salmon in the Columbia was initiated early in the history of basin development. The supporters of hatcheries placed a lot of confidence in the ability of artificial production to provide immediate bonanzas in returning fish. The first salmon hatchery in the Columbia River basin was built on the Clackamas River in Oregon in 1876. By the end of the century, there were seven hatcheries in Washington and several in Oregon. By 1909, there were at least 24 hatcheries in the basin in Washington and Oregon. Hatchery propagation efforts in Idaho, however, were limited until recent years.

The need for hatchery facilities was emphasized in the first report of the Washington State Fish Commission in 1890:

> To foster and replenish the streams of our state with salmon and trout, the establishment of a hatchery is a positive necessity. While though much could be done by the passage and enforcement of a stringent law protecting our fish during the spawning, still, as has been demonstrated in the older states without the aid of artificial propagation, the stock of wild fish will eventually be exhausted. (Cited in Wahle and Smith 1979).

The public gave a great deal of credit to these early efforts. In 1905, hatchery releases totaled 62 million fry and eggs. Through 1910, these stations had released some 550,000 salmon and steelhead fry into tributaries of the Columbia River (Ortmann *et al* 1976). The *Pacific Fisherman* extolled the virtues of these releases in a number of issues in the early 1900s. This publication credited the good August returns in 1903 and 1904 to the increased releases, stating, "There seems no question but that 75 percent of the salmon entering the river are directly attributable to artificial propagation." (cited in Smith 1979). Smith notes that the Oregon master fish warden ". . . argued that the increase in the salmon pack from 266,000 cases in 1913 to 454,000 cases in 1914 resulted from the return of salmon released from ponds in 1910." (Smith 1979). While it was undoubtedly the vageries of nature—not the efforts of man—that caused these resurgences, the hatchery propagation efforts were well on their way to becoming a permanent fixture in the efforts to maintain and restore the salmon resources.

Initial propagation efforts involved only the collection and incubation of eggs. Newly hatched fry were planted directly into the recipient streams without any efforts to feed the fish before release. In several instances, salmon runs virtually were destroyed in the hatchery stream before the effort was abandoned for lack of eggs. Soon, ponds were added to the hatcheries and fish were reared for short periods of time before release. Gradually, as technology improved, efforts began truly to bear fruit. Major breakthroughs in diet, disease, water-quality needs, and understanding of early life histories led to the development of techniques that today play a major role in the production of chinook, Steelhead, and coho in the Columbia, and these and other species elsewhere.

Passage of the Mitchell Act in 1938 and subsequent amendments to it led to the present development of hatcheries in the basin. This act provided funding of hatchery construction and operation as compensation for habitat destroyed by various activities on the basin. Additional facilities were constructed and are operated through other funding sources. In 1960, there were 22 anadromous-fish rearing stations in the basins. This number had grown to more than 40 by 1976 (Wahle and Smith 1979). Even more stations have been added since.

In 1960, the hatcheries in the basin alone released nearly 100 million chinook, with a total production of a half million pounds. (Wahle and Smith 1979). In 1980, hatcheries released 94 million fall chinook, 27,600,000 spring chinook, and 3,060,000 summer chinook into the Columbia River basin (Smith pers. comm.).

Estimates of the total contribution of hatchery-produced chinook to the fisheries of the Columbia River and the Pacific Ocean were derived from the first large-scale evaluation program, initiated in 1962. Fish were marked by the removal of a combination of fins so they could be identified later. The evaluation was conducted at 12 hatcheries, which produced 90 percent of the fall chinook released in the basin from 1963 through 1966. Extensive sampling of the fisheries from California to Alaska, including those within the Columbia, indicated a total catch of nearly 1.4 million fall chinook at stations included in the study (Worland *et al* 1969).

## Significance of the Species

Because salmon of the Columbia River basin range widely across state and national boundaries, they are of both national and international importance. Perhaps of greater importance, however, is the historical role that salmon played in the past and continues to play today in Indian tribal culture:

> "The right to resort to the fishing places in controversy was a part of the larger rights possessed by the Indians . . . which were not much less necessary to the Indians than the atmosphere they breathed." This statement, made by Supreme Justice McKenna in the case of *U.S. vs. Winans,* 198 U.S. 370 in 1905, rings as true in 1984 as it did then. The Columbia River and its waters play as large a role in the culture of its Indian people today as they did prior

to the coming of the white man. While "progress" on the Columbia destroyed much of what once was for the Indian people, "The River" still provides the heart of our culture and a significant portion of our economy (Yallup 1985).

# Historical Perspective

## Prehistoric and Early Settlement Period

The salmonid resource, prior to white settlement of the Pacific Northwest, was the basis of the cultures of many of the Indian peoples who lived throughout the region. Indians gathered yearly at traditional fishing grounds throughout the basin to catch the fish which often meant the difference between starvation and life. Early explorers marveled at both the abundance of the resource and its significance to the native inhabitants.

Chinook fed to the Lewis and Clark expedition by a band of Shoshoni Indians in 1805 provided Lewis with the first clue that he had, indeed, crossed over from the Missouri River drainage into the Pacific Coast (cited in Wilkinson and Conner 1983). As the expedition traveled from the headwaters of the Snake River basin toward the ocean, they subsisted on roots and dried salmon provided by Indians encountered along the way. Wilkinson and Conner credit this generous provision of fish as the primary reason that the expedition was able to continue to its completion.

Radiocarbon dating techniques indicate that Indians probably were living along the Columbia as early as 11,000 B.C. (Netboy 1974). The Indian population of the Columbia River basin prior to white immigration from the east is estimated to have been approximately 50,000. By the 1840s, the native population had declined to less than 9,000, decimated by diseases contracted from the settlers. The subsistence catch of salmon and steelhead by the Indians, prior to the white invasion, is estimated at from 18 million (Craig and Hacker 1940) to nearly 42 million pounds yearly (Northwest Power Planning Council 1985). These estimates all far exceed the take of salmon and steelhead in the basin by all fishers in recent years.

Celilo Falls, on the mainstem of the Columbia some 200 miles above the ocean, probably was the most important of the many aboriginal fishing sites in the basin. In its undisturbed state, the Columbia River dropped steeply through this area over a series of cascades and water falls through narrow river channels. This area extended for some eight miles and provided a number of delays to the upstream migration of salmon and steelhead. These obstacles provided the Indians an opportunity to collect fish through a variety of means. One of the most common methods of capture was the use of a large hoop dip net held in the turbulence until an exhausted fish was swept into it by the current. Chinook salmon were the most important species to the fishers at Celilo Falls. Fish were consumed fresh or dried and pounded into pemmican. This area attracted Indians from bands throughout the Columbia basin. As many as 3,000 people gathered at the site during the peak of the run. Major tribal fisheries also were found at Willamette Falls, Kettle Falls on the upper Columbia River, the confluence of the Methow and Columbia rivers, the Snake and Columbia rivers, Spokane Falls, and Salmon Falls on the upper Snake River (Smith 1979). Celilo Falls continued to be the site of important tribal commercial, ceremonial, and subsistence fisheries until it was inundated by the Dalles Dam in the mid-1950s.

In other areas, the Indians constructed artificial barriers, or weirs, to delay the passage of salmon and make them vulnerable to capture. Fish were also gaffed, seined, gill-netted, and speared along their migration routes and on the spawning grounds. Smith (1979), Netboy (1974 and 1980), and Wilkinson and Conner (1983) provide excellent summaries of the Indian fishing techniques and historical accounts of the fisheries.

## Commercial and Recreational Exploitation

The Indians not only used salmon for personal use but traded fish with other tribes and early settlers as well. The commercial exploitation of salmon and steelhead slowly grew as the settlers sought ways to market the seemingly unlimited resource so readily available to them. Pemmican was not an acceptable product in the outside markets. Attempts at exporting salted salmon, commencing in the 1820s, also were generally unsuccessful. Canning of salmon began in 1864 on the Sacramento River, California, and opened the door to intensive commercial exploitation.

The canning process was moved north to the Columbia in 1866. The salteries soon shifted to the canning of salmon. Within a few years, canneries were located all along the river and their impact already was being felt. Initially, only the highest quality salmon—the summer chinook runs—were exploited. As this resource declined, other species, as well as spring and fall chinook, gained importance. From its start in 1866, the annual pack increased by 1883 to some 600,000 cases of 48 one-pound cans. The estimated total catch exceeded 42 million pounds in 1883 and 1884. Despite branching out rapidly to fish in other runs in the river, the pack declined steadily after that (Smith 1979).

In the early days of the commercial fishery, sail-powered gill-net boats, traps, fish wheels, and horse-pulled seines were the primary fishing gear. Eventually, stationary gear was outlawed and legal gear limited to drift gill nets. Historical accounts of the commercial fisheries of the river are found in Smith (1979) and Seufert (1980).

As the Columbia River salmon runs began to decline, fishermen moved outside the river and began the interception of the runs on their ocean feeding grounds and migratory routes. By 1910, trolling gear was being used off Cape Flattery on the north coast of Washington and off the west coast of Vancouver Island to catch chinook and coho. The fishery off the mouth of the Columbia began in about 1912 and expanded rapidly from about 500 boats in 1915 to at least 1,500 vessels by 1920 (Phinney 1976). By the mid-1970s, more than

3,000 vessels were licensed to fish off the coast of Washington alone (Wright 1976). Total ocean-troll catch in waters extending from central California to southeast Alaska have been reduced gradually from an average of approximately 2.5 million yearly in the early 1970s to less than 1.1 million from 1983 through 1985. While many production areas contribute to these catches, the Columbia River basin is the largest single contributor. The Pacific Fishery Management Council (1985) states that catch declines are related to both more restrictive regulations and reduced populations of fish.

Recreational fishing in the Columbia River and its tributaries began late in the 19th century. Fishing activity was concentrated in and near the mouths of the tributaries. Chinook salmon have always been the most sought of the Columbia River salmon, though coho play an important role. As larger, motorized boats became available, the fishery expanded to the lower river near the confluence with the ocean (Haw *et al* 1967). The Columbia River mouth provided the first major access to ocean waters for the recreational fishery. By the early 1950s, recreationalists were beginning to explore the marine areas off the mouth of the river. As vessels continued to improve, the fishery expanded rapidly both here and at access points all along the Washington and Oregon coast (Phinney and Miller 1977). Soon, far more Columbia River chinook and coho were being taken in the ocean fisheries than in the river.

In recent years, because of the generally depressed status of the upriver runs, recreational fisheries have been limited primarily to the hatchery runs of the lower-river tributaries. Regulations of the mainstem fisheries have restricted efforts to times and areas where the upriver spring and summer chinook runs are only incidentally affected. The lower-river tributaries continue to provide excellent recreational fisheries for spring and fall chinook and coho. In 1983, for example, some 45,000 salmon, primarily chinook and coho, were taken by Washington-licensed anglers in the Columbia River and it tributaries. Nearly half of these came out of the Cowlitz river alone (Washington Department of Fisheries 1984). In that same year, more than 36,000 salmon were caught by Oregon-licensed anglers in the Columbia River and its tributaries. Some 27,500 of these, primarily spring chinook, were landed in the Willamette River and its tributaries (Oregon Department of Fish and Wildlife 1985). Prior to the declines in upriver runs, as many as 39,000 salmon were caught yearly in the state of Idaho alone (Chaney and Perry 1976). In recent years, recreational fishing in Idaho has been restricted to hatchery returns in the hatchery tributary.

# Current Trends

## Prehistoric Abundance

Several estimates have been made of the prehistoric abundance of salmon and steelhead in the Columbia River basin. The Pacific Fishery Management

Council (1979) estimated that prior to the influence of water-development projects and other habitat losses the basin produced 3.44 million chinook, 1.20 million coho, 0.65 million sockeye, and 0.95 million chum annually. These estimates were based on available habitat prior to developments. The Northwest Power Planning Council (1985), based on that same data, judged the prehistoric steelhead production to be 2.04 million fish. Based on maximum catches by species and race during the history of commercial fishing and application of a range of catch rates, the power planning council estimates the total run to have ranged from 11 million and 16 million salmon and steelhead. Chinook account for 4.8 million to 8.5 million of these.

## Trends During Early Period of Exploitation

As noted previously, commercial fishing for chinook began in earnest in the 1870s and slowly shifted to other species as the chinook runs declined. Chinook landings peaked during the period of 1881-85, prior to any recorded catches of other species. Coho landings reached their peak in the 1920s and fell off

Five-year mean commercial catches in Columbia River, 1886-1980 (in 1,000s of fish).

| Period | Chinook | Coho | Sockeye | Chum |
|---|---|---|---|---|
| 1866-1870 | 220 | * | * | * |
| 1871-1875 | 1,045 | * | * | * |
| 1876-1880 | 1,687 | * | * | * |
| 1881-1885 | 2,122 | * | * | * |
| 1886-1890 | 1,304 | * | 734[1] | * |
| 1891-1895 | 1,307 | 334[2] | 447 | * |
| 1896-1900 | 1,254 | 372 | 523 | * |
| 1901-1905[3] | 1,560 | 154 | 225 | 93 |
| 1906-1910 | 1,255 | 328 | 208 | 177 |
| 1911-1915 | 1,455 | 389 | 258 | 247 |
| 1916-1920 | 1,641 | 506 | 232 | 285 |
| 1921-1925 | 1,187 | 698 | 344 | 170 |
| 1926-1930 | 1,095 | 671 | 208 | 326 |
| 1931-1935 | 980 | 380 | 84 | 91 |
| 1936-1940 | 798 | 195 | 97 | 181 |
| 1941-1945 | 867 | 128 | 54 | 183 |
| 1946-1950 | 756 | 126 | 68 | 61 |
| 1951-1955 | 412 | 76 | 76 | 25 |
| 1955-1960 | 313 | 30 | 130 | 4 |
| 1961-1965 | 265 | 122 | 19 | 2 |
| 1966-1970 | 269 | 355 | 26 | 1 |
| 1971-1975 | 321 | 209 | 33 | 1 |

Source: Modified from Beiningen (1976) for the period 1866-1970. Oregon Department of Fish and Wildlife and Washington Department of Fisheries (1984) for the period 1976-1980.
* No landings recorded.
[1] No data for 1886-1888.
[2] No data for 1891.
[3] No data for 1901.

sharply by the 1950s. A resurgence in landings in the 1960s and 1970s is credited to improved hatchery production. Sockeye and chum abundance, following initial exploitation, also declined to low levels.

## Recent Trends

Combining commercial and recreational catches with dam counts and hatchery returns provides a minimal estimate of the inriver run size of salmon and steelhead. These estimates do not include the numbers of naturally spawning fish in tributaries below Bonneville Dam, except those included in the fishway counts at Willamette River Falls. Lower-river spring chinook runs have shown significant improvement, primarily because of increased hatchery production. Upper-river runs of spring and summer chinook have declined sharply. This decline stems almost entirely from the cumulative impacts of hydroelectric-

Best estimates of chinook salmon returns to Columbia River, 1960-1983 (in 1,000s of fish).

| Year | Spring chinook | | | Summer chinook | Fall chinook | | | Total chinook |
|------|------|------|------|------|------|------|------|------|
| | Lower river[1] | Upper river[2] | Total | Total | Lower river | Upper river | Total | |
| 1960 | 28.8 | 133.9 | 162.7 | 142.6 | 16.1 | 230.0 | 246.1 | 551.4 |
| 1961 | 32.4 | 161.5 | 193.9 | 129.2 | 45.9 | 206.4 | 252.3 | 575.4 |
| 1962 | 44.7 | 199.8 | 244.5 | 108.0 | 45.4 | 245.2 | 290.6 | 643.1 |
| 1963 | 58.3 | 147.3 | 205.6 | 100.0 | 58.4 | 206.7 | 265.1 | 570.7 |
| 1964 | 78.7 | 168.5 | 247.2 | 97.0 | 92.4 | 279.8 | 372.2 | 716.4 |
| 1965 | 66.4 | 175.5 | 241.9 | 82.1 | 95.3 | 303.9 | 399.2 | 723.2 |
| 1966 | 60.9 | 175.2 | 236.1 | 74.8 | 80.0 | 267.8 | 347.8 | 658.7 |
| 1967 | 89.5 | 151.0 | 240.5 | 100.7 | 77.5 | 307.5 | 385.0 | 726.2 |
| 1968 | 66.0 | 133.5 | 199.5 | 89.4 | 136.5 | 209.6 | 346.1 | 635.0 |
| 1969 | 78.5 | 216.5 | 295.0 | 106.2 | 130.5 | 340.5 | 471.0 | 872.2 |
| 1970 | 81.6 | 171.2 | 252.8 | 72.9 | 172.9 | 359.3 | 532.2 | 857.9 |
| 1971 | 98.9 | 168.0 | 266.9 | 89.5 | 192.3 | 296.3 | 488.6 | 845.0 |
| 1972 | 72.9 | 280.4 | 353.3 | 77.5 | 103.5 | 234.8 | 338.3 | 769.1 |
| 1973 | 93.2 | 232.9 | 326.1 | 48.9 | 244.4 | 317.6 | 562.0 | 937.0 |
| 1974 | 115.6 | 108.5 | 224.1 | 34.0 | 117.8 | 239.3 | 357.1 | 615.2 |
| 1975 | 71.6 | 104.1 | 175.7 | 44.4 | 152.2 | 373.7 | 525.9 | 746.0 |
| 1976 | 86.6 | 78.3 | 164.9 | 42.1 | 204.3 | 359.4 | 563.7 | 770.7 |
| 1977 | 95.4 | 143.6 | 239.0 | 41.4 | 173.1 | 275.6 | 448.7 | 729.1 |
| 1978 | 112.1 | 129.0 | 241.1 | 43.6 | 154.1 | 240.7 | 394.8 | 679.5 |
| 1979 | 73.8 | 51.4 | 125.2 | 34.5 | 135.5 | 219.9 | 355.4 | 515.1 |
| 1980 | 75.4 | 61.0 | 136.4 | 31.2 | 126.7 | 192.8 | 319.5 | 487.1 |
| 1981 | 100.2 | 65.8 | 166.0 | 27.1 | 105.0 | 200.9 | 305.9 | 499.0 |
| 1982[3] | 117.7 | 77.1 | 194.8 | 26.7 | 135.3 | 261.1 | 396.4 | 617.9 |
| 1983[3] | 99.0 | 57.8 | 156.8 | 23.7 | 76.9 | 170.8 | 247.7 | 428.2 |

Source: Oregon Department of Fish and Wildlife; Washington Department of Fisheries (1984)

[1] Lower river: below Bonneville Dam.

[2] Upper river: above Bonneville Dam.

[3] Preliminary estimates.

project construction and operation in the upper basin, though mid-Columbia summer chinook are caught extensively in the ocean waters.

Steelhead of upriver origin declined into the late 1970s and early 1980s. These runs have rebounded strongly in 1983, 1984, and 1985. Sockeye have shown similar encouraging run strength the past three years after sharp declines in the 1970s. Chum salmon have not shown any recovery. Catches are generally less than 1,000 fish yearly. Escapement estimates are not made, though data indicate a continued general decline. Run-size estimates are not available for winter and summer steelhead runs below Bonneville Dam (Oregon Department of Fish and Wildlife and Washington Department of Fisheries 1984). The average run size for 1977-86, including the ocean catch, is estimated at 2.6 million salmon and steelhead, including 1.6 million chinook (Northwest Power Planning Council 1985). The past several years have witnessed a strong resurgence in the upriver runs of fall chinook.

Best estimate of total salmonid returns to the Columbia River by species, 1960-1983 (in 1,000s of fish).

| Year | Steelhead[1] | Coho | Sockeye | Chinook[3] | Total[2] |
|------|-----------|------|---------|---------|--------|
| 1960 | 199.8 | 47.7 | 179.1 | 551.4 | 978.0 |
| 1961 | 227.9 | 112.4 | 57.7 | 575.4 | 973.4 |
| 1962 | 251.7 | 184.7 | 38.7 | 643.1 | 1,118.2 |
| 1963 | 228.8 | 161.9 | 65.4 | 570.7 | 1,026.8 |
| 1964 | 178.6 | 453.9 | 104.9 | 716.4 | 1,453.8 |
| 1965 | 227.3 | 519.0 | 55.2 | 723.2 | 1,524.7 |
| 1966 | 209.2 | 785.9 | 169.2 | 658.7 | 1,823.0 |
| 1967 | 167.3 | 694.2 | 165.4 | 726.2 | 1,753.1 |
| 1968 | 161.6 | 423.9 | 134.7 | 635.0 | 1,355.2 |
| 1969 | 171.9 | 463.4 | 75.8 | 872.2 | 1,583.3 |
| 1970 | 138.5 | 1,057.1 | 95.3 | 857.9 | 2,148.8 |
| 1971 | 224.6 | 632.7 | 150.5 | 845.0 | 1,852.8 |
| 1972 | 225.6 | 353.0 | 123.3 | 769.1 | 1,471.0 |
| 1973 | 187.8 | 415.5 | 61.3 | 937.0 | 1,601.6 |
| 1974 | 144.8 | 521.5 | 43.9 | 615.2 | 1,325.4 |
| 1975 | 84.1 | 427.6 | 58.2 | 746.0 | 1,315.9 |
| 1976 | 122.4 | 372.1 | 43.7 | 770.7 | 1,308.9 |
| 1977 | 195.4 | 193.0 | 99.8 | 729.1 | 1,217.3 |
| 1978 | 103.8 | 373.5 | 18.4 | 679.5 | 1,175.2 |
| 1979 | 113.6 | 316.7 | 52.6 | 515.1 | 998.0 |
| 1980 | 129.6 | 330.1 | 58.9 | 487.1 | 1,005.7 |
| 1981 | 161.1 | 200.3 | 56.0 | 499.0 | 916.4 |
| 1982[4] | 158.8 | 482.1 | 50.2 | 617.9 | 1,309.0 |
| 1983[4] | 220.4 | 135.7 | 100.5 | 428.2 | 884.8 |

Source: Oregon Department of Fish and Wildlife; Washington Department of Fisheries (1984)
[1]Above Bonneville runs only.
[2]Excludes steelhead below Bonneville Dam and chum.
[3]From Table
[4]Preliminary estimates.

# Management

## Causes of Decline

It has taken virtually all the timber harvested by Paul Bunyon to produce the paper used to document the causes of the demise of the Columbia River salmon and steelhead runs (see Blumm 1985a and 1985b; Netboy 1958, 1974, and 1980; Chaney and Perry 1976; Northwest Power Planning Council 1981, 1984, and 1985; Pacific Fishery Management Council 1979; Seufert 1980; Smith 1979; Schwiebert 1977; Van Hyning 1973; and Wilkinson 1983). Virtually all authors point at the development of water-use projects as the primary block to anadromous-fish production in the basin.

The development of the hydroelectric resources of the basin began late in the last century. The initial growth was slow and the impacts relatively minor, though several tributaries had been developed heavily by the late 1910s. In the 1930s, however, the construction of Rock Island, Bonneville, and Grand Coulee dams had a pronounced effect on the anadromous-fish resource. The late 1950s and early 1960s saw the upper Snake basin lost through the construction of Brownlee, Oxbow, and Hells Canyon dams. Four mainstem projects were developed on the lower Snake River commencing in 1961. Four public-utility-district projects and a major federal project were completed on the Columbia River between Grand Coulee Dam and the mouth of the Snake River between 1955 and 1967. Today, the main stems of the Columbia and Snake rivers have a total of 19 dams. These dams have reduced or eliminated the production of salmonids. A total of 128 hydroelectric and multiple-purpose projects are scattered throughout the basin. Their combined storage exceeds 67 million acre-feet (Northwest Power Planning Council 1985).

The Pacific Fishery Management Council (1979) in its review of habitat losses in the basin concluded that the stream habitat available for chinook production had declined from nearly 12,000 miles to less than 6,400 miles. The largest portion of this loss is in the Snake River basin, where Hell's Canyon Dam on the Snake River and Dworshak Dam on the North Fork Clearwater River block access to nearly 3,500 miles of former production area. The construction of Grand Coulee Dam, followed by Chief Joseph Dam, blocked migrants to the upper Columbia River. The upper Columbian basin, above the Snake River, has lost more than 1,000 miles of stream habitat. While a number of areas have been opened to production through the provision of fish-passage facilities at former natural barriers, these new production areas have not offset the major losses due to the construction of storage and hydroelectric projects.

The operation of storage and hydroelectric projects has compounded the problem of habitat losses due to their construction. The Columbia River and many of its tributaries have seen drastic changes in the seasonal runoff patterns. Storage has reduced sharply the flow during the spring and early sum-

Maximum regulated and unregulated flood peak in Columbia River at The Dalles, Oregon, in 1,000's cubic feet per second and completion of major storage facilities in the upper Columbia Basin.

| Year | Unregulated Flow | Regulated Flow | Proportion Reduced | Storage Initiated (in 1000 AF) |
|------|------|------|------|------|
| 1910-32 | | | | 5-Yakima R. [1066] |
| 1914 | | | | Arrowrock [287] |
| 1916 | | | | Jackson Lake [847] |
| 1926 | | | | American Falls [1125] |
| 1927 | | | | Lake Chelan [676] |
| 1930 | | | | Deadwood [162] |
| 1932 | | | | Owyhee [715] |
| 1938 | | | | Grand Coulee [5232] |
| 1938 | | | | Flathead Lake [1219] |
| 1945 | | | | Anderson Ranch [423] |
| 1947 | | | | Cascade [653] |
| 1949 | 660 | 624 | 0.05 | |
| 1950 | 823 | 744 | 0.10 | |
| 1951 | 652 | 602 | 0.08 | Hungry Horse [2982] |
| 1952 | 597 | 561 | 0.06 | Albeni Falls [1155] |
| 1953 | 672 | 612 | 0.09 | |
| 1954 | 590 | 560 | 0.05 | |
| 1955 | 614 | 551 | 0.10 | |
| 1956 | 940 | 823 | 0.12 | Palisades [1200] Lucky Peak [278] |
| 1957 | 820 | 705 | 0.14 | |
| 1958 | 735 | 593 | 0.19 | Brownlee [980] |
| 1959 | 642 | 555 | 0.14 | Noxon [231] |
| 1960 | 493 | 470 | 0.05 | |
| 1961 | 789 | 699 | 0.11 | |
| 1962 | 503 | 460 | 0.09 | |
| 1963 | 481 | 437 | 0.09 | |
| 1964 | 764 | 662 | 0.13 | |
| 1965 | 669 | 520 | 0.22 | |
| 1966 | 455 | 396 | 0.13 | |
| 1967 | 781 | 622 | 0.20 | Duncan Lake [1411] |
| 1968 | 533 | 404 | 0.24 | Arrow Lakes [7145] John Day Res. [535] |
| 1969 | 628 | 449 | 0.29 | |
| 1970 | 634 | 426 | 0.33 | |
| 1971 | 740 | 557 | 0.25 | |
| 1972 | 1053 | 618 | 0.41 | Libby [4934] Dworshak [2016] |
| 1973 | 402 | 221 | 0.45 | Kinbasket Lake [12000] |
| 1974 | 1010 | 590 | 0.42 | |
| 1975 | 669 | 423 | 0.37 | |
| 1976 | 637 | 419 | 0.34 | |
| 1977 | 276 | 183 | 0.34 | |
| 1978 | 565 | 313 | 0.45 | |
| 1979 | 482 | 306 | 0.37 | |
| 1980 | 544 | 341 | 0.37 | |
| 1981 | 579 | 436 | 0.25 | |
| 1982 | 759 | 422 | 0.56 | |

Source: modified from Tables 19 and 20, Columbia River Water Group, 1983

mer months of smolt migration. At least 27 major storage projects in the basin impound water for flood control and for release at a more opportune time for the production of electricity. The largest of these, Kinbasket Lake in British Columbia, has a storage capacity of 12,000 acre-feet. The combined effect of these storage projects became a system-wide problem in the early 1970s, though local impacts caused immediate problems upon the completion of each of them. Following 1969, flood peaks were reduced by 25 to 56 percent (Columbia River Water Group 1983).

With increased upstream storage, generating capacity at many mainstem hydroelectric projects was increased. Consequently, smolt journey to the sea was prolonged because of decreased water velocity in what had become a long series of lakes in their migration path. The route is more hazardous because the amount of spill was reduced, and the fish were forced to exit the reservoirs through the turbines. Ebel *et al* (1979) show that juvenile chinook migrants are delayed 40 to 50 days during low-water years. This delay increases their susceptibility to predation and impedes their ability to convert from a fresh to a salt-water environment. Passage through the turbines, rather than over the relatively safe spillways, causes a mortality of 15 to 20 percent per project (Chaney and Perry 1976), though higher mortalities have been discovered in some studies (Northwest Power Planning Council 1985). During low-flow years, the cumulative impact of losses of migrating juveniles can be staggering. Sims *et al* (1978) documented the loss of 95 percent of all chinook and steelhead migrants during the low-flow year of 1973 as the fish journeyed through the four lower Snake River projects and the McNary and John Day dams. They estimated the loss at 99 percent in the low-flow year of 1977.

Excessive fishing rates also are blamed for part of the demise of the salmon and steelhead runs of the Columbia River. Ocean fisheries all along the Pacific Coast had expanded rapidly by the 1950s. Inriver fisheries, alone, imposed excessively high take on some runs. After the completion of Bonneville Dam, when estimates of upriver salmon escaping the commercial fisheries became possible, inriver catch rates on spring chinook commonly exceeded 60 percent and were estimated to have been as high as 86 percent in some years. Less than 20 percent of the summer chinook that entered the river from 1938 through 1944 passed upstream above Bonneville Dam. Sockeye, caught only within the river, suffered catch rates as high as 86 percent (Fish Commission of Oregon and Washington Department of Fisheries 1975). Estimates made by the Northwest Power Planning Council (1985) of historic run size and the catch level of the Indian tribes in the basin suggest that Indian take alone may have averaged 40 percent. Some runs were likely in danger at that rate, and imposition of additional catches once the lower-river commercial fisheries began possibly destroyed less-productive runs.

A number of other factors can be associated with the decline of runs in the basin. Logging and the transportation of logs to the mills temporarily destroyed some habitat. Mining activities, particularly placer dredger mining, had its impact on many of the tributaries. Grazing in the watersheds destroyed the riparian vegetation and resulted in increased siltation and higher water temperatures. Diversion of flow for irrigation and associated storage projects destroyed many runs and caused serious declines in others. Urbanization and the pollutants associated with human environmental encroachment were severe in many areas. The Northwest Power Planning Council (1985) provides a summary of these impacts.

Many of these effects are reversible, and in many cases they have been reversed. Fishing rates have been reduced significantly. Logging practices have improved. Pollution abatement has occurred. Minimum flows have been established in some streams to protect at least some segment of the stream's productivity. Nature has flushed out of the environment many of the sediments that resulted from logging, mining, and overgrazing. The habitat inundated or permanently blocked by dams is irretrievably lost.

## Indian Treaty Rights

Following the non-Indian settlement of the Columbia basin, conflicts between settlers and Indians were frequent. These conflicts culminated in the establishment of a number of treaties that established reservation areas for the Indians. Common in the language of these treaties is the guarantee to the tribes of the "right of taking fish at all usual and accustomed stations, in common with citizens of the United States" (cited in Wilkinson and Conner 1983). The interpretation of this language, particularly with respect to the rights of treaty Indians outside the boundaries of their reservations, has caused almost continual court litigation since the early 1960s. Essentially, the federal courts have held that the treaty Indians have a right to a "fair share" of the anadromous-fisheries resource and that the right includes the protection of the environment necessary to produce that resource. Wilkinson and Conner (1983), Blumm and Johnson (1981), Heinemann and Rosenbaum (1983), Blumm (1985a), and others provide accounts of treaty rights issues.

In 1968, the federal government filed suit against the state of Oregon over closures imposed on treaty fishing above Bonneville Dam. The case still continues and, it is to be hoped, will culminate in 1986 with agreed upon catch management and production goals for salmon and steelhead in the upper Columbia basin.

## Major Legislative Action

Efforts to rehabilitate the salmon steelhead runs of the basin have been assisted by several recent federal actions.

***Northwest Power Planning Act.*** Until passage of the Northwest Power Planning Act, (Public Law 96-501 [16 U.S.C. 839 *et seq*]), the fish and wildlife agencies and Indian tribes lacked many of the tools necessary to properly address problems associated with the Columbia River hydroelectric system. Efforts previously had been on a project-by-project basis, often with only limited success. Passage of the act provided necessary new tools with which the impacts of the Columbia River hydroelectric dams can be addressed. The Northwest Power Planning Council, established by the act, was directed to develop a fish and wildlife program. The intent of the act for the program was stated in Section 4(h)(1)(A):

> The Northwest Power Planning Council shall promptly develop and adopt pursuant to the subsection, a program to protect, mitigate and enhance fish and wildlife, including related spawning grounds and habitat, on the Columbia River and its tributaries. Because of the unique history, problems and opportunity presented by the development and operation of hydroelectric facilities on the Columbia River and its tributaries, the program to the greatest extent possible shall be designed to deal with that river and its tributaries as a system.

Perhaps most importantly, the act [Section 4(h)(10)(A)] directs the Bonneville Power Administration to use its legal and financial resources to:

> . . . protect, mitigate and enhance fish and wildlife to the extent affected by the development and operation of any hydroelectric project of the Columbia River and its tributaries in a manner consistent with . . . the program adopted by the Northwest Power Planning Council . . . and the purposes of this act.

The Fish and Wildlife Program (Northwest Power Planning Council 1984) was adopted in November 1982 and amended in 1984. It was developed from some 400 recommendations provided to the Northwest Power Planning Council by the appropriate Indian tribes, fish and wildlife agencies, and other interested parties—including the power-facility operators (Northwest Power Planning Council 1981). The program places a major emphasis on the restoration of the upriver runs of salmon and steelhead and provides water to be used at the direction of the fish and wildlife agencies and tribes to improve spring passage conditions for downstream migrants. It directs the installation of by-pass facilities, including the provision of spill, to increase survival at the dams. Additional investigations are identified to determine the best means of improving survival in the reservoirs and at the dams. A number of habitat-improvement and passage-restoration projects are included in the program to increase spawning and rearing success and to offset the irretrievable loss of habitat due to dam construction.

*United States-Canada Salmon Interception Treaty.* Following nearly two decades of difficult negotiations, the United States/Canada Pacific Salmon Interception Treaty was signed by the two nations in 1985. This represents a significant step forward in the management of North American Pacific salmon resources. The Columbia River salmon, particularly chinook, and the U.S. users of that valuable resource will benefit significantly from the implementation of the treaty. As noted previously, much of the catch of the Columbia River chinook occurs in ocean waters. Of that, the majority of the catch of certain stocks of fall and summer chinook takes place in the waters off Canada and Alaska—far outside the management authority of the Columbia basin states or the treaty tribes. As a consequence, little could be done under the previously existing management frameworks for additional protection of the depleted stocks of Columbia River chinook short of total closure of all fisheries in the basin and off the coasts of Washington and northern Oregon.

Coastwide management and enhancement plans will be provided in order to rebuild the depressed chinook stocks to optimum production by 1998. The treaty places a lid on take in 1985 and 1986 in certain waters where interceptions commonly occur. Catches in subsequent years will be reduced as necessary to maintain the rebuilding schedule. It is the obligation of each country to assure that fish saved by catch reductions are allowed to escape to the spawning grounds. Once the stocks are rebuilt, catch limits will be adjusted to provide for maximum sustained take and to assure that each country and fishery receives a fair allocation of the catch.

Ocean take of chinook in the waters of British Columbia and Alaska will be reduced approximately 25 percent from 1984 levels. For 1985 and 1986, this amounts to a reduction of 400,000 chinook. Not all of these are of Columbia River origin. Nonetheless, this will result in significant increases in the returns of mid-Columbia summer chinook, upriver bright fall chinook, and Bonneville Pool hatchery fish, and a lesser, but important, benefit to the lower-river hatchery and wild stocks. It is estimated, for example, that the 1984 fishing patterns allowed for 73 percent of the catch of upriver bright fall chinook to be taken in British Columbia and Alaska waters. With implementation of the treaty, that level will be reduced to 30 percent by 1998. The catch of tule-stock fall chinook in these northern waters will be reduced from an estimated 38 percent in 1984 to 26 percent in 1998 (U.S.-Canada Treaty Coalition et al 1985).

Without the treaty, many chinook stocks were faced with continued overfishing and some stocks with the threat of virtual extinction. The catch size in the ocean fisheries of Canada and Alaska has not declined at the same rate at which chinook populations have declined. This relative stability was only possible through increasingly high catch rates and alarmingly low escapement levels (U.S./Canada Chinook Technical Committee 1983).

Columbia River coho stocks will receive minimal protection under the treaty. These stocks generally do not enter fisheries north of coastal Washington to any significant degree. Columbia River chum and sockeye salmon and steelhead trout are not taken in any ocean fisheries, except for an occasional incidental capture. Certain other chinook stocks will receive little noticeable benefit, since the present information on their distribution indicates only limited ocean take in any fishery. These include the various spring chinook stocks originating above Bonneville Dam and the Snake River summer chinook.

*The Salmon and Steelhead Conservation and Enhancement Act.* This 1980 law [16 U.S.C. Section 3301 *et seq* (Public Law 96-561)] authorized the establishment of the Salmon and Steelhead Advisory Commission, which recommends administrative structures for the development and coordination of research, enhancement, and enforcement policies for the steelhead and salmon resources of the Columbia River and most of western Washington. The need for a change in administrative structure is evidenced by the multiple state, tribal, and federal jurisdictions involved in the region's salmon and steelhead management. This structure also is to include dispute-resolution procedures. The Salmon and Steelhead Advisory Commission has completed its recommendations and submitted its report to the secretary of Commerce for approval. Final acceptance of the report and the implementation of its recommendations will greatly improve interjurisdictional coordination throughout the range of fish produced in the waters of the Columbia River and Western Washington (Salmon and Steelhead Advisory Commission 1984).

## Fishing Management

Because of the depleted upriver runs of chinook and sockeye, commercial and recreational take of spring and summer chinook and sockeye within the Columbia Basin have been restricted severely or eliminated entirely in recent years. No fisheries have been permitted to focus purposefully on upriver spring runs since 1977. Summer chinook have not been taken as a target species since 1963. Sockeye fisheries were closed until the summer of 1983, when the first commercial fishery since 1972 was conducted. Commercial take of steelhead by non-treaty fishers has been prohibited by state laws since 1975, though Indian and recreational fishing of upriver runs has continued on a limited scale. Limited tribal fisheries for ceremonial and subsistence purposes continued during this era.

Returns of fall chinook and coho have continued to be sufficiently strong to allow annual inriver commercial, recreational, and tribal take. Ocean fisheries, including those in southern Alaska, have faced reductions in fishing time and allowable catch to permit rebuilding of Columbia River stocks of chinook and coho as well as other depressed stocks. Adjustments have been necessary to provide for proper escapement levels of critical stocks and to meet court-ordered sharing requirements with the treaty tribes.

# Prognosis

The past history of the Columbia River Basin and its salmon and steelhead resource has not been encouraging. It is hoped, however, that the education taught by that history will be put to full use in the restoration of that resource.

Through implementation of many of the measures of the Fish and Wildlife Program, improved survival of juvenile and adult fish on their journey to and from the sea may be anticipated. Improved habitat conditions, along with the opening of new production areas, may result in increased total production. Additional protection afforded the fish as they approach maturity in the ocean has been provided through the imposition of more restrictive fishing regulations. With the enactment of the Salmon Interception Treaty, and the additional savings of critical chinook stocks that will result from its implementation, these runs should begin to ascend to some semblance of their former importance. Full restoration is not a reasonable expectation because of the tremendous losses in production habitat and the hydro-related losses that will remain despite the best efforts to reduce passage mortalities.

These fish also must be provided adequate protection from excessive take once they enter the Columbia River. This appears to be rapidly coming about, though management errors can be expected. The treaty tribes and the fisheries-management agencies now are resolving issues through face-to-face negotiations, rather than through litigation in the federal court, to develop a joint cooperative-management endeavor. Resource management is more directly in the hands of the appropriate fisheries-management experts and left less to the whims of the legal system. The fisheries-management agencies and tribes, along with the other entities that long have affected the status of the resource without being held accountable for that impact, are working together in better concert than has ever occurred in the past. This spirit of cooperation is founded both on recognition of a need for protection and on the value of the fisheries resources. A catalyst for these efforts is the constant threat of court action on the part of the Indian tribes and the fisheries managers if many past practices detrimental to the salmon resource are not modified. Controversy between the sport and commercial fisheries, Indian and non-Indian, ocean versus river will not end magically, but should have more clearly defined routes toward a satisfactory solution.

The past several years have seen a reversal in the trends of several runs of Columbia River salmon and steelhead. Sockeye runs have shown considerable strength over the past three years. Summer steelhead returns have been extremely good, although supported to a large degree by substantial releases of hatchery production. Some improvement has been seen in the upriver spring chinook runs. There have been substantial increases in the returns of fall chinook destined for the mid-Columbia. It is hoped that these are omens of the future, not just vagaries of nature.

# Recommendations

The equipment necessary for the restoration of the Columbia River salmon and steelhead runs should now be available. The most effective use of these tools will be necessary if this effort is to be successful. It is imperative that:

(1) the intent of the Salmon Interception Treaty be fully implemented, including the passing of the fish "saved" from the northern fisheries into escapements as needed to meet spawning escapement needs;

(2) the treaty tribes and the fisheries management agencies in the Columbia River Basin successfully conclude deliberations on catch and production objectives for the resource and that these objectives be compatible with the efforts of the Northwest Power Planning Council in its implementation of the Fish and Wildlife Program;

(3) these deliberations adequately provide for the rebuilding of the depressed resources, meeting the treaty and non-treaty fishery needs only when the resource itself can do so without being harmed;

(4) survival and total production from the tributaries of the basin be improved significantly through the implementation of measures within the Fish and Wildlife Program;

(5) a comprehensive management plan be developed for each of the river's sub-basins and that these be melded into a single, basin-wide approach considering the needs of all interested parties, and

(6) a new inriver management approach be developed to overcome the present problems inherent with a fisheries management system that includes the interests and concerns of two federal fisheries agencies, four state fish and wildlife management authorities, and four treaty Indian tribes.

# References

Bauersfeld, K.B. 1978. *The effect of daily flow fluctuations on spawning fall chinook in the Columbia River.* Technical Report No. 38. Washington Department of Fisheries. 32 pp.

Beninigen, K.T. 1976. "Fish runs," in *Investigative Reports of Columbia River Fisheries Projects.* Prepared for the Pacific Northwest Regional Commission. July 1976. 65 pp.

Blumm, M. and B. Johnson. 1981. Indian treaty fishing rights and protection of the environment. *Anadromous Fish Law Memo.* Issue 12. April 1981. Lewis and Clark Law School. Portland, Oregon. 28 pp.

Blumm, M. 1985a. Workshop on the late, great Columbia River Fishery (Part I)—History of the fishery and ongoing restoration efforts. *Anadromous Fish Law Memo.* Issue 32. August 1985. Lewis and Clark Law School. Portland, Oregon. 11 pp.

Blumm, M. 1985b. Workshop of the late, great Columbia River Fishery (Part II)—Salmon and the law. Anadromous Fish Law Memo. Issue 32. August 1985. Lewis and Clark Law School. Portland, Oregon. 15 pp.

Bonneville Power Administration. 1985. *1984 Fish and Wildlife Annual Project Summary.* Bonneville Power Administration. Portland, Oregon. 15 pp.

Burner, C.J. 1951. "Characteristics of spawning nests of Columbia River salmon." *Fisheries Research Bulletin* No. 61. U.S. Department of Interior. 21 pp.

Chaney E. and L.E. Perry. 1976. *Columbia River Basin Salmon and Steelhead Analysis.* Summary report. Pacific Northwest Regional Commission. 74 pp.

Chapman, D.W., D.E. Weitkamp, T.L. Welsh, and T.H. Schadt. 1984. *Effects of Minimum Flow Regimes on Fall Chinook Spawning at Vernita Bar, 1978-82.* Final report to Grant County Public Utility District. 123 + appendices.

Columbia River Water Management Group. 1983. *Columbia River Water Management Report for Water Year 1982.* Columbia River Water Management Group. Portland, Oregon. 173 pp.

Craig, J.A. and R.L. Hacker. 1940. "Histories and development of the fisheries of the Columbia River." *Bureau of Fisheries Bulletin* No. 32, Vol. XLIX.

Dawley, E.M., R.D. Ledgerwood, T.H. Blahm, R.A. Kirn, A.E. Rankis, and F.J. Ossiander. 1984. *Migrational Characteristics and Survival of Juvenile Salmonids Entering the Columbia River Estuary During 1982.* National Marine Fisheries Service. Seattle, Washington. 49 pp. + appendices.

Delarm, M.R., L.R. Basham, S.W. Pettit, J.B. Athearn, and J.V. Barker. 1984. *Fish Transportation Oversight Team Annual Report—FY 1983. Transport Operations on the Snake and Columbia Rivers.* National Oceanic and Atmospheric Administration Technical Memorandum National Marine Fisheries Service F/NWR-7. National Marine Fisheries Service. 87 pp. + appendix.

Ebel W.J., G.K. Tanonaka, G.E. Monan, H.L. Raymond, and D.L. Park. 1979. *Status report—1978. The Snake River Salmon and Steelhead Crisis: Its Relation to Dams and the National Energy Shortage.* Processed Report 79-9. Northwest and Alaska Fisheries Center, National Marine Fisheries Service.

Fish Commission of Oregon and Washington Department of Fisheries. 1975. *Status Report—Columbia River Fish Runs and Commercial Fisheries, 1938-1979.* 1974 addendum. 44 pp.

Fulton, L.A. 1968. "Spawning areas and abundance of chinook salmon (*Oncorhynchus tshawytscha*) in the Columbia River basin—past and present." U.S. Fish and Wildlife Service, *Specialized Scientific Report Fisheries* No. 571. 26 pp. + maps.

Galbreath, J.L. and R.L. Ridenhour. 1964. "Fecundity of Columbia River chinook salmon." Fish Commission of Oregon. *Research Briefs* 10(1):16-27.

Haw, F., Wendler, H.O., and G. Deschamps. 1967. "Development of Washington state salmon sport fishery through 1964." *Research Bulletin* No. 7. May 1967. Washington Department of Fisheries. 192 pp.

Hasler, A.D. 1966. *Underwater Guideposts: Homing of Salmon.* University of Wisconsin Press. Madison, Wisconsin.

Heinemann, L. and K. Rosenbaum. 1983. "Securing a fair share: Indian treaty rights and the 'comprehensive' plan for the Columbia River." *Anadromous Fish Law Memorandum* Issue 21. March 1983. Lewis and Clark Law School. Portland, Oregon. 16 pp.

Hewes, G.W. 1973. "Indian fisheries productivity in precontact times in the Pacific salmon area." *Northwest Anthropological Research Notes* 7(2):133-155.

Howell, P., L. LaVoy, W. Kendra, and D. Ortmann. 1985. *Stock Assessments of*

*Columbia River Anadromous Salmonids. Vol. 1 Chinook, Coho, Chum, and Sockeye Salmon.* Prepared for BPA Project No. 84-335. July 1985.

Major, R.L., J. Ito, S. Ito, and H. Godfrey. 1978. "Distribution and abundance of chinook salmon (*Oncorhynchus tshawytscha*) in offshore waters of the north Pacific Ocean." *International North Pacific Fisheries Commission Bulletin* No. 38. Vancouver, Canada. 54 pp.

Mason, J.E. 1965. "Salmon of the North Pacific Ocean—Part IX. Coho, chinook, and masu salmon in offshore waters." *North Pacific Fisheries Commission Bulletin* 16. 135 pp.

Meekin, T.K. 1967. *Report on the 1966 Wells Dam Chinook Tagging Study.* Washington Department of Fisheries. 41 pp.

Netboy, A. 1958. *Salmon of the Pacific Northwest—Fish vs. Dams.* Binfords & Mort, Publishers. Portland, Oregon. 122 pp.

Northwest Power Planning Council. 1981. *Recommendations for the Fish and Wildlife Program under the Pacific Northwest Electric Power Planning and Conservation Act.* Volumes I-IV. Northwest Power Planning Council. Portland, Oregon.

Northwest Power Planning Council. 1984. *Columbia River Basin Fish and Wildlife Program.* Adopted November 15, 1982. Amended October 10, 1984. Portland, Oregon.

Northwest Power Planning Council. 1985. *Compilation of Information on Salmon and Steelhead Losses in the Columbia River Basin.* Revised draft. December 2, 1985. Portland, Oregon. 253 pp. + appendices.

Oregon Department of Fish and Wildlife and Washington Department of Fisheries. 1984. *Status Report. Columbia River Fish Runs and Fisheries,* 1960-83. 76 pp.

Oregon Department of Fish and Wildlife. 1985. *Oregon's Salmon and Steelhead Catch Data, 1974-1983.* Processed report. June 1985. 13 pp.

Ortmann, D.W., F. Cleaver, and K.R. Higgs. 1976. "Artificial propagation," in *Investigative Reports of Columbia River Fish Runs and Fisheries, 1960-83.* 76 pp.

Pacific Fishery Management Council. 1979. *Freshwater Habitat, Salmon Produced, and Escapements for Natural Spawning Along the Pacific Coast of the U.S.* A report prepared by the Anadromous Salmonid Environmental Task Force. 68 pp.

Pacific Fishery Management Council. 1985. *1984 Ocean Salmon Fisheries Review.* Pacific Fishery Management Council. Portland, Oregon.

Phinney, L.A. 1976. "Commercial fishery regulations and management objectives, with observations on sport fishery catch statistics," in *Investigative Reports of the Columbia River Fisheries Project for the Pacific Northwest Regional Commission.* 48 pp.

Phinney, L.A. and M.C. Miller. 1977. *Status of Washington's Ocean Sport Fishery in the Mid-1970's.* Washington Department of Fisheries Technical Report No. 24. 72 pp.

Pulford, E.F. 1964. "Analysis of average-weight sampling of commercial catches of Columbia River chinook salmon." Fish Commission of Oregon. *Research Briefs* (10)1:5-15.

Royce, W.F., L.S. Smith, and A.C. Hartt. 1968. "Models of oceanic migrations of Pacific salmon and comments on guidance mechanisms." U.S. Fish and Wildlife Service *Fishery Bulletin* 66(3).

Salmon and Steelhead Advisory Commission. 1984. *A New Management Structure for Anadromous Salmon and Steelhead Resources and Fisheries of the Washington and Columbia River Conservation Areas.* National Marine Fisheries Service. July 31, 1984. 71 pp.

Schwiebert, E., ed. 1977. *Columbia River Salmon and Steelhead: Proceedings of a symposium.* Special Publication No. 10. American Fisheries Society. Washington, D.C. 214 pp.

Seufert, F. 1980. *Wheels of Fortune.* Oregon Historical Society. Publishers Press. Salt Lake City, Utah. 259 pp.

Shelton, J.M. 1955. "The hatching of chinook salmon eggs under simulated stream conditions." *Progressive Fish-Culturist* 17(1):20-35.

Shelton, J.M. and R.D. Pollock. 1966. "Siltation and egg survival in incubation channels." *Transactions of the American Fisheries Society* 95(2):183-187.

Sims, C.W., W.W. Bentley, and R.C. Johnsen. 1978. *Effects of Power Peaking Operations on Juvenile Salmon and Steelhead Trout Migrations Progress 1977.* Northwest and Alaska Fisheries Center. National Marine Fisheries Center. 52 pp.

Smith, C.L. 1979. *Salmon Fishers of the Columbia.* Oregon State University Press. Corvallis, Oregon. 117 pp.

U.S.-Canada Chinook Technical Committee. 1983. Report of the U.S./Canada Chinook Technical Committee, prepared for the advisors to the U.S./Canada negotiations on the limitation of salmon interceptions. Unpublished manuscript. 18 pp.

U.S.-Canada Treaty Coalition. Northwest Indian Fisheries Commission, Columbia River Inter-Tribal Fish Commission, Washington State Department of Fisheries, Oregon Department of Fish and Wildlife. 1985. The U.S.-Canada salmon interception treaty. Unpublished brief. 15 pp.

Van Hyning, J.M. 1973. "Factors affecting the abundance of fall chinook salmon in the Columbia River." Fish Commission of Oregon. *Research Reports* (4)1. 87 pp.

Wahle, R.J. and R.Z. Smith. 1979. *A Historical and Descriptive Account of Pacific Coast Anadromous Salmonid Tearing Facilities and a Summary of Their Releases by Region, 1960-76.* National Oceanic and Atmospheric Administration Technical Report. National Marine Fisheries Service SSRF-736. 26 pp.

Washington Department of Fisheries. 1984. *Washington State Sport Catch Report, 1983.* Washington Department of Fisheries. 5 pp.

Wasserman, L., J. Hubble, and B. Watson. 1985. "Yakima River spring chinook enhancement study." *Annual Report FY 1984.* Project No. 82-16. Bonneville Power Administration. 115 pp.

Wilkinson, C.F. and D.K. Conner. 1983. The law of the Pacific salmon fishery: conservation and allocation of a transboundary common property resource. *Kansas Law Review.* University of Kansas. 109 pp.

Worland, D.D., R.J. Wahle, and P.D. Zimmer. 1969. "Contribution of Columbia River hatcheries to harvest of fall chinook salmon (*Oncorhynchus tshawytscha*)." *Fishery Bulletin* Vol. 67, No. 2. National Marine Fisheries Service.

Wright, S.G. 1976. *Status of Washington's Commercial Troll Salmon Fishery in the Mid-1970s.* Technical Report No. 21. Washington Department of Fisheries. 50 pp.

Wydoski, R.S. and R.R. Whitney. 1979. *Inland Fishes of Washington.* University of Washington Press. Seattle, Washington. 220 pp.

Yallup, W.F. 1985. "River use: A tribal viewpoint," in *Proceedings of a conference.* Washington Sea Grant Marine Advisory Publication. University of Washington. Seattle, Washington. pp. 73-78.

*Lloyd A. Phinney has worked as a fisheries biologist for the State of Washington Department of Fisheries for 23 years. For the past 10 years his research has focused primarily on the salmon of the Columbia River.*

Survival for the spotted owl, a native of Pacific Northwest old-growth forest, is dependent upon the controversial logging policies of the Bureau of Land Management and the Forest Service.

*Gary Braasch*

# The Spotted Owl

## Eric Forsman

Independent Consultant

## and
## E. Charles Meslow

Oregon Cooperative Wildlife Research Unit

## Species Description and Natural History

T HE SPOTTED OWL is an inconspicuous resident of the forested mountains of western North America. In the Pacific Northwest and northern California it is restricted primarily to old-growth forests or mixed forests of old-growth and mature trees. It is declining in numbers as old-growth forests are harvested and converted to intensively managed second-growth forests (Forsman et al 1984, Gould 1977, Marcot and Gardetto 1980, U.S. Fish and Wildlife Service 1982). Efforts to protect or manage habitat for the spotted owl have met with considerable opposition from timber interests, primarily because such management involves the retention of large tracts of old-growth forest (Heinrichs 1983, Hayward 1982). Because of the magnitude of the economic decisions involved, managers are reluctant to adopt conservative management plans for the spotted owl. Consequently, the management offered is the minimum believed to be essential to maintain a viable owl population. This controversy is still far from resolved.

### Physical Characteristics

The spotted owl is a medium-sized owl with round head, dark brown plummage, and dark eyes. It has white spots on the head and nape and white mottling on the breast and abdomen, thus the name spotted owl. Aside from

743

its appearance, the most distinctive feature of the spotted owl is its extremely unwary behavior around humans. Spotted owls are so tame, in fact, that it is easy to capture them with noose poles (Forsman 1983). The sexes are much alike, although females have higher-pitched calls. Females average approximately 22 ounces, males 20 ounces (Earhart and Johnson 1970).

Juvenile spotted owls go through a series of downy plumages during their first summer, but thereafter are distinguishable from adults only because their tail feathers are tipped with pure white bars rather than the mottled bars typical of adults (Forsman *et al* 1984). The juvenile rectrices are not molted until the owls are approximately 27 months old (Forsman *et al* 1984).

The only species with which the spotted owl might be confused is the closely related barred owl (*Strix varia*). Barred owls are slightly larger than spotted owls and have a distinct pattern of horizontal bars on the breast and vertical streaks on the abdomen. Unlike spotted owls, barred owls are wary and usually fly away when approached. Once geographically isolated from the spotted owl, the barred owl has extended its range in recent years, invading the Pacific Northwest and northern California (Taylor and Forsman 1976). In some areas, it appears that barred owls are displacing spotted owls.

## Taxonomy and Distribution

The American Ornithologists' Union presently recognizes three subspecies of the spotted owl: the northern spotted owl (*Strix occidentalis caurina*), California spotted owl (*S.o. occidentalis*), and Mexican spotted owl (*S.o. lucida*) (American Ornithologists' Union 1957, 1983). These subdivisions are based primarily on slight differences in plumage color and have not been verified by substantive studies. It is not clear whether the northern and California subspecies are distinct or simply represent a gradual change from north to south within the range of the species (Oberholser 1915).

The range of the northern spotted owl includes southwestern British Columbia, western Washington, western Oregon, and northwestern California (Bent 1938). This subspecies is confined primarily to the coastal mountains and the Cascade Range of Oregon and Washington and to the coastal mountains of California north of San Francisco. Its neighboring geographic group, the California spotted owl, is confined to the Sierra Nevada Mountains and coastal mountains of California south of San Francisco and possibly northern Baja, California.

The Mexican spotted owl occurs from Colorado and central Utah south in the higher mountains through Arizona, New Mexico, extreme west Texas, and Mexico. In Mexico, this subspecies apparently is resident in the higher mountains at least as far south as Jalisco, Michoacan, and Guanajuato (American Ornithologists' Union 1983). Although the northern and California spotted owls have been studied intensively in recent years, the Mexican spotted owl has received little attention.

## Population Size

Intensive calling surveys in Washington, Oregon, and California during the past 15 years have revealed that the spotted owl is fairly common in old-growth forests (Forsman *et al* 1984, Marcot and Gardetto 1980, Gould 1979). In suitable habitat, pairs typically are spaced one to two miles apart (Forsman *et al* 1984, Marcot and Gardetto 1980, Marshall 1942). Total population size is unknown, but pairs or individual birds have been observed at some 1,502 sites in Oregon and 1,450 sites in California (Forsman unpubl. data, Gould, California Department of Fish and Game, pers. comm.). Data on spotted owl sightings in Washington have not been fully compiled, but preliminary information indicates that pairs or individual adult birds have been observed at approximately 300 sites (Owens, Washington Department of Natural Resources, pers. comm.).

## Home Range Characteristics and Habitat Use

Spotted owls occupy relatively large home ranges used for foraging, nesting, and roosting. Most individuals are relatively sedentary, spending the entire year in the same general area (Forsman *et al* 1984, Solis 1983, Sisco and Gutiẽrrez 1984). However, recent information from California's Sierra Nevada Mountains indicates that some adults undertake winter movements into areas up to 20 miles from their summer home ranges (Laymon 1985).

The home ranges of 14 radio-tagged adult spotted owls in Oregon varied in size from 1,356 to 8,349 acres, with a mean of 3,816 acres (Forsman *et al* 1984). A similar study of seven adults in northern California yielded home ranges of 600 to 3,301 acres, with a mean of 1,594 acres (Sisco and Gutiẽrrez 1984, Solis 1983). Data from these studies are not directly comparable because owls were not observed with equal frequency or for equal periods of time.

Because paired individuals use many areas that do not overlap, their combined home ranges usually are much larger than their individual home ranges. The combined home ranges of six pairs studied in Oregon averaged 6,614 acres, with a range of 2,840 to 10,440 acres (Forsman and Meslow 1985). Two pairs studied in northern California had combined home ranges of 1,258 and 2,126 acres (Solis 1983, Sisco and Gutiẽrrez 1984).

Radiotelemetry studies in Washington, Oregon, and northern California have indicated that spotted owls show a strong preference for foraging and roosting in old-growth forests or in mixed stands of old-growth and mature forest. Cut-over areas and young second-growth forests are used occasionally, but not nearly as frequently as are older forests (Solis 1983, Sisco and Gutiẽrrez 1984, Forsman *et al* 1984, Allen, Washington Department of Game, pers. comm.). The amount of old-growth within spotted owl home ranges varies considerably. In Oregon, the amount of old-growth in the combined home ranges of paired individuals ranged from 1,008 acres to 3,786 acres, with a mean of 2,264 acres (Forsman and Meslow 1985).

Why spotted owls prefer older forests is unknown, but several possible explanations have been suggested (Forsman et al 1984, Barrows 1981, Carey 1985, Gutiérrez 1985). It is possible, for instance, that the owls forage and nest in older forests because preferred prey or suitable nest sites are most abundant there. It has also been argued that spotted owls prefer to roost in older stands because the unique structure of such stands provides the best protection from both hot and cold temperatures and from precipitation. Other theories are that the owls avoid cut-over areas because suitable foraging perches are lacking or because they are more susceptible to predation in such areas. It is entirely possible that all of these factors act together.

## Site Tenacity and Adult Longevity

Adult spotted owls tend to occupy the same areas year after year and to associate with the same mate each year (Forsman et al 1984, Miller 1974). Adult mortality rates and longevity are poorly documented. However, available information suggests that most individuals that survive long enough to acquire territories are relatively long-lived (Barrowclough and Coats 1985). Several banded adults in Oregon have survived at least 10 years in the wild (Forsman unpubl. data). A captive bird in our possession is 15 years old and continues to lay eggs almost every year.

## Reproduction

In the Pacific Northwest, spotted owls nest almost exclusively in cavities or platforms in trees (Forsman et al 1984). They do not build their own nests. Cavity nests typically are located in large old-growth coniferous trees with broken tops. A variety of platform nests are used, including nests built by other birds or mammals and natural platforms in deformed clumps of limbs.

In the southwestern United States and southern California, spotted owls nest on ledges in caves or on cliffs, as well as in cavities or platforms in trees (Bendire 1892, Dunn 1901, Dickey 1914, Ligon 1926). In contrast to cavity nests in the Pacific Northwest, cavity nests in southern California and the southwestern United States often are located in oak trees or other hardwoods (Dunn 1901, Bendire 1892).

Spotted owl nests in the Pacific Northwest and northwestern California most commonly are located in old-growth forests or in mixed forests of old growth and mature trees. These forests typically are multi-layered, with an overstory of large old-growth trees and one or more understory layers of smaller trees (Forsman et al 1984, Solis 1983).

Like many other owls, spotted owls exhibit dramatic fluctuations in reproduction from year to year. Reproductive performance in recent years has been relatively poor, with few pairs nesting in most years (Forsman et al 1984, Barrows 1985, Gutierrez et al 1985a,b, Allen, Washington Department of

Game, unpubl. data, Miller and Meslow, Oregon Cooperative Wildlife Research Unit, unpubl. data). As in other owls, reproductive performance is likely related to prey abundance, but this has yet to be demonstrated for the spotted owl.

Nesting pairs typically begin to roost together near their nest sites in late February or March, two to three weeks before the eggs are laid. Soon after they begin to roost together, they begin a nightly ritual in which they copulate and display near the nest (Forsman *et al* 1984).

Eggs are laid at three day intervals in March or early April. The usual clutch is two, but clutches of one or three are not uncommon. Clutches of four are extremely rare (Dunn 1901, Bendire 1892). Incubation, performed entirely by the female, lasts approximately 32 days. During incubation and brooding periods, the male feeds the female and young. The young leave the nest when they are approximately 35 days old and subsequently are fed by their parents in the vicinity of the nest until late summer or fall. Most young begin to disperse from their natal areas in September or October. Straight-line dispersal distances of 0.6 to 62 miles have been reported (Gutierrez *et al* 1985b). However, all dispersal data collected thus far have been incomplete because the marked young either died or were lost before they became successful breeders (Forsman *et al* 1984, Laymon 1985, Gutierrez *et al* 1985a,b, Miller and Meslow 1985).

## Juvenile Mortality

Recent studies of juvenile dispersal in Oregon, Washington, and California indicate that few of the juvenile spotted owls produced in a given year survive to reproduce (Forsman *et al* 1984, Laymon 1985, Gutiẽrrez *et al* 1985a,b, Miller and Meslow 1985). Most mortality appears to be due to starvation and predation. If the high rate of juvenile mortality, nearly 100 percent, observed in these studies were to persist, it could result in a rapid population decline. The other alternative is that the juvenile survival data collected thus far are atypical. The years during which the dispersal studies were conducted—1982, 1983, and 1984—included two years in which few pairs nested. This could indicate a period of reduced prey populations or some other deleterious factor in which dispersing juveniles were subjected to extremely rigorous conditions. Another alternative is that the radio transmitters used to monitor dispersing juveniles reduced the mobility, foraging efficiency, or thermoregulatory efficiency of the owls, thereby making the marked individuals more susceptible to death by starvation or predation. The latter possibility seems unlikely considering that numerous adult spotted owls have been radio-tracked without suffering suspiciously high mortality rates. In summer, 1985, 17 juvenile spotted owls were radio-tagged in Oregon. As of December 31, 1985, six still were alive. These preliminary data indicate that the 1985 cohort may be experiencing a reduced mortality rate.

## Food and Foraging Behavior

Spotted owls forage primarily by sitting on elevated perches and diving on their prey. They forage mainly at night, but also will attempt to capture prey during the day if the opportunity presents itself. The diet includes a variety of mammals, birds, insects, and reptiles, but the core of the diet in most areas is comprised of small mammals, especially arboreal and semi-arboreal mammals such as the northern flying squirrel, red tree vole, and woodrats (Forsman *et al* 1984, Marshall 1942, Solis 1983, Barrows 1980, Kertell 1977, Wagner *et al* 1982).

# Significance of the Species

Because of its habitat needs, the spotted owl has become a symbol in the effort to retain viable remnants of old-growth forests (Heinrichs 1983). In particular, it has become a symbol of the era before the arrival of the European settlers, when primeval forests blanketed much of North America, and natural events, rather than economics, controlled the fate of the forest and its creatures.

From an economic standpoint, the spotted owl is significant because of the timber-harvest income foregone to protect its habitat. It is unclear exactly how much spotted owl management will cost, but undoubtedly it will involve many millions of dollars in foregone timber revenues (Heinrichs 1983, Hayward 1982).

# Historical Perspective

The invasion of the western United States by European settlers resulted in rapid clearing of forests from extensive areas, especially low-lying areas and the foothills of the major mountain ranges. This apparently resulted in the extirpation of the spotted owl in many areas (Forsman *et al* 1977, Gould 1977, Phillips *et al* 1964). Exact estimates of this population decline are impossible because much of the habitat destruction occurred before the range of the species was documented. The result, however, is that spotted owls are restricted now primarily to the more rugged mountain ranges, away from areas where the virgin forest has been eliminated.

# Current Trends

In the Pacific Northwest and California, the spotted owl is still fairly common but declining (Forsman *et al* 1984, Gould 1977, Postovit 1977). The rate of population decline has been estimated at 0.8 percent per year in Oregon

(Forsman *et al* 1984), and 0.45 percent per year in California (Gould 1985). The primary reason for the decline is harvest of old-growth forests. Population trends in the southwestern United States and Mexico are unknown.

# Management

## Oregon

In 1973, at the request of the director of the Oregon Department of Fish and Wildlife, an interagency committee was formed to coordinate the mangement of the spotted owl and other sensitive wildife in Oregon. One of the first goals of this committee, composed of biologists from the Oregon Department of Fish and Wildlife, U.S. Forest Service, Bureau of Land Management (BLM), U.S. Fish and Wildlife Service (FWS), and Oregon State University, was to develop a spotted owl management plan for Oregon.

The major questions that confronted this committee were: (1) For how many pairs of owls should habitat be protected? (2) How should sites with protected habitat be distributed? and (3) How should the habitat on the protected sites be managed? At the outset, the committee felt constrained to advise the minimum number of pairs and habitat necessary to sustain a viable population. Managing for more than a minimum viable population was not considered because of the intense pressure to reduce conflicts with timber management. Unfortunately, no one knew for sure what constituted a minimum viable population of spotted owls (and we still do not)(Barrowclough and Coats 1985). As a result, the committee decided that the best approach would be to maintain a population of pairs spaced at uniform intervals throughout the range of the owl, such that no pairs or groups of pairs became isolated from other segments of the population. The committee recommended, therefore, that spotted owl management areas be spaced at three-mile to 12-mile intervals on Forest Service and BLM lands, with an average spacing of about six miles (Oregon Endangered Species Task Force 1977). Wider spacing between pairs was deemed undesirable because the inventory data indicated that spotted owl pairs rarely were isolated from other pairs by more than a few miles. To achieve the desired spacing between pairs, the committee recommended that 400 pairs of owls be protected in Oregon (Oregon Endangered Species Task Force 1977).

In regard to the amount of old-growth habitat managed for each pair of spotted owls, the spotted owl committee again felt constrained by one overriding imperative: The amount recommended would be the minimum necessary to sustain each pair of owls. Again, however, no one knew what the minimum was. The committee initially estimated that 300 acres of old growth per pair should be adequate (Oregon Endangered Species Task Force 1977). This was increased to 1,000 acres in the 1981 revised plan, after radiotelemetry studies indicated that most pairs used large home ranges that encompassed at least 1,000 acres of old growth (Forsman and Meslow 1985, Oregon and Washington Interagency Wildlife Committee 1981). The revised spotted owl management plan further stipulated that the 1,000 acres of old growth should include a core area of at least 300 acres centered around the nest area, with the remaining old growth located within a one-and-a-half-mile radius of the nest. The one-and-a-half-mile limit was added because the available radiotelemetry data indicated that nesting pairs restricted most of their foraging to within a one-and-a-half-mile radius of their nests (Forsman *et al* 1984).

The plan did not specify how old-growth forests within spotted owl mangement areas were to be managed, other than to state that the objective ". . . should be to maintain dense multi-layered stands in which overstory trees are at least 250 years old, and understory trees range in age from saplings to 200 years old, i.e., uneven-aged understory. The salvage of down or dead material should not be conducted in old-growth stands managed for spotted owls. Stands intended as replacements for existing old-growth stands should be managed to duplicate conditions in natural old-growth stands already present in the area" (Oregon and Washington Interagency Wildlife Committee 1981).

Although the Forest Service and BLM accepted the spotted owl management plan as an interim guideline, they did so with conditions attached. Both agencies balked at accepting the 1,000-acre guideline, opting instead to manage for only 300 acres of old growth. However, the Forest Service did agree to "retain the option" to manage for an additional 700 acres of old growth in each spotted owl management area if it eventually became apparent that 300 acres was not enough.

Both agencies insisted that the interim guidelines should apply only until they completed their long-range timber management plans, at which time they would spell out their final decisions concerning spotted owls. One of the first of these plans that was forthcoming was the 10-year timber management plan for BLM's Coos Bay District, released in 1981. In this plan, the district proposed to protect 16 pairs of spotted owls (Bureau of Land Management 1981). This decision conformed fairly closely with the interim numbers proposed in the spotted owl management plan, except that the amount of old-growth habitat managed for each pair was only 300 acres rather than 1,000. Because the proposed timber management alternative in the final environmental impact statement reduced the allowable cut on the Coos Bay District by approximately seven percent, the proposed alternative was very unpopular with the timber industry and local groups that relied on income from timber harvest. Apparently in response to intense pressure from these groups, BLM proposed to modify the final environmental impact statement by eliminating most of the protective measures that had been proposed for spotted owls and other old-growth-dependent wildlife. This would have reduced the number of spotted owls on the district to three to four pairs at most (Bureau of Land Management 1982). This proposal, which amounted to a complete rejection of the spotted owl management plan, resulted in an immediate storm of protest from the Oregon Department of Fish and Wildlife, the U.S. Fish and Wildlife Service, and various environmental groups. As a result, the district again reversed its decision and agreed to manage for 16 pairs of spotted owls (Bureau of Land Management 1983).

The Coos Bay experience apparently convinced BLM that it was not going to be possible to depart significantly from the interim spotted owl agreement without serious political and legal repercussions. As a result, the 10-year management plans for the rest of the western Oregon districts have followed the interim spotted owl guidelines fairly closely, a notable exception being that BLM still has not accepted the 1,000-acre old-growth minimum for managing spotted owl pairs.

The proposed final decision of the Forest Service concerning spotted owl management in Oregon was described in the 1984 *Regional Guide for the Pacific Northwest Region*. The decision was to manage for only 263 pairs rather than the 290 pairs specified in the interim agreement (U.S. Forest Service 1984a).

The decision to reduce the number of managed pairs on Forest Service lands was justified in the regional guide on the grounds that the required spacing between pairs could be obtained with only 263 pairs. While this sounds like reasonable justification for altering the plan, the fact is that the number of pairs needed to achieve the required spacing varies tremendously depending on the type of spacing pattern used and the positioning of the spacing grid relative to forest boundaries. For instance, to achieve a truly uniform spacing of six miles between all pairs on federal lands would require a hexagonal spacing pattern (Barlow 1974). To achieve such a pattern would require a much greater number of pairs than was chosen in the regional guide or in the spotted owl management plan. The decision to reduce the number of pairs that are managed on Forest Service land will result in wider spacing between pairs.

Upon release, the 1984 regional guide was almost immediately appealed by the National Wildlife Federation and several other environmental groups on the grounds that the spotted owl management plan was a major environmental action that required an environmental impact statement (National Wildlife Federation, Oregon Wildlife Federation, Lane County Audubon Society, Oregon Natural Resources Council 1984). The appeal was successful and, as a result, the Forest Service Pacific Northwest Regional Office presently is preparing a supplemental environmental impact statement for the 1984 regional guide that deals specifically with spotted owl management. The supplemental environmental impact statement will examine a number of alternatives for spotted owl management that were not considered in the regional plan and could result in modifications to the final decision in the regional plan. The supplemental environmental impact statement is scheduled for release in draft form in March 1986.

Although it is a beginning, the Oregon spotted owl mangement plan is fraught with problems. From the outset, management of the spotted owl has been designed to maintain only a minimum viable population of owls, thereby avoiding federal listing of the species as threatened or endangered. Given the management objective of maintaining a minimum population size, it is doubtful that it will be possible to sustain a viable population of owls if each pair is provided with only a minimum amount of old-growth habitat, especially if that habitat also is of minimal quality. And yet, that is exactly how the spotted owl management plan is being implemented in many instances in the Pacific Northwest. To minimize the impact of spotted owl management on the allowable cut, many spotted owl management areas have been placed in poor quality habitat where spotted owls probably will find it difficult or impossible to exist. In fact, it appears that many spotted owl management areas are not even occupied by spotted owls. In a recent study in Washington, researchers could not verify the presence of spotted owl pairs in 48 percent of the spotted owl management areas surveyed on national forests (Allen and Brewer 1985). On BLM lands in Oregon, surveys in 1984 and 1985 failed to demonstrate the presence of pairs in nearly 50 percent of the spotted owl management areas surveyed (Neitro, Bureau of Land Management, unpubl. data).

The low occupancy rate of spotted owl management areas reflects two problems. First, the owl survey data used to establish management areas were, in many cases, inadequate. As a result, management areas often were located in the wrong place relative to areas used by spotted owls. Second, the low occupancy rate of spotted owl management areas often reflects the poor quality of sites selected for management. In selecting sites for management, there is a strong temptation for forest managers to pass over high timber-yield sites with a long history of spotted owl occupancy in favor of low-yield sites with an inconsistent or non-existent record of spotted owl occupancy. Far too often, potential timber yields appear to be the primary criteria for site selection, rather than demonstrated occupancy by spotted owls.

Maintaining uniform spacing between spotted owl management areas has become a particularly difficult problem for two reasons. First, some national forests and BLM districts have persisted in concentrating their owl management areas in wilderness areas, scenic areas, and other reserved areas, often creating a sparse distribution of managed pairs on commercial forest lands. The objective of the Spotted Owl Management Plan was to maintain a uniform distribution of owls throughout the range of the species, regardless of land-use allocations. The second problem with the distribution of managed pairs is that the interagency committee underestimated the number of pairs necessary to maintain uniform spacing on BLM lands. As a result, large tracts of forest on most BLM districts contain no spotted owl management areas. For example, out of approximately 274 townships (a township is a 36-square-mile area) that include major BLM holdings in Oregon, only 64 townships have spotted owl management areas (Bruce, Oregon Department of Fish and Wildlife, pers. comm.).

Another factor that makes the successful outcome of the current spotted owl management plan in Oregon especially risky is BLM's decision to manage for only 300 acres of old growth per pair. The Forest Service position relative to the amount of old growth to be managed for each pair is at present unclear, but presumably will be clarified in the supplemental environmental impact statement to the 1984 regional plan. Still another problem with implementation of the Spotted Owl Management Plan is that timber sales frequently are intermingled with forest stands reserved for spotted owl management before the nests and principal roost areas of the resident owls are located. In situations where the primary spotted owl use areas have not been determined, it is possible that timber sales will accidently include the nest sites or major roost areas of the resident owls.

Even if the problems cited above did not exist, many spotted owl management areas eventually may become unsuitable for spotted owls because of chance environmental events such as fire, windthrow, and disease. For this reason alone, the spotted owl management effort may be doomed in the long run unless the management agencies initiate a program to grow replacement stands of old-growth on areas adjacent to the existing management areas. How this problem will be resolved is at present unclear.

A variety of methods have been proposed for managing old-growth forests within spotted owl management areas in Oregon. Most of these methods fall into one of three alternatives: (1) preservation, (2) long-term rotation, or (3) uneven-aged management. The preservation approach is a minimal management approach—the area is left alone for the most part. The majority of national forests and BLM districts in Oregon appear to be leaning toward the preservation approach to spotted owl management (U.S. Forest Service 1984b, Neitro, Bureau of Land Managment, pers. comm.). Whether this option will continue to be the preferred option in the forthcoming Forest Service supplemental environmental impact statement remains to be seen. The long-term rotation alternative involves setting up a harvest regime in which new old-growth stands are produced as others are harvested. While this alternative offers a continuous supply of appropriate habitat, it is not particularly popular with forest managers because it results in reduced timber yields on up to three times more forest acreage than does the preservation alternative. However, long-term rotations are being planned for some spotted owl management areas (Neitro, Bureau of Land Management, pers. comm.). The uneven-aged management alternative has been proposed for at least one national forest in Oregon (U.S. Forest Service 1984b). This approach would involve the selective removal of trees within spotted owl management areas on a regular basis, such that as much as 60 percent of the potential timber yield could be obtained. Whether this can be accomplished without seriously degrading the habitat for owls has not been demonstrated.

Private timber owners and the Oregon Department of Forestry have shown little interest in protecting spotted owl habitat in Oregon. In response to an invitation to participate in the implementation of the spotted owl management plan, the state forester promised in 1978 that ". . . the philosophy embodied in the Plan will be implemented on State land through a continued monitoring for the presence of owls within second-growth forests. At the time such populations are found, further implementation can be considered." (Schroeder 1978). Despite this promise, the Department of Forestry has never implemented any monitoring program for spotted owls nor made any effort to protect the habitat of spotted owls that have been observed on state lands subsequent to 1978. The irony of this situation is that while the Oregon Department of Fish and Wildlife is deeply involved in the effort to protect the spotted owl, its sister agency, the Department of Forestry, is systematically eliminating spotted owl habitat on state-owned lands. This situation is especially unfortunate because state lands offer the only hope for maintaining spotted owls in the northern coast ranges of Oregon, where there are essentially no federally owned lands.

Although the initial selection of spotted owl management areas has been left up to the Forest Service and BLM, the Oregon Department of Fish and Wildlife has assumed the responsibility of evaluating all sites selected for management in the state. The review process involves an assessment of each site based on (1) quantity and distribution of old growth (2) placement of the core area relative to the nest area or major roost areas, (3) history of occupancy by spotted owls, and (4) spacing of the site relative to other spotted owl management areas. The Oregon Department of Fish and Wildlife plans to recommend that management areas that fail the review process be replaced by better management sites, if such sites are available (Bruce, Oregon Department of Fish and Wildlife, pers. comm.). It remains to be seen if the managing agencies will agree to the changes recommended by the Oregon Department of Fish and Wildlife.

## Washington

Spotted owl management in Washington has been modeled after the Oregon plan. BLM administers little land in western Washington and has no plans to manage for spotted owls there. The Forest Service has tentatively opted to manage for 112 pairs in the state (U.S. Forest Service 1984a). This decision could, of course, be modified in the forthcoming supplemental environmental impact statement. As in Oregon, private landowners and the state forestry agency—the Department of Natural Resources—have shown little interest in managing habitat for spotted owls. A recent request to put several spotted owl management areas on Department of Natural Resources lands is encountering considerable opposition from within the agency (Brewer, Washington Department of Game, pers. comm.). It appears, therefore, that aside from the 112 management areas on Forest Service lands, few spotted owls will be protected intentionally in Washington. However, Washington has an extensive system of national parks and wilderness areas that have not been thoroughly searched for spotted owls. While additional pairs undoubtedly will be protected by their inclusion in these reserved areas, the distribution and numbers involved are unclear.

As a result of recent radiotelemetry studies in Washington, the Washington Department of Game is now considering a recommendation that spotted owl management areas should include in excess of 2,000 acres of old growth (Brewer, Washington Department of Game, pers. comm.). This recommendation is based on the fact that the radio-tagged owls that were observed in Washington had larger home ranges and used larger areas of old growth than owls that have been observed in Oregon and northwestern California. This suggests that management plans for spotted owls need to be somewhat flexible to allow for regional differences in habitat use.

## California

Spotted owl management in California also had been modeled after the plan developed in Oregon, with some significant differences. First, the number of pairs to be managed was left up to the individual national forests. The result was that the forests in northern California and the Sierra Nevada Mountains chose to manage for a total of 500 to 550 pairs of owls (Carrier 1985, U.S. Forest Service 1984c). The forests in the coastal ranges of southern California chose to protect all known owl pairs, at least for the time being. The second major difference is that most forests in California plan to manage a minimum of 1,000 acres of old growth and/or mature forest for each pair of spotted owls selected for management (Carrier, U.S. Forest Service, pers. comm., Carrier *et al* 1984). Some national forests in California plan to create and manage spotted owl habitat by selectively thinning stands that develop on cutover areas (Smith 1982). At present, this approach is experimental.

The Bureau of Land Management does not have extensive spotted owl habitat in California, but does plan to manage appoximately 15 old-growth reserve areas that contain blocks of old-growth forest. Some of these areas currently provide habitat for spotted owls (Neitro, Bureau of Land Management, pers. comm.). There are no plans at present to manage for spotted owls on state-owned lands in California (Gould, California Department of Fish and Game, pers. comm.).

## Prognosis

Even if they are successful, the spotted owl management programs currently being implemented in Washington, Oregon, and California will allow a large reduction in the total population of spotted owls. In addition, the spotted owl is facing a potential new threat—the invasion of its traditional range by a closely related species, the barred owl. In some areas, it appears that barred owls are displacing spotted owls (Brewer, Washington Department of Game, pers. comm.). These factors do not bode well for the future of the spotted owl. About the best that can be expected is that management for the species will result in a greatly reduced, but viable, population of owls.

## Recommendations

Implementation of the spotted owl management plan has not achieved the objectives envisioned by the interagency team of biologists who drafted the plan. Current spotted owl management provides the minimum number of owls with habitat that is frequently minimial or less than minimal in terms of quality and/or quantity. This approach does not bode well for the continued viability of the owl. A positive first step to mitigate this situation would be to select management sites that include the best available habitat and that are known to be occupied consistently by spotted owls. Sites that have a poor or undocumented history of occupancy by spotted owls should be selected as spotted owl management areas only if no alternatives exist.

Two actions can help insure that management areas are occupied by spotted owls and are placed correctly relative to areas used by resident owls. First, a thorough field investigation needs to be conducted to locate the nests and principal roost areas of each pair selected for managment. Second, timber-sale layout in areas adjacent to spotted owl management areas should proceed only after the nest areas and principal roost areas of the managed pairs are located. These actions will ensure that nests and roost areas are not harvested accidentally.

Land management agencies in the Pacific Northwest and California need to develop a consistently funded program for surveying spotted owls and monitoring spotted owl management areas. In the past, intensity of spotted owl survey work has fluctuated radically from year to year, apparently in response to funding levels. As a result, survey data are limited in many areas and inconsistent between years. Even as late as 1985, agencies were still relying, in many instances, on volunteers to survey spotted owls, presumably because of funding constraints. Although we do not wish to belittle the contributions of volunteers, critical resource programs which require professional training or experience should be staffed by accountable employees who receive adequate compensation.

Because the number of management areas on BLM lands in Oregon are not adequate to maintain a uniformly distributed owl population, the number of spotted owl management areas on BLM lands should be increased. The director of the Oregon Department of Fish and Wildlife has made such a proposal in a letter to the BLM state director (Donaldson 1985). On all public forest lands, the emphasis should be on maintaining a uniform distribution of pairs regardless of land allocations. Forest-managing agencies should do everything possible to ensure that spotted owls do not become separated in a series of isolated populations. Where timber harvest has produced large gaps in the range of the species (e.g., the Columbia Gorge, the Olympia Peninsula, and the coastal ranges of northwest Oregon and southwest Washington), a high priority should be to regenerate suitable habitat for the species as soon as possible. State and federal lands in these areas are key to re-establishing the continuous distribution of the spotted owl in a significant portion of its range.

Because it is inevitable that some spotted owl management sites will be destroyed by fire or other chance environmental events, a series of occupied replacement sites needs to be retained. The required number and distribution of replacement sites could be estimated based on historical rates of habitat loss to fire and other environmental perturbations. Such precautionary action can help ensure that region-wide spotted owl populations do not fall below critical minimal levels. Experimental silvicultural efforts offer the potential to create suitable habitat for spotted owls in a shorter time than is required with natural succession. Research in this area may ameliorate the economic impacts of spotted owl management.

It has been argued that the amount of old growth managed for each pair of spotted owls in Oregon should be the mean acreage used by radio-marked birds (2,264 acres) rather than the minimum (1,008 acres) (Carey 1985, National Wildlife Federation *et al* 1985). From a biological standpoint, this argument is reasonable because it is unlikely that any species can thrive if it is provided only with a minimum of habitat, especially if that habitat is of less than optimal quality. In all likelihood, however, the minimum amount of old-growth or mature-forest habitat required by pairs of spotted owls probably varies from site to site and year to year depending on site quality, prey abundance, regional differences in habitat, and many other factors. Two recently completed studies in California and ongoing studies of habitat use by adult spotted owls in Washington and Oregon undoubtedly will help to resolve this issue (Sisco and Gutiérrez 1984, Solis 1983, Brewer and Allen, study in progress, Laymon, manuscript in preparation, Miller and Meslow, study in progress). A prudent course of action in the interim would be to constrain old-growth harvest adjacent to spotted owl management areas until the adequacy of the 1,000-acre (or other) prescription is fully demonstrated—keep the options open.

Because no explicit plan has been developed for old-growth management on BLM or Forest Service lands in the Pacific Northwest or California, the Spotted Owl Management Plan is viewed by some conservation groups as a surrogate old-growth management plan. It was not designed to function in this capacity. The Spotted Owl Management Plan addresses the specific needs of the spotted owl and is inadequate as a plan for protecting the other plants and animals that may occupy specialized old-growth communities or that require closer spacing of habitat areas. The challenge to the forest management agencies is to develop and display generalized old-growth management plans that encompass the needs of the spotted owl as well as the needs of other plants and animals that occupy old-growth habitat (Harris 1984).

# References

Allen, H. and L. Brewer. 1985. *A Progress Report for the Cooperative Administrative Study to Monitor Spotted Owl Management Areas in National Forests in Washington.* Unpublished report. Washington Department of Game. Olympia, Washington. 138 pp.

American Ornithologists' Union. 1957. *Check-List of North American Birds,* 5th ed. Lord Baltimore Press, Maryland. 691 pp.

American Ornithologists' Union. 1983. *Check-List of North American Birds,* 6th ed. Allen Press, Inc., Lawrence, Kansas. 877 pp.

Barlow, G. 1974. "Hexagonal territories." *Animal Behavior* 22, no. 4:876-878.

Barrowclough, G.F., and S.L. Coats. 1985. "The demography and population genetics of owls, with special reference to the conservation of the spotted owl (*Strix occidentalis*)," in R.J. Gutiérrez and A.B. Carey eds., *Ecology and Management of Spotted Owls in the Pacific Northwest.* United States Department of Agriculture Forest Service, Pacific Northwest Forest and Range Experiment Station. General Technical Report PNW-185. Portland, Oregon. Pp. 74-85.

Barrows, C. 1980. "Feeding ecology of the spotted owl in California." *Raptor Research* 14, no. 3:73-78.

Barrows, C.W. 1981. "Roost selection by spotted owls: an adaptation to heat stress." *Condor* 83, no. 4:302-309.

Barrows, C.W. 1985. "Breeding success relative to fluctuations in diet for spotted owls in California," *in* R.J. Gutiérrez and A.B. Carey eds., *Ecology and Management of Spotted Owls in the Pacific Northwest,* United States Department of Agriculture Forest Service, Pacific Northwest Forest and Range Experiment Station. General Technical Report PNW-185. Portland, Oregon. Pp. 50-54.

Bendire, C.E. 1892. *Life Histories of North American Birds with Special Reference to Their Breeding Habits and Eggs.* United States National Museum Special Bulletin no 1. 446 pp.

Bent, A.C. 1938. *Life Histories of North American Birds of Prey, Part II.* U.S. National Museum Bulletin no. 170. 482 pp.

Bureau of Land Management. 1981. *South Coast-Curry Final Timber Management Environmental Impact Statement.* Bureau of Land Management. Portland, Oregon.

Bureau of Land Management. 1982. *South Coast-Curry Timber Management Plan Proposed Decision.* Bureau of Land Management. Portland, Oregon. 26 pp.

Bureau of Land Management. 1983. *South Coast-Curry Timber Management Plan Record of Decision.* Bureau of Land Management. Portland, Oregon. 16 pp.

Carey, A.B. 1985. "A summary of the scientific basis for spotted owl management," *in* R.J. Gutierrez and A.B. Carey eds., *Ecology and Management of Spotted Owls in the Pacific Northwest.* U.S. Department of Agriculture, Forest Service, Pacific Northwest Forest and Range Experiment Station. General Technical Report PNW-185. Pp. 100-114.

Carrier, D.W., D.M. Solis and E.F. Toth. 1984. "Providing habitat for spotted owls through a managed forest ecosystem on California's national forests," in W.C. McComb ed., *Proceedings of the Workshop on Management of Nongame Species and Ecological Communities*. Department of Forestry, University of Kentucky. Lexington, Kentucky. pp. 283-291.

Dickey, D.R. 1914. "The nesting of the spotted owl." *Condor* 16, no. 5:193-202.

Letter from J.R. Donaldson to William Lavelle, Oregon State Director, Bureau of Management, September 6, 1985.

Dunn, H.H. 1901. "The spotted owl (*Syrnium occcidentale*)." *Oologist* 18, no. 11:165-167.

Earhart, C.M. and N.K. Johnson. 1970. "Size dimorphism and food habits of North American owls." *Condor* 72, no. 3:251-264.

Forsman, E.D., E.C. Meslow and M.J. Strub. 1977. Spotted owl abundance in young versus old-growth forests, Oregon. *Wildlife Society Bulletin* 5, no. 2:43-47.

Forsman, E.D. 1983. *Methods and Materials for Locating and Studying Spotted Owls*. U.S. Department of Agriculture Forest Service, Pacific Northwest Forest and Range Experiment Station. General Technical Report PNW-162, Portland, Oregon. 8 pp.

Forsman, E.D., E.C. Meslow and H.M. Wight. 1984. "Distribution and biology of the spotted owl in Oregon." *Wildlife Monographs* no. 87. 64 pp.

Forsman, E.D. and E.C. Meslow. 1985. "Old-growth retention for spotted owls—how much do they need?" in R.J. Gutiérrez and A.B. Carey eds., *Ecology and Management of Spotted Owls in the Pacific Northwest*. U.S. Department of Agriculture, Forest Service, Pacific Northwest Forest and Range Experiment Station. General Technical Report PNW-185. Pp. 58–59.

Gould, G.I., Jr. 1985. "Management of spotted owls by the Calfornia Department of Fish and Game," in R.J. Gutiérrez and A.B. Carey eds., *Ecology and Management of Spotted Owls in the Pacific Northwest*. U.S. Department of Agriculture, Forest Service, Pacific Northwest Forest and Range Experiment Station. General Technical Report PNW-185. Pp. 21–26.

Gould, G.I., Jr. 1977. "Distribution of the spotted owl in California." *Western Birds* 8, no. 4:131-146.

Gould, G.I. Jr. 1979. "Status and management of elf and spotted owls in California," in P.P. Schaeffer and S.M. Ehlers eds., *Proceedings of the Symposium on Owls of the West: Their Ecology and Conservation*. National Audubon Society Western Education Center. Tiburon, California. pp. 86-97.

Gutiérrez, R.J. 1985. "An overview of recent research on the spotted owl," in R.J. Gutierrez and A.B. Carey eds., *Ecology and Management of Spotted Owls in the Pacific Northwest*. U.S. Department of Agriculture, Forest Service, Pacific Northwest Forest and Range Experiment Station. General Technical Report PNW-185. Pp. 39–49.

Gutiérrez, R.J., J.P. Ward, A.B. Franklin, W. Lahaye and V. Meretsky. 1985b. "Dispersal ecology of juvenile northern spotted owls (*Strix occidentalis caurina*) in Northwestern California." Unpublished Report. Humboldt State University. Arcata, California. 48 pp.

Gutiêrrez, R.J., A.B. Franklin, W. Lahaye, V.J. Meretsky and J.P. Ward. 1985a. "Juvenile spotted owl dispersal in Northwestern California, preliminary results," *in* R.J. Gutierrez and A.B. Carey eds., *Ecology and Management of Spotted Owl in the Pacific Northwest.* U.S. Department of Agriculture, Forest Service, Pacific Northwest Forest and Range Experiment Station. General Technical Report PNW-185. Pp. 60-65.

Hayward, D.R. 1982. "Will the spotted owl become our billion dollar bird?" *The Log* 6, no. 1:14-17.

Harris, L.D. 1984. *The Fragmented Forest: Island Biogeography Theory and the Preservation of Biotic Diversity.* University of Chicago Press, Chicago, Illinois. 211 pp.

Heinrichs, J. 1983. "The winged snail darter." *Journal of Forestry* 81, no. 4:212-215, 262.

Kertell, K. 1977. "The spotted owl at Zion National Park, Utah." *Western Birds* 8, no. 4:147-150.

Laymon, S.A. 1985. "General habitats and movements of spotted owls in the Sierra Nevada," *in* R.J. Gutiêrrez and A.B. Carey eds., *Ecology and Management of Spotted Owls in the Pacific Northwest.* U.S. Department of Agriculture, Forest Service, Pacific Northwest Forest and Range Experiment Station. General Technical Report PNW-185. Pp. 66-68.

Ligon, J.S. 1926. "Habits of the spotted owl." *Auk* 43, no. 4:421-427.

Marcot, B.G. and J. Gardetto. 1980. "Status of the spotted owl in Six Rivers National Forest, California." *Western Birds* 11, no. 2:79-87.

Marshall, J.T., Jr. 1942. "Food and habitat of the spotted owl." *Condor,* vol. 44, no. 2. pp. 66-67.

Miller, G.M. 1974. "Grace Miller on spotted owls," *in* L.W. Walker ed., *The Book of Owls.* Alfred A. Knopf. New York, New York. pp. 130-146.

Miller, G.S. and E.C. Meslow. 1985. "Dispersal data for juvenile spotted owls: the problem of small sample size," *in* R.J. Gutiêrrez and A.B. Carey eds., *Ecology and Management of Spotted Owls in the Pacific Northwest.* U.S. Department of Agriculture, Forest Service, Pacific Northwest Forest and Range Experiment Station. General Technical Report PNW-185. Pp. 69-73.

National Wildlife Federation, Oregon Wildlife Federation, Lane County Audubon Society and Oregon Natural Resources Council. 1985. "Reply of Appellants to Chief's Responsive Statement." Unpublished legal document submitted to Chief, U.S. Forest Service, January 1985. 15 pp.

National Wildlife Federation, Oregon Wildlife Federation, Lane County Audubon Society and the Oregon Natural Resources Council. 1984. "Notice of Appeal of Final Regional Guide and EIS for Region 6." Unpublished legal document submitted to Chief, U.S. Forest Service, July 1984. 2 pp.

Oberholser, H.C. 1915. "Critical notes on the subspecies of the spotted owl (*Strix occidentalis* [Xantus])," *in* *Proceeding of the U.S. National Museum,* vol. 49, no. 2106. pp. 251-257.

Oregon Endangered Species Task Force. 1977. *Oregon Interagency Spotted Owl Management Plan.* Oregon Department of Fish and Wildlife. Portland, Oregon. 3 pp.

Oregon and Washington Interagency Wildlife Committee. 1981. *Revised Oregon Interagency Spotted Owl Management Plan.* Oregon Department of Fish and Wildlife. Portland, Oregon. 3 pp.

Phillips, A.R., J.T. Marshall, Jr., and G. Monson. 1964. *The Birds of Arizona.* University of Arizona Press. Tucson, Arizona. 212 pp.

Postovit, H.R. 1977. *A Survey of the spotted owl in northwest Washington.* National Forest Products Association. Washington, D.C. 15 pp.

Letter from J.E. Schroeder to Robert Stein, Chairman of the Oregon Endangered Species Task Force, February 3, 1978.

Sisco, C. and R.J. Gutiërrez. 1984. *Winter Ecology of Radio-Tagged Spotted Owls on Six Rivers National Forest, Humboldt Co.,* California. Unpublished report. Humboldt State University. Arcata, California. 140 pp.

Letter from Z.G. Smith Jr. to Region 5 Forest Supervisors and Staff Directors, December 17, 1982.

Solis, D.M. Jr. 1983. "Summer habitat ecology of spotted owls in Northwest California." Master's thesis. Humboldt State University, Arcata, California. 168 pp.

Taylor, A.L. and E.D. Forsman. 1976. "Recent range extensions of the barred owl in Western North America, including the first record for Oregon." *Condor* 78, no. 4:560-561.

U.S. Department of Agriculture, Forest Service. 1984a. *Regional Guide for the Pacific Northwest Region.* U.S. Department of Agriculture Forest Service, Pacific Northwest Region, Portland, Oregon. pp. 3-12 to 3-15.

U.S. Department of Agriculture, Forest Service. 1984b. Unpublished working paper. Pacific Northwest Region, Portland, Oregon. 7 pp.

U.S. Department of Agriculture, Forest Service. 1984c. *Land Management Planning Direction.* Pacific Southwest Region, San Francisco, California. pp. 4-15 to 4-22.

U.S. Fish and Wildlife Service. 1982. *The Northern Spotted Owl: A Status Review.* U.S. Fish and Wildlife Service, Portland, Oregon. 29 pp.

Wagner, P.W., C.D. Marti and T.C. Borer. 1982. "Food of the spotted owl in Utah." *Raptor Research* 16, no. 1:27-28.

*Eric Forsman conducted pioneering ecological investigations of the spotted owl in Oregon while earning his M.S. and Ph.D. degrees at Oregon State University.*

*Charles Meslow is Professor of Wildlife Ecology and Leader of the Cooperative Wildlife Research Unit at Oregon State University. During 1984-86, he served as President of The Wildlife Society.*

*For reviewing various drafts of this manuscript, the authors would like to thank Dean Carrier, Andy Carey, Reid Goforth, Gordon Gould, Kirk Horn, Gary Miller, Bill Neitro, Len Ruggiero, and Hal Salwasser. Opinions expressed in the manuscript do not necessarily reflect the views of the reviewers.*

A male sage grouse fans his tail in a courtship display. Grazing on public lands and
habitat alteration projects by the Bureau of Land Management and the Forest
Service jeopardize the grouse.

*Leonard Lee Rue III*

# Sage Grouse

## Robert E. Autenrieth

Idaho Department of Fish and Game

## Species Description and Natural History

THE SAGE GROUSE was first described in 1827 and was given its current scientific name, *Centrocercus urophasianus* (Latin for spiny-tailed pheasant), in 1831 (Patterson 1952). It is grouped with the gallinaceous birds, all of which have a specialized stomach or gizzard. However, the sage grouse gizzard is thin walled and unsuited for digesting seeds. Sage grouse are a mottled, brownish-gray with only subtle sexual dimorphism during nonbreeding periods, except that adult males weigh up to six pounds and adult females 50 percent less. The white chest feathers and specialized head feathers (filoplumes) easily distinguish males during the March-through-May breeding period. Tail feathers are mostly black with white tips, while those on females are mottled black, brown, and white. Female appearance generally is more drab.

### Range

Sage grouse have inhabited the northwestern United States and southern Canada since the Pleistocene epoch (Wetmore 1951). Their historic range conformed closely to the distribution of big sagebrush on the climax sagebrush-prairie ecosystem. This ecosystem originally extended from western Kansas, western Nebraska, and western North and South Dakota westward to include northeastern Arizona, northwestern New Mexico, the northeastern sections of

Colorado, and practically all of Montana, Idaho, Wyoming, Nevada, and Utah, excluding the forested mountainous regions. It is also extended into the east-central portion of California, the eastern halves of Oregon and Washington, and the southern border of the three southwestern Canadian provinces (Patterson 1952).

The sage grouse currently is found in parts of Washington, Oregon, Idaho, Montana, Alberta, Saskatchewan, North Dakota, California, Nevada, Utah, Colorado, and Nebraska. Historically it also occurred in British Columbia, New Mexico, and Oklahoma (Patterson 1952).

## Leks

The annual cycle begins in late February, when males leave wintering areas and return to traditional breeding grounds, known as strutting grounds or leks. The same leks may be used for many years. For example, the Muddy Springs lek near Laramie, Wyoming, has been active and in the same location since 1940 (Wiley Jr. 1978). In Idaho, a broken bird-point arrowhead found at one of the strutting grounds indicates use during the time of Indian occupancy, at least 105 to 110 years ago (Dalke *et al* 1963). Leks characteristically are open areas such as meadows, low-sage zones, or roads surrounded by big-sage cover. In Montana, leks are bare areas adjacent to dense stands of sagebrush (Wallestad 1975). Many strutting grounds in central Montana were found on old homestead sites where sagebrush had been cleared. Other disturbance areas, such as livestock salt sites, temporary sheep camps, and back-country air strips, often are used. Leks vary in size from one to 40 acres (Scott 1942). Often the leks are located on or within one to two miles of the winter range. However, in Idaho sage grouse are known to move up to 50 miles from wintering areas to leks (Pyrah 1954).

Leks usually are surrounded by sagebrush cover. Big sage (*Artemisia tridentata*) is used as a food source and for loafing and escape cover. Following strutting each morning, cocks begin feeding, followed by dusting and loafing. Seventy-six percent of transmittered cocks in Montana remained within less than a mile of the lek during the day. Data collected on transmittered adult cocks in Idaho also showed daily moves of less than a mile from the lek (Autenrieth 1981).

Eighty percent of cock locations in Idaho occurred in sagebrush stands where canopy cover ranged from 20 to 50 percent. Adult birds used early spring forb growth but relied primarily on sagebrush. Sagebrush canopy coverage averaged 30 percent on a cock use area during the breeding season in Montana, and cocks were not observed in areas of less than 10 percent canopy coverage (Eng and Schladweiler 1972).

As the peak of breeding passes and strutting interest declines, cocks begin leaving the lek. The cocks move to areas of succulent vegetation and are later followed by hens with broods (Patterson 1952).

## Lek Attendance by Hens

Hens usually arrive on the leks beginning in March. Their relatively small size, mottled coloration, and secretive behavior make their presence easily missed by a casual observer. They may feed on the periphery of the lek and appear to ignore the nearby strutting cocks until physiologically ready to breed. At that time the hen will posture near a strutting cock with wings outstretched on the ground. The cock immediately assumes the tail-on-tail posture and breeding is completed in a matter of seconds. Adult hens attended the lek for one to three days. Yearling hens attended in diminishing numbers from one to five days. Most yearling hens attended for two days (Petersen 1980). Peak of hen attendance in Idaho usually is the first week of April for the Snake River plains populations and about a week later for high-elevation populations. The number of copulations in one day is variable, but an individual hen on a southwest Idaho lek was observed to breed eight times in one morning with the same cock (Autenrieth 1981).

## Nesting

Within a week to 10 days following breeding the hen builds a nest in the vicinity of the lek. The nest is a depression in the ground lined with twigs, grass, and feathers. Nesting radius studies conducted on five Idaho sage grouse populations indicated that when good nesting cover was available near the lek, the nesting radius tended to be less than when cover was sparse and only found in clumps. The nesting radius of 306 nests ranged from zero to seven and a half miles from the nearest lek (Autenrieth 1981). Nest location appeared to be related to cover selection. No relationship with proximity of water, meadows, or a brood food source such as anthills was found.

In many areas, nesting sage grouse use the maximum big sagebrush height and canopy cover available, although Idaho studies indicate that hens select something less than the greatest canopy cover (Keller *et al* 1941, Trueblood 1954, Gray 1967, Klebenow 1969, Wallestad and Pyrah 1974, Autenrieth 1981). This is not surprising when the height and density of southern Idaho sagebrush range is compared with the relatively sparse cover found in Montana. Big-sage canopy per tenth acre surrounding the nest bush ranged from 23.4 percent to 38.1 percent for five study areas, with height ranging between nine and 31 inches. The fact that in all cases the nest bush was taller and had a greater average diameter than surrounding brush indicates that the hen is, in fact, selecting for a nest bush. It ranged from 22 to 31 miles, with a diameter between three and three and a half feet.

Differences in sagebrush characteristics around 31 successful and 10 unsuccessful nests were measured in Montana (Wallestad and Pyrah 1974). Successful nests had greater than average sagebrush cover surrounding the nest and were located in stands with a higher average canopy than unsuccessful nests. The average height of sagebrush cover over all nests was 16 inches, compared to an average height of nine inches in adjacent areas.

The hens usually select a bush that provided an umbrella. The lowest limbs above the nests ranged from seven to 10 inches, providing protective camouflage. On better ranges, litter and grass-forb understory contributed to successful nesting by further camouflaging the site. Understory also contributed to a microclimate warmer than the air temperature a yard above the nest (Autenrieth 1981). Nest temperature dropped less during hen absence where understory was greatest. The importance of big sage cover for nesting cannot be overestimated (Girad 1937, Keller *et al* 1941, Patterson 1952, Gill 1965, Gray 1967, Wallestad and Pyrah 1974). A continuous temperature-monitoring study on a nesting hen in 1973 and another in 1974 indicated that absences from the nest are of short duration and usually occur twice a day (Autenrieth 1981).

## Brood Rearing

Broods are located mostly in sagebrush types through June, moving to meadow areas in July (Gill 1965, Savage 1969). Brood observations indicated vegetation averaged 14 percent sagebrush canopy coverage in June, 12 percent for July, 10 percent for August, and 21 percent in September (Wallestad 1971). The greatest number of brood observations in Idaho were in open stands of sagebrush. As the summer progresses, the broods moved up in elevation following a gradient of succulent food plants (Klebenow 1969).

Brood moves are dictated by vegetation desiccation. Movements of 30 miles to summer areas are not uncommon for migratory populations and appear to be associated with habitat requirements (Crawford Jr. 1960). The dry lowland breeding complex, characterized by vast stands of big sagebrush with little forb production or water, dictate a move to moister zones where insects and forbs are available.

Average daily movements appear to be random and associated with feeding in the meadows, shading during the heat of the day, and roosting (Wallestad 1971). Broods make progressively longer moves as they grow older and stronger. The location of broods in any year is tied to forb and insect availability. Broods in Idaho move to traditional areas as dictated by general range condition, so the timing of arrival on wet meadows and irrigated alfalfa fields varies. Some ranchers in Idaho believe lack of sage grouse broods in their fields by early August is a sign of low brood production, but often this absence reflects the fact that good forb production on the range has negated the use of dry-year concentration areas.

Daily undisturbed moves of unsuccessful yearling females varies little from the movement pattern of brood hens. Habitat preferences also are similar. A monitored yearling remained on or near an irrigated meadow for 26 days (Autenrieth 1981).

The importance of foothill meadows to sage grouse is becoming increasingly apparent. Workers have long noted the heavy use of meadows in late summer and fall (Savage 1969). Where broods do not migrate to upland meadows as the lower range desiccates, they are dependent on springs and stream meadows. High brood success is due to the continual availability of succulent forbs. Broods in sedentary populations must compete with livestock on lowland meadows and generally these broods exhibit lower success and wide production fluctuations. They do well when a wet spring and summer make forbs widely available throughout the range. They do poorly when a dry spring and summer limits forb availability to spring and meadow areas. Livestock always out-competes them.

Dandelions, Chinese lettuce, common salsify, western yarrow, alfalfa, and sweet clover head the list of important forbs for broods. Insect availability is critical during the first three weeks of life.

## Winter

Sage grouse winter ranges are traditional to the degree that as snow accumulates on summer-fall ranges, migrations to lowlands occur in a predictable pattern. This is particularly true of migratory populations. Little difference is found in sedentary populations, except that flock size increases and use areas change from meadow to sagebrush habitats. The extent of seasonal movements varies with the severity of winter weather, topography, and vegetative cover. The predictable moves probably are directed initially to areas of most palatable sagebrush and secondarily, as snow depth increases, to areas where brush is still available. Wintering sage grouse flocks concentrate where low sage (*A. arbuscula* or *nova*) occurs, as in Idaho (Crawford 1960). Slope and aspect also control winter-range use (Beck 1977). Sage grouse use areas of less than 15 percent slope and prefer southwest exposures. The use of greatest available canopy cover is common in Montana (Eng and Scladweiler 1972). The majority of winter observations were in sagebrush with more than a 20 percent canopy coverage. Flocks segregated by sex during winter in Colorado, where hens used denser stands of sage than did males (Beck 1977).

Winter food habits are relatively simple. A total of 99.7 percent of the diet is sagebrush during December, January, and February (Patterson 1952, Wallestad 1975). The principle brush species on an eastern Idaho winter range are big, low, and three-tip sage (*A. tripartita*) and rabbitbrush (*Chrysothamus* spp.) (Bean 1941). Sage grouse feed almost entirely on sagebrush leaves from January through March and only occasionally on rabbitbrush.

## Parasites, Diseases, and Poisons

The importance of parasites has received little attention mostly because an outbreak usually must be widespread before it is documented. Early accounts of sage grouse during the settlement years reported dead birds found around waterholes during high-population years. Cause of death was not documented, but more recently has been attributed to coccidiosis (Thorne 1969). Symptoms are weakness, possibly an inability to fly, emaciation, diarrhea, and possibly death. Most cases have been in the vicinity of drying waterholes. Diseased birds occasionally were seen in Montana in areas near irrigation ditches and alfalfa fields. July and August, when water sources became limited, were the outbreak periods. The problem was alleviated as fall and winter dispersal occurred (Wallestad 1975).

The parasite most often reported by sportsmen is tapeworms (*Raillietina*). They probably are the most common sage grouse parasite. However, birds with apparently heavy intestinal infestations usually appear in good body condition and are fit for consumption.

Ectoparasites such as lice, ticks, and mites are infrequently observed but were reported on sage grouse in Wyoming (Simon 1940). They generally are unimportant to the health of their host.

Diseases that might be important to sage grouse are: salmonellosis, botulism or limberneck, avian tuberculosis, pasteurellosis, and aspergillosis (Thorne 1969), although avian tuberculosis and pasteurellosis have not been diagnosed in sage grouse.

During periods of drought, remnant water supplies may be toxic because of high concentrations of dissolved solids. Dissolved solid concentrations of 3,807 parts per million are toxic to sage grouse (Post 1960).

The use of insecticides on alfalfa fields and sagebrush range during grasshopper infestations prompted a study on the effects on sage grouse (Eng 1952). The work showed chlordane and aldrin had little direct effects on the birds, but their food supply certainly was reduced.

The herbicide 2,4-D has been sprayed on thousands of acres of sagebrush as a part of range rehabilitation programs. Proper use of 2,4-D normally will not result in either an acute or a chronic hazard to nontarget organisms (Norris 1971). Residues of 2,4-D, sprayed on sagebrush at two pounds per acre, were found in sage grouse muscle and tissue, but sage grouse were not seriously harmed by inhabiting recently sprayed ranges (Carr and Glover 1970).

## Predation

Predation is a decimating force throughout the annual sage grouse cycle. Use of open, difficult to approach leks and roosting areas and the secretive nature of hens while nesting are adaptations that help reduce predation pressure. However, one of the greatest restraints on population increases is nest predation.

The hen is present on the nest only while actually laying eggs during the 10 to 14 day laying period, and is absent from one-half hour after sunrise to one hour before sunset (Gill 1965). Nest vulnerability was greatest during this period.

A dummy-nest study was conducted in south-central Idaho during the spring of 1975 (Autenrieth 1981). A total of 200 nests were established in typical nesting habitat. The objectives were to simulate the unattended nests of laying hens, compare predation between habitat types, and determine important nest predators.

Care was taken to closely simulate sage grouse nests. Seven infertile pheasant (*Phasianus colchicus*) eggs were placed in the dummy nests. Number one Victor steel traps were concealed at each nest. Ravens (*Corvus corax*) were the most important nest predators for this sage grouse population.

The importance of ravens or crows (*Corvus brachyrhynchos*) as nest predators also was shown by extensive nest studies in Oregon, where raven predation was the greatest single sage grouse limiting factor (Batterson and Morse 1948). Magpies (*Pica pica*) also are opportunistic in their feeding habits and feed on eggs. During the time that magpies are feeding their young, they are serious nest predators within a quarter-mile radius of the magpie nesting site (Greene 1948).

Badgers (*Taxidea taxus*) are important nest predators on sage grouse in Oregon (Nelson 1955). Badgers destroyed 17 (33 percent) of 51 known nests, ravens destroyed four (eight percent), Belding's ground squirrels (*Spermophilus beldingi*) two (four percent), and unknown predators three (six percent). A 44 percent sage grouse nest loss to badgers was documented in Colorado (Gill 1965). A 42 percent predation of sage grouse nests was due to the Richardson's ground squirrel (*S. richardsonii*) and striped ground squirrel in Wyoming (Patterson 1952). Richardson's ground squirrels accounted for 50 percent of sage grouse nests lost in Colorado (Gill 1965). Squirrel-destroyed nests averaged 2.9 eggs per clutch, compared with five eggs per clutch on badger-destroyed nests. This difference occurred because ground squirrels visited unattended nests during the laying period, while badgers flushed incubating hens from the nests after incubation had begun.

Sage grouse predation the rest of the year is less important when compared with recruitment lost to nest predation. However, 40 percent of the hatch succumbed to some form of mortality between hatching and hunting season in Montana (Wallestad 1975).The percent loss attributable to predators is unknown, but golden eagles (*Aquila chrysaetos*) and hawks, including marsh (*Circus cyaneus*), Swainson's (*Buteo swainsoni*), red-tailed (*Buteo jamaicenis*), and rough-legged (*Buteo lagopus*), were common. The importance of raven predation on young chicks in Idaho is unmeasured but also must be significant. Red-tailed hawks and ferruginous hawks (*Buteo regalis*) are important predators on juvenile sage grouse in Wyoming (Patterson 1952).

Adult sage grouse probably are not a primary prey species during the summer months, but become more vulnerable in winter concentrations when snow cover makes them more visible. Golden eagles were observed testing sage grouse during January and February in eastern Idaho (Bean 1941). Attempts to take a grouse were unsuccessful. In Colorado, only one attack on wintering grouse by a golden eagle was observed during the 383 hours of observations

(Beck 1977). Sage grouse may be a secondary prey species for golden eagles and coyotes, (*Canis latrans*) with cottontail rabbits (*Sylvilagus spp.*) and jackrabbits (*Lepus spp.*) the primary prey species (Hogue 1954). Winter predator pressure on sage grouse undoubtedly is less during the years of peak rabbit and small rodent populations.

That golden eagles frequent leks is common knowledge among those who make trend surveys. Cocks usually are flushed from the lek by the presence of an eagle. The limited dawn and dusk strutting periods may be an adaptation to diurnal raptor pressure and nocturnal mammalian predator activity (Hartzler 1974). In summary, nest predation appears to be the most important population constraint, followed by brood losses and adult predation. However, predator control programs have a history of great expense with little success. To promote the destruction of one or several predator species to benefit sage grouse is not a viable alternative and, with the possible exception of raven control, would have little success.

## Significance of the Species

The sage grouse is an indicator species for quality sagebrush habitats, the only habitat in which the species occurs. Populations have been extirpated from sagebrush lands converted to agriculture, urban zones, and exotic grasslands for livestock grazing. The perpetuation of sage grouse populations is a challenge for enlightened land managers who recognize the value of the often-maligned sagebrush ranges and of habitat diversity, since wildlife abundance and diversity are the best measures of management success.

Sage grouse are an important part of western history, including Indian folklore and pioneer table fare. Their demise would leave an unfillable void. An economic survey conducted in Idaho in 1972 indicated some $600,000 were spent for two days of sage grouse hunting (Autenrieth 1981). That figure would increase to over a million dollars today and total several million for all sage grouse states.

## Historical Perspective

The Lewis and Clark expedition in the early 1800s reported that sage grouse were plentiful in Montana and parts of Wyoming. No total population estimates are found in historic accounts, but high densities of birds commonly were found in parts of at least 12 western states (Patterson 1952). Approximately 90 million acres of habitat were available. It was estimated in 1951 that more than 50 percent of the original habitat had been lost to the settlement and development of the western United States and Canada (Martin *et al* 1951).

Settlement of the West brought intensive agricultural, grazing, and hunting activities. Sage grouse were eaten by settlers moving through on the Oregon Trail. Prior to 1900 little protection from hunting was afforded the birds, and they were shot year-round. In 1900, a liberal first season was set in Idaho to extend fom August 1 to November 1, with a limit of 15 to 20 sage grouse. By 1937, many wildlife biologists and conservationists believed that sage grouse were headed for extinction (Girard 1937). No sage grouse hunting was allowed in many of the states during the 1940s. However, by the 1950s population numbers increased significantly, and conservative hunting seasons were allowed and have continued through today. Habitat losses continue to be the major concern.

## Current Trends

Sage grouse numbers have diminished in historic times to the degree that only eight states currently have populations that can withstand hunting. While periodic and seasonal factors, such as unusually harsh winter and spring weather and predation, may affect sage grouse, the long-term problems are caused by livestock overgrazing and sagebrush-range conversion to crested-wheat fields and agriculture. Some individuals in the livestock industry promote the idea that western rangeland originally consisted mostly of grass and that past grazing abuses created grouse habitat by coverting thousands of acres to predominantly sagebrush. While few would deny past grazing abuses, a study of 29 journals and diaries left by early 19th century travelers indicates that the intermountain region was dominated by sagebrush, with stands of grass confined mostly to wet valley bottoms, moist canyons, and mountain slopes (Vale 1975). Cross (1851) indicated that the Snake River country in Idaho west to the Cascade Mountains, a distance of 700 miles, was "entirely destitute of grass." Sage grouse research conducted in Idaho, Montana, Wyoming, Nevada, and Colorado within the past 20 years has defined year-round habitat requirements and documented the dependence of sage grouse on sagebrush through all seasons (Patterson 1952).

Generally stated, their findings are as follows:

1. The lek is a key area because it is a traditional breeding site and provides wildlife managers with trend data for over-winter survival. It is also the hub from which nesting occurs.
2. The quality of nesting habitat surrounding the lek is the single most important factor in population success. Where a 35-percent sagebrush (*Artemisia* spp.) canopy and 24-inch height are combined with residual grass cover, the probability of predator detection is reduced significantly. The percentage of successfully nesting hens and the ratio of juveniles to adult females are significantly higher in areas with robust shrub-grass production and where forbs are a common component of the spring range.

3. Broods require forbs, insects, and cover for concealment, growth, and shade. Where these requirements are met at or near the nest site, the brood moves less, reducing exposure to predation and conserving energy. On dry ranges, however, broods are forced to move to the nearest meadow to meet their needs. Competition with livestock is most significant under these conditions. Although water availability in meadows is the critical factor for livestock, the associated grazing and trampling reduces the availability of forbs for sage grouse broods.

4. Sage grouse consume mostly sagebrush in winter and also use it for protection from cold. Their migration to traditional winter ranges is governed by snow depth. During the 1977 winter drought, when little snow accumulated in southern Idaho, sage grouse were widely distributed. During recent severe winters, sage grouse were documented in large groups on low-elevation ranges where they had not been observed before. In some areas, agriculture has removed the sagebrush on these historic winter ranges, previously used only during severe conditions.

Sage grouse population trends have been monitored yearly since the mid-1950s by the Western States Sage Grouse Committee via a questionnaire to 12 western states and Canadian provinces. Population fluctuations are a common occurrence in all states mostly in relation to weather and habitat quality during the nesting and brood-rearing periods. More serious than fluctuations is habitat loss from wildfires, energy development, sodbusting for crops, and sagebrush eradication to enhance livestock production.

Some states have suffered greater habitat and sage grouse population losses than others. The trend is clear and has not changed in the past 30 years. Sage grouse habitat continues to be reduced yearly, causing a drop in sage grouse numbers in all states. The sage grouse is on New Mexico's state endangered bird list. At the 1983 Sage Grouse Workshop, Colorado reported sage grouse declines caused by sagebrush eradication programs. In Idaho, some population decline was caused by wildfires. Utah reported "massive" habitat losses, with 12 or 13 strutting grounds declining in bird numbers where range plowing or spraying had occurred. Wyoming reported that mining activity currently is the greatest source of habitat loss in that state.

# Management

The majority of sage grouse habitat occurs on public lands administered by the federal Bureau of Land Management (BLM). From the 1950s through the mid-1970s, an estimated five to six million acres of sagebrush range have been treated by burning, spraying, plowing, disking, chaining, cutting, and beating to convert these ranges to grasslands. When land managers expressed a need for guidelines for sagebrush control projects, the Western States Sage Grouse

Workshop Committee in 1977 provided recommendations outlining sage grouse life history and the effects of sagebrush control, particularly the use of the herbicide 2,4-D, on sage grouse and their habitat. The herbicide kills not only sagebrush, but the forbs on which juvenile sage grouse are highly dependent.

The guidelines call for a two-year notice to wildlife agencies for all treatment proposals, no control work where sagebrush cover is less than 20 percent, and no control on winter ranges or within two miles of the breeding-nesting complex. These guidelines provided consideration for the sage grouse resource and, while not always followed, gave impetus to the multiple-use concept.

Law suits filed against federal land management agencies in the early 1980s halted all spraying on public lands. For this reason, and partly to reduce adverse effects on wildlife, controlled burning has become popular. The results are similar to those of spraying, i.e. removal of sagebrush to enhance grass production, but burning also favors forb production, vital to brood production. No technique is problem free, however. In some areas, burning results in the invasion of an exotic annual, cheatgrass, which usually out-competes other grasses and forbs. Controlled burns also remove the more dense areas of sagebrush, which often are the best nesting cover, and leave only sparse areas with limited cover value. Consequently, researchers again found themselves attempting to provide data on sagebrush-control impacts subsequent to BLM implementation of the program on thousands of acres of sage grouse habitat. Research currently is being conducted in Idaho on how prescribed burns affect sage grouse and their habitat. Information on where hens nest after fire removes their traditional nesting cover and whether they successfully nest elsewhere are among the research objectives.

Sage grouse management is critically affected by habitat and hunting management. Habitat management is both the greatest challenge and the greatest frustration. State wildlife agencies are responsible for perpetuating wildlife species, while the U.S. Forest Service and BLM are responsible for the habitat. The Federal Land Policy and Management Act of 1976 states that public lands will be managed in a manner that will protect the quality of the air, water, and atmosphere as well as the quality of scientific, scenic, historical, ecological, environmental, and archaelogical resources that, where appropriate, certain public lands will be preserved in their natural condition; and that public lands will provide food and habitat for fish and wildlife and domestic animals.

The directive to manage habitat for both wildlife and livestock seems clear. The Public Rangelands Improvements Act of 1978 authorized a stewardship program, that requires the improvement of leased range lands to provide productive wildlife habitat. However, in practice the stewardship program results in business as usual, with the rancher-controlled board dictating range projects to enhance livestock grazing with little if any concern for wildlife needs. A recent example is the preferred plan selected by BLM in Utah's

Rich County to burn or spray 65,187 acres, 46 percent, of BLM holdings in Rich County, causing major reductions or removal of seven known sage grouse populations. This story is repeated in every state with public lands. This incongruity is difficult to understand, considering that only four percent of the red meat and 25 percent of the wool produced in the United States come from using public lands. As long as livestocksmen dictate BLM and Forest Service policy and as long as the people of the United States subsidize the ranchers, who pay only $1.35 for one month's grazing per cow (a fifth the value paid on similar private lands), sage grouse and other wildlife habitat will continue to decline. Wildlife agencies are relegated to an advisory role on habitat manipulation proposals and usually are left to minimizing detrimental impacts. Seldom, if ever, is a project designed to benefit wildlife. Until this changes, the outlook for sage grouse is not bright. Without suitable habitat, little else matters in sage grouse management.

The impact of hunting has been a concern of fish and game departments and sportsman groups since early times. The opinion that hunting is the primary population control is difficult to counter. It is the obvious impact, while more important factors, such as weather, nest predation, competition with livestock, and habitat loss, go virtually unnoticed.

Early data indicated that sage grouse hunting was harmful only when seasons extended from July to October with no bag limit (Patterson 1952). Seasons in July and August permitted hunters to be selective in their shooting, significantly increasing the number of young birds harvested. This created a disparity in population age ratios that may have been detrimental to good production.

Montana recognizes that sage grouse populations fluctuate, but the state maintains a three or four bird bag limit with a six or eight possession limit (Wallestad 1975). These limits are based on the following factors: high annual turnover, law of diminishing returns (hunters soon quit hunting when their success is low, ensuring maintenance of breeding stock), and the fact that total kill is a factor of opening day success and not season length. Montana seasons vary from 16 to 63 days.

Studies in Colorado indicate that only about 10 percent of the fall populations are taken annually and that yearling males are most vulnerable to the gun (Braun and Hoffman no date). Adult males and yearling and adult females are less vulnerable. These findings provide little or no support for conservative seasons and bag limits.

Past studies in Idaho provide little indications of overhunting in spite of the fact that often more sage grouse are bagged there yearly than in other states. In 1969, during a sage grouse population peak in Idaho, hunter-questionnaire data indicated that 31,394 hunters killed 81,729 birds. Colorado fielded 9,126 hunters who killed 21,922 birds. Montana had 37,690 hunters (including all bird hunters) who took 53,462 birds. Wyoming's 13,417 sage grouse hunters took 61,311 birds.

The economic impact of a sage grouse season was studied in Idaho in 1972. A total of 7,719 hunters was interviewed at check stations regarding their expenses, including miles traveled, motels, meals, groceries, beverages, arms, shotgun shells, and miscellaneous purchases such as game vests and flashlights. Figures were compiled only for the opening weekend. Subsequent hunting trips would increase the figures by a unknown but doubtedly significant figure. The cost per hunter varied from $6.25 to $43.78. The statewide average was $19.45 per hunter. Cost differences usually reflected the remoteness of the hunting area and whether the hunt was for one day or a weekend. A total of 30,913 hunters killed 72,100 sage grouse. At $19.45 cost per hunter, $601,258 was spent. The cost per bird was $8.34.

Since 1972, fuel costs have more than tripled and other costs are at least double. The two days of hunting in 1972 projected to 1985 would be well over a million dollars. The economic values of sage grouse and other wildlife have not received full consideration in past range-management decisions.

## Prognosis

The future of sage grouse depends on public land programs that adhere to sage grouse habitat management needs. Sage grouse are completely tied to sagebrush habitat and are extirpated wherever it is removed. Sagebrush removal usually is a priority on these lands, and it is for this reason that few private lands support year-round sage grouse populations.

It would be too optimistic to presume that BLM and the Forest Service will provide sufficient sage grouse habitat. The Federal Land Policy and Management Act has done little but produce an array of alternatives for habitat-alteration proposals. Selecting the best alternative for wildlife is so rare that it is almost non-existent.

The hope that the Public Land Grazing Committee recommendations will be adopted to reduce overgrazing on public lands seems unlikely to be fulfilled. Already, western congressmen are proposing a *status quo* bill that will perpetuate subsidized grazing on public lands. While the current administration emphasizes less government and promotes the idea that each program should pay its way, grazing on public range lands continues to be a sacred cow. Competitive bidding, the best way to establish fair market value for grazing lands, is needed. The most important need, however, is to place livestock grazing on an equal level with other uses of the public range. Only then will wildlife needs be given more than token notice. Sage grouse are an important indicator species of habitat diversity and quality on the western sagebrush-dominated rangelands. However, the future of the viable populations that still exist is not certain and will not be until sage grouse habitat needs become a priority with BLM and the Forest Service.

# Recommendations

Sage grouse and habitat requirements have been well documented during the past 30 years, and realistic recommendations for perpetuating the species are available. State wildlife agencies are eager to work on designing habitat-alteration projects that will benefit both sage grouse and livestock, but until the federal land agencies commit themselves to such an approach, state wildlife agencies can do little more than attempt to lessen the impacts of various projects.

Further research is warranted into the exact mechanisms of population reduction following a sagebrush eradication project. This knowledge will aid in working with BLM and the Forest Service. Studies comparing weather and population trends will be important in understanding the population fluctuations observed in all states that have sage grouse. Further work on the impact of hunting on sage grouse also will provide an important basis for establishing long-term management plans.

Most states are writing five- to 10-year management plans for all wildlife species, including sage grouse. These plans explain the problem and programs that currently are important. Their distribution to interested individuals, states, and federal agencies is an attempt to aid wildlife management through communication.

The Sage Grouse Workshop Committee recommends the following guidelines for use in sage grouse habitat to minimize the detrimental effects of sagebrush control:

1. The state wildlife agencies should be notified, by means of an environmental assessment, of each specific proposal to control vegetation a minimum of two years in advance of treatment. In situations where it is not possible to provide a two-year notice, as on private lands, the state wildlife agency should be notified as soon as the project is proposed. An adequate amount of lead time is necessary to properly evaluate control projects during all seasons of the year.
2. No control work will be considered where live sagebrush cover is less than 20 percent or on steep (20 percent or more gradient) upper slopes with skeletal soils where big sagebrush is a foot tall or less.
3. The breeding complex (leks and nesting areas) will be defined as all lands within a two-mile radius of an occupied lek. In areas with poor-quality nesting habitat, the radius may well exceed two miles. Control of vegetation will not be undertaken within the breeding complex or on nesting and brood areas. On-site investigations by land management and state wildlife agency personnel will be essential to determine inviolate areas. Areas to be protected from treatment will be clearly defined on maps.
4. No control will be attempted in any area known to have supported important wintering concentrations of sage grouse within the past 10 years.

5. No control will be attempted along streams, meadows, or secondary drainages, both dry and intermittent. A strip of living sage no less than 400 yards wide will be retained along the edges of meadows and drainages. On-site inspections by land management and wildlife agency personnel will be made to assess the desirability of increasing or decreasing the width of untreated strips in specific areas.

6. When sagebrush control is found to be unavoidable in sage grouse range, all treatment measures should be applied in irregular patterns using topography and other ecological considerations to minimize adverse effects on the sage grouse resource. Widths of treated and untreated areas can vary for the convenience of application techniques except that treated areas should be no wider than 100 yards and untreated areas will be at least as wide as treated areas. The untreated areas should not be treated until food and cover plants in the treated areas attain a composition comparable to that of the untreated areas.

7. Where possible, spraying should be done with a helicopter or ground equipment. No spraying should be done when wind velocity exceeds five miles per hour.

8. Whenever possible, complete kill or removal of sagebrush in treated areas should be avoided. Partial kill or removal of sagebrush may enhance the area for livestock, prevent loss of all snow cover in winter, and allow for some use of the disturbed area by sage grouse.

# References

Autenrieth, R.E. 1981. *Sage Grouse Management in Idaho.* Idaho Department of Fish and Game Wildlife Bulletin 9. 238 pp.

Batterson, W.M. and W.B. Morse. 1948. *Oregon Sage Grouse.* Oregon Fauna Series 1. Oregon Game Committee, Portland. 29 pp.

Bean, R.W. 1941. Life History Studies of the Sage Grouse (*Centrocercus urophasianus*) in Clark County, Idaho. M.S. Thesis. Utah State College, Logan. 44 pp.

Beck, T.D.I. 1975. Attributes of a Wintering Population of Sage Grouse, North Park, Colorado. M.S. Thesis. Colorado State University, Fort Collins. 49 pp.

Braun, C.E. and D.M. Hoffman. *Vulnerability and Population Characteristics of Sage Grouse in Moffat County.* Colorado Division of Wildlife, Federal Aid Wildlife Rest. Project W-37-R-32. pp. 163-199.

Carr, H.D. and F.A. Glover. 1970. "Effects of sagebrush control on sage grouse," *Transactions of the North American Wildlife Conference* 35:205-215.

Crawford, J.E. Jr. 1960. The Movements, Productivity, and Management of Sage Grouse in Clark and Fremont Counties, Idaho. M.S. Thesis. University of Idaho, Moscow. 85 pp.

Cross, O. 1851. *A Report in the Form of a Journal to the Quartermaster General of the March of the Regiment of Mounted Riflemen to Oregon From May 10 to October 5, 1849*. Senate Executive Documents, 31st Congress, 2nd Session, Vol. 1, pt. 2. Government Printing Office, Washington, D.C. 126-231.

Dalke, P.D., D.B. Pyrah, D.C. Stanton, J.E. Crawford, and E. Schlatterer. 1963. "Ecology, productivity, and management of sage grouse in Idaho," *Journal of Wildlife Management* 27:811-841.

Eng, R.L. 1952. "A two-summer study of the effects on bird populations of chlordane bait and aldrin spray as used for grasshopper control," *Journal of Wildlife Management* 16:326-337.

Eng, R.L. and P. Schladweiler. 1972. "Sage grouse winter movements and habitat use in central Montana," *Journal of Wildlife Management* 36:141-146.

Girard, G.L. 1937. "Life history, habits and food of sage grouse (*Centrocerus urophasianus*) Bonaparte," *University of Wyoming Publication* 3:1-56.

Gray, G.M. 1967. An Ecological Study of Sage Grouse Broods with Reference to Nesting, Movements, Food Habits, and Sagebrush Strip Spraying in the Medicine Lodge Drainage, Clark County, Idaho. M.S. Thesis. University of Idaho, Moscow. 200 pp.

Greene, R.J. 1948. *Statewide Pheasant Nest Predation by Magpies*. Montana Fish and Game Department Federal Aid Wildlife Rest. Project 21-R-2. pp. 171-179.

Hartzler, J.E. 1974. "Predation and the daily timing of sage grouse leks," *Auk* 91:532-536.

Hogue, J. 1954. *The Grouse and the Eagle*. Colorado Conservation 3(6):8-11.

Keller, R.J., H.R. Shepard, and R.N. Randall. 1941. *Survey of 1941: North Park, Jackson County, Moffat County*. Colorado Game and Fish Commission Sage Grouse Survey 3. 31 pp.

Klebenow, D.A. 1969. "Sage grouse nesting and brood habitat in Idaho," *Journal of Wildlife Management* 33:649-662.

Martin, A.C., H.S. Zim and A.L. Nelson. 1951. *American Wildlife and Plants*. McGraw-Hill Book Co., Inc., New York. 500 pp.

Nelson, O.C. 1955. A Field Study of the Sage Grouse in Southeastern Oregon With Special Reference to Reproduction and Survival. M.S. Thesis. Oregon State College, Corvallis. 113 pp.

Norris, L.A. 1971. *Chemical Brush Control: Assessing the Hazard*. Society of American Foresters National Convention. Washington, D.C. pp. 715-720.

Patterson, R.L. 1952. *The Sage Grouse in Wyoming*. Sage Books, Inc., Denver. 341 pp.

Peterson, B.E. 1980. *Evaluation of the Effects of Changes in Hunting Regulations on Sage Grouse Populations: Evaluation of Census of Females*. Colorado Division of Wildlife, Federal Aid Wildlife Restoration Project W-37-R-33. pp. 115-116.

Post, G. 1960. *Salmonella Species Isolated From Intestinal Contents of Five Sage Grouse*. Wildlife Disease Survey FW-3-R-7, Wyoming Fish and Game Commission. 23 pp.

Pyrah, D.B. 1954. A Preliminary Study Toward Sage Grouse Management in Clark and Fremont Counties Based on Seasonal Movements. M.S. Thesis. University of Idaho, Moscow. 90 pp.

Savage, D.E. 1969. *The Relationship of Sage Grouse to Upland Meadows in Nevada.* Nevada Cooperation Wildlife Restoration Unit, Reno. 101 pp.

Scott, J.W. 1942. "Mating behavior of the sage grouse," *Auk* 59:477-498.

Simon, F. 1940. "The parasites of the sage grouse," *University of Wyoming Publication* 7(5):77-100.

Thorne, E.T. 1969. "Diseases in Wyoming sage grouse," *Proceedings of the Western States Sage Grouse Workshop* 6:192-198.

Trueblood, R.W. 1954. "Sage grouse grass reseeding studies," *Utah Fish and Game Bulletin* 9(8):1-7.

Vale, T.R. 1975. "Presettlement vegetation in the sagebrush grass areas of the intermountain west," *Journal of Range Management* 28:32-36.

Wallestad, R.O. 1975. *Life History and Habitat Requirements of Sage Grouse in Central Montana.* Montana Department of Fish and Game, Helena. 65 pp.

Wetmore, A. 1951. Secretary, Smithsonian Institution. Personal Letter, May 8, 1951.

Wiley, R.H. Jr. 1978. "The lek mating system of the sage grouse," *Scientific American* 238(5):114-125.

*Robert Autenreith, at the time of the writing of this chapter, was ending his fifteenth year as a research biologist with the Idaho Fish and Game Department.*

Discovery of several new populations of small whorled pogonias has led botanists to conclude that the rare plant's chances for survival are fairly secure.

*Richard W. Dyer*

# Small Whorled Pogonia

## Richard W. Dyer
### U.S. Fish and Wildlife Service

## Species Description and Natural History

ALTHOUGH IT IS a member of the orchid family, the small whorled pogonia (*Isotria medeoloides*), a perennial herb, does not have a vividly colored, striking flower. This inconspicuous, light-green orchid could be confused with other more common woodland plants, but careful observation will reveal noticeable differences. The plant grows from slender hairy roots and a single stems emerges from a short vertical rhizome. Mature plants are three and a half to 10 inches tall, and have five or six light-green, elliptical, somewhat pointed leaves one to three inches long and about two to two and a half inches wide positioned in a whorl at the top of a light-green stem. The hollow stem is about the thickness of a pencil, its waxy surface covered with a whitish powder. One or occasionally two light-yellowish-green flowers, or seed pods if plants are in fruit, emerge from the center of the whorl of leaves. The flowers appear in late May in the South and early to mid-June in the North (Correll 1950). The flowers are self-pollinating, lack nectar guides, and have no detectable fragrance (Mehroff 1980).

The length of the sepals and the pedicel of the flower distinguish the small whorled pogonia from the other more common North America member of the genus, *I. verticillata,* the large whorled pogonia. The ranges of both species overlap, and the plants may even occur in the same habitat, particularly from southern New England southward to Georgia. The purplish sepals of the more common large whorled pogonia are widely spreading and exceed more than an inch length. The flowers are borne on a noticeable pedicel. The sepals of the endangered small whorled pogonia are greenish, not as widely spread, and no more than an inch long. The flowers appear to be sissile but actually have a very short pedicel (Correll 1950). The seed pods are erect capsules and produce numerous brown dust-like seeds.

## Range

The small whorled pogonia is found only in eastern North America, from Ontario, Canada, to northern Georgia. Seventeen states are included in the species distribution. The plant was first discovered by Frederich Pursh in 1814. Officially listed as an endangered species in 1982, it is one of approximately 119 plants legally protected under the Endangered Species Act.

Endangered and threatened plants are often associated with unique or specialized habitats such as serpentine outcrops, calcareous wetlands, or alpine meadows. This is not the case, however, with the small whorled pogonia. Although it is often referred to as one of the rarest orchids in the eastern United States, it can be found in a variety of forest habitats that typify the transitional northern hardwood and temperate forests of eastern North America.

Deciduous hardwood forests—beech, birch, maple, oak, and hickory—with a mix of pine and hemlock, characterize most known *Isotria* sites. The spectrum of habitats includes dry, rocky, wooded slopes to rich moist streambanks. The plants potentially could occur most anywhere. The chances, however, of finding a new population at a given site are extremely remote. Many field botanists, naturalists, and biologists have looked for this orchid for many years without finding one. One common characteristic of a number of known sites seems to be the stage of forest succession. Relatively open areas in 50- to 60-year-old forests are preferred habitats. Known sites also typically are free of thick underbrush and dense competing forbs that keep sunlight from reaching the forest floor. These general parameters are useful guidelines in searching for new populations. Unfortunately no reliable indicator species have been associated with *Isotria medeoloides*.

The lakes region and rolling foothills of the White Mountains in Maine and New Hampshire appear to be the major center of the species distributon. Several new large colonies of more than 100 plants each have been found in this region in the past five years. These new populations have been discovered by focusing on areas adjacent to meandering vernal or ephemeral stream beds and the up-slope gullies and depressions that give rise to small streams. Rich, decaying leaf mold on acid soils provide ideal substrate. Recent discoveries in this area, however, could be a function of intensive field surveys using improved techniques rather than a true indication of the species geographical abundance. Additional field work in the southern half of the species' range is needed to clarify the true distribution and abundance.

Much remains to be learned about the pogonia's biology, particularly regarding its physical, chemical, and biological requirements for germination, growth, development, and reproduction. Past studies investigating several widely separated populations with less than five plants per population have indicated that the pogonia's reproduction and survival are inversely related to increases in such variables as the density of associated trees, tree basal area, and shrub and herb cover (Mehrhoff 1980). These variables are in effect the factors controlling the intensity of light reaching the forest floor. More recent, detailed investigation, however, on large, vigorous colonies of more than 100 plants have shown no correlation between any single variable and the plants reproductive status, i.e. flowering vs. non-flowering plants (Brumback and Fyler 1983).

Doubtlessly there are particular conditions of such factors as filtered light, temperature, and composition of soil substrate under which the plants would be most successful, and certainly the stage of forest succession is an important factor in creating these conditions. These variables, however, have yet to be fully understood and incorporated in scientifically sound management activities.

Few known populations, such as those in Rhode Island and Virginia, have been or were monitored for many years (Grimes 1921, Baldwin 1967). Although expected fluctuations have occurred in the number of plants annually appearing at these sites, the long-term trend has been one of gradual decline, with fewer flowering plants appearing each year until the population eventually disappears.

Long-term dormancy of some orchids is well documented, and published literature suggests that the small whorled pogonia may remain dormant for 10 to 20 years (Correll 1950). This is a matter of speculation, however, as recent field studies do not support this theory. Detailed observations including the marking and mapping of many individual plants indicate the pogonias generally do not remain dormant for more that one or two years (Brumback and Fyler 1984).

## Growth

Detailed long-term studies were begun in 1982 at a large *Isotria* population in central New Hampshire. Approximately 200 plants have been marked and plotted within the population to assess development and population dynamics, including date of emergence, sequence of floristic development, natural mortality factors, age to maturity, and other phenomena. Based on this detailed study and other ongoing investigations, several interesting facets of the pogonia's biology are beginning to be understood. For example, there appear to be three or four distinct developmental stages, with the majority of the plants within a population slowly progressing concurrently through these stages. Young plants within a population appear as small, completely sterile vegetative plants. They also tend to appear later in the growing season and thus may not be observed in early census counts. As much as 20 percent of a colony may be in this category. The second stage of maturity seems to be an "arrested" stage in which individual plants produce non-functional flowering buds that abort and eventually whither away. Approximately a third of the plants in the study populations fall in this category. Mature plants, which can be nearly 50 percent of a colony, produce one or sometimes two flowers. Of those that do flower, however, only about half fully develop and produce seed pods.

Some individual plants do not follow this sequential development, i.e., they may be "arrested" one year, dormant the next, and appear the next year in flower. The number of years a given plant might remain at one of these stages is not fully understood, but ongoing studies should provide insights to these and other questions.

## Significance of the Species

Although the small whorled pogonia is of extreme scientific interest, it has no known economic value and its ecological significance appears to have little unique importance. It is also an unlikely source for as yet undiscovered drugs or medicines. Because it is difficult to propagate successfully, it is presently of little horticultural value. Its most apparent value is one of public education and the unique ability it has to increase public awareness on the plight of endangered and threatened plants in general and the need for rare-plant conservation. Because it is such a wide-ranging species and can occur most anywhere, it is often the subject of popular articles and local media attention.

Why it occurs where it does and how it maintains itself in such low numbers are the subjects of much interest to the scientist. There is a need, however, for the general public to understand the overall importance of plants and society's dependence on them for existing and future sources of food, energy, chemicals, and medicines. The extinction of any single species further reduces the opportunities for these future, yet critically important, discoveries. Whether a plant occurs in the hardwood forests of the northeastern United States or the tropical jungles of South America, every species' extinction is a genetic loss that can never be replaced.

## Historical Perspective

When the small whorled pogonia was officially proposed for listing under the Endangered Species Act, more dried specimens of the plant existed in institutional herbaria than were known to exist in the wild. Various scientific publications, journals, popular articles, and books on the orchids of North America referred to the species as one of the rarest, most elusive orchids in the eastern United States (Crow 1982). Historically, it was known to occur in 48 counties in 16 eastern states and Canada. Botanical records, some dating back to the late 1880s, verified the species occurrence in approximately 60 locations. Based on intensive field work in the mid-70s to early 1980s, it was determined that many of these sites are now occupied by golf courses, shopping malls, highways, housing developments, and general suburban sprawl.

When the species was listed in the fall of 1982, the total known population was approximately 600 plants at 18 locations in 17 counties in 10 different states and Ontario, Canada. Three large populations in Maine and New Hampshire accounted for nearly 80 percent of the total known number of plants, andmore than half of the populations consisted of less than 10 plants. Based on the gradual decline of plants within known populations and the inadvertent loss of many historical sites, the species clearly needed the kind of assistance and protection offered by the Endangered Species Act. Many public comments were received in response to the listing proposal, and state natural resource agencies, national, state, and local conservation organizations, and other interested parties were unanimous in their concurrence with the need to officially list the species as endangered.

## Current Trends

Primarily because of intensive field work in the past three years, knowledge of the status of the small whorled pogonia has greatly improved. In the spring of 1985, approximately 3,200 plants were estimated to exist in 49 different populations in 13 states. Twenty-one of the known populations occur in central New Hampshire.

Ten of the populations are considered exceptionally large colonies, with more than 100 plants each. Two populations in New Hampshire have more than 500 plants.

It is generally agreed among New England botanists most familiar with the species that the plant is not as rare as originally believed and that more populations will be discovered. It is particularly important that additional populations be found before they are inadvertently destroyed, as has happened all too often in the past. It is significant to note that some of the largest colonies discovered in the past five years might well have been partially or totally destroyed had they not been found and protected with the help of cooperative landowners.

## Management

The protection and management of the small whorled pogonia are responsibilities shared among federal and state natural resource agencies, private conser-

## Historical and Current Distribution of the Small Whorled Pogonia (1985)

| State | County | State | County |
|-------|--------|-------|--------|
| Connecticut | Fairfield | New Jersey | Bergen |
| | Hartford | | Hunterdon |
| | New Haven | | Monmouth |
| | New London | | Passaic |
| | Tolland | | *Sussex (2) |
| | Windham | | |
| | *Litchfield (1) | | |
| | | New York | Nassau |
| Georgia | Habersham | | Onondaga |
| | *Rabun (1) | | Rockland |
| | | | Suffolk |
| | | | Ulster |
| | | | Washington |
| Illinois | *Randolph (1) | | |
| | | North Carolina | |
| | | | Harnett |
| | | | *Henderson (1) |
| | | | *Macon (1) |
| | | | Surry |
| Maine | *Cumberland (4) | | |
| | Kennebec | | |
| | Oxford | | |
| | *York (2) | | |
| Maryland | Montgomery | Pennsylvania | Berks |
| | | | *Centre (1) |
| | | | Chester |
| | | | Greene |
| | | | Monroe |
| | | | Montgomery |
| | | | Philadelphia |
| | | | *Venango (1) |
| Massachusetts | *Essex (1) | | |
| | *Hampden (1) | | |
| | Hampshire | | |
| Michigan | *Berrien (1) | | |
| | | Rhode Island | *Providence (1) |
| | | | Kent |
| Missouri | Bollinger | | |
| New Hampshire | *Belknap (2) | South Carolina | *Oconee (5) |
| | *Carroll (5) | | |
| | Grafton | | |
| | *Merrimack (2) | Vermont | Chittenden |
| | *Rockingham (1) | | |
| | *Strafford (11) | | |
| Virginia | Buckingham | Canada | *Elgin, Ontario (1) |
| | *Caroline (1) | | |
| | Gloucester | | |
| | *James City (1) | | |
| | *Prince William (1) | | |

* Counties with extant populations; number of known sites in parenthesis.

vation organizations, and, perhaps most important of all, individual landowners. The implementation of scientifically sound management actions, such as habitat manipulation, to maintain the optimum state of forest succession requires a thorough understanding of the pogonia's biology. Research currently is under way to increase knowledge of the species' growth and reproduction. These biological investigations are being supported by the U.S. Fish and Wildlife Service, state natural resource agencies, The Nature Conservancy, and the New England Wildflower Society.

In addition to the scientific studies, a crucial need exists for better coordinated protection. Protection strategies do not need to be complicated. Often needed protection can be accomplished by simply informing landowners of the species existence on their property, making them aware of the significance of the plant, and seeking their cooperation in protecting the site. In the past, many populations have been inadvertently lost because people that need to be informed were not aware of the plants and their significance. Recently, the efforts of cooperative landowners and concerned citizens have resulted in the protection of some sites. Most landowners are very interested in the plants and more than willing to help. A sense of pride seems to develop once landowners are made aware of how they can help preserve an endangered species. There are instances, however, when a more formalized protection strategy might be needed. The Nature Conservancy has played a key role in working to protect known populations through various protection strategies, such as easements and acquisitions. This kind of strategy has been particularly appropriate when the site was threatened by private development.

Needed protection also can be provided by the Endangered Species Act. Section 7 of the law prohibits federal agencies from authorizing, funding, or carrying out actions likely to jeopardize the continued existence of listed species. In instances where known populations may be affected by federal projects such as highways and power dams, the consultation process called for in the law can be extremely helpful in resolving potential conflicts.

## Prognosis

There is no question in the minds of those most familiar with this species that additional undiscovered populations have yet to be found. Although the lakes region of central New Hampshire and Maine now appears to be a major center of species distribution, Connecticut, western Massachusetts, New York, Pennsylvania, and northern New Jersey offer great hope for finding new colonies.

The official recovery plan for the small whorled pogonia was approved in January 1985 (Poulos 1985). The primary objective of the plan is to "locate and protect 30 populations of at least 20 individuals each throughout the range of the species." That objective can be successfully achieved if the commitment is made to look for intensively and protect the new sites. The plant is not difficult to properly identify. Detailed, helpful descriptions can be found in most popular wildflower books. The major ingredient for success in finding these new sites is more people looking and knowing what to look for. FWS currently is cooperating with the University of Maine Cooperative Extension Service to develop an informational brochure to assist in this endeavor. Thirty thousand copies of the brochure will be printed and distributed throughout the range of the species. The objectives of the brochure are to increase public awareness on the status of the small whorled pogonia and to encourage public cooperation in finding new populations and protecting existing sites.

In the past three years, several new colonies, some in excess of 100 plants, have been found. These discoveries have played a major role in advancing our understanding of the species and insuring the species continued existence. Interestingly, some of the largest colonies would have been destroyed had they not been found on the property of willing cooperative landowners. With increasing public awareness and concern for endangered and threatened plants, there is every reason to believe that the small whorled pogonia will remain a part of our heritage.

## Recommendations

The FWS recovery plan is a summary of the best expert opinion on effective pogonia conservation and protection. If implemented, it will lead to the successful recovery of the species and its removal from the Endangered Species List. The single greatest need in successfully achieving the recovery goal is the commitment to search intensively for new sites—to find them before they are unknowingly destroyed. Intricate research or common sense protection schemes can only be undertaken if there are plants to protect. The best chance of finding new sites is to expand field surveys near existing populations. Several populations have been found by searching similar habitats in the vicinity of existing populations.

Beyond additional field searches and implementations of protection strategies, other recommendations in the recovery plan are studies on the species' biology. Investigation of the species' possible dormancy, its relationship with an associated mycorrhizal fungi, and methods of natural dispersal will help lead to sound management actions. Monitoring existing colonies and educational activities such as the wide dissemination of information leaflets or brochures hold particular promise for increasing public awareness and concern on behalf of the endangered small whorled pogonia.

## References

Baldwin, J.T. Jr. 1967. "*Isotria medeoloides* at the Grimes station in Virginia." *America Orchid Society Bulletin.* 36:803-805.

Brumback, W.E. and C.W. Fyler. 1983. Monitoring study of *Isotria medeoloides* in East Alton, New Hampshire. Unpublished study funded by the U.S. Fish and Wildlife Service, Newton Corner, Massachusetts. 23 pp.

Brumback, W.E. and C.W. Fyler. 1984. Monitoring study of *Isotria medeoloides* in East Alton, New Hampshire. Unpublished study funded by the U.S. Fish and Wildlife Service, Newton Corner, Massachusetts. 39 pp.

Correll, P.S. 1950. *Native Orchids of North America North of Mexico.* Chronica Botanica Company, Waltham, Massachusetts. pp. 143-145.

Crow, G.E. 1982. *New Englands Rare, Threatened and Endangered Plants.* U.S. Government Printing Office, Washington, D.C. pp. 6-7.

Grimes, E.J. 1921 "A new station for *Pogonia affinis.*" Rhodora 23:195-197.

Homoya, M.A. 1977. Distribution and ecology of the genus *Isotria* in Illinois. Master's Thesis. Southern Illinois University, Carbondale, Illinois. 104 pp.

Luer, C.A. 1975. *The Native Orchids of the United States and Canada Excluding Florida.* The New York Botanical Garden, Bronx, New York. pp. 252-254.

Mehrhoff, L.A. 1980. The reproductive biology of the genus *Isotria* (Orchidaceae) and the ecology of *Isotria medeoloides.* Master's Thesis. University of North Carolina, Chapel Hill, North Carolina. 64 pp.

Poulos, P.G. 1985. *Small Whorled Pogonia Recovery Plan.* U.S. Fish and Wildlife Service, Newton Corner, Massachusetts. 40 pp.

*Richard W. Dyer is with the Fish and Wildlife Service's Region 5 Office of Endangered Species in Newton Corner, Massachusetts where he has worked as a biologist for nine years. He has spent three years as research coordinator for the small whorled pogonia.*

A polar bear glowers across arctic ice. Poorly managed subsistence hunting, which takes almost the maximum allowable number of females yearly, is a major threat to the bear.

*Steven C. Amstrup*

# Polar Bear

## Steven C. Amstrup

U.S. Fish and Wildlife Service

## Species Description and Natural History

NORTH OF ALASKA, Canada, and Eurasia lies the polar ice cap, a floating plate of frozen sea up to 2,500 miles across. The ice cap is not solid. Rather, under the influence of differential currents, winds, and temperatures the ice splits into slabs a few feet to many miles across. These slabs collide with one another until their surfaces are littered with rubble and ribbed with pressure ridges. In summer, freshwater lakes spread across the surface of the ice, and larger leads open up between the separating floes.

The overlord of this ever-moving expanse of snow, ice, and sky is the polar bear (*Ursus maritimus*), a fitting master indeed. Polar bears are the largest nonaquatic predators on the globe. Adult females weigh from 300 to 700 pounds, depending on season and reproductive status. Adult males are often twice that, and weights exceeding half a ton are common. One bear recently captured in Canada weighed 1,700 pounds, nearly four times the weight of a lion or tiger. A large male polar bear is commonly eight feet or more from nose to tail, stands more than 12 feet tall on its hind legs, has a neck 45 inches in circumference, and leaves a footprint 10 inches wide. Only severe climatic events and man can threaten the security of this great predator.

Polar bears evolved from the predecessors of today's brown bears between 100,000 and 250,000 years ago (Kurten 1964). Although that seems a long time, it is quite brief in evolutionary terms. In fact, polar bears are one of the newest distinct forms of large mammal. However, they have made substantial changes in a relatively short time. Long, gently curved claws previously used for unearthing roots, insects, and small mammals became short, strongly curved, and very sharp for clinging to ice and to large prey such as seals. The flat cheek teeth formerly used for grinding plant material gradually became more pointed and developed sharper surfaces for shearing meat, blubber, and hide. The fur increased in density, became hollow for better warding off the incessant cold, and, most noticeably, assumed a creamy white color providing better camouflage in the monotonously white environment.

These adaptations must have been successful, for polar bears currently occupy the entire sea-ice-covered region of the northern hemisphere (DeMaster and Stirling 1981). The polar bear is in fact one of the most appropriate symbols of the arctic.

## Distribution

Polar bears occur on lands and seas controlled by Denmark, Norway, Canada, the Soviet Union, and the United States. Their distribution in the United States is limited to Alaska.

The Norwegians call the polar bear "Isbjorn" or "ice bear," a most fitting name since the species distribution is closely tied to that of the sea ice. For example, polar bears frequent the Alaskan land area mainly between late September and June when the sea ice dominates the coastal environments of northwestern and northern Alaska. When the sea ice expands to its maximum in late winter, polar bears can be found in coastal areas as far south as the Bering Strait between North America and Asia. In summer, the ice retreats to the north (Lentfer 1972), and most of the bears go with it. The distribution of Alaska's polar bears during summer is not well known. However, biologists presume the bears occupy the edge of the polar ice cap where most of the sea remains ice covered year round.

Perhaps because there are few geographical barriers on the sea ice, polar bears are quintessential wanderers. In fact, scientists thought for a long time that bears traveled indiscriminately around the globe and that if one waited long enough, individual bears seen in the Alaskan arctic would ultimately appear in the Soviet Union and, later, as they drifted with the ice, in Spitzbergen (Pederson 1945, Scott et al 1959). However, tag and recovery studies conducted in Canada, Alaska, Svalbard, and Greenland since the late 1960s have suggested that most individual bears travel within restricted areas (Stirling et al 1978, DeMaster and Stirling 1981, Lentfer 1983). These descriptions of polar bear movements are necessarily fragmentary, though, because an enormous number of tags are required to provide very few reobservations. Furthermore, polar bears can be captured and tagged only during certain times of the year, so reobservations are often spatially clustered and widely separated in time.

During the past four years, I have studied polar bear ecology in Alaska's arctic region. A principal objective of that research has been to better describe the seasonal and annual movements of polar bears in this part of the world. By radio collaring 50 bears and relocating them from aircraft, I have confirmed, among other things, that most Alaskan bears maintain activity areas within which they move about according to the rhythm of the seasons. It is not yet clear whether these activity areas are comparable to the home ranges of terrestrial mammals and birds, but the areas are large by almost any measure. During a single year, some Alaskan polar bears have traveled throughout some 50,000 square miles of sea ice, an area nearly the size of the state of Washington.

Some wanderings may result from movements of the sea ice, a dynamic platform upon which to live. One spring I learned how significantly the cold, currents, and winds can alter the distribution of polar bears as well as that of other mammals that call the ice their home. My colleagues and I spent five weeks during April and May 1983 trying to capture, mark, and instrument bears near Prudhoe Bay and Barter Island in Alaska's eastern Beaufort Sea. Although we flew many hours and looked over a lot of sea ice, we encountered only about a third as many bears as during the same period in 1982. Our radio tracking and ice surveys suggested that the difference did not reflect a reduction of bear numbers in the Beaufort Sea, but rather a different distribution. On the sea's eastern side the ice was continually opening and refreezing, more suitable for polar bears than the solidly frozen ice of our study area. Consequently, most collared bears (and presumably most other bears) were east of the areas we could effectively search from headquarters at Barter Island or Prudhoe Bay. While we were having such poor success, Canadian researchers in the Beaufort Sea, working only 100 or 200 miles east of us, were catching lots of bears. Ice conditions differed again in 1984, and that spring we encountered the highest number of bears ever. That increase was impossible to explain by reproduction among resident bears, verifying that distributional rather than numerical changes were the root of our problem in 1983. Even greater annual changes in bear distribution have been recorded in parts of Canada (DeMaster et al 1980).

Even discounting extremes of weather, the more predictable seasonal motion of the ice requires corresponding movements from the bears. Polar bears that in winter occupy the Southern Chukchi and Bering seas, which separate Alaska from Asia, must move north hundreds of miles as their ice home melts in summer. We now know that bears of the Beaufort Sea (North Slope), animals that may move seasonally 150 miles or more north or south, may also move east and west more than 400 miles during the course of a single year.

## Feeding Habits

Although all bears are classified as meat eaters (Carnivora), only the polar bear is ecologically a carnivore or true predator. Polar bears will feed upon beached whales and other carrion when available. They also have been known to take walruses and white whales, and one Labrador population, now apparently extinct, reputedly fed on fish much as brown bears do (Stirling and Kiliaan 1980). Over most of the polar bear's range, however, ringed seals (*Phoca hispida*) and bearded seals (*Erignathus barbatus*) form the bulk of the diet (DeMaster and Stirling 1981).

Seals are large and difficult to catch. A bear may kill two or three seals in one day, then none for a couple of weeks or more. However, polar bears are well adapted to such a feast or famine diet. They can store considerable energy as fat, which also insulates against the arctic cold, and they can consume large quantities of food rapidly to take advantage of short-term abundance. Polar bears can eat some 10 percent of their weight within 30 minutes. The stomach of a large bear may hold 200 pounds of food (Best 1977).

Information about long-term food consumption is difficult to gather and varies with sex, age, condition, and size of the bear. However, it appears that a polar bear must kill a ringed seal every five or six days on the average to maintain its body condition (Best 1977). Eley (1976) found that polar bears walked nearly 100 miles for each seal killed. Theoretically, a bear could feed for several days on the carcass of a bearded seal, which is much larger than a ringed seal. However, evidence suggests that scavenging by foxes and other bears quickly eliminates any bearded seal remains in excess of what a successful hunter can eat at first sitting (Stirling 1974, Stirling and Archibald 1977).

Bears commonly catch seals by waiting patiently beside a breathing hole in the ice. One ringed seal will alternately use several breathing holes. During cold weather the seal must visit each hole regularly to assure it does not freeze over. When a seal surfaces and sticks its nose through the hole to breathe, a waiting bear will spring forward, catch the seal's head in its jaws, and kill or disable the seal while pulling it from the water. One bear was observed waiting motionlessly at an open seal hole for more than 14 hours. It is said that Eskimos, armed with harpoons rather than teeth and claws, learned from the polar bear how to catch seals by waiting patiently at breathing holes.

In spring, bears sometimes break into the subnivian (under snow) lairs of seals. These lairs are created late in winter, when the breathing holes become covered with the snow that incessantly drifts across the arctic ice surface. When the snow is sufficient, the seals will carve out hollows in which they haul out to rest. Adult female seals enlarge them to form birthing lairs.

Two years ago I saw a four-year-old female polar bear attempt to break into such a lair. Three times she stretched on hind legs to her greatest height and fell forward on her front paws right above the lair. Just before impact with the snow, she would thrust her front limbs forward "pushup" style, increasing the velocity and force of the impact. In this case, the pavement-like snow was too thick for her to break through, and she did not enter the lair. Had the snow crust been thinner, the bear, having pinpointed the seal's location under the snow by smell, would have broken the roof of the lair and tried to pin the seal to the ice before it could slide into its hole.

Newborn seal pups, or "whitecoats" as they are often called, cannot enter the water because their fat layer does not yet provide sufficient insulation. These animals are vulnerable to predation by polar bears regardless of snow thickness. Several times I have observed where bears, unable to break through the roofs of birthing lairs, dug through several feet of snow or ice and caught white-coated pups. Pups are not the preferred prey, however, since they provide the bear with far less energy per unit of effort than do larger, fatter seals.

Polar bears also stalk seals basking on the ice surface in spring and summer. The classic situation occurs when a bear spots a basking seal from some distance and sneaks closer by using pressure ridges in the ice for cover. The stalk culminates with a wild charge over the last several yards as the bear tries to grab and disable the seal before it can enter the water. If successful, the bear is quick to remove its catch from the water's edge, leaving extensive blood trails in the snow. An aquatic stalk is less common, but has been observed on several occasions. In this case, a bear swims underwater to the edge of an ice floe where a seal rests and explodes onto the floe, attempting to cut off the seal's escape route (Stirling 1974).

Like the explorers' tales of encounters with the plains grizzly bear (*Ursus arctos horribilis*), many early accounts of polar bears describe ferocious beasts that devoured humans and could not be killed with the primitive weapons of the day. In 1596, Willem Barents and his men reportedly fought a terrible battle with a polar bear near what is now called Bear Island in the Svalbard Archipelago (Larsen 1978). The Norwegian explorer Fridtjof Nansen also described frightening encounters with polar bears occurring in the Greenland expedition around 1870 (Larsen 1978).

During the heydey of Alaskan polar bear trophy hunting in the mid-1960s, stories of polar bears stalking humans who ventured onto the ice were common, and the polar bear's awesome reputation grew. Biologists have discovered, however, that polar bears, although not benign towards humans, are not the marauding killers many early stories and recent television programs have made them out to be. Curious and often unafraid, they may sometimes be aggressive but are not blatantly antagonistic toward people. Their reactions to humans mostly reflect the circumstances of the encounter. Polar bears must be respected because of their size, speed, and strength. When in the bear's world, humans must take extreme care to stay out of their way. It must be remembered that the things polar bears usually eat are about the size of people. More often than not, however, any attention they pay to humans is a matter of curiosity rather than aggression.

Accounts of polar bears stalking humans that are out walking on the ice probably reflects this curiosity, as well as basic behavior patterns that have evolved for thousands of years. Other than an occasional human visitor, bears are the only things that make large tracks on the ice surface, and bears tend to follow the tracks of other bears. Young bears do this so they can scavenge on the kills of more experienced hunters. Big males follow tracks because they sometimes drive smaller bears off of kills and occasionally even kill and eat smaller bears. In the spring, males follow tracks in hope of finding estrous females. Human tracks in the snow resemble bear tracks, and, to a bear, probably smell strange and worth investigating. The hunter who turns to find a bear walking in his tracks may indeed be in danger. However, he has probably experienced this track following behavior, rather than an instinct to prey upon humans.

## Breeding

Polar bears have one of the slowest mammalian reproductive rates. Females usually breed for the first time at five or six years of age, producing cubs about eight months later (DeMaster and Stirling 1981). Because young bears remain with their mothers for more than two years, learning to hunt and survive, litters are produced no more frequently than every three years. Moreover, although some bears aged 25 to 30 years have been captured, most probably do not live beyond 20. Therefore, most females theoretically produce no more than five litters. In fact, recent population analyses, although not definitive, suggest that most females live long enough to produce only one or two litters. Although our knowledge of reproduction and survival is still incomplete, it is abundantly clear that polar bear populations cannot increase rapidly. This necessitates careful scrutiny of actions that might reduce either reproduction or survival rates.

Although any polar bear may construct a temporary den in order to escape cold or a severe storm, only pregnant females regularly den for extended periods. Maternity dens typically consist of tunnels dug into snow banks and enlarged by the mother and cubs as winter progresses. We have observed pregnant females entering dens between mid-October and the end of November. This seems appropriate, since the sun sets in the polar bear's Alaskan habitat in mid-November and does not clear the horizon again until mid-January.

In many parts of the world, polar bears den in large concentrations or core areas. Among the largest are those found on Wrangel Island in the Soviet Union, on some of the islands comprising the Svalbard Archipelago north of the Norwegian mainland, and near the west coast of Hudson Bay in Canada (Uspenski and Kistchinskii 1972, Stirling et al 1977, Larsen 1985). Several other areas where polar bears regularly den also have been identified, but biologists have been unable to locate such areas in Alaska, where as many as 200 female polar bears may enter maternity dens each fall. Every couple of years a few dens are reported in Alaska, but they usually are in remote locations and so far have not demonstrated the clumping that seems to be the rule in other areas. Until recently fewer than 50 dens had even been located in Alaska.

For many years, considerable research and survey effort failed to shed light on the distribution of Alaskan polar bear dens, and biologists were left to speculate. The dearth of known recent dens in Alaska has caused some biologists to hypothesize that Alaskan bears may now den elsewhere. Banks Island in Canada and Wrangel Island in the Soviet Union have long been recognized as polar bear maternity denning areas (Harrington 1968, Uspenski and Kistchinskii 1972). Because the sites are relatively close, in terms of potential polar bear movements, to Alaska, it has been suggested that the Alaskan bears den there. Now, however, we may be on the verge of a long-awaited breakthrough. During the winters of 1983 and 1984, I radio-tracked instrumented bears to 26 maternity den sites. This in itself seemed a breakthrough, increasing by 50 percent the known Alaskan dens. But the real news was the distribution of those dens. Only three were found on land. A fourth was thought to have been on or near land, although the den site was not pinpointed. The others were on the high arctic pack ice. Further, several other instrumented bears assumed to be pregnant were last observed heading north and west onto the high-pack ice in late summer. Since polar bears from all other known populations seem to have their roots on land, the possibility that most Beaufort Sea bears den on the ice pack could provide the explanation we have long sought. Data are needed from additional years to verify that this trend is real.

On land or ice, cubs typically are born in December or January (Harrington 1968, DeMaster and Stirling 1981). Litters of two cubs occur most frequently. Single cubs are less common, and litters of three are rare except in Hudson Bay, Canada. Polar bear cubs have fur at birth, but weigh only one and a half pounds and are blind and helpless. By spring, however, they weigh about 25 pounds and continue to grow rapidly. At one year they weigh 200 pounds, at two years nearly 400 pounds.

Polar bear families denning on land, and probably those denning at sea as well, typically remain in the vicinity of the den for several days after emergence (Larsen 1985). During this time the cubs romp and play and explore the outside world. This period of acclimation must be of great survival value, because female bears that have not eaten since fall extend the lengthy fasting period to allow for it. When the time is right the family moves onto the ice, and sometimes the cubs must keep up a rigorous pace. One female that denned in Alaska led her two young cubs on a trek covering at least seven miles per day (assuming she moved in a straight line, which is not likely) during each of the first 17 days away from the den.

# Significance of the Species

As a top predator, polar bears have greatly influenced the evolution of other arctic species. This is demonstrated by the biological contrasts between arctic and Antarctic sea ice. Flightless penguins and other birds occupy the Antarctic ice surface for much of the year, as do several species of seals. Many of these animals can be approached and even touched before becoming alarmed (Stirling 1977). On the northern ice, where the white bear stalks, only the wariest of animals are found. Although both ringed and bearded seals do haul out on the ice surface at times, they are never far from a hole or lead in the ice. They are ever vigilant and retreat into the water at the first sign of danger. This is in stark contrast to Weddell seals (*Leptonychotes weddelli*), the Southern Hemisphere's equivilent to ringed seals. Unaccustomed to predators, Weddell seals can be touched and marked for scientific studies without an overt avoidance response. They even give birth on the exposed surface of the ice. They simply have not needed any anti-predator defensive behaviors while on the ice surface.

# Historical Perspective

Polar bear furs have been prized since the days of the Roman Empire, particularly by nobility (Larsen 1978). In some parts of the world, the history of early interactions with polar bears was dominated by commercial interest in furs, and commercial exploitation left an indelible mark on current polar bear distribution. Originally, a population of polar bears occupied St. Matthew Island in Alaska's Bering Sea. When the explorer Henry Elliot anchored at St. Matthew in the summer of 1874, he saw polar bears, "yea hundreds of them," and over the course of his nine-day survey of the island was never out of sight of one or more the great beasts (Elliot 1898). Unlike most of Alaska's polar bears, many of these individuals spent the summer on the island instead of following the sea ice as it retreated to the north. Unfortunately, by 1900, commercial hunters in search of seal skins and whale oil had all but eliminated the St. Matthew bears (Hanna 1920). Today, only a few old bones and trails worn into the tundra attest to the great bears' reign on St. Matthew Island.

Around the turn of the century, local Eskimos apparently removed many bears from dens in the Canning River region of Alaska's north slope (Leffingwell 1919). It would not be surprising if bears were removed from other areas as well. Also around the turn of the century many bears were killed by whalers wintering in the region of Herschel Island just east of the border between Alaska and Canada. The introduction of modern firearms increased the Eskimos' ability to kill polar bears. We know that Eskimo hunters today still remove some bears from dens near Alaska's coast and that even a low level of removal of bears looking for or occupying maternity dens could prevent re-establishment of denning areas if their use had previously been disrupted as a result of heavy hunting by Yankee whalers or coastal residents.

Local reductions in polar bear numbers also occurred in other parts of the world as bears were trapped, shot, and otherwise killed at almost every opportunity. Perhaps only the remoteness and unpredictability of the polar bear's habitat, and the inability of early man-made machines to traverse it, saved the great white bears from extinction during the era of unregulated commercial hunting that extended through the mid 1900s in some areas. Today, possibly 40,000 bears remain. About 3,000 to 5,000 occur in Alaska.

## Current Trends

Approximately 1,200 polar bears worldwide were being killed yearly in the 1950s and 1960s (Scott *et al* 1959). However, new hunting restrictions (see below) stopped the severe declines that had been evident in some areas. Some polar bear populations are now actually increasing (Larsen 1985). Although polar bear kills in Europe and Asia are dramatically lower now, hunting has not declined as significantly in North America. However, hunting is strictly controlled in Canada, where most of the North American take occurs. There appear to be about as many Alaskan polar bears today as there were 25 years ago, and numbers seem stable. However, because of impending changes in arctic Alaska, the prospect that U.S. populations are only stable is not really comforting since the bear's slow reproductive rate makes it vulnerable to natural and man-caused population reductions.

Finally, evidence suggests that the Alaskan polar bear population is relatively small and widely dispersed. Off the coast of Alaska, about one bear occurs for every 50 to 70 square miles of ice habitat. Because the population is small and individuals mature and reproduce slowly, a small margin of safety surrounds any activity affecting polar bears or their habitats. Although the Marine Mammal Protection Act limits hunting of polar bears to local residents of native descent, it allows those peoples to hunt polar bears at any time and to kill any number without regard to sex or age. Further, such hunting currently cannot be restricted unless populations of the species become depleted or in danger of extinction.

## Management

In recognition of the polar bear's increasing vulnerability to modern man's presence in the arctic, the five nations within whose boundaries polar bears occur ratified in 1976 the International Agreement for the Conservation of

Polar Bears. By signing this polar bear treaty, these nations agreed to conduct national research programs to learn more about polar bears. They also agreed to regulate hunts within safe limits, to protect females and young, and to protect polar bear ecosystems.

Independently, or as a result of the polar bear treaty, each jurisdiction has implemented actions to protect and properly manage polar bears. DeMaster and Stirling (1981) outlined existing worldwide hunting regulations. The Soviet Union ended all polar bear hunting in 1955. Since then, the only reported takings of polar bears in the USSR have been a few cubs yearly for circuses, zoos, and other forms of public display. In 1970, Norway dramatically reduced the level of commercial and trophy hunting in the Svalbard area. This action was followed in 1973 by a complete ban on killing polar bears in Svalbard, except for defense of life and property.

In Canada, female bears and their young are protected by specific statutes and by season closures which make them less available to hunters. The total take is regulated by a nationwide quota system that operates in each village that has access to polar bears, and trends in the sex and age composition of the take are closely monitored. Denmark has eliminated commercial hunting of polar bears in Greenland, where only subsistence hunting by native residents is allowed now. This hunting is further restricted by the requirement that hunters use only traditional means, including kayaks and dog sleds but not including snow machines or other motorized vehicles (C. Vibe pers. comm.). Recent history has shown that these regulations effectively limit the kill in Greenland to acceptable levels.

The United States chose to implement the provisions of the polar bear treaty via the Marine Mammal Protection Act of 1972. This law, which went into effect in 1973, leaves polar bear hunting open only to coastal Indians, Aleuts, and Eskimos who live within polar bear range. Unfortunately, the act forbids any regulation of subsistence hunting by these poeple.

## Prognosis

The Polar Bear Specialists Group of the International Union for the Conservation of Nature and Natural Resources and the Canadian Polar Bear Technical Committee—the two most prestigious bodies of polar bear knowledge in the world—have concluded that unregulated or inadequately regulated hunting is the most important of the two critical threats to the polar bear. Unregulated hunting can quickly eliminate entire populations or portions of them, as occurred on St. Matthew Island. On the other hand, a properly managed hunt can assure perpetual survival of polar bears by recruiting popular and political support for maintaining bear populations at high levels. Records kept when trophy hunting occurred in Alaska (1956 to 1972) verify that a well-managed hunt could assure a stable level of human utilization and maintain an optimum polar bear population.

Unfortunately, subsistence polar bear hunting in Alaska currently is not well managed. The average polar bear take in Alaska has declined since the passage of the Marine Mammal Protection Act, but the size of the female take remains high. In fact, during the July 1, 1983 to June 30, 1984 recording season, more females may have been killed than in any other year on record. Available evidence indicates, at least in the Beaufort Sea, that the annual loss of females from the population is currently about the maximum allowable. Estimates of survival and recruitment derived from the age structure of nearly 1,000 polar bears captured live in the Beaufort Sea during the last decade suggest that as many as 61 adult females may be lost to natural and other causes yearly, while perhaps only 56 are recruited. It would be best if removal of females from the population would decline, and it certainly must not increase. Yet, females are more vulnerable than males to the coastal-based hunting strategies used by Eskimo hunters (Stirling *et al* 1975), and regulations to correct the availability bias do not exist.

# Recommendations

An uncontrolled polar bear hunt was perhaps tolerable when few people lived in Alaska's arctic and when there was little human activity, but things have changed. Mainly because of the increased affluence following discovery of oil and natural gas, human populations in the arctic are burgeoning, and increasing numbers of people want the opportunity to hunt bears. The increased affluence that has allowed the rapid increase in numbers of local people also has increased the mobility of those people. Snow machines, power boats, and even aircraft enable residents of the north to move quickly when pursuing game and permit them to establish and maintain camps far from home. This has created an unprecedented ability to affect polar bears and other wildlife resources. Impacts related to hunting could be managed with a few simple and straightforward regulations. For example, quotas setting a limit on the numbers of polar bears that each village could kill during any given year would keep the kill within what the bear population could sustain regardless of the growth in human numbers within the villages. This approach currently is used with good results in Canada.

Since protection of female polar bears is the most important aim, an even simpler approach might work just as well. Most adult females are either pregnant or encumbered by cubs during most of their lives (recall that they keep cubs with them for more than two years). Thus, if it were illegal to kill females with young and their young, and also illegal to kill bears in dens, most females would be protected. Further, if hunting seasons did not open until after pregnant females entered dens, say December 15 of each year, the majority of females without cubs also would be protected. With these restraints, hunters possibly could go about their business without concern for a quota limitation. Regardless of how it is done, changes in the numbers of people in the arctic and in their abilities to kill polar bears must be addressed if polar bears are to survive. Unfortunately, managers cannot currently take any of these measures because the Marine Mammal Protection Act mandates unrestricted hunting by Aleuts, Eskimos, and Indians.

The second potential threat to bears and their habitats is the direct effect of the current wave of arctic industrialization. We lack the knowledge to predict or even understand how the search for and development of petroleum and other nonrenewable resources may affect polar bears. In addition to increasing numbers of permanent residents, several thousand people presently occupy work camps in the Alaskan and adjacent Canadian arctic. Vessels ply arctic waters in summer, trucks and other vehicles pound over ice roads in winter, and aircraft abound year-round. Bear-human interactions are increasing and will continue to do so, resulting in added direct losses from bear populations.

Many impacts of industrialization are likely to be more nebulous, however. A major concern has been whether pipelines and access roads parallel to the coast would discourage female bears from moving ashore to traditional denning areas. Whether seismic testing and other exploration and development activities would disturb bears in dens also has been a major concern. The period of maternal denning is likely the phase of the polar bear's life cycle in which the animals are most vulnerable to human or other disturbances. However, if subsequent data confirm that most Alaskan bears den at sea, where they are not as likely to be influenced by the activities of man as are bears denning on land, this major management concern may be diminished.

Other concerns remain unanswered, however. We do not know if seismic testing will reduce the abundance of seals, ultimately lowering polar bear hunting success. We know that oil spills are highly unlikely, but they can occur. We know that treatment of "oiled" bears is too expensive for anything other than demonstration purposes and that prior knowledge of bear distribution and movements could be of greater value in allowing us to minimize the opportunities for bears to contact oil in the first place. But our knowledge is far from complete. In fact, we have a long way to go to obtain the information necessary to answer most questions regarding polar bear interactions with arctic developments. That places us at a real disadvantage when designing management efforts to maintain polar bear populations.

With intensified research and management, most potential conflicts between polar bears and man probably can be resolved. However, the challenges are as immense as the arctic itself. We must learn more about the basic ecological needs of polar bears and how those needs may be affected by increasing levels of human activities. We must possess the maximum possible regulatory flexibility to respond to natural or man-caused fluctuations in polar bear numbers. We must be willing and able to react positively to increased interest in both consumptive and nonconsumptive uses of polar bears and other arctic wildlife. And we must be innovative if we are to simultaneously develop Alaska's valuable mineral and energy resources and allow the polar bear to remain master of the northern ice.

# References

Best, R.C. 1975. "Ecological aspects of polar bear nutrition." *in* R.L. Phillips and C. Jonkel, eds. *Proceedings of the 1985 Predator Symposium.* Montana Forest and Range Experiment Station, Missoula. pp. 203-211.

DeMaster, D.P., M.C.S. Kingsley, and I. Stirling. 1980. "A multiple mark and recapture estimate applied to polar bears." *Canadian Journal of Zoology* 58(4):633-638.

DeMaster, D.P. and I. Stirling. 1981. *"Ursus maritimus."* Mammalian Species No. 145:1-7 American Society of Mammalology.

Eley, T.J. 1976. *An Analysis of Polar Bear Predation on Ice Pinniped Populations of Alaska.* Internal Report, U.S. Fish and Wildlife Service, Anchorage, Alaska 27 pp.

Elliott, H.W. 1898. *Seal and Salmon Fisheries and General Resources of Alaska.* U.S. Government Printing Office, Washington, D.C. Vol. 111.

Harrington, C.R. 1978. *Denning Habits of the Polar Bear* (Ursus maritumus Phipps). Canadian Wildlife Service Report Series No. 5. 30 pp.

Hanna, G.D. 1920. "Mammals of the St. Matthew Island, Bering Sea." *Journal of Mammalology* 1:118-122.

Kurtén, B. 1964. "The evolution of the polar bear, *Ursus maritimus* Phipps." *Acta. Zoologica Fennica.* 108:1-30.

Larsen T. 1978. *The World of the Polar Bear.* Hamlyn Publishing Group, Ltd. 96 pp.

Larsen, T. 1985. "Polar bear denning and cub production in Svalbard, Norway." *Journal of Wildlife Management* 49(2):320-326.

Leffingwell, E. 1919. *The Canning River Region, Northern Alaska.* U.S. Geological Survey Professional Paper 109. U.S. Government Printing office, Washington, D.C. 247 pp.

Lentfer, J.W. 1972. "Polar bear—sea ice relationships," *in* S. Herrero, ed., *Bears—Their Biology and Management.* IUCN, New Series 23. pp. 165-171.

Lentfer, J.W. 1983. "Alaskan polar bear movements from mark and recovery." *Arctic.* 36(3):282-288.

Pederson, A. 1945. *Der Eisbar, Verbreitung und Lebensweise.* E Brunn and Co., Kovenhaven. 166 pp.

Scott, R.F., K.W. Kenyon, J.L. Buckley, and S.T. Olson. 1959. "Status and management of the polar bear and Pacific walrus." *Transactions of the North American Wildlife Conference* 24:366-373.

Stirling, I. 1974. "Midsummer observations on the behavior of wild polar bears *(Ursus maritimus)." Canadian Journal of Zoology* 52:1191-1198.

Stirling, I. 1977. "Adaptations of Weddell and ringed seals to exploit the polar fast ice habitat in absence or presence of surface predators." Smithsonian Institution SCAR *Symposium on Anarctic Biology* 3:741-748.

Stirling, I., D. Andriashek, P. Latour, and W. Calvert. 1975. *Distribution and Abundance of Polar Bears in the Eastern Beaufort Sea.* Canadian Wildlife Service Technology Report 2. 59 pp.

Stirling I. and W.R. Archiblad. 1977. "Aspects of predation of seals by polar bears." *Journal of Fish Research Board of Canada* 34:1126-1129.

Stirling, I., C. Jonkel, P. Smith, R. Robertson and D. Cross. 1977. *The Ecology of the Polar Bear* (Ursus maritimus) *Along the Western Coast of Hudson Bay."* Occasional Paper No. 33. Canadian Wildlife Service. 64 pp.

Stirling, I and H.P.L. Kiliaan. 1980. *Population Ecology Studies of the Polar Bears in Northern Labrador.* Canadian Wildlife Service Occasional Paper 42:5-18.

Stirling, I., R.E. Schweinburg, W. Calvert and H.P.L. Kiliaan. 1978. *Population Ecology of the Polar Bear Along the Proposed Arctic Islands Gas Pipeline Route.* Final Report to Environmental Management Service. Department of Environment, Edmonton, Alberta. 93 pp.

Uspenski, S.M. and A.A. Kistchinskii. 1972. "New data on the winter ecology of the polar bear *(U. martimus)* on Wrangel Island," *in* S. Herrero, ed., *Bears—Their Biology and Management.* IUNC, New Series. 23. pp. 181-197.

*Steven C. Amstrup, project leader for the Fish and Wildlife Service's polar bear project, has studied polar bears since 1981.*

Cause for concern about the peregrine will remain as along as chlorinated-hydrocarbon pesticides are used in Latin America, but currently the falcon population seems to be recovering.

*George Galioz/Photo Researchers*

# Peregrine Falcon

## Gerald Craig

Colorado Division of Wildlife

## Species Description and Natural History

THE TERM "PEREGRINE," derived from the Latin word connoting someone traveling abroad, accurately describes this species' mobility and tendency to wander, a tendency which may account for the falcon's nearly cosmopolitan occurrence. Breeding peregrines occupy all the world's major land masses, excluding Antarctica (Hickey 1969, Brown and Amadon 1968). Three subspecies of peregrines inhabit North America. The tundra peregrine (*Falco peregrinus tundrius*) nests in the North American arctic tundra and migrates as far south as Argentina to winter (Cade 1982, White 1968). The tundra form is generally recognized as a subspecies by biologists (U.S. Fish and Wildlife Service 1984, 1983, Ratcliffe 1963), but presently is not officially acknowledged as such by the American Ornithologists' Union. The *anatum* subspecies (*Falco peregrinus anatum*) occupies the tiaga zone southward into central Mexico, and the nonmigratory Peales's peregrine (*Falco peregrinus pealei*) resides in the coastal regions from the Aleutians to northern Washington (Fyfe *et al* 1976, Cade 1982).

### Physical Characteristics

Peregrines are slightly larger than crows and, as is typical of most raptors, females average a quarter to a third larger than their mates (Lewin 1985). The

807

females weigh 26 to 35 ounces and have wingspans of 43 to 46 inches, while males weigh from 19 to 23 ounces and have wingspans of 38 to 43 inches. Both sexes possess very similar plumages, however. The most prominent adult plumage characteristics are the feathers on the crown of the head, the broad moustachial stripe, and the ear patches, which form a black helmet. The breast is cream or buff liberally marked with horizontal bars. The upper breast in the crop region tends to have fewer markings on the male and may appear nearly white at a distance. The upper tail, back, and wing coverts are blue-grey barred with dark slate. As with all members of the falcon family, the eye is dark brown. Flesh around the eyes, the area at the base of the beak, and the feet are waxy yellow (Brown and Amadon 1968).

Juveniles are browner than adults, with most feather margins edged in buff. Although they retain the helmet of the adult, it is dark brown, and the moustachial stripes usually are narrower. The breast is heavily streaked and the flesh around the eyes, cere, and feet usually is blue-gray to greenish yellow. While adult plumage is distinctive, immature peregrines may be confused with prairie falcons (*Falco mexicanus*) where they coexist, although the latter may be distinguished by its dark underwing auxillaries (Brown and Amadon 1968).

The plumages of the southern-breeding tundra peregrine and tiaga-breeding *anatum* peregrine gradate where the ranges of the subspecies meet. As a rule, the tundra form is typified by narrow moustachial and cheek markings and the whitish ground color of the upper breast. The *anatum* form possesses wide moustachial and cheek markings that may form a solid helmet, and the upper breast often is tinged with pinkish or salmon. The Peale's form tends to be larger than the other two subspecies, is darker, and tends to have small vertical streaks on the upper breast (White 1968, Brown and Amadon 1968).

## Migration

The three subspecies differ in their migratory habits. The Peale's is almost sedentary, while the tundra form regularly migrates as far south as Argentina. In the tiaga zone, *anatum* peregrines exhibit migratory behavior similar to that of the tundra form. The central Rocky Mountain population appears to winter at least as far away as central Mexico, but peregrines in the Southwest and southern California may be nearly sedentary, occupying their breeding territories year-round.

Plumage variability of individuals and the subtle nature of the plumage differences among the subspecies make it difficult to impossible to unequivocally identify the origin of particular peregrines. Thus the "similarity of appearance" clause of the Endangered Species Act is imposed wherever the nonendangered Peale's peregrine or threatened tundra subspecies overlaps the range of the endangered *anatum* subspecies (U.S. Fish and Wildlife Service 1983, 1984).

## Diet

Peregrines feed almost exclusively upon other birds but, contrary to their former misnomer of "duck hawk," waterfowl do not constitute the bulk of their diet. Peregrines prefer shorebirds pigeons, doves, robins, flickers, jays, swifts, swallows, and other passerines that opportunity presents. The falcon's hunting tactics usually preclude the killing of birds that frequent undergrowth or occupy coniferous habitats. Marshes and riparian zones are important hunting habitats since they serve to attract and concentrate prey.

Peregrines are spectacular fliers capable of sustaining speeds of 50 to 60 miles per hour in level flight and of achieving speeds in excess of 200 miles per hour in a stoop (dive) initiated several hundred feet above their quarry (Hickey 1969, Cade 1982). Their mode of hunting by stooping is not particu-

Historic breeding range of peregrine falcons in North America

larly efficient, however. If it keeps its wits, the intended quarry often avoids the stoop by maintaining its flight course until the last possible moment, then shifting and dodging out of the falcon's trajectory. Although some individuals may become particularly adept hunters, it is estimated that peregrines succeed in making kills only 10 to 40 percent of the time (Roalkam 1985, Cade 1982). The falcons compensate for this inefficiency by traveling extensively when hunting. During the breeding season, a peregrine may range up to 18 miles (Porter *et al* 1973) from its eyrie in search of prey, so a hunting range of 10 miles may be considered typical (Rocky Mountain/Southwestern Recovery Team 1977).

## Breeding

Where the opportunity presents itself, peregrines prefer to nest on high escarpments that dominate the topography. Frequently, such sites were the last to be abandoned during population declines (Hickey 1942, 1969) and are the first to be reoccupied upon recovery (Ratcliffe 1980). Where records exist, these 'first class' sites often show a history of occupancy spanning several centuries (Hickey 1969, Cade 1982). Although they typically prefer inaccessible ledges on cliffs, the species occasionally nests on river cutbanks or, in the arctic, in cliff nests abandoned by ravens (*Corvus corax*) and rough-legged hawks (*Buteo lagopus*) (Hickey 1969). Elsewhere, they have occupied man-made structures such as castles, bridge abutments, and office towers (Hickey 1969, Cade 1982). Indeed, it appears that falcons recently established in the East seem to prefer nesting upon bridge abutments and office buildings. This may be due to a propensity among birds released upon man-made structures to nest upon similar structures.

Onset of breeding is delayed with increasing latitude. In temperate zones, territories typically are established in March, and in the arctic pairs begin courting as early as mid-April. At the southern extent of their range, pairs may even loosely maintain territories throughout the year (Rocky Mountain/Southwestern Recovery Team 1977).

The escarpment upon which the eyrie will be located is the focus for breeding falcons. While they may not intentionally mate for life, pairs demonstrate fidelity to the breeding sites they frequented in previous years. The male usually arrives at the cliff first and defends his territory while courting passing females. If she survived the winter, his mate often arrives several weeks later and courtship begins. Should the female arrive and the male fail to return, she will maintain the territory and endeavor to attract a new mate.

Like other members of the falcon family, peregrines do not build nests of sticks. They merely form a hollow, called a 'scrape,' in the soil or sand substrate and deposit their eggs. Typically, three to four eggs are laid, and the female assumes the majority of the incubation chores while the male periodically relieves her so she can stretch her wings and feed. The male maintains vigilance against intruders and provides prey for his mate during incubation and early brooding. The eggs typically take 33 days to hatch, and the young fledge at 40 to 45 days of age. During the latter half of young-rearing, both adults forage for prey.

The length of time that young are dependent upon their parents after fledging appears to vary with individual hunting ability, tolerance of the parents, and migratory habits. Family groups remained together up to migration time (five to six weeks) in Greenland, while nonmigratory Australian peregrines were still in family groups nine weeks after fledging (Sherrod 1983). Young usually make their own kills two to four weeks after fledging and probably are capable of independently supporting themselves four to six weeks after fledging. However, since they are conditioned to seek food from the adults, they are likely to remain with the parents until they migrate or are driven away.

It is believed that peregrines of both sexes first breed when two years old. Nesting attempts by subadult females usually produce infertile eggs, although several subadult females recently produced young in Colorado. The increased incidence of subadult breeding may be indicative of an expanding population comprised of young falcons that do not have to compete for sites with experienced adults. Although peregrines may live 18 to 22 years (Enderson 1969), their average life span is probably nearer to six to eight years. As would be expected of a predator, peregrines have low productivity, and the young experience relatively high mortality. The average brood size of normally reproducing falcons is 2.5 young per successful pair (Ratcliffe 1980). Only one out of four young survive to their first year, after which they face an annual mortality of 20 percent (Rocky Mountain/Southwestern Recovery Team 1977, Ratcliffe 1980, Enderson 1969). Although golden eagles and great horned owls are quick to take advantage of recently fledged young and unwary adults, the greatest cause of mortality among peregrines is not predators but collision with twigs, limbs, and wire while in flight.

## Significance of the Species

The peregrine signifies clearly the impact that man has had upon his environment and the extraordinary efforts that are being taken to rectify the problems. The peregrine's worldwide population decline dramatically focused attention on the effects the chlorinated-hydrocarbon pesticides have upon nontarget organisms in areas remote from the point of application. Peregrine studies provided the basis for key testimonies in the 1968-69 Wisconsin court case that led to the first statewide ban on DDT use and in the Environmental Protection Agency hearings that ultimately resulted in the 1972 ban on the application of certain chlorinated-hydrocarbon pesticides throughout the United States (Dunlop 1981). The peregrine's position at the apex of a complex food chain renders the species sensitive to subtle perturbations that normally would not be documented at the primary levels but are magnified and apparent at higher trophic levels. Indeed, the only way to monitor the extent and intensity of deleterious pesticides in the environment may be by monitoring contaminant levels in peregrines and their eggs. Finally, recent successes with captive propagation and re-establishment of wild peregrines have encouraged similar recovery efforts for bald eagles and California condors.

## Historical Perspective

The peregrine has had a stormy relationship with mankind. In medieval times, peregrines were cherished by the nobility for falconry, and harsh penalties awaited those caught destroying a falcon or owning a peregrine out of their station. After the advent of gunpowder and the uprising of the masses, the aristocratic sport of falconry fell into disfavor and peregrines, viewed as competitors for game birds, were exterminated as the opportunity arose. Transplanted Europeans gave the name "duck hawk" to the peregrine in America, and up to the middle of this century the falcon was considered vermin by game-bird farmers and most wildlife management agencies. Paintings by Fuertes and Audubon of peregrines attacking ducks did not improve the public's opinion of the falcon. During World War II it became necessary for the British Air Ministry to eliminate 600 peregrines that nested on the Dover cliffs along the English coast because the falcons were killing homing pigeons that downed airmen released to signal their location to rescuers (Ratcliffe 1980).

Historically, peregrines nested throughout North America and northern Mexico, although they apparently were not breeding occupants of the Great Plains and most of the Southeast (Hickey 1969). Compared to other raptors, however, the peregrine probably never was a common breeding bird. Prior to the population decline in the 1950s and 1960s, 350 breeding territories were estimated east of the Mississippi River (Eastern Peregrine Falcon Recovery Team 1979), another 215 nesting pairs were known for the Rocky Mountain and southwestern United States (Rocky Mountain/Southwestern Recovery Team 1977), and 153 nest sites were recorded for the West Coast (The Pacific Coast Recovery Team 1982). To the North, it has been estimated that 250 *anatum* peregrines occupied the tiaga region of Alaska, and perhaps 100 additional pairs bred in the boreal regions of Canada. Although estimates are imprecise, at least 75 pairs inhabited Baja California and another 100 pairs may have bred in the Mexican highlands (U.S. Fish and Wildlife Service 1983). Since additional, unrecorded nesting pairs undoubtedly existed throughout North America in historic times, an estimate of 1,500 to 2,000 pairs of *anatum* peregrines may be accurate. Also no record exists of the historic population levels of the tundra subspecies, but broad estimates of between 2,000 and 3,000 pairs have been projected for the population distributed throughout the tundra regions of Greenland, Canada, and Alaska (Ratcliffe 1980). The Alaskan peregrine recovery team believes that 150 pairs probably occurred north of the tiaga in Alaska. The Peale's peregrine probably numbered 450 to 600 pairs distributed along the coast of British Columbia and the Aleutian Islands (U.S. Fish and Wildlife Service 1983, Cade 1982).

A severe decline in Great Britain's peregrine population was first documented in the early 1960s (Ratcliffe 1963). It was suggested subsequently that DDT was causing reproductive failure and affecting recruitment into wild breeding territories throughout eastern North America (Berger et al 1969). The survey team could not find a single territory occupied by breeding peregrines, and the population was considered extirpated. At the same time, similar population declines were observed in ospreys nesting in the lake states (Peterson 1969, Postupalsky 1969, Berger and Mueller 1969) and along the eastern seaboard (Stickel 1969) and in bald eagles in Florida (Sprunt 1969). In 1965, Hickey convened an international conference at Madison, Wisconsin, to discuss the problem, suggest causes, and develop a coordinated research approach (Hickey 1969). The conferees noted that peregrine population declines in North America and western Europe followed a similar pattern—the gradual loss of productive sites over a period of years. As pairs failed to produce adequate numbers of young, recruitment was insufficient to offset natural adult mortality, and site occupancy declined. Chlorinated-hydrocarbon pesticide levels correlated to eggshell thinning in wild peregrines, but cause and effect could not be proved by field evidence (Cade et al 1971). Subsequent laboratory investigations of captive kestrels (Wiemeyer and Porter 1970), black ducks (Heath et al 1969), and ringed doves (Peakall et al 1973) provided the evidence that DDT and several other chlorinated hydrocarbons induced sufficient eggshell thinning to cause hatch failure. Eggshell thinning was first documented in 1947. Prior to that time, eggshells were of normal thickness (Anderson and Hickey 1972). Severe population declines were associated with a thinning of 18 to 20 percent (Ratcliffe 1980). The pesticides also may induce behavioral abnormalities such as decreased nest attentiveness, reduced territoriality, and failure to complete essential phases of the reproductive cycle (Peakall et al 1975).

By 1972, the *anatum* and tundra subspecies were placed on the endangered species list, making it illegal for anyone, including falconers, to take birds from the wild. A continent-wide survey in 1975 concluded that the *anatum* population was extirpated east of the Mississippi as well as in Idaho, Montana, and Wyoming and that only 47 occupied sites could be documented for the western United States. The tundra peregrine had regained slightly from its lowest levels in the early 1970s, but still less than 40 percent (69) of the known breeding sites (184) were occupied in the Alaskan and Canadian arctic, and only half of those pairs produced young.

## Current Trends

In 1983, the U.S. Fish and Wildlife Service (FWS) estimated that between 500 and 550 pairs of *anatum* peregrines existed in North America. Nesting pairs were distributed as follows: 125 pairs in Alaska, 30 to 40 pairs in Canada, 50 pairs along the West Coast, 53 pairs in the Rocky Mountain/Southwest region, 17 pairs in the East, and 175 possible, but mostly unconfirmed, pairs in Mexico (U.S. Fish and Wildlife Service 1983). The peregrines breeding in the East must be subtracted from these estimates, since they are not truly *anatum* (see below) and thus do not contribute to recovery of that subspecies. Although the figures of 75 pairs for Baja and the Gulf of California may be reasonable, the estimate of 100 pairs in the Mexican highlands is conjectural since only 20 to 30 pairs are known (Cade 1982). Thus, an overall population estimate of 400 to 425 pairs is conservative but probably more accurate than the FWS estimate.

Management efforts have sustained and expanded the populations in northern Alberta (Fyfe *et al* 1978), Colorado (Enderson *et al* 1982), and California (Cade 1984), but continued eggshell thinning in these regions are causes for concern. Reintroduction efforts are re-establishing the species in Idaho, Montana, and Wyoming (Cade and Dague 1985), but if experiences in Alberta and Colorado are any indication it is likely that these pairs also may accumulate levels of DDT high enough to affect reproduction. If so, these birds will require artificial augmentation. Recent surveys in the Colorado Plateau region of Utah (Cade 1984) have located previously undocumented pairs in that area, but the pairs must be monitored yearly in order to establish reproductive trends. Inconsistent and piecemeal investigations in Arizona suggest that a substantial population of up to 40 pairs may reside there, but occupancy rates, reproductive trends, and pesticide residue levels must be monitored before population status can be established. Reoccupancy of vacant territories is one of the indicators of population recovery, but this appears not to have occurred in either Arizona or New Mexico.

The Canadian Wildlife Service and provincial governments have undertaken captive propagation and release programs to re-establish the *anatum* subspecies in the northern Rocky Mountains of Alberta. Hacking efforts also have established pairs that are breeding successfully on building ledges in Edmonton and Montreal.

The tundra-peregrine population had recovered sufficiently by 1983 for FWS to "downlist" it to threatened status (U.S. Fish and Wildlife Service 1983). Sampling of pairs breeding along the various Alaskan rivers revealed nearly normal reproduction, and DDT levels in blood samples taken from migrating falcons trapped on the Gulf and Atlantic seaboards were reduced sufficiently for an estimated 90 percent of the falcons to reproduce normally. In addition, the numbers of migrant peregrines observed at census stations along the coasts had increased from .25 per hour in the early 1970s to .56 per hour in the mid-1970s. By 1981, sightings averaged 1.08 per hour.

Statistical study of peregrine data suggests that annual production reached 13,550 young from 1976 through 1981. If each wild breeding pair had an average production of 1.25 young (considered typical of a normally reproducing population) there would have to be at least 10,840 pairs to produce them. This is well over the 2,000 to 3,000 pairs estimated to exist historically (Cade 1982). Although several factors can affect the statistical method used to reach this population estimation, the results, even if imprecise, demonstrate that the tundra peregrine is not in any immediate danger of extinction (U.S. Fish and Wildlife Service 1984). Consequently, recovery efforts now concentrate primarily upon monitoring the status and reproduction of wild breeding peregrines (U.S. Fish and Wildlife Service 1983).

The Peale's peregrine population remains nearly unchanged since historic times. Its sedentary habits and preference for marine fowl seem to protect it from the impacts of DDT. Thickness measurements of a sample of Aleutian peregrine eggs yielded an average of eight percent thinning, apparently not sufficient to diminish hatch success (White *et al* 1973).

Although the release efforts in the East do not contribute to recovery of the *anatum* subspecies, it is appropriate to summarize the results of the program. Release efforts were first undertaken in 1975, when six young were hacked successfully (Barclay and Cade 1983). By 1985, more than 700 young had been released successfully, and 38 to 40 pairs were breeding in mountain as well as urban settings (Cade and Dague 1985). If the current rate of increase persists (the population doubles approximately every two years), the eastern goal of 150 reproducing pairs may be achieved by 1990 (Eastern Peregrine Falcon Recovery Team 1979).

# Management

Recovery plans have been developed for the Alaska populations (tundra- and tiaga-dwelling forms of the *anatum*) (Alaskan Peregrine Falcon Recovery Team 1982), the East (the extirpated eastern form of the *anatum*) (Eastern Peregrine Falcon Recovery Team 1979), the Rocky Mountain/Southwest *anatum* populations (Rocky mountain/Southeast Recovery Team 1977), and the West Coast *anatum* population (The Pacific Coast Recovery Team 1982). The plans were formulated by FWS-appointed teams of wildlife biologists from federal and state agencies as well as from private conservation groups. Once approved, the plans serve as guidelines for recovery actions to be implemented by wildlife conservation and land management agencies (Roter and Marshall 1975, Marshall 1978).

The Eastern recovery plan concentrates upon establishing a peregrine type to replace the extirpated eastern *anatum* subspecies. The recovery efforts for Rocky Mountain and Southwestern populations are directed toward reestablishing the subspecies in vacant regions, maintaining and expanding wild populations experiencing reproductive difficulties, and monitoring apparently stable populations in portions of Arizona, New Mexico, and southern Utah. The Pacific Coast and Alaska recovery plans likewise direct efforts toward maintaining existing wild pairs and restoring the population. Each of the plans recognizes the need to maintain suitable nesting and foraging habitats and encourages international efforts to curtail harmful pesticide use.

Expanding urbanization, water and energy development, and recreational activities continue to shrink important wildlife habitats. All the recovery plans emphasize the need to preserve the breeding sites and associated hunting habitats required to sustain the falcons and their young. Aside from direct disturbance or harrassment of breeding pairs, the greatest impacts are those that sufficiently alter the character of key hunting habitats so as to reduce the prey upon which the pair is dependent. Hunting forays of 18 miles and greater from the eyrie make it difficult to unequivocally document all critical foraging areas or prove that a particular amount of habitat loss will be tolerated before a site's occupancy is jeopardized. As a rule, recovery plans recommend protection of key hunting areas within 10 miles (Rocky Mountain/Southwestern Recovery Team 1977) and 15 miles (Alaskan Peregrine Falcon Recovery Team 1982) of the breeding site.

Captive propagation is an essential component of peregrine recovery efforts within Canada and the United States. In 1970 and 1971, two propagation projects were initiated almost simultaneously within both countries. The Canadian Wildlife Service established a propagation project directed primarily toward producing *anatum* peregrines for release in Alberta (Fyfe 1976). The U.S. project, the Peregrine Fund, was initially created at Cornell University to produce falcons for release in the East (Cade and Temple 1977). The program expanded into a western project devoted to production of *anatum* peregrines for release in the Rocky Mountain region. A West Coast operation was added to produce falcons for release in California, Washington, and Oregon. Peregrine Fund operations are partially funded with federal and state monies, but also receive substantial support from private grants and donations. Several private breeding projects have sprung up, but they are incapable of producing the appropriate gene pools in the quantities required for large-scale releases. A program at McGill University in Toronto has furnished small numbers of falcons for release by private interests along the upper Mississippi River.

Pioneering propagation efforts were motivated by falconers seeking ways to obtain stock for falconry. Although successes were few and productivity was inconsistent, the falconers provided an important nucleus of the breeding stock for the Peregrine Fund. Private breeders and falconers succeeded in amending the Endangered Species Act in 1978 to exclude from protection any peregrines held in captivity prior to 1978 as well as any progeny produced by the exempted falcons (U.S. Fish and Wildlife Service 1984). This permitted the sale of exempted falcons by falconers and others. The justification presented was that the Endangered Species Act impeded captive production by the private sector and that the amendment would result in a significant increase in falcons for release in the wild. The same argument also was used to justify a 1984 Migratory Bird Act amendment that permitted sale of captive-produced raptors (U.S. Fish and Wildlife Service 1983). To date, these amendments have not appreciably increased the number of peregrines available for release to the wild (Leape unpubl.). In fact, the few successful propagators often hybridize peregrines with other species and subspecies, rendering their stock unsuitable for release anywhere except in the East. The sale amendment has commercialized falconry, fostering suspicion and distrust of propagators and falconers.

Captive-produced peregrines are being re-established into vacant territories primarily through the technique of "hacking" (Sherrod *et al* 1981). This release technique evolved from a falconry method of conditioning fledglings so that they would be more effective hunters. Hacking involves confining in a large box (usually four feet high, four feet wide, and six feet long with wire and bars on one side) young that are nearly ready to fledge. The hack boxes may be placed on cliff ledges, towers, or buildings, wherever it is desirable to establish a pair of breeding falcons. The young are fed in the box by attendants for a week before release and become familiar with their surroundings. Upon the release, the fledglings should recognize their surroundings and return to the hack box for food and protection at night. The falcons are kept under surveillance by hack-site attendants until they are hunting successfully for themselves. This technique has established all the falcons currently breeding in the East and has re-established pairs at vacant sites in the Rocky Mountains and the West Coast.

Wild populations that have experienced pesticide-induced reproductive difficulties are supplemented with captive-produced young (Burnham *et al* 1978, Fyfe *et al* 1978). The terms for this activity are augmentation or fostering. Typically, plastic replicas replace the thin-shelled wild eggs, which are removed and artificially incubated. Prior to the expected hatch of the wild eggs, a brood of up to four captive-produced young are placed in the nest to be reared by the wild pair. This approach reduces the possibility of nest failure due to egg breakage or infertility and assures that the pair has the opportunity to fledge a maximum number of young. The improved hatch success of wild eggs through artificial incubation also assures that additional falcons are available for release to the wild. The technique of fostering has proved effective in bolstering wild production in Colorado (Burnham *et al* 1978, Enderson *et al* 1982), Alberta (Fyfe 1978), and California (Cade 1984) and may have to be implemented as a remedial measure at some sites where reintroduced falcons show pesticide-induced reproductive difficulties. Although it is depressing to consider, should the pesticide problem persist, wild breeding peregrines can be maintained in perpetuity by fostering captive-produced young to pairs experiencing eggshell-thinning difficulties. The alternative to this would be to maintain a captive colony in the hopes of re-establishing falcons in the wild at a future time when pesticides are no longer a threat. Such a captive colony risks severe gene-pool reduction along with a loss of the ability to adapt in the wild

(Seal 1978). Maintaining a captive colony should be considered the final step after all other actions fail.

Several attempts were made to release young peregrines by cross-fostering them to other wild raptors. The technique simply involves replacing the foster parents' brood with a brood of captive-produced peregrines (Fyfe 1978). Although the cross-fostering offered potential, hacking proved to be a more effective method of re-establishing peregrines. Efforts using prairie falcons as foster parents in Colorado and Idaho were discontinued because of unusually high nestling mortality. Biologists also feared that the young peregrines might imprint upon their foster parents and fail to seek peregrines as mates when they matured.

The extirpated eastern population of the *anatum* subspecies is being replaced through captive propagation and release of a conglomeration of peregrine subspecies, including falcons originating from North and South America, Australia, Scotland, and Spain (Barclay and Cade 1983). This approach is predicated on a belief, developed at a conference hosted by the National Audubon Society (Clement 1974), that the gene pool of the eastern *anatum* is extinct and that even if the birds were available, the habitat has been altered so drastically that they probably would not be able to survive. Hence, the biologists chose to release a variety of subspecies and let natural selection develop the appropriate form of peregrine.

Re-establishment of peregrines in the East and recovery of the tundra subspecies have had an unexpected side effect: as recovery occurs, administrators reason that the falcon is no longer in immediate jeopardy and redirect resources to species they perceive to be in greater danger of extinction. Hence, federal resources needed to maintain captive propagation and to provide assistance to the states have been reduced or withdrawn before the populations are secure, thus jeopardizing recovery efforts.

Illegal take of nestlings continues to be a problem that may increase as population recovery provides more opportunities. Despite vigorous surveillance by eyrie wardens, in 1981 nestlings and eggs were robbed from 47 eyries in Great Britain, and 84 additional nesting failures were attributed to the same cause. Thus, human robberies accounted for failure of 21 percent of the nesting attempts in the United Kingdom in a single year (Ratcliffe 1984). Every year, at least 50 eyries have been cleaned of nestlings or eggs (Cade unpubl. data).

A joint "sting" operation by FWS and the Canadian Wildlife Service in 1984 yielded controversial evidence that in excess of 100 *anatum* peregrines had been taken illegally from the wild from 1982 through 1984 (Leape unpubl. data). The methods and publicity given to the operation by FWS have been contested bitterly by the falconry community (Shor 1984), and arguments have been voiced that because the wild populations were increasing at the time, the illegal take was not an adverse impact (Cade unpubl. data). Regardless of the methods used to obtain the indictments, those indicted were aware that their actions were illegal. The National Audubon Society has asked Congress to remove a major legal loophole by repealing the 1978 Endangered Species Act Amendment that permitted falconers to keep endangered subspecies held in possession prior to 1978 (Leape unpubl. data). Regardless of the final outcome, wild peregrine populations can ill afford human-caused attrition at their current levels. Illegal take through nest robbing and trapping will continue to be a management problem that must be addressed through effective law enforcement and surveillance of vulnerable wild nests.

# Prognosis

Regardless of the successes with reintroduction and augmentation of wild pairs, the peregrine will continue to be threatened with extinction until deleterious chlorinated-hydrocarbon pesticides are removed from ecosystems occupied by the birds. It is possible that the ban on DDT use in the United States and Canada may have been responsible for the improved productivity of tundra peregrines. The ban also may account for preliminary evidence that eastern peregrines are producing eggshells of normal thickness. This would imply that the peregrines are feeding upon predominantly uncontaminated prey that either is nonmigratory or is not migrating into regions where deleterious pesticides are being applied. While the continued pesticide application in Latin America may not occur in regions frequented by the tundra peregrine's prey, it appears to have affected the prey of western-breeding peregrines, especially those intermountain-region peregrines that survived local pesticide application in North America.

Colonization of the tropics has increased the incidence of malaria and led to an increase in the application of DDT for public health as well as for agricultural purposes (Martin 1985). In 1984, Brazil alone applied more than 30,000 metric tons of DDT. Application will expand as the human population increases and the mosquitoes become more resistant to the pesticide. As DDT application programs shift, expand, and decline throughout North and South America, it will be impossible to predict which prey and which peregrine predators will be affected.

All is not darkness, however. Biologists have tackled a very difficult species and demonstrated that peregrines can be captively propagated in sufficient numbers to re-establish breeding pairs in vacant territories and sustain declining populations. It has been demonstrated in California, Colorado and Alberta that it is possible to sustain some wild populations in spite of poor natural reproduction. It also may be possible to induce some pairs to become sedentary and feed upon resident, noncontaminated prey, such as pigeons in metropolitan areas.

Finally, chlorinated-hyrdocarbon pesticides have been used for more than 40 years, and experience has shown that these poisons have serious side effects upon beneficial, nontarget organisms and become less effective upon subsequent applications. It is inevitable that more economically and ecologically sound substitutes will come on the market. The problem will be to maintain peregrines as well as other affected bird life until that occurs.

# Recommendations

It is critical to document the sources and extent of chlorinated-hydrocarbon pesticide application within the United States and Central and South America. Recent evidence indicates that kelthane, a compound regularly applied to citrus and cotton crops in the United States, may be a significant source of DDT. Indirect evidence also indicates that DDT is being smuggled from Mexico and applied in the Southwest. Sources of the chemical within the United States must be eliminated first, then vigorous negotiations must take place with our neighbors to alert them to the harm DDT causes within their own countries.

Inevitably, important nesting and hunting habitats will be lost as land development expands. When this occurs, it is important to document and quantify the impacts upon the resident peregrines. The resulting information will assist in developing mitigative measures for similar actions proposed elsewhere.

Recovery efforts have been under way in some localities for more than a decade, and significant progress has been made. The activities have varied among the states, sometimes without regard to the priorities recommended in the recovery plans. It is time to evaluate progress toward recovery goals on a regional, national, and international basis. Are the recovery plans still pertinent? If so, are recovery plans being followed by FWS when prioritizing annual funding allocations? As various populations expand and more states become involved with peregrines, it is important that standardized monitoring programs be implemented so that data is comparable. Although periodic sampling of potential prey for evidence of pesticide contamination may yield a general idea of contaminant levels in the falcon's environment, the only reliable method of determining impacts of pesticides upon breeding peregrines is to monitor eggshell-thinning changes.

The eastern peregrine recovery plan is philosophically controversial. It is a noble plan to re-establish a peregrine type to replace the extinct *anatum* population, but is it truly directed toward recovery of an endangered species? This was a topic of much discussion and debate when the eastern recovery team first tackled the problem, and the controversy has persisted to the present. The administrators finally accepted arguments that the work qualified for funding under the Endangered Species Act. If the re-creation philosophy is accepted as justifiable endangered species action, what priority is it? With limited funding available, should the program be given a priority lower than that of programs devoted to sustaining and recovering endangered populations that still exist in the wild state? After all, creation of an eastern *anatum* has no urgency. The eastern release activities are an important breakthrough in nongame wildlife management and should be continued through to the logical conclusion. However, they should be funded from other sources and not compete for limited federal funding for endangered species.

Despite the tundra peregrine's extended ecosystem, stretching from the arctic to the tropics, the subspecies remains highly vulnerable to activities throughout its range. Rapid changes in the South American wintering areas may have profound effects. It is obvious that counting migrant peregrines on the Gulf and Atlantic beaches is far too imprecise a method of monitoring distant arctic subpopulations. Hence, it is important that arctic breeding inventories be expanded in order to document breeding areas and develop sampling schemes to monitor reproduction yearly and document contaminant levels in the eggs.

# References

Alaskan Peregrine Falcon Recovery Team. 1982. *Recovery Plan for the Peregrine Falcon—Alaska Population* (Falco peregrinus tundrius and F.p. anatum). U.S. Fish and Wildlife Service. Anchorage, Alaska.

Anderson, D.W. and J.J. Hickey. 1972. "Eggshell changes in certain North American birds." *Proceedings of the International Ornithological Congress* 15:514-540.

Barclay, J.H. and T.J. Cade. 1983. "Restoration of the Peregrine Falcon in the Eastern United States." *Bird Conservation* 1:3-39.

Berger, D.D. and H.C. Mueller. 1969. "Ospreys in Northern Wisconsin," *in* J.J. Hickey ed., *Peregrine Falcon Populations: Their Biology and Decline*. University of Wisconsin Press. Madison, Wisconsin. pp. 340-341.

Berger, D.D., C.R. Sindelar, Jr., and K.E. Gamble. 1969. "The status of breeding peregrines in the eastern United States," *in* J.J. Hickey ed., *Peregrine Falcon Populations: Their Biology and Decline*. University of Wisconsin Press. Madison, Wisconsin. pp. 165-173.

Brown, L. and D. Amadon. 1968. *Eagles, Hawks and Falcons of the World*. McGraw Hill. New York, New York. 945 pp.

Burnham, W.A., G.R. Craig, J.H. Enderson, and W.R. Heinrich. 1978. "Artificial increase in reproduction of wild peregrine falcons." *Journal of Wildlife Management* 42(3):625-628.

Cade, T.J., J.L. Lincer, C.M. White, D.G. Roseneau, and L.G. Swartz. 1971. "DDE residues and eggshell changes in Alaskan falcons and hawks." *Science* 172:955-957.

Cade, T.J. and S.A. Temple. 1977. "The Cornell University falcon programme," *in* R.D. Chancellor ed., *Report on Proceedings, World Conference on Birds of Prey, Vienna 1975*. Taylor and Francis, Ltd. Great Britain. pp. 353-369.

Cade, T.J. 1982. *The Falcons of the World.* Cornell University Press. Ithaca, New York. 192 pp.

Cade, T.J. 1984. *The Peregrine Fund Newsletter.* Ithaca, New York. (Fall).

Cade, T.J. and P.R. Dague. 1985. *The Peregrine Fund Special Spring Report.* (Spring).

Cade, T.J. 1985. Statement of Dr. Tom J. Cade, before the House Committee on Merchant Marine and Fisheries, Subcommittee on Fisheries and Wildlife Conservation, on reauthorization of the Endangered Species Act and the raptor exemption. Unpublished. 7 pp.

Clement, R.C. 1974. "Proceedings of a conference on peregrine falcon recovery." *Audubon Society Conservation Report* No. 4. National Audubon Society. New York, New York.

Dunlop, T.R. 1981. *DDT: Scientists, Citizens and Public Policy.* Princeton University Press. Princeton, New Jersey.

Eastern Peregrine Falcon Recovery Team. 1979. *Peregrine Falcon Recovery Plan—Eastern Population.* U.S. Fish and Wildlife Service. Newton Corner, Massachusetts. 147 pp.

Enderson, J.H. 1969. "Peregrine and prairie falcon life tables based upon band-recovery data," *in* J.J. Hickey ed., *Peregrine Falcon Populations: Their Biology and Decline.* University of Wisconsin Press. Madison, Wisconsin. pp. 505-509.

Enderson, J.H., G.R. Craig, W.A. Burnham, and D.D Berger. "Eggshell thinning and organo-chlorine residues in Rocky Mountain peregrines (*Falco peregrinius*) and their prey." *Canadian Field-Naturalist* 96(3):255-264.

Fyfe, R.W., S.A. Temple, and T.J. Cade. 1976. "The 1975 North American peregrine falcon survey." *Canadian Field-Naturalist* 90(3):28-273.

Fyfe, R.W. 1976. "Rationale and success of the Canadian Wildlife Service peregrine breeding project." *Canadian Field-Naturalist* 90(3):308-319.

Fyfe, R.W., H. Armbruster, U. Banasch, and L.J. Beaver. 1978. "Fostering and cross-fostering of birds of prey," *in* S.A. Temple ed., *Endangered Birds: Management Techniques for Preserving Threatened Species.* University of Wisconsin Press. Madison, Wisconsin. pp. 183-193.

Heath, R.G., J.W. Spann, and J.F. Kreitzer. 1969. "Marked DDE impairment of mallard reproduction in controlled studies." *Nature* 224:47-48.

Hickey, J.J. 1942. "Eastern population of the duck hawk." *The Auk* 59(2):174-204.

Hickey, J.J. 1969. *Peregrine Falcon Populations: Their Biology and Decline.* University of Wisconsin Press. Madison, Wisconsin.

Leape, J.P. 1985. Statement of the National Audubon Society on the raptor exemption H.R. 2767 before the Subcommittee on Fish and Wildlife of the House Committee on Merchant Marine and Fisheries. Unpublished. 18 pp.

Lewin, R. 1985. "Why are male hawks so small?" *Science* 28(June):1299-1300.

Lincer, J.L. 1975. "DDE-induced eggshell thinning in the American kestrels: a comparison of field and laboratory results." *Journal of Applied Ecology* 12:781-794.

Marshall, D.B. 1978. "The recovery plan approach to endangered species restoration in the United States," *in* S.A. Temple ed., *Endangered Birds: Management Techniques for Preserving Threatened Species.* University of Wisconsin Press. Madison, Wisconsin. pp. 429-434.

Martin, E.G. 1985. "Resurgent use of DDT in world's malaria war is worrying ecologists." *Wall Street Journal* (May).

Peakall, D.B., J.L. Lincer, R.W. Risebrough, J.B. Pritchard, and W.B. Kinter. 1973. "DDE-induced eggshell thinning: structural and physiological effects in three species." *Comparative General Pharmacology* 4:305-315.

Peakall, D.B., T.J. Cade, C.M. White, and J.R. Haugh. 1975. "Organo-chlorine residues in Alaskan Peregrines." *Pesticides Monitoring Journal* 8:225-260.

Peterson, R.T. 1969. "Population trends of ospreys in the northeastern United States," *in* J.J. Hickey ed., *Peregrine Falcon Populations: Their Biology and Decline.* University of Wisconsin Press. Madison, Wisconsin. pp. 333-337.

Porter, R.D., C.M. White, and R.J. Erwin. 1973. "The peregrine falcon in Utah, emphasizing ecology and competition with the prairie falcon." *Brigham Young University Science Bulletin of Biological Serials* 18(1):1-74.

Porter, R.D. and D.B. Marshall. 1977. "The recovery team approach to restoration of endangered species," *in* R.D. Chancellor ed., *World Conference on Birds of Prey: Held in Vienna, 1975.* Taylor and Francis Ltd. Great Britain. pp. 314-319.

Postupalsky, S. 1969. "The status of the osprey in Michigan in 1965," *in* J.J. Hickey ed., *Peregrine Falcon Populations: Their Biology and Decline.* University of Wisconsin Press. Madison, Wisconsin. pp. 338-340.

Ratcliffe, D.A. 1963. "The status of the peregrine in Great Britain." *Bird Study* 10:56-90.

Ratcliffe, D.A. 1980. *The Peregrine Falcon.* Buteo Books. Vermillion, South Dakota. 416 pp.

Ratcliffe, D.A. 1984. "The peregrine breeding population of the United Kingdom in 1981." *Bird Study* 31(1):1-18.

Roalkvam, R. 1985. "How effective are hunting peregrines?" *Raptor Research* 19(1):27-29.

Rocky Mountain/Southwestern Recovery Team. 1977. *American Peregrine Recovery Plan (Rocky Mountain Southwest Populations).* U.S. Fish and Wildlife Service. Denver, Colorado. 183 pp.

Seal, U.S. 1978. "The Noah's ark problem: multigeneration management of wild species in captivity," *in* S.A. Temple ed., *Endangered Birds: Management Techniques for Preserving Threatened Species.* University of Wisconsin Press. Madison, Wisconsin. pp. 303-313.

Sherrod, S.K., W.R. Heinrich, W.A. Burnham, J.H. Barclay, and T.J. Cade. 1981. *Hacking: A Method for Releasing Peregrine Falcons and Other Birds of Prey.* The Peregrine Fund. 61 pp.

Sherrod, S.K. 1983. *Behavior of Fledgling Peregrines.* The Peregrine Fund, Inc. p. 202.

Shor, W. 1984. "Operation falcon." *Hawk Chalk* 23(2):25-50.

Sprunt, A. IV. 1969. "Population trends of the bald eagle in North America," *in* J.J. Hickey ed., *Peregrine Falcon Populations: Their Biology and Decline*. University of Wisconsin Press. Madison, Wisconsin. pp. 347-351.

Stickel, W.H. 1969. "Ospreys in the Chesapeake Bay area," *in* J.J. Hickey ed., *Peregrine Falcon Populations: Their Biology and Decline*. University of Wisconsin Press. Madison, Wisconsin. p. 337.

The Pacific Coast Recovery Team. 1982. *Pacific Coast Recovery Plan for the American Peregrine Falcon*. U.S. Fish and Wildlife Service. Portland, Oregon.

U.S. Fish and Wildlife Service. 1983. "Implementation of the Endangered Species Act exemption for certain raptors; raptor propagation permits; federal falconry standards final rule." *Federal Register* 48(32):31600-31610.

U.S. Fish and Wildlife Service. 1983. "Proposed reclassification of the peregrine falcons in North America." *Federal Register* 48(41):8796-8802.

U.S. Fish and Wildlife Service. 1984. "Endangered and threatened wildlife and plants; reclassification of the Arctic peregrine falcon in the coterminous United States." *Federal Register* 49(55):10520-10526.

Weimeyer, S.E. and R.D. Porter. 1970. "DDE thins eggshells of captive American kestrels." *Nature* 227:737.

White, C.M. 1968. "Diagnosis and relationship of the North American tundra-inhabiting peregrine falcons." *The Auk* 85(2):179-191.

White, C.M, W.B. Emison, and F.S.L. Williamson. 1973. "DDE in the resident Aleutian Island peregrine population." *Condor* 75(3):306-311.

*Gerald Craig, a raptor specialist with the Colorado Division of Wildlife since 1972, monitors peregrine falcon reproduction, pesticide levels, and brood occupancy.*

Hooded warblers bring food to nestlings in Ohio. The hooded warbler may soon face extirpation as a result of rapid deforestation in its Central American wintering ground.

*Ron Austing/Photo Researchers*

# The Hooded Warbler

## George V.N. Powell
National Audubon Society

## and
## John H. Rappole
Caesar Kleberg Wildlife Research Institute

## Species Description and Natural History

Hooded WARBLERS (*Wilsonia citrina*) are sexually dimorphic. The adult male is easily recognized by the presence of a solid black hood that covers the back of the head, neck, throat, and upper breast. The remainder of the head and underparts are bright yellow. The back, wings, and tail are olive green. Aside from the hood, the only distinctive markings are large white spots on the inner webs of the outer tail feathers. Unlike many warbler species, the male hooded warbler retains its breeding coloration throughout the winter months. The coloration of females is similar to that of the males, but duller and lacking all but a hint of the black hood and tail spots (Terres 1980).

### Range

The breeding range of the hooded warbler is restricted primarily to the eastern United States, with localized populations breeding just west of the Mississippi River and in eastern Texas (Bent 1963, Oberholser 1974). The northern limit extends from Illinois across central New York and casually into southern New England. The southern limit includes northern Florida and the Gulf states.

On the breeding range, hooded warblers occupy mature deciduous forests that contain well-developed understories. They are particularly attracted to damp areas formed by seeps, streams, or swamps. In the forest they restrict themselves primarily to the understory and rarely move more than 15 feet above ground while foraging. Males, however, do make use of tree-top song perches early in the breeding season.

Species that depend on mature forest, as do hooded warblers, are categorized as forest-interior species (Whitcomb *et al* 1976). They avoid second growth and edge habitats and must have relatively large tracts of uninterrupted forest for breeding. Forest-interior species tend to disappear from forests that become fragmented even though the fragments are larger than several breeding territories (Bond 1957, Moore and Hooper 1975). Based on breeding-bird data from Maryland, Robbins (1979) calculated that 50 acres was the minimum forest area required to sustain populations of hooded warblers. However, he suspected this number erred on the low side because of the rarity of hooded warblers on his study sites. Most of the other 15 forest-interior species on his study sites required 250 acres for maximum population density. In the Washington D.C. area, hooded warblers became extinct in forest fragments that were up to 1,200 acres (Briggs and Criswell 1978, Robbins 1979).

As yet, the warbler's need for large areas of forest has not been explained fully. One possibility is that forest fragmentation may give nest predators greater access to the forest interior. According to this hypothesis, the resultant

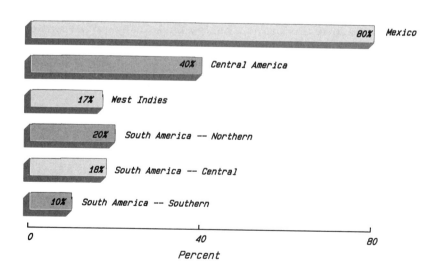

Distribution of Forest Migrants Wintering In the Neotropics. Wide-ranging Species are Represented in more than a Single Region.

80% Mexico
40% Central America
17% West Indies
20% South America -- Northern
18% South America -- Central
10% South America -- Southern

Percent

decline in breeding success leads returning migrants to avoid fragmented areas. An alternative explanation is that migrants returning from the tropics fail to discover isolated forest fragments, so the fragments remain unoccupied (Whitcomb *et al* 1981).

The hooded warbler's winter range extends from southern Veracruz and the Yucatan Peninsula of Mexico south to southern Coast Rica and (rarely) into western Panama (Rappole *et al* 1983). The winter ranges of 99 species of forest migrants from North America are concentrated in Mexico, Central America, and the Caribbean Islands. Only 53 species range as far as South America, excluding Panama, combined here with Central America. Of these, only 19 species have wintering distributions centered in South America (Rappole *et al* 1983). The vast Amazon Basin is unexploited by most North American migrants.

The warblers (Parulinae) clearly demonstrate the concentration of winter ranges in southern Mexico. Twenty-nine of 43 migrant warblers include southern Mexico in their winter range, while only six species winter primarily

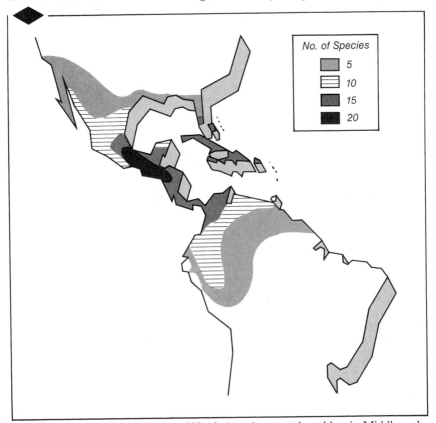

Winter distribution of 43 species of North American wood warblers in Middle and South American forest habitats. See table for species.

in South America. As a result of their concentration in the relatively small area of Middle America, and particularly southern Mexico, forest migrants of all species become a major component of the avifauna in those areas. They average 30 percent of the total avifauna at seven sites in Mexico, 12 percent at eight locations in Central America, and one to 30 percent (averaged by island) at 28 locations in the Antilles, but only seven percent at four sites in South America (summarized by Rappole *et al* 1983: 9-10, Terborgh and Faaborg 1980).

## Breeding

Hooded warblers are monogamous during the breeding season. Pairs defend a territory that includes both the nest site and feeding area. Territories range from one and a half to more than five acres per pair (Stewart and Robinson 1958). When successful, pairs usually are single brooded, but a pair will make multiple attempts if necessary to produce a successful nest.

The female constructs a compact nest made of woven plant fibers with a fine grass lining. Nests generally are located one to five feet above the ground. The three to four eggs are incubated by both sexes (Odum 1931). After 12 days the young hatch virtually naked, but within eight days are fully feathered and ready to leave the nest. After fledging they remain with the adults for several weeks, following them through the forest begging noisily.

## Migration

Hooded warblers, along with most neotropical migrants, leave the United States in early fall. Virtually all are gone by October. They follow a trans-Gulf route in fall and a more westerly route north over the western Gulf of Mexico and coastal plain of Mexico and Texas in spring (Rappole *et al* 1979). Habitat use during migration has not been well studied, but migrants probably have specific requirements for forested areas during stopovers. At these sites, they feed intensively to rebuild fat reserves before continuing their journeys (Rappole and Warner 1976).

The habitat requirements of hooded warblers and forest migrants in general on their wintering grounds are poorly understood. Until recently, migrants were considered essentially as invaders from the north that were not as well adapted for tropical habitats as were permanent residents. Because they were outcompeted by permanent tropical residents at food concentrations (Willis 1966, Leck 1972), wintering migrants were thought to be excluded from primary habitats and forced into second growth, isolated scrub, or forest edges. Newer studies of interactions between migrants and permanent tropical residents (Chipley 1976, Barlow 1980) and between migrants and their habitats (Bennett 1980, Rabenold 1980, Stiles 1980) have tended to disprove this hypothesis. Migrants are now recognized as an integral part of the neotropical ecosystem. Furthermore, recent studies indicate that wintering migrants have specific needs in tropical habitat just as they do in northern forests during the breeding season. While these habitat requirements remain largely unidentified, their existence is indicated by the ecological separation of migrant species (Fitzpatrick 1980, Keast 1980) by such factors as geography, elevation (highland vs. lowland), habitat type (broad-leafed vs. coniferous, dry vs. wet, seasonal vs. aseasonal), seral stage (second growth vs. mature), diet (fugivory, insectivory, or gramnivory), and foraging guild (flycatcher, foliage gleaner, etc.).

Hooded warblers are restricted to areas below 3,000 feet in mature broad-leafed forests with well-developed understories or older second growth (Wetmore 1943). Lynch *et al* (1985) have shown that wintering hooded warblers are segregated by habitat type, with males occupying more mature forests than females. Their data suggests that females are excluded from the more mature stands into less preferred habitat with second-growth features. Hooded

Percent of forest-bird species that migrate to Middle or South America for winter. Numbers indicate locations of long-term studies that have shown significant declines in neotropical migrant populations. (1) Ambuel and Temple 1982; (2) Serrao and Smiley 1982; (3) Leck *et al.* 1981; (4) Hall 1984; (5) Wilcove and Whitcomb 1983. At these locations, forest areas remained constant and migrant declines were attributed primarily to destruction of winter habitat.

warblers feed primarily in the understory and make short, hawking flights either to capture flying insects or to glean them from the vegetation. Individuals will take advantage of army ant swarms, capturing insects that are fleeing from the swarms (Willis 1966).

A long-standing question regarding winter-habitat use by migrant birds is whether species such as the hooded warbler require primary, undisturbed forest or whether second growth, scrub, or forest edges actually are better habitats. To help determine migrant sensitivity to forest disturbance, Rappole and Morton (1985) quantified migrant distributions on a study area in southern Mexico before and after partial logging and clearing. They found that the number of hooded warblers using the study area decreased after the disturbance. Other migrants categorized as mature-forest species also showed significant declines, indicating that mature forest species are, in fact, dependent on relatively undisturbed forest.

Many migrant species, including hooded warblers, are territorial on the wintering ground (Schwartz 1964, Rappole and Warner 1980, Powell unpublished data). Hooded warblers establish territories upon arriving and maintain

Number of forest migrants captured in mist nests before and after a forested study area in Veracruz, Mexico, was disturbed by logging and partial clearing (Taken from Rappole & Morton 1985). Figures adjusted for equal net hours.

| Species | Pre-disturbance (1973-4 & 1974-5) | Post-disturbance (1980 & 1981) |
|---|---|---|
| Sharp-skinned Hawk | 0 | 0.9 |
| Yellow-bellied Flycatcher* | 8.0 | 12.0 |
| Least Flycatcher* | 2.5 | 4.6 |
| Swainsons's Thrush* | 1.0 | 0 |
| Hermit Thrush* | 0.5 | 0 |
| Wood Thrush* | 45.0 | 18.0 |
| Gray Catbird | 6.5 | 4.6 |
| White-eyed Vireo | 8.0 | 5.5 |
| Yellow Warbler | 0.5 | 0.9 |
| Magnolia Warbler* | 10.5 | 4.6 |
| Yellow-rumped Warbler | 0 | 4.6 |
| Black-and-white Warbler* | 10.0 | 0 |
| American Redstart | 0.5 | 5.5 |
| Worm-eating Warbler* | 8.5 | 0.9 |
| Ovenbird* | 1.0 | 3.7 |
| Northern Waterthrush* | 1.0 | 3.7 |
| Louisiana Waterthrush* | 3.0 | 0.9 |
| Kentucky Warbler* | 22.5 | 15.7 |
| Hooded Warbler* | 22.5 | 17.5 |
| Wilson's Warbler | 12.0 | 15.7 |
| Summer Tanager* | 0 | 2.9 |

* Mature forest species

them throughout the winter months. Males and females establish separate territories and defend them against all conspecific trespassers regardless of sex. Methods of territorial defense include call notes, agonistic displays, and chasing. Intruders that fail to retreat are physically attacked and driven off. At one site in Mexico, territories were about 0.7 acres (Rappole and Warner 1980). Limited data from banding studies indicate that migrants return to the same territories year after year (Schwartz 1964, Loftin *et al* 1966, Nickell 1968, Rappole and Warner 1980, Robbins pers. commun.). Current studies with radio-telemetered wood thrushes (*Hylocichla mustelina*), a mature-forest species, are revealing that, on the wintering ground, individuals that establish territories in mature forest are more sedentary and have a significantly lower mortality rate than individuals that are unable to establish territories. Individuals without territories, called floaters, tend to occupy second growth and edge habitats (Winker and Rappole unpublished data).

## Significance of the Species

Taken as an individual species, it is difficult to attach a high level of either ecological or human importance to the hooded warbler. Aside from its aesthetic value as one of the more visually and acoustically pleasing species in eastern deciduous forests, it seems unlikely that this species performs any irreplaceable function for humans. Considered alone, its loss or rarefaction is not likely to elicit much reaction from the human community. Perhaps a valid analogy to the loss of hooded warblers is the virtual extinction of Bachman's warbler, another parulid warbler of the eastern United States. The Bachman's warbler (*Vermivora bachmanii*) has disappeared from forests of the southeast during this century without demonstrable impact on the forest ecosystem, and most people are not even aware of its demise.

While loss of the hooded warbler as a single species would likely pass without major repercussions, its decline as part of a general disappearance of neotropical forest migrants is extremely significant. The potential loss or major decline in populations of upwards of 90 or 100 species of North American songbirds undoubtedly will have major consequences. These species include many of the prettiest and most sought after birds, such as hummingbirds, warblers, and tanagers. The 50 million people in the United States with a professed interest in birding (U.S. Department of the Interior 1977, Keller 1980) would be directly affected by the rarefaction of these species.

A second major avenue by which forest migrants may contribute directly to human well being is through their impact on insect pests. Quantitative data are insufficient to assess the importance of forest migrants to insect pest control (Plunkett 1979). Perhaps the clearest example of forest migrants attacking a pest is that of the bay-breasted (*Dendroica castanea*), blackburnian (*D. Fusca*), and Tennessee warblers (*Vermivora peregrina*), species that concentrate at spruce budworm outbreaks (Kendeigh 1947). Even in this case, however, their role in actually controlling the outbreak is debatable (Morris *et al* 1958). That forest birds have an impact on pest species is certain, but attaching a specific value to this function is not possible at present.

A final function of forest migrants as benefactors to mankind is through their potential role as indicator species. The importance of forest migrants as indicators will be derived from the link that they provide between the developed nations centered in temperate habitats and the developing nations of the tropical habitats. While most of the developed nations have evolved fairly stringent policies against internal environmental degradation, they still maintain a largely laissez-faire attitude toward environmental destruction in areas outside their borders. As a result, the developed nations are party to the drastically accelerating destruction of tropical forests and the movement by mankind toward what may well become the greatest man-induced disaster of all time (Myers 1979).

The dimensions of this approaching disaster are still being elucidated, particularly with respect to potential impacts on the global environment brought about by elevated world temperatures (Bolin 1977, Sagan *et al* 1979, Lovejoy 1981, Emanuel *et al* 1984, Henderson-Sellers and Gornitz 1984, Hobbie *et al* 1984, Schneider 1984). However, there is no argument over the predicted loss in genetic diversity and its cost to mankind in terms of access to future commercial and medical products (Gomez-Pompa *et al* 1972, Myers 1979, Ehrlich 1981, *The Global 2000 Report* 1980, Wilson 1982, Iltis 1983, Caufield 1985). While the costs of tropical habitat destruction are recognized, the lack of tangible impacts within the developed nations has resulted in relative inaction in regard to mitigating the problem. Migrants that depend on tropical forests for their survival may serve to bring visual results of tropical deforestation to the United States. Publicizing declines of up to a third of United States avifauna may well do more to stimulate an outcry and subsequent actions against tropical deforestation than the far more serious, but more removed, predictions of global disaster. As Talbot (1980) states, "It seems to be virtually a law of nature that people are not moved to action until they see a problem clearly with their own eyes."

# Historical Perspective

When Europeans first reached America, the status of habitats used by neotropical migrants was at two extremes. Breeding-ground habitats were virtually pristine, while wintering grounds in Central America were heavily modified by agriculture.

At the onset of the 16th century, migrant breeding grounds in the future United States consisted of more than a billion acres of mostly undisturbed

Forest Area in the United States by Region (in thousand of acres).

| Region | Pre-Colonial[A] | 1872[B] | 1920[A] | 1930[A] | 1945[C] | 1953[C] | 1963[C] | 1970[C] | 1977[D] |
|---|---|---|---|---|---|---|---|---|---|
| New England[1] | 38,908 | 17,415 | 25,708 | 27,273 | 31,092 | 31,378 | 31,886 | 33,411 | 32,460 |
| Mid-Atlantic[2] | 69,610 | 24,406 | 28,678 | 27,139 | 34,260 | 34,987 | 35,177 | 41,024 | 39,017 |
| Central[3] | 170,560 | 80,967 | 60,182 | 64,249 | 69,271 | 68,431 | 70,073 | 71,236 | 67,700 |
| South[4] | 298,640 | 203,591 | 177,865 | 190,758 | 174,631 | 184,707 | 206,397 | 198,749 | 193,715 |
| Lakes[5] | 104,320 | 29,186 | 57,100 | 55,895 | 55,700 | 55,201 | 54,334 | 53,960 | 50,887 |
| West[6] | 340,830 | 95,509 | 129,584 | 140,840 | 225,271 | 241,561 | 239,652 | 240,386 | 230,889 |
| TOTAL USA | 1,022,000 | 451,108 | 479,117 | 505,898 | 590,225 | 616,265 | 637,519 | 657,182 | 617,414 |

[A]U.S. Dept. of Commerce 1924, 1935
[B]Agricultural Report 1872
[C]U.S. Bureau of the Census 1950, 1962, 1965, 1976
[D]U.S. Dept. of Agriculture 1982

[1]Maine, New Hampshire, Vermont, Massachusetts, Rhode Island, and Connecticut
[2]New York, New Jersey, Pennsylvania, Delaware, and Maryland
[3]Ohio, Indiana, Illinois, West Virginia, Kentucky, Tennessee, Iowa, Missouri, e. Kansas and e. Nebraska
[4]Virginia, North Carolina, South Carolina, Georgia, Florida, Alabama, Mississippi, Arkansas, Louisiana, e. Texas, and e. Oklahoma
[5]Michigan, Wisconsin, and Minnesota
[6]Idaho, Montana, Wyoming, Colorado, w. South Dakota, New Mexico, Arizona, Utah, Nevada, California, Oregon and Washington

forest habitat (Farb 1961). For the next 200 years these forests remained largely intact except for relatively localized deforestation on the eastern seaboard. By the 1800s, man was making major inroads into eastern forests, and by the 1860s alarm was was being raised about the possibility that America would soon run out of forest products (Marsh 1864, Starr 1865, Lapham *et al* 1867). Widespread concern sparked the federal government to make its first nationwide survey of American forests (Agricultural Report 1872). This study revealed that more than half of the U.S. forests were gone, and much that remained existed as small woodlots. Concern over the rate of forest destruction gave rise to the National Forest System and marked the beginning of a return of forests (Trefethen 1976, Williams 1983).

While no analysis of the status of hooded warblers in particular or forest migrants in general was recorded for the mid-1800s, they very likely suffered major population declines in conjuction with the loss of forest habitat. At that time, America was losing its most abundant forest bird, the passenger pigeon (*Ectopistes migratorius*), and the wild turkey (*Meleagris gallopavo*) was being extirpated from many parts of its range. Loss of forest habitat may have played a major role in decline of these species (Schorger 1955, Aldrich 1967).

Forest habitat in the United States reached its low point sometime between the 1870s and 1920s. By 1920, when the next survey of forests was made, considerable recovery had occurred (Farb 1961). From that time until at least the 1970s the amount of forest habitat in the United States has continued to increase (U.S. Department of Commerce 1935, 1965, 1976, U.S. Census Bureau 1950, 1962). In the New England, Mid-Atlantic, and Western regions, forest habitat has almost doubled since the late 1800s. The midwestern farm belt and the South have shown close to a 15-percent increase in forest coverage.

For forest migrants, regrowth of eastern forests is more significant than is indicated by these figures. In the late 1800s, when forest coverage was at its lowest point, a greater percentage of the forested land existed as small woodlots than is the case today. For example, farm woodlots accounted for 60 percent of forest in 1872, but currently account for only 40 percent (Agricultural Report 1872, U.S. Department of Agriculture 1958). Farm woodlots tend to be small and therefore less attractive as breeding sites for hooded warblers and other forest interior species. In contrast, forests outside of farms tend to be larger (U.S. Department of Agriculture 1958) and of greater value to forest species.

Not all of the regrowth of forest land has been beneficial to forest birds. In some areas, particularly the South, much of the regrowth of forest includes forest plantations, which are less valuable to forest migrants. However, the increase in total forest acreage and particularly the increase in larger forest tracts following the turn of the century probably allowed a resurgence of forest interior species on the breeding grounds.

This resurgence may now be threatened by the growth of a relatively new application for forested sites, i.e., second-home development. The use of forested sites for second homes has grown dramatically in the last decade, and a decline in forested areas in the eastern United States between 1970 and 1977 may reflect this change (Ragatz 1969). If the move for second homes continues, the loss of forest habitat could once again become a serious threat to forest migrants.

The historical record for hooded warbler winter habitat follows a markedly different pattern from that found on the breeding grounds. Europeans arriving in Middle America encountered major civilizations with a combined population estimated at more than 40 million people (Cook and Borah 1971, Woodward 1985). The agricultural backbone of the Mayan and Aztec cultures was a combination of permanent agriculture in major population centers and shifting slash-and-burn cultivation in less densely populated areas (Culbert 1974). No statistics exist to show the forest or agricultural acreages in 1500, but historical evidence indicates that the clearing was fairly extensive (Gordon 1957, Sauer 1966, Bennett 1968, Parsons 1975, Culbert 1985) and would have affected wintering migrant populations. However, the nature of the slash-and-burn agricultural practices used outside the major population centers would have mitigated to some extent the impacts of deforestation because clearings were small and temporary. The cycle consisted of clearing, cropping, and then abandoning sites that regenerated to forest. The resulting second growth returned to productive habitat for wintering migrants. Furthermore, clearings were situated to avoid poor soils and rugged topography, leaving large areas of mountainous regions undisturbed.

Percent of Original Forest Coverage Present in the United States and Middle America Since 1500

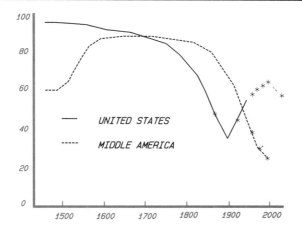

Sources of data points for the U.S. are given in Table 3.
Data points for Middle America are from FAO (1947, 1956).
For periods where no data were available, X forest was
estimated on the basis of human population and its
expected impact on forest coverage (see text for details).

Following European contact with Middle America, the intensity of land use changed markedly. Diseases that accompanied the Europeans quickly decimated native populations, reducing them by as much as 95 percent. The result was large scale abandonment of agricultural lands and regeneration of forests throughout much of Middle America (Bennett 1968, Denevan 1976, Parsons 1975, Boucher *et al* 1983). Slash-and-burn continued to be the dominant agricultural practice, but at a much reduced intensity. The overall decline in human population and the subsequent forest regeneration that quickly followed the European arrival would have increased habitat availability greatly for most forest migrants, including the hooded warbler. Deforestation probably did not become a serious widespread threat to migrant habitats in Middle America until the 1900s, since Middle American populations probably did not return to pre-Columbian levels until as late as 1930. Figures on forest coverage are non-existent for Middle America before 1940 and then only partial coverage is available until 1950. At that time 60 percent of the area already had been deforested. Thirty percent of the forest remaining in 1950 was removed by 1982 (Food and Agricultural Organization 1947, 1956).

## Current Trends

In southern Mexico, the principal wintering ground for hooded warblers and many other tropical migrants, deforestation is rapidly translating into a complete loss of lowland rainforest.

Perhaps even more important than the absolute decline in forest is the fact that much of the forest destruction, particularly in the last three decades, has been to allow for the introduction of cash crops grown for export. Most significant of these export crops is beef. Cattle ranching has grown to be a major factor in the rate of deforestation in Middle America (Myers 1980). The number of head has reached 56 million, more than double 1940 production. Cattle ranching is particularly detrimental to forest migrants because it requires permanent pasture. The production of pasture for cattle has interrupted the cyclical pattern of slash-and-burn agriculture. Once forests are removed and replaced with pastures, they tend to remain as pastures indefinitely. Furthermore, pastures generally are maintained through annual burning. Hedgerows, remnants of forest, and scrub adjacent to pastures also tend to burn because little effort is made to contain the fires. Consequently, the pastures are constantly expanding at the expense of even second-growth migrant habitat.

The rapid decline in forest habitat that Middle America currently is experiencing, coupled with the shift in land-use patterns to a focus on export crops, particularly cattle, can only result in severe pressures on wintering populations of forest migrants. Lowland habitats used by hooded warblers are being lost at a particularly high rate, making this species likely to be among the first forest migrants to experience population declines.

While declines in the hooded warbler population are expected, it is difficult to document changes in species, such as the hooded warbler, that have wide distributions. Problems originate from two main sources. First, few surveys have been continued over enough years to differentiate between normal fluctuations and long-term declines. Second, even where such surveys exist they are based mostly on singing-bird counts that tend to be inaccurate. Singing-male counts do not account for the floating birds that may make up 20 to 30 percent of the total population (Wilcove and Terborgh 1984). A decline in population will first result in the elimination of floaters prior to any reduction in singing males. Furthermore, these counts assume that each singing bird represents a mated pair. This assumption is not true even in healthy populations, because unmated first-year males will sing as much or more than mated males (Nice 1943). The problem is exacerbated in declining populations that may contain increasing proportions of unmated birds.

The problem of detecting a declining population is exemplified clearly by E.S. Morton's studies of summer Kentucky warblers at Front Royal, Virginia (Morton pers. comm.). Morton found that while singing-bird counts indicated no change in the population, his band return rates were only 10 to 20 percent. Normal returns for many forest-related species are 50 to 60 percent (Roberts 1971). Morton's low return rates are the kind of insidious decline that will pass unnoticed until critical levels of disappearance are reached and the woods actually fall silent.

Despite the difficulties involved in attempting to investigate long-term changes in bird populations, a number of studies in the northeastern and north-central United States have documented significant declines in forest migrants. These studies incorporate a sufficiently wide geographic region to suggest that these declines are indicative of general trends. Leck *et al* (1981) concluded that all of the 11 migrant species that historically bred on a forest tract in central New Jersey had declined significantly since 1959. Ambuel and Temple (1982) reported significant declines in most migrant forest species on forest tracts in Wisconsin. These forest tracts had remained unaltered by man since the initial surveys in 1954. Serrao and Smiley (1982) reported declines in migrant populations on large forest tracts in northeastern New Jersey and southern New York. At one of these sites, precipitous declines were recorded in hooded warbler density. Another study that compared migrant populations in 1947 and 1982 at a site in the Smoky Mountains (Wilcove and Whitcomb 1983) found that the hooded warbler was among 10 of 16 forest migrants that had declined. Hall (1984) analyzed breeding bird populations on a tract of virgin forest in West Virginia. He found that there had been significant declines in populations of most neotropical migrants over a 35-year period.

All of the above studies involved sufficiently large tracts of forest to eliminate forest fragmentation as the cause for migrant population declines. In each case, populations of permanent residents remained constant, indicating that habitat quality on the sites themselves had not changed. In each study, loss of winter habitat was hypothesized as the primary cause for declines in migrant species.

The silencing of the temperate woodlands cannot be expected to occur all at once throughout the bird's range. Populations from a given part of the breeding range tend to winter together as well (Ramos and Warner 1980). Certain parts of the winter range are being deforested more rapidly than others. El Salvador is almost completely deforested, as are vast areas of Mexico. In contrast, Honduras still has significant forest reserves (Myers 1980).

# Management

The U.S. Fish and Wildlife Service (FWS) has financed the collection of information on migratory species in the tropics, as have the Canadian Wildlife Service and the World Wildlife Fund (Rappole et al 1983). FWS also holds summer workshops for Latin American wildlife professionals in which it includes some discussion of problems confronting migratory species. However, very little basic research or implementation of programs derived from research findings has been done. The World Wildlife Fund has the most ambitious, though still modest, program, one that involves a number of innovative ways of addressing the problems of migratory bird decline, including: local tropical conservation education programs; agricultural improvement programs; alternative land-use programs to reduce pressure on tropical forested regions; identification of critical size for forest preserves; and basic research on the effects of forest removal on winter migrants. The International Council for Bird Preservation particularly through the Panamanian section, has a number of small programs designed to raise local awareness concerning tropical bird conservation, as does the International Union for Conservation of Nature and Natural Resources. The U.S. Nature Conservancy has initiated a program for the establishment of conservation data centers in Latin American countries to help identify areas that should be preserved.

Unfortunately, the magnitude of the problem dwarfs current efforts to solve it. Considerably more interest by government and nongovernment organizations is needed if anything other than token resistance to an overwhelming problem is to be presented.

# Prognosis

At present rates of forest destruction, the long-term prognosis for forest migratory species is poor. Some of the species can survive in degraded forest habitats or second growth, but few if any can survive in the pastures, agricultural fields, or urban sprawl now replacing forests.

It has long been assumed that, because birds have wings and are highly mobile, they can simply move elsewhere to avoid the most serious effects of habitat destruction. Basic research, however, has shown that "moving elsewhere" is a poor option at best. "Elsewhere" presumably means to other areas of suitable habitat. However, searching for these new areas requires increasing the risk of starvation and predation. Furthermore, new habitat, once located, is likely to be occupied by a conspecific unwilling to share or give up its ground. Thus, forest reduction results in the loss of the animals that lived in the destroyed forest.

For forest migrants on the breeding grounds, suitable forest habitat (more than 500 acres) was reduced by more than 80 percent at its lowest point around the turn of the century. Therefore, it is likely that migrant populations were reduced by 80 percent or more below precolonial levels. Since that time, a significant increase in forest coverage probably has allowed migrant populations to increase substantially. However, even today parts of the United States, particularly the mid-Atlantic and midwestern states, still have less than 20 percent of their area covered by forest suitable for migrants. Therefore, while in general migrant populations are far more secure on their breeding grounds than they were 80 to 100 years ago, the recovery has been spotty and only partial. It is now possible that the trend of forest regeneration has been reversed, with increasing suburbs around population centers causing forest fragmentation and subsequent declines in forest migrant populations in those areas. While this trend is troubling, there should be sufficient forest holdings in public ownership to guarantee continued availability of prime breeding habitat for forest species. It is critical to forest migrant species that these large forest tracts remain unbroken. It is hoped that a growing awareness of the problem of forest fragmentation can lead to the adoption of mitigation techniques to lessen the detrimental impacts of forest exploitation (Robbins 1979).

On the wintering grounds the prognosis is far more threatening. Human population growth in most relevant countries is very high at an average 2.2 percent annual increase, and the need for an improved balance of payment ever increases the demand for the production of exportable crops. While in the past, slash-and-burn agricultural practices partially mitigated the impact of development of migrant habitat (see Buechner and Buechner 1970), the present growth of beef industries in virtually all Middle American countries has short-circuited the normal process of cultivation, abandonment, and regeneration, and resulted in a proliferation of burned-over pastures. These areas offer virtually no habitat value for forest migrants. This change has rendered moot the long-standing controversy over whether expanding agriculture in the tropics benefited wintering migrants. Even second-growth habitats will become increasingly scarce if the conversion to pasture continues unabated.

Under current trends, primary forests in Middle America are falling at a rate estimated to be as high as one percent per year (Bolin 1977). This drastic decline is likely to continue until parks and reserves, currently amounting to

Forest species that breed in the United States and migrate to Middle or South America for winter.

| Common Name | Scientific Name | Winters in Forest Habitat* | Winters in Mature Forest |
|---|---|---|---|
| | ACCIPITRIDAE | | |
| Swallow-tailed Kite | *Elanoides forficatus* | X | X |
| Mississippi Kite | *Ictinia mississippiensis* | | X |
| Sharp-shinned Hawk | *Accipiter striatus* | X | |
| Cooper's Hawk | *A. cooperii* | X | |
| Black-Hawk | *Buteogallus anthracinus* | | |
| Broad-winged Hawk | *B. platypterus* | X | |
| Red-tailed Hawk | *Buteo jamaicensus* | | |
| | COLUMBIDAE | | |
| White-crowned Pigeon | Columba leucocephala | X | |
| Red-billed Pigeon | *C. flavirostris* | X | |
| Band-tailed Pigeon | *C. fasciata* | X | |
| | *CUCULIDAE* | | |
| Black-billed Cuckoo | *Coccyzus erythropthalmus* | X | X |
| Yellow-billed Cuckoo | *C. americanus* | X | X |
| Mangrove Cuckoo | *C. minor* | X | |
| | CAPRIMULGIDAE | | |
| Poor-will | *Phalaenoptilus nuttallii* | X | |
| Chuck-will's widow | *Caprimulgus carolinensis* | X | X |
| Whip-poor-will | *C. vociferus* | X | X |
| | *APODIDAE* | | |
| Chimney Swift | *Chaetura pelagica* | X | |
| Vaux's Swift | *C. vauxi* | X | |
| | TROCHILIDAE | | |
| Broad-billed Hummingbird | *Cyanthus latirostris* | | |
| Buff-Bellied Hummingbird | *Amazilia yacatanensis* | | |
| Violet-crowned Hummingbird | *A. verticalis* | | |
| Blue-throated Hummingbird | *Lampornis clemenciae* | | |
| Magnificent Hummingbird | *Eugenes fulgens* | X | |
| Ruby-throated Hummingbird | *Archilochus colubris* | X | |
| Calliope Hummingbird | *Stellula calliope* | X | |
| | TROGONIDAE | | |
| Elegant Trogan | *Trogon elegans* | X | |
| | PICIDAE | | |
| Yellow-bellied Sapsucker | *Sphyrapicus varius* | X | |
| Williamson's Sapsucker | *S. thyroideus* | X | |
| | TYRANNIDAE | | |
| Olive-sided Flycatcher | *Contopus borealis* | X | |
| Great Pewee | *C. pertinax* | X | |
| Western Wood Pewee | *C. sordidulus* | X | X |
| Eastern Wood Pewee | *C. virens* | X | X |
| Yellow-bellied Flycatcher | *Empidonax flaviventris* | X | X |
| Acadian Flycatcher | *E. virescens* | X | X |
| Willow Flycatcher | *E. trailii* | X | |

* Includes mature forest, second growth, forest edge & forest fragments.

Forest species that breed in the United States and migrate to Middle or South America for winter.—continued

| Common Name | Scientific Name | Winters in Forest Habitat* | Winters in Mature Forest |
|---|---|---|---|
| Least Flycatcher | E. minimus | X | |
| Hammond's Flycatcher | E. hammondii | X | |
| Dusky Flycatcher | E. oberholseri | X | |
| Gray Flycatcher | E. wrightii | X | |
| Western Flycatcher | E. difficilis | X | X |
| Buff-breasted Flycatcher | E. fulvifrons | X | |
| Eastern Phoebe | Sayornis phoebe | X | |
| Dusky-capped Flycatcher | Myiarchus tuberculifer | X | |
| Great Crested Flycatcher | M. crinitus | X | X |
| Brown-crested Flycatcher | M. tyrannulus | X | |
| Great Kiskadee | Pitangus sulphuratus | X | |
| Sulphur-bellied Flycatcher | Miodynastes luteiventris | X | |
| Eastern Kingbird | Tyrannus tyrannus | | |
| | T. dominicensis | | |
| | MUSCICAPIDAE | | |
| Gray Kingbird | SYLVIINAE | | |
| Ruby-crowned Kinglet | Regulus calendula | X | |
| Blue-gray Gnatcatcher | Polioptila caerulea | X | X |
| | TURDINAE | | |
| Veery | Catharus fuscescens | X | X |
| Gray-cheeked Thrush | C. minimus | X | X |
| Swainson's Thrush | C. ustulatus | X | X |
| Hermit Thrush | C. guttatus | X | |
| Wood Thrush | Hylocichla mustelina | X | X |
| | MIMIDAE | | |
| Gray Catbird | Dumetella carolinensis | X | |
| | BOMBYCILLIDAE | | |
| Cedar Waxwing | Bombycilla cedrorum | X | |
| | VIREONIDAE | | |
| White-eyed Vireo | Vireo griseus | X | |
| Bell's Vireo | V. bellii | | |
| Black-capped Vireo | OV. atricapilla | | |
| Solitary Vireo | V. solitarius | X | X |
| Yellow-throated Vireo | V. flavifrons | X | X |
| Warbling Vireo | V. gilvus | X | X |
| Philadelphia Vireo | V. philadelphicus | X | X |
| Red-eyed Vireo | V. olivaceus | X | |
| Black-whiskered Vireo | V. altiloaguus | X | |
| | EMBERIZIDAE | | |
| | PARULINAE | | |
| Bachman's Warbler | Vermivora bachmanii | X | X |
| Blue-winged Warbler | V. pinus | X | |
| Golden-winged Warbler | V. chrysoptera | X | X |

* Includes mature forest, second growth, forest edge & forest fragments.

Forest species that breed in the United States and migrate to Middle or South America for winter.—continued

| Common Name | Scientific Name | Winters in Forest Habitat* | Winters in Mature Forest |
|---|---|---|---|
| Tennessee Warbler | *V. peregrina* | X | |
| Orange-crowned Warbler | *V. celata* | X | |
| Nashville Warbler | *V. ruficappila* | X | |
| Virginia's Warbler | *V. virginiae* | X | |
| Lucy's Warbler | *V. luciae* | X | |
| Northern Parula | *Parula americana* | X | X |
| Yellow Warbler | *Dendroica petechia* | | |
| Chestnut-sided Warbler | *D. pensylvanica* | X | X |
| Magnolia Warbler | *D. magnolia* | X | X |
| Cape May Warbler | *D. tigrinan* | X | X |
| Black-throated Blue Warbler | *D. caerulescens* | X | X |
| Yellow-rumped Warbler | *D. coronata* | | |
| Black-throated Gray Warbler | *D. nigrescens* | X | |
| Townsend's Warbler | *D. townsendi* | X | X |
| Hermit warbler | *D. occidentalis* | X | |
| Black-throated Green Warbler | *D. virens* | X | X |
| Blackburnian Warbler | *D. fusca* | X | X |
| Yellow-throated Warbler | *D. dominica* | X | |
| Pine Warbler | *D. pinus* | X | |
| Kirtland's Warbler | *D. kirtlandii* | X | |
| Prairie Warbler | *D. discolor* | X | |
| Bay-breasted Warbler | *D. castanea* | X | X |
| Blackpoll Warbler | *D. striata* | X | X |
| Cerulean Warbler | *D. cerulea* | X | X |
| Black-and-White Warbler | *Mniotilta varia* | X | X |
| American Redstart | *Setophaga ruticilla* | X | X |
| Prothonotary Warbler | *Protonotaria citrea* | X | |
| Worm-eating Warbler | *Helmitheros vermivorus* | X | X |
| Swainson's Warbler | *Limnothlypis swainsonii* | X | X |
| Ovenbird | *Seiurus aurocapillus* | X | X |
| Northern Waterthrush | *S. noveboracensis* | X | X |
| Louisiana Waterthrush | *S. motacilla* | X | X |
| Kentucky Warbler | *Oporornis formosus* | X | X |
| Connecticut Warbler | *O. agilis* | X | |
| Mourning Warbler | *O. philadelphia* | X | |
| Hooded Warbler | *Wilsonia citrina* | X | X |
| Wilson's Warbler | *W. pusilla* | X | |
| Canada Warbler | *W. canadensis* | X | X |
| Red-faced Warbler | *Cardellina rubrifrons* | X | |
| Painted Redstart | *Myioborus pictus* | X | |
| | **THRAUPINAE** | | |
| Hepatic Tanager | *Piranga flava* | X | X |

* Includes mature forest, second growth, forest edge & forest fragments.

Forest species that breed in the United States and migrate to Middle or South America for winter.—continued

| Common Name | Scientific Name | Winters in Forest Habitat* | Winters in Mature Forest |
|---|---|---|---|
| Summer Tanager | P. rubra | X | |
| Scarlet Tanager | P. olivacea | X | X |
| Western Tanager | P. ludoviciana | X | X |
| | CARDINALINAE | | |
| Rose-breasted Grosbeak | Pheucticus ludovicianus | X | |
| Black-headed Grosbeak | P. melanocephalus | X | |
| | EMBERIZINAE | | |
| Green-tailed Towhee | Pipilo chlorurus | | |
| | P. erythrophthalmus | | |
| Rufous-sided Towhee | ICTERINAE | | |
| Northern Oriole | Icterus galbula | | |

* Includes mature forest, second growth, forest edge & forest fragments.

less than five percent of the original forests, remain as the only major stands of undisturbed habitat. The amount of younger second growth and disturbed forests ultimately will decline too as population growth and uncontrolled burning of pastures take their toll. Even where slash-and-burn agriculture continues as the principal land-use practice, crowding by rapidly increasing agricultural populations forces farmers into shorter rotation cycles, leaving less time for regeneration of second growth.

The first species to show the effects of forest destruction will be those requiring mature forest habitat. In general, these species are not expected to become extinct, but they will become increasingly uncommon and ultimately rare. Forest species that do not require primary forest also are expected to decline, but over a longer time frame. In all, major declines may occur in some 90 or 100 species. This decline certainly will mark the greatest change in North American avifauna since plume hunting and market gunning were at their peaks.

One species of forest migrant that already may have gone this route is the Bachman's warbler. Never an abundant species, the Bachman's warbler has declined in numbers until it is now virtually extinct. The winter range of the Bachman's warbler apparently was restricted to the lowland forests of Cuba, a habitat all but eliminated for sugar cane production in the early 1900s (Smith 1954). Loss of this habitat is thought to be a major cause for the Bachman's warbler decline (Terborgh 1974).

The hooded warbler is at a crossroads. Indications are that it already has begun to decline. Predictions are that the decline will become precipitous. This charmingly beautiful songbird is the unlikely carrier of a sobering message. If we wish to continue to experience North American forests as we know them today, with their full compliment of songbirds, we must act immediately to forestall the loss of the tropical forests. Tragically, the demise of the hooded warbler and of all our forest migrants, amounts to just a tip of a disasterous iceberg, a warning that hundreds of thousands, perhaps a million, tropical species may soon face extinction. The loss of so many and so varied a range of organisms would far outstrip the significance of precipitous declines in neo-tropical migrants.

# Recommendations

For a species requiring at least two distinct habitats, it is necessary to consider recommendations for each habitat independently. Management recommendations for hooded warblers and forest interior species in general on their breeding grounds are thoroughly outlined by Robbins (1979: 210). The principal recommendation is to avoid unnecessary fragmentation of forests. The remaining 15 recommendations present management applications to maximize that goal while still exploiting the forest for commercial purposes. To this we add the recommendations that this information be distributed to all government agencies, from local to national, so that a maximum effort can be made to save as many large forest tracts as possible.

Recommendations to enhance the protection of migration and winter habitat are far more complicated because they involve dealings at an international level.

## Federal Government Responsibility

1. Foreign Aid: Through foreign aid and quasi-government loaning institutions (i.e., World Bank, Inter-American Development Bank, Organization of American States, Agency for International Development, Export-Import Bank, etc; see Shane [1980] for full discussion of these institutions), the U.S. government exerts a major influence on development in Middle American countries. Government agencies that administer foreign aid programs should be required to comply with the National Environmental Policy Act since their actions are directly affecting U.S. songbirds.
2. Beef Imports: A major cause for the rapid growth in Middle American cattle industries is the import of beef into the United States (Myers 1981). Unless it can be shown that cattle ranching in the neotropics is a sustainable activity that does not inevitably lead to environmental degradation, the United States should ban the importation of beef produced in humid tropical countries.
3. International Agreements: The United States government should seek further multilateral commitments with other Western Hemisphere nations for

the protection of migratory birds, an internationally shared resource. Such agreements should emphasize the need for habitat-management policies that minimize effects on avian resources and provide incentives for protecting critical habitats.

4. Research: A program should be established to assess the amounts of various forest habitats in the neotropics. In conjunction with this, studies should be initiated to identify areas of critical habitat for wintering migrants. These data should be made available to local governments and for use in environmental assessments and impact statements.

5. Alternate Land Use: Government and quasi-government foreign aid should be redirected to encourage and support forest preservation. Greater financial support also should be made available for environmental education, wildlands management, natural history tourism, and agricultural research designed to provide alternatives to the destructive practices currently employed.

## Corporate Responsibility

United States corporations play an important role in providing the necessary capital and expertise for economic development in virtually all Middle American countries. Corporations should be required to follow environmental guidelines. United States businesses operating abroad should be required to adhere to the National Environmental Policy Act whenever they request U.S. import or export permits.

## Individual Responsibility

It is the responsibility of individuals as consumers, voters, stockholders, and members of conservation organizations to initiate responsible attitudes and policies toward the conservation of forest migrant habitat in Middle America.

# References

Agricultural Report. 1872. Report of the Commissioner of Agriculure for the Year 1872. Government Printing Office, Washington, D.C.

Aldrich, J.W. 1967. "Historical Background," *in* O.H. Hewitt ed., *The Wild Turkey and its Management*. Wildlife Society, Washington, D.C.

Ambuel, B., and S.A. Temple. 1982. "Songbird populations in southern Wisconsin forests: 1954-1979." *Journal of Field Ornithology* 53:149-158.

Barlow, J.C. 1980. "Patterns of ecological interactions among migrant and resident vireos on the wintering ground," *in* A. Keast and E.S. Morton eds., *Migrant Birds in the Neotropics: Ecology, Behavior, Distribution, and Conservation*. Smithsonian Institution Press, Washington, D.C. pp. 79-107.

Bennett, C.F. 1968. "Human influence on the zoogeography of Panama." *Ibero-Americana* 51.

Bennett, S.E. 1980. "Interspecific competition and the niche of the American redstart (*Setophaga ruticilla*) in wintering and breeding communities," *in* A. Keast and E.S. Morton eds., *Migrant Birds in the Neotropics: Ecology, Behavior, Distribution, and Conservation,* Smithsonian Institution Press, Washington, D.C. pp. 319-35.

Bent, A.C. 1963. *Life Histories of North American Wood Warblers.* Two vols. Dover, New York.

Bolin, B. 1977. "Changes of land biota and their importance for the carbon cycle." *Science* 196:613-15.

Bond, R.R. 1957. "Ecological distribution of breeding birds in the upland forests of southern Wisconsin." *Ecology Monograph* 27:351-84.

Boucher, D.H., M. Hansen, S. Risch, and J.H. Vandermeer. 1983. "Agriculture," in *Costa Rican Natural History.* University of Chicago Press, Chicago, Illinois.

Buechner, H.K. and J.H. Buechner. 1970. "The avifauna of northern Latin America: a symposium held at the Smithsonian Institution 13-15 April 1966." *Smithsonian Contributions to Zoology* 26:1-119.

Caufield, C. 1985. *In the Rainforest.* A.A. Knopf, New York.

Chapman, F.M. 1907. *The Warblers of North America.* D. Appleton and Co., New York.

Chipley, R.M. 1976. "The impact of wintering migrant wood warblers on resident insectivorous passerines in a subtropical Columbian oak woods." *Living Bird* 15:119-141.

Cook, S. and W. Borah. 1971. *Essays on Population, History, Mexico, and the Caribbean.* University of California Press, Berkeley, California.

Culbert, T.P. 1974. *The Lost Civilization: The Story of the Classic Maya.* Harper and Row, New York.

Culbert, T.P. 1985. "The Maya enter history." *Natural History* 94(4):42-48.

Denevan, W.M. 1976. *The Native Population of the Americas 1492.* University of Wisconsin Press, Madison, Wisconsin.

Ehrlich, P.R. and A.H. Ehrlich. 1981. *Extinction: The Causes and Consequences of the Disappearance of Species.* Random House, New York. 305 pp.

Emanuel, W.R., G.T. Killough, W.M. Post, and H.H. Shuggart. 1984. "Modeling terrestrial ecosytems in the global carbon cycle with shifts in carbon storage capacity by land use change." *Ecology* 65:970-83.

Farb, P. 1961. *The Forest.* Time Inc., New York.

Fitzpatrick, J.W. 1980. "Wintering of North American tyrant flycatchers," *in* A. Keast and E.S. Morton eds., *Migrant Birds in the Neotropics: Ecology, Behavior, Distribution, and Conservation.* Smithsonian Institution Press, Washington, D.C.

Food and Agricultural Organization. 1984. *FAO Production Yearbook, 1983,* vol. 37. FAO Statistics Series No. 55., FAO, Rome.

Food and Agricultural Organization. 1948. *Forest Resources of the World.* FAO, Washington, D.C.

Food and Agricultural Organization. 1974. *Production yearbook 1973,* vol. 27. FAO, Rome.

Food and Agricultural Organization. 1947. *Yearbook of Food and Agricultural Statistics 1947.* FAO, Washington, D.C.

Food and Agricultural Organization. 1956. *Yearbook of Food and Agricultural Statistics 1955,* vol IX, part 1. FAO, Rome.

Forman, R.T.T., A.E. Galli and C.F. Leck. 1976. "Forest size and avian diversity in New Jersey woodlots with some land-use implications." *Oecologica* 26:1-8.

Galli, A.E., C.F. Leck, and R.T.T. Forman. 1976. "Avian distribution patterns in forest islands of different sizes in central New Jersey." *Auk* 93:356-64.

*The Global 2000 Report to the President: Entering the Twenty-first Century,* vol. 2, Technical Report. 1980. Gerald O. Barney, Study Director. Government Printing Office, Washington D.C.

Gomez-Pompa A., C. Vasquez-Yanes, and S. Guevara. 1972. "The tropical rain forest: a non-renewable resource." *Science* 177:762-65.

Gordon, B.L. 1957. "Human geography and ecology in the Sinu country of Colombia." *Ibero-Americana* 39.

Hall, G.A. 1984. "Population decline of neotropical migrants in an Appalachian forest." *American Birds* 38(1):14-18.

Henderson-Sellers, A. and V. Gornitz. 1984. "Possible climatic impacts of land cover transformations, with particular emphasis on tropical deforestation." *Climatic Change* 6:231-57.

Hobbie, J., J. Cole, J. Dugan, R.A. Houghton, and B. Peterson. 1984. "Role of biota in global CO balance: the controversy." *BioScience* 34:492-8.

Iltis, H.H. 1983. "What will be their fate? Tropical forests." *Environment* 25:55-60.

Keast, A. 1980. "Spatial relationships between migratory parulid warblers and their ecological counterparts in the neotropics," *in* A Keast and E.S. Morton eds., *Migrant Birds in the Neotropics: Ecology, Behavior, Distribution, and Conservation,* Smithsonian Institution Press, Washington, D.C.

Kellert, S.R. 1980. *Phase II: Activities of the American Public Relating to Animals.* U.S. Fish and Wildlife Service. Washington, D.C.

Kendeigh, S.C. 1947. "Bird population studies in the coniferous forest biome during a spruce budworm outbreak." Ontario Department Lands. *Forest Biology Bulletin* 1:1-100.

Lapham, I. A., J.G. Knapp, and H. Crocker. 1867. *Report of the Disasterous Effects of the Destruction of Forest Trees Now Going on the State of Wisconsin.* Madison, Wisonsin.

Leck, C.F. 1972. "The impact of some North American migrants at fruiting trees in Panama." *Auk* 89:842-50.

Leck, C.F., B.G. Murray, and J. Swinebroad. 1981. "Changes in breeding bird populations at Hutcheson Memorial Forest since 1958." *William L. Hutcheson Memorial Forest Bulletin* 6:8-15.

Loftin, H.D., J. Rogers, and D.L. Hicks. 1966. "Repeats, returns, and recoveries of North American migrant birds banded in Panama." *Bird-Banding* 37:35-44.

Lovejoy, T. 1981. "A world less green." *Defenders* 56:2-5.

Lynch, J.F., E.S. Morton, and M.E. Van der Voort. 1985. "Habitat segregation between the sexes of wintering hooded warblers (*Wilsonia citrina*)." *Auk* 102:714-21.

Marsh, G.P. 1864. *Man and Nature: or Physical Geography as Modified by Human Action.* New York.

Moore, N.W. and R.O. Hooper. 1975. "On the number of bird species in British woods." *Biology Conservation* 3:239-50.

Morris, R.F., W.F. Cheshire, C.A. Miller, and D.G. Mott. 1958. "The numerical response of avian and mammalian predators during a graduation of the spruce budworm." *Ecology* 39:487-94.

Myers, N. 1979. *The Sinking Ark.* Pergamon Press, New York.

Myers, N. 1980. *Conversion of Tropical Moist Forests.* National Academy of Science, Washington, D.C.

Nice, M.M. 1943. "Studies in the life history of the Song Sparrow, vol II. Behavior." *Transactions of the Linnean Society.* New York 6:1-328.

Nickell, W.P. 1968. "Return of northern migrants to tropical winter quarters and banded birds recovered in the United States." *Bird-Banding* 39:107-16.

Oberholser, H.C. 1974. *The Bird Life of Texas.* University of Texas Press, Austin, Texas.

Odum, E.P. 1931. "Notes on the nesting habits of the hooded warbler." *Wilson Bulletin* 43:316-7.

Parsons, J.J. 1975. "The changing nature of New World tropical forests since European colonization," in *The Use of Ecological Guidelines for Development in the American Humid Tropics.* International Union for the Conservation of Nature and Natural Resources Pub. 31:28-37.

Plunkett, R.L. 1979. "The importance of birds in forest communities," in *Workshop Proceedings Management of North Central and Northeastern Forests for Nongame Birds.* U.S. Department of Agriculture Forest Service General Technical Report NC-51.

Rabenhold, K.N. 1980. "The black-throated green warbler in Panama: geographic and seasonal comparison of foraging," in A. Keast and E.S. Morton eds., *Migrant Birds in the Neotropics: Ecology, Behavior, Distribution, and Conservation.* Smithsonian Institution Press, Washington, D.C.

Ragatz, R.L. 1969. The Vacation Home Market: An Analysis of the Spatial Distribution of Population on a seasonal Basis. Dissertation. Cornell University, Ithaca, New York.

Ramos, M.A. and D.W. Warner. 1980. "Analysis of North American subspecies of migrant birds wintering in Los Tuxtlas, southern Mexico," *in* A. Keast and E.S. Morton ed., *Migrant Birds in the Neotropics: Ecology, Behavior, Distribution, and Conservation.* Smithsonian Institution Press, Washington, D.C.

Rappole, J.H. and E.S. Morton. 1985. "Effects of habitat alternation on a tropical avian forest community," *in* P.A. Buckley, M.S. Foster, E.S. Morton, R.S. Ridgely, and F.G. Buckley eds., *Neotropical Ornithology.* Ornithology Monograph no. 36.

Rappole, J.H. and D.W. Warner. 1976. "Relationships between behavior, physiology and weather in avian transients at a migration stopover site." *Oecologia* 26:193-212.

Rappole, J.H., E.S. Morton, T.E. Lovejoy, III, and J.L. Rous. 1983. *Nearctic Avian Migrants in the Neotropics.* U.S. Department of the Interior, Fish and Wildlife Service. Washington, D.C. 646 pp.

Rappole, J.H., M.A. Ramos, R.J. Oehlenschlager, D.W. Warner, and C.D. Berkan. 1979. "Timing of migration and route selection in North American songbirds," *in* D.L. Drawe ed., *Proceedings of the First Welder Wildlife Foundation Symposium.* Welder Wildlife Foundation, Sinton, Texas.

Robbins, C.S. 1979. "Effect of forest fragmentation on bird populations," *in* R.M. DeGraaf and K.E. Evans eds., *Proceedings of the Workshop on Management of North Central and Northeastern Forests for Nongame Birds.* U.S. Department of Agriculture Forest Service General Technical report NC-51. Washington, D.C.

Sagan, C., O.B. Toon, and J.B. Pollock. 1979. "Anthropogenic albedo changes and the earth's climate." *Science* 206:1363-8

Sauer, C.O. 1966. *The Early Spanish Main.* University of California Press, Berkeley, California. 112 pp.

Schneider, S.H. 1984. "Deforestation and climatic modification-an editorial." *Climatic Change* 6:227-9.

Schorger, A.W. 1955. *The Passenger Pigeon, Its Natural History and Extinction.* University of Oklahoma Press, Norman, Oklahoma.

Schwartz, P. 1964. "The northern waterthrush in Venezuela." *Living Bird* 3:169-84.

Serrao, J. and D. Smiley. 1982. *Trends in Populations of Breeding Birds at Three Separate Natural Areas in the Eastern U.S.* Research Report. Mohonk Preserve, Inc.

Smith, E.E. 1954. *The Forests of Cuba.* Maria Moors Cabot Foundation Publication no. 2. 98 pp.

Sprunt, A. Jr. 1954. *Florida Bird Life.* Coward-McCann, Inc., New York.

Starr, T. 1865. *American Forests: Their Destruction and Preservation.* Annual Report of 1865. United States Department of Agriculture. Washington, D.C. pp. 210-34.

Steinhart, P. 1983. "Trouble in the Tropics." *National Wildlife* 22(1):16-20.

Stewart, R.E. and C.S. Robbins. 1958. *Birds of Maryland and the District of Columbia.* U.S. Department of the Interior, Fish and Wildlife Service. Washington, D.C. North American Fauna no. 62.

Stiles, F.G. 1980. "Evolutionary implications of habitat relations between permanent and winter resident landbirds in Costa Rica," *in* A. Keast and E.S. Morton eds., *Migrant Birds in the Neotropics: Ecology, Behavior, Distribution, and Conservation.* Smithsonian Institution Press, Washington, D.C. pp. 421-35.

Talbot, L.M. 1980. "The world's conservation strategy." *Environmental Conservation* 7(4):259-68.

Terborgh, J. 1974. "Preservation of natural diversity: the problems of extinction prone species." *BioScience* 24(12):715-22.

Terborgh, J.W. and J.R. Faaborg. 1980. "Factors affecting the distribution of North American migrants in the Eastern Caribbean region," *in* A. Keast and E.S. Morton eds., *Migrant Birds in the Neotropics: Ecology, Behavior, Distribution, and Conservation.* Smithsonian Institution Press, Washington, D.C. pp. 145-155.

Terres, J.K. 1980. *The Audubon Society Encyclopedia of North American Birds.* Alfred A. Knopf, New York.

Trefethen, J.B. 1976. *The American Landscape: 1776-1976 Two Centuries of Change.* Wildlife Management Institute, New York. 99 pp.

U.S. Bureau of the Census. *Statistical Abstract of the United States: 1950.* (71st ed.) Washington, D.C.

U.S. Bureau of the Census. *Statistical Abstract of the United States: 1962.* (83rd ed.) Washington, D.C..

U.S. Bureau of the Census. *Statistical Abstract of the United States: 1965.* (86th ed.) Washington, D.C.

U.S. Bureau of the Census. *Statistical Abstract of the United States: 1976.* (97th ed.) Washington, D.C.

U.S. Department of Agriculture. 1958. *Timber Resources for America's Future.* Forest Service, U.S. Department of Agriculture forest Resource Report No. 14.

U.S. Department of Agriculture. 1982 *An Analysis of the Timber Situation in the United States 1952-2030.* U.S. Forest Service. Washington, D.C. Forest Resource Report No.23.

U.S. Department of Commerce. 1924. *Statistical Abstract of the United States: 1923.* (46th ed.). Bureau of Foreign and Domestic Commerce. Washington, D.C.

U.S. Department of Commerce 1935. *Statistical Abstract of the United States: 1935.* (57th ed.). Bureau of Foreign and Domestic Commerce, Washington, D.C.

U.S. Department of the Interior. 1977. *The 1975 National Survey of Hunting, Fishing and Wildlife Associated Recreation.* Washington, D.C. 91 pp.

Wetmore, A. 1943. "Birds of southern Veracruz, Mexico." *Proceedings of the United States National Museum* 93:215-340.

Whitcomb, R.F., J.F.Lynch, P.A. Opler, and C.S. Robbins. 1976. "Island biogeography and conservation: strategy and limitations." *Science* 193:1030-32.

Whitcomb, R.F., C.S. Robbins, J.F. Lynch, B.L. Whitcomb, M.K. Klimkiewicz, and D. Bystrak. 1981. "Effects of forest fragmentation on avifauna of the eastern deciduous forest," *in* R.L. Burgess and D.M. Sharpe eds., *Forest Island Dynamics in Man-Dominated Landscapes.* Springer Verlag, New York. 3110 pp.

Wilcove, D.S. and J.W. Terborgh. 1984. "Patterns of population decline in birds." *American Birds* 38(1):10-13.

Wilcove, D.S. and R.F. Whitcomb. 1983. "Gone with the trees." *Natural History* 92:82-91.

Willis, E.O. 1966. "The role of migrant birds at swarms of army ants." *Living Bird* 5:187-231.

Wilson, E.O. 1982. *Proceedings of the U.S. Strategy Conference on Biological Diversity.* Department of State. Washington, D.C.

Woodward, R.L. 1985. *Central America: A Nation Divided.* Oxford Press, New York.

*George V. N. Powell is a field biologist for the National Audubon Society.*
*John H. Rappole, an ornithologist, has spent more than a decade studying the loss of migratory-bird habitat in the New World tropics.*

The decline of the black duck in recent decades makes its future dubious unless the
hunter kill is reduced significantly in the near future.
*Leonard Lee Rue III*

# Black Duck

## Howard E. Spencer Jr.

Maine Department of Inland Fisheries and Wildlife, Retired

## Species Description and Natural History

THE BLACK DUCK (*Anas rubripes*), also known as the black mallard and red legs, is a large dabbling duck very much like its close relative the green-headed mallard. Like other dabblers it springs directly from the water when flushed and commonly tips or "dabbles" for its food in less than two feet of water. Superficially, at least, and unlike the mallard, the sexes are similar in appearance, particularly in regard to plumage. Young and immatures of both sexes have olive-green bills, but bill color varies in the adults and usually is distinctive between the sexes. The yellowish color of the males' bills becomes stronger and more pronounced as the birds mature and reach breeding condition. Females have olive-greenish bills with nearly black blotches on the upper mandible. Females also characteristically, though not always, have one or more large pin-head-size black spots at the base of the upper and/or lower mandibles. The tarsus and feet, except for dark webs, vary from olive in the young to pale pinkish orange in adult females and a strong red in the adult males ("red legs").

Although named "black" duck, the species does not give an impression of being truly black except at a distance in poor light. In the hand or in good light, the bird is a rich dusky brown with lighter buffy patterns on the feather tips. The under wings are silvery with white linings and flash distinctively as the bird flies. The head and neck are a much lighter buffy gray with small, very dark, flecking. A dark eye stripe is prominent. Both sexes bear a superficial resemblance to the female mallard but actually are much darker, sport a lighter head and neck, and lack the hen mallard's light upper tail coverts. The wing speculum is an irridescent metallic blue with, at most, a slight white trailing margin. There is no white on the leading edge of the speculum.

Plumage changes in the black duck follow patterns similar to those of other dabbling ducks. Natal down is replaced at approximately two months with the first adult-like plumage. This is followed by the first breeding plumage a month or so later, which actually produces little difference in appearance and is retained until after the first breeding season the following spring or summer. In post-breeding molts, primary wing feathers are shed at essentially the same period, and the birds are temporarily flightless. The timing of this post-breeding or "eclipse" molt varies between males and females. It occurs first among the males, which may leave their nesting mates as soon as early June or late May. Molting males tend to flock together and seek seclusion during the flightless period. Nesting females commonly molt individually at about the time their young are achieving flight. Some females may remain flightless into late September. After the first year, plumage changes occur twice yearly throughout the life of the bird.

Although the longevity of black ducks varies in the wild and captivity, band-recovery records of wild-trapped birds suggest an average life span of two to three years. At least two records exist, however, for Maine-banded black ducks recovered by hunters or found dead more than 25 years after banding.

Palmer (1976) gives the following size and weight statistics for black ducks: length 22 to 26 inches, wingspread 33 to 37 inches, second-year males 2.5 to 3.25 pounds, females 2.25 to 2.75 pounds. Certainly these are good average size ranges, but under winter stress conditions birds may weigh considerably less. Conversely, adult males in late fall prime may approach four pounds. One killed December 4, 1947, in Frankfort, Maine, weighed three pounds 13 ounces, and another killed in December 1967 in Falmouth, Maine, weighed three pounds 15 ounces (Personal file data).

## Diet

The food habits of black ducks vary greatly with age, season, and location. Although the diet is typical of dabbling ducks in general, the black is perhaps more dependent on animal matter than are many other species. Aquatic invertebrates are a major constituent in the diet of nesting females and fulfill the egg-laying birds' increased protein need. Similarly, young up to six to eight weeks old feed heavily on aquatic invertebrates, presumably to provide the protein required for rapid growth.

During late summer and early fall, most black ducks feed heavily on maturing aquatic vegetation. They also are known to be upland feeders, on occasion making use of agricultural crops such as blueberries, potatoes, oats, buckwheat, corn, etc. In the late fall and winter, animal matter again becomes important. In salt or brackish habitat, snails (gastropods), clams, mussels, and amphipods are important constituents. Some fin fish also are consumed (mummichogs in tidal environments, gizzard shad inland). When and where available, the following aquatic plants are extensively used: wild rice, bulrushes, smartweed, burreed, arrowhead, pond weeds, millets, coontail, acorns, and the seeds of button brush, bald cypress, and tupelo gum. Marine species include eelgrass, wigeon grass, horned pondweed, bulrushes, and sedges.

## Range

Black duck range covers most of eastern North America south and east of Hudson Bay. Breeding range extends from Cape Hatteras, North Carolina, to the northern limit of the boreal forest. Westward, the black breeds to Wisconsin and Ontario. In recent decades the greatest densities probably have occurred within a band 50 miles north and south of the St. Lawrence River. Breeding densities in the Chesapeake Bay area reportedly have declined drastically since the Stotts/Davis study of the late fifties (Stotts 1960). The southern limits of the breeding range are overlapped by the wintering range. On the

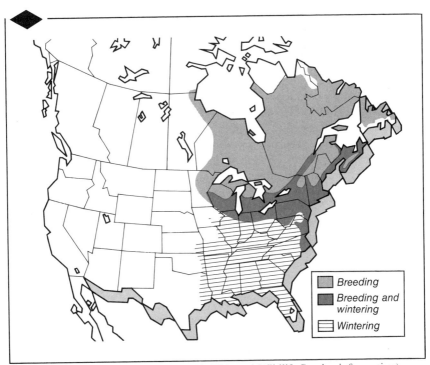

Range of the black duck (after U.S. Fish and Wildlife Service information)

Atlantic Coast, black ducks winter northward to Nova Scotia, Prince Edward Island, and Newfoundland. The southern wintering limits extend to the Gulf Coast and west to east Texas. Tropical Florida probably is excluded.

## Behavior

Black ducks mature during the first year. Young females probably begin pairing when six to seven months old during December and January of their first year. Young males mature one to two months later (Stotts and Davis 1960). Adult birds begin pair formation in early September and most have established pair bonds by mid-December. By April, nearly all birds have found mates. Male blacks remain in attendance on their mates from seven to 22 days into the incubation period. In the case of renesting females, males may remain from four to 16 days. Pair bonds may on occasion be more enduring, however. Barclay (1970) observed a marked pair in the spring of 1969 that also were together in November of the following fall. An appreciable percentage of females return to the same area in which they previously nested (Coulter and Miller 1968, and others).

Home range size during the breeding season varies among individuals. Coulter and Miller (1968) indicated that in New England it may encompass up to five square miles. In other regions it may be less. Drakes commonly establish open-water waiting sites within the home range. They occupy these sites while the hen is on the nest.

Black ducks nest on or adjacent to many wetland types. In Maine, they have been found nesting in blueberry/conifer uplands nearly a half mile from water, but by far the majority nest within 75 yards of water. Except for a limited number of unique situations, blacks rarely nest in great density. Two to five pairs has been about the maximum on most Maine marshes, regardless of the size of the marsh. Beaver ponds are optimum nesting habitat for black ducks, but the ducks also use shorelines of slow-moving rivers and streams, tidal estuaries, marshy lake shores, sedge meadow/bog types, islands in large bodies of open water, and other similar sites.

Actual nest sites are selected within one to three weeks after arrival on the breeding area. Most are ground nests, but elevated natural cavities may be used, particularly in flood-plain areas. The vegetative cover surrounding nest sites varies greatly, but nests usually are very well hidden despite the fact that blacks are early nesters.

## Nesting

Duck broods often hatch before spring vegetation is appreciably advanced. Egg laying commences three to four days after nest construction and proceeds at a rate of one egg per day. Clutch size ranges from seven to 12, and incubation requires from 23 to 33 days depending on latitude, ambient temperatures, and other factors. Nests may be lost to many factors—flooding and predation are especially important. Nest success rates of 38 percent in the Chesapeake Bay area and 49 percent on the St. Lawrence estuary have been reported (Bellrose 1976). Some blacks will renest a second time after losing a nest, but a third attempt rarely will be made. Second and third nests usually contain fewer eggs. Despite reduced clutch sizes, renesting is an important factor in overall production. Stotts (1968) estimated that in the same area and time that nest success was 38 percent, 62 percent of the pairs eventually produced broods. Estimating survival from hatching to flying is extremely difficult. Many studies suggest a wide range in success from one area to another. In Maine, eight to 10 young per brood at hatching usually is reduced to four to six by flight stage (58 to 60 days). More valid estimates of survival can be determined through banding programs after the young reach an age of about five weeks (large enough to hold the band).

## Fall Migration

Fall migration begins with the post-breeding-season dispersal period. Black ducks wander widely during this period and also begin to gather (stage) in larger groups prior to the definitive move southward. More northern breeders probably tend to begin southward movement earlier. Black ducks have been recovered at Maine banding stations in mid-August of the same year that they were banded in Canada as young. Whether this represents post-breeding dispersal or migration is a moot point. The build-up of staging birds is well under way by mid-September, and banded young of the year have been recovered at Merrymeeting Bay, Maine, from the length and breadth of Maine during the first week of October.

In many areas, the opening of the hunting season traditionally has provided a stimulus to push staged birds southward. Weather patterns also stimulate black duck movements in the fall when the ducks seem to move in waves of small to moderate flocks across New England. Five hundred is a *big* flock, 1,000 to 5,000 unusual—particularly in recent years. By mid-December, most inland blacks have passed through and reached their wintering grounds. Maritime birds have drifted down the coast and with great fidelity situated themselves on the wintering areas of the previous year. In the past few decades, intensified banding programs and increasingly sophisticated analyses of recoveries have provided a wealth of both qualitative and quantitative data on migration. This information is discussed further below.

## Wintering

As with most species, winter is a critical period for black ducks. The degree of stress they undergo is not necessarily a function of how far north they remain. For example, blacks wintering on the coast of Maine or Nova Scotia may have more available food, and sometimes shelter, than those on the Jersey salt marshes. Tidal fluctuation in the northern areas plus estuaries and near-shore islands can provide an abundance of invertebrate foods and wind breaks that more southern areas lack once the marshes freeze. Conversely, prolonged extreme temperatures down to minus 25 degrees in northern latitudes can reduce both the availability of foods at accessible depths as well as the birds' ability to fly to more favorable feeding sites. On the coast of Maine, many black ducks winter on tidal estuaries and depend upon invertebrates in littoral mud flats for sustenance. When extremely cold temperatures persist for several days and the salt-water temperatures approach freezing, the tidal flats freeze during low tide and do *not* thaw while covered by the tide. This reduces the available feeding area to a narrow band of water a few feet wide along the margins of the low-tide line. The available feeding time is thus also restricted to a very few hours twice in every 24 hour period. The duration of extreme weather patterns, their frequency, and when they occur is important, e.g. early in January, when birds are in good condition, or in March, after winter stress has taken its toll. The latter pertains also in New Jersey. Although black ducks currently winter at least as far south as Georgia, winter starvation south of New Jersey or perhaps Delaware has not been documented.

At the present time, the largest numbers of wintering black ducks are found in New Jersey.

## Spring Migration

The northward shift of black ducks starts in March and is complete by June or before. In the Atlantic Flyway many birds move along the coast first, then move inland to breeding areas as "ice out" occurs. Breeding pairs have been observed in residence on beaver flowages in the Bangor, Maine, area when snow in the woods was still hip deep and only a few square feet of open water was available. Aged broods observed later indicated that successful nesting and laying may be initiated in such conditions.

## Habitat Requirements

Habitat requirements for the black duck are difficult to define because of the very broad range of wetland and water types they use. Perhaps the only generalized statement that can be made is that the species does not tolerate human disturbance well. In a broad view, it is a species of the eastern forests north to the tree line and west to the prairies. During migration and winter, black ducks may be found on nearly any sized body of unfrozen water, even well-wooded swamps. There is a strong tendency to gather on large water areas during the fall and winter. Conversely, the small beaver ponds that provided such important breeding habitat in summer are used rather rarely in the fall. The tidal/salt marshes of the eastern seaboard are important wintering areas as far south as Georgia. However, flooded, wooded swamps also may be used in the lower end of both the Atlantic and Mississippi flyways. Atlantic Flyway blacks wintering in the northern end of the range usually find salt marshes frozen and resort to more marine environments, such as estuaries, bays and sounds.

The blacks need for seclusion is particularly notable during the breeding season. Rarely in the Northeast are more than two to three breeding pairs observed on the average area. Exceptions occur of course, as on the islands studied by Coulter and Miller (1968), Stotts and Davis (1960), and Reed (1975).

## Limiting Factors

Black ducks are in decline, and nearly everyone familiar with the black duck has an opinion on the cause. Many factors play a role, but whether or not they are truly limiting is debatable. Some decimating influences affect the black and other species, too. Among these are blood parasites and lead poisoning, red tide and oil spills, habitat losses and shooting, pesticide residues and predators, weather conditions and heavy metals. The list goes on, but last and perhaps by no means least comes evolution and hybridization with the mallard. The role and significance of hunting is discussed in more detail elsewhere.

# Significance of the Species

Sought by native peoples in northern latitudes for subsistence food; sought by hundreds of thousands of hunters for food and recreation; sought by uncounted photographers, birdwatchers, and artists; studied by scientists; surveyed by international agencies and managed jointly by the United States and Canada, the black duck must by considered highly significant. The black's wariness, large size, and palatability have made it traditionally the number one game duck of eastern Canada and the Atlantic Coast of the United States.

In 1951, the black duck made up three percent of waterfowl-hunter bag checks in the Mississippi Flyway and 24 percent in the Atlantic Flyway. In New England, the black ducks made up nearly half the bag (Addy 1953). In the 1980s, the status changed radically. Hunter numbers and total days of hunting have increased dramatically. Scientific survey data for the United States and Canada, available only since 1968, show the annual kill ranging from high of 772,000 in 1976 to a low of 523,000 in 1983. Significantly, the proportionate kill between the United States and Canada almost has reversed itself since 1976. That year the United States retrieved kill was 55 percent of the total and Canada's 45 percent. Similar figures exist for every year since the initiation of Canadian kill surveys in 1968. Then, in 1977, the United States took 43 percent, Canada 57 percent. From 1977 through 1983, Canada accounted for more than half of the annual kill of black ducks each year except 1980, when it took 49 percent. Canadian hunting pressure is less than that of the United States, but has increased moderately since 1968 (Spencer *et al* 1981).

Other than man, the black duck is not a significant prey species for any predator. It does not form a major portion of the diet nor is it particularly or regularly taken by any species.

## Historical Perspective

Various references describe the use of black ducks as food by the aborigines, and some writers refer to the ducks' presence during coastal exploration in the 17th century. It appears that the black duck has been common on the eastern seaboard since the days of European colonization. Addy (1953) states, "about 60 years ago the black began to extend its range westward (Griscom 1949). Today there are reports of broods in North Dakota (Hammond 1950) . . . and [it] now occurs rather frequently in Manitoba in the late summer and fall."

Despite a paucity of reliable population estimates, various early observers, including well-qualified biologists, became concerned about declining black duck populations. For the May 1947 issue of *Field and Stream*, imminent New Brunswick biologist Bruce Wright wrote an article entitled, "Can We Restore the Black Duck?" Similarly, in February of that year Ira Gabrielson called attention to the "slowly and steadily decreasing" numbers of black ducks. In the early 1950s, concerned wildlife-management leaders on the eastern seaboard formed the Joint Black Duck Committee to attack the problem of declining black ducks. This group matured into the Atlantic Flyway Council. In 1967, the council established a standing Black Duck Committee that in March 1968 sponsored a symposium on the black duck problem. Participation was flyway-wide, with contributions from many of the best in the business at that time. Results of the meetings included well-documented, published proceedings and the recommendation that negotiations with Canada be initiated for the purpose of developing a unified management program and that in the interim the flyway maintain a one-black-duck daily bag limit (two in possession) within the general framework of season length and bag limit for all ducks (Barske 1968).

Modern scientific population surveys and inventories were developed and initiated in the United States during the mid-1950s and in Canada about 10 years later. Prior to this time, observations had been predominantly qualitative. The first nationwide survey was the mid-winter waterfowl inventory, generally considered to have been operational by 1955. Since that year, efforts and coverage have been reasonably consistent. This inventory provides an estimate of black duck numbers over the entire United States. It normally is conducted the first two weeks of January. It is essentially an aerial survey.

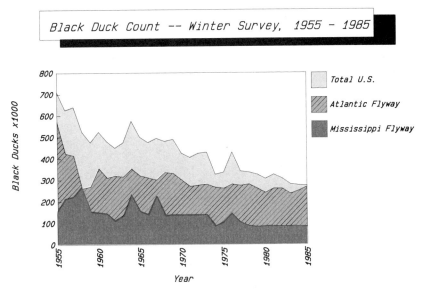

Black Duck Count -- Winter Survey, 1955 - 1985

Estimates are that the Winter Survey (Winter Inventory) records
1/3 to 1/5 of all black ducks (Martinson et al., 1968: 48;
Martin et al., 1967; Anon. 1976: 8). The validity of using the
winter inventory as an indicator of population trend is
discussed by Smith (1983: 3). Crissey (1976. 2), and Heusmann (1980).

Resultant data provide the longest continuous record of black duck populations available. Although the numerical estimates may be debatable, the
trends revealed appear to be bona fide. The average decline has been about
two percent yearly, with a 60 percent decline from 1955 to 1983 (Grandy
1983). In addition to the overall decline, changes in distribution have occurred. It appears that a larger proportion of the population is wintering
farther north in the Atlantic Flyway, while the reverse is true in the Mississippi
Flyway. The southeastern and Canadian populations have remained about
the same. A factor having some influence on Mississippi Flyway distribution
may be the notable decline of breeding black ducks in southwestern Ontario.

## Current Trends

Ever since the advent of modern inventories, winter surveys have indicated a
declining black duck population. This is the only direct range-wide count
available. Other population estimates and/or indices have been developed
from indirect sources, such as harvest surveys and band recovery analysis.
Spencer (1982) calculated a 76 percent decline in the numbers of black duck
broods produced in Maine between the periods 1956-65 vs. 1977-81. Although
data are limited, other waterfowl biologists southward and westward in the
Atlantic Flyway also report serious declines in breeding populations (Per.

comm.). The Black Duck Management Plan (Spencer *et al* 1980) reported North American pre-hunting season population estimates, developed by extrapolation, of approximately 2.5 million blacks in 1980. Current wintering populations over the 1981-85 period have ranged from 201,000 to 241,000 in the Atlantic Flyway and 58,000 to 90,000 in the Mississippi Flyway (279,000 to 331,000 United States total). Canadian wintering populations are estimated at 20,000 to 25,000 (Black Duck Management Plan and U.S. Fish and Wildlife Service data). In January 1985, the winter inventory recorded the smallest number of black ducks in its 31-year history. Only 279,000 blacks were tallied in the entire United States.

Over a period of three decades, at least three increasingly sophisticated and comprehensive analyses of black duck band recoveries have been completed. Addy (1953) analysed 15,481 shooting recoveries from 1918 through January 1951, plus an additional 2,037 recoveries through the spring of 1952. Addy's study, the most comprehensive study at that time, provided a tremendous amount of concrete information on migration routes, timing, and numbers of birds using various routes. He showed that some of the most northern breeders went the farthest south and moved the greatest distances. He also suggested that some populations had relatively sedentary habits, nesting and wintering within the same limited area. For example, a few blacks nest in inland Maine and winter on the Maine Coast.

Geis, Smith, and Rogers (1971) also studied black duck band recoveries and developed survival rates for different components of the populations. They presented data showing the breeding-ground origins of birds killed by hunters in various geographic areas. Additionally, they examined the hypothesis that the hunting kill is not totally additive to nonhunting mortality because a portion of the hunting take would die in any event as a result of natural factors. Their calculations suggest that slightly more than half of the hunting mortality on first-year blacks banded in summer *is* additive to nonhunting mortality. For summer-banded adults, the additive proportion is considerably higher.

In the following decade, new discoveries and advances occurred in the mathematical methodology and computer technology for analysing band recoveries. Using these new techniques, Blandin (1982) was able to appraise mortality/survival rates for various segments of the black duck population throughout its range. He demonstrated that survival rates of adult males exceeded all other sex and age groups and that immature females had the lowest survival potential. Rates varied considerably from different regions within the black duck range, but overall the data suggested that young female black ducks were being killed by hunters at an annual rate that precluded their recruitment into the breeding population in sufficient numbers to replenish and maintain the population. This finding supports the validity of the decline illustrated by winter inventory records.

## Percent Distribution of Wintering Black Ducks By Management Regions*

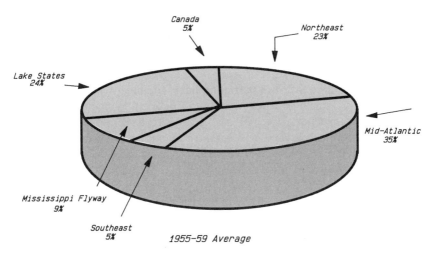

Canada
5%

Northeast
23%

Lake States
24%

Mid-Atlantic
35%

Mississippi Flyway
9%

Southeast
5%

1955-59 Average

* Area of the Circle is Proportionate to the Average Total
Population for each Period.
** Estimated average 22,000

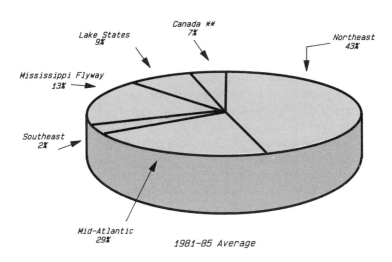

Lake States
9%

Canada **
7%

Northeast
43%

Mississippi Flyway
13%

Southeast
2%

Mid-Atlantic
29%

1981-85 Average

It would seem that there can be little doubt of a serious decline in the North American black duck population. The causes of this decline probably are many, but the one significant cause that can be controlled by man at will is the legal hunting take. A moratorium on black duck hunting has been recommended many times, but the failure of the politicians who control hunting regulations to act upon these recommendations will in all likelihood result in continued reduction of black duck numbers.

# Management

Black duck management is but part of broader wildlife or waterfowl management problems. It can be categorized into "population management," the results of which depend to a major degree upon resource-use regulation, and "habitat management," dealing with man's attempt to control, improve, or increase the quantity and quality of available black duck habitat. With respect to populations, the United States government bears the ultimate responsibility, by law, for the wise use and preservation of this renewable resource. This is under the jurisdiction of the U.S. Fish and Wildlife Service (FWS) in the Department of Interior. Management measures currently in use consist principally of establishing annual hunting regulations safeguarded by an extremely limited enforcement staff. To provide a basis for hunting regulations, hunters are asked to mail in a completed questionnaire about their success and to send in a wing from each bird shot. These two surveys provide detailed information on the magnitude and distribution of the black duck kill. Distribution is measured by periods within the season, by geographic areas (states), and by four sex and age groups (adult males, adult females, immature males, and immature females).

Although there have been strong local or regional hunter kill trends, no clearly discernible trend in the North American take exists between 1968 and 1983. The change in distribution of the major take from the United States to Canada and increased hunting pressure during this period make interpretation of North American data difficult. It is notable that black duck hunting success, measured by the number of blacks killed per 1,000 hunter days, has declined (Spencer et al 1981).

Unfortunately, little use has been made of the various data that have been collected and analysed. Wildlife managers believe that the annual regulations governing hunting-season length and daily bag limit are the major determinants controlling the overall take. In 1953-54, season length was 60 days. It rose to 70 days from 1955 through 1957. In 1958 it was cut to 60 days and in 1959 to 40. Since 1959 it has increased to 50 days. Black duck bag limits were four from 1953 through 1960, two from 1961-63, four from 1964-66, and finally two in 1967. They remained at two through 1983, except for a one bird limit in 1972 (for a more detailed review of hunting regulations see Grandy 1983).

The states may set more restrictive hunting seasons than are called for in federal regulations, but not less. In 1983, Maine's concern for the black duck resulted in greater restrictions on black duck hunting than those promulgated by FWS. Several other states took similar actions. Finally, in 1984, federal regulations were designed to reduce the U.S. kill by 25 percent. Analyses of results are not yet available.

On the Canadian side of the border, where the major portion of the kill occurs, regulations traditionally have been more liberal, with four-to-six-bird daily bag limits. In 1984, slightly more restrictive regulations were put into effect.

A possible third category of waterfowl management might be termed "administrative management." This includes the four flyway councils, made up of state and provincial biologists, and their work, plus the support and recognition accorded them by federal, state, dominion and provincial wildlife administrators. Although it took at least six years to produce, the Black Duck Management Plan for North America 1980-2000, Vols. I & II (Spencer *et al* 1981) by the Atlantic Flyway Council was truly the result of a cooperative effort by all the above concerned agencies plus private groups such as Ducks Unlimited and various university researchers. It is to be hoped that it will provide guide lines for re-establishing a viable black duck population. Its stated long-range goal is to increase the population and to provide for the continued use of the resource at or above present levels on a sustained basis.

Long-term management objectives are to establish an increasing population as measured by the five-year running averages of the winter inventory and to maintain recreational and subsistence use at or above present levels. Strategies to achieve these objectives through management include proposals to reduce mortality, increase productivity, and improve population status evaluation.

The habitat management aspects of the black duck problem also have been and are being addressed at various levels. Habitat inventories have been completed by state, provincial, federal and dominion agencies. In the United States, pertinent national wildlife refuges where feasible will be managed to benefit black ducks. The same can be said of state management areas. The problem of adequate wintering habitat is being considered, and FWS has developed a plan for winter-habitat acquisition and management. On the breeding grounds, Ducks Unlimited has intensified eastern Canadian habitat development in behalf of black ducks. In addition to these organized efforts, individual researchers are endeavoring to determine what makes quality black duck habitat. However, in the final analysis habitat management and research is a time consuming and expensive operation and results will be years in coming, if they come at all.

## Prognosis

At the present level of management the future of the black duck is questionable and may even be in serious jeopardy. Unless the hunter kill is reduced significantly in the very near future, particularly in Canada, the black duck may not survive as a game species to the year 2000. As numbers become reduced, increased frequency of hybridization with mallards will occur and perhaps ultimately only mongrels will remain. Conversely, an immediate and significant reduction in the hunter take may enable the residual population to rebuild. The productivity of individual pairs is good. If and when an adequate kill reduction occurs, new methods of controlling the total take must be employed or the cycle will repeat itself. As pointed out previously, the present population is less than half what it was 30 years ago and continues to decline.

## Recommendations

Achieving the goals, objectives, and strategies outlined in the Black Duck Management Plan for North America is crucial to black duck management. Specific programs also recommended by the plan include but are not limited to:

- reduction of hunting mortality
- increase productivity through habitat management
- control of competition with mallards as appropriate
- local control of predation where desirable and feasible
- improved appraisal of survival through banding
- improvement of the winter inventory
- continued research and development of production surveys
- improved measurement of the U.S. hunter take.

These recommendations are useful primarily for black duck managers and/or administrators. However, anyone concerned about black duck survival should seek to disseminate information concerning black duck status and to support politically at all levels the initiation and aggressive implementation of the Black Duck Management Plan for North America.

## References

Addy, C.E. 1953. *Fall Migration of the Black Duck.* Special Science Report: Wildlife No. 19. Fish and Wildlife Service. U.S. Department of Interior. 63 pp.

Barclay, J.S. 1970. Ecological aspects of defensive behavior in breeding mallards and black ducks. Ph.D Thesis. Ohio State University. Columbus, Ohio. 176 pp.

Barski, P. (ed.) 1968. *The Black Duck, Evaluation, Management and Research: A Symposium.* Atlantic Waterfowl Council and Wildlife Management Institute (pub.) 193 pp.

Blandin, W.W. 1982. Population characteristics and simulation modelling of black ducks. Ph.D Dissertation. Clark University. Worchester, Massachusetts. 345 pp.

Bellrose, F.C. 1976. *Ducks, Geese and Swans of North America.* Stackpole Books. 544 pp.

Coulter, M.W. and W.R. Miller. 1968. "Nesting biology of black ducks and mallards in northern New England." *Vermont Fish and Game Department Bulletin* 68-2. 74 pp.

Geis, A.D., R.I. Smith and J.P. Rogers. 1971. *Black Duck Distribution, Harvest Characteristics, and Survival.* U.S. Fish and Wildlife Service Special Science Report: Wildlife 139. 241 pp.

Grandy, J.W. 1983. "The North American black duck (*Anas rubripes*); a case study of 28 years of failure in American wildlife management." *International Journal for the Study of Animal Problems.* Supplementary Volume 4, No. 4. 35 pp.

Palmer, R.S. (ed.) 1976. *Handbook of North American Birds. Vol. 2.* Yale University Press. New Haven, Connecticut. 521 pp.

Reed, A. 1975. "Reproductive output of black ducks in the St. Lawrence estuary." *Journal of Wildlife Management* 39(2):243-255.

Spencer, H.E. *et al.* 1981. Black Duck Management Plan for North America 1980-2000. Vol. I. Vol. II. Atlantic Waterfowl Council Unpublished. Mimeographed. 42 pp. V. I, 124 pp. V II.

Stotts, V.D. and D.E. Davis. 1960. "The black duck in the Chesapeake Bay of Maryland: Breeding behavior and biology." *Chesapeake Science* 1:127-154.

Stotts, V.D. 1968. "Habitat and breeding ecology. East Central United States," *in* P. Barske ed., *The Black Duck: Evaluation, Management, and Research Atlantic Flyway Council.* pp. 102-112.

Wright, B.S. 1947. *The Black Duck in Eastern Canada: A Study of the Breeding Biology.* Report to Chief Naturalist, Ducks Unlimited (Canada). Frederickton, N.B. April 1947.

*Howard E. Spencer, Jr., retired as director of wildlife research after 30 years with the Maine Department of Inland Fish and Wildlife. He has studied black ducks for more than 25 years.*

Red knots congregate during migration at central staging areas. Protection of these areas is vital to surival of the knot and other shorebird migrants.

*Frank Schleicher/Photo Researchers*

# Red Knot

## Brian A. Harrington

Manomet Bird Observatory

## Species Description and Natural History

RED KNOTS (*Calidris canutus*) are the largest of the true sandpipers in North America, yet are not much larger than an American robin (*Turdus migratorius*). Males tend to be slightly smaller than females, as is common among shorebirds (Johnsgard 1981). Breeding plumage includes a rich, russet breast and a dorsal coloration ranging from dark brown to orange-russet. Males tend to be more richly colored than females. Breeding feathers start appearing as early as February, but molt rarely is completed before April. Molt from breeding into nonbreeding plumage begins before the south migration commences, but most adults still retain roughly half the breeding plumage from July through mid-September. Full winter plumage usually is present by early November. In nonbreeding plumage, knots are notably nondescript: light gray dorsally and dirty white ventrally.

The bill of the red knot is typical of that found in the true sandpipers—medium length (about 1.4 to 1.6 inches), stocky, straight. Females tend to have slightly longer bills than males. The knot's legs are proportionately shorter than those of most sandpipers, perhaps a reflection of the knot's tendency to forage above the waterline in its principal habitats. Wing length typically ranges from six to seven inches, a greater length than is found in otherwise similar-sized birds. American robins, blue jays (*Cyanocitta cristata*), and mourning doves (*Zenaida macroura*), for example, normally have wing

871

lengths less than five and a half inches long. Such long and narrow wings are commonplace among shorebirds and other birds that undertake long, nonstop migratory flights.

The knot's weight varies greatly among individuals. The average fat-free weight is about four ounces, but migratory knots caught at staging areas weighed about half a pound.

## Range and Migration

Although knots are found worldwide, the North American race (*C.c. rufa*) nests in the central Canadian arctic and winters between southern North America and southern South America. The so-called European race (*C.c. canutus*) nests on high-arctic islands in eastern Canada and on Greenland, but migrates across the Atlantic Ocean to winter on European marine coasts. A third and smaller breeding group, also considered to be *C.c. canutus* (American Ornithologists' Union 1957) breeds in Siberia and winters on the African West Coast, principally in Mauritania, but also in South Africa and in New Zealand and Australia.

Knots have some of the longest migrations known to science, and in recent years have been intensively studied in both the New and Old World. Some fly 2,000 to 3,000 miles over water nonstop at high altitudes (Richardson 1979). These distances are crossed in an estimated 50 to 80 hours. Other shorebird species and other populations within species migrate over varying distances (McNeil and Cadieux 1972). The lengths of the nonstop segments also vary.

## Migration of Old World Knots

Knots that nest in Siberia and winter in western and southern Africa depart the eastern Siberian Coast in a westerly direction, apparently flying southwest over the polar sea toward the Baltic and North Sea coasts of Finland, Denmark, and the Netherlands and perhaps the Barents Sea Coast of Norway (Dick *et al* 1976). Little is known of this flight save for fragmentary information from the New Siberia Islands, the Taymyr Peninsula, and northeastern Norway. Pleske (1928) noted that flocks were seen traveling southwestward along the western Taymyr Coast during late August, a season considerably later than the main autumn flight (see below). In northeastern Norway, small flocks were reported during late July (Dick *et al* 1976), flocks that probably were coming from Siberia via a trans-polar ocean route.

Knots commonly are reported on the Baltic Sea coasts of Finland, Norway, Sweden, and Denmark in late July. Evidence from banding (e.g. Dick *et al* 1976) suggests that these also are from Siberia and that the migration continues from the Baltic to a staging area on the Waddensee coasts of Germany and the Netherlands during late July and early August. Banding here, in Iceland, in Great Britain, and on the West African coast has shown that Siberian knots on the Waddensee are joined by others from Greenland and eastern Canada traveling by way of Iceland and southern Norway. The Siberian knots continue to western European coasts and veer southward to Mauritania, with some continuing to South Africa. Meanwhile, most of the knots from the western Atlantic move to spend winter in the British Isles.

Another Old World group of knots spends the boreal winter in Australasia, especially in New Zealand. Little information has been published on the breeding origins or the migration routes of these birds, but circumstantial evidence suggests that they come from the Wrangel Island breeding group off eastern Siberia. A recently discovered major spring staging area in Alaska's Copper River Delta (Isleib 1979) probably is used by birds of this group, but how they get there is unknown. The principal southward route also is unknown, but apparently differs from the spring route inasmuch as knots are scarce in Alaska at that season (Kessel and Gibson 1978).

## Migrations of New World Knots

***South Migration.*** Accounts from the breeding grounds suggest that adult knots begin leaving nesting areas in Alaska and Canada during mid-July. The southward migration must commence quickly, because knots also begin appearing at Atlantic staging grounds in southern Canada and the United States at the same time. Counts by cooperators in the International Shorebird Surveys, a project operated by the Manomet Bird Observatory in Massachusetts, along with information in the National Audubon Society's journal *American Birds,* have provided the basis for this description of the autumn migration of *rufa.* Other information is drawn from the banding and survey programs of the Manomet Bird Observatory and the Canadian Wildlife Service.

The fall migration in eastern North America (Harrington 1983) begins with an overland flight by adults in a narrow front between James Bay, Ontario, and the U.S. Atlantic Coast in late July and early August, followed by an overwater flight toward South America. The majority of birds in the first leg of this flight visit coastal stopover sites on James Bay and on the Atlantic Coast between Chesapeake Bay and Cape Cod Bay (Morrison and Harrington 1979), with principal areas in Massachusetts and New Jersey.

The pattern of knot migration in eastern North America changes after mid-August with the appearance of the first juvenile birds, including many scattered at inland locations where the species earlier was rare (Manomet Bird Observatory unpub.). Inland, the passage zone is much broader, while on the coast numbers dwindle at northeastern sites and tend to increase at mid-Atlantic sites. In southeastern states and on the Gulf Coast numbers increase throughout September and October.

Taken together, the information from mid-August suggests that juvenile knots fly across a broad overland front to coastal sites south of New England, where they mix with adults that have not migrated to South America. The migratory route of juveniles after this stage is not clear, but the recovery in southern Brazil during early November of one banded in Massachusetts (Manomet Bird Observatory unpubl.) shows that some, at least, probably migrate to the southern Argentine wintering area.

Peak numbers of *rufa* arrive on the U.S. Gulf Coast between late September and early November. Although their origin is unclear, banding has shown that some had visited New England during July and August. Others apparently arrived by direct flights originating in Canada. After November (Texas) or February (Florida), the Gulf Coast group disappears to unknown areas.

Most of the knots leaving Massachusetts and, presumably, New Jersey, fly overwater to South America. Evidence of this flight comes from several sources. First, as numbers dwindle during early August in New England and New Jersey, no increase occurs in the southeastern and Gulf Coast states. Second, knots banded in Massachusetts have been found in South America soon after they were banded. For example, one banded on August 13 was found 16 days later on the Guyana coast (Morrison and Spaans 1979). Another, marked with dye on August 7, was seen 16 days later on Anegada Island, British West Indies, and three banded at James Bay, Canada, were found in Surinam just 23 days later (Morrison and Spaans 1979). Four additional birds, marked in Massachusetts during late July, were recorded in the Guianas during August or September in years following their original banding.

Surveys of the Guyana and Surinam coastline during August and September suggest that knots fly steadily eastward along the Atlantic Coast, apparently traveling toward staging areas east of Surinam and French Guiana. Spaans (1978) found few knots in Surinam after October.

The southward flight from northeastern South America apparently continues 2,500 miles directly across Amazonia to coastal Argentina south of La Plata River, and then down the Argentine Coast to the wintering grounds in southern Argentina and Tierra del Fuego (Harrington 1983). The passage along the Argentine Coast occurs during early October, which means that the knots' location between Surinam and Argentina is unknown for about a month. The birds probably are somewhere on the northeastern Brazilian Coast, probably on sandy sections east of the Amazon River mouth.

The principal wintering zone of knots in South America is between Peninsula Valdez in northern Chubut and Tierra del Fuego (Harrington and Morrison 1980). Recent aerial surveys by the Canadian Wildlife Service (Morrison 1983) found the largest numbers at Bahia Lomos at the eastern end of the Strait of Magellan. Other concentrations were on the eastern Tierra del Fuego coast, particularly near Rio Grande, and on the coast of Golfo San Jorge. This whole section of the Atlantic Coast is a zone of intense offshore oil development and also borders a major supertanker route. Oiling of shorebirds and other birds is commonplace (Harrington and Morrison 1980).

*North Migration.* The northward migration of *rufa* in Argentina was under way at Peninsula Valdez when researchers from Manomet Bird Observatory arrived in mid-March 1981. Peak numbers passed during the first third of April, and most were gone by the 20th. Weights of captured birds indicated that knots at Peninsula Valdez had sufficient fat to fly 600 to 1,500 miles without stopping. This, combined with the fact that few knots were found for 600 miles north of Peninsula Valdez, suggests that the flight passed directly to southern Brazil.

In 1984, a second Manomet Bird Observatory research team was assembled from Argentina, Uruguay, Brazil, the United States, and Canada with funding provided by the World Wildlife Fund-U.S. One of the team's goals was to survey the south Brazilian Coast during April and May. They found a major knot staging area along a remote Atlantic beach and coastal lagoon, Lagoa do Peixe, south of Porto Alegre. The weights of knots caught at Lagoa do Peixe were the heaviest ever recorded and suggested that the birds were capable of flying, nonstop, several thousand miles, perhaps even to the United States (Harrington *et al,* in press).

Incredibly, just 13 days after knots were first seen leaving Lagoa do Peixe, marked individuals were found on the Delaware Bay shoreline of New Jersey, 5,000 miles from where they had been marked. Circumstantial evidence suggests they may have flown this distance without stopping, for no other staging area has been found between Brazil and the United States in spite of dedicated searches in Surinam (Spaans 1978), eastern Venezuela (McNeil 1970, Mercier, *in lit.*), western Venezuela (Casler and Lira 1979, Casler, *in lit.*), and Colombia (Rusk 1959). Whatever means are employed, knot migration between 32 south and 39 north latitude is very rapid. If the flight is interrupted, it cannot be for long, for the air travel would require at least five days, leaving eight days available for stops along the way.

The passage of most northbound knots through the United States takes place between May 15 and 31. Work of International Shorebird Survey cooperators shows a flight in some years along the Atlantic shore of Georgia and South Carolina, but in most years landfall apparently is made on the mid-Atlantic Coast. Here tens of thousands of knots collect at Delaware Bay to feed on horseshoe crab eggs (*Limulus polyphemus*) when the crabs come ashore on spring tides to breed during the second half of May (Bidderman 1983). The buildup of knots is complete by the end of the month, when as many as 95,000 have been counted (Dunne *et al* 1983), more *rufa* than are known from any other location in the Western Hemisphere.

From Delaware Bay the remaining northward migration evidently is completed in a single flight, except for occasions when adverse weather is encountered. The major exodus from Delaware Bay has been observed during the last few days of May and the first few days of June, shortly before adults appear on the breeding grounds (see above).

## Breeding

A precise description of the breeding ranges of the two knot races in North America is not possible, because knots nest in remote areas infrequently visited by biologists and because the racial distinctions of the adults are based on vague characters that change with the age of the feathers, exposure to sunlight, etc. Genetic and protein studies could possibly clarify these distinctions.

Given the taxonomic difficulties, in this summary the North American knot breeding areas are divided into three zones.

*Northern Alaska.* According to Kessel and Gibson (1978), knots breed in Alaska north and west from the Seward Peninsula to Barrow and Cooper Island. Breeding is unknown between Cooper Island and the Mackenzie River Delta in Canada. Conover (1943) believed the Alaskan knots are *canutus,* most likely an eastern extension of the Wrangel Island breeding group (Dement'ev *et al* 1969).

*The Low Canadian Arctic.* This area of the Canadian shield includes the mainland tundra and the islands of the central Canadian archipelago south of 70 north latitude. Here knots, *rufa* in all cases, nest in small numbers on southeastern Victoria Island and nearby on Jenny Lind and Taylor islands (Brenard 1925, Parmelee *et al* 1967). Circumstantial evidence also suggests nesting on Southampton Island in Hudson's Bay (Sutton 1932, Manning in Bray 1943, Parker and Ross 1973). To summarize, *rufa's* breeding range is poorly known but apparently is centered on the central arctic islands of the Canadian shield.

*The Middle and High Canadian Arctic.* The distribution of knots across the northern islands of the Candian archipelago also is poorly known. In cases where taxonomic distinction has been made, the race was *canutus,* including birds at Prince of Wales Island (Manning and Macpherson 1961), Devon Island (Hussell and Holroyd 1974), Axel Heiberg Island (Morrison 1977), and Ellesmere Island (Parmelee and MacDonald 1960). *Canutus* also nests in Greenland (Hobson 1972).

Several accounts exist of knot biology in the arctic, but the most complete reports (Pleske 1928, Parmelee and MacDonald 1960, Nettleship 1974, Hobson 1972) all deal with the race *canutus.* Unless otherwise noted, information here comes from one or a combination of these works.

In almost all accounts, knots arrive on the nesting grounds during late May and early June, with both sexes returning together in an advanced reproductive condition. According to some accounts, knots are paired when they return, but more likely they pair so quickly that this appears to be the case. Nesting begins about two weeks after arrival. Incubation lasts 21 to 23 days, and highly precocious, downy chicks hatch during the first half of July.

Parents and chicks leave the nesting sites within a few days and move as far as a half mile to lower ground, where they can find tundra pools, or to lake or marine shorelines. Here they join bands of young adults of their own and other species, particularly ruddy turnstones (*Arenaria interpres*), thus attaining some protection from predators through safety in numbers. It is unclear whether females stay with broods after this stage (Parmelee and MacDonald 1960, but see Hobson 1972), but the low numbers in museum collections suggest that the females depart, leaving males to tend the brood. Departure of females before males is commonplace in other arctic shorebirds.

Juvenile knots first fly 18 to 20 days after hatching. Males apparently then leave the broods, and the young depart from the breeding grounds about two weeks later.

Nettleship (1974) prefaced his description of knot nesting habitat by saying, "it seems clear that the choice of nest site varies widely and would be difficult to describe in any useful general way." Nevertheless, a few general points from various accounts are worth review.

Knots breed only in arctic tundra, using habitats ranging from wet, low, and well-vegetated areas to dry slopes and ridges. Nests are located on tussocks or hummocks of grass near tundra pools, usually more than half a mile from the coasts. In western Ellesmere, more nests were found in wet habitats than on dry slopes and ridges, but in north-central Ellesmere they were on slopes, near marshes and pools. Pleske (1928) found nests mostly on sunny slopes or hill summits where snow melted first.

Knot nests are deep scrapes four to four and a half inches in diameter by two inches deep, lined with willow leaves and/or lichens, and usually well hidden among stunted willows or rocks. Normal clutches are four eggs laid at about daily intervals, but sometimes fewer are laid. A typical clutch of eggs weighs 50 to 60 percent of the female's weight. Eggs are closely incubated by both sexes.

The strongest influences on knot nesting ecology are weather, geographic location, and climate. For example, Hobson (1972) believed that knots failed to breed in years of low precipitation because lowered water reduced the aquatic-larvae and other insect-larvae populations upon which knots feed.

## Diet

Morrison (1975) and Parmelee and MacDonald (1960) found that knots at Ellesmere and Greenland return in spring before invertebrate animal prey is readily available. If late snow should fall, as often happens, the fat reserves remaining at the end of the migration probably are critical to survival and to the success of early breeding biology. In some springs, knots must resort to eating vegetation until animal food is available. Nettleship (1974) describes a characteristic probing and jabbing used to find grass shoots, seeds, sedges, and mosses in marshes and wet tundra. By mid-June, foraging changes to pecking for insects, particularly caterpillars, larval flies, and chironomids. The latter were locally abundant through most of the season, first in shoreward and permanent ponds during late June, then further inland during the first half of July and at large lakes during July and early August.

Pleske (1928) found that insects, arachnids, and oligochaete worms were major knot foods in Siberia.

## Significance of the Species

The major significance of red knots is their representation of the many shorebirds that depend upon critical staging sites during migrations between North and South America. Although not a widely recognized problem, the protection and management, where warranted, of critical stopover sites should be given a high conservation priority, for a variety of shorebirds including knots are threatened by the loss of migration staging areas.

The ecological importance of knots is not well understood. No studies exist to show what direct effect they may have on horseshoe-crab populations in Delaware Bay, or of indirect effects on shellfish or other invertebrate animals which are eaten by horseshoe crabs. Similarly, no information exists on relationships between knots and edible mussel populations in Massachusetts, New Jersey, or Argentina.

Knots themselves are the prey of other wildlife, including at least one endangered species, the peregrine falcon (*Falco peregrinus*) (pers. obser.).

## Historical Perspective

During the late 1800s and early 1900s, shorebirds were hunted legally in almost all parts of the Western Hemisphere. Although numerous anecdotal accounts exist of the numbers taken by sportsmen and of wasteful slaughter by market-hunters, none of the accounts allow precise comparisons to be made with numbers today. Nevertheless, it is clear that many species were affected severely by unregulated gunning and loss of suitable habitat. One formerly abundant species, the Eskimo curlew (*Numenius borealis*), has never recovered from its virtual extirpation, but others, whose numbers also were reduced, have recovered substantially today. Red knots are in the latter category.

Perhaps the best accounts of the knot's dramatic decline was given by George Mackay, a shorebird hunter who was among the first to publicize dwindling shorebird numbers. Mackay (1893) wrote that before 1850, knots were found in "immense number" in the Cape Cod region of Massachusetts, where they were so abundant that "estimates of their number were useless." Knot sport and market hunting were intense in Massachusetts and also in Virginia, where thousands were shot in spring for New York City markets (Mackay 1893). In 1893, Mackay concluded that "the knots in a great measure have been killed off." He also wrote, however, that they "have learned what invariably awaits them in certain localities, [and] the remnants of the once large numbers pass on, carrying their companions with them, being unwilling to risk the death of persecution that awaits them at all times . . . "

Another Massachusetts naturalist, Joseph A. Hager (pers. comm.), suggests that the knot's wariness may partly explain why their numbers appeared so low. Nevertheless, almost all accounts agree that populations were reduced greatly, perhaps by half according to some accounts and by more than 95 percent according to others (Forbush 1912). Today, populations have recovered from the low levels of the 1890s, although it is impossible to determine to what extent.

The arctic shorebirds most reduced in numbers during the 1800s were those that concentrated at migration staging areas. The simple act of concentrating, at any part of the life cycle, renders large proportions vulnerable to catastrophe. Today, many of the traditional shorebird coastal staging areas are increasingly disrupted by recreational and commercial activities, a problem that often could be reduced through careful management.

## Current Trends

Although red knot populations have recovered substantially since the 1890s, lack of information makes it impossible to show whether the populations now are stable. Information from the International Shorebird Surveys indicate no significant declines between 1974 and 1981 (Howe and Geissler, in lit.), but numbers apparently dropped substantially between 1981 and 1984 and then increased in 1985. Statistical evaluations of trends since 1981 have not been made, but assuming the trends are verified, causes of the change still remain unknown. It is reasonable to expect numbers to fluctuate when extensive breeding failures occur from time to time. Evaluation of long-term trends, using data collected over decades, will clarify some of these points, but no program has yet been maintained long enough to enable this to be done.

## Management

In the Western Hemisphere, no less than 14 species of shorebirds, including red knots, breed north of the tree line in Canada, Alaska, and Siberia, and winter chiefly in South America, some as far south as Tierra del Fuego, the southernmost land of the continent. These species are highly vulnerable to loss of critical migration staging areas. Protection of these birds cannot be accomplished in North America alone. It requires an internationally coordinated effort, such as the sister-reserve system recently proposed by the World Wildlife Fund and others. Under this system, a series of important stopover areas would be protected cooperatively by nations throughout the hemisphere.

The crux of the conservation problem is that a majority of the shorebird species that migrate between North and South America tend to concentrate in enormous numbers at a relatively small number of migration staging areas. In some cases, perhaps more than half the population may gather at single sites, attracted by predictably abundant but ephemeral food resources. While at stopover areas, shorebirds feed intensively, sometimes almost doubling their weight in less than two weeks. The accrued fat is then metabolized during flights to successive staging areas, usually a thousand or more miles away. In general, these long flights traverse biomes unsuitable to shorebirds, such as broad expanses of boreal forest, neotropical jungle, large stretches of ocean, deserts, and so forth. Thus, fat accrued at the stopover sites is critical to successful completion of the flight.

Expanding human populations and intense commercial and recreational development in North and South America have reduced the number of staging sites. Today, it is estimated that half, and in some cases perhaps 90 percent, of the individuals of 12 species use one or the other of two major North American spring stopover sites—one in Kansas and one on the mid Atlantic Coast. Similar areas exist on the West Coast. The conservation priority is clear—major staging sites in North and South America must be protected.

Responsibility for the management and protection of red knots and other North American shorebirds falls within the purview of national, provincial, and state governments. A review of the law and conventions germane to red knots is given by Senner and Howe (1984). The strongest legal protection is provided by the Migratory Bird Treaty Act. A few international agreements in the Western Hemisphere also aim to protect critical migratory-bird staging or wintering areas.

In the United States, shorebirds are incidental beneficiaries of legislation such as the National Environmental Policy Act of 1969, the Clean Water Act, and the Coastal Zone Management Act, as well as many state efforts to protect locally rare and endangered species such as terns and beach-nesting shorebirds. Furthermore, shorebirds in many nations benefit from national, state, and local parks, wildlife management areas, and similar reserves.

No active management has been initiated on behalf of knots or most other coastal shorebirds, with the notable exception of commendable efforts by the states of New Jersey and Delaware and by the New Jersey Conservation Foundation to protect key sections of the Delaware Bay shoreline. This coastal zone is used heavily by several shorebird species (Dunne *et al* 1983), including a very high but imprecisely known proportion of *rufa*. Incidental protection is provided to several of the knot's remaining coastal-migration staging areas that have been set aside as wildlife refuges or other reservations. This list includes Monomoy National Wildlife Refuge and the Cape Cod National Seashore in Massachusetts, Jamaica Bay National Wildlife Refuge in New York, the Brigantine Unit of the Edwin B. Forsythe National Wildlife Refuge in New Jersey, Bombay Hook National Wildlife Refuge in Delaware, Chincoteague National Wildlife Refuge in Virginia, the Virginia Coastal Reserve, Huntington Beach State Park in South Carolina, Padre Island National Seashore in Texas, and the Chugach National Forest in Alaska. Finally, the Wia Wia Nature Reserve in Surinam and the Argentine national park at Peninsula Valdez are important to *rufa*.

In many of the existing reserves, active management for knots and other shorebirds could be accomplished by maintaining resting-area sanctuaries free of human disturbance during appropriate seasons. In many instances, resting sanctuaries are needed only for parts of the tidal cycle, for example for two hours either side of high tide.

## Prognosis

Knots and many other shorebirds lead a perilous existence because of their dependence upon a few unprotected key migration staging areas. Furthermore, many species have relatively small, unprotected wintering zones (cf. Morrison 1984, Morrison *et al* 1985). Coastal resources throughout the western Atlantic are used intensively for commerce and recreation, and threats to wildlife, including knots, are pervasive and growing. Efforts by organizations such as the World Wildlife Fund are prompting new proposals, but governments have been slow to respond, a matter complicated because coordination is needed between many governments. However, the sister-reserve concept can be managed within nations but informally coordinated between them, thus offering hope that conservation measures can be achieved soon. Without such efforts, and without cooperation between governments, the future of the knots and their allies will remain clouded.

## Recommendations

Although information from the International Shorebird Surveys has identified some key migration staging areas used by knots and other shorebirds in the eastern United States, similar work is needed west of the 105th longitude. The International Shorebird Survey has not adequately identified key migration areas in Central and South America, largely because there are few capable naturalists who can volunteer the substantial commitments involved in the project. Improved information is needed.

The Canadian Wildlife Service has made a substantial commitment to identifying key shorebird areas not only in Canada, but cooperatively with other governments in South America. This work should be translated to active management goals and should be joined more actively by the United States government as well as by Central and South American governments, including Mexico, Panama, Venezuela, Surinam, Guyana, Brazil, Ecuador, Argentina, and Chile, all of which are known to host major shorebird stopover or wintering areas.

An international administrative framework is needed to identify and protect the critical migration staging sites and wintering zones used by knots and other shorebirds. Identification of other threats, especially spills of harmful petrochemical substances or chronic oil pollution in wintering zones, is needed along with contingency plans to deal with them.

In the United States, protection is needed for key knot stopover areas in Alaska, Massachusetts, New Jersey, and Texas and for wintering areas in Florida. In Alaska, the Copper River Delta is used by as many as 100,000 knots in spring (Isleib 1979) and is susceptible to spills from trans-Alaskan oil pipeline tankers (Senner 1979, Senner and Howe 1984). The key site in Massachusetts is Third Cliff Beach in Scituate. In New Jersey, knots and other shorebirds concentrate to an extraordinary degree on the Delaware Bay shoreline (Dunne *et al* 1983, Bidderman 1983). The importance of Delaware Bay to migratory shorebirds should be considered in contingency plans designed for responses to commercial tanker or industrial accidents. The food attracting the shorebirds—horseshoe crab eggs—also should be reviewed. Delaware Bay serves one of the largest petrochemical complexes in the world, and therefore has an extraordinary volume of tanker traffic. Accidents could decimate New World shorebird populations. Developing plans for dealing with even some of the more likely chemical accidents may require extraordinary measures, so methods of risk reduction should be reviewed in light of the region's immense importance to migratory shorebirds.

Great Egg Harbor Inlet on the New Jersey Atlantic shore is a major autumn stopover. While knots and other shorebirds benefit there from coastal protection laws, they also need protected resting areas during high tides.

Knots also use the Texas Gulf Coast during spring and autumn migration, especially Bolivar Flats near Galveston, Mustang Island at Port Aransas, and the Padre Island shore. Mustang Island is under intense condominium development, and regional planning there should include protection of habitats needed by knots and other wildlife. Bolivar Flats, adjacent to the shipping channel serving Houston, a particularly important area to migratory shorebirds, is unmanaged but should be protected.

In Florida, about 15,000 knots winter on the intensively developed west coast between St. Petersburg and Naples. Although recreational use of this coast is intense, knots seem to persevere, at least until the peak of the winter tourist season in March (Harrington *et al* 1982). But now some of the few remaining resting areas are falling to commercial and recreational development. Resting-area sanctuaries are urgently needed.

As for South America, major concentrations of knots spend the boreal winter between Tierra del Fuego and Peninsula Valdez (Morrison 1983). The highest concentrations exist along the southern coast, where offshore oil development is intense and where there are major supertanker routes. Oiling of shorebirds (Harrington and Morrison 1980) and other birds needs to be reduced. In addition, establishment of coastal reserves in critical wintering areas in Surinam and Tierra del Fuego would benefit native and migratory shorebirds, knots included.

During northward migration, the first major staging areas used by knots are at Peninsula Valdez on the central Argentine Coast. It is unclear how long individual knots remain there, but the turnover rate may be fairly rapid as the birds continue toward staging areas in southern Brazil. Peninsula Valdez is an Argentine national park, but much of the land is cattle and sheep rangeland, including land that surrounds a shallow lake used as a resting area by knots at night. It is not clear whether this rangeland should be protected as park property or if in fact it represents private inholdings in the park.

Knots also use major staging areas in southern Brazil about 600 miles north of Peninsula Valdez, especially a shallow lagoon called Lagoa do Peixe and nearby Atlantic shoreline in the state of Rio Grande do Sul. Lagoa do Peixe is not protected, but conservation organizations, including the World Wildlife Fund, the International Council for Bird Preservation, and the International Waterfowl Research Bureau, have begun discussions with agencies of the Brazilian government. There is some urgency to develop shoreline management plans because mariculture projects and development of tourism in the area are being planned.

Knots currently are taken for food in Guyana and for food and sport at gunning clubs in Barbados. Wherever shorebird hunting is not essential for human nutrition, it should be made illegal and the laws enforced.

Finally, a rather weak but symbolically important international agreement, the Ramsar Convention, already exists to encourage protection of internationally important wetlands (Senner and Howe 1984) and could lead to improved shorebird protection. Unfortunately, only two Western Hemisphere governments, Chile and Canada, have ratified it. As of December 1985, the United States, Uruguay, and Suriname had signed but not yet ratified the convention, and Costa Rica and Panama were preparing to sign it. Shorebirds and many other wetland birds could benefit by broader ratification and strengthening of the Ramsar Convention in the Western Hemisphere.

A second convention, the Bonn Convention, also could be important to shorebird conservation worldwide. Its focus on migratory animals of all habitats is broader than the Ramsar Convention's focus on wetlands. The United

States has balked at sending policy-making delegates to the Bonn Convention, but has sent observers.

Nations such as the United States and others mentioned above should strongly support and help strengthen the Ramsar Convention. Careful consideration should also be given to the Bonn Convention.

# References

American Ornithologists' Union. 1957. *Check-list of North American birds*. American Ornithologists' Union. Washington, D.C. 691 pp.

Bidderman, J.O. 1983. "Food for flight." *Audubon* 85:112-119.

Bray, R. 1943. "Notes on the birds of Southampton Island, Baffin Island, and the Melville Peninsula." *Auk* 60:504-536.

Brenard, J.F. 1925. "Unusual circumstance of Sabine Gull (*Xema sabini*) burying dead gull for protection from enemies." *Murrelet* 1925:4-5.

Casler, C.L. and J.R. Lira. 1979. "Censos poblacionales de aves marinas de la costa occidental del Golfo de Venezuela." *Boletin Centro Invest. Biol.* 13:37-85.

Conover, B. 1943. "The races of the knot (*Calidris canutus*)." *Auk* 45:226-228.

Dement'ev, G.P., N.A. Gladkov, and E.P. Spangenberg. 1969. *Birds of the Soviet Union, v. 3*. Israel Program for Scientific Translations. Jerusalem. 756 pp.

Dick, W.J.A., M.W. Pienkowski, M. Waltner and C.D.T. Minton. 1976. "Distribution and geographical origins of knot *Calidris canutus* wintering in Europe and Africa." *Ardea* 64:22-47.

Dunne, P., D. Sibley, C. Sutton, and W. Wander. 1983. "1982 aerial shorebird survey of Delaware Bay." *Records of New Jersey Birds* 8:68-75.

Forbush, E.H. 1912. *Game Birds, Wild-fowl, and Shore Birds*. Massachusetts State Board of Agriculture. Boston, Massachusetts. 622 pp.

Forbush, E.H. 1925. *Birds of Massachusetts and Other New England States*. Commonwealth of Massachusetts Department of Agriculture. Boston, Massachusetts.

Harrington, B. 1983. "The migration of the red knot." *Oceanus* 26:44-48.

Harrington, B.A. and R.I.G. Morrison. 1980. "Notes on the wintering areas of Red Knot *Calidris canutus rufa* in Argentina, South America." *Wader Study Group Bulletin* 28:40-42.

Harrington, B.A., D.C. Twichell, and L.E. Leddy. 1982. "Knots in Florida—a migration mystery." *The Florida Field Naturalist* 55 No. 5:4-5.

Hobson, W. 1972. "The breeding biology of the knot (*Calidris c. canutus*)." *Western Foundation of Vertebrate Zoology* 2:5-25.

Hussell, D.J.T. and G.L. Holroyd. 1974. "Birds of the Truelove Lowland and adjacent areas of northeastern Devon Island, N.W.T." *Canadian Field Naturalist* 88:197-212.

Isleib, M.E. 1979. "Migratory shorebird populations on the Copper River

Delta and eastern Prince William Sound, Alaska." *Studies in Avian Biology* 2:125-129.

Johnsgard, P.A. 1981. *The Plovers, Sandpipers, and Snipes of the World.* University of Nebraska Press. Lincoln, Nebraska. 493 pp.

Kessel, B. and D.D. Gibson. 1978. "Status and distribution of Alaska birds." *Studies in Avian Biology* 1:1-100.

Mackay, G.H. 1893. "Observations on the knot (*Tringa canutus*)." *Auk* 10:25-35.

Manning, T.H. and A.H. Macpherson. 1961. "A biological investigation of Prince of Wales Island, N.W.T." *Transactions of the Royal Canadian Institute* 33(part 2):116-239.

McNeil, R. 1970. "Hivernage et estivage d'oiseaux aquatiques Nord-Americains dans le Nord-est du Venezuela (mue, accumulation de graisse, capacite de vol et routes de migration)." *L'Oiseau et la Revue Francaise D'ornithologie* 40:185-302.

McNeil, R. and F. Cadieux. 1972. "Fat content and flight range of some adult spring and fall migrant North American shorebirds in relation to migration routes on the Atlantic Coast." *Naturalist Canada* 99:589-606.

Morrison, R.I.G. 1975. "Migration and morphometrics of European knot and turnstone on Ellesmere Island, Canada." *Bird-Banding* 46:290-301.

Morrison, R.I.G. 1977. "Migration of arctic waders wintering in Europe." *Polar Record* 18 No. 116:475-486.

Morrison, R.I.G. and B.A. Harrington. 1979. "Critical shorebird resources in James Bay and eastern North America." *Transactions of the 44th North American Wildlife and Natural Resources Conference, 1979.* Wildlife Management Institute of Washington, D.C. pp. 498-507.

Morrison, R.I.G. and A.L. Spaans. 1979. "National Geographic mini-expedition to Surinam, 1978." *Wader Study Group Bulletin* 26:37-41.

Morrison, R.I.G. 1983. "Aerial surveys of shorebirds in South America—some preliminary results." *Wader Study Group Bulletin* 37:41-45.

Morrison, R.I.G. 1984. "Migration systems of some New World shorebirds," *in* J. Burger and B.L. Olla eds., *Behavior of Marine Animals.* Plenum Press. New York. pp. 125-202.

Morrison, R.I.G., R.K. Ross, P. Canevari, P.deT.Z. Antas, B. deJong, B. Ramdial, F. Espinosa, M. Madriz T., and J.M. de Perez. 1985. "Aerial surveys of shorebirds and other wildlife in South America: some preliminary results." *Canadian Wildlife Service Progress Notes* 148:1-22.

Nettleship, D. 1974. "The breeding of the knot *Calidris canutus* at Hazen Camp, Ellesmere Island, N.W.T." *Polarforschung* 44:8-26.

Parker, G.R. and R.K. Ross. 1973. "Notes on the birds of Southampton Island, N.W.T." *Arctic* 26:123-129.

Parmelee, D.F. and S.D. MacDonald. 1960. "The birds of west-central Ellesmere Island and adjacent areas." *National Museum of Canada Bulletin No. 169, Biological Series* 63:1-103.

Parmelee, D.F., H.A. Stephens, and R.H. Schmidt. 1967. The birds of south-eastern Victoria Island and adjacent small islands." *National Museum of Canada, Biological Series* 78 No. 222. Ottawa, Canada. 229 pp.

Pleske, T. 1928. "Birds of the Eurasian tundra." *Memorandum of the Boston Society of Natural History* 6:111-485.

Richardson, W.J. 1979. "Southeastward shorebird migration over Nova Scotia and New Brunswick in autumn: a radar study." *Canadian Journal of Zoology* 57:107-124.

Rusk, M. 1959. "New York State Birds in Colombia." *The Kingbird* 9:12-18.

Senner, S.E. 1979. "An evaluation of the Copper River Delta as critical habitat for migrating shorebirds." *Studies in Avian Biology* 2:131-145.

Senner, S.E. and M.A. Howe. 1984. "Conservation of nearctic shorebirds," *in* J. Burger and B.L. Olla eds., *Behavior of Marine Animals*. Plenum Press. New York. pp. 379-421.

Spaans, A.L. 1978. "Status and numerical fluctuations of some North American waders along the Surinam coast." *Wilson Bulletin* 90:60-83.

Sutton, G.M. 1932. "The birds of Southampton Island." *Memorandum of the Carnegie Museum* 12:1-275.

*Brian A. Harrington is the ornithologist in charge of coastal-bird research at the Manomet Bird Observatory in Massachusetts, where he has worked since 1972.*

The future for the osprey looks promising now that organochloride-pesticide use has declined and wildlife managers have undertaken reintroduction projects.

*Leonard Lee Rue III*

# Osprey

## Mark A. Westall

President, The International Osprey Foundation

## Species Description and Natural History

THE OSPREY (*Pandion haliaetus*), found on every continent except Antarctica, is one of the most widely distributed bird species. In certain anatomical features, the osprey is similar to kites, falcons, hawks, eagles, and even Old and New World vultures (Grossman and Hamlet 1964). In many other ways, however, the osprey is very different. For example, its unusually long talons, curved into about a third of a circle, are completely round. The talons of other raptors are concave and grooved on the underside. It is also the only hawk that can reverse its outer toe, as in owls, in order to grasp its prey with two toes in front and two in back (Terres 1980).

In the Western Hemisphere, ospreys are divided into two subspecies: the North American osprey (*P.h. carolinensis*) and the Bahaman osprey (*P.h. ridgwayi*) (Prevost 1982, 1983). The relationship between these two subspecies remains unclear. Present-day Bahaman ospreys may be the survivors of an ancient North American population which was displaced by ospreys that disbursed from Europe by unknown natural means and formed the present North American population. Or they may be a more recent offshoot from North American ospreys, better adapted to breeding in subtropical habitats. Whatever the case, apparently secondary contact occurs between the two populations in south Florida (Allen 1962, Odgen 1977, Poole pers. comm.). The question of the subspecies relationship probably will remain unanswered until complicated genetic research can be accomplished to determine how closely related the two populations are (Prevost 1982, 1983).

## North American Distribution

Ospreys are distributed throughout North America and are seen regularly along its seacoasts, rivers, and major lakes and waterways during migration. These migrants winter in the West Indies and in Central and South America as far south as Argentina and Chile (Worth 1936, Henny and Van Velzen 1972, Kennedy 1973, Melquist *et al* 1979).

Current breeding populations, however, are restricted to the coasts and larger lakes, leaving much of the interior of the continent noticeably devoid of occupied nesting territories. Although some reports of past breeding populations within the interior region where ospreys now are absent may be debated, historical records presented by Henny (1983) show that ospreys did occasionally nest there. The reasons behind their disappearance is unknown, but a few researchers presently are working to reintroduce the species within the interior of North America primarily through the establishment of "hacking" programs (Hammer 1982, Schaadt and Rymon 1983, Brown 1984) (See Management).

Ospreys that breed south of the 29th parallel in south Florida, Baja California, and the Pacific Coast of Mexico generally are considered nonmigratory or resident birds. These birds may disperse during the nonbreeding season, but do not migrate farther south as their more northern relatives do (Ogden 1977, Judge 1983, Westall 1983).

## Physical Characteristics

Bald eagles and ospreys are commonly confused because both birds are large raptors with chocolate to fudge brown upperparts and white heads. Upon closer examination, however, ospreys are distinguished easily from all other birds of prey. The osprey, 21 to 24 inches long with a wingspan of 54 to 72 inches, is larger than most hawks but not as large as the bald eagle. The white head and neck have a broad dark streak along the cheeks and down the sides, with occasional streaks of brown on the crown. The eyes are bright yellow to pale brown. The bill is black and the cere, pale blue.

The underparts are white with some brown streaks on the breast depending on sexual and breeding characteristics. The tail is lightly colored and exhibits fine dark bands with a broad terminal bar edged in white. The legs and feet are bluish-gray to greenish-white, and the talons are black. In flight, ospreys are distinguished by white underparts and narrow, almost gull-like wings with a dark patch at the sharp bend or "wrist" of the wings (Brown and Amadon 1968, Zarn 1974, Terres 1980). Male and female ospreys are very similar in appearance except that males tend to have less streaking on the breast and crown than do females and usually are smaller, although there is a substantial amount of overlap (Terres 1980). Immature ospreys resemble adults except that the feathers of the brown upperparts of the immature are tipped in white, and the eyes are orange.

## Diet

The osprey commonly is called the fish hawk, and for good reason: It feeds almost exclusively on fish. Terres' (1980) list of prey species includes alewives, bluefish, blowfish, bonito, bowfin, carp, catfish, eels, flounders, flying fishes, goldfish, herring, horned pout, jacks, menhaden, mullet, perch, pickeral, pike, salmon, shad, sheephead, squeteague, suckers, and trout. The osprey preys upon whichever species is most available. Rarely, the osprey will take prey such as small mammals, birds, reptiles, amphibians, and some invertebrates (Sindelar and Schluter 1968, Tait *et al* 1972, Wiley and Lohrer 1973, Layher 1984).

## Voice

Vocal communication in ospreys is accomplished by a series of melodious calls or whistles that have yet to be adequately put into words, though many have tried (Bent 1937). Suffice it to say that these calls represent various feelings or desires that the caller is communicating to others in the area.

The most commonly heard call is the "greeting" given from one osprey to another when they are near one another. These calls are heard particularly around nesting sites when a bird on a nest advertises its presence to an approaching bird.

The "triumphant" or "courtship" call generally is expressed by the male during the mating ritual. It also is heard during similar behavioral displays upon the return of the male after a successful fishing foray and during periods of danger, such as when an eagle is in the area or an intruder is at the nest.

While the female waits for the male to return to the nest, she quite often will give the "anxious" call in anticipation of receiving another meal, either for herself or her young. The young, as they mature and become more vocal, give a similar call that only the most trained observer can discern.

As a prelude to another call, ospreys sometimes emit a comparatively quiet, short call known as the "confused" call. This call is heard quite often when one bird is alone on the nest studying a particular problem, such as realigning a displaced piece of nesting material.

Occasionally beginning as the "confused" call, the "alarm" call typically is heard at the first appearance of danger. If the danger continues to increase, the alarm call invariably transcends into the "very angry" or "really mad" call. The latter call generally is heard only after the birds have made several attempts to alleviate the threat and the danger has not disappeared.

## Hunting Behavior

While fishing, the osprey flies over the water at altitudes usually ranging from 30 to 100 feet. Upon sighting its prey, the bird hovers momentarily, trailing its legs, and then makes a powerful, falcon-like stoop toward the water. At approximately six feet above the surface, the osprey thrusts its feet forward, striking the water and sometimes completely disappearing below the surface. Occasionally, ospreys have been known never to rise again after one of these dives. Their carcasses, or at least their talons, have been found later still attached to the backs of their potential prey. Consequently, the osprey has the dubious distinction of being an extremely "stubborn" bird prone to sacrificing its life rather than releasing a fish too large to overcome (Bent 1937). It is more likely that the osprey is so thoroughly adapted to holding onto its slippery prey that if too large a fish is grasped, the bird is pulled under and eventually drowned before it can let go.

After rising from the water, with or without its prey, the osprey pauses in mid-flight to shake off water. It then either continues the hunt or returns to its nest or a favorite feeding perch, its prey clasped in its talons and carried torpedo fashion to lessen wind resistance.

Studies indicate that the osprey has an average hunting success rate of 76 percent (Lambert 1943, MacCarter 1972, Garber 1972, French 1972, Ueoka and Koplin 1973). Although ospreys clearly are proficient predators, the amount of time and energy they expend on a fishing foray is dependent on many factors. Abundance of prey is one such factor. Ospreys breeding on lakes low in dissolved nutrients and primary productivity have lower productivity rates than those nesting on lakes with moderate dissolved-nutrient levels and primary productivity. The lower lake productivity diminishes the male's ability to capture prey (MacCarter 1972, Garber 1972, Collopy 1984). Warmer surface-water temperatures or tidal activity, factors that drive fish to lower depths, also can affect the osprey's ability to capture prey (Lambert 1943, Ueoka and Koplin 1973). Hunting success is affected by weather, too (MacCarter 1972, Grubb 1977).

## Breeding

Generally, ospreys mate for life, though a certain amount of promiscuity occurs (French 1972, Westall pers. obser.). The pair bond is re-established each year at the beginning of the mating season through the courtship ritual. During courtship, the male displays with a series of spectacular upward climbs and dives. He hovers momentarily at the top of each climb and then dives from heights up to 1,000 feet with wings closed, sometimes while carrying a fish. The female watches from the nest or somewhere nearby, or both members of the pair may fly above the nest with the male chasing the female. Copulation occurs at the nest or on a nearby perch (Johnson and Melquist 1973, Zarn

1974). The male lands on the back of the female with his talons closed, so as not to injure her, and copulation is completed. Mating begins soon after re-establishment of the pair bond and may continue for several weeks (Garber 1972). This behavior sometimes occurs toward the end of the nesting season, too, especially among pairs that lost their nests or young before fledging.

As the pair bond is being established, the male usually brings nesting material to a site he has chosen and creates the foundation of the nest. If the pair has bred in previous years, the male will begin to refurbish the old nest, which may be in poor shape from lack of use or storms that occurred during the nonbreeding season.

## Nesting

After the female decides the chosen nesting site suits her needs, she too helps provide nesting material. As the nest approaches completion, the female be-comes more lethargic and spends more and more time at the nest creating the nest cup and making final preparations for the arrival of the eggs. The male during this period begins providing most of the food (Garber and Koplin 1972, Green 1974). This division of duties permits efficient raising of the young. It also may have evolutionary significance in that female ospreys would place themselves and their eggs in serious jeopardy if they caught fish immediately prior to egg-laying.

Ospreys build their nests singly or in colonies depending on the abun-dance of prey and suitable nesting sites. Historically, ospreys nested in large colonies of 200 to 300 nests, as on Plum and Gardiners islands in New York state (Allen 1892, Chapman 1908, Abbott 1911, Knight 1932). In recent dec-ades, however, such large colonies became almost unheard of and colonial nesting only just now is beginning to occur once again (Hagan 1984).

Generally, nests are built in standing trees near water, though in some areas they may be as far as 12 miles from the nearest fishing grounds (Jamie-son et al 1982, Hagan 1984). However, osprey nests have been built on top of duck blinds, channel markers, roots of upturned trees, giant cactus, aban-doned quarry draglines, inactive fire station alarm sirens, artificial platforms, microwave towers, chimneys, school buildings, active utility poles, windmills, weather vanes, on rocks, rock pinnacles and beach dunes (Terres 1980, Wes-tall pers. obser.).

Established pairs of ospreys use the same nest year after year unless it is destroyed. If the nest is destroyed, the pair usually rebuilds a new nest as close to the old site as possible. Nest size averages three feet in diameter and one to two feet in depth (Bent 1937, Brown and Amadon 1968, Roberts 1969, Garber 1972), but nests have been known to weigh as much as a half a ton (Abbott 1911). Although constructed primarily of sticks one-half to one inch in diam-eter and up to two or three feet long, the osprey incorporates just about anything that is not tied down. Examples include seaweed, cornstalks, shingles, small pieces of boards from boxes, parts of oars, a broken boat hook, a boat tiller, a small rudder, parts of life preservers, parts of fish nets, discarded tangles of fishing line, rope, charred wood, a toy boat with one sail still attached, a pair of shorts, one glove, an empty garbage bag, shellfish egg cases, a rubber boot, old shoes, a straw hat, empty aluminum cans, oyster shells, a rag doll, parts of dead birds, bones, and dried cow manure (Allen 1892, Westall pers. obser.).

## Eggs and Young

For resident populations of ospreys south of the 29th parallel, egg-laying begins in December and continues into April. Farther north, in the temperate regions of the United States and Canada, gradual delay occurs because the beginning of egg-laying correlates with the increasing temperatures associated with the coming of spring. This change is accompanied by a shortening of the actual egg-laying period. Egg-laying does not begin in northern Canada until mid-May and continues no later than June (Bent 1937).

Clutch size also varies slightly moving from the tropics to temperate regions. In south Florida, ospreys usually lay three eggs, sometimes two, and rarely four (Westall 1983, Phillips *et al* 1984). In comparison, ospreys in Massachusetts usually lay three eggs, but quite often four and very rarely two (Poole 1982, 1983).

Bent (1937) called osprey eggs "the handsomest of all the hawks' eggs." They usually are more elongated than other raptor eggs and have a fairly smooth and finely granulated shell. The underlying color, often largely or wholly concealed, may be white to creamy white with heavy blotches of rich, dark browns. The markings are sometimes concentrated at one end, leaving much of the underlying color exposed. Rarely an egg will lack all or almost all of the brown blotches. Incubation averages 30 to 35 days, perhaps longer in western North America (Zarn 1974).

After incubation has begun, the female incubates approximately 70 percent of the time, the male the rest of the time. Male incubation always occurs during the daylight hours and usually while the female is perched nearby eating whatever food the male has provided (Garber and Koplin 1972, Green 1974).

Only one brood is produced during a breeding season. Hatching occurs asynchronously, and the young remain in the nest for approximately eight weeks before fledging. Once the young have hatched, the male spends very little time on the nest except for the transfer of fish to the female. The female feeds the young, usually one at a time, small pieces of fish in fairly rapid succession, alternately feeding the young and herself (Bent 1937, Brown and Amadon 1968, Zarn 1974). The female protects the young from intruders more aggressively than the male and shields them from the sun and during rain showers. After the young are mature enough to regulate their body temperatures sufficiently, the female will spend less and less time on the nest. By six weeks of age, the young may be left alone completely for short periods while both parents spend more time hunting to provide the necessary food for the growing family (Garber and Koplin 1972, Green 1974).

During periods of poor food availability, the youngest or smallest chick will succumb to starvation. Very little sibling aggression occurs among young ospreys, though it has been observed in south Florida (Poole 1979, 1982, Westall pers. obser.). Young ospreys, when first hatched, are covered completely with very short, soft down. They are well camouflaged and easily overlooked by an intruder at the nest. They also are masters of playing dead. At the first sound of the parents' alarm calls, the young lie flat in the nest with wings partly extended and neck outstretched on the floor of the nest. They will even allow themselves to be handled without showing any signs of life.

Unlike many other raptors, the young ospreys lack secondary down and look more reptilian than birdlike. By three weeks of age, short feathers have appeared on the back of the neck and wings. By four weeks the plumage becomes more distinct, and by five weeks the young bird looks more like an immature osprey should (Bent 1937). A few months after fledging, the young osprey is indistinguishable from the adult.

By the time the young are five to six weeks old, they are able to stand and to feed themselves. The female still assists at feeding, but spends an ever-increasing amount of time away from the nest helping the male procure fish.

At about two weeks before fledging, the young begin exercising and testing their flying capabilities by flapping their wings, sometimes for several minutes. Their first flights usually are short with awkward, uncertain landings on a nearby perch. They quickly become more daring, and during a post-fledgling period, which lasts from two to six weeks, the young ospreys stay with the family unit and improve their flying and hunting skills.

Very little is known about the post-fledgling behavior of either the young or the adults (Zarn 1974, Schaadt and Rymon 1982). Meinertzhagen (1954) portrayed ospreys almost anthropomorphically in describing the parents' attempts to teach the young to fish, while other authors believe the young have an innate hunting instinct without which hacking projects (see below) could not succeed (Schaadt and Rymon 1982, Hammer and Beddow 1984, Brown 1984).

Before the fall migration begins, the family unit breaks up (Stinson 1977). Immature ospreys remain on their wintering grounds throughout their first summer and return to the breeding grounds as two-year-olds, usually within 200 miles of where they fledged (Spitzer 1978, 1979).

Resident populations of ospreys do not migrate, so their young may be seen for several months after fledging in the general area where they were produced. Eventually, as these birds become sexually mature, their breeding dispersal patterns correlate with those of migratory populations.

## Enemies

Man can be the osprey's most dangerous enemy. Careless or intentional shootings still occur. Egg collectors caused severe declines in the past, but no longer threaten osprey populations in North America. Of course, loss of habitat is the most destructive force of all.

Man also can be the osprey's most avid benefactor. In many local areas today, ospreys represent a stable, healthy environment and are protected and monitored to ensure their well-being. Many communities have even established artificial nesting programs for the birds (See Management).

Perhaps the osprey's most infamous enemy is the bald eagle (*Haliaetus leucocephalus*). Bent (1937) and others have described quite dramatically the eagle's tactics of dive-bombing the osprey to force the smaller bird to drop its catch in order to defend itself. Magnificent frigate birds (*Fregata magnificens*) also are adept at stealing food from ospreys (Bent 1937, Peck 1967).

Crows (*Corvus brachyrhynchos* and *C. ossifragus*), ravens (*Corvus corax*), magpies (*Pica pica*) and gulls have been accused of preying on osprey eggs (Bent 1937, Zarn 1974), while great blue herons (*Ardea lineatus*), great horned owls (*Bubo virginianus*), red-shouldered hawks (*Buteo lineatus*) and bald eagles may prey on the young (Bent 1937, Ogden 1975, Hammer 1982, Brown 1984).

## Longevity

The first year of an osprey's life appears to be the most crucial. Henny and Wight (1969) calculated first year survival rates for ospreys banded during the period 1926-47 as ranging from only 43 percent to 49 percent. Survival rates increased after the first year to as high as 84 percent. After the eighteenth year, survival again decreased.

Although the average lifespan is 18 years, ospreys have been known to live much longer. An osprey banded in 1914 on Gardiners Island, New York was found dead at the same location 21 years later, and another osprey banded at North Cedar Branch, Delaware, was found shot along Herring Creek, Delaware, when it was 32 years old (Kennard 1975).

# Significance of the Species

Ospreys have been widely recognized for many years as an indicator of the health and well-being of their natural environment (Ogden 1977, Henny 1983). The species' susceptibility to persistent pesticide poisoning, the relative ease with which it can be monitored, and its successful adaptation in many communities to a human-altered environment makes it especially valuable as an indicator species. Baseline data collected from earlier studies during the DDT era (see Historical Perspective) and from monitoring projects that are continuing today play an important role in our ability to recognize and evaluate future threats to the natural system. The fact that ospreys readily accept artificial nesting sites also has increased their popularity with the general public and indirectly improved the relationship between humans and all raptor species.

## Historical Perspective

As mentioned earlier in this report, ospreys historically nested along North America's seacoasts, lakes, and major waterways except within the interior of the conterminous United States. Although there are occasional records of ospreys nesting in the interior, these records are sporadic, and it is impossible to determine the extent and abundance of nesting activity within the region prior to European settlement.

Where ospreys were known to breed, they nested either in solitary nests, small groups, or large colonies. The largest concentrations of nesting ospreys occurred until the middle of this century between Virginia and Massachusetts (Bent 1937, Spitzer and Poole 1980). An example of these high concentrations was Gardiners Island, New York, which had an estimated 300-plus nests on its 3,300 acres during the 1930s and 1940s (Knight 1932, Wilcox 1944, Puleston 1977).

Beginning in the late 1800s, ospreys gradually declined in abundance because of direct and indirect human disturbance. Birds of prey in general, including ospreys, suffered from shooting and egg collecting. Loss of habitat through logging, agricultural and urban development, and other land uses exacerbated the species' decline (Bent 1937, Zarn 1974).

After World War II and the advent of more modern pesticides, primarily DDT and other organochlorines, ospreys began a drastic decline, especially in the northeastern United States (Emerson and Davenport 1963, Dunstan 1970). It was not until the mid-1960s, however, when Ames and Mersereau (1964) documented the crash of the Connecticut River colony and implicated these pesticides, that much attention was given to the species (Henny 1983). Research on the status of ospreys in North America increased exponentially during the next several years, and reproductive failure due to pesticide poisoning was confirmed (Hickey and Anderson 1968, Peterson 1969b, Postupalsky 1971, Koplin 1971).

DDT and its metabolites affect ospreys in at least two ways. First, they induce abnormal breeding behaviors such as delayed breeding, failure to lay eggs or second clutches, and egg-eating by the parent birds. Second, organochlorines can inhibit the ability of the female osprey to mobilize carbonate ions, essential to normal eggshell production (Zarn 1974). Eggshell thinning causes increased egg breakage or embryo mortality. Only a few populations of nesting ospreys in North America did not suffer from DDT poisoning (Reese 1970, Ogden 1977, Westall 1983).

# Current Trends

In 1972, the Environmental Protection Agency outlawed the use of DDT in the United States, and osprey populations began a gradual return to their pre-DDT-era productivity rates. Most populations today have stabilized or are, in fact, increasing. Eastern Canada and Maine are maintaining healthy numbers of nesting ospreys (Henny 1983, Seymour and Bancroft 1983, Stocek and Pearce 1983). The population nesting from New York City to Boston, which suffered so severely during the 1950s and 1960s, has not only regained the ability to sustain itself, but also has the potential for significant growth as well (Spitzer and Poole 1980). Although this population and others in New Jersey have stabilized, they are still a fraction of their former abundance (Henny 1983), and there is no indication that these highly developed areas will ever support population levels similar to those once sustained.

Ironically, Florida's Everglades population has suffered some recent declines, possibly due to food stress (Kushlan and Bass 1983), while the rest of the southeastern United States appears to be doing well (Henny and Noltemeier 1975, Westall 1983, Collopy 1984, Reinman 1984, Whittemore 1984).

The status of osprey populations in central Canada remains uncertain, and further research in this area is badly needed. Ospreys nesting in the Great Lakes region have stabilized and are increasing slightly (Henny 1983). Nesting ospreys within the U.S. interior may be increasing because of reservoir development (Henny 1983) and several hacking projects recently established or planned throughout the region (Hammer 1982, Schaadt and Rymon 1983, Brown 1984).

Although ospreys historically nested all along the Pacific Coast from Alaska to southern California, they are today greatly restricted in central and southern California (Diamond 1969). Henny *et al* (1978a) believe birds nesting in central and southern California may be either remnants of the larger population that previously nested in the region or recent pioneers from elsewhere.

# Management

## Laws and Regulations

Two legislative or regulatory actions enacted in 1972 stand out as landmarks in measures taken to protect ospreys. On March 10, 1972, the osprey was added to the list of bird species protected by the treaty between the United States and Mexico for the protection of migratory birds and game animals. This gave federal protection to the osprey under the Migratory Bird Treaty.

As mentioned above, on December 31, 1972, the use of DDT was banned in the United States. This action was absolutely necessary to the survival of the osprey and many other raptor species. Unfortunately, use of the pesticide has not been banned on the osprey's wintering grounds so the species still faces the threat of pesticide contamination south of the United States (Johnson and Melquist 1973).

Perhaps the most important form of governmental protection concerning ospreys today, however, comes from the individual states themselves. Ospreys are classified as endangered in eight states and threatened, or similarly listed, in 20 states (Le Franc 1984). Many states also are establishing nongame programs funded by small, usually voluntary donations made by people filing tax returns or by special taxes on automobile license tags. The success of these programs is imperative if funding for enforcement of laws and research projects within the states is to continue.

## Egg and Young Manipulations

It has long been known that if eggs are removed from the nest early enough, adult ospreys will lay a second clutch of eggs in about 14 days (Olendorff *et al* 1980). Double-clutching had an added benefit during the DDT era. Beginning in the mid-1970s, Kennedy (1977a) showed that second clutches had thicker shells with lower residue levels of pesticides and, thus, were more productive.

Further work by Spitzer (1978) illustrated the ease with which osprey eggs could be transferred from less polluted areas (Chesapeake Bay) to heavily contaminated areas such as Long Island Sound. He also moved 53 nestlings three to 30 days old from Maryland to Connecticut. Forty-five of these young fledged successfully. In two separate cases, osprey nests with two young three to four weeks old were given three new young only one week old without rejection problems.

Hacking, however, appears to be the newest management technique for ospreys in the 1980s. "Hacking" is a falconer's term for removing young raptors from their nests and fledging them from artificial structures to give the young birds a degree of natural experience before being taken into captivity for falconry training (Michell 1900). By altering the procedure slightly, food is supplied for the young osprey for several weeks past fledging so they can be released into the wild at a predetermined location. This has great management potential because ospreys show strong fidelity to their nesting area. Only a small number are long-distance dispersers (Henny 1983). The significance of this form of management is that historical osprey populations can be restored and enhanced and new, previously unused but suitable habitat, such as reservoirs, can be colonized more quickly (Schaadt and Rymon 1983, Brown 1984, Hammer and Beddow 1984, Jones 1984).

## Habitat Management

A little used but still valuable tool for osprey management is the designation of important habitat as osprey management areas. The U.S. Forest Service established two such areas in 1969 and 1971.

In 1969, the Forest Service and the Oregon Department of Fish and Wildlife entered into an agreement to set aside some 10,000 acres on the Deschutes National Forest, Oregon, for the establishment of the Crane Prairie Reservoir Osprey Management Area (Anderson and Gates 1983). It has as its primary objectives the protection and improvement of osprey habitat, protection of the species, and provision of opportunities for public enjoyment (Roberts 1969).

In fall 1971, an osprey management area was set aside at Eagle Lake in Lassen National Forest in northern California (Kahl 1971). The objectives at this management area were similar to those at Crane Prairie Reservoir. The timber management guidelines established at these two areas to protect osprey nesting habitat could be used wherever similar conditions exist. The guidelines are: 1) cut no timber or snags within approximately 200 feet of water bodies where ospreys nest; 2) beyond the 200-foot "no-cut" zone, restrict cutting for the next 1,120 feet, where at least two dominant trees per acre must be left standing; 3) around each individual nest, create another 132-foot wide "no-cut" zone; 4) allow only restricted activity 660 feet on all sides of the nest; 5) allow no hunting from April 1 to September 30 within the management area; 6) mark nest trees with metal signs to prevent the inadvertent destruction of the sites by uninformed individuals.

## Artificial Nest Sites

Artificial-platform programs have been more successful for ospreys than for any other raptor species. The earliest available reference to erecting artificial nesting platforms for ospreys is in Ames and Mersereau (1964), who erected 24 platforms over a three-year period in southern Connecticut. Of these 24 platforms, 23 were used by ospreys before the end of the project.

Since that time, hundreds of structures have been erected for ospreys throughout North America. Martin et al (in prep.) state that the benefits of artificial platforms include: 1) provision of nests in areas that lack sufficient natural nest sites, 2) replacement of insecure natural nests, 3) relocation of nests away from excessive disturbance, and 4) substitution of nests located on hazardous or conflicting man-made structures.

Several studies have shown artificial platforms to be readily accepted by ospreys. Occupancy rates of 27 percent have been recorded in Oregon (Henny et al 1978b), 32 percent (Airola and Shubert 1981) and 60 percent (Garber et al 1974) in California, 55 percent in Michigan (Postupalsky 1978), 70 percent in Florida (Westall 1983), and from 58 percent (Reese 1977) to 82 percent (Rhodes 1972) in Chesapeake Bay, Maryland.

Some of these studies reported that artificial nest sites produced almost twice as many young as did natural sites (Postupalsky 1978, Van Daele and Van Daele 1982, Westall 1983). Although not all studies reported such increased productivity for artificial sites, they were all well within the minimum standards necessary to maintain osprey-population stability (Henny and Wight 1969).

# Prognosis

The future for ospreys in North America looks very promising. With the gradual decline in the use of organochlorine pesticides during the 1970s, ospreys began a slow return to pre-DDT-era productivity rates and stability. The return to stability was accomplished much faster by ospreys than by other birds of prey because of their own population dynamics and because of human resource management techniques.

Whether osprey population levels in the Northeast will ever return to those at the turn of the century is subject to debate. However, these populations should continue to remain stable and to serve as indicators of the overall well-being of the natural environment. Through education and artificial nesting programs, the Southeast also should remain stable.

Hacking programs in the interior of the conterminous United States should enhance existing osprey populations in the region and accelerate the colonization of new and previously unused habitats. Western North America populations, though never as dense as those of the East, probably will continue to flourish as long as incidental shootings and logging practices do not undermine productivity. Even recolonization of southern California by ospreys may be accomplished through hacking projects to be proposed in the near future.

Recently, two new factors have been discussed that may have future impacts on osprey populations. Acid rain may prove severely detrimental to habitat suitability over some of the osprey's range because of its impact on lake ecosystems and the osprey's prey base. Shooting of ospreys at fish hatcheries also has the potential to cause significant local or migratory mortalities. It is impossible to predict at the present time the effect these two factors will have on osprey populations.

Nevertheless, the osprey's future looks brighter and brighter because of its increased association with man. Perhaps partially because ospreys prey on species that man still considers plentiful and because ospreys have learned to adapt to a man-altered environment, the osprey is quickly becoming popular with the general public. This means that its management is not left solely to researchers and government bureaucracies. Entire communities are participating in osprey-management projects, such as artificial-nesting programs and reintroduction projects.

A note of caution, however, should be expressed concerning this "popularity". Great care should be taken to ensure that all criteria necessary for osprey breeding success can be satisfied before a project is begun. Additionally, the effect on the prey base and on other competing species and human reactions to an osprey nesting on every street corner must be considered. If sound, professional osprey management in North America is realized, the species should continue to prosper and share the continent with its human neighbors.

# Recommendations

Osprey populations in most regions of North America are well on their way to recovering from the decline of the past several decades. Nonetheless, ospreys remain a species sensitive to many forms of environmental calamity. Zarn (1974) identified several recommendations that are still valid today with only minor revisions, and some of them are incorporated in the discussion below.

Research into all aspects of osprey biology is needed in order to better understand the species population dynamics. Monitoring of populations should continue not only in the urban and suburban environment, but also in the wilder, less accessible habitats. More studies concerning artificial and natural populations are necessary. Hacking projects have heightened the need for better understanding of post-fledgling behavior and the effects on donor populations.

Large nesting colonies that are not on protected lands need to be identified and measures taken to ensure the stability of the prey base and other supporting factors. Areas that have abundant fish resources, but are lacking in suitable nesting sites, might benefit from the establishment of artificial-nesting programs. Projects of this type, however, should be thoroughly planned before being initiated.

Human activity can influence osprey productivity significantly, especially in areas where the birds are not used to human interference. In these areas, access to nesting ospreys should be limited. Even in urban and suburban environments, some ospreys are more sensitive than others to the close proximity of human activity. Signs warning the public to maintain respectable distances from oversensitive birds should be erected. If these signs are ignored, all regulations protecting ospreys should be enforced.

The sensitivity of ospreys to pesticide contamination is well known. Because of the deleterious effects of pesticides on osprey reproductive success, no organochlorine pesticides should be used in North America. Measures also should be taken to prohibit their use in Central and South America and their importation into the United States as hidden ingredients in pesticides manufactured in foreign countries.

Finally, public awareness programs should be developed and maintained wherever ospreys are found. The species will interact with humans more and more as time progresses, and an educated public will be vital to osprey survival.

# References

Abbott, C.G. 1911. *The Home-Life of the Osprey.* H.F. Witherby and Company. London. 54 pp.

Airola, D.A. and N. Shubert. 1981. "Reproductive success, nest site selection, and management of ospreys at Lake Almanor, California 1969-1980." *California-Nevada Wildlife Transactions* 1981:79-85.

Allen, C.S. 1892. "Breeding habits of the fish hawk on Plum Island, New York." *Auk* 9(4):313-321.

Allen, R.P. 1962. *Birds of the Caribbean.* Thames and Hudson. London. 256 pp.

Ames, P.L. and G.S. Mersereau. 1964. "Some factors in the decline of the osprey in Connecticut." *Auk* 81:173-185.

Anderson, J. and G. Gates. 1983. *An Investigation of the Osprey and Cormorant Populations of Crane Prairie Reservoir.* Unpublished report. Oregon Department of Fish and Wildlife, Non-game Division. 80 pp.

Beddow, T.E. 1984. "Recovery of natural nesting osprey in the Tennessee Valley," *in* M.A. Westall ed., *Proceedings of the Southwestern U.S. and Caribbean Osprey Symposium.* The International Osprey Foundation. Sanibel Island, Florida. pp. 67-73.

Bent, A.C. 1937. "Life histories of North American birds of prey, Part 1." *United States National Museum Bulletin 167.*

Bogener, D.J. 1979. *Osprey Inventory and Management Study for Shasta Lake Ranger District (1979).* Unpublished report. U.S. Forest Service. Redding, California. 13 pp.

Brown, L.H. and D. Amadon. 1968. *Eagles, Hawks, and Falcons of the World.* McGraw-Hill Book Company. New York. 945 pp.

Brown, R.D. 1984. "Carolina Raptor Center's osprey introduction project in Piedmont, North Carolina," *in* M.A. Westall ed., *Proceedings of the Southeastern U.S. and Caribbean Osprey Symposium.* The International Osprey Foundation. Sanibel Island, Florida. pp. 119-132.

Chapman, F.M. 1908. "Fish-hawks of Gardiners Island." *Bird Lore* 10:59-68.

Collopy, M.W. 1984. "Parental care, productivity, and predator-prey relationships of ospreys in three North Florida lakes: preliminary report," *in* M.A. Westall ed., *Proceedings of the Southeastern U.S. and Caribbean Osprey Symposium.* The International Osprey Foundation. Sanibel Island, Florida. pp. 85-98.

Detrich, P.J. 1978. *Osprey Inventory and Management Study for Shasta Lake Ranger District.* Unpublished report. U.S. Forest Service. Redding, California. 17 pp.

Diamond, J.M. 1969. "Avifauna equilibria and species turnover rates on the Channel Islands of California." *Proceedings of the National Academy of Science* 64:57-63.

Dunstan, T.C. 1970. "Raptor research foundation continental osprey status survey-1969." *Raptor Research News* 4:81-103.

Eckstein, R.G., P.V. Vanderschaeger and F.L. Johnson. 1979. "Osprey nesting platforms in north central Wisconsin." *Passenger Pigeon* 41:145-148.

Emerson, D. and M. Davenport. 1963. "Profile of the Osprey." *Naragansett Naturalist* 6:56-58.

French, J.M. 1972. Distribution, abundance, and breeding status of ospreys in northwestern California. M.S. Thesis. Humboldt State University. Arcata, California. 58 pp.

Friedmann, H. 1950. *The Birds of North and Middle America.* Smithsonian Institute U.S. National Museum Bulletin 50.

Garber, D.P. 1972. Osprey nesting ecology in Lassen and Plumas counties, California. M.S. Thesis. Humboldt State University. Arcata, California. 59 pp.

Garber, D.P. and J.R. Koplin. 1972. "Prolonged and bisexual incubation by California ospreys." *Condor* 74(2):201-202.

Garber, D.P., J.R. Koplin and J.R. Kahl. 1974. "Osprey management on the Lassen National Forest, California," *in* F.N. Hamerstrom, Jr., B.E. Harrell and R.R. Olendorff eds., *Management of Raptors.* Raptor Research Report No. 2. pp. 119-122.

Green, R. 1974. "Breeding behavior of ospreys *Pandion haliaetus* in Scotland." *Ibis* 118(4):475-490.

Grossman, M.L. and J. Hamlet. 1964. *Birds of Prey of the World.* Bonanza Books. New York. pp. 368-370.

Grubb, T.G. 1977. "Weather dependent foraging in ospreys." *Auk* 94(1):146-149.

Hagan, J.M. 1984. "A North Carolina osprey population: social group or breeding aggregation?" *in* M.A. Westall ed., *Proceedings of the Southeastern U.S. Caribbean Osprey Symposium.* The International Osprey Foundation. Sanibel Island, Florida. pp. 43-60.

Hammer, D.A. 1982. Osprey reintroduction in the Tennessee Valley," *in* R.R. Odom and J.W. Guthrie eds., *Proceedings of the Nongame and Endangered Wildlife Symposium, Technical Bulletin WL 5.* Georgia Department of Natural Resources. Athens, Georgia. pp. 75-83.

Hammer, D.A. and T.E. Beddow. 1984. "Hacking young ospreys to restore Tennessee Valley populations," *in* M.A. Westall ed., *Proceedings of the Southeastern U.S. Caribbean Osprey Symposium.* The International Osprey Foundation. Sanibel Island, Florida pp. 75-83.

Henny, C.J. 1977. "Research, management and status of the osprey in North America," *in* R.D. Chancellor ed., *Proceedings of the World Birds of Prey Conference. International Council for Bird Preservation.* Vienna. pp. 199-222.

Henny, C.J. 1983. "Distribution and abundance of nesting ospreys in the United States," *in* D.M. Bird ed., *Biology and Management of Bald Eagles and Ospreys.* Harpell Press. Ste. Anne de Bellevue, Quebec. pp. 175-186.

Henny, C.J. and H.M. Wight. 1969. "An endangered osprey population: estimates of mortality and production." *Auk* 86(2):188-198.

Henny, C.J. and W.T. Van Velzen. 1972. "Migration patterns and wintering localities of American ospreys." *Journal of Wildlife Management* 36(4):1133-1141.

Henny, C.J. and D.P. Noltemeier. 1975. "Osprey nesting populations in the coastal Carolinas." *American Birds* 29(6):1073-1079.

Henny, C.J., D.J. Dunaway, R.D. Mallette and J.R. Koplin. 1978a. "Osprey distribution, abundance, and status in western North America: I. The northern California population." *Northwest Scientist* 52:261-271.

Henny, C.J., J.A. Collins and W.J. Diebert. 1978b. "Osprey distribution, abundance, and status in western North America, II: the Oregon population." *The Murrelet* 59:14-25.

Hickey, J.J. and D.W. Anderson. 1968. "Chlorinated hydrocarbons and eggshell changes in raptorial and fish-eating birds." *Science* 162:271-273.

Jacobs, J. 1977. "Comparison of osprey nesting success between the 1940s and 1970s in Cape May County," *in* J.C. Odgen ed., *Transactions of the North American Osprey Research Conference*. U.S. National Park Service Proceedings, Series 2. Washington, D.C. pp. 101-103.

Jamieson, I., N.R. Seymour and R.P. Bancroft. 1982. "Time and activity budgets of ospreys nesting in northeastern Nova Scotia." *Condor* 84(4):439-441.

Johnson, D.R. and W.E. Melquist. 1973. *Unique, Rare and Endangered Raptorial Birds of Northern Idaho: Nesting Success and Management Recommendations*. University of Idaho and U.S. Department of Agriculture Forest Service. Publication no. RI-73-021. 42 pp.

Jones, W.L. 1984. "Hacking ospreys in West Virginia." *Redstart* 51(4):122-129.

Judge, D.S. 1983. "Productivity of ospreys in the Gulf of California. *Wilson Bulletin* 95(2):243-255.

Kahl, J.R. 1971. *Osprey Habitat Management Plan, Lassen National Forest, 1971*. Lassen National Forest. Susanville, California. 33 pp.

Kahl, J.R. 1972a. "Better homes for feathered fishermen." *Outdoor California* 33(3):4-6.

Kahl, J.R. 1972b. "Osprey management on the Lassen National Forest." *Transactions of the California-Nevada Section of the Wildlife Society* 1972:7-13.

Kennard, J.H. 1975. "Longevity records of North American birds." *Bird Banding* 46(1):55-73.

Kennedy, R.S. 1973. "Notes on the migration of juvenile ospreys from Maryland and Virginia." *Bird Banding* 44(3):180-186.

Kennedy, R.S. 1977a. "Method for increasing osprey productivity," *in* J.C. Ogden ed., *Transactions of the North American Osprey Research Conference*. U.S. National Park Service Proceedings, Series 2. Washington, D.C. pp. 35-42.

Kennedy, R.S. 1977b. "Status of the osprey in tidewater Virginia, 1970-

1971," *in* J.C. Ogden ed., *Transactions of the North American Osprey Research Conference.* U.S. National Park Service Proceedings, Series 2. Washington, D.C. pp. 121-133.

Knight, C.W.R. 1932. "Photographing the nest life of the osprey." *National Geographic Magazine* 62:247-260.

Koplin, J.R. ed., 1971. *Osprey Workshop: Summary of Research Findings and Management Recommedations.* California-Nevada Section of the Wildlife Society. 1971 Transactions. pp. 114-122.

Kushlan, J.A. and O.L. Bass, Jr. 1983. "Decreases in the southern Florida osprey population, a possible result of food stress," *in* D.M. Bird ed., *Biology and Management of Bald Eagles and Ospreys.* Harpell Press. Ste. Anne de Belle-vue, Quebec. pp. 187-200.

Lambert, G. 1943. "Predation efficiency of the osprey." *Canadian Field-Naturalist* 57:87-88.

Layher, W.G. 1984. "Osprey preys on canada goose gosling." *Wilson Bulletin* 96(3):469-470.

Le Franc, M.N. Jr., ed. 1984. "Status reports: state endangered and threatened raptor species." *The Eyas* 7(3):17-20.

MacCarter, D.L. 1972. Reproductive performance and population trends of ospreys at Flathead Lake, Montana. M.S. Thesis. Humboldt State University. Arcata, California. 80 pp.

Martin, C.O., W.A. Mitchell and D.A. Hammer. In prep. "Osprey nest platforms. Section 5.2.7." *in* C.O. Martin ed., *The U.S. Army Corps of Engineers Wildlife Resources Management Manual.*

Melquist, W.E., D.R. Johnson and W.D. Carrier. 1979. "Migration patterns of northern Idaho and eastern Washington ospreys." *Bird Banding* 49(3):234-236.

Michell, E.B. 1900. *The Art and Practice of Hawking.* Methuen and Company. London. 291 pp.

Ogden, J.C. 1975. "Effects of bald eagle territoriality on nesting ospreys." *Wilson Bulletin* 87(4):496-505.

Ogden, J.C. 1977. "Preliminary report of a study of Florida ospreys," *in* J.C. Ogden ed., *Transactions of the North American Osprey Research Conference.* U.S. National Park Service Proceedings Series 2. Washington, D.C. pp. 143-152.

Olendorff, R.R., R.S. Motroni and M.W. Call. 1980. *Raptor Management—The State of the Art in 1970.* U.S. Department of Interior Bureau of Land Management Technical Note 345.

Peck, F.B. 1967. "Skyway robbery: osprey attack by frigate bird." *Audubon Magazine* 69(3):58-60.

Peterson, R.T. 1969a. "Osprey—endangered world citizen." *National Geographic* 136(1):52-67.

Peterson, R.T. 1969b. "Population trends of ospreys in the northeastern United States," *in* J.J. Hickey ed., *Peregrine Populations: Their Biology and Decline.* University of Wisconsin Press. Madison, Wisconsin. pp. 340-341.

Phillips, S.R., M.A. Westall, and P.W. Zajicek. 1984. "The winter of 1983: poor productivity for ospreys on Sanibel Island, Florida," *in* M.A. Westall ed., *Proceedings of the Southeastern U.S. and Caribbean Osprey Symposium.* The International Osprey Foundation. Sanibel Island, Florida. pp. 61-66.

Poole, A. 1979. "Sibling aggression among nestling ospreys in Florida Bay." *Auk* 96(2):415-417.

Poole, A. 1982. "Brood reduction in temperate and sub-tropical ospreys." *Oecologia* 53:111-119.

Poole, A. 1983. "Courtship feeding, clutch size, and egg size in ospreys: A preliminary report," *in* D.M. Bird ed., *Biology and Management of Bald Eagles and Ospreys.* Harpell Press. Ste. Anne de Bellevue, Quebec. pp. 243-256.

Postupalsky, S. 1971. "Bald eagle and osprey study in Michigan and Ontario: a report of the 1969 and 1970 nesting season." *California Condor* 6(1):1-3.

Postupalsky, S. 1978. "Artificial nesting platforms for ospreys and bald eagles. *In* S.A. Temple (ed.) *Endangered Birds: Management Techniques for Preserving Threatened Species.* University of Wisconsin Press, Madison. Pp. 33-45.

Postupalsky, S. and S.M. Stackpole. 1974. "Artificial nesting platforms for ospreys in Michigan," *in* F.N. Hamerstrom, Jr., B.E. Harrell and R.R. Olendorff eds., *Management of Raptors.* Raptor Research Report no. 2. pp. 105-117.

Prevost, Y.A. 1982. The wintering ecology of ospreys in Senegambia. Ph.D dissertation. University of Edinburgh. 159 pp.

Prevost, Y.A. 1983. "Osprey distribution and subspecies taxonomy." *In* D.M. Bird (ed.) *Biology and Management of Bald Eagles and Ospreys.* Harpell Press, Ste. Anne de Bellevuer, Quebec. Pp. 157-174.

Puleston, D. 1977. "Osprey population studies on Gardiner's Island, N.Y." *in* J.C. Ogden ed., *Transactions of the North American Osprey Research Conference.* U.S. National Park Service Proceedings, Series 2. Washington, D.C. pp. 95-99.

Reese, J.G. 1965. "Breeding status of the osprey in central Chesapeake Bay." *Maryland Birdlife* 21(4):105-107.

Reese, J.G. 1977. "Reproductive success of ospreys in central Chesapeake Bay." *Auk* 94:202-221.

Reese, J.G. 1977. "Nesting success of ospreys in central Chesapeake Bay," *in* J.C. Ogden ed., *Transactions of the North American Osprey Research Conference.* U.S. National Park Service Proceedings, Series 2. Washington, D.C. pp. 109-113.

Reinman, J.P. 1984. "The status of osprey populations of the central and northern Gulf Coasts of Florida," *in* M.A. Westall ed., *Proceedings of the Southeastern U.S. and Caribbean Osprey Symposium.* The International Osprey Foundation. Sanibel Island, Florida. pp. 109-117.

Rhodes, L.I. 1972. "Success of osprey nest structures at Martin National Wildlife Refuge." *Journal of Wildlife Management* 36:1296-1299.

Rhodes, L.I. 1977. "Osprey population aided by nest structures," *in* J.C. Ogden ed., *Transactions of the North American Osprey Research Conference*. U.S. National Park Service Proceedings, Series 2. Washington, D.C. pp. 77-83.

Roberts, H.B. 1969. *Management Plan for the Crane Prairie Reservoir Osprey Management Area*. U.S. Department of Agriculture Forest Service and Oregon State Game Commission. 20 pp.

Schaadt, C.P. and L.M. Rymon. 1982. "Innate fishing behavior of ospreys." *Raptor Research* 16(2):61-62.

Schaadt, C.P. and L.M. Rymon. 1983. "The restoration of ospreys by hacking," D.M. Bird ed., *Biology and Management of Bald Eagles and Ospreys*. Harpell Press. Ste. Anne de Bellevue, Quebec. pp. 299-305.

Seymour, N.R. and R.P. Bancroft. 1983. "The status and use of two habitats by ospreys in northeastern Nova Scotia," *in* D.M. Bird ed., *Biology and Management of Bald Eagles and Ospreys*. Harpell Press. Ste. Anne de Bellevue, Quebec. pp. 275-280.

Sindelar, C. and E. Schluter. 1968. "Osprey carrying a bird." *Wilson Bulletin* 80:103.

Spitzer, P.R. 1978. "Osprey egg and nestling transfers: Their value as ecological experiments and as management procedures," *in* S.A. Temple ed., *Endangered Birds: Management Techniques for Preserving Threatened Species*. University of Wisconsin Press. Madison, Wisconsin. pp. 171-182.

Spitzer, R.R. 1979. Dynamics of a Discrete Coastal Breeding Population of Ospreys in Northeastern U.S., 1969-1979. Ph.D. thesis (unpubl.). Graduate School of Cornell University, Ithaca, N.Y. 55 Pp.

Spitzer, P.R. and A. Poole. 1980. "Coastal ospreys between New York City and Boston: a decade of reproductive recovery 1969-1979." *American Birds* 34:234-241.

Stinson, C.H. 1977. "Familial longevity in ospreys." *Bird Banding* 48(1):72-73.

Stocek, R.F. and P.A. Pearce. 1983. "Distribution and reproductive success of ospreys in New Brunswick, 1974-1980," *in* D.M. Bird ed., *Biology and Management of Bald Eagles and Ospreys*. Harpell Press. Ste. Anne de Bellevue, Quebec. pp. 215-221.

Tait, W.W., H.M. Johnson, and W.D. Courser. 1972. "Osprey carrying a small mammal." *Wilson Bulletin* 84:341.

Terres, J.K. 1980. *The Audubon Encyclopedia of North American Birds*. Alfred A. Knopf, Inc. New York. pp. 644-646.

Ueoka, M.L. and J.R. Koplin. 1973. "Foraging behavior of ospreys in northwestern California." *Raptor Research* 7(2):32-38.

Valentine, A. 1967. "Man-made osprey nesting sites a success." *Michigan Audubon Newsletter* 14(4):4-5.

VanDaele, L.J. and H.A. VanDaele. 1982. "Factors affecting the productivity of ospreys nesting in west-central Idaho." *Condor* 84:292-299.

Webb, W.L. and A.H. Lloyd. 1984. "Design and use of tripods as osprey nest platforms," *in* M.A. Westall ed., *Proceedings of the Southeastern U.S. and Carib-*

*bean Osprey Symposium.* The International Osprey Foundation. Sanibel Island, Florida. pp. 99-107.

Westall, M.A. 1983. "An osprey population aided by nest structures on Sanibel Island, Florida," *in* D.M. Bird ed., *Biology and Management of Bald Eagles and Ospreys.* Harpell Press. Ste. Anne de Bellevue, Quebec. pp. 287-291.

Whittemore, R.E. 1984. "Historical overview of osprey at the the Mattamuskeet National Wildlife Refuge: results from ten years of nest and productivity surveys," *in* M.A. Westall ed., *Proceedings of the Southeastern U.S. and Caribbean Osprey Symposium.* The International Osprey Foundation. Sanibel Island, Florida. pp. 17-41.

Wilcox, S.L. 1944. "Banding ospreys on Long Island." *New York State Bulletin to the Schools.* March 1944. pp. 262-264.

Wiley, J.W. and F.E. Lohrer. 1973. "Additional records of non-fish prey taken by ospreys." *Wilson Bulletin* 85:468-470.

Worth, C.B. 1936. "Summary and analysis of some records of banded ospreys." *Bird Banding* 7:156-160.

Zarn, M. 1974. *Habitat Management Series for Unique or Endangered Species. Report no. 12: Osprey,* Pandion Haliaetus carolinensis. U.S. Department of Interior Bureau of Land Management Technical Note 254.

*Mark A. Westall, who has studied ospreys for nearly a decade, founded the International Osprey Foundation in 1981.*

Although the endangered Lange's metalmark butterfly now numbers only some 600 individuals, the outlook for the insect is good because its habitat is protected and managed.

*Edward Ross*

# Lange's Metalmark Butterfly

## Paul A. Opler
### and
## Lee Robinson
U.S. Fish and Wildlife Service

## Species Description And Natural History

Lange's metalmark butterfly (*Apodemia mormo langei*) is one of nine subspecies of the western North American Mormon metalmark (Opler and Powell 1961). The adult butterflies are small, with wingspans varying from one to one and a half inches. The dorsal wings are primarily black with a pattern of white spots. The inner forward half of the forewing has red-orange background. A small central patch, subtended by black, is also red-orange, instead of white as in all other *A. mormo* subspecies. The hindwing bases also are invaded by red-orange scaling. Below, the wings have a more muted pattern of gray, white, black, and orange.

### Breeding

The Lange's metalmark butterfly's life cycle centers around the one food plant used by the caterpillar, auriculate buckwheat (*Eriogonum nudum* variety *auriculatum*). The adults depend on the buckwheat and two other plants for the nectar that fulfills their energy and water needs (Arnold 1983). The other plants are Douglas' ragwort (*Senecio douglasii*) and divergent snakeweed (*Gutierrezia divergens*).

The adult butterflies, the reproductive phase of the metalmark, have one flight during August and September each year. The males take up "perches" on plants, especially their host buckwheat, from which they fly out to locate receptive females. Males remain within a very small area. Mated pairs may be seen perched on deerbrush (*Lotus scoparius*). The total life span of the adults is about a week. Female Lange's metalmarks lay a single egg under a host buckwheat leaf, then move on before selecting another leaf. In all, probably several hundred eggs are laid. Eggs hatch in early spring, and the caterpillars require several months to complete feeding on host leaves and stems. The chrysalis is formed in litter under the host buckwheat (Arnold 1983).

### Range

The Lange's metalmark, once restricted to riverine sand dunes along the southern bank of the Sacramento-San Joaquin River just east of Antioch, Contra Costa County, California, is now found only on the Antioch Dunes National Wildlife Refuge and a few adjacent parcels. Occasional individuals showing *langei* features are found within some variable south-coast range populations, such as those in eastern San Luis Obispo County (Opler and Powell 1961).

## Significance of the Species

The Lange's metalmark was among the first insects listed as endangered by the U.S. Fish and Wildlife Service (FWS) under protection of the Endangered Species Act of 1973 (U.S. Fish and Wildlife Service 1976). It is the only insect for which the Department of the Interior has acquired a specific refuge.

The butterfly's significance includes its potential for evolutionary, genetic, and population studies, together with the fact that it and two endangered plants (Antioch Dunes evening primrose [*Oenothera deltoides* var. *howellii*]—see *Audubon* July 1985 issue—and the Contra Costa wallflower [*Erysimum capitatum* var. *angustatum*]) share an endangered ecosystem (U.S. Fish and Wildlife Service 1978).

Few other river-associated sand dune systems exist in North America, and the Antioch Dunes has the largest number of unique species now limited to such a small area (Powell 1983). At least 27 insect species and subspecies were described from specimens collected at the Antioch Dunes, and about 13 appear to be endemic. About half of these insect endemics now may be extinct—the largest such loss of native insects on the continent (Powell 1983).

The geographic variation of Lange's metalmark and its other related subspecies already has been studied (Opler and Powell 1961). Extensive collections and notes at the University of California at Berkeley suggest the species would be an excellent subject for investigations into population genetics and evolutionary processes. Annual population monitoring and mark-recapture studies from 1976 to 1985 make the Lange's metalmark one of the most closely monitored insect populations in the world (Arnold 1983, 1984).

# Historical Perspective

The Lange's metalmark was first collected at the Antioch Dunes in 1936 by W.H. Lange, a University of California at Davis entomologist. A few museum specimens are labelled "Oakley," a small town about 10 miles east of the Antioch Dunes National Wildlife Refuge (Opler and Powell 1961). Originally, the native sand-dune habitat at Antioch comprised about one square mile, but because of active sand mining and industrialization, any semblance of native dune habitat now is limited to about a tenth of a square mile (Howard 1983). Lange's metalmark probably was able to use much of the original area because its buckwheat host plant was one of the community dominants. Population numbers may have reached 10,000 individuals prior to commercial activities. Even in the mid-1950s, a time when the available habitat was reduced greatly, about 20 lepidopterists took more than 200 specimens during an organized field trip. Even then the annual population probably was at least several thousand.

# Current Trends

The Lange's metalmark butterfly was listed as endangered under the U.S. Endangered Species Act in June, 1976 (U.S. Fish and Wildlife Service 1976). In 1977, critical habitat was proposed (U.S. Fish and Wildlife Service 1977) but later withdrawn (U.S. Fish and Wildlife Service 1979). The butterfly's population status has been monitored for the past nine years by Drs. Richard A. Arnold and Jerry A. Powell. The adult population size, based on capture-recapture sampling, in 1984 was estimated at 659 individuals (Arnold 1984, 1985).

Arnold (1984) stated that butterfly and buckwheat food-plant numbers show a strong and positive correlation, suggesting that the habitat is at its carrying capacity. Invasion of exotic vegetation, primarily European grasses, is stabilizing the little remaining sand-dune habitat and is reducing the establishment of natural seedlings and possibly stressing the mature buckwheat plants. Fire is a threat to the butterfly, although it appears to rejuvenate the buckwheat. However, crown-sprouting buckwheat generally is not suitable to the larvae for three to four years.

# Management

Antioch Dunes National Wildlife Refuge, administered by FWS and managed by the San Francisco Bay National Wildlife Refuge, was established in 1980 specifically to preserve the habitat of the Lange's metalmark butterfly and two other endangered species—the Contra Costa wallflower and the Antioch Dunes evening-primrose. The only other known sites for the butterfly include two strips of land, owned by Pacific Gas and Electric as right-of-way land for their transmission lines and an adjacent strip owned by the Wm. McCullough & Sons Co. These parcels comprising only a few thousand square feet, border on a section of Antioch Dunes National Wildlife Refuge. FWS currently has a cooperative agreement with Pacific Gas and Electric that allows FWS to manage the lands for the three endangered species and the unique habitat.

Since acquisition, FWS has been working with scientists and interested individuals to improve the habitat for the endangered species. Most of the work has involved hand-clearing (weeding) areas to open up the habitat to the native plant species, particularly the buckwheat. For example, in February 1984 an old car body was removed from the refuge. The area was severely disturbed from dragging the vehicle out. Once the vehicle was removed the area was raked smooth and left alone. The following spring and summer numerous buckwheat seedlings sprouted at the site. The seeds apparently were dormant in the soil but unable to sprout, possibly because they were suppressed by the heavy covering of European grasses. Since then that area has remained essentially weed-free, with only minor weeding required in the spring and summer. The young buckwheat plants continue to grow well, and it is anticipated that the butterflies will start using this buckwheat colony in the near future.

Since 1979 buckwheat has been grown from seed at a nursery and then planted at the refuge and adjacent properties. Some of the plants were set out in a "wagon-wheel" configuration on the theory that the increased density of plants would "confuse" the butterflies into thinking more plant material was available for the larvae, thus stimulating the females to lay their eggs on the young plants. The success of this planting scheme has not been reported.

FWS is in the process of removing part of an old vineyard on the refuge and recontouring the land to form relatively small sand-dune areas. Those recontoured areas will be seeded and planted with native species, particularly the buckwheat.

Private individuals, the University of California at Berkeley, and the California Conservation Corps have been cultivating buckwheat as well as other native plants for the refuge from seed gathered from the refuge and adjacent properties.

## Prognosis

The long-term outlook for the Lange's metalmark is guardedly positive despite the current low population level. FWS has completed consultation on needed management actions, and funds are available for fencing, recontouring of a former vineyard, and reintroduction of natural sand to areas previously mined down to hardpan. These actions, when carried out, should allow formation of wind-blown drift dunes, natural regeneration of the buckwheat host plants, and rebound in butterfly numbers.

## Recommendations

Clearly, two major problems need to be addressed, both in the short and long runs, to help stabilize and preserve this endangered butterfly: human-caused problems, e.g. fires and trampling, and exotic vegetation. It would be naive to think the entire refuge could ever be restored to its pristine condition. Instead, work will be concentrated in areas that show a potential for restoration. Some areas will be allowed to go to the climax vegetation type of oak woodland, while other areas will be held artificially to early successional stages. The two endangered plants and the auriculate buckwheat grow better in the early successional stages and, in fact, may require open or disturbed sandy soils to survive.

Arnold (1985) has recommended that at least 1,500 buckwheat seedlings be planted yearly to solidify and expand the butterfly population. This will involve a great amount of time in preparing an area to receive this number of seedlings. Fall/winter 1985-86 will be the first time that a large number of buckwheat seedlings will be planted on the refuge.

Human-caused problems will be controlled by temporarily closing certain parts of the refuge to the public. The effect of the closure on the endangered species and the habitat in general will be assessed after five years, and a decision will be made then on whether to re-open the area. Educational programs given by refuge personnel will continue among local school and community organizations with the hope that understanding of the uniqueness and fragility of the refuge will promote cooperation and preservation.

In the long run it is hoped that auriculate buckwheat/Lange's metalmark butterfly colonies can be established in noncontiguous areas nearby the refuge to reduce the possibility of extinction by fire or disease. This would involve contracting and working with private landowners and local park officials.

## References

Arnold, R.A. 1983. "Ecological studies of six endangered butterflies (Lepidopters, Lycaenidae): Island biogeography, patch dynamics, and the design of habitat preserves." *University of California Publications in Entomology* 99: 1-161.

————1984. *Monitoring of the Endangered Lange's Metalmark Butterfly in 1983 at the Antioch Dunes.* Contract report to San Francisco Bay National Wildlife Refuge, P.O. 524, Newark, CA 94560, Contract # 10181-9726, 7 figures.

————1985. *Ecological Studies of the Endangered Lange's Metalmark Butterfly at the Antioch Dunes.* Final report to San Francisco National Wildlife Refuge, P.O. Box 524, Newark, CA 94560, Project NR-81-1. 10pp, 2 figures.

Howard, A.Q. 1983. *The Antioch Dunes.* Contract report to San Franscisco Bay National Wildlife Refuge, P.O. Box 524, Newark, Ca 94560, Contract # 11640-0333-1, 118 pp; 3 appendices.

Opler, P.A. and J.A. Powell. 1961. "Taxonomic and distributional studies on the western components of the *Apodemia mormo* complex (Riodinidae)." *Journal of Lepidoptist's Society* 15:145-171.

Powell, J.A. 1983. Changes in the insect fauna of a deteriorating riverine sand dune community during 50 years of human exploitation. Unpublished report. Division of Entomology, University of California, Berkeley, 94720. 79 pp.

U.S. Fish and Wildlife Service. 1976. "Final rulemaking-6 California butterflies as Endangered species." *Federal Register* 41: 22041-22044.

————1977. "Proposed critical habitat for six California butterflies." *Federal Register* 42:12381.

————1978. "Final rulemaking-13 Endangered and Threatened U.S. plants." *Federal Register* 43:40685.

————1979. "Withdrawal of critical habitat proposals." *Federal Register* 44:

*Paul A. Opler, hired by the Fish and Wildlife Service in 1974 to list endangered and threatened butterflies, is now with the FWS office in Fort Collins, Colorado, where he is chief of the Land Section of the Office of Information Transfer.*

*Lee Robinson is a wildlife biologist for the San Francisco Bay wildlife refuge complex, where she oversees development and implementation of the management plan for the Antioch Dunes unit of the refuge.*

A Kemp's ridley sea turtle lays its eggs. Exploitation of the turtles has so decimated them that some scientists believe the species will never recover.

*Peter Pritchard*

◆ ———————————————————————————— ◆

# Kemp's Ridley Sea Turtle

## Jack B. Woody

U.S. Fish and Wildlife Service

## Species Description and Natural History

THE KEMP'S RIDLEY sea turtle (*Lepidochelys kempi*) is one of the smallest of the eight species of sea turtles, with an average adult weight of 70 to 90 pounds and an average straight-line carapace length of 23 to 27 inches. (Chavez *et al* 1967). Visually, the carapace of the adult may be as wide as it is long, giving the impression of a distinctly round shell. Coloration of the upper shell, or carapace, is grey-olive while the underside is cream-to-white, with the limbs similar to the grey-olive of the carapace. Carapace scutes are not distinctive and have none of the "tortoise shell" appearance found in some species of sea turtles. Hatchlings are dark grey top and bottom, but when wet appear jet black. They may have a narrow white line along the trailing edge of the flippers. Hatchling shells are rather soft, but harden during the first year's growth. Color also changes during the first year to a rather attractive light olive-brown with obvious scute patterns. The underside lightens to become similar to that of the adult.

Adult sexes are similar, except males have a distinctly longer and thicker tail than do females. Males also have a strongly developed claw on the fore-flippers that enables them to better grip the female during copulation at sea. The carapace normally has five pairs of relatively large lateral scutes and 12 pairs of marginals. The head is rather triangular and broad, with a distinctive "beak" and powerful jaws. The hooked-beak appearance of the jaw gave this species its common Mexican name, "tortuga lora," or parrot turtle (Pritchard and Marquez 1973).

## Range

The Kemp's ridley has the most restricted range of any sea turtle species in the Western Hemisphere, with only one recognized nesting beach in the world. This beach is located in the Mexican state of Tamaulipas, in the Municipio de Aldama, near the village of Rancho Nuevo, approximately 250 miles south of the U.S./Mexican border on the western Gulf of Mexico (Hildebrand 1963). Although the entire coastline from Padre Island, Texas, to south of Tampico, Mexico, encompassing hundreds of miles, appears quite similar, the Kemp's ridley confines its nesting activities to this small, isolated stretch of beach no more than 15 miles long. Nothing indicates that this nesting location has varied. Occasionally, one to a few Kemp's ridleys nest outside of this key nesting zone, the most recent report being a female Kemp's coming ashore on Padre Island National Seashore, Texas, in June 1985 and laying a clutch of 96 eggs (King 1985). However, significant nesting of this species either to the north or south of the Rancho Nuevo beach has never been recorded.

Juveniles and subadults are more widely distributed than are adults, a situation that has generated opposing theories. Young and adult Kemp's are found in the same areas of the Gulf, but young turtles also are relatively common along the New England coast (Lazell 1980) and in Chesapeake Bay (Byles 1985). Records of occurrence diminish rapidly north of the United States, but young Kemp's have been recorded in the waters of Nova Scotia, the Irish Republic, the British mainland, the Netherlands, and the Atlantic coast of France. Records south of this area exist, including the Mediterranean and African coasts, but are questionable. The species has never been reported from the Caribbean.

Two theories (Carr 1980, Hendrickson 1980) explain why adults are not found along the East Coast. One theory is that hatchlings that leave the natal beach in Mexico begin to move, possibly with prevailing currents, in a clockwise pattern up along the Gulf and then down along Florida's west coast. At this point, some of these small turtles pass through the straits of Florida, enter the Atlantic and the northward-moving Gulf Stream currents, and drift or swim northward with the current until they enter feeding areas such as Chesapeake Bay or even into New England areas during warmer periods. As the waters begin to cool in the fall, the turtles, which have gained in both size and strength, move southward, eventually re-entering the Gulf of Mexico, where they mature along with that segment of the population that remained in the Gulf.

The other theory is that the young turtles that leave the Gulf of Mexico and are taken up along the East Coast do not return to the Gulf of Mexico and are lost to the reproductive population. They are either taken further north into colder waters, where they die, or further east, where they exist as lone waifs in foreign seas with little or no contact with others of the species. Which of these theories is correct remains to be determined. Both appear reasonable, and perhaps future investigations will settle this long-standing question. It does appear that the great majority of young Kemp's, as well as the adults, remain in the U.S. or Mexican waters of the Gulf of Mexico and do not enter the Atlantic.

## Diet

The favored diet of the carnivorous, mature Kemp's appears to be various species of crabs, but they also take crustaceans, mollusks, jellyfish, fish, gastropods, and echinoderms (Pritchard and Marquez 1973). The powerful jaws allow the animal to crush almost anything it can get into its mouth, be it crab or thick-shelled clams. Hatchlings are thought to be omnivorous feeders, using both plant and animal matter. Little is known of the food habits of juveniles, but the animals become more carnivorous as they become larger and more mobile. Although female Kemp's that come ashore to nest at Rancho Nuevo are docile and seldom, if ever, attempt to bite, old-time fishermen report that when caught and taken aboard a boat, this species was noted for being vicious and would thrash about wildly, attempting to bite the nearest thing at hand.

## Breeding

The Kemp's nests from early April into July, with peak numbers nesting from May through June. Hatching begins in July and continues into mid-August. Hatchling emergence occurs in early morning, before dawn, and extends for a relatively short period beyond.

The Kemp's ridley is unique among sea turtles in nesting during daylight hours. Whereas other species come ashore to nest at night, it is very unusual for a Kemp's to be seen ashore after dark. However, it is possible that when there were large numbers of this species 40 years or so ago, nesting did extend into the night and prior to dawn. Why the Kemp's, of all sea turtles, is a daylight nester can only be surmised. It has been theorized that less natural nest predation may occur during daylight as opposed to darkness, but this is questionable. Coyotes work the nesting area during daylight and, even with the presence of turtle-beach workers, still take a few nests. Daylight nesting certainly makes the species more susceptible to human predation.

Nesting usually occurs during periods of relatively strong winds, often in the afternoon period, and may consist of a few turtles or a few hundred. Why the turtles select windy days to come ashore is not known. It has been suggested that the winds cover the tracks and nest sites of these relatively lightweight turtles, making it more difficult for predators to locate the nests.

Historically, the Kemp's would come ashore to nest in large aggregations, known in Spanish as "arribadas" (arrivals). We know from a film made by a Mexican engineer, Andres Herrera of Tampico (Hildebrand 1963), that on June 18, 1947, an arribada of approximately 40,000 Kemp's nested on this relatively short stretch of beach. Unfortunately, these numbers no longer occur, and a large arribada today is 150 to 250 animals.

The female Kemp's emerges from the water and proceeds, in almost a straight line, to the dune area above the normal high-tide zone. She will pause one or more times to push her snout into the sand as if testing or searching for some indication that the site meets her criteria for satisfactory nesting. Whether she is smelling, testing sand grain size, moisture content, chemical aspects, or a combination of many factors remains a mystery. In contrast to the larger species of sea turtles, the small ridley is a rapid nester, and usually completes the nesting cycle in less than an hour.

The nest site most often selected is at the base or slightly up the side of the first row of dunes. Some animals crawl up the first dune and nest in the trough between dunes or on the upper dune area. The nest site selected is first swept clean with the foreflippers, which are then planted in the sand as an anchor while the nesting proceeds. The nest cavity is dug by the hind flippers, which act as small shovels as each flipper alternately digs out small amounts of sand, which are thrown forward. This digging continues until the nest cavity, which averages about 14 to 18 inches deep, is completed. The turtle then positions herself so that the rear of the carapace conceals the hole and begins to deposit her eggs one to three at a time, until the clutch is completed. Normally, the mouth is slightly open and the sound of the animal's breathing is quite audible (Pritchard 1979). Usually, the entire clutch of white, ping-pong-ball-size eggs is deposited in less than 15 minutes. The total number of leathery-shelled eggs laid averages 104 and ranges from approximately 60 to 140 (U.S. Fish and Wildlife Service 1984).

Once the clutch is completed, the female moves her hind flippers in a curling motion along the sand surface toward her tail, thereby filling the hole. She then flattens the sand under her through a vigorous side-to-side thumping of her shell on the sand, while using the hind flippers to pull additional sand over the nest and smooth it. She also begins using the front flippers to throw sand to the rear between periods of thumping the sand flat with her shell. Gradually, the animal begins to move from the site, still throwing sand alternately with one front and hind flipper until finally she ceases and heads back to sea (Pritchard 1979). Once an individual turtle begins nest digging, it is generally quite oblivious to activities around it, including man. Each female may nest three times in a season, laying more than 300 eggs. Unlike most other turtle species, a number of the Kemp's females will nest in consecutive years.

Depending on temperature, hatching occurs 50 to 70 days after laying. Survival of hatchlings to maturity is believed to be quite low. Predation of hatchlings begins upon emergence from the nest cavity as ghost crabs, birds, or other terrestrial and avian predators take their toll. Once they enter the sea, turtles are taken by a number of predators. Sharks appear to be the primary natural predator of adult turtles, and it is not unusual to find severely mutilated females attempting to crawl up the beach and nest. In some cases, the hind flippers are gone, along with part of the carapace, but the flipperless animal still goes through the motions of digging a nest and eventually deposits the eggs on the sand surface.

How many years are required for a wild Kemp's ridley, or any other species of sea turtle, to reach sexual maturity is not known. Until recently, it was widely accepted that it probably took six to eight years for this species to reach reproductive maturity in the wild (Pritchard and Marquez 1973). However, based on bits and pieces of information becoming available for some of the other species, it appears reasonable to assume that the time required is considerably longer than first surmised—perhaps 15 years may be a closer guess. Ridleys held in captivity and maintained on relatively high protein diets grow rapidly. Eggs were laid by six-year-old Kemp's bred at the Cayman Turtle Farm in 1984 (Wood and Wood 1984), but only three hatched, and the young did not survive. As of July 1985, these same turtles had not attempted to nest again (Wood 1985). Regardless of the success or failure of captive growth and reproductive efforts, captive turtles should not be assumed to mirror growth and development of wild sea turtles. However, it does indicate that onset of maturity is size-dependent, not age-dependent.

## Significance of the Species

At one time in the past, and potentially today, this species, like sea turtles in general, was important as both a source of protein to local Mexican villagers and as a saleable product generating currency for a primarily agrarian society. Until 1965, both adult turtles and their eggs were exploited heavily. Pack trains reportedly hauled hundreds of thousands of eggs from the nesting beach to markets in Tampico and elsewhere (Hildebrand 1963). In some cases, adults were butchered for their meat, probably for local consumption as well as for sale to local markets.

Because of the very low number of turtles remaining and the protective measures of the Mexican Fisheries Department, little take of eggs or turtles has occurred in the past 20 years. The species presently has no economic importance.

## Historical Perspective

Prior to the film made by Andres Herrera in 1947 and his verbal account of what he learned and witnessed at that time, the world knew little of this species. Indeed, as an engineer Herrera did not realize the value of his film until it was discovered by a herpatologist doing research in Mexico. Consequently, the Kemp's was the last sea turtle to have its nesting beach discovered by the outside world, when Herrera's film was revealed to the scientific world in 1961 during a meeting of the American Society of Ichthyologists and Herpetologists in Austin, Texas (Hildebrand 1963, Carr 1967).

In the mid-1940s, the species probably numbered at least 100,000 adults, perhaps considerably more. However, other than the 1947 film of approximately 40,000 females nesting at one time along a mile of beach, little else is known.

The historical distribution and range of the species is believed to be similar to what it is today. The decline in numbers was a direct result of annual human exploitation of adults and eggs at the nesting beach into the mid-1960s.

In addition to direct exploitation, the species was, and is, taken incidental to other commercial and sport-fishing activities in both U.S. and Mexican waters. Trawling activities and the expanding shrimp fleets of both countries added to the take at the nesting beach. The species has declined to very low numbers despite considerable protective efforts by both the United States and Mexico and is now considered to be the most endangered species of sea turtle in the world. It was listed as endangered in 1970 (35 FR 18320; December 2, 1970) under the U.S. Endangered Species Act and is on Appendix I of the Convention on International Trade in Endangered Species of Wild Fauna and Flora (CITES).

## Current Trends

Although estimates vary, it is unlikely that more than 600 to 900 mature females and an equal number of males survive. Even with protection, the species has continued to decline. Research completed this year indicates a 30 percent decline over the past decade. The population probably numbers no more than 400 nesting females.

At such a low number, extinction becomes a real possibility in spite of the efforts of two nations. The species has declined to the point where otherwise minor environmental problems could prove crucial, and any loss is significant. At this time, the impact of oil spills, other chemical pollutants, commercial and recreational fishing, dredging, and other factors on this species is not known.

A major oil-well blowout, Intox I, that occurred in the Bay of Campeche during the spring of 1979 may have had major adverse impacts on Kemp's hatchling survival and perhaps on all age classes. Currents carried the oil northwesterly to the beaches of Tamaulipas and Texas. During the 1979 hatching period, the oil drifted throughout the offshore area and washed ashore. Although emergency measures were taken to protect the hatchlings (U.S. Fish and Wildlife Service 1979), losses could have been substantial to this year class. Oil on the nesting beach and offshore slicks continue to be an annual concern throughout the western Gulf.

The Mississippi Delta region, where Kemp's concentrate, deposits unknown quantities and kinds of contaminants into the Gulf every day of the year, as do all United States and Mexican drainages that empty into the Gulf. What effect this is having, directly or indirectly, can only be surmised. The accidental drowning of an adult Kemp's in a shrimp trawl 30 years ago was of relatively minor concern. Today it is of major concern, for that single adult may have produced 300 eggs during the nesting season, perhaps enough for the species to remain above the threshold of no return. Sea turtles, once they reach maturity, are believed to be potentially long-lived. Because of this, subtle changes in populations that might be fairly obvious in relatively short-lived terrestrial wildlife are not discernible in sea turtles. Present ignorance of the life history of these animals also compounds the difficulty of understanding and managing the species. Suffice it to say that information does not exist to determine whether this species can or cannot be maintained as a viable wild animal.

## Management

Because of the heavy exploitation of this animal and the identification in the early 1960s of its nesting area, the Mexican government, through its Departamento de Pesca, instituted in 1966 a program for the protection of the nesting beach and offshore waters. This project has continued, and within the past 10 years the beach has become one of the most intensely patrolled and actively managed nesting sites in the world. Although Mexico establishes annual regulations and take quotas for other species of sea turtles, complete protection is provided for the Kemp's ridley.

The Mexican fisheries department has established a seasonal turtle camp immediately adjacent to the midway point of the nesting beach. Beginning in early April each year since 1966 and extending through the hatching period of mid-August, the camp is occupied by biologists, technicians, students, support personnel, and armed Mexican marines. In 1978, an informal agreement was reached between representatives of the Mexican fisheries department, the U.S. Fish and Wildlife Service (FWS), National Marine Fisheries Service, National Park Service, and the Texas Parks and Wildlife Department to cooperate on a 10-year program. Under this agreement, the United States assists Mexico in Kemp's management and research efforts in exchange for permitting the yearly removal to the United States of approximately 2,000 to 3,000 eggs (U.S. Fish and Wildlife Service 1978). This has amounted to approximately two to three percent of the total eggs laid each year.

Taking these eggs is an experimental effort to establish, in the United States, a second nesting population to further safeguard the species. The site chosen was the Padre Island National Seashore in south Texas, which is approximately 250 miles up the coast from the Rancho Nuevo nesting beach. This barrier beach area is under the jurisdiction of the National Park Service, which can protect both the site and the turtles should this experiment be successful. The area has a history of only occasional nesting by individual Kemp's ridleys and loggerheads, the most recent being in June 1985, when a female Kemp's reportedly laid 96 eggs.

The eggs destined for Padre Island are collected in sterile plastic bags as they drop from the cloaca, preventing contact with Rancho Nuevo beach sand. The eggs are then placed in individual styrofoam boxes containing sand brought from Padre Island. This is done on the premise that some unknown mechanism "imprints" the location of the natal beach on the hatchlings so that those that survive to maturity will return to the natal beach nest. Placing of the Padre Island eggs into Padre Island sand for the incubation period is done in case the imprinting may be tied to idiosyncrasies of a particular beach sand and its chemistry. The 20 or so clutches collected in this fashion are flown out of Mexico by FWS, usually in late June, to Padre Island, where incubation is completed under the care of the National Park Service. Upon hatching, the hatchlings are allowed to crawl down the beach and into the sea, but are then captured and "headstarted" until approximately one year of age by the National Marine Fisheries Service at its Galveston laboratory. The following spring the turtles, now about the size of dinner plates, are released into the Gulf off Padre Island.

All of this transplant phase of the project is highly experimental, and the chance of successfully establishing a second nesting population on Padre Island is minimal. However, this experiment has provided sound data and techniques on how to maintain and raise healthy ridleys in captivity, diagnose and treat various diseases and viruses, and obtain maximum hatches of eggs, and has resulted in a better understanding of the at-sea movements of released animals.

Parties of both countries recognize that because of the very low population, extraordinary steps are in order, even though untried and untested, which may help to stem the decline and ultimately recover the species. Headstarting is being done on the assumption that survival of wild hatchlings is extremely low, but that survival increases as the individual turtle grows. As hatchlings, the turtles are the potential victims of a very wide range of factors, including ingestion of tar balls that plug the gullet and kill the animal, and being eaten by relatively small fish, birds, etc. Headstarting attempts to overcome this high initial loss by maintaining the animals until they have grown to a size that may substantially limit what could eat them or otherwise lessen their survival. Headstarted and released Kemp's that have been recaptured in areas frequented by wild juvenile ridleys exhibit normal growth and behavior

(Klima and McVey 1982). Where they will eventually go to nest remains to be answered. The oldest animals released would now be seven years old (1978 year class).

As stated previously, the nesting beach at Rancho Nuevo is protected and managed by the Mexican fisheries department. A squad of Mexican marines is assigned to provide patrol and protection throughout the season. However, because of predators and poachers, it is still necessary to relocate all nests to protected corrals adjacent to the base camp.

The 15 miles of nesting beaches are checked at least twice a day, seven days a week, for tracks and turtles. Frequency of patrols is increased on days of strong winds because high winds increase chances that turtles will come ashore. If patrols determine that turtle activity is building and an arribada may be in the offing, the marines are strategically placed to discourage poachers (who also know when to expect turtles), and assignments are given to all personnel for egg collecting, tagging, corral work, communications, etc. Activity at these times is intense but well organized. An arribada may occur in the early afternoon, but the field people may work late into the night until all nests have been documented and relocated into the protected corrals. Two fenced corrals are maintained adjacent to the base camp, and most of the nests collected are transplanted to these corrals, which are protected from human and other predators. Annual hatch rate has varied from approximately 50 to 70 percent over the past eight years. All turtles encountered are flipper-tagged, and other pertinent data is recorded.

Since the 1977 agreement between U.S. and Mexican agencies, FWS has provided direct on-site assistance to Mexico by furnishing additional beach workers, scientific equipment, all-terrain cycles for beach patrol, and other forms of assistance. Depending on available annual funds, FWS has often kept a light, single-engine aircraft at camp, which is used to back up beach patrols along the nesting beach and north and south of the area and to search for occurrences of other possible nesting. The aircraft also has been used to search for and locate female turtles fitted with radio transmitters, to alert the marines, and to harass poachers, who are usually on horseback.

Combining the resources of the Departamento de Pesca and FWS has resulted in increased effectiveness and efficiency of protection and management on the nesting beach. Development by the National Marine Fisheries Service of the Trawling Efficiency Device and its hoped-for use by U.S. commercial shrimp trawlers would reduce the accidental take of turtles in commercial shrimp-trawling operations within U.S. waters. The device, placed at the entrance of the trawl nets, prevents turtles and many other marine organisms from entering the bag at the trawl. Turtles, fish, and other large material are caught on a frame of angled metal bars and ejected up and out of the net. Shrimp catch is not reduced.

In addition to actions by the government, the private sector has been very active in the conservation of this species. A number of local and national groups, such as HEART in the Houston area, Sea Turtles, Inc. of South Padre Island, and the Center for Environmental Education in Washington, D.C., have provided funds and equipment to FWS for Rancho Nuevo and to the National Marine Fisheries Service for headstarting. Several aquaria in the United States are holding and raising a limited number of Kemp's that could be used in captive breeding or in a longer period of headstarting should this action become necessary. Cayman Turtle Farm, a program run by the Cayman Government, British West Indies, also is maintaining a small number of Kemp's. The 1984 nesting attempts of two of these animals may indicate that this turtle eventually will provide hatchlings.

Satellite tracking of adult females began in June 1985, when transmitters were attached to two females as they completed their nesting at Rancho Nuevo. Unfortunately, this satellite-tracking effort ended in about one month. In July, one animal was taken by a shrimp trawler off Freeport, Texas. It was reported that this turtle was released alive. The transmitter was returned to the National Marine Fisheries Service. The second transmitter was found beached south of Tampico, Mexico. The fate of the turtle is unknown (Mysing 1985). FWS and the National Marine Fisheries Service, in cooperation with Mexico, plan to put transmitters on 25 or more animals in 1986 at Rancho Nuevo. This will provide more definitive information on the annual movements of reproducing females and lend support to further identification and management of key sites offshore.

## Prognosis

It has been suggested that the Kemp's ridley has declined to such a low level that it cannot recover and that although individuals will exist for quite some time, the species eventually will disappear from the wild. Opposed to the pessimistic theory is the hypothesis that with protection efforts increases will be observed within the next five to 10 years, and the species will slowly recover.

## Recommendations

No reduction in the current protective efforts of the United States and Mexico can be allowed if the species is to have any chance at survival. Current economic problems in Mexico could force a reduction in funding for this project, a potentially disastrous development. Any reduction in nesting-beach protection means loss of nests and reproductive females, losses the species can least withstand. Mexico must continue its current program, and the United States, through FWS, should continue to provide personnel and equipment to assist Mexico in this endeavor. This cooperative effort should be formalized by both countries in a written agreement for a time period of not less than 10 years beyond 1988.

Additional investigation is needed into the role of incubation temperatures in sex determination. It is known that incubation temperatures determine the sex of most, if not all, sea turtle species. Movement of eggs to protected corrals or transplanting into styrofoam boxes could alter normal sex ratios (Morreale *et al* 1982), and this altering, if it produces a preponderance of males, is not the intent of management efforts. Work currently is under way on this question as it relates to Kemp's, but it must be clarified as soon as possible.

Through the National Marine Fisheries Service, increased efforts must be made to gain acceptance and routine use of the Trawling Efficiency Device by the U.S. shrimp-trawling industry of the Gulf of Mexico. Mexico's department of fisheries should initiate similar efforts in the Mexican shrimp industry, with the U.S. National Marine Fisheries Service providing initial technical assistance.

Headstarting efforts with Kemp's have been under way since 1978 and should continue for the full 10-year agreement period, but prior to extending the effort, a complete and thorough evaluation needs to be done. By the summer of 1989, 10,000 to 15,000 headstarted Kemp's presumably "imprinted" on Padre Island, will have been released. Headstarting for Padre Island beyond the 10-year period is somewhat tentative until more is known about the factors involved in imprinting and about what turtles already headstarted and released will do when maturity is reached.

Two of the greatest needs in the management of sea turtle stocks are development of an accurate aging technique—preferably one that can be used for live animals—and a permanent external marking method. Without these two methodologies, many of the questions about population structure, including recruitment and survival, will remain educated guesses.

A better understanding of the species' behavior and habitat preferences at sea must be developed and, with this, identification and protection of key use areas in the United States and Mexico. The National Marine Fisheries Service presently is studying this subject and has no additional plans for more research. Efforts to improve reproduction in captive turtles should continue on a limited and selected basis. This should be done to ensure that a representative sample of the live animals survives should the wild population be lost. Whether this type of project could ever be used to re-establish a wild population is debatable, but the magnitude of the sea turtle decline demands that no possible means for increasing turtle numbers be ignored. Captive propagation, which has not yet been successful for this species, and headstarting are experimental endeavors and should not, under any circumstances, be considered as viable practices to prevent extinction in the wild until their value has been demonstrated. Stringent enforcement in both Mexico and the United States to prevent taking of this species must continue and, in some cases, be increased.

All of these measures require funding. Although government agencies in both countries, with support from private individuals and organizations, have made vital contributions, private industry so far has helped little with conservation and management. Moreover, industry represents a potential or existing threat to the species' survival. The petroleum industry of both the United States and Mexico has been and will remain responsible for the loss of some turtles. Researchers continue to collect dead hatchlings choked by tar balls in their gullets or rolled up in wads of tar. The tar came from offshore sources—ships, drilling operations, blowouts, or spills. But whatever the point source, the tar is in the waters and on the beaches of the two nations every day of the year.

Shrimp trawlers are still taking turtles incidental to their operations. Some of these turtles live, some die. It is illegal under the Endangered Species Act to take this species, in U.S. waters either intentionally or accidentally. The shrimp industry has been asked to adopt the relatively inexpensive device that will prevent turtle deaths in trawl nets, but unfortunately has been slow to adopt the devices even though instructions for building and installing them are available free from the National Marine Fisheries Service (National Marine Fisheries Service 1983). Hook-and-line sport fisherman also take an unknown number of young ridleys in bays and estuaries.

Industry in the United States has a responsibility, either by existing state and federal laws or as a moral obligation, to help correct the environmental problems they have created and to which they are contributing. They have yet to come forward to protect the Kemp's ridley, and their help and cooperation is badly needed.

The Kemp's ridley, as with all sea turtles, takes many years to mature—as long or longer than humans—and subtle adverse changes in populations are not easily detected or reversed in the short-run. The success or failure of efforts to increase or in other ways manage sea turtles cannot be assessed in a few years' time. A deer population may turn over four, five, or six times before a hatchling sea turtle reaches maturity, while a quail population may be in its twentieth or older generation in the same amount of time. Past efforts of Mexico and the United States cannot be easily evaluated before another 10 years have passed. Because of the embarrassing lack of knowledge and limited resources devoted to this species, any future prognosis as to the species' survival or extinction must remain theoretical.

# References

Byels, R. 1985. Personal Communication.

Carr, A. 1967. *So Excellent A Fish*. Natural History Press. Garden City, New York.

Carr, A. 1980. "Some problems of sea turtle ecology." *American Zoology* 20:489-498.

Chavez, H., G.M. Contreras, D.T.P. 1967. Eduardo Hernandez. "Aspectos biologicos y protecion de la tortuga lora. *Lepidochelys kempi* (Garman), en la Costa de Tamaulipas, Mexico." *Institute Nacional Investigation Biology Pesqu.* No. 17, Mexico City.

Hendrickson, J.R. 1980. "The ecological strategies of sea turtles." *American Zoology* 20:597-608.

Hildebrand, H.H. 1963. "Hallazgo del area de amidacion de la tortuga marina 'lora,' *Lepidochelys kempi* (Garman) en la costa occidental del Golfo de Mexico." *Ciencia* 22(4):105-112.

King, R. 1985. Personal Communication.

Klima, E.F. and James P. McVey. 1982. "Headstarting the Kemp's ridley turtle, *Lepidochelys kempi,*" in K.A. Bjorndal, ed., *Biology and Conservation, Proceedings of the World Conference on Sea Turtle Conservation.* Smithsonian Institution Press. Washington, D.C. 585 pp.

Lazell, J.D. 1980. "New England waters: critical habitat for marine turtles." *Copea* 1980(2):290-295.

Morreale, S.J., Georgita J. Ruiz, James R. Spotila, and Edward A. Standora. 1982. "Temperature-dependent sex determination: Current practices threaten conservation of sea turtles." *Science* 216:1245-1247.

Mrosovsky, N. 1982. "Sex ratio bias in hatchling sea turtles from artificially incubated eggs." *Biological Conservation* 23:309-314.

Mysing, J. 1985. Personal Communication.

National Marine Fisheries Service. 1983. *Construction and Installation Instructions for the Trawling Efficiency Device.* SEFC, Mississippi Laboratories, Pascagoula, Mississippi. 15 pp.

Pritchard, P.C.H., and M.R. Marquez. 1973. "Kemp's ridley turtle or the Atlantic ridley, *Lepidochelys kempi.*" *International Union for the Conservation of Nature and Natural Resources Monograph* No. 2. Marine Turtle Series. IUCN, Morges.

Pritchard, P.C.H. 1979. *Encyclopedia of Turtles.* T.F.H. Publications, New Jersey and Hong Kong. pp. 672-747.

U.S. Fish and Wildlife Service. 1978 through 1984. Annual Reports on United States/Mexico Conservation of Kemp's Ridley Sea Turtle at Rancho Nuevo, Tamaulipas, Mexico. U.S. Fish and Wildlife Service, Albuquerque, New Mexico.

Wood, J.R. and Fern E. Wood. 1984. "Captive breeding of the Kemp's ridley." *Marine Turtle Newsletter* No. 30:12.

Wood, J. 1985. Personal Communication.

*Jack B. Woody is the Fish and Wildlife Service's national sea turtle coordinator. He is stationed in the Region 2 Office in Albuquerque and has studied sea turtles for 12 years.*

The loggerhead shrike apparently is declining nationwide, with the most severe declines in the central states. The cause for the decline is uncertain and the subject of continuing study.

*Bill Dyer/Photo Researchers*

# The Loggerhead Shrike

## James D. Fraser
## and
## David R. Luukkonen

Virginia Polytechnic Institute

## Species Description and Natural History

THE LOGGERHEAD SHRIKE (*Lanius ludovicianus*) is a perching bird of pasture, savannah, and open brushland. At nine inches and one and one-half ounces, it is slightly smaller than the American robin (*Turdus migratorius*), yet it routinely preys upon vertebrates such as snakes, sparrows, and mice. Its habit of impaling prey on thorns or other projections, and the fact that it was first described in the Louisiana territory, earned the shrike its scientific name, which means "the butcher of Louisiana." It is commonly known as the butcherbird.

Like northern mockingbirds (*Mimus polyglottos*), loggerhead shrikes have gray backs, light breasts, and white wing spots and tail bars. They can be distinguished from mockingbirds, however, by their black facial masks, larger heads, heavier bills, and plumper silhouettes. In flight, the loggerhead has very rapid wingbeats compared to those of the mockingbird.

The loggerhead shrike also is very similar to the northern shrike (*Lanius excubitor*), which occasionally enters the loggerhead's winter range. The northern shrike, however, is slightly larger, has a faintly barred breast, a light-colored mandible, and an interrupted, rather than continuous, face mask (Miller 1931).

933

## Range

Loggerhead shrike range extends from southern Canada to Mexico, and from coast to coast. Where snow covers the ground less than 10 days per year, shrikes tend to be resilient; further north they are at least partially migratory (Miller 1931). The loggerhead shrike is territorial in winter as well as summer and aggressively defends nest sites, feeding areas, and roost trees from intruding shrikes and other competing species (Miller 191, Bent 1950, Williams 1958).

## Breeding

Shrikes nest earlier than most other passerine birds, in much of their range laying their first eggs in April and May and as early as February and March in the South. Males tend to return to the same territories year after year, but there is no evidence that females do (Kridelbaugh 1983). Both sexes participate in nest building (Kridelbaugh 1982). Nests are placed in any of a variety of trees, shrubs, or vines, including willows (*Salix* spp.), eastern red cedars (*Juniperus virginiana*), osage orange (*Maclura pomifera*), hackberry (*Celtis occidentalis*), hawthornes (*Crataegus* spp.), apples (*Pyrus malus*), locusts (*Robinia* spp.), honeylocusts (*Gleditsia* spp.), and roses (*Rosa* spp.). Most nests are built between three and 30 feet above the ground in a crotch or on top of an old nest, often in dense twigs or foliage. Construction varies with local materials, but most are built of coarse twigs and are lined with herbaceous vegetation and animal hair (Miller 1931, Bent 1950, Kridelbaugh 1983).

Loggerhead shrikes usually lay five or six eggs, although extremes of three and eight have been reported. Incubation usually begins after laying the second to last egg. Although there have been some reports to the contrary (Bent 1950), recent observers agree that only the female incubates (Siegel 1980, Kridelbaugh 1982) and that the male feeds the incubating female. Incubation lasts about 17 days, a relatively long period for a passerine (Miller 1930, Lohrer 1974, Porter *et al.* 1975, Kridelbaugh 1983). Southern birds may raise two, possibly three, broods yearly, and birds from all localities are likely to renest after a nesting failure (Miller 1931, Bent 1950, Lohrer 1974, Siegel 1980).

Young are fed in the nest by both parents for 17 to 21 days (Miller 1931, Lohrer 1974, Porter *et al.* 1975, Siegel 1980, Kridelbaugh 1983). They then spend two or three days exploring the nest tree by hopping from branch to branch before they begin flying. The young are fed by the parents for three or four weeks after fledging.

## Diet

Perhaps more has been written about shrike food habits than about any other aspect of the species' natural history. This is undoubtedly because shrikes are the only passerine bird that regularly kills and consumes large vertebrate prey and because they engage in the unusual practice of impaling their prey. Although the oft-pictured impaled mouse has conveyed the impression that shrikes specialize on rodents, the fact is that they are extremely catholic in their feeding habits and will apparently take any animal they are capable of subduing. Mammals taken include voles (*Microtus* spp.), white-footed mice (*Peromyscus* spp.), house mice (*Mus musculus*), harvest mice (*Reithrodontomys* spp.), pocket mice (*Perognathus* spp.), kangaroo rats (*Dipodomys* spp.), and shrew (*Sorex* spp.). One record exists of a loggerhead shrike taking a full-grown cotton rat (*Sigmodon hispidus;* Hoxie 1889).

A variety of small birds are taken, including chimney swifts (*Chaetura pelagica*), sparrows, warblers, buntings, and finches. When shrikes were common in residential areas, it was not unusual for them to attack caged canaries. Frightened by the aggressors, canaries often thrust their heads through the cage bars, only to be decapitated by the hungry shrikes. Lizards, snakes, and frogs are captured in some areas, and fish were recorded in one instance.

Insects often constitute the bulk of the loggerhead's diet. Grasshoppers, crickets, and beetles are favorites—particularly when they are present in great numbers. Butterflies, moths, bees, and spiders are taken somewhat less frequently. Shrikes occasionally take carrion and have been observed scavenging meat scraps left by northern harriers (*Circus cyaneus*) and rough-legged hawks (*Buteo lagopus*) (Judd 1898, Beal and McAtee 1912, Miller 1931, Bent 1950, Chapman and Casto 1972, Anderson 1976, Kridelbaugh 1982).

The adaptive significance of impaling behavior has long been a matter of speculation among naturalists. One plausible explanation for this behavior is that, lacking the strong feet of raptors, shrikes impale prey as an aid in food handling. Another possible explanation is that the impaled animals serve as a cache to which shrikes can return when they require food. Caching prey near the nest also allows the female to feed herself during short breaks in incubation without leaving the vicinity of the nest and without expending a great deal of energy foraging (Applegate 1977).

## Significance of the Species

Public opinion about shrikes has changed with changes in general attitudes toward predators. When predators were villified by the public, shrikes took more than their share of acrimony. Not only did they kill treasured songbirds, they also impaled their victims, a behavior wrongfully perceived as a vengeful or sadistic streak. More recently, the image of predators in general, and shrikes in particular, has improved. Indeed, some people now view predators as guardians of the ecological balance and, by virtue of their predation on pests, as friends of the farmer.

Neither viewpoint is correct. There is no reason to believe that predation and impaling are anything more or less than naturally evolved adaptive behaviors. Moreover, little evidence exists to suggest that shrikes have a significant impact on prey populations. Indeed, this seems quite unlikely. A more enlightened view considers that these interesting birds occupy a unique ecological niche; give pleasure to those who value the bird's ecological role and to those who enjoy observing beautiful birds; are scientifically valuable because they represent one of only two North American passerines that prey regularly on vertebrates; and give pleasure to those who study animal behavior. These intangible values give the bird a significance impossible to quantify.

Shrikes may one day be among those species that have an important impact on wildlife management. As one of five federally recognized national species of special emphasis, the declining loggerhead shrike should be the subject of heightened effort to alleviate its problems. However, the current political and bureaucratic climate tends to ignore nongame species such as the shrike. Greater public awareness of the shrike could help change this attitude.

In the future, shrikes may, like other species, fill some unanticipated human need. The shrike's greatest value to man, however, may be the ability to signal problems in the ecosystem upon which man depends. If we can discover why loggerhead shrike populations are declining, might we not also find a threat to human health or to the health of our domestic animals?

## Historical Perspective

Little is known about the distribution and abundance of loggerhead shrikes in presettlement North America. We may assume, however, that because of its preference for open country, the shrike was rare in eastern North America and in the mountainous West, both largely forested in pristine times. Because they require trees and bushes for nesting, roosting, and hunting, they probably were uncommon in the pristine prairie of the central United States. When European settlers began clearing the eastern forest and bringing trees to the plains, shrikes probably responded by expanding into the newly created habitat (Butler 1897). Thus Palmer (1898) wrote that the loggerhead shrike "is considered a fairly common bird over most of the region between Maine and Florida and Ohio and Illinois to Louisiana." Perhaps they reached their greatest numbers in the brushlands and deserts of the southwestern and south-central United States, where they still are relatively abundant.

## Current Trends

Local shrike declines were reported as early as the beginning of the century (Hess 1910, Eifrig 1919), and several lines of evidence indicate a precipitous decline in recent years. FWS (the U.S. Fish and Wildlife Service) coordinates a yearly nationwide survey of breeding birds on some 2,400 routes. This survey has shown a four percent annual decline in continental shrike populations since the first routes were established in 1968 (Bystrak and Robbins 1977, Bystrak 1981). Detailed analyses of these data suggest that the decline is most severe in the central states (Geissler and Noon 1981).

Analyses of Audubon Society Christmas bird counts indicate serious declines in wintering populations in the eastern United States (Morrison 1981). Christmas counts also suggest that Pacific Coast populations are stable or slowly declining.

A third line of evidence for shrike declines comes from the subjective opinions of local experts, summarized annually in Audubon's Blue List. Birds included on this list are species that have shown noncyclical population declines or range contractions (Tate 1981). The shrike has been included in every edition of this list since it was first published in 1972 (Arbib 1972-1980, Tate 1981, Tate and Tate 1982), with the most serious declines again reported from the eastern states.

More detailed regional studies support these reports. In the northeastern United States, Milburn (1981) examined museum collections, Christmas bird counts, ornithological literature, five different compilations of breeding bird records, and the unpublished notes of numerous amateur and professional ornithologists. She concluded that the loggerhead shrike is declining and in jeopardy in the northeastern United States. In Illinois, a 36-square-mile study area was surveyed periodically from 1957 to 1966. During that period, pairs of nesting shrikes declined from 13 to zero (Graber *et al.* 1973). In Missouri, Kridelbaugh (1982) found a 60 percent reduction in the numbers of observed shrikes between 1967 and 1979. Additionally, shrikes observed on Missouri Christmas bird counts declined 82 percent between 1960 and 1977.

Habitat destruction has been suggested as a possible explanation for the decline. As the tractor replaced the horse, the amount of pasture in the United States was reduced rapidly. Some was converted to other agricultural uses. Other tracts, particularly in the Northeast, reverted to forest. Land planted to rowcrops offers little habitat for the vertebrate prey of shrikes, and forest is simply not shrike habitat. Additionally, the recent trend has been toward larger fields and "clean" farming. These practices result in reduction of the fencerow vegetation used by shrikes and their prey.

Despite the fact that habitat loss has likely had an impact on shrike populations, it may not be the sole reason for the decline. Indeed, shrikes have disappeared from areas where fencerow-pasture habitat is still available. Graber et al. (1973) suggested two phases of the decline in Illinois. They attributed a slow decline from 1900 to the middle 1950s to habitat loss, and a rapid and ultimately disastrous decline from 1957 to 1965 to unknown causes.

Contamination by pesticides has been suggested as another explanation for the decline. Analyses of loggerhead shrikes in southern Illinois showed concentrations of DDE, a metabolite of DDT, in subcutaneous fat and eggs (Anderson and Duzan 1978). Moreover, shrike eggshells collected in 1971 and

1972 were significantly thinner than shells collected before 1900. These results are similar to those for the peregrine falcon (*Falco peregrinus*), bald eagle (*Haliaeetus leucocephalus*), and brown pelican (*Pelecanus occidentalis*), species known to have experienced reproductive failures and population declines due to ingesting DDT or DDE (Ratcliffe 1970, Anderson and Hickey 1972, Cooke 1973, Faber and Hickey 1973, Blus et al. 1974). Shrike shell thickness showed smaller changes in California and Florida (Morrison 1979), where shrike populations apparently are not decreasing as rapidly as elsewhere. Despite this, the reproductive rate of loggerhead shrikes, even in declining populations, has been relatively high (Graber *et al.* 1973, Porter *et al.* 1975, Anderson and Duzan 1978, Siegel 1980, Kridelbaugh 1982, 1983), and the crushed eggs associated with DDE-induced reproductive failures in other species have not been reported. Thus the actual effect of DDT on shrike populations is not fully understood.

Another chemical that has been shown to affect bird populations is dieldrin. This chemical, like other pesticides, can result in toxicosis and death and, at sublethal levels in shrikes, can interfere with the normal development of hunting behavior (Busbee 1977). This type of influence could have an impact on fledging survival and, ultimately, on shrike populations.

Fortunately, DDT and dieldrin have been banned from most applications since the early 1970s, and a number of species have shown evidence of recovering from their effects. There is no evidence that shrike populations are increasing, however, which supports the contention that DDT and dieldrin may not have been responsible for recent shrike declines. At present, the cause of the shrike decline is imperfectly understood.

## Management

The loggerhead shrike is currently on state threatened lists in Illinois, Iowa, Michigan, and Wisconsin. The Missouri Conservation Department, FWS, and the Virginia Commission of Game and Inland Fisheries have sponsored studies aimed at determining the status of shrikes and making management recommendations. Milburn (1981) and Kridelbaugh (1982) suggested that the species be included in the federal list of threatened and endangered species. Kridelbaugh also recommended continued monitoring and management of nesting cover. Despite these recommendations, we are unaware of any existing efforts to manage loggerhead shrike populations or their habitats. Indeed, until the cause for the decline is thoroughly understood, such efforts may be futile.

## Prognosis

The future of the loggerhead shrike is uncertain. It is clear that the destiny of shrike habitat will be tied closely to the management of pasture and rangeland. While prime shrike habitat is disappearing, particularly in the northeastern United States, it is not clear that this is the main factor limiting shrike populations. The abundance of seemingly suitable but unoccupied habitat patches suggests that it is not, although this idea should be tested. Reliable predictions about the future of the loggerhead shrike will have to await incontrovertible identification of the factor or factors responsible for the decline.

## Recommendations

The situation demands immediate study. Shrike populations studies should be coordinated both in the eastern United States, where populations have declined rapidly, and in the south-central or southwestern United States, where populations are stable or declining more slowly. Only such studies will determine clearly the reasons for the shrike decline and provide sound recommendations for the recovery of the species.

## References

Anderson, D.W., and J.J. Hickey. 1972. "Eggshell changes in North American Birds." *Proceedings of the XV Ornithological Congress:* 514-540.

Anderson, R.M. 1976. "Shrikes feed on prey remains left by hawks." *Condor* 78:269.

Anderson, W.C., and R.E. Duzan. 1978. "DDE residues and eggshell thinning in loggerhead shrikes." *Wilson Bulletin* 90:215-220.

Applegate, R.D. 1977. "Possible ecological role of food caches of loggerhead shrikes." *Auk* 94:391-392.

Arbib, R. 1972. "The blue list for 1973." *American Birds* 26:932-933.

Arbib, R. 1973. "The blue list for 1974." *American Birds* 27:943-945.

Arbib, R. 1974. "The blue list for 1975." *American Birds* 28:971-974.

Arbib, R. 1975. "The blue list for 1976." *American Birds* 29:1067-1072.

Arbib, R. 1976. "The blue list for 1977." *American Birds* 30:1031-1039.

Arbib, R. 1977. "The blue list for 1978." *American Birds* 31:1087-1096.

Arbib, R. 1978. "The blue list for 1979." *American Birds* 32:1106-1113.

Arbib, R. 1979. "The blue list for 1980." *American Birds* 33:830-835.

Beal, F.E.L., and W.L. McAtee. 1912. "Food of some well known birds of forest, farm, and, garden." *U.S. Department of Agriculture Farmers Bulletin* 506:1-35.

Bent, A.C. 1950. "Life histories of North American wagtails, shrikes, vireos, and their allies." *U.S. National Museum Publication* 197. 411 pp.

Blus, L., A.A. Belisle, and R.M. Prouty. 1974. "Relations of the brown pelican to certain environmental pollutants." *Pesticide Monitoring Journal* 7:181-194.

Busbee, E.L. 1977. "The effects of dieldrin on the behavior of young loggerhead shrikes." *Auk* 94:28-35.

Butler, A.W. 1897. "The birds of Indiana." *Twenty-second Report of the Department of Geology and Natural Resources of Indiana:* 515-1187.

Bystrak, D. 1981. "The North American breeding bird survey." *in* C.J. Ralph and M. Scott, eds. *Estimating Numbers of Terrestrial Birds.* Studies in Avian Biology No. 6. Cooper Ornithological Society.

Bystrak, D., and C.S. Robbins. 1977. "Bird populations trends detected by the North American breeding bird survey." *Political Ecological Studies* 3: 131-143.

Chapman, B.R., and S.D. Casto. 1972. "Additional vertebrate prey of the loggerhead shrike." *Wilson Bulletin* 84:496-497.

Cooke, A.S. 1973. "Shell thinning in avian eggs by environmental pollutants." *Environmental Pollution* 4:85-152.

Eifrig, G. 1919. "Birds of the Chicago area." *Auk* 36;513-524.

Faber, R.A. and J.J. Hickey. 1973. "Eggshell thinning, chlorinated hydrocarbons, and mercury in inland aquatic bird eggs, 1967 and 1970." *Pesticide Monitoring Journal* 7:27-36.

Geissler, P.H., and B.R. Noon. 1981. "Estimates of avian populations trends from the North American Breeding Bird Survey." Pages 42-51 *in* C.J. Ralph and M. Scott, eds., *Estimating the Numbers of Terrestrial Birds.* Studies in Avian Biology No. 6 Cooper Ornithologist Society.

Graber, R.R., J.W. Graber, and E.L. Kirk. 1973. "Illinois birds: Laniidae." *Illinois Natural History Survey Biological Notes* 83. Illinois Natural History Survey. 18 pp.

Hess, G.K. 1980. "Summary of the status of shrikes in Delaware." *Delmarva Ornithology* 15: 8-9.

Hoxie, W. 1889. "Food of the loggerhead shrike." *Ornithology and Oology* 14:72.

Judd, S.D. 1898. "The food of shrikes." *U.S. Department of Agriculture Division of Biological Survey Bulletin* 9:15-26.

Kridelbaugh, A.L. 1982. "An ecological study of loggerhead shrikes in central Missouri." Unpublished M.S. Thesis. University of Missouri, Columbia. 114 pp.

Kridelbaugh, A.L. 1983. "Nesting ecology of the loggerhead shrike in central Missouri." *Wilson Bulletin* 95:303-308.

Lohrer, F.E. 1974. "Post-hatching growth and development of the loggerhead shrike in Florida." Unpublished M.S. thesis. University of Southern Florida. 62 pp.

Milburn, T. 1981. "Status and distribution of the loggerhead shrike *Lanius ludovicianus* in the northeastern United States." U.S. Department of the Interior Fish and Wildlife Service office of Endangered Species, unpublished report.

Miller, A.H. 1931. "Systematic revision and natural history of the American shrikes *(Lanius).*" *University of California Publication of Zoology* 38:11-242.

Morrison, M.L. 1981. "Population trends of the loggerhead shrike in the United States." *American Birds* 35:754-757.

Palmer, W. 1898. "Our small eastern shrike." *Auk* 15:244-258.

Porter, D.K., M.A. Strong, J.B. Giezenntanner, and R.A. Ryder. 1975. "Nest ecology, productivity, and growth of the loggerhead shrike on the shortgrass prairie." *Southwestern Naturalist* 19:429-436.

Ratcliffe, D.A. 1970. "Changes attributable to pesticides in egg breakage frequency and eggshell thickness in some British birds." *Journal of Applied Ecology* 7:67-115.

Siegel, M.S. 1980. "The nesting ecology and population dynamics of the loggerhead shrike in the blackbelt of Alabama." Unpublished M.S. thesis. University of Alabama. 30 pp.

Tate, J. Jr. "The blue list for 1981." *American Birds* 35:3-10.

Tate, J. Jr. and D.J. Tate. 1982 "The blue list for 1982." *American Birds* 36:126-135.

Williams, F.M. 1958. "Interspecific defense of roost site by loggerhead shrike." *Wilson Bulletin* 70:95.

*James D. Fraser, an assistant professor of wildlife science at Virginia Polytechnic Institute, specializes in research on declining species. His work on the loggerhead shrike is funded by the Fish and Wildlife Service and by the Virginia Game Commission's nongame program.*

*David R. Luukkonen is a graduate student at Virginia Polytechnic Insitute who is studying loggerhead shrikes.*

Chances for recovery of the endangered Knowlton cactus, currently numbering 9,000 plants in the wild, seem good if federal, state, and private cooperation in its protection continues.
*Peggy Olwell/U.S. Fish and Wildlife Service*

# The Knowlton Cactus

## Peggy Olwell

U.S. Fish and Wildlife Service

## Species Description and Life History

THE KNOWLTON CACTUS (*Pediocactus knowltonii*), smallest member of the genus (Heil *et al* 1981), was also once the rarest member as well. This diminutive plant grows either as a solitary stem or in a cluster of up to 19 stems, which are globular and range from 0.3 to two inches tall and a half to one inch in diameter. The light gray-green stem is relatively inconspicuous, blending in with the surrounding soil and rock. The stem is dotted with small projections, each capped with usually 18 to 23 dense white spines (Benson 1982). Although the plant scarcely protrudes above soil level most of the year, from mid-April through early May the yellow-centered, pink flowers, generally bigger than the plant itself, make the cactus more conspicuous. As with other members of the genus, the Knowlton cactus has a non-persistent perianth and the fruit opens along a vertical slit on the ovary wall (Heil *et al* 1981). Fruit formation occurs between late May and early June resulting in two to three green to tannish fruits per plant and 10-12 seeds per fruit (U.S. Fish and Wildlife Service 1985).

## Range

The Knowlton cactus is limited to a small area in the pinyon-juniper woodland of northwestern New Mexico. Extension of the population into La Plata

943

County, Colorado, has been reported, but has not been relocated since first discovered in 1958. The type locality for the Knowlton cactus is south of La Boca, Colorado, in San Juan County, New Mexico (Benson 1961). This site, on privately owned land, contains the only known viable population of Knowlton cactus, an estimated 9,000 plants. This population covers an area of about 12 acres, with the highest densities occurring within less than two and a half acres (Knight 1985). The only other known occurrence, consisting of two plants, is located in Reece Canyon about four miles from the type locality on Bureau of Land Management (BLM) land. It is uncertain whether this population is natural or the result of transplantation by the New Mexico Cactus and Succulent Society in 1960 (U.S. Fish and Wildlife Service 1985).

The habitat is at the eastern edge of the Colorado Plateau, adjacent to the San Juan Mountains. The species grows on Tertiary alluvial deposits that form rolling gravelly hills covered with Colorado pinyon, Rocky Mountain juniper, and sagebrush. The type-locality population grows on the top and slopes of a single hill at an elevation of 6,250 feet.

## Significance of the Species

All species of *Pediocactus*, except *Pediocactus simpsonii*, are of limited geographic range and restricted to small areas of specialized habitat (Benson 1962b). Benson (1962b) considers *Pediocactus* to be the "keystone of the arch" of U.S. cactus genera—it and a few other genera are intermediate between the genus *Echinocactus*, and the genera *Coryphantha* and *Mammillaria*. Therefore, this genus is important in the taxonomic realignment of the Cactaceae.

In addition to the taxonomic significance of *Pediocactus knowltonii*, preliminary data from tissue culturing of the Knowlton cactus indicate that mass propagation of genetically identical clones can be produced in less time than any other propagation technique (Clayton 1985). Because of the genetic consistency of the various clonal strains, this species may prove to be a good model with which to conduct ecological and physiological experiments. Data from these studies may prove useful in developing recovery and management strategies for this and other threatened and endangered cacti.

## Historical Perspective

The Knowlton cactus was first discovered in 1958 by F.G. Knowlton, who sent a specimen of the cactus to Lyman Benson. The spines of the Knowlton cactus differed from juvenile plants of *Pediocactus simpsonii*, but publication of the new species was considered unwise until more evidence on the maturity of the Knowlton cactus could be obtained. In 1960, a second collection of the cactus was made by Prince Pierce; the largest specimens were the same size as those collected by Knowlton (Benson 1961). Benson (1960) first described the species briefly in 1960 and with additional information and specimens, completed the description later (Benson 1961, 1962a).

There is some question as to whether all the collected specimens were from the type locality, since three population localities were cited in the publications. Two of these localities either never existed or have been extirpated over the years. It is presumed that the historic range of the species is the same as the present range except for the Reece Canyon locality.

The geographic range of the Knowlton cactus always has been limited, and overcollection has caused the number of plants in the population to fluctuate greatly. In 1960, members of the New Mexico Cactus and Succulent Society set out to "rescue" the Knowlton cactus from flooding due to construction of the Navajo Dam (Murphey 1961). Society members collected all the plants they could from the type locality. It was only after this mass collection was made that it was realized that the habitat of the Knowlton cactus was above the floodwaters of Navajo Lake.

The Knowlton cactus declined from 1965 to 1979 because of overcollection by cactus enthusiasts. The population dropped to less than 100 individual plants in 1978 (Arp 1979), the species virtually extirpated by collectors within two decades. By the late 1970s, some collectors believed that the natural population had been eliminated. Since 1980, the collecting pressure is thought to have lessened as collectors turned to propagation. Seeds in the soil have germinated, and the present wild population numbers 9,000 individuals, a marked increase.

## Current Trends

The Knowlton cactus was given endangered status by the U.S. Fish and Wildlife Service (FWS) under the Endangered Species Act on November 28, 1979 (U.S. Fish and Wildlife Service 1979). The act protects listed plants by prohibiting their removal from federal lands. It also prohibits the sale, import, export, or transport in interstate or foreign commerce of any listed plant species (Public Law 93-205, 1973). The Lacey Act, as amended in 1981, also provides some protection for the Knowlton cactus. Under this act, interstate or foreign commerce of any plant taken in violation of any federal or state law is illegal (Public Law 97-79, 1981).

On July 29, 1983, *Pediocactus knowltonii* was placed on Appendix I of the Convention on International Trade in Endangered Species of Wild Fauna and Flora (CITES), which requires permits from both the importing and exporting countries before shipment may occur. Only scientific trade benefitting the species' survival is allowed (U.S. Fish and Wildlife Service 1983).

The New Mexico Endangered Plant Law (Section 9-10-10 NMSA 1978 [Laws of NM 1985, Chapter 143]), effective November 1, 1985, recognizes *Pediocactus knowltonii* as endangered and prohibits its collection on public lands or its transportation within the State without a permit.

TRAFFIC (U.S.A.) investigated the U.S. cactus trade and demonstrated that the trade has undergone a positive change since the late 1970s. It appears that propagation has replaced wild collection as a means of obtaining most species of cacti (Fuller 1985). The increase in the number of individual Knowlton cacti in the wild suggests that collection of the species may have decreased.

Though the pressure from U.S cactus collectors may have lessened somewhat, a very active interest in this and other U.S. cacti still survives among European and Japanese collectors. A case in point is an article in a recent German cactus and succulent journal that described the habitat and gave exact directions to the type localities of *Pediocactus* and *Sclerocactus* (Gerhart and Menzel 1983). Commercial trade in these species is occurring in Europe and Japan. If collecting of reproducing adults from the type locality of *Pediocactus knowltonii* increases, then annual recruitment and establishment of seedlings may significantly decrease. This would result in a rapid and steadily diminishing population.

The Nature Conservancy in 1984 raised $5,000 from private sources to protect the population from further impacts, including illegal collectors. A fence was constructed in May 1984 to keep out domestic livestock and to deter collectors. It is illegal to collect Knowlton's cactus without permission of the landowner, and The Nature Conservancy is not permitting collection of the plant (Egbert 1985).

Although collecting is the foremost threat to the Knowlton cactus, oil and gas exploration and recreational development also pose potential problems. No gas wells are located directly on the type locality, although a gas well is situated at the edge of the hill where the plants occur. Because this site is in an area of proven oil and gas deposits, the potential exists for oil and gas exploration (U.S. Fish and Wildlife Service 1985). In an effort to protect this population of the Knowlton cactus, the Public Service Company of New Mexico donated 25 acres of land surrounding the center of the population to The Nature Conservancy in August 1983. The Nature Conservancy was given only the surface rights, not the mineral rights, to the land, but the group hopes to obtain cooperation from those holding mineral rights beneath the land sometime soon (Egbert 1985).

The Los Pinos River Valley, which includes Knowlton cactus habitat, is an excellent area for recreation and development of vacation land. Although there is no possibility of The Nature Conservancy land being sold to developers, development of the surrounding area and the subsequent influx of people may have a strong negative effect on the Knowlton cactus because of additional collection and off-road vehicle traffic (U.S. Fish and Wildlife Service 1985).

# Management

As part of the requirements of the Endangered Species Act, a recovery plan for the Knowlton cactus was developed and approved by FWS in March 1985.

Protection from further collection and disturbance, inventory and maintenance of viable populations in their natural habitat, and development of a comprehensive trade management plan are the main emphases of the recovery plan. Several measures necessary to ensure the survival of the Knowlton cactus and to aid in its recovery are: development of a cooperative agreement with The Nature Conservancy, reintroduction of the cactus into sites within its historic range, and monitoring the species and its habitat to obtain population data. Since only one known viable population of the Knowlton cactus exists, the need to implement these measures is urgent.

Because *Pediocactus knowltonii* essentially exists at this one locality, and the locality is on private land and very well known to cactus collectors, its survival is tenuous. Locating additional populations is a major concern. Habitat adjacent to the population has been searched innumerable times, but no new populations have been found. In addition, BLM in July 1985 ended a two-year intensive field survey of potential habitat along the Los Pinos, the La Plata, and the San Juan rivers south of Arboles, Colorado. Unfortunately, no additional sites were located. However, prime habitat was mapped, and this can be considered for future reintroduction (Bureau of Land Management 1985).

Reintroduction of the Knowlton cactus to sites within its historic range is especially important to recovery of the species. Several areas on federal and state lands were surveyed in March 1985 to identify an adequate reintroduction site. The area selected duplicates most of the environmental parameters that exist at the type locality, and access to the site is restricted.

Reintroduction began in May 1985, when 250 cuttings were taken from wild plants and hardened in a greenhouse over the summer. About half the individuals were planted at an undisclosed reintroduction site the following September. The remaining plants will be planted in the spring of 1986. The population will be monitored intensively to determine the fecundity and stability of the population. If the project is successful, the data will be used for future reintroductions of the Knowlton cactus. This project is a cooperative effort between FWS, BLM, Bureau of Reclamation, The Nature Conservancy, and the State of New Mexico.

Because the Endangered Species Act protects listed plants from collection only on federal lands, the single viable population of Knowlton cactus lacks any federal protection. Thus, a cooperative agreement between FWS and The Nature Conservancy is being developed. Negotiations are under way for FWS to acquire an easement on the The Nature Conservancy property so that Endangered Species Act protection would apply to the Knowlton cactus. This agreement is in the developmental stage, but all parties probably will concur.

Also of importance to the ultimate success of the recovery of the Knowlton cactus is the development of a cactus-trade management plan. Prior to its development, studies are necessary to determine what species are in the trade, the overall trend of trade in listed cacti, and the feasibility of reducing the collecting pressure on the wild populations by promoting a commercial, artificial propagation program. Development of strategies for effective implementation of law enforcement responsiblities under the Endangered Species Act, Convention on International Trade in Endangered Species of Wild Fauna and Flora, Lacey Act, and state native plant laws also is necessary. These measures will result in a comprehensive cactus trade management plan (U.S. Fish and Wildlife Service 1985). With collection as the major threat to Knowlton cactus, it is a high priority task for the recovery of this species.

Tissue culturing of the Knowlton cactus has been developed by the New Mexico State University Plant Genetic Engineering Laboratory. Preliminary results indicate a successful technique to produce a large number of Knowlton cactus (Clayton 1985). Having large quantities of propagated Knowlton cacti available will enable studies to be conducted on the species growth requirements and limiting factors. In addition to ecological studies, FWS can determine the feasibility of reducing the collecting pressure on the wild populations by placing these artificially propagated plants into the trade.

It is the intention of FWS to establish a monitoring study at the type locality to collect data on population size, dynamics, density, structure, and community composition. This study will be ongoing and will provide baseline data from which other recovery strategies can be determined.

Less urgent, but still essential to the success of the recovery process, is the development of a public education program. Such a program will not only expose the public to the status of the Knowlton cactus, but also will serve to focus attention on problems associated with endangered plants in general.

## Prognosis

At this point in the recovery of the Knowlton cactus it is difficult to give a definitive forecast. If the population continues to increase and collection continues to decrease along with the successful establishment of the reintroduced population, then the future for the Knowlton cactus is optimistic. Substantial efforts have been made by PNM, The Nature Conservancy, New Mexico, BLM and FWS to alleviate the threats and protect the habitat of the Knowlton cactus. With the implementation of the recovery plan and the continued active cooperation of federal and state agencies and private organizations, it is believed that the species will survive and recover.

## Recommendations

To ensure the species' survival, several actions need to be implemented. These actions, however, are dependent upon the result and success of studies presently under way. Fundamental to the species survival and recovery is the reintroduction of several populations into the species' historic range. Before undertaking any more reintroductions, FWS would like to determine the success of the trial efforts. Population biology and ecological studies will provide data from which future recovery and management strategies can be developed.

# References

Benson, L. 1960. *"Pediocactus knowltonii* L. Benson." *Cactus and Succulent Journal of America* 32:193.

———— 1961. "A revision and amplification of Pediocactus I." *Cactus and Succulent Journal of America* 33:49-54.

———— 1962a. "A revision and amplification of Pediocactus II." *Cactus and Succulent Journal of America* 34:17-19.

———— 1962b. "A revision and amplification of Pediocactus IV." *Cactus and Succulent Journal of America* 34:163-168.

———— 1982. *The Cacti of the United States and Canada.* Stanford University Press. Stanford, California.

Bureau of Land Management. 1985. Endangered and Threatened Plant Inventory: *Pediocactus knowltonii* Distribution and Habitat. Contract #NM010-CT4-0010. Farmington, New Mexico.

Egbert, J. 1985. New Mexico Nature Conservancy. Personal Communication with U.S. Fish and Wildlife Service.

Fuller, D. 1985. "U.S. cactus and succulent business moves toward propagation." *TRAFFIC* (U.S.A.)6:1-11.

Gerhart, F. and J. Menzel. 1983. "Zu den standorten winter kakteen in den sudwestlichen vereinigten stadten." *Kakteen und ander Succulenten.* pp. 140-190.

Heil, K., B. Armstrong and D. Schlesser. 1981. "A review of the genus Pediocactus." *Cactus and Succulent Journal of America* 53:17-39.

Letter from G.K. Arp, ARCO Oil and Gas Company, to U.S. Fish and Wildlife Service, March 26, 1979.

Letter from P.W. Clayton, New Mexico State University, to U.S. Fish and Wildlife Service, September 25, 1985.

Knight, P. 1985. New Mexico Natural Resources Dept. Personal Communication with U.S. Fish and Wildlife Service.

Murphey, B.F. 1961. "A new cactus for New Mexico." *Cactus and Succulent Journal of America* 33:28.

U.S. Fish and Wildlife Service. 1979. "Determination that *Pediocactus knowltonii* is an endangered species." *Federal Register* 44:62244-62246.

U.S. Fish and Wildlife Service. 1983. "Appendices to the Convention on International Trade in Endangered Species of Wild Fauna and Flora." *Federal Register* 48:45259-45263.

U.S. Fish and Wildlife Service. 1985. Knowlton Cactus Recovery Plan. Albuquerque, N.M.

*Peggy Olwell is the endangered species botanist for Arizona and New Mexico. She works for the Fish and Wildlife Service's Region 2 Office of Endangered Species in Albuquerque, New Mexico.*

Although still fairly abundant in Alaska and Canada, only about 1,200 wolves, primarily in Minnesota, still survive in the lower 48 states.

*Leonard Lee Rue III*

# Gray Wolf

## Rolf O. Peterson
Michigan Technological University

## Species Description and Natural History

ASIDE FROM THE human species, the wolf (*Canis lupus*) was the most widespread of all modern mammals, occurring throughout the Northern Hemisphere on the continents of North America and Eurasia (Nowak 1983). Since the entry of Europeans into North America, the wolf has been forced from its original continent-wide distribution to a remnant range limited to northern areas sparsely populated by humans.

In the United States, wolves are limited today mainly to Alaska and northeastern Minnesota, with perhaps 20 in northwestern Wisconsin (Thiel unpubl. data) and about two dozen in Michigan's Isle Royale National Park (Mech 1966, Peterson 1977, Allen 1979). Wolves persist throughout Canada except in New Brunswick, Nova Scotia, and Newfoundland in the east; the prairie portion of Manitoba and Saskatchewan; and cultivated and populated areas in Alberta and British Columbia. The total number of wolves in North America is unknown, but Minnesota is thought to contain about 1,200 (Anderson 1985), Alaska about 10,000 (Skoog 1983), and British Columbia, Alberta, and Manitoba a combined total of about 15,000 (Carbyn 1983). A total North American estimate of 30,000 to 40,000 wolves probably is conservative.

It is ironic that the wolf, ancestor of the beloved dog, has been the object of human persecution throughout recorded history. This has not changed even though the wolf is perhaps the most-studied and best-understood North American carnivore.

## Physical Characteristics

The dog-like appearance of the wolf is familiar to most people, although the range in size and color is suprisingly variable. Most wolves are gray, dark dorsally and lighter on the ventral side. A new coat of long guard hairs grows annually prior to the winter season, with additional warmth provided by dense underfur. The attractive color patterns along the back, side, and head of the typical gray wolf are formed by four alternating bands of light and dark on individual guard hairs, a characteristic distinguishing wild canids such as the wolf and coyote from domestic dogs that have similar coloration (Gier pers. comm.). Wolf color can range from completely white, common on Arctic islands, to completely black, a frequent color in western Canada and Alaska.

Wolves range in weight from about 60 pounds in eastern North America (Mech 1970) up to 130 pounds or more in Alaska (Ballard *et al* 1981). Wolves generally increase in size in northern and western portions of their present range, with the largest individuals occurring in northern Alberta (Nowak 1983). Adult males generally average about 10 pounds more than adult females.

## Taxonomy

The red wolf, (*C. rufus*) is intermediate in size between wolves and coyotes and originally occurred as the sole wolf-like form in the southeastern United States. When the few remaining red wolves were threatened with extinction by hybridization with coyotes (*C. latrans*) in the late 1970s, (Shaw 1977), the U.S. Fish and Wildlife Service (FWS) live-trapped and brought into captivity as many pure red wolves as possible. FWS in 1979 declared the red wolf extinct in the wild.

Goldman (1944) originally divided *Canis lupus* in North America into 24 subspecies based on skull characteristics. Almost half the subspecies probably are extinct (Nowak 1983). Modern students of wolf taxonomy generally agree that too many subspecies originally were described. Indeed, many of Goldman's distinctions have not held up under the scrutiny of a more sophisticated analysis of a much larger number of samples. In a preliminary study, Nowak (1983) identified five major groups, with a split between a northern and southern type occurring at about the U.S.-Canada border. A third variety, the eastern wolf of southern Ontario, probably was widespread through the eastern United States and may have had affinities with the red wolf (Novak 1983). The fourth and fifth groups comprised wolves in Mexico and on the high arctic islands. Nowak's five groups are logically linked with the distinct glacial refugia dating from the most recent North American glaciation.

Wolves in forested areas often are called "timber wolves." "Brush wolves," a name commonly attached to coyotes in the Midwest, are, of course, not wolves at all. In New England a canid intermediate in size between wolf and coyote may be a coyote with some wolf genes from hybridization (Schmitz and Kolenosky 1985).

## Ecology and Behavior

The wolf is a major predator of hoofed mammals, or ungulates, such as deer, moose, elk, caribou, mountain sheep, and musk-ox. Until the 1870s, bison provided an exceptionally abundant prey species on the North American prairies. In spite of a popular book suggesting otherwise (Mowat 1963), wolves cannot thrive on small rodents (Kuyt 1972). Remains of beavers and occasionally of snowshoe hares appear in wolf droppings at times and may be seasonally important, but the overall contribution to total prey biomass by these smaller prey usually is not prominent (Hall 1971, Peterson 1977, Ballard *et al* 1981).

Wolf populations are organized into packs—family groups that number from two to 20 animals. Reproducing packs inhabit territories that are defended from other wolves and that range in size from 40 to 1,000 square miles (Van Ballenberghe *et al* 1975, Peterson 1977, Fuller and Keith 1980, Ballard *et al* 1981, Fritts and Mech 1981, Mech and Hertel 1983, Peterson *et al* 1984b), depending on pack size and prey density.

Like other group-living mammals, wolves have highly developed and fascinating patterns of social behavior. Packs are organized around a dominance hierarchy that exists among both males and females, with leadership provided by an alpha male and an alpha female. These co-dominant wolves commonly lead packs while traveling and direct all important activities (Fox 1971, Haber 1977, Peterson 1977). Alpha wolves are responsible for virtually all scent-marking, which serves to demarcate the pack's territory (Peters and Mech 1975), and defend the pack from any perceived dangers.

The alpha male and female are thought to mate for life, although new mates are sought whenever an alpha dies. One female at Isle Royale remained in the alpha position for 11 years, during which time she had four different mates in succession (Peterson 1977 and unpubl. data). Alpha wolves are commonly the parents of other wolves in the pack and usually will produce the only pups. Wolves usually mate in February and bear young 63 days later (Mech 1970). Pups thus are born in early spring, usually in an underground den, abandoned beaver lodge, or hollow log.

Periodically during their first summer the pups are moved through a succession of summer homesites or "rendezvous areas" (Murie 1944), but otherwise lead a rather sedentary existence as wide-ranging adults bring back food for them. If pups are well-fed, they can reach adult size by September or October, when they must begin the winter pattern of continuous travel within the pack's territory. Yearlings and two-year-old wolves commonly explore areas outside this territory on their own, and some disperse permanently as young adults. Most wolves are sexually immature until they are at least 22 months old. Reproduction after that age depends to a large extent on social status, with alpha wolves responsible for most successful matings (Packard *et al* 1983).

Wolf population size depends on food abundance. Pack size seems to be a function of prey size, with larger prey supporting larger packs. Limited food is thought to increase aggression within a pack dependent on small prey, prompting subordinate wolves to disperse (Zimen 1976). Territory size is responsive to changes in food supply—abundant food brings about shrinkage in pack territories, while food shortage prompts trespassing as packs attempt to increase their territories (Peterson and Page 1983, Peterson 1977, Mech 1977a, b). Such trespassing can lead to direct conflicts and mortality, especially among alpha wolves.

# Significance of the Species

As a top carnivore, wolves have had a far-reaching influence. Wolf predation can be thought of as largely responsible for much of the behavior of hoofed big game in North America. Since wolf predation can have a powerful depressant effect on ungulate population growth rates and probably on ungulate density, wolf predation has prevented explosive growth rates in ungulate populations and subsequent damage to forage plants. Leopold (1949) considered wolves and other large predators to be "protectors" of the mountains, which are vulnerable to overuse by browsing mammals.

The role of wolf predation in regulating prey is still the subject of considerable scientific debate. While wolf predation is undeniably a dominant cause of mortality for prey species, the kill rates of a similar number of wolves can be highly variable. This realization has prompted some biologists to argue that the physical condition of prey animals, and indirectly prey food supply, influences the magnitude of wolf predation (Peterson 1977). In two major studies of wolf-moose interaction, more than a third of the adult moose killed by wolves showed evidence of skeletal pathology in the form of tooth infections, fat-depleted bone marrow, and arthritis (Peterson *et al* 1984b, Peterson 1977). Others (e.g. Bergerud *et al* 1983) argue that prey condition is not a relevant issue, especially for ungulate prey less than a year old, when mortality is highest.

Most studies have indicated that wolf predation selectively removes certain sex and age groups from prey populations. Pimlott (1967) pointed out long ago that the significance of predation in regulating prey will increase in direct proportion to the extent that prereproductive young are taken. Wolf predation commonly is focused on such young prey. More data of this type are available for moose than any other prey (Peterson *et al* 1984b), and these data show a distinct pattern of selection for moose less than a year old and those older than seven years.

It is clear that wolf predation can greatly reduce prey populations at times. Mech and Karns (1977) reported that wolf predation was instrumental in eliminating deer from hundreds of square miles in northeastern Minnesota. Peterson and Page (1983) concluded that wolf-caused mortality maintained the Isle Royale moose population at a low plateau for several years in the late 1970s. Bergerud (1980) has argued that wolf predation typically maintains wild caribou populations at a low equilibrium. Gasaway et al (1983) demonstrated with a wolf-removal experiment that wolf predation was the major cause of low moose calf survival in interior Alaska. Finally, Peterson et al (1984) suggested that the influence of wolf predation on Isle Royale moose varied over a 30-year period, producing fluctuations that might occur regularly.

One senses in the recent literature a lack of consensus that probably stems from the complexity typical of wolf-prey relationships, still an active area of research that has immediate applicability to wildlife management issues. Studies of wolves and wild prey indicate that wolves and humans are likely to compete directly, since the addition of human hunting to natural predation might be sufficient to lead a decline in prey.

Competition between humans and wolves for wild prey is a rather recent concern, but wolf predation on domestic stock has occurred for thousands of years. This, together with fear of the wolf, largely explain man's antipathy for wolves. During the Middle Ages, wolves became the embodiment of evil, as shown in Biblical analogies of the predator and the lamb.

Without a doubt, wolves readily kill domesticated animals. Also doubtless is the damage that wolves can cause individual livestock owners. Yet wolf depredation is insignificant for the livestock industry as a whole, even in Minnesota where Fritts (1982) found that the highest cattle loss claimed for any single year by farmers from 1977 through 1980 were .45 per 1,000 in 1979. The highest sheep losses for the same period were 1.18 per 1,000 in 1980. Even these losses can be greatly reduced by more intensive animal husbandry. Most states and provinces with a depredation problem have a compensation program for affected individuals in addition to various types of wolf removal strategies (Carbyn 1983).

Fear of the wolf remains a significant influence, hampering effective wolf conservation throughout the world (Hook and Robinson 1982, Shahi 1983, Bjarvall 1983, Voskar 1983). It is likely that wolves did eat and kill humans during the long-lasting and widespread wars in Europe after the Middle Ages (Zimen 1981), adding some substance to the werewolf legends that had been handed down from earlier centuries. And although there are no records in North America of a healthy wild wolf attacking a human (Mech 1970), European settlers brought their traditional fears with them to North America. Such beliefs appear to be partially responsible for the negative attitudes toward wolves among some residents of Michigan, where a small group of introduced wolves were all killed by humans within a few months (Wiese et al 1975).

For millions of urban residents in North America, however, wolves are a symbol of wilderness and an important part of our wildlife heritage. As more people become aware of ecological principles, especially the important role predation plays in natural selection, wolves gain popular respect. The majority of citizens in states with wolves, such as Michigan, Minnesota, and Alaska, have a positive attitude toward the wolf (Hook and Robinson 1982, Kellert 1985 and pers. comm.).

From an ecological perspective, wolves in North America are associated with reasonably intact ecosystems where natural forces predominate. As such, wolves can be thought of as indicative of a healthy ecosystem. This is largely an artifact, not a characteristic of the species, arising from the fact that in North America wolf elimination has been so effective that wolves have been relegated to wilderness and other sparsely populated areas. In other parts of the world, notably where wolves themselves are smaller, the species has survived in ecosystems where all wild prey have been eliminated and domestic animals and garbage constitute the major wolf "prey" (Boitani 1982, Mendelssohn 1982).

## Historical Perspective

The wolf in North America, indeed throughout the world, has been relentlessly persecuted by humans. Bounties were paid for dead wolves in the American colonies some 300 years ago (Mech 1970). Methods used to kill wolves remained rather primitive—guns and traps, primarily—until late in the 19th century. Efforts were persistent enough, however, to eliminate wolves from eastern North America by 1900, with the exception of portions of the Great Lakes and northern Appalachians (Nowak 1983).

The introduction of strychnine about 100 years ago made it possible to exterminate wolves. By 1900, poison became the control agent of choice for private individuals and the government alike. In 1915, the federal government began a wolf control program in the western United States, and the program was carried out with such zeal that wolves were virtually extinct throughout the West by 1930. Through the use of poison, wolves were eliminated even from vast areas of Alaska, such as the Kenai Peninsula (Peterson and Woolington 1982). Wolves likewise disappeared from much of southwest Canada, and the species reached a low ebb just prior to the Great Depression (Nowak 1983). Economic hard times and World War II dominated the next two decades, and wolf populations were able to recover. In the early 1950s aerial gunning made its appearance and, combined with the use of poison, threatened wolves in their remnant range (Stenlund 1955, Harbo and Dean 1983). By the late 1950s, wolves continued to exist in the United States only in Alaska and northern Minnesota and on Isle Royale in Lake Superior. Even in these areas, wolves were unprotected and considered vermin, except in national parks.

# Current Trends

The status of wolves in both Alaska and Minnesota improved in the late 1960s as poison was banned, aerial gunning declined, and bounties were eliminated. The wolf was designated as a big game animal and furbearer in Alaska, and federal endangered species legislation in 1966, 1969, and 1973 led eventually to complete legal protection for the wolf in Minnesota (Anderson 1985), where it is listed as threatened under the federal endangered species act. All other lower-48 wolves are listed as endangered, including the Mexican wolf. By the early 1970s, the status of wolves in most Canadian provinces was upgraded to that of game animal or furbearer, and normal control programs became rare.

Protection allowed wolves to recolonize areas in Alaska such as the Seward and Kenai peninsulas (Harbo and Dean 1983), and an increased distribution in Minnesota led to re-establishment in northwestern Wisconsin (Mech and Nowak 1981) during the 1970s. A litter of wolf pups has been produced on the Montana-British Columbia border yearly since 1982, resulting in 15 to 20 resident wolves near Glacier National Park (Ream pers. comm.).

Wolf distribution now is probably greater than at any time in the past 50 years, although significant declines have occurred. Wolves disappeared from Michigan's Upper Peninsula in the 1960s (Robinson 1973), and the red wolf became extinct in the wild during the late 1970s (Carbyn in press). Wolves in Mexico have declined to just a few individuals in the face of burgeoning human population growth. Wolf declines have been linked invariably to excessive human-caused mortality. The distribution of the species in North America is not expected to change greatly through the end of the 20th century, although a retreat to the north in some Canadian provinces and possibly Minnesota is likely as human use of the landscape increases.

Most North American wolves are managed as game or furbearing animals. A few hundred in Canada receive total legal protection while inside national parks (Carbyn, in press). Reported annual kill in Canada currently is about 4,000 wolves, with about 15 percent of that total taken for predator control purposes (Carbyn 1983).

The estimated 1,200 wolves in Minnesota are legally protected, but the illegal kill may amount to 200 yearly (Mech pers. comm.). Even though completely protected, Minnesota wolves older than six months die almost as often from human-related causes as from natural deaths (Mech pers. comm.). Wolves exist in only two U.S. national parks outside of Alaska—Voyageurs and Isle Royale.

# Management

In the United States, FWS has directed efforts to draw up and finalize a recovery plan for the eastern timber wolf, the Rocky Mountain wolf, the Mexican wolf, and the red wolf. This provides the foundation for future management of the most seriously jeopardized wolves in North America, those listed as endangered or threatened.

Without a doubt the most controversial aspect of wolf management in Alaska and Canada today is wolf reduction in order to increase big game numbers for sport and subsistence use by humans. Research during the 1970s indicated that wolves often are responsible for low recruitment rates among ungulate prey and that even where big game has declined for other reasons, wolves can nevertheless maintain prey at low densities for many years (Gasaway *et al* 1983). The realization that big game restoration could be facilitated by wolf reduction recently has led to expensive and large-scale control programs carried out by or with the assistance of state or provincial wildlife biologists in Alaska and Canada. Wildlife managers in northern areas often view wolf control as the only feasible management alternative.

In the past decade the state of Alaska, in an effort to increase moose populations, has spent about $1 million to kill wolves, with per capita cost exceeding $1,000 per wolf removed (Anchorage *Daily News* 1985). Dramatic increases in the survival of young moose and other species have been recorded in some cases (Gasaway *et al* 1983). However, wolf control for the benefit of game species has met heated opposition from conservationists and many professional biologists. In 1984, the Alaska Department of Fish and Game dropped its plans for an aerial wolf hunt in the brunt of public opposition. Opponents said the hunt raised biological as well as ethical questions because some research suggests wolves are not the only cause of low moose populations (*Defenders of Wildlife* 1985a). Citing severe winters and human hunting, opponents said the wolves should not be controlled until human hunting is further limited (*Defenders of Wildlife* 1984a and 1985b).

Controversy over wolves in Minnesota is equally intense but of a different character. FWS has been responsible for wolf management in Minnesota for the past decade, with federal control agents taking a few dozen wolves each year where depredation on domestic animals has occurred. The Minnesota Department of Natural Resources has consistently maintained that a limited sport hunting and trapping season should be initiated, reasoning that this should lead to reduced depredation problems, reduced illegal kill, and reduced animosity among local citizens. The state's proposal finally found a sympathetic ear in the Interior Department in the early 1980s, but an Interior move to return management authority to Minnesota was blocked in 1984 and 1985 in a U.S. District Court and by the Eighth U.S. Circuit Court of Appeals after a coalition of environmental groups filed suit (Anderson 1985). The position of the courts was that management of the eastern timber wolf in Minnesota, where the animal is federally listed as threatened, could not be turned over to the state.

Minnesota's wolf management proposal, which included a sport trapping season, was consistent with the recovery plan for the eastern timber wolf, approved in 1978. The recovery plan provided for complete sanctuaries (Zones 1-3), centered in the Boundary Waters Canoe Area wilderness of northeastern Minnesota and in a region near Voyageurs National Park along the Canadian border to the west. Surrounding these sanctuaries was Zone 4, where controlled hunting and trapping could occur within well-defined limits. Zone 5 was the agricultural and heavily settled remainder of the state, where wolves would not be protected. Court decisions, however, have prohibited the recreational taking of wolves as proposed by Minnesota. The courts have ruled that the Endangered Species Act does not permit the taking of listed species except in cases of extreme population pressure.

Wolves border on areas with domestic livestock in Minnesota and in several Canadian provinces, with the inevitable consequence that domestic animals are taken as prey. Depredating wolves in Minnesota can be killed by federal trappers. Minnesota and most Canadian provinces have a compensation program for validated livestock losses to wolves. In Alaska, carnivores can be killed legally at any time of the year in order to protect private property, but no significant depredation occurs on the comparatively scarce stocks of domestic animals.

For the eastern timber wolf, the major chance for enlargement of its current range is in northern Wisconsin and Upper Michigan. Excessive human-caused mortality, has kept the small Wisconsin population from expanding. About 2,700 miles of suitable wolf range (i.e. with a road density of less than one lineal mile per square mile of habitat) exists in northern Wisconsin, primarily on national forests, and likely even more habitat remains in Upper Michigan. Legal protection, however, has not been sufficient to repopulate these areas.

The wolf is, of course, a high-profile species that attracts considerable public interest. Several private orgainzations in the United States devote all their efforts to wolf-related issues, and private rearing facilities are critical for the continued maintenance of a remnant breeding stock for red and Mexican wolves. Because of broad public interest, virtually all nationally important conservation organizations have dealt with wolf management controversies to some extent.

## Prognosis

The future of wolves in North America is almost entirely in human hands. Adequate prey populations are present throughout the remaining range of the wolf on this continent. It is likely that over the majority of its range in North America, human-caused mortality dominates wolf population dynamics. With only a few exceptions, it is unlikely that wolf distribution will increase significantly, so questions about the future of wolves can be reduced to 1) how much will wolf range and population levels decline, and 2) how fast will this occur.

There is little doubt that the Mexican wolf will soon be extinct in the wild (Carley per. comm., in Carbyn, in press). Captive breeding stock is so limited for this subspecies that the full range of its genetic heritage already has been diminished.

Elsewhere in North America the future of wolves is more favorable. While wolf control programs have grown quickly in scope over the past decade, none of these are intended to permanently reduce the distribution of the species. However, some northward retreat of wolves probably will occur in the western Canadian provinces and perhaps in Minnesota as human pressures grow. In the Great Lakes states, wolf survival depends on the presence of adequate refugia from humans, usually areas with less than a mile of road per square mile of habitat (Thiel 1985). Even if wolf distribution can be maintained, it is doubtful that wolf density will occur at naturally determined levels. Legal and illegal kill by humans is high enough to reduce wolf density over much of its current range in North America.

Concern about the rapid growth of wolf reductions as a "routine" wildlife management technique is justified (Carbyn in press). Because of continuing uncertainty over the role of wolf predation and other factors in regulating prey density, the outcome of wolf removal programs is highly unpredictable. It is obvious that wolf control can rapidly become institutionalized, and increasing demand for hunting opportunities for humans will produce continued pressure to enlarge the scope of wolf reduction programs. The Wolf Specialist Group/Species Survival Commission of the International Union for Conservation of Nature and Natural Resources acknowledges that wolf control may at times be required in order to speed recovery of prey populations, but recommends that such control be initiated only when hunting by humans also is eliminated.

Carbyn (in press) pointed out that the wildlife managers busily laying plans to reduce wolf populations usually are doing nothing whatsoever to ensure that adequately large areas also are set aside for wolf protection. He stated that it is likely that "there is not a wolf pack anywhere in the wilds of western or northern Canada that can find complete sanctuary from man's direct persecution in any of our wilderness reserves." Wolves already are absent from almost all U.S. national parks, and it is unlikely that many wolf packs on the entire continent are not significantly affected by human-caused mortality. Most national parks and equivalent preserves are too small to provide protection for wide-ranging wolves, since individual packs may travel across hundreds of square miles. As *de facto* wilderness disappears in the North, formal preserves will assume a more important role in providing adequate reservoirs of genetic material for all species, including wolves.

A substantial portion of North American wolves live in the northern fringes of the continent, where native peoples have considerable influence over land and wildlife management decisions. Treaty Indians in Canada have unrestricted hunting privileges and often kill large numbers of game animals in many areas. The future way of life for both wild wolves and Inuit peoples in northern Canada is linked directly to the maintenance of large herds of caribou, herds vulnerable to excessive human hunting (Heard 1983). Innovative management programs that ensure survival of large caribou herds will be required.

The most important long-term threat to wolves in Alaska, and therefore in the United States, is permanent occupation of the land by increasing numbers of people plus associated agricultural and domestic animals. Substitution of domestic animals for wild ungulates threatens Alaskan wolves that currently inhabit the fringes of settled land. Alaska is attempting to develop a local cattle industry that will provide more self-sufficiency for the fastest growing human population of any state. This will displace the wild prey of the wolf and encourage depredation on domestic stock.

# Recommendations

A combination of strategies will be required to maintain wild wolves in North America, as exemplified by the zone designations of the Eastern Timber Wolf Recovery Plan (Bailey *et al* 1978). Areas must be set aside where wolves are not allowed, where they are subject to control, and where they are guarded from all possible human intervention. The concerned human constituency is diverse and clashes are inevitable between national and local interests and between hunters and nonhunters. The five general recommendations that follow will prove vital to the survival of wolves in North America. Accompanying these recommendations are several specific plans that can be acted upon immediately.

## Reintroduction

Restoration of wolves to parts of their former range is possible in only a few parts of the United States, as outlined below. These restorations will be high-profile projects generating considerable public interest, and none will be accomplished without controversy. It is critical that there be an extensive opportunity for public involvement, especially at the local level.

The wolf in Mexico is all but extinct and, under the terms of a cooperative agreement between FWS and Mexico's Fauna Silvestre, Mexico has first choice of captive wolves in the event of a release of wolves in the wild (Malloy pers. comm.). As a first step toward restoration in the United States, FWS could, in cooperation with Mexico, identify possible release sites in southern Arizona, New Mexico, and southwestern Texas. Restoration in Mexico probably is not currently feasible.

The red wolf should be introduced to suitable portions of the southeastern coastal plain, in accordance with the FWS Red Wolf Recovery plan. This should be done without unnecessary delay so that wolves that were wild-caught or are first generation captives can be used. Of the original 44 wolves captured in the wild, only four remain (Malloy pers. comm.).

Wolves should be released in Yellowstone National Park, the center of a prime wilderness ecosystem, where they can be maintained in their natural state and assist in regulation of elk populations.

## Research

The major need in future research is to understand the role of wolf predation in regulating ungulate prey. In addition to surveys and applied research projects in local areas where wolves are managed, hunted, and trapped, continuation of long-term research on wolves and their prey under natural conditions is vitally needed, including the continuation of 28 years of research in Isle Royale National Park and 20 years in northern Minnesota. Wolves and their prey are long lived (Peterson *et al* 1984), so unraveling predator-prey dynamics requires a long-term research commitment.

Only one wolf study in Canada has exceeded a decade and that is a project in Riding Mountain National Park that was initiated in the early 1970s by the Canadian Wildlife Service in cooperation with Parks Canada. The Canadian Wildlife Service has, until recently, been at the forefront of wolf research in Canada. The service's research capabilities need to be maintained and enhanced as soon as possible.

## Reserves

A strategy for long-term wolf survival in North America must include establishment of major areas of protection so that the natural genetic diversity of wolves and other forms of life can be perpetuated under a regime of natural selection and so that there will be adequate natural areas to serve for comparison with areas where wolves are managed or reduced. It is already difficult to locate undisturbed wolf populations that provide comparable baseline data for the various predator-prey systems.

More large preserves in North America, on the scale of those established in Alaska in 1980, are needed. Designated areas must be large enough for natural ecological processes to function, including predation by such large carnivores as the wolf. It is already too late for this in the lower-48 states, and the newly established parks and refuges in Alaska are inadequately protected from poaching. National parks and refuges in Alaska need more protection, both from illegal hunting of wildlife and from development that threatens or restricts wildlife.

Pristine wilderness is not required for the continued existence of wolves. Any land-management program in Alaska that provides priority consideration for wildlife and effective protection will help ensure long-term wolf conservation. Alaska recently designated portions of the Talkeetna Mountains and Kenai Peninsula as critical habitats for caribou and moose. Such initiatives, prohibiting settlement and intensive agriculture, should be encouraged.

Canada needs a reawakening of interest in the establishment of an adequate system of natural reserves. Only two International Biosphere Reserves exist in Canada, and neither supports wolves. Canada lacks a system of national wildlife refuges, but the national park system should be expanded to encompass large wilderness reserves in representative habitats, areas that will be maintained as wilderness. Resolutions of native land claims and hunting rights must precede any expansion of the parks system.

"Reserves" of a different sort—areas with a road density of less than one mile of road per square mile of habitat—will be required in the Great Lakes states in order to maintain wolf habitat in Minnesota and to allow for reestablishment of wolves in Wisconsin and Upper Michigan. Much of the appropriate land in Wisconsin and Michigan lies within national forests. Forest management plans for the next 50 years, now being drawn up by the U.S. Forest Service, should provide for wolf recovery by ensuring that there is one large area (more than 1,000 square miles) or several smaller areas (each at least 200 square miles) with low road density. Similar measures should be encouraged in suitable forests in Idaho and Montana.

## Management

Existing populations of wolves will have to be managed with more sensitivity to the diverse citizen constituency interested in this species. Wolf control programs have, in the past, often been based on poor data, undermining public confidence in wildlife management. Control methods viewed by managers as "efficient," such as aerial gunning and poison, usually are regarded as highly unacceptable by a substantial portion of the public. The demand for wolf reduction will increase in direct proportion to hunting effort, which can only increase as more people settle in the fringe areas of Alaska and Canada. Management of big game populations should be accomplished as often as possible with the aim of conserving natural predators.

Where wolves are trapped, management agencies must take the lead in prohibiting inhumane trapping practices (in some jurisdictions wolf traps are often checked only on weekends and abandoned snares continue to snare wolves and other wildlife). Where wolves are hunted for sport, the same rules of fair chase used for other game should apply. "Land-and-shoot trapping" in Alaska, particularly, is officially regarded as an appropriate means of taking furbearers. A type of hunting that requires only a trapping permit, it involves locating wolves from aircraft and then landing to shoot them. It often leads to wolf reductions comparable to formal control programs and is prohibited for virtually all other game animals. In areas where land-and-shoot trapping is permitted, traditional hunting by individuals without aircraft often is precluded.

Although hunting pressure surely will increase on species currently preyed upon by wolves, the proportion of hunters and trappers in North America probably will decline. As this occurs, it is possible that the strong advances made in wildlife management with the support and funding of sportsmen may stagnate. Nonconsumptive users must begin to show equal motivation and marshall more resources to maintain and enhance wildlife (Carbyn in press).

## Education

Increased urbanization in North America will produce a populace that is divorced from the land, from hunting, from trapping, and often from any direct contact with wolves and other wildlife. Basic facts of wolf ecology need to be communicated to the urban masses, who often have an unrealistic attitude toward this species.

Likewise, rural citizens in frequent contact with wolves seldom have other than a strictly utilitarian attitude toward all wildlife, often resenting any competition from carnivores. The rich history of human-wolf interaction needs to be more widely understood so that present-day efforts to maintain the species can be viewed in proper perspective.

Without doubt the finest single effort to provide the public with a balanced understanding of the wolf is the "Wolves and Humans" museum exhibit produced by the Science Museum of Minnesota in 1983 and now traveling to other museums. This exhibit needs to be continually exposed to the public in an area where wolf conservation is important, such as northern Minnesota. A wolf interpretive center should be established to house the exhibit and provide continuing opportunity for increased public understanding.

Writing of the challenge to maintain species diversity, E. O. Wilson (1984) declared, "When very little is known about an important subject, the questions people raise are almost invariably ethical. Then as knowledge grows, they become more concerned with information and amoral, in other words more narrowly intellectual. Finally, as understanding becomes sufficiently complete, the questions turn ethical again." Wolf conservation appears to be at this moral/intellectual crossroads. The future of wolves in North America will depend on the extent to which humans are willing to compromise and coexist for the benefit of another species.

## References

Allen, D.L. 1979. *Wolves of Minong.* Houghton-Mifflin, Boston. 499 pp.

Anderson, C. 1985. "Can people and timber wolves co-exist?" *Minnesota Volunteer* 48(280):26-31.

Bailey, R. 1978. ed. *Recovery Plan for the Eastern Timber Wolf.* U.S. Fish and Wildlife Service, Washington, D.C. 79 pp.

Ballard, W.R., R.O. Stephenson, and T.H. Spraker. 1981. *Nelchina Basin Wolf Studies.* Alaska Department of Fish and Game, Federal aid in Wilderness Restoration Final Report, Project W-17-8 through W-17-11. 201 pp. (mimeograph).

Bergerud, A.T. 1980. "Review of the population dynamics of caribou in North America." *International Caribou-Reindeer Symposium* 2:556-581.

Bergerud, A.T., W. Wyett and B. Snider. 1983. "The role of wolf predation in limiting a moose population." *Journal of Wildlife Management* 47:977-988.

Bjarvall, A. 1983. "Scandinavia's response to a natural repopulation of wolves." *Acta Zoologica Fennica* 174:273-275.

Boitani, L. 1982. "Wolf Management in intensively used areas of Italy," *in* F.H. Harrington and P.C. Paquet eds. *Wolves of the World.* Noyes Publications, Park Ridge, New Jersey. pp. 158-172.

Carbyn, L.N. ed. 1983. *Wolves in Canada and Alaska: Their Status, Biology, and Managment.* Canadian Wildlife Service Report Serial No. 45:1-135.

Carbyn, L.N. "Wolves," *in* M. Novale ed., *Wild Furbearer Management and Conservation in North America.* In press.

*Defenders.* 1984a. "Alaska's aerial wolf war." Defenders of Wildlife, Washington D.C. March/April:35-36.

*Defenders.* 1984b. "Alaska's board of game schedules another winter aerial wolf hunt." Defenders of Wildlife, Washington D.C. November/December 1984:40.

*Defenders.* 1985. "Board expands Alaska wolf hunt." Defenders of Wildlife, Washington D.C. January/February 1985:40-41, 46.

Fox, M.W. 1971. *Behavior of Wolves, Dogs and Related Canids.* Harper and Row, New York.

Fuller, T.K. and L.B. Keith. 1980. "Wolf population dynamics and prey relationships in northeastern Alberta." *Journal of Wildlife Managment* 44:583-602.

Fritts, S.H. 1982. *Wolf Depredation on Livestock in Minnesota.* U.S. Department of the Interior Fish and Wildlife Service Research Publication 145, Washington D.C.

Fritts, S.H. and L.D. Mech. 1981. "Dynamics, movements, and feeding ecology of a newly protected wolf population in northwestern Minnesota." *Wildlife Monograph* 80:1-79.

Gasaway, W.C., R.O. Stephenson, J.C. Davis, P.E.K. Shepard, and O.E. Burris, 1983. "Interrelationships of wolves, prey, and man in interior Alaska." *Wildlife Monograph* 84:1-50.

Goldman, E.A. 1944. *The Wolves of North America. Pt. II.* American Wildlife Institute, Washington, D.C. pp. 398-636.

Haber, G.C. 1977. Socio-ecological dynamics of wolves and prey in a subarctic ecosystem. Ph.D Thesis, University of British Columbia, Vancouver. 785 pp.

Hall, A.M. 1971. Ecology of beaver and selection of prey by wolves in central Ontario. Master of Science Thesis, University of Toronto. 116 pp.

Harbo, S.J. and F.C. Dean. 1978. "Historical and current perspectives on wolf management in Alaska." pp. 51-64 *in* Carbyn (1983).

Heard, D.C. 1983. "Historical and present status of wolves in the Northeast Territories." pp. 44-47 *in* Carbyn (1983).

Hook, R.A. and W.L. Robinson. 1982. "Attitudes of Michigan citizens toward predators," *in* F.H. Harrington and P.C. Paquet eds., *Wolves of the World.* Noyes Publications, Park Ridge, New Jersey. pp. 382-394.

Kellert, S. 1985. *The Public and the Timber Wolf in Minnesota.* Yale School of Forestry and Environmental Studies.

Kuyt, E. 1972. "Food habits and ecology of wolves on barren-ground caribou range in the Northwest Territories." *Canadian Wildlife Service Report* No. 21, Ottawa. 36 pp.

Leopold, A. 1949. *A Sand County Almanac.* Oxford University Press, Oxford.

Mech, L.D. 1966. *The Wolves of Isle Royale.* U.S. Park Service Fauna Serial No. 7., Washington, D.C. 210 pp.

Mech, L.D. 1970. *The Wolf.* Natural History Press, New York. 384 pp.

Mech, L.D. 1977a. "Productivity, mortality, and population trends of wolves in northeastern Minnesota." *Journal of Mammalology* 58:559-574.

Mech, L.D. 1977b. "Population trend and winter deer consumption in a Minnesota wolf pack," *in* R. Phillips and C. Jonkel eds., *Proceedings of the 1975 Predator Symposium.* Montana Forest Conservation Experiment Station. Missoula, Montana. 268 pp.

Mech, L.D. and P.D. Karns. 1977. "Role of the wolf in a deer decline in the Superior Natural Forest." *U.S. Department of Agriculture Forest Service Research Paper* NC-148. North Center Forestry Experiment Station. St. Paul, Minnesota. 23 pp.

Mech, L.D. and H.H. Hertel. 1983. "An eight-year demography of a Minnesota wolf pack." *Acta Zoological Fennica* 174:249-250.

Mech, L.D. and R.M. Nowak. 1981. "Return of the grey wolf to Wisconsin." *American Midlands Naturalist* 105:408-409.

Mendelssohn, H. 1982. "Wolves in Israel," *in* F.H. Harrington and P.C. Paquet eds., *Wolves of the World.* Noyes Publications, Park Ridge, New Jersey. pp. 173-195.

Mowat, F. 1963. *Never Cry Wolf.* Little, Brown Co., Boston, Massachusetts. 247 pp.

Murie, A. 1944. *The Wolves of Mount McKinley.* U.S. National Park Service Fauna Serial No. 5, Washington, D.C. 238 pp.

Nowak, R.M. 1983. "A perspective on the taxonomy of wolves in North America." *in* Carbyn (1983). pp. 10-19.

Packard, J.M., L.D. Mech and U.S. Seal. 1983. "Social influences on reproduction in wolves," *in* Carbyn (1983). pp. 78-85.

Peters, R.P. and L.D. Mech. 1975. "Scent-marking in wolves." *American Scientist* 63:628-637.

Peterson, R.O. 1977. "Wolf ecology and prey relationships on Isle Royale." *U.S. National Park Service Science Monograph Serial* 11. 210 pp.

Peterson, R.O. and J.D. Woolington. 1982. "The apparent extirpation and reappearance of wolves on the Kenai Peninsula, Alaska," *in* F.H. Harrington and P.C. Paquet eds., *Wolves of the World.* Noyes Publications, Park Ridge, New Jersey. pp. 334-344.

Peterson, R.O. and R.E. Page 1983. "Wolf and moose population fluctuations in Isle Royale National Park, U.S.A." *Acta Zoological Fennica* 174:265-266.

Peterson, R.O., R.E. Page and K.M. Dodge. 1984a. "Wolves, moose and the allometry of population cycles." *Science* 224:1350-1352.

Peterson, R.O., J.D. Woolington, and T.N. Bailey. 1984b. "Wolves of the Kenai Peninsula, Alaska." *Wildlife Monograph* 88:1-52.

Pimlott, D.H. 1967. "Wolf predation and ungulate populations." *American Zoologist* 7:267-233.

Robinson, W.L. 1973. "Status of the wolf in Michigan." *American Midlands Naturalist* 94:226-233.

Schmitz, O.J. and G.B. Kolenosky. 1985. "Hybridization between wolf and coyote in captivity." *Journal of Mammalogy* 66:402-405.

Shahi, S.P. 1983. "Status of grey wolf *(Canis lupus pallipes,* Sykes) in India." *Acta Zoologica Fennica* 174:282-286.

Shaw, J.H. 1977. "The wolf that lost its genes." *Natural History* 86:80-88.

Skoog, R.O. 1983. "Results of Alaska's attempts to increase prey by controlling wolves." *Acta Zoological Fennica* 174:245-247.

Stenlund, M.H. 1955. "A field study of the timber wolf *(Canis lupus)* on the Superior National Forest, Minnesota." *Minnesota Department of Conservation Bulletin* 4:1-55.

Thiel, R.P. 1985. "Relationship between road densities and wolf habitat suitability in Wisconsin." *American Midlands Naturalist* 113:404-407.

Van Ballenberghe, V., A.W. Erickson, and D. Byman. 1975. "Ecology of the timber wolf in northeastern Minnesota." *Wildlife Monograph* 43:1-43.

Voskar, J. 1983. "Present problems of wolf preservation in Czechoslavakia." *Acta Zoologica Fennica* 174:287-288.

Weise, T.F., W.L. Robinson, and L.D. Mech. 1975. "An experimental translocation of the eastern timber wolf." *Audubon Conservation Report* No. 5.

Wilson, E.O. 1984. *Biophilia.* Harvard University Press, Cambridge, Massachusetts. 157 pp.

Zimen, E. 1976. "On the regulation of pack size in wolves." *Z. Tierpsychologie* 40:300-341.

Zimen, E. 1981. *The Wolf: A Species in Danger.* Delacourt Press, New York.

*Rolf O. Peterson, an associate biology professor at Michigan Technical University, started his wolf studies in 1970 with research on wolf/moose population dynamics at Isle Royale National Park. He also studied wolf/moose interactions in the Kenai for three years.*

# PART 5

# Appendices

# Appendix A

# Forest Service Directory

## WASHINGTON HEADQUARTERS

Mailing Address:
Forest Service-USDA
P.O. Box 2417
Washington, D.C. 20013

General Information:
  (202) 655-4000
Public Inquiries
  (202) 447-3957

| Title | Name | Phone |
|---|---|---|
| Chief | R. Max Peterson | 202 447-6661 |
| Associate Chief | F. Dale Robertson | 202 447-7491 |

### National Forest System

| | | |
|---|---|---|
| Depute Chief | J. Lamar Beasley | 202 447-3523 |
| Director, Aviation and Fire Management | John A. Hafterson | 202 235-8666 |
| Director, Engineering | Vacant | 202 235-8035 |
| Director, Lands | Richard D. Hall | 202 235-8212 |
| Director, Land Management Planning | Everett L. Towle | 202 447-6697 |
| Director, Minerals and Geology Mgmt. | Howard E. Banta | 202 235-8105 |
| Director, Range Management | Robert M. Williamson | 202 235-8139 |
| Director, Recreation Management | Roy W. Feuchler | 202 447-3706 |
| Director, Timber Management | George M. Leonard | 202 447-6893 |
| Director, Watershed and Air Management | David G. Unger | 202 235-8096 |
| Director, Wildlife and Fisheries | Robert D. Nelson | 202 235-8015 |

971

## State and Private Forestry

| | | |
|---|---|---|
| Deputy Chief | John H. Ohman | 202 447-6657 |
| Director, Cooperative Fire Protection | Lawrence A. Amicarella | 202 235-8039 |
| Director, Cooperative Forestry | Tony Dorrell | 202 235-2212 |
| Director, Forest Pest Management | James L. Stewart | 202 235-1560 |

## Research

| | | |
|---|---|---|
| Deputy Chief | Robert E. Buckman | 202 447-6665 |
| Director, Forest Environmental Research | Ronald D. Lindmark | 202 235-1071 |
| Director, Forest Fire and Atmospheric Sciences Research | Charles W. Philpot | 202 235-8195 |
| Director, Forest Insect and Disease Research | Gerald W. Anderson | 202 235-8065 |
| Director, Forest Products and Harvesting Research | Stanley O. Bean, Jr. | 202 235-1203 |
| Director, Forest Resources Economics Research | H. Fred Kuiser, Jr. | 202 447-2747 |
| Director, International Forestry | David A. Harcharik | 202 235-2743 |
| Director, Timber Management Research | Stanley L. Krugman | 202 235-8200 |

## Programs and Legislation

| | | |
|---|---|---|
| Deputy Chief | Jeff M. Sirmon | 202 447-6663 |
| Director, Environmental Coordination | David E. Ketcham | 202 447-4708 |
| Director, Legislative Affairs | Mark A. Reimers | 202 447-4708 |
| Director, Policy Analysis | Christopher Risbrudt | 202 447-2775 |
| Director, Program Development and Budget | John A. Leasure | 202 447-6987 |
| Director, Resources Program and Assessment | Thomas E. Hamilton | 202 382-8235 |

## Administration

| | | |
|---|---|---|
| Deputy Chief | Jerome A. Miles | 202 447-6707 |

## Office of General Council-USDA

| | | |
|---|---|---|
| Assistant General Council, Natural Resources Division | Clarence W. Brizee | 202 447-7121 |

# Regional Headquarters and National Forests

## Region 1-Northern Region

Federal Building                                  406 329-3011
P.O. Box 7669
Missoula, MT 59807

Regional Forester                    James C. Overbay
Director, Wildlife and Fisheries     Barbara L. Holder

## Region 2-Rocky Mountain

11177 West 8th Ave.                               303 236-3711
P.O. Box 25127
Lakewood, CO 80225
Regional Forester                    James F. Torrence
Director, Range, Wildlife Fisheries
   and Ecology                       Glen Hetzel

## Region 3-Southwestern

Federal Building                                  505 842-2401
517 Gold Ave., SW
Albuquerque, NM 87102

Regional Forester                    Milo Jean Hussell
Director, Wildlife Management        William D. Zeedyk

## Region 4—Intermountain

Federal Building                                  801 625-5412
324 25th Street
Odgen, UT 84401

Regional Forester                    J.S. Tixier
Director, Wildlife Management        William R. Barbridge

## Region 5-Pacific Southwest

630 Sansome Street                                415 556-4310
San Francisco, CA 94111

Regional Forester                    Zane G. Smith, Jr.
Director, Fisheries and Wildlife
   Management                        Joseph H. Harn

## Region 6—Pacific Northwest

319 S.W. Pine St.                              503 221-3625
P.O. Box 3623
Portland, OR 97208

Regional Forester                    Charles T. Coston
Director, Fish and Wildlife          Hugh Black

## Region 8—Southern

1720 Peachtree Rd, N.W.                        404 881-4177
Atlanta, GA 30367

Regional Forester                    John E. Alcock
Director, Fisheries, Wildlife, and
  Range                              Jerry P. McIlwain

## Region 9—Eastern

310 West Wisconsin Ave.                        414 291-3693
Milwaukee, WI 53203

Regional Forester                    Larry Henson
Director, Range, Wildlife, and
  Landscape Management               Bruce Hronek

## Region 10—Alaska

Federal Office Building                        907 586-7263
P.O. Box 1628
Juneau, AK 99802

Regional Forester                    Michael A. Barton
Director, Wildlife and Fisheries     Philip J. Janik

# Forest and Range Experiment Stations

Intermountain Station                North Central Station
Laurence E. Lassen, Director         Robert A. Hann, Director
502 25th Street                      1992 Folwell Ave.
Ogden, UT 84401                      St. Paul, MN 56108
(801) 625-5412                       (612) 642-5207

Northeastern Station
Denver P. Burns, Director
370 Reed Road
Broomall, PA 19008
(215) 461-3006

Pacific Northwest Station
Robert L. Ethington, Director
P.O. Box 3890
Portland, OR 97208
(503) 294-2052

Pacific Southwest Station
Roger R. Bay, Director
1960 Addison Street
Box 245
Berkeley, CA 94701
(415) 486-3291

Rocky Mountain Station
Charles M. Loveless, Director
240 W. Prospect
Fort Collins, CO 80526
(303) 221-4390

Southeastern Station
Jerry Cisco, Director
200 Weaver Blvd
Asheville, NC 28804
(704) 259-6758

Southern Station
Thomas H. Ellis, Director
T-10210, U.S. Postal Service Bldg.
701 Loyola Ave.
New Orleans, LA 70113
(504) 589-6787

Forest Products Labratory
Robert L. Youngs, Director
Gifford Pinchot Drive
Box 5130
Madison, WI 53705
(608) 264-5600

## State and Private Forestry Offices

are located in the Regional Headquarters, except for the Eastern Region, where it is at:

Northeastern Area
370 Reed Road
Broomall, PA 19008
(215) 461-1660

# Appendix B

# U.S. Fish and Wildlife Service Directory

## Washington Headquarters

Mailing Address:
Fish and Wildlife Service
Department of the Interior
18th and C Streets, NW
Washington, D.C. 20240

| Title | Name | Phone |
|-------|------|-------|
| Director (Acting) | F. Eugene Hester | 202-343-4717 |
| Deputy Director (Acting) | Ronald E. Lambertson | 202-343-4545 |
| Office of Legislative Services, Chief | Steven R. Robinson | 202-343-5403 |
| Office of International Affairs, Chief | Lawrence N. Mason | 202-343-5188 |

## Wildlife Resources Program

| | | |
|-------|------|-------|
| Associate Director, (Acting) | Walter O. Stieglitz | 202-343-5333 |

| | | |
|---|---|---|
| Deputy Associate Director, National Wildlife Refuge System | Vacant | 202-343-5333 |
| Deputy Associate Director, Wildlife Management | Don W. Minnich | 202-343-5333 |
| Program Development Staff, Chief | Russel D. Earnest | 202-343-6351 |
| Division of Law Enforcement, Chief | Clark R. Bavin | 202-343-9242 |

Law Enforcement: Special Agents-in-Charge

Loren K. Parcher (District 1)
Lloyd 500 Building, Suite 1490
500 NE Multnomah Street
Portland, OR 97232
(503) 231-6125

John E. Cross (District 2)
P.O. Box 329
Albuquerque, NM 87103
(505) 766-2091

Robert A. Hodgins (District 3)
Bishop Henry Whipple Building
Fort Snelling
Twin Cities, MN 55111
(612) 725-3530.

Dan M. Searcy (District 4)
P.O. Box 4839
Atlanta, GA 30302
(404) 221-5872

James V. Sheridan (District 5)
P.O. Box 129
New Town Branch
Boston, MA 02258
(617) 965-2298

Terry L. Grosz (District 6)
P.O. Box 25486
Denver Federal Center
Denver, CO 80225
(303) 234-4612

James H. Hogue (District 7)
P.O. Box 4-2597
Anchorage, AK 99509-2597
(907) 276-3800

| | | |
|---|---|---|
| Office of Migratory Bird Management, Chief | Rollin D. Sparrowe | 202-254-3207 |
| Office of Public Use Management, Chief | Conley L. Moffett | 202-653-2220 |
| Division of Realty, Chief | Vacant | 202-653-8750 |
| Division of Refuge Management, Chief | James F. Gillett | 202-343-4311 |
| Division of Wildlife Management, Chief | LeRoy W. Sowl | 202-632-7463 |
| Office of Youth Activities, Chief | Donald H. Boyd | 202-343-4404 |

## Fishery Resources Program

| | | |
|---|---|---|
| Associate Director | Dr. Joseph H. Kutkuhn | 202-343-6394 |
| Deputy Associate Director | Gary Edwards | 202-343-4266 |
| Office of Program Development, Chief | William P. Atchison | 202-343-6307 |
| Office of Facility Services, Chief | G. Donald Weathers | 202-653-8232 |
| Division of Program Operations, Chief | John T. Brown | 202-653-8746 |

## Regional Offices

Assistant Regional Directors-Fisheries Resources

Wally Steucke (Region 1)
Lloyd 500 Building, Suite 1692
500 NE Multnomah Street
Portland, OR 97232
(503) 231-5967

Conrad Fjetland (Region 2)
P.O. Box 1306
Albuquerque, NM 87103
(505) 766-2323

John Popowski (Region 3)
Bishop Henry Whipple Building
Fort Snelling Twin Cities, MN
   55111
(612) 725-3505

Frank Richardson (Region 4)
R.B. Russell Federal Bldg.
75 Spring Street SW
Atlanta, GA 30303
(404) 221-3576

Dr. James Weaver (Region 5)
One Gateway Center, Suite 700
Newton Corner, MA 02158
(617) 965-5100

Jon Nelson (Region 7)
1011 E. Tudor Road
Anchorage, AK 99503
(907) 786-3539

Danny Regan (Region 6)
P.O. Box 25486
Denver Federal Center
Denver, CO 80225
(303) 236-8154

## Habitat Resources Program

| | | |
|---|---|---|
| Associate Director | Harold J. O'Connor | 202-343-4767 |
| Deputy Associate Director | Suzanne Mayer | 202-343-4767 |
| Office of Program Development, Chief | Larry R. Shanks | 202-343-5000 |
| Division of Ecological Services, Chief | Stephanie Caswell | 202-343-2618 |
| Division of Environmental Coordination, Chief | Columbus H. Brown | 202-343-5685 |
| Division of Resource Contaminant Assessment, Chief | Clarence E. Faulkner | 202-343-5452 |

## Federal Assistance Program

| | | |
|---|---|---|
| Associate Director | Rolf Wallenstrom | 202-343-4646 |
| Deputy Associate Director | Roman H. Koenigs | 202-343-4646 |
| Office of Program Development and Administration, Chief | John M. Murphy | 703-235-1726 |
| Office of Endangered Species, Chief | John L. Spinks, Jr. | 703-235-2771 |
| Federal Wildlife Permit Office, Chief (acting) | Richard K. Robinson | 703-235-1937 |
| Division of Federal Aid, Chief | Vacant | 703-235-1526 |
| Federal Aid, Management Operations | Robert N. Bartel | 703-235-1526 |
| Federal Aid, Planning | William M. Conlin | 703-235-1526 |

| Federal Aid, Wildlife Management | C. Phillip Agee | 703-235-1526 |
| Federal Aid, Fishery Management | Robert J. Sousa | 703-235-1526 |
| Federal Aid, Lands Management and Construction | Thomas W. Taylor | 703-235-1526 |
| Federal Aid, Hunter Education | Robert G. Nelson | 703-235-1526 |

## Research and Development

| Associate Director | Richard N. Smith | 202-343-5715 |
| Deputy Associate Director | John D. Buffington | 202-653-8791 |
| Division of Planning and Information Mgmt, Chief | Vacant | 202-653-8791 |
| Division of Biological Services, Chief | Edward T. Laroe | 202-653-8723 |
| Division of Cooperative Fish and Wildlife Research Units, Chief | John G. Rogers | 202-653-8766 |
| Division of Fishery Research, Chief | Robert E. Stevens | 202-653-8772 |
| Office of Scientific Authority, Chief | Charles Dane | 202-653-5948 |
| Division of Wildlife Research, Chief | Jan E. Riffe | 202-653-8762 |

## Planning and Budget

| Assistant Director | Edwin A. Verburg | 202-343-4329 |
| Division of Program Analysis, Chief | James C. Leupold | 202-343-2444 |
| Division of Program Plans, Chief | Willard Spaulding, Jr. | 202-343-4633 |

## Administration

| Assistant Director | Edward L. Davis | 202-343-4888 |
| Division of Contracting and General Services, Chief | Joel Greenstein | 202-653-8703 |

| Division of Finance, Chief | H. Howard Hulbert | 202-343-8991 |
| Office of Information Resources Management, Chief (acting) | Claude Christensen | 202-653-7558 |
| Division of Personnel, Chief | John R. Caracciolo | 202-343-6104 |
| Public Affairs, Assistant Director | Phil Million | 202-343-5634 |

# REGIONAL OFFICES

*Region 1: California, Hawaii, Idaho, Nevada, Oregon, Washington, Pacific Trust Territories.*
Fish and Wildlife Service
Lloyd 500 Building, Suite 1692
500 NE Multnomah Street
Portland, OR 97232

| Regional Director | Richard J. Myshak | 503-231-6118 |
| Assistant Regional Director, Wildlife Resources | Lawrence W. Debates | 503-231-6214 |
| Assistant Regional Director, Fishery Resources | Erwin W. Steuke | 503-231-5967 |
| Assistant Regional Director, Habitat Resources | David Riley | 503-231-6159 |
| Habitat Resources, Wetlands Coordinator | Dennis Peters | 503-231-6154 |
| Assistant Regional Director, Federal Assistance | William F. Shake | 503-231-6121 |
| Federal Assistance, Federal Aid Specialist | Donald Friberg | 503-231-6121 |
| Federal Assistance, Endangered Species Specialist | Wayne White | 503-231-6131 |
| Law Enforcement, Special Agent-in-Charge | David L. McMullen | 503-231-6125 |

*Region 2: Arizona, New Mexico, Oklahoma, Texas*
Fish and Wildlife Service
P.O. Box 1306
Albuquerque, NM 87103

| | | |
|---|---|---|
| Regional Director | Michael J. Spear | 505-766-2321 |
| Assistant Regional Director, Wildlife Resources | W. Ellis Klett | 505-766-2327 |
| Assistant Regional Director, Federal Assistance and Fishery Resources | Conrad A. Fjetland | 505-766-2323 |
| Federal Assistance, Federal Aid Specialist | Donald G. Kuntzelman | 505-766-2321 |
| Federal Assistance, Endangered Species Specialist | James Johnson | 505-766-2323 |
| Assistant Regional Director, Habitat Resources | James A. Young | 505-766-2324 |
| Habitat Resources, Wetlands Coordinator | Warren Hagenbuck | 505-766-2914 |
| Law Enforcement, Special Agent-in-Charge | John E. Cross | 505-766-2091 |

*Region 3: Iowa, Illinois, Indiana, Michigan, Minnesota, Missouri, Ohio, Wisconsin.*
Fish and Wildlife Service
Bishop Henry Whipple Building
Fort Snelling Twin Cities, MN 55111

| | | |
|---|---|---|
| Regional Director | Harvey K. Nelson | 612-725-3563 |
| Assistant Regional Director, Wildlife Resources | Harold W. Benson | 612-725-3507 |
| Assistant Regional Director, Fishery Resources and Federal Management | John S. Popowski | 612-725-3505 |
| Federal Assistance, Federal Aid Specialist | Joseph W. Artmann | 612-725-3500 |
| Federal Assistance, Endangered Species Specialist | James Engel | 612-725-3503 |

| Assistant Regional Director, Habitat Resources | Gerald Lowry | 612-725-3510 |
| Habitat Resources, Wetlands Coordinator | Ronald Erickson | 612-725-3593 |
| Law Enforcement, Special Agent-in-Charge | Robert A. Hodgins | 612-725-3530 |

*Region 4: Alabama, Arkansas, Florida, Georgia, Kentucky, Louisiana, Mississippi, North Carolina, South Carolina, Tennessee, Puerto Rico, Virgin Islands.*
Fish and Wildlife Service
R.B. Russell Building
75 Spring Street, SW
Atlanta, GA 30303

| Regional Director | James W. Pulliam, Jr. | 404-331-3588 |
| Assistant Regional Director, Wildlife Resources | Crayton J. Lankford | 404-331-3538 |
| Assistant Regional Director, Fishery Resources | Frank R. Richardson | 404-331-3576 |
| Assistant Regional Director, Habitat Resources | Warren T. Olds, Jr. | 404-331-6343 |
| Habitat Resources, Wetlands Coordinator | John Hefner | 404-331-6343 |
| Assistant Regional Director, Federal Assistance | John I. Christian | 404-331-3580 |
| Federal Assistance, Federal Aid Specialist | John Hall | 404-331-3588 |
| Federal Assistance, Endangered Species Specialist | Marshall Jones | 404-331-3583 |
| Law Enforcement, Special Agent-in-Charge | Dan M. Searcy | 404-331-5872 |

*Region 5: Connecticut, Delaware, Maine, Maryland, Massachusetts, New Hampshire, New Jersey, New York, Pennsylvania, Rhode Island, Vermont, Virginia, West Virginia*
Fish and Wildlife Service
One Gateway Center, Suite 700
Newton Corner, MA 02158

| Regional Director | Howard N. Larsen | 617-965-5100 ext. 200 |
| Assistant Regional Director, Wildlife Resources | Donald Young | 617 965-5100 ext. 222 |
| Assistant Regional Director, Fishery Resources | James E. Weaver | 617-965-5100 ext. 208 |
| Assistant Regional Director, Habitat Resources | Donald W. Woodlard | 617-965-5100 ext. 217 |
| Habitat Resources, Wetlands Coordinator | Ralph Tiner | 617-965-5100 ext. 379 |
| Assistant Regional Director, Federal Assistance | Stephen W. Parry | 617-965-5100 ext. 212 |
| Federal Assistance, Federal Aid Specialist | William T. Hesselton | 617-965-5100 |
| Federal Assistance, Endangered Species Specialist | Paul Nickerson | 617-965-5100 ext. 316 |
| Law Enforcement, Special Agent-in-Charge | James V. Sheridan | 617-965-5100 ext. 254 |

*Region 6: Colorado, Kansas, Montana, Nebraska, North Dakota, South Dakota, Utah, Wyoming*
Fish and Wildlife Service
P.O. Box 25486
Denver Federal Center
Denver, CO 80225

| Regional Director | Galen L. Buterbaugh | 303-236-7920 |
| Assistant Regional Director, Wildlife Resources | Nelson B. Kverno | 303-236-8145 |
| Assistant Regional Director, Fishery Resources | Danny M. Regan | 303-236-8154 |
| Assistant Regional Director, Habitat Resources | William E. Marten | 303-236-8189 |
| Habitat Resources, Wetlands Coordinator | Charles Elliot | 303-236-8180 |

| Assistant Regional Director, Federal Assistance | John D. Green | 303-236-5416 |
| Federal Assistance, Federal Aid Specialist | Jerry J. Blackard | 303-236-7920 |
| Federal Assistance, Endangered Species Specialist | David Fleming and Barry Mulder | 303-236-7398 |
| Law Enforcement, Special Agent-in-Charge | Terry L. Grosz | 303-236-7540 |

*Region 7: Alaska*
Fish and Wildlife Service
1011 E. Tudor Road
Anchorage, AK 99503

| Regional Director | Robert E. Gilmore | 907-786-3542 |
| Assistant Regional Director, Wildlife Resources | John P. Rogers | 907-786-3538 |
| Assistant Regional Director, Fishery Resources and Federal Assistance | Jon M. Nelson | 907-786-3539 |
| Federal Assistance, Federal Aid Specialist | William H. Martin | 907-786-3542 |
| Federal Assistance, Endangered Species Specialist | Dennis Money | 907-786-3435 |
| Assistant Regional Director, Habitat Resources | Robert D. Jacobsen | 907-786-3522 |
| Habitat Resources, Wetlands Coordinator | John Hall | 907-786-3403 |
| Law Enforcement, Special Agent-in-Charge | James H. Hogue | 907-786-3311 |

# Appendix C

# National Park Service Directory

## WASHINGTON HEADQUARTERS

National Park Service
Interior Building
Washington, D.C. 20240

General Information:
202 343-4747

| Title | Name | Phone |
|---|---|---|
| Director | Wm. Penn Mott | 202 343-4621 |
| Deputy Director | Denis Galvin | 202 343-5081 |
| Special Asst. for Policy Development | Dwight Rettie | 202 343-7456 |
| Public Affairs | George J. Berklacy | 202 343-6843 |
| Leg. & Congressional | James "Mike" Lambe | 202 343-1326 |
| Equal Opport. Officer | Marshall Brookes | 202 343-6738 |
| Minority Businesses | Barbara Guillard-Payn | 202 343-3884 |
| *Associate Directors:* | | |
| Natural Resources | Richard Briceland | 202 343-5193 |
| Park Operations | Stanley Albright | 202 343-5651 |
| Cultural Resources | Jerry Rogers | 202 343-7625 |

| | | |
|---|---|---|
| Planning and Development | David Wright | 202 343-6741 |
| Financial Systems | Stan Salisbury | 202 343-2002 |
| Personnel and Administrative Services | Dick Powers | 202 343-8855 |

*Natural Resources Division:*

| | | |
|---|---|---|
| Air Quality | Barbara Brown | 202 343-4911 |
| Special Science Projects | Al Greene | 202 343-8114 |
| Energy, Mining, & Minerals | Carol McCoy | 202 343-4650 |
| Biological Resources | John Reed | 202 343-8125 |
| Water Resources | Tom Lucke | 303 221-5341 |

# Regional Offices

*North Atlantic Regional Office*
National Park Service
15 State Street
Boston, MA 02109
(617) 223-3793

Chief Scientist:
Dr. Michael Soukup
Natural Resource Specialist:
Dr. Michael Soukup

The region includes Connecticut, Maine, Massachusetts, New Hampshire, New Jersey, New York, Rhode Island, and Vermont.

\*  \*  \*  \*  \*

*Mid-Atlantic Regional Office*
National Park Service
143 South Third Street
Philadelphia, PA 19106
(215) 597-3679

Chief Scientist:
John Karish
Natural Resource Specialist:
Mike Maule

The region includes Delaware, Maryland, Pennsylvania, Virginia, and West Virginia.

\*  \*  \*  \*  \*

*National Capital Region*
National Park Service
1100 Ohio Drive, SW
Washington, D.C. 20242
(202) 426-6700

Chief Scientist:
Dr. William Anderson
Natural Resource Specialist:
Stan Locke

The National Capital Region covers parks in the metropolitan area of Washington, D.C. and certain field areas in Maryland, Virginia, and West Virginia.

\*  \*  \*  \*  \*

*Southeast Regional Office*
National Park Service
75 Spring SW. Street
Atlanta, GA 30303
(404) 331-3448

Chief Scientist:
Dr. G. Jay Gogue
Natural Resource Specialist:
Dr. G. Jay Gogue

The region includes Alabama, Georgia, Kentucky, Mississippi, North Carolina, South Carolina, Tennessee, Puerto Rico, and the Virgin Islands.

\* \* \* \* \*

*Midwest Regional Office*
National Park Service
1709 Jackson Street
Omaha, NE 68102
(402) 221-3448

Chief Scientist:
Dr. Michael Ruggiero
Natural Resource Specialist:
Ben Holmes

The region includes Illinois, Indiana, Iowa, Kansas, Minnesota, Michigan, Missouri, Nebraska, Ohio, and Wisconsin.

\* \* \* \* \*

*Rocky Mountain Regional Office*
National Park Service
655 Parfet Street
Denver, CO 80225
(303) 236-4648

Chief Scientist:
Dan Huff
Natural Resource Specialist:
Jim Olson

The region includes Colorado, Montana, North Dakota, South Dakota, Utah, and Wyoming.

\* \* \* \* \*

*Southwest Regional Office*
National Park Service
Old Santa Fe Trail
P.O. Box 728
Santa Fe, NM 87501
(505) 988-6375

Chief Scientist:
Dr. Milford Fletcher
Natural Resource Specialist:
Dr. Milford Fletcher

The region includes part of Arizona, Arkansas, Louisiana, New Mexico, Oklahoma, and Texas.

\* \* \* \* \*

*Western Regional Office*
National Park Service
450 Golden Gate Avenue
P.O. Box 36063
San Francisco, CA 94102
(415) 556-5186

Chief Scientist (Acting)
Gene Wehunt
Natural Resource Specialist:
Francis Jacot

The region includes part of Arizona, California, Hawaii, and Nevada.

\* \* \* \* \*

*Pacific Northwest Regional Office*
National Park Service
Westin Building
2001 Sixth Avenue, Room 1920
Seattle, WA 98121
(206) 442-4830

Chief Scientist:
James Larson
Natural Resources Specialist:
Dick Praisl

The region includes Idaho, Oregon, and Washington.

*Alaska Regional Office*
National Park Service
2525 Gambell Street, Room 107
Anchorage, AK 99503
(907) 271-4196

The region includes Alaska.

Chief Scientist:
Al Lovass
Natural Resource Specialist:
Al Lovass

National Park Service Cooperative Park Study Units

| REGION | CPSU | NPS CONTACT | UNIVERSITY CONTACT | STATUS |
|---|---|---|---|---|
| North Atlantic Region | College of the Atlantic Bar Harbor, ME 04609 | Dr. Michael Soukup 8-223-7765 | Dr. William Drury (207) 288-5015 | Active |
| | Rutgers University Center for Coastal and Environmental Studies The State University of New Jersey Doolittle Hall New Brunswick, NJ 08903 | Dr. Paul Buckley 8-342-5389 or commercial no. (201) 221-1824 | Dr. Norbert Psuty (201) 932-3738 | Active |
| | State University of New York College of Environmental Science and Forestry Syracuse, NY 13210 | Dr. Michael Soukup 8-223-7765 | Dr. Bill Porter (315) 470-6798 | Active |
| | University of Massachusetts Department of Forestry & Wildlife Mgmt. Holdsworth Hall Amherst, MA 01003 | Dr. Michael Soukup 8-223-7765 | Dr. Bill Patterson (413) 545-2666 | Active |
| Mid-Atlantic Region | University of Pennsylvania Morris Arboretum 9914 Meadowbrook Avenue Philadelphia, PA 19118 | None | Dr. Ann Rhoads (215) 247-5777 | Active |
| | University of Virginia Department of Environmental Sciences Charlottesville, VA 22903 | None | Dr. Robert Dolan (804) 924-7761 | Active |
| | Pennsylvania State University 208 Ferguson Building University Park, PA 16802 | Mr. John F. Karish (814) 865-7974 | Dr. Brian J. Turner (814) 865-1602 | Active |

| Region | Institution | Contact 1 | Contact 2 | Status |
|---|---|---|---|---|
| National Capital Region | None | None | None | None |
| Southeast Region | Clemson University<br>Department Head<br>Parks, Recreation, and Tourism Mgmt.<br>Clemson, SC 29631 | Dominic Dottavio<br>(803) 656–2182 | Dr. Herbert Brantley<br>(803) 656–3036 | Active |
| | University of Georgia<br>Institute of Ecology<br>Athens, GA 30608 | Susan P. Bratton<br>(404) 542–2968 | Dr. James Cooley<br>(404) 542–2968 | Active |
| Midwest Region | Michigan Technological University<br>Houghton, MI 49931 | Dr. J. Robert Stottlemyer | None | Active |
| Southwest Region | Texas A&M University<br>Department of Recreation & Parks<br>College Station, TX 77843 | Dr. Denny Fenn<br>(409) 845–5369 | Dr. Leslie Reid<br>(713) 845–7323 | Active |
| Rocky Mountain Region | Colorado State University<br>College of Forestry and Natural Resources<br>Ft. Collins, CO 80523 | None | Dr. Harry E. Troxell<br>(303) 491–6675 | Active |
| | University of Wyoming<br>Box 3166<br>University Station<br>Laramie, WY 82071 | None | Dr. Kenneth L. Diem<br>(307) 766–4207 | Active |
| | Utah State University<br>Department of Forest Resource<br>College of Natural Resources UMC 52<br>Logan, UT 84322 | None | Dr. Richard F. Fisher<br>(801) 750–2455 | Inactive |

National Park Service Cooperative Park Study Units—continued

| REGION | CPSU | NPS CONTACT | UNIVERSITY CONTACT | STATUS |
|---|---|---|---|---|
| Pacific Northwest Region | University of Idaho College of Forestry Moscow, ID 83843 | Dr. R. Gerald Wright 8–554-1111 ask for # (208) 885–7990 Dr. Gary E. Machlis 8–554-1111 ask for # (208) 885–7129 | Dr. John R. Erhenriech, Dean (208) 885–6442 | Active |
| | Oregon State University School of Forestry Corvallis, OR 97331 | Dr. Edward E. Starkey (503) 754–2056 Dr. Donald R. Field (503) 754–2056 Dr. Gary Larson (503) 757–4668 | Dean Carl H. Stoltenberg (503) 754–2221 | Active |
| | University of Washington College of Forest Resources Seattle, WA 98195 | Dr. James K. Agee (206) 543–2688 Mr. Darryll R. Johnson (206) 545–7404 | Dean David B. Thorud (206) 545–1928 | Active |
| Western Region | University of Arizona 125 Biological Science (East) Building 43 Tucson, AR 85821 | Dr. R. Roy Johnson 8–762-6886 Dr. Heaton Underhill 8–762-6919 Mr. Peter Bennett (602) 629–6985 Dr. Steven Carothers (602) 774–5500 | None | Active |
| | University of Nevada Department of Biological Science Las Vegas, NV 89154 | Dr. Charles Douglass 8–598-6468 | None | Active |

| University of Hawaii<br>Department of Botany<br>Honolulu, HI 96822 | Dr. Donald Gardner<br>(808) 948-8218<br>Dr. Lloyd Loope<br>(808) 572-1983<br>Dr. Charles Stone<br>(808) 967-8211 | Dr. Clifford W. Smith<br>(808) 948-8218 | Active |
|---|---|---|---|
| University of California<br>Department of Land, Air & Water<br>Resources<br>Davis, CA 95616 | Dr. Charles Van Ripper III<br>(916) 752-7119<br>Dr. Christine<br>Schoenwald-Cox<br>(916) 752-7119 ext. 2088<br>Dr. Gary Davis<br>(805) 644-8157<br>Dr. David Parsons<br>(209) 565-3341<br>Dr. David Graber<br>(209) 565-3341<br>Dr. Gary Fellers<br>(415) 663-8522<br>Dr. Jan van Wagtendonk<br>8-448-4465<br>Mr. Stephen Viers<br>(707) 822-7611<br>Dr. William Halvorson<br>(805) 644-8157<br>None | Dr. Lynn D. Whittig<br>(916) 752-0765 | Active |
| AK | None | None | None |

Source: National Park Service, 12/27/84

# Appendix D

# Bureau of Land Management Directory

## WASHINGTON HEADQUARTERS

Bureau of Land Management
U.S. Department of the Interior
Washington, D.C. 20240

Robert Burford, Director
Bureau of Land Management
202-343-3801

David Almand, Chief
Division of Wildlife, BLM
202-653-9202

## State Office Directors and Biologists

*Alaska*
Mike Penfold, State Director
*Laun Buoy, State Office Biologist
Bureau of Land Management
701 C Street
Anchorage, AK 99513
Commercial: (907) 271-3349
FTS: 8-907-271-3349

*Arizona*
Dean Bibles, State Director
*John Costellano, State Off. Bio.
Bureau of Land Management
3707 North 7th Street
Phoenix, AZ 85011
Com: (602) 261-5512
FTS: 8-261-5512

*Biologist for Endangered Species

994

*California*
Ed Hasley, State Director
*Mike Ferguson, State Office Bio.
Bureau of Land Management
Federal Office Building
2800 Cottage Way
Sacramento, CA 95825
Com: (916) 484-4701
FTS: 8-468-4701

*Colorado*
Kannan Richards, State Director
*Lee Upham, State Office Bio.
Bureau of Land Management
2020 Arapahoe Street
Denver, CO 80205
Com: (303) 837-4325
FTS: 8-546-4325

*Denver Service Ctr.*
*Allen Cooperrider, Svc. Ctr. Bio.
Bureau of Land Management
Denver Service Center
Bldg. 50, Denver Federal Ctr.
Denver, CO 80225
Com: (303) 236-0161
FTS: 8-776-0161

*Eastern States Office*
Curtis Jones, Director
*Gene Ludlow, State Office
  Biologist
Bureau of Land Management
Eastern States Office
350 South Pickett Street
Alexandria, VA 22304
Com: (703) 274-0069
FTS: 8-274-0069

*Idaho*
Clair Whitlock, State Director
*Allen Thomas, State Office
  Biologist
Bureau of Land Management
3380 Americana Terrace
Boise, ID 83706
Com: (208) 334-1835
FTS: 8-554-1835

*Montana* (MT, SD, ND)
Dean Stepanek, State Director
Ray Hoem, State Office Bio.
*Dan Hinckley
Bureau of Land Management
222 North 32nd Street
Billings, MT 59107
Commercial: (406) 657-6655
FTS: 8-585-6655

*Nevada*
Ed Spang, State Director
David Goicoechea, State Off. Bio.
*Osborne Casey
Bureau of Land Management
300 Booth Street/Room 3038
Reno, NV 89520
Com: (702) 784-5455
FTS: 8-470-5455

*New Mexico* (NM, OK, TX)
Charles Luscher, State Director
*Brian Mills, State Office Biologist
Bureau of Land Management
Montoya Federal Bldg.
South Federal Place
Santa Fe, NM 87501
Com: (505) 988-6231
FTS: 8-476-6231

*Biologist for Endangered Species

*Oregon* (OR, WA)
William Leavell, State Director
Art Oakley, State Office Bio.
*Bill Nietro
Bureau of Land Management
825 NE. Multnomah Street
Portland, OR 97208
Com: (503) 231-6866
FTS: 8-429-6866

*Utah*
Roland Robinson, State Director
*Jerry Farringer, State Off. Bio.
Bureau of Land Management
324 South State Street
Salt Lake City, UT 84111-2303
Com: (801) 524-3123
FTS: 8-588-3123

*Wyoming* (WY, KS, NE)
Hillary Oden, State Director
*Dick Felthousen, State Off. Bio.
Bureau of Land Management
2515 Warren Avenue
Cheyenne, WY 82003
Com: (307) 778-2086
FTS: 8-328-2086

*Biologist for Endangered Species

# Appendix E

# Wetlands Management Directory

Locations for Obtaining National Wetlands Inventory Maps

## State Distribution Centers

*California*
CA Dept of Fish and Game
Natural Heritage Section
1416 Ninth Street
Sacramento, CA 95814
(916) 322-2493

*Connecticut*
Dept. of Env. Protection
Natural Resources Center
State Office Building
Hartford, CT 06115
(203) 566-3540

*Delaware*
State of Delaware
Dept. of Natural Resources and
    Environmental Control
Wetlands Section
Edward Tatnall Building
P.O. Box 1401
Dover, DE 19903

*Guam*
Director
Bureau of Planning
Government of Guam
Agna, Guam 96910

*Hawaii*
Board of Land and Nat'l Res.
Div. of Forestry and Wildlife
Technical Services
P.O. Box 621
Honolulu, HI 96889

*Maine*
Maine Geological Survey
Maine Station 22, State House
Augusta, ME 04333
(207) 289-2801

*Maryland*
Maryland Dept. of Natural Res.
Wetlands Division
Water Resources Administration
Tawes State Office Building
Annapolis, MD 21401
(301) 269-3871

*Massachusetts*
MA Assoc. of Conservation Comm.
Lincoln Filene Center
Tufts University
Medford, MA 02155

*Mississippi*
Tech. Transfer Office
Building 11000
NSTL Station, MS 39529

*Nebraska*
Dr. Vincent Dreezen, Director
Conservation and Survey Division
University of Nebraska
113 Nebraska Hall
Lincoln, NE 68588-0517

*New Hampshire*
Office of State Planning
State of New Hampshire
2½ Beacon Street
Concord, MA 03301
(603) 271-2155

*New Jersey*
N.J. Dept. of Envir. Protection
Bureau of Collection and Licensing
Maps and Publications
CN-402
Trenton, NJ 08625
(609) 292-2578

*New York*
CLEARS
Resource Information Laboratory
464 Hellister Hall
Cornell University
Ithaca, NY 14853
(607) 256-6520

*Oregon*
Oregon Dept. of Fish and Wildlife
506 SW Mill Street
Portland, OR 97208
(503) 229-5249

*Pennsylvania*
Coastal Zone Management
Office of Resource Mgmt.
Dept. of Envir. Resources
P.O. Box 1467
Harrisburg, PA 17120

*Rhode Island*
Dept. of Environmental Mgmt.
Freshwater Wetlands Section
38 State Street
Providence, RI 02908
(401) 277-6820

*Vermont*
Vermont Dept. of Water Resources
Montpelier, VT 05602
(802) 828–2761

*Washington*
Chief Cartographic
Washington Dept. of Ecology
Mail Stop PV-11
Olympia, WA 98504
(206) 459–6201

## U.S. Geologic Survey Mapping Centers

National Cartographic
Information Center
U.S. Geological Survey
507 National Center
Reston, VA 22092
1–800–USA–MAPS

# REGIONAL OFFICES

Eastern Mapping Center-NCIC
U.S. Geological Survey
536 National Center
Reston, VA 22092
Com: (703) 860–6336
FTS: 928–6336

Nat'l Cartographic Info. Ctr.
U.S. Geological Survey
Skyline Building
218 E. Street
Anchorage, AK 99501
Com: (907) 271–4159
FTS: 271–4159

Mid-Continent Mapping Center-
  NCIC
U.S. Geological Survey
1400 Independence Road
Rolla, MO 65401
Com: (314) 341–0851
FTS: 227–0851

Rocky Mount. Mapping Center-
  NCIC
U.S. Geological Survey
Box 25046, Stop 504 Federal Center
Denver, CO 80225
Com: (303) 236–5829
FTS: 776–5829

Nat'l Cartographic Info. Center
U.S. Geological Survey
Nat'l Space Technology Labs
Building 3101
NSTL Station, MS 39529
Com: (601) 688–3544
FTS: 467–2427

Tennessee Valley Authority
200 Haney Building
311 Broad Street
Chattanooga, TN 37401
Com: (615) 755–2148
FTS: 857–2148

Western Mapping Center-NCIC
U.S. Geological Survey
345 Middlefield Road
Menlo Park, CA 94025
Com: (415) 323-8111, ext. 2427
FTS: 467-2427

## FWS Regional Wetland Coordinators

Dennis Peters (Region 1)
U.S. Fish and Wildlife Service
Lloyd 500 Bldg., Suite 1692
500 NE Multnomah Street
Portland, OR 97232
(503) 231-6154

Warren Hagenbuck (Region 2)
U.S. Fish and Wildlife Service
P.O. Box 1306
Albuquerque, NM 87103
(505) 766-2914

Ron Erickson (Region 3)
U.S. Fish and Wildlife Service
Bishop Henry Whipple Federal
  Bldg.
Twin Cities, MN 55111
(612) 725-3536

John Hefner (Region 4)
U.S. Fish and Wildlife Service
R.B. Russell Federal Bldg.
75 Spring Street SW.
Atlanta, GA 30303
(404) 221-6343

Ralph Tiner (Region 5)
U.S. Fish and Wildlife Service
One Gateway Center, Suite 700
Newton Corner, MA 02158
(617) 965-5100 ext. 379

Charles Elliott (Region 6)
U.S. Fish and Wildlife Service
P.O. Box 2548
Denver Federal Center
Denver, CO 80225
(303) 234-5586

John Hall (Region 7)
U.S. Fish and Wildlife Service
1011 E. Tudor Road
Anchorage, AK 99503
(907) 786-3403

## Information on the Wetlands Database

Database Administrator
Western Energy and Land Use Team
U.S. Fish and Wildlife Service
Drake Creekside One, 2627 Redwing Road
Fort Collins, CO 80526-2899

Location for Obtaining Wetlands Plant List
(Availability scheduled for end of 1986)

Fish and Wildlife Service
9720 Executive Center Drive
Monroe Building, Suite 101
St. Petersburg, FL 33702

# KEY 404 CONTACTS

Four key agencies are involved in the review and processing of 404 permits:
the Army Corps of Engineers, the Environmental Protection Agency, the Fish
and Wildlife Service, and the National Marine Fisheries Service. Permit applications are reviewed in the field as follows: in the Fish and Wildlife Service by
the Ecological Services field offices; in the National Marine Fisheries Service
by the Habitat Conservation offices; in the Environmental Protection Agency
at the regional offices; and in the Corps at the district offices. FWS field offices
are listed in Appendix B; the other agencies' field offices are listed below.

Other key contacts in the Corps also are given below: key policy-level
officials in the Washington headquarters, including the Regulatory Branch
that has direct oversight over 404 operations; and the division offices, which
oversee the district offices but are not normally involved in permit decisions.
Questions on permit applications should be directed to the district offices, not
these other contacts.

## Environmental Protection Agency

Headquarters
U.S. Environmental Protection Agency
401 M St., SW.
Washington, D.C. 20360

Lee Thomas, Administrator
(202) 382-4700

Jennifer Joy Manson, Assistant Administrator
Office of External Affairs
(202) 382-5654

Allan Hirsch, Director
Office of Federal Activities
(202) 382-5053

John Meagher, Chief
Division of Aquatic Resources
(202) 382-5043

*Region I*
Michael DeLand, Administrator
John F. Kennedy Federal Bldg.,
Room 2203
Boston, MA 02203
(617) 223-7210

*Region II*
Richard Dewling, Acting Admin.
26 Federal Plaza
Room 1009
New York, NY 10007
(212) 264-2525

*Region III*
Thomas Eichler, Administrator
Curtis Building
6th and Walnut Streets
Philadelphia, PA 19106
(215) 597-9814

*Region IV*
Charles R. Jeter, Administrator
345 Courtland St., NE.
Atlanta, GA 30308
(404) 881-4727

*Region V*
Valdas V. Adamkus, Administrator
230 S. Dearborn
Chicago, IL 60604
(312) 353-2000

*Region VI*
Dick Whittington, Administrator
First International Bldg.
1201 S. Elm Street
Dallas, TX 75270
(214) 767-2600

*Region VII*
Morris Kay, Administrator
1735 Baltimore Street
Kansas City, MO 64108
(816) 374-5493

*Region VIII*
Lincoln Tower Bldg., Room 900
1860 Lincoln Street
Denver, CO 80203

*Region IX*
Judith E. Ayers, Acting Admin.
215 Freemont Street
San Francisco, CA 94105
(415) 974-8135

*Region X*
Ernesta Barnes, Administrator
1200 Sixth Avenue
Seattle, WA 98101
(206) 442-1220

## Army Corps of Engineers

Robert K. Dawson
Assistant Secretary of the Army for Civil Works
(202) 697-3365

Lieutenant General E.R. Heiberg III
Chief, Corps of Engineers, (CECG/DAEN-ZA)
(202) 272-0000

Major General H.J. Hatch
Director of Civil Works (DAEN-CWZ)
(202) 272-0099

Bernard N. Goode
Chief, Regulatory Branch (DAEN-CWO-N)
(202) 272-0199

# Division and District Offices

The codes listed for the district offices and the phone numbers given for both district and division offices are for the regulatory branches, which handle 404 permits.

**Lower Mississippi Valley Division**
P.O. Box 80
Vicksburg, MS 39180
(601) 634-5818

*Memphis District*
Clifford Davis Federal Bldg.
Room B-202
Memphis, TN 38103-1894
ATTN: LMMCO-G
(901) 521-3471

*St. Louis District*
210 Tucker Blvd., N.
St. Louis, MO 63101-1986
ATTN: LMSOD-F
(314) 263-5703

*New Orleans District*
P.O. Box 60267
New Orleans, LA 70160-0267
ATTN: LMNOD-S
(504) 838-2255

*Vicksburg District*
P.O. Box 60
Vicksburg, MS 39180-0060
ATTN: LMKOD-F
(601) 634-5276

**Missouri River Division**
P.O. Box 103 Downtown Station
Omaha, NE 68101
(402) 221-7290

*Kansas City District*
700 Federal Building
601 E. 12th Street
Kansas City, MO 64106-2896
ATTN: MRKOD-P
(816) 374-3645

*Omaha District*
P.O. Box 5
Omaha, NE 68101-0005
ATTN: MROOP-N
(402) 221-4133

**New England Division**
424 Trapelo Road
Waltham, MA 02254
(617) 647-8338
(No district offices.)

**North Atlantic Division**
90 Church Street
New York, NY 10077
(212) 264-7535

*Baltimore District*
P.O. Box 1715
Baltimore, MD 21203–1715
ATTN: NABOP-R
(301) 962–3670

*New York District*
26 Federal Plaza
New York, NY 10278–0090
ATTN: NANOP-R
(212) 264–3996

*Norfolk District*
803 Front Street
Norfolk, VA 23510–1096
ATTN: NAOOP-P
(804) 446–3652

*Philadelphia District*
U.S. Custom House
2nd and Chestnut Street
Philadelphia, PA 19106–2991
ATTN: NAPOP-R
(215) 597–2812

### North Central Division
536 S. Clark Street
Chicago, IL 60605–1592
(312) 353–6379

*Buffalo District*
1776 Niagara Street
Buffalo, NY 14207–3199
ATTN: NCBCO-S
(716) 876–5454

*Chicago District*
219 S. Dearborn Street
Chicago, IL 60604–1797
ATTN: NCCCO-R
(312) 353–6428

*Detroit District*
P.O. Box 1027
Detroit, MI 48231–1027
ATTN: NCECO-L
(313) 226–2218

*Rock Island District*
Clock Tower Building
Rock Island, IL 51201–2004
ATTN: NCROD-S
(309) 788–6361 ext. 6370

*St. Paul District*
1135 USPO and Custom House
St. Paul, MN 55101–1479
ATTN: NCSCO-RF
(612) 725–5819

### North Pacific Division
P.O. Box 2870
Portland, OR 97208
(503) 221–3780

*Alaska District*
P.O. Box 898
Anchorage, AK 99506–0898
ATTN: NPACO-RF
(907) 753–2712

*Portland District*
P.O. Box 2946
Portland, OR 97208–2946
ATTN: NPPND-RF
(503) 221–6995

*Seattle District*
P.O. Box C-3755
Seattle, WA 98124-2252
ATTN: NPSOP-RF
(206) 764-3495

*Walla Walla District*
Building 602, City-County Airport
Walla Walla, WA 99362-9265
ATTN: NPWOP-RF
(509) 522-6718

**Ohio River Division**
P.O. Box 1159
Cincinnati, OH 45201-1159
(513) 684-3972

*Honolulu District*
Building 230, Fort Shafter
Honolulu, HI 96858-5440
ATTN: PODCO-O
(808) 438-9258

*Nashville District*
P.O. Box 1070
Nashville, TN 37202-1070
ATTN: ORNOR-F
(615) 251-5181

*Huntington District*
502 8th Street
Huntington, WV 25701-2070
ATTN: ORHOP-F
(304) 529-5487

*Pacific Ocean Division*
Building T-1
Fort Shafter,
Honolulu, HI 96858-5440
(808) 438-9258

*Louisville District*
P.O. Box 59
Louisville, KY 40201-0059
ATTN: ORLOP-F
(502) 582-5452

*Pittsburgh District*
Federal Building
1000 Liberty Avenue
Pittsburgh, PA 15222-4186
ATTN: ORPOR-F
(412) 644-4204

**South Atlantic Division**
510 Title Building
30 Pryor St., SW.
Atlanta, GA 30303
(404) 331-6744

*Charleston District*
P.O. Box 919
Charleston, SC 29402-0919
ATTN: SACCO-P
(803) 724-4330

*Mobile District*
P.O. Box 2288
Mobile, AL 36628-0001
ATTN: SAMOP-S
(205) 690-2658

*Jacksonville District*
P.O. Box 4970
Jacksonville, FL 32232-0019
ATTN: SAJRD
(904) 791-1659

*Savannah District*
P.O. Box 889
Savannah, GA 31402-0889
ATTN: SASOP-F
(912) 994-5347

*Wilmington District*
P.O. Box 1890
Wilmington, NC 28402-4511
ATTN: SAWCO-E
(919) 343-4511

### South Pacific Division
630 Sansome Street, Room 1216
San Francisco, CA 94111
(415) 556-2648

*Los Angeles District*
P.O. Box 2711
Los Angeles, CA 90053-2325
ATTN: SPLCO-R
(213) 688-5606

*San Francisco District*
211 Main Street
San Francisco, CA 94105
(415) 974-0416

*Sacramento District*
650 Capitol Mall
Sacramento, CA 95814-4797
ATTN: SPKCO-O
(916) 440-2842

### Southwestern Division
1114 Commerce Street
Dallas, TX 75242
(214) 767-2432

*Albuquerque District*
P.O. Box 1580
Albuquerque, NM 87103-1580
ATTN: SWACO-OR
(505) 766-2776

*Little Rock District*
P.O. Box 867
Little Rock, AR 72203-0867
ATTN: SWLCO-P
(501) 378-5295

*Fort Worth District*
P.O. Box 17300
Ft. Worth, TX 76102-0300
ATTN: SWFOD-O
(817) 334-2681

*Tulsa District*
P.O. Box 61
Tulsa, OK 74121-0061
ATTN: SWTOD-RF
(918) 581-7261

*Galveston District*
P.O. Box 1229
Galveston, TX 77553-1229
ATTN: SWGCO-R
(409) 766-3925

# ARMY RESEARCH CONTACTS

U.S. Army Engineers Water Resources Support Center
Casey Building
Ft. Belvoir, VA 22060
Dredging Division, Environmental Management Team (WRSC-D)
Institute for Water Resources (WRSC-IWR)

U.S. Army Waterways Experiment Station (WES)
Environmental Laboratory
P.O. Box 631
Vicksburg, MS 39180-0631
Chief, Environmental Laboratory: John Harrison
Chief, Environmental Resources Division: Conrad J. Kirby
Chief, Ecosystem Res. and Stimulation Division: Donald L. Robey
Chief, Environmental Systems Division: Lewis E. Link

## National Marine Fisheries Service

## NORTHEAST REGION

(includes area from Maine to North Carolina)

*Main Offices*
(ME, NH, MA, RI)
Thomas E. Bigford, Branch Chief
Fish Pier
Gloucester, MA 01930
(617) 281-3600

*Field Offices*
(NY, CT)
Milford Laboratory
Michael Ludwig, Area Supervisor
Rogers Avenue
Milford, CT 06460
(203) 783-4228

(MD, VA, PA, DE)
Oxford Laboratory
Edward W. Christoffers, Area
  Supervisor
Railroad Avenue
Oxford, MD 21654
(301) 226-5771

(NJ)
Sandy Hook Laboratory
Stanley W. Gorski, Area Supervisor
P.O. Box 428
Highlands, NJ 07732
(201) 342-8237

## SOUTHEAST REGION

(includes area from North Carolina to Mexico)

*Regional Offices*
Richard J. Hoogland, Asst. Regional
    Director
9450 Koger Blvd.
St. Petersburg, FL 33702
(813) 893-3503

*Field Offices*
(NC, SC, GA)
Pivers Island
Randall Cheek, Area Supervisor
P.O. Box 570
Beaufort, NC 28516
(919) 728-5090

(FL, AL, MS, VI, PR)
Edwin Keppner, Area Supervisor
3500 Dellwood Beach Rd.
Panama City, FL 32407
(904) 234-5061

(LA, TX)
Daniel Moore, Area Supervisor
4700 Avenue U
Galveston, TX 77550
(409) 766-3699

## SOUTHWEST REGION

(California and U.S. Pacific Islands)

*Regional Office*
James J. Slawson, Branch Chief
300 South Ferry Street
Terminal Island, CA 90731
(213) 548-2518

*Field Offices*
(Northern California)
James R. Bybee, Area Supervisor
3150 Paradis Drive
Tiburon, CA 94920
(415) 435-3149

(HI and West Pacific)
John J. Naughton, Area Supervisor
2570 Dole St.
P.O. Box 3830
Honolulu, HI 96812
(808) 955-8831

## NORTHWEST REGION

(Oregon, Washington, Idaho)

*Portland Office*
(OR, ID)
Dale Evans, Division Chief
Merrit E. Tuttle, Branch Chief
847 N.E. 19th Avenue, #350
Portland, OR 97232-2279
(503) 230-5400

*Field Office*
(Washington)
Alan B. Groves, Area Supervisor
7600 Sand Point Way, NE
BIN: C15700
Seattle, WA 98115
(206) 526-6172

## ALASKA REGION

(Southern Alaska)

*Regional Office*
Theodore F. Meyers, Division Chief
P.O. Box 1668
Juneau, AK 99802
(907) 586-7235

*Anchorage Field Office*
(Northern Alaska)
Ronald J. Morris, Area Supervisor
Federal Bldg. & U.S. Court House
701 C St., Box 43
Anchorage, AK 99513
(907) 271-5006

# HOW TO APPLY FOR A 404 PERMIT

A 404 permit is required for the disposal of dredged or fill material in the "waters of the United States," a broad term that applies to most of the nation's lakes, rivers, streams, wetlands, and coastal waters. Certain activities are exempt and do not need a Corps permit; other activities can proceed without an individual 404 permit if they are covered by a regional or nationwide permit and if certain conditions are followed. Contact the regulatory branch of the Corps district office in your area for specific information about location, exemptions, and regional and nationwide general permits.

The basic criteria used by the Corps in reviewing 404 permit applications and the involvement of the resource agencies is discussed in the chapter on wetlands. The basic steps in applying for a 404 permit are as follows:

(1) *Preapplication consultation.* This is an optional step involving one or more meetings between the district engineer's staff and the permit applicant and usually is related to applications for major activities that require the preparation of detailed environmental documents.

(2) *Submission of application.* Obtain appropriate forms from the district regulatory office. Most districts use ENG Form 4345, but some may use slightly modified forms for joint processing with a state agency. You will be asked to include, among other information, a complete description of the proposed activity and drawings, sketches, plans, location, purpose and in-

tended use, work schedule, and names and addresses of adjoining property owners.

(3) *Permit Review.* When the application is received, it is assigned an identification number to be referred to in all inquiries about your application. The Corps issues public notice of the application within 15 days of receiving it and provides for a 15- to 30-day comment period, depending upon the nature of the activity. The proposal is reviewed by the Corps, the public, special-interest groups, and local, state, and federal agencies. Those interested in reviewing permit applications for their area should be sure to get on the mailing list of the local Corps district regulatory office. The review period may be extended if the applicant fails to submit information or if the requirements of other laws make an extension necessary.

(4) *Public hearing.* Public hearings may be held to acquire information and give the public the opportunity to present views and opinions. Any person may request in writing during the comment period that a hearing be held and must give specific reasons as to the need for a hearing. Hearings are held at the discretion of the district engineer. Very few applications involve a public hearing.

(5) *Permit decision.* The district engineer determines whether the permit complies with the 404(b)(1) guidelines. If he determines it does, he determines whether the project is in the public interest. 404 regulations require the Corps to deny a permit if it does not comply with the 404(b)(1) guidelines, but if it does comply, the permit is to be issued unless it would not be in the public interest to do so. The permit applicant is notified of the permit decision.

For more information, contact the Corps district office in your area or write for the following pamphlet: U.S. Army Corps of Engineers Regulatory Program: Applicant Information, EP 1145-2-1, May 1985.

# Appendix F

# Federal Offices Involved in the Management of Marine Fisheries and the Conservation of Marine Mammals

## DEPARTMENT OF COMMERCE

Department of Commerce
National Oceanic and Atmospheric Administration
National Marine Fisheries Service
Page Building 2
3300 Whitehaven St., NW
Washington, D.C. 20235

Assistant Administrator for Fisheries
Room 400, Page Building 2
(202) 634-7283

Chief, Management and Budget Staff
Room 350, Page Building 2
(202) 634-7405

Chief, Constituent Affairs Staff
Room 430D, Page Building 2
(202) 634-7220

Chief, Policy and Planning Staff
Room 358, Page Building 2
(202) 634-7430

Deputy Assistant Administrator for Fisheries Resource Management
Room 428, Page Building 2
(202) 634-7514

Director, Office of Fisheries Management
Room 418, Page Building 2
(202) 634-7218

Chief, Fishery Management Operations Division
Room 420, Page Building 2
(202) 634-7449

Chief, Fees, Permits & Regulations Division
Room 428, Page Building 2
(202) 634-7432

Director, Office of Industry Services
Room 300, Page Building 2
(202) 634-7261

Chief, Industry Development Division
Room 328A, Page Building 2
(202) 634-7451

Chief, Financial Services Division
Room 312, Page Building 2
(202) 634-4697

Director, Office of International Fisheries
Room 240, Page Building 2
(202) 634-7267

Chief, International Organization and Agreements Division
Room 240, Page Building 2
(202) 634-7357

Chief, International Fisheries Development and Services Division
Room 220, Page Building 2
(202) 634-7263

Director, Office of Protected Species and Habitat Conservation
Room 168, Page Building 2
(202) 634-7461

Chief, Protected Species Division
Room 172, Page Building 2
(202) 634-7529

Chief, Permits & Documentation Branch
Room 172, Page Building 2
(202) 634-7529

Chief, Protected Species Management Branch
Room 168, Page Building 2
(202) 634-7471

Chief, Habitat Conservation Division
Room 168, Page Building 2
(202) 634-7490

Director, Office of Enforcement
Room 280, Page Building 1
(202) 634-7265

## REGIONAL OFFICES

Director, Northeast Region (ME, NH, MA, CT, RI, NY, NJ, DE, MA, VA,
WV, PA, VT, OH, IN, IL, MI, WI, MN)
National Marine Fisheries Service
14 Elm Street, Federal Building
Gloucester, MA 01930
(617) 281-3600

Director, Southeast Region (NC, SC, GA, FL, AL, MS, LA, TX, OK, NE,
NM, KS, IA, MO, AR, TN, KY)
National Marine Fisheries Service
9450 Koger Boulevard
St. Petersburg, FL 33702
(813) 893-3141

Director, Northwest Region (OR, WA, ID, MT, ND, SD, CO, WY, UT)
National Marine Fisheries Service
7600 Sand Point Way, NE.
BIN C15700
Seattle, WA 98115-0070
(206) 527-6150

Director, Southwest Region (CA, NV, AZ, HI)
National Marine Fisheries Service
300 S. Ferry Street
Terminal Island, CA 90731
(213) 548-2575

Director, Alaska Region
National Marine Fisheries Service
P.O. Box 1668
Juneau, AK 99802
(907) 586-7221

# DEPARTMENT OF THE INTERIOR

## U.S. Fish and Wildlife Service

Chief, Office of Endangered Species
U.S. Fish and Wildlife Service
18th & C Streets, NW
Washington, D.C. 20240
(703) 235-2771

Chief, Division of Wildlife
  Management
U.S. Fish and Wildlife Service
18th & C Streets, NW
Washington, D.C. 20240
(703) 632-7463

## Regional and Field Offices

Director, Alaska Region
U.S. Fish and Wildlife Service
1011 E. Tudor Road
Anchorage, AK 99503
(907) 786-3542

Manatee Coordinator
Endangered Species Field Station
2747 Art Museum Drive
Jacksonville, FL 32207
(904) 791-2580

Sea Otter Coordinator
Endangered Species Field Station
2800 Cottage Way, Room E-2727
Sacramento, CA 95825
(916) 484-4731

## Marine Mammal Commission

1625 Eye Street, NW
Washington, D.C. 20006
(202) 653-6237

# Appendix G

# Budget Information Contacts on Federal Fish and Wildlife Programs

| Title | Name | Phone |
|---|---|---|
| *Army Corps of Engineers (Wetlands 1404 Program)* | | |
| Chief, Director of Civil Works | Don B. Cluff | (202) 272–0191 |
| *Bureau of Land Management* | | |
| Chief, Office of Budget | Roger L. Hildeberdel | (202) 343–8571 |
| Budget Analyst, Division of Wildlife | Nancy F. Green | (202) 653–9202 |
| *Environmental Protection Agency (Wetlands/404 Program)* | | |
| Director, Budget Office | David P. Ryan | (202) 475–8340 |
| Budget Analyst, 404 Program | James F. Horn | (202) 382–4170 |
| *Fish and Wildlife Service* | | |
| Assistant Director, Planning and Budget | Edwin A. Verburg | (202) 343–4329 |
| Chief, Division of Program Analysis | James C. Leupold | (202) 343–2444 |
| *Forest Service* | | |
| Director, Program Development and Budget | John A. Leasure | (202) 447–6987 |
| Leader, Program, Planning, and Development Team | John Rich | (202) 447–6987 |
| *Marine Mammal Commission* | | |
| Executive Director | John R. Twiss, Jr. | (202) 653–6237 |
| *National Marine Fisheries Service* | | |
| Budget Analyst, Office of Policy and Planning | Donald A. Wickham | (202) 634–7430 |
| *National Park Service* | | |
| Chief, Budget Division | C. Bruce Sheaffer | (202) 343–4566 |
| Supervisory Budget Analyst | Rory D. Westberg | (202) 343–4566 |

# Appendix H

# Congressional Contacts and Addresses

## Bill Status

To determine the status of legislation in the House or Senate, call the Bill Status Office at (202) 225-1772

## Copies of Legislation and Reports

To obtain copies of bills, committee reports, or public laws, write the appropriate congressional document office. All requests should list documents in numerical order, lowest to highest, and must include a self-addressed mailing label.

> House Document Room (202) 225-3456
> H-226 Capitol
> Washington, D.C. 20515
> (You may obtain up to one copy of six different documents)
>
> \* \* \* \*
>
> Senate Document Room (202) 224-7860
> B04, Hart Building
> Washington, D.C. 20510
> (You may obtain up to three copies of six different documents)

# Congressional Committees

To obtain detailed information about pending wildlife legislation or congressional oversight activity contact the appropriate House or Senate Committee.

## HOUSE OF REPRESENTATIVES

*Committee on Agriculture,* Rm. 1301, Longworth House
Office Bldg., Washington, D.C. 20515 (202, 225-2171)
Chairman: E (Kika) de la Garza (TX)
Consists of 41 Members: adulteration of seeds, insect pests, and protection of birds and animals in forest reserves; agriculture generally; agricultural and industrial chemistry; agricultural colleges and experiment stations; agricultural economics and research; agricultural education extension services; agricultural production and marketing and stabilization of prices of agricultural products; animal industry and diseases of animals; crop insurance and soil conservation; dairy industry; entomology and plant quarantine; extension of farm credit and farm security; forestry in general, and forest reserves other than those created from the public domain; human nutrition and home economics; inspection of livestock and meat products; plant industry, soils, and agricultural engineering; rural electrification; commodities exchanges and rural development.

Subcommittee on Forests, Family Farms, and Energy Majority Staff: Charlie R. Rawls (202) 225-9381

*Committee on Appropriations,* Rm H-218, Capitol Bldg.,
Washington, D.C. 20515 (202, 225-2771)
Chairman: Jamie L. Whitten (MS)
Consists of 57 Members: appropriation of the revenue for the support of the government, recissions of appropriations contained in appropriation acts, and transfers of unexpended balances.

Subcommittee for Interior Appropriations (Interior and Forest Service) Majority Staff: D. Neal Sigmon (202) 225-3081
Minority Staff: Barbara Wainman (202) 225-1882

Subcommittee for Commerce, Justice, State and Judiciary appropriations (National Marine Fisheries Service) Majority Staff: John G. Shank (202) 224-7244

*Committee on Interior and Insular Affairs,* Rm. 1324, Longworth
House Office Bldg., Washington, D.C. 20515 (202, 225-2761)
Chairman: Morris K. Udall (AZ)
Consists of 42 Members: forest reserves and national parks created from the public domain; forfeiture of land grant and alien ownership, including alien ownership of mineral lands; geological survey; interstate compacts relating to

apportionment of waters for irrigation purposes; irrigation and reclamation, including water supply for reclamation projects, and easements of public lands for irrigation projects, and acquisition of private lands when necessary to complete irrigation projects; measures relation to the care and management of Indians, including the care and allotment of Indian lands and general and special measures relating to claims which are paid out of Indian funds; measures relating generally to the insular possessions of the U.S., except matters affecting their revenue and appropriations; military parks and battlefields; national cemeteries administered by the secretary of the Interior, and parks within the District of Columbia; mineral land laws and claims and entries thereunder; mineral resources of the public lands; mining interests generally; mining schools and experimental stations; petroleum conservation on the public lands and conservation of the radium supply in the U.S.; preservation of prehistoric ruins and objects of interest on the public domain; public lands generally, including entry, easements, and grazing thereon; relations of the U.S. with the Indians and the Indian tribes; regulation of the domestic nuclear energy industry, including regulation of research and development reactors and nuclear regulatory research. Also special oversight functions with respect to all programs affecting Indians and non-military nuclear energy and research and development including the disposal of nuclear waste.

Subcommittee on Public Lands
Majority Staff: Russ Shay (202) 226-7735
                Stanly Sloss (202) 226-7730

Subcommittee on National Parks and Recreation
Majority Staff: Dale Crane (202) 226-7736

*Committee on Merchant Marine and Fisheries*, Rm. 1334, Longworth House Office Bldg., Washington, D.C. 20515 (202, 225-4047)
Chairman: Walter B. Jones (NC)
Consists of 42 Members: merchant marine generally; oceanography and marine affairs, including coastal zone management; Coast Guard, including lifesaving service, lighthouses, lightships, and ocean derelicts; fisheries and wildlife, including research, restoration, refuges, and conservation; measures relating to the regulation of common carriers by water (except matters subject to the jurisdiction of the Interstate Commerce Commission) and to the inspection of merchant marine vessels, lights and signals, lifesaving equipment, and fire protection on such vessels; Merchant Marine officers and seamen; navigation and the laws relating thereto, including pilotage, Panama Canal and the maintenance and operation of the Panama Canal consistent with the treaty with Panama and the implementation legislation enacted pursuant to such treaty; and interoceanic canals generally; primary oversight jurisdiction over the Outer Continental Shelf Lands Act and legislative jurisdiction over any proposed amendments. Registering and licensing of vessels and small boats;

rules and international arrangements to prevent collisions at sea; United States Coast Guard and Merchant Marine Academies, and State Maritime Academies; international fishing agreements.

Majority Staff: John Dentler (Fisheries) (202) 226-3547
Full Committee: Katherine Skinner (Wildlife) (202) 226-3547

Subcommittee on Fisheries, Wildlife Conservation and the Environment

Majority Staff: Jeffery Curtis (Wildlife)  (202) 226-3522
Paul Carothers  (202) 226-3522
Glen Delaney (Fisheries)  (202) 226-3522
Tim Smith  (202) 226-3522

Minority Staff: Tom Melius (Wildlife)  (202) 226-3520
Jeff Kaelin (Fisheries)  (202) 226-3520

## SENATE

*Committee on Agriculture, Nutrition and Forestry,* Rm 328-A, Russell Bldg., Washington, D.C. 20510 (202, 224-2035)
Chairman: Jesse Helms (NC)
Ranking Minority Member: Edward Zorinsky (NE)
Concerned with Agriculture and agricultural commodities; inspection of livestock, meat and agricultural products; animal industry and diseases of animals; pests and pesticides; agricultural extension services and experiment station; forestry, forest reserves and wilderness areas other than those created from the public domain; agricultural economics and research; human nutrition; home economics; extension of farm credit and farm security; rural development, rural electrification and watersheds; agricultural production and marketing and stabilization of prices of agricultural products; crop insurance and soil conservation; school nutrition programs; food stamp programs; food from fresh waters; plant industry, soils, and agricultural engineering; the committee also studies and reviews, on a comprehensive basis, matters relating to food, nutrition and hunger, both in the U.S. and in foreign countries, and rural affairs and reports on them from time to time.

Majority Staff: Charles M. Ollerman  (202) 224-6901

*Committee on Appropriations,* S-128, The Capitol, Washington, D.C. 20510 (202, 224-3471)
Chairman: Mark O. Hatfield (OR)
Concerned with all proposed legislation, messages, petitions, memorials, and other matters relating to appropriation of the revenue for the support of the government.

Majority Staff: Donald Knowles (Interior/Forest Service)  (202) 224-7257
Minority Staff: Charles Estes  (202) 224-7214

*Committee on Commerce, Science and Transportation*, US Senate, SD-508, Washington, D.C. 20510 (202, 224-5115)
Chairman: John C. Danforth (MO)
Concerned with interstate commerce; transportation; regulation of interstate common carriers, including railroads, buses, trucks, vessels, pipelines and civil aviation; merchant marine and navigation; marine and ocean navigation, safety and transportation, including navigational aspects of deepwater ports; Coast Guard; inland waterways, except construction; communications; regulation of consumer products and services, except for credit, financial services and housing; the Panama Canal, except for maintenance, operation, administration, sanitation and government, and interoceanic canals generally; standards and measurements; highway safety; science, engineering and technology research and development and policy; nonmilitary aeronautical and space sciences; transportation and commerce aspects of Outer Continental Shelf lands; marine fisheries; coastal zone management; oceans, weather and atmospheric activities; sports.

National Ocean Policy Study
Majority Staff: Bob Eisenbud    (202) 224-8170
Minority Staff: J. Michael Nussman    (202) 224-4912

*Committee on Energy and Natural Resources*, Rm. SD-358, Dirksen Bldg., Washington, D.C. 20510 (202, 224-4971)
Chairman: James A. McClure (ID)
Jurisdiction: Coal production, distribution utilization; energy policy, regulation, conservation, and research; hydroelectric power; irrigation and reclamation; national parks; wilderness areas; historical sites; public lands and forest; oil and gas production and distribution; mining, mineral lands, mining claims; solar energy systems; extraction of minerals from oceans and Outer Continental Shelf lands.

Subcommittee Public Lands, Reserved Water and Resource Conservation.
Majority Staff: Tony Bevinetto    (202) 224-0613
Minority Staff: Tom Williams    (202) 224-7145

*Committee on Environmental and Public Works*, Rm. SD-410, Dirksen Bldg., Washington, D.C. 20510 (202, 224-6176)
Chairman: Robert T. Stafford (VT)
Jurisdiction: All proposed legislation, messages, petitions, memorials, and other matters relating to the following subjects: environmental policy; environmental research and development; ocean dumping; fisheries and wildlife; environmental aspects of Outer Continental Shelf lands; solid waste disposal and recycling; environmental effects of toxic substances, other than pesticides; water resources; flood control and improvements of rivers and harbors, including environmental aspects of deepwater ports; public works, bridges, and dams; water pollution; air pollution; noise pollution; nonmilitary environ-

mental regulation and control of nuclear energy; regional economic development; construction and maintenance of highways; public buildings and improved grounds of the United States generally, including federal buildings in the District of Columbia. The committee also studies and reviews, on a comprehensive basis, matters relating to environmental protection and resource utilization and conservation, and report on them from time to time.

Subcommittee on Environmental Pollution (Wildlife)
Majority Staff: Robert Davison   (202) 224-6691
Minority Staff: Helen Kalbaugh   (202) 224-2331

# Appendix I

# Major Population Objectives, Status and Trends of Migratory Bird Species of Special Management Emphasis[a]

| Species or Population | Major Objective(s) | Status and Trends |
|---|---|---|
| 1. Black Duck[b] | Mid-winter index of 450,000. | Mid-winter index presently under 280,000. Population has declined slowly but rather steadily for over 20 years. |
| Brant: | | |
| 2. Atlantic Population | Mid-winter index of at least 100,000. | In the early 1980s, the mid-winter index has ranged from 97,000 to 124,000 birds. Wide annual variation in population sizes occur with mid-winter indices of 200,000 in the 1950s and 1960s, and a low of 42,000 in 1972-73. |

[a]Prepared by MBMO from NSSE plans and available trend information
[b]Below management objective

| Species or Population | Major Objective(s) | Status and Trends |
|---|---|---|
| 3. Pacific Population | Mid-winter index of 185,000. brant (58,000 in USA). | Mid-winter indices have ranged from 46,000 in 1959 to more than 190,000 in the early 1980s. The overall population appears stable, but breeding and wintering segments are changing in number. Some major nesting colonies in Alaska are undergoing serious declines. |
| Canada Goose: | | |
| 4. Atlantic Flyway Population[a] | Mid-winter index of 850,000 north of Virginia-North Carolina line. By 1990, 200,000 birds south of Maryland during late December. | Index averaged approximately 830,000 during the early 1980s. The population has been increasing since the 1950s, with a progressively smaller percentage wintering in southern areas. |
| 5. Tennessee Valley Population[b] | Mid-winter objective is 150,000. | The 1969-83 average index is 126,000. The population is stable to slowly increasing with a concern to keep a high percentage of the population wintering in southern areas. |
| 6. Mississippi Valley Population[b] | Mid-winter index of 500,000 birds by 1988. | Current index is 400,000 or so geese. Population was at a peak in the late 1970s (450,000+). Concern to increase wintering in southern areas. |
| 7. Great Plains Population[b] | Breeding index in U.S. of 15,000 breeding pairs by the year 1990. | Current estimate is 7,500 breeding pairs. |
| 8. Eastern Prairie Population | Short-term objective is a mid-winter index of 200,000± 10%; long-term is 300,000 with at least 100,000 of these south of Missouri. | Population is at or slightly below objective. Overall stable population with attempts being made to increase numbers in southern wintering areas. |
| 9. Western Prairie Population | Fall index of at least 200,000. | Population apparently stable averaging over 200,000 in the early 1980s. A large portion of the population winters north of historically used sites. |

[a]Prepared by MBMO from NSSE plans and available trend information
[b]Below management objective

| Species or Population | Major Objective(s) | Status and Trends |
|---|---|---|
| 10. Tall Grass Prairie Population | Mid-December index of 225,000 | Population slowly increasing, averaging above management objective in early 1980s. |
| 11. Short Grass Prairie Population | Breeding population index of at least 150,000 geese as measured by the mid-winter index. | Population relatively stable with mid-winter counts in the early 1980s ranging from 150,000 to almost 200,000 geese. |
| 12. Hi-Line Population | Attain a mid-winter index of 80,000 birds by 1990, with 8,000 of these in New Mexico. | Population is increasing, but still below the 1990 objective. Compared to historic distribution, a higher percentage of the population wintering in northern areas (Colorado vs. New Mexico). |
| 13. Rocky Mountain Population | Maintain mid-winter index above 50,000. | In the early 1980s indices above 60,000 and still increasing. A progressively larger percentage of the population winters in northern areas. |
| 14. Pacific Population | Maintain the estimated breeding index of at least 12,400 pairs (10,000 in USA) | In the early 1980s, the index was 12,380. Overall, the population is stable or slightly increasing. |
| 15. Pacific Flyway Population (Lessers and Taverner's) | Mid-winter index of between 100,000 to 150,000 geese in eastern Oregon and eastern Washington. | Population relatively stable but may be increasing slightly in distribution and numbers. |
| 16. Vancouver | Maintain fall population of 90,000 birds (approximate figure, not based on survey data). | Population apparently is stable. |
| 17. Dusky[b] | Maintain mid-winter index of 20,000. | Mid-winter index averaged 17,000 in early 1980s (down from 20,000 in early 1970s), and has declined to about 7,500 in 1985. |
| 18. Cackling[b] | Fall index of 250,000. | Fall counts in Klamath Basin of California currently less than 30,000. Steady and long-term decline from peak counts of almost 400,000 in the mid-1950s. |

[a]Prepared by MBMO from NSSE plans and available trend information
[b]Below management objective

| Species or Population | Major Objective(s) | Status and Trends |
|---|---|---|
| Canvasback Duck: | | |
| 19. Eastern Population[b] | Spring breeding index of 450,000 birds in principal production areas. | In the early 1980s, the average index was slightly below 400,000, compared to the 1963–82 mean of 418,000. |
| 20. Western Population | Spring breeding index of 175,000 ducks (90,000 nesting in United States). | In the early 1980s, the average index was at the objective level, with the 1963-82 mean at 163,000. |
| 21. Mallard[b] | Spring breeding index of 10.9 million ducks (4.8 million in United States). | Index is currently below 6 million, with long-term mean index of approximately 8 million. |
| 22. Pintail[b] | Spring breeding index of 6.9 million birds (3 million in United States). | Current index is below 4 million birds, compared to a long-term (1962–83 mean of 5.6 million. |
| 23. Redhead[b] | Spring breeding index of 875,000 birds. | Current index is slightly below management objective. Population was at a low point in the early 1960s. |
| 24. Ring-necked[b] | Maintain a breeding population index of at least 666,500 in surveyed areas. | Population slightly below objective level and stable. |
| Snow goose: | | |
| 25. Atlantic Flyway Population (Greater) | Spring population (pre-breeding) of at least 120,000 and not more than 180,000. | Population has increased from a few thousand in the early 1900s to more than 200,000 in recent falls. |
| 26. Mid-Continent Population (lesser) | Breeding population ranging from 800,000 to 1.2 million birds. | Stable population, with some nesting colonies at or above habitat carrying capacity. |
| 27. Western Central Flyway Population (Lesser and Ross) | Mid-December index in United States of 54,200 birds. | Population is at management objective and increasing rapidly. |
| 28. Western Canadian Arctic Population (Lesser) | Breeding population index of 200,000 birds. | No annual data on breeding population, but estimates made during the past 20 years range from 100,000 to 200,000 nesting birds. |
| 29. Wrangel Island Population (Lesser)[b] | Breeding population of at least 120,000 geese. | Currently below management objective and stable to slowly decreasing, but fluctuates widely because of weather related factors affecting production. |

[a]Prepared by MBMO from NSSE plans and available trend information
[b]Below management objective

1025

| Species or Population | Major Objective(s) | Status and Trends |
|---|---|---|
| **Trumpeter Swan:** | | |
| 30. Pacific Coast Population | Late summer index of 6,000 birds. | Current population is slightly above objective, and population is increasing. |
| 31. Interior Population[b] | Achieve 30 breeding pairs by 2000 at Hennepin, Minnesota, maintain 50 breeding pairs in Lacreek population and winter 400 swans at Lacreek Northwest Region by 1990. | Restoration effort affords potential for achieving objective. |
| 32. Rocky Mountain Population | Winter population of at least 1,100 swans (Idaho, Montana, Wyoming). | Population is currently at management objective and stable. However, poor survival of United States cygnets may be related to winter habitat being used at carrying capacity. |
| **Tundra Swan:** | | |
| 33. Eastern Population | Mid-winter index of 60,000 to 80,000 birds. | In the early 1980s the index averaged more than 80,000. Population is slowly increasing. |
| 34. Western Population | Mid-winter index of at least 38,000 swans. | Population is currently well above the management objective and increasing. |
| **White-Fronted Goose:** | | |
| 35: Tule[b] | Fall flights of 5,000 or more. | In the early 1980s, the post-season population was estimated to be more than 4,000 birds. This small population is increasing slowly. |
| 36. Eastern Midcontinent Population | Mid-December index of 50,000 to 80,000 birds. | In the early 1980s, the index averaged 65,000, compared to less than 45,000 in the early 1970s. |
| 37. Western Midcontinent Population | March index of 200,000 to 300,000 birds. | In recent years, the index is approaching the 300,000 level compared to a level of under 30,000 in the late 1950s. |
| 38. Pacific Flyway Population | Fall index of 300,000 birds. | Current counts in Klamath Basin under 100,000 compared to peak indices of more than 400,000 in the late 1950s. |

[a]Prepared by MBMO from NSSE plans and available trend information
[b]Below management objective

| Species or Population | Major Objective(s) | Status and Trends |
|---|---|---|
| 39. Wood Duck | Maintain a sufficient breeding population (3.2 million by indirect estimate) to sustain an annual take of 1.3 million in the U.S. and 123,000 in Canada. | Population at objective level and apparently stable. |
| 40. Interior Least Tern Population[c] | Maintain breeding population of 1,500 to 2,000 birds (periodic rangewide census) | In 1975, approximately 1,250 nesting birds were counted. Trend is unknown as too few counts have been conducted. |
| 41. Mourning Dove[b] | Achieve spring indices (average doves heard per route) in the Management Units as follows: Eastern, 17.2; Central, 25.6; Western; 12.7. | Populations below management objectives. Downward trends have been documented in the Eastern and Western units, and in the Central Unit for the past five years. |
| 42. Northern Spotted Owl | Maintain breeding population of at least 1,200 pairs in Washington, Oregon, and California. (periodic rangewide census; draft objective.) | Current estimates indicate 3,000 pairs. Because habitat is being lost, trend probably is downward. |
| 43. Osprey | Maintain at least 7,400 breeding pairs within the contiguous United States, and 200 pairs in Alaska. | At or near management objective. Population is stable to slightly increasing in historic range. |
| 44. Piping Plover[b] | Maintain or increase current 500+ breeding pairs on Atlantic Coast.<br><br>Maintain or increase current 600+ breeding pairs in Great Plains States.<br>Restore Great Lakes States breeding pairs to 50 by 1995. | Species much reduced in Northeast coastal areas and Great Lakes because of loss of undisturbed beach nesting habitat. |
| 45. Roseate Tern[b] | Restore breeding populations in the northeastern United States to 4,500 pairs by 1990, including at least three colonies at formerly occupied sites. Restore nesting colonies at Dry Tortugas and Florida Keys to at least 200 pairs by 1990. Maintain a nesting population of 1,500 to 1,800 pairs in Eastern Puerto Rico and the Virgin Islands. | Species underwent serious population decline in coastal New England during the past half century. Loss of undisturbed beach nesting habitat and competition/ predation by gulls are principal factors. |

[a]Prepared by MBMO from NSSE plans and available trend information
[b]Below management objective

| Species or Population | Major Objective(s) | Status and Trends |
|---|---|---|
| Sandhill Crane: | | |
| 46. Easter Population (Greater) | Fall index of at least 14,700. | Currently exceeds 16,000. [c]Eastern Population below management level |
| 47. Midcontinent Population[b] (Lesser, Canadian, Greater) | March index of at least 480,000, and not more than 590,000. | In the early 1980s, the population was slightly under the management objective. The population has increased steadily from under 200,000 during the mid-1970s (spring migration levels). |
| 48. Rocky Mountain Population (Greater) | Maintain spring index of between 12,000 and 16,000 cranes (San Luis Valley, CO) | Population is at objective level and slowly increasing. |
| 49. Lower Colorado Population (Greater)[b] | Winter index of 2,600 by the year 2000. | In 1979, winter index was approximately 2,000. The population is relatively stable. |
| 50. Pacific Flyway Population (Lesser) | Mid-winter index of 20,000 to 25,000. | At objective level and population is stable. |
| 51. Central Valley Population (Greater)[b] | Fall index of a minimum of 4,000. | Presently at 3,400 cranes. Overall, population is stable. |
| 52. White-winged Dove[b] | Increase spring index in Arizona to 40 doves/route; in California and Nevada maintain nesting at 1984 level; in Texas 800,000 nesting doves by 1997; in Florida and Puerto Rico increase nesting; in Mexico, fall population of 12 million to 16 million birds in Tamaulipas. | Arizona and Texas whitewings are down and decreasing. California and Nevada populations probably are stable. In Florida this introduced species is increasing slowly. Mexican population of whitewings is relatively stable. |
| 53. Woodcock[c] | Spring indices of 2.25 and 3.50 males per route in the Eastern and Central Woodcock Regions (Atlantic and Mississippi Flyways), respectively. | Eastern population below objective level and decreasing. Western population is decreasing but currently is at objective level. |
| 54. Golden Eagle, Western Population | Plan under preparation | |

[a]Prepared by MBMO from NSSE plans and available trend information
[b]Below management objective

1028

# Appendix J

# The Development of Annual Waterfowl Hunting Regulations*

Annual regulations development begins with the gathering of population information. This information is developed and analyzed prior to initiation of an extensive administrative process that finalizes the regulations for an ensuing hunting season.

## Biological Surveys

Experimental surveys of the waterfowl breeding grounds were initiated in 1947 to develop statistically sound ways of measuring annual changes in breeding populations and production. The surveys continued experimentally through 1950. In 1951 the breeding-ground surveys became an operational waterfowl-management tool. The continental breeding range has been divided into units of a size that can be conveniently surveyed by one aerial crew in a short period. The southern half of Alberta is an example. Nine of these units cover all of the major breeding grounds there. These survey units are further divided into strata that are areas with similar characteristics of habitat and waterfowl density. Within these strata, transects (census lines) are established in an east-west direction, from seven to 20 miles apart on the prairies, where the duck population is greatest, to as much as 60 miles apart in northern areas where the breeding duck population is less dense. Nearly 33,000 miles of transects are

* Source: Office of Migratory Bird Management, FWS.

covered during each of two surveys, in May and in July. Observations of ducks, water areas, broods, etc., on these transects are recorded separately on 18-mile segments along the census lines to facilitate analysis of data. The crew, consisting of a pilot-biologist and an observer, flies the same straight-line transects every year during both the May and July surveys. The aircraft is flown at an altitude of 100–150 feet, depending upon terrain. The pilot and observer count birds on each side of the plane, in a strip 220 yards wide in the May survey and 110 yards wide in July, recording their observations on transistorized dictating machines. Thus, the average number of ducks per square mile can be calculated and then expanded to the total number present in each survey stratum.

*Breeding Population Survey* This survey begins early in May and ends by mid-June. The purpose is to determine the number of potential breeding birds for the various species and the ratio of single drakes to pairs, which gives an index to nesting progress. The number of water areas present in May throughout the prairie pothole country of southern Canada, Montana, the Dakotas, and western Minnesota also is determined from the early survey. Aerial counts of ducks are corrected with "visibility rates" derived from sample transects censused from both the air and on the ground. This procedure determines the proportion of ducks present but not seen by the aerial survey crew. Some species are less visible and harder to identify from the air than others. Scaup and canvasback, for instance, are at the top of the visibility scale, whereas green-winged teal are the most difficult to see. Waterfowl breeding populations in several states are determined either from aerial surveys or ground counts made by state personnel. These population estimates are added to service estimates to determine the size of breeding populations of ten species of ducks on a continental basis.

*Production Survey* This survey is conducted during July, when both broods and adult birds are still on nesting territory and can be counted. The number of adults gives an indication of how much nesting is still in progress. Data on age class and number of young per brood are recorded to determine the progress and success of the season. The number of water areas remaining in July compared with the number present in May gives an index of the relative stability or deterioration of the habitat.

Particularly with mallards, data on the size of the breeding population, the number of broods observed, and the number of water areas in May and in July can be used to predict production prospects and the size of the fall flight for a given year. These data are analyzed statistically in a formula that yields an estimate of the number of mallard young that will be produced.

Because breeding-ground surveys for geese, wood ducks, and black ducks, which breed in remote areas or heavily forested habitat, are too expensive or have not yet been perfected, fall flights for these species must be estimated using results from winter, banding, and hunter-kill surveys, plus limited observations on breeding grounds.

Additional information bearing on production and probable fall flights is obtained from Canadian Wildlife Service and U.S. Fish and Wildlife Service personnel at key points throughout the duck and goose breeding areas, and from Ducks Unlimited and other private and state conservation agencies that conduct various types of waterfowl surveys. All of this information is used in developing a fall-flight forecast.

*Harvest Survey*   The results of a mail questionnaire survey of waterfowl hunters, a duck-wing and goose-tail collection survey, and banding of waterfowl provide an "after-the-fact" check of aerial survey data. By mid-July of each year, the responses to a questionnaire mailed to hunters, the study of duck wings sent in by cooperating hunters, and the analysis of recoveries of ducks banded the previous summer have been completed. This work provides information on the numbers of ducks bagged by hunters; the species, age and sex of the birds killed; and the timing and distribution of harvests. Band-recovery data gives a measure of the vulnerability to hunting of young versus old ducks, allowing the young:adult ratio in the previous fall population to be determined. The young:adult ratio reflects the production of the previous summer and allows the accuracy of the prediction of production made from the May and July aerial surveys to be checked. In this manner the accuracy of the fall-flight forecasts can be refined from year to year.

## Administrative Actions

The development of annual regulations is based on population data, but the final regulations are a result of a series of exchanges of information that occur throughout the year. For the purpose of this discussion, a calendar year will be used and the discussion will address the process in a general manner, recognizing that there are a number of other meetings that occur both within the service, the states, and in private groups that have an input into the development of waterfowl hunting regulations.

## January

The service provides the states with an activities schedule for development of migratory-game-bird regulations for the coming year. Also, during January the Service Regulations Committee meets to consider proposed changes in basic hunting regulations and annual regulations relating to migratory game-bird seasons.

# February

Initial regulation proposals are prepared and reviewed by FWS, the Interior Department, and the Office of Management and Budget.

# March

A proposed rulemaking is published in the *Federal Register* inviting public comments on proposed migratory-game-bird hunting regulations. Separate comment periods are established for the proposed rules for Alaska, Puerto Rico and the Virgin Islands, and for early season regulations (beginning before October 1) and for late-season regulations. The published regulations proposals sent to the states and flyway councils in early March are reviewed at the flyway council meetings held in conjunction with the North American Wildlife and Natural Resources Conference.

# April

The service reviews all recommendations and comments received from flyway councils, states, private and professional groups, service units, and the public concerning the migratory-game-bird hunting regulations.

# May

Proposed amendments to the migratory-game-bird hunting regulations are developed and published in the *Federal Register* as a "Supplemental Proposal." Comment periods for the supplemental proposals are as stated in the March *Federal Register* document.

The service continues to receive comments as a result of publication in the *Federal Register* of proposed changes in migratory-game-bird regulations.

# June

The Service Regulations Committee meets to consider early season regulation proposals. These are then presented at a public hearing where further comment is obtained. The committee considers all comments and recommends to the director season lengths, bag limits, and shooting hours for migratory game birds in Alaska, Puerto Rico, and the Virgin Islands. The committee also considers proposals for other early season regulations (mourning and white-winged doves, band-tailed pigeons, woodcocks, snipe, rails, gallinules, September teal, experimental September seasons, and some goose and sandhill crane seasons). The comment period continues for both early and late season proposals. Two *Federal Register* documents—final frameworks for Alaska, Puerto Rico, and the Virgin Islands and proposed frameworks for early seasons—are prepared. Proposed early season frameworks are mailed to the states so they make tentative season decisions.

# July

In early July, the service publishes proposed early season frameworks and final frameworks for Alaska, Puerto Rico, and the Virgin Islands.

In late July, the service publishes the final early season frameworks in the *Federal Register*, establishing outside dates, bag limits, and shooting hours for early season migratory game birds. The comment period continues for late season proposals. Early season dates are received from the states.

The Service Regulations Committee and representatives of the flyway councils meet in Denver to review data on the status of waterfowl populations and the fall-flight forecasts that are developed from survey and census data collected up until the time of the meeting. Harvest and population objectives are developed.

Flyway councils meet and develop their recommendations on the late-season frameworks that are considered by the Service Regulations Committee.

# August

The Service Regulations Committee meets on or about August 1 to develop regulations recommendations for consideration by the director. Consultants from the flyway councils meet with the committee to provide technical information pertinent to these recommendations, based on survey and other information collected by state wildlife agencies. The recommendations are presented at a public hearing in Washington D.C. the next day.

Comments received at the public hearing are reviewed and considered by the Service Regulations Committee immediately after the public hearing. The committee forwards its final recommendations to the director for consideration. Upon his approval, proposed late-season frameworks are prepared, sent immediately to the states, and published in the *Federal Register* in early August. A 10-day comment period is provided.

# September

After considering any further public comments on the proposed regulations, final late-season regulations are published in the *Federal Register* in early September.

States select seasons, bag limits, and other regulatory provisions within the frameworks established for each flyway. The selections are transmitted to the Fish and Wildlife Service for publication in the *Federal Register* in late September. The states publish these regulations in their hunting-regulation leaflets. This is the final step in the regulations process.

# Appendix K

# Permit Requirements for Federally Protected Fish and Wildlife Species

For General Permit Information Contact:

Federal Wildlife Permit Office    or    Office of Protected Species
Fish and Wildlife Service                   National Marine Fisheries Service
U.S. Department of the Interior        Department of Commerce
Washington, D.C. 20240             Washington, D.C. 20235
(703) 235–1903                  (202) 634–7529

## Marine Mammals

All species of marine mammals are protected under the Marine Mammal Protection Act, and some also are protected under the U.S. Endangered Species Act and the Convention on International Trade in Endangered Species. These animals include whales, dolphins, porpoises, seals, sea lions, polar bears, sea otters, dugongs, and manatees.

1034

## The Marine Mammal Protection Act

The U.S. Fish and Wildlife Service has jurisdiction over the following marine mammals under the Marine Mammal Protection Act and the Endangered Species Act:

| Species | Common name | Marine Mammal Protection Act | Endangered Species Act |
|---|---|---|---|
| Ursus maritumus | polar bear | YES | Not Listed |
| Enhydra Lutris | sea otter | YES | Threatened* |
| Odobenus rosmarus | walrus | YES | Not Listed |
| Dugong dugon | dugong | YES | Endangered |
| Trichechus manatus | West Indian manatee | YES | Endangered |
| Trichechus inunguis | Amazonian manatee | YES | Endangered |
| Trichechus senegalensis | West African | YES | Threatened |
| Lutra felina | marine otter | YES | Endangered |

*southern population (California) only

The National Marine Fisheries Service has jurisdiction of all other marine mammals under these laws.

In general, it is prohibited under the Marine Mammal Protection Act to (1) TAKE marine mammals; (2) IMPORT marine mammals; and (3) POSSESS, TRANSPORT, SELL OR OFFER FOR SALE unlawfully taken marine mammals.

Exceptions may be made for (1) PRE-ACT specimens taken before December 21, 1972; (2) INTERNATIONAL AGREEMENTS ENTERED INTO BY THE UNITED STATES before December 21, 1972; (3) ALASKAN NATIVES; (4) BY PERMIT for scientific research, public display, and incidental take in commercial fisheries; and (5) IF A WAIVER is granted by the Federal Government.

## The U.S. Endangered Species Act

In general, it is prohibited under the Endangered Species Act to (1) TAKE listed species; (2) IMPORT listed species; (3) EXPORT listed species; (4) SELL OR OFFER FOR SALE listed species, and (5) POSSESS OR TRANSPORT unlawfully taken specimens.

Exceptions may be made for (1) PRE-ACT specimens acquired on or before December 28, 1973; and (2) BY PERMIT for scientific research and/or enhancement of propagation or survival if this species is ENDANGERED, and also for zoological exhibition, educational purposes, and special purposes consistent with the Act if the species is THREATENED.

## The Convention of International Trade in Endangered Species (CITES)

All cetaceans (whales, dolphins, and porpoises), all sirenians (manatees and dugongs) and several marine carnivores (seals, otters, walrus, and polar bears) are protected under CITES.

CITES applies to international shipments of listed species. It does not apply to activities conducted solely within the United States. The U.S. Fish and Wildlife Service has jurisdiction for import and export of all marine mammals listed under CITES.

Animals listed on Appendix I of CITES may be shipped internationally under a permit issued by the country of import AND a permit issued by the country of export. Animals listed on Appendix II of CITES may be shipped internationally under a permit issued by the country of export. Imports from the sea of Appendix I and II species may be made under permit from the country of import. Certificates of exception may be used in lieu of permits if animals are bred in captivity or were acquired before the date that CITES applied to them.

Polar bears are provided additional protection under a five-nation international agreement. In the United States this agreement is implemented by the provisions of the Marine Mammal Protection Act (discussed above).

For further permit information about CITES and species under jurisdiction of the U.S. Fish and Wildlife Service, call (703/235-1903) or write: U.S. Fish and Wildlife Service, Federal Wildlife Permit Office, P.O. Box 3654, Arlington, VA 22203.

For further permit information about species under jurisdiction of the National Marine Fisheries Service, call (202/634-7529) or write: Permit Program Manager, Office of Marine Mammals and Endangered Species, National Marine Fisheries Service, Department of Commerce, Washington, D.C. 20235.

# NMFS Application Instructions for Wildlife Permits

The National Marine Fisheries Service (NMFS) has the responsibility for oceanic species under the Marine Mammal Protection Act of 1972, Endangered Species of 1973, and Fur Seal Act of 1966. Under established regulations, NMFS may issue permits for the possession and transportation of northern fur seals for public display (50 CFR Part 215); the taking and importing of marine mammals for scientific research and public display (50 CFR Part 216); and the taking, importing, and exportation of threatened or endangered species for scientific purposes or to enhance the propagation or survival of such species (50 CFR Parts 217-222). These regulations apply to parts, products, and specimens as well as live animals. A list of species under the jurisdiction of

NMFS for which permits may be issued is attached; it indicates the status of each animal under the Endangered Species Act and the Convention on International Trade in Endangered Species.

# Supplemental Information

*Atlantic Bottlenose Dolphins.*   The taking of bottlenose dolphins in the Southeastern United States is limited to certain areas, and quotas have been established limiting the number that may be taken each year. Permit Holders are required to consult the Southeast Regional Director at least one week prior to collection for approval of the specific dates and locations. If the requested collection area is closed at the time you wish to collect, you will have the option of changing the location of taking to an area where the annual quota has not been filled. If this requires a change in collectors, you must first request and receive written authorization from the Assistant Administrator for Fisheries.

*Northern Fur Seals.*   Northern fur seals may be taken only by employees of the Federal Government. If you want to obtain this species for public display, contact the Pribilof Islands Program Director, National Marine Fisheries Service, Northwest Region, 7600 Sand Point Way, N.E., BIN C15700, Seattle, WA 98115 (telephone 206/527-6110), for further information concerning availability before submitting your application. Research on this species is the responsibility of the Director, National Marine Mammal Laboratory, Building 32, 7600 Sand Point Way, N.E. Seattle, WA 98115 (telephone 206/442-4711), who should be contacted directly on research requests. Although no permit is required, all research must be authorized, normally through a cooperative research agreement.

*Beached/Stranded Animals.*   NMFS encourages the use of healthy beached/stranded animals in place of taking animals from the wild. In the case of U.S. coastal pinnipeds, such as California sea lions, applicants are required to justify the need for taking animals from the wild rather than obtaining rehabilitated beached/stranded ones. For information on the availability of these animals, contact the appropriate NMFS Regional Office (see attached list).

*Foreign Applications.*   Applications from foreign facilities to take live animals for export from the United States must comply with the attached export policy statement. The application must be submitted through the appropriate agency of the foreign government, and this agency should (1) verify the information set forth in the application; (2) certify that they will enforce the terms and conditions of a permit if issued; and (3) certify that they will afford comity to a National Marine Fisheries Service decision to amend, suspend, or revoke a permit.

Foreign applications that involve the maintenance of live animals must also include a written emergency plan. This plan should outline provisions to ensure that all marine mammals will be adequately maintained in all reasonably foreseeable emergencies, such as loss of power or water, or natural disasters. It should include plans for adequate care in event of a strike or illness of personnel. If there are laws prohibiting strikes by animal-care staff, this should be specified in the plan. A description of emergency sources of water and power should be included. If plans do not exist, they must be developed. Further, the approving government agency should review and provide a statement that the plans have been found adequate. That agency should also include any government policies or regulations for ensuring the continued well-being of the animals.

*Animal Welfare Act.* The Animal and Plant Health Inspection Service (APHIS), Department of Agriculture, has responsibilities under the Animal Welfare Act for captive marine mammals and has established regulations and standards, "Marine Mammals; Humane Handling, Care, Treatment, and Transportation." Most U.S. facilities maintaining marine mammals are required to be licensed or registered by APHIS, and this requirement must be satisfied before a permit would be issued. U.S. facilities that are exempt from the provisions may voluntarily request to be licensed or registered. If a facility is not licensed or registered (which includes all foreign facilities), Section VII.D. of these instructions must be answered completely. If the application is for public display, compliance with the standards must be documented before any permit can be issued. Further, the standards are incorporated as conditions to all permits involving captive marine mammals. For information concerning the Animal Welfare Act and its requirements, you should contact the Animal Care Staff, Animal and Plant Health Inspection Service, Department of Agriculture, Room 703, Federal Building, 6505 Belcrest Road, Hyattsville, MD 20782 (telephone 301/436-7933).

*CITES Import/Export Permits.* U.S. regulations require that imports or exports of wildlife listed on the appendices to the Convention on International Trade in Endangered Species of Wild Fauna and Flora (CITES) be accompanied by the proper CITES permit or documentation. This is in addition to the required permits under the Marine Mammal Protection Act and the Endangered Species Act. The U.S. agency responsible for implementing CITES is the Federal Wildlife Permit Office, Fish and Wildlife Service, P.O. Box 3654, Arlington, VA 22203 (telephone 703/235-1903). The CITES status of marine mammals and endangered species under NMFS jurisdiction is indicated on the attached species list. Please note that all cetaceans are included on either Appendix I or II.

*Modifications to Permits.* Requests for modifications to permits should include the reasons for the proposed modification and a detailed description of the proposed changes. Requests should address all applicable sections of these instructions. Modification requests involving an increased number of animals, additional species, or an increased risk to the animals are subject to both 30-day public and Marine Mammal Commission reviews, and are granted at the discretion of the Assistant Administrator for Fisheries.

*Replacement Animals.* If any marine mammal is killed during the course of taking or importing, or is later determined to be unacceptable, this animal will be considered as having been taken or imported. However, a Permit Holder may submit a request for a permit modification to allow an additional animal to be taken. This request should include causes of death, including necropsy (or reasons found unacceptable), clinical history, detailed capture report, and disposition of the animal. Replacement requests, which are subject to 30-day public and Marine Mammal Commission reviews, are granted at the discretion of the Assistant Administrator for Fisheries.

*Marine Mammal Inventory System.* The Office of Marine Mammals and Endangered Species, NMFS, maintains a running inventory of all marine mammals maintained by Permit Holders. These inventories include all species of marine mammals under the jurisdiction of NMFS (cetaceans and pinnipeds, except walrus) that were taken under the authority of the Marine Mammal Protection Act or that were held or acquired since the date of the first permit application. Beached/stranded animals being maintained for rehabilitation purposes only and that will be returned to the wild need not be included. However, if these animals are to be retained either by your facility or another facility (which requires a federally issued permit or Letter of Agreement), they should be included in the inventory.

Since these inventory reports are updated throughout the year, mortality and other reports should be submitted as required by permits. In January of each year, the inventories are sent out to all facilities for verification and correction. The return of the corrected inventory serves as the annual report on the health and condition of the animals, which is required by permits and Letters of Agreement. (Research and other special reports required by permit must also be submitted). Further, the updated report, along with necropsy reports not previously submitted, should be used to satisfy Section VII. E.1. of these application instructions. An additional copy of an inventory can be obtained by calling the Office of Marine Mammals and Endangered Species (telephone 202/634-7529).

# INSTRUCTIONS

*Where to Send Applications:* Submit an original and two signed copies of the completed application to the Assistant Administrator for Fisheries, National Marine Fisheries Service, U.S. Department of Commerce, Washington, D.C. 20235. If you have questions or need assistance, please contact the Office of Marine Mammals and Endangered Species (telephone 202/634-7529).

*Give Complete Information:* NMFS endeavors to process all applications as quickly as possible. An application must be complete before it is forwarded to reviewers and before a Notice of Receipt is published in the *Federal Register*. Incomplete applications will not be processed; additional information will be requested or the application returned.

Therefore, it is in your interest to furnish complete and specific information. Review time is shorter when the proposed methods, objectives, and potential adverse impacts are clearly addressed.

The sufficiency of a permit application will be determined by NMFS based on the requirements of the appropriate regulations. The information outlined below will be used to determine whether the application is complete and whether a permit should be issued. Reports required under previous permits must be up-to-date for a new application to be considered.

Information should be presented in the following categories. If a question does not apply, indicate not applicable (N/A).

I. One of the titles below as appropriate—
   A. Application for Permit for Public Display under the Fur Seal Act;
   B. Application for Permit for Public Display under the Marine Mammal Protection Act;
   C. Application for Permit for Scientific Research under the Marine Mammal Protection Act;
   D. Application for Permit for Public Display and Scientific Research under the Marine Mammal Protection Act;
   E. Application for Permit for Scientific Purposes under the Endangered Species Act;
   F. Application for Permit to Enhance the Propagation or Survival of the Endangered Species under the Endangered Species Act;
   G. Application for Permit for Scientific Research under the Marine Mammal Protection Act, and Scientific Purposes under the Endangered Species Act;
   H. Application for Permit for Scientific Research under the Marine Mammal Protection Act, and to Enhance the Propagation or Survival of the Endangered Species under the Endangered Species Act.

II. The date of the application.
III. The identity of the Applicant, including complete name, address, and

telephone number. If the Applicant is a partnership or corporation, include the details of the business relationship.

IV. A description of the animals, parts, or products to be taken, imported, or exported, including:

    A. The number of animals by species (common and scientific names) and type of taking (e.g., harassment, tag/release, capture/maintain). Clearly indicate if an animal will be taken more than once or in more than one manner. If take by harassment is being requested, indicate the maximum number of animals that may be harassed and the number of times they may be harassed;

    B. The size, sex, age, and reproductive condition of the animals at the time of taking;

    C. The dates and locations of the proposed taking, as specifically as possible, and the requested duration of the permit;

    D. A description of the status of the stock of each species as it relates to the area of taking (cite sources);

    E. The reason for removing a live animal from the wild rather than using a beached/stranded one;

    F. In the case of imported animals, the country from which the animal was taken, whether taken in a lawful manner, the manner of taking, and the management and protection programs of the country from which the animals originate. The Marine Mammal Protection Act prohibits the import for public display of any animal that was pregnant, nursing, or less than eight months old when taken.

V. If the Application is for public display, provide an estimate of the numbers and types of people who will visit the display annually and a list of any educational or scientific programs associated with the display.

VI. If the application is for scientific research or to enhance the propagation or survival of a species, provide the following:

    A. A detailed description of the proposed project, including

        1. The background and a review of the current knowledge of the problem under investigation;

        2. A discussion of the objectives of the proposed project and, if endangered or threatened species are involved, a statement of how the project will enhance or benefit the wild population;

        3. A detailed discussion of the procedures and research techniques that will be used to carry out the projects and the background and test experience for using them. This discussion should include: a description of any tags, method, location and duration of attachment, and method of release; kind and dosage of any drugs to be used, purpose of use, and method of application; holding time prior to release of animals; and,

biological sampling methods and number and types of samples to be taken from each animal;

4. The potential for temporary or permanent adverse impact on the individual animals, and the steps that will be taken to minimize adverse effects and to insure that the animals will be taken in humane manner.

B. A copy of the formal research proposal or contract, if one has been prepared. Please note that activities discussed in the research proposal that require a permit will not be considered unless they have been specifically requested in the application.

C. The experience and qualifications of the investigators (curriculum vitae previously submitted are not required).

D. The names and addresses of sponsors or cooperating institutions.

E. A description of the arrangements, if any, for the disposition of specimen materials in a museum or other institutional collection for the continual benefit to science.

F. If you have been issued previous permits for marine mammals or endangered species, provide an update to the last research permit report, including numbers of animals taken, mortalities, causes of such mortalities, and steps taken to avoid similar mortalities.

G. If live animals are to be maintained under conditions not complying with Animal Welfare Act standards, provide a copy of the research protocol review by the university's or institution's animal-care committee.

VII. If the requested live animals will be maintained in captivity either for public display or scientific research, provide the following as appropriate:

A. If the collector is a NMFS designated Collector of Record, provide

1. The name of the collector;

2. The length of time for the transfer of the animals from the initial holding facility to the permanent facility.

B. If the collector is not a Collector of Record, provide

1. The name and qualifications of the personnel who will capture the animals;

2. A detailed description of the manner of capture, including gear to be used;

3. A description of the pen, tank, container, cradle, or other device used during capture, transportation, or as an initial holding facility;

4. Mode of transportation, special care during transport, and the length of time for the transfer of the animals from the capture site to the initial holding facility and from the initial holding facility to the permanent facility;

5. A statement as to whether the animals will be accompanied during transport by a veterinarian or other knowledgeable person and the qualifications of that person;

6. A written certification from the doctor of veterinary medicine responsible for the animals, stating that the methods of capture, transport, and care will be adequate to ensure the well-being of the animals.

C. If the facility is a licensed or registered facility under the Animal Welfare Act provide

1. The USDA license or registration number, and a copy of the last USDA inspection report for marine mammals;

2. The terms of any variance granted by the Department of Agriculture that is currently in effect;

3. A statement that the facilities are adequate for the additional requested animals.

D. If the facility is not a licensed or registered facility under the Animal Welfare Act (this includes non-registered research and all foreign facilities), provide sufficient information for a determination on compliance with the regulations and standards "Marine Mammals; Humane Handling, Care, Treatment, and Transportation" for all species of marine mammals maintained, including the following information:

1. A description of the animal enclosures, including construction materials, water and power supply, vertical air space, protection from the weather, and protection from the public (SS.3.101—3.103);

2. Specific dimensions of all pools, dry resting areas, and other holding facilities, and the number, sex, and species to be held in each; provide a diagram indicating all dimensions, including variations in depths of the pools (SS.3.104);

3. The amount and type of diet, who feeds the animals, and how the food is stored (SS.3.105);

4. Bacterial standards, a record of recent coliform counts and how often they are made, chemicals added, pH level maintained, salinity, temperature, and a description of the filtration system (SS.3.106);

5. How often the pools and food preparation areas are cleaned and sanitized, and any provisions for pest control (SS.3.107);

6. A written emergency plan that includes provisions to ensure that all marine mammals will be adequately maintained under all reasonably foreseeable circumstances, such as loss of power or water, or natural disasters. It should include plans for adequate care in the event of a strike or illness of personnel. If there are laws prohibiting strikes by animal-care staff, this

should be specified in the plan (SS.3.108). A description of emergency sources of water and power should be included (SS.3.101);

7. The names and qualifications of the animal-care staff, including the curator and veterinarian responsible for the animals (SS.3.108 and SS.3.110), and a written certification from the veterinarian stating that the facilities and the methods of care and maintenance are adequate to ensure the well-being of the animals.

E. Provide the following information for all marine mammals captured or maintained by or for the Applicant:

1. An updated marine mammal inventory, including new acquisitions, transfers/sales of animals, and mortalities. Include necropsy reports that have not previously been submitted. If this is a first application, provide a list of all marine mammals maintained during the previous year (previous five years for endangered species) and information on the age, sex, acquisition, mortality, and causes of mortality, including necropsy reports. This information should be submitted on the attached inventory forms;

2. If mortalities have occurred, the steps taken by the Applicant to avoid or decrease similar mortalities.

VIII. One of the following certifications, as appropriate:

A. For applications involving fur seals: "I hereby certify that the foregoing information is complete, true, and correct to the best of my knowledge and belief. I understand that this information is submitted for the purposes of obtaining a permit under the Fur Seal Act of 1966 and regulations promulgated thereunder, and that any false statement may subject me to the criminal penalties of 18 U.S.C. 1001."

B. For applications involving marine mammals: "I hereby certify that the foregoing information is complete, true, and correct to the best of my knowledge and belief. I understand that this information is submitted for the purpose of obtaining a permit under the Marine Mammal Protection Act of 1972 (16 U.S.C. 1361-1407) and regulations promulgated thereunder, and that any false statement may subject me to the criminal penalties of 18 U.S.C. 1001, or to penalties provided under the Marine Mammal Protection Act of 1972."

C. For applications involving endangered species: "I hereby certify that the foregoing information is complete, true, and correct to the best of my knowledge and belief. I understand that this information is submitted for the purpose of obtaining a permit under the Endangered Species Act of 1973 (16 U.S.C. 1531-1543) and regulations promulgated thereunder, and that any false statement may subject me to the criminal penalties of 18 U.S.C. 1001, or penalties provided under the Endangered Species Act of 1973."

D. For applications involving marine mammals and endangered species: "I hereby certify that the foregoing information is complete, true, and correct to the best of my knowledge and belief. I understand that this information is submitted for the purpose of obtaining a permit under the Marine Mammal Protection Act of 1972 (16 U.S.C. 1361–1407) and regulations promulgated thereunder, and the Endangered Species Act of 1973 (16 U.S.C. 1531–1543) and regulations promulgated thereunder, and that any false statement may subject me to the criminal penalties of 18 U.S.C. 1001, or to penalties provided under the Marine Mammal Protection Act of 1972 and under the Endangered Species Act of 1973."

IX. Name, title, and signature of Applicant or responsible party.

# Policy—Export of Marine Mammals

Policy and Procedures on Applying for Permits to Take Living Marine Mammals to be Maintained in Areas Outside Jurisdiction of the United States (as abstracted from a statement of National Marine Fisheries Service policy—40 *Federal Register* 11619, March 12, 1975).

The National Marine Fisheries Service (NMFS) has determined that, under the Marine Mammal Protection Act of 1972 (16 U.S.C. 1361–1407), its responsibilities with respect to the care and maintenance of animals in facilities outside the jurisdiction of the United States can be met only if there is independent evidence upon which to base a conclusion as to the reliability of statements concerning existing or planned facilities set forth in an application, as well as independent evidence that the government having jurisdiction over the facility has the appropriate laws and regulations to ensure compliance with permit conditions (and will do so) and will provide to NMFS essential periodic reports.

Therefore, no application from a foreign facility for a permit to take marine mammals for export from the United States will be considered unless:

(a) it is submitted to the Assistant Administrator for Fisheries, NMFS, through an appropriate agency of a foreign government;

(b) it includes, in addition to the information required by pertinent regulations (39 F.R. 14348, April 23, 1974):

   i. a certification from such appropriate government agency verifying the information set forth in the application;

   ii. a certification from such government agency that the laws and regulations of the government involved permit enforcement of the teams of the conditions of the permit, and that the government will enforce such terms;

iii. a statement that the government concerned will afford comity to a NMFS decision to amend, suspend, or revoke a permit.

For the purposes of obtaining certification from the appropriate government agency, a foreign facility may obtain a copy of the general conditions to a permit by writing to: The Assistant Administrator for Fisheries, National Marine Fisheries Service, National Oceanic and Atmospheric Administration, U.S. Department of Commerce, Washington, D.C. 20235.

For the purposes of this policy and the processing of all applications from a foreign facility for a permit, "appropriate government agency" means an agency or agencies of a foreign government that perform functions and activities similar to the functions performed by the National Marine Fisheries Service under the Marine Mammal Protection Act.

NOTE: In addition to the above requirements, the appropriate government agency should also:

(1) review and provide a statement that the emergency plan submitted by the Applicant has been found adequate; and

(2) include any government policies or regulations for ensuring the continued well-being of the marine mammals.

# THE U.S. ENDANGERED SPECIES ACT

The U.S. Endangered Species Act was passed on December 28, 1973, to prevent the extinction of many species of animals and plants. The Act provides strong measures to help alleviate the loss of species and their habitats. It places restrictions on a wide range of activities involving endangered and threatened animals or plants to help ensure their continued survival. With limited exceptions, the Act prohibits activities with these protected species unless authorized by a permit from the U.S. Fish and Wildlife Service.

By definition, an "endangered species" is any animal or plant listed by regulation as being in danger of extinction. A "threatened species" is any animal or plant that is likely to become endangered within the foreseeable future. The U.S. List of Endangered and Threatened Wildlife and Plants includes both native and foreign species.

## A. WHAT IS PROHIBITED BY THE ENDANGERED SPECIES ACT

Without a permit, it is unlawful for any person subject to the jurisdiction of the United States to commit, attempt to commit, solicit another to commit, or cause to be committed any of the following activities:

### *For all Endangered and Most Threatened Wildlife*

—Import or export.
—Deliver, receive, carry, transport, or ship in interstate or foreign commerce in the course of a commercial activity.
—Sell or offer for sale in interstate or foreign commerce.
—Take within the United States and its territorial seas or upon the high seas ("take" means to harm, harass, pursue, hunt, shoot, wound, kill, trap, capture, or collect, or attempt to engage in any such conduct).
—Possess, ship, deliver, carry, transport, sell, or receive unlawfully taken wildlife.

### *For all Endangered and Most Threatened Plants*

—Import or Export
—Deliver, receive, carry, transport, or ship in interstate or foreign commerce in the course of a commercial activity.
—Sell or offer for sale in interstate or foreign commerce.
—Remove and reduce to possession from areas under federal jurisdiction.

The prohibitions apply equally to live or dead animals or plants, their progeny (or seeds in the case of plants), and any parts or products derived from them.

## B. PERMITS

The U.S. Fish and Wildlife Service's Federal Wildlife Permit Office (FWPO) may issue permits for prohibited activities for the following purposes:

*Endangered Species Permits*
—Scientific research.
—Enhancement of propagation or survival of the species.
—Incidental taking.

*Threatened Species Permits*
—Scientific research.
—Enhancement of propagation or survival of the species.
—Zoological, horticultural, or botanical exhibition.
—Educational purposes.
—Special purposes consistent with the purposes and policy of the Act.
—Incidental taking.

*Captive-Bred Wildlife*
Qualified persons who register with the U.S. Fish and Wildlife Service may buy and sell live endangered or threatened animals not native to the United States, that have been born in the United States, for enhancement of propagation provided the other person is registered for the same species. A "Fact Sheet" on this procedure is available from FWPO.

*Pets* Permits are not issued for keeping or breeding endangered or threatened animals for pet purposes. The use of protected species as pets is not consistent with the purposes of the Act, which is aimed at conservation of the species and recovery of wild populations.

*Applying for a Permit* Permit applications and instructions may be obtained from the FWPO. A $25 application processing fee is required, and applicants should allow at least 60 days for processing of these applications.

## C. PERMIT EXEMPTIONS

Certain situations are exempt from the prohibitions of the Act:

*Pre-act or "Grandfather" Clause* Species held in captivity or in a controlled environment on (a) December 28, 1973, or (b) the date of publication in the *Federal Register* for final listing, whichever is later, are exempt from prohibitions of the Act PROVIDED such holding or any subsequent holding or use of the specimen was not in the course of a commercial activity. Commercial activity includes any activity that is intended for profit or gain. An affadavit and supporting documentary evidence of pre-Act status must accompany the shipment of listed species between states and between the United States and another country. (Any endangered or threatened specimens born in captivity from pre-Act parents are fully protected and not considered pre-Act.)

*Antiques* Certain antiques, including scrimshaw, can be imported into the United States if they are more than 100 years old and have not been repaired or modified since December 28, 1973, with any part of a listed species. Such antiques must enter through a port designated by the U.S. Customs Service and must be accompanied by authenticating documentation.

*Special Rules* If a species is listed as threatened or as an experimental population, special rules designated to cover unique situations may allow otherwise prohibited activities. Some species covered by special rules include certain kangaroos, several primates, the grizzly bear, gray wolf, African elephant, American alligator, and leopard.

*Intrastate Commerce* Commercial activities involving legally acquired endangered or threatened species that take place entirely within one State are not prohibited by the Act. However, many states regulate activities involving protected species. Individuals should contact the appropriate state fish and wildlife agency before undertaking any activities involving endangered or threatened wildlife and plants.

*Offer for sale*   Endangered and threatened species may be advertised for sale PROVIDED the advertisement contains a statement that no sale may be consummated until a permit has been obtained from the U.S. Fish and Wildlife Service. However, keep in mind that the Act prohibits the sale of a listed species in interstate or foreign commerce unless a permit is obtained PRIOR to the sale.

*Loans and Gifts*   Lawfully taken and held endangered and threatened species may be shipped interstate as a *bona fide* gift or loan if there is no barter, credit, other form of compensation, or intent to profit or gain. A standard breeding loan, where no money or other consideration changes hands but some offspring are returned to the lender of a breeding animal, is not considered a commercial activity and, thus, is not prohibited by the Act and does not require a permit. Documentation of such an activity should accompany the shipment.

*Hybrids*   Hybrids, defined as offspring of two animals or two plants where each parent is from a different species and where at least one parent is listed under the Act, are not protected by the Act. However, it is recommended that breeding records be maintained to show parentage and hybrid status of offspring. Note that other laws such as the Migratory Bird Treaty Act (MBTA) and the Convention on International Trade in Endangered Species of Wild Fauna and Flora (CITES) consider hybrids protected.

*Alaska Natives*   Alaska natives who reside in Alaska, and non-natives who are permanent residents of native villages and are primarily dependent upon the taking of listed wildlife, may import or take endangered or threatened wildlife for subsistence purposes, or as raw material for the production of authentic native handicrafts, if the take is not done in a wasteful manner. These articles of handicrafts and clothing may be sold in interstate commerce without federal permits.

*Raptors*   Prohibitions under the Act do not apply to any endangered or threatened raptors (except the bald eagle) legally held in captivity or in a controlled environment on November 10, 1978, or to any progeny thereof PROVIDED that are possessed and banded under the terms of a valid permit issued under MBTA and are identified in the earliest applicable annual report required under such permit as meeting their criteria. (It does not apply to any raptor intentionally returned to the wild.)

*Seeds from Artificially Propagated Threatened Plants*   No permits are required for interstate or foreign commerce, import, and export of seeds from artificially propagated specimens of threatened plants. However, seeds must be accompanied by label stating that they are of cultivated origin.

## D. SHARED JURISDICTION

The National Marine Fisheries Service (NMFS) has jurisdiction over certain marine species as outlined in 50 CFR 222.23. It shares jurisdiction for sea turtles; NMFS has jurisdiction for sea turtles while in the water and the U.S. Fish and Wildlife Service for sea turtles on land. For further information about species under NMFS jurisdiction, contact: Permit Program Manager, Office of Marine Mammals and Endangered Species, NMFS, Department of Commerce, Washington, D.C. 20235, telephone (202) 634-7529.

## E. COMPLIANCE WITH OTHER LAWS

Requirements of other laws also must be met. Depending on the species involved, other requirements may include import and export documents under CITES, possession permits under MBTA, permits under the Marine Mammal Protection Act, and compliance with federal, state, and foreign laws under the Lacey Act.

For more information write: Federal Wildlife Permit Office
1000 N. Glebe Road, Room 611
Arlington, VA 22201

# Convention on International Trade in Endangered Species of Wild Fauna and Flora

Regulations to enforce the Convention on International Trade in Endangered Species of Wild Fauna and Flora (CITES) took effect in May, 1977. The United States and more than 70 other nations are party to the Convention and have established procedures to regulate the import and export of imperiled species covered by the treaty. The Convention imposes no restrictions or controls on shipments between states or U.S. territories, including the District of Columbia, Guam, the Commonwealth of Puerto Rico, the Trust Territories, U.S. Virgin Islands, and American Samoa.

U.S. regulations require that imports or exports of wildlife and plants listed on any of the three appendices of the Convention be accompanied by proper permits or certificates of exception. CITES export documentation is always required; import permits are necessary only for species listed in Appendix I. This is explained in more detail below, along with certain exceptions.

The Federal Wildlife Permit Office (WPO) acts as the U.S. Management Authority for CITES. This office accepts permit applications, coordinates their review, and determines whether a permit or certificate should be issued. WPO also will provide the addresses for permit issuing offices in foreign countries upon request. Please feel free to contact WPO if you have any questions (see address and phone number below).

IMPORTANT: Some Convention species are also protected by other

U.S. laws under which permit requirements may be more stringent—for example, the U.S. Endangered Species Act and the Marine Mammal Protection Act. Permit applicants must satisfy the requirements of all laws under which a particular species is protected. WPO will provide information to help you understand these requirements.

## Appendix I Permits

Appendix I includes species presently threatened with extinction. The Convention's most stringent controls are directed at activities involving these animals and plants. All shipments of such species, their parts, and derivatives (including manufactured products), require two permits—one from the importing country (obtained first) and another from the exporting country. Such permits will be issued only when the purpose for import is not primarily commercial and will not be detrimental to the survival of the species. Permit applications should be submitted to the Management (permit issuing) Authority of both countries.

## Appendix II Permits

Appendix II species are not presently threatened with extinction but may become so unless their trade is regulated. CITES controls are less stringent for Appendix II species than Appendix I. Import permits are not needed for Appendix II species, but an export permit or reexport certificate must accompany each shipment. Export permits can be issued for any purpose as long as the export will not be detrimental to the survival of the species. Reexport certificates are required for items previously imported, including items subsequently converted to manufactured goods. Please remember that some Appendix II species are also covered under the Endangered Species Act (ESA) and you must comply with its regulations.

A "Letter of Authorization" (LOA) system has been implemented in the United States to facilitate the issuance of Appendix II export permits for shipments of skins, fur pelts, or products of bobcat, lynx, river otter, Alaskan gray wolf, Alaskan brown bear, American alligator, and for reexport of all Appendix or III species. This system reduces the amount of paperwork for the exporter and expedites the issuance of an original permit for each shipment. LOA's may be valid for two years and are renewable.

## Appendix III

Appendix III includes species that do not fall in the Appendix I or II categories, but are regulated for conservation purposes by a Party nation. International shipments of these species requires either an export permit from the country that listed the species or a reexport certificate or certificate of origin from any other country. No import permit is necessary.

## Certificates of Exception

Certificates of exception may be issued by the country of export for artificially propagated plants, captive-bred animals, items acquired before the Convention applied to them, and noncommercial exchanges between registered scientific institutions. Wildlife and plants exempted under these certificates may be traded internationally without being subject to the strict permit requirements of the Convention. The certificates must be displayed, but are not collected, at U.S. ports of entry or exit.

## Other Exceptions—Personal and Household Goods

Wildlife and plants may be exempt from CITES regulations in certain other situations that do not require the issuance of a certificate of exception. Pets and other personal and household goods that you took with you when you left the United States may be reentered with appropriate U.S. Customs documentation. Appendix II and III specimens acquired abroad may be imported without CITES documents if they are accompanying personal baggage or are part of the household effects of someone moving his/her residence to the United States and the exporting country does not require a permit for this type of export. Appendix II species also listed on the ESA do not qualify for this exemption and a permit under the ESA is needed. However, specimens of Appendix I species that you acquire abroad may not be brought back without the required CITES permits. Convention documents are not required for wildlife or plants being transshipped through the United States if they remain in Customs control.

If you are not sure whether your situation falls into one of these categories, you should contact WPO or a local office of the Law Enforcement Division of the Fish and Wildlife Service.

## Foreign Documentation

If you are importing protected wildlife or plants from a nation that is not a Party to CITES, you must still obtain from that nation documents that contain all the information normally required in CITES export permits. On request, WPO will provide you with sample documents and addresses of the proper authorities to contact in non-CITES nations to obtain such documents.

## Your Application

Your application for U.S. document consists of two parts—the Fish and Wildlife Service Standard Permit Application (Form 3-200) and specific information required by the Convention. Specific questions should be found on the back of the appropriate application. If no questions are found on the back, please contact WPO and we will send them to you. A $25 fee is required with the application.

Incomplete applications are the most frequent and time-consuming cause for delay in reviewing permit applications. You can help expedite review of your application by taking care that you supply all of the requested information. The Permit Branch staff of WPO will be glad to assist you.

## The Shipment

All wildlife shipments must enter and leave this country through Customs ports designated by the U.S. Fish and Wildlife Service (New York, NY; Miami, FL; New Orleans, LA; Dallas/Ft. Worth, TX; Los Angeles and San Francisco, CA; Chicago, IL; Seattle, WA; and Honolulu, HI) unless, because of special circumstances, an Exception to Designated Port permit is obtained. Shipment containers must be marked on the outside with the names and addresses of the sender and receiver, and an accurate statement of the species (and the numbers of each species) in the container. Also, a "Declaration for Importation or Exportation of Fish and Wildlife" (Form 3-177) must be filed at the Customs port of entry.

All plant shipments must be made through ports designated by the U.S. Department of Agriculture (USDA) and, in addition, must comply with other USDA requirements. You may obtain information about USDA requirements by writing: Permit Unit, USDA, Room 638 Federal Building, Hyattsville, MD 20782 (301/436-8645).

### Permit and Certificate Requirements

| ACTIVITY | APPENDIX I | APPENDIX II | APPENDIX III |
|---|---|---|---|
| Import from a foreign country | U.S. import permit foreign export or reexport permit | Foreign export or reexport permit | Foreign export or reexport permit or certificate of origin |
| Import from the sea Export from the U.S. | U.S. import permit U.S. export permit & foreign import permit | U.S. import permit U.S. export permit | Not applicable U.S. certificate of origin (or export permit if U.S. listed) |
| Reexport from the U.S. | U.S. reexport cert. & foreign import permit | U.S. reexport certificate | U.S. reexport certificate |

### Exception to Permit Requirements

| | |
|---|---|
| Transshipment | No permit or certificate needed if under Customs control |
| Pre-Convention | Certificate for pre-Convention specimens needed for all above activities |
| Captive-bred wildlife or artificially propagated plants | Certificate for captive-bred wildlife or artificially propagated plants needed for all above activities |

Exception to Permit Requirements—continued

| | | |
|---|---|---|
| Personal or household effects | No permits or certificates needed for App. I unless being imported by a U.S. resident | No permits or certificates needed for App. II or III unless being imported by U.S. resident from country where taken from wild if country requires export permit |
| Scientific exchange | U.S. certificate for scientific exchange needed by U.S. institutions for import, export, or reexport of accessioned specimens not being shipped under other exception | |

For more information write:

Federal Wildlife Permit Office
1000 N. Glebe Road, Room 611
Arlington, VA 22201

## Summary of CITES Permit Requirements

| | EXPORT | RE-EXPORT | IMPORT |
|---|---|---|---|
| Appendix I | • Export permit by WPO<br>• Prior issuance of import permit by MA of importing country<br>OR<br>• Certificate of exception by WPC<br>—Pre CITES<br>—Captive Bred/ Artificial Propagation | • Reexport certificate by WPO<br>• Prior issuance of import permit by MA of importing country | • Import permit by WPO<br>• Export permit or reexport certificate from exporting country OR<br>• Certificate of exception from exporting or reexporting country |
| Appendix II | • Export permit by WPO<br>OR<br>• Certificate of exception | • Reexport certificate by WPO (evidence of legal importation) | • Export permit OR reexport certificate OR certificate of exception from exporting/ reexporting country. |
| Appendix III | Certificates or origin by WPO<br>NOTE: U.S. lists no Appendix III species | • Reexport certificate by WPO (evidence of legal importation | • Export permit from "listing" country<br>• Certificate of origin OR reexport certificate from "non-listing" country |

WPO = Wildlife Permit Office, Fish and Wildlife Service
MA = Management Authority

# Permits for Protected Plants

Certain plants and animals that are now or may become threatened with extinction are protected under the U.S. Endangered Species Act of 1973

(ESA) and/or the Convention on International Trade in Endangered Species of Wild Fauna and Flora (CITES). The ESA places restrictions on the import, export, interstate and foreign commerce of listed species. CITES is an international agreement that places restrictions on import, export, and reexport of listed species. Please note that all orchids, cacti, and cycads are listed under CITES, some on Appendix I (the most restrictive category), the remainder on Appendix II. Some species, including several cacti, are listed under both ESA and CITES, and the restrictions of both laws apply.

Permits may be required by the country of import, export, or both, as outlined below. Applications and information on ESA and CITES permit requirements are available from the Federal Wildlife Permit Office (WPO). This office coordinates the review of applications and determines whether or not a U.S. permit can be issued. WPO will provide the addresses of Management Authorities in foreign countries upon request.

## The Endangered Species Act

Import, export, interstate, and foreign commerce (including delivery, receipt, transportation, shipping, sale or offer for sale, trade, barter, or any similar transfer or ownership for profit or gain) of wild or cultivated endangered plants are fully protected by the Act. Permits are issued for scientific purposes and for the enhancement of survival and propagation of the species. Individuals applying for artificially propagated endangered/threatened species permits must submit additional information on the methods of propagation and source of parental stock. If a species is listed as threatened, these activities also may be authorized: botanical or horticultural exhibition, educational purposes, or other activities consistent with the purposes and policy of the Act. Seeds of artificially propagated specimens of threatened species do not require a permit from WPO, however, all such seeds must be labeled as of artificially propagated origin. In all other cases threatened species are afforded the same protection provided to endangered species.

For further information, contact:
        Federal Wildlife Permit Office
        Fish and Wildlife Service
        U.S. Dept. of the Interior
        Washington, D.C. 20240

Please refer to FWS F-018 when making inquiries.

## CITES—APPENDIX I

Permits are required from the Management Authorities of both the importing and exporting countries. The import permit must be obtained prior to requesting the export permit from the country of origin. Seeds, parts and products, and hybrids are afforded full protection as Appendix I specimens. Artificially propagated Appendix I plants are given special consideration, depending on whether they were propagated for commercial purposes.

## CITES—Appendix II & III

A permit is required only from the country of export or reexport. The export of seeds, parts, and products of species listed on Appendix II or III *do not* require CITES documents unless such parts are specified in the Appendices, i.e., unless the word "seeds" or "roots" appears in parentheses after the species listing.

## CITES—CERTIFICATES OF EXCEPTION

Specimens grown entirely from seeds or cuttings (artificially propagated) or specimens acquired before the date CITES applied to that species (pre-Convention) may qualify for a Certificate of Exception. Plants exempted under these certificates may be traded internationally under a streamlined document system. WPO will help determine if your specimens qualify.

## The U.S. Department of Agriculture (USDA)

Plants may be imported and exported only through ports designated by the USDA. All CITES and ESA certificates and permits authorizing plant import or export must be signed and stamped by a port inspector of the USDA Animal and Plant Health Inspection Service, Division of Plant Protection and Quarantine (APHIS-PPQ). The USDA has additional regulations that apply to plant imports. You should contact an APHIS-PPQ port inspector, or write to the USDA for more information: USDA, APHIS-PPQ, Federal Center Building, Hyattsville, MD 20782 (301/436-8645).

Correction: The 1982 Amendments to the ESA added the provision that it is unlawful for any person subject to the jurisdiction of the United States to *remove and reduce to possession any such species [listed plants] from areas under Federal jurisdiction.*

# CAPTIVE-BRED WILDLIFE REGISTRATION SYSTEM

The Captive-bred Wildlife (CBW) regulation [50 CFR 17.21 (g)] became effective in September 1979, making it easier to conduct activities that enhance the propagation or survival of eligible captive-bred wildlife listed under the U.S. Endangered Species Act. The CBW regulation permits a wider range of activities with a greater number of species than was possible under the previous Captive Self-Sustaining Population (CSSP) regulation.

## Who may register?

Persons subject to the jurisdiction of the United States may register with the U.S. Fish and Wildlife Service (FWS) under the CBW regulation. The term "persons" includes, but is not limited to, individuals such as game breeders, corporations such as private game farms, and organizations such as zoos and circuses.

## What types of wildlife are covered?

The CBW regulation covers only LIVING, EXOTIC (i.e., non-native) wildlife listed under the U.S. Endangered Species Act that are born in captivity in the United States. The FWS Director may determine if certain native species are eligible under the CBW registration; currently only the Laysan duck (*Anas laysanensis*) is eligible. NOTE: The jaguar, margay, ocelot, wolf, nene goose, and Hawaiian duck and other *native* species are NOT covered under the CBW system. For native species not covered under the CBW registration system, an Endangered or Threatened Species permit is required for *each* transaction that deals with interstate or foreign commerce, import and export.

## What activities may be conducted?

To transport, deliver, receive, sell, or offer for sale in *interstate commerce,* BOTH the buyer and seller must be registered for the family/families of wildlife involved. Each transaction must document that the animal was born in captivity in the United States and the buyer's and seller's CBW permit numbers. Registrants must comply with any applicable state laws.

    *Export and reimport of the same animals* are allowed only when the animals remain under the registrant's care and are uniquely identified to the FWS employee at the time of export. The registrant (usually circuses and other live animal acts) must have a valid CBW permit, which allows for this activity, in his/her possession *and* must have all permits under regulations that might include import and export documents under the Convention on International Trade in Endangered Species (CITES), possession permits under the Migratory Bird Treaty Act, permits under the Marine Mammal Protection Act, and requirements under the Lacey Act, including marking of containers, filing a Wildlife Declaration (Form 3-177), and obtaining foreign documents when necessary.

    For *export* where the animal will leave registrant's care, the CBW registrant must provide the Federal Wildlife Permit Office (WPO) with written evidence that the foreign recipient will use the wildlife for enhancement of propagation or survival and that the foreign facilities and expertise to care for the animal are adequate. Permits covering other regulations (see above) must also be obtained.

    *Take* (meaning harm or harass) is allowed in the context of normal animal husbandry, including euthanasia. It does NOT imply removal from the wild.

NOTE: No "first-time" *imports* are allowed under the CBW registration.

## How does one register?

Permit applications and instructions are available from the WPO. A $25 application fee is required, and applicants should allow at least 30 days for processing the application. The CBW registration permit is valid for two years and is renewable. More species or families may be added at a later date by requesting an amendment to the registration, if the registrant qualifies for the species/family.

# Appendix L

# Species and Special Groups for Which National Resource Plans are Prepared by FWS

**(As of January 1, 1986)**

## Mammals

Grizzly bear (*Ursus arctos horribilis*)
   (Lower 48 states population)
Polar bear (*Ursus maritumus*)
Black-footed ferret (*Mustela nigripes*)
Sea otter (*Enhydra lutris*)
Coyote (*Canis latrans*)
Gray wolf (*Canis lupus*)
   (Eastern and Rocky Mt. populations)
Walrus (*Odobenus rosmarus*)
West Indian manatee (*Trichechus manatus*)

## Birds

Brown pelican (*Pelecanus occidentalis*)
Tundra swan (*Cygnus columbianus*)
Trumpeter (*Cygnus buccinator*)
White-fronted goose (*Anser albifrons*)

Seabird group

Snow goose (*Chen caerulescens*)
Brant (*Branta bernicla*)
Canada goose (*Branta canadensis*)
Wood duck (*Aix sponsa*)
Black duck (*Anas rubripes*)                          Surface feeding duck group
Mallard (*Anas platyrhynchos*)
Pintail (*Anas acuta*)
Canvasback (*Aythya valisineris*)
Redhead (*Aythya americana*)                          Bay duck group
Ring-necked duck (*Aythya collaris*)
California condor (*Gymnogyps californianus*)
Osprey (*Pandion haliaetus*)
Bald eagle (*Haliaeetus leucocephalus*)
Golden eagle (*Aquila chrysaetos*)
Peregrine falcon (*Falco peregrinus*)
Attwater's greater prairie-chicken (*Tympanuchus
    cupido attwateri*)
Masked bobwhite (*Colinus virginianus ridgwayi*)
Yuma clapper rail (*Rallus longirostris
    yumanensis*)
Light-footed clapper rail (*Rallus longirostris
    levipes*)
Sandhill crane (*Grus canadensis*)
Whooping crane (*Grus americana*)
Piping plover (*Charadrius melodus*)
American woodcock (*Scolopax minor*)                  Shorebird group
Roseate tern (*Sterna dougallii*)
Eastern least tern (*Sterna antillarum antillarum*)
Interior least tern (*Sterna antillarum athalassos*)  Gull and Tern group
California least tern (*Sterna antillarum brownii*)
White-winged dove (*Zenaida asciatica*)
Mourning dove (*Zenaida macroura*)
Spotted owl (*Strix occidentalis*)
Red-cockaded woodpecker (*Picoides borealis*)
Kirtland's warbler (*Dendroica kirtlandii*)

## Reptiles

American alligator (*Alligator mississippiensis*)

## Fish

Sea lamprey (*Petromyzon marinus*) (Great Lakes)
Coho salmon (*Oncorhynchus kisutch*)
    (Anadromous populations—Pacific Coast/
    Alaska)

Sockeye salmon (*Oncorhynchus nerka*)
(Alaska populations)

Chinook salmon (*Oncorhynchus tshawytscha*)
(Anadromous populations—Pacific Coast/
Alaska)

Cutthroat trout (*Salmo clarki*)
(Western U.S.)

Steelhead (Anadromous populations—Pacific
Coast/Alaska/Rainbow trout (*Salmo
gairdneri*)

Atlantic salmon (*Salmo salar*)
(Anadromous populations)

Lake trout (*Salvelinus namaycush*)
(Great Lakes)

Cui-ui (*Chasmistes cujus*)
(Historical range)

Striped bass (*Morone saxatilis*)
(*Anadromous populations—Atlantic/Gulf coasts*)

Great Lakes Percidae

Pacific salmon group

Stream trout group

## Molluscs

(No specific species identified)

## PLANTS

(No specific species identified)

Total number of species or species groups: 56

# Appendix M

# Fish and Wildlife Species for Which Regional Resources Plans are Prepared

**(As of January 1986)**

## REGION 1

Lahontan Cutthroat Trout

## REGION 2

Rainbow Trout
Humpback Chub
Woundfin
Gilla Topminnow
Knowlton Cactus
Peebles Navajo Cactus

## REGION 3

Common Tern
Great Blue Heron
Higgin's Eye Pearly Mussel

Indiana Bat
Gray Bat
Ozark Big-eared Bat
Iowa Pleistocene Snail
Northern Monkshod

## REGION 4

Brook Trout
Rainbow Trout
Brown Trout
Snail (Everglade) Kite
Tennessee Coneflower
Wood Stork
Yellow-shouldered Blackbird
Eastern Bluebird
Florida Duck

1062

Audubon Wildlife Report
National Audubon Society
950 3rd Avenue
New York, New York, 10022

Audubon Wildlife Report
National Audubon Society
950 3rd Avenue
New York, New York, 10022

## ORDER FORM

Please send me _____ copies of the *1986 AUDUBON WILD-LIFE REPORT*. Enclosed is a check or money order for $34.95 plus $2.50 postage and handling for each copy.

Please send me _____ copies of the *1985 AUDUBON WILD-LIFE REPORT*. Enclosed is a check or money order for $24.95 plus $2.50 postage and handling for each copy.

Please send me _____ copies of both the 1985 and 1986 volumes. Enclosed is a check or money order for $49.95 plus $2.50 postage and handling.

Name_____
Organization_____
Address_____
City_____ State_____ Zip_____

*Please make check or money order payable to*
*the National Audubon Society. Allow four weeks for delivery.*

## ORDER FORM

Please send me _____ copies of the *1986 AUDUBON WILD-LIFE REPORT*. Enclosed is a check or money order for $34.95 plus $2.50 postage and handling for each copy.

Please send me _____ copies of the *1985 AUDUBON WILD-LIFE REPORT*. Enclosed is a check or money order for $24.95 plus $2.50 postage and handling for each copy.

Please send me _____ copies of both the 1985 and 1986 volumes. Enclosed is a check or money order for $49.95 plus $2.50 postage and handling.

Name_____
Organization_____
Address_____
City_____ State_____ Zip_____

*Please make check or money order payable to*
*the National Audubon Society. Allow four weeks for delivery.*

Mottled Duck
Caribbean Waterfowl Group:
  —West Indian Whistling Duck
  —Masked Duck
  —West Indian Ruddy Duck
  —White-cheeked Pintail
Red-headed Woodpecker
Seaside Sparrow
White-crowned Pigeon

## REGION 5

Colonial Nesting Waterbirds
American Shad

## REGION 6

Paddlefish

## REGION 7

Emperor Goose

# Appendix N

# National Forest System Acreage by State as of September 30, 1984 (in acres)

| State | National Forest | Natl. Grasslands | Other* | Total |
|-------|----------------|------------------|--------|-------|
| AL | 646,216 | — | 100 | 646,316 |
| AK | 22,938,652 | — | — | 22,938,652 |
| AZ | 11,218,403 | — | 51,003 | 11,269,406 |
| AR | 2,478,454 | — | 1,993 | 2,480,447 |
| CA | 20,426,092 | — | 31,066 | 20,457,158 |
| CO | 13,817,859 | 611,930 | 560 | 14,430,349 |
| CT | — | — | 24 | 24 |
| FL | 1,099,109 | — | — | 1,099,109 |
| GA | 869,911 | — | 9,568 | 872,479 |
| HI | — | — | 1 | 1 |
| ID | 20,385,566 | 47,658 | — | 20,433,224 |
| IL | 253,378 | — | 8,214 | 261,592 |
| IN | 187,523 | — | 1,012 | 188,535 |
| KS | — | 108,177 | — | 108,177 |
| KY | 530,082 | — | 144,184 | 674,266 |
| LA | 597,933 | — | — | 597,933 |
| ME | 41,833 | — | 9,404 | 51,237 |
| MI | 2,758,650 | — | 4,982 | 2,763,632 |
| MN | 2,715,240 | — | 88,413 | 2,803,653 |

*Includes Purchase Units, Land Utilization Projects, Research and Experimental Areas, and other miscellaneous areas.

| State | National Forest | Natl. Grasslands | Other* | Total |
|-------|----------------:|-----------------:|-------:|------:|
| MS | 1,148,261 | — | 330 | 1,148,591 |
| MO | 1,453,743 | — | 15,745 | 1,469,488 |
| MT | 16,796,582 | — | 121 | 16,796,703 |
| NE | 257,260 | 94,332 | 144 | 351,736 |
| NV | 5,150,156 | — | — | 5,150,156 |
| NH | 686,790 | — | 18,884 | 705,674 |
| NM | 9,085,663 | 136,412 | 103,414 | 9,325,489 |
| NY | 13,232 | — | — | 13,232 |
| NC | 1,215,467 | — | 772 | 1,216,239 |
| ND | — | 1,104,819 | 796 | 1,105,615 |
| OH | 177,485 | — | 464 | 177,949 |
| OK | 248,965 | 46,300 | — | 295,265 |
| OR | 15,491,324 | 105,224 | 1,124 | 15,597,672 |
| PA | 510,406 | — | 227 | 510,633 |
| SC | 609,656 | — | 1,080 | 610,736 |
| SD | 1,134,185 | 862,871 | — | 1,997,056 |
| TN | 625,279 | — | 325 | 625,604 |
| TX | 665,114 | 117,542 | — | 782,656 |
| UT | 7,989,733 | — | 55,630 | 8,045,363 |
| VT | 294,610 | — | 499 | 295,109 |
| VA | 1,634,062 | — | — | 1,634,062 |
| WA | 9,055,485 | — | 738 | 9,056,223 |
| WV | 968,270 | — | 6,235 | 974,505 |
| WI | 1,504,202 | — | 199 | 1,504,401 |
| WY | 8,682,125 | 571,885 | — | 9,254,010 |
| PR | 27,846 | — | — | 27,846 |
| VI | — | — | 147 | 147 |
| TOTAL | 186,383,802 | 3,807,150 | 557,398 | 190,748,350 |

*Includes Purchase Units, Land Utilization Projects, Research and Experimental Areas, and other miscellaneous areas.

Source: U.S. Department of Agriculture, Forest Service, *Land Areas of the National Forest System,* September 30, 1984.

# Index

*Abby Dodge* case, 271
Accelerated Refuge Maintenance and Management Program, 429-430, 459
Acid rain
  implications for loons, 685-686
  osprey habitat, 901
  problem areas, 483
  water quality effect, 135
Act of February 9, 1871, 270-271
Act of March 4, 1917, 91
Administrative Procedure Act, Bureau of Land Management violations, 536-537
Adopt-a-Horse program, 79
African ice plants, Channel Islands National Park, 487
Agency for International Development, 551
Agreement on Cooperation in the Field of Environmental Protection, 554-555, 557
Agricultural Conservation program, 148
Agricultural Stabilization and Conservation Service, 380
Agricultural Trade Development and Assistance Act of 1954, 278, 548
Air Management, 133-134; *see also* Soil, Water and Air Management Program
'Akoko plant, 368
Alaska
  Alaska Native Claims Settlement Act, 449
  fishery resource, 339-340
  history, 448-449
  mining operations in national parks, 492
  refuges, 448-455
    acreage, 450

Alaska Lands Act, 451
Alaska National Interest Lands Conservation Act, 449, 451
  budget, 453-454
  compatibility determintions, 451-452
  current program emphasis, 452-453
  history, 449
  management, 449, 451-452
  planning, 454-455
  problems and issues, 453
*Alaska Fish and Wildlife Federation and Outdoor Council, Inc. v. Jantzen*, 242, 560-561, 574
Alaska king crab, 266, 339
Alaska Lands Act, 451
  compatibility determinations, 451-452
  land exchanges, 452
  provisions for Arctic National Wildlife Refuge, 452
Alaska Land Use Council, 453
Alaska Lumber and Pulp, 164-165
Alaska National Interest Lands Conservation Act of 1980, 164-165, 426, 449, 451
Alaska Native Claims Settlement Act, 449
Alaska natives, *see* Hunting, subsistence
Alaskan pollock, fishery resource, 340
Alaska Peninsula National Wildlife Refuge, management plan, 455
Alaska Sport Hunting bill, 489
Albacore, resource status, 338
American Committee for International Wildlife Protection, 563-564
American Fisheries Promotion Act, 289-290, 293

American Fisheries Society, 303
American Game Conference, 631
Anadromous fish
  Forest Service role, 110-111
  habitat research, 140
  wetlands, 112-113
  *see also* specific species
Anadromous Fish Conservation Act of 1965, 277, 586
*Anas rubripes, see* Black duck
Animal and Plant Health Inspection Service, 1038
Animal Welfare Act, marine mammals, 1038
Antarctic Treaty, 292
Antioch Dunes evening primrose, 912, 914
Antioch Dunes National Wildlife Refuge, 912-913, 915
*Apodemia mormo langei, see* Lange's metalmark butterfly
Applachian Trail, 123
Aquaculture, 293-294, 320
Aquatic Resources Trust Fund, 204-205
Aransas National Wildlife Refuge, 660, 665, 667
Archeological Resources Preservation Act of 1979, 124
Arctic National Wildlife Refuge, 452, 454
Areas of critical environmental concern, 518-521
  areas already designated, 520
  confusion with natural area designations, 519
  defined, 518
  designation, 519
  failure of high-level Bureau of Land Management officials to give priority to, 519
Army
  Corps of Engineers, *see* Corps of Engineers
  research contacts, 1007
Atlantic Coast Fish Study for Development and Protection of Fish Resources, 273
Atlantic Flyway, numbers of geese, 257-258
Atlantic Flyway Council, 862, 867
Atlantic Ocean
  international fisheries, 291-292
  resource status, 333-336
Atlantic salmon, 697-709
  adult return records, 707
  anadromy and homing, 698-699
  artificial propagation program, 706
  commercial fishing, 701, 703, 705
  current trends, 702-704
  declining populations worldwide, 702-703
  diet, 698
  freshwater habitat, 700
  historical perspective, 701-702
  holding pools, 700
  impact of hydroelectric dams, 706-707
  management complexities in New England, 705-707
  Native American fishing, 700-701
  prognosis, 707-708
  range, 697-698
  recommendations, 708-709
  recreational fishing, 701, 705
  restoration efforts, 704-706, 708
  significance of species, 700-701

size of returning salmon, 698
smolt stocking, 707
spawning, 699-700
species description, 697
worldwide management, 704-705
Atlantic Salmon Convention Act of 1982, 292
Atlantic striped bass, decline in population, 326
Atlantic Striped Bass Conservation Act, 294, 326
Atlantic Tuna Commission, 280
Atlantic Tuna Convention Act, amendment, 288
Attelboro Mall Permit, 399-401, 408-409
Audubon's Blue List, 937
Australian pine, Everglades National Park, 487

Bachman's warbler, 833, 845
Bald eagle
  and lead shot, 238-239
  osprey enemy, 896
  recovery, 369
  *U. S. v. Dion*, 248, 360-361, 367-368
Bandelier, feral burros, 485-486
Bankhead-Jones Farm Tenant Act of 1937, 48, 74, 77, 83
Bartlett Act, 273
*Bergen v. Lawrence*, 538
Big-game animals, population, 538-539
Bighorn sheep, Bureau of Land Management, 508
Billfish, resource status, 335
Bill status office, 1016
Biosphere Reserve network, 479
Birds
  forest-interior species, 828
  migratory, *see* Migratory birds
  migratory shore birds, 229, 259
  species for which Fish and Wildlife Service prepares resource plans, 1059-1060
Bison
  hunting outside of Yellowstone National Park, 480
  population decline, 349
Black duck, 855-868
  band recoveries, 864
  behavior, 858
  current trends, 863-866
  diet, 856-857
  fall migration, 859
  habitat
    management, 867
    requirements, 860-861
  historical perspective, 862-863
  hunting, 861-862, 864, 866-867
  limiting factors, 861
  management, 866-867
  nesting, 858-859
  population objectives, status and trends, 256, 863, 1022
  prognosis, 868
  range, 857-858
  recommendations, 868
  renesting, 859
  significance of species, 861-862

size, 856
species description, 855-856
spring migration, 860
wintering, 859-860
Black Duck Committee, 862
Black Duck Management Plan for North America, 864, 867-868
Black-footed ferret, declining population, 370-371
Bluefin tuna, population, 333
Boars, Great Smoky Mountains, 484-485
Boating Safety Account, 204
Bobcats, export and CITES, 570-571
Bonn Convention, 572, 883-884
Bonneville Power Administration, 733
Bonytail chub, 363
Bosque del Apache National Wildlife Refuge, 661, 665
Bottlenose dolphins, permits for taking, 1037
Bottomfish, incidental catch, 336
Bottomland hardwoods, 382, 383, 408
Brant, population objectives, status and trends, 233, 241, 258-259, 1022-1023
Brazilian pepper, Everglades National Park, 487
Bristol Bay Cooperative Management plan, 222
Brook trout, eastern, in Yellowstone Lake, 486
Buenos Aires National Wildlife Refuge, hunting controversy, 433-434
Bureau of Land Management, 497-540
   acreage, 497, 498-499
   budget and personnel, 504-506
      information contacts, 1015
      wildlife habitat management appropriations, 505
      wildlife-related scientists, 504
   changing policies, 512
   Classification and Multiple-Use Act, 500
   commercial forests, 499
   cooperative management agreements, 534-536
   current issues, 511-512
   definition of affected interests, 537
   dilution of allotment management plans, 536
   dilution of land-use plans, 536-537
   diversity of wildlife on lands, 497
   endangered and threatened species, 507-508
   Endangered Species Act, 501
   E. O. 11988 and 11990, 501
   Federal Land Policy and Management Act, 498, 500
   fencing of public lands, 538
   Forest Service land swap, 101-102, 528-529
   FY 1985 appropriations, 32
   general accomplishments, 506-507
   grazing, see Grazing
   habitat management plans, 508-509
   key offices involved in fish and wildlife management, 502
   land base and uses, 498-499
   land-use planning, 503
   lawsuit to reinstate protective withdrawals and classifications, 522-524
   legal authority, 499-501

low priority for areas of environmental concern, 518-521
   Management Framework Plans, 503, 516-517
   Migratory Bird Conservation Act, 501
   Military Lands Withdrawal Act of 1985, 533-534
   nonfederal contributions, 510
   northern spotted owl
      low amounts of old-growth habitat, 750, 752-753
      number of management areas, 750, 756
      Oregon and California Grant Lands, 521-522
      underestimation of pairs needed, 752
   oil and gas leasing, 94
   Oregon and California Grant Lands Act, 501
   organization, 501-502
   penalties for violators and supplemental feeding, 537
   priority to commodity uses, 498
   Public Rangelands Improvement Act, 501
   rangelands, see Range management
   recovery plans, 507
   research and development, 510
   Resource Management Plans, 503, 515-518
      areas of critical environmental concern, 519
      federal court action and, 517
      status, 516
      supplemental program guidance, 517-518
      termination of land classifications without, 517, 524
   riparian policy, 510-511
   sagebrush control projects, 772-774
   Sikes Act Extension, 501
   state office personnel, 994-996
   status of resource, 538-540
   Taylor Grazing Act, 500
   Washington headquarters, 994
   wilderness study and management, 524-528
      charges of inadequacy, 526-527
      complaint that potential areas are not being protected, 525
      designation of new areas, 527
      mining in, 527-528
   Wild Free-Roaming Horses and Burros Act, 501, 532
   wild horses and burros, 77, 532-533
   wildlife habitat management, 503-504
      appropriations, 505
   wildlife program accomplishments, 506
Burning, prescribed, 109
   particulate matter from, 134
   research, 139
   sagebrush-control, 773-774
Burros, feral
   on Bureau of Land Management land, 77, 532-533
   Grand Canyon, Death Valley, and Bandelier, 485-486
   see also Wild Free-Roaming Horses and Burros Act

Cackling Canada goose, population declines, 241

Cactus, trade management plan, 948
*Calidris canutus, see* Red knot
California, spotted owl management, 755
California condor, declining population, 371
California sea otter, establishing new population, 364-367
*California v. Block*, 126
Canada, lack of wildlife refuges, 963
Canada goose, population objectives, status and trends, 233, 241, 257-258, 1023-1024
Canadian Polar Bear Technical Committee, 800
Canadian Wildlife Service, 882
    peregrine falcon propagation programs, 814, 816
*Canfield v. United States*, 538
*Canis lupus, see* Gray wolf
Canvasback duck, population objectives, status and trends, 232, 1025
Canyonlands National Park, proposed nuclear-waste dump, 482
Capital Construction Fund for Fishing Vessels, 281, 325
Captive-bred Wildlife Registration System, 1056-1058
Caribou, 169-172
Cayman Turtle Farm, 928
Celilo Falls, 723-724
Central Flyway, numbers of geese, 257-258
*Centrocerus urophasianus, see* Sage grouse
Channel Islands National Park
    African ice plants, 487
    combating exotic rodents, 478
Cheyenne Bottoms State Waterfowl Management Area, 668
Chincoteague National Wildlife Refuge, conflicts with development, 447-448
Chinook salmon, 715-737
    age at spawning, 717-718
    artificial production, 721-722
    causes of decline, 729-732
    commercial fishing, 731
        1886-1980, 726
    commerical and recreational exploitation, 724-725
    current trends, 727-728
    distribution of stock as percent of total catch, 720
    egg incubation and fry emergence, 719
    fecundity, 718-719
    fishing management, 735
    freshwater residence and downstream migration, 719-720
    historical perspective, 723-725
    homing, 716-717
    hydroelectric dams impact, 729
    Indian treaty rights, 732
    Native American fishing, 722-723
    Northwest Power Planning Act, 732-733
    ocean distribution, 720-721
    passage through turbines, 731
    prehistoric abundance, 725-726
    prehistoric and early settlement period, 723-724
    prognosis, 735-736
    range, 716
    recommendations, 736-737

resource status, 337, 339-340
    returns, 1960-1983, 727
    runs of Columbia, 716
    Salmon and Steelhead Conservation and Enhancement Act, 735
    sex ratio, 718
    significance of species, 722-723
    size, 718
    spawning, 717, 719
    storage projects, 729, 731
    trends during early period of exploitation, 726-727
    U. S.-Canada Samon Interception Treaty, 733-734
Chlorinated-hydrocarbon pesticides, *see* DDT
Christmans berry, Hawaii Volcanoes National Park, 487
Chugach National Forest, budget, 454
Chum salmon, commercial fishing, 1886-1980, 728
CITES, *see* Convention of International Trade in Endangered Species of Wild Fauna and Flora
Civilian Conservation Corps, 8
Clarke-McNary Act of 1924, 8, 130, 146
Classification and Multiple-Use Act, 500, 523
Clean Air Act of 1977, 131-132
    Class I airsheds
        National Forest System, 131, 134
        National Park Service, 475
Clean Water Act of 1977, 131, 384; *see also* Section 404 permit program
Clearcutting, 14, 53-54; *see also* Timber harvest
Coal Leasing Amendments Act of 1975, 91
Coal mining
    National Forest System, 91-92
    trends, 101
Coastal Barrier Resources Act, wetlands, 374
Coastal Zone Management Act of 1972, 202, 385
    spotted owl management, 521
    wetlands, 374
Coast Guard, enforcement of Fishery Conservation and Management Act, 302
Coho salmon
    commercial fishing, 1886-1980, 728
    resource status, 339-340
    returns, 1960-1983, 728
Colorado
    enforcement program, 608
    incidence of fish and wildlife violations, 614
    nongame wildlife management, 644-645, 649-650
        check-off, 645, 650
        encompassing all wildlife, 645
        funding, 645, 650
        projects, 649
        reorganization, 650
        river otter reintroduction, 649
Colorado River, water depletion and endangered fish, 363
Columbia River, maximum flood peak, 730
Columbia River Basin
    area, 715
    Chinook salmon, *see* Chinook salmon
Columbia River Basin Fishery Development Program, 272

Commerce Clause, 398-399
Commercial Fisheries Research and Development Act, 277
Commercial forests
  acreage, 144
  Bureau of Land Management, 499
  defined, 47
  Tongass National Forest, 163
Commission on Marine Science, Engineering, and Resources, 279-281
  recommendations, 279-280
Common loon, see Loon
Common Varieties of Mineral Materials Act of 1947, 95
Common variety minerals, 95
Comprehensive Environmental Response, Compensation, and Liability Act, 441
Condor, California, declining population, 371
Congressional Research Service, workshops on grazing fees, 514
Connecticut River, restoration programs, 705-706
Conservation Practices Program, 83
Conservation Reserve Program, 248
Contra Costa wallflower, 912-913
Convention Concerning Conservation of Migratory Birds and Their Environment, 555
Convention for the Conservation of Antarctic Marine Living Resources, 292
Convention for the Conservation of Salmon in the North Atlantic Ocean, 292, 704
Convention for the Preservation of the Halibut Fishery of the North Pacific Ocean and Bering Sea, 272
Convention for the Preservation of Wild Animals, Birds and Fish in Africa, 563
Convention for the Protection of Birds Useful to Agriculture, 563
Convention for the Protection of Migratory Birds, 231, 243, 553-554
Convention for the Protection, Preservation, and Extension of the Sockeye Salmon Fishery of the Fraser River System, 272
Convention for the Regulation of Whaling, 546
Convention on Fishing and Conservation of the Living Resources of the High Seas, 273
Convention on Future Multilateral Cooperation in the Northwest Atlantic Fisheries, 291-292
Convention on International Trade in Endangered Species of Wild Fauna and Flora, 1050-1055, 546, 566-574
  Appendix I, 568, 1051, 1053, 1055-1056
  Appendix II, 568, 1051, 1053, 1056
  Appendix III, 568, 1051, 1053, 1056
  application for permit, 1052-1053
  Berne criteria, 572
  certificates of exception, 1052, 1056
  current concerns, 570-571
  and Endangered Species Act, 1055
  exception to permit requirements, 1053-1054
  farming and ranching, 571-572
  Federal Wildlife Permit, 1050
  Fish and Wildlife Service preparation for biennial meetings, 568
  group listings controversy, 570

history and legislative authority, 566-567
  import/export permits, 1038-1039
  judging success of CITES, 573
  Kemp's Ridley Sea Turtle, 924
  Knowlton cactus, 945
  legislation, 573-574
  organization and operations, 567-569
  participation of nongovernmental organizations, 569
  permits for protected plants, 1054-1056
  personal and household goods, 1052
  shipments, 1053
  species protected, 1036
  staff and budget, 569-570
  USDA and, 1056
  see also Federal Wildlife Permit Office
Convention on Nature Protection and Wildlife Preservation in the Western Hemisphere, 546, 574
  control of markets for wild animal products, 567
  current concerns, 565-566
  history and legislative authority, 563-564
  moneys appropriated, 565
  organization and operations, 564-565
Convention on the Conservation of Migratory Species of Wild Animals, 572
Convention on the Territorial Sea and Contiguous Zone, 273
Convention on Wetlands of International Importance Especially as Waterfowl Habitat, 562-563, 883
Cooperative Farm Forestry Act of 1937, 148
Cooperative Fire Management, 149
Cooperative Forest Management Act of 1950, 148
Cooperative Forestry Assistance Act of 1978, 148-149, 152
Cooperative Forestry Program, 150-151
  budget, 152
  wildlife and fisheries, 152
Cooperative Management Agreements, 534-536
Coordination areas, 415
Coos Bay District, timber management plan and spotted owl, 750-751
Copeland Report, 147
Copper Report, 146
Corps of Engineers
  budget information contacts, 1015
  memoranda of agreement, 395-397
  projects that affect commercial and recreational fisheries, 302
  Section 404 responsibilities, 384-385; see also Section 404 permit program
Coyote, predator control on Malheur National Wildlife Refuge, 439
Crane Prairie Reservoir Osprey Management Area, 900
Critical habitat, see Habitat, critical
Current Federal Aid Research System, 203

Dall's porpoise, incidental catch, 327
Dams
  environmental impact, 47-48

prohibition on wild and scenic river system, 122
D'Arbonne National Wildlife Refuge, oil and gas exploration, 435-438
Davis Canyon, proposed nuclear-waste dump, 482
DDT
  effects on peregrine falcon, 811, 813, 819-820
  eggshell thinning, 897, 937-938
  loggerhead shrike, 937-938
  osprey, 896-898
  Wheeler National Wildlife Refuge contamination, 447
Death Valley, feral burros, 485-486
Defenders of Wildlife, 571
Defenders of Wildlife v. Endangered Species Scientific Authority, 571, 574
Deficit Reduction Act, 204
Deforestation, tropical, effect on U. S. migratory birds, 240-241
Delaware Bay
  red knot, migration, 875
  shoreline protection, 880, 882
Denver Wildlife Research Center, 223
Department of Agriculture
  CITES and, 1056
  educational information for fishing community, 301
Department of Agriculture Organic Act of 1956, 44
Department of Commerce
  endangered species, 354
  inspection programs for fishery products, 302
Department of State
  international conservation treaties, 547
  offices having international conservation responsibilities, 548
  participation in deliberations of fishery agreements, 301
Department of the Interior
  international wildlife conservation, 548-550
  leasable minerals, see Leasable minerals
  offices having international conservation responsibilities, 549
  position on use of reserved right, 436
  pressure for development of oil and gas in Alaska, 453
  Special Foreign Currency Program obligations, 550
  violation of duties, cooperative management agreements, 535
Desert bighorn sheep, Bureau of Land Management, 508
Desert tortoise, Bureau of Land Management, 508
Desert Tortoise Council, 508
Dingell-Johnson Act, see Federal Aid in Fish Restoration Act
Dinosaur National Monument, cricket-control programs and peregrine falcon populations, 481-482
Division of Federal Aid, program structure, 221
Division of Law Enforcement, program structure, 220

Division of Realty, program structure, 220
Division of Refuge Management, 220, 419
Division of Wildlife Management, 220, 226
Division of Wildlife Research, 220, 223
Dogfish, 327, 333-334
Dove, mourning, population, 1028
Duck
  breeding population, 250-256
  1985-1986 hunting regulations, 234-236
  see also specific species
Duck hawk, see Peregrine falcon
Duck stamp, 375-376, 418
Ducks Unlimited, 216, 867
  opposition to hunting take restrictions, 235
  wetlands preservation, 113
Dworshak Dam, 729

East-Coast Poaching, 616-617
Eastern national forests, 19, 21, 7-8
Eastern Pacific Ocean Tuna Fishing Agreement, 291
Eastern Wildnerness Act of 1975, 12, 44, 121
Eighth International Conference of American States, 564
Elk, 71, 480
Emergency Wetlands Acquisition Act, 406
Emergency Wetlands Conservation Act, 380
Emergency Wetlands Resources Act, 244-245
Emperor goose, population, 241, 258
Endangered species
  bald eagle, 238-239
  Bureau of Land Management responsibilities, 507-508
  defined, 349
  desert tortoise, 508
  Forest Service role, 109-110
  illegal taking or possesion, 614
  Kemp's Ridley sea turtle, see Kemp's Ridley sea turtle
  Knowlton cactus, see Knowlton cactus
  Land Acquisition Priority System, 430-431
  Lange's metalmark butterfly, see Lange's metalmark butterfly
  loon, see Loon
  1985-1986 state budgets, 642-644
  in National Park System, 493
  osprey, see Osprey
  peregrine falcon, see Peregrine falcon
  permits for prohibited activities, 1047-1048
  prohibited activities, 1047
  red-cockaded woodpecker, 161-162
  research, 140
  small whorled pogonia, see Small whorled pogonia
  state nongame research, 636
  whooping crane, see Whooping crane
  woodland caribou, 169-172
Endangered Species Act of 1973, 44, 501, 567, 580, 586
  adequacy of protection for candidate species, 359-360
  amendments, 565, 829
  authority for endangered species program, 349-350
  and CITES, 1055
  critical habitat, whooping crane, 668

current and proposed authorization ceilings, 366
exceptions allowed, 1035
exemption of captive-bred raptors, 361-362, 816
inconsistencies with Marine Mammal Protection Act, 366
Knowlton cactus, protection, 947
marine fisheries, 281
marine mammals protected, 1035
peregrine falcon
    exclusion of captive falcon, 816
    similarity of appearance clause, 808
permit exemptions, 1048-1049
permits for prohibited activities, 1047-1048
prohibited activities, 1046-1047
reauthorization, 363, 365-367
Section 6 cooperative agreements, 356-358
Section 7, 357, 359
shared jurisdiction, 1050
steel shot prohibition, 238
uncertainty over application to American Indians, 360-361
whooping crane recovery team, 670
wildlife management, 105
wildlife refuge establishment, 417-418
*see also* Endangered species program
Endangered Species Conservation Act, 567
Endangered species program, 347-371
    appropriations, 353, 367
    backlog of candidate species, 354
    budget and staff, 352-353
    declining species, 370-371
    Department of Agriculture, 352
    division of responsibility, 350
    establishing new population of California sea otters, 364-367
    illegal trade in peregrine falcons, 361-362
    interagency consultation, 357, 359
    legal authority, 349-350
    legal developments, 367-369
    National Marine Fisheries Service, 352
    new species listings, 353-354
    Office of Endangered Species, Fish and Wildlife Service, 352
    organizational chart, 348
    principal elements, 349
    program administration, 350-352
    protection for threatened predators, 364
    recovering species, 353, 369-370
    recovery plans, 354, 356
    Section 6 cooperative agreements, 356-358
    species added to endangered and threatened lists in 1985, 355-356
    species subject to Department of Commerce jurisdiction, 354
    western water conflicts, 362-364
    *see also* Endangered Species Act, 365
Endangered Species Scientific Authority, 570
Energy and minerals management, 85-102
    accelerated mineral activity, 99-100
    common variety minerals, 95
    General Mining Law of 1872, 87, 99
    impacts on fish and wildlife, 86
    leasable minerals, *see* Leasable minerals
    locatable minerals, 87-89
    mineral patent applications, 88
    mineral resources types, 86
    mining administration on National Forest System, 90
    mining in Bureau of Land Management wilderness areas, 527-528
    outstanding and reserved rights, 97-98, 436
    planning, 98-99
    potential acreage, 85
    protected areas, 95-97
    prudent man and marketability test, 88
    roles of Forest Service and Interior Department, 86-87
    workload and production, fiscal years 1980-1984, 99
    *see also* Oil and gas drilling and exploration
*Enos. v. Marsh*, 368
Environmental Protection Agency
    acid rain, 135
    budget information contacts, 1015
    fish research, 310
    memoranda of agreement, 395-397
    Section 404 responsibilities, 384-385
    upgrading of 404 program, 392-394
        404(c) veto power, 392-393
        emphasis on bottomland hardwoods and isolated wetlands, 393
        enforcement, 393-394
        identifying high-priority wetlands, 393
        wetlands research, 394
Environmental zone, defined, 245-246
Environmental Zone Deductions, 490-491
Everglades National Park
    diversion of freshwater flows, 482
    exotic plants, 487
    groundwater depletion, 483
Executive Order 11644, 128
Executive Order 11988, 374, 501
Executive Order 11989, 128
Executive Order 11990, 374-375, 501
Executive Re-organization Plan No. 4 of 1970, 280, 288

*Falco peregrinus, see* Perergrine falcon
Farm and Rural Development Act, 405
Farm Bill, *see* Food Security Act of 1985
Farmers Home Administration, conservation easements, 405
Federal Aid in Fish Restoration Act, 178, 182-183, 197, 580
    amendments, 198-199, 587
    apportionment of funds, 183
    budget and staff, 187
        expenditures by state, 191
        research funding, 586
    eligible projects, 182
    fish restoration and management project definition, 182
    habitat acquisition, 588
    increased support to fisheries management and boating programs, 294
    law enforcement, 608
    new stocking and hatchery guidelines, 199-200
    Reagan initiative to cut spending, 204-205
    research expenditures, 193-195
    revenues sources, 183

state wildlife conservation funds, 583
Federal Aid in Wildlife Restoration Act, 178-181, 197, 579-580
  amendments to promote formal planning, 587
  apportionment of funds, 181
  budget and staff, 187
    nongame funds, 632
    research funding, 191-193, 586
  eligible projects, 180-181
  game emphasis, 179
  habitat acquisition, 588
  land acquisition, 195
  law enforcement, 608
  purpose, 178-179
  restoration project definition, 179-180
  revenue sources, 181
  state use of funds by project type, 189-191
  state wildlife conservation funds, 583
  trapper education, 201
  use of grants, 178
Federal Aid Program, 177-210
  biological achievements, 188-189
  budget and staff, 177, 187
  Dingell-Johnson Act
    expenditures by state, 191
    Reagan initiative to cut spending, 204-205
    research expenditures, 193-195
    new uses, 198-199
  diversion of license revenues, 201-202
  expenditures for waterfowl, 195, 197
  fishing lakes, 195
  Fish and Wildlife Service' inactive role in setting guidelines, 189
  goals, 185-186
  grant process, 186-187
  hunter education, 200-201
  incompatible use of areas acquired with federal aid funds, 202-203
  land acqusition expenditures, 194-195
  legal authorities, *see* Federal Aid in Fish Restoration Act; Federal Aid in Wildlife Restoration Act; Fish and Wildlife Conservation Act
  legal developments, 210
  new stocking and hatchery guidelines, 199-200
  organization and operations, 184-188
  Pittman-Robertson Act
    research expenditures, 191-193
    state use by project type, 189-191
  program implementation, 185
  project review process, 186
  reliance on state administration, 198
  research coordination, 203-204
  resource status, 208-210
  status of state planning efforts, 196-198
  substantial project, definition, 186
  trapper education, 201
Federal Assistance Program, personnel, 979-980
Federal Land Policy and Management Act of 1976, 45-46, 74, 96-97, 500, 773, 775
  areas of critical environmental concern, 518-521

Bureau of Land Management requirements, 498, 503
cooperative management agreements and, 535
grazing fees, 513
instant study areas, 525, 527
range betterment funds, 76, 82, 85
range management, 75-76
refuge establishment, 415
Resource Management Plans, *see* Bureau of Land Management, Resource Management Plans
wilderness studies, 524-525
withdrawals and classifications, 523
Federal marine fisheries management, 267-340
aquaculture, 293-294
Congressional committees, 303-304
federal agencies other than National Marine Fisheries Service, 301-303
federal waters, *see* Federal waters
Fishery Conservation and Management Act, *see* Fishery Conservation and Management Act
fishery management plans, 286-287, 305-309
  amendments, 308-309
  fisheries under consideration, 316
  framework plans, 308
  in effect, 315-316
  need for environmental impact statements, 305-306
  need for in fishery, 305
  optional features, 308
  preliminary plans in effect, 315
  procedural requirements of other acts, 307
  proposed fisheries, 316
  proposed rules, 306
  recreational fisheries, 319
  required elements, 307
  striped bass, 326
  swordfish, 325
  unenforceable regulations, 329
foreign competition, 321-323
foreign fishing, 287
incidental catch, 326-328
industry assistance, 275-278
international fisheries agreements after Fishery Conservation and Management Act, 290-291
  Antarctic Treaty, 292
  Atlantic Ocean, 291-292
  Pacific Ocean, 291
jurisdictional controversies, 325-326
legislation, 329-331
  Congressional action in 1984, 294-295
  fishery marketing councils, 330-331
  Interjurisdictional Fisheries Research Act, 331
  National Aquaculture Improvement Act, 331
  reauthorizaton of Magnuson Fishery Conservation and Management Act, 329-330
  since Fishery Conservation and Management Act, 292-293
legislative history, 270-278
  Act of February 9, 1871, 270-271

Agricultural Trade Development and Assistance Act, 278
American Fisheries Promotion Act, 289-290
Anadromous Fish Conservation Act, 277
Coastal Zone Management Act, 282
Commercial Fisheries Research and Development Act, 277
Fish and Wildlife Act, 277
Fish and Wildlife Coordination Act, 278
Fishermen's Protective Act, 276
Fishery Conservation and Management Act, 282-283
Fishery Conservation Zone Act, 288
halibut fishery, 271-272
Lacey Act amendment, 278
Magnuson Fishery Conservation and Management Act, 283
management jurisdiction, 272-273
Marine Mammal Protection Act, 281
National Marine Sanctuary Program, 282
National Sea Grant College and Program Act, 277-278
Northwest Atlantic and North Pacific fisheries, 274-275
Pacific salmon treaties, 272
Pacific tuna fisheries, 274
Pelly Amendment, 276
Section 404 permit program, 278, 281-282
Sponge Act, 271
Treaty for the Preservation and Protection of Fur Seals, 271
Truman proclamation, 273
U. S. Fishing Fleet Improvment Act, 277
limiting access to domestic fisheries, 323-325
management under the Magnuson Fishery Conservation and Management Act, 315-317
marine recreational fisheries, 318-319
maximum sustainable yield concept, 286
National Marine Fisheries Service, see National Marine Fisheries Service
nonfederal agencies and organizations, 303
optimum yield, 286
planning, 304-309
    fishery management plans, see Federal marine fisheries management, fishing management plans
    National Marine Fisheries Service, 304-305
problem-causing features, 270
research, 310-311
    National Marine Fisheries Service, 309-310
status of resource, 332-340
    Alaska Region, 339-340
    Northeast Region, 332-334
    Northwest Region, 338-339
    Southeast Region, 334-336
    Southwest Region, 336-338
Stratton Commission, 279-281
transboundary fish stocks, 326
transition years, 279
Federal Power Act, 275
Federal Water Pollution Control Act of 1972, 131, 384
Federal waters, 283

defined, 268
exclusive management over, 283
foreign catch, 269-270
joint ventures, 322
jurisdiction management, 273
map, 284-285
Federal Wildlife Permit Office
    CITES responsibilities, 569-570, 1050
    moneys appropriated, 569
Fees, Permits, and Regulations Division, 297
Ferret, black-footed, declining population, 370-371
Fish
    Fish and Wildlife Service propagation species, 1064-1065
    habitat
        National Forest System, 111
        research, 140
        see also Habitat management
    species for which Fish and Wildlife Service prepares resource plans, 1060-1061
    stocking, 199-200
    see also Anadromous fish; Federal Aid in Fish Restoration Act; specific species
Fish and Wildlife Act of 1956, 350
    marine fisheries, 277
    wildlife refuge establishment, 417
Fish and Wildlife Conservation Act of 1980, 178, 183-184, 197, 580, 587, 632
    financing, 184
    Fish and Wildlife Service report on funding, 205-206
    nongame wildlife conservation, 183
    reauthorization legislation, 207
Fish and Wildlife Coordination Act, 217, 278, 350, 385, 389, 418
    amendments, 246-247, 405-406
    requirement of state pln for nongame management, 638
Fish and Wildlife Program, 733
Fish and Wildlife Reference Service, 203-204
Fish and Wildlife Service
    administration, 980-981
    budget information contacts, 1015
    cooperative agreement with states, 580
    endangered species program, see Endangered species program
    Federal Aid Program, see Federal Aid Program
    Federal Assistance Program, personnel, 979-980
    Fishery Resources Program, 978, 1064-1065
    Habitat Resources Program, personnel, 979
    increased hunting on wildlife refuges, 433-434
    management of inland fisheries, 302
    Marine Mammal Conservation, personnel, 1014
    memoranda of agreement, 395-397
    mitigation recomendations and Section 404 permit program, 389-390
    National Wetlands Inventory, see National Wetlands Inventory
    new criteria for identification of lead-shot problem areas, 239
    Office of International Activities, 565
    Office of the Scientific Authority, 569

offices responsible for migratory birds activities, 220-221
permits for prohibited activities, 1047-1048
planning and budget personnel, 980
recovery plan, 787-788
Regional offices, 351, 978-979, 981-985
Regional Wetland Coordinators, 1000
research and development personnel, 980
Resource Contamination Division, 446
Section 6 agreements, 634
Section 404 permit reviews, 385
species for which regional resources plans are prepared, 1062-1063
species for which resource plans are prepared, 1059-1061
undercover training for conservation officers, 606
Washington headquarters, 976
Wildlife Resources Program, *see* Wildlife Resources Program
*see also* National Wildlife Refuge System
Fisheries Loan Fund, 314
extension, 293
Fishermen's Contingency Fund, 293, 314
Fishermen's Guaranty Fund, 314
Fishermen's Protective Act, 276
amendments, 288, 292-293
Fishery Conservation and Management Act of 1976, 268, 270, 275, 282-283
amendments, 288-290
deep-seabed mining, 289
exclusions from management provisions, 283
fishery management plans, 286-287
maximum sustainable yield concept, 286
optimum yield, 286
Packwood-Magnuson Amendment, 289
*see also* Magnuson Fishery Conservation and Management Act
Fishery conservation zone, *see* Federal waters
Fishery Conservation Zone Act of 1977, 288
Fishery Management Operations Division, 297
Fishery products, U.S. trade deficit, 269
Fishery Resources Program, 978, 1064-1065
Fish hawk, *see* Osprey
Fishing
commercial
Atlantic salmon, 701, 703, 705
Chinook salmon, 724-726, 731, 735
chum salmon, 726
coho salmon, 726
impact on loons, 687, 689
sockeye salmon, 726
foreign, 306-307, 321, 287
incidental catch, 269, 326-328
marine recreational, 269, 318-319
put-and-take stocking, 200
recreational
Atlantic salmon, 701, 705
Chinook salmon, 724, 735
state regulations, 588
*see also* Federal marine fisheries management
Fishing Bridge, 483
Fishing Vessel and Gear Damage Compensation Fund, 314
Fishing Vessel Obligation Fund, 325
Florida, nongame wildlife programs, 650-652
funding, 651

Nongame Wildlife Advisory Council, 650-651
public education, 651
research projects, 651
Florida Panther National Wildlife Refuge, 456
*Florida Rock Industries,Inc. v. United States*, 407-408
Flyways, administrative, 10-11
Food and Drug Administration, safety of fish and shellfish products, 302
Food Security Act of 1985, 375, 403-405
conservation easements, 405
conservation reserve, 403-404
sodbusters and swampbusters, 247-248, 404-405
Foreign Assistance Act of 1961, 551
Foreign Fishing Observer Fund, 314
Forensics, wildlife, 627
Forest and Rangeland Renewable Resources Research Act of 1978, *see* Resources Planning Act
Forest habitat
impact of second-home development, 836-837
regrowth, 836
Forest Pest Management Program, 149-150
Forest plans
habitat for endangered and threatened species, 107
mineral planning, 98-99
proposed roads in roadless areas, 127
timber sales, 55, 66-67
Forest Research Program, 135-144, 18
budget, 137, 139
expansion and increased complexity of research needs, 142-143
Forest and Rangeland Renewable Resources Research Act, 137
functional areas, 136
funding, 143-144
FY 1985 appropriations, 33
history, 136-137
legal authority and requirements, 136-137
planning and management, 137-142
experimental forests and ranges, 141
fire and atmospheric sciences, 139
fish, 140-141
forest environmental research, 138-139
forest products and harvesting, 139
general research efforts, 138-139
insects and diseases, 139
international forestry, 139
range, 140
research natural areas, 141-142
research planning, 138
resource economics, 139
timber management, 139
wildlife, 140-141
trends and issues, 142-144
Forest Reserve Act of 1891, 4, 103, 145
Forest reserves
history, 4-7
Pinchot's philosophy, 6
purpose, Organic Act, 5
transfer from Interior to Agriculture, 5

Forest Road Program, 62-63
Forestry
    international, 139
    *see also* State and Private Forestry Program
Forestry Incentives Program, 148
Forests
    commercial, *see* Commercial forest
    historical acreage, 835
    nonindustrial private, 148
    private ownership, 144
Forest Service
    Adopt-a-Horse program, 79
    adoption of European forestry concepts, 6
    authority over administration of energy and
        mineral activities, 528
    budget, 30-44
        categories, 32-33
        full-time equivalents, 32-33
        FY 1985 appropriations, 32-34, 36
        information contacts, 1015
        management funding, 36
        permanent and trust funds, 33, 35
        resource-protection programs, 36
        setting appropriations, 30-31
        timber program funding, 49
        trends, 38-40
        *see also* Resources Planning Act; specific
            agencies
    Bureau of Land Management land swap,
        101-102, 528-529
    congressional oversight of programs, 22-23
    controversy, 15
    criticisms of mismanagement, 2-3
    early reserves, 4-7
    environmental laws affecting forest manage-
        ment, 13
    feuding with Park Service, 8-9
    field staff organization, 20
    fish and wildlife habitats, *see* Habitat man-
        agement
    forest and range experiment stations, 974-
        975
    grizzly bear management, 168-169
    history and legislative authority, 3-6
    Human Resources Program, 18
    Job Corps, 18
    major programs, 18-19
    moratorium on destroying healthy animals,
        80
    multiple use, 12-13
    National Forest Management Act, 14-15
    organization, 15-18
    planning
        appeals, 27
        developing alternativs, 25-26
        forest plans, 23-25
        FORPLAN, 26
        implementation, 27-28
        irrelevance of Resources Planning Act
            programs to decision-making process,
            28
        national planning, 23-24
        plan amendment, 27
        regional guides, 23-24
        Resources Planning Act in practice, 28-30
    proposed management for spotted owl, 751
    recreation and wilderness, 9, 12
    regional headquarters, 973-974
    road constrution and management, 61-64
    Roadless Area Review and Evaluation, 125-
        127
    Senior Community Service Employment
        Program, 18
    setting grazing levels, 81
    state and private forestry, 972, 975
    supplemental environmental impact state-
        ment, spotted owl, 751
    timber management, *see* Timber manage-
        ment
    Touch America Project, 19
    Volunteers in the National Forests, 18-19
    Washington headquarters, 971
    woodland caribou management, 169-172
    Youth Conservation Corps, 18
    *see also* National Forest System; specific pro-
        grams
FORPLAN, 26
Forsythe-Chafee Act, *see* Fish and Wildlife
    Conservation Act
Fur seals
    permits for taking, 1037
    Treaty for Preservation and Protection of
        Fur Seals, 545-546

Gadwall, population status, trends, and objec-
    tives, 232
Game
    birds, management, 229
    emphasis of Pittman-Robertson Act, 179
    illegal method of taking, 609
    illegal possession, 609
    population in southeastern states, 208-209
    wildlife violations, 609
Game refuge
    establishment on federal land, 103
    hunting on, 104
Gas leasing, *see* Oil and gas leasing
Gateway National Recreation Area, herpeto-
    fauna restoration at Jamaica Bay, 476-477
*Gavia, see* Loon
*Geer v. Connecticut,* 581
General Land Office, land frauds, 5
General Exchange Act, 45
General Mining Law of 1872, 87-88, 99, 522
Geological Survey, National Water Quality
    Assessment Program, 445
Georges Bank, haddock populations, 333
Geothermal steam, 92-93
Geothermal Steam Act of 1970, 92-93
Gila National Forest, 9
Gillnet fishery, incidental catch of seabirds,
    327
Glacier National Park, problems with adjacent
    lands, 482
Golden eagle, population objectives, status and
    trends, 1028
Goose
    emperor, 241, 258
    Pacific Flyway, reversing decline of, 241-243
    population estimates, 257-259
    ross, 233
    snow goose, 233, 258, 1025

subsistence hunting by Alaskan natives, 242-243, 259
white-fronted, 241, 1026
Grand Canyon, feral burros, 485-486
Grand Coulee Dam, 729
Granger-Thye Act of 1950, 75
Grant Village, 483
Grasslands, see National grasslands
Grays Lake National Wildlife Refuge, 660, 664, 671
Gray wolf, 951-964
    current trends, 957
    domestic stock predation, 955
    ecology and behavior, 953-954
    education, 964
    fear of, 955
    hunting, 364, 958-960
    management, 957-959
        control and ungulate populations, 958
        recommendations, 963-964
        use of poison to control, 956
    physical characteristics, 952
    population, 951
    prognosis, 959-961
    recommendations, 961
    recovery plan, 957-959
    reintroduction, 961-962
    research, 962
    reserves, 962-963
    role in regulating prey, 954-955
    species description, 951
    taxonomy, 952
Grazing, 529-532
    allotments, 72-73
    agreements, 83
    Bureau of Land Management lands, 499
    decline in Bureau of Land Management funding, 506
    definition of affected interests, 537
    delay in making adjustments, 530
    dilution of allotment management plans, 536
    dilution of land-use plans, 536-537
    effect on soil and water quality, 135
    environmental impact statements, 530
    fees, 76, 83, 85
        reauthorization, 513-515
    increases in potential wilderness areas, 526
    interrelationships of wildlife and fish with livestock, 140
    Malheur National Wildlife Refuge, 438-439
    management, 82-83
    penalties for violators and supplemental feeding, 537
    permits, 75, 80-81
        western states, 83
    revised grazing rules, 534-535
    grazing trends, 83-84
    see also Range management
Grazing Service, 500
Great Basin National Park, legislation for, 491
Great Egg Harbor Inlet, 882
Great Smoky National Park, wild boars, 484-485
Green sea turtles, Surinamese plan, 572
Grizzly bear, 168-169
    hunting, 364

Interagency Grizzly Bear Committee, 110
Groundfish, 337, 340
Grus americana, see Whooping crane
Guava, Hawaii Volcanoes National Park, 487
Gulf States Marine Fisheries Commission, 273

Habitat
    acquisition
        nationally significant, Land Acquisition Priority System, 431-432
        by states, 588
        see also National Wildlife Refuge System; Wetlands
    conservation, National Marine Fisheries Service, 317-318
    critical, defined, 668
    improvement, drop in, 112
Habitat destruction
    declining whooping crane population, 667
    loggerhead shrike, 937
    loons, 686-687
    peregrine falcon, 816
    tropical, 834
Habitat management, 102-113
    anadromous fish, 110
    direct habitat improvement, 108-109
    drop in habitat improvement, 112
    endangered, threatened and sensitive species, 109-110
    funding, 37
    indicator species, 107
    legal authority and requirements, 103-106
        Endangered Species Act, 105
        Forest Reserve Act, 103
        game refuges, 103-104
        National Environmental Policy Act of 1969, 104-105
        National Forest Management Act of 1976, 105-106
        Organic Act, 103
        Sikes Act, 105-106
    maintaining viable populations, 107
    National Forest System, funding, 172-173
    planning and management, 106
    resident fish, 111
    trends and issues, 112-113
    wetlands and anadromous fish, 112-113
    wildlife coordination, 108
    wildlife damage control, 111-112
Habitat Resources Program
    Office of Ecological Services, 220-221
    personnel, 979
Haddock, population, 333
Halibut fishery, 271-272
Harbor seals, 339
Hawaii Volcanoes National Park, exotic plant species, 487
Hell's Canyon Dam, 729
Herpetofauna, restoration at Jamaica Bay, 476-477
Historic Preservation Act of 1966, 124
Hooded warbler, 827-847
    breeding, 827-828, 830
    corporate responsibility, 847
    current trends, 838-840
    declines in population, 839, 845

federal government responsibility, 846-847
individual responsibility, 847
management, 840
migration, 830-833
    interactions with permanent tropical residents, 830-831
    territoriality, 832-833
    winter-habitat use, 832
minimum forest area required, 828
prognosis, 840-841, 845-846
    breeding grounds, 841
    wintering grounds, 841
range, 827-830
    winter, 829-830
recommendations, 846-847
significance of species, 833-834
species description, 827
winter habitat
    historical record, 837
Hooper Bay Agreement, 241-242, 561
Horses, wild, on Bureau of Land Management land, 532-533; see also Wild Free-Roaming Horses and Burros Act
House of Representatives, committees, 1017-1019
H.R. 1533, 329
H.R. 2122, 489
H.R. 2483, 491
H.R. 2935, 330
H.R. 3302, 491
H.R. 3804, 490
H.R. 4962, 489
Humane Society of the United States v. Hodel, 434
Humane Society of the United States v. Watt, 249
Human Resources Program, 18
Humpback chub, 363
Hunting
    black duck, 861-862, 864, 866-867
    buddy, 626
    ducks, 1985-1986 regulations, 234-236
    education
        Federal Aid Program, 200-201
        funded by Pittman-Robertson grants, 181
    gray wolf, 364, 958-960
    grizzly bear, 364
    illegal, 614-615, 626-627
        see also State wildlife law enforcement
    impact on sage grouse, 774-775
    land-and-shoot trapping, 963
    on refuges, 433-434
    polar bear, 799-802
    red knot, 879
    shorebirds, 878
    stabilized regulations, 228-229, 232
    state regulations, 588
    subsistence
        Alaska Lands Act, 451
        amending international treaties to allow, 557-562
        average annual harvest, 561
        effect on Pacific Flyway, 559
        Endangered Species Act, 360-361
        goose, 242-243, 259
        Hooper Bay Agreement, 561
        legitimization, 560
        loon, 687, 689

nonenforcement of Migratory Bird Treaty Act, 558
    polar bear, 802
    taking of listed wildlife, 1049
    swan, 259
    trapper education, 201
    trapping and steel-jaw traps, 435
        in National Parks, 489-490
    woodcock, 262
Hybrids, protection, 1049
Hydroelectric dams, 46-47
    Chinook salmon, decline, 729
    impact on Atlantic salmon, 706-707

Ickes, Harold, 8-9
Idaho Panhandle National Forest Plan, 170-171
Illinois Natural History Survey, 634
Indian treaty rights, Chinook salmon, 732
In Re: Permanent Surface Mining Regulation Litigation, 92
Interagency Coordinating Committee, 383
Interagency Grizzly Bear Committee, 110, 169
Interagency Spotted Owl Management Plan, 521
Inter-American Tropical Tuna Commission, 274, 291
Interior Appropriations Bill, Stevens amendment, 237
Interior Department, see Department of the Interior
Interior least tern, population objectives, status and trends, 1027
Interjurisdictional Fisheries Research Act, 331
International Agreement for the Conservation of Polar Bears, 799-800
International American Tropical Tuna Commission, 551
International Association of Fish and Wildlife Agencies, 303, 560
International Commission for the Conservation of Atlantic Tunas, 280, 298
International Commission for the Northwest Atlantic Fisheries, 282
International Conference on the Law of the Sea, 273
International Convention Advisory Commission, 572
International Convention for the Conservation of Atlantic Tuna, 280
International Convention for the High Seas Fisheries of the North Pacific Ocean, 275
    amendments, 291
International Convention for the Northwest Atlantic Fisheries, 275, 288
International Convention for the Regulation of Whaling, 546
International Council for Bird Preservation, 840
International North Pacific Fisheries Commission, 298
International Pacific Halibut Commission, 298
International Shorebird Survey, 873, 875, 879, 881
International Trade Commission, 322-323
International Union for the Conservation of

Nature and Natural Resources, 562, 567, 569, 800, 960
International wildlife conservation, 543-575
  acceding to Ramsar Convention, 562-563
  agencies and programs, 547-552
    Interior Department, 548-550
  amending treaties to allow subsistence taking, 557-562
  CITES, see Convention on International Trade in Endangered Species of Wild Fauna and Flora
  history and legislative authority, 545-546
  legal developments, 574
  migratory bird treaties, see Migratory birds, treaties
  necessity of international cooperation, 543-544
  special setting for international cooperation, 544-545
  status of resource, 574-574
  Third World assistance, 551
  treaties
    halibut fishery, 271-272
    Pacific salmon, 272
    treaty-making process, 546-547
  Treaty for Preservation and Protection of Fur Seals, 545-546
  U. S. influence on multilateral lending institutions, 551-552
  Western Hemisphere Convention, 563-566
*Isotria Medeoloides, see* Small whorled pogonia

Jamaica Bay Wildlife Refuge, herpetofauna restoration, 476-477
Job Corps, 18
Joint Black Duck Committee, 862
Joint Congressional Committee on Forestry, 147

Kemp's Ridley sea turtle, 919-930
  breeding, 921-923
  captive propagation, 923, 929
  cooperation between U. S. agencies and Mexico, 925, 928
  current trends, 924-925
  diet, 921
  experiment to establish second nesting population, 926
  headstarting, 926, 929
  historical perspective, 923-924
  incidental catch, 328
  management, 925-928
  oil on nesting beach, 924-925
  population declines, 924
  predators, 922-923
  prognosis, 928
  protection of nesting beach, 925, 927
  range, 920-921
  recommendations, 928-930
  significance of species, 923
  species description, 919-920
Kesterson National Wildlife Refuge, contaminants, 440-441, 445-447
Ketchikan Pulp Co., 164
Kinbasket Lake, 731
Kirwin National Wildlife Refuge, 668

Knowlton cactus, 943-949
  current trends, 945-946
  historical perspective, 944-945, 956
  management, 946-948
  prognosis, 948
  range, 943-949
  recommendations, 948-949
  recovery plan, 946-947
  reintroduction to historical sites, 947
  significance of species, 944, 954-956
  species description, 943
  tissue culturing, 944, 948
Knutson-Vandenberg Act of 1930, 8
  amendment, 106
Knutson-Vandenberg Fund, 35, 37
  receipts, 58
  reforestation, 57, 60

L-20 regulations, 9
Lacey Act, 945
  amendment, 62, 278
Land Acquisition Priority System, 430-432
Land-and-shoot trapping, 963
Land and Water Conservation Fund, 44, 105, 123, 244, 418-419
  acquisition and appropriation history, 380
  land acquisition, 378-379
  proposed amendment, 125
  wetlands, acquisition, 377
Land and Water Conservation Fund Act, 44, 123, 350, 353
  refuge acquisition, 418
Lange's metalmark butterfly, 911-915
  breeding, 911-912
  current trends, 913
  habitat improvement, 914
  historical perspective, 913
  management, 913-914
  prognosis, 914-915
  range, 912
  recommendations, 915
  shared endangered ecosystem, 912
  significance of species, 912
  species description, 911
*Lanius ludovicianus, see* Loggerhead shrike
Lantana, Hawaii Volcanoes National Park, 487
Large whorled pogonia, 781-782
Lassen National Forest, 900
Lead shot, toxic poisoning
  bald eagles, 238-239
  criteria for identification of problem areas, 239-240
  death rate, 236-237
  migratory birds, 236-240
  *NWF v. Hodel*, 238, 368-369
  partial ban on lead shot, 237
  Stevens amendment, 237
  Supplemental Environmental Impact Statement, 240
Leasable minerals, 89, 91-95
  acquired lands, 91
  coal mining, 91-92, 101
  existing licenses, prospecting permits and leases, 93
  geothermal steam, 92-93

management, 93-95
Mineral Leasing Act of 1920, 89
preference right lease, 93
prohibition under Wilderness Act, 127
public domain, 89
Legislation
bill status office, 1016
congressional document offices, 1016
Lehman Cave National Monument, 491
*Lepidochelys kempi, see* Kemp's Ridley sea turtle
Lichens, as indicator for airborne pollutants,
134
Lillian Annette Rowe National Audubon
Sanctuary, 672
Livestock, grazing, *see* Grazing; Range management
Lobster, resource status, 334
Locatable minerals, 87-89
regulations, 88-89
Loggerhead shrike, 933-939
breeding, 934
current trends, 936-938
DDT, 937-938
diet, 934-935
habitat destruction, 937
historical perspective, 936
management, 938
population declines, 936-937
prognosis, 938-939
range, 934
recommendations, 939
significance of species, 935-936
species description, 933
Loon, 679-692
adaptation to human intrustion, 6890690
artificial nesting platforms, 688
breeding, 680-681, 691
competition with man for habitats, 686
current trends, 684-687
environmental pollutants, 684-686, 691
foods, 680
historical perspective, 683-684
hunting by Native Americans, 687, 689
impact of commercial fishing, 687, 689
indicator of heavy metal pollution, 683
locomotion, 680
management, 687
migration, 681-683
nesting habitat destruction, 686-687
populations, 685, 691
productivity, 684
prognosis, 689-690
public education, 688, 691-692
recommendations, 690-692
significance of species, 683
species description, 679-680
status in states, 688
volunteer loon watchers, 688
Loon Preservation Committee, 687
Louisiana Pacific-Ketchikan, 164-165
*Louisiana Wildlife Federation v. York*, 408
Lumber Code, 147-148

Mackerels, resource status, 335-336
Magnuson Fishery Conservation and Management Act, 283, 290
amendments, 321
conflicting jurisdiction in state waters, 325
efficient implementation, 328-329
enforcement, 302
fishery management plans, *see* Federal marine fisheries management, fishery management plans
management of fisheries under, 315-317
preliminary management plans, 315
reauthorization, 329-330
State Department, 301
Maine rivers, restoration programs, 705-706
Malheur National Wildlife Refuge, predator control and grazing, 438-439
Mallard
black, *see* Black duck
population status, trends, and objectives, 232, 234, 1030
Mammals, species for which Fish and Wildlife Service prepares resource plans, 1059
Manomet Bird Observatory, 873, 875
Marine fisheries
Canadian import impact, 322
economic and cultural role, 267-268
management, federal offices involved in, 1011-1014
trade deficit, 322
*see also* Federal marine fisheries management
Marine Fisheries Commissions, 303
Marine Mammal Commission, 1014
budget information contacts, 1015
research, 310
Marine Mammal Protection Act of 1972, 328, 801, 1045
amendment, 288
exceptions allowed, 1035
inconsistencies with Endangered Species Act, 366
marine fisheries, 281
polar bear, 799-800
unrestricted hunting by Alaskan natives, 802
reauthorization, 289, 295
species protected, 1035
Marine mammals
Animal Welfare Act, 1038
beached/stranded animals, 1037
conservation, federal offices involved in, 1014
Convention of International Trade in Endangered Species, 1036, 1038-1039
Endangered Species Act, 1035
export policy, 1045-1046
foreign application for taking, 1037-1038
inventory system, 1039
Marine Mammal Protection Act, 1035
modifications, 1039
National Marine Fisheries Service, wildlife permits, 1036-1037, 1040-1045
permits for taking, 1034
replacement animals, 1039
*see also* specific species
Marine Protection, Research, and Sanctuaries Act of 1972, 282, 294
Marine recreational fishing, 269
Marine Resources and Engineering Development Act, 279

Marine Sanctuaries Reauthorization Bill, 289
McIntyre-Stennis Act, 137
McSweeney-McNary Research Act, 136-137
*Melaleuca*, Everglades National Park, 487
Menhaden, 268, 335
Merchant Marine Act of 1936
  amendments, 281, 293
Merchant Marine and Fisheries Committee, 207
Merrimack River, restoration programs, 705-706
Mexican duck, 575
Mexican wolf, 960
Mid-Continent Waterfowl Management Project, 226
Middle America
  deforestation and cattle ranching, 838, 841
  European contact, 837-838
  U. S. government responsibility, 846-847
Midwest Fur Poaching, 617
Migratory Bird Act, amendment, captive-bred raptors, 817
Migratory Bird Conservation Act of 1929, 217, 350, 375, 377, 501
  inviolate sanctuaries, 433
  wildlife refuge establishment, 416
Migratory Bird Conservation Fund, 416
  appropriations, 376
  land acquisition, 378
  refuge acquisition, 418
  wetlands acquisition, 375-376
Migratory Bird Hunting and Conservation Stamp Act of 1934, 217, 375-376
  refuge acquisition, 418
  wildlife refuge establishment, 416
Migratory birds, 215-263
  1985-1986 duck-hunting regulations, 234-236
  Agreement on Cooperation in the Field of Environmental Protection, 554-555, 557
  average annual subsistence harvest, 561
  banding project, 214
  breeding-bird survey, 250
  budget and staff, 224
  categories, 215
  Convention Concerning Conservation of Migratory Birds and Their Environment, 555
  Convention for the Protection of Migratory Birds, 553-554
  declines in forest migrants, 839
  effect of logging and partial clearance, 832
  effects of tropical deforestation, 240-241
  Emergency Wetlands Resources Act, 244-245
  Farm Bill provisions for land conservation, 247-248
  field plans, 222
  Fish and Wildlife Coordination Act amendments, 246
  Fish and Wildlife Service agency structure, 220-221
  forest species breeding in U. S. and migrating to Middle or South America, 842-845
  historical perspective, 834-838
  history and legislative authority, 216-217
  Hooper Bay Agreement, 561

impact on insect pests, 833-834
increasing waterfowl production, 226
as indicator species, 834
interaction with permanent tropical residents, 830-831
international agreements, 546
Japanese treaty, 554-555, 561-562
Land Acquisition Priority System, 431
lead shot poisoning, 236-240
  *NWF v. Hodel*, 238, 368-369
legal developments, 248-249
management plans, 220
Mexican treaty, 554, 561-562
Migratory Bird Treaty Act, *see* Migratory Bird Treaty Act
migratory shore and upland game species management, 229
nongame
  management, 229-231
  population, 262-263
  unstable or decreasing population, 260-261
North American Waterfowl Management Plan, 231-234, 556
organization and operations, 217
partnership between Fish and Wildlife Service and states, 215-216
plans, 221-222
population objectives, status and trends, 226, 839, 1022-1028
regionally significant species, 230
regional plans, 222
requiring mature forest habitat and deforestation, 845
research, 222-223
restructuring waterfowl management, 224-225
reversing the decline of Pacific Flyway Geese, 241-243
stabilized hunting regulations study, 228-229
tax-code changes that promote conservation, 245-246
treaties, 552-557
  history, 552-555
  implementation, 555
  legislative authority, 553-555
  organization and operations, 555-557
U.S.-Mexico Joint Committee on Wildlife Conservation, 556-557
waterfowl, *see* Waterfowl
wetlands, *see* Wetlands
Yukon-Kuskokwim Delta Management Agreement, 561
*see also* specific species
Migratory Bird Treaty Act, 216-217, 399, 553, 666-667, 880
  amendment, 560
  challenge to, 553-554
  court cases, 248-249
  implementation of international treaties, 555
  nonenforcement against subsistence hunters, 558
  osprey, 898
  steel shot use, 238-239
Migratory shore birds, 229, 259

Military Lands Withdrawal Act of 1985, 533-534
Mineral deposit, budget trends, 38
Mineral Leasing Act for Acquired Lands, 91
Mineral Leasing Act of 1920, 89, 99
Mineral materials, 95
Minerals management, *see* Energy and minerals management
Minerals Management Service, 310
Mining and Minerals Policy Act, 99
Mississippi Flyway, numbers of geese, 257-258
*Missouri v. Holland*, 554, 581
Mitchell Act, 722
Mountain goats, Olympic Mountains, 485
Mourning dove, population objectives, status and trends, 1027
Multiple use, definition, 13
Multiple-Use Sustained-Yield Act of 1960, 12-13, 30, 51, 74-75, 104, 114

Nassau River Valley Ecological Preserve, legislation for, 491
Nantahala National Forest, stocking with wild boars, 485
National Aquaculture Act of 1980, 293-294
National Aquaculture Improvement Act, 331
National Audubon Society, 216
National Environmental Policy Act of 1969, 13, 23, 390, 524
  Bureau of Land Management violations, 537
  cooperative management agreements and, 535
  draft documents, 306
  fish and wildlife protection, 104-105
  leasing requirements, 101
  locatable minerals, 88
  mitigation banking, 246
  road building, 167
  sale-area design, 56
  wetlands, 374
National Federation of Fishermen, 303, 325
National Fish and Wildlife Service Training Center, 456
National Fisheries Institute, 303
National Forest Management Act of 1976, 8, 14-15, 23, 51, 58-60, 70, 74-75, 114
  alternative formulation requirement, 26
  clearcutting, 53-54
  diversity, 54
  drafts of forest plans, 3
  even-aged harvest methods, 53
  fish and wildlife management, 105-106
  forest research, 137
  grasslands, 77
  Knutson-Vandenberg deposits, 106
  maintaining viable populations, 107
  non-declining flow, 51-52
  Purchaser Election Program, 62
  riparian zone protection, 54
  road construction goal, 63-64
  rotation age, 54
  soil and water management, 130-131
  suitability, 52-53
  timber sales, 54-55
National Forest System, 28

acreage, 19, 1066-1067
activities, 114
attacks on the system, 6-7
below-cost timber sales, 165-167
Class I air quality areas, 131, 134
coal mining, 91-92
commodity used, 1-2
competing and conflicting demands, 2
critical decisions about fish and wildlife management, 3
Depression, 8
eastern forests, 7-8
  versus western forests, 19, 21
fish and wildlife recreational activities, 102
forest plans, 23-25
funding for wildlife and fish habitat management, 172-173
important timber area, 48-49
L-20 regulations, 9
land acquisition, 41, 44-45
  budget trends, 39
  choice of lands, 44
  by condemnation, 45
  by exchange, 44-45
  Federal Aid Program, 194-195
  funding, 45
  land disposal, 45-46
livestock grazing, *see* Grazing; Range management
Mining Administration, 90
old-growth timber harvest and wildlife, *see* Old-growth forests
organization, 19-22
outstanding and reserved rights, 97-98
overgrazing, 73
personnel, 971-972
population estimated for wild horses and burros, 79
primitive areas, 9, 12
protected areas, 95-97
range, *see* Range management
ranger districts, 22
receipts from recreation use, 124-125
recreational visitor days, 113, 115
regions, 21-22
road building, 167-168
  budget, 168
special use permits, 46-47, 124
summary of total recreational use, 116-119
territories, wild horses and burros, 78
timber cut, 48
unresolved RARE II acreage, 127
U-regulations, 9, 12
wilderness areas, *see* Wilderness
wildlife and recreation, 1
withdrawls, 46, 96-97
World War I to World War II, 8-9
*see also* Energy and minerals management
National grasslands, 76-77
  grazing agreements, 83
  grazing management, 82-83
  grazing permits, 81
National Industrial Recovery Act, 147
National Landmark Program, 490
National Marine Fisheries Service, 295-301
  budget, 311-315
  information contacts, 1015

research, 310
state and industry assistance programs, 314
current issues, 320-321
enforcement of Fishery Conservation and Management Act, 302
export policy for marine mammals, 1045-1046
Fees, Permits, and Regulations Division, 297
Financial Services Division, 297
fisheries, 295, 297
fisheries centers, 300, 310
Fisheries Resource Management, 297-298
habitat conservation, 317-318
international wildlife conservation, 550-551
jurisdiction, 1050
marine recreational fisheries, 318-319
memoranda of agreement, 395-397
Office of Enforcement, 298
Office of International Fisheries, 297
Office of Protected Species and Habitat Conservation, 298, 352
organizational chart, 296
personnel, 1011-1013
planning, 304-305
policy for marine recreational fisheries, 319
preliminary management plans, foreign fishing, 306-307
regional fishery management councils, 299-301
regional offices, 1007-1009, 1013-1014
regional organization, 299-300
research, 309-310
science and technology, 298-299
shifts in activities, 319-320
Strategic Plan, 267
wildlife permits, 1036-1037, 1040-1045
National Marine Sanctuary Program, reauthorization, 294
National Oceanic and Atmospheric Administration
budget, 311
fisheries management, 301
National Sea Grant Office, 301
National Park Service, 463-493
accomplishments, 474-476
acreage, 466
agency structure, 466-468
associate director for Natural Resources, 466
Biological Resources Division, 466, 468
budget, 470-471
information contacts, 1015
Class I airsheds, 475
combating exotic rodents at Channel Islands, 478
cooperative park study units, 472, 990-993
current issues, 478-479
Digital Cartography, 493
eastern brook trout in yellowstone, 486
exotic plant species, 486-487
exotic species, 484-486
feral burros in Grand Canyon, Death Valley, and Bandelier, 485-486
feuding with Forest Service, 8-9
field units, 466
general management plan, 469
Geographic Information Systems, 493

herpetofauna restoration at Jamaica Bay, 476-477
history, 463
land acquisition, 473-474
legal developments, 492
legislation, 488-491
   Alaska Sport Hunting bill, 489
   Great Basin National Park, 491
   H. R. 2122 and 4962, 489
   H. R. 3804, 490
   Nassau River Valley Ecological Preserve, 491
   Park Protection and Resources Management Act, 489
   S. 1839 Environmental Zone deductions, 490-491
   Wildlife and the National Parks Act of 1984, 489
legislative authority, 464
management of overabundant prairie dog populations, 481
management philosophy, 464-465
mountain goats at Olympic Mountains, 485
National Park System Organic Act, 464
natural resource management, low priority, 488
natural resource specialist trainee program, 475-476
new director and his 12-point plan, 472-473
NPFLORA, 493
Office of International Parks Affairs, 550, 564, 566
organization headquarters chart, 467
oryx at White Sands National Monument, 477
peregrine falcon program, 477-478
planning, 468-470
predator control on adjacent lands, 480-481
pressures from adjacent lands, 480-484
privately owned land within park boundaries, 481
recreational visitor days, 114
regional offices, 987-989
research, 471-472
resource-management plans, 469
statement for management, 469
status of resource, 492-493
Status of the Parks Report, 479
trapping in, legislation, 489-490
units with natural resource specialists, 468
Washington headquarters, 986-987
wild boars at Great Smoky Mountains, 484-485
National Park System Organic Act, 46, 74, 103, 130, 464
water rights, 132
National recreation areas, prohibition of mineral mining, 96
National Rifle Association, suit to allow trapping in National Parks, 489-490
National Sea Grant College and Program Act, 277-278
National Sea Grant College Program, 310
National Trails System
budget, 130
deterioration, 129-130
management, 125

National Trails System Act of 1968, 44, 123-124

National Water Quality Assessment Program, 445

National Wetlands Inventory, 374, 381-384
assessments and evaluations, 383-384
data collection efforts, 382
hydric soils, 382
mapping, 381
studies on federal incentives for wetlands destruction, 382-383

National Wetlands Inventory Project, 244

National Wetlands Technical Council, 383

National Wilderness Preservation Act, 12

National Wilderness Preservation System, 120

National wildlife Federation
lead-shot opposition, 237
steel shot proponents, 238

*National Wildlife Federation v. Burford*, 517

*National Wildlife Federation v. Coston*, 167

*National Wildlife Federation v. Hodel*, 238, 368-369

*National Wildlife Federation v. Marsh*, 391, 394, 398, 400, 402

National Wildlife Health Laboratory, 223

National Wildlife Preservation Act of 1964, 96

National Wildlife Refuge System, 413-460
Accelerated Refuge Maintenance and Management Program, 429-430, 459
acreage and facilities, 414
Alaska refuges, *see* Alaska, refuges
biological monitoring, 432
budget, 426-428
Alaska refuges, 453-454
Cape Charles Training Center, 456
Chincoteague National Wildlife Refuge, 447-448
contaminants, 440-447
Kesterson National Wildlife Refuge, 440-441, 445-447
master list of service lands with contaminant studies, 442-445
Wheeler National Wildlife Refuge, 447
coordination areas, 415
Fish and Wildlife Service master plans, 421
Florida Panther National Wildlife Refuge, 456
increased hunting, 433-434
increased public use, 428-429
increased use of volunteers, 430
Land Acquisition Priority System, 430-432
management, 422
National Wildlife Refuge System Administration Act, 423
oil and gas exploration, 435-438
organization and operations, 419-420
planning and inventory, 420-422
predator control and grazing, 438-439
changes to predator control policy, 440
refuge acquisition
extension of authority, 455
funding and priorities, 418-419
interagency land transfers, 417-418
refuge establishment, 415-418
Endangered Species Act, 417

Fish and Wildlife Act, 417
Migratory Bird Conservation Act, 416
Migratory Bird Hunting and Conservation Stamp Act, 416
National Wildlife Refuge System Administration Act, 418417
Refuge Recreation Act, 423
research, 425-426
resource management, 422-425
compatibility determinations, 424-425
croplands, 423
fire, 423
grasslands, 422-423
marsh and water management, 422
public-use and economic-use, 423-424
status of resource, 456-460
problems reported by units of system, 458-459
trapping and steel-jaw traps, 435
types of areas, 413, 415
waterfowl production areas, 415
wetlands, 374
wilderness, 426

National Wildlife Refuge System Administration Act of 1966, 350, 418, 423

Natural Resources Defense Council, 166

*Natural Resources Defense Council v. Calloway*, 387, 398

*Natural Resources Defense Council v. Hodel*, 535

*Natural Resources Defense Council v. Morton*, 500

Nature Conservancy, 216, 787, 840, 946

*Nevada v. United States*, 249

Nevada Wilderness Bill, 491

New Jersey conservation Foundation, 880

New Mexico
Operation Game Thief, 617-619
Endangered Plant Law, 945

*Newport Galleria Group v. Deland*, 408-409

New York, nongame wildlife programs, 652-653

Non-declining flow, 51-52
departures, trends, 70

Nongame Act, *see* Fish and Wildlife Conservation Act

Nongame, Endangered and threated Species Conservation Act, 645

Nongame wildlife
defined, 633-634
*see also* Migratory birds, nongame; State nongame wildlife programs

Nongame Wildlife Act, 650

Nongame Wildlife Trust Fund, Florida, 651

North American Loon Fund, 688

North American Waterfowl Management Plan, 222, 231-234, 556
added habitat, 232
population objectives, 231-232
stabilized hunting regulations, 232

North Atlantic Salmon Conservation Organization, 298, 703-704

*North Dakota v. United States*, 249

Northeast Atlantic, status of resource, 333

*Northern Alaska Environmental Center v. Hodel*, 492

Northern fur seals, permits for taking, 1037

Northern Pacific Halibut Act, 272

Northern Prairie Wildlife Research Center, 223

North Pacific Fisheries Act of 1954, 275
  amendments, 291
North Pacific Fishery Management Council,
  restriction on authority to limit access, 324
North Pacific Halibut Act, 272
Northwest Atlantic, overfishing, 282
Northwest Atlantic fisheries, 274-275
Northwest Atlantic Fisheries Act, 275
Northwest Atlantic Fisheries Organization, 291
*Northwest Indian Cemetary Protective Associatin, et
  al., v. Peterson*, 167-168
Northwest Power Planning Act, 732-733
NPFLORA, 493

*Odocoileus hemionus sitkensis, see* Sitka black-
  tailed deer
Office of Endangered Species, 352, 550
Office of Industry Services, 297
Office of International Activities, moneys ap-
  propriated, 565
Office of International Affairs, 549, 564
Office of International Fisheries, 297
Office of Marine Mammals and Endangered
  Species, inventory system, 1039
Office of Migratory Bird Management, 549-
  550
  changing role, 224-225
  data collection, 226
  nongame migratory bird report, 230
  North American Waterfowl Plan, 556
  plans, 221-222
  program structure, 220
Office of Protected Species and Habitat Conservation, 298, 352
Office of Territorial and International Affairs
  resolving fishing violations, 302-303
Off-road vehicles, in National Forest System,
  128-129
Oil and gas drilling and exploration
  Alaska Lands Act, 451-452
  geophysical permits, 93-94
  increase in activity, 100-101
  initiation of lease, 94
  National Wildlife Refuge System, 435-438
  pressure for in Alaska, 453
Oil spill, effect on polar bear, 802
Old-growth forests, 159-165
  caribou, 171
  loss, 71
  managing, 753
  red-cockaded woodpecker, 161-162
  Sitka black-tailed deer, 162-165
  spotted owl and timber harvesting, 159-161
  *see also* Spotted owl
Olympic Mountains, mountain goats, 485
*Oncorhynchus tshawytscha, see* Chinook salmon
Operation Falcon, 617
Operation Game Thief, 617-619
Operation Gillnet, 616
Operation Outdoors, 12
Operation Trophy Kill, 616
Oregon, spotted owl, management, 521-522,
  749-754
Oregon and California Grant Lands, spotted
  owl, 521-522

Oregon and California Grant Lands Act of
  1937, 501
Organic Act, *see* National Park System Organic Act
Organic Administration Act of 1897, 4, 145
Oryx, management in White Sands National
  Monument, 477
Osprey, 889-902
  artificial nest sites, 630, 900-901
  breeding, 892-893
  current trends, 898
  diet, 891
  double-clutching, 899
  egg and young manipulations, 899
  eggs, 894
  enemies, 896
  habitat management, 899-900
  hacking, 899, 901
  historical perspective, 897-898
  hunting behavior, 892
  impact of acid rain, 901
  laws and regulations, 898-899
  longevity, 896
  nesting, 893-894
  North American distribution, 890
  physical characteristics, 890-891
  population objectives, status and trends,
    1027
  productivity and human activity, 902
  prognosis, 901-902
  recommendations, 902
  significance of species, 896-897
  species description, 889-890
  subspecies, 889
  voice, 891
  young, 894-895
Otters
  California sea, 364-367
  river, reintroduction, 649
Ouachita National Wildlife Refuge, natural-
  gas drilling, 437
Outer Continental Shelf Lands Act, 293
Outstanding rights, 97-98

Pacific brant, population, 258-259
Pacific Crest Trail, 123
Pacific Fishery Management Council, 729
Pacific Flyway
  effect of subsistence hunting, 559
  numbers of geese, 257-258
  reversing decline of geese, 241-243
Pacific Ocean
  international fisheries, 291
  resource status, 336-338
Pacific Salmon Treaty Act of 1985, 291
Pacific States Marine Fishery Commission, 273
Packwood-Magnuson Amendment, 289
Padre Island National seashore, experimental
  Kemp's Ridley sea turtle nesting population,
  926
Pan American Union, 564
*Pandion haliaetus, see* Osprey
Park Protection and Resources Management
  Act, 489
Passenger pigeon, population decline, 349
Patuxent Wildlife Research Center, 223

captive whooping crane flock, 669
Pawcatuck River, restoration programs, 705-706
Peales's peregrine falcon, *see* Perergrine falcon
*Pediocactus knowltonii, see* Knowlton cactus
Pelagic sealing, 545-546
Pelican, white, delisting, 649
Pelly Amendment, 276
Peregrine falcon, 807-821
  augmentation, 817
  breeding, 810-820
    in Colorado, 649
  captive produced, 816-817
  cross-fostering, 818
  current trends, 814-815
  diet, 809-810
  effects of DDT, 811, 813, 819-820
  effects of Dinosaur National Monument's cricket-control program, 481-482
  eggshell thinning, 813-814
  fostering, 817
  habitat destruction, 816
  hacking, 478, 814, 817
  historical perspective, 812-813
  illegal take of nestlings, 818-819
  illegal trade, 361-362
  management, 815-819
  migration, 808
  National Park Service program, 477-478
  physical characteristics, 807-808
  population, 815
  production, 815
  prognosis, 819-820
  propagation programs, 814, 816
  recommendations, 820-821
  recovery plans, 815-816, 820
  re-establishment in the East, 818, 820-821
  significance of species, 811-812
  species description, 807
Peregrine Fund, 477, 816
Pesticides
  decline in use by Forest Service, 150
  *see also* DDT
*Picoides borealis,* 161-162
Pinchot, Gifford, 5-6
Pink salmon, fishery resource, 340
Pintail, population status, trends, and objectives, 232, 234
Piping plover, 363
  population objectives, status and trends, 1027
Pittman-Robertson Act, *see* Federal Aid in Wildlife Restoration Act
P.L. 96-510, 441
P.L. 98-369, 294
P.L. 98-371, 294
P.L. 98-454, 294
P.L. 98-541, 294
P.L. 98-595, 294
P.L. 98-623, 294
P.L. 99-191, 455
P.L. 480, 548
Plants, exotic, 486-487
Platte River, 363, 668
Pogonia
  large whorled, 781-782
  *see also* Small whorled pogonia

Polar bear, 791-803
  breeding, 796-797
  current trends, 799
  dens, 796-797
  distribution, 792-793
  effect of artic industrialization, 802
  feeding habits, 794-796
  historical perspective, 798-799
  hunting, 799-802
  management, 799-800
  prognosis, 800-801
  protection of females, 801-802
  recommendations, 801-803
  significance of species, 798
  species description, 791-792
  subsistence hunting, 801
  track following, 796
Polar Bear Specialists Group, 800
Population and Habitat Management, 225
Porpoise, incidental catch in tuna fishery, 327-328
Prairie dogs, management of overabundant populations, 481
Predator control
  changes to policy in National Wildlife Refuge System, 440
  lands adjacent to National Parks, 480-481
  Malheur National Wildlife Refuge, 438-439
Preference right lease, 93
Private land
  tax incentives for conservation measures, 245
  waterfowl conservation, 226
Pronghorn, 496
  fencing off of Bureau of Land Management lands, 538
Protect Our Wetlands and Duck Resources Act, 244
Public Land Grazing Committee, 775
Public lands, fencing, 538
Public Rangelands Improvement Act of 1978, 501, 74, 76, 773
  cooperative management agreements and, 535
  expiration of grazing-fee formula, 515
  grazing fees, 83, 513
  wild horses and burros, 78
Public Utilities Regulatory Policies Act of 1978, 46
Purchaser Credit Program, 62
Purchaser Election Program, 62

Quivira National Wildlife Refuge, 668

Ramsar Convention, 562-563, 883
Rangelands
  condition by percentages, 539
  monitoring, 529-532
    problems with, 531
Range management, 72-85
  allotments, 84
    management plans, 81-82
  condition, 73
    condition by percentage, 539
  conflict between livestock and wildlife, 73
  improvements, 73, 82
  reductions in, 84-85

legal authority and requirements, 74-80
early grazing administration, 74-75
Federal Land Policy and Management
Act, 75-76
Granger-Thye Act of 1950, 75
national grasslands, 76-77
Public Rangelands Improvement Act, 76
range betterment fund, 76, 82, 85
Wild Free-Roaming Horses and Burros
Act, 77-80
monitoring/grazing modifications, 529-532
overgrazing, 73
World War I, 74
range conditions, 73
role of National Forest System, 72
setting grazing levels, 81
see also Grazing; National Grasslands
*Rangifer tarandus caribou*, 169-172
Raptors
Endangered Species Act, 361-362, 808, 816
population, 262-263
see also specific species
Recovery plans, endangered species program,
354, 356
Recreation and wilderness management, 113-
130
legal authority and requirements, 114, 120-
124
Archeological Resources Preservation Act,
124
Eastern Wilderness Act, 121
Historic Preservation Act, 124
Land and Water Conservation Act, 123
Multiple-Use Sustained Yield Act, 114
National Trails System, 123-124
Wild and Scenic Rivers Act, 121-123
Wilderness Act, 120-121
planning and management
funding, 130
general recreational use , 124-125
off-road vehicles, 128-129
reduced management, 129
trails, 125
wilderness, 125-128
trends and issues, 129-130
Red-cockaded woodpecker, 161-162, 436-437
Redhead duck, population status, trends, and
objectives, 232
Red knot, 871-884
breeding, 876-877
current trends, 879
diet, 877-878
historical perspective, 878-879
hunting, 879
management, 879-881
migration, 872
New World knots, 873-876
north, 875
Old World knots, 872-873
south, 873-875
prognosis, 881
range, 872
recommendations, 881-884
significance of species, 878
species description, 871-872
staging areas, 883
staging sites, 880, 882

wildlife refuges, 881
Red wolf, 952, 961-962
Redwood National Park, 462
Reforestation, 59-60
Knutson-Vandenberg Fund, 57, 60
Reforestation Trust Fund, 60
Refuge Recreation Act of 1962, 423
Regional Guides, 23-24
Regulatory Policies Act, see Public Utilities
Regulatory Policies Act of 1978
*Reis Brothers v. Ketchikan Pulp Co. and Alaska
Lumber and Pulp Co.*, 164
Reports, congressional document offices, 1016
Reptiles, species for which Fish and Wildlife
Service prepares resource plans, 1060
Reserved rights, 97-98
Resource plans, nongame migratory birds, 230
Resources Planning Act, 13-14, 23, 66, 74, 75,
105, 114
attempt to put dollar values on benefits of
wildlife use, 29-30
disparity between goals and actual spending
levels, 28-29
federal-state-private cooperative programs,
145
forest research, 137
Forest Service budget, 40-41
goals, 41
compared to Forest System accomplishments, 42
fish and wildlife habitiat improvement,
102-103
grazing use, 84
minerals program, 100
National Trails System, 130
recreation in Forest System, 129
soil, water, and air, 134
timber program, 49-50, 55
grasslands, 77
increased timber harvest, 65
indicator species, 107
irrelevance of programs to decision-making
process, 28
lack of meeting national objectives, 29
mineral activity, 99-100
national planning requirements, 24
regional guides, 23-24
soil and water management, 130-131
Resources Planning Act Assessment, 24, 65
Resources Planning Act Program, 24
Restoration project, defined, 179-180
Right of Eminent Domain Act of August 1,
1885, 45
Ringed seals, polar bear diet, 794-795
Riparian zones
Bureau of Land Management policy, 510-
511
effects of livestock grazing, 73, 135
management, 85
protection, National Forest Management
Act, 54
River otters, reintroduction, 649
Rivers and Harbors Act, 397
Rivers, see Wild and Scenic River System; spe-
cific rivers
Road, construction and management, 61-64
categories of roads, 61

elk habitat, 71
Forest Road Program, 62
funding, 62-63
in National Forest System, 167-168
planning, 63-64
projected miles, 69
Purchaser Credit Program, 35, 62
Purchaser Election Program, 62
RARE, 125-127
roadless areas, 69-70
trends, 68-70
wildlife implications, 61, 64
Rocky Mountain National Park, 480-481
Rodents, exotic, Channel Islands National Park, 478
Roseate tern, population objectives, status and trends, 1027
Ross goose, population status and objectives, 233

S. 747, 330
S. 1245, 330
S. 1386, 330
S. 1839, 490-491
Sage grouse, 763-777
brood rearing, 766-767
current trends, 771-772
economic impact of hunting season, 775
historical perspective, 770-771
hunting impact, 774-775
leks, 764-765
management, 772-775
nesting, 765-766
parasites, diseases and poisons, 767-768
predation, 768-770
prognosis, 775
quality of nesting habitat, 771
range, 763-764
recommendations, 776-777
significance of species, 770
species description, 763
winter, 767, 772
Sage Grouse Workshop Committee, 776-777
Salmon
Atlantic Salmon Convention Act, 292
Atlantic, *see* Atlantic salmon
Chinook, *see* Chinook salmon
chum, 728
Forest Service role, 110-111
Pacific salmon treaties, 272
Pacific Salmon Treaty Act, 291
Salmon and Steelhead Advisory Commission, 735
Salmon and Steelhead Conservation and Enhancement Act, 735
*Salmo salar, see* Atlantic salmon
Saltonstall-Kennedy Act of 1954, 276
amendments, 293
Fund, 314
funding of private fishery research, 311
private fisheries development foundations funding, 303
Salt Plains National Wildlife Refuge, 668
Sandhill crane
nesting area in Malheur National Wildlife Refuge, 438-439

population objectives, status and trends, 439, 1028
Sandpiper, *see* Red knot
Sawtimber
defined, 48
inventories, 60
in national forests, 48
private lands, 72
Scaup, population status, trends, and objectives, 232
Sea Grant Advisory Program, 301
Seals, and polar bears, 794-795, 798
Sea otter, California, establishing new population, 364-367
Sea-turtles
incidental catch, 328
Surinamese plan, 572
Section 404 permit program, 278, 281-282, 302, 384-403
404(b)(1) guidelines, 386
agency responsibilities, 384-385
application procedure, 1009-1010
Army research contacts, 1007
definition of wetlands, 387
division and district offices, 1003-1006
Forest System, 131
key contacts, 1001
legal developments, 407-409
National Marine Fisheries Service, 317
regional offices, 1002, 1007-1009
permit issuance, 386
problems and issues, 394-403
404(q) memoranda of agreement, 395-397
Attelboro Mall permit and water dependency test, 399-401
consolidated regulations, 402
EPA steamlined procedures, 402
isolated waters and interstate commerce, 397-399
regulation of solid waste disposal in waters, 403
regulatory relief efforts, 394
revisions to National Environmental Policy Act regulations, 402-403
scope of program, 397-398
South Carolina coastal wetlands, 401-402
program accomplishments and trends, 387-394
fish and wildlife mitigation, 389-390
permits issued and denied, 388-389
pre-discharge notification requirement, 390-392
project modifications, 388
upgrading of EPA 404 program, 392-394
wetlands delineation, 392
scope of program, 386-387
statutory authority, 384
violations, 385
wetland coverage, 387
Selenium, poisoning of waterfowl, 440-441, 445-446
Senate, committees, 207, 1019-1021
Senior Community Service Employment Program, 28
Sensitive species
Forest Service role, 110
research, 140

Shellfish, population, 334
Shorebirds
  hunting, 878
  management, 880
Shoveler, population status, trends, and objectives, 232
Shrimp, resource status, 335
Shrimp fishery, incidental catch, 328
Sierra Club, attempts to block drilling on D'Arbonne National Wildlife Refuge, 436-437
*Sierra Club and the Wilderness Society v. Block, et al*, 162
*Sierra Club et al v. Block, et al*, 162
*Sierra Club v. Clark*, 364
Sikes Act
 agreements, 106
  amendments, 105
  habitat improvement, 112
  user fee, 105
Sisk Act of 1967, 45
Sitka black-tailed deer, 162-165
  Tongass timber harvest controversy, 164
Sleeping Bear Dunes National Lakeshore, timber harvesting, 482
Small Tracts Act of 1983, 45
Small whorled pogonia, 781-788
  current trends, 785
  dormancy, 783
  growth, 783-784
  historical and current distribution, 786
  historical perspective, 784-785
  management, 785, 787
  private lands, 787
  prognosis, 787-788
  range, 782-783
  recommendations, 788
  significance of species, 784
  species description, 781-782
  wild boars in Great Smoky National Park, 485
Snail kite, recovery, 370-371
Snow goose, population objectives, status and trends, 233, 258, 1025
Society of American Foresters, 145-146
Sockeye salmon
  commercial fishing, 731
    1886-1980, 728
  fishery resource, 340
  returns, 1960-1983, 728
Sockeye Salmon or Pink Salmon Fishing Act of 1947, 272
Soil,inventory, 135
Soil Conservation and Domestic Allotment Act of 1936, 148
Soil Conservation Service, 382, 77
Soil, Water and Air Management Program, 130-135
  acid rain, 135
  air management, 133-134
  Clean Air Act, 131-132
  Clean Water Act, 131
  funding decline, 134-135
  legal authority and requirements, 130-132
  National Forest Management Act, 130-131
  resource conditions, 135
  Resources Planning Act, 130-131

  soil management, 133
  trends and issues, 134-135
  water rights, 132-133
  watershed management, 132
South Atlantic Fishery Management Council, Swordfish Fishery Management Plan, 325
South Carolina Coastal Wetlands, 401-402
Special Use Permits, 46-47
Sponge Act, 271
Sport Fishing and Boating Enhancement Committee, 205
Sport Fishing Institute, 303
Sport Fish Restoration Account, 204
Spotted Owl, 159-161, 743-757
  amount of necessary old-growth habitat, 749-750
  current trends, 748-749
  distribution, 744
  food and foraging behavior, 748
  historical perspective, 748
  home range characteristics and habitat use, 745-746
 interim guidelines, 749-750
  juvenile mortality, 747
  low occupancy management areas, 752
  management, 749-755
    California, 755
    Oregon, 749-754
    Washington, 754-755
  nests, 746
  old-growth forest management, 753, 757
  Oregon and California Grant Lands, 521-522
  physical characteristics, 743-744
  population objectives, status and trends, 745, 1027
  prognosis, 160-161, 755-756
  recommendations, 756-757
  replacement sites, 757
  reproduction, 746-747
  significance of species, 748
  site tenacity and adult longevity, 746
  species description, 743
  surveying, 756
  taxonomy, 744
  viable population, 160, 749, 752
Squawfish, 363
Stamp Act of 1934, *see* Migratory Bird Hunting and Conservation Stamp Act of 1934
State and Private Forestry Program, 18, 144-153
  funding, 149, 152
    congressional rejection of administration proposals to cut, 31
    FY 1985 appropriations, 33
 history and legal authority, 145-149
    cooperation vs. regulation, 145-146
    Cooperative Forestry Assistance, 148-149
    Lumber Code, 147-148
    nonindustrial private forests, 148
  program management, 149-152
    Cooperative Fire Management, 149
    Cooperative Forestry, 150-152
    Forest Pest Management, 149-150
  trends and issues, 152-153
State Department, *see* Department of State
State Forest Resource Plans, 151

Statement of Policy, 24
State nongame wildlife programs, 631-655
  history, 631-632
  adequacy of goals and objectives, 654
  Colorado, 644-645, 649-650
  definition of nongame, 633-634
  education and information, 637
  Florida, 650-652
  funding, 638-644
    check-offs, 632-633, 638-639, 653-654
    Colorado, 645, 650
    current issues, 653-654
    Florida, 651
    New York, 652-653
    1983 tax year results, 640-641
    1985-1986 budgets, 642-644
    sale of auto tags, 639
    sales tax, 639
  integration of game and nongame conservation, 654-655
  inventory, 634-635
  lack of authority over plants, 634
  land acquisition, 636-637
  management, 636-637
  New York, 652-653
  planning and evaluation, 638
  program goals, 634
  research, 635-636
  survey, 646-648
  urban wildlife, 637-638
State waters
  defined, 268
  jurisdictional controversy, 325
  jurisdiction management, 273
State wildlife conservation, 579-589
  agency functions, 582-583
  consultation, 589
  federal grants, see Federal Aid Program
  financing, 583-586
    revenue sources, 584-585
  habitat acquisition, 588
  history, 579
  information and education, 588-589
  interest in serving sportsmen, 631-632
  law enforcement, 589
  planning, 586-587
  professionalization of state wildlife agencies, 579-581
  reasons for failure to adopt formal planning processes, 198
  research, 586
  species management, 587-588
  state authority, 581-582
  status of planning efforts, 196-198
State wildlife law enforcement, 589, 593-627
  agency assigned to, 595
  allocation of resources, 606-608
  arrests and violations, 610-615
    arrests and convictions, state conservation officers, 610-612
    incidence of violations in Colorado and Virginia, 614
    percent of arrests by category, 1984, 613
  assaults on conservation officers, 621
  commercialization of wildlife, 615-617, 626-627
  definition, 594

dilution of enforcement programs, 623-625
expenditure of time, 595, 598-599
fines, 617
history, 593
illegal importation or exportation, 609, 614
major federal-state investigations, 616-617
officers killed in line of duty, 622
operation game thief, 617-619
organization, 594-595
patrol, 594
personnel qualification, selection, and training, 606
planning and record keeping, 625-626
poacher reporting programs, 619-621
public indifference, 622-623
research, 608-609
selective enforcement policies, 607
staff and budget, 595, 600-605
  basic information on state conservation officers, 602-604
  Fish and Wildlife agency, 600-601
types of laws enforced, 624
wildlife forensics, 627
wildlife violations, 609, 614
Statutes, table, 154-156
Steelhead
  current trends, 728
  Forest Service role, 110-111
  returns, 1960-1983, 728
St. Matthew Island, polar bear, 798
Stock, defined, 716
Stratton Commission, see Commission on Marine Science, Engineering, and Resources
Striped bass, population, 334
Striped Bass Fishery Management Plan, 326
*Strix occidentalis*, see Spotted owl
Subsistence hunting, see Hunting, subsistence
Superfund law, 441
Supplemental Appropriations Act of 1985, 529
Supplemental environmental impact statement, lead poisoning, 240
Surface Mining Control and Reclamation Act of 1977, 91-92, 96
Swans, 259
  population, 259, 1026
Sweedens Swamp permit decision, 400
Swordfish, resource status, 335
Swordfish Fishery Management Plan, jurisdiction problems, 325

Tamarisk, desert parks, 487
Tanner crab, fishery resource, 339
Taylor Grazing Act, 500, 535
Teal, population status, trends, and objectives, 232
Territorial sea, see State waters
Texas Gulf Coast, 882
Third Conference on the Law of the Sea, 283
*Thomas v. Peterson*, 56
Threatened species
  bald eagle, 238-239
  Bureau of Land Management responsibilities, 507-508
  California sea otter, 364-367
  controversy in Minnesota, 958-959
  defined, 349

Forest Service role, 109-110
gray wolf, *see* Gray wolf
loggerhead shrike, *see* Loggerhead shrike
loon, *see* Loon
in National Park System, 493
osprey, *see* Osprey
peregrine, *see* Peregrine
permits for prohibited activities, 1047-1048
prohibited activities, 1047
research, 140
Timber
buy-back, 57
Forest Service report, 146
planning, 55-56
Timber Contract Modification Act, 57
Timber harvest, 13-14
clearcutting, 14
forest plans, 55
increased, 65-68
1950-1984, 66
non-industrial private forests, 153
old-growth forests, 159-165
red-cockaded woodpecker, 161-162
Sitka black-tailed deer, 162-165
spotted owl, 159-161
practices, Tongass National Forest, 165
private lands, 72
question of wildlife benefits from, 166
RARE I and RARE II, 126
reduction proposed by environmental
groups, 71
research, 139
soil management, 133
Tongass, 163-164
Timber management, 47-51
achievement of Resources Planning Act
goals, 49-50
Forest Service, 2
funding, 49
legal authority and requirements, 51-55
clearcutting, 53-54
cost-efficiency requirement, 53
departures, 51-52
diversity, 54
even-aged harvest methods, 53
harvesting constraints, 53-55
non-declining flow, 51-52
'not appropriate' lands, 53
riparian zone protection, 54
rotation age, 54
sales, 54-55
suitability, 52-53
plans, spotted owl and, 750-751
research, 139
wildlife implications, 50-51
Timber sales, 57
below-cost, 59, 165-167
budget trends, 38
conflict between goals and other resource
goals, 65
contracts, 57
fuelwood, 58
funding support, 36-37
FY 1984, 37, 56
Knutson-Vandenberg deposits, 35, 37
long-term projections, 67
National Forest Management Act, 54-55

1980 revised RPA offering goals, 67
receipts, 58-59
road credits , 35
salvage, 58
Timber-stand-improvement, 61
Tongass National Forest, 162-163
fraud in timber sales, 164
timber harvest practices, 165
Tortoise, desert, Bureau of Land Management,
508
Touch America Project, 19
Townsite Act, 46
Toxic contaminants, National Wildlife Refuge
System, *see* National Wildlife Refuge Sys-
tem, contaminants
TRAFFIC(U.S.A.), 946
Trapping in Pictured Rocks National Lake-
shore, 489
Trapping in the New River Gorge National
Riverway, 489
Trapping in the Ozarks National Scenic
Riverways, 489
Trawling Efficiency Device, 328, 927, 929
Treaty for the Preservation and Protection of
Fur Seals, 271, 545-546
Trinity River Basin Fish and Wildlife Restora-
tion Act, 294
Trout Unlimited, 112
Trumpeter swan, 259
population objectives, status and trends,
1026
*Tulalip Tribes* v. *The Federal Energy and Regula-
tory Commission*, 47
Tuna
Atlantic Tuna Commission, 280
incidental catch of porpoises, 327-328
Pacific fisheries, 274
resource status, 338
Tuna Conventions Act of 1950, 274
Tundra peregrine falcon, *see* Peregrine falcon
Tundra swan, 259
population objectives, status and trends,
1026
Turtle excluder device, 328, 927, 929

Ungulates
wolf predation, 954-955
*see also* specific species
United Nations Environment Program, 569
United States-Canada Salmon Interception
Treaty, 733-734
United States Fishing Fleet Improvement Act
of 1960, 277
*United States* v. *Brant*, 249
*United States* v. *Chandler*, 248-249
*United States* v. *Dion*, 248, 360-361, 367-368
*United States* v. *Huebner*, 408
*United States* v. *McCullagh*, 553
*United States* v. *New Mexico*, 132
*United States* v. *Riverside Bayview Homes*, 407
*United States* v. *Seest*, 249
*United States* v. *Shawmer*, 553
*United States* v. *Wulff*, 248
Unlawful Inclosures Act, 538
Upland game birds, population, 259, 262
Urban wildlife, 637-638

U-Regulations, 9, 12
*Ursus actos horribilus*, 168-169
*Ursus maritimus, see* Polar bear
U.S.-Canada Halibut Convention, 324
U. S. Fish and Wildlife Service, *see* Fish and Wildlife Service
U.S. Forest Service, *see* Forest Service
U.S.-Japan Natural Resources Panel, 557
U.S.-Mexico Joint Committee on Wildlife Conservation, 556-557
U.S. Sea Turtle Recovery Team, 328

Virginia
   Commission of Game and Inland Fisheries, organizational chart, 596-597
   incidence of fish and wildlife violations, 614
Volunteers in the National Forest, 18-19
*Voyageurs National Park Association v. Arnett*, 492
Voyageurs National Park, trapping, 492

Washington, spotted owl management, 754-755
Washington Convention, *see* Convention on International Trade in Endangered Species of Wild Fauna and Flora, 567
Washita National Wildlife Refuge, 668
Water
   diversion, 47
   management, *see also* Soil, Water and Air Management Program
   western conflict between conservation needs and water diversion, 362-364
Water Bank Act of 1970, 377
Water Bank Program, 377-378
   elimination of 1986 funding, 380
   status of agreements, 379
   wetlands leasing, 379-380
Water-dependency test, 400-401
Waterfowl
   biological surveys, 1029-1031
   breeding population survey, 1030
   disease research, 227
   Federal Aid Program expenditures, 195, 197
   habitat acquisition objectives, 228
   harvest survey, 1031
   hunting regulations development, 1029-1033
   increasing production, 226
   international surveys, 555-556
   management restructuring, 224-225
   North American Waterfowl Management Plan, 222, 231-234, 556
   production areas, 249, 415
   production survey, 1030-1031
   relationship of Alaskan populations to continental populations, 559
   *see also* specific species
Water rights, national forest, 132-133
Watershed, management, 130, 132
Weddell seals, 798
Weeks Act of 1911, 7-8, 44-45, 130, 145
Western Hemisphere Convention, *see* Convention on Nature Protection and Wildlife Conservation in the Western Hemisphere
Western national forests, 19, 21
Western States Sage Grouse Committee, 772-773

Wetland Loan Act, 249
Wetlands, 373-410
   acquisition and leasing, 227-228, 375-381
      accomplishments and trends, 378-381
      Land and Water Conservation Fund, 377-379
      Migratory Bird Conservation Fund, 375-376, 378
      nationally significant, Land Acquisition Priority System, 432
      Water Bank Program, 377-379
      Wetlands Loan Act, 379
   acreage, 373-374
   Adamus system of evaluation, 383
   anadromous fish, 112-113
   Army research contacts, 1007
   Barrier Resources, 374
   Clean Water Act Amendments, 407
   Coastal Zone Management Act, 374
   conservation, 113
   database, 382, 1000
   delineation, 392
   destruction
      federal incentives, 382-383
      federal programs and policies, 375
   Emergency Wetland Acquisition Act, 406
   Emergency Wetland Resources Act, 244-245
   Fish and Wildlife Coordination Act amendments, 405-406
   Fish and Wildlife Service Regional Wetland Coordinators, 1000
   Food Security Act, 403-405
   functions, 383
   identifying high-priority, 393
   inventory maps
      Geologic Survey Mapping Centers, 999-1000
      state distribution centers, 997-999
   isolated, 393
      Section 404 program, 397-399
   legal developments, 407-409
   losses, 374, 409
   National Environmental Policy Act, 374
   National Marine Fisheries Service, 1007-1009
   National Wetlands Inventory, *see* National Wetlands Inventory
   National Wildlife Refuges, 374
   plant list, 382
   problem areas, 409-410
   Ramsar Convention, 562-563, 883
   research, 394
   status of resource, 409-410
   *see also* National Wildlife Refuse System; Section 404 permit program
Wetlands Conservation Fund, 244
Wetlands Loan Act, 217, 245, 376
   land acquisition, 379, 418
Wheeler National Wildlife Refuge, contaminants, 447
White-fronted goose, population objectives, status and trends, 241, 1026
White pelican, delisting, 649
White Sands National Monument, oryx, 477
White-winged dove, population objectives, status and trends, 1028
Whooping crane, 363, 659-674

bio-accumulation as indicator of environmental conditions, 665
breeding, 661-663
captive production, 669
collision with powerlines, 672
composite nesting area, 662
current trends, 670-671
diet, 663
fossil records, 665
habitat
  destruction, 667
  maintenance, 672
historical migration routes, 666
historical perspective, 665-670
losses, 666
management, 671-672
migration, 660-661
monitoring of movements during migration, 671
nonmigratory flock, 665-666
placing eggs in nests of sandhill cranes, 669
plan for downlisting to threatened status, 673
prognosis, 673
range, 660-661
recommendations, 673-674
recovery, 370
refuge establishment, 667-668
roosting, 663
sexual maturity, 661-662
significance of species, 664-665
species description, 659-660
territoriality, 663-664
value, 664
water management, 672
Whooping Crane Recovery Plan, 673
Wigeon, population status, trends, and objectives, 232
Wild and Scenic Rivers Act of 1968, 44-45, 96, 121-123
Wild and Scenic River System, 121-123
designated rivers, 122
prohibition of mineral mining, 96
Wilderness
acreage, 126
Bureau of Land Management study and management, 524-528
defined, 120
designation of new Bureau of Land Management areas, 527
Federal Land Policy and Management Act, 524-525
grazing increase in potential areas, 526
legal authority and requirements, 120-121
management, 125-128
management limitations, 127
management of roadless areas not designated as wilderness, 127
mining in, Bureau of Land Management, 527-528
prohibition of mineral mining, 96
in refuge system, 426
Roadless Area Review and Evaluation, 125-127
*see also* Recreation and wildnerness management

Wilderness Act, 45, 104, 120-121, 426, 525
prohibited activities, 121, 128
Wilderness Society, military lands withdrawal, 534
Wild Free-Roaming Horses and Burros Act of 1971, 74, 501, 532
range management, 77-80
  amendment, 79
  excess animals, 78
  population estimates, 79
Wildlife
captive-bred, 1047
illegal taking for commercial purposes, 615-617, 626-627
research, *see* Forest Research Program
Wildlife and Fish Habitat Relationship Program, 108, 141
Wildlife and the National Parks Act of 1984, 489
Wildlife damage control, 111-112
jurisdiction division, 111
migratory birds, 223
Wildlife forensics, 627
Wildlife Management Institute, 632
Wildlife products, increasing market values, 616, 626
Wildlife Protection Project, 557
Wildlife refuges
lack of in Canada, 963
red knot, 881
*see also* National Wildlife Refuge System
Wildlife Resources Program
budget, 224-225
organization, 218-219
personnel, 976-978
program structure, 220
research needs and objectives, 223
*see also* National Wildlife Refuge System
Wildnerness Act of 1964, 44
*Wilson citrina, see* Hooded warbler
Wolf Specialist Group/Species Survival Commission, 960
Wood Buffalo National Park, 660, 663, 667
Woodcock, population objectives, status and trends, 262, 1028
Wood duck, population objectives, status and trends, 1027
Woodland caribou, 169-172
Wood thrushes, territoriality, 833
World Wildlife Fund, 840, 880-881

Yellowstone National Park
development on adjacent lands, 482-483
eastern brook trout, 486
Fishing Bridge, 483
Grant Village, 483
hunting of bison outside of, 480
reintroduction of wolves, 962
Youth Conservation Corps, 18
Yukon-Kuskokwim Delta Goose Management Plan, 241-243
Yukon-Kuskokwim Delta Management Agreement, 561